# www.wadsworth.com

*www.wadsworth.com* is the World Wide Web site for Thomson Wadsworth and is your direct source to dozens of online resources.

At *www.wadsworth.com* you can find out about supplements, demonstration software, and student resources. You can also send email to many of our authors and preview new publications and exciting new technologies.

**www.wadsworth.com**
Changing the way the world learns®

# PHILOSOPHY
# A NEW INTRODUCTION

**Douglas Mann**
*University of Western Ontario*

**G. Elijah Dann**
*University of Toronto & University of Waterloo*

THOMSON

WADSWORTH

Australia • Canada • Mexico • Singapore • Spain
United Kingdom • United States

THOMSON
WADSWORTH

Publisher: Holly J. Allen
Philosophy Editor: Steve Wainwright
Assistant Editors: Lee McCracken and Anna Lustig
Editorial Assistant: Barbara Hillaker
Marketing Manager: Worth Hawes
Advertising Project Manager: Bryan Vann
Print/Media Buyer: Rebecca Cross
Permissions Editor: Bob Kauser
Composition Buyer: Ben Schroeter

Production Service: G&S Typesetters, Inc.
Text Designer: Jan Faulstich
Photo Researcher: Sue Howard
Copy Editor: Cynthia Lindlof
Cover Designer: Yvo Riezebos
Cover Image: Waterhouse, *The Sorceress*. The Leicester Galleries, London.
Compositor: G&S Typesetters, Inc.
Printer: Maple-Vail Book Manufacturing Group

Printed in the United States of America
1   2   3   4   5   6   7   08   07   06   05   04

For more information about our products, contact us at:
**Thomson Learning Academic Resource Center**
**1-800-423-0563**

For permission to use material from this text, contact us at
**Web: http://www.thomsonrights.com**

Library of Congress Control Number: 2004100570

ISBN 0-534-60057-3

**Wadsworth/Thomson Learning**
**10 Davis Drive**
**Belmont, CA 94002-3098**
**USA**

**Asia**
Thomson Learning
5 Shenton Way #01-01
UIC Building
Singapore 068808

**Australia/New Zealand**
Thomson Learning
102 Dodds Street
Southbank, Victoria 3006
Australia

**Canada**
Nelson
1120 Birchmount Road
Toronto, Ontario M1K 5G4
Canada

**Europe/Middle East/Africa**
Thomson Learning
High Holborn House
50/51 Bedford Row
London WC1R 4LR
United Kingdom

**Latin America**
Thomson Learning
Seneca, 53
Colonia Polanco
11560 Mexico D.F.
Mexico

**Spain/Portugal**
Paraninfo
Calle Magallanes, 25
28015 Madrid, Spain

# Contents

# 3  MIND, BODY, AND SELF   193

# 4  KNOWING OUR WORLD   299

## 5  ETHICS   394

## 6  POLITICAL THEORY   463

# 9 THE PHILOSOPHY OF CULTURE    719

# Preface

There are quite a few introductory philosophy texts in print, many of them with merit. Yet we thought the others all lacked some vital component. Some of them focus almost exclusively on metaphysics and epistemology and include few or no reflections on aesthetics, political theory, and culture. Many introductory texts are merely collections of readings prefaced by a short paragraph on the author, thus leaving the students to fend for themselves regarding basic terminology, ideas, and historical connections between philosophers. Other texts do a good job of introducing ideas and thinkers but offer only the briefest selections from the authors discussed.

In this text we tried to steer a path between several extremes, starting each chapter with a substantial introduction to the field of philosophy dealt with in it, and appending to each reading a commentary that gives students some background on the author they are about to read, along with a summary of some of the main issues the reading raises. Although we have included a few heavily edited selections, some are complete essays or chapters from books (or essays or chapters with very minor deletions).

Part of our goal is to expand the philosophical canon by including full chapters on the philosophy of religion, political theory, feminist theory, aesthetics, and the philosophy of culture, and by including selections from a variety of schools of thought—analytic philosophy, existentialism, idealism, Romanticism, and pragmatism. We've also included a substantial chapter on Greek philosophy, including short essays linking the fragments of six pre-Socratic thinkers.

Many of the authors included are central to the canon as conceived by traditionalists: Plato, Descartes, Locke, Hume, Mill, and Sartre all make a substantial appearance. Other authors selected are lesser-known philosophers, and some are usually not considered to be philosophers at all. Once again, our goal is to loosen up the philosophical canon, to give it more of an interdisciplinary context. In addition, as you'll no doubt notice after scanning the publication dates of the selections, a substantial portion come from works published in the last twenty years. In sum, we hope our text gives students a picture of philosophy as a living conversation, one in which a diversity of voices can be heard.

Douglas Mann would like to thank Heidi Hochenedel for reading over and commenting on Chapter 1, and Andrea Moe for reading over and offering her advice on parts of Chapters 6 and 7. G. Elijah Dann would like to thank Douglas Mann for his help in completing various chapters included in this text.

We would also like to thank Peter Adams for getting this whole project started, and the Wadsworth staff, notably Steven Wainwright and Lee McCracken, for helping us to finish it. Jamie Armstrong, of G&S Typesetters, also showed great patience and skill in the final editing and typesetting.

As far as the division of labor goes, we cowrote all sections except those specified here. G. Elijah Dann wrote and edited Chapters 2, 4, and 5, the Aristotle commentaries in Chapter 1, and the Chapter 8 section on Tolstoy. We cowrote the section on Hume in Chapter 2.

Douglas Mann wrote and edited Chapters 1, 3, 6, 7, and 9, along with the "Meta-Narrative of the History of Philosophy" section of the introduction; the section on Collingwood's idea of history in Chapter 4; "What Is Art?" and the sections on Edmund Burke, Romanticism, Walter Benjamin, Herbert Marcuse, Arthur Danto, Harold Bloom in Chapter 8; and all the study questions and bibliographies.

Finally, we would like to thank the following reviewers who commented on earlier drafts of the manuscript:

- Ted Toadvine, Emporia State University
- Ronald L. Jackson, Clayton College and State University
- William deVries, University of New Hampshire
- Eric Kraemer, University of Wisconsin, La Crosse
- Peter Hutcheson, Southwest Texas State University
- Mark Alfino, Gonzaga University
- Kent Baldner, Western Michigan University
- Bruce Morito, Athabasca University
- Prof. Thomas A. Baker, Niagara University
- Dr. Bernard den Ouden, University of Hartford
- Dr. Ronald R. Cox, San Antonio College
- Barbara Montero, Georgia State University
- Kelly C. Smith, Clemson University
- Micheal Pelt, Ph.D., University of Arkansas at Little Rock
- Paulette Kidder, Seattle University
- Cleavis Headley, Florida Atlantic University
- Kate Mehuron, Eastern Michigan University
- Bruce B. Janz, Augustana College
- Lynne Tirrell, University of Massachusetts, Boston
- John M. Carvalho, Villanova University
- T.A. Torgerson, University of Minnesota, Duluth

Douglas Mann
London, Ontario

G. Elijah Dann
Waterloo, Ontario

April 2004

# An Introduction to the Great Conversation of Philosophy

## PHILOSOPHY AND ITS PROBLEMS _____

### Some Basic Terminology

#### PHILOSOPHY: THE LOVE OF WISDOM

We start at the beginning: What does "philosophy" mean? As we discuss the various terms in this textbook, we'll make a habit of noting the *etymology* of the word in question. Etymology is the study of the origin and source of words. The English language derives many of its words from Greek and Latin, often by way of medieval or early modern French. The word "philosophy" is no exception. *Philia* means "love," *sophia* "wisdom": Hence, philosophy is "the love of wisdom." Although there are various Greek words for love, such as *eros* for erotic love and *agape* for spiritual love, *philia* is the most appropriate term to describe the love of wisdom. The Greek word *philia* can certainly refer to the affection between people, especially friends or family, but it can also refer to the benefit that comes from this sort of loving. Loving wisdom brings an important benefit to the lover. By loving wisdom, and as a result becoming wise, one's life can be full of thoughtful decisions and meaningful acts.

The ancient Greek philosopher Socrates remains the best example of someone who was a "lover of wisdom." Although you may think that acquiring wisdom is a matter of having all the right answers, Socrates thought that it was more a matter of *asking the right questions*. By knowing the proper questions when faced with a problem, debate, or issue, one can find good answers more easily than someone who starts off without such a foundation. By trying to ask the right questions ourselves, we could also show how others don't really know what they're saying or demanding of us. The most famous example, illustrated by Socrates, is the nature of "justice." He asked his friends, "How can you try to do just deeds before you even know what justice is?"

As you read the nine chapters that follow this introduction, you'll see how philosophy over the centuries has gone far beyond Socrates' personal and direct style of discussing philosophy with those around him. As you read through the selections in this text, you may wonder how each of them contributes to the quest for wisdom. Yet each of them *will* leave you with new questions to ask, with new ideas that will help you to understand the world. Although each chapter contributes only in part to this quest, if you take the contribution seriously, you'll be on your way to becoming a lover of wisdom, a philosopher.

## METAPHYSICS

If philosophy is the love of wisdom, then part of the task of being philosophical is the matter of understanding the world around us. We normally consider scientists, such as biologists, physicists, and geneticists, to be best suited to undertake this examination. They inspect the physical world.

Metaphysicians, in contrast to scientists, believe there is more to reality than just what we can physically examine. So when metaphysicians take up the task of understanding the world, they ask the question, "What makes up the world?" Even more ambitiously, they ask, "What makes up reality?" or, "What are the basic properties of the world?" This is the task of metaphysics—literally from the Greek *meta,* meaning "after" or "beyond," and *physics.* Hence, "beyond physics."

There are many different sorts of metaphysicians, assembled into different schools of thought. Yet painting with broad strokes, we can say that all metaphysicians think we need to try to get at the underlying substance of reality. To really understand the order of the world, we need to think abstractly and profoundly about the world and its objects (including people). So metaphysicians talk about "essence," "being," "universals," and "the mind."

These questions are actually not as weird as they may first appear. For instance, if you believe in God, have you ever thought about what God must be like in order to be eternal, all good, all knowing, and all powerful? Although you undoubtedly talk about your mind all the time, do you see it as the same thing as your brain, or separate from it? Is it a substance different from your body? Complicating matters more, do you believe you have a soul that leaves the body at death? If so, what is its nature, and how, as a spirit, can it connect to or have any influence over the material part of your person while you are physically alive? Do we have free will, or are we determined by our physical and social environment? For good or ill, metaphysicians try to show us how complicated these matters can be.

## EPISTEMOLOGY

Of course, we hope that studying philosophy will do more than just get you to ask the right questions. We hope you'll gain new knowledge about the world around you as well. But in line with the philosophical spirit described previously, and some of the problems metaphysicians are engrossed in, we first have to ask exactly what something is before we can go looking for it. For example, if someone asked you to find a "smirk," how would you know what to look for or know when you have actually found one?

Before we talk about *attaining* knowledge, we must first ask, "What *is* 'knowledge'?" This is the question that philosophers, called "epistemologists" ask. Epistemologists study epistemology. This word comes from two Greek words: *epistēmē,* "knowledge," and *logos,* "the study of." This should be plain enough. But how exactly does one study *knowledge?*

Although we use words such as "belief" and "knowledge" synonymously, there is quite a difference in their proper use. When we say we *know* something, we are claiming a greater degree of certainty for that claim than we would for a mere *belief* about it. Yet how do we get a sense of this certainty in order to be sure when we should use the word "know," as opposed to the word "belief"? Can this certainty be somehow measured or quantified?

Another issue that epistemologists deal with is the nature of truth. What exactly makes a claim true? Are there degrees of truthfulness? Is truthfulness somehow associated with certainty? If so, how?

Although these questions may appear to be quite esoteric and of little use in our day-to-day lives, nothing could be further from the case. Think about how often people on television, in magazines and newspapers, and even at your university or college try to get you to believe something. Each time you need to ask a question such as: "Why should I believe this person?" "Is what this person saying true?" and "How do I go about determining whether they are right?" You could find yourself believing something whole-heartedly, only to discover later that you didn't ask yourself these questions carefully enough. Given the almost infinite number of belief systems looking for new converts and adherents, this can be a very important matter. If you get better at asking the right questions, understanding the differences between them, and learning how to sort out good from bad criteria for believing something, you'll be better off negotiating through the competing claims you encounter at school and in society at large.

## ETHICS

Ethics governs our moral behavior, helping us to decide whether our actions are right or wrong. The problem, however, is that we often have deep disagreements with each other over what precise actions and ideas are right and which ones are wrong. When we say that someone is acting rightly or wrongly, on what do we base our decision?

For 2,500 years, philosophers have been developing theories about how we should behave in order to be ethical. Even though they have had an enormous amount of time to come up with an adequate ethical theory, they have produced only a few that are worthy of serious consideration.

When we think something is right or wrong, are we making our decision based on general rules that we think we must always follow? Rules such as, "always keep your promises," "always tell the truth," or "do to others what you would want done to yourself"? As we'll see later, this notion that we have to stick to general moral rules regardless of the consequences is called *deontology,* from the Greek word for "duty."

Perhaps instead of following your duty in moral decision making, you think about the *consequences* of your actions. This is called *consequentialism* for obvious reasons. Do you only consider how *you* will be affected by your decisions, or do you also consider everyone who will benefit or suffer as a result of your actions? If the former, then ethicists would call you an *egoist;* if you take everyone into account, and seek to promote their happiness as far as you can, then you're a *utilitarian.*

There are other ways of justifying and condemning actions. We can appeal to virtues such as honesty, friendship, kindness, and patience. Instead of thinking either of abstract principles or of the consequences of our actions, *virtue ethicists* argue that we should continually practice virtuous acts in order to develop our character.

A fourth major option is the appeal to natural law. Just as physical laws govern physical bodies and objects, some thinkers believe that there are "natural laws" in place to order our moral behavior. They believe that we should act according to the natural laws ordained by God, who designed both the physical and the moral world in specific ways. When we frustrate the natural ends given us by our Creator, we act immorally. Naturally, this view of ethics is difficult for atheists to embrace.

## POLITICAL THEORY

Political theory has to do with such things as freedom, equality, justice, and power. Although sometimes seen as a branch of ethics because it has to do with the rightness and wrongness of political actions and political institutions (notably the state), it is more useful to see it as an independent field within philosophy, given its concern not only with right and wrong but also with the nature of power and government, which brings in practical political questions.

Political theorists want to know such things as what basic rights people can legitimately claim; whether the state should promote social and economic equality between its citizens, or emphasize individual freedom instead; what is the most just form of the state; and how rulers can best guarantee social peace or their positions of power. They are also very interested in the moral foundation of the state—how its existence can be justified. Some theorists, called *contractarians*, believe that the state is founded on some sort of social contract between the citizenry and their rulers; others, such as Karl Marx, believe that the state is an organ of class domination.

Political theory, unlike some of the other areas of philosophy, is grounded in a number of "canonical" or essential works that have grown only slightly over the last century or so (despite the vast number of books and articles written on the subject). These include Plato's *Republic*, Aristotle's *Politics*, Machiavelli's *The Prince*, Hobbes's *Leviathan*, Locke's *Second Treatise on Government*, Marx and Engels's *The Communist Manifesto*, Mill's *On Liberty*, and Rawls's *A Theory of Justice*. We'll visit selections from all of these works in this reader and explore how the basic terminology of political theory has changed over the last three millennia.

## AESTHETICS

As we saw previously, ethics deals with moral values. Most ethicists argue that these values come about, more or less, through rational deliberation. But we have other sorts of values as well. Some may like hip-hop, whereas others like industrial music. Some may like contemporary art; others may like more classical pieces. Some may like beer, others wine. We usually see these values as matters of taste as opposed to the outcomes of rational processes of deliberation. Some of us, for example, can't listen to country and western music longer than five minutes. But this isn't because we've come to logically believe that jazz is preferable. In fact, if asked, "Why do you hate country music?" we may have no really good answer. It is a matter of what we *feel* to be good music. In contrast to moral values, aesthetic values (indirectly from the Greek word *aisthanomai*) come to us through our senses.

There are two main types of questions that aesthetics grapples with. The first deals with the question "What is art?" and everything that follows from it. The second sort of question deals more generally with what we call the "aesthetic experience," including the nature of beauty. These are related but distinct sorts of questions.

The issues raised by aesthetics are numerous. One is the controversial debate over what exactly constitutes art. Some people might look at a work by Picasso and say, "A child could do the same with watercolors and paper." Some pieces of art that depict controversial scenes provoke strong reactions among the public. Certainly the debate over sexually explicit writings or photographs is a good example here: Recall the recent debate over the photographs of Robert Mapplethorpe, which often featured nude male models in explicitly sexual poses. Is there a difference between art and pornography? If so, what is it? Are there some types of artistic expression that are politically incorrect and best banned? Can we rationally argue about differences in artistic taste? Can we "show" someone who doesn't like fried cow brain and turnips that these things are actually quite tasty, or at least productive of a hardy constitution?

There are some other equally difficult questions related to the cultivation of taste. Can the language of aesthetics also use the "should" of ethics? That is, should people like classical music? Should people like a rare wine as opposed to a bottle of beer? Should culturally refined people go to art museums instead of hockey and baseball games? Should people like poetry? Is there such a thing as a "higher" sort of aesthetic appreciation? We'll revisit many of these questions in our chapter on aesthetics.

## Why Don't Philosophers Agree?

Philosophers rarely agree with each other. Why?

For one reason, because of what the English philosopher R. G. Collingwood called "the logic of question and answer." Collingwood thought that all propositions (or statements) were answers to some sort of question. So if you say, "It's warm outside," the question connected to this is "What's the weather like?"

Further, the sort of question we're asked limits the answer we can give. To use a simple example, if someone asked you "What time is it?" to answer "green" or "chocolate ice cream" would be wrong, no matter how passionately you uttered the answers. The field of possible good answers is severely limited by the question itself: you either give an answer based on the 24-hour 60-minute scale of time currently popular, or say something like "I don't know," or if you're in a bad mood, "It's time you bought a watch!"

This logic of question and answer also applies to philosophical speculation. The sort of questions philosophers ask limits the answers that can be sought or given. In addition, not all philosophers are interested in the same questions. For example, when looking at social life, an ethicist might be interested in moral issues such as capital punishment and abortion, whereas an epistemologist might be interested in how people use words like "knowledge" and "belief." A political theorist might want to know how people create political institutions or what they think about justice. A philosopher of religion will be interested in whether proofs for the existence of God actually do the trick, and what effect this has on social issues. So the types of questions that the ethicist asks about social life will be different from those asked by the epistemologist, and will have a different range of answers. We can't say that the ethicist is "wrong" to be interested in moral issues, any more than we can say that you're "mistaken" to admire Beethoven's Ninth Symphony.

In addition to asking a variety of potentially distinct questions, philosophers disagree about their methods of philosophizing. This is tied to what Thomas Kuhn calls "paradigms." Paradigms are comprehensive and highly articulated views of the world. Some examples include how a religious fundamentalist would think about the world around him or her, or how the Cambridge astrophysicist Stephen Hawking understands the universe. Each of us has our own little paradigms, too, though their range of sophistication, detail, and coherence varies widely from person to person. Some people's paradigms or worldviews are coherent and well developed, whereas those of less philosophical types might be a jumble of contradictory and half-articulated beliefs. In the context of science, however, a paradigm clarifies for the scientist what counts as a valid problem to be researched, and how to conduct that research. Each such paradigm is made up of a series of assumptions, for instance, that the universe is expanding, that light is made out of waves or particles, or that space is three dimensional.

Applying this to philosophy, if we make some basic moral or metaphysical assumptions before we start philosophizing, these will obviously color our thinking. For example, if we assume that a powerful, just God exists, it's more likely that we'll believe that the universe has a purpose and that there are objectively valid moral rules that guide our lives. This belief in God is what Collingwood called an *absolute presupposition:* It's something that we assume absolutely, that no amount of empirical evidence will shake. Philosophy is founded on a series of such presuppositions that philosophers, even today, don't always agree about. And because they can't get their presuppositions straightened out, they naturally disagree about specific issues. To use a silly example: If a group of philosophers were to hold a debate on the issue "which fruit tastes the best?" and one group of debaters insisted that apples and oranges weren't really fruits at all, yet chocolate and ice cream counted as fruits, then the debate would probably not be too fruitful (excuse the pun). We have to define the field of our debate in a way that all debaters agree to before the debate becomes meaningful. Unfortunately, this isn't always possible with a cantankerous lot of philosophers.

As a second example, a physicist or biologist might prefer, due to his or her training, to explain things in purely physical terms. Such a scientist could be adamant that there is no immaterial soul that can live forever that is somehow attached to our physical body. The absolute presupposition here is what philosophers call materialism: that there is nothing outside the material world. Needless to say, modern science is dominated by this assumption.

A noted split in philosophy departments in the last half century in the Western world is that between "analytic" philosophers, largely of British and American origin, who emphasize the logical analysis of philosophical language in their work and who tend to focus on logical and epistemological problems, and "continental" thinkers, largely from Germany and France, who lean toward basic metaphysical and moral issues in their work, especially the nature of human existence. Mind you, not every

British and American thinker can be fitted into the analytic camp, nor is every European thinker a "continentalist." Further, each group of thinkers has tackled aspects of all six of the major areas of philosophy outlined previously, despite the leanings mentioned above. We'll meet representatives of both camps in this text, for example, A. J. Ayer and Gilbert Ryle from the analytic camp, and Jean-Paul Sartre and Jean Baudrillard from the continental camp.

This split between analytic and continental approaches to philosophy involves not only a split between different fields of interest, but also between different notions of what counts as a good foundation for a belief. Analytic philosophers usually insist on rigorously constructed, strictly logical arguments, backed up by sound scientific evidence. The price they pay for this logical rigor is that they tend to be seen as a bit stuffy and removed from the everyday world, as less able to deal with the complexities of human emotions and basic values.

Continental philosophers try to construct good arguments, too, yet are less concerned with formal logic and the natural sciences as the foundation of philosophical argument. To this end, their philosophical interests may seem more relevant to our ordinary, day-to-day lives and problems, including the popular culture that surrounds us. They are more open to using literature to express their views; for example, Jean-Paul Sartre wrote not only philosophical treatises, but plays and novels too. Yet for this very reason they are looked down upon by analytics as too fluffy and lacking rigor, an unjust opinion in our view.

We do well to remember that philosophers (like everyone else) have egos. Despite the fact that throughout their research and teaching they write and talk about how to be rational, objective, critical thinkers, they are often reluctant to admit blind spots and errors in their own thinking, even when there is good evidence they are misinformed or in error. They may be concerned with defending a sacred position within their field of specialization against hostile outsiders, or simply defending something they've said in the past even though good arguments have been made against it (and they know it).

So for all of these reasons, philosophers disagree. But that doesn't mean that the great philosophical conversation isn't worthwhile. Instead these disagreements help us to understand the issues, allowing us to see things from various positions. Our various beliefs and ideas about things, even those that seem relatively innocent and trivial, are connected to all sorts of other beliefs, convictions, and prejudices. When we are talking about one particular belief, say our belief in God, such a belief is connected to all sorts of other beliefs that reach deeply into our semiconscious thought processes. We also need to recognize that our logical reasons for holding a belief are not always so easy to distinguish from the emotional or psychological reasons that we accept the belief in question. Certainly we've all experienced those moments when in the heat of the battle we've argued something that seemed to us at the time perfectly rational and self-evident, only to realize later, in a cool moment of reflection, that our position depended more on our emotional reaction to our opponent than any objective, detached logic.

These considerations shouldn't discourage us from philosophical engagement, research, and inquiry. If we restricted ourselves to conversations where everyone always agreed, we'd live pretty silent lives. Perhaps most important, we wouldn't have written this book unless we believed that philosophy is a profitable and highly intriguing discipline. Indeed, these cautionary notes aren't meant to scare you away from the discipline, but to help you to become a better philosopher by starting from a foundation of self-awareness. To paraphrase Socrates, an unexamined philosophy is not worth knowing.

## Philosophy and Conversation

We can see Western philosophy as one great conversation, one between the living, the dead, and the yet to be born, to borrow Edmund Burke's phrase. This view is similar to that held by the contemporary American philosopher Richard Rorty. Although dubious that philosophers can come up with as many valid answers as they think they have, Rorty holds that the history of philosophy has a very interesting and important story to tell us all the same. Think what kind of discussion would erupt if we were able to put all the philosophers who have ever lived into a great hall. We would meet the pre-Socratics, Socrates, Plato, and Aristotle, the medieval scholastics, Descartes, Hume, Kant, Marx, and Nietzsche, just to name a few luminaries. If you've ever seen the United Nations debate a contentious issue, it might be something quite similar. Translators would interpret each of the thinker's speeches into the hall's intercom; philosophy graduate students would scurry back and forth between the philosophers, delivering personal messages, some of them containing hastily scrawled ideas, others personal attacks and threats; and as each prominent speaker went to the podium to expound his or her own views, a group of philosophers representing an opposed school of thought would walk out in indignation. We can only imagine what Aquinas would have made of Nietzsche, or if Descartes and Marx would have had anything to say to each other in such a scenario.

Although this can't happen, the next best thing is a common occurrence. Philosophers separated by centuries, thousands of miles, and completely different cultures do participate in a lively, collective conversation on a daily basis. First, by building upon each other's work and ideas, philosophical schools of thought are slowly built up, reformulated, and corrected. This continual construction is possible because there are philosophers living today who hold closely to the respective views of practically every important philosopher who has made a worthy contribution to the discipline (or at minimum, they are still intrigued by the same problems as their predecessors). A good example in this regard is Plato: There are still philosophers today who are very sympathetic to his views, even though others regard his notion of the "forms" and his picture of the ideal state as dangerous nonsense.

As you work your way through this text, you should get a sense of this conversation. You should notice how philosophers usually do their own philosophical musing either in reaction to another philosopher's work or by building on the work of their predecessors. The influence of the philosophical tradition will always be evident in each thinker's work. We could hardly expect anything different. We all know that nothing is ruder than someone who jumps into the middle of a serious conversation without knowing anything about what is being argued. This person might be more than ready to offer his opinions and his advice, and, more often than not, a resolution to the debate. But just as it is important to know something about what is being argued or discussed between disputants in an everyday conversation, we also need to know something about the history, issues, and problems of the great philosophical conversation before we can make a helpful contribution to it. The aim of our text is to do precisely this.

# A META-NARRATIVE OF THE HISTORY OF PHILOSOPHY

We can divide up the great conversation of Western philosophy into fifteen major moments or periods, with some of them overlapping each other. There are, of course, a bewildering variety of minor movements and secondary tributaries branching off from the central stream of this great conversation, but these are best left for more advanced studies.

Each of these moments presented a distinctive way of talking about philosophical problems. We can divide these fifteen moments into three great historical eras, the ancient, medieval, and modern periods, and see their progress as one big story, or "meta-narrative," of the history of this conversation. Even though some of the following dates are fairly precise, remember that many of these moments in the great conversation got started before the dates listed, or lingered on long after most of their central supporters were dead and gone. As we mentioned previously, there are still a few Platonists and Aristotelians lurking about in the darker corners of university and college philosophy departments over two millennia after this moment in the great conversation ended who no doubt run into Marxists, feminists, and postmodernists at the coffee machine on a daily basis.

The time frames of each moment can instead be seen as the period when the conversation that the great thinkers mentioned below was liveliest. Here are these moments, with some indication of where in this text you can listen to fragments of each of these moments in the great conversation of Western philosophy:

## Ancient Philosophy (750 BC–AD 312)

**Myths and Legends (750–546 BC): From Homer to Thales.** This period can be thought of as "prephilosophical" in that there's nothing from it that looks anything like a philosophical text in the modern sense. Yet the religious poetry of Homer, Hesiod, and other lesser Greek lights contains some basic metaphysical notions about how the universe works. In the simplest terms, Homer and others saw the world as controlled by the will of the gods, though they recognized that wily human beings like Odysseus could upon occasion thwart that will. Natural processes and events such as earthquakes and hurricanes were in some sense the product of divine fury, just as a bountiful harvest or a good catch of fish were the product of the gods' pleasure.

**Greek Cosmological Philosophy (546–428 BC): From Thales to Anaxagoras.** This is the beginning of philosophy proper. We'll deal with the thinkers of this period in much greater detail in Chapter 1. Suffice it to say for now that the great cosmological or "pre-Socratic" (i.e., before Socrates) philosophers were mainly concerned with the nature of the physical universe, and less so with human nature and moral issues. To mention but three of their many ideas about the cosmos: Thales thought that its basic element was water; Heraclitus thought that everything was regulated by a world fire; and Empedocles believed that the great cosmic forces were Love and Strife. Their ideas may have been wild and woolly, but the pre-Socratics laid the groundwork for Western philosophy with their daring speculations.

**Greek Anthropological Philosophy (450–322 BC): Socrates, Plato, and Aristotle.** These three great thinkers, all Athenians for at least part of their lives, moved the focus of Greek philosophy away from the physical universe (though Aristotle was still very much interested in biology and physics) to the human world. Socrates lived and breathed in his dialectical method, going around Athens's public places asking the citizens about their ideas of morality, beauty, and justice. Plato built his ideal state in his most famous work *The Republic,* whereas Aristotle proposed that we should settle moral dilemmas by adhering to the "golden mean," and all behave like good Athenian gentlemen. This was the first great moment in the philosophical conversation, not to be matched at least until the seventeenth century, if then. We'll have a look at it in detail in the next chapter.

**Hellenistic and Roman Philosophy (322 BC–AD 312): From the Death of Aristotle to the Edict of Constantine.** This period is characterized by a continuing concern with anthropological issues, especially ethics and the good life. It is in large part a series of reflections on the work of earlier Greek thinkers, with the notable exception of the Stoics, who argued that the best life is one of moderation and of resignation to the way the world is. Less fatalistic was Epicurus, who advocated a life of mild pleasures and the avoidance of suffering. We can conveniently end this moment in the history of Western philosophy with the Edict of Constantine in AD 312, which made Christianity the official religion of the Roman Empire.

## Medieval Philosophy (AD 312–1450)

**Early Medieval Thought (AD 312–ca. 1000).** This period, comprising the last century or so of the Roman Empire and the so-called Dark Ages, was not extremely productive philosophically for political, economic, and religious reasons. The empire was invaded by wave after wave of barbarian hordes: the Goths, Huns, Saxons, and Celts. Trade and commerce fell apart in the wake of these invasions, as Europe fell into chaos. Against this chaotic backdrop, Christianity took root as the dominant religion of the Western world. The first great thinker of the Christian age was St. Augustine, a North African bishop. He proposed, influenced no doubt by the sorry state of affairs in the last days of the Roman Empire, that there was a "City of God" that was infinitely more important than the mundane concerns of the "City of Man." Also worthy of note is Boethius, who took consolation in philosophy as the love of wisdom while rotting in prison, put there by the Byzantine (Eastern) Emperor Theodoric.

**Scholasticism (ca. AD 1000–1450).** Things eventually settled down in Europe starting in the eleventh century AD (although the Vikings took another century or so to change their marauding habits), allowing for relative peace and the renewal of trade. During this period, the great conversation took place mostly in monasteries between religious scholars: hence the term "scholasticism." It owed a debt to the Muslim world and the Arab philosophers Avicenna and Averroës, who transmitted

Aristotle's ideas to the West early in this period. Scholasticism flowered in the twelfth and thirteenth centuries. Aristotle became the guiding light of late medieval philosophy, usually referred to simply as "The Philosopher."

Scholasticism's main concerns had to do with reconciling Christian faith with reason, in making philosophy a handmaiden of theology. The towering figure of scholasticism was St. Thomas Aquinas, whose philosophical system became the official doctrine of the Catholic Church (later known as *Thomism*). Also of importance were Duns Scotus, a Scottish or Irish monk, and William of Occam, who invented a philosophical "razor" that compelled us to shave away unnecessary entities when constructing philosophical arguments. See Chapter 2 for some of the scholastic attempts to prove the existence of God.

The abstract theological speculations of the Scholastics came to a crashing halt with the Renaissance, which got started in Italy around the middle of the fifteenth century. Philosophy returned to the spirit of Socrates and Plato, and started to ask embarrassing (for the Church at least) questions about the nature of the world.

## Modern Philosophy (AD 1450–present)

**The Renaissance (AD 1450–1600).** The Renaissance was a great flowering of philosophy, art, science, literature, technology, and exploration. It got started in Italy, being associated with names like Raphael, Michelangelo, Leonardo da Vinci, and Machiavelli, but soon spread throughout Western Europe. Columbus sailed to America in 1492, disproving the "flat earth" theory popular in medieval geography. Gutenberg developed the printing press early in the sixteenth century, while around the same time Copernicus disproved the medieval idea that the sun went around the earth, establishing the reverse to be true. This was also a time of rediscovery of ancient Greek literature, philosophy, and architecture, with Renaissance "humanists" such as Erasmus and Thomas More reading Plato and other ancient authors as correctives to Aristotle.

A greater skepticism about medieval views of religion was in the air, along with the sense that one had to check the scientific claims made by authorities like Aristotle and Aquinas with physical experiments, like Galileo's famous dropping of objects of different weights from the Leaning Tower of Pisa to disprove Aristotle's idea that objects fall with a speed proportional to their weight. This may or may not have really happened, though it is certainly a powerful parable in the modern history of science about how a simple experiment can erode traditional beliefs. Parallel to this philosophical skepticism came the Protestant Reformation of the early sixteenth century, which rejected the authority of the pope and established a series of reformed Christian churches, mostly in Northern European countries. Martin Luther started the Reformation in Germany, later aided by John Calvin in Geneva and John Knox in Scotland (not to mention King Henry VIII's establishment of the Church of England due to a dispute with the pope). See Chapter 6 for selections from Machiavelli's short book *The Prince,* with its typically humanist enthusiasm for political realism.

**The Scientific Revolution and Continental Rationalism (1600–1715).** Out of the Renaissance's skepticism about the authority of the Church and its official philosophers came the Scientific Revolution of the seventeenth century. This was also a philosophical revolution, one that got started with René Descartes' methodical doubt and embracing of clear and distinct ideas as the road to truth (see Chapter 3 for selections from Descartes' *Meditations*). He said that there was, to start with, only one thing we could be sure of: that we exist as thinking beings. Needless to say, this way of thinking worried many religious leaders (although Descartes also tried to prove the existence of God using quasi-medieval arguments). Baruch Spinoza and G. W. Leibniz, the other two great continental European rationalists, picked up Descartes' focus on human reason as the foundation for knowledge.

On the scientific side of things, Galileo (who got *started* before 1600) developed laws of motion from experimental data, whereas Johannes Kepler worked out some of the laws of planetary motion from astronomical observations. In England, the seventeenth century took on a more empirical flavor than in France, with Francis Bacon insisting that we have to put nature "to the question" (i.e., to torture it) for answers. He meant that we have to perform experiments and accumulate data to understand the world. Thomas Hobbes argued for a materialist view of things: He saw human beings as "matter in motion," and in his *Leviathan* showed how political society evolves out of the chaos of a war of each against all by means of a social contract between selfish parties. See Chapter 6 for selections from Hobbes's *Leviathan*.

**The Enlightenment and British Empiricism (1688–1798): From Locke's *Two Treatises of Government* to Kant's Last Works.** This was an incredibly rich period for ideas in France, Scotland, and England, the centers of the Enlightenment. Alternatively, this period could be dated as falling between two revolutions: the Glorious Revolution of 1688 in England, more of a coup d'état than a full-fledged revolution, which installed the constitutional monarch King William in the place of the more autocratic King James II, and the end of the French First Republic and thus symbolically the French Revolution owing to another coup d'état, that of Napoleon Bonaparte in 1800. It was truly an age of great revolutions, of both the political and the intellectual varieties. The American colonists threw off the yoke of the British Empire, citing John Locke's argument that a people had a right to revolt against unjust kings; the French people got rid of the last vestiges of feudalism, not to mention the heads of King Louis, his wife Marie Antoinette, and hundreds of aristocrats in their own revolution; while the authority of the Church was questioned by philosophers throughout the Western world, as technology and science seemed to promise an unending progress for the human race. Indeed, at the end of this era, in 1794, the Marquis de Condorcet wrote that "the perfectibility of man is indefinite," despite the fact that he was in a French jail cell at the time, condemned by his Jacobin enemies for being a member of the wrong political party.

At the center of the philosophical conversation in this period was British empiricism. John Locke, George Berkeley, and David Hume each put forward their own version of empiricism, the notion that all knowledge comes from the senses. Locke also put forward a kinder and gentler version of Thomas Hobbes's social contract theory, where the state of nature was a fairly peaceful place that people sought to escape from only to guarantee the fruits of their labors. See Chapter 4 for Locke's epistemology, and Chapter 6 for his political theory. Hume helped to shape modern ethical theory by championing a view of morality as grounded in human sympathy and sentiments of utility. Hume's philosophy of religion can be found in Chapter 2, his view of the self in Chapter 3, and his epistemological skepticism in Chapter 4.

The French philosophes, such as Voltaire, Denis Diderot, and Baron Montes-quieu, questioned aristocratic privilege and the power of the Church, for the most part defending an empiricist view of knowledge. They believed that ignorance and superstition held the human race back, problems that could be alleviated by a calm philosophical spirit and scientific investigation. Jean Jacques Rousseau, in his heart a romantic, condemned modern civilization for robbing human beings of their primitive organic connection to nature, arguing for a return to a simpler way of life. At the end of this era, Mary Wollstonecraft criticized the failure of Enlightenment thinkers to take women into account in their battle against privilege and inequality. See Chapter 6 for more on Wollstonecraft.

The crown of Enlightenment philosophy can be found in the work of Immanuel Kant. He called himself a "transcendental idealist," but in fact tried to combine idealism and empiricism in his philosophy. It's true that all knowledge starts with experience, says Kant, but our minds structure that experience in an active way, imposing structures like space and time on our sense data. Thus, he looks ahead to romanticism in seeing the self not as a passive recipient of sense data, but as actively involved in the construction of knowledge. See Chapter 5 for Kant's ethics, and the Introduction to Chapter 8 for his view of aesthetic judgment.

**Romanticism and Idealism (1774–1889): From Goethe's *The Sorrows of Young Werther* to Yeats's *Crossways*.** These are two distinct movements that shared some common ideas. Romanticism championed the passions and the imagination over reason; the need to commune with nature; the idea of a creative, active self with a deep inner life; and the notion that everything is in flux, always changing. These last two ideas, especially the latter, are the foundation of German idealism. Its greatest exponent, G. W. F. Hegel, argued that ideas are what make the world go around, and that these ideas are connected by something he called the "dialectic." By the dialectic he meant that our ideas are always in conflict, always changing; as they battle with each other, they produce new ideas, which fight new battles, and so on. As these battles go on, we get closer and closer to the absolute truth. For Hegel, the meaning of history is the progress of the idea of freedom, a progress that culminated in the Prussian state for which he worked (see Chapter 6 for an idea of how Karl Marx picked up the dialectic and used it for his own purposes).

Hegel's most famous compatriots in the heyday of German idealism, from the 1790s to the 1830s, were J. G. Ficthe and Friedrich von Schelling, two thinkers often referred to in philosophy textbooks, but seldom read today. The poet Friedrich von Schiller was associated with both romanticism and idealism, putting forward an account of the beautiful that developed Kant's ideas. Francis Fukuyama has attempted to revive Hegel's idealism in our own day: See Chapter 6 for more on this attempt.

Romanticism is mainly a movement in European literature. Johann Wolfgang von Goethe, William Wordsworth, Samuel Taylor Coleridge, Percy Bysshe Shelley, and William Butler Yeats are some of its greatest exponents. It's important as a critique of the rationalism and empiricism that dominated Western thought until the end of the eighteenth century. See Chapter 3 for a discussion of the romantic idea of the self and Chapter 8 for the romantic view of beauty and the nature of artistic creation.

**Liberalism, Utilitarianism, and Their Critics (1789–1890): From the French Revolution to Nietzsche's Madness.** This moment in the history of Western philosophy is admittedly something of a hodgepodge of ideas. We can center it around the ideas that came out of the democratic revolutions of the eighteenth century, notably the French Revolution of 1789–1795. Indeed, 1789 was an auspicious year. In July the French people revolted against the feudal regime that ruled their country, their National Assembly passing a Declaration of the Rights of Man in October that enshrined such human rights as liberty, property, and security of person from arbitrary arrest. In the same year Jeremy Bentham published his *Principles of Morals and Legislation,* which defended a utilitarian account of ethics and politics: We should always act so as to ensure a maximum of pleasure and a minimum of pain for all sentient beings. Naturally, this called into question aristocratic privilege, not to mention forms of oppression based on race or sex.

John Stuart Mill, educated at Bentham's knee, continued the British empiricist tradition. He was also the most important exponent of liberalism in the nineteenth century. He defended a more refined utilitarian ethic than Bentham's: We have to take both the quantity *and* the quality of pleasures into account in making moral decisions. Mill also championed a wide liberty of thought and action, worried about the "tyranny of the majority" he saw as emerging from democratic societies, and argued for the rights of women. See Chapter 5 for Mill's take on utilitarianism, and Chapter 6 for his defense of liberty of thought.

Karl Marx argued that liberal ideas were merely a clever ruse used by the new capitalist class to ensure their economic domination of a free marketplace. In fact, all of history was a struggle between economic classes, said Marx. Liberalism was merely the latest installment in a long series of ideologies used by the ruling class to justify its power. See Chapter 6 for Marx's critique of capitalism.

At the end of the moment of the conversation, Friedrich Nietzsche attacked liberal moral codes and Christianity as parts of a "slave morality" that celebrated the will to power of the herd, the general mass of sheep who made up modern societies. Nietzsche's work came to an abrupt halt in 1890, when he succumbed to madness. See Chapter 2 for Nietzsche's attack on Christianity, and Chapter 5 for his critique of morality.

**Pragmatism (1878–present): From Peirce to Rorty.** Largely an American phenomenon, the pragmatists argued that the value of a thing depended on how useful it was. Obviously, this was a very practical philosophy, and very convenient to a society with a certain faith in the progress of science and technology. It started with Charles Sanders Peirce's invention of the term "pragmaticism" to describe a theory of meaning where the truth of a statement depended on its practical consequences. William James popularized pragmatism, arguing that true ideas are those that get us into satisfactory relationships with other parts of our experience, while John Dewey applied the pragmatic idea of truth to a number of fields, including politics, education policy, and aesthetics. Taking his cue from Dewey, Richard Rorty came up with his ironism, where we "ironically" hold on to our philosophical beliefs only as long as they work. See Chapter 4 for selections from William James and Richard Rorty.

**Analytic Philosophy (1890–present): From Frege and Russell to the Modern Academy.** Analytic philosophy has tended to focus on the logical analysis of language as a way of solving philosophical problems. It got started in the late nineteenth century with the work of Gottlob Frege, who wanted to apply mathematical logic to language, making it a precise instrument of meaning. Bertrand Russell, who took many philosophical positions during his long career, developed analytic thought further with his early- and mid-twentieth-century work in logic and epistemology.

A. J. Ayer took analytic philosophy to its extreme with his positivism, which insisted that the only meaningful statements were those that could be verified by experience. Thus, ethics and metaphysics were nonsense, because they couldn't be verified by any facts.

The Austrian thinker Ludwig Wittgenstein, probably the most imposing figure among the analytical philosophers, started out sympathetic to the positivist position. He argued that the point of language is either to picture facts in the world or to express logical relationships. Later, in his "ordinary language" philosophy, he concluded that the meaning of words could be found in the way they are used in the many language games we play in everyday life (which sounds a bit like pragmatism). In this later philosophy he saw philosophy as therapeutic, as helping us to get rid of false problems by analyzing the way we use philosophical concepts. Gilbert Ryle picked up on Wittgenstein's ordinary language philosophy, introducing the idea of the "category mistake" to show how "mind" and "body" belong to different logical categories, and thus to analyze away the mind/body problem. See Chapter 3 for Ryle's criticism of Descartes, and Chapter 4 for Ayer's positivism.

**Existentialism and Phenomenology (1843–1855, 1900–1980): From Kierkegaard's *Fear and Trembling* to the Death of Sartre.** Søren Kierkegaard can be seen as the grandfather of existentialism, with his idea that religious belief was a leap of faith over an existential void into a purely subjective truth. Existentialism took something of a holiday in the late nineteenth century, though the Russian novelist Dostoevsky used existential themes such as the absurdity of human existence in his works in the 1870s and 1880s, with Nietzsche writing about human self-creation and the death of God in the same period. See Chapter 2 for Kierkegaard's critique of the Christianity of his day.

This moment of the conversation got started again at the dawn of the twentieth century owing to phenomenology, which looks at human consciousness as a pure phenomenon, bracketing out any moral or metaphysical assumptions about its contents, including the existence or nonexistence of its objects. Edmund Husserl started off the movement in earnest with his 1900 book *Logical Investigations.* Martin Heidegger developed phenomenology in his groundbreaking 1927 book *Being and Time,* which he termed an "ontological analytic of Dasein," or in ordinary English, a study of human being. Jean-Paul Sartre continued Heidegger's basic project of analyzing human existence in arguing that human existence precedes essence in the philosophical order of things, and that all human beings are "condemned to be free." Sartre said that our conscious being is a nothingness, a void we fill in with our life projects.

Albert Camus brought existential ideas to literature, painting pictures of alienated strangers who rolled meaningless rocks up the meaningless hills of their absurd lives. Simone de Beauvoir, Sartre's lifelong friend, applied existential ideas to the inequality of the sexes. See Chapter 3 for Sartre's defense of the existential idea of human freedom and Camus' idea of how we can overcome the absurdity of life.

**Postmodernism (1966–present): From Derrida's Johns Hopkins University Lecture to the Future.** The word "postmodern" can be used in at least two senses: (1) as a description of the historical era we're currently living through, one where high tech and mass media penetrate into every corner of our lives; or (2) to describe a type of theorizing that puts objective truth and reality into question. Obviously, we're interested in the second definition here, though it very much depends on the first.

Michel Foucault's work acts as a sort of overture to postmodernism: His books on the history of madness, the clinic, the prison, and the human sciences between 1961 and 1971 all attempt to show how our Western notions of scientific knowledge are tied up with attempts to exert control over those people who the ruling powers define as "mad," "sick," or "criminal." In the 1970s and 1980s, he extended the same sort of analysis to sexuality, arguing that our view of sexual deviancy is just a construction used to control certain forms of practice.

Yet if there's a moment we isolate as the beginning of the postmodern conversation, it's Jacques Derrida's 1966 address at Johns Hopkins University in Baltimore, "Structure, Sign, and Play in the Discourse of the Human Sciences." In this essay, Derrida announces to America the core of his deconstructive method: He rejects the idea that there are metaphysical "centers" around which we can build structures of truth (as Descartes had tried to do), seeing language as wrapped up in an endless play of meanings. The French postmodernist invasion had begun. See Chapters 4 and 9 for more on deconstruction.

At the end of the 1970s, Jean-François Lyotard identified what made the present era "postmodern": our collective loss of faith in meta-narratives such as liberal progress, the proletarian revolution, or Christian redemption. Marshall McLuhan, though no postmodernist, gave succor to the movement by analyzing how modern media shape and reshape the way we perceive our world. This made some philosophers take popular culture and the technology associated with it more seriously when thinking about epistemological issues. By the early 1980s, Jean Baudrillard had translated McLuhan's aphorism "the medium is the message" into a whole critique of modern life, arguing that consumer culture and new media such as television and computers have produced a "hyperreal" world where we've lost touch with the underlying reality that these simulations supposedly represent.

See Chapter 9 for discussions of McLuhan, Lyotard, and Baudrillard, and of the impact of postmodernism on the philosophy of culture.

Our quick journey through the various moments in the great conversation of Western philosophy has come to an end. At the current time, the great conversation, at least in the Anglo-American world, is dominated by analytic philosophy, sometimes with a bit of pragmatism and liberalism mixed in. From time to time, one can hear scattered discussions of continental philosophy, notably existentialism, phenomenology, and postmodernism, interrupting this main stream of the conversation. In this reader we'll try to give students of philosophy a sampling of all these contemporary debates. However, first we have to do the hard work of filling in the details of some of the past moments in the great conversation. We'll start in the next chapter by returning to the place where the whole thing got started, ancient Greece in the sixth century BC.

## General Bibliography for Readers

Following are some of the better dictionaries, encyclopedias, and introductions to philosophy. In the bibliographies that follow each of the chapters, we'll assume that you've already consulted some of these sources before going into greater depth with the works listed there.

Audi, Robert, ed. *The Cambridge Dictionary of Philosophy.* Cambridge, UK: Cambridge University Press, 1999. A hefty (1,000-page) one-volume dictionary with 4,000 articles by 436 contributors that perhaps puts too much emphasis on twentieth-century analytic philosophy and logic, but a substantial work all the same.

Blackburn, Simon. *The Oxford Dictionary of Philosophy.* Oxford: Oxford University Press, 1996. Less than half the length of the Cambridge dictionary, but less parochially analytic.

Copleston, Frederick. *A History of Philosophy.* New York: Image Doubleday, various dates. A standard multivolume history of philosophy by a Catholic scholar who is usually, but not always, able to prevent his religious worldview from interfering with a fair treatment of the thinker in question.

Craig, Edward, ed. *The Routledge Encyclopedia of Philosophy.* 10 volumes. London: Routledge, 1998. The new kid on the encyclopedic block, but probably now the standard longer reference work for serious students of philosophy. It contains over 2,000 articles on all aspects of philosophy, ranging from Buddhism to deconstruction. Each article contains cross-references to other articles, along with an extensive bibliography. It is also available on CD-ROM.

Edwards, Paul, ed. *The Encyclopedia of Philosophy.* New York: The Free Press/Macmillan, 1967. The old standard reference work for serious philosophers until Routledge came along with its encyclopedia. Articles on all the major thinkers and concepts, including bibliographies.

Honderich, Ted, ed. *The Oxford Companion to Philosophy.* Oxford: Oxford University Press, 1995. Another 1,000+ page philosophical dictionary with short articles on all important thinkers and concepts, along with maps of the various branches of philosophy and a chronological table. The articles were written by a diverse collection of dozens of scholars.

Osborne, Richard. *Philosophy for Beginners.* New York: Writers and Readers, 1992. A surprisingly comprehensive treatment of the subject, with some of the best comic art in either the "Beginners" or "Introducing" series. Yes, philosophy can be fun.

Reese, William L. *Dictionary of Philosophy and Religion: Eastern and Western Thought.* Atlantic Highlands, NJ: Humanities Press, 1996. This dictionary offers pithy summaries of the biographies and main doctrines of the great and not-so-great thinkers, along with definitions of key terms. Very useful.

Weiner, Philip P., ed. *Dictionary of the History of Ideas: Studies of Selected Pivotal Ideas.* New York: Scribner's, 1968, 1973. A four-volume work with fairly detailed articles on the central ideas and movements in science, philosophy, religion, history, politics, art, and literature by many different scholars. A bit dated, but includes nice bibliographies.

## Internet Resources

*The Internet Encyclopedia of Philosophy:* www.utm.edu/research/iep
An ongoing project with many very noticeable gaps. This site features a collection of medium-length and longer articles on individual philosophers. What is there is pretty reliable. It also features a timeline and a small collection of philosophical texts. Edited by James Fieser.

*A Dictionary of Philosophical Terms and Names:* www.philosophypages.com/dy/index.htm
This database is very extensive, featuring many short entries on philosophical terms, movements, and thinkers, with about forty of the greatest philosophers getting a full-page treatment (with nice bibliographies linked to Internet booksellers). There are internal links be-

tween elements of the dictionary and external ones to other Web sites, a synopsis of the history of Western philosophy, along with a timeline of the great thinkers and even a study guide. Very useful.

*Episteme Links to Philosophical Texts:* www.EpistemeLinks.com
A meta-database of links to over 900 philosophical texts available on the Web, along with book and job lists, journal descriptions with Web page links, a list of academic publishers, and discussion groups.

*Guide to Philosophy on the Internet:* http://www.earlham.edu/~peters/philinks.htm
Exhaustive list of links to Internet pages, plus the Hippias search engine, which is geared to cover philosophy pages only. Divided according to general guides, philosophers, philosophical topics, associations, journals, course outlines, e-texts, bibliographies, dictionaries, and a few more things. From Peter Suber of Earlham College.

*xrefer:* http://www.xrefer.com
A meta search engine that links to dictionaries and encyclopedias from prominent publishers such as Oxford University Press, Penguin, Macmillan, and Bloomsbury. Included are the *Oxford Companion to Philosophy* and *The Bloomsbury Guide to Human Thought*.

*Island of Freedom:* http://www.island-of-freedom.com/index.htm
An interesting, attractive site with snapshots of nineteen major philosophers. It also contains sections on major poets, artists, and theologians, along with sections on several aspects of Eastern religion and philosophy.

## CHAPTER ONE

*The unexamined life is not worth living.*
SOCRATES

# The Ancient Greek Origins of Western Philosophy

## INTRODUCTION: THE BIRTH OF PHILOSOPHY IN ANCIENT GREECE

Philosophy greeted its dawn in the West somewhere around 600 BC in the city-states of mainland Greece and the Greek part of Asia Minor. The Egyptians may have perfected pyramid building and mummification, while the Babylonians may have delved deeply into astronomy and mathematics, but it was the ancient Greeks who first began to think about the universe in philosophical terms. To do so, they had to develop a whole new vocabulary to describe their new ideas, a vocabulary that shaped the Western conversation of philosophy. Here is some of that new vocabulary.

### New Words Appear

Our English word "philosophy" comes from the combination of two ancient Greek words, *philia* and *sophia,* which mean "love" and "wisdom." Philosophy is therefore the "love of wisdom," and a philosopher is a "lover of wisdom." We also have the Greeks to thank for providing the roots and meanings of the six major divisions of modern philosophy:

**1. Metaphysics:** From *metaphusika,* literally "that which comes after the *Physics.*" This was the title given to Aristotle's work on metaphysical issues by Andronicus of Rhodes, who edited his scattered writings into book form around 50 BC. It was the book that came after the *Physics* (which dealt with natural scientific matters), so Andronicus called it the *Metaphysics.* Metaphysics didn't exist as a separate study, so a term had to be coined to cover the range of issues it deals with: the nature of the universe (*cosmology,* the theory of the *kosmos),* the existence and nature of God (*theology,* the theory of *theos,* God), the relationship between the body and the mind, and the nature of causality, to mention just the main issues. Metaphysics, thus, has to do with questions at the basis or outside of the realm of physical science.

**2. Epistemology:** This word comes from *epistēmē* and *logos*, words meaning "knowledge" and "reason or word or discourse." Epistemology is therefore the *logos* of *epistēmē*, the theory of knowledge.

**3. Ethics:** This comes from *ethikos*, which means rules of right conduct. Aristotle wrote the first systematic book on this area, called the *Nicomachean Ethics*.

**4. Political Theory:** This comes from the Greek word *politikē*, politics. Aristotle also wrote a book on this subject, aptly named the *Politics*.

**5. Aesthetics:** Derived from the Greek word *aisthetikos*, the philosophy of beauty. The root of this word comes from the Greek verb for perception. We *perceive* the beautiful, while we *think* about things such as ethics, mathematics, and logic.

**6. Logic:** From *logikē*, a systematic way of thinking and arguing. Aristotle helped to formalize this by inventing the syllogism, a three-part form of reasoning like the following: "(1) All men are mortal. (2) Socrates is a man. (3) Therefore, Socrates is mortal."

## The Mythological Period: The Gods as the Causes of Material Change

The first attempt by the ancient Greeks to come to grips with the nature of the cosmos in writing came in Homer's epic poems the *Iliad* and the *Odyssey*. These epic poems recount the Trojan War and Odysseus's eventful return voyage to his home in Ithaca. In them, Homer, who wrote (assuming that he didn't just piece together other poets' works, and that he existed at all) some time in the eighth century BC, interwove his story of the human side of the events with accounts of the gods' internal debates, quarrels, and interventions into these events. His is the best picture we have of the worldview of the preclassical Greeks of the period 900–600 BC, before the birth of philosophy and science in Ionia (western Asia Minor). According to this worldview, lightning comes from Zeus, floods come from Poseidon, the rising sun is really Apollo's chariot, and the Fates rule over our lives. Natural events are connected to the will of the gods, with no independent and constant laws governing them.

In Homer's account of the Trojan War in the *Iliad*, the gods hold councils to decide the fate of Achilles, Hector, and the other Greek and Trojan warriors. Yet even here there is an element of later Greek humanism, for the city is taken not by the will of the gods, but by the cunning of Odysseus, who builds a giant wooden horse that the Trojans mistake for a gift and symbol of the Greeks' admission of defeat. The Greeks pretend to sail off in their ships, and the Trojans move the horse within their gates. As legend has it, Odysseus and a few men, hiding inside the horse, leave by a trap door and open the gates of the besotted city (the citizens had just had a party to celebrate their imagined victory) to the hiding Greek warriors. The Greeks sack the city, and win the ten-year war against Troy.

In Part II of Homer's epic story of the Trojan War and its aftermath, the *Odyssey*, Odysseus has to deal with all sorts of divine and semidivine beings on his voyage home, ranging from his mortal enemy the sea god Poseidon, the benefactor of the Trojans during the war, who throws storms at Odysseus's ships, to the divine nymph Calypso, who uses her beauty and wiles to keep Odysseus on her enchanted isle for ten years. After many trials and tribulations, Odysseus triumphs over all of this divine host and returns home to Ithaca to exact revenge on some local aristocrats who want to marry his wife Penelope and steal his kingdom.

The lesson of Homer's epic poems is ambiguous. Yes, the gods control natural processes such as the weather and oceans, influence human fate, and can dispatch less wary humans with ease. Nevertheless, cunning heroes like Odysseus can actually outwit them, although he did have some help from Athena, his patron on Mount Olympus, when he returned to Ithaca. Homer's gods are not omnipotent or omniscient. There are limits to both their powers and their knowledge.

After Homer came the poet Hesiod, who in his poem the *Theogony* (written about 725 BC) describes the origins of the cosmos and the gods. Here is a brief selection from his account of creation:

> Hail, daughters of Zeus! Give me sweet song,
> To celebrate the holy race of gods
> Who live forever, sons of starry Heaven
> And Earth, and gloomy Night, and salty Sea.
> Tell how the gods and the earth arose at first,
> And rivers and the boundless swollen sea
> And shining stars, and the broad heaven above,
> And how the gods divided up their wealth
> And how they shared their honours, how they first
> Captured Olympus with its many folds.
> Tell me things, Olympian Muses, tell
> From the beginning, which first came to be?
> Chaos was first of all, but next appeared
> Broad-bosomed Earth, sure standing-place for all
> The gods who live on snowy Olympus' peak,
> And misty Tartarus, in a recess
> Of broad-pathed earth, and Love, most beautiful
> Of all the deathless gods. He makes men weak,
> He overpowers the clever mind, and tames
> The spirit in the breasts of men and gods.
> From Chaos came black night and Erebos.*
> And Night in turn gave birth to Day and Space
> Whom she conceived in love to Erebos.
> And Earth bore starry Heaven, first, to be
> An equal to herself, to cover her
> All over, and to be a resting-place,
> Always secure, for all the blessed gods.
> Then she brought forth long hills, the lovely homes
> Of goddesses, the Nymphs who live among
> The mountain clefts. Then, without pleasant love,
> She bore the barren sea with its swollen waves,
> Pontus . . .†

As we can see, Hesiod uses the gods as stand-ins for natural processes, calling the primal condition of the universe Chaos, out of which our world was born. He equates human forces like love with physical things such as night, day, and the oceans. In Hesiod, as in Homer, divine and natural forces are tightly intertwined. The

*Part of the underworld.
†*Theogony,* lines 104–133, from *Hesiod and Theogonis,* trans. Dorothea Wender (Penguin Books, 1973).

sharp blade of rational thinking first provided by some ponderers who lived in a non-descript Greek town in Asia Minor would be required to start the long slow process of separating the gods from nature.

To help you navigate your way through this chapter (hopefully in less time than Odysseus took to get home to Ithaca), there follows a chart of all the major Greek philosophers from the beginning of philosophical thinking beginning around 600 BC to the death of Alexander the Great in 323 BC.* Note that where the philosopher's dates are only rough guesses, they are enclosed in square brackets.

## Ancient Greek Philosophers from the Beginning until the Time of Alexander the Great

| PHILOSOPHER | DATES (BC) | "SCHOOL" | MAIN IDEAS |
|---|---|---|---|
| *Cosmological Period* | *600–425* | | *Investigated nature, the kosmos. Explained natural phenomena without bringing in the gods.* |
| Thales of Miletus | [625–545] | Milesian | Astronomer. Predicted 585 BC eclipse of sun. Basic element is water. Earth a disk floating on a vast sea. |
| Anaximander of Miletus | [610–547] | Milesian | Things come and go from *apeiron,* a state of boundless indeterminancy. World a drum floating in space. Higher life evolved from the sea. |
| Anaximenes of Miletus | [588–524] | Milesian | Air the primary element. Change caused by rarefaction and condensation. World rests on air. |
| Pythagoras of Samos | [570–500] | Pythagorean and Milesian | Founder of mystic sect practicing vegetarianism, purification rites. All things are numbers. Believed in metempsychosis, the transmigration of the souls. |
| Heraclitus of Ephesus | [540–475] | None (Ionian) | Everything in flux. Can't step in the same river twice. The world an everlasting fire. War or strife the father of all. The unity of opposites (the *Logos).* |
| Parmenides of Elea | [515–450] | Eleatic | True Being is a static, unchanging, eternal, homogeneous sphere. Reason tells us motion, change, and the world of the senses are illusions. |
| Zeno of Elea | [488–430] | Eleatic | Paradoxes of space, time, and motion disproved common sense idea of cosmos as always changing. |
| Empedocles of Acragas | [490–430] | Semi-Eleatic | Accepted Parmenides' view of Being, but wanted to explain change. Love and Strife the great cosmic forces, uniting and separating the "roots": earth, air, fire, water. Theory of evolution from the fishes. |
| Anaxagoras of Clazomenae | [500–428] | Materialist (Atomist) | World made up of tiny indivisible "seeds" of different sizes, shapes, colors. Generation and destruction from spatial rearrangement |

*As we've seen in the Introduction, there were important Greek thinkers such as Epicurus and the Stoics who lived during the "Hellenistic" period (the third and second centuries BC) who we won't cover here.

| PHILOSOPHER | DATES (BC) | "SCHOOL" | MAIN IDEAS |
|---|---|---|---|
| | | | of seeds. *Nous* (mind) are the purest seeds, governing all. There is a mixture of everything in everything else. |
| Democritus of Abdera | [460–370] | Atomist | Follower of Leucippus. World made up of uncuttable, indestructible atoms. Change caused by their mechanical movement. Soul atoms made of fire; consciousness comes from inhaling them. |
| *Anthropological Period* | *425–300* | | *Focus turns away from physical nature to ethical, political, and aesthetic questions.* |
| Protagoras of Abdera | [480–411] | Sophist | "Man is the measure of all things": the individual the sole source of truth. Ethical relativist, agnostic. Took money to teach sons of the rich how to argue. |
| Socrates of Athens | 470–399 | Socratic | Truth gained through reason and dialogue. Used a "dialectical method" to challenge orthodox beliefs. The unexamined life not worth living. Be a gadfly. Questioned traditional views of the gods. |
| Plato of Athens | 427–327 | Socratic/ Pythagorean (Platonist) | Revered mathematics. Theory of forms: conceptual knowledge higher than opinions based on senses. Tripartite soul (reason, spirit, animal passions). Justice as harmony of the whole. Philosopher-kings. |
| Aristotle of Stagira | 384–322 | Aristotelian | More empirical than Plato. Invented logical syllogism. Ten categories of judgment. Four types of causes. Substance = matter + form. God as Unmoved Mover. Virtue in ethics: follow the golden mean. "Man is a political animal." |

## The Cosmological Period of Ancient Greek Thought: The Pre-Socratics

The early Greek philosophers, who started their thinking about 600 BC in Ionia, the southwest coast of Asia Minor (modern Turkey), were *"phusikoi"*—from which the English word "physicist" evolved—speculators about science and nature. They were interested in the "nature" of things and thus were both philosophers and scientists. Modern scholars call this group of thinkers *pre-Socratics,* as they lived, for the most part, before Socrates.

The pre-Socratics were interested not only in the material processes of nature but also in the origin of the *kosmos* or universe as a whole and how human beings relate to it. They were also very practical men. Thales is reputed to have made a killing in the olive oil market, Anaximander drew the first map and founded a colony, while Thales, Heraclitus, Parmenides, and Empedocles were all, at least for a time, active politicians. In fact, Empedocles was reputed to have magical powers that could cure the sick, which made him very popular in his hometown of Acragas in Sicily.

It's difficult to speculate on the degree to which these thinkers were influenced by each other's ideas. The ancient writers who recounted their ideas in the centuries after the pre-Socratics' lifetimes certainly believed that they were familiar with each other's ideas, and formed them into schools. In some cases there were quite solid connections between them. The three Milesian philosophers, Thales, Anaximander, and Anaximenes, were closely associated: Thales taught Anaximander, who then taught Anaximenes. In addition, Pythagoras is reputed to have been a follower of Anaximenes; Parmenides was almost certainly reacting against Heraclitus's doctrines; and Zeno was clearly a follower of Parmenides.

In the readings we'll look in some detail at the fragments and secondhand accounts of two key triads of pre-Socratic thought: first, the Milesian school of Thales, Anaximander, and Anaximenes; then the "Great Speculators" on Being and Becoming: Heraclitus, Parmenides, and Empedocles. First, however, we shall take a quick look at all the major pre-Socratics and at the three great thinkers in the period that immediately followed them, namely, Socrates, Plato, and Aristotle.*

## THE IONIAN PHYSICISTS: THALES, ANAXIMANDER, ANAXIMENES, AND PYTHAGORAS

The first philosopher in Western history was Thales of Miletus. We know that he was active in the early sixth century, because he predicted the eclipse of 585 BC. Thales taught his fellow Milesian Anaximander, who, in turn, taught Anaximenes. We'll learn more about Thales and the Milesians later. Suffice it to say here that each of these early Ionian thinkers searched for a single material cause, an *archē,* for the cosmos. Thales suggested water, Anaximenes air, while Anaximander thought that the physical world came from the *apeiron,* a boundless indeterminancy. Anaximander also put forward a theory of evolution of land animals from sea life.

A fourth pre-Socratic thinker loosely related to the Milesians was Pythagoras (ca. 570–500 BC). He was born on the island of Samos in the Aegean Sea (and was thus Ionian) and was reputed to be a follower of Anaximenes. Pythagoras left Samos for Croton in Italy when he was thirty, forming a secret society there with strange rules like not eating beans, and less strange ones like not eating animal flesh. These practices were based on his idea of *metempsychosis,* the transmigration of souls. According to this idea, at death the soul is released from the body and migrates into a new one, which could be an animal body. This depends on how one lived one's life. This idea resembles the ancient Indian idea of a cycle of rebirth based on accumulated karma, though we have no evidence that Pythagoras had any knowledge of Eastern religion.

Pythagoras was a shadowy figure. He apparently wrote no books. His philosophy was transmitted to us by his pupils, who usually prefaced their account with the phrase "as the master says." So we can't really distinguish Pythagoras's own ideas from the elaborations of his disciples. One important theme should be mentioned, however: the idea that the cosmos is made up of numbers, or can be understood in purely quantitative terms. The Pythagoreans apparently got this idea from observing the mathematical relationship between notes produced by a lute and where on the fret board one fingers it. They reasoned that perhaps the universe as a whole follows

---

*We will cover these six pre-Socratic thinkers only very briefly here; they will be discussed in more detail later in this chapter.

this principle and is regulated by a cosmic harmony. This mysticism concerning numbers and mathematics eventually found its way to Athens and into Plato's philosophy. Plato believed that mathematical ideas were a higher form of knowledge than sense perceptions, and he forbade entrance to his Academy to anyone who didn't have at least a smattering of mathematical knowledge.

## THE GREAT SPECULATORS: HERACLITUS, PARMENIDES, ZENO, AND EMPEDOCLES

The second phase of pre-Socratic thought can be characterized as a great debate between the advocates of Becoming and Being, and the related question of the One and the Many.* Heraclitus of Ephesus, a city in Ionia, argued that all things in nature were constantly in flux and that the primary material element in the cosmos was fire. He also argued that a rational principle he called the *Logos* ruled over this change.

Parmenides of Elea used logic and reason to argue that Being (everything, that is) was a static, eternal, and perfect Sphere, despite the changes in nature that we think we witness by means of our senses. Something can't come from nothing, he said, so everything must already exist, already *be.* The separate nature of things, time, space, and motion are all illusions that disappear once we realize that all things are One.

His follower Zeno of Elea provided his patron with several paradoxes of multiplicity and motion that supported Parmenides' idea of an unchanging Being. Here are three of them:

1. If you cut a line in half, you get two sections; if you cut each section in half, you get four subsections; and so forth, to infinity. Because we cannot come to an end point in this process, Zeno felt that this proves that the line can't be made up of a multiplicity of points.
2. More famously, he said that, to get to point $X$, one must first get halfway there, to $Y$. But to get halfway there, to $Y$, one must first get a quarter of the way there, to $Z$. And to get to $Z$, one must first. . . . In short, in a finite amount time one would have to pass by an infinite number of points in space, which is impossible. Hence, motion is an illusion.
3. Achilles, a fast runner, and a turtle are racing. The turtle takes an early lead, no doubt due to Achilles' disdain for the turtle's racing prowess. Achilles tries to catch up. However, by the time he reaches the point where the turtle presently is, let's call it $X$, the crafty turtle has moved forward some finite distance, to point $Y$. When Achilles tries to reach point $Y$, the turtle has already moved on to $Z$, and so on. According to Zeno, Achilles never catches the turtle, because the plucky reptile always moves at least a small finite distance forward in any given amount of time.

The message of Zeno's paradoxes was that change, motion, and the identity of distinct things in the cosmos are illusions and, thus, that Parmenides was right: Being is, unchanging, and eternal. The One truly exists, whereas the many-natured appearance of things in the world is an illusion.

Empedocles of Acragas, a city in Sicily, tried to combine both Being and Becoming by agreeing with Parmenides that Being is, that nothing new comes into the

*That is to say, whether reality was one big whole, or made up of disparate substances.

cosmos, but that things inside of Being change owing to the efforts of Love and Strife, cosmic principles of attraction and repulsion. He also formalized the various elements of nature into four: earth, air, fire, and water, suggesting the idea that all things in the cosmos are various combinations of these elements. Lastly, he was reputed to have had mysterious powers of healing and proposed once again the idea that land animals evolved from marine life.

## THE LATER PHYSICISTS: ANAXAGORAS, LEUCIPPUS, AND DEMOCRITUS

We will not cover this later group of pre-Socratics (who weren't strictly speaking pre-Socratics at all, because they were all still alive during Socrates' lifetime) in the readings below. All the same, they represent the last, most developed phase in ancient Greek cosmological thinking. Anaxagoras of Clamonzae was known chiefly for his idea that all things were made up of various combinations of indivisible, imperishable "seeds." For him, all things contained at least trace amounts of all the different types of seeds. We name things according to their predominant element; for example, a gold ring is called "gold" because most of the seeds that make it up are gold seeds.

Anaxagoras's real innovation was the introduction of the idea of *nous* (Mind), which he believed was a thin, unmixed fluid that caused change and motion in the cosmos. He generally agreed with Parmenides' idea that nothing new comes into existence and that material things in the world are merely recombinations of old matter. Anaxagoras was charged with impiety by opponents of his friend Pericles shortly after the outbreak of the Peloponnesian War for his belief that the moon, sun, and stars were just rocks in the sky and not gods. He was right about this, by the way.

Leucippus, whose birthplace and dates are unknown, founded the atomist school. We know very little about his individual ideas, so for an account of atomism we have to look at his follower Democritus's work. In chronological terms, Democritus is not a true pre-Socratic, because he lived for almost three decades after Socrates' death. However, in terms of his interest in explaining the physical cosmos, he certainly was.

Democritus, who was thought to have visited Egypt, Persia, and India, was from Abdera, in Thrace. He thought that the world was made up of indivisible, indestructible atoms and that things changed due to their mechanical movement, their attractions, repulsions, collisions, sticking together, falling apart. He thought that we perceive external objects because of the images (perhaps bundles of atoms) they emanate and that our souls are made up of globe-shaped atoms of fire, further refining Heraclitus's old view. With the atomists, we come to the end of pre-Socratic thought, and its goal of trying to understand the physical cosmos.

# The Anthropological Period: Man as the Measure of All Things

## THE GREAT SHIFT

From about 425 to 300 BC, most of the important Greek thinkers turned their attention away from explaining physical nature toward a rigorous investigation of human life and the values associated with it. This included investigations of morality, politics, religion, and aesthetics; but it also included a study of the human thought process itself, including the basis of knowledge (epistemology) and the best way to think through philosophical problems (logic). Plato and Aristotle discussed all these issues, often in great detail. Before we get to them, however, we should first mention the thinkers who formed the foundation of their thought, the Sophists and Socrates.

## THE SOPHISTS

The Sophists were teachers of rhetoric who taught the sons of rich Athenian families how to speak and argue in the law courts and assembly, for which efforts they were handsomely rewarded with cold cash. In some cases, they did the arguing themselves, as a modern lawyer would for a client. Generally speaking, they were relativists. Like lawyers, their moral position depended on who was paying them.

The best-known Sophist was Protagoras of Abdera, Democritus's hometown. His most famous pronouncement was "Man [i.e., the individual person] is the measure of all things, of what is, that it is; of what is not, that it is not." In other words, everyone was his or her own best judge of the truth. Like most of the Sophists, Protagoras was an ethical relativist: Right and wrong depended on context. For him, there were no universal moral truths.

Protagoras visited Athens in the 440s and 430s, and debated with Pericles. He wrote many books, including *Truth* and *On the Gods.* In 411 BC, he was charged with impiety because in *On the Gods* he admitted that he didn't know whether the gods existed. As his punishment, he was banished. Socrates' view of philosophy was in part a reaction against the Sophists' cynicism and relativism.

## SOCRATES

The greatest minds of ancient Greece were the trinity of Socrates, Plato, and Aristotle, with whom we'll become better acquainted in later sections of this chapter. Socrates lived his entire life in Athens. His example created the image of the philosopher as a pesky gadfly who questioned his fellow Athenians about moral, political, and religious questions using a "dialectical" method. In this process, he often appeared to be a skeptic, questioning the validity of popular religious, social, and political beliefs. He opposed the Sophists both because they took money for what they did and because they pretended to give valuable knowledge to their pupils.

Socrates claimed that the oracle of Delphi told a friend of his that he was the wisest man in all of Greece because he knew that he knew nothing, or, in positive terms, that he was critical of not only others' beliefs but of his own as well. He was convinced that the "unexamined life was not worth living." He paid for his convictions in 399 BC when he was found guilty of impiety toward the gods and of corrupting the youth of Athens, and was sentenced to death when he suggested the ironic alternative penalty of free meals in the city gymnasium for life. Socrates was fond of irony, which is often lost on dim-witted and overly serious people. He willingly drank a cup of hemlock to carry out his own punishment, and left behind a noble example of a philosopher who courageously pursued rational knowledge in the face of popular hostility. Socrates wrote no books, but he had a number of friends who did, including Plato, who made him the hero of most of his philosophical dialogues.

## PLATO

Socrates' most illustrious follower was Plato, who wrote a series of dialogues in which Socrates was usually the main character (although they also contained other historical figures, including other philosophers, statesmen, and Plato's brothers). Plato was influenced by Socrates' dialectical method of question and answer, thinking that rational truth was attainable by means of this method. In addition, he was influenced by the Pythagoreans' notion that the cosmos could be understood as a collection of numbers, and by the Eleatics' idea that the senses are unreliable guides to the truth, which can only be known by reason.

He combined these insights into his theory of forms or ideas. Our senses, said Plato, show us many distinct things—chairs, dogs, tables, rivers, and so on. Yet connecting these distinct things, he argued, there must be basic concepts that allow us to recognize them as members of classes of things, concepts that he called "forms." These forms he took as real, not just as human inventions. We recognize that Rover, Fido, and Spot are all "dogs" because the form of "dogginess" presides over them, in some ethereal realm beyond our senses.

Not surprisingly, Plato thought that the purest forms of knowledge were mathematics and geometry, for the truths contained in these sciences didn't seem to depend on the senses at all. We don't have to sketch out a myriad of triangles to know that they will all have three sides, or that all have three angles that add up to 180 degrees. In the same way, 2+3 will always equal 5, regardless of whether the moon is purple or monkeys develop the ability to speak French. Insofar as Plato believed in the absolute reality of these forms or ideas, we can call him an "idealist."

As for his ethics and politics, he believed that the human soul could be divided into three parts: our reason, our higher emotions (such as courage), and our animal appetites. Naturally, we should desire that reason control the chariot of the soul and not let the wild horses of our animal passions carry us away (as he outlines in his dialogue *Phaedrus*). Similarly, the best political state would be one that is divided into three classes: the philosopher-kings, who use reason in their deliberations; the soldiers, who evoke courage in their duties; and the artisans and workers, whose highest virtue is self-control. If these classes were to learn to work and live in harmony, then we could call such a state "just." We'll learn more about Plato's epistemological and political views when we read selections from *The Republic,* his masterwork.

## ARISTOTLE

The last of the great Greek philosophers of antiquity is Aristotle, who, like Democritus and Protagoras, came from Thrace, in northeastern Greece. Aristotle was more empirical than his teacher Plato. He performed many scientific studies, including ones on the parts of animals, marine life, human biology, psychology, and political constitutions. He and his students catalogued and described 158 different constitutions of current and past states, of which only the *Constitution of Athens* remains—a copy of it written on papyrus was found in the Egyptian desert in the nineteenth century.

Aristotle criticized Plato's theory of forms. He didn't believe that the forms of things were separable from their physical matter, existing in a pure realm of ideas. Instead, the form of Fido, that he's a dog, can be seen in his barking, his general shape, his smelly paws, and so on. These things can't be separated from the matter that makes him up.

In addition, Aristotle invented the logical syllogism, and argued that there were four types of causes: the material, formal, efficient, and final causes. Science today would only recognize efficient causes as, properly speaking, causes at all. His notion of "final causes," the idea that things in nature have goals and purposes (e.g., an acorn has the *telos* or goal of becoming an oak tree), made him very popular in the Middle Ages, when he was referred to simply as "The Philosopher." The medieval mind relished his idea that nature was teleological, for it saw purpose as implanted in things by God.

Speaking of God, for Aristotle he was an "unmoved mover," not a curmudgeonly old fellow with a beard who hurled thunderbolts at mortals that didn't propitiate him. Aristotle's God was rather colorless, a vague force that started the whole cosmic ball rolling, but didn't do too much on a day-to-day basis.

In ethics, Aristotle promoted the virtuous life, which he defined largely as the pursuit of the "golden mean." By this, he meant taking a middle course between two extremes. For example, Aristotle would have advocated not being either a drunkard or a total abstainer, but being a moderate consumer of alcoholic beverages. Similarly, courage is the golden mean between cowardice, on the one hand, and rashness in the face of enormous odds against you, on the other.

Aristotle lived much of his life in Athens, and founded the Lyceum, a rival university to Plato's Academy. He also tutored Alexander the Great. When Alexander died in 323 BC, the Athenians revolted against Macedon. Aristotle was accused of impiety for his connection to Alexander, so he left town, saving the Athenians (as he put it) from sinning against philosophy a second time.

# AN OVERVIEW OF THE PRE-SOCRATICS

## *Some General Comments*

The pre-Socratic philosophers, as we've already seen, were those ancient Greek thinkers who were active up to Socrates' heyday, from roughly 600 to 430 BC. We can make a number of generalizations about their goals and methods:

1. Their main goal was to examine, in what they took to be a rational and scientific way, the nature of the *kosmos,* the physical universe. This included inanimate physical nature, the weather, astronomical bodies, plants and animal life, and the human body. They asked questions such as, Where did all this come from? How does it change? Can it be resolved into one or a finite number of basic physical elements, what Aristotle would later call an *archē?*
2. They asked these questions without making reference to the pagan gods of the Greek tradition. Saying that lightning bolts came from Zeus or that tidal waves were caused by the angry sea god Poseidon wasn't very useful to the pre-Socratics. They wanted an entirely *natural* explanation of these phenomena.

3. They were fascinated by change in nature, and slowly began to see change as the product of natural laws. This paradigm shift to the notion that nature acts in regular and comprehensible ways, and that sacrificing goats to Apollo or praying to Athena will have no effect on these changes, is perhaps the most profound one ever made in the history of our species.

4. Further, they started to link scientific explanations of natural phenomena with the ability to use technology to improve human life: Thales used astronomy and mathematics to aid in navigation, Anaximander drew a map of the Greek world, and Empedocles developed human medicine (though most of it was little better than quackery). They were, in short, practical men, in addition to being philosophers and scientists.

## The Sources

None of the complete original books written by the pre-Socratic philosophers has survived intact, so a bit of archeological work must be done to unearth their ideas. There are several sources we can call on:

*Fragments* of their original works directly quoted in various ancient philosophers and writers, collected and numbered in Diels and Kranz's *The Presocratics*. The numbers in square brackets below refer to the fragment numbers used by Deils and Kranz in their "B" edition, which has become the standard system for numbering the pre-Socratic fragments.

The *doxographers*. These are ancient writers who have quoted from Theophrastrus's work *Physicorum opioniones (Opinions of the Physicists)* more or less accurately. Theophrastrus (371–287 BC) was Aristotle's most eminent student; but only his essay *On the Senses* from the *Opinions* survives intact. His *Opinions* was used as a standard "textbook" for early Greek philosophy for centuries, and was quoted by many later authors. The doxographers include:

- Simplicius (ca. AD 600–640), author of a *Commentary on the Physics* of Aristotle, a valuable book of about 1,000 pages, which contains many references to the pre-Socratics
- Hippolytus (ca. AD 180–235), the Christian author of *Refutation of All Heresies,* another important source for the pre-Socratics
- Plutarch (ca. AD 45–120), the author of various moral essays
- A shady figure referred to as the "pseudo-Plutarch" (second century AD), author of *The Scientific Beliefs of the Philosophers*

In the few cases where we've quoted the doxographers, we've included their name and the book from which the quotation was taken.

The *biographers,* the most famous being Diogenes Laertius (third century AD), author of a chatty, but not entirely reliable book called *Lives of the Philosophers.* Also, we get glimpses of some of the pre-Socratics (notably Thales and Pythagoras) in Herodotus's *Histories,* which are ostensibly about the Persian invasions of the early fifth century BC, but which also contain many digressions on the myths, history, and customs of various ancient cultures. Herodotus (ca. 485–420 BC) seems to have recorded just about every interesting story he was ever told, including some on other thinkers and writers up to his own day.

Descriptions of the doctrines of the pre-Socratics in complete philosophical works, notably those of Plato and Aristotle (his *Metaphysics* and *Physics* are especially useful).

Unless otherwise noted, the translations of the pre-Socratics in this chapter (including both the fragments and the ancient commentaries) are based on those in John Burnet's *Early Greek Philosophy,* 3rd ed. (London, 1920). We've compared Burnet's translations with the following sources, in many cases making minor alterations: (1) G. S. Kirk and J. E. Raven's *The Presocratic Philosophers* (Cambridge University Press, 1957), an extensive source which contains both the original Greek and English translations; (2) Jonathan Barnes's *Early Greek Philosophy* (Penguin, 1987), which includes much doxography and puts the existing fragments back into the secondary texts they were extracted from (remember that we have none of the original works of the pre-Socratics); (3) Kathleen Freeman's *Ancilla to the Presocratics Philosophers* (1948); and (4) several secondary sources on ancient Greek thought. We've eliminated Burnet's use of old English flourishes, re-inserted a few original Greek terms with suggested translations, and reconstructed a sentence here and there for greater clarity.

Now let's turn back the clock to around 600 BC, and visit the town of Miletus in Asia Minor to see what the fuss about this new thing called "philosophy" is all about.

# THALES AND THE MILESIANS CONTEMPLATE THE COSMOS

## *Prologue on Ionia*

The Ionians, who spoke a distinct dialect of Greek and dominated the coasts of the Aegean Sea, including its islands and the western coast of Asia Minor (now Turkey), saw themselves, not entirely without justification, to be the sophisticates of seventh- and sixth-century BC Greece. They were more refined and cultured than their "boorish" Dorian cousins on the Greek mainland: Indeed, of the major ancient Greek thinkers, only Empedocles came from a city speaking the Dorian dialect. Later this role would shift to the Athenians, who themselves spoke the Ionian dialect. To begin the story of philosophy, we have to turn to Ionia, specifically to the city-state of Miletus, in southwestern Asia Minor.

Ionia lived in an uneasy relationship with its more powerful neighbors, first with the Kingdom of Lydia, a minor empire that controlled much of central Asia Minor between the early seventh century and 546 BC, then with Lydia's conqueror, the mighty Persian Empire, which dominated Asia Minor, Syria, Mesopotamia, and Persia itself in the last half of the sixth century and the early part of the fifth century BC. Yet despite this uneasy relationship with its neighbors, the Ionian cities were vital, vibrant places, centers of trade, art, science, and philosophy from the revival of Greek civilization around 700 BC until the collapse of the Ionian Revolt against Persia and the destruction of Miletus by the Persians in 494 BC.

Because most of the information we have on the early Ionian philosophers isn't directly from their fragments, but from secondary sources, we will indicate what purport to be direct quotations from them with italics and fragment numbers in [square brackets]. Remember, with the Milesians we are dealing as much with legend as with fact.

## Thales' Wet Cosmos

Thales (ca. 625–545 BC) was a native of Miletus, in the southwest corner of Asia Minor, in Ionia. He was the first real philosopher in Western history. He was also an engineer, inventor, mathematician, politician, and financial speculator, among other things, being considered one of the Seven Wise Men of the day. Depending on whom one reads, he either wrote nothing or wrote a book called *Nautical Astronomy*. We can date his life with some accuracy thanks to Herodotus, who said that he predicted the eclipse of 585 BC, putting an end to the war between the Lydians and the Medes. He may have gotten his eclipse-predicting skills from Babylonian astronomy, though predicting an eclipse at any exact point on the planet's surface was a tricky business in Thales' day. His prediction may have been as much a lucky guess as precise astronomical calculation.

Many stories, some of them no doubt wild exaggerations, about Thales can be found in the work of ancient writers. He was reported to have made a killing in the olive oil market when he bought up all the olive presses in his area, anticipating a bumper crop. He is also reported by Herodotus to have proposed a federation of Ionian city-states with its capital at Teos in order to defend the area against the Ionians' more powerful, unfriendly neighbors. He is said to have visited Egypt, and introduced Egyptian geometry to Greece. In fact, he apparently used triangulation to determine the distance of ships out at sea. He is also said to have taught Milesian sailors how to steer their ships by the constellation Ursa Minor (the Little Bear). One day, according to one writer of ancient tabloids, he fell down a well while staring up at the heavens, making astronomical observations.

Thales started the Ionian tradition of attributing the structure of the cosmos to a single material cause or foundational principle, what Aristotle would over 200 years later call an *archē* (from which comes the English word "archeology," the study of early or "founding" civilizations). In his case, this basic substance was water, as Aristotle tells us:

> Of the first philosophers, then, most thought the principles which were of the nature of matter were the only principles of all things . . . [they thought that] there must be some entity—either one or more than one—from which all other things come to be, it being conserved.
>
> Yet they do not all agree as to the number and the nature of these principles. Thales, the founder of this type of philosophy, says the *archē* [first principle or material cause] is water (for which reason he declared that the earth rests on water), getting the notion perhaps from seeing that the nutriment of all things is moist, and that heat itself is generated from the moist and kept alive by it (and that from which they come to be is a principle of all things). He got his notion from this fact, and from the fact that the seeds of all things have a moist nature, and that water is the origin of the nature of moist things. (Aristotle, *Metaphysics* 983b, W. D. Ross translation)

As Aristotle suggests, the idea that everything came from water isn't as crazy as it sounds. After all, water can take various forms: As ice, it is solid; as steam or a mist, it is gaseous; while in its "natural" state, it is liquid. Most of the earth is covered with water. In fact, humans are roughly 70 percent water, with some flesh and bones mixed in to keep all that gushing liquid in place. As a first guess at the basic substance of the universe, Thales' idea of a wet cosmos was a reasonable one.

Further, Thales (according to Aristotle) thought that the earth was a flat disk floating on a great sea, like a log. Aristotle goes on to ask (in *On the Heavens)* if this is true, then what holds up this vast sea which, in turn, supports the earth?

The only other inkling we have of Thales' ideas are secondary reports that he believed that "all things are full of gods," which may have meant that he was a pantheist. He was also reported to have said that magnets are alive, for they have the power of moving iron. Whatever he meant by these last two cryptic remarks, we can be reasonably sure that Thales was the first thinker in Western history who tried to explain natural phenomena such as eclipses, lightning, earthquakes, rainbows, and clouds on their own terms, without bringing in the gods. With Thales, we enter the "cosmological" period of ancient Greek thought. The gods recede into the background, as natural science is born, the Milesian philosophers acting as its midwife.

## Anaximander's Unbounded Cosmos

Anaximander (ca. 610–547 BC) was also a native of Miletus, and was a student of Thales. He is credited with making the first map (to help out Milesian mariners), introducing the sundial to the Greeks, and founding a colony at Apollonia on the Black Sea. He wrote a book on nature of which only one very slim fragment remains.

Anaximander wasn't satisfied with attributing all physical things and changes in the universe to one substance, as Thales did with water. Instead, he claimed that underlying all physical things was an *indefinite, infinite, or unbounded substance* called the *apeiron.* Here is Simplicius's account of Anaximander's first cause or principle, the *apeiron,* which contains the first fragment of philosophical writing in Western history that remains to us:

> Anaximander of Miletus, son of Praxiades, a fellow citizen and associate of Thales, said that the *archē* [material cause or principle] and first element of things was the *apeiron* [infinite, indefinite, unbounded], he being the first to introduce this name of the material principle. He says it is neither water nor any other of the so-called elements, but a substance different from them which is infinite, from which arise all the heavens and the worlds within them. And into that from which things take their rise they pass away once more, as is proper; for [1] *"they make reparation and satisfaction to one another for their injustice according to the ordering of time,"* as he says in these somewhat poetical terms. (Simplicius, *Commentary on the Physics* 24.13–25)

Simplicius goes on to note that Anaximander noticed how the four "elements" (of earth, air, fire, and water) turned into each other, yet didn't want to make any one of them the basic element of the cosmos (the *archē*), choosing instead the *apeiron.* They turn into each other by some vague process of "eternal motion," the cause of the origin of worlds, too. However, it wasn't until Empedocles that the Greeks distinguished these elements as individual substances. The Milesians would mix in other substances such as clouds, wind, or ether from time to time with the four "basic" elements (earth, air, fire, water) in their descriptions of natural phenomena.

One could easily argue that Anaximander's idea of the *apeiron* is a more satisfying explanation of the cosmos than Thales' water-centered position. After all, if everything came from water, given an infinite amount of time, wouldn't cold and wet things eventually win the day over dry and hot things, and create an eternally cold and wet cosmos? Where did air and fire come from in the first place? The idea of a boundless, infinite, indestructible "substratum" (to use Aristotle's term) for the cosmos accounted for the variety of things in the universe somewhat better than did a massive pool of water.

Reconstructing his ideas a bit from the available secondhand reports, Anaximander seems to have thought that at first there was only the *apeiron,* the unbounded. Then eddies or vortices in the *apeiron* formed, with the heavier elements—as is natural in a spinning cone or swirling eddy—tending toward the center. Thus, the hot (fire) and cold (earth and water) elements were separated off, the fire forming a sort of force field around the colder planet earth at the center of the great cosmic eddy. In fact, at first the planet was covered entirely with water; but the sun burned off some of this water, creating winds. The hot region of space formed itself into rings or wheels of fire, surrounded by air, these rings "breathing out flames at a certain point through orifices" (as the doxographer Aetius puts it), which we see as the moon, sun, and stars. The earth was at the center of the great cosmic eddy, and is shaped like a cylinder or drum, its depth one-third of its breadth.

Lastly, we can reasonably assign to Anaximander a primitive theory of human evolution from lower life-forms, long before Charles Darwin had any such notion. Here are some secondary reports that sketch Anaximander's fantastic fable of the fish people:

> Living creatures arose from the moist element as it was evaporated by the sun. Man was like another animal, namely, a fish, in the beginning. (Hippolytus, *Refutations of All Heresies* I.6)

> The first animals were produced in the moisture, each enclosed in a prickly bark. As they advanced in age, they came out upon the drier part. When the bark broke off, they survived for a short time. (Pseudo-Plutarch, *On the Scientific Beliefs of the Philosophers* 908D)

> He declares that at first human beings arose in the inside of fishes, and after having been reared like sharks, and become capable of protecting themselves, they were finally cast ashore and took to land. (Plutarch, *Table Talk* 730)

How did he come to the startling conclusion that human beings had evolved from fishes? He reasoned if human beings always had to nurse as long as they do now, they would never have survived the struggle for existence:

> Further, he says that originally man was born from animals of another species. His reason is that while other animals quickly find food by themselves, man alone requires a lengthy period of suckling. Hence, had he been originally as he is now, he would never have survived. (Pseudo-Plutarch, *Miscellanies* 179.2)

Thus, Anaximander improved upon Thales' wet cosmos by offering the *apeiron* as its material cause, adding to this a fairly complex account of the earth, moon, sun, and other heavenly bodies, along with a theory of human evolution that was primitive yet pregnant with future possibilities.

## *Anaximenes' Airy Cosmos*

The third Milesian philosopher we will consider here is the most lightly regarded by contemporary scholars, even though he was held in high regard in antiquity. Anaximenes (ca. 588–524 BC) reverted to Thales' notion that one could point to a basic material principle or cause to explain the cosmos. In his case, he chose *air.*

His real innovation was his theory of rarefaction and condensation to explain how things in the cosmos change. Hippolytus, after discussing how air is invisible when most uniform, yet always in motion, says of Anaximenes' view of air:

> When it is dilated so as to be rarer, it becomes fire; while winds, on the other hand, are condensed Air. Cloud is formed from Air by compression; and this, still further condensed, becomes water. Water, condensed still more, turns to earth; and when condensed as much as it can be, to stones. (Hippolytus, *Refutations of All Heresies* I.7)

We can construct a simple linear diagram to show how this process of rarefaction and condensation worked:

← *Rarefaction*            *Condensation* →

Fire ← Air ← Winds ← Clouds ← Water ← Earth ← Stones

This view, though perhaps a retreat from Anaximander's more sophisticated view of the cosmos as grounded in the *apeiron,* still had some merit. After all, our souls are made of air (as Anaximenes tells us directly), so air is connected with the human principle of intelligence. Why shouldn't air be the basic principle of the cosmos?

> [2] *Just as . . . our soul, being air, holds us together, so do breath and air encompass the whole world.* (Quoted in the Pseudo-Plutarch, *Scientific Beliefs*)

Further, the earth is like a disk and the sun, moon, and stars like "leaves" floating on the great mass of air. We return to Hippolytus's account of Anaximenes' ideas:

> The earth is flat and rides on air. In the same way the sun and the moon and the other heavenly bodies, which are of a fiery nature, are supported by the air because of their breadth. The heavenly bodies were produced from the earth by moisture rising from it. When this is rarefied, fire comes into being, and the stars are composed of the fire thus raised aloft. There were also bodies of earthy substance in the region of the heavenly bodies, revolving along with them. And he says that the heavenly bodies do not move under the earth, as others suppose, but round it, as a felt cap turns round our head. The sun is hidden from sight, not because it goes under the earth, but because it is concealed by the higher parts of the earth, and because its distance from us becomes greater. The heavenly bodies give no heat because of the greatness of their distance.
>
> Winds are produced when air is condensed and rushes along under propulsion; but when it is concentrated and thickened still more, clouds are generated; and, lastly, it turns to water. (Hippolytus, *Refutations of All Heresies* I.7)

Lastly, Anaximenes offers some fairly scientific accounts of earthly natural phenomena. He says that hail is water from clouds that has solidified; that lightning comes from a parting of the clouds by strong winds, a fiery flash resulting; that rainbows form when sunlight shines on thick, condensed air (water vapor, perhaps), causing different colors; and that earthquakes result when the earth is heated (or dried) and cooled (or made moist) in quick succession. These were pretty good guesses of how these phenomena operate. Anaximenes, although not as original as his predecessors at Miletus, sounds even more "scientific" to the modern ear than Thales and Anaximander, at least if we forgive him his air-centered picture of the cosmos.

All three of the Milesian philosophers shared the same goal: to explain the nature of the cosmos. All three put forward some sort of basic material cause of all things: water, the unbounded, or air. All three framed their explanations in at least crudely scientific terms: Changes in nature were the product of natural forces and not divine intervention.

We now turn away from these early physicists to the much more complex picture offered by three Great Speculators about the nature of the universe.

# THE GREAT SPECULATORS ON BEING AND BECOMING: HERACLITUS, PARMENIDES, AND EMPEDOCLES

## *Heraclitus's Flux*

Heraclitus of Ephesus (ca. 540–475 BC) was a haughty aristocrat who had great contempt both for his fellow citizens and for other Greek writers and thinkers. He wrote a book on nature, theology, and politics probably called *On Nature* that he deposited in the temple of Artemis in his hometown for the benefit of his fellow Ephesians. After the defeat of the Persians by the Greeks, he withdrew to the countryside because he didn't think very highly of the democratic regime that took power in Ephesus. He was known as "The Obscure" for his difficult writing style. Some of his fragments (we'll dispense with italicizing direct quotations from the pre-Socratics from now on) give us a picture of his haughtiness. Here's what he thought of some of his contemporaries:

> [40] The learning of many things does not teach understanding, or else it would have taught Hesiod and Pythagoras, and again Xenophanes and Hecataeus.*

Here's what he thought of the universe as a whole:

> [124] The fairest universe is but a dust-heap piled up at random.

We get more evidence of this haughtiness in the opening lines of *On Nature*:

> [1] Though this *Logos* [word] is forever true, yet men are as unable to understand it when they hear it for the first time as before they have heard it at all. For, though all

---

*Xenophanes of Colophon (about 560–478 BC) was an early Greek poet and philosopher who influenced Parmenides and his followers. He argued against the existence of the immoral, limited gods of pagan Greece in favor of a single all-powerful, all-knowing, moral deity, thus anticipating Parmenides' unlimited, unchanging Sphere of Being.

Hecataeus of Miletus (about 550–480) was an early Greek historian, travel writer, and ambassador who developed map making further from Anaximander's first forays into cartography, and who tried to convince the Ionian cities not to revolt against the Persians. His well-known (at least in ancient times) book *Tour of the World* described the local customs of various cities and peoples throughout Europe and Asia.

things come to pass in accordance with this *Logos* [word or law], men seem as if they had no experience of them, when they make trial of the words and deeds which I expound as I divide each thing according to its kind and show how it truly is. But other men do not know what they are doing when awake, even as they forget what they do when asleep.

Heraclitus was a much more complex thinker than any of the Milesians, and in many ways is the most interesting of the pre-Socratics. He emphasized the reality of change in the cosmos, advocated the unity of opposites (cold and hot, wet and dry, etc.), and put forward what sounds to us today like a theory of moral relativism.

He seems to attach special meaning to the Greek word *logos,* which meant, in general, "word," speech," "reason," "discourse," or "measure." He used it to mean both "word" and "measure," but also as a law-governed process of change that gave order to the cosmos (as we saw previously in Fragment 1). This hidden *Logos* couldn't be discerned by just anyone: It required the special sort of mystical wisdom that Heraclitus himself laid claim to. This *Logos* or law of nature could not be easily perceived:

[2] So we must follow that which is common [i.e., universal]. Yet although my *Logos* [word] is universal, the majority live as if they had a wisdom of their own.

[108] Of all whose discussions I have heard, there is not one who attains to understanding that wisdom is set apart from all.

[107] Eyes and ears are bad witnesses to men if they have barbarian souls [i.e., ones that don't understand their language].

[22] Those who seek for gold dig up much earth and find little.

[123] Nature loves to hide.

Heraclitus is best known for his observation that one cannot step in the same river twice, because the waters making up the river change from second to second. His wider point was that the material world is always in *flux,* always changing, at least according to our senses. This is literally true: Even as you read this text, the cells in your body are slowly changing, plants and animals are growing and dying, and so on. The bigger question here is whether there is any underlying structure or set of laws governing this flux. Here are the relevant fragments from Heraclitus:

[91] You cannot step into the same river twice; for fresh waters are ever flowing in upon you.

[49a] We step and do not step into the same rivers; we are and are not.

As we'll see in the next section, Parmenides took this to mean that the senses couldn't be trusted. Our reason tells us that Being cannot change, even if our senses tell us that rivers flow, winds blow, and people are born, grow old, and die. The Eleatics (Parmenides and his followers) argued against the reality of change. Heraclitus, however, argued that change is real, but is part of a larger "unity of opposites," as we shall soon see. He also argued for the general reliability of the senses, even if he was skeptical about how the masses interpreted their sensory knowledge.

[55] I honour most those things learned by sight and hearing.

Heraclitus returned in part to the Milesian tradition of nominating one of the basic elements as the material cause, the *archē*, of the cosmos. He chose *fire*. He also thought that some sort of cosmic rule governed how this cosmic fire causes change in our world:

> [30] This *kosmos,* which is the same for all, no one of gods or men has made; but it was ever, is now, and ever shall be an ever-living Fire, with measures kindling, and measures going out.

> [90] All things are an exchange for Fire, and Fire for all things, even as wares for gold and gold for wares.

> [76] Fire lives the death of air, and air lives the death of fire; water lives the death of earth, earth that of water.

Furthermore, he seemed to take the idea of fire ruling the cosmos quite literally, viewing it as both a material entity *and* a moral force. It is the agent of the cosmic *Logos.* He writes:

> [16] [Speaking of the invisible fire:] How can one hide from that which never sets?

> [66] Fire in its advance will judge and convict all things.

> [64] [Fire is . . .] the thunderbolt that steers the course of all things.

With his emphasis on flux and fire as the great cosmic forces, and his hostility to democracy and the common folk, it should come as no surprise that Heraclitus thought that strife and war were never-ending phenomena, at the heart of both cosmic and human changes:

> [80] We must know that war is common to all and justice is strife, and that all things come into being and pass away through strife.

> [53] War is the father of all and the king of all; and some he has made gods and some men, some slaves and some free.

> [24] Gods and men honour those who are slain in battle.

Heraclitus's most interesting gambit was to invent the concept of the *unity of opposites,* a concept that would become very important in the nineteenth century as used by G.W. F. Hegel and Karl Marx, two of the leading lights of modern German philosophy. Heraclitus thought that at the basis of cosmic changes was a unity:

> [69] The way up and the way down is one and the same.

> [41] Wisdom is one thing. It is to know the purpose by which all things are steered through all things.

> [50] When you have listened not to me but to the *Logos,* it is wise to agree that all things are one.

The various opposites in the world—hot and cold, wet and dry, heavy and light, good and evil—were parts of this hidden unity. In fact, even when things were hostile or in disagreement with each other, this was only more proof of their hidden unity, just as we must use opposing tension in drawing a bow string to make it fire the arrow in the opposite direction:

[51] Men do not know how what is at variance with itself is in agreement. It is an *harmonia* [attunement] of opposite tensions, like that of the bow and the lyre.

[54] The hidden *harmonia* [attunement] is better than the open.

Similarly, even things that *appear* to be bad, such as sickness, hunger, weariness, injustice, and evil, are just the other side of the coin of their "good" opposites. In fact, without these bad things, their good equivalents would be meaningless*:

[110] It is not good for men to get all they wish to get.

[111] It is sickness that makes health pleasant; evil, good; hunger, plenty; weariness, rest.

[23] They would not know the name of Justice if these things [i.e., unjust things] did not exist.

Heraclitus also had a vague and mystical notion of the gods. He seems to question the anthropomorphic† picture of the gods given by the pagan Greek fables:

[93] The lord [i.e., Apollo] whose oracle is at Delphi neither utters nor hides his meaning, but shows it by a sign.

[32] The wise is one only, unwilling and willing to be called by the name of Zeus.

He even hints at the monotheistic idea of God, a single deity that is all knowing, all wise, and all powerful. Further, he ridicules the polytheist Greek practices of animal sacrifice and praying to idols:

[78] The way of man has no wisdom, but that of God has.

[79] Man is called a baby by God, even as a child by a man.

[83] The wisest person is an ape compared to God, just as the most beautiful ape is ugly compared to man.

[5] They vainly purify themselves by defiling themselves with blood, just as if one who had stepped into the mud were to wash his feet in mud. Any man who perceived him doing this would deem him mad. Moreover, they pray to these statues as if one were to talk with houses, not knowing what gods or heroes are.

Heraclitus was quite Ionian in his belief that psychological changes result from a change in the basic material elements within a person. Because our souls are made of fire, it is deadly to them to become wet or intoxicated, even though we may enjoy this wetness when we have a few glasses of wine. Heraclitus thus offers what seems to be a purely physiological account of human psychology:

---

*Most people would agree that happiness is a good thing. As a thought experiment, suppose that scientists invented a "happy pill" with no negative side effects that would make you happy all of the time, regardless of what happened to you. Would you take it? If so, would your pill-induced happiness be genuine or meaningful? This experiment illustrates Heraclitus's point about opposites needing each other to exist.

†"Anthropomorphic" means the inappropriate attribution of human ideas or images to something that is not human. The Greeks saw their gods as powerful beings that looked and acted like we human beings, except with the arrogance and freedom that resulted from their immortality and superhuman powers.

[36] For it is death to souls to become water, and death to water to become earth. But water comes from earth; and from water, soul.

[77] It is pleasure to souls to become moist.

[117] A man, when he gets drunk, is led stumbling by a beardless lad, knowing not where he steps, having his soul wet.

[118] The dry soul is the wisest and best.

However, he adds a mystical touch to this physiology of the soul. Its *Logos* is very deep:

[45] You will not find the boundaries of the soul by travelling in any direction, so deep is its *Logos* [measure, account].

Lastly, when we look at his moral ideas, we find that Heraclitus puts forward what sounds at first like *relativism*. The goodness or badness of something depends on the context in which one finds it:

[9] Donkeys prefer straw to gold.

[61] Sea water is the purest and the most polluted. Fish can drink it, and it is good for them; to men it is undrinkable and destructive.

[97] Dogs bark at those they do not know.

Even if human beings hold to this idea of relativity, there is a divine order in the cosmos in which all things are equally good:

[102] To God all things are beautiful, good and just; but men hold some things wrong, and some right.

This divine order of things feeds all the human systems of law and morality. Once again, we see the unity of opposites in effect. Even if the laws of Sparta and Athens or of the Greeks and the Persians differ totally, they are both the product of the *Logos:*

[114] Those who speak with understanding must hold fast to what is common to all as a city holds fast to its law *[Nomos]*, and even more strongly. For all human laws are fed by the one divine law. It governs as much as it will, and suffices for all things with something to spare.

Heraclitus had great contempt for democracy and the common person. The masses follow popular singers, and glut themselves like beasts on food, drink, and possessions. Could he have had a vision of our consumer society?

[104] [Speaking of the common folk:] For what thought or wisdom have they? They follow the poets and take the crowd as their teacher, knowing not that there are many bad and few good.

[29] For even the best of them choose one thing above all others, immortal glory among mortals; while most of them satisfy themselves like beasts.

We leave Heraclitus behind with these two short fragments, which speak for themselves:

[49] One man is ten thousand to me, if he be the best.

[119] Man's character is his fate.

With Heraclitus we have the great philosopher of the flux, fire, strife, and war among the pre-Socratics. He was the apostle of Becoming, of change. Yet even he recognized that there was an underlying order beneath all this strife, flux, and measures of fire being kindled and going out, an order he christened the *Logos.* The philosophers of Elea attempted to quench Heraclitus's cosmic fire with the cool logic of Being, arguing that all this change, this strife, these ever-flowing rivers of Becoming were illusions provided by our senses. Instead, argued the Eleatics, we must look to Reason, which tells us that *all things are One.*

## Parmenides' Unchanging Cosmos

In Elea, a Greek colony in southern Italy, there arose a school of thought in the sixth century BC that challenged Heraclitus's vision of cosmic flux with its own vision of an unchanging cosmos, one propelled by what the Eleatics took to be the clearest of logics. Their founder was reputed to be Xenophanes, a poet and religious reformer whose poetry hinted that there was a single cosmic unity, ruled by a single divine Being. The two great thinkers of this school were Parmenides of Elea (ca. 515–450 BC), whose philosophical poem, written in ungainly hexameter verse in the Ionian dialect, laid out this unchanging cosmos quite clearly, and his friend and follower Zeno of Elea, whose paradoxes, as described in the introduction to this chapter, seemed to prove that change, motion, and the multiplicity of things were just illusions created by our undisciplined senses.*

Parmenides' great poem was divided into two parts: *The Way of Truth* and *The Way of Opinion.* Two large pieces, plus a number of smaller pieces, of *The Way of Truth* have been handed down to us by the doxographers. In the Prologue to *The Way of Truth,* Parmenides tells the fanciful story of his trip to visit a goddess who gives him the wisdom he seeks:

> [1] [lines 1–32] The chariot that bears me carried me as far as my heart desired, when it had brought me and set me on the renowned way of the goddess, which leads the man who knows through all the towns. On that way was I borne along; for on it the wise steeds carried me, straining at my chariot, the maidens showing the way. And the axle, glowing in the socket—for it was urged round by the whirling wheels at each end—gave out a sound like a pipe, when the daughters of the Sun, hastening to convey me into the light, threw back their veils from off their faces and left the abode of Night. . . .

Parmenides goes on to describe how the maidens guided his chariot into the presence of the goddess, who greets him:

> "Welcome, O youth, who comes to my abode on the chariot that bears you tended by immortal charioteers! It is no evil fate, but Right and Justice that has sent you forth to travel on this path. Far, indeed, does it lie from the beaten track of men! You must learn all things, both the unshaken heart of well-rounded truth, as well as the opinions of mortals in which there is no true belief. Yet nonetheless you will learn these

* Interestingly enough, one could see the debate between Heraclitus and the Eleatics as akin to the twentieth-century debate between continental and analytic philosophers. The former emphasize the ambiguity of life, morality, perception, and beauty, while the latter prefer cool, clear logical thinking and analysis as ways of understanding the world.

things too, how passing right through all things one should judge the things that seem to be.

But avoid thinking about this path of inquiry, nor let habit, born of much experience, force you to cast upon this way a wandering eye or sounding ear or tongue; but judge by argument the much disputed proof uttered by me. There is only one way left that can be spoken of. . . ."

. . . which is, of course, "the way of truth." This way could only be taken by the gods and those they chose to honor with special wisdom, or at least by those who chose to use their reason and ignore the swirling world of illusions produced by the senses. This phenomenal realm could be described by a lower sort of wisdom, the Way of Opinion. This division between two types of knowledge—that produced by reason and that which comes from the senses—would greatly influence Plato. Thus, Plato's theory of knowledge can be called, at least in part, "Parmenidean."

In a fragment from somewhere in *The Way of Truth,* Parmenides lays out a distinction between Being and Nothingness in terms of two paths: one that leads to true knowledge, and another that leads nowhere, for one cannot "know" that which doesn't exist:

[2, 3] Come now, I will tell you—and preserve my account and carry it away—the only two paths of inquiry that can be thought of. The first, namely, that *It is,* and that it is impossible for it not to be, is the path of persuasion, for truth is its companion. The other, namely, that *It is not,* and that it must not be—that, I tell you, is a path devoid of knowledge. For you cannot know what is not—that is impossible—nor utter it; for the same things that can be thought of, can be.

We can only have knowledge of things that exist. Nonexistence, Nothingness, is a meaningless concept, an empty category:

[7.1-2] It shall never be proven, that the things that are not, are; restrain your thought from that path of inquiry.

The core of Parmenides' picture of the unchanging cosmos is given in the second long fragment from *The Way of Truth* that we still have, preserved by Simplicius. The goddess continues her oration to the young Parmenides:

[8 lines 1–52] "One path only is left for us to speak of, namely, that *It is.* In this path there are very many signs that what is is uncreated and indestructible; for it is complete, immovable, and without end. Nor was it ever, nor will it be; for now it is, all at once, a continuous one. For what kind of origin for it will you look for? In what way and from what source could it have drawn its increase? . . . I shall not let you say or think that it came from what is not; for it can neither be thought nor uttered that anything is not. And, if it came from nothing, what need could have made it arise later rather than sooner? Therefore must it either be altogether or not be at all. Nor will the force of truth suffer anything to arise besides itself from that which is not. Therefore Justice does not loose her fetters and let anything come into being or pass away, but holds it fast. Our judgment in these matters depends on this: "Is it or is it not?" Surely it has been decided, as it must be, that we are to set aside the one path as unthinkable and nameless (for it is no true path), and that the other path is real and true. How, then, can what *is* perish? Or how could it come into being? If it came into being, it is not; nor is it if it is going to be in the future. Thus generation and passing away are not to be heard of.

Nor is it divisible, since it is all alike, and there is no more of it in one place than in another, to hinder it from holding together, nor less of it, but everything is full of what is. Therefore it is wholly continuous; for what is, is in contact with what is.

Moreover, it is immovable in the bonds of mighty chains, without beginning and without end; since coming into being and passing away have been driven afar, and true belief has cast them away. It is the same, and it rests in the self-same place, abiding in itself. And thus it remains constant in its place; for hard necessity keeps it in the bonds of the limit that holds it fast on every side, since it is not permitted for what is to be incomplete, for it is in need of nothing; if it were, it would stand in need of everything.

The thing that can be thought and that for the sake of which the thought exists is the same; for you cannot find thought without something that is, as to which it is uttered. And there is not, and never shall be, anything besides what is, since fate has chained it so as to be whole and immovable. Hence all these things are but names which mortals have given, believing them to be true—coming into being and passing away, being and not being, change of place and alteration of bright colour.

Since, then, it has a furthest limit, it is complete on every side, like the mass of a rounded sphere, equally poised from the centre in every direction; for it cannot be greater or smaller in one place than in another. For there is no nothing that could keep it from reaching out equally, nor can anything that is be more here and less there than what is, since it is all inviolable. For the point from which it is equal in every direction tends equally to the limits.

Here shall I close my trustworthy speech and thought about the truth. Henceforward learn the beliefs of mortals, giving ear to the deceptive ordering of my words."

We can summarize Parmenides' view of Being in the preceding fragment as follows:

- It is *unchanging.* If it did change, this would imply that *something* could come from *nothing,* which Parmenides takes as logically impossible.
- It is *complete* or *perfect,* requiring nothing to be added or taken away from it.
- It is *immovable:* After all, where would Being go?
- It is *eternal* and *uncreated,* existing for all time just as it is now.
- It is *continuous* and *indivisible:* there isn't more of it in some places, less in others.
- It is a *sphere,* its limits equidistant from the center.
- It is *finite,* and there is *no empty space* beyond it.*
- Thinking something proves that it exists, at least as a thought. In other words, *thought equals existence,* thinking equals Being.

The core of Parmenides' argument for the Sphere of Being is purely logical: Everything must already exist in some form, for things cannot just pop into existence out of nothing. Being as a whole cannot be incomplete, for then things could, in theory, be added to it. Being cannot go anywhere: There is no realm of "non-Being" (the idea that Parmenides ridicules in his poem) for Being to go to for a metaphysical walkabout. And it couldn't have come into existence or have been created, for once again we run into the problem of something—namely, our reality—coming from nothing. In short, *Being is,* even if our senses witness things appearing to change.

---

* Later, Parmenides' follower Melissus (fifth century BC) argued that Being must be infinite to preserve the Eleatic idea of Being as eternal, complete, and immovable.

As a thought experiment, try to think of something that *does not* exist. It will not do any good to think of things like unicorns or fairies: Unicorns are just horses with an imaginary horn, while we've all seen images of fairies in picture books and movies. Remember: Parmenides is not restricting Being to physical things (although at times he seems to speak in these terms). Even if you were to dream up something that you've never seen pictures of, or heard of from others or films or books, for example, a fictional character like the mighty Zondar, King of the Selucians, the second that you start to attribute characteristics to Zondar—for example, that he wears a purple robe, speaks in a booming deep voice, is married to the ravishing Xalaxia, Queen of the Fruggites—Zondar *exists,* at least as an imaginary character in your mind. Parmenides' point, if pushed to the limit, consists of this: Nonexistence and non-Being are empty and meaningless ideas. We cannot perceive *or* think of things that don't exist. Therefore, Being is a complete, eternal, unchanging, and immovable sphere.

To support Parmenides' view of the unchanging cosmos, his friend and collaborator Zeno put forward his famous paradoxes of multiplicity and motion, some of which were described earlier in this chapter. In fact, if we extend Zeno's arguments to what you're doing right now, you'll quickly realize that you can't even *really* be reading this text. For to read the second sentence in this paragraph, you must read the first one; but to get to the end of the first sentence, you must get halfway through it; to get to the last word in the first sentence, you must read the next to last word; and so on. According to Zeno, you'll take an infinite amount of time to get through even a single sentence (this is a good excuse for handing in essays late, by the way).

However, this notion is absurd. Of course, we can finish reading texts, walk down the street, or drive across town. Things really do move and change. How do we critique Zeno's paradoxes? One way we can do so is by seeing space and time not as a series of discrete points, but as "flows" (thus returning to Heraclitus). Then the problem of trying to move through an infinite series of points in a finite amount of time never arises.

Further, when we examine how people actually experience the passage of time, Zeno's paradoxical concerns seem to vanish. When we say things like "my bicycle wheel is twenty-six inches wide," or "our class is fifty minutes long," we are applying human conventions of measurements to things that are in themselves not broken up into bits of space or time. We can draw a distinction between "objective time," the sort of time we measure with a clock, and "subjective time," the time we actually feel passing. A boring lecture may seem to last forever, while an interesting one is over before you know it. When we live in subjective space and time, we *feel* time passing, though at rates that may or may not match that recorded by objective time. We don't divide up subjective time into discrete, mathematically measurable units. In subjective time, we can fire arrows at targets, catch up to slow-moving tortoises, and get to the end of sentences in philosophy texts. We can do it in objective time, too, but only if Zeno isn't standing beside us, chiding us for our foolishness.*

---

*This is a simple refutation of Zeno. More sophisticated mathematical refutations based on an infinitesimal calculus were introduced in the eighteenth century.

# Empedocles on Love and Strife

Empedocles (ca. 490–430 BC) was the third of the great speculators about the relationship between Being and Becoming among the pre-Socratics. He was a philosopher, natural historian, doctor, poet, and politician from the town of Acragas in Sicily. He was a lively character, a supporter of the democratic faction in Acragas who wore a purple robe and a crown to show off his special status within the state, claiming (with some apparent success) that he could heal the sick with medical miracles. According to one story, he threw himself into the volcano at Etna so that no one would know how he died, thereby taking his disappearance as the ascent of a god. Later he was found out when a citizen discovered his bronze sandals, spewed out by Etna in an eruption.

He wrote two major works: *On Nature* and *Purifications.* The former contains most of his cosmological speculations. He seems to have adhered to a combination of the mystical Orphic religion and Pythagoreanism, notably the vegetarianism of the latter sect. Philosophically, he tried to solve the problem presented by Parmenides and the Eleatics. Our reason tells us that Being doesn't change, yet our senses show us that individual things change constantly. To solve this problem, he introduced Love and Strife as the cosmic forces regulating this change (subbing for Heraclitus's monistic principle of the *Logos*), and four distinct material elements—earth, air, fire, and water—as the constituents of the things that undergo change.

In the following fragments, Empedocles agrees with Parmenides' notion of Being as complete, unchanging, eternal, and uncreated, at least as a starting point. Something cannot come from nothing, so change is just a mixing of the various elements of what already exists:

> [8] And I shall tell you another thing. There is no substance of any of the things that perish, nor any cessation for them in baneful death. They are only a mixing and interchange of what has been mixed. Substance is but a name given to these things by men.

> [11] Fools!—for they have no far-reaching thoughts—who think that what did not exist before comes into being, or that anything can perish and be utterly destroyed. [12] For it cannot be that anything can arise from what in no way is, and it is impossible and unheard of that what is should perish; for it will always be, wherever one may keep putting it. . . . [13] In the All there is nothing empty. Whence, then, could anything come to increase it? [14] And in the All there is nothing empty and nothing too full.

Further, Empedocles agrees with Parmenides' depiction of Being as a perfect sphere:

> [27] There [in the sphere] are distinguished neither the swift limbs of the sun, no, nor the shaggy earth in its might, nor the sea—so fast was the god bound in the close covering of Harmony, spherical and round, rejoicing in his circular solitude.

> [29] [When the world was ruled by Love:] Two branches did not spring from its back, it had no feet, no swift knees, no fruitful parts; but it was a Sphere, equal on every side.

> [28] But he was equal on every side and quite without end, spherical and round, rejoicing in his circular solitude.

This perfect sphere existed, according to Empedocles, in a Golden Age when Love reigned supreme. Since that day, we've suffered a fall from grace, as Strife came along and split up the perfect sphere into various combinations of elements. Fragment 17 from *On Nature* is central for an understanding of how Empedocles saw Love and Strife as taking turns bringing together and forcing apart the four elements that make up the physical universe. In it, we learn that Love is the great principle of attraction in the cosmos (including the attraction felt between male and female halves of all animal species), while Strife is the great principle of repulsion. Empedocles, like Parmenides, believed that one needed to use reason to achieve an intellectual understanding of the cosmos, for all we witness with our senses is never-ending change without purpose:

> [17] I shall tell a twofold tale. At one time it grew to be one only out of many; at another, it divided up to be many instead of one. There is a double becoming of perishable things and a double passing away. The coming together of all things brings one generation into being and destroys it; the other grows up and is scattered as things become divided. And these things never cease continually changing places, at one time all uniting in one through Love, at another each borne in different directions by the repulsion of Strife. Thus, as far as it is their nature to grow into one out of many, and to become many once more, when the one is parted asunder, so far they come into being and their life abides not. But, inasmuch as they never cease changing their places continually, so far they are ever immovable as they go round the circle of existence.
>
> But come, hearken to my words, for learning increases wisdom. As I said before, when I revealed the limits of my discourse, I shall tell a twofold tale. At one time it grew together to be one only out of many, at another it parted asunder so as to be many instead of one; Fire and Water and Earth and the mighty height of Air; dread Strife, too, apart from these, of equal weight to each, and Love in their midst, equal in length and breadth. Her you must contemplate with your mind; do not sit with dazed eyes. It is she that is known as being implanted in the frame of mortals. It is she that makes them have thoughts of love and perform deeds of union. They call her by the names of Joy and Aphrodite. Her no mortal has yet marked moving round among them.
>
> But listen to the undeceitful ordering of my discourse. For all these are equal and alike in age, yet each has a different prerogative and its own peculiar nature, but they gain the upper hand in turn when the time comes round. And nothing comes into being besides these, nor do they pass away; for, if they had been passing away continually, they would not be now, and what could increase this universe and whence could it come? How, too, could it perish, since no place is empty of these things? There are these alone; but, running through one another, they become different at different times—and are forever and always the same.

From this fragment, we can conclude that Empedocles saw the universe as cycling through four great cosmic ages: (1) the Age of the Perfect Sphere, when Love reigns supreme; (2) an age when Strife begins to break up the sphere of Love, separating off some of the elements; (3) an Age of Strife, when the elements are all separated; and (4) an age when Love is returning, bringing back together some of the elements. At present, we live in either the second or fourth age.

In the following fragments, we learn that Love and Strife are eternal forces and that their never-ending conflict brings about all things in nature, including gods, men and women, birds, bees, and fishes. This process is like the mixing of colors on a painter's palette: A bit of blue paint added to some yellow produces a green; similarly, a mixing of certain proportions of certain elements might produce a dolphin, while some other mixture produces an olive tree:

> [16] For even as they [i.e., Strife and Love] were before, so too they shall be; nor ever, I think, will boundless time be emptied of that pair.

> [21] Come now, look at the things that bear witness to my earlier discourse, if anything I said before was incomplete in form, behold the sun, everywhere bright and warm, and all the immortal things that are bathed in heat and bright radiance. Behold the rain, everywhere dark and cold; and from the earth issue forth things firm and solid. When in Strife they are different in form and separated; but they come together in Love, and are desired by one another.
> For out of these have sprung all things that were and are and shall be—trees and men and women, beasts and birds and the fishes that dwell in the waters, even the gods that live long lives and are exalted in honour.
> For there are these alone; but, running through one another, they take different shapes—so much does mixture change them.

> [23] Just as when painters are decorating temple-offerings, men whom wisdom has taught well their art—they, when they have taken pigments of many colours with their hands, mixed them in due proportion, more of some and less of others, and from them produce shapes like all things, making trees and men and women, beasts and birds and fishes that dwell in the waters, and even gods that live long lives, and are exalted in honour—so let not the error prevail over your mind, that there is any other source of all the perishable creatures that appear in countless numbers. Know this for sure, for you have heard the tale from a god.

As already mentioned, Empedocles was the first of the pre-Socratics to formalize the physical elements of nature into four "roots" (as he called them): earth, air, fire, and water. It is as though he had a chemist's periodic table that consisted of only four elements. The following fragment outlines the four elements and how Love combines them into "mortal things":

> [71] But if your assurance of these things was in any way deficient as to how, out of Water and Earth and Air and Fire mingled together, arose the forms and colours of all those mortal things that have been fitted together by Aphrodite, and so are now come into being. . . .

Empedocles also made a number of geophysical observations that explain the origin of eclipses, the world's oceans, and salt:

> [42] And she [the moon] cuts off his rays [i.e., the sun's] as he goes above her, and casts a shadow on as much of the earth as is the breadth of the pale-faced moon.

> [55] Sea is the sweat of the earth.

> [56] Salt was solidified by the impact of the sun's beams.

Like Anaximander, Empedocles put forward a theory of evolution. But his was a very strange one: He thought that the parts of plants, animals, and human beings wandered around separately—imagine heads and arms and legs bouncing around a field looking for each other—eventually urged by Love to seek each other out. But when they came together, it was by pure chance how things turned out, for they didn't always combine in a very efficient or aesthetically pleasing manner. There were headless bodies, ox-headed human beings, and sexually ambiguous creatures of all sorts. Eventually, the inefficient combinations died out, the fittest survived, and we have the plant and animal species that exist today:

[20] This [the contest between Love and Strife] is manifest in the mass of mortal limbs. At one time all the limbs that are the body's portion are brought together by Love in blooming life's high season; at another, severed by cruel Strife, they wander each alone by the breakers of life's sea. It is the same with plants and the fish that make their homes in the waters, with the beasts that have their lairs on the hills and the seabirds that sail on wings.

[57] On it [the earth] many heads sprung up without necks and arms wandered bare and bereft of shoulders. Eyes wandered alone, in want of foreheads.

[58] Solitary limbs wandered seeking for union.

[61] Many creatures with faces and breasts looking in different directions were born; some, offspring of oxen with faces of men, while others, again, arose as offspring of men with the heads of oxen, and creatures in whom the nature of women and men was mingled, furnished with sterile parts.

Empedocles also had a few things to say about human biology. He thought that sight was the cause of sexual desire, that male children were born from the "warmer part" of a woman's womb, and that the organ of thought was not the brain, but the heart:

[64] And upon him came [sexual] desire, reminding him through sight.

[67] For in its warmer part the womb brings forth males, and that is why men are dark and more manly and shaggy.

[105] [The heart], dwelling in the sea of blood that runs in opposite directions, where what men call thought is chiefly found; for the blood round the heart is the thought of men.

His main contribution to understanding human physiology was his theory of effluences, which he used to explain perception. All things give off "effluences," which are what we might think of as waves or particles:

[89] Know that effluences flow from all things that have come into being.

Further, our bodies are covered with pores of various sizes, small enough to hold the blood in our bodies, but large enough to allow air and fire to enter. He compares sight to the way that a lantern lets out a light through the glass shield surrounding it, yet doesn't allow the wind to come in and blow out the flame. Similarly, our pupils are made out of fire, and surrounded by membranes made out of earth and air. The effluences of fire given off by material objects can pass through these membranes because their pores are wide enough to let the finer fire particles in. When they reach the fiery center of our eyes, our pupils, they're recognized as fiery images of what they are (i.e., pictures of the objects that gave off the effluences in question):

[84] And even as when a man thinking to sally forth through a stormy night, prepares a lantern, a flame of blazing fire, fastening to it horn plates to keep out all manner of winds, and they scatter the blast of the winds that blow, but the light leaping out through them, shines across the threshold with unfailing beams, inasmuch as it is finer; even so did she [Love] then entrap the elemental fire, the round pupil, confined

within membranes and delicate tissues, which are pierced through and through with wondrous passages. They keep out the deep water that surrounds the pupil, but they let through the fire, inasmuch as it is finer.

[109] For it is with earth that we see Earth, and Water with water; by air we see bright Air, by fire flaming Fire. By love do we see Love, and Hate by grievous hate.

Empedocles' second major work, also a poem, was called *Purifications.* Less of it is available to us, though enough to get a picture of Empedocles' moral and religious ideas. In *Purifications,* Empedocles suggests that there was once a Golden Age when Love ruled supreme, before the Olympian gods were worshipped and when all beasts were tame. It was a sort of Garden of Eden:

[128] Nor had they any Ares for a god nor Cydimus [Tumult], nor was Zeus king nor Cronos nor Poseidon, but Cypris [Love] the Queen. . . . They worshipped her with holy gifts, with painted figures and perfumes of cunning fragrancy, with offerings of pure myrrh and sweet-smelling frankincense, casting on the ground libations of brown honey. And the altar did not reek with pure bull's blood, but this was held in the greatest abomination among men, to eat the noble limbs after tearing out the life.

[130] For all things were tame and gentle to man, both beasts and birds, and friendly feelings were kindled everywhere.

Paralleling the Christian story, Empedocles talks about a fall from grace when the reign of Love ends and that of Strife begins. When the spirits that lived in this time of bliss polluted themselves, they re-entered the cycle of reincarnation, taking on one mortal body after another. Again, this sounds suspiciously like the ancient Indian notion of karma and the cycle of rebirth, which holds that the performance of bad actions will prevent one from escaping an endless series of physical lives. Empedocles himself was caught in this cycle:

[115] There is an oracle of Necessity, an ancient decree of the gods, eternal and sealed fast by broad oaths, that whenever one of the *daimons* [spirits], who have been given long-lasting life, has sinfully polluted his hands with blood, or followed strife and swore a false oath, he must wander thrice ten thousand seasons from the abodes of the blessed, being born throughout the time in all manners of mortal forms, changing one toilsome path of life for another. For the mighty Air drives him into the Sea, and the Sea spews him forth onto the dry Earth; Earth tosses him into the beams of the blazing Sun, and he flings him back to the eddies of Air. One takes him from the other, and all reject him. One of these I now am, an exile and a wanderer from the gods, for I put my trust in mad Strife.

[119] From what honour, from what a height of bliss have I fallen to go about among mortals here on earth.

Empedocles seems to have been influenced by the rites and ideas of the Pythagoreans. We find some evidence of this in *Purifications* where he repeats a couple of typically Pythagorean rules of conduct:

[140] Abstain wholly from laurel leaves.

[141] Wretches, utter wretches, keep your hands from beans!

Further, he believed in the Pythagorean doctrine of *metempsychosis,* the transmigration of souls. In Fragment 126, he talks about the goddess "clothing them with a strange garment of flesh," referring to the reincarnation of someone's spirit into a new body. In fact, Empedocles himself claimed special knowledge of his own past lives:

> [117] For I have already been a boy and a girl, a bush and a bird and a dumb fish in the sea.

Speaking of the souls of the wise:

> [146] But, at the last, they appear among mortal men as prophets, song-writers, physicians, and princes; and thence they rise up as gods exalted in honour, [147] sharing the hearth of the other gods and the same table, free from human woes, safe from destiny, and incapable of hurt.

This idea of transmigration of souls, he felt, made *vegetarianism* morally imperative, for by sacrificing or eating animals, one may, in fact, be feasting on one's friends and relatives reincarnated into a new, nonhuman form:

> [136] Will you not cease from this ill-sounding slaughter? Do you not see that you are devouring one another in the thoughtlessness of your hearts?

> [137] And the father lifts up his own son in a changed form and slays as he prays. Infatuated fool! And they run up to the sacrificers, begging mercy, while he, deaf to their cries, slaughters them in his halls and gets ready the evil feast. In like manner does the son seize his father, and children their mother, tear out their life and eat the kindred flesh.

Empedocles was a strange mixture of cosmological philosopher, medical doctor, and religious oddball. However, he made a serious attempt to reconcile the metaphysical conflict of Being and Becoming by introducing the cosmological forces of Love and Strife and by dividing up physical nature into four basic elements. He was the last of the bold speculators on this issue in the cosmological period of Greek thought, though not the last of the pre-Socratics of note (see the introduction to this chapter concerning Anaxagoras and Democritus).

Empedocles' systematization of nature into four distinct elements, although crude by the standards of modern science, showed a finer appreciation of nature than did the monistic picture of the Ionian philosophers. Empedocles didn't try to reduce all of nature to a single material principle, be it water, air, or fire. And though his cosmic forces of Love and Strife might seem to be fanciful poetic inventions, keep in mind that, according to modern physics, atoms are made up of various arrangements of protons and electrons, or positively and negatively charged particles, and that electromagnetic forces—forces of attraction and repulsion—are at the core of our modern understanding of how matter is held together in discrete bundles. So, at least in a metaphorical sense, Love and Strife—attraction and repulsion—*are* the basic forces that hold together and cause change in the universe.

# THE PHILOSOPHER AS PESKY GADFLY: SOCRATES' APOLOGY

Socrates (470–399 BC) had a favorite pastime: to go about the town barefoot, taking self-important people aside and engaging them in philosophical dialogue. He saw himself as a "gadfly" who stung the lazy beast of the *polis* (city-state) by engaging the rich, powerful, and supposedly wise in philosophical debate, forcing them either to justify their moral, political, and religious prejudices or to give them up as irrational and ungrounded. He was married to Xanthippe, who apparently gave poor Socrates a hard time for giving up his glamorous career as a stonecutter for philosophy. They had three sons.

Socrates had a number of young aristocratic friends who followed him around the city as he sought out partners in dialogue. However, he also made many enemies by exposing the hypocrisy and ignorance of those with whom he conversed. He was widely thought to be skeptical about the traditional religious beliefs of the Athenians. After they suffered defeat in 404 BC at the hands of the Spartan-led coalition, many conservatives in the city blamed the defeat on the city's neglecting its religious duties (and on the resulting loss of divine favor). To even up old scores, three of them accused Socrates of impiety toward the gods of Olympus and of corrupting the youth of the city.

*The Apology* is a record of Socrates' defense in the law court of Athens against charges brought against him by Meletus, Anytus, and Lycon. The trial took place in 399 BC. Socrates' words were recorded, a few years later, by Plato, no doubt with *some* artistic freedom. Because many of the audience were still alive and could check Plato's account of the trial against their own memories, he probably took care not to embellish Socrates' actual words *too* much. *The Apology* is the best picture we have of Socrates' ideas and way of life, since he wrote nothing himself.

Any citizen in Athens could bring a case to the court against any other citizen. There were no permanent judges: 501 citizens were selected by lot to act as jurors in the case. Appeals to rhetoric and emotion were common in these trials. The accused would often break down in tears or parade his family before the court to secure a dismissal. If the person bringing the complaint didn't get at least 20 percent of the vote, he was fined 1,000 drachmas, a hefty sum. If the accused were found guilty of the charge, each side was given the opportunity to propose a suitable penalty, and the jury chose which of the two it found the fairest. This procedure had a tendency of making both prosecution and defense propose reasonable penalties, to avoid their immediate rejection by the jury as either too punitive or too lenient.

Socrates' most famous pupil was Plato. Plato's extant works are in dialogue form, consisting of discussions between several characters, with Socrates usually being the main speaker. It is difficult to know to what extent Socrates would have agreed with Plato's ideas. However, Socrates' method was indeed the *dialectic:* He would ironically pretend ignorance of a subject, and ask people for definitions of things like goodness, justice, truth, and beauty. After listening to their definitions, he would probe these definitions for weaknesses by asking his partner in dialogue a series of penetrating questions. After agreeing that the first definition wasn't very good, a new one would be sought, and the whole process would start over again (that is, if they had the patience to put up with him).

## A Summary of the Dialogue

*The Old Charges against Socrates (17a–20c):* In this section of his defense, Socrates says that not only does he have to fight the accusations made against him in the courtroom itself, but also those made against him by the "Old Accusers" that have haunted him for years. Socrates defends himself against the charges that he is a "nature philosopher" (i.e., a cosmologist) and a Sophist. He replies by saying that he's not interested in physical science, and that since he does not take any money for his philosophical "teaching," he could not be a Sophist.

*Socrates' Defense Part 1: The Oracle of Delphi and the New Charges (20d–30d):* Before tackling the actual accusations made against him by the "New Accusers," he talks about how when his friend Chairephon visited the oracle of Delphi, the priestess told him that there was no man wiser than Socrates. Because he didn't know what this meant at first, he talked to politicians, poets, and artisans, and although they knew some things, they were ignorant of things outside their expertise. He concluded that the oracle meant that he was wise because he realized that he really knew nothing, for it's better to be in this state than to believe you know things that you really don't. He decided that the god of Delphi (Apollo) had given him the duty of talking to people who thought they were wise in order to expose their ignorance.

He then goes on to address the charges made against him in the current trial, of impiety and of corrupting the youth. These, he says, are untrue, and based on the resentment felt by his accusers caused by their humiliation at having been exposed as ignorant through the dialectical method. He says that he wouldn't corrupt the youth, for to do so would only harm the city and thus himself. To counter the charge of impiety, he says that a *daimon,* or friendly spirit, followed him around, telling him when he was doing something wrong. This proved that he couldn't be an atheist, as Meletus had suggested.

He finishes this section by noting that when he was a soldier he never deserted his post, so it would be improper for him to desert his post now by changing his philosophical way of life. We have no real knowledge of life after death, he says, but we can be sure that injustice in this world is wrong. It's wiser to fear doing a certain wrong than to worry about what happens to us after we die.

*Socrates' Defense Part 2: The Gadfly (30e–35d):* In continuing his defense, Socrates compares himself to a gadfly, a type of horsefly that stung the rump of that "great and noble horse," the city of Athens, which needed to be, from time to time, awoken from its dogmatic slumbers. He talks about his refusal to cooperate with the Thirty Tyrants* during their rule. He asks his accusers, why some of his former "students" haven't come forward to accuse him, especially given the fact that some of them are present in the courtroom? Finally, he says that he refuses to parade his family before the court to ask for mercy, although this would certainly have aided his case.

*The End of the Trial (35e–42a):* The vote is close, but goes against Socrates. Meletus proposes death as a penalty, while Socrates, who feels he has spent his whole lifetime helping the state, counterproposes the ironic penalty of free meals in the Prytaneum, where the Olympian athletes trained. He is too poor to pay a fine, and exile would be pointless, for he'd only continue his mission in whatever city he was exiled to. After all, "the unexamined life is not worth living."

Finally, he suggests a minor fine of 30 minae to be paid by his friends Plato, Crito, and others. The jury rejects this idea and votes for death.

In his concluding remarks, he tells the jurors who voted against him that he won't run away like a coward or weep and wail. He prophesizes that after he's gone

---

*They ruled Athens with an iron fist after the city was defeated by Sparta and its allies in the Peloponnesian War (431–404 BC).

a far greater punishment will be inflicted on his accusers, and that it would be far more noble and honorable for them to improve themselves than to kill gadflies like Socrates who call their cherished dogmas into question. He then tells his supporters not to worry since his *daimon* has been quiet, reassuring him that he is acting properly.

For Socrates, death is either a long sleep or a migration of the soul to another world. If the former, what could be nicer? If the latter, he could think of nothing more interesting than to speak to the shades of Homer, Hesiod, Odysseus, and other famous individuals in Hades. No evil can happen to a good man, he says, for the gods will care for him, even if he is killed. He ends by bidding the jurors farewell. A few days later, after his friends have failed to convince him to try to escape to another city, he drinks a cup of hemlock and dies.

*The Apology* presents a seductive picture of the ideal philosopher. This is someone who pursues true knowledge by a dialectical process of asking questions, forming definitions, and then critically examining them. He is also someone who acts as a gadfly, challenging those who claim wisdom or power to defend their ethical and political views, even at the risk of his own career and life. Needless to say, not many philosophers can claim to have lived up to Socrates' challenge.

# The Apology

## PLATO

I DO NOT KNOW, men of Athens, how my accusers affected you; as for me, I was almost carried away in spite of myself, so persuasively did they speak. And yet, hardly anything of what they said is true. Of the many lies they told, one in particular surprised me, namely that you should be careful not to be deceived by an accomplished speaker like me. That they were not ashamed to be immediately proved wrong by the facts, when I show myself not to be an accomplished speaker at all, that I thought was most shameless on their part—unless indeed they call an accomplished speaker the man who speaks the truth. If they mean that, I would agree that I am an orator, but not after their manner, for indeed, as I say, practically nothing they said was true. From me you will hear the whole truth, though

not, by Zeus, gentlemen, expressed in embroidered and stylized phrases like theirs, but things spoken at random and expressed in the first words that come to mind, for I put my trust in the justice of what I say, and let none of you expect anything else. It would not be fitting at my age, as it might be for a young man, to toy with words when I appear before you.

One thing I do ask and beg of you, gentlemen: if you hear me making my defence in the same kind of language as I am accustomed to use in the market place by the bankers' tables,[1] where many of you have heard me, and elsewhere, do

[1] The bankers or money-changers had their counters in the market place. It seems that this was a favorite place for gossip.

SOURCE: Plato, *The Apology*, in *The Trial and Death of Socrates*, trans. G. M. A. Grube (Indianapolis: Hackett, 1975), pp. 22–42 (complete). Reprinted by permission of Hackett Publishing Company, Inc. All rights reserved.

not be surprised or create a disturbance on that account. The position is this: this is my first appearance in a lawcourt, at the age of seventy; I am therefore simply a stranger to the manner of speaking here. Just as if I were really a stranger, you would certainly excuse me if I spoke in that dialect and manner in which I had been brought up, so too my present request seems a just one, for you to pay no attention to my manner of speech—be it better or worse—but to concentrate your attention on whether what I say is just or not, for the excellence of a judge lies in this, as that of a speaker lies in telling the truth.

It is right for me, gentlemen, to defend myself first against the first lying accusations made against me and my first accusers, and then against the later accusations and the later accusers. There have been many who have accused me to you for many years now, and none of their accusations are true. These I fear much more than I fear Anytus and his friends, though they too are formidable. These earlier ones, however, are more so, gentlemen; they got hold of most of you from childhood, persuaded you and accused me quite falsely, saying that there is a man called Socrates, a wise man, a student of all things in the sky and below the earth, who makes the worse argument the stronger. Those who spread that rumour, gentlemen, are my dangerous accusers, for their hearers believe that those who study these things do not even believe in the gods. Moreover, these accusers are numerous, and have been at it a long time; also, they spoke to you at an age when you would most readily believe them, some of you being children and adolescents, and they won their case by default, as there was no defence.

What is most absurd in all this is that one cannot even know or mention their names unless one of them is a writer of comedies.[2] Those who maliciously and slanderously persuaded you—who also, when persuaded themselves then persuaded others—all those are most difficult to deal with: one cannot bring one of them into court or

refute him; one must simply fight with shadows, as it were, in making one's defence, and cross-examine when no one answers. I want you to realize too that my accusers are of two kinds: those who have accused me recently, and the old ones I mention; and to think that I must first defend myself against the latter, for you have also heard their accusations first, and to a much greater extent than the more recent.

Very well then. I must surely defend myself and attempt to uproot from your minds in so short a time the slander that has resided there so long. I wish this may happen, if it is in any way better for you and me, and that my defence may be successful, but I think this is very difficult and I am fully aware of how difficult it is. Even so, let the matter proceed as the god may wish, but I must obey the law and make my defence.

Let us then take up the case from its beginning. What is the accusation from which arose the slander in which Meletus trusted when he wrote out the charge against me? What did they say when they slandered me? I must, as if they were my actual prosecutors, read the affidavit they would have sworn. It goes something like this: Socrates is guilty of wrongdoing in that he busies himself studying things in the sky and below the earth; he makes the worse into the stronger argument, and he teaches these same things to others. You have seen this yourselves in the comedy of Aristophanes, a Socrates swinging about there, saying he was walking on air and talking a lot of other nonsense about things of which I know nothing at all. I do not speak in contempt of such knowledge, if someone is wise in these things—lest Meletus bring more cases against me—but, gentlemen, I have no part in it, and on this point I call upon the majority of you as witnesses. I think it right that all those of you who have heard me conversing, and many of you have, should tell each other if anyone of you has ever heard me discussing such subjects to any extent at all. From this you will learn that the other things said about me by the majority are of the same kind.

Not one of them is true. And if you have heard from anyone that I undertake to teach peo-

[2] This refers in particular to Aristophanes, whose comedy, *The Clouds,* produced in 423 BC, ridiculed the (imaginary) school of Socrates.

ple and charge a fee for it, that is not true either. Yet I think it a fine thing to be able to teach people as Gorgias of Leontini does, and Prodicus of Ceos, and Hippias of Elis.[3] Each of these men can go to any city and persuade the young, who can keep company with anyone of their own fellow-citizens they want without paying, to leave the company of these, to join with themselves, pay them a fee, and be grateful to them besides. Indeed, I learned that there is another wise man from Paros who is visiting us, for I met a man who has spent more money on Sophists than everybody else put together, Callias, the son of Hipponicus. So I asked him—he has two sons— "Callias," I said, "if your sons were colts or calves, we could find and engage a supervisor for them who would make them excel in their proper qualities, some horse breeder or farmer. Now since they are men, whom do you have in mind to supervise them? Who is an expert in this kind of excellence, the human and social kind? I think you must have given thought to this since you have sons. Is there such a person," I asked, "or is there not?" "Certainly there is," he said. "Who is he?" I asked, "What is his name, where is he from? and what is his fee?" "His name, Socrates, is Evenus, he comes from Paros, and his fee is five minas." I thought Evenus a happy man, if he really possesses this art, and teaches for so moderate a fee. Certainly I would pride and preen myself if I had this knowledge, but I do not have it, gentlemen.

One of you might perhaps interrupt me and say: "But Socrates, what is your occupation? From where have these slanders come? For surely if you did not busy yourself with something out of the common, all these rumours and talk would not have arisen unless you did something other

than most people. Tell us what it is, that we may not speak inadvisedly about you." Anyone who says that seems to be right, and I will try to show you what has caused this reputation and slander. Listen then. Perhaps some of you will think I am jesting, but be sure that all that I shall say is true. What has caused my reputation is none other than a certain kind of wisdom. What kind of wisdom? Human wisdom, perhaps. It may be that I really possess this, while those whom I mentioned just now are wise with a wisdom more than human; else I cannot explain it, for I certainly do not possess it, and whoever says I do is lying and speaks to slander me. Do not create a disturbance, gentlemen, even if you think I am boasting, for the story I shall tell does not originate with me, but I will refer you to a trustworthy source. I shall call upon the god at Delphi as witness to the existence and nature of my wisdom, if it be such. You know Chairephon. He was my friend from youth, and the friend of most of you, as he shared your exile and your return. You surely know the kind of man he was, how impulsive in any course of action. He went to Delphi at one time and ventured to ask the oracle—as I say, gentlemen, do not create a disturbance—he asked if any man was wiser than I, and the Pythian replied that no one was wiser. Chairephon is dead, but his brother will testify to you about this.

Consider that I tell you this because I would inform you about the origin of the slander. When I heard of this reply I asked myself: "Whatever does the god mean? What is his riddle? I am very conscious that I am not wise at all; what then does he mean by saying that I am the wisest? For surely he does not lie; it is not legitimate for him to do so." For a long time I was at a loss as to his meaning; then I very reluctantly turned to some such investigation as this: I went to one of those reputed wise, thinking that there, if anywhere, I could refute the oracle and say to it: "This man is wiser than I, but you said I was." Then, when I examined this man—there is no need for me to tell you his name, he was one of our public men—my experience was something like this: I thought that he appeared wise to many people

---

[3] These were all well-known Sophists. Gorgias, after whom Plato named one of his dialogues, was a celebrated rhetorician and teacher of rhetoric. He came to Athens in 427 BC, and his rhetorical tricks took the city by storm. Two dialogues, the authenticity of which has been doubted, are named after Hippias, whose knowledge was encyclopedic. Prodicus was known for his insistence on the precise meaning of words. Both he and Hippias are characters in the *Protagoras* (named after another famous Sophist).

and especially to himself, but he was not. I then tried to show him that he thought himself wise, but that he was not. As a result he came to dislike me, and so did many of the bystanders. So I withdrew and thought to myself: "I am wiser than this man; it is likely that neither of us knows anything worthwhile, but he thinks he knows something when he does not, whereas when I do not know, neither do I think I know; so I am likely to be wiser than he to this small extent, that I do not think I know what I do not know." After this I approached another man, one of those thought to be wiser than he, and I thought the same thing, and so I came to be disliked both by him and by many others.

After that I proceeded systematically. I realized, to my sorrow and alarm, that I was getting unpopular, but I thought that I must attach the greatest importance to the god's oracle, so I must go to all those who had any reputation for knowledge to examine its meaning. And by the dog,[4] gentlemen of the jury—for I must tell you the truth—I experienced something like this: in my investigation in the service of the god I found that those who had the highest reputation were nearly the most deficient, while those who were thought to be inferior were more knowledgeable. I must give you an account of my journeyings as if they were labours I had undertaken to prove the oracle irrefutable. After the politicians, I went to the poets, the writers of tragedies and dithyrambs and the others, intending in their case to catch myself being more ignorant then they. So I took up those poems with which they seemed to have taken most trouble and asked them what they meant, in order that I might at the same time learn something from them. I am ashamed to tell you the truth, gentlemen, but I must. Almost all the bystanders might have explained the poems better than their authors could. I soon realized that poets do not compose their poems with knowledge, but by some inborn talent and by inspiration, like seers and prophets

who also say many fine things without any understanding of what they say. The poets seemed to me to have had a similar experience. At the same time I saw that, because of their poetry, they thought themselves very wise men in other respects, which they were not. So there again I withdrew, thinking that I had the same advantage over them as I had over the politicians.

Finally I went to the craftsmen, for I was conscious of knowing practically nothing, and I knew that I would find that they had knowledge of many fine things. In this I was not mistaken; they knew things I did not know, and to that extent they were wiser than I. But, gentlemen of the jury, the good craftsmen seemed to me to have the same fault as the poets: each of them, because of his success at his craft, thought himself very wise in other most important pursuits, and this error of theirs overshadowed the wisdom they had, so that I asked myself, on behalf of the oracle, whether I should prefer to be as I am, with neither their wisdom nor their ignorance, or to have both. The answer I gave myself and the oracle was that it was to my advantage to be as I am.

As a result of this investigation, gentlemen of the jury, I acquired much unpopularity, of a kind that is hard to deal with and is a heavy burden; many slanders came from these people and a reputation for wisdom, for in each case the bystanders thought that I myself possessed the wisdom that I proved that my interlocutor did not have. What is probable, gentlemen, is that in fact the god is wise and that his oracular response meant that human wisdom is worth little or nothing, and that when he says this man, Socrates, he is using my name as an example, as if he said: "This man among you, mortals, is wisest who, like Socrates, understands that his wisdom is worthless." So even now I continue this investigation as the god bade me—and I go around seeking out anyone, citizen or stranger, whom I think wise. Then if I do not think he is, I come to the assistance of the god and show him that he is not wise. Because of this occupation, I do not have the leisure to engage in public affairs to any extent, nor indeed to look after my own, but

[4] A curious oath, occasionally used by Socrates, it appears in a longer form in the *Gorgias* (482b) as "by the dog, the god of the Egyptians."

I live in great poverty because of my service to the god.

Furthermore, the young men who follow me around of their own free will, those who have most leisure, the sons of the very rich, take pleasure in hearing people questioned; they themselves often imitate me and try to question others. I think they find an abundance of men who believe they have some knowledge but know little or nothing. The result is that those whom they question are angry, not with themselves but with me. They say: "That man Socrates is a pestilential fellow who corrupts the young." If one asks them what he does and what he teaches to corrupt them, they are silent, as they do not know, but, so as not to appear at a loss, they mention those accusations that are available against all philosophers, about "things in the sky and things below the earth," about "not believing in the gods" and "making the worse the stronger argument"; they would not want to tell the truth, I'm sure, that they have been proved to lay claim to knowledge when they know nothing. These people are ambitious, violent and numerous; they are continually and convincingly talking about me; they have been filling your ears for a long time with vehement slanders against me. From them Meletus attacked me, and Anytus and Lycon, Meletus being vexed on behalf of the poets, Anytus on behalf of the craftsmen and the politicians, Lycon on behalf of the orators, so that, as I started out by saying, I should be surprised if I could rid you of so much slander in so short a time. That, gentlemen of the jury, is the truth for you. I have hidden or disguised nothing. I know well enough that this very conduct makes me unpopular, and this is proof that what I say is true, that such is the slander against me, and that such are its causes. If you look into this either now or later, this is what you will find.

Let this suffice as a defence against the charges of my earlier accusers. After this I shall try to defend myself against Meletus, that good and patriotic man, as he says he is, and my later accusers. As these are a different lot of accusers, let us again take up their sworn deposition. It goes something like this: Socrates is guilty of corrupting the young and of not believing in the gods in whom the city believes, but in other new divinities. Such is their charge. Let us examine it point by point.

He says that I am guilty of corrupting the young, but I say that Meletus is guilty of dealing frivolously with serious matters, of irresponsibly bringing people into court, and of professing to be seriously concerned with things about none of which he has ever cared, and I shall try to prove that this is so. Come here and tell me, Meletus. Surely you consider it of the greatest importance that our young men be as good as possible?[5]—Indeed I do.

Come then, tell the jury who improves them. You obviously know, in view of your concern. You say you have discovered the one who corrupts them, namely me, and you bring me here and accuse me to the jury. Come, inform the jury and tell them who it is. You see, Meletus, that you are silent and know not what to say. Does this not seem shameful to you and a sufficient proof of what I say, that you have not been concerned with any of this? Tell me, my good sir, who improves our young men?—The laws.

That is not what I am asking, but what person who has knowledge of the laws to begin with?—These jurymen, Socrates.

How do you mean, Meletus? Are these able to educate the young and improve them?—Certainly.

All of them, or some but not others?—All of them.

Very good, by Hera. You mention a great abundance of benefactors. But what about the audience? Do they improve the young or not?—They do, too.

What about the members of Council?—The Councillors, also.

But, Meletus, what about the assembly? Do members of the assembly corrupt the young, or do they all improve them?—They improve them.

---

[5] Socrates here drops into his usual method of discussion by question and answer. This, no doubt, is what Plato had in mind, at least in part, when he made him ask the indulgence of the jury if he spoke "in his usual manner."

All the Athenians, it seems, make the young into fine good men, except me, and I alone corrupt them. Is that what you mean?—That is most definitely what I mean.

You condemn me to a great misfortune. Tell me: does this also apply to horses do you think? That all men improve them and one individual corrupts them? Or is quite the contrary true, one individual is able to improve them, or very few, namely the horse breeders, whereas the majority, if they have horses and use them, corrupt them? Is that not the case, Meletus, both with horses and all other animals? Of course it is, whether you and Anytus say so or not. It would be a very happy state of affairs if only one person corrupted our youth, while the others improved them.

You have made it sufficiently obvious, Meletus, that you have never had any concern for our youth; you show your indifference clearly; that you have given no thought to the subjects about which you bring me to trial.

And by Zeus, Meletus, tell us also whether it is better for a man to live among good or wicked fellow-citizens. Answer, my good man, for I am not asking a difficult question. Do not the wicked do some harm to those who are ever closest to them, whereas good people benefit them?—Certainly.

And does the man exist who would rather be harmed than benefited by his associates? Answer, my good sir, for the law orders you to answer. Is there any man who wants to be harmed?—Of course not.

Come now, do you accuse me here of corrupting the young and making them worse deliberately or unwillingly?—Deliberately.

What follows, Meletus? Are you so much wiser at your age than I am at mine that you understand that wicked people always do some harm to their closest neighbours while good people do them good, but I have reached such a pitch of ignorance that I do not realize this, namely that if I make one of my associates wicked I run the risk of being harmed by him so that I do such a great evil deliberately, as you say? I do not believe you, Meletus, and I do not think anyone else will. Either I do not corrupt the young or, if I do, it is unwillingly, and you are lying in either

case. Now if I corrupt them unwillingly, the law does not require you to bring people to court for such unwilling wrong-doings, but to get hold of them privately, to instruct them and exhort them; for clearly, if I learn better, I shall cease to do what I am doing unwillingly. You, however, have avoided my company and were unwilling to instruct me, but you bring me here, where the law requires one to bring those who are in need of punishment, not of instruction.

And so, gentlemen of the jury, what I said is clearly true: Meletus has never been at all concerned with these matters. Nonetheless tell us, Meletus, how you say that I corrupt the young; or is it obvious from your deposition that it is by teaching them not to believe in the gods in whom the city believes but in other new divinities? Is this not what you say I teach and so corrupt them?—That is most certainly what I do say.

Then by those very gods about whom we are talking, Meletus, make this clearer to me and to the jury: I cannot be sure whether you mean that I teach the belief that there are some gods—and therefore I myself believe that there are gods and am not altogether an atheist, nor am I guilty of that—not, however, the gods in whom the city believes, but others, and that this is the charge against me, that they are others. Or whether you mean that I do not believe in gods at all, and that this is what I teach to others.—This is what I mean, that you do not believe in gods at all.

You are a strange fellow, Meletus. Why do you say this? Do I not believe, as other men do, that the sun and the moon are gods?—No, by Zeus, jurymen, for he says that the sun is stone, and the moon earth.

My dear Meletus, do you think you are prosecuting Anaxagoras? Are you so contemptuous of the jury and think them so ignorant of letters as not to know that the books of Anaxagoras[6] of Clazomenae are full of those theories, and further, that the young men learn from me what

---

[6] Anaxagoras of Clazomenae, born about the beginning of the fifth century BC, came to Athens as a young man and spent his time in the pursuit of natural philosophy. He claimed that the universe was directed by Nous (Mind), and that matter was indestructible but always combining in various ways. He left Athens after being prosecuted for impiety.

they can buy from time to time for a drachma, at most, in the bookshops, and ridicule Socrates if he pretends that these theories are his own, especially as they are so absurd? Is that, by Zeus, what you think of me, Meletus, that I do not believe that there are any gods?—That is what I say, that you do not believe in the gods at all.

You cannot be believed, Meletus, even, I think, by yourself. The man appears to me, gentlemen of the jury, highly insolent and uncontrolled. He seems to have made this deposition out of insolence, violence and youthful zeal. He is like one who composed a riddle and is trying it out: "Will the wise Socrates realize that I am jesting and contradicting myself, or shall I deceive him and others?" I think he contradicts himself in the affidavit, as if he said: "Socrates is guilty of not believing in gods but believing in gods," and surely that is the part of a jester!

Examine with me, gentlemen, how he appears to contradict himself, and you, Meletus, answer us. Remember, gentlemen, what I asked you when I began, not to create a disturbance if I proceed in my usual manner.

Does any man, Meletus, believe in human affairs who does not believe in human beings? Make him answer, and not again and again create a disturbance. Does any man who does not believe in horses believe in equine affairs? Or in flute music but not in flute-players? No, my good sir, no man could. If you are not willing to answer, I will tell you and the jury. Answer the next question, however. Does any man believe in divine activities who does not believe in divinities?— No one.

Thank you for answering, if reluctantly, when the jury made you. Now you say that I believe in divine activities and teach about them, whether new or old, but at any rate divine activities according to what you say, and to this you have sworn in your deposition. But if I believe in divine activities I must quite inevitably believe in divine beings. Is that not so? It is indeed. I shall assume that you agree, as you do not answer. Do we not believe divine beings to be either gods or the children of gods? Yes or no?— Of course.

Then since I do believe in divine beings, as you admit, if divine beings are gods, this is what I mean when I say you speak in riddles and in jest, as you state that I do not believe in gods and then again that I do, since I believe in divine beings. If on the other hand the divine beings are children of the gods, bastard children of the gods by nymphs or some other mothers, as they are said to be, what man would believe children of the gods to exist, but not gods? That would be just as absurd as to believe the young of horses and asses, namely mules, to exist, but not to believe in the existence of horses and asses. You must have made this deposition, Meletus, either to test us or because you were at a loss to find any true wrongdoing of which to accuse me. There is no way in which you could persuade anyone of even small intelligence that it is not the part of one and the same man to believe in the activities of divine beings and gods, and then again the part of one and the same man not to believe in the existence of divinities and gods and heroes.

I do not think, gentlemen of the jury, that it requires a prolonged defence to prove that I am not guilty of the charges in Meletus' deposition, but this is sufficient. On the other hand, you know that what I said earlier is true, that I am very unpopular with many people. This will be my undoing, if I am undone, not Meletus or Anytus but the slanders and envy of many people. This has destroyed many other good men and will, I think, continue to do so. There is no danger that it will stop at me.

Someone might say: "Are you not ashamed, Socrates, to have followed the kind of occupation that has led to your being now in danger of death?" However, I should be right to reply to him: "You are wrong, sir, if you think that a man who is any good at all should take into account the risk of life or death; he should look to this only in his actions, whether what he does is right or wrong, whether he is acting like a good or a bad man." According to your view, all the heroes who died at Troy were inferior people, especially the son of Thetis who was so contemptuous of danger compared with disgrace.[7] When he was eager to kill Hector, his goddess mother warned

---

[7] The scene between Thetis and Achilles is from the *Iliad* (18, 94ff.).

him, as I believe, in some such words as these: "My child, if you avenge the death of your comrade, Patroclus, and you kill Hector, you will die yourself, for your death is to follow immediately after Hector's." Hearing this, he despised death and danger and was much more afraid to live a coward who did not avenge his friends. "Let me die at once," he said, "when once I have given the wrongdoer his deserts, rather than remain here, a laughing-stock by the curved ships, a burden upon the earth." Do you think he gave thought to death and danger?

This is the truth of the matter, gentlemen of the jury: wherever a man has taken a position that he believes to be best, or has been placed by his commander, there he must I think remain and face danger, without a thought for death or anything else, rather than disgrace. It would have been a dreadful way to behave, gentlemen of the jury, if, at Potidaea, Amphipolis and Delium, I had, at the risk of death, like anyone else, remained at my post where those you had elected to command had ordered me, and then, when the god ordered me, as I thought and believed, to live the life of a philosopher, to examine myself and others, I had abandoned my post for fear of death or anything else. That would have been a dreadful thing, and then I might truly have justly been brought here for not believing that there are gods, disobeying the oracle, fearing death, and thinking I was wise when I was not. To fear death, gentlemen, is no other than to think oneself wise when one is not, to think one knows what one does not know. No one knows whether death may not be the greatest of all blessings for a man, yet men fear it as if they knew that it is the greatest of evils. And surely it is the most blameworthy ignorance to believe that one knows what one does not know. It is perhaps on this point and in this respect, gentlemen, that I differ from the majority of men, and if I were to claim that I am wiser than anyone in anything, it would be in this, that, as I have no adequate knowledge of things in the underworld, so I do not think I have. I do know, however, that it is wicked and shameful to do wrong, to disobey one's superior, be he god or man. I

shall never fear or avoid things of which I do not know, whether they may not be good rather than things that I know to be bad. Even if you acquitted me now and did not believe Anytus, who said to you that either I should not have been brought here in the first place, or that now I am here, you cannot avoid executing me, for if I should be acquitted, your sons would practise the teachings of Socrates and all be thoroughly corrupted; if you said to me in this regard: "Socrates, we do not believe Anytus now; we acquit you, but only on condition that you spend no more time on this investigation and do not practise philosophy, and if you are caught doing so you will die"; if, as I say, you were to acquit me on those terms, I would say to you: "Gentlemen of the jury, I am grateful and I am your friend, but I will obey the god rather than you, and as long as I draw breath and am able, I shall not cease to practise philosophy, to exhort you and in my usual way to point out to any one of you whom I happen to meet: Good Sir, you are an Athenian, a citizen of the greatest city with the greatest reputation for both wisdom and power; are you not ashamed of your eagerness to possess as much wealth, reputation and honours as possible, while you do not care for nor give thought to wisdom or truth, or the best possible state of your soul?" Then, if one of you disputes this and says he does care, I shall not let him go at once or leave him, but I shall question him, examine him and test him, and if I do not think he has attained the goodness that he says he has, I shall reproach him because he attaches little importance to the most important things and greater importance to inferior things. I shall treat in this way anyone I happen to meet, young and old, citizen and stranger, and more so the citizens because you are more kindred to me. Be sure that this is what the god orders me to do, and I think there is no greater blessing for the city than my service to the god. For I go around doing nothing but persuading both young and old among you not to care for your body or your wealth in preference to or as strongly as for the best possible state of your soul, as I say to you: "Wealth does not bring about excellence, but excellence brings about wealth and all other public and private blessings for men."

Now if by saying this I corrupt the young, this advice must be harmful, but if anyone says that I give different advice, he is talking nonsense. On this point I would say to you, gentlemen of the jury: "Whether you believe Anytus or not, whether you acquit me or not, do so on the understanding that this is my course of action, even if I am to face death many times." Do not create a disturbance, gentlemen, but abide by my request not to cry out at what I say but to listen, for I think it will be to your advantage to listen, and I am about to say other things at which you will perhaps cry out. By no means do this. Be sure that if you kill the sort of man I say I am, you will not harm me more than yourselves. Neither Meletus nor Anytus can harm me in any way; he could not harm me, for I do not think it is permitted that a better man be harmed by a worse; certainly he might kill me, or perhaps banish or disfranchise me, which he and maybe others think to be great harm, but I do not think so. I think he is doing himself much greater harm doing what he is doing now, attempting to have a man executed unjustly. Indeed, gentlemen of the jury, I am far from making a defence now on my own behalf, as might be thought, but on yours, to prevent you from wrongdoing by mistreating the god's gift to you by condemning me; for if you kill me you will not easily find another like me. I was attached to this city by the god—though it seems a ridiculous thing to say—as upon a great and noble horse which was somewhat sluggish because of its size and needed to be stirred up by a kind of gadfly. It is to fulfill some such function that I believe the god has placed me in the city. I never cease to rouse each and every one of you, to persuade and reproach you all day long and everywhere I find myself in your company.

Another such man will not easily come to be among you, gentlemen, and if you believe me you will spare me. You might easily be annoyed with me as people are when they are aroused from a doze, and strike out at me; if convinced by Anytus you could easily kill me, and then you could

sleep on for the rest of your days, unless the god, in his care for you, sent you someone else. That I am the kind of person to be a gift of the god to the city you might realize from the fact that it does not seem like human nature for me to have neglected all my own affairs and to have tolerated this neglect now for so many years while I was always concerned with you, approaching each one of you like a father or an elder brother to persuade you to care for virtue. Now if I profited from this by charging a fee for my advice, there would be some sense to it, but you can see for yourselves that, for all their shameless accusations, my accusers have not been able in their impudence to bring forward a witness to say that I have ever received a fee or ever asked for one. I, on the other hand, have a convincing witness that I speak the truth, my poverty.

It may seem strange that while I go around and give this advice privately and interfere in private affairs, I do not venture to go to the assembly and there advise the city. You have heard me give the reason for this in many places. I have a divine sign from the god which Meletus has ridiculed in his deposition. This began when I was a child. It is a voice, and whenever it speaks it turns me away from something I am about to do, but it never encourages me to do anything. This is what has prevented me from taking part in public affairs, and I think it was quite right to prevent me. Be sure, gentlemen of the jury, that if I had long ago attempted to take part in politics, I should have died long ago, and benefited neither you nor myself. Do not be angry with me for speaking the truth; no man will survive who genuinely opposes you or any other crowd and prevents the occurrence of many unjust and illegal happenings in the city. A man who really fights for justice must lead a private, not a public, life if he is to survive for even a short time.

I shall give you great proofs of this, not words but what you esteem, deeds. Listen to what happened to me, that you may know that I will not yield to any man contrary to what is right, for fear of death, even if I should die at once for not yielding. The things I shall tell you are commonplace and smack of the lawcourts, but they are true. I have never held any other office in the city, but I served as a member of the Council, and our tribe Antiochis was presiding at the time when you wanted to try as a body the ten generals who had failed to pick up the survivors of the naval battle.[8] This was illegal, as you all recognized later. I was the only member of the presiding committee to oppose your doing something contrary to the laws, and I voted against it. The orators were ready to prosecute me and take me away, and your shouts were egging them on, but I thought I should run any risk on the side of law and justice rather than join you, for fear of prison or death, when you were engaged in an unjust course.

This happened when the city was still a democracy. When the oligarchy was established, the Thirty[9] summoned me to the Hall, along with four others, and ordered us to bring Leon from Salamis, that he might be executed. They gave many such orders to many people, in order to implicate as many as possible in their guilt. Then I showed again, not in words but in action, that, if it were not rather vulgar to say so, death is something I couldn't care less about, but that my whole concern is not to do anything unjust or impious. That government, powerful as it was, did not frighten me into any wrongdoing. When we left the Hall, the other four went to Salamis and brought in Leon, but I went home. I might have been put to death for this, had not the government fallen shortly afterwards. There are many who will witness to these events.

Do you think I would have survived all these years if I were engaged in public affairs and, acting as a good man must, came to the help of justice and considered this the most important thing? Far from it, gentlemen of the jury, nor would any other man. Throughout my life, in any public activity I may have engaged in, I am the same man as I am in private life. I have never come to an agreement with anyone to act unjustly, neither with anyone else nor with any one of those who they slanderously say are my pupils. I have never been anyone's teacher. If anyone, young or old, desires to listen to me when I am talking and dealing with my own concerns, I have never begrudged this to anyone, but I do not converse when I receive a fee and not when I do not. I am equally ready to question the rich and the poor if anyone is willing to answer my questions and listen to what I say. And I cannot justly be held responsible for the good or bad conduct of these people, as I never promised to teach them anything and have not done so. If anyone says that he has learned anything from me, or that he heard anything privately that the others did not hear, be assured that he is not telling the truth.

Why then do some people enjoy spending considerable time in my company? You have heard why, gentlemen of the jury, I have told you the whole truth. They enjoy hearing those being questioned who think they are wise, but are not. And this is not unpleasant. To do this has, as I say, been enjoined upon me by the god, by means of oracles and dreams, and in every other way that a divine manifestation has ever ordered a man to do anything. This is true, gentlemen, and can easily be established.

If I corrupt some young men and have corrupted others, then surely some of them who have grown older and realized that I gave them bad advice when they were young should now themselves come up here to accuse me and avenge themselves. If they were unwilling to do so themselves, then some of their kindred, their fathers or brothers or other relations should recall it now if their family had been harmed by me. I see many of these present here, first Crito, my contemporary and fellow demesman, the father of Critoboulos here; next Lysanias of Sphettus, the father of Aeschines here; also Antiphon the Cephisian, the father of Epigenes; and others

---

[8] This was the battle of Arginusae (south of Lesbos) in 406 BC, the last Athenian victory of the war. A violent storm prevented the Athenian generals from rescuing their survivors. For this they were tried in Athens and sentenced to death by the assembly. They were tried in a body, and it is this to which Socrates objected in the Council's presiding committee which prepared the business of the assembly. He obstinately persisted in his opposition, in which he stood alone, and was overruled by the majority. Six generals who were in Athens were executed.

[9] This was the harsh oligarchy that was set up after the final defeat of Athens in 404 BC and that ruled Athens for some nine months in 404 – 403 before the democracy was restored.

whose brothers spent their time in this way; Nicostratus, the son of Theozotides, brother of Theodotus, and Theodotus has died so he could not influence him; Paralios here, son of Demodocus, whose brother was Theages; there is Adeimantus, son of Ariston, brother of Plato here; Acantidorus, brother of Apollodorus here.

I could mention many others, some one of whom surely Meletus should have brought in as witness in his own speech. If he forgot to do so, then let him do it now; I will yield time if he has anything of the kind to say. You will find quite the contrary, gentlemen. These men are all ready to come to the help of the corruptor, the man who has harmed their kindred, as Meletus and Anytus say. Now those who were corrupted might well have reason to help me, but the uncorrupted, their kindred who are older men, have no reason to help me except the right and proper one, that they know that Meletus is lying and that I am telling the truth.

Very well, gentlemen of the jury. This, and maybe other similar things, is what I have to say in my defence. Perhaps one of you might be angry as he recalls that when he himself stood trial on a less dangerous charge, he begged and implored the jury with many tears, that he brought his children and many of his friends and family into court to arouse as much pity as he could, but that I do none of these things, even though I may seem to be running the ultimate risk. Thinking of this, he might feel resentful toward me and, angry about this, cast his vote in anger. If there is such a one among you—I do not deem there is, but if there is—I think it would be right to say in reply: My good sir, I too have a household and, in Homer's phrase, I am not born "from oak or rock" but from men, so that I have a family, indeed three sons, gentlemen of the jury, of whom one is an adolescent while two are children. Nevertheless, I will not beg you to acquit me by bringing them here. Why do I do none of these things? Not through arrogance, gentlemen, nor through lack of respect for you. Whether I am brave in the face of death is another matter, but with regard to my reputation and yours and that of the whole city, it does not seem right to me to do these things, especially at my age and with my reputation. For it is generally believed, whether it be true or false, that in certain respects Socrates is superior to the majority of men. Now if those of you who are considered superior, be it in wisdom or courage or whatever other virtue makes them so, are seen behaving like that, it would be a disgrace. Yet I have often seen them do this sort of thing when standing trial, men who are thought to be somebody, doing amazing things as if they thought it a terrible thing to die, and as if they were to be immortal if you did not execute them. I think these men bring shame upon the city so that a stranger, too, would assume that those who are outstanding in virtue among the Athenians, whom they themselves select from themselves to fill offices of state and receive other honours, are in no way better than women. You should not act like that, gentlemen of the jury, those of you who have any reputation at all, and if we do, you should not allow it. You should make it very clear that you will more readily convict a man who performs these pitiful dramatics in court and so makes the city a laughingstock, than a man who keeps quiet.

Quite apart from the question of reputation, gentlemen, I do not think it right to supplicate the jury and to be acquitted because of this, but to teach and persuade them. It is not the purpose of a juryman's office to give justice as a favour to whoever seems good to him, but to judge according to law, and this he has sworn to do. We should not accustom you to perjure yourselves, nor should you make a habit of it. This is irreverent conduct for either of us.

Do not deem it right for me, gentlemen of the jury, that I should act towards you in a way that I do not consider to be good or just or pious, especially, by Zeus, as I am being prosecuted by Meletus here for impiety; clearly, if I convinced you by my supplication to do violence to your oath of office, I would be teaching you not to believe that there are gods, and my defence would convict me of not believing in them. This is far from being the case, gentlemen, for I do believe in them as none of my accusers do. I leave it to you and the god to judge me in the way that will be best for me and for you.

[*The jury now gives its verdict of guilty, and Meletus asks for the penalty of death.*]

There are many other reasons for my not being angry with you for convicting me, gentlemen of the jury, and what happened was not unexpected. I am much more surprised at the number of votes cast on each side, for I did not think the decision would be by so few votes but by a great many. As it is, a switch of only thirty votes would have acquitted me. I think myself that I have been cleared on Meletus' charges, and not only this, but it is clear to all that, if Anytus and Lycon had not joined him in accusing me, he would have been fined a thousand drachmas for not receiving a fifth of the votes.

He assesses the penalty at death. So be it. What counter-assessment should I propose to you, gentlemen of the jury? Clearly it should be a penalty I deserve, and what do I deserve to suffer or to pay because I have deliberately not led a quiet life but have neglected what occupies most people: wealth, household affairs, the position of general or public orator or the other offices, the political clubs and factions that exist in the city? I thought myself too honest to survive if I occupied myself with those things. I did not follow that path that would have made me of no use either to you or to myself, but I went to each of you privately and conferred upon him what I say is the greatest benefit, by trying to persuade him not to care for any of his belongings before caring that he himself should be as good and as wise as possible, not to care for the city's possessions more than for the city itself, and to care for other things in the same way. What do I deserve for being such a man? Some good, gentlemen of the jury, if I must truly make an assessment according to my deserts, and something suitable. What is suitable for a poor benefactor who needs leisure to exhort you? Nothing is more suitable, gentlemen, than for such a man to be fed in the Prytaneum,[10] much more suitable for him than for any one of you who has won a victory at Olympia with a pair or a team of horses. The Olympian victor makes you think yourself happy; I make you be happy. Besides, he does not need food, but I do. So if I must make a just assessment of what I deserve, I assess it at this: free meals in the Prytaneum.

When I say this you may think, as when I spoke of appeals to pity and entreaties, that I speak arrogantly, but that is not the case, gentlemen of the jury; rather it is like this: I am convinced that I never willingly wrong anyone, but I am not convincing you of this, for we have talked together but a short time. If it were the law with us, as it is elsewhere, that a trial for life should not last one but many days, you would be convinced, but now it is not easy to dispel great slanders in a short time. Since I am convinced that I wrong no one, I am not likely to wrong myself, to say that I deserve some evil and to make some such assessment against myself. What should I fear? That I should suffer the penalty Meletus has assessed against me, of which I say I do not know whether it is good or bad? Am I then to choose in preference to this something that I know very well to be an evil and assess the penalty at that? Imprisonment? Why should I live in prison, always subjected to the ruling magistrates the Eleven? A fine, and imprisonment until I pay it? That would be the same thing for me, as I have no money. Exile? for perhaps you might accept that assessment.

I should have to be inordinately fond of life, gentlemen of the jury, to be so unreasonable as to suppose that other men will easily tolerate my company and conversation when you, my fellow citizens, have been unable to endure them, but found them a burden and resented them so that you are now seeking to get rid of them. Far from it, gentlemen. It would be a fine life at my age to be driven out of one city after another, for I know very well that wherever I go the young men will listen to my talk as they do here. If I drive them away, they will themselves persuade their elders to drive me out; if I do not drive them away, their fathers and relations will drive me out on their behalf.

Perhaps someone might say: But Socrates, if you leave us will you not be able to live quietly, without talking? Now this is the most difficult

---

[10] The Prytaneum was the magistrates' hall or town hall of Athens in which public entertainments were given, particularly to Olympian victors on their return home.

point on which to convince some of you. If I say that it is impossible for me to keep quiet because that means disobeying the god, you will not believe me and will think I am being ironical. On the other hand, if I say that it is the greatest good for a man to discuss virtue every day and those other things about which you hear me conversing and testing myself and others, for the unexamined life is not worth living for man, you will believe me even less.

What I say is true, gentlemen, but it is not easy to convince you. At the same time, I am not accustomed to think that I deserve any penalty. If I had money, I would assess the penalty at the amount I could pay, for that would not hurt me, but I have none, unless you are willing to set the penalty at the amount I can pay, and perhaps I could pay you one mina of silver.[11] So that is my assessment.

Plato here, gentlemen of the jury, and Crito and Critoboulus and Apollodorus bid me put the penalty at thirty minae, and they will stand surety for the money. Well then, that is my assessment, and they will be sufficient guarantee of payment.

[*The jury now votes again and sentences Socrates to death.*]

It is for the sake of a short time, gentlemen of the jury, that you will acquire the reputation and the guilt, in the eyes of those who want to denigrate the city, of having killed Socrates, a wise man, for they who want to revile you will say that I am wise even if I am not. If you had waited but a little while, this would have happened of its own accord. You see my age, that I am already advanced in years and close to death. I am saying this not to all of you but to those who condemned me to death, and to these same jurors I say: Perhaps you think that I was convicted for lack of such words as might have convinced you, if I thought I should say or do all I could to avoid my sentence. Far from it. I was convicted because I lacked not words but boldness and shamelessness and the willingness to say to you what you

would most gladly have heard from me, lamentations and tears and my saying and doing many things that I say are unworthy of me but that you are accustomed to hear from others. I did not think then that the danger I ran should make me do anything mean, nor do I now regret the nature of my defence. I would much rather die after this kind of defence than live after making the other kind. Neither I nor any other man should, on trial or in war, contrive to avoid death at any cost. Indeed it is often obvious in battle that one could escape death by throwing away one's weapons and by turning to supplicate one's pursuers, and there are many ways to avoid death in every kind of danger if one will venture to do or say anything to avoid it. It is not difficult to avoid death, gentlemen of the jury, it is much more difficult to avoid wickedness, for it runs faster than death. Slow and elderly as I am, I have been caught by the slower pursuer, whereas my accusers, being clever and sharp, have been caught by the quicker, wickedness. I leave you now, condemned to death by you, but they are condemned by truth to wickedness and injustice. So I maintain my assessment, and they maintain theirs. This perhaps had to happen, and I think it is as it should be.

Now I want to prophesy to those who convicted me, for I am at the point when men prophesy most, when they are about to die. I say gentlemen, to those who voted to kill me, that vengeance will come upon you immediately after my death, a vengeance much harder to bear than that which you took in killing me. You did this in the belief that you would avoid giving an account of your life, but I maintain that quite the opposite will happen to you. There will be more people to test you, whom I now held back, but you did not notice it. They will be more difficult to deal with as they will be younger and you will resent them more. You are wrong if you believe that by killing people you will prevent anyone from reproaching you for not living in the right way. To escape such tests is neither possible nor good, but it is best and easiest not to discredit others but to prepare oneself to be as good as possible. With this prophecy to you who convicted me, I part from you.

[11] One mina was 100 drachmas, equivalent to, say, twenty-five dollars, though in purchasing power probably five times greater. In any case, a ridiculously small sum under the circumstances.

I should be glad to discuss what has happened with those who voted for my acquittal during the time that the officers of the court are busy and I do not yet have to depart to my death. So, gentlemen, stay with me awhile, for nothing prevents us from talking to each other while it is allowed. To you, as being my friends, I want to show the meaning of what has occurred. A surprising thing has happened to me, judges—you I would rightly call judges. At all previous times my usual mantic sign frequently opposed me, even in small matters, when I was about to do something wrong, but now that, as you can see for yourselves, I was faced with what one might think, and what is generally thought to be, the worst of evils, my divine sign has not opposed me, either when I left home at dawn, or when I came into court, or at any time that I was about to say something during my speech. Yet in other talks it often held me back in the middle of my speaking, but now it has opposed no word or deed of mine. What do I think is the reason for this? I will tell you. What has happened to me may well be a good thing, and those of us who believe death to be an evil are certainly mistaken. I have convincing proof of this, for it is impossible that my customary sign did not oppose me if I was not about to do what was right.

Let us reflect in this way, too, that there is good hope that death is a blessing, for it is one of two things: either the dead are nothing and have no perception of anything, or it is, as we are told, a change and a relocating for the soul from here to another place. If it is complete lack of perception, like a dreamless sleep, then death would be a great advantage. For I think that if one had to pick out that night during which a man slept soundly and did not dream, put beside it the other nights and days of his life, and then see how many days and nights had been better and more pleasant than that night, not only a private person but the great king would find them easy to count compared with the other days and nights. If death is like this I say it is an advantage, for all eternity would then seem to be no more than a single night. If, on the other hand, death is a change from here to another place, and what we are told is true and all who

have died are there, what greater blessing could there be, gentlemen of the jury? If anyone arriving in Hades will have escaped from those who call themselves judges here, and will find those true judges who are said to sit in judgement there, Minos and Radamanthus and Aeacus and Triptolemus and the other demi-gods who have been upright in their own life, would that be a poor kind of change? Again, what would one of you give to keep company with Orpheus and Musaeus, Hesiod and Homer? I am willing to die many times if that is true. It would be a wonderful way for me to spend my time whenever I met Palamedes and Ajax, the son of Telamon, and any other of the men of old who died through an unjust conviction, to compare my experience with theirs. I think it would be pleasant. Most important, I could spend my time testing and examining people there, as I do here, as to who among them is wise, and who thinks he is, but is not.

What would one not give, gentlemen of the jury, for the opportunity to examine the man who led the great expedition against Troy, or Odysseus, or Sisyphus, and innumerable other men and women one could mention. It would be an extraordinary happiness to talk with them, to keep company with them and examine them. In any case, they would certainly not put one to death for doing so. They are happier there than we are here in other respects, and for the rest of time they are deathless, if indeed what we are told is true.

You too must be of good hope as regards death, gentlemen of the jury, and keep this one truth in mind, that a good man cannot be harmed either in life or in death, and that his affairs are not neglected by the gods. What has happened to me now has not happened of itself, but it is clear to me that it was better for me to die now and to escape from trouble. That is why my divine sign did not oppose me at any point. So I am certainly not angry with those who convicted me, or with my accusers. Of course that was not their purpose when they accused and convicted me, but they thought they were hurting me, and for this they deserve blame. This much I ask from them: when my sons grow up, avenge yourselves by causing them the same kind of grief that I caused you, if you think they care for money or anything else more than they care for virtue, or if they think they are somebody when they are nobody. Reproach them as I reproach you, that they do not care for the right things and think they are worthy when they are not worthy of anything. If you do this, I shall have been justly treated by you, and my sons also.

Now the hour to part has come. I go to die, you go to live. Which of us goes to the better lot is known to no one, except the god.

# PLATO'S REPUBLIC

## *Background on Plato: The Justice Debate*

The greatest philosophical work that remains from the ancient world is undoubtedly Plato's *Republic.* In it he paints his picture of a utopian republic, discussing not only political questions, but epistemological, psychological, ethical, and aesthetic ones as well. It is set immediately after a civic celebration in the house of Cephalus, who lives in Athens's port city, the Piraeus. Socrates describes the conversation the next day to a number of people who weren't actually there. The purpose of the dialogue is to define *justice,* which Socrates believes requires a full description of the just state. This description will give us evidence not only of what the just individual is like, but also of the essence of justice in general, what Plato calls the "form" of justice.

Plato (427–347 BC) was from an aristocratic family in Athens. His father Ariston was a descendent of Athens's ancient kings, and his uncles Critias and Charmenides were part of an aristocratic uprising against Athenian democracy. Plato was well connected and unsympathetic to democracy. He wrote either 26 or 28 dialogues (the authenticity of two of them is in question) on various philosophical issues, including *The Republic.*

He was a student of Socrates. His early writings show great admiration for the famous philosophical gadfly. He was present at Socrates' defense, which he recorded in the *Apology.* He traveled to Italy and Sicily when he was forty, to Italy probably to meet with some followers of Pythagoras, and to Sicily to visit the tyrant Dionysius I of Syracuse in the hopes (false, as it turned out) of implementing some of his utopian political ideas there. One story has it that he was briefly sold into slavery. In any case, he returned to Athens after his failure to influence Dionysius.

Plato then founded a school called the Academy in Athens. Over its portal was the inscription "Let No One Ignorant of Mathematics Enter Here." Plato was influenced by the mathematical mysticism of Pythagoras. He believed that geometry and mathematics in general represented the purest form of reasoning, that form which was most free from the polluting world of the senses. As a result, the Academy (in a sense the first university) taught arithmetic, geometry, astronomy, harmonics, and, of course, philosophy. It had scientific equipment and a library, and lasted 300 years. Aristotle was a student of the Academy for many years.

Book 1 and the opening parts of book 2 of *The Republic* involve the only truly dialectical part of the dialogue, the only part where Socrates is forced to take seriously the objections of his audience. Later the book degenerates into a monologue by Socrates, interrupted by remarks from his audience like "clearly" or "yes" or "I dare say." In it Socrates critically examines a series of definitions of justice given by his friends.

1. The dialogue starts after a religious festival when Socrates and Glaucon are pulled aside by Polemarchus and invited to stay for the evening in his home (this section is omitted from the readings below). Over dinner, they strike up a conversation. Polemarchus's father Cephalus starts by spending some time reflecting on old age. Socrates then pulls a definition of justice out of him. Cephalus suggests that **justice is telling the truth and paying back debts** [which we can designate definition "J1"] (331d). Socrates asks, "Is it right to give back a weapon to a madman who is threatening to kill everyone?" It would seem not, so they reject this definition. Cephalus leaves, handing the dialectical baton to his son Polemarchus.

2. Polemarchus then suggests that justice is giving everyone his or her due—**justice is helping friends and harming enemies** [J2] (332d). But Socrates asks, "Who are one's friends? Those he *believes* to be so, or those who *really are* good?" If it's those we merely *believe* to be good, then it's possible that justice demands that we help bad people and harm innocent ones. Moreover, it's never just to harm people. Treating people badly doesn't improve them. So this definition is rejected.

3. The first really serious definition comes from Thrasymachus, a Sophist. He suggests that **justice is what's in the interest of the stronger party** [J3A] (337c). He says, paraphrasing somewhat, "Look around at all the states in the world. They each have their own sets of laws made by the state's rulers to protect their private interests. Thus all laws are just reflections of the interests of the powerful."

Socrates responds by noting that even rulers sometimes make mistakes, and so, as just citizens—even under Thrasymachus's own definition of justice—we are sometimes compelled to disobey the commands of those in power. Thrasymachus attempts to save his J3A argument by saying that a ruler acting *as* a ruler cannot make mistakes, but Socrates counters this by trying to show that a ruler's interests lie in doing what's good for his subjects.

4. Thrasymachus replies to this by claiming that the only reason people behave well is because they fear punishment. Real leaders, he says, treat their subjects like sheep. His new claim is something like the following:

> **People are just only because they fear suffering wrong. Injustice, on a grand scale, is the best course of action for a ruler, if he is wise.** [J3B] (343–344)

Socrates first replies with a tricky argument that tries to show that the just are good and wise, while the unjust are evil and ignorant (this has been omitted from the readings below). He then makes the more substantial argument that the unjust person and the unjust state will lack any unity of purpose, as both will suffer from endless internal quarrels. So they will be neither strong nor happy.

5. Glaucon vigorously defends Thrasymachus's way of thinking by recounting the story of the Ring of Gyges, which had the magical power of rendering one invisible. If we gave one such ring to a just person, and another to an unjust one, they would behave in the same way. Further, a perfectly just man who is *seen* as unjust will be persecuted, while an unjust man who cunningly hides his evil acts will be applauded by the multitude. So Thrasymachus was right: people behave justly out of fear of being caught (359c–360d).

Adeimantus adds that even if the gods are angry at the unjust, it's better to become rich and buy them off with sacrifices. So justice is useless to those superior in wealth or power. Real justice is thus **whatever one can get away with** [J4].

Plato's general answer to the Ring of Gyges problem is that only a harmonious soul is truly just. To prove this, he suggests that we look for the meaning of justice in an ideal state, for the justice in such a state will give us the "big picture" of what justice in the soul looks like. It takes him the rest of the dialogue to describe the outlines of such a state.

# The Republic, Part 1

## PLATO

### PERSONS OF THE DIALOGUE

SOCRATES, the narrator.
GLAUCON, Plato's brother.
ADEIMANTUS, Plato's brother.
POLEMARCHUS, Cephalus's son.
CEPHALUS, the host.
THRASYMACHUS, a Sophist.
CLEITOPHON.

. . . and others who are mute auditors. The dialogue takes place in the house of Cephalus at the Piraeus, the port of Athens, just after a city festival.

*[Part 1. The Justice Debate.*
*Book 1–Book 2, 367e]*

[CHAPTER 2. POLEMARCHUS: JUSTICE AS HELPING FRIENDS AND HARMING ENEMIES. BOOK I, 331E–336A]

[331e] Tell me then, heir of the argument, what did Simonides[1] say, and according to you truly say, about justice?

[1] Simonides (ca. 556–468 BC) was a lyric poet from the Aegean island of Ceos.

He said that the repayment of a debt is just, and in saying so he appears to me to be right.

I should be sorry to doubt the word of such a wise and inspired man, but his meaning, though probably clear to you, is the reverse of clear to me. For he certainly does not mean, as we were just now saying, that I ought to return a deposit of arms or of anything else to one who asks for it when he is not in his right senses; and yet a deposit [332a] cannot be denied to be a debt.

True.

Then when the person who asks me is not in his right mind I am by no means to make the return?

Certainly not.

When Simonides said that the repayment of a debt was justice, he did not mean to include that case?

Certainly not; for he thinks that a friend ought always to do good to a friend and never evil.

You mean that the return of a deposit of gold [332b] which is to the injury of the receiver, if the two parties are friends, is not the repayment of a debt—that is what you would imagine him to say?

Yes.

And are enemies also to receive what we owe to them?

SOURCE: *The Republic of Plato,* 3rd ed., trans. Benjamin Jowett (1871; Oxford: Clarendon Press, 1888). The readings from *The Republic* are based on Benjamin Jowett's 1871 translation. The spelling and punctuation have been modernized; in a small number of cases we have also modernized Jowett's language. We've followed J. M. Cornford's division of *The Republic* into 5 parts and 40 chapters, although we've shifted his division between parts 1 and 2 forward and changed a few of his chapter titles slightly. Our readings consist of most of part 1, three selections from part 2, and two from part 3. The part and chapter titles have been enclosed in square brackets to emphasize the fact that these divisions didn't exist in the original work. All footnotes are ours—ED.

To be sure, he said, they are to receive what we owe them, and an enemy, as I take it, owes to an enemy that which is due or proper to him—that is to say, evil.

Simonides, then, after the manner of poets, would seem to have spoken darkly of the nature of justice; [332c] for he really meant to say that justice is the giving to each man what is proper to him, and this he termed a debt.

That must have been his meaning, he said.

By heaven! I replied; and if we asked him what due or proper thing is given by medicine, and to whom, what answer do you think that he would make to us?

He would surely reply that medicine gives drugs and meat and drink to human bodies.

And what due or proper thing is given by cookery, and to what?

[332d] Seasoning to food.

And what is that which justice gives, and to whom?

If, Socrates, we are to be guided at all by the analogy of the preceding instances, then justice is the art which gives good to friends and evil to enemies.

That is his meaning then?

I think so.

And who is best able to do good to his friends and evil to his enemies in time of sickness?

The physician.

[332e] Or when they are on a voyage, amid the perils of the sea?

The pilot.

And in what sort of actions or with a view to what result is the just man most able to do harm to his enemy and good to his friends?

In going to war against the one and in making alliances with the other.

But when a man is well, my dear Polemarchus, there is no need of a physician?

No.

And he who is not on a voyage has no need of a pilot?

No.

Then in time of peace justice will be of no use?

I am very far from thinking so.

You think that justice may be of use in peace as well as in war?

[333a] Yes.

Like farming for the acquisition of grain?

Yes.

Or like shoemaking for the acquisition of shoes—that is what you mean?

Yes.

And what similar use or power of acquisition has justice in time of peace?

In contracts, Socrates, justice is of use.

And by contracts you mean partnerships?

Exactly.

But is the just man [333b] or the skilful player a more useful and better partner at a game of draughts?

The skilful player.

And in the laying of bricks and stones is the just man a more useful or better partner than the builder?

Quite the reverse.

Then in what sort of partnership is the just man a better partner than the harp-player, as in playing the harp the harp-player is certainly a better partner than the just man?

In a money partnership.

Yes, Polemarchus, but surely not in the use of money; for you do not want a just man to be your counsellor in the purchase [333c] or sale of a horse; a man who is knowing about horses would be better for that, would he not?

Certainly.

And when you want to buy a ship, the shipwright or the pilot would be better?

True.

Then what is that joint use of silver or gold in which the just man is to be preferred?

When you want a deposit to be kept safely.

You mean when money is not wanted, but allowed to lie?

Precisely.

That is to say, justice is useful when money is useless?

[333d] That is the inference.

And when you want to keep a pruning-hook safe, then justice is useful to the individual and to the state; but when you want to use it, then the art of the vine-dresser?

Clearly.

And when you want to keep a shield or a lyre,

and not to use them, you would say that justice is useful; but when you want to use them, then the art of the soldier or of the musician?

Certainly.

And so of all the other things; justice is useful when they are useless, and useless when they are useful?

That is the inference.

[333e] Then justice is not good for much. But let us consider this further point: Is not he who can best strike a blow in a boxing match or in any kind of fighting best able to ward off a blow?

Certainly.

And he who is most skilful in preventing or escaping from a disease is best able to create one?

True.

And [334a] he is the best guard of a camp who is best able to steal a march upon the enemy?

Certainly.

Then he who is a good keeper of anything is also a good thief?

That, I suppose, is to be inferred.

Then if the just man is good at keeping money, he is good at stealing it.

That is implied in the argument.

Then after all the just man has turned out to be a thief. And this is a lesson which I suspect you must have learnt out of Homer; for he, speaking of Autolycus, [334b] the maternal grandfather of Odysseus, who is a favourite of his, affirms that

"He was excellent above all men in theft and perjury."

And so, you and Homer and Simonides are agreed that justice is an art of theft; to be practiced however "for the good of friends and for the harm of enemies," that was what you were saying?

No, certainly not that, though I do not now know what I did say; but I still stand by the latter words.

[334c] Well, there is another question: By friends and enemies do we mean those who are so really, or only in seeming?

Surely, he said, a man may be expected to love those whom he thinks good, and to hate those whom he thinks evil.

Yes, but do not persons often err about good and evil: many who are not good seem to be so, and conversely?

That is true.

Then to them the good will be enemies and the evil will be their friends?

True.

And in that case they will be right in doing good to the evil [334d] and evil to the good?

Clearly.

But the good are just and would not do an injustice?

True.

Then according to your argument it is just to injure those who do no wrong?

No, Socrates; the doctrine is immoral.

Then I suppose that we ought to do good to the just and harm to the unjust?

I like that better.

But see the consequence—Many a man who is ignorant of human nature has friends who are bad friends, [334e] and in that case he ought to do harm to them; and he has good enemies whom he ought to benefit; but, if so, we shall be saying the very opposite of that which we affirmed to be the meaning of Simonides.

Very true, he said: and I think that we had better correct an error into which we seem to have fallen in the use of the words "friend" and "enemy."

What was the error, Polemarchus? I asked.

We assumed that he is a friend who seems to be or who is thought good.

And how is the error to be corrected?

We should rather say that he is a friend who is, as well as seems, good; and that he who seems only, [335a] and is not good, only seems to be and is not a friend; and of an enemy the same may be said.

You would argue that the good are our friends and the bad our enemies?

Yes.

And instead of saying simply as we did at first, that it is just to do good to our friends and harm to our enemies, we should further say: It is just to do good to our friends when they are good and harm to our enemies when they are evil?

[335b] Yes, that appears to me to be the truth.

But ought the just to injure any one at all?

Undoubtedly he ought to injure those who are both wicked and his enemies.

When horses are injured, are they improved or deteriorated?

The latter.

Deteriorated, that is to say, in the good qualities of horses, not of dogs?

Yes, of horses.

And dogs are deteriorated in the good qualities of dogs, and not of horses?

Of course.

[335c] And will not men who are injured be deteriorated in that which is the proper virtue of man?

Certainly.

And that human virtue is justice?

To be sure.

Then men who are injured are of necessity made unjust?

That is the result.

But can the musician by his art make men unmusical?

Certainly not.

Or the horseman by his art make them bad horsemen?

Impossible.

And can the just by justice make men unjust, [335d] or speaking generally, can the good by virtue make them bad?

Assuredly not.

Any more than heat can produce cold?

It cannot.

Or drought moisture?

Clearly not.

Nor can the good harm any one?

Impossible.

And the just is the good?

Certainly.

Then to injure a friend or any one else is not the act of a just man, but of the opposite, who is the unjust?

I think that what you say is quite true, [335e] Socrates.

Then if a man says that justice consists in the repayment of debts, and that good is the debt which a man owes to his friends, and evil the debt which he owes to his enemies,—to say this is not wise; for it is not true, if, as has been clearly shown, the injuring of another can be in no case just.

I agree with you, said Polemarchus.

Then you and I are prepared to take up arms against any one who attributes such a saying to Simonides or Bias or Pittacus, or any other wise man or seer?

I am quite ready to do battle at your side, he said.

[336a] Shall I tell you whose I believe the saying to be?

Whose?

I believe that Periander or Perdiccas or Xerxes or Ismenias the Theban, or some other rich and mighty man, who had a great opinion of his own power, was the first to say that justice is "doing good to your friends and harm to your enemies."

Most true, he said.

Yes, I said; but if this definition of justice also breaks down, what other can be offered?

## [CHAPTER 3. THRASYMACHUS: JUSTICE AS THE INTEREST OF THE STRONGER. BOOK 2, 336B–347E]

[336b] Several times in the course of the discussion Thrasymachus had made an attempt to get the argument into his own hands, and had been put down by the rest of the company, who wanted to hear the end. But when Polemarchus and I had done speaking and there was a pause, he could no longer hold his peace; and, gathering himself up, he came at us like a wild beast, seeking to devour us. We were quite panic-stricken at the sight of him.

He roared out to the whole company: [336c] What folly, Socrates, has taken possession of you all? And why, sillybillies, do you knuckle under to one another? I say that if you want really to know what justice is, you should not only ask but answer, and you should not seek honour to yourself from the refutation of an opponent, but have your own answer; for there is many a one who can ask and cannot answer. [336d] And now I will not have you say that justice is duty or advantage or profit or gain or interest, for this sort of nonsense will not do for me; I must have clearness and accuracy.

I was panic-stricken at his words, and could not look at him without trembling. Indeed I believe that if I had not fixed my eye upon him, I should have been struck dumb: but when I saw his fury rising, [336e] I looked at him first, and was therefore able to reply to him.

Thrasymachus, I said, with a quiver, don't be hard upon us. Polemarchus and I may have been guilty of a little mistake in the argument, but I can assure you that the error was not intentional. If we were seeking for a piece of gold, you would not imagine that we were "knuckling under to one another," and so losing our chance of finding it. And why, when we are seeking for justice, a thing more precious than many pieces of gold, do you say that we are weakly yielding to one another and not doing our utmost to get at the truth? No, my good friend, we are most willing and anxious to do so, but the fact is that we cannot. And if so, you people who know all things should pity us [337a] and not be angry with us.

How characteristic of Socrates! he replied, with a bitter laugh—that's your ironical style! Did I not foresee—have I not already told you, that whatever he was asked he would refuse to answer, and try irony or any other shuffle, in order that he might avoid answering?

You are a philosopher, Thrasymachus, I replied, and well know that if you ask a person what numbers make up twelve, [337b] taking care to prohibit him whom you ask from answering twice six, or three times four, or six times two, or four times three, "for this sort of nonsense will not do for me," then obviously, that is your way of putting the question, no one can answer you. But suppose that he were to retort, "Thrasymachus, what do you mean? If one of these numbers which you forbid be the true answer to the question, am I falsely to say some other number which is not the right one?—[337c] is that your meaning?" How would you answer him?

Just as if the two cases were at all alike! he said.

Why should they not be? I replied; and even if they are not, but only appear to be so to the person who is asked, ought he not to say what he thinks, whether you and I forbid him or not?

I presume then that you are going to make one of the forbidden answers?

I dare say that I may, notwithstanding the danger, if upon reflection I approve of any of them.

But what [337d] if I give you an answer about justice other and better, he said, than any of these? What do you deserve to have done to you?

Done to me!—as becomes the ignorant, I must learn from the wise—that is what I deserve to have done to me.

What, and no payment! a pleasant notion!

I will pay when I have the money, I replied.

But you have, Socrates, said Glaucon: and you, Thrasymachus, need be under no anxiety about money, for we will all make a contribution for Socrates.

Yes, [337e] he replied, and then Socrates will do as he always does—refuse to answer himself, but take and pull to pieces the answer of some one else.

Why, my good friend, I said, how can any one answer who knows, and says that he knows, just nothing; and who, even if he has some faint notions of his own, is told by a man of authority not to utter them? [338a] The natural thing is, that the speaker should be some one like yourself who professes to know and can tell what he knows. Will you then kindly answer, for the edification of the company and of myself?

Glaucon and the rest of the company joined in my request and Thrasymachus, as any one might see, was in reality eager to speak; for he thought that he had an excellent answer, and would distinguish himself. But at first he pretended to insist on my answering; at length he consented to begin. [338b] Behold, he said, the wisdom of Socrates; he refuses to teach himself, and goes about learning of others, to whom he never even says Thank you.

That I learn of others, I replied, is quite true; but that I am ungrateful I wholly deny. I have no money, and therefore I pay in praise, which is all I have: and how ready I am to praise any one who appears to me to speak well you will very soon find out when you answer; [338c] for I expect that you will answer well.

Listen, then, he said; I proclaim that justice is nothing else than the interest of the stronger. And now why do you not praise me? But of course you won't.

Let me first understand you, I replied. Justice, as you say, is the interest of the stronger. What, Thrasymachus, is the meaning of this? You cannot mean to say that because Polydamas, the wrestler, is stronger than we are, and finds the eating of beef conducive to his [338d] bodily strength, that to eat beef is therefore equally for our good who are weaker than he is, and right and just for us?

That's abominable of you, Socrates; you take the words in the sense which is most damaging to the argument.

Not at all, my good sir, I said; I am trying to understand them; and I wish that you would be a little clearer.

Well, he said, have you never heard that forms of government differ; there are tyrannies, and there are democracies, and there are aristocracies?

Yes, I know.

And the government is the ruling power in each state?

Certainly.

[338e] And the different forms of government make laws democratic, aristocratic, tyrannical, with a view to their several interests; and these laws, which are made by them for their own interests, are the justice which they deliver to their subjects, and him who transgresses them they punish as a breaker of the law, and unjust. And that is what I mean when I say that in all states there is the same principle of justice, [339a] which is the interest of the government; and as the government must be supposed to have power, the only reasonable conclusion is, that everywhere there is one principle of justice, which is the interest of the stronger.

Now I understand you, I said; and whether you are right or not I will try to discover. But let me remark, that in defining justice you have yourself used the word "interest" which you forbade me to use. [339b] It is true, however, that in

your definition the words "of the stronger" are added.

A small addition, you must allow, he said.

Great or small, never mind about that: we must first enquire whether what you are saying is the truth. Now we are both agreed that justice is interest of some sort, but you go on to say "of the stronger"; about this addition I am not so sure, and must therefore consider further.

Proceed.

I will; and first tell me, Do you admit that it is just for subjects to obey their rulers?

[339c] I do.

But are the rulers of states absolutely infallible, or are they sometimes liable to err?

To be sure, he replied, they are liable to err.

Then in making their laws they may sometimes make them rightly, and sometimes not?

True.

When they make them rightly, they make them agreeably to their interest; when they are mistaken, contrary to their interest; you admit that?

Yes.

And the laws which they make must be obeyed by their subjects,—and that is what you call justice?

Doubtless.

[339d] Then justice, according to your argument, is not only obedience to the interest of the stronger but the reverse?

What is that you are saying? he asked.

I am only repeating what you are saying, I believe. But let us consider: Have we not admitted that the rulers may be mistaken about their own interest in what they command, and also that to obey them is justice? Has not that been admitted?

Yes.

[339e] Then you must also have acknowledged justice not to be for the interest of the stronger, when the rulers unintentionally command things to be done which are to their own injury. For if, as you say, justice is the obedience which the subject renders to their commands, in that case, O wisest of men, is there any escape from the conclusion that the weaker are commanded to do, not what is for the interest, [340a] but what is for the injury of the stronger?

Nothing can be clearer, Socrates, said Polemarchus.

Yes, said Cleitophon, interposing, if you are allowed to be his witness.

But there is no need of any witness, said Polemarchus, for Thrasymachus himself acknowledges that rulers may sometimes command what is not for their own interest, and that for subjects to obey them is justice.

Yes, Polemarchus—Thrasymachus said that for subjects to do what was commanded by their rulers is just.

Yes, Cleitophon, but he also said that justice is the interest of the stronger, and, [340b] while admitting both these propositions, he further acknowledged that the stronger may command the weaker who are his subjects to do what is not for his own interest; whence follows that justice is the injury quite as much as the interest of the stronger.

But, said Cleitophon, he meant by the interest of the stronger what the stronger thought to be his interest—this was what the weaker had to do; and this was affirmed by him to be justice.

Those were not his words, [340c] rejoined Polemarchus.

Never mind, I replied, if he now says that they are, let us accept his statement. Tell me, Thrasymachus, I said, did you mean by justice what the stronger thought to be his interest, whether really so or not?

Certainly not, he said. Do you suppose that I call him who is mistaken the stronger at the time when he is mistaken?

Yes, I said, my impression was that you did so, when you admitted that the ruler was not infallible [340d] but might be sometimes mistaken.

You argue like an informer, Socrates. Do you mean, for example, that he who is mistaken about the sick is a physician in that he is mistaken? or that he who errs in arithmetic or grammar is an arithmetician or grammarian at the time when he is making the mistake, in respect of the mistake? True, we say that the physician or arithmetician or grammarian has made a mistake, but this is only a way of speaking; for the fact is that [340e] neither the grammarian nor any other person of skill ever makes a mistake in so far as he is what his name implies; they none of them err unless their skill fails them, and then they cease to be skilled artists. No artist or sage or ruler errs at the time when he is what his name implies; though he is commonly said to err, and I adopted the common mode of speaking. But to be perfectly accurate, since you are such a lover of accuracy, we should say that the ruler, [341a] in so far as he is a ruler, is unerring, and, being unerring, always commands that which is for his own interest; and the subject is required to execute his commands; and therefore, as I said at first and now repeat, justice is the interest of the stronger.

Indeed, Thrasymachus, and do I really appear to you to argue like an informer?

Certainly, he replied.

And you suppose that I ask these questions with any design of injuring you in the argument?

No, he replied, "suppose" is not the word—I know it; but you will be found out, and [341b] by sheer force of argument you will never prevail.

I shall not make the attempt, my dear man; but to avoid any misunderstanding occurring between us in future, let me ask, in what sense do you speak of a ruler or stronger whose interest, as you were saying, he being the superior, it is just that the inferior should execute—is he a ruler in the popular or in the strict sense of the term?

In the strictest of all senses, he said. And now cheat and play the informer if you can; [341c] I ask no quarter at your hands. But you never will be able, never.

And do you imagine, I said, that I am such a madman as to try and cheat Thrasymachus? I might as well shave a lion.

Why, he said, you made the attempt a minute ago, and you failed.

Enough, I said, of these civilities. It will be better that I should ask you a question: Is the physician, taken in that strict sense of which you are speaking, a healer of the sick or a maker of money? And remember that I am now speaking of the true physician.

A healer of the sick, he replied.

And the pilot—that is to say, the true pilot—is he a captain of sailors or a mere sailor?

[341d] A captain of sailors.

The circumstance that he sails in the ship is not to be taken into account; neither is he to be called a sailor; the name pilot by which he is distinguished has nothing to do with sailing, but is significant of his skill and of his authority over the sailors.

Very true, he said.

Now, I said, every art has an interest?

Certainly.

For which the art has to consider and provide?

Yes, that is the aim of art.

And the interest of any art is the perfection of it—this and nothing else?

[341e] What do you mean?

I mean what I may illustrate negatively by the example of the body. Suppose you were to ask me whether the body is self-sufficing or has wants, I should reply: Certainly the body has wants; for the body may be ill and require to be cured, and has therefore interests to which the art of medicine ministers; and this is the origin and intention of medicine, as you will acknowledge. Am I not right?

[342a] Quite right, he replied.

But is the art of medicine or any other art faulty or deficient in any quality in the same way that the eye may be deficient in sight or the ear fail of hearing, and therefore requires another art to provide for the interests of seeing and hearing—has art in itself, I say, any similar liability to fault or defect, and does every art require another supplementary art to provide for its interests, and that another and another without end? Or have the arts to look only after their own interests? [342b] Or have they no need either of themselves or of another?—having no faults or defects, they have no need to correct them, either by the exercise of their own art or of any other; they have only to consider the interest of their subject-matter. For every art remains pure and faultless while remaining true—that is to say, while perfect and unimpaired. Take the words in your precise sense, and tell me whether I am not right.

Yes, clearly.

Then medicine [342c] does not consider the interest of medicine, but the interest of the body?

True, he said.

Nor does the art of horsemanship consider the interests of the art of horsemanship, but the interests of the horse; neither do any other arts care for themselves, for they have no needs; they care only for that which is the subject of their art?

True, he said.

But surely, Thrasymachus, the arts are the superiors and rulers [342d] of their own subjects?

To this he assented with a good deal of reluctance.

Then, I said, no science or art considers or enjoins the interest of the stronger or superior, but only the interest of the subject and weaker?

He made an attempt to contest this proposition also, but finally acquiesced.

Then, I continued, no physician, in so far as he is a physician, considers his own good in what he prescribes, but the good of his patient; for the true physician is also a ruler having the human body as a subject, and is not a mere money-maker; that has been admitted?

Yes.

And the pilot likewise, in the strict sense of the term, is a ruler of sailors and [342e] not a mere sailor?

That has been admitted.

And such a pilot and ruler will provide and prescribe for the interest of the sailor who is under him, and not for his own or the ruler's interest?

He gave a reluctant "Yes."

Then, I said, Thrasymachus, there is no one in any rule who, in so far as he is a ruler, considers or enjoins what is for his own interest, but always what is for the interest of his subject or suitable to his art; to that he looks, and that alone he considers in everything which he says and does.

[343a] When we had got to this point in the argument, and every one saw that the definition of justice had been completely upset, Thrasymachus, instead of replying to me, said: Tell me, Socrates, have you got a nurse?

Why do you ask such a question, I said, when you ought rather to be answering?

Because she leaves you to snivel, and never wipes your nose: she has not even taught you to know the shepherd from the sheep.

What makes you say that? I replied.

Because you fancy that the shepherd or [343b] cowherd fattens or tends the sheep or oxen with a view to their own good and not to the good of himself or his master; and you further imagine that the rulers of states, if they are true rulers, never think of their subjects as sheep, and that they are not studying [343c] their own advantage day and night. Oh, no; and so entirely astray are you in your ideas about the just and unjust as not even to know that justice and the just are in reality another's good; that is to say, the interest of the ruler and stronger, and the loss of the subject and servant; and injustice the opposite; for the unjust is lord over the truly simple and just: he is the stronger, and his subjects do what is for his interest, and minister to his happiness, [343d] which is very far from being their own. Consider further, most foolish Socrates, that the just is always a loser in comparison with the unjust. First of all, in private contracts: wherever the unjust is the partner of the just you will find that, when the partnership is dissolved, the unjust man has always more and the just less. Secondly, in their dealings with the State: when there is an income tax, the just man will pay more and the unjust less on the same amount of income; and when there is anything to be received [343e] the one gains nothing and the other much. Observe also what happens when they take an office; there is the just man neglecting his affairs and perhaps suffering other losses, and getting nothing out of the public, because he is just; moreover he is hated by his friends and acquaintance for refusing to serve them in unlawful ways. But all this is reversed in the case of the unjust man. I am speaking, as before, [344a] of injustice on a large scale in which the advantage of the unjust is more apparent; and my meaning will be most clearly seen if we turn to that highest form of injustice in which the criminal is the happiest of men, and the sufferers or those who refuse to do injustice are the most miserable—that is to say tyranny, which by fraud and force takes away the property of others, not little by little but wholesale; comprehending in one, things sacred as well as profane, private and public; [344b] for which acts of wrong, if he were detected perpetrating

any one of them singly, he would be punished and incur great disgrace—they who do such wrong in particular cases are called robbers of temples, and man-stealers and burglars and swindlers and thieves. But when a man besides taking away the money of the citizens has made slaves of them, then, instead of these names of reproach, he is termed happy and blessed, not only by the citizens [344c] but by all who hear of his having achieved the consummation of injustice. For mankind censure injustice, fearing that they may be the victims of it and not because they shrink from committing it. And thus, as I have shown, Socrates, injustice, when on a sufficient scale, has more strength and freedom and mastery than justice; and, as I said at first, justice is the interest of the stronger, whereas injustice is a man's own profit and interest.

[344d] Thrasymachus, when he had thus spoken, having, like a bathman, deluged our ears with his words, had a mind to go away. But the company would not let him; they insisted that he should remain and defend his position; and I myself added my own humble request that he would not leave us. Thrasymachus, I said to him, excellent man, how suggestive are your remarks! And are you going to run away before you have fairly taught or learned whether they are true or not? Is the attempt to determine the way of man's life so small a matter in your eyes [344e]— to determine how life may be passed by each one of us to the greatest advantage?

And do I differ from you, he said, as to the importance of the enquiry?

You appear rather, I replied, to have no care or thought about us, Thrasymachus—whether we live better or worse from not knowing what you say you know, is to you a matter of indifference. Please, friend, do not keep your knowledge to yourself; we are a large party; [345a] and any benefit which you confer upon us will be amply rewarded. For my own part I openly declare that I am not convinced, and that I do not believe injustice to be more gainful than justice, even if uncontrolled and allowed to have free play. For, granting that there may be an unjust man who is able to commit injustice either by fraud or force, still this does not convince me of the superior advantage of injustice, [345b] and there may be others who are in the same predicament with myself. Perhaps we may be wrong; if so, you in your wisdom should convince us that we are mistaken in preferring justice to injustice.

And how am I to convince you, he said, if you are not already convinced by what I have just said; what more can I do for you? Would you have me put the proof bodily into your souls?

Heaven forbid! I said; I would only ask you to be consistent; or, if you change, change openly and let there be no deception. [345c] For I must remark, Thrasymachus, if you will recall what was previously said, that although you began by defining the true physician in an exact sense, you did not observe a like exactness when speaking of the shepherd; you thought that the shepherd as a shepherd tends the sheep not with a view to their own good, but like a mere diner or banqueter with a view to the pleasures of the table; or, again, [345d] as a trader for sale in the market, and not as a shepherd. Yet surely the art of the shepherd is concerned only with the good of his subjects; he has only to provide the best for them, since the perfection of the art is already ensured whenever all the requirements of it are satisfied. And that was what I was saying just now about the ruler. I conceived that the art of the ruler, considered as ruler, whether in a state or in private life, [345e] could only regard the good of his flock or subjects; whereas you seem to think that the rulers in states, that is to say, the true rulers, like being in authority.

Think! No, I am sure of it.

Then why in the case of lesser offices do men never take them willingly without payment, unless under the idea that they govern for the advantage not of themselves but of others? [346a] Let me ask you a question: Are not the several arts different, by reason of their each having a separate function? And, my dear illustrious friend, do say what you think, that we may make a little progress.

Yes, that is the difference, he replied.

And each art gives us a particular good and not merely a general one—medicine, for example, gives us health; navigation, safety at sea, and so on?

Yes, he said.

And the art of payment has the special function of giving pay: but we do not confuse this with other arts, [346b] any more than the art of the pilot is to be confused with the art of medicine, because the health of the pilot may be improved by a sea voyage. You would not be inclined to say, would you, that navigation is the art of medicine, at least if we are to adopt your exact use of language?

Certainly not.

Or because a man is in good health when he receives pay you would not say that the art of payment is medicine?

I should say not.

[346c] Nor would you say that medicine is the art of receiving pay because a man takes fees when he is engaged in healing?

Certainly not.

And we have admitted, I said, that the good of each art is specially confined to the art?

Yes.

Then, if there be any good which all artists have in common, that is to be attributed to something of which they all have the common use?

True, he replied.

And when the artist is benefited by receiving pay the advantage is gained by an additional use of the art of pay, which is not the art professed by him?

He gave a reluctant assent to this.

Then the pay [346d] is not derived by the several artists from their respective arts. But the truth is, that while the art of medicine gives health, and the art of the builder builds a house, another art attends them which is the art of pay. The various arts may be doing their own business and benefiting that over which they preside, but would the artist receive any benefit from his art unless he were paid as well?

I suppose not.

But does he therefore confer no benefit [346e] when he works for nothing?

Certainly, he confers a benefit.

Then now, Thrasymachus, there is no longer any doubt that neither arts nor governments provide for their own interests; but, as we were before saying, they rule and provide for the interests of their subjects who are the weaker and not the stronger—to their good they attend and not to the good of the superior. And this is the reason, my dear Thrasymachus, why, as I was just now saying, no one is willing to govern; because no one likes to take in hand the reformation of evils which are not his concern without remuneration. [347a] For, in the execution of his work, and in giving his orders to another, the true artist does not regard his own interest, but always that of his subjects; and therefore in order that rulers may be willing to rule, they must be paid in one of three modes of payment: money, or honour, or a penalty for refusing.

What do you mean, Socrates? said Glaucon. The first two modes of payment are intelligible enough, but what the penalty is I do not understand, or how a penalty can be a payment.

You mean that you do not understand the nature of this payment which to the best men [347b] is the great inducement to rule? Of course you know that ambition and avarice are held to be, as indeed they are, a disgrace?

Very true.

And for this reason, I said, money and honour have no attraction for them; good men do not wish to be openly demanding payment for governing and so to get the name of hirelings, nor by secretly helping themselves out of the public revenues to get the name of thieves. And not being ambitious [347c] they do not care about honour. Wherefore necessity must be laid upon them, and they must be induced to serve from the fear of punishment. And this, as I imagine, is the reason why the forwardness to take office, instead of waiting to be compelled, has been deemed dishonourable. Now the worst part of the punishment is that he who refuses to rule is liable to be ruled by one who is worse than himself. And the fear of this, as I conceive, induces the good to take office, not because they would, but because they cannot help—not under the idea that they are going to have any benefit or enjoyment themselves, but as a necessity, and because they are not able to commit the task of ruling to any one who is better than themselves, [347d] or indeed as good. For there is reason to think that if a city were composed entirely of

good men, then to avoid office would be as much an object of contention as to obtain office is at present; then we should have plain proof that the true ruler is not meant by nature to regard his own interest, but that of his subjects; and every one who knew this would choose rather to receive a benefit from another than to have the trouble of conferring one. So far am I [347e] from agreeing with Thrasymachus that justice is the interest of the stronger. This latter question need not be further discussed at present.

## [CHAPTER 4, EDITED. THRASYMACHUS: JUSTICE IS MORE PROFITABLE THAN INJUSTICE. BOOK I, 350C–354C]

[350c] . . . Then the just has turned out to be wise and good and the unjust evil and ignorant.

Thrasymachus made all these admissions, [350d] not fluently, as I repeat them, but with extreme reluctance; it was a hot summer's day, and the perspiration poured from him in torrents; and then I saw what I had never seen before, Thrasymachus blushing. As we were now agreed that justice was virtue and wisdom, and injustice vice and ignorance, I proceeded to another point:

Well, I said, Thrasymachus, that matter is now settled; but were we not also saying that injustice had strength; do you remember?

Yes, I remember, he said, but do not suppose that I approve of what you are saying or have no answer; [350e] if however I were to answer, you would be quite certain to accuse me of haranguing; therefore either permit me to have my say out, or if you would rather ask, do so, and I will answer "Very good," as they say to story-telling old women, and will nod "Yes" and "No."

Certainly not, I said, if contrary to your real opinion.

Yes, he said, I will, to please you, since you will not let me speak. What else would you have?

Nothing in the world, I said; and if you are so disposed I will ask and you shall answer.

Proceed.

Then I will repeat the question which I asked before, in order that our examination of [351a] the relative nature of justice and injustice may be carried on regularly. A statement was made that injustice is stronger and more powerful than justice, but now justice, having been identified with wisdom and virtue, is easily shown to be stronger than injustice, if injustice is ignorance; this can no longer be questioned by any one. But I want to view the matter, Thrasymachus, in a different way: You would not deny that a state may be unjust and [351b] may be unjustly attempting to enslave other states, or may have already enslaved them, and may be holding many of them in subjection?

True, he replied; and I will add the best and perfectly unjust state will be most likely to do so.

I know, I said, that such was your position; but what I would further consider is, whether this power which is possessed by the superior state can exist or be exercised without justice or only with justice.

[351c] If you are right in your view, and justice is wisdom, then only with justice; but if I am right, then without justice.

I am delighted, Thrasymachus, to see you not only nodding assent and dissent, but making answers which are quite excellent.

That is out of civility to you, he replied.

You are very kind, I said; and would you have the goodness also to inform me, whether you think that a state, or an army, or a band of robbers and thieves, or any other gang of evil-doers could act at all if they injured one another?

[351d] No indeed, he said, they could not.

But if they abstained from injuring one another, then they might act together better?

Yes.

And this is because injustice creates divisions and hatreds and fighting, and justice imparts harmony and friendship; is not that true, Thrasymachus?

I agree, he said, because I do not wish to quarrel with you.

How good of you, I said; but I should like to know also whether injustice, having this tendency to arouse hatred, wherever existing, among slaves or among freemen, will not make them hate one another and set them at variance and render them incapable [351e] of common action?

Certainly.

And even if injustice be found in two only, will they not quarrel and fight, and become enemies to one another and to the just?

They will.

And suppose injustice abiding in a single person, would your wisdom say that she loses or that she retains her natural power?

Let us assume that she retains her power.

Yet is not the power which injustice exercises of such a nature that wherever she takes up her abode, whether in a city, in an army, in a family, or in any other body, [352a] that body is, to begin with, rendered incapable of united action by reason of sedition and distraction; and does it not become its own enemy and at variance with all that opposes it, and with the just? Is not this the case?

Yes, certainly.

And is not injustice equally fatal when existing in a single person; in the first place rendering him incapable of action because he is not at unity with himself, and in the second place making him an enemy to himself and the just? Is not that true, Thrasymachus?

Yes.

And my friend, I said, [352b] surely the gods are just?

Granted that they are.

But if so, the unjust will be the enemy of the gods, and the just will be their friend?

Feast away in triumph, and take your fill of the argument; I will not oppose you, lest I should displease the company.

Well then, proceed with your answers, and let me have the remainder of my repast. For we have already shown that the just are clearly wiser and better and abler than the unjust, [352c] and that the unjust are incapable of common action; nay more, that to speak as we did of men who are evil acting at any time vigorously together, is not strictly true, for if they had been perfectly evil, they would have laid hands upon one another; but it is evident that there must have been some remnant of justice in them, which enabled them to combine; if there had not been they would have injured one another as well as their victims; they were but half-villains in their enterprises; for had they been whole villains, and utterly unjust, [352d] they would have been utterly incapable of action. That, as I believe, is the truth of the matter, and not what you said at first. But whether the just have a better and happier life than the unjust is a further question which we also proposed to consider. I think that they have, and for the reasons which to have given; but still I should like to examine further, for no light matter is at stake, nothing less than the rule of human life.

Proceed.

I will proceed by asking a question: Would you not say [352e] that a horse has some end?

I should.

And the end or use of a horse or of anything would be that which could not be accomplished, or not so well accomplished, by any other thing?

I do not understand, he said.

Let me explain: Can you see, except with the eye?

Certainly not.

Or hear, except with the ear?

No.

These then may be truly said to be the ends of these organs?

They may.

But you [353a] can cut off a vine-branch with a dagger or with a chisel, and in many other ways?

Of course.

And yet not so well as with a pruning-hook made for the purpose?

True.

May we not say that this is the end of a pruning-hook?

We may.

Then now I think you will have no difficulty in understanding my meaning when I asked the question whether the end of anything would be that which could not be accomplished, or not so well accomplished, by any other thing?

I understand your meaning, he said, and assent.

[353b] And that to which an end is appointed has also an excellence? Need I ask again whether the eye has an end?

It has.

And has not the eye an excellence?

Yes.

And the ear has an end and an excellence also?

True.

And the same is true of all other things; they have each of them an end and a special excellence?

That is so.

Well, and can the eyes fulfill their end [353c] if they are wanting in their own proper excellence and have a defect instead?

How can they, he said, if they are blind and cannot see?

You mean to say, if they have lost their proper excellence, which is sight; but I have not arrived at that point yet. I would rather ask the question more generally, and only enquire whether the things which fulfill their ends fulfill them by their own proper excellence, and fall of fulfilling them by their own defect?

Certainly, he replied.

I might say the same of the ears; when deprived of their own proper excellence they cannot fulfill their end?

True.

And the same observation will apply [353d] to all other things?

I agree.

Well; and has not the soul an end which nothing else can fulfill? for example, to superintend and command and deliberate and the like. Are not these functions proper to the soul, and can they rightly be assigned to any other?

To no other.

And is not life to be reckoned among the ends of the soul?

Assuredly, he said.

And has not the soul an excellence also? [353e] Yes.

And can she or can she not fulfill her own ends when deprived of that excellence?

She cannot.

Then an evil soul must necessarily be an evil ruler and superintendent, and the good soul a good ruler?

Yes, necessarily.

And we have admitted that justice is the excellence of the soul, and injustice the defect of the soul?

That has been admitted.

Then the just soul and the just man will live well, and the unjust man will live ill?

That is what your argument proves.

[354a] And he who lives well is blessed and happy, and he who lives ill the reverse of happy?

Certainly.

Then the just is happy, and the unjust miserable?

So be it.

But happiness and not misery is profitable.

Of course.

Then, my blessed Thrasymachus, injustice can never be more profitable than justice.

Let this, Socrates, he said, be your entertainment at the Bendidea.[2]

For which I am indebted to you, I said, now that you have grown gentle towards me and have left off scolding. Nevertheless, I have not been well entertained; [354b] but that was my own fault and not yours. As an epicure snatches a taste of every dish which is successively brought to table, he not having allowed himself time to enjoy the one before, so have I gone from one subject to another without having discovered what I sought at first, the nature of justice. I left that enquiry and turned away to consider whether justice is virtue and wisdom or evil and folly; and when there arose a further question about the comparative advantages of justice and injustice, I could not refrain from passing on to that. [354c] And the result of the whole discussion has been that I know nothing at all. For I know not what justice is, and therefore I am not likely to know whether it is or is not a virtue, nor can I say whether the just man is happy or unhappy.

## [CHAPTER 5. GLAUCON AND ADEIMANTUS: THE RING OF GYGES; JUSTICE AS EXPEDIENCY. BOOK 2, 357A–367E]

[357a] With these words I was thinking that I had made an end of the discussion; but the end, in truth, proved to be only a beginning. For Glaucon, who is always the most pugnacious of men, was dissatisfied at Thrasymachus' retirement; he wanted to have the battle out. So he said to me: Socrates, do you wish really to persuade us, [357b] or only to seem to have persuaded us, that to be just is always better than to be unjust?

I should wish really to persuade you, I replied, if I could.

Then you certainly have not succeeded. Let me ask you now:—How would you arrange goods—are there not some which we welcome for their own sakes, and independently of their consequences, as, for example, harmless pleasures and enjoyments, which delight us at the time, although nothing follows from them?

[357c] I agree in thinking that there is such a class, I replied.

Is there not also a second class of goods, such as knowledge, sight, health, which are desirable not only in themselves, but also for their results?

Certainly, I said.

And would you not recognize a third class, such as gymnastic, and the care of the sick, and the physician's art; also the various ways of money-making—these do us good but we regard them as disagreeable; [357d] and no one would choose them for their own sakes, but only for the sake of some reward or result which flows from them?

There is, I said, this third class also. But why do you ask?

Because I want to know in which of the three classes you would place justice?

[358a] In the highest class, I replied,—among those goods which he who would be happy desires both for their own sake and for the sake of their results.

Then the many are of another mind; they think that justice is to be reckoned in the troublesome class, among goods which are to be pursued for the sake of rewards and of reputation, but in themselves are disagreeable and rather to be avoided.

I know, I said, that this is their manner of thinking, and that this was the thesis which Thrasymachus was maintaining just now, when

---

[2] The horseback torch races that the company was going to attend after supper.

he censured justice and praised injustice. But I am too stupid to be convinced by him.

I wish, [358b] he said, that you would hear me as well as him, and then I shall see whether you and I agree. For Thrasymachus seems to me, like a snake, to have been charmed by your voice sooner than he ought to have been; but to my mind the nature of justice and injustice have not yet been made clear. Setting aside their rewards and results, I want to know what they are in themselves, and how they inwardly work in the soul. If you, please, then, I will revive [358c] the argument of Thrasymachus. And first I will speak of the nature and origin of justice according to the common view of them. Secondly, I will show that all men who practice justice do so against their will, of necessity, but not as a good. And thirdly, I will argue that there is reason in this view, for the life of the unjust is after all better far than the life of the just—if what they say is true, Socrates, since I myself am not of their opinion. But still I acknowledge that I am perplexed when I hear the voices of Thrasymachus and myriads of others dinning in my ears; and, on the other hand, [358d] I have never yet heard the superiority of justice to injustice maintained by any one in a satisfactory way. I want to hear justice praised in respect of itself; then I shall be satisfied, and you are the person from whom I think that I am most likely to hear this; and therefore I will praise the unjust life to the utmost of my power, and my manner of speaking will indicate the manner in which I desire to hear you too praising justice and censuring injustice. Will you say whether you approve of my proposal?

Indeed I do; [358e] nor can I imagine any theme about which a man of sense would more often wish to converse.

I am delighted, he replied, to hear you say so, and shall begin by speaking, as I proposed, of the nature and origin of justice.

They say that to do injustice is, by nature, good; to suffer injustice, evil; but that the evil is greater than the good. And so when men have both done and suffered injustice and have had experience of both, not being able [359a] to avoid the one and obtain the other, they think

that they had better agree among themselves to have neither; hence there arise laws and mutual covenants; and that which is ordained by law is termed by them lawful and just. This they affirm to be the origin and nature of justice;—it is a mean or compromise, between the best of all, which is to do injustice and not be punished, and the worst of all, which is to suffer injustice without the power of retaliation; and justice, being at a middle point between the two, is tolerated not as a good, [359b] but as the lesser evil, and honoured by reason of the inability of men to do injustice. For no man who is worthy to be called a man would ever submit to such an agreement if he were able to resist; he would be mad if he did. Such is the traditional received account, Socrates, of the nature and origin of justice.

Now that those who practice justice do so involuntarily and because they have not the power to be unjust will best appear if we imagine something of this kind: [359c] having given both to the just and the unjust power to do what they will, let us watch and see where desire will lead them; then we shall discover in the very act the just and unjust man to be proceeding along the same road, following their interest, which all natures deem to be their good, and are only diverted into the path of justice by the force of law. The liberty which we are supposing may be most completely given to them in the form of such a power [359d] as is said to have been possessed by Gyges the ancestor of Croesus the Lydian.[3] According to the tradition, Gyges was a shepherd in the service of the king of Lydia; there was a great storm, and an earthquake made an opening in the earth at the place where he was feeding his flock. Amazed at the sight, he descended into the opening, where, among other marvels, he beheld a hollow brazen horse, having doors, at which he stooping and looking in saw a dead

[3] Croesus was the last king of Lydia, a kingdom in Asia Minor. He ruled from about 560 to 546 BC, and was known for his great riches. Jealous of Persian power, he asked the oracle of Dodona what would happen if he attacked the Persians. The oracle told him that "a great empire will fall." So he went to war with Persia, was defeated, and his kingdom destroyed, thus proving the oracle right.

body of stature, as appeared to him, more than human, [359e] and having nothing on but a gold ring; this he took from the finger of the dead and went back up. Now the shepherds met together, according to custom, that they might send their monthly report about the flocks to the king; into their assembly he came having the ring on his finger, and as he was sitting among them he chanced to turn the collet of the ring inside his hand, when instantly he became invisible [360a] to the rest of the company and they began to speak of him as if he were no longer present. He was astonished at this, and again touching the ring he turned the collet outwards and reappeared; he made several trials of the ring, and always with the same result—when he turned the collet inwards he became invisible, when outwards he reappeared. Whereupon he contrived to be chosen one of the messengers [360b] who were sent to the court; where as soon as he arrived he seduced the queen, and with her help conspired against the king and slew him, and took the kingdom. Suppose now that there were two such magic rings, and the just put on one of them and the unjust the other; no man can be imagined to be of such an iron nature that he would stand fast in justice. No man would keep his hands off what was not his own when he could safely take what he liked out of the market, [360c] or go into houses and lie with any one at his pleasure, or kill or release from prison whom he would, and in all respects be like a God among men. Then the actions of the just would be as the actions of the unjust; they would both come at last to the same point. And this we may truly affirm to be a great proof that a man is just, not willingly or because he thinks that justice is any good to him individually, but of necessity, for wherever any one thinks that he can safely be unjust, there he is unjust. [360d] For all men believe in their hearts that injustice is far more profitable to the individual than justice, and he who argues as I have been supposing, will say that they are right. If you could imagine any one obtaining this power of becoming invisible, and never doing any wrong or touching what was another's, he would be thought by the lookers-on to be a most wretched idiot, although they would praise him to one another's faces, and keep up appearances with one another from a fear that they too might suffer injustice. Enough of this.

[360e] Now, if we are to form a real judgment of the life of the just and unjust, we must isolate them; there is no other way; and how is the isolation to be effected? I answer: Let the unjust man be entirely unjust, and the just man entirely just; nothing is to be taken away from either of them, and both are to be perfectly furnished for the work of their respective lives. First, let the unjust be like other distinguished masters of craft; like the skilful pilot or physician, who knows intuitively his own powers and keeps within their limits, [361a] and who, if he fails at any point, is able to recover himself. So let the unjust make his unjust attempts in the right way, and lie hidden if he means to be great in his injustice (he who is found out is nobody): for the highest reach of injustice is: to be deemed just when you are not. Therefore I say that in the perfectly unjust man we must assume the most perfect injustice; there is to be no deduction, but we must allow him, while doing the most unjust acts, to have acquired the greatest reputation for justice. [361b] If he have taken a false step he must be able to recover himself; he must be one who can speak with effect, if any of his deeds come to light, and who can force his way where force is required his courage and strength, and command of money and friends. And at his side let us place the just man in his nobleness and simplicity, wishing, as Aeschylus[4] says, to be and not to seem good. There must be no seeming, for if he seem to be just [361c] he will be honoured and rewarded, and then we shall not know whether he is just for the sake of justice or for the sake of honours and rewards; therefore, let him be clothed in justice only, and have no other covering; and he must be imagined in a state of life the opposite of the former. Let him be the best

---

[4] Aeschylus (ca. 525–456 BC) was the first of the great Greek tragedians. He wrote about 90 plays, of which 7 survive. He presented them at competitive drama festivals in Athens. His most well known plays are *Seven against Thebes*, *Agamemnon*, and *Prometheus Bound*.

of men, and let him be thought the worst; then he will have been put to the proof; and we shall see whether he will be affected by the fear of infamy and its consequences. And let him continue thus to the hour of death; [361d] being just and seeming to be unjust. When both have reached the uttermost extreme, the one of justice and the other of injustice, let judgment be given which of them is the happier of the two.

Heavens! my dear Glaucon, I said, how energetically you polish them up for the decision, first one and then the other, as if they were two statues.

I do my best, he said. And now that we know what they are like there is no difficulty in tracing out the sort of life which awaits either of them. [361e] This I will proceed to describe; but as you may think the description a little too coarse, I ask you to suppose, Socrates, that the words which follow are not mine.—Let me put them into the mouths of the eulogists of injustice: They will tell you that the just man who is thought unjust will be scourged, racked, bound—[362a] will have his eyes burnt out; and, at last, after suffering every kind of evil, he will be impaled: Then he will understand that he ought to seem only, and not to be, just; the words of Aeschylus may be more truly spoken of the unjust than of the just. For the unjust is pursuing a reality; he does not live with a view to appearances—he wants to be really unjust and not to seem only:

"His mind has a soil deep and fertile, [362b]
Out of which spring his prudent counsels."

In the first place, he is thought just, and therefore bears rule in the city; he can marry whom he will, and give in marriage to whom he will; also he can trade and deal where he likes, and always to his own advantage, because he has no misgivings about injustice; and at every contest, whether in public or private, he gets the better of his antagonists, and gains at their expense, and is rich, and out of his gains he can benefit his friends, [362c] and harm his enemies; moreover, he can offer sacrifices, and dedicate gifts to the gods abundantly and magnificently, and can honour the gods or any man whom he wants to honour in a far better style than the just, and therefore he is likely to be dearer than they are to the gods. And thus, Socrates, gods and men are said to unite in making the life of the unjust better than the life of the just.

I was going to say something in answer to Glaucon, [362d] when Adeimantus, his brother, interposed: Socrates, he said, you do not suppose that there is nothing more to be urged?

Why, what else is there? I answered.

The strongest point of all has not been even mentioned, he replied.

Well, then, according to the proverb, "Let brother help brother"—if he fails in any part do you assist him; although I must confess that Glaucon has already said quite enough to lay me in the dust, [362e] and take from me the power of helping justice.

Nonsense, he replied. But let me add something more: There is another side to Glaucon's argument about the praise and censure of justice and injustice, which is equally required in order to bring out what I believe to be his meaning. Parents and tutors are always telling their sons and their wards [363a] that they are to be just; but why? not for the sake of justice, but for the sake of character and reputation; in the hope of obtaining for him who is reputed just some of those offices, marriages, and the like which Glaucon has enumerated among the advantages accruing to the unjust from the reputation of justice. More, however, is made of appearances by this class of persons than by the others; for they throw in the good opinion of the gods, and will tell you of a shower of benefits which the heavens, as they say, rain upon the pious; and this accords with the testimony of the noble Hesiod and Homer, [363b] the first of whom says, that the gods make the oaks of the just—

"To bear acorns at their summit, and bees in the middle;
And the sheep are bowed down with the weight of their fleeces."

and many other blessings of a like kind are provided for them. And Homer has a very similar strain; for he speaks of one whose fame is:

"As the fame of some blameless king who, like a god,
Maintains justice; to whom the black earth brings forth [363c]
Wheat and barley, whose trees are bowed with fruit,
And his sheep never fail to bear, and the sea gives him fish."

Still grander are the gifts of heaven which Musaeus and his son assign to the just; they take them down into the world below, where they have the saints lying on couches at a feast, everlastingly drunk, crowned with garlands; [363d] their idea seems to be that an immortality of drunkenness is the highest meed of virtue. Some extend their rewards yet further; the posterity, as they say, of the faithful and just shall survive to the third and fourth generation. This is the style in which they praise justice. But about the wicked there is another strain; they bury them in a swamp in Hades, and make them carry water in a sieve; also while they are yet living [363e] they bring them to infamy, and inflict upon them the punishments which Glaucon described as the portion of the just who are reputed to be unjust; nothing else does their invention supply. Such is their manner of praising the one and censuring the other.

Once more, Socrates, I will ask you to consider another way of speaking about justice and injustice, [364a] which is not confined to the poets, but is found in prose writers. The universal voice of mankind is always declaring that justice and virtue are honourable, but grievous and toilsome; and that the pleasures of vice and injustice are easy of attainment, and are only censured by law and opinion. They say also that honesty is for the most part less profitable than dishonesty; and they are quite ready to call wicked men happy, and to honour them both in public and private when they are rich or in any other way influential, [364b] while they despise and overlook those who may be weak and poor, even though acknowledging them to be better than the others. But most extraordinary of all is their mode of speaking about virtue and the gods: they say that the gods apportion calamity and misery to many good men, and good and happiness to the wicked. And begging prophets go to rich men's doors and persuade them that they have a power committed to them by the gods [364c] of making an atonement for a man's own or his ancestor's sins by sacrifices or charms, with rejoicings and feasts; and they promise to harm an enemy, whether just or unjust, at a small cost; with magic arts and incantations binding heaven, as they say, to execute their will. And the poets are the authorities to whom they appeal, now smoothing the path of vice with the words of Hesiod;—

"Vice may be had in abundance without trouble; [364d]
the way is smooth and her dwelling-place is near.
But before virtue the gods have set toil,"

and a tedious and uphill road: then citing Homer as a witness that the gods may be influenced by men; for he also says:

"The gods, too, may be turned from their purpose;
and men pray to them and avert their wrath by sacrifices and soothing entreaties, [364e]
and by libations and the odour of fat,
when they have sinned and transgressed."

And they produce a host of books written by Musaeus and Orpheus, who were children of the Moon and the Muses—that is what they say—according to which they perform their ritual, and persuade not only individuals, but whole cities, that expiations and atonements for sin may be made by sacrifices and amusements which fill a vacant hour, and are equally at the service of the living and the dead; [365a] the latter sort they call mysteries, and they redeem us from the pains of hell, but if we neglect them no one knows what awaits us.

He continued: And now when the young hear all this said about virtue and vice, and the way in which gods and men regard them, how are their minds likely to be affected, my dear Socrates,—those of them, I mean, who are quick witted, and, like bees on the wing, light on every flower, and from all that they hear are prone to draw conclusions as to [365b] what manner of persons they should be and in what way they should walk if they would make the best of life? Probably the youth will say to himself in the words of Pindar—

"Can I by justice or by crooked ways of deceit ascend a loftier tower which may be a fortress to me all my days?"

For what men say is that, if I am really just and am not also thought just, profit there is none, but the pain and loss on the other hand are unmistakable. But if, though unjust, I acquire the reputation of justice, a heavenly life is promised to me. Since then, [365c] as philosophers prove, appearance tyrannizes over truth and is lord of happiness, to appearance I must devote myself. I will describe around me a picture and shadow of virtue to be the vestibule and exterior of my house; behind I will trail the subtle and crafty fox, as Archilochus,[5] greatest of sages, recommends. But I hear some one exclaiming that the concealment of wickedness is often difficult; to which I answer, Nothing great is easy. [365d] Nevertheless, the argument indicates this, if we would be happy, to be the path along which we should proceed. With a view to concealment we will establish secret brotherhoods and political clubs. And there are professors of rhetoric[6] who teach the art of persuading courts and assemblies; and so, partly by persuasion and partly by force, I shall make unlawful gains and not be punished. Still I hear a voice saying that the gods cannot be deceived, neither can they be compelled. But what if there are no gods? or, suppose them to have no care of human things—[365e] why in either case should we mind about concealment? And even if there are gods, and they do care about us, yet we know of them only from tradition and the genealogies of the poets; and these are the very persons who say that they may be influenced and turned by "sacrifices and soothing entreaties and by offerings." Let us be consistent then, and believe both or neither. If the poets speak truly, why then we

had better be unjust, and offer of the [366a] fruits of injustice; for if we are just, although we may escape the vengeance of heaven, we shall lose the gains of injustice; but, if we are unjust, we shall keep the gains, and by our sinning and praying, and praying and sinning, the gods will be propitiated, and we shall not be punished. "But there is a world below in which either we or our posterity will suffer for our unjust deeds." Yes, my friend, will be the reflection, but there are mysteries and atoning deities, and these have great power. [366b] That is what mighty cities declare; and the children of the gods, who were their poets and prophets, bear a like testimony.

On what principle, then, shall we any longer choose justice rather than the worst injustice? when, if we only unite the latter with a deceitful regard to appearances, we shall fare to our mind both with gods and men, in life and after death, as the most numerous and the highest authorities tell us. Knowing all this, Socrates, how can a man [366c] who has any superiority of mind or person or rank or wealth, be willing to honour justice; or indeed to refrain from laughing when he hears justice praised? And even if there should be some one who is able to disprove the truth of my words, and who is satisfied that justice is best, still he is not angry with the unjust, but is very ready to forgive them, because he also knows that men are not just of their own free will; unless, by chance, there is some one whom the divinity within him may have inspired with a hatred of injustice, or who has attained knowledge of the truth—[366d] but no other man. He only blames injustice who, owing to cowardice or age or some weakness, has not the power of being unjust. And this is proved by the fact that when he obtains the power, he immediately becomes unjust as far as he can be.

The cause of all this, Socrates, was indicated by us at the beginning of the argument, when my brother and I told you how astonished we were to find that of all [366e] the professing panegyrists of justice—beginning with the ancient heroes of whom any memorial has been preserved to us, and ending with the men of our own time—no one has ever blamed injustice or

[5] Archilochus, who lived in the seventh century BC, was considered the first lyrical poet. He wrote satirical poems that often attacked prominent individuals.
[6] The Sophists.

praised justice except with a view to the glories, honours, and benefits which flow from them. No one has ever adequately described either in verse or prose the true essential nature of either of them abiding in the soul, and invisible to any human or divine eye; or shown that of all the things of a man's soul which he has within him, justice is the greatest good, and injustice the greatest evil. [367a] Had this been the universal strain, had you sought to persuade us of this from our youth upwards, we should not have been on the watch to keep one another from doing wrong, but every one would have been his own watchman, because afraid, if he did wrong, of harbouring in himself the greatest of evils. I dare say that Thrasymachus and others would seriously hold the language which I have been merely repeating, and words even stronger than these about justice and injustice, grossly, as I conceive, perverting their true nature. But I [367b] speak in this vehement manner, as I must frankly confess to you, because I want to hear from you the opposite side; and I would ask you to show not only the superiority which justice has over injustice, but what effect they have on the possessor of them which makes the one to be a good and the other an evil to him. And please, as Glaucon requested of you, to exclude reputations; for unless you take away from each of them his true reputation and add on the false, we shall say that you do not praise justice, but the appearance of it; [367c] we shall think that you are only exhorting us to keep injustice dark, and that you really agree with Thrasymachus in thinking that justice is another's good and the interest of the stronger, and that injustice is a man's own profit and interest, though injurious to the weaker. Now as you have admitted that justice is one of that highest class of goods which are desired indeed for their results, but in a far greater degree for their own sakes—like sight or hearing or knowledge or health, [367d] or any other real and natural and not merely conventional good—I would ask you in your praise of justice to regard one point only: I mean the essential good and evil which justice and injustice work in the possessors of them. Let others praise justice and censure injustice, magnifying the rewards and honours of the one and abusing the other; that is a manner of arguing which, coming from them, I am ready to tolerate, but from you who have spent your whole life in the consideration of this question, unless I hear the contrary from your own lips, [367e] I expect something better. And therefore, I say, not only prove to us that justice is better than injustice, but show what they either of them do to the possessor of them, which makes the one to be a good and the other an evil, whether seen or unseen by gods and men.

## The Just State and the Just Individual

The ancient Greeks believed that there were four basic virtues: *temperance, courage, wisdom,* and *justice.* Plato sought these virtues in his ideal state. He believed that the human soul could be divided up into three parts: *the bodily appetites,* such as hunger, thirst, lust, and greed; *the higher emotions, or spirit;* and *the intellect, or reason.* Our bodily appetites form the greatest part of the soul, and are by nature insatiable, so they have to be closely monitored by the rational elements of our soul.

Justice in the soul comes about when each of its parts fulfills its proper function. The proper function of reason is to rule the other parts. The proper function of the spirited part of the soul is to act like a good soldier, protecting reason against the appetites and doing reason's bidding. The proper function of the appetites is to be the servant of reason, to be temperate, and to know their place. So the highest virtue of the appetites is *obedience* to reason and spirit (i.e., *temperance*); of spirit, *courage;* of the intellect, *wisdom.* Each part of the soul reflects one of the first three of the traditional Greek virtues.

This leads Socrates to propose the following as a final definition of justice:

> Justice is the harmony of the whole, where every element (in a soul or a state) performs its proper function [J5].

Only if this is true can we have a just soul or state. This virtuous soul or state is *healthy,* whereas an unjust soul or state is full of strife, and thus *diseased.* Plato's view of justice thus involves seeing every element in the soul or state as having a *natural* role or function.

Following is Plato's model of the just soul and the ideal state and the corresponding virtues in each:

## Plato's Model of the Just Soul and the Ideal State

| ELEMENT OF THE SOUL | CORRESPONDING ELEMENT IN THE STATE | VIRTUE |
|---|---|---|
| Reason | Guardians (Philosopher-Kings) | Wisdom (Temperance) |
| Spirit | Soldiers (Auxiliaries) | Courage (Temperance) |
| Appetites | Craftsmen | Obedience (Temperance) |
| *Result* | | |
| The Healthy Soul | The Healthy State | Justice |

Plato divides the population of his ideal republic into three classes reflecting the three basic functions of the state: the *craftsmen* to do manual labor and to build things; the *auxiliaries* or soldiers, to protect the state; and the *philosopher-kings,* or *guardians,* to perform the executive function within the state. This division reflects the tripartite division of the soul.

Plato wanted his philosopher-kings to justify the class division of the republic with a *"noble lie."* Its purpose was to naturalize the division of citizens into classes. They should tell the citizens that the masses of artisans, farmers, and so forth had *bronze* mixed with their soul, and thus deserved their lower status; that the soldiers had *silver* in their soul, and thus deserved a middle status; and that the elite guardians of the republic had *gold* in their souls, and thus deserved to rule. The rulers would be wise, the soldiers courageous, and all of them temperate, thus resulting in a *just* society.

The basic economic needs of the state require a division of labor among various craft occupations, for example, farmers, weavers, merchants, shopkeepers, and hired laborers. These are the "bronze" folk of the *polis.* The craftsmen have no general virtue to themselves, although in so far as they perform their work well and accept the rule of their "betters," they partake of the general virtue of *justice;* while in so far as they control their appetites, they share *temperance* with the other classes of the state.

Plato's republic was modeled on the severe oligarchy of ancient Sparta, a state organized for war. He prescribed a rigid training of the youth destined to be guardians as preparation for their rule. Gymnastics, music, and military training were all part of the guardians' education. They were tested for their strength and courage. Some of these "guardians" were destined to be only soldiers, those who police the state internally and who protect it against other states. They are like watchdogs who are fierce to enemies, but kind and loyal toward their masters, the shepherds of the state. Because war would inevitably come if the state had any resources at all, these watchdogs would protect the state against its enemies with their highest virtue, *courage.*

Very few in the state have the wisdom to rule. Those guardians destined by their skills to rule must first and foremost have a philosophical element in their nature, a love of wisdom. They are the ones capable of knowing the Form of the Good. But they must also go through the same tests of courage as the soldiers, so they are fighting philosophers. They will live simply, in a military organization, without private property or permanent family connections, sharing everything and everyone (including their sexual partners). There would be no discrimination against women in this class. Plato hoped that this *communism,* aided by reason, would free the guardians from being ruled by their appetites.

# The Republic, Selections from Part 2

## PLATO

*[Part 2. Justice in the State and in the Individual. Book 2, 367e– Book 5, 471c]*

[CHAPTER 10, EDITED. THE SELECTION OF RULERS AND THE NOBLE LIE. BOOK 3, 414B–BOOK 4, 421C]

. . . HOW THEN MAY WE devise one of those needful falsehoods of which we lately spoke— [414c] just one royal lie which may deceive the rulers, if that be possible, and at any rate the rest of the city?

What sort of lie? he said.

Nothing new, I replied; only an old Phoenician tale of what has often occurred before now in other places (as the poets say, and have made the world believe), though not in our time, and I do not know whether such an event could ever happen again, or could now even be made probable, if it did.

How your words seem to hesitate on your lips!

You will not wonder, I replied, at my hesitation when you have heard.

[414d] Speak, he said, and fear not.

Well then, I will speak, although I really know not how to look you in the face, or in what words to utter the audacious fiction, which I propose to communicate gradually, first to the rulers, then to the soldiers, and lastly to the people. They are to be told that their youth was a dream, and the education and training which they received from us, an appearance only; in reality during all that time they were being formed and fed in the womb of the earth, where they themselves [414e] and their arms and appurtenances were manufactured; when they were completed, the earth, their mother, sent them up; and so, their country being their mother and also their nurse, they are bound to advise for her good, and to defend her against attacks, and her citizens they are to regard as children of the earth and their own brothers.

You had good reason, he said, to be ashamed of the lie which you were going to tell.

True, I replied, [415a] but there is more coming; I have only told you half. Citizens, we shall say to them in our tale, you are brothers, yet God has framed you differently. Some of you have the power of command, and in the composition of these he has mingled gold, wherefore also they

SOURCE: See note on page 69.

have the greatest honour; others he has made of silver, to be auxiliaries; others again who are to be farmers and craftsmen he has composed of brass and iron; and the species will generally be preserved in the children. But as all are of the same original stock, [415b] a golden parent will sometimes have a silver son, or a silver parent a golden son. And God proclaims as a first principle to the rulers, and above all else, that there is nothing which should so anxiously guard, or of which they are to be such good guardians, as of the purity of the race. They should observe what elements mingle in their offspring; for if the son of a golden or silver parent has an added element of brass and iron, [415c] then nature orders a transposition of ranks, and the eye of the ruler must not be pitiful towards the child because he has to descend in the scale and become a farmer or artisan, just as there may be sons of artisans who having an element of gold or silver in them are raised to honour, and become guardians or auxiliaries. For an oracle says that when a man of brass or iron guards the State, it will be destroyed. Such is the tale; is there any possibility of making our citizens believe in it?

[415d] Not in the present generation, he replied; there is no way of accomplishing this; but their sons may be made to believe in the tale, and their sons' sons, and posterity after them.

I see the difficulty, I replied; yet the fostering of such a belief will make them care more for the city and for one another. Enough, however, of the fiction, which may now fly abroad upon the wings of rumour, while we arm our earth-born heroes, and lead them forth under the command of their rulers. Let them look round and select a spot [415e] from which they can best suppress insurrection, if any prove troublesome within, and also defend themselves against enemies, who like wolves may come down on the fold from without; there let them encamp, and when they have encamped, let them sacrifice to the proper Gods and prepare their dwellings.

Just so, he said.

And their dwellings must be such as will shield them against the cold of winter and the heat of summer.

I suppose that you mean houses, he replied.

Yes, I said; but they must be the houses of soldiers, and not of shop-keepers.

[416a] What is the difference? he said.

That I will endeavour to explain, I replied. To keep watchdogs, who, from want of discipline or hunger, or some evil habit or other, would turn upon the sheep and worry them, and behave not like dogs but wolves, would be a foul and monstrous thing in a shepherd?

Truly monstrous, he said.

[416b] And therefore every care must be taken that our auxiliaries, being stronger than our citizens, may not grow to be too much for them and become savage tyrants instead of friends and allies?

Yes, great care should be taken.

And would not a really good education furnish the best safeguard?

But they are well-educated already, he replied.

I cannot be so confident, my dear Glaucon, I said; I am much certain [416c] that they ought to be, and that true education, whatever that may be, will have the greatest tendency to civilize and humanize them in their relations to one another, and to those who are under their protection.

Very true, he replied.

And not only their education, but their habitations, and all that belongs to them, should be such as will neither impair their virtue as guardians, nor tempt them to prey upon the other citizens. Any man of sense must acknowledge that.

[416d] He must.

Then let us consider what will be their way of life, if they are to realize our idea of them. In the first place, none of them should have any property of his own beyond what is absolutely necessary; neither should they have a private house or store closed against any one who has a mind to enter; their provisions should be only such as are required by trained warriors, who are men of temperance and courage; [416e] they should agree to receive from the citizens a fixed rate of pay, enough to meet the expenses of the year and no more; and they will go to mess and live together like soldiers in a camp. We will tell them that they received gold and silver from God; the diviner metal is within them, and they have therefore no need of the dross which is current among men, and ought not to pollute the divine by any such earthly added element; for that commoner metal has been the source [417a] of many unholy deeds, but their own is undefiled. And they alone of all the citizens may not touch or handle silver or gold, or be under the same roof with them, or wear them, or drink from them. And this will be their salvation, and they will be the saviours of the State. But should they ever acquire homes or lands or moneys of their own, they will become housekeepers and farmers instead of guardians, [417b] enemies and tyrants instead of allies of the other citizens; hating and being hated, plotting and being plotted against, they will pass their whole life in much greater terror of internal than of external enemies, and the hour of ruin, both to themselves and to the rest of the State, will be at hand. For all which reasons may we not say that thus shall our State be ordered, and that these shall be the regulations appointed by us for our guardians concerning their houses and all other matters?

Yes, said Glaucon.

[419a] Here Adeimantus interposed a question: How would you answer, Socrates, said he, if a person were to say that you are making these people miserable, and that they are the cause of their own unhappiness; the city in fact belongs to them, but they are none the better for it; whereas other men acquire lands, and build large and handsome houses, and have everything handsome about them, offering sacrifices to the gods on their own account, and practising hospitality; moreover, as you were saying just now, they have gold and silver, and all that is usual among the favourites of fortune; but our poor citizens are no better than mercenaries [420a] who are quartered in the city and are always mounting guard?

Yes, I said; and you may add that they are only fed, and not paid in addition to their food, like other men; and therefore they cannot, if they would, take a journey of pleasure; they have no money to spend on a mistress or any other luxurious fancy, which, as the world goes, is thought to be happiness; and many other accusations of the same nature might be added.

But, said he, let us suppose all this to be included in the charge.

[420b] You mean to ask, I said, what will be our answer?

Yes.

If we proceed along the old path, my belief, I said, is that we shall find the answer. And our answer will be that, even as they are, our guardians may very likely be the happiest of men; but that our aim in founding the State was not the disproportionate happiness of any one class, but the greatest happiness of the whole; we thought that in a State which is ordered with a view to the good of the whole we should be most likely to find Justice, and [420c] in the ill-ordered State injustice: and, having found them, we might then decide which of the two is the happier. At present, I take it, we are fashioning the happy State, not piecemeal, or with a view of making a few happy citizens, but as a whole; and by-and-by we will proceed to view the opposite kind of State. Suppose that we were painting a statue, and some one came up to us and said, Why do you not put the most beautiful colours on the most beautiful parts of the body—the eyes ought to be purple, but you have made them black—[420d] to him we might fairly answer, Sir, you would not surely have us beautify the eyes to such a degree that they are no longer eyes; consider rather whether, by giving this and the other features their due proportion, we make the whole beautiful. And so I say to you, do not compel us to assign to the guardians a sort of happiness which will make them anything but guardians; [420e] for we too can clothe our farmers in royal apparel, and set crowns of gold on their heads, and bid them till the ground as much as they like, an no more. Our potters also might be allowed to repose on couches, and feast by the fireside, passing round the wine cup, while their wheel is conveniently at hand, and working at pottery only as much as they like; in this way we might make every class happy—and then, as you imagine, the whole State would be happy. But do not put this idea into our heads; [421a] for, if we listen to you, the farmer will be no longer a farmer, the potter will cease to be a potter, and no one will have the character of any distinct class in the State. Now this is not of much consequence where the corruption of society, and pretension to be what you are not, is confined to cobblers; but when the guardians of the laws and of the government are only seemingly and not real guardians, then see how they turn the State upside down; and on the other hand they alone have the power of giving order and happiness to the State. We mean our guardians to be true saviours [421b] and not the destroyers of the State, whereas our opponent is thinking of peasants at a festival, who are enjoying a life of revelry, not of citizens who are doing their duty to the State. But, if so, we mean different things, and he is speaking of something which is not a State. And therefore we must consider whether in appointing our guardians we would look to their greatest happiness individually, or whether this principle of happiness does not rather reside in the State as a whole. But if the latter be the truth, then the guardians and auxiliaries, [421c] and all others equally with them, must be compelled or induced to do their own work in the best way. And thus the whole State will grow up in a noble order, and the several classes will receive the proportion of happiness which nature assigns to them.

I think that you are quite right.

## [CHAPTER 12. THE VIRTUES IN THE STATE. BOOK 4, 427D–434D]

[427d] But where, amid all this, is justice? son of Ariston, tell me where. Now that our city has been made habitable, light a candle and search, and get your brother and Polemarchus and the rest of our friends to help, and let us see where in it we can discover justice and where injustice, and in what they differ from one another, and which of them the man who would be happy should have for his portion, whether seen or unseen by gods and men.

Nonsense, said Glaucon: did you not promise to search yourself, [427e] saying that for you not to help justice in her need would be an impiety?

I do not deny that I said so; and as you remind me, I will be as good as my word; but you must join.

We will, he replied.

Well, then, I hope to make the discovery in this way: I mean to begin with the assumption that our State, if rightly ordered, is perfect.

That is most certain.

And being perfect, is therefore wise and valiant and temperate and just.

That is likewise clear.

And whichever of these qualities we find in the State, the one which is not found will be the residue?

[428a] Very good.

If there were four things, and we were searching for one of them, wherever it might be, the one sought for might be known to us from the first, and there would be no further trouble; or we might know the other three first, and then the fourth would clearly be the one left.

Very true, he said.

And is not a similar method to be pursued about the virtues, which are also four in number?

Clearly.

[428b] First among the virtues found in the State, wisdom comes into view, and in this I detect a certain peculiarity.

What is that?

The State which we have been describing is said to be wise as being good in counsel?

Very true.

And good counsel is clearly a kind of knowledge, for not by ignorance, but by knowledge, do men counsel well?

Clearly.

And the kinds of knowledge in a State are many and diverse?

Of course.

There is the knowledge of the carpenter; but is that the sort of knowledge [428c] which gives a city the title of wise and good in counsel?

Certainly not; that would only give a city the reputation of skill in carpentering.

Then a city is not to be called wise because possessing a knowledge which counsels for the best about wooden implements?

Certainly not.

Nor by reason of a knowledge which advises about brazen pots, I said, nor as possessing any other similar knowledge?

Not by reason of any of them, he said.

Nor yet by reason of a knowledge which cultivates the earth; that would give the city the name of agricultural?

Yes.

Well, I said, and is there any knowledge in our recently-founded State among any of the citizens which advises, not about any particular thing [428d] in the State, but about the whole, and considers how a State can best deal with itself and with other States?

There certainly is.

And what is this knowledge, and among whom is it found? I asked.

It is the knowledge of the guardians, he replied, and is found among those whom we were just now describing as perfect guardians.

And what is the name which the city derives from the possession of this sort of knowledge?

The name of good in counsel and truly wise.

[428e] And will there be in our city more of these true guardians or more blacksmiths?

The blacksmiths, he replied, will be far more numerous.

Will not the guardians be the smallest of all the classes who receive a name from the profession of some kind of knowledge?

Much the smallest.

And so by reason of the smallest part or class, and of the knowledge which resides in this presiding and ruling part of itself, the whole State, being thus constituted according to nature, will be wise; [429a] and this, which has the only knowledge worthy to be called wisdom, has been ordained by nature to be of all classes the least.

Most true.

Thus, then, I said, the nature and place in the State of one of the four virtues has somehow or other been discovered.

And, in my humble opinion, very satisfactorily discovered, he replied.

Again, I said, there is no difficulty in seeing the nature of courage, and in what part that quality resides which gives the name of courageous to the State.

How do you mean?

Why, I said, every one [429b] who calls any

State courageous or cowardly, will be thinking of the part which fights and goes out to war on the State's behalf.

No one, he replied, would ever think of any other.

The rest of the citizens may be courageous or may be cowardly, but their courage or cowardice will not, as I conceive, have the effect of making the city either the one or the other.

Certainly not.

The city will be courageous in virtue of a portion of herself which preserves under all circumstances that opinion [429c] about the nature of things to be feared and not to be feared in which our legislator educated them; and this is what you term courage.

I should like to hear what you are saying once more, for I do not think that I perfectly understand you.

I mean that courage is a kind of salvation.

Salvation of what?

Of the opinion respecting things to be feared, what they are and of what nature, which the law implants through education; and I mean by the words "under all circumstances" to intimate that in pleasure [429d] or in pain, or under the influence of desire or fear, a man preserves, and does not lose this opinion. Shall I give you an illustration?

If you please.

You know, I said, that dyers, when they want to dye wool for making the true sea-purple, begin by selecting their white colour first; this they prepare and dress with much care and pains, in order that the white ground may take the purple hue in full perfection. The dyeing then proceeds; [429e] and whatever is dyed in this manner becomes a fast colour, and no washing either with lyes or without them can take away the bloom. But, when the ground has not been duly prepared, you will have noticed how poor is the look either of purple or of any other colour.

Yes, he said; I know that they have a washed-out and ridiculous appearance.

Then now, I said, you will understand what our object was in selecting our soldiers, and educating them in music [430a] and gymnastics; we were contriving influences which would prepare them to take the dye of the laws in perfection, and the colour of their opinion about dangers and of every other opinion was to be indelibly fixed by their nurture and training, not to be washed away by such potent lyes as pleasure—mightier agent far in washing the soul than any soda or lye; [430b] or by sorrow, fear, and desire, the mightiest of all other solvents. And this sort of universal saving power of true opinion in conformity with law about real and false dangers I call and maintain to be courage, unless you disagree.

But I agree, he replied; for I suppose that you mean to exclude mere uninstructed courage, such as that of a wild beast or of a slave—this, in your opinion, is not the courage which the law ordains, and ought to have another name.

[430c] Most certainly.

Then I may infer courage to be such as you describe?

Why, yes, said I, you may, and if you add the words "of a citizen," you will not be far wrong;—hereafter, if you like, we will carry the examination further, but at present we are seeking not for courage but justice; and for the purpose of our enquiry we have said enough.

You are right, he replied.

[430d] Two virtues remain to be discovered in the State—first temperance, and then justice which is the end of our search.

Very true.

Now, can we find justice without troubling ourselves about temperance?

I do not know how that can be accomplished, he said, nor do I desire that justice should be brought to light and temperance lost sight of; and therefore I wish that you would do me the favour of considering temperance first.

Certainly, [430e] I replied, I should not be justified in refusing your request.

Then consider, he said.

Yes, I replied; I will; and as far as I can at present see, the virtue of temperance has more of the nature of harmony and symphony than the preceding.

How so? he asked.

Temperance, I replied, is the ordering or controlling of certain pleasures and desires; this is curiously enough implied in the saying of "a man being his own master"; and other traces of the same notion may be found in language.

No doubt, he said.

There is something ridiculous in the expression "master of himself"; for the master is also the servant [431a] and the servant the master; and in all these modes of speaking the same person is denoted.

Certainly.

The meaning is, I believe, that in the human soul there is a better and also a worse principle; and when the better has the worse under control, then a man is said to be master of himself; and this is a term of praise: but when, owing to evil education or association, the better principle, which is also the smaller, is overwhelmed by the greater mass of the worse—in this case [431b] he is blamed and is called the slave of self and unprincipled.

Yes, there is reason in that.

And now, I said, look at our newly-created State, and there you will find one of these two conditions realized; for the State, as you will acknowledge, may be justly called master of itself, if the words "temperance" and "self-mastery" truly express the rule of the better part over the worse.

Yes, he said, I see that what you say is true.

Let me further note that the manifold [431c] and complex pleasures and desires and pains are generally found in children and women and servants, and in the freemen so called who are of the lowest and more numerous class.

Certainly, he said.

Whereas the simple and moderate desires which follow reason, and are under the guidance of mind and true opinion, are to be found only in a few, and those the best born and best educated.

Very true.

These two, as you may perceive, have a place in our State; and the meaner desires of the many [431d] are held down by the virtuous desires and wisdom of the few.

That I perceive, he said.

Then if there be any city which may be described as master of its own pleasures and desires, and master of itself, ours may claim such a designation?

Certainly, he replied.

It may also be called temperate, and for the same reasons?

Yes.

And if there be any State in which [431e] rulers and subjects will be agreed as to the question who are to rule, that again will be our State?

Undoubtedly.

And the citizens being thus agreed among themselves, in which class will temperance be found—in the rulers or in the subjects?

In both, as I should imagine, he replied.

Do you observe that we were not far wrong in our guess that temperance was a sort of harmony?

Why so?

Why, because temperance is unlike courage and wisdom, each of which resides in a part only, [432a] the one making the State wise and the other valiant; not so temperance, which extends to the whole, and runs through all the notes of the scale, and produces a harmony of the weaker and the stronger and the middle class, whether you suppose them to be stronger or weaker in wisdom or power or numbers or wealth, or anything else. Most truly then may we deem temperance to be the agreement of the naturally superior and inferior, [432b] as to the right to rule of either, both in states and individuals.

I entirely agree with you.

And so, I said, we may consider three out of the four virtues to have been discovered in our State. The last of those qualities which make a state virtuous must be justice, if we only knew what that was.

The inference is obvious.

The time then has arrived, Glaucon, when, like huntsmen, we should surround the cover, and look sharp that justice does not steal away, and pass [432c] out of sight and escape us; for beyond a doubt she is somewhere in this country: watch therefore and strive to catch a sight of her, and if you see her first, let me know.

Would that I could! but you should regard me

rather as a follower who has just eyes enough to see what you show him—that is about as much as I am good for.

Offer up a prayer with me and follow.

I will, but you must show me the way.

Here is no path, I said, and the wood is dark and perplexing; [432d] still we must push on.

Let us push on.

Here I saw something: Halloo! I said, I begin to perceive a track, and I believe that the quarry will not escape.

Good news, he said.

Truly, I said, we are stupid fellows.

Why so?

Why, my good sir, at the beginning of our enquiry, ages ago, there was justice tumbling out at our feet, and we never saw her; nothing could be more ridiculous. Like [432e] people who go about looking for what they have in their hands—that was the way with us—we looked not at what we were seeking, but at what was far off in the distance; and therefore, I suppose, we missed her.

What do you mean?

I mean to say that in reality for a long time past we have been talking of justice, and have failed to recognise her.

I grow impatient at the length of your prelude. Move on!

[433a] Well then, tell me, I said, whether I am right or not: You remember the original principle which we were always laying down at the foundation of the State, that one man should practise one thing only, the thing to which his nature was best adapted;—now justice is this principle or a part of it.

Yes, we often said that one man should do one thing only.

Further, we affirmed that justice was doing one's own business, and not being a busybody; [433b] we said so again and again, and many others have said the same to us.

Yes, we said so.

Then to do one's own business in a certain way may be assumed to be justice. Can you tell me whence I derive this inference?

I cannot, but I should like to be told.

Because I think that this is the only virtue which remains in the State when the other virtues of temperance and courage and wisdom are abstracted; and, that this is the ultimate cause and condition of the existence of all of them, and while remaining in them is also their preservative; and [433c] we were saying that if the three were discovered by us, justice would be the fourth or remaining one.

That follows of necessity.

If we are asked to determine which of these four qualities by its presence contributes most to the excellence of the State, whether the agreement of rulers and subjects, or the preservation in the soldiers of the opinion which the law ordains about the true nature of dangers, or wisdom and watchfulness [433d] in the rulers, or whether this other which I am mentioning, and which is found in children and women, slave and freeman, artisan, ruler, subject,—the quality, I mean, of every one doing his own work, and not being a busybody, would claim the palm—the question is not so easily answered.

Certainly, he replied, there would be a difficulty in saying which.

Then the power of each individual in the State to do his own work appears to compete with the other political virtues, wisdom, temperance, courage.

Yes, he said.

And the virtue which enters into this competition is justice?

[433e] Exactly.

Let us look at the question from another point of view: Are not the rulers in a State those to whom you would entrust the office of determining suits at law?

Certainly.

And are suits decided on any other ground but that a man may neither take what is another's, nor be deprived of what is his own?

Yes; that is their principle.

Which is a just principle?

Yes.

Then on this view also justice will be admitted to be the having and doing [434a] what is a man's own, and belongs to him?

Very true.

Think, now, and say whether you agree with me or not. Suppose a carpenter to be doing the business of a cobbler, or a cobbler of a carpenter; and suppose them to exchange their implements or their duties, or the same person to be doing the work of both, or whatever be the change; do you think that any great harm would result to the State?

Not much.

But when the cobbler or any other man whom nature designed to be a trader, [434b] having his heart lifted up by wealth or strength or the number of his followers, or any like advantage, attempts to force his way into the class of warriors, or a warrior into that of legislators and guardians, for which he is unfitted, and either to take the implements or the duties of the other; or when one man is trader, legislator, and warrior all in one, then I think you will agree with me in saying that this interchange and this meddling of one with another is the ruin of the State.

Most true.

Seeing then, I said, that there are three distinct classes, any meddling of one with another, or the change of one into another, [434c] is the greatest harm to the State, and may be most justly termed evil-doing?

Precisely.

And the greatest degree of evil-doing to one's own city would be termed by you injustice?

Certainly.

This then is injustice; and on the other hand when the trader, the auxiliary, and the guardian each do their own business, that is justice, and will make the city just.

[434d] I agree with you.

## [CHAPTER 14. THE VIRTUES IN THE INDIVIDUAL. BOOK 4, 441C–445B]

[441c] And so, after much tossing, we have reached land, and are fairly agreed that the same principles which exist in the State exist also in the individual, and that they are three in number.

Exactly.

Must we not then infer that the individual is wise in the same way, and in virtue of the same quality which makes the State wise?

Certainly.

Also that [441d] the same quality which constitutes courage in the State constitutes courage in the individual, and that both the State and the individual bear the same relation to all the other virtues?

Assuredly.

And the individual will be acknowledged by us to be just in the same way in which the State is just?

That follows, of course.

We cannot but remember that the justice of the State consisted in each of the three classes doing the work of its own class?

We are not very likely to have forgotten, he said.

We must recollect that the individual in whom the several qualities of his nature [441e] do their own work will be just, and will do his own work?

Yes, he said, we must remember that too.

And ought not the rational principle, which is wise, and has the care of the whole soul, to rule, and the passionate or spirited principle to be the subject and ally?

Certainly.

And, as we were saying, the united influence of music and gymnastic will bring them into accord, nerving [442a] and sustaining the reason with noble words and lessons, and moderating and soothing and civilizing the wildness of passion by harmony and rhythm?

Quite true, he said.

And these two, thus nurtured and educated, and having learned truly to know their own functions, will rule over the appetitive, which in each of us is the largest part of the soul and by nature most insatiable of gain; over this they will keep guard, lest, waxing great and strong with the fullness of bodily pleasures, as they are termed, the appetitive, no longer confined to her own sphere, [442b] should attempt to enslave and rule those who are not her natural-born subjects, and overturn the whole life of man?

Very true, he said.

Both together will they not be the best defenders of the whole soul and the whole body against attacks from without; the one counselling, and the other fighting under his leader, and courageously executing his commands and counsels?

True.

And he is to be deemed courageous [442c] whose spirit retains in pleasure and in pain the commands of reason about what he ought or ought not to fear?

Right, he replied.

And him we call wise who has in him that little part which rules, and which proclaims these commands; that part too being supposed to have a knowledge of what is for the interest of each of the three parts and of the whole?

Assuredly.

And would you not say that he is temperate [442d] who has these same elements in friendly harmony, in whom the one ruling principle of reason, and the two subject ones of spirit and desire are equally agreed that reason ought to rule, and do not rebel?

Certainly, he said, that is the true account of temperance whether in the State or individual.

And surely, I said, we have explained again and again how and by virtue of what quality a man will be just.

That is very certain.

And is justice dimmer in the individual, and is her form different, or is she the same which we found her to be in the State?

There is no difference in my opinion, he said.

[442e] Because, if any doubt is still lingering in our minds, a few commonplace instances will satisfy us of the truth of what I am saying.

What sort of instances do you mean?

If the case is put to us, must we not admit that the just State, or the man who is trained in the principles of such a State, will be less likely than the unjust to make away with a deposit of gold or silver? Would any one deny this?

[443a] No one, he replied.

Will the just man or citizen ever be guilty of sacrilege or theft, or treachery either to his friends or to his country?

Never.

Neither will he ever break faith where there have been oaths or agreements?

Impossible.

No one will be less likely to commit adultery, or to dishonour his father and mother, or to fail in his religious duties?

No one.

[443b] And the reason is that each part of him is doing its own business, whether in ruling or being ruled?

Exactly so.

Are you satisfied then that the quality which makes such men and such states is justice, or do you hope to discover some other?

Not I, indeed.

Then our dream has been realized; and the suspicion which we entertained at the beginning of our work of construction, that some divine power must have [443c] conducted us to a primary form of justice, has now been verified?

Yes, certainly.

And the division of labour which required the carpenter and the shoemaker and the rest of the citizens to be doing each his own business, and not another's, [443d] was a shadow of justice, and for that reason it was of use?

Clearly.

But in reality justice was such as we were describing, being concerned however, not with the outward man, but with the inward, which is the true self and concern of man: for the just man does not permit the several elements within him to interfere with one another, or any of them to do the work of others, he sets in order his own inner life, and is his own master and his own law, and at peace with himself; and when he has bound together the three principles within him, which may be compared to the higher, lower, and middle notes of the scale, [443e] and the intermediate intervals—when he has bound all these together, and is no longer many, but has become one entirely temperate and perfectly adjusted nature, then he proceeds to act, if he has to act, whether in a matter of property, or in the treatment of the body, or in some affair of politics or private business; always thinking and calling that which preserves and co-operates with this har-

monious condition, just and good action, and the knowledge [444a] which presides over it, wisdom, and that which at any time impairs this condition, he will call unjust action, and the opinion which presides over it ignorance.

You have said the exact truth, Socrates.

Very good; and if we were to affirm that we had discovered the just man and the just State, and the nature of justice in each of them, we should not be telling a falsehood?

Most certainly not.

May we say so, then?

Let us say so.

And now, I said, injustice has to be considered.

Clearly.

[444b] Must not injustice be a strife which arises among the three principles—a meddlesomeness, and interference, and rising up of a part of the soul against the whole, an assertion of unlawful authority, which is made by a rebellious subject against a true prince, of whom he is the natural vassal, what is all this confusion and delusion but injustice, and intemperance and cowardice and ignorance, and every form of vice?

Exactly so.

[444c] And if the nature of justice and injustice be known, then the meaning of acting unjustly and being unjust, or, again, of acting justly, will also be perfectly clear?

What do you mean? he said.

Why, I said, they are like disease and health; being in the soul just what disease and health are in the body.

How so? he said.

Why, I said, that which is healthy causes health, and that which is unhealthy causes disease.

Yes.

And just actions cause justice, [444d] and unjust actions cause injustice?

That is certain.

And the creation of health is the institution of a natural order and government of one by another in the parts of the body; and the creation of disease is the production of a state of things at variance with this natural order?

True.

And is not the creation of justice the institution of a natural order and government of one by another in the parts of the soul, and the creation of injustice the production of a state of things at variance with the natural order?

Exactly so, he said.

Then virtue is the health [444e] and beauty and well-being of the soul, and vice the disease and weakness and deformity of the same?

True.

And do not good practices lead to virtue, and evil practices to vice?

Assuredly.

Still our old question of the comparative advantage of justice and injustice has not been answered: Which is the more profitable, to be just [445a] and act justly and practice virtue, whether seen or unseen of gods and men, or to be unjust and act unjustly, if only unpunished and unreformed?

In my judgment, Socrates, the question has now become ridiculous. We know that, when the bodily constitution is gone, life is no longer endurable, though pampered with all kinds of meats and drinks, and having all wealth and all power; and shall we be told that when the very essence of the vital principle is undermined and [445b] corrupted, life is still worth having to a man, if only he be allowed to do whatever he likes with the single exception that he is not to acquire justice and virtue, or to escape from injustice and vice; assuming them both to be such as we have described?

Yes, I said, the question is, as you say, ridiculous.

## The Philosopher-Kings and the Allegory of the Cave

In our first selection from part 3 of *The Republic,* Socrates proclaimed that there will never be a just society until kings became philosophers and philosophers kings. Put in simple terms, Plato believed in *the rule of the wise.** This idea of philosophers ruling the state is Plato at his most beguiling—it has certainly intrigued philosophy students for hundreds of years.

Our more substantial selection from part 3 is the Allegory of the Cave. This illuminates Plato's theory of knowledge, his *epistemology.* Imagine, he says, a cave where a group of prisoners is chained in such a fashion that they can only see the cave's back wall. Behind them is a fire, and behind the fire, in the mouth of the cave, there's a low wall behind which walk passersby carrying various statues and animal figures. The sun casts shadows of these people and their statues onto the back wall of the cave, and the prisoners take these shadows for reality. They represent, of course, the majority of humanity.

One day, one of the prisoners is set free from the cave. He is dazzled by the light at first, but later comes to realize that the shadows he formerly took as real were no more than illusions. At first he sees the real objects held by the passersby, and eventually the sun itself, which symbolizes the Good. But when he goes back to the cave, he can no longer see in the dark, and his old comrades (who only believe in the shadow world they live in) ridicule his talk about the greater reality of the sunlit world.

This is, of course, a parable. The unphilosophical masses can only see the shadow world of the senses; only the philosopher, by using his or her critical reason, can escape the cave and see reality. Plato thus believed we can divide our beliefs between

---

* A less generous interpretation of the philosopher-kings has been given by Karl Popper in his *The Open Society and Its Enemies,* where he suggests that Plato is advocating a quasi-fascist dictatorship in *The Republic.*

opinion, in Greek *doxa,* based on the senses, and *true knowledge,* in Greek *epistēmē,* which we arrive at through reason.

This story of the cave and its implication that there are two types of knowledge is connected to Plato's epistemology, his theory of forms. Plato believed that for every real entity in the world there was a formal, ideal image that represented its objective reality, that is; there is a *form* or *idea* of the cat that allows us to recognize all individual cats *as* cats, a form of beauty to help us recognize all beautiful things, and so on. We can think of a form as a sort of *objective essence.*

The common interpretation of this theory of forms is that sensible things are just copies of universal realities that Plato thought existed in some sort of heaven. A looser interpretation suggests that the forms are essentially an *epistemological device* invented to explain how particular things appear to our senses as isolated entities, yet nevertheless seem to participate in some universal essence. In either case, Plato does seem to accord the forms some "ontological" reality outside the minds of individuals accessing them. The forms are "true knowledge," accessible only through the use of reason.

The ultimate form in *The Republic* is the Form of the Good. It was symbolized by the sun, from which shone the light of reason. Only the philosopher could "see" this form. This special wisdom—the ability to know the intellectual form of things—is the main reason that Plato feels that in a just state, philosopher-kings must rule.

# The Republic, Selections from Part 3

## PLATO

*[Part 3. The Philosopher-Kings. Book 5, 471c–Book 7, end]*

[CHAPTER 18, EDITED. THE NEED FOR PHILOSOPHER-KINGS. BOOK 5, 473B–E]

[SOCRATES SPEAKING:] Then you must not insist on my proving that the actual State will in every respect coincide with the ideal: if we are only able to discover how a city may be governed nearly as we proposed, you will admit that we have discovered the possibility which you demand; [473b] and will be contented. I am sure that I should be contented—will not you?

Yes, I will.

Let me next endeavour to show what is that fault in States which is the cause of their present

bad administration, and what is the least change which will enable a State to pass into the truer form; and let the change, if possible, be of one thing only, or, if not, of two; at any rate, let the changes be as few and slight as possible.

[473c] Certainly, he replied.

I think, I said, that there might be a reform of the State if only one change were made, which is not a slight or easy though still a possible one.

What is it? he said.

Now then, I said, I go to meet that which I liken to the greatest of the waves; yet shall the word be spoken, even though the wave break and drown me in laughter and dishonour; and do you mark my words.

Proceed.

I said: Until philosophers are kings, [473d] or the kings and princes of this world have the spirit

SOURCE: See note on page 69.

and power of philosophy, and political greatness and wisdom meet in one, and those commoner natures who pursue either to the exclusion of the other are compelled to stand aside, cities will never have rest from their evils—nor the human race, as I believe—and then only will this our State [473e] have a possibility of life and behold the light of day. Such was the thought, my dear Glaucon, which I would have avoided saying if it had not seemed too extravagant; for to be convinced that in no other State can there be happiness private or public is indeed a hard thing.

Socrates, what do you mean? I would have you consider that the word which you have uttered is one at which numerous persons, and very respectable persons too, in a figure pulling off their coats all in a moment, [474a] and seizing any weapon that comes to hand, will run at you might and main, before you know where you are, intending to do heaven knows what; and if you don't prepare an answer, and put yourself in motion, you will be "pared by their fine wits," and no mistake.

You got me into the scrape, I said.

And I was quite right; however, I will do all I can to get you out of it; but I can only give you good-will and good advice, and, perhaps, I may be able to fit answers to your questions better than another—that is all. [474b] And now, having such an auxiliary, you must do your best to show the unbelievers that you are right.

## [CHAPTER 25. THE ALLEGORY OF THE CAVE. BOOK 7, 514A–521B]

[514a] And now, I said, let me show in a figure how far our nature is enlightened or unenlightened: Behold! human beings living in a underground den, which has a mouth open towards the light and reaching all along the den; here they have been from their childhood, and have their legs and necks chained so that they cannot move, [514b] and can only see before them, being prevented by the chains from turning round their heads. Above and behind them a fire is blazing at a distance, and between the fire and the

prisoners there is a raised way; and you will see, if you look, a low wall built along the way, like the screen which marionette players have in front of them, over which they show the puppets.

I see.

And do you see, I said, men passing along the wall carrying [514c] all sorts of vessels, and statues and figures of animals made of wood and stone and various materials, [515a] which appear over the wall? Some of them are talking, others silent.

You have shown me a strange image, and they are strange prisoners.

Like ourselves, I replied; and they see only their own shadows, or the shadows of one another, which the fire throws on the opposite wall of the cave?

True, he said; how could they see anything but the shadows if they were never allowed [515b] to move their heads?

And of the objects which are being carried in like manner they would only see the shadows?

Yes, he said.

And if they were able to converse with one another, would they not suppose that they were naming what was actually before them?

Very true.

And suppose further that the prison had an echo which came from the other side, would they not be sure to fancy when one of the passers-by spoke that the voice which they heard came from the passing shadow?

No question, he replied.

[515c] To them, I said, the truth would be literally nothing but the shadows of the images.

That is certain.

And now look again, and see what will naturally follow if the prisoners are released and disabused of their error. At first, when any of them is liberated and compelled suddenly to stand up and turn his neck round and walk and look towards the light, he will suffer sharp pains; the glare will distress him, and he will be unable to see the realities of which in his former state he had seen the shadows; [515d] and then conceive some one saying to him, that what he saw before was an illusion, but that now, when he is approaching nearer to being and his eye is turned towards more real existence, he has a clearer vision,—what will be his reply? And you may further imagine that his instructor is pointing to the objects as they pass and requiring him to name them,—will he not be perplexed? Will he not fancy that the shadows which he formerly saw are truer than the objects which are now shown to him?

Far truer.

And if he is compelled to look straight at the light, [515e] will he not have a pain in his eyes which will make him turn away to take and take in the objects of vision which he can see, and which he will conceive to be in reality clearer than the things which are now being shown to him?

True, he said.

And suppose once more, that he is reluctantly dragged up a steep and rugged ascent, and held fast until he's forced into the presence of the sun himself, is he not likely to be pained and irritated? [516a] When he approaches the light his eyes will be dazzled, and he will not be able to see anything at all of what are now called realities.

Not all in a moment, he said.

He will require to grow accustomed to the sight of the upper world. And first he will see the shadows best, next the reflections of men and other objects in the water, and then the objects themselves; then he will gaze upon the light of the moon and the stars and the spangled heaven; and he will see the sky and the stars [516b] by night better than the sun or the light of the sun by day?

Certainly.

Last of he will be able to see the sun, and not mere reflections of him in the water, but he will see him in his own proper place, and not in another; and he will contemplate him as he is.

Certainly.

He will then proceed to argue that this is he who gives the season and the years, and is the guardian of all that is in the visible world, [516c] and in a certain way the cause of all things which he and his fellows have been accustomed to behold?

Clearly, he said, he would first see the sun and then reason about him.

And when he remembered his old habitation, and the wisdom of the den and his fellow-prisoners, do you not suppose that he would felicitate himself on the change, and pity them?

Certainly, he would.

And if they were in the habit of conferring honours among themselves on those who were quickest to observe the passing shadows and to remark which of them went before, [516d] and which followed after, and which were together; and who were therefore best able to draw conclusions as to the future, do you think that he would care for such honours and glories, or envy the possessors of them? Would he not say with Homer,

"Better to be the poor servant of a poor master,"

and to endure anything, rather than think as they do [516e] and live after their manner?

Yes, he said, I think that he would rather suffer anything than entertain these false notions and live in this miserable manner.

Imagine once more, I said, such a one coming suddenly out of the sun to be replaced in his old situation; would he not be certain to have his eyes full of darkness?

To be sure, he said.

And if there were a contest, and he had to compete [517a] in measuring the shadows with the prisoners who had never moved out of the den, while his sight was still weak, and before his eyes had become steady (and the time which would be needed to acquire this new habit of sight might be very considerable) would he not be ridiculous? Men would say of him that up he went and down he came without his eyes; and that it was better not even to think of ascending; and if any one tried to loose another and lead him up to the light, let them only catch the offender, and they would put him to death.

No question, he said.

This entire allegory, I said, you may now append, dear Glaucon, to the previous argument; [517b] the prison-house is the world of sight, the light of the fire is the sun, and you will not misapprehend me if you interpret the journey upwards to be the ascent of the soul into the intellectual world according to my poor belief, which, at your desire, I have expressed—whether rightly or wrongly God knows. But, whether true or false, my opinion is that in the world of knowledge the idea of good appears last of all, and is seen only with an effort; [517c] and, when seen, is also inferred to be the universal author of all things beautiful and right, parent of light and of the lord of light in this visible world, and the immediate source of reason and truth in the intellectual; and that this is the power upon which he who would act rationally, either in public or private life must have his eye fixed.

I agree, he said, as far as I am able to understand you.

Moreover, I said, you must not wonder that those who attain to this beatific vision are unwilling to descend to human affairs; for their souls are ever hastening into the upper world [517d] where they desire to dwell; which desire of theirs is very natural, if our allegory may be trusted.

Yes, very natural.

And is there anything surprising in one who passes from divine contemplations to the evil state of man, misbehaving himself in a ridiculous manner; if, while his eyes are blinking and before he has become accustomed to the surrounding darkness, he is compelled to fight in courts of law, or in other places, about the images or the shadows of images of justice, and is endeavouring to meet [517e] the conceptions of those who have never yet seen absolute justice?

Anything but surprising, he replied.

Any one who has common sense [518a] will remember that the bewilderments of the eyes are of two kinds, and arise from two causes, either from coming out of the light or from going into the light, which is true of the mind's eye, quite as much as of the bodily eye; and he who remembers this when he sees any one whose vision is perplexed and weak, will not be too ready to laugh; he will first ask whether that soul of man has come out of the brighter light, and is unable to see because unaccustomed to the dark, [518b] or having turned from darkness to the day is dazzled by excess of light. And he will count the one happy in his condition and state of being, and he will

pity the other; or, if he have a mind to laugh at the soul which comes from below into the light, there will be more reason in this than in the laugh which greets him who returns from above out of the light into the den.

That, he said, is a very just distinction.

But then, if I am right, certain professors of education must be wrong [518c] when they say that they can put a knowledge into the soul which was not there before, like sight into blind eyes.

They undoubtedly say this, he replied.

Whereas, our argument shows that the power and capacity of learning exists in the soul already; and that just as the eye was unable to turn from darkness to light without the whole body, so too the instrument of knowledge can only by the movement of the whole soul be turned from the world of becoming into that of being, and learn by degrees to endure the sight of being, and of the brightest and best of being, [518d] or in other words, of the good.

Very true.

And must there not be some art which will effect conversion in the easiest and quickest manner; not implanting the faculty of sight, for that exists already, but has been turned in the wrong direction, and is looking away from the truth?

Yes, he said, such an art may be presumed.

And whereas the other so-called virtues of the soul seem to be akin to bodily qualities, [518e] for even when they are not originally innate they can be implanted later by habit and exercise, the virtue of wisdom more than anything else contains a divine element which always remains, and by this conversion is rendered useful and profitable; [519a] or, on the other hand, hurtful and useless. Did you never observe the narrow intelligence flashing from the keen eye of a clever rogue—how eager he is, how clearly his paltry soul sees the way to his end; he is the reverse of blind, but his keen eye-sight is forced into the service of evil, and he is mischievous in proportion to his cleverness.

Very true, he said.

But what if there had been a circumcision of such natures in the days of their youth; and they had been severed from those sensual pleasures, such as eating and drinking, [519b] which, like leaden weights, were attached to them at their birth, and which drag them down and turn the vision of their souls upon the things that are below—if, I say, they had been released from these impediments and turned in the opposite direction, the very same faculty in them would have seen the truth as keenly as they see what their eyes are turned to now.

Very likely.

Yes, I said; and there is another thing which is likely, or rather a necessary inference from what has preceded, that neither the uneducated and uninformed of the truth, [519c] nor yet those who never make an end of their education, will be able ministers of State; not the former, because they have no single aim of duty which is the rule of all their actions, private as well as public; nor the latter, because they will not act at all except upon compulsion, fancying that they are already dwelling apart in the Islands of the Blest.

Very true, he replied.

Then, I said, the business of us who are the founders of the State will be to compel the best minds to attain that knowledge which we have already shown to be the greatest of all—they must continue to ascend [519d] until they arrive at the good; but when they have ascended and seen enough we must not allow them to do as they do now.

What do you mean?

I mean that they remain in the upper world: but this must not be allowed; they must be made to descend again among the prisoners in the den, and partake of their labours and honours, whether they are worth having or not.

But is not this unjust? he said; ought we to give them a worse life, when they might have a better?

[519e] You have again forgotten, my friend, I said, the intention of the legislator, who did not aim at making any one class in the State happy above the rest; the happiness was to be in the whole State, and he held the citizens together by persuasion and necessity, making them benefactors of the State, [520a] and therefore benefactors of one another; to this end he created them,

not to please themselves, but to be his instruments in binding up the State.

True, he said, I had forgotten.

Observe, Glaucon, that there will be no injustice in compelling our philosophers to have a care and providence of others; [520b] we shall explain to them that in other States, men of their class are not obliged to share in the toils of politics: and this is reasonable, for they grow up at their own sweet will, and the government would rather not have them. Being self-taught, they cannot be expected to show any gratitude for a culture which they have never received. But we have brought you into the world to be rulers of the hive, kings of yourselves and of the other citizens, and have educated you far better [520c] and more perfectly than they have been educated, and you are better able to share in the double duty. Wherefore each of you, when his turn comes, must go down to the general underground abode, and get the habit of seeing in the dark. When you have acquired the habit, you will see ten thousand times better than the inhabitants of the den, and you will know what the several images are, and what they represent, because you have seen the beautiful and just and good in their truth. And thus our State which is also yours will be a reality, and not a dream only, and will be administered in a spirit unlike that of other States, in which men fight with one another [520d] about shadows only and are distracted in the struggle for power, which in their eyes is a great good. Whereas the truth is that the State in which the rulers are most reluctant to govern is always the best and most quietly governed, and the State in which they are most eager, the worst.

Quite true, he replied.

And will our pupils, when they hear this, refuse to take their turn at the toils of State, when they are allowed to spend the greater part of their time with one another in the heavenly light?

[520e] Impossible, he answered; for they are just men, and the commands which we impose upon them are just; there can be no doubt that every one of them will take office as a stern ne-

cessity, and not after the fashion of our present rulers of State.

Yes, my friend, I said; and there lies the point. You must contrive for your future rulers another and a better life [521a] than that of a ruler, and then you may have a well-ordered State; for only in the State which offers this, will they rule who are truly rich, not in silver and gold, but in virtue and wisdom, which are the true blessings of life. Whereas if they go to the administration of public affairs, poor and hungering after their own private advantage, thinking that hence they are to snatch the chief good, order there can never be; for they will be fighting about office, and the civil and domestic broils which thus arise will be the ruin of the rulers themselves and of the whole State.

[521b] Most true, he replied.

And the only life which looks down upon the life of political ambition is that of true philosophy. Do you know of any other?

Indeed, I do not, he said.

And those who govern ought not to be lovers of the task? For, if they are, there will be rival lovers, and they will fight.

No question.

Who then are those whom we shall compel to be guardians? Surely they will be the men who are wisest about affairs of State, and by whom the State is best administered, and who at the same time have other honours and another and a better life than that of politics?

They are the men, and I will choose them, he replied.

# ARISTOTLE

## *Aristotle on Ethics: What Is the Good Life?*

The astonishing thing about Aristotle's (384–322 BC) account of ethics is that it still influences present-day thinking on ethics and moral theory. "Virtue ethics" (which will be described in Chapter 5) is a good example of Aristotle's lingering influence.

In his account of ethics, Aristotle spoke of human teleology. The word "teleology" is derived from two Greek words: *telos*, meaning "end" or "goal," and *logos*, meaning "the study of." Teleology, then, involves the ends of all things, from rocks to human beings. Although Socrates and Plato were familiar with the concept of teleology, Aristotle made it an important part of his philosophy.

When applied to human or animal activity, the notion of teleology can be easily appreciated. We see animals carrying out activities that appear to be goal oriented all the time. They feed themselves, build nests and dens, and procreate. Human beings often do the same sorts of things—albeit we build houses instead of nests. In addition to carrying out these animal-like activities, we have the ability to reflect on these goals, to have aspirations, and to make decisions.

Aristotle maintained teleology was due to our physiology and not just our ability for rational and emotional decisions. In the Middle Ages, St. Thomas Aquinas gave Aristotle's teleology a Christian twist. Today this is why the Roman Catholic Church believes that the human *telos* is most fully expressed in a man and a woman joining in holy matrimony and only then procreating. Because methods of birth control frustrate human teleology, the Church sees these methods as morally wrong.

The main feature of Aristotle's moral philosophy was his insistence that the end of all human activity, all human action, was to achieve *eudaimonia,* often translated as "happiness." "Well-being," another possible translation, denotes a complete general satisfactoriness, and gives a more accurate sense of Aristotle's position.

Now the question is, "How is one to achieve this well-being?" We typically ask this question today without connecting it to ethics. We just assume, for instance, that pursuing a business degree is good for us, and that we will be happy when we graduate and get a managerial position in high-tech industry with a hefty salary. Why should we bring ethics into the discussion?

Virtue, from the Greek *areté,* means to be good at something. Aristotle took its meaning a bit further. In his book *Nicomachean Ethics* (1106a 14) he says:

> Virtue is a disposition relating to choice, being in a mean relative to us, which is determined by a rule, and as a man of good sense would determine it.

To have virtue is a matter of practicing moderation, of finding the "mean" between two extremes. Virtues can either be intellectual or ethical in nature. Examples of intellectual virtues are things like wisdom or intelligence. Ethical virtues, which concern us here, are those characteristics we find praiseworthy in the ethical sphere of human activity. The four primary virtues of ancient philosophy were temperance, courage, wisdom, and justice. Later, when Aristotle became the main classical source of inspiration for Christian theologians during the Middle Ages, the virtues of faith, hope, and love were added to this list. Intellectual virtues were related to ethical virtues because the intellect allows us to find this ethical *mean* (i.e., a middle ethical position).

In describing what is virtuous, Aristotle spoke of a mean between competing options or extremes. Aristotle was concerned with how extreme human behavior can be. This can show itself in two ways: Either we overreact to a situation, or we do not adequately react to a situation that demands our moral attention.

Think of someone drowning in a lake, not far from the shore. A passerby, in order to act within the mean, must quickly evaluate the situation. She must quickly consider her ability to save the drowning person. What kind of swimmer is she? How deep is the water, and what kind of current might there be? One might be forced to think through these considerations in a split second, making the decision without being absolutely certain that it's the right one.

Aristotle wants to show us that it's not always ethically correct or virtuous to try to save the drowning person. The judgment whether or not we should save this person depends on the circumstances surrounding the incident, circumstances that will vary depending on the people involved. In this case, if the passerby isn't a strong swimmer and still attempts a rescue, she will most likely lose her life in her effort to save the drowning person. For Aristotle, this attempt would be foolhardy because of its excess. Her decision was not made in accordance with reason.

But let's change the circumstances a bit: The drowning person has slipped into a shallow lake, and is face down in the water. This time the passerby happens to be a gold-medal Olympic swimmer. Under these conditions we would consider not doing anything as cowardice on the swimmer's part. In fact, the failure to aid someone in danger when one is capable of doing so is a crime in most countries.

These examples all draw on Aristotle's definition of the mean, which he saw as "a mean relative to us." "Relative" doesn't mean that "everything is relative" or there are no moral truths. Aristotle means rather we should judge our handling of a moral dilemma relative to our ability to resolve it. However, Aristotle does point out that while some actions may be relative to the context that we face, certain actions are never ethically right. The clearest cases of such actions are adultery and cold-blooded murder.

To summarize, we become virtuous over time by consistently acting according to reason, and by choosing a mean between extremes, knowing that the ultimate end of all human activity is well-being. Aristotle draws the analogy between ethical behavior and the life of an artist. Just as an artist must practice his or her art in order to become skillful, we must practice virtue to become virtuous. A person who wants to be courageous appropriately practices courage; a person desiring a generous character practices generosity within the mean, and so on through all the virtues.

Aristotle's *Nicomachean Ethics* captures many of our basic intuitions about how to be ethical. The ethical life demands careful reflection on our part. We cannot rush headlong into a moral decision without running the risk of making things worse. The virtues, our moral dispositions, must be developed and nurtured over time. Through continued practice, we can bring about our most desired goal—to have well-being, to live the good life.

# On Virtue and the Ethical Mean

## ARISTOTLE

### *Book 2*

#### CHAPTER 5

CONCERNING VIRTUE we should state not only this, that it is a habit, but also the kind of habit it is. It should be noted that every virtue (a) makes that of which it is the virtue be well disposed and (b) makes it perform its function well; e.g., the virtue of an eye both makes the eye a good eye and makes it perform its function well, for it is by the virtue of the eye that we see well. Similarly, the virtue of a horse makes (a) the horse a good horse and also (b) good at running and carrying its rider and facing the enemy. So if such is the case in every instance, the virtue of a man, too, would be the habit from which he becomes good and performs his function well. How this can be done has already been stated, but it may become evident also if we view the kind of nature possessed by virtue. Now in everything which is continuous and divisible it is possible to take an amount which is greater than or less than or equal to the amount required, and the amounts taken may be so related either with respect to the thing itself or in relation to us; and the equal is a mean between excess and deficiency. By "the mean," in the case of the thing itself, I mean that which lies at equal intervals from the extremes, and this mean is just one thing and is the same for everyone; but, when related to us, it neither

SOURCE: Aristotle, *Nicomachean Ethics,* trans. Hippocrates G. Apostle, bk. 2, 1106a 14–1107b 30; 1108a 5–9, 20–36; 1108b 11–20; 1109a 20–b 26, in *Aristotle: Selected Works,* 2nd ed., trans. Hippocrates G. Apostle and Lloyd P. Gerson (Grinnell, IA: Peripatetic Press, 1986), pp. 444–450 (edited). The subtitles to the Aristotle readings were added by us and aren't in the original.

exceeds nor falls short [of what is proper to each of us], and this is neither just one thing nor the same for everyone. For example, if ten is many and two is few, then six is taken as the mean with respect to the thing itself, for six exceeds two and is exceeded by ten by equal amounts; and this is the mean according to an arithmetic proportion. But the mean relative to us should not be taken in this manner; for if ten pounds are too much and two pounds are too little for someone to eat, the trainer will not [necessarily] order six pounds, since this is perhaps too much or too little for the one who is to take it; for Milo[1] it is too little, but for a beginner in athletics it is too much. It is likewise in running and wrestling. And this is the way in which every scientist avoids excess and deficiency but seeks and chooses the mean, not the mean with respect to the thing itself but the one in relation to a given person.

If, then, this is the manner in which every science performs its function well, namely, by keeping an eye on the mean and working towards it (whence arises the usual remark concerning excellent works, that nothing can be subtracted from or added to them, since both excess and deficiency destroy the excellence in them while the mean preserves it), and if, as is our manner of saying, it is with an eye on this that good artists do their work, and if virtue, like nature, is more precise and better than any art, then virtue would be aiming at the mean. I am speaking here of ethical virtue, for it is this which is concerned with feelings and *actions,* in which there is excess, deficiency, and moderation. For example, we may have the feelings of fear, courage, *desire,* anger, pity, and any pleasure or pain in general either more or less than we should, and in both cases this is not a good thing; but to have these feelings at the right times and for the right things and towards the right men and for the right purpose and in the right manner, this is the mean and the best, and it is precisely this which belongs to virtue. In *actions,* too, there is excess, deficiency, and moderation in a similar manner.

Now an [ethical] virtue is concerned with feelings and *actions,* in which excess and deficiency are errors and are blamed, while moderation is a *success* and is praised; and both *success* and praise belong to virtue. Virtue, then, is a kind of moderation, at least having the mean as its aim. Also, a man may make an error in many ways (for evil, as the Pythagoreans conjectured, belongs to the infinite, while goodness belongs to the finite), but he may *succeed* in one way only; and in view of this, one of them is easy but the other hard. It is easy to miss the mark but hard to hit it. So it is because of these, too, that excess and deficiency belong to vice, but moderation to virtue.

For men are good in one way, bad in many.

## CHAPTER 6

[Ethical] virtue, then, is a habit, disposed toward *action* by deliberate choice, being at the mean relative to us, and defined by reason and as a prudent man would define it. It is a mean between two vices, one by excess and the other by deficiency; and while some of the vices exceed while the others are deficient in what is right in feelings and *actions,* virtue finds and chooses the mean. Thus, according to its *substance* or the definition stating its essence, virtue is a mean [of a certain kind], but with respect to the highest good and to excellence, it is an extreme.

Not every *action* nor every feeling, however, admits of the mean, for some of them have names which directly include badness, e.g., such feelings as malicious gladness, shamelessness, and envy, and, in the case of *actions,* adultery, theft, and murder; for all of these and others like them are blamed for being bad, not [just] their excesses or deficiencies. Accordingly, one is never right in performing these but is always mistaken; and there is no problem of whether it is good or not to do them, e.g., whether to commit adultery with the right woman, at the right time, in the right manner, etc., for to perform any of these is without qualification to be mistaken. If this were not so, we would be maintaining that in *acting* unjustly or in a cowardly way or intemperately,

[1] A great wrestler.

too, there is moderation and excess and deficiency; for according to such a view there would be also a moderation of excess and of deficiency, an excess of excess, and a deficiency of deficiency. But just as there is no excess or deficiency of temperance or of bravery, because the mean is in a certain way an extreme, so, too, there is no moderation or excess or deficiency in the vices mentioned above but only a mistake, regardless of the manner in which one *acts;* for, universally, there is no moderation of excess or of deficiency, nor an excess or a deficiency of moderation.

## CHAPTER 7

We must not only state this universally, however, but also apply it to particular cases; for, among statements about *actions,* those which are [more] universal are rather empty while those which are [more] particular tend to be more true; for *actions* deal with particulars, and it is with these that our statements should be in harmony. So let us consider each of these virtues and vices from our table.

With regard to fear and courage, the mean is bravery. He who exceeds in not fearing has no name (many virtues and vices have no names), but he who exceeds in courage is rash; and he who exceeds in fear and is deficient in courage is a coward.

With regard to pleasures and pains—not all of them [but mainly of the bodily senses], and less with regard to pains than with regard to pleasures—the mean is temperance while the excess is intemperance. Men deficient with regard to pleasures hardly exist, and for this reason such men happen to have no name; but let them be called "insensible."

With regard to giving and taking property, the mean is generosity, while the excess and deficiency are, respectively, wastefulness and stinginess. Excess and deficiency in these two vices are present in contrary ways; for the wasteful man exceeds in giving away and is deficient in taking, while the stingy man exceeds in taking but is deficient in giving away. (At present we are giving a sketchy and summary account of these, and this

is sufficient; later[2] we shall specify them more precisely.) With regard to property there are also certain other dispositions. The mean is munificence, for a munificent man differs from a generous man in that he deals with large amounts, while a generous man deals with small amounts [also]. The excess in large donations is extravagance or conspicuous consumption, and the deficiency is meanness; but these vices differ from the vices opposed to generosity, and the manner in which they differ will be stated later.

With regard to honor and dishonor, the mean is high-mindedness, the excess is said to be a sort of vanity, and the deficiency is low-mindedness. And just as generosity was said to be related to munificence by being concerned with smaller amounts, so too there is a virtue which is concerned with smaller honors and is similarly related to high-mindedness, which is concerned with great honors; for it is possible to desire honor as one should, or more than one should, or less than one should. Now he who exceeds in his desires is called "ambitious," he who is deficient is called "unambitious," but he who desires honor in moderation has no name. . . .

With regard to anger, too, there is excess, deficiency, and moderation. These habits are almost nameless, but since we say that the moderate man is good-tempered, let us call the mean "good temper." As for the extremes, let the man who exceeds be called "irascible" and the corresponding vice "irascibility," and let the man who is deficient be called "inirascible" and the corresponding deficiency "inirascibility." . . .

With regard to truth, then, the moderate man is a sort of truthful man and the mean may be called "truthfulness"; but pretense which exaggerates is boastfulness and the possessor of it is boastful, while pretense which understates is self-depreciation and the possessor of it is self-depreciatory.

With regard to what is pleasant in amusing others, the moderate man is witty and the corresponding disposition is wit, but the disposition which tends to exceed is buffoonery and the pos-

[2] Book 4.

sessor of it is a buffoon, while he who is deficient is a sort of boor and the corresponding habit is boorishness.

With regard to what is pleasant in the other manner, the one found in [all] situations of life, the man who is pleasant as he should be is friendly and the mean is friendliness; but he who behaves excessively is complaisant, if he does this not for the sake of anything else, but is a flatterer, if he does it for his personal benefit, while he who is deficient and is unpleasant in all situations is a quarrelsome sort of man or a man hard to get along with.

There are moderations in feelings, too, and in what concerns feelings. Thus a sense of shame is not a virtue, but a man with a sense of shame is praised also; for here, too, one man is said to be moderate, i.e., he who has a sense of shame, another behaves excessively, like the abashed man who is ashamed of everything, and a third is deficient or is not ashamed at all; and he is called "shameless." . . .

## CHAPTER 8

Since the kinds of habits are three, and since two of them are vices, one with respect to excess but the other with respect to deficiency, while the third is a virtue, which is a mean, each of them is opposed to each of the others in some manner; for the extremes [the vices] are contrary both to the mean and to each other, while the mean is contrary to the extremes; for just as the equal is greater when related to the less but less when related to the greater, so in both feelings and *actions* the middle habits [the moderations] exceed when related to the deficiencies but are deficient when related to the excesses. For the brave man appears rash to the coward but a coward to the rash man. . . .

## CHAPTER 9

We have sufficiently discussed the following: that ethical virtue is a mean; the manner in which it is a mean; that it is a mean between two vices, one with respect to excess and the other with respect

to deficiency; and that it is such a mean because it aims at what is moderate in feelings and *actions*.

In view of what has been said, it is a difficult task to become a virtuous man, for in each case it is a difficult task to attain the mean; for example, not everyone can find the mean [the center] of a circle but only he who knows geometry. So, too, anyone can get angry or give money or spend it, and it is easy. But to give to the right person, the right amount, at the right time, for the right purpose, and in the right manner, this is not something that anyone can do nor is it easy to do; and it is in view of this that excellence is rare and praiseworthy and noble. Accordingly, he who aims at the mean should first keep himself away from that vice which is more contrary to the mean, as Calypso recommends also: "keep the ship away from the surf and spray";[3] for one of the two extremes is more subject to mistake, while the other is less so. So since it is difficult to attain the mean exactly, we should choose as a second best, as the saying goes, that which has the least of what is bad; and this will most likely be effected in the manner stated.

We should take into consideration also the vices to which we are easily drawn, for some of us are by nature inclined towards some of them, others towards others; and we come to know these by our pains and pleasures. We should then drag ourselves towards the contrary extreme, for by drawing ourselves well away from our disposition to error, we shall be more likely to arrive at the mean, like those who straighten warped sticks by bending them in the contrary direction.

On every occasion, what we should guard against most is the pleasurable or pleasure, for we do not judge pleasure impartially. Thus towards pleasure we should feel just as the elders of the people felt towards Helen, and we should repeat their saying[4] on every occasion; for by getting rid of pleasure in this manner we are less likely to be mistaken. To sum up, then, if we do all these things, we shall best be able to attain the mean.

[3] Homer, *Odyssey,* xii 108, 219 ff.
[4] Homer, *Iliad,* iii 156–160.

Perhaps all this is difficult, and especially in individual cases, for it is not easy to specify, for example, how and with whom and on what kinds of provocations and how long a man should be angry; for we do sometimes praise those who are deficient and call them "good-tempered" but at other times speak of those who are harsh as being manly. Nevertheless, the man who is blamed is not he who deviates from goodness only a little, whether towards excess or deficiency, but he who deviates much, for the latter does not escape our notice. Nor is it easy to specify by a formula the limits beyond which one becomes blameworthy and the extent to which one should be blamed, for this is not easy for any sensible object; such specifications depend on individual situations, and judgement depends on the sensation of these. So much, then, is clear, that the intermediate habit is in all cases praiseworthy, and that we should lean sometimes in the direction of excess and sometimes in the direction of deficiency, for by so doing we shall most easily attain the mean and goodness.

## Aristotle on Politics: What Is the Best Form of Government?

Aristotle's political theory follows logically from his discussion of ethics. The connection was intended. If we wish to have well-being, there is greater chance we will achieve it being part of a community instead of acting individually. The *polis* (the city-state) organizes collections of such individuals to aid in the production of their well-being.

Aristotle notes that human beings are more political than any other animal, including the highly organized honeybees. So he begins by describing how the city-state first comes together. It starts with the individual, who by virtue of birth is part of a family. Families, in turn, create associations with each other in order to help sustain their individual well-being. These associations give birth to village life. When a number of villages join together for economic reasons or self-protection, a state comes into being. This natural evolution from individual families to the state proves Aristotle's idea that human beings are "political animals."

What, then, is the role of the state once it comes into existence from these associations of villages? Recall Aristotle's conception of how individual well-being is brought about: The good life was the *telos* of human activity. The state, as a collection of individuals, was a natural result of this *telos* for a large group of individuals. From this way of thinking about things, it followed that the state is morally prior to the individual. The individual is not self-sufficient—we need the family to sustain us. Yet unlike the individual, however, the state is self-sufficient. The whole is prior to its parts. The state served to enable its citizens to achieve *eudaimonia*. This well-being is holistic: It includes all aspects of an individual's life, its political, physical, moral, and intellectual components.

Although Aristotle conceived the state as coming together from an original collection of individuals, not all individuals in the city-state were created equal. To be a full *citizen* in Aristotle's state was a status open to only a select few, and only these select few had the right to participate in a legislative or judicial office of the state.

Aristotle's vision of the state was not the sort of representative government we find in modern democratic societies. The few men selected to be citizens were to be completely and wholly devoted to the state, with their service beginning as young soldiers and continuing with their later joining the political assembly and playing a role in the courts. After learning how to be ruled as a youth, in the latter part of life, the citizen serves in the state's priesthood. For Aristotle, learning how to be ruled was a necessary condition for knowing how to rule. This sort of life was reserved exclusively for the "leisured class." These were the minority of men who had the time to devote themselves to the highly demanding training regimen required by Aristotle for membership in his ruling class.

By today's standards this was a highly elitist and sexist understanding of who was capable of ruling the state. Women were certainly excluded from the process. Men who labored manually, whether as farmers or artisans, were also excluded from ruling the state. Manual labor was thought to make one unfit for the intellectual task of governing. Despite this dim view of manual labor, Aristotle recognized that such labor on the part of the citizenry was indispensable to the functioning of the state, as it provided leisure for the elite. This leisure, in turn, was required in order for young men to develop the necessary skills for them to play their eventual leadership roles.

Having answered the question, "Who is to govern?" we now need to ask the question, "Exactly what form should the state take?" For Aristotle, this question was practical as well as theoretical. We may envision a government which, in a perfect or ideal world, would be the best and most effective. But given that a state must exist in the real world, a world that is far from ideal, we must be practical in conceptualizing it.

Aristotle analyzed six possible states, which he thought could be further split up. States that have the interests of all citizens in mind are to be preferred to distorted forms—those where the rulers serve only their own interests. Aristotle lays this out below in book 2, 1279b. We can see how his six basic forms of the state are distinguished in the following chart, which makes obvious its parallel to the "mean" in ethics:

| NUMBER OF RULERS | TRUE FORM OF THE STATE | DISTORTED FORM OF THE STATE |
|---|---|---|
| One | Monarchy (Kingship) | Tyranny |
| Few | Aristocracy | Oligarchy |
| Many | Democracy (Polity) | People's Rule |

Aristotle understood *polity* as the "true" from of democracy. Here the middle class governs the many in the interests of the state. Similar to his balance in ethics, Aristotle strikes a balance between the very rich and the very poor. Within the middle class lay moderation. Again, balance or the mean is the key conceptual device for Aristotle. The distorted form of polity was the so-called "people's rule." This was a deviant form of government as it involved mob rule, the rule of the poor. The government's interest was focused only on them, not on the common interest of all. As you read through the *Politics*, keeping this scheme in mind should help you to follow Aristotle's various combinations and divisions.

# The State's Origin in the Household

## ARISTOTLE

### *Book 1*

#### CHAPTER I

WE OBSERVE THAT every state is a sort of association, and that every association is formed for the sake of some good (for all men always *act* in order to attain what they think to be good). So it is clear that, while all associations aim at some good, the association which aims in the highest degree and at the supreme good is the one which is the most authoritative and includes all the others. Now this is called "a state," and it is a political association.

Those who think[1] that a statesman, a king, a ruler of a household, and a master of slaves are all the same do not speak well, for they hold that these [rulers] differ not in kind but with respect to the number of their subjects. Thus they regard a master as a ruler of few, a householder as a ruler of a somewhat greater number, and a statesman or a king as a ruler of a still greater number, as if there were no difference between a large household and a small state; and [they distinguish] a king from a statesman [only] in this, that the first is the sole authority of the state but the second rules and is ruled in turn according to the truths of political science.

Now these views are not true, and this will be clear if we examine what has just been said according to our usual method of inquiry. For, just as in every other discipline it is necessary to analyze a composite subject into its elements, which are the smallest parts of the whole, so by looking closely at the elements of a state, we will be better placed to observe how these elements differ

from one another and, if possible, to grasp something about each of the above-mentioned arts [royal art, political art, etc.].

#### CHAPTER 2

If one were to look at the growth of things from their beginning, one would also be, as in other disciplines, in the best position to speculate on these matters. First, there must be a union of those who cannot exist without each other, that is, a union of male and female for the sake of procreation (and the tendency in men, as in the other animals and in plants, to leave behind their own kind is natural and not the result of deliberate choice). Second, there must be a union of that which by nature can rule and that which [by nature should be] ruled, for the sake of their preservation; for that which can foresee by *thought* is by nature a ruler or by nature a master, whereas that which [cannot foresee by *thought* but] can carry out the orders with the body is by nature a subject or a slave. In view of this, the master and the slave have the same interest [i.e., preservation].

Now there is a distinction by nature between the female and the slave. For nature is never niggardly like the smiths who make the Delphian knife: she makes a thing to serve only one thing, for an instrument can best accomplish its task by serving one and not many functions. Yet among the barbarians the female and the slave are placed in the same rank; and the *reason* for this is the fact that they do not have rulers by nature but their association consists of slaves, both male and female. It is in view of this that poets say,

[1] Plato, *Statesman*, 258E–259D.

SOURCE: Aristotle, *Politics*, bk. 1, 1252a–1253b 12; 1259a 37–b 17, in *Aristotle: Selected Works*, 2nd ed., trans. Hippocrates G. Apostle and Lloyd P. Gerson (Grinnell, IA: Peripatetic Press, 1986), pp. 547–550, 562–563 (edited).

"It is meet that Greeks should rule barbarians,"

implying that a barbarian and a slave are the same by nature. Out of these two associations [male-female, master-slave] a household is formed first, and Hesiod was right when he said,

"First a house and a wife and an ox for the plough,"

for a poor man uses an ox instead of a house slave. An association formed by nature for the daily needs of life, then, is a household, and its members are called by Charondas "companions of the hearth," and by Epimenides the Cretan "companions of the manger." But the first association formed from many households for other than daily needs is the village, and the most natural form of a village seems to be a colony of a household, comprised of the children and grandchildren, those who are called by some "suckled with the same milk"; and it is in view of this that the first states were at first ruled by kings (and nations are still so governed nowadays), for they were formed of persons [already] governed by kings. For every household is ruled royally by the eldest, so the [early] colonies, too, were similarly ruled because of their kinship. And this is Homer's meaning [concerning the Cyclopes] when he says,[2] "each of them rules over children and wife," for they lived in scattered groups, as in ancient times. And it is because of this, too, that all men say that the Gods are ruled by kings, for men were ruled by kings in ancient days, and are still so ruled now; just as the forms of the Gods were thought to resemble those of men, so were the living habits of the Gods.

Finally, a complete association composed of many villages is a state, an association which (a) has reached the limit of every self-sufficiency, so to speak, (b) was formed for the sake of living, but (c) exists for the sake of living well. For this reason, every state exists by nature, if indeed the first associations too existed by nature; for the latter associations have the state as their end, and

nature is the end [of becoming]. For the kind of thing which a subject becomes at the end of a generation is said to be the nature of that subject, as in the case of a man or a horse or a house. Besides, the final cause or the end is the best, and the self-sufficiency [of an association] is the end and the best.

From the above remarks, then, it is evident that a state exists by nature and that man is by nature a political animal; but [he] who exists outside a state because of [his] nature and not by luck is either [bad] or superior to man: [he] is like the man denounced by Homer[3] as being "tribeless, lawless, hearthless." In addition, such a [man] by [his] nature *desires* war inasmuch as [he] is solitary, like an isolated piece in a game of draughts. It is clear, then, why man is more of a political animal than a bee or any other gregarious animal; for nature, as we say, does nothing in vain, and man alone of all animals has the power of reason.

Voice, of course, serves as a sign of the painful and the pleasurable, and for this reason it belongs to other animals also; for the nature of these advances only up to the point of sensing the painful and the pleasurable and of communicating these to one another. But speech serves to make known what is beneficial or harmful, and so what is just or unjust; for what is proper to man compared to the other animals is this: he alone has the sense of what is good or evil, just or unjust, and the like, and it is an association of beings with this sense which makes possible a household and a state. Further, a state is prior by nature to a household or each man, since the whole is of necessity prior to each of its parts. For if the whole [man] ceases to exist, his foot or hand will exist only equivocally, and such a hand will then be like a hand made of stone. Indeed every part, such as [a hand or a foot], is defined by its function or power, so if the [power and the function] are lacking, one should not say that what remains is the same as a hand unless one uses the term "hand" equivocally.

[2] *Odyssey,* ix 114.

[3] *Iliad,* ix 63.

It is clear, then, that a state exists by nature and is prior to each [of its parts]; for if each man is not self-sufficient when existing apart from a state, he will be like a part when separated from the whole; and one who cannot associate with others or does not need association with others because of self-sufficiency is no part of a state but is either a brute or a God.

Now there is a natural tendency in all men to form such an association [i.e., a state], and he who was the first to do so was the cause of the greatest good; for just as man when perfected is the best of all animals, so he is the worst of all when separated from law and judgement. For the most cruel injustice is the one which has weapons to carry it out; and a man, born with weapons [e.g., speech, hands, ability to reason, etc.] to be used with prudence and virtue, can misuse these [weapons through folly and vice] for contrary ends most of all. For this reason, a man without virtue can be the most unholy, the most savage, and the worst [of animals] for lust and gluttony. Justice, on the other hand, is political [i.e., belongs to the state]; for judgement about matters requiring justice, that is, the discernment of what is just, is the principle of ordering in a political association.

## CHAPTER 3

Since it is evident of what parts a state is composed, we must discuss household management first, for every state is made up of households. The parts of a household are those of which a household is in turn composed, and a complete household is composed of freemen and slaves; and since our inquiry should begin with the smallest parts, which are master and slave, husband and wife, and parent and children, we should consider what each of these three [associations] is and what kind of thing it should be; the three are: the master-slave association, the mari-tal association (the union of *man* and woman has no name), and thirdly the parent-child association (for this association, too, has no special name). So let these three be the associations of a household. . . .

## CHAPTER 12

As already stated, the art of household management has three parts: (a) that of the rule of a master over slaves, already discussed, (b) that of the rule of a father over children, and (c) that of the rule of a husband over his wife. The ruler of a household, as a husband and a father, rules both his wife and his children, who are free, but he does this not in the same manner; he rules politically over his wife but royally over his children. For the male is by nature more able to lead than the female, except in some cases where there is a departure from nature, and so is the elder and mature man compared to the younger and immature. But in most political states the citizens rule and are ruled in turns, for it is the nature of such a state to aim at equality of its members and show no difference. On the other hand, whenever one citizen rules and another is ruled, we expect a difference in outward form and manner of address and honors, as illustrated by a speech of Amasis about his foot-pan.[4] The rule of the male over the female is of this kind, and it is permanent; but his rule over children is royal; for a father rules [his children] by virtue of his affection and by right of his seniority, and this is indeed a form of royal rule. It is in view of this that Homer, in using the expression "father of both *men* and Gods," spoke well of Zeus, who is the king of them all. For a king, although of the same race as his subjects, should be by nature superior to them; and such indeed is the relation of the elder to the younger and of a father to his child.

---

[4] Herodotus, II 172.

# Forms of the State

## ARISTOTLE

### *Book 3*

#### CHAPTER 6

HAVING SETTLED THESE THINGS, let us consider next whether we should posit only one or many forms of government, and if many, what they are and how many there are, and what the differences among them are.

A government is the arrangement of the various offices of a state, and especially of the most authoritative of all the others, for the authority over each of the others is the ruling body, and this is [the main part of] the government. I mean, for example, that the authority in popular governments is the common people, whereas in oligarchies it is the few [wealthy]; so we speak of these two governments as being different, and we may speak of the other forms of government in the same way.

First, let us lay down the purpose for which a state has been formed and also the kinds of rule which govern men and their social life. Now we have stated also at the start of this treatise, where we described household management and the rule of a master, that men are by nature political animals, and for this reason, even when they have no need of each other's help, they desire no less to live with each other; and, moreover, common expediency brings them together to the extent that it contributes to the good life of each. In fact, the good life is the end in the highest degree for all men taken together and for each of them taken separately; and they come together for the sake of mere living also (for perhaps there is in [mere] living itself something fine), and they maintain their political association even for the sake of mere living, as long as life's hardships are not excessive. Clearly, most men cling to life

at the cost of enduring many ills, which shows that there is some contentment and a natural sweetness in mere living. . . .

It is evident, then, that the forms of government which aim at the common interest happen to be right with respect to what is just without qualification; but those forms which aim only at the interest of the rulers are all erroneous and deviations from the right forms, for they are despotic, whereas a state is an association of freemen.

#### CHAPTER 7

Having settled these matters, we shall next examine the forms of government, their number and what each of them is, starting first with the right forms, for when these have been described, the deviations from them, too, will become evident.

The terms "government" and "ruling body" are [generically] the same in meaning, the ruling body being the authoritative part of a state, and this part must be either one ruler or few or the majority; and whenever the ruling body, whether one or few or the majority, rules for the common interest, the corresponding form of government is necessarily right, but whenever the ruling body rules for its own interest, whether it be one ruler or few or the majority, the corresponding form of government is a deviation from the right form. For we should say that either those who do not partake [of benefits] are not citizens, or that they [as citizens] should get a share of those benefits.

We usually employ the name "kingship" for a monarchy which aims at the common interest, the name "aristocracy" for a government by the few but more than one, either because the rulers are the best *men*, or because they aim at the best interest of the state or of those who participate in

SOURCE: Aristotle, *Politics,* bk. 3, 1278b 6–30; 1279a 17–b 19; 1279b 40–1280a 8; 1280b 40–1281a 36, in *Aristotle: Selected Works,* 2nd ed., trans. Hippocrates G. Apostle and Lloyd P. Gerson (Grinnell, IA: Peripatetic Press, 1986), pp. 573–576, 578–579 (edited).

it, and the common name πομτεία [i.e., "democracy"] for a government by the many if it governs for the common interest. And there is a good reason for this [use of language]; for it is possible for one *man* or a few to excel in virtue but very difficult for the majority to become perfect in every virtue, unless this be military virtue, which is most likely to exist in the majority. It is in view of this that, in this form of government, the military men have the greatest authority and those who share in the government are those who possess arms.

Of governments which deviate from the right forms, tyranny is opposed to kingship, oligarchy is opposed to aristocracy, and people's rule is opposed to democracy. For tyranny is a monarchy which aims at the interest of the monarch [only], oligarchy aims at the interest of the prosperous [only], people's rule aims at the interest of the poor [only], but none of them aims at the common interest.

## CHAPTER 8

But we should state what each of the above governments is at greater length, for there are some difficulties; and it is appropriate for one, who makes a philosophical inquiry into a subject but does not attend only to the practical side of it, not to overlook or omit anything but to bring out the truth concerning each point.

As already stated, tyranny is a monarchy, and its rule is despotic over the political association; oligarchy is a government ruled by those who possess [much] property; people's rule, on the contrary, is a government ruled by those who do not possess much property but are needy.

. . . The difference between people's rule and oligarchy is that between poverty and wealth. So the government in which few or the majority hold office because of wealth must be an oligarchy, and that in which the poor, whether few or many, hold office must be a people's rule, although it happens [always or most of the time], as already stated, that the rulers in an oligarchy are few whereas those in a people's rule are the majority; for those who are prosperous are [usu-

ally] few, but sharing in freedom belongs to all, and it is because of prosperity and freedom that disputes arise between the wealthy and the free as to the form of government.

## CHAPTER 9

. . . The end of a state, then, is the good life, and the associations and activities just mentioned are for the sake of that end. And a state is an association of families and villages for the sake of a perfect and self-sufficient life, which is, in our way of saying, a happy and noble life. We should posit, then, that a political association exists for the sake of noble *actions* and not for the sake of [merely] living together. It is indeed for this reason that those who contribute most to such an association are a greater part of the state than those who are equal or greater in freedom or birthright but inferior in political virtue, or than those who exceed in wealth but are exceeded in virtue.

It is evident from what has been said, then, that all those who disagree about governments are speaking only of a part of what is just.

## CHAPTER 10

A problem arises, however, as to what part of the state should have authority. Should it be the multitude, or the wealthy, or the equitable, or the one best man, or the tyrant? There appears to be a difficulty regardless of which of these alternatives is taken.

If the poor because of their superior number distribute the property of the wealthy, would it not be unjust? "No, by Zeus," it will be answered, "for this would be justly decreed by the part which has authority." But if not this, what should we call the height of injustice? For if the majority of all citizens once more distribute among themselves the property of the minority, etc., it is evident that the state will be eventually ruined. Moreover, virtue certainly does not destroy its possessor, nor is that which is just destructive of the state; so it is clear that this law, too, cannot be just. Further, all the *actions* of a tyrant, too, would of necessity be just; for, being stronger, he coerces all the others just as the majority coerce the wealthy. But then, is it just for the few or the wealthy to rule? If they, too, plunder or confiscate the possessions of the majority, is this just? If it is, so will it be in the previous cases. It is evident, then, that all of these *actions* are bad and not just.

But should the equitable hold office and have authority over all matters? Then all the others, not being honored by being excluded from political rule, will live without honor; for we call the offices of the state its "honors," and if the same men always rule, all the others must be always without honor. Again, is it better for the most virtuous man alone to hold office? But this will be even more oligarchical, for those without honor will be even more numerous. Perhaps one might say that, in general, it is bad for a man and not the law to have authority, seeing that a man is subject to the passions of the soul. . . .

# The Best State

## ARISTOTLE

### *Book 4*

#### CHAPTER II

WE SHOULD NOW INQUIRE what is the best form of government and the best way of life for most states and most men, using as a principle of judgment not virtue which is far above ordinary men, nor the kind of education which requires a [gifted] nature and fortunate circumstances, nor yet a form of government held up as an ideal, but rather a way of life in which most men can share and a form of government in which most states can participate. . . .

Now in every state there are three parts: the very prosperous, the very needy, and the middle class. So since it is agreed that the moderate and the mean are the best, it is evident that the best possession of goods which comes from fortune, too, is the one which is moderate, for this is the easiest to deal with in a rational manner; for he who greatly excels in beauty or strength or noble birth or wealth, or in the contraries of these, i.e., in ugliness or weakness or low birth or poverty, finds it difficult to follow reason. The former tend to become insolent or great criminals, but the latter rather mischievous and petty rascals; for, of unjust treatments, some come about because of insolence, others because of mischief. Again, these [the middle class] are least given to an [inordinate] love of power or rule, both of which are harmful to states. In addition, those who excel in good fortune—those who are strong and wealthy and have friends and the like—neither wish nor *know* how to be ruled (and they are brought up in this way at home during their childhood, for, living in luxury, they do not acquire the habit of submitting to instruction), while those who lack excessively these goods of fortune are too humble [either to wish or to *know* how to rule]. So the latter *know* not how to rule but only how to be ruled despotically, while the former *know* not how to be ruled at all but only how to rule despotically. Accordingly, what results is not a state of freemen but one of despots and of slaves, of envious and of contemptuous men. Such a "state" is farthest removed from being a political and a friendly association; for an association is characterized by friendliness,

SOURCE: Aristotle, *Politics*, 1295a 25–1296a 9; 1326b 8–26; 1332b 12–1333a 16, in *Aristotle: Selected Works,* trans. Hippocrates G. Apostle and Lloyd P. Gerson (Grinnell, IA: Peripatetic Press, 1986), pp. 588–589, 597, 599–600 (edited).

whereas enemies do not wish to share even the same path.

Anyway, a state aims at being an association of men who are equal and alike as far as possible, and such is an association composed of middle-class citizens most of all. So a state which is, as we maintain, by nature composed of such men will necessarily be best governed, and such citizens are the ones most secure in the state; for neither do they, unlike poor men, *desire* what belongs to others, nor others *desire* what belongs to them, as poor men *desire* what belongs to the wealthy. And because of the fact that they neither plot against others nor others plot against them, they lead a life free from danger. It is for this *reason* that the prayer of Phocylides was well expressed when he said,

> "Many things are best in the middle;
> And there, in a state, I care to be."

It is clear, then, that the best political association, too, is the one which consists of the middle class. And states in which the middle class is large can be well governed; and best so, if the middle class is stronger than those of the wealthy and the poor combined, but [less so], if the middle class is stronger than either one of the two classes, for, in the latter case, the addition of the middle class to one of the other two classes tips the scale and prevents the remaining extreme class from becoming dominant.

It is for this reason that the most fortunate state is that in which its citizens have moderate and sufficient property. A state where some citizens have excessive property and the rest nothing at all becomes either an extreme people's rule or an impetuous oligarchy or a tyranny because both parts are extremes; for from an uncontrolled people's rule or an oligarchy there arises a tyranny, but from moderate forms of government or those close to them this is much less likely to occur, and the *reasons* for these will be given when the changes of forms of government are discussed.

Evidently, then, the moderate form of government is the best, since it alone is free from rebellion; for where the middle class is large, rebellions

or factions in such a government are least likely to occur. . . .

## Book 7

### CHAPTER 4

. . . In view of the above discussion, a state in the primary sense must be a political association which first becomes large enough to be self-sufficient for a good life. There may be a state even with a larger population, but, as we stated, not without a limit. As for what that limit is, it can be easily seen from the facts. For the *actions* of the state are those of the rulers and those of the ruled, and the function of a ruler is to command and to judge. Now in judging what is just and distributing offices according to merit, the citizens must know each other's characters; for, wherever this does not happen to occur, both the election to offices and the judgments of what is just, being done without adequate preparation and so unjustly, are necessarily bad (and evidently such happens to be the case whenever populations are very large). Further, foreigners and resident aliens would easily be able to participate in the government; for it is not difficult to do so without being detected because of an excess of population.

Clearly, then, the best [upper] limit of the population of a state is the greatest number which, being easily seen at a glance, suffices for a [good] life of its citizens. So concerning the size of a state, let the above remarks be sufficient.

### CHAPTER 14

Since every political association is composed of rulers and those ruled, let us consider whether these should interchange or remain the same throughout life; for clearly it will follow that the education of citizens should differ according to each of the two alternatives.

Now if there were some citizens who surpassed the rest as much as Gods and heroes are believed to surpass ordinary men (first, being far superior to them in their bodies, and second, in their souls), and in a way that the superiority of the rulers over the subjects would be evident without dispute, it is clear that it would be decidedly better for the rulers and those ruled to be always the same. But since this is not easily attainable and kings do not surpass their subjects as much as, according to Scylax, the kings of India do their subjects, it is evident that for many *reasons* all must alike share in government by ruling and being ruled by turns. For "equality" means that similar people [should have] the same; and it is difficult to maintain a government constituted contrary to justice, for all those in the country who wish a change will join with those who are ruled, and then it will be quite impossible for the ruling body to be stronger than those who oppose them.

On the other hand, it cannot be disputed that the rulers should be at least superior to the ruled. So the lawgiver should attend to these matters and to the manner in which sharing [by all citizens] should take place. But we have considered this problem earlier; for nature herself has furnished us with the distinction by making within the same species some members young but other members older, the former meant to be ruled but the latter to rule. Now the young never resent being ruled while young nor regard themselves as being better [rulers] than their elders, especially when they expect that they will make up for being ruled when they reach the proper age. So one should say that in one sense the rulers and the ruled are the same, but in another sense that they are different, and that their education must be in one sense the same, but in another sense different; for, as it is said, he who is to rule well should first [learn to] be ruled.

As we stated at the beginning of this treatise, one kind of rule is for the sake of the rulers, another is for the sake of those who are ruled. We call the first rule "despotic"; the second is a rule over freemen. So some commands differ, not in the things which are to be done but in the purpose for which they are to be done. For this reason, many duties which are thought to be menial are also duties which are noble for the children of freemen to perform; for the nobility or lack of nobility of *actions* does not consist so much in the *actions* themselves as in the end or purpose [for which they are performed]. So since we maintain that [in the best state] the virtue of a citizen and of a ruler is the same as that of the best *man,* and since the same *man* should become first one who is ruled and later a ruler, the task of a lawgiver would be (a) to see that *men* become good, (b) to find the appropriate means by which this can be accomplished, and (c) to know what the end of the best life is. . . .

## Study Questions

These questions serve several purposes: They can be used to review the chapter, as topics to be discussed or formally presented at seminars, or as essay topics.

1. What were the Milesian philosophers trying to explain? Why did Thales think that the *archē*, the first principle, of the cosmos was water? Why did Anaximenes think it was air? Were their positions reasonable?

2. What did Anaximander mean by his idea of the *apeiron?* Can this be seen as an improvement on Thales' cosmology? Why or why not?

3. What was Anaximander's theory of evolution? Is it similar to Darwin's theory?

4. What did Anaximenes mean by "rarefaction and condensation"? Does Anaximenes' theory of material change represent an improvement on Thales and Anaximander? Why or why not?

5. How did Heraclitus reconcile his theory of universal flux with his notion of a cosmic order? Was he successful?

6. What element did Heraclitus think was the *archē* of the cosmos? Why? How was his choice connected to his idea that you can't step into the same river twice?

7. Why did Parmenides think that Being was an eternal, perfect, unchanging Sphere? How was his view a critique of Heraclitus?

8. What did Zeno's paradoxes attempt to prove? Can they be refuted?

9. What basic forces did Empedocles see as behind cosmic change? How can we relate these forces to modern physics?

10. How did Empedocles improve on the earlier pre-Socratics' attempt to divide the physical world into distinct types of substances?

11. What, in general, distinguished pre-Socratic philosophy from the earlier mythological period and from the later anthropological philosophers?

12. What specific charges were made against Socrates at his trial? How did he refute each charge? Was his refutation successful?

13. What picture of the philosopher do we get from Socrates' *Apology?* Can we hold this picture up as one that all philosophers should attempt to embody?

14. What general method of inquiry does Socrates employ in the *Apology?* Can such a method produce true knowledge? Why or why not?

15. What are Polemarchus's and Cephalus's definitions of justice in the justice debate in book 1 of *The Republic?* How does Socrates defeat each one?

16. What basic challenge (or challenges) to objective moral truth do Thrasymachus and Glaucon offer in the second half of the justice debate in *The Republic?* How does Socrates answer them? Can you think of any good answers, other than those given by Socrates himself, to this challenge?

17. Into what elements does Plato divide the human soul? Is he right to assume that justice in the soul will be mirrored by a parallel justice in a rightly ordered state?

18. What sort of class structure does Plato establish in his ideal state? How does he suggest this class structure be explained to the members of the state? Do hierarchical societies need such a founding myth in order to justify themselves?

19. Was Plato right that there can be no justice in the state until kings become philosophers, and philosophers become kings? Is this a good idea in the modern world? Why or why not?

20. Is it fair to call Plato's republic an oppressive authoritarian state, one where freedom is squelched in favor of social harmony?

21. What does Plato's "Allegory of the Cave" tell us about his theory of knowledge? Does Plato's basic epistemological distinction make sense?

22. What does Aristotle mean by "teleology"? What evidence for teleology did he find in the animal world and in human life? What problems, if any, are associated with a teleological view of human life?

23. What does Aristotle mean by a "virtue"? How does he figure out what is virtuous in a specific moral situation? Is such a method practical?

24. Which virtues should we practice in contemporary life if we want to achieve well-being? Would Aristotle agree with your list? Why or why not?

25. To whom did Aristotle limit political citizenship? How did he justify this limitation? What did he think of women and slaves?

26. What are the six forms of the state that Aristotle distinguishes? Which form did he think was the best one? How did his choice conflict with Plato's picture of the best state? Who do you think makes the better case?

## Bibliography

Barnes, Jonathan. *Aristotle.* Oxford: Oxford University Press, 1982. A short book, part of the usually reliable Past Masters series.

Barnes, Jonathan. *Early Greek Philosophy.* Penguin, 1987. A good (but not complete) selection of the pre-Socratic fragments, doxography, and biography, with an excellent introduction and a short synopsis of each thinker.

Barnes, Jonathan. *The Presocratic Philosophers.* 2nd ed., 2 volumes. London: Routledge and Kegan Paul, 1988.

Boardman, John, Jasper Griffin, and Oswyn Murray. *Greece and the Hellenistic World.* Oxford: Oxford University Press, 1988. Part of the *Oxford History of the Classical World,* this book contains separate chapters on early Greek Philosophy, Classical Greek philosophy, and Hellenistic philosophy and science.

Burnet, John. *Early Greek Philosophy.* 4th ed. London: A. and C. Black, 1930. An older source for the pre-Socratics, with detailed commentaries on the fragments and doxography.

Cavalier, Robert. *Plato for Beginners.* London/New York: Writers and Readers, 1990.

Copleston, Frederick. *A History of Philosophy: Volume I. Greece and Rome.* Garden City, NY: Image Books, 1963. Copleston's history offers a good clear summary of the Greeks' main doctrines, although his Catholicism occasionally intrudes to muddy the clear Aegean waters.

Diels, Hermann, and W. Kranz. *Die Fragmente der Vorsokratiker (Fragments of the Presocratics).* 10th ed. Berlin: Weidmann, 1952. The standard edition of the pre-Socratic fragments, with a handy numbering system to boot.

Diogenes Laertius. *Lives of the Eminent Philosophers.* Trans. R. D. Hicks. 2 volumes. New York: Putnam's, 1925. All the dirt on the ancient Greeks.

Freeman, Kathleen. *Ancilla to the Presocratic Philosophers.* Oxford: Blackwell, 1948. Bare-bones translations of the pre-Socratic fragments.

Guthrie, W. K. C. *A History of Greek Philosophy.* Cambridge, UK: Cambridge University Press, 1962–1981. 6 volumes. The mother of all works on the ancient Greeks.

Hussey, Edward. *The Presocratics.* Indianapolis: Hackett, 1995.

Kirk, G. S., and J. E. Raven. *The Presocratic Philosophers.* 3rd ed. with M. Schofield. Cambridge, UK: Cambridge University Press, 1983. Extensive collection of the pre-Socratic fragments and doxography in Greek, with summaries and English translations.

Plato. *The Collected Dialogues of Plato.* Edith Hamilton and Huntington Cairns, eds. Princeton, NJ: Princeton University Press, 1961. A complete collection of Plato's works.

Ross, W. D. *Aristotle.* 5th ed. London: Methuen, 1955.

Taylor, A. E. *Plato, The Man and His Work.* 6th ed. New York: Humanities Press, 1952.

Taylor, A. E. *Socrates.* New York: Anchor, 1952.

Vlastos, Gregory. *Platonic Studies.* 2nd ed. Princeton, NJ: Princeton University Press, 1981.

## Internet Resources

*The Last Days of Socrates:* http://socrates.clarke.edu/
This site features Plato's dialogues *Euthyphro, Apology, Crito,* and *Phaedo,* with synopses, lots of pictures, maps, and other graphics, and hypertext links to brief biographies and descriptions of historical events and philosophical concepts. Highly recommended.

*Exploring Plato's Dialogues:* http://plato.evansville.edu/intro.htm
This site features a biography of Plato, the Jowett translations of five dialogues, an e-text of John Burnet's *Early Greek Philosophy,* and a short bibliography.

*The Perseus Project:* http://www.perseus.tufts.edu/
A massive searchable library of classical texts, including Plato and Aristotle. The texts are available in both Greek and English.

*The Internet Classics Library:* http://classics.mit.edu/index.html
Contains over 400 texts by classical authors, including Plato and Aristotle, in English.

*Ancient Greek Sites on the Web:* http://www.webcom.com/shownet/medea/grklink.html
A page of links to sites on all aspects of the study of ancient Greece, including texts, art, maps, religion, and philosophy.

*God is dead.*
FRIEDRICH NIETZSCHE
*Nietzsche's dead.*
GOD

# CHAPTER TWO

# The Philosophy of Religion

## AN INTRODUCTION TO THE PHILOSOPHY OF RELIGION

In philosophy the big questions come before the big answers. The philosophy of religion is no different. Some of the big questions it asks are: Does God exist? Can his existence be proven? What is the relationship between faith and reason? Is belief in God a matter of calculated arguments or "a leap of faith"? Is God necessary for morality? If God is all good and all powerful, why is there evil in the world?

In the readings that follow we will introduce the main combatants in the various disputes found in the philosophy of religion. The philosophical issues raised in these arguments and exchanges have been debated for centuries largely because of their respective ability to provoke strong feelings across a wide range of thinkers. Although you may make up your mind very quickly on some of the matters raised, remember there are equally sincere detractors and defenders engaged in the debate.

It may seem odd that the central problems in the philosophy of religion, after centuries of discussion, remain unsolved. To accept this lack of consensus is one of the first steps toward becoming a philosopher—to realize truths and answers to philosophical questions are not easy to come by, despite the efforts of great thinkers. The twentieth-century theologian Paul Tillich noted that the worth of these debates lies in their ability to get our thinking processes going, rather than actually giving us concrete proofs.

We begin the readings with perhaps the most famous and controversial proof for the existence of God: the so-called *ontological argument.* In a few carefully worded

ILLUSTRATION © Royalty-Free/Getty Images

premises, its architect, St. Anselm of Canterbury (AD 1033–1109), believed he could show that God's existence is necessary. If you wish, take a brief look at it now to get a first impression.

As you look over his argument with more care, you'll notice you don't have to leave your room to see how and if it works. You can sit in your chair and simply think about whether its premises lead to the conclusion. This is why Anselm's argument is often described as being *a priori*. Something argued a priori means that the given argument doesn't depend on evidence based on sensory experience. In the case of Anselm's argument, you can think it through without having to check what is claimed with the world around you. Depending on how your mind works, this quality will make the argument either easier or more difficult to follow.

Anselm's argument is indeed unique. Today we are generally not used to thinking as rigorously as a devoted scholar from the eleventh century. We're more likely to use our gut instincts when thinking about the existence or nonexistence of God. Having gone through Anselm's argument with students on a number of occasions, I've noticed a few mistakes students can make.

It may be tempting to quickly criticize Anselm without cautiously going through the various premises leading to the conclusion that God exists. It is important to spend some time working through each of the steps in Anselm's argument before making up your mind about whether or not he is successful.

Second, after understanding Anselm's argument, it may be tempting to quickly discount its merit. It could very well be his argument does not prove God's existence. But it is not so easy to show how it fails. Even today, centuries after he first presented this argument, philosophers and theologians still hotly dispute its worth. A former professor of mine once told us that Anselm's argument may put our head in a bit of a spin: One day we'll wake up thinking Anselm had it all wrong; the next day we'll wake up thinking there really is something to the argument. You might be more confident in evaluating the argument. Whatever you think, Anselm's ontological argument represents one of most important moments in the philosophy of religion.

About two centuries later, St. Thomas Aquinas (AD 1224–1274) presented a number of arguments for the existence of God quite different from Anselm's. As you go through them, you may wonder what kind of mind could be so imaginative (in the good sense of the word!). At least part of the explanation lies in the fact that Aquinas's childhood and life were not particularly typical. Born in a castle in the south of Italy, at the age of ten he attended the University of Naples. Later, becoming a monk of the Dominican Order, Thomas spent most of his short life studying and writing about theology and philosophy. He died at the age of fifty.

In 1879, Pope Leo XIII pronounced St. Thomas's views, and the various interpretations of his views known as "Thomism," to be the accepted doctrinal framework of the Roman Catholic Church. This acceptance, centuries after his death, shows that Thomas's views were not readily accepted by the scholars of Catholicism. Because he tried to show how Aristotle and the Christian worldview were compatible, his work was initially viewed with suspicion. After his death, like-minded attempts for this reconciliation were condemned by the two most notable centers of theological study of the time, the universities of Oxford and Paris.

After a lifetime of writing volumes on topics such as the nature and knowledge of God, Aquinas had a mystical vision. After this dramatic experience, he declared his thoughts on theological and philosophical subjects were like straw worthy of being fed to the flames.

Despite this vision, Aquinas, like Anselm, had been very interested in showing how belief in God could be supported by the powers of human reason. The role reason plays vis-à-vis faith was a lively debate, and went back to the early Church fathers. Namely: Is it possible to have knowledge about God through the unaided powers of human reasoning, or can we only know God through faith? Isn't faith a matter of believing something without proof?

For his part, Aquinas distinguished between two different ways of doing theology. First, "revealed theology," as its name suggests, gives us knowledge about God directly revealed, either through prophets such as Moses (and, as a consequence, the Ten Commandments), or through scripture. But because Aquinas believed that humans are created in the image of God and that our ability to reason is part of this image, he thought there are some things we can learn about God through our ability to reflect and reason. Aquinas described this as "natural theology." Aquinas's argument for the existence of God by appeal to the world's design is a good example of how we can know something about God through our powers of reflection.

Although Aquinas wrote a handbook on how to convert nonbelievers, it was not so much the case Anselm and Aquinas, living between the eleventh and thirteenth centuries, needed to prove the existence of God to the unbelievers and skeptics of their time. Christian faith infused Europe during the medieval period, and due to the political climate freethinkers and atheists would have been quickly dealt with. As a result, few people expressed any open skepticism about the existence of God.

Even though skepticism about God was dangerous, this was quite different from doubting the worth of certain proofs for the existence of God. Interestingly, Aquinas was one of the first to forcibly argue against Anselm's ontological proof for the existence of God. We've included Aquinas's criticism in our readings. Philosophers since have thought Aquinas was right, while others were convinced he missed the force of Anselm's position. The debate continues to this day.

In any case, the lesson we can learn from Aquinas here is one of intellectual integrity: That is, one should not accept an argument merely because it favors one's beliefs. It is more important to hold to arguments that are sound.

While Anselm had only one argument for God's existence, Aquinas formulated *five ways* (*quinque viae*) God could be known. As philosophically controversial as Anselm's argument, Aquinas's demonstrations were quite a different sort.

First, Aquinas stated his arguments from an empirical or *a posteriori* starting point. Aquinas's demonstrations start from our observations of the world and the way it works, and end with the existence of God being the logical explanation.

Second, due to this a posteriori methodology, to appreciate the strength of Aquinas's arguments we have to leave our place of study and go out and observe the world to check out his claims. As some see it, this demand for contact with the empirical world places Aquinas's arguments at a clear advantage to that of Anselm.

Whatever their relative merits, Anselm's and Aquinas's proofs still fascinate many present-day philosophers. There are, however, different ways of analyzing issues central to the philosophy of religion. The Danish philosopher Søren Kierkegaard (1813–1855) presents one of these alternatives. Similar to Anselm and Aquinas, Kierkegaard had both philosophical and theological concerns in mind. And, again like Anselm and Aquinas, he was a devout Christian (a Protestant in his case).

Despite these similarities, there are important differences between Kierkegaard and his predecessors. Kierkegaard marks a distinct shift from thinkers who debate the proofs over the existence of God, to those who think these traditional arguments are a serious distortion of religious faith. Kierkegaard believed it was the very mark of impiety to think that belief in God could somehow be reduced to arguments or demonstrations. For him, faith is a matter of making a decision—the most profound of our human existence.

Kierkegaard believed that the power of human reason was one thing; faith in God, however, was something else. Faith was a matter of deep passion and conviction. Kierkegaard was thus closer to the church father Tertullian than he was to Anselm and Aquinas, closer to Jerusalem—the City of God, than Rome—the City of the Philosophers. Kierkegaard thought religious belief was a matter of personal, subjective faith. It was not the conclusion brought about by an objective, rational process.

The polarized views of Anselm, Aquinas, and Kierkegaard are still fairly well represented in contemporary goings on in the philosophy of religion. As King Solomon said in *Ecclesiastes,* there is nothing new under the sun. While different combatants come and go, the battles remain basically the same.

Of course, not all philosophers are interested in showing how God's existence can be revealed or experienced. One of the marks of the modern age was not only the desire to be free from political and ecclesiastical control, but to be free to dissent from religious belief. The next two selections in this chapter, from David Hume and Friedrich Nietzsche, are good examples of philosophers who took this sharp turn in the philosophy of religion.

David Hume (1711–1776), a Scottish philosopher, took exception to Anselm's and Aquinas's arguments for God's existence. Along with his criticisms of these sorts of arguments, he included a strong case against the reasonability of miracles. He was not, however, always on the defensive. On the offense, he raised the problem of evil as a serious objection to religious belief.

As noted in the chapter on epistemology, Hume argued that beliefs and knowledge could only come from sense experience. For Hume, the only legitimate way of determining whether God exists is to examine the empirical world. With Hume's emphasis on the empirical world, Anselm's a priori argument proves nothing.

But things are not better for Aquinas's a posteriori arguments. Although Aquinas refers to the empirical world in his arguments, Hume argued that there is nothing in the nature of the world that compels us to see it as the product of divine design. In addition, Hume thought that because this empirical world operates according to physical laws, when we see a strange occurrence, instead of thinking it is a miracle, it is far more reasonable to believe it a natural process we don't fully understand.

Along with his criticisms of the traditional proofs, Hume posed extremely difficult questions for Christians and other theists. The toughest of these questions was the problem of evil. In a nutshell, Hume said an all-powerful and wholly good God would remove, or at least alleviate, the suffering that has been present throughout human history. Because horrible things still happen, it was therefore reasonable to believe either God doesn't care enough about human and animal suffering to do something about it or he isn't powerful enough to impede it. On either count, such a God doesn't fit with the description given by the Judeo-Christian tradition. Hume was satisfied with the third alternative that the problem of evil offered: God simply does not exist.

Hume wasn't the first to use the problem of evil as a defeater for the existence of God. The eighteenth-century French novelist and philosopher François Marie Arouet Voltaire (1694–1778) also used it as a powerful weapon against religious believers. In a little book still very popular today, *Candide,* Voltaire satirized another philosopher's view, Gottfried Leibniz (1646–1716), who advocated that ours is the "best of all possible worlds." Voltaire's book came about because of how he was shaken by the carnage and human suffering caused by the Lisbon earthquake of 1755. Such a terrible event seemed to serve no comprehensible divine purpose. How could a good God allow such meaningless pain and death, and how could one then conclude this world is the best of all worlds that could be? Hume's formulation of the problem remains a forceful consideration for theists who believe in both the omnipotence (all powerfulness) and omnibenevolence (all goodness) of God.

Of the foregoing philosophers, Friedrich Wilhelm Nietzsche (1844–1900) is a more difficult figure to understand and categorize. A classical philologist by training, he made significant contributions in philosophy, particularly in the latter part of his life. To appreciate his writings, we need to understand the cultural tensions of his time.

Religious skepticism and the outright denial of Christianity had been around prior to Nietzsche, but he was particularly acerbic in his rejection of the Christian worldview—what he described as the "God-hypothesis." He rejected all the religious talk of Christianity: the soul, the resurrection, the world beyond, and, as we will see in the chapter on ethics, Christian values.

Nietzsche first wondered about the Christian story. How could the account of a virgin birth producing God's son and all the recordings of miracles culminating in his crucifixion have captured, for two millennia, the imagination of an entire civilization? His reaction to the Christian story and its values is best understood by looking at Nietzsche's philosophy of life.

Nietzsche had been greatly influenced by the atheism of the philosopher Arthur Schopenhauer (1788–1860). Schopenhauer was himself influenced by Eastern philosophy and religion, notably Buddhism. He held the view that the world was filled with suffering and pain. The world had no rationale or plan behind it. In short, we live in a godless and irrational world.

Nietzsche appreciated Schopenhauer's atheism except for one detail; he was put-off by the pessimism Schopenhauer's view evoked: That God is necessary for human happiness and purpose. Nietzsche rejected this brand of nihilism. He believed that even if our activities are without ultimate purpose (or teleology), we could still accept and affirm our temporal and mortal purposes and condition. Indeed, in order to truly do so, Christian values had to be rejected because they promoted weakness and a denial of the reality of our physical and spiritual natures.

What we strive for, in our human activities, falls under Nietzsche's description of "the will to power." The will to power is our desire to strive for mastery, whether with ourselves or with others. The sort of power Nietzsche was thinking about is the fundamental drive for happiness. Of course how mastery is pursued, as will to power, can be a double-edged sword. Used one way, it could result in terrible destructiveness; the other, in great feats and accomplishments.

Will to power contrasts with Christian morality, which, as Nietzsche saw it, only encourages an unhealthy humility and *ressentiment*. "Higher types" were set in contrast to the "herd" or "slave" morality that Christianity encouraged. These higher types wished to affirm this godless world, a world without teleology or ultimate purpose. Their "will to power" was more forthright and honest than the sneaky and subterranean will to power of the self-denying herd shepherded by their ascetic priests.

This rejection of Christian values and the Christian worldview will be further explored in the chapter on ethics. Suffice to say Nietzsche's critique of Christianity followed largely from his belief that it denied our true nature, a denial that led us to repudiate our physical and spiritual strength in favor of Christian-inspired weakness.

Nietzsche's criticisms of Christianity are highly barbed. Yet some commentators have asked: "Was he a vicious detractor of Christianity, a hero for atheists? Or, was he an iconoclast, whose criticisms of Christianity helped to reaffirm the meaning of what it meant to be a Christian?" While more Christians have probably been offended than impressed by Nietzsche, some have even maintained there is nothing particularly incompatible in agreeing with Nietzsche (at least on some major points) and still being a Christian. This thought becomes thornier when trying to reconcile Christian belief with Nietzsche's well-known claim that "God is dead" or his notion that the Christian ethic of humility was a "slave morality."

No discussion in the philosophy of religion would be complete without looking at the problem of evil. As mentioned previously, David Hume addressed this problem. To review: If God is indeed all good and all powerful, why does he allow evil to exist? For Hume, the answer was clear: Evil exists, therefore God doesn't. As you might guess by now, not all philosophers of religion have agreed with Hume's conclusion.

The attempt by philosophers and theologians to reconcile the goodness of God with the existence of evil is called *theodicy*. It is a subject that can raise tempers on both sides, especially when thinking about the terrible atrocities of the past century. Witness the Holocaust, Stalin's gulags, Hiroshima and Nagasaki, Rwanda, and the racial strife in the United States.

All these terrible events make it difficult for some to believe that God could be a loving being, a being interested in human affairs. Some Jewish scholars, in particular, have argued that the Holocaust makes it impossible to think God is concerned with our welfare.

There are a number of ways the debate over the problem of evil may unfold. Our readings offer two, well-articulated, views of the problem of evil. The first article, written by B. C. Johnson (a pseudonym), forcefully argues that, given the terrible things that happen in our world, it follows that "it is unlikely God is all good." The value of Johnson's article lies in how he carefully and critically examines the various attempts by theists to show how God's benevolence and the presence of evil in our world are compatible.

John Hick's article delves into the problem of evil from a Christian perspective.

His response, which considers various attempts to reconcile the problem of evil with the Christian worldview, can be seen as a partial response to Johnson.

Hick argues that critics such as Johnson wrongly assume God's intention in the creation of the world was to craft a place "whose inhabitants would experience a maximum of pleasure and a minimum of pain." As Hick sees it, the pain, difficulties, and even terrible suffering we experience in the world are all part of what he describes as "soul-making." Soul-making is only possible in an imperfect world. Only in a world where we are confronted with tough decisions and forced to come to grips with our human failings will we also experience God's creative purpose for humankind.

Hick makes every attempt to take the problem of evil seriously, although not everybody will be satisfied with his response. Yet the point of being exposed to these arguments is not to necessarily provide a solution to age-old problems. It is rather to appreciate the complexity involved in working through the various issues on each side of the debate.

Our last reading, which focuses on more contemporary issues in the philosophy of religion, rounds out the chapter. Alvin Plantinga is a professor of philosophy and former director of the Center for Philosophy of Religion at the University of Notre Dame. He has written a number of books on evidence for the existence of God (including on the ontological argument and the problem of evil). He is a devout evangelical, well respected among Christian conservatives, both Protestant and Catholic, in the United States and abroad.

His well-known paper "Christian Philosophy at the End of the Twentieth Century" has become a touchstone for many Christian philosophers. In his paper he draws a line in the sand between the interests of religious believers and what he describes as "secular culture." With this distinction adamantly established, Plantinga argues it then follows that Christian philosophers of religion must, according to their own very different set of beliefs, set their own questions and issues within this discipline. They should not, for example, be so quick to jump on every new philosophical bandwagon that comes along.

# MEDIEVAL PROOFS FOR THE EXISTENCE OF GOD _____

## *St. Anselm and the Ontological Argument*

St. Anselm's ontological proof for the existence of God is one of the shortest and most provocative arguments ever formulated by a philosopher. With just a few seemingly innocent steps Anselm has taken generations of unwary readers by surprise.

This is not to say his reasoning is easy to follow. Keep in mind the steps he takes the reader through are well thought out and carefully planned. To appreciate the full force of his argument, it's important to go through each of the premises cautiously. Afterwards we will put his argument into a form easier to follow. The key phrases in Anselm's argument have been placed in italics.

# God Truly Is

## ANSELM

AND SO, O LORD, since you give knowledge of the faith, give me understanding—as much knowledge as you know to be good for me—that you exist, and you are who we believe you to be.

### CHAPTER 2

And, indeed, we believe you *to be a being than which none greater can be thought.* Or can it be that there is no such being, for "the fool said in his heart, 'there is no God'" (Ps. 13:1, 52:1)? Yet, when this same fool hears me say "a being greater than which cannot be thought," he understands what he heard, even if he does not think such a being exists.

For it is one thing for an object to be in the understanding, and another thing for that object to exist. When a painter thinks about what he is going to paint, he has it in his understanding, but he does not suppose that the painting already exists. But after he has made the painting, he has it in his thought and thinks that it exists because he has just painted it.

So even the fool, then, must be willing to admit that *a being than which none greater can be thought* exists at least in his understanding, since when he hears this he understands it, and whatever is understood exists in thought.

Yet clearly that *than which a greater being cannot be thought* cannot exist in the understanding alone. For if it is in the understanding alone, it can be thought of as existing also in reality, and this is greater. Therefore a being who exists both in the understanding and in reality would be a greater being. That is, if *that than which a greater cannot be thought* is in the understanding alone,

this same thing than which a greater being cannot be thought is that than which a greater can be thought. But obviously this is impossible. Without doubt, therefore, there exists, both in the understanding and in reality, something than which a greater being cannot be thought.

### CHAPTER 3

And it assuredly exists so truly, that it cannot be conceived not to exist. For, it is possible to conceive of a being which cannot be conceived not to exist; and this is greater than one which can be conceived not to exist. Hence, if that than which nothing greater can be conceived can be conceived not to exist, it is not that than which nothing greater can be conceived. But this is an irreconcilable contradiction. There is, then, so truly a being than which nothing greater can be conceived to exist, that it cannot even be conceived not to exist; and this being you are, O Lord, our God.

You so truly are, then, O Lord, my God, that you cannot even be thought of as not existing. And this is right. For if one could think of something better than you, that creature would rise above the Creator and judge its Creator; but this is altogether absurd. And indeed, whatever else there is, except you alone can be thought of as not existing. You alone, therefore, of all beings, has being in the truest and highest sense, since no other being so truly exists, and thus every being has less being. Why, then, has "the fool said in his heart, 'There is no God,'" when it is so evident, to a rational mind, you exist supremely? Why, except that he is a stupid fool?

SOURCE: Anselm, *Proslogium,* chaps. 2 and 3, trans. S. N. Deane (1903; La Salle, IL: Open Court, 1962), pp. 7–9.

Let's rephrase Anselm's argument to clarify how he thinks this proof works. To begin with, everyone can imagine a very powerful being whom we normally call "God." At least at this point, Anselm doesn't mean to say you *should* believe this being exists. He only means to point out it is possible to *think* of such a being. For the sake of argument, even an atheist or agnostic can admit she can at least imagine such a being. It is important to note that whether you think this being actually exists is beside the point at this stage of the argument.

Next, our conception of God should be such that it is the greatest being one could imagine. Judaism, Islam, and Christianity have all understood God as the most powerful and perfect being that exists. To meet this definition, they have assigned God the following attributes:

1. Omnipotence: God is all powerful.
2. Omnipresence: God is present everywhere.
3. Omniscience: God knows all things.
4. Omnibenevolence: God is all good.

Once we give our conception of God all these attributes, we have in our minds an understanding of a being that cannot be made greater. For example, one cannot add any extra power to an already all-powerful being. (For the sake of argument, if for some reason you think you can add any extra attribute of perfection we've left out, Anselm wouldn't necessarily oppose you doing so. The important point is that you arrive at a conception of a being greater than which none greater can be conceived.)

The crux of the argument comes at this point. Having ascribed all these attributes to this being, making him the greatest that can be thought of, did you think of adding the attribute of "existence"? It is essential to Anselm's argument that you do.

This is the clincher to his argument: Isn't a being that exists in reality greater than a being that exists only in the imagination? Put another way, think of the greatest being that can be thought of, one who has all the attributes of greatness. Seeing that a being that exists is greater than a being that doesn't, you have to give your conception of God the attribute of existence. When you do so, voila! God exists!

Keeping in mind Anselm believes God's existence is a matter of logical certainty, is he successful in demonstrating God exists? Can you explain in your own words why or why not? The premises seemed innocent enough, but the conclusion is rather surprising. What happened?

Fortunately for us, a thousand years have passed since Anselm presented his argument. During this time a number of responses have been raised, considerations that may help us sort through his position.

The common objections to Anselm's argument include the following:

1. Anselm is quite wrong suggesting we can actually have an understanding of those attributes of God listed by theologians. How can we begin to understand, for example, omnipresence? How could a being be everywhere at the same time? Can we indeed really conceive such a thing?
2. Why believe "existence" makes an object greater than one that exists only in our imagination? Are some of the things we imagine not greater than things that ac-

tually exist? Isn't my idea of the perfect vacation better than any vacation I can actually have?

3. Does attributing existence to something indeed lead to that thing existing? In the preceding example, just because I can *imagine* a perfect vacation, attributing existence to it in my mind hardly makes it real.

Interestingly, most of the objections raised against Anselm's argument were given in his own day.

Anselm's defenders, however, argue that we speak of things such as "infinity" even though we are not fully able to comprehend this concept. We are still able to have some sense of its meaning because we use it quite often in common talk. Think of the car named *Infinity*. It must evoke some kind of image for the consumer or the car company wouldn't have used the name in the first place. The same applies to definitions of the concepts "time" and "justice." We have difficulty coming up with an exact definition and understanding of these words, but we can still use the terms meaningfully in everyday discourse.

To appreciate the sense of "greatest" as Anselm uses it, it may help to know he held the belief, going back to Plato and St. Augustine, that if something is good then it must exist. In today's world this may seem a little strange. But now that you've studied Plato's theory of the Forms, it is easier to see how this made sense to Anselm.

Irrespective of Anselm's Platonism, isn't it the case that a real thing is greater than an imagined thing? This goes not only for our imagined vacation but also for things such as world peace. Isn't real world peace greater than imagined world peace? What about our relationships? Isn't a friend who really exists greater than an imaginary friend? Who can help us more, an imaginary friend or a real one?

There are further issues to consider. On the question of whether we can attribute *existence* to this being in the same way we attribute other characteristics to God, we should turn to Anselm's first major detractor, the monk Gaunilo.

Gaunilo argued that one doesn't have to accept the first premise. The atheist, skeptic, freethinker, or agnostic may from the start deny we can have an idea of the most perfect being. Anselm had a reply to this criticism.

In the first premise, Anselm doesn't ask whether you believe in God or not. He just asks you to conduct a *thought experiment*—an experiment that takes place in your mind rather than in a laboratory. Anselm, following his Platonism, thinks that the logic of his argument is a matter of merely taking what we know about other "degrees of perfection" and applying it to God's perfection.

For example, Anselm would argue we are able to see some objects as more beautiful than others because in our understanding we have a standard of absolute beauty. Similarly, we have a sense of the perfection (or lack thereof) of objects in the real world because we have a standard of absolute perfection in our minds.

Gaunilo, not so easily defeated, shifts to his second objection. Even if we were to grant Anselm's premises, does it follow that just because we have an idea of a particular thing such a thing must then exist? Think of our wonderful imaginary vacation mentioned before. Here Gaunilo also argues from analogy. He asks us to think of a perfect island—one with lots of fresh water, fruit, palm trees, and sandy beaches. Gaunilo points out it doesn't follow that being able to have an idea of this island means this island actually exists. Gaunilo's criticism is important, and it is restated later by the eighteenth-century philosopher Immanuel Kant.

Maybe to Gaunilo's chagrin, Anselm actually agreed with him. It indeed doesn't follow that because we can imagine such an island, the island actually exists. Anselm rather argues that ideas of islands and other physical things are quite different from our idea of God. And God is the one being to whom Gaunilo's island argument does *not* apply.

Now we turn to the French philosopher René Descartes who, in his own formulation of the argument, focused his attention on whether existence was something that is necessarily part of a perfect thing.

# The Ontological Argument Restated

## RENÉ DESCARTES

BUT IF THE MERE FACT that I can produce from my thought the idea of something entails that everything which I clearly and distinctly perceive to belong to that thing really does belong to it, is not this a possible basis for another argument to prove the existence of God? . . . At first sight, however, this is not transparently clear, but has some appearance of being a sophism. Since I have been accustomed to distinguish between existence and essence in everything else, I find it easy to persuade myself that existence can also be separated from the essence of God, and hence that God can be thought of as not existing. But when I concentrate more carefully, it is quite evident that existence can no more be separated from the essence of God than the fact that its three angles equal two right angles can be separated from the essence of a triangle, or than the idea of a mountain can be separated from the idea of a valley. Hence it is just as much of a contradiction to think of God (that is, a supremely perfect being) lacking existence (that is, lacking a perfection), as it is to think of a mountain without a valley.

However, even granted that I cannot think of God except as existing, just as I cannot think of a mountain without a valley, it certainly does not follow from the fact that I think of a mountain with a valley that there is any mountain in the world; and similarly, it does not seem to follow from the fact that I think of God as existing that he does exist. For my thought does not impose any necessity on things; and just as I may imagine a winged horse even though no horse has wings, so I may be able to attach existence to God even though no God exists.

But there is a sophism concealed here. From the fact that I cannot think of a mountain without a valley, it does not follow that a mountain and valley exist anywhere, but simply that a mountain and a valley, whether they exist or not, are mutually inseparable. But from the fact that I cannot think of God except as existing, it follows that existence is inseparable from God, and hence that he really exists. It is not that my thought makes it so, or imposes any necessity on any thing; on the contrary, it is the necessity of

SOURCE: "Fifth Meditation: The Essence of Material Things, and the Existence of God Considered a Second Time," in *Meditations on First Philosophy* (1641); reprinted in *The Philosophical Writings of Descartes,* rev. ed., vol. 2, trans. John Cottingham, Robert Stoothoff, and Dugald Murdoch (Cambridge, UK: Cambridge University Press, 1996), pp. 45–47.

the thing itself, namely the existence of God, which determines my thinking in this respect. For I am not free to think of God without existence (that is, a supremely perfect being without a supreme perfection) as I am free to imagine a horse with or without wings.

And it must not be objected at this point that while it is indeed necessary for me to suppose God exists, once I have made the supposition that he has all perfections (since existence is one of the perfections), nevertheless the original supposition was not necessary. Similarly, the objection would run, it is not necessary for me to think that all quadrilaterals can be inscribed in a circle; but given this supposition, it will be necessary for me to admit that a rhombus can be inscribed in a circle—which is patently false. Now admittedly, it is not necessary that I ever light upon any thought of God; but whenever I do choose to think of the first and supreme being, and bring forth the idea of God from the treasure house of my mind as it were, it is necessary that I attribute all perfections to him, even if I do not at that time enumerate them or attend to them individually. And this necessity plainly guarantees that, when I later realize that existence is a perfection, I am correct in inferring that the first and supreme being exists.

Descartes' restatement of Anselm's ontological argument has the advantage of being almost as short as Anselm's original proof. Descartes takes up Anselm's argument by emphasizing the relationship between God's essence and his existence.

Descartes again raises the question: Just because we can think of something, does it follow that this thing must exist? Even when it comes to God, Descartes, at least at first, answers "no." One can quite easily, it seems, separate God's essence from his existence. One can *think* of God, yet at the same time believe he does not exist.

After more reflection, however, Descartes changes his mind, arguing that one can no more think of God as not existing as one can conceive of a triangle without having its three angles equal to two right angles. To use another example, just as it is impossible to think of a mountain without a valley, so Descartes concludes that God's existence is inseparable from his essence.

It remains open to debate whether Descartes reinforces Anselm's original argument or just repeats the same mistake. In any case, this restatement of the ontological argument is an important moment in the history of the philosophy of religion. The ontological argument will most certainly continue to provoke thought and argument.

## St. Thomas Aquinas and the Five Proofs for the Existence of God

It comes as no surprise that atheists and agnostics are critical of arguments that attempt to prove the existence of God. What may come as a surprise is that even theists consider some of these arguments unsuccessful. Similar to St. Anselm, St. Thomas Aquinas (1224–1274), the Church's most celebrated thinker, was very interested in developing proofs for the existence of God. But, like Gaunilo, he was also highly critical of Anselm's argument.

There is quite a sense of moral and intellectual integrity on Aquinas's part for voicing this disagreement. While some may be cynically willing to use every argument in their favor, even a believer shouldn't accept a proof for God's existence if it doesn't work.

As we have just seen, Anselm argues that because it is greater to exist than not to exist (at least in the case of God), God must exist, since he is the greatest being imaginable. Aquinas, from the start, did not believe everyone has a clear and distinct idea of God. Even assuming we could have an idea of this sort, it wouldn't follow that the object the idea is supposed to represent existed. As Aquinas put it, we may be able to think of God existing "mentally," but this is far from God existing "actually."

Aquinas had further criticisms of Anselm. He wondered whether existence could be considered a characteristic or a quality. Even if this were possible, does any being, even God, *necessarily* exist outside the philosopher's mind? Aquinas disagreed that the property of existence can necessarily be assigned to God.

Regardless of the strength of Aquinas's objections to Anselm's ontological argument, he certainly wasn't opposed to all proofs for the existence of God. In fact, Aquinas developed five of his own.

As we have already seen, Anselm's argument was based on what could be described as *pure rational reflection*. He formulated his argument without stepping outside of his study. It was a thought experiment. In contrast, Aquinas developed his arguments by observing the world around him or, to be more accurate, what he considered to be the effects of God on the world we live in.

First, Aquinas asked us to take note of the fact that the things we see around us do not contain within themselves a sufficient explanation for their existence. In our earthly realm, the explanation of things must refer to some prior action on the part of natural or human forces and intentions. For example, people owe their existence to the prior existence and actions of their parents.

Second, quite different from Anselm, Aquinas maintained that no matter how successful his proofs might be they cannot give us perfect knowledge of God. Whatever we learn by reflection and observation about the material world and its objects will be imperfect and inadequate. Such imperfection, in turn, cannot reveal God in all his perfection. There will always be a gulf between the material and the spiritual, the finite and the infinite.

Despite this gulf Aquinas still believed some "natural" knowledge of God's existence and nature was possible. If carefully developed, arguments for the existence of God were of value. All his proofs begin with some phenomenon in the natural world on which he bases an argument for the existence of God. Following is a summary of his five arguments.

## ARGUMENT FROM MOTION

Other philosophers, notably Aristotle, used the argument from motion. Aquinas observed that someone or something has put all moving things into motion. Think of an object that moves. What caused it to move? Once decided, what caused this second object to move the first one? Because an infinite series is impossible, this moving and being moved must come to an end at some point. Aquinas describes the thing at the end of this series of movers as the "unmoved mover" or "first mover." This first mover, he says, is God.

## ARGUMENT FROM EFFICIENT CAUSES

Aquinas's second argument examines a somewhat technical notion called "efficient causes." He notes once again, from observation of the natural world, nothing can be the cause of itself.

Looking at the world around us, this seems to make sense. For something to be the cause of itself, it would have to exist before itself in order to cause itself. But this is absurd because nothing can cause itself. So something else caused it. And a third thing must have caused the second thing to exist, and so on to infinity. But there cannot be an infinite series of causes, says Aquinas. There must be a first efficient cause. We call this cause God.

## ARGUMENT FROM NECESSITY AND CONTINGENCY

The third proof examines the difference between necessary and contingent existence. Observing the world around us, we see that living things are either born or come into existence, and then perish over time. Whether plants, animals, or human beings—living things are all mortal. There was a time when they were not, and there will be a time in the future when they will no longer be. Philosophers have described this mortal state, this kind of existence as "contingent existence."

Aquinas continues. Now, because at one time all that exists did not exist, how did things first come to be? No thing can create itself. If there were only contingent beings in the world, at one time there would have been nothing at all. And nothing could have come into being out of this primal nothingness. But because things obviously now exist, namely our world and everything in it, these things must have come from something noncontingent. But from what?

To resolve this question Aquinas brings into the picture the idea of a "necessary being." In contrast to a contingent being, a necessary being does not owe its existence to anything else. That's why it is "necessary." At some point in our reasoning backward, we will have to admit such a necessary being—a being that has within itself its own necessity, and is thus able to cause contingent beings to come into existence. We call this necessary being God.

As a footnote to this proof, some have asked whether there can be many necessary beings. Although Aquinas believed this was not logically possible, for the sake of argument he points out even if a necessary being causes other necessary beings, we cannot trace these necessary beings back into infinity (as he showed in his argument of efficient causes). So there must still be an "ultimate" necessary being, the prime cause of all other necessary beings.

## ARGUMENT FROM GRADATION

The fourth proof has a somewhat different flavor. To begin with, think about how each day we make evaluations about things: We say that a movie, song, or Web site is better than all others. We may even come to the conclusion we have seen the perfect movie or heard the perfect song (although we can often say this each month with a new movie or song we've seen or heard).

Aquinas saw this ability on our part to judge gradations or degrees of perfection as an important human quality. Of course, when we speak of the "perfect song," we are usually just talking about relative perfection. Nevertheless, we assume we have some objective basis from which to make these judgments. We assume these judgments are not irrational; we believe we have a good basis to justify our claims about the superiority of the film, song, or Web site that has caught our fancy.

Aquinas believed we are able to make these comparisons because the qualities we are judging are in reference to some perfect conception we have in mind. Aquinas concludes there is a being who has these greatest perfections, perfections that allow us mortal beings to make judgments of goodness and the like. We call this greatest being God. (Remember he bases this reasoning on the scholastic belief that the greatest being must have the greatest perfection in goodness, nobility, and truth.)

## THE ARGUMENT FROM TELEOLOGY

This argument for God's existence was held by Aquinas to be one of the most persuasive. We saw in our discussion of Aristotle's ethics the ancient origins of the idea of teleology, a term derived from two Greek words: *telos,* meaning "end" or "goal," and *logos,* meaning "reason" or "word" or, more generally, "the study of."

Understanding how human beings and animals have goals or ends is one thing. But Aquinas thought there was a sort of *telos* applicable even to inorganic objects. His best example was an archer and an arrow. It is clear an arrow moves through the air to its target not because of its own intention or decision, but because of the decision and skill of the archer who launched it from his or her bow. This intention to fire the arrow implies a decision. The intention can be traced to some person with knowledge and intelligence. The arrow's hitting its target is the product of a human *telos.*

On a larger scale, Aquinas thought he saw a general teleology or intention connected to the existence of the earth and its surrounding universe. This grand intention was the product of a Divine Intellect or Intelligent Cause. Things are the way they are because a supremely powerful and intelligent designer made them that way. Fish have gills and fins to swim through water; birds have wings to fly with; human beings have minds to think with. These things aren't accidental: They were planned. In other words, the universe shows strong evidence of intelligent design. This argument is appropriately called "the design argument."

Looking back at these arguments from what we know today, we can see there are considerations Aquinas could not have anticipated. When thinking about teleology, for example, Darwin's theory of evolution offers a naturalistic and materialist explanation for how the natural world came to be. The requirement that there must be a Divine Intelligence or Cosmic Architect behind the universe is not as scientifically and philosophically evident today as it was in Aquinas's time.

Another important consideration here is that Aquinas's proofs only demonstrate, at best, the existence of some sort of Divine Intelligence or Designer. There is still a long way to go to arrive at the God of medieval Catholicism. These arguments may establish the existence of *a* god, but not necessarily Aquinas's Christian God. In today's global village, now that we know there are many different views of who God is—whether from the perspective of the Muslim, Hindu, Jew, or Christian—once we prove God's existence, how are we then to decide which God in particular is the existing God?

# Reasons in Proof of the Existence of God

## THOMAS AQUINAS

### Article 2. Whether the Existence of God Is Demonstrable

LET US PROCEED to the second point. It is objected (1) that the existence of God is not demonstrable: that God's existence is an article of faith, and that articles of faith are not demonstratable, because the office of demonstration is to prove, but faith pertains (only) to things that are not to be proven, as is evident from the Epistle to the Hebrews, 11. Hence that God's existence is not demonstratable. Again, (2) that the subject matter of demonstration is that something exists, but in the case of God we cannot know what exists, but only what does not, as Damascenus says (Of the Orthodox Faith, I., 4) Hence that we cannot demonstrate God's existence. Again, (3) that if God's existence is to be proved it must be from what He causes, and that what He effects is not sufficient for His supposed nature, since He is infinite, but the effects finite, and the finite is not proportional to the infinite. Since, therefore, a cause cannot be proved through an effect not proportional to itself, it is said that God's existence cannot be proved.

But against this argument the apostle says (Rom. I., 20), "The unseen things of God are visible through His manifest works." But this would not be so unless it were possible to demonstrate God's existence through His works. What ought to be understood concerning anything, is first of all, whether it exists. *Conclusion.* It is possible to demonstrate God's existence, although not *a priori* (by pure reason), yet *a posteriori* from some work of His more surely known to us.

In answer I must say that the proof is double. One is through the nature of a cause and is called *propter quid:* this is through the nature of preceding events simply. The other is through the nature of the effect, and is called *quia,* and is through the nature of preceding things as respects us. Since the effect is better known to us than the cause, we proceed from the effect to the knowledge of the cause. From any effect whatsoever it can be proved that a corresponding cause exists, if only the effects of it are sufficiently known to us, for since effects depend on causes, the effect being given, it is necessary that a preceding cause exists. Whence, that God exists, although this is not itself known to us, is provable through effects that are known to us.

To the first objection above, I reply, therefore, that God's existence, and those other things of this nature that can be known through natural reason concerning God, as is said in Rom. I., are not articles of faith, but preambles to these articles. So faith presupposes natural knowledge, so grace nature, and perfection a perfectible thing. Nothing prevents a thing that is in itself demonstratable and knowable, from being accepted as an article of faith by someone that does not accept the proof of it.

To the second objection, I reply that, since the cause is proven from the effect, one must use the effect in the place of a definition of the cause in demonstrating that the cause exists; and that this applies especially in the case of God, because for proving that anything exists, it is necessary to accept in this method what the name signifies, not however that anything exists, because the question what it is is secondary to the question whether it exists at all. . . . Whence by proving that God exists through His works, we are able by this very method to see what the name God signifies.

To the third objection, I reply that, although a perfect knowledge of the cause cannot be had from inadequate effects, yet that from any effect

SOURCE: Oliver J. Thatcher, ed., *The Library of Original Sources* (Milwaukee: University Research Extension, 1907), vol. 5: *The Early Medieval World*, pp. 359–363; reprinted in Paul Halsall, *The Medieval Sourcebook* (http://www.fordham.edu/halsall/sbook.html).

manifest to us it can be shown that a cause does exist, as has been said. And thus from the works of God His existence can be proved, although we cannot in this way know Him perfectly in accordance with His own essence.

## Article 3. Whether God Exists

Let us proceed to the third article. It is objected (1) that God does not exist, because if one of two contradictory things is infinite, the other will be totally destroyed; that it is implied in the name God that there is a certain infinite goodness: if then God existed, no evil would be found. But evil is found in the world; therefore it is objected that God does not exist. Again, that what can be accomplished through a less number of principles will not be accomplished through more. It is objected that all things that appear on the earth can be accounted for through other principles, without supposing that God exists, since what is natural can be traced to a natural principle, and what proceeds from a proposition can be traced to the human reason or will. Therefore that there is no necessity to suppose that God exists. But as against this note what is said of the person of God (Exod. III., 14) I am that I am. *Conclusion*. There must be found in the nature of things one first immovable Being, a primary cause, necessarily existing, not created; existing the most widely, good, even the best possible; the first ruler through the intellect, and the ultimate end of all things, which is God.

**I answer that it can be proved in five ways that God exists.**

The **first** and plainest is the method that proceeds from the point of view of motion. It is certain and in accord with experience, that things on earth undergo change. Now, everything that is moved is moved by something; nothing, indeed, is changed, except it is changed to something which it is in potentiality. Moreover, anything moves in accordance with something actually existing; change itself, is nothing else than to bring forth something from potentiality into actuality. Now, nothing can be brought from potentiality to actual existence except through something actually existing: thus heat in action, as fire, makes fire-wood, which is hot in potentiality, to be hot actually, and through this process, changes itself. The same thing cannot at the same time be actually and potentially the same thing, but only in regard to different things. What is actually hot cannot be at the same time potentially hot, but it is possible for it at the same time to be potentially cold. It is impossible, then, that anything should be both mover and the thing moved, in regard to the same thing and in the same way, or that it should move itself. Everything, therefore, is moved by something else. If, then, that by which it is moved, is also moved, this must be moved by something still different, and this, again, by something else. But this process cannot go on to infinity because there would not be any first mover, nor, because of this fact, anything else in motion, as the succeeding things would not move except because of what is moved by the first mover, just as a stick is not moved except through what is moved from the hand. Therefore it is necessary to go back to some first mover, which is itself moved by nothing—and this all men know as God.

**The second proof** is from the nature of the efficient cause. We find in our experience that there is a chain of causes: nor is it found possible for anything to be the efficient cause of itself, since it would have to exist before itself, which is impossible. Nor in the case of efficient causes can the chain go back indefinitely, because in all chains of efficient causes, the first is the cause of the middle, and these of the last, whether they be one or many. If the cause is removed, the effect is removed. Hence if there is not a first cause, there will not be a last, nor a middle. But if the chain were to go back infinitely, there would be no first cause, and thus no ultimate effect, nor middle causes, which is admittedly false. Hence we must presuppose some first efficient cause—which all call God.

**The third proof** is taken from the natures of the merely possible and necessary. We find that certain things either may or may not exist, since they are found to come into being and be destroyed, and in consequence potentially, either existent or non-existent. But it is impossible for all things that are of this character to exist eternally, because what may not exist, at length will not. If, then, all things were merely possible (mere accidents), eventually nothing among things would exist. If this is true, even now there would be nothing, because what does not exist, does not take its beginning except through something that does exist. If then nothing existed, it would be impossible for anything to begin, and there would now be nothing existing, which is admittedly false. Hence not all things are mere accidents, but there must be one necessarily existing being. Now every necessary thing either has a cause of its necessary existence, or has not. In the case of necessary things that have a cause for their necessary existence, the chain of causes cannot go back infinitely, just as not in the case of efficient causes, as proved. Hence there must be presupposed something necessarily existing through its own nature, not having a cause elsewhere but being itself the cause of the necessary existence of other things—which all call God.

**The fourth proof** arises from the degrees that are found in things. For there is found a greater and a less degree of goodness, truth, nobility, and the like. But more or less are terms spoken of various things as they approach in diverse ways toward something that is the greatest, just as in the case of hotter (more hot) which approaches nearer the greatest heat. There exists therefore something that is the truest, and best, and most noble, and in consequence, the greatest being. For what are the greatest truths are the greatest beings, as is said in the *Metaphysics* Bk. II. 2. What moreover is the greatest in its way, in another way is the cause of all things of its own kind (or genus); thus fire, which is the greatest heat, is the cause of all heat, as is said in the same book (cf. Plato and Aristotle). Therefore there exists something that is the cause of the existence of all things and of the goodness and of every perfection whatsoever—and this we call God.

**The fifth proof** arises from the ordering of things for we see that some things which lack reason, such as natural bodies, are operated in accordance with a plan. It appears from this that they are operated always or the more frequently in this same way the closer they follow what is the Highest; whence it is clear that they do not arrive at the result by chance but because of a purpose. The things, moreover, that do not have intelligence do not tend toward a result unless directed by some one knowing and intelligent; just as an arrow is sent by an archer. Therefore there is something intelligent by which all natural things are arranged in accordance with a plan —and this we call God.

In response to the first objection, then, I reply what Augustine says; that since God is entirely good, He would permit evil to exist in His works only if He were so good and omnipotent that He might bring forth good even from the evil. It therefore pertains to the infinite goodness of God that he permits evil to exist and from this brings forth good.

My reply to the second objection is that since nature is ordered in accordance with some defined purpose by the direction of some superior agent, those things that spring from nature must be dependent upon God, just as upon a first cause. Likewise, what springs from a proposition must be traceable to some higher cause which is not the human reason or will, because this is changeable and defective and everything changeable and liable to non-existence is dependent upon some unchangeable first principle that is necessarily self-existent as has been shown.

# SØREN KIERKEGAARD ON THE CHRISTIAN CHURCH

The Christian church has had many detractors over the centuries whether from freethinkers, skeptics, or atheists. Criticism, coming from outside the church, isn't particularly surprising. Some of the most stringent judgment, however, has come from within its own ranks. The most notable were the Protestant Reformers John Calvin and Martin Luther.

Given all the disparagement from within and without the church, few critics of organized religion have equaled the tenacity of Søren Aabye Kierkegaard (1813–1855). The fact that he was a Christian didn't make him shy away from challenging some of the theological and philosophical teachings of the church. Kierkegaard's personal life gives us an indication of how events can influence one's philosophy. Growing up in Copenhagen, Søren was the youngest of seven children. By the age of twenty-one, he had witnessed the death of his parents and five of his siblings. While alive, Søren's father had a great deal of influence over his son. This effect was not particularly positive, as his father was extremely heavy handed enforcing his son's religious beliefs.

One of Kierkegaard's major frustrations was what he saw to be the deep contradiction between what was supposed to exemplify the Christian's life of faith and the public expression of that faith in the Denmark of his day. As a deeply religious individual, Kierkegaard was particularly disturbed by the spiritual condition of the Protestant state church. He viewed it as a shallow reflection of the Christian faith.

In the following essay, Kierkegaard writes how both the church and its ministers have become corrupt, forgetting their original task. He describes this corruption as "a forgery." He said this because the church's aspiration, as described in the Christian scriptures, the New Testament, is to emulate the teachings of Christ. By Kierkegaard's time, this reflection had dimmed to the point of obscurity. He pejoratively named the organized church of his day "Christendom."

In his appraisal, Kierkegaard repeated what Christ described to be the true purpose and mission of the church. Christ's message of salvation for all, rich and poor, had been replaced by ornate cathedrals with ministers who saw their main task as the consolation of the affluent members of the congregation. Kierkegaard muses that if Christ entered the cathedrals of Denmark, as he did in the synagogue of his own time, he would drive its priests and ministers out into the streets with a homemade whip.

There is a story about Kierkegaard entering a beautiful cathedral, one surrounded by abject poverty. That Sunday the minister of this ornate cathedral, dressed in his colorful robes, reads a passage from a gold-leafed Bible. The passage, from the Gospel of Luke, was where Christ told the people: "Blessed are you who are poor, for yours is the kingdom of God." (6: 20) Kierkegaard said that this Bible verse, read in the middle of such terrible poverty, was so bizarre and ridiculous he couldn't understand why the parishioners didn't burst out in laughter after hearing it.

Kierkegaard wasn't against ministers who selected and read passages from the Bible for their parishioners. What bothered him was rather the discrepancy between what the Bible verses said and the actual lives of the church members. The other problem was that after reading from the Bible the minister would then go on to "explain" for the congregation what the passage meant.

Kierkegaard believed that a very simple church service was best. A prayer and a song would be given, and then the minister would read a passage from the scripture. Upon reading the passage, the minister would then allow the congregation to think and decide for themselves how the words of Christ should be understood. The passage from the Bible, that Kierkegaard criticizes the church with, is not exactly the meekest he could have chosen. The verse records Christ talking to the religious leaders of his day, the Pharisees. The Pharisees were a pious group of religious leaders who interpreted the Judaic Law for the Jewish community. They were described by the writers of the New Testament as having become self-righteous and hypocritical by the time of Christ. In the passage that Kierkegaard refers to, Christ accuses some of them of trying to destroy the very religious faith that they were entrusted to protect and nurture.

Kierkegaard applies this passage to his own day. As a devout Christian, he wanted the churches in Denmark to reassess their role vis-à-vis their spiritual flock.

Even though Kierkegaard lived 150 years ago, it is interesting to think about how his criticism of the church might still hold today. Many of you are undoubtedly aware of the religious programs on television on Sunday mornings, urging viewers to contribute to the various ministries. Think about how some churches are built today—they can be massive structures costing millions of dollars. The Christian scriptures are clear that Christians should not try to spend their way into heaven. The same scriptures, moreover, hold up poverty as a noble ideal. The New Testament even says that the true temple of God is not built with human hands (Acts 17:24). Shouldn't the money Christians spend for opulent churches instead be sent to poverty-stricken countries or given to unemployed people or to hospitals and care centers for the elderly in our own communities? Kierkegaard would no doubt opt for the latter course of action if he were alive today.

What do these questions and criticisms have to do with the philosophy of religion? The behavior of people who claim to know God and his will frequently come under scrutiny by atheists, agnostics, and other critics of religion. If religious people claim to know God, yet live in a way that seems inconsistent with their own descriptions of godly behavior, what does this say about the truthfulness of their religious beliefs? For example, how do Christians justify building luxurious expensive churches when there is such poverty and want in the world?

This essay by Kierkegaard is also relevant to the way some Christian ministers seek political power. Consider how various Christian coalitions in the United States have come to have a powerful voice in the electoral process. Think also of how some of these religious leaders have made strong moral claims upon the country as a whole. For example, consider the Christian conservative Jerry Falwell, who, after the terrorist attacks in New York and Washington, DC, in September 2001, said that American society brought this upon itself because of the country's growing acceptance of secularism, homosexuality, feminism, and abortion. Although he later said that he made his comment in an untimely fashion, he didn't recant his view. How does this pronouncement from a prominent Christian minister reflect upon Christ's original message to "love one's neighbor"?

In a broader sense, we can ask whether we need religion at all in order to be able to judge right from wrong. Can we have a clear sense of morality without God? Historically speaking, theologians have argued we need God in order to have an objective basis of right and wrong. But do we? If Christians themselves do not act in a way that we, as unbelievers, find rightful and decent, how can we be persuaded that the religious beliefs of Christians (or of any other religious believers) are right? This is the philosophical question lurking in the background of Kierkegaard's essay.

# Attack upon "Christendom"

## SØREN KIERKEGAARD

### What Christ's Judgment Is about Official Christianity

IT MIGHT SEEM STRANGE that not till now do I come out with this; for Christ's judgment after all is surely decisive, inopportune as it must seem to the clerical gang of swindlers who have taken forcible possession of the firm "Jesus Christ" and done a flourishing business under the name of Christianity.

It is not without reason, however, that I educe this testimony now, and he who has followed with attention my whole work as an author will not have failed completely to observe that there is a certain method in the way I set to work, that in the first place it is determined by the fact that this whole thing about "Christendom" is, as I have said, a criminal case, corresponding to what ordinarily is known as forgery, imposture, except that here it is religion which is thus made use of; and in the second place by the fact that I really have, as I have said, a talent for detective work.

. . . For though it is true that I know with God that I have spoken truly and spoken as I ought to speak, and though what I have said is true and ought to be said, even if there were no words to this effect from Christ himself, yet it is always a good thing that we know from the New Testament how Christ judges official Christianity.

And that we do know from the New Testament, His judgment is found there. But naturally I am fully convinced that thou, whoever thou art, if thou knowest nothing about what Christianity is except what is to be learned from the Sunday sermons of the "witnesses to the truth," thou mayest go year after year to three churches every Sunday, hear, broadly speaking, every one of the royal functionaries—and never hear the words of Christ which I have in view.

Presumably the witnesses to the truth think about it in this way: The proverb says not to speak of rope in the house of a man that was hanged; so also it would be madness to bring forward in the church these words from God's Word which bear witness before high heaven against the juggling tricks of the priests. Indeed I might be tempted to make the following requirement, which, equitable and mild as it is, yet the only punishment I desire to inflict upon the priests. Certain passages from the New Testament would be selected, and the priest be obliged to read them aloud before the congregation. Of course I should have to make one stipulation, that after he had knocked off reading such a passage from the New Testament the priest should not, as he usually does, put the New Testament aside and proceed thereupon to "explain" what he had read. No, many thanks. No, what I might be tempted to propose is the following order of service: the congregation assembles; a prayer is said at the church door; a hymn is sung; then the priest goes up to the speaker's seat, takes out the New Testament, pronounces the name of God, and thereupon reads from it before the congregation that definite passage, loudly and distinctly, whereupon he has to be silent and to remain standing silently for five minutes in the pulpit, and then he can go. This I would regard as exceedingly profitable. I am not thinking of making the priest blush. He who is conscious of willing to understand by Christianity what he understands by Christianity, and without blushing has been capable of taking an oath upon the New Testament, is not a man one can easily cause to blush; and it may indeed be said to be an essential part of the preparation of an official priest that he has weaned himself from the childish habits of youth and innocence, like blushing, etc. But I assume that

SOURCE: Søren Kierkegaard, *Attack upon "Christendom"* (1854–1855), trans. Walter Lowrie (1944; Boston: Beacon Press, 1956), pp. 117–124. Reprinted by permission of Princeton University Press.

the congregation would blush on behalf of the priest.

And now for the words of Christ to which I refer.

They are found in Matthew 23:29–33; Luke 11:47, 48; and they read as follows:

> Woe unto you, scribes and Pharisees, hypocrites! for ye build the sepulchers of the prophets and garnish the tombs of the righteous, and say, If we had been in the days of our fathers, we should not have been partakers with them in the blood of the prophets. Wherefore ye witness to yourselves, that ye are sons of them that slew the prophets. Fill up then the measure of your fathers. Ye serpents, ye offspring of vipers, how shall ye escape the judgment of hell?

> Woe unto you! for ye build the tombs of the prophets, and your fathers killed them. So ye are witnesses and consent unto the works of your fathers: for they killed them, and ye build their tombs.

But what then is "Christendom"? Is not "Christendom" the most colossal attempt at serving God, not by following Christ, as He required, and suffering for the doctrine, but instead of that, by "building the sepulchers of the prophets and garnishing the tombs of the righteous" and saying, "If we had been in the days of our fathers, we should not have been partakers with them in the blood of the prophets"?

It is of this sort of divine service I used the expression that, in comparison with the Christianity of the New Testament, it is playing Christianity. The expression is essentially true and characterizes the thing perfectly. For what does it mean to play, when one reflects how the word must be understood in this connection? It means to imitate, to counterfeit, a danger when there is no danger, and to do it in such a way that the more art is applied to it, the more delusive the pretense is that the danger is present. So it is that soldiers play war on the parade grounds: there is no danger, one only pretends that there is, and the art essentially consists in making everything deceptive, just as if it were a matter of life and death. And thus Christianity is played in "Christendom." Artists in dramatic costumes make their appearance in artistic buildings—there really is no danger at all, anything but that: the teacher is a royal functionary, steadily promoted, making a career—and now he dramatically plays Christianity, in short, he plays comedy. He lectures about renunciation, but he himself is being steadily promoted; he teaches all that about despising worldly titles and rank, but he himself is making a career; he describes the glorious ones ("the prophets") who were killed, and the constant refrain is: If we had been in the days of our fathers, we should not have been partakers with them in the blood of the prophets—we who build their sepulchers and garnish their tombs. So they will not go so far even as to do what I have constantly, insistently and imploringly proposed, that they should at least be so truthful as to admit that they are not a bit better than those who killed the prophets. No, they take advantage of the circumstance that they are not in fact contemporary with them to assert mendaciously of themselves that they are far, far better than those who killed the prophets, entirely different beings from those monsters—they in fact build the sepulchers of the men so unjustly killed and garnish their tombs.

However, this expression, "to play Christianity," could not be used by the Authoritative Teacher; He has a different way of talking about it.

Christ calls it (O give heed!), He calls it "hypocrisy." And not only that, but He says (now shudder!), He says that this guilt of hypocrisy is as great, precisely as great a crime as that of killing the prophets, so it is blood-guilt. Yea, if one could question Him, He would perhaps make answer that this guilt of hypocrisy, precisely because it is adroitly hidden and deliberately carried on through a whole lifetime, is a greater crime than theirs who in an outburst of rage killed the prophets.

This then is the judgment, Christ's judgment upon "Christendom." Shudder; for if you do not, you are implicated in it. It is so deceptive: must not we be nice people, true Christians, we who build the sepulchers of the prophets and garnish the tombs of the righteous, must not we be nice people, especially in comparison with those monsters who killed them? And besides, what else shall we do? We surely cannot do more than be willing to give of our money to build churches, etc., not be stingy with the priest, and go ourselves to hear him. The New Testament answers: What thou shalt do is to follow Christ, to suffer, suffer for the doctrine; the divine service thou wouldst like to carry on is hypocrisy; what the priests, with family, live on is that thou art a hypocrite, or they live by making thee a hypocrite, by keeping thee a hypocrite.

"Your fathers killed them, and ye build their tombs: so ye are witnesses and consent unto the works of your fathers." Luke 11:48.

Yes, Sunday Christianity and the huge gang of tradesmen-priests may indeed become furious at such a speech, which with one single word closes all their shops, quashes all this royally authorized trade, and not only that, but warns against their divine worship as against blood-guilt.

However, it is Christ who speaks. So profoundly does hypocrisy inhere in human nature that just when the natural man feels at his best, has got a divine worship fixed up entirely to his own linking, Christ's judgment is heard: This is hypocrisy, it is blood-guilt. It is not true that while on weekdays thy life is worldliness, the good thing about thee is that after all on Sundays thou goest to church, the church of official Christianity. No, no, official Christianity is much worse than all thy weekday worldliness, it is hypocrisy, it is blood-guilt.

At the bottom of "Christendom" there is this truth, that man is a born hypocrite. The Christianity of the New Testament was truth. But man shrewdly and knavishly invented a new kind of Christianity which builds the sepulchers of the prophets and garnishes the tombs of the righteous, and says, "If we had been in the days of our fathers." And this is what Christ calls blood-guilt.

What Christianity wants is . . . the following of Christ. What man does not want is suffering, least of all the kind of suffering which is properly the Christian sort, suffering at the hands of men. So he dispenses with "following," and consequently with suffering, the peculiarly Christian

suffering, and then builds the sepulchers of the prophets. That is one thing. And then he says, lyingly before God, to himself and to others, that he is better than those who killed the prophets. That is the second thing. Hypocrisy first and hypocrisy last—and according to the judgment of Christ . . . blood-guilt.

Imagine that the people are assembled in a church in Christendom, and Christ suddenly enters the assembly. What does thou think He would do?

He would turn upon the *teachers* (for of the *congregation* He would judge as He did of yore, that they were led astray), He would turn upon them who "walk in long robes," tradesmen, jugglers, who have made God's house, if not a den of robbers, at least a shop, a peddler's stall, and would say, "Ye hypocrites, ye serpents, ye generation of vipers"; and likely as of yore He would make a whip of small cords and drive them out of the temple.

Thou who readest this, if thou knowest nothing more about Christianity than is to be learned from the Sunday twaddle—I am thoroughly prepared for thee to be shocked at me, as though I were guilty of the cruelest mockery of God by representing Christ in this way, "putting such words into His mouth: serpents, generation of vipers. That is so dreadful. These indeed are words one never hears from the mouth of a cultivated person; and to make Him repeat them several times, that is so dreadfully common; and to turn Christ into a man who uses violence."

My friend, thou canst look it up in the New Testament. But when what has to be attained by preaching and teaching Christianity is an agreeable, a pleasurable life in a position of prestige, then the picture of Christ must be altered considerably. As for "garnishing"—no, there will be no sparing on that: gold, diamonds, rubies, etc. No, the priest is glad to see that and makes men believe that this is Christianity. But severity, the severity which is inseparable from the seriousness of eternity, that must go. Christ thus becomes a languishing figure, the impersonation of insipid human kindliness. This is related to the consideration that the plate must be passed during the sermon and the congregation must be in a mood to spend something, to shell out freely; and above all it is related to the desire prompted by fear of men to be on good terms with people, whereas the Christianity of the New Testament is: in the fear of God to suffer for the doctrine at the hands of men.

But "woe unto you, who build the sepulchers of the prophets" (teaching the people that this is the Christianity of the New Testament) "and garnish the tombs of the righteous" (constantly setting Money and Christianity together by the ears) and say, "If we"—yea, if ye had lived in the time of the prophets, ye would have put them to death, that is, ye would have done, as actually was done, hiddenly prompted the people to do it and bear the guilt. But in vain ye hide yourselves behind "Christendom," for what is hidden be-

comes revealed when the Truth pronounces the judgment: "Wherefore ye bear witness to yourselves that ye are the sons of them that killed the prophets, and ye fill up the measure of your fathers; for they killed the prophets, and ye garnish their tombs." In vain ye set yourselves up as holy, in vain ye think that precisely by building the tombs of the righteous ye prove yourselves better than the ungodly men who put them to death. Ah, the impotence of hypocrisy to hide itself! Ye are seen through and through. Precisely the building of the tombs of the righteous and saying, "If we," precisely this is to kill them, to be the true children of those ungodly men, doing the same thing as they, it is to bear witness to the fathers' deeds and to consent to them, to fill up the measure of your fathers, that is, to do what is far worse.

# DAVID HUME'S SKEPTICAL ATTACKS ON RELIGION

Besides talking and writing about philosophy, similar to most other philosophers of the day, David Hume (1711–1776) was involved in many other activities. Besides his philosophical work, he wrote essays on literature and politics, produced a six-volume history of England, and was a librarian to the Faculty of Advocates in Edinburgh.

Despite being very busy with other matters, Hume wrote some of the most important philosophical works in the English language. These writings covered a number of important issues, including the nature of human reason, personal identity, skepticism, and morality.

He is also well known for his highly provocative and influential writings on the philosophy of religion. His two most important works in this field are *An Enquiry Concerning Human Understanding* (1748) and his posthumously published *Dialogues Concerning Natural Religion* (1779). Given the current interest in the debate over euthanasia, Hume's essay "Of Suicide," also published after his death, should be of special interest to the religious believer. In it he defends the right of a person suffering from great pain or old age to end it all, arguing that committing suicide is no more an infringement on the rights of the Almighty than avoiding falling rocks or using medicine to cure an illness.

Hume was an empiricist. He believed that all knowledge comes either directly or indirectly from our perceptions, from our five senses. When we are born our minds contain no information about the world. He agreed with John Locke that the mind at birth was a *tabula rasa,* a "blank tablet." You'll read more about Locke's and Hume's epistemological views in Chapter 4. Suffice here to note that their views on how we can know things provided certain difficulties for theism.

Hume rejected arguments such as Anselm's on the grounds that there is no such thing as a priori knowledge. Actual knowledge can only come from our expe-

rience of the world around us. We cannot draw any conclusions about this world before investigating it empirically through our senses. Moreover, whatever we extrapolate from knowledge gained this way could never constitute a certain "proof" of anything. For Hume, empirical knowledge is never 100 percent true. It is, at best, highly
probable. If we let go of a hundred objects, and they all fall down, this doesn't "prove"
all objects in the future we let go of will always fall down—merely that it is highly
likely they will. We come to our beliefs because of "custom" and "habit."

So much for a priori arguments for God's existence. Aquinas's a posteriori proofs,
however, fare no better. In his *Dialogues Concerning Natural Religion* (excerpted below), Hume puts a modernized version of Aquinas's design argument into the mouth
of the character Cleanthes, the defender of "natural religion" (i.e., religious belief
based not on miracles but scientific evidence), and what most scholars take as Hume's
own critique of this argument into the mouth of the skeptic Philo. Cleanthes sees nature as one huge machine in which all the parts function together perfectly, therefore
proving the existence of a Divine Designer. He points to the human eye and sexual
desire as examples of things that had to be designed by some greater power to fulfill
the functions they do—they couldn't have come about from a series of accidental
material causes.

Yet Philo is skeptical one can jump from glimpses of bits and pieces of order in
the world to a view that includes a Grand Order and, thus, a Grand Designer. What
order we see within nature can only be described as regularities produced by material causes. Any "design" we see and imagine is the result of our very human desire
to give order to a world that is more accurately a matter of chaos mixed with order.
Indeed, Darwin's theory of evolution has added force to Hume's critique of the design argument, and taken much of the wind out of the sails of Aquinas's argument
that the world shows evidence of a divine teleology. The most Philo can admit to
Cleanthes is that the design argument proves only there is some vague evidence of
design in nature, but that this design could just as easily have been the "first rude essay of some infant deity," a bungled attempt at world making by an aged god, or
even the result of a team effort on the behalf of several deities.

The second major issue Hume dealt with in the *Dialogues* is the problem of evil.
In Part 10, Philo puts the issue rather starkly, along the following lines:

1. There is suffering and evil in the world. Yet as God is usually pictured as all good,
   this leads us to a contradiction: Why would a good God allow this evil to exist in
   the first place? There are several ways to explain away this contradiction (and because God is also seen as all knowing, we can't say that he's unaware of this evil).
2. One possibility is that God is not omnipotent and cannot stop this evil from existing. But with such limited powers he's not really much of a god, is he?
3. Another possibility is that he *is* omnipotent, but is unwilling to stop human suffering. In this case, he's at least bad (or "malevolent," as Philo puts it).
4. The third possibility is that God is able to stop evil, but deliberately wills it to happen. Then he is an evil God, hardly worthy of our worship!
5. Yet the most reasonable conclusion to draw is either we finite mortal beings cannot understand the nature of an infinite being such as God (Philo calls this his
   "mysticism") or that God does not exist at all and evil is the result of purely natural and human forces. Scholars have debated which of these conclusions Hume
   wanted us to draw from the *Dialogues*, although it is far more likely he wanted us

to draw the latter, and waffled about it to escape the very practical repercussions of being charged as an atheist by the Scottish authorities.

Besides these criticisms of the arguments for the existence of God, Hume also had difficulty with the miracles normally associated with religions.

A miracle can be defined as a contravention of a law of nature by God's will. Let's say your friend Molly tells you that while attending church last Sunday she saw a miracle: real blood dripping from the wounds on a statue of Christ. In his famous "Essay on Miracles" (really a section from *An Enquiry Concerning Human Understanding*), he put forward what he believed to be the supreme proof that the miracles purported to have taken place by the world's religions are all delusions or shams. He starts by noting "A wise man . . . proportions his belief to the evidence." Hume argues in the case above, where you are faced with the choice between believing Molly's testimony that a miracle had in fact occurred *and* believing she is either lying, deluded, or being tricked, the latter is far more likely. After all, you've witnessed countless instances of the laws of nature being observed in your daily life, knowing, as well, they are observed in other parts of the world, yet few if any verifiable reports of miracles. It's far more reasonable to reject the reality of this miracle and to look for a naturalistic explanation of the event.

In Part 2 of the "Essay on Miracles," Hume offers four more concrete reasons for refusing to believe in the reality of miracles:

1. The miracles we hear of in religious texts and stories have not been witnessed by enough men of "unquestioned good-sense, education, and learning" for us to take them seriously. In other words, the witnesses of most miracles are simple, gullible, or unscrupulous people.

2. People have a natural tendency to believe strange and wondrous stories about things both natural and supernatural. Hume gives examples of sea monsters, prophecies, and even gossip about couples who are seen together by villagers soon getting married. In our own day, people still read astrology columns in the newspaper, study the prophecies of Nostradamus and L. Ron Hubbard, and read entertainment magazines for gossip about the love lives of their favorite celebrities. This love of wondrous stories is obviously still alive and well.

3. Miracles are mostly prevalent in the tales of "ignorant and barbarous nations," and rarely in more civilized ones. Ancient histories abound with stories of miraculous divine interventions into battles and plagues, of the gods communicating through omens, oracles, and prophecies. Perhaps you've read Homer's poems and seen this yourself. Yet as we get closer and closer to the present day, these divine interventions tend to disappear. Why? Presumably because they never happened in the first place, but were the product of a superstitious terror felt by primitive peoples.

4. Finally, the credibility of a miracle in one religion is destroyed by all those attested to by other religions. This is similar to a criminal trial: If Mike insists that the accused William was nowhere near the scene of the crime on the day in question, while Kathy insists that he was there, both testimonies cannot be true (in the absence of any other evidence). Maybe one is right and the other wrong, or maybe both are wrong, but they both most certainly cannot be right. The same goes for the various miracles claimed by each of the world's religions.

All the major religions use their respective miracles and proofs to show that their religion is right. But they all can't be right, because they disagree about major points of doctrine. For example, Judaism maintains that God exists as one Person, and his name is Yahweh. Traditional Christianity holds that God exists as a Trinity, with three divine Persons making up the Godhead. Islam maintains, similar to Judaism, that God exists as one Person, but His name is Allah and his Prophet is Mohammed. These beliefs are extremely diverse. The miracles and proofs of the different religions, which supposedly attest to the truthfulness of each, cannot all be right. So either only one of the religions is right, or, as Hume thought, all of them are wrong.

It was this last reason for rejecting the reality of miracles where Hume saw a major violation of the principle of contradiction. (The principle of contradiction says that something cannot be A and not A simultaneously. To deny this principle could get you into a lot of trouble. Think about how you'd do getting across a busy intersection thinking that the bus is approaching and not approaching at the same time. Either the bus is heading toward you or it is not. Making the wrong decision could land you in the hospital where more time would be afforded to think about the principles of logic!)

There is much disagreement today as to the force of Hume's criticisms against arguments for the existence of God. Some philosophers believe Hume has ended any discussion over whether God exists by plainly showing he does not. Yet other philosophers of religion disagree with his assessment. In light of contemporary trends in philosophy and culture, they have moved the parameters of the discussion over God's existence into a different frame of reference. These philosophers argue we can no longer discuss religious questions the way Anselm, Aquinas, Descartes, and Hume did. The sophisticated French philosopher Paul Ricoeur, for example, looks to the problem of evil as a metaphor that sheds light on the discussion of God's existence and not as a literal challenge to that existence.

Hume's critiques of religion are certainly telling. But reports of the death of God are probably, at least at this time in our human history, still premature.

# Dialogues Concerning Natural Religion

## DAVID HUME

NOTE: THERE ARE THREE characters in Hume's *Dialogues* (excluding the narrator Pamphilus)—Demea, the least important of the three, who bases his simple religious belief on faith and tradition; Cleanthes, the supporter of the "natural religion" referred to in the title, who defends the argument from design for God's existence; and Philo, the skeptic, who attacks this argument as a false analogy between the natural and divine worlds, and who presents the prob-

SOURCE: David Hume, *Dialogues Concerning Natural Religion* (1779); reprinted in *The Library of Liberal Arts*, ed. Norman Kemp Smith (New York: Bobbs-Merrill, 1947), pp. 143–144, 146–148, 154, 167–169, 180–181, 191–192, 193–195, 198–202.

lem of evil as putting God's existence into doubt. Parts 2 and 9 below deal with the argument from design, Part 10 with the problem of evil.

## Part 2

*Cleanthes:* . . . Look round the world: contemplate the whole and every part of it: You will find it to be nothing but one great machine, subdivided into an infinite number of lesser machines, which again admit of subdivisions, to a degree beyond what human senses and faculties can trace and explain. All these various machines, and even their most minute parts, are adjusted to each other with an accuracy, which ravishes into admiration all men, who have ever contemplated them. The curious adapting of means to ends, throughout all nature, resembles exactly, though it much exceeds, the productions of human contrivance; of human design, thought, wisdom, and intelligence. Since therefore the effects resemble each other, we are led to infer, by all the rules of analogy, that the causes also resemble; and that the Author of Nature is somewhat similar to the mind of man; though possessed of much larger faculties, proportioned to the grandeur of the work, which he has executed. By this argument *a posteriori*,[1] and by this argument alone, do we prove at once the existence of a Deity, and his similarity to human mind and intelligence.

*Demea:* I shall be so free, CLEANTHES, said DEMEA, as to tell you, that from the beginning I could not approve of your conclusion concerning the similarity of the Deity to men; still less can I approve of the mediums, by which you endeavour to establish it. What! No demonstration of the Being of a God! No abstract arguments! No proofs *a priori*! Are these, which have hitherto been so much insisted on by philosophers, all fallacy, all sophism? Can we reach no farther in this subject than experience and probability? I will not say, that this is betraying the cause of a Deity: But surely, by this affected candour, you give advantages to Atheists, which they never

could obtain, by the mere dint of argument and reasoning.

*Philo:* What I chiefly scruple in this subject, said PHILO, is not so much, that all religious arguments are by CLEANTHES reduced to experience, as that they appear not to be even the most certain and irrefragable of that inferior kind. That a stone will fall, that fire will burn, that the earth has solidity, we have observed a thousand and a thousand times; and when any new instance of this nature is presented, we draw without hesitation the accustomed inference. The exact similarity of the cases gives us a perfect assurance of a similar event; and a stronger evidence is never desired nor sought after. But where-ever you depart, in the least, from the similarity of the cases, you diminish proportionably the evidence; and may at last bring it to a very weak *analogy,* which is confessedly liable to error and uncertainty. After having experienced the circulation of the blood in human creatures, we make no doubt, that it takes place in TITIUS and MAEVIUS: But from its circulation in frogs and fishes, it is only a presumption, though a strong one, from analogy, that it takes place in men and other animals. The analogical reasoning is much weaker, when we infer the circulation of the sap in vegetables from our experience, that the blood circulates in animals; and those, who hastily followed that imperfect analogy, are found, by more accurate experiments, to have been mistaken.

If we see a house, CLEANTHES, we conclude, with the greatest certainty, that it had an architect or builder; because this is precisely that species of effect, which we have experienced to proceed from that species of cause. But surely you will not affirm, that the universe bears such a resemblance to a house, that we can with the same certainty infer a similar cause, or that the analogy is here entire and perfect. The dissimilitude is so striking, that the utmost you can here pretend to is a guess, a conjecture, a presumption concerning a similar cause; and how that pretension will be received in the world, I leave you to consider.

[*Philo continues after a brief interruption*] . . . Now according to this method of reasoning,

---

[1] From experience, as opposed to a priori, meaning logically prior to experience.

DEMEA, it follows (and is, indeed, tacitly allowed by CLEANTHES himself) that order, arrangement, or the adjustment of final causes is not, of itself, any proof of design; but only so far as it has been experienced to proceed from that principle. For aught we can know *a priori*, matter may contain the source or spring of order originally, within itself, as well as mind does; and there is no more difficulty in conceiving, that the several elements, from an internal unknown cause, may fall into the most exquisite arrangement, than to conceive that their ideas, in the great, universal mind, from a like internal, unknown cause, fall into that arrangement . . .

. . . But can you think, CLEANTHES, that your usual phlegm and philosophy have been preserved in so wide a step as you have taken, when you compared to the universe houses, ships, furniture, machines; and from their similarity in some circumstances inferred a similarity in their causes? Thought, design, intelligence, such as we discover in men and other animals, is no more than one of the springs and principles of the universe, as well as heat or cold, attraction or repulsion, and a hundred others, which fall under daily observation. It is an active cause, by which some particular parts of nature, we find, produce alterations on other parts. But can a conclusion, with any propriety, be transferred from parts to the whole? Does not the great disproportion bar all comparison and inference? From observing the growth of a hair, can we learn any thing concerning the generation of a man? Would the manner of a leaf's blowing, even though perfectly known, afford us any instruction concerning the vegetation of a tree?

But allowing that we were to take the *operations* of one part of nature upon another for the foundation of our judgement concerning the *origin* of the whole (which never can be admitted) yet why select so minute, so weak, so bounded a principle as the reason and design of animals is found to be upon this planet? What peculiar privilege has this little agitation of the brain which we call *thought,* that we must thus make it the model of the whole universe? Our partiality in our own favour does indeed present it on all occasions; but sound philosophy ought carefully to guard against so natural an illusion.

## Part 3

*Cleanthes:* . . . Let me here observe too . . . that this religious argument, instead of being weakened by that scepticism, so much affected by you, rather acquires force from it, and becomes more firm and undisputed. To exclude all argument or reasoning of every kind is either affectation or madness. The declared profession of every reasonable sceptic is only to reject abstruse, remote and refined arguments; to adhere to common sense and the plain instincts of nature; and to assent, where-ever any reasons strike him with so full a force, that he cannot, without the greatest violence, prevent it. Now the arguments for natural religion are plainly of this kind; and nothing but the most perverse, obstinate metaphysics can reject them. Consider, anatomize the eye: Survey its structure and contrivance; and tell me, from your own feeling, if the idea of a contriver does not immediately flow in upon you with a force like that of sensation. The most obvious conclusion surely is in favour of design; and it requires time, reflection and study to summon up those frivolous, though abstruse objections, which can support Infidelity. Who can behold the male and female of each species, the correspondence of their parts and instincts, their passions and whole course of life before and after generation, but must be sensible, that the propagation of the species is intended by Nature? Millions and millions of such instances present themselves through every part of the universe; and no language can convey a more intelligible, irresistible meaning, than the curious adjustment of final causes. To what degree, therefore, of blind dogmatism must one have attained, to reject such natural and such convincing arguments?

## Part 5

*Philo [after pointing out to Cleanthes the problems of assuming a perfect God in an imperfect world]:* . . . But were this world ever so perfect a production, it must still remain uncertain, whether all the excellencies of the work can justly be ascribed to the workman. If we survey a ship, what an exalted idea must we form of the ingenuity of the carpenter, who framed so complicated, useful and beautiful a machine? And what surprise must we feel, when we find him a stupid mechanic, who imitated others, and copied an art, which, through a long succession of ages, after multiplied trials, mistakes, corrections, deliberations, and controversies, had been gradually improving? Many worlds might have been botched and bungled, throughout an eternity, ere this system was struck out: much labour lost: many fruitless trials made: and a slow, but continued improvement carried on during infinite ages in the art of world-making. In such subjects, who can determine, where the truth; nay, who can conjecture where the probability, lies; amidst a great number of hypotheses which may be proposed, and a still greater number, which may be imagined?

And what shadow of an argument, continued PHILO, can you produce, from your hypothesis, to prove the unity of the Deity? A great number of men join in building a house or ship, in rearing a city, in framing a commonwealth: Why may not several deities combine in contriving and framing a world? This is only so much greater similarity to human affairs. By sharing the work among several, we may so much farther limit the attributes of each, and get rid of that extensive power and knowledge, which must be supposed in one deity, and which, according to you, can only serve to weaken the proof of his existence. And if such foolish, such vicious creatures as man can yet often unite in framing and executing one plan; how much more those deities or daemons, whom we may suppose several degrees more perfect?

But farther, CLEANTHES; men are mortal, and renew their species by generation; and this is common to all living creatures. The two great sexes of male and female, says MILTON, animate the world. Why must this circumstance, so universal, so essential, be excluded from those numerous and limited deities? Behold then

the theogony[2] of ancient times brought back upon us.

And why not become a perfect Anthropomorphite?[3] Why not assert the deity or deities to be corporeal, and to have eyes, a nose, mouth, and ears? EPICURUS maintained, that no man had ever seen reason but in a human figure; therefore the gods must have a human figure. And this argument, which is deservedly so much ridiculed by CICERO, becomes, according to you, solid and philosophical.

In a word, CLEANTHES, a man, who follows your hypothesis, is able, perhaps, to assert, or conjecture, that the universe, sometime, arose from something like design: but beyond that position he cannot ascertain one single circumstance, and is left afterwards to fix every point of his theology, by the utmost licence of fancy and hypothesis. This world, for aught he knows, is very faulty and imperfect, compared to a superior standard; and was only the first rude essay of some infant deity, who afterwards abandoned it, ashamed of his lame performance: it is the work only of some dependent, inferior deity; and it the object of derision to his superiors: it is the production of old age and dotage in some superannuated deity; and ever since his death, has run on at adventures, from the first impulse and active force, which it received from him. You justly give signs of horror, DEMEA, at these strange suppositions: but these, and a thousand more of the same kind, are CLEANTHES's suppositions, not mine. From the moment the attributes of the Deity are supposed finite, all these have place. And I cannot, for my part, think, that so wild and unsettled a system of theology is, in any respect, preferable to none at all. . . .

## Part 7

*Philo:* . . . The BRAMINS[4] assert, that the world arose from an infinite spider, who spun this whole complicated mass from his bowels, and

[2] A genealogy of the gods.
[3] Someone who attributes human characteristics to non-human things, in this case God.
[4] Hindu priests of the upper caste.

annihilates afterwards the whole or any part of it, by absorbing it again, and resolving it into his own essence. Here is a species of cosmogony,[5] which appears to us ridiculous; because a spider is a little contemptible animal, whose operations we are never likely to take for a model of the whole universe. But still here is a new species of analogy, even in our globe. And were there a planet, wholly inhabited by spiders, (which is very possible) this inference would there appear as natural and irrefragable as that which in our planet ascribes the origin of all things to design and intelligence, as explained by CLEANTHES. Why an orderly system may not be spun from the belly as well as from the brain, it will be difficult for him to give a satisfactory reason.

## Part 9

*Philo* [*last paragraph*]: . . . But dropping all these abstractions, continued PHILO; and confining ourselves to more familiar topics; I shall venture to add an observation, that the argument *a priori* has seldom been found very convincing, except to people of a metaphysical head, who have accustomed themselves to abstract reasoning, and who finding from mathematics, that the understanding frequently leads to truth, through obscurity, and contrary to first appearances, have transferred the same habit of thinking to subjects, where it ought not to have place. Other people, even of good sense and the best inclined to religion, feel always some deficiency in such arguments, though they are not perhaps able to explain distinctly where it lies. A certain proof, that men ever did, and ever will derive their religion from other sources than from this species of reasoning.

## Part 10

*Demea:* It is my opinion, I own, replied DEMEA, that each man feels, in a manner, the truth of religion within his own breast; and from a consciousness of his imbecility and misery, rather

than from any reasoning, is led to seek protection from that Being, on whom he and all nature is dependent. So anxious or so tedious are even the best scenes of life, that futurity is still the object of all our hopes and fears. We incessantly look forward, and endeavour, by prayers, adoration, and sacrifice, to appease those unknown powers, whom we find, by experience, so able to afflict and oppress us. Wretched creatures that we are! what resource for us amidst the innumerable ills of life, did not Religion suggest some methods of atonement, and appease those terrors, with which we are incessantly agitated and tormented?

*Philo:* I am indeed persuaded, said PHILO, that the best and indeed the only method of bringing every one to a due sense of religion, is by just representations of the misery and wickedness of men. And for that purpose a talent of eloquence and strong imagery is more requisite than that of reasoning and argument. For is it necessary to prove, what every one feels within himself? 'Tis only necessary to make us feel it, if possible, more intimately and sensibly.

*Demea:* . . . And why should man, added he, pretend to an exemption from the lot of all other animals? The whole earth, believe me PHILO, is cursed and polluted. A perpetual war is kindled amongst all living creatures. Necessity, hunger, want, stimulate the strong and courageous: Fear, anxiety, terror, agitate the weak and infirm. The first entrance into life gives anguish to the new-born infant and to its wretched parent: Weakness, impotence, distress, attend each stage of that life: and 'tis at last finished in agony and horror.

*Philo:* Observe too, says PHILO, the curious artifices of Nature, in order to imbitter the life of every living being. The stronger prey upon the weaker, and keep them in perpetual terror and anxiety. The weaker too, in their turn, often prey upon the stronger, and vex and molest them without relaxation. Consider that innumerable race of insects, which either are bred on the body of each animal, or flying about infix their stings in him. These insects have others still less than themselves, which torment them. And thus on

---

[5] An account of the origin of the universe.

each hand, before and behind, above and below, every animal is surrounded with enemies, which incessantly seek his misery and destruction.

*Demea:* Man alone, said DEMEA, seems to be, in part, an exception to this rule. For by combination in society, he can easily master lions, tygers, and bears, whose greater strength and agility naturally enable them to prey upon him.

*Philo:* On the contrary, it is here chiefly, cried PHILO, that the uniform and equal maxims of Nature are most apparent. Man, it is true, can, by combination, surmount all his *real* enemies, and become master of the whole animal creation: but does he not immediately raise up to himself *imaginary* enemies, the daemons of his fancy, who haunt him with superstitious terrors, and blast every enjoyment of life? His pleasure, as he imagines, becomes, in their eyes, a crime: his food and repose give them umbrage and offence: his very sleep and dreams furnish new materials to anxious fear: and even death, his refuge from every other ill, presents only the dread of endless and innumerable woes. Nor does the wolf molest more the timid flock, than superstition does the anxious breast of wretched mortals.

Besides, consider, DEMEA; this very society, by which we surmount those wild beasts, our natural enemies; what new enemies does it not raise to us? What woe and misery does it not occasion? Man is the greatest enemy of man. Oppression, injustice, contempt, contumely, violence, sedition, war, calumny, treachery, fraud; by these they mutually torment each other: and they would soon dissolve that society which they had formed, were it not for the dread of still greater ills, which must attend their separation.

[*a few pages later*] . . . And is it possible, CLEANTHES, said PHILO, that after all these reflections, and infinitely more, which might be suggested, you can still persevere in your Anthropomorphism, and assert the moral attributes of the Deity, his justice, benevolence, mercy, and rectitude, to be of the same nature with these virtues in human creatures? His power we allow infinite: whatever he wills is executed: but neither man nor any other animal are happy: therefore he does not will their happiness. His wisdom is infinite: he is never mistaken in choosing the means to any end: but the course of Nature tends not to human or animal felicity: therefore it is not established for that purpose. Through the whole compass of human knowledge, there are no inferences more certain and infallible than these. In what respect, then, do his benevolence and mercy resemble the benevolence and mercy of men?

EPICURUS's old questions are yet unanswered. Is he willing to prevent evil, but not able? then is he impotent. Is he able, but not willing? then is he malevolent. Is he both able and willing? whence then is evil?[6]

You ascribe, CLEANTHES, (and I believe justly) a purpose and intention to Nature. But what, I beseech you, is the object of that curious artifice and machinery, which she has displayed in all animals? The preservation alone of individuals and propagation of the species. It seems enough for her purpose, if such a rank be barely upheld in the universe, without any care or concern for the happiness of the members that compose it. No resource for this purpose: no machinery, in order merely to give pleasure or ease: no fund of pure joy and contentment: no indulgence without some want or necessity, accompanying it. At least, the few phenomena of this nature are over-balanced by opposite phenomena of still greater importance.

Our sense of music, harmony, and indeed beauty of all kinds gives satisfaction, without being absolutely necessary to the preservation and propagation of the species. But what racking pains, on the other hand, arise from gouts, gravels, megrims, tooth-aches, rheumatisms; where the injury to the animal-machinery is either small or incurable? Mirth, laughter, play, frolic, seem gratuitous satisfactions, which have no farther tendency: spleen, melancholy, discontent, superstition, are pains of the same nature. How then does the divine benevolence display itself, in the sense of you Anthropomorphites? None but we

---

[6] Epicurus (341–270 BC) was an ancient Greek philosopher noted for his materialism and his defense of a life full of simple pleasures.

Mystics, as you were pleased to call us, can account for this strange mixture of phenomena, by deriving it from attributes, infinitely perfect, but incomprehensible.

*Cleanthes:* And have you at last, said CLEANTHES smiling, betrayed your intentions, PHILO? Your long agreement with DEMEA did indeed a little surprise me; but I find you were all the while erecting a concealed battery against me. And I must confess, that you have now fallen upon a subject, worthy of your noble spirit of opposition and controversy. If you can make out the present point, and prove mankind to be unhappy or corrupted, there is an end at once of all religion. For to what purpose establish the natural attributes of the Deity, while the moral are still doubtful and uncertain? . . .

The only method of supporting divine benevolence (and it is what I willingly embrace) is to deny absolutely the misery and wickedness of man. Your representations are exaggerated: Your melancholy views mostly fictitious: Your inferences contrary to fact and experience. Health is more common than sickness: Pleasure than pain: Happiness than misery. And for one vexation, which we meet with, we attain, upon computation, a hundred enjoyments.

*Philo:* Admitting your position, replied PHILO, which yet is extremely doubtful; you must, at the same time, allow, that, if pain be less frequent than pleasure, it is infinitely more violent and durable. One hour of it is often able to outweigh a day, a week, a month of our common insipid enjoyments: And how many days, weeks, and months are passed by several in the most acute torments? Pleasure, scarcely in one instance, is ever able to reach ecstasy and rapture: And in no one instance can it continue for any time at its highest pitch and altitude. The spirits evaporate; the nerves relax; the fabric is disordered; and the enjoyment quickly degenerates into fatigue and uneasiness. But pain often, good God, how often! rises to torture and agony; and the longer it continues, it becomes still more genuine agony and torture. Patience is exhausted; courage languishes; melancholy seizes us; and nothing terminates our misery but the removal of its cause, or another event, which is the sole cure of all evil, but which, from our natural folly, we regard with still greater horror and consternation.

But not to insist upon these topics, continued PHILO, though most obvious, certain, and important; I must use the freedom to admonish you, CLEANTHES, that you have put the controversy upon a most dangerous issue, and are, unawares introducing a total Scepticism into the most essential articles of natural and revealed theology. What! no method of fixing a just foundation for religion, unless we allow the happiness of human life, and maintain a continued existence even in this world, with all our present pains, infirmities, vexations, and follies, to be eligible and desireable! But this is contrary to every one's feeling and experience: It is contrary to an authority so established as nothing can subvert: No decisive proofs can ever be produced against this authority; nor is it possible for you to compute, estimate, and compare all the pains and all the pleasures in the lives of all men and of all animals: And thus by your resting the whole system of religion on a point, which, from its very nature, must for ever be uncertain, you tacitly confess, that that system is equally uncertain.

But allowing you, what never will be believed; at least, what you never possibly can prove, that animal, or at least, human happiness in this life exceeds its misery; you have yet done nothing: For this is not, by any means, what we expect from infinite power, infinite wisdom, and infinite goodness. Why is there any misery at all in the world? Not by chance surely. From some cause then. Is it from the intention of the Deity? But he is perfectly benevolent. Is it contrary to his intention? But he is almighty. Nothing can shake the solidity of this reasoning, so short, so clear, so decisive; except we assert, that these subjects exceed all human capacity, and that our common measures of truth and falsehood are not applicable to them; a topic, which I have all along insisted on, but which you have, from the beginning, rejected with scorn and indignation. . . .

Here, CLEANTHES, I find myself at ease in my argument. Here I triumph. Formerly, when we argued concerning the natural attributes of intelligence and design, I needed all my sceptical and metaphysical subtilty to elude your grasp. In many views of the universe, and of its parts, particularly the latter, the beauty and fitness of final causes strike us with such irresistible force, that all objections appear (what I believe they really are) mere cavils and sophisms; nor can we then imagine how it was ever possible for us to repose any weight on them. But there is no view of human life or of the condition of mankind, from which, without the greatest violence, we can infer the moral attributes, or learn that infinite benevolence, conjoined with infinite power and infinite wisdom, which we must discover by the eyes of faith alone. . . .

# FRIEDRICH NIETZSCHE AND THE DEATH OF GOD

The following selections from Friedrich Nietzsche's (1844–1900) reflections on Christianity may appear to be overly acerbic. After all, he made the famous pronouncement that "God is dead." This comment was not designed by Nietzsche to endear him to religious believers. He certainly made them feel quite uncomfortable with his ideas. The important issue here is to rather think about *why* we have such feelings. Some of us may have this response because we are not used to hearing people speak so harshly about other people's religious views.

We may not agree with the abruptness of Nietzsche's assessment of Christianity. Most philosophers would nevertheless agree that he is at least being true to the philosophical tradition, going back to Socrates, trying to uncover prejudices and false beliefs. So, whatever feelings of disdain Nietzsche may rouse in us, we are still compelled to assess whether his verdict on religion is right or wrong.

Given the importance Christianity has played within Western civilization, at least from the fourth century AD onward, Nietzsche was brave to challenge the major precepts, values, and doctrines of the Christian religion. Criticism of this sort doesn't come without paying a price. He was not in danger of extreme legal or political retaliation in his day, but he still encountered social reprisals. Even in the late nineteenth century, most Europeans would not have received outward rejection and criticism of Christianity very kindly. Consider what reaction his views would evoke even today if they were read over the radio or presented on television during prime time.

As mentioned in the introduction to this chapter, Nietzsche was convinced there was no God, and, as a result, there was no overarching purpose for our being here. With no grand purpose or design for our lives, we are left to create our own meaning.

This lack of teleology in our individual and collective existence led some, such as Schopenhauer, to develop a philosophy of gloominess and pessimism. Nietzsche maintains, to the contrary, that this need not be the consequence of our condition. Rather, we should affirm our lives, squarely facing the challenge by creating our own values without the aid of religious leaders or scriptures.

There were a number of reasons Nietzsche was so antagonistic toward Christianity. First, there was the false belief that there is a Creator who lovingly and purposefully created the earth and all that inhabits it. He also thought it amazing at best, absurd at worst, to imagine the truth of all the events contained in the Christian story: the creation of Adam and Eve, the begetting of the Son of God by a virgin, the various miracles recounted in the New Testament, the crucifixion and resurrection of Christ, and the events that immediately followed involving the life of the Apostle Paul and the foundation of the Church.

Nietzsche had particular disdain for the teachings of Jesus and the Church he supposedly founded. These teachings flew in the face of Nietzsche's worldview. We are not here, he maintained, to extol life-draining behavior such as humility, pity, peaceful contentment, and brotherly love. When we live out these virtues, Nietzsche argued, we are stripped of any capacity for earthly happiness. We ought instead to embrace the chaotic and sometimes violent conditions of our lives, to embrace the noble aspect of our will to power. It is only by doing this we will be able to face our actual human, earthly condition.

These themes are all raised in the following selections from Nietzsche. His discussion of Christianity is not philosophical in the same way as Anselm, Aquinas, and Descartes when they put forward arguments for the existence of God. But his evaluation *is* philosophical in the sense that he brings into question the believability of Christian beliefs and doctrine. Here Nietzsche echoes David Hume.

Although not well known in his own day, Nietzsche has of late stimulated a great deal of renewed interest not only among philosophers but also among academics in other disciplines, particularly in literature. His work shows a richness of thought, as well as being something of a prophetic nature. He anticipated what he thought lay ahead for Western culture and society, predicting a period of nihilism and great political and military struggles in the twentieth century (he was certainly right about this). As you explore his other writings, you will most likely find that he is not as difficult as some other philosophers to understand. Some think that his most valuable musings are his aphorisms—short, proverbial thoughts on a wide field of issues. His lively and accessible style is conducive to reading him at leisure and reflecting on his thought, whether in the classroom, café, or on the sand of some beach. Nietzsche is not only a profound philosopher, but a poet and sage to boot. It is good to keep in mind that Nietzsche was, and remains, an enigmatic figure in philosophy.

The selections chosen from him for this chapter are divided into three sections. In the first set of selections, Nietzsche makes his famous claim that God is dead. He then goes on to probe the idea that the "good" God of Christianity is pale and decadent as compared to the proud, so-called "immoral" national gods of the ancient pagans. In the second set, Nietzsche argues that there was, at best, only one Christian, Christ himself. The whole ecclesiastical structure that arose after his death was a denial of his very message that worldly political structures didn't matter when it came to our purity of heart and the eternal salvation it leads to. He also ridicules Christian beliefs such as the miracle of a virgin birth and the blood sacrifice of the "Son of God" as leftover pieces of antiquity. In the third group of readings, taken from his sketches of a work he never completed, titled *The Will to Power,* we hear Nietzsche outline how he sees Christianity as a sheepish and pessimistic herd morality, a revolt of the oppressed, mediocre, and sick against their opposites. We'll revisit this theme of herd or slave morality in Chapter 5.

# Nietzsche on God

## FRIEDRICH NIETZSCHE

### *From* The Gay Science

125

*The madman.*—Have you not heard of that madman who lit a lantern in the bright morning hours, ran to the market place, and cried incessantly: "I seek God! I seek God!"—As many of those who did not believe in God were standing around just then, he provoked much laughter. Has he got lost? asked one. Did he lose his way like a child? asked another. Or is he hiding? Is he afraid of us? Has he gone on a voyage? emigrated?—Thus they yelled and laughed.

The madman jumped into their midst and pierced them with his eyes. "Whither is God?" he cried; "I will tell you. *We have killed him*— you and I. All of us are his murderers. But how did we do this? How could we drink up the sea? Who gave us the sponge to wipe away the entire horizon? What were we doing when we unchained this earth from its sun? Whither is it moving now? Whither are we moving? Away from all suns? Are we not plunging continually? Backward, sideward, forward, in all directions? Is there still any up or down? Are we not straying as through an infinite nothing? Do we not feel the breath of empty space? Has it not become colder? Is not night continually closing in on us? Do we not need to light lanterns in the morning? Do we hear nothing as yet of the noise of the gravediggers who are burying God? Do we smell nothing as yet of the divine decomposition? Gods, too, decompose. God is dead. God remains dead. And we have killed him.

"How shall we comfort ourselves, the murderers of all murderers? What was holiest and mightiest of all that the world has yet owned has bled to death under our knives: who will wipe this blood off us? What water is there for us to clean ourselves? What festivals of atonement, what sacred games shall we have to invent? Is not the greatness of this deed too great for us? Must we ourselves not become gods simply to appear worthy of it? There has never been a greater deed; and whoever is born after us—for the sake of this deed he will belong to a higher history than all history hitherto."

Here the madman fell silent and looked again at his listeners; and they, too, were silent and stared at him in astonishment. At last he threw his lantern on the ground, and it broke into pieces and went out. "I have come too early," he said then; "my time is not yet. This tremendous event is still on its way, still wandering; it has not yet reached the ears of men. Lightning and thunder require time; the light of the stars requires time; deeds, though done, still require time to be seen and heard. This deed is still more distant from them than the most distant stars—*and yet they have done it themselves.*"

It has been related further that on the same day the madman forced his way into several churches and there struck up his *requiem aeternam deo*. Led out and called to account, he is said always to have replied nothing but: "What after all are these churches now if they are not the tombs and sepulchers of God?"

### *From* Daybreak

91

*God's honesty.*—A god who is all-knowing and all-powerful and who does not even make sure that his creatures understand his intention—

SOURCES: Friedrich Nietzsche, *The Gay Science* (1882), trans. Walter Kaufmann (New York: Vintage Books, 1974), pp. 181–182. Copyright 1974 Random House, Inc. Used by permission of Random House, Inc. Friedrich Nietzsche, *Daybreak: Thoughts on the Prejudices of Morality* (1881), ed. Maude Marie Clark and Brian Leiter, trans. R. J. Hollingdale (New York: Cambridge University Press, 1982), pp. 52–54. Reprinted by permission of Cambridge University Press.

could that be a god of goodness? Who allows countless doubts and dubieties to persist, for thousands of years, as though the salvation of mankind were unaffected by them, and who on the other hand holds out the prospect of frightful consequences if any mistake is made as to the nature of the truth? Would he not be a cruel god if he possessed the truth and could behold mankind miserably tormenting itself over the truth? —But perhaps he is a god of goodness notwithstanding—and merely *could* not express himself more clearly! Did he perhaps lack the intelligence to do so? Or the eloquence? So much the worse! For then he was perhaps also in error as to that which he calls his "truth," and is himself not so very far from being the "poor deluded devil"! Must he not then endure almost the torments of Hell to have to see his creatures suffer so, and go on suffering even more through all eternity, for the sake of knowledge of him, and *not* be able to help and counsel them, except in the manner of a deaf-and-dumb man making all kinds of ambiguous signs when the most fearful danger is about to fall on his child or his dog?—A believer who reaches this oppressive conclusion ought truly to be forgiven if he feels more pity for this suffering god than he does for his "neighbours"—for they are no longer his neighbours if that most solitary and most primeval being is also the most suffering being of all and the one most in need of comfort.—All religions exhibit traces of the fact that they owe their origin to an early, immature intellectuality in man—they all take astonishingly *lightly* the duty to tell the truth: they as yet know nothing of a *duty of God* to be truthful towards mankind and clear in the manner of his communications.— On the "hidden god," and on the reasons for keeping himself thus hidden and never emerging more than half-way into the light of speech, no one has been more eloquent than Pascal—a sign that he was never able to calm his mind on this matter: but his voice rings as confidently as if he had at one time sat behind the curtain with this hidden god. He sensed a piece of immorality in the "*deus*

*absconditus*" and was very fearful and ashamed of admitting it to himself: and thus, like one who is afraid, he talked as loudly as he could.

## 93

*What is truth?*—Who would not acquiesce in the *conclusion* the faithful like to draw: "Science cannot be true, for it denies God. Consequently it does not come from God; consequently it is not true—for God is the truth." It is not the conclusion but the premise which contains the error: how if God were *not* the truth and it were precisely this which is proved? if he were the vanity, the lust for power, the impatience, the terror, the enraptured and fearful delusion of men?

## 95

*Historical refutation as the definitive refutation.* —In former times, one sought to prove that there is no God—today one indicates how the belief that there is a God could *arise* and how this belief acquired its weight and importance: a counter-proof that there is no God thereby becomes superfluous.—When in former times one had refuted the "proofs of the existence of God" put forward, there always remained the doubt whether better proofs might not be adduced than those just refuted: in those days atheists did not know how to make a clean sweep.

## *From* The Anti-Christ

### 15

In Christianity neither morality nor religion come into contact with reality at any point. Nothing but imaginary *causes* ("God," "soul," "ego," "spirit," "free will"—or "unfree will"): nothing but imaginary *effects* ("sin," "redemption," "grace," "punishment," "forgiveness of sins"). A traffic between imaginary *beings* ("God," "spirits," "souls"); an imaginary *natural* science (an-

SOURCE: Friedrich Nietzsche, *Twilight of the Idols; and The Anti-Christ* (1885), trans. R. J. Hollingdale (1968; Harmondsworth, UK: Penguin Books, 1997), pp. 125–128. Copyright R. J. Hollingdale, 1968.

thropocentric; complete lack of the concept of natural causes); an imaginary *psychology* (nothing but self-misunderstandings, interpretations of pleasant or unpleasant general feelings, for example the condition of the *nervus sympathicus*, with the aid of the sign-language of religio-moral idiosyncrasy—"repentance," "sting of conscience," "temptation by the Devil," "the proximity of God"); an imaginary *teleology* ("the kingdom of God," "the Last Judgement," "eternal life").—This purely fictitious world is distinguished from the world of dreams, very much to its disadvantage, by the fact that the latter *mirrors* actuality, while the former falsifies, disvalues and denies actuality. Once the concept "nature" had been devised as the concept antithetical to "God," "natural" had to be the word for "reprehensible"—this entire fictional world has its roots in *hatred* of the natural (—actuality!—), it is the expression of a profound discontent with the actual. . . . *But that explains everything.* Who alone has reason to *lie himself out* of actuality? He who *suffers* from it. But to suffer from actuality means to be an abortive actuality. . . . The preponderance of feelings of displeasure over feelings of pleasure is the *cause* of a fictitious morality and religion: such a preponderance, however, provides the *formula* for *décadence* . . .

16

A critical examination of the *Christian concept of God* invites a similar conclusion.—A people which still believes in itself still also has its own God. In him it venerates the conditions through which it has prospered, its virtues—it projects its joy in itself, its feeling of power on to a being whom one can thank for them. He who is rich wants to bestow; a proud people needs a God in order to *sacrifice*. . . . Within the bounds of such presuppositions religion is a form of gratitude. One is grateful for oneself: for that one needs a God.—Such a God must be able to be both useful and harmful, both friend and foe—he is admired in good and bad alike. The *anti-natural* castration of a God into a God of the merely

good would be totally undesirable here. One has as much need of the evil God as of the good God: for one does not owe one's existence to philanthropy or tolerance precisely. . . . Of what consequence would a God be who knew nothing of anger, revengefulness, envy, mockery, cunning, acts of violence? to whom even the rapturous *ardeurs* of victory and destruction were unknown? One would not understand such a God: why should one have him?—To be sure: when a people is perishing; when it feels its faith in the future, its hope of freedom vanish completely; when it becomes conscious that the most profitable thing of all is submissiveness and that the virtues of submissiveness are a condition of its survival, then its God *has* to alter too. He now becomes a dissembler, timid, modest, counsels "peace of soul," no more hatred, forbearance, "love" even towards friend and foe. He is continually moralizing, he creeps into the cave of every private virtue, becomes a God for everybody, becomes a private man, becomes a cosmopolitan. . . . Formerly he represented a people, the strength of a people, everything aggressive and thirsting for power in the soul of a people: now he is merely the good God. . . . There is in fact no other alternative for Gods: *either* they are the will to power—and so long as they are that they will be national Gods—*or* else the impotence for power—and then they necessarily become *good* . . .

18

The Christian conception of God—God as God of the sick, God as spider, God as spirit—is one of the most corrupt conceptions of God arrived at on earth: perhaps it even represents the low-water mark in the descending development of the God type. God degenerated to the *contradiction of life,* instead of being its transfiguration and eternal *Yes!* In God a declaration of hostility towards life, nature, the will to life! God the formula for every calumny of "this world" for every lie about "the next world"! In God nothingness deified, the will to nothingness sanctified! . . .

# Nietzsche on Christian Belief and the Christian Church

## FRIEDRICH NIETZSCHE

### *From* Human, All Too Human

#### 52

*The point of honesty in deception.*—With all great deceivers there is a noteworthy occurrence to which they owe their power. In the actual act of deception, with all its preparations, its enthralling in voice, expression and gesture, in the midst of the scenery designed to give it effect, they are overcome by *belief in themselves:* it is this which then speaks so miraculously and compellingly to those who surround them. The founders of religions are distinguished from these great deceivers by the fact that they never emerge from this state of self-deception: or very rarely they experience for once that moment of clarity when doubt overcomes them; usually, however, they comfort themselves by ascribing these moments of clarity to the evil antagonist. Self-deception has to exist if a grand *effect* is to be produced. For men believe in the truth of that which is plainly strongly believed.

#### 113

*Christianity and antiquity.*—When on a Sunday morning we hear the bells ringing we ask ourselves: is it possible! this is going on because of a Jew crucified 2000 years ago who said he was the son of God. The proof of such an assertion is lacking.—In the context of our age the Christian religion is certainly a piece of antiquity intruding out of distant ages past, and that the above-mentioned assertion is believed—while one is otherwise so rigorous in the testing of claims—is perhaps the most ancient piece of this inheritance. A god who begets children on a mortal woman; a sage who calls upon us no longer to work, no longer to sit in judgement, but to heed the signs of the imminent end of the world; a justice which accepts an innocent man as a substitute sacrifice; someone who bids his disciples drink his blood; prayers for miraculous interventions; sin perpetrated against a god atoned for by a god; fear of a Beyond to which death is the gateway; the figure of the Cross as a symbol in an age which no longer knows the meaning and shame of the Cross—how gruesomely all this is wafted to us, as if out of the grave of a primeval past! Can one believe that things of this soft are still believed in?

#### 116

*The everyday Christian.*—If the Christian dogmas of a revengeful God, universal sinfulness, election by divine grace and the danger of everlasting damnation were true, it would be a sign of weakmindedness and lack of character *not* to become a priest, apostle or hermit and, in fear and trembling, to work solely on one's own salvation; it would be senseless to lose sight of one's eternal advantage for the sake of temporal comfort. If we may assume that these things are at any rate *believed* true, then the everyday Christian cuts a miserable figure; he is a man who really cannot count to three, and who precisely on account of his spiritual imbecility does not deserve to be punished so harshly as Christianity promises to punish him.

#### 117

*Of the prudence of Christianity.*—Among the artifices of Christianity is that of proclaiming the

SOURCE: Friedrich Nietzsche, *Human, All Too Human,* trans. R. J. Hollingdale (New York: Cambridge University Press, 1986), pp. 40, 65–67. Reprinted with permission of Cambridge University Press.

complete unworthiness, sinfulness and despicableness of man in general so loudly that to despise one's fellow man becomes impossible. "Let him sin as he may, he is nonetheless not essentially different from me: it is I who am in every degree unworthy and despicable": thus says the Christian to himself. But this feeling too has lost its sharpest sting, because the Christian does not believe in his individual despicableness: he is evil as a man as such and quietens his mind a little with the proposition: we are all of *one* kind.

## *From* The Anti-Christ

### 36

—Only we, we *emancipated* spirits, possess the prerequisite for understanding something nineteen centuries have misunderstood—that integrity become instinct and passion which makes war on the "holy lie" even more than on any other lie. . . . One has been unspeakably far from our benevolent and cautious neutrality, from that discipline of the spirit through which alone the divining of such strange, such delicate things is made possible: at all times one has, with shameless self-seeking, desired only *one's own* advantage in these things, one constructed the *Church* out of the antithesis to the Gospel.

If anyone were looking for a sign that an ironical divinity was at work behind the great universal drama he would find no small support in the *tremendous question-mark* called Christianity. That mankind should fall on its knees before the opposite of what was the origin, the meaning, the *right* of the Gospel, that it should have sanctified in the concept "Church" precisely what the "bringer of glad tidings" regarded as *beneath him, behind* him—one seeks in vain a grander form of *world-historical irony*—

### 39

—To resume, I shall now relate the *real* history of Christianity.

—The word "Christianity" is already a misunderstanding—in reality there has been only one Christian, and he died on the Cross. The "Evangel" *died* on the Cross. What was called "Evangel" from this moment onwards was already the opposite of what *he* had lived: "*bad* tidings," a *dysangel*. It is false to the point of absurdity to see in a "belief," perchance the belief in redemption through Christ, the distinguishing characteristic of the Christian: only Christian *practice*, a life such as he who died on the Cross *lived*, is Christian. . . . Even today *such* a life is possible, for *certain* men even necessary: genuine, primitive Christianity will be possible at all times. . . . *Not* a belief but a doing, above all a *not*-doing of many things, a different *being*. . . . States of consciousness, beliefs of any kind, holding something to be true for example—every psychologist know this—are a matter of complete indifference and of the fifth rank compared with the value of the instincts: to speak more strictly, the whole concept of spiritual causality is false. To reduce being a Christian, Christianness, to a holding something to be true, to a mere phenomenality of consciousness, means to negate Christianness. *In fact there have been no Christians at all.* The "Christian," that which has been called Christian for two millennia, is merely a psychological self-misunderstanding. Regarded more closely, that which has ruled in him, *in spite of* all his "faith," has been *merely* the instincts—and what instincts! "Faith" has been at all times, with Luther for instance, only a cloak, a pretext, a *screen*, behind which the instincts played their game—a shrewd *blindness* to the dominance of *certain* instincts. . . . "Faith"—I have already called it the true Christian *shrewdness*—one has always *spoken* of faith, one has always *acted* from instinct. . . . The Christian's world of ideas contains nothing which so much as touches upon actuality: on the other hand, we have recognized in instinctive hatred *for* actuality the driving element, the only driving element in the roots of Christianity.

SOURCE: Friedrich Nietzsche, *Twilight of the Idols; and The Anti-Christ* (1885), trans. R. J. Hollingdale (1968; Harmondsworth, UK: Penguin Books, 1997), pp. 148, 151. Copyright R. J. Hollingdale, 1968.

# Nietzsche on Christianity as Herd Morality

## FRIEDRICH NIETZSCHE

### *From* The Will to Power

#### 195 (NOV. 1887–MARCH 1888)

"CHRISTIANITY" HAS BECOME something fundamentally different from what its founder did and desired. It is the great antipagan movement of antiquity, formulated through the employment of the life, teaching and "words" of the founder of Christianity but interpreted in an absolutely arbitrary way after the pattern of fundamentally different needs: translated into the language of every already existing subterranean religion—

It is the rise of pessimism (—while Jesus wanted to bring peace and the happiness of lambs): and moreover the pessimism of the weak, the inferior, the suffering, the oppressed.

Its mortal enemy is (1) power in character, spirit and taste; "worldliness"; (2) classical "happiness," the noble levity and skepticism, the hard pride, the eccentric intemperance and the cool self-sufficiency of the sage, Greek refinement in gesture, word, and form. Its mortal enemy is the Roman just as much as the Greek.

#### 210 (SPRING–FALL 1887)

Read the New Testament as a book of seduction: virtue is appropriated in the instinct that with it one can capture public opinion—and indeed the most modest virtue, which recognizes the ideal sheep and nothing further (including the shepherd—): a little, sweet, well-meaning, helpful, and enthusiastically cheerful kind of virtue that expects absolutely nothing from the outside—that sets itself altogether apart from "the world." The most absurd arrogance, as if on one hand the community represented all that is right, and on the other the world all that is false, eternally reprehensible, and rejected, and as if the destiny of mankind revolved about this fact. The most absurd hatred toward everything in power: but without touching it! A kind of inner detachment that outwardly leaves everything as it was (servitude and slavery; to know how to turn *everything* into a means of serving God and virtue).

#### 215 (SPRING–FALL 1887)

Christianity as a denaturalization of herd-animal morality: accompanied by absolute misunderstanding and self-deception. Democratization is a more natural form of it, one less mendacious.

Datum: the oppressed, the lowly, the great masses of slaves and semi-slaves *desire power.*

First step: they make themselves free—they ransom themselves, in imagination at first, they recognize one another, they prevail.

Second step: they enter into battle, they demand recognition, equal rights, "justice."

Third step: they demand privileges (—they draw the representatives of power over to their side).

Fourth step: they demand *exclusive* power, and they get it—

In Christianity, three elements must be distinguished: (a) the oppressed of all kinds, (b) the mediocre of all kinds, (c) the discontented and sick of all kinds. With the first element Christianity fights against the political nobility and its ideal; with the second element, against the exceptional and privileged (spiritually, physically—) of all kinds; with the third element, against the natural instinct of the healthy and happy.

When a victory is won, the second element steps into the foreground; for then Christianity

SOURCE: Friedrich Nietzsche, *The Will to Power* (1906), ed. Walter Kaufmann, trans. Walter Kaufmann and R. J. Hollingdale (New York: Random House, 1967), pp. 114–115, 124, 126–127. Used by permission of Random House, Inc.

has persuaded the healthy and happy to its side (as warriors in its cause), likewise the powerful (as interested parties on account of the conquest of the mob)—and now it is the herd instinct, the mediocre nature which is of value from any point of view, which gets its supreme sanction through Christianity. This mediocre nature at last grows so conscious of itself (—acquires courage for itself—) that it arrogates even *political* power to itself—

Democracy is Christianity made natural: a kind of "return to nature" after, on account of its extreme antinaturalness, it could be overcome by the opposite values.—Consequence: the aristocratic ideal henceforth loses its naturalness ("the higher man," "noble," "artist," "passion," "knowledge," etc.; romanticism as cult of the exception, the genius, etc.).

216 (SPRING–FALL 1887;
REV. SPRING–FALL 1888)

*When the "masters" could also become Christians.*—It lies in the instinct of a community (family, race, herd, tribe) to feel that the conditions and desires to which it owes its survival are valuable in themselves, e.g., obedience, reciprocity, consideration, moderation, sympathy—consequently to suppress everything that contradicts or stands in the way of them.

Likewise, it lies in the instinct of the rulers (be they individuals or classes) to patronize and applaud the virtues that make their subjects useful and submissive (—conditions and affects which may be as different as can be from their own).

The herd instinct and the instinct of the rulers agree in praising a certain number of qualities and conditions—but for differing reasons: the former from direct egoism, the latter from indirect egoism.

Submission of the master races to Christianity is essentially the consequence of the insight that Christianity is a herd religion, that it teaches obedience: in short, that Christians are easier to rule than non-Christians. With this hint, the pope recommends Christian propaganda to the emperor of China even today.

# THE PROBLEM OF EVIL

## *Taking Seriously the Problem of Evil*

The problem of evil has always been a vexing paradox for theologians and Christian philosophers. If God is all powerful and all good, how can he permit evil—torture, war, plagues, and natural disasters? A number of ideas have been put forward to resolve this apparent contradiction, as we've seen from our look at Hume:

1. God is not all powerful; therefore, he cannot prevent any evil that happens.
2. God is not all good; therefore, he allows some evil to exist, being not really too concerned with it.
3. God doesn't exist.
4. God is all good and all powerful, but there are reasons he allows evil to exist.

Religious apologists (*apologia,* from the Greek meaning "to give a defense") have traditionally argued for the fourth option. Attacking this position, B. C. Johnson (a pseudonym) argues one cannot reconcile belief in the existence of God with all the terrible things we see in the world around us.

For example, how can a good God allow a house with a family inside it to burn to the ground? If someone other than God had the ability to stop the house from burning down, and stood by watching, wouldn't we condemn this person's inaction as cowardice? So if God can stop terrible things from happening, why doesn't he?

Some have responded by bringing into the conversation the philosophical notion of *free will*. Free will refers to the human ability to make choices with at least some degree of individual liberty and self-determination. It refers to the idea that our actions haven't been predetermined, whether physically, psychologically, sociologically, or spiritually. When we choose to do something, we make our choice freely, without coercion. (That's not to say that all people *actually* act according to their free will all of the time; merely that they have that capacity in the abstract. For instance, people who join a religious cult or become addicted to a drug are usually seen as having their free will taken away from them: They can no longer make autonomous choices, acting under psychological coercion in the first case, and the physical coercion of their own body in the second. Yet before they joined the cult or became addicted to the drug, they *were* free to choose to avoid going down either of these paths.)

The notion of free will has a theological interpretation as well. God didn't create humanity to be mindless robots, programmed to follow His directives without reflection and desire. Instead, God made us free agents with the ability to decide for ourselves how to act. So we can't blame God for our all-too-human evils. For example, the Holocaust was not God's fault, but rather that of Hitler and his Nazi henchmen.

Johnson responds to this by asking how this evil, even if it is caused by men and women, should absolve God's responsibility for not coming to the aid of those who suffer. Moreover, even if humans bear full responsibility for human evils, this doesn't explain why God allows natural evils—volcanoes, hurricanes, tornadoes, and famines.

Johnson also deals with a number of other arguments given by theists that attempt to resolve the problem of evil. In each case he offers one or several strong counter-arguments to the theist's position.

Johnson's position has a powerful emotional and philosophical resonance to it. When terrible things happen to us or our community, we can well dispute how to reconcile these events with the belief that God is good. His article presents an exacting and terse battery of arguments that the theist must carefully sort through.

# God and the Problem of Evil

## B. C. JOHNSON

*B. C. Johnson is a pen name for the author who wishes to remain anonymous.*

HERE IS A COMMON situation: a house catches on fire and a six-month-old baby is painfully burned to death. Could we possibly describe as "good" any person who had the power to save this child and yet refused to do so? God undoubtedly has this power and yet in many cases

SOURCE: B. C. Johnson, *The Atheist Debater's Handbook* (Buffalo: Prometheus Press, 1981). Copyright 1981. Reprinted by permission of Prometheus Books. Anthologized in *Philosophy and Contemporary Issues*, 5th ed., ed. John R. Burr and Milton Goldinger (New York: Macmillan, 1981), pp. 135–140.

of this sort he has refused to help. Can we call God "good"? Are there adequate excuses for his behavior?

First, it will not do to claim that the baby will go to heaven. It was either necessary for the baby to suffer or it was not. If it was not, then it was wrong to allow it. The child's ascent to heaven does not change this fact. If it was necessary, the fact that the baby will go to heaven does not explain why it was necessary, and we are still left without an excuse for God's inaction.

It is not enough to say that the baby's painful death would in the long run have good results and therefore should have happened, otherwise God would not have permitted it. For if we know this to be true, then we know—just as God knows—that every action successfully performed must in the end be good and therefore the right thing to do, otherwise God would not have allowed it to happen. We could deliberately set houses ablaze to kill innocent people and if successful we would then know we had a duty to do it. A defense of God's goodness which takes as its foundation duties known only after the fact would result in a morality unworthy of the name. Furthermore, this argument does not explain why God allowed the child to burn to death. It merely claims that there is some reason discoverable in the long run. But the belief that such a reason is within our grasp must rest upon the additional belief that God is good. This is just to counter evidence against such a belief by assuming the belief to be true. It is not unlike a lawyer defending his client by claiming that the client is innocent and therefore the evidence against him must be misleading—that proof vindicating the defendant will be found in the long run. No jury of reasonable men and women would accept such a defense and the theist cannot expect a more favorable outcome.

The theist often claims that man has been given free will so that if he accidentally or purposefully causes fires, killing small children, it is his fault alone. Consider a bystander who had nothing to do with starting the fire but who refused to help even though he could have saved the child with no harm to himself. Could such a bystander be called good? Certainly not. If we would not consider a mortal human being good under these circumstances, what grounds could we possibly have for continuing to assert the goodness of an all-powerful God?

The suggestion is sometimes made that it is best for us to face disasters without assistance, otherwise we would become dependent on an outside power for aid. Should we then abolish modern medical care or do away with efficient fire departments? Are we not dependent on their help? Is it not the case that their presence transforms us into soft, dependent creatures? The vast majority are not physicians or firemen. These people help in their capacity as professional outside sources of aid in much the same way that we would expect God to be helpful. Theists refer to aid from firemen and physicians as cases of man helping himself. In reality, it is a tiny minority of men helping a great many. We can become just as dependent on them as we can on God. Now the existence of this kind of outside help is either wrong or right. If it is right, then God should assist those areas of the world which do not have this kind of help. In fact, throughout history, such help has not been available. If aid ought to have been provided, then God should have provided it. On the other hand, if it is wrong to provide this kind of assistance, then we should abolish the aid altogether. But we obviously do not believe it is wrong.

Similar considerations apply to the claim that if God interferes in disasters, he would destroy a considerable amount of moral urgency to make things right. Once again, note that such institutions as modern medicine and fire departments are relatively recent. They function irrespective of whether we as individuals feel any moral urgency to support them. To the extent that they help others, opportunities to feel moral urgency are destroyed because they reduce the number of cases which appeal to us for help. Since we have not always had such institutions, there must have been a time when there was greater moral urgency than there is now. If such a situation is morally desirable, then we should abolish modern medical care and fire departments. If the situation is not morally desirable, then God should have remedied it.

Besides this point, we should note that God is represented as one who tolerates disasters, such as infants burning to death, in order to create moral urgency. It follows that God approves of these disasters as a means to encourage the creation of moral urgency. Furthermore, if there were no such disasters occurring, God would have to see to it that they occur. If it so happened that we lived in a world in which babies never perished in burning houses, God would be morally obliged to take an active hand in setting fire to houses with infants in them. In fact, if the frequency of infant mortality due to fire should happen to fall below a level necessary for the creation of maximum moral urgency in our real world, God would be justified in setting a few fires of his own. This may well be happening right now, for there is no guarantee that the maximum number of infant deaths necessary for moral urgency are occurring.

All of this is of course absurd. If I see an opportunity to create otherwise nonexistent opportunities for moral urgency by burning an infant or two, then I should *not* do so. But if it is good to maximize moral urgency, then I *should* do so. Therefore, it is not good to maximize moral urgency. Plainly we do not in general believe that it is a good thing to maximize moral urgency. The fact that we approve of modern medical care and applaud medical advances is proof enough of this.

The theist may point out that in a world without suffering there would be no occasion for the production of such virtues as courage, sympathy, and the like. This may be true, but the atheist need not demand a world without suffering. He need only claim that there is suffering which is in excess of that needed for the production of various virtues. For example, God's active attempts to save six-month-old infants from fires would not in itself create a world without suffering. But no one could sincerely doubt that it would improve the world.

The two arguments against the previous theistic excuse apply here also. "Moral urgency" and "building virtue" are susceptible to the same criticisms. It is worthwhile to emphasize, however, that we encourage efforts to eliminate evils; we approve of efforts to promote peace, prevent famine, and wipe out disease. In other words, we do value a world with fewer or (if possible) no opportunities for the development of virtue (when "virtue" is understood to mean the reduction of suffering). If we produce such a world for succeeding generations, how will they develop virtues? Without war, disease, and famine, they will not be virtuous. Should we then cease our attempts to wipe out war, disease, and famine? If we do not believe that it is right to cease attempts at improving the world, then by implication we admit that virtue-building is not an excuse for God to permit disasters. For we admit that the development of virtue is no excuse for permitting disasters.

It might be said that God allows innocent people to suffer in order to deflate man's ego so that the latter will not be proud of his apparently deserved good fortune. But this excuse succumbs to the arguments used against the preceding excuses and we need discuss them no further.

Theists may claim that evil is a necessary by-product of the laws of nature and therefore it is irrational for God to interfere every time a disaster happens. Such a state of affairs would alter the whole causal order and we would then find it impossible to predict anything. But the death of a child caused by an electrical fire could have been prevented by a miracle and no one would ever have known. Only a minor alteration in electrical equipment would have been necessary. A very large disaster could have been avoided simply by producing in Hitler a miraculous heart attack—and no one would have known it was a miracle. To argue that continued miraculous intervention by God would be wrong is like insisting that one should never use salt because ingesting five pounds of it would be fatal. No one is requesting that God interfere all of the time. He should, however, intervene to prevent especially horrible disasters. Of course, the question arises: where does one draw the line? Well, certainly the line should be drawn somewhere this side of infants burning to death. To argue that we do not know where the line should be drawn is no excuse for failing to interfere in those instances that would be called clear cases of evil.

It will not do to claim that evil exists as a necessary contrast to good so that we might know what good is. A very small amount of evil, such as a toothache, would allow that. It is not necessary to destroy innocent human beings.

The claim could be made that God has a "higher morality" by which his actions are to be judged. But it is a strange "higher morality" which claims that what we call "bad" is good and what we call "good" is bad. Such a morality can have no meaning to us. It would be like calling black "white" and white "black." In reply the theist may say that God is the wise Father and we are ignorant children. How can we judge God any more than a child is able to judge his parent? It is true that a child may be puzzled by his parents' conduct, but his basis for deciding that their conduct is nevertheless good would be the many instances of good behavior he has observed. Even so, this could be misleading. Hitler, by all accounts, loved animals and children of the proper race; but if Hitler had had a child, this offspring would hardly have been justified in arguing that his father was a good man. At any rate, God's "higher morality," being the opposite of ours, cannot offer any grounds for deciding that he is somehow good.

Perhaps the main problem with the solutions to the problem of evil we have thus far considered is that no matter how convincing they may be in the abstract, they are implausible in certain particular cases. Picture an infant dying in a burning house and then imagine God simply observing from afar. Perhaps God is reciting excuses in his own behalf. As the child succumbs to the smoke and flames, God may be pictured as saying: "Sorry, but if I helped you I would have considerable trouble deflating the ego of your parents. And don't forget I have

to keep those laws of nature consistent. And anyway if you weren't dying in that fire, a lot of moral urgency would just go down the drain. Besides, I didn't start this fire, so you can't blame *me*."

It does no good to assert that God may not be all-powerful and thus not able to prevent evil. He can create a universe and yet is conveniently unable to do what the fire department can do—rescue a baby from a burning building. God should at least be as powerful as a man. A man, if he had been at the right place and time, could have killed Hitler. Was this beyond God's abilities? If God knew in 1910 how to produce polio vaccine and if he was able to communicate with somebody, he should have communicated this knowledge. He must be incredibly limited if he could not have managed this modest accomplishment. Such a God if not dead, is the next thing to it. And a person who believes in such a ghost of a God is practically an atheist. To call such a thing a god would be to strain the meaning of the word.

The theist, as usual, may retreat to faith. He may say that he has faith in God's goodness and therefore the Christian Deity's existence has not been disproved. "Faith" is here understood as being much like confidence in a friend's innocence despite the evidence against him. Now in order to have confidence in a friend one must know him well enough to justify faith in his goodness. We cannot have justifiable faith in the supreme goodness of strangers. Moreover, such confidence must come not just from a speaking acquaintance. The friend may continually assure us with his words that he is good but if he does not act like a good person, we would have no reason to trust him. A person who says he has faith in God's goodness is speaking as if he had known God for a long time and during that time had never seen Him do any serious evil. But we know that throughout history God has allowed numerous atrocities to occur. No one can have justifiable faith in the goodness of such a God. This faith would have to be based on a close friendship wherein God was never found to do anything wrong. But a person would have to be blind and deaf to have had such a relationship with God. Suppose a friend of yours had always claimed to be good yet refused to help people when he was in a position to render aid. Could you have justifiable faith in his goodness?

You can of course say that you trust God anyway—that no arguments can undermine your faith. But this is just a statement describing how stubborn you are; it has no bearing whatsoever on the question of God's goodness.

The various excuses theists offer for why God has allowed evil to exist have been demonstrated to be inadequate. However, the conclusive objection to these excuses does not depend on their inadequacy.

First, we should note that every possible excuse making the actual world consistent with the existence of a good God could be used in reverse to make that same world consistent with an evil God. For example, we could say that God is evil and that he allows free will so that we can freely do evil things, which would make us more truly evil than we would be if forced to perform evil acts. Or we could say that natural disasters occur in order to make people more selfish and bitter, for most people tend to have a "me-first" attitude in a disaster (note, for example, stampedes to leave burning buildings). Even though some people achieve virtue from disasters, this outcome is necessary if persons are to react freely to disaster—necessary if the development of moral degeneracy is to continue freely. But, enough; the point is made. Every excuse we could provide to make the world consistent with a good God can be paralleled by an excuse to make the world consistent with an evil God. This is so because the world is a mixture of both good and bad.

Now there are only three possibilities concerning God's moral character. Considering the world as it actually is, we may believe: (a) that God is more likely to be all evil than he is to be all good; (b) that God is less likely to be all evil than he is to be all good; or (c) that God is

equally as likely to be all evil as he is to be all good. In case (a) it would be admitted that God is unlikely to be all good. Case (b) cannot be true at all, since—as we have seen—the belief that God is all evil can be justified to precisely the same extent as the belief that God is all good. Case (c) leaves us with no reasonable excuses for a good God to permit evil. The reason is as follows: if an excuse is to be a reasonable excuse, the circumstances it identifies as excusing conditions must be actual. For example, if I run over a pedestrian and my excuse is that the brakes failed because someone tampered with them, then the facts had better bear this out. Otherwise the excuse will not hold. Now if case (c) is correct and, given the facts of the actual world, God is as likely to be all evil as he is to be all good, then these facts do not support the excuses which could be made for a good God permitting evil. Consider an analogous example. If my excuse for running over the pedestrian is that my brakes were tampered with, and if the actual facts lead us to believe that it is no more likely that they were tampered with than that they were not, the excuse is no longer reasonable. To make good my excuse, I must show that it is a fact or at least highly probable that my brakes were tampered with—not that it is just a possibility. The same point holds for God. His excuse must not be a possible excuse, but an actual one. But case (c), in maintaining that it is just as likely that God is all evil as that he is all good, rules this out. For if case (c) is true, then the facts of the actual world do not make it any more likely that God is all good than that he is all evil. Therefore, they do not make it any more likely that his excuses are good than that they are not. But, as we have seen, good excuses have a higher probability of being true.

Cases (a) and (c) conclude that it is unlikely that God is all good, and case (b) cannot be true. Since these are the only possible cases, there is no escape from the conclusion that it is unlikely that God is all good. Thus the problem of evil triumphs over traditional theism.

# John Hick's Attempted Theodicy

The problem of evil is a serious problem for theists. Simply put, how could a good God allow such terrible things as wars, genocide, and famine to happen, things we can see on our nightly news? From a broadly construed Christian perspective, John Hick deals with the problem of evil in an interesting way. It may indeed be compatible with the thinking of an Islamic or Jewish apologist.

Hick pays attention to one of the central issues related to the problem of evil—the relationship between human freedom and responsibility. Our freedom of the will, our capacity for doing evil as well as good, was a necessary part of God's creation. In order to become "children of God," He had to create us with the freedom to choose to act as we wish. Hick then takes some time discussing some of the objections raised against this view.

An important point in the traditional theist's theodicy is that much of the evil that occurs in our world is specifically due to the wrongful actions of human beings. When we think about human and animal suffering, past and present, how much of it can we say is the result of human actions? Aren't wars, famine, murders, and pollution all the results of human decisions and human actions? Hick argues that human beings must take responsibility for a large portion of the evil in the world.

Evil, however, is not only a matter of human intention. There are also natural evils—things such as earthquakes, floods, hurricanes, tornadoes, and droughts. How do theists explain evils of this sort?

Hick argues that the atheist or skeptic is wrong to assume that an all-loving, all-good God should create a world where everything is perfect—a world void of pain and suffering. A world where there could be no pain would also be a world where there can be no uniform laws of nature. For instance, if a speeding car broke through a road barricade and plunged over a cliff, in such a perfect world, the car would just rebound safely back on the road, thus violating various laws of gravity. There would be no storms on the ocean, no drowning at sea, no turbulence around airplanes. A thug attempting to attack someone would have his knife disintegrate in his hand. A world such as this would turn out to be very different from our own. Hick points out that a world with no wrong actions would as well be a world where there are no right actions. How could one be courageous in a world where no one ever faced danger? We would have no opportunity for moral development. As the old song goes, life would be a dream.

As Hick sees it, humans would not be able to show their capacity for good in a world such as B. C. Johnson's. In the world that we actually live in, where evil exists alongside the human capacity for good, humans are free to choose between good and evil. This is what Hick describes as "soul-making." Soul-making, the process by which we mature and grow morally and spiritually, can only be possible in a world where there are real choices with real consequences.

Many of the points raised by Hick have been around for centuries. The considerations do, however, take on a new tone with each generation. Hick tries to address the problem of evil in light of the modern world, offering a nice counterpoint to Johnson's atheism.

# The Problem of Evil

## JOHN HICK

To MANY, the most powerful positive objection to belief in God is the fact of evil. Probably for most agnostics it is the appalling depth and extent of human suffering, more than anything else, that makes the idea of a loving Creator seem so implausible and disposes them toward one or another of the various naturalistic theories of religion.

As a challenge to theism, the problem of evil has traditionally been posed in the form of a dilemma: if God is perfectly loving, he must wish to abolish evil; and if he is all-powerful, he must be able to abolish evil. But evil exists; therefore God cannot be both omnipotent and perfectly loving.

Certain solutions, which at once suggest themselves, have to be ruled out so far as the Judaic-Christian faith is concerned.

To say, for example (with contemporary Christian Science), that *evil is an illusion of* the human mind, is impossible within a religion based upon the stark realism of the Bible. Its pages faithfully reflect the characteristic mixture of good and evil in human experience. They record every kind of sorrow and suffering, every mode of man's inhumanity to man and of his painfully insecure existence in the world. There is no attempt to regard evil as anything but dark, menacingly ugly, heart-rending, and crushing. In the Christian scriptures, the climax of this history of evil is the crucifixion of Jesus, which is presented not only as a case of utterly unjust suffering, but as the violent and murderous rejection of God's Messiah. There can be no doubt, then, that for biblical faith, evil is unambiguously evil, and stands in direct opposition to God's will.

Again, to solve the problem of evil by means of the theory (sponsored for example, by the Boston "Personalist" School) *of a finite deity* who does the best he can with a material, intractable and coeternal with himself, is to have abandoned the basic premise of Hebrew-Christian monotheism; for the theory amounts to rejecting belief in the infinity and sovereignty of God.

Indeed, any theory which would *avoid the problem of the origin of evil by depicting it as an ultimate constituent of the universe,* coordinate with good, has been repudiated in advance by the classic Christian teaching, first developed by Augustine, that evil represents the going wrong of something which in itself is good. Augustine holds firmly to the Hebrew-Christian conviction that the universe is *good*—that is to say, it is the creation of a good God for a good purpose. He completely rejects the ancient prejudice, widespread in his day, that matter is evil. There are, according to Augustine, higher and lower, greater and lesser goods in immense abundance and variety; but everything which has being is good in its own way and degree, except in so far as it may have become spoiled or corrupted. Evil—whether it be an evil will, an instance of pain, or some disorder or decay in nature—has not been set there by God, but represents the distortion of something that is inherently valuable. Whatever exists is, as such, and in its proper place, good; evil is essentially parasitic upon good, being disorder and perversion in a fundamentally good creation. This understanding of evil as something negative means that it is not willed and created by God; but it does not mean (as some have supposed) that evil is unreal and can be disregarded. On the contrary, the first effect of this doctrine is to accentuate even more the question of the origin of evil.

SOURCE: John Hick, "The Problem of Evil," *Philosophy of Religion* (Englewood Cliffs, NJ: Prentice-Hall, 1963), pp. 40–46. Copyright 1963. Reprinted by permission of Prentice Education, Inc., Upper Saddle River, NJ. Reprinted in *Philosophy and Contemporary Issues,* 5th ed., ed. John R. Burr and Milton Goldinger (New York: Macmillan, 1992), pp. 140–145.

Theodicy,[1] as many modern Christian thinkers see it, is a modest enterprise, negative rather than positive in its conclusions. It does not claim to explain, nor to explain away, every instance of evil in human experience, but only to point to certain considerations which prevent the fact of evil (largely incomprehensible though it remains) from constituting a final and insuperable bar to rational belief in God.

In indicating these considerations it will be useful to follow the traditional division of the subject. There is the problem of *moral evil* or wickedness: why does an all-good and all-powerful God permit this? And there is the problem of the *nonmoral evil* of suffering or pain, both physical and mental: why has an all-good and all-powerful God created a world in which this occurs?

Christian thought has always considered moral evil in its relation to *human freedom and responsibility*. To be a person is to be a finite center of freedom, a (relatively) free and self-directing agent responsible for one's own decisions. *This involves being free to act wrongly as well as to act rightly.* The idea of a person who can be infallibly guaranteed always to act rightly is self-contradictory. There can be no guarantee in advance that a genuinely free moral agent will never choose amiss. Consequently, the possibility of wrong-doing or sin is logically inseparable from the creation of finite persons, and to say that God should not have created beings who might sin amounts to saying that he should not have created people.

This thesis has been challenged in some recent philosophical discussions of the problem of evil, in which it is claimed that no contradiction is involved in saying that God might have made people who would be genuinely free and who could yet be guaranteed always to act rightly. A quote from one of these discussions follows:

> If there is no logical impossibility in a man's freely choosing the good on one, or on several occasions, there cannot be a logical impossibility in his freely choosing the good on every occasion. God was not, then, faced with a choice between making innocent automata and making beings who, in acting freely, would sometimes go wrong: there was open to him the obviously better possibility of making beings who would act freely but always go right. Clearly, his failure to avail himself of this possibility is inconsistent with his being both omnipotent and wholly good.[2]

A reply to this argument is suggested in another recent contribution to the discussion.[3] *If by a free action* we mean an action which is not externally compelled but which flows from the nature of the agent as he reacts to the circumstances in which he finds himself, there is, indeed, no contradiction between our being free and our actions being "caused" (by our own nature) and therefore being in principle predictable. *There is a contradiction, however, in saying that God is the cause of our acting as we do but that we are free beings in relation to God.* There is, in other words, a contradiction in saying that God has made us so that we shall of necessity act in a certain way, and that we are genuinely independent persons in relation to him. If all our thoughts and actions are divinely predestined, however free and morally responsible we may seem to be to ourselves, we cannot be free and morally responsible in the sight of God, but must instead be his helpless puppets. Such "freedom" is like that of a patient acting out a series of post-hypnotic suggestions: he appears, even to himself, to be free, but his volitions have actually been pre-determined by another will, that of the hypnotist, in relation to whom the patient is not a free agent.

A different objector might raise the question of whether or not we deny God's omnipotence if we admit that he is unable to create persons who are free from the risks inherent in personal freedom. The answer that has always been given is that to create such beings is logically impossible. *It is no limitation upon God's power that he can-*

---

[1] The word "theodicy," from the Greek *theos* (God) and *dike* (righteous), means the justification of God's goodness in the face of the fact of evil.

[2] J. L. Mackie, "Evil and Omnipotence," *Mind* (April 1955), 209.

[3] Flew, in *New Essays in Philosophical Theology.*

*not accomplish the logically impossible, since there is nothing here to accomplish, but only a meaningless conjunction of words—in this case "person who is not a person."* God is able to create beings of any and every conceivable kind; but creatures who lack moral freedom, however superior they might be to human beings in other respects, would not be what we mean by persons. They would constitute a different form of life which God might have brought into existence instead of persons. When we ask why God did not create such beings in place of persons, the traditional answer is that only persons could, in any meaningful sense, become "children of God," capable of entering into a personal relationship with their Creator by a free and uncompelled response to his love.

When we turn from the possibility of moral evil as a correlate of man's personal freedom to its actuality, we face something which must remain inexplicable even when it can be seen to be possible. For we can never provide a complete causal explanation of a free act; if we could, it would not be a free act. The origin of moral evil lies forever concealed within the mystery of human freedom.

The necessary connection between moral freedom and the possibility, now actualized, of sin throws light upon a great deal of the suffering which afflicts mankind. *For an enormous amount of human pain arises either from the inhumanity or the culpable incompetence of mankind.* This includes such major scourges as poverty, oppression and persecution, war, and all the injustice, indignity, and inequity which occur even in the most advanced societies. These evils are manifestations of human sin. Even disease is fostered to an extent, the limits of which have not yet been determined by psychosomatic medicine, by moral and emotional factors seated both in the individual and in his social environment. To the extent that all of these evils stem from human failures and wrong decisions, their possibility is inherent in the creation of free persons inhabiting a world which presents them with real choices which are followed by real consequences.

We may now turn more directly to the problem of suffering. Even though the major bulk of actual human pain is traceable to man's misused freedom as a sole or part cause, there remain other sources of pain which are entirely independent of the human will, for example, earthquake, hurricane, storm, flood, drought, and blight. In practice it is often impossible to trace a boundary between the suffering which results from human wickedness and folly and that which falls upon mankind from without. Both kinds of suffering are inextricably mingled together in human experience. For our present purpose, however, it is important to note that the latter category does exist and *that it seems to be built into the very structure of our world*. In response to it, theodicy, if it is wisely conducted, follows a negative path. It is not possible to show positively that each item of human pain serves the divine purpose of good; but, on the other hand, it does seem possible to show that the divine purpose as it is understood in Judaism and Christianity could not be forwarded in a world which was designed as a permanent hedonistic paradise.

An essential premise of this argument concerns the divine purpose in creating the world. The skeptic's assumption is that man is to be viewed as a completed creation and that God's purpose in making the world was to provide a suitable dwelling-place for this fully-formed creature. Since God is good and loving, the environment which he has created for human life to inhabit is naturally as pleasant and comfortable as possible. The problem is essentially similar to that of a man who builds a cage for some pet animal. Since our world, in fact, contains sources of hardship, inconvenience, and danger of innumerable kinds, the conclusion follows that this world cannot have been created by a perfectly benevolent and all-powerful deity.

Christianity, however, has never supposed that God's purpose in the creation of the world was to construct a paradise whose inhabitants would experience a maximum of pleasure and a minimum of pain. The world is seen, instead, as a place of "*soul-making*" in which free beings, grappling with the tasks and challenges of their existence in a common environment, may become "children of God" and "heirs of eternal life." A way of thinking theologically of God's continuing creative purpose for man was suggested by some of the early Hellenistic Fathers of the Christian Church, especially Irenaeus. Following hints from St. Paul, Irenaeus taught that man has been made as a person in the image of God but has not yet been brought as a free and responsible agent into the finite likeness of God, which is revealed in Christ. Our world, with all its rough edges, is the sphere in which this second and harder stage of the creative process is taking place.

This conception of the world (whether or not set in Irenaeus' theological framework) can be supported by the method of negative theodicy. Suppose, contrary to fact, that this world were a paradise from which all possibility of pain and suffering were excluded. The consequences would be very far-reaching. For example, no one could ever injure anyone else: the murderer's knife would turn to paper or his bullets to thin air; the bank safe, robbed of a million dollars, would miraculously become filled with another million dollars (without this device, on however large a scale, proving inflationary); fraud, deceit, conspiracy, and treason would somehow always leave the fabric of society undamaged. Again, no one would ever be injured by accident: the mountain-climber, steeplejack, or playing child falling from a height would float unharmed to the ground; the reckless driver would never meet with disaster. There would be no need to work, since no harm could result from avoiding work; there would be no call to be concerned for others in time of need or danger, for in such a world there could be no real needs or dangers.

To make possible this continual series of individual adjustments, nature would have to work by "special providences" instead of running according to general laws which men must learn to respect on penalty of pain or death. The laws of nature would have to be extremely flexible: sometimes gravity would operate, sometimes not; sometimes an object would be hard and solid, sometimes soft. There could be no sci-

ences, for there would be no enduring world structure to investigate. In eliminating the problems and hardships of an objective environment, with its own laws, life would become like a dream in which, delightfully but aimlessly, we would float and drift at ease.

One can at least begin to imagine such a world. It is evident that our present ethical concepts would have no meaning in it. If, for example, the notion of harming someone is an essential element in the concept of a wrong action, in our hedonistic paradise there could be no wrong actions—nor any right actions in distinction from wrong. Courage and fortitude would have no point in an environment in which there is, by definition, no danger or difficulty. Generosity, kindness, the *agape* aspect of love, prudence, unselfishness, and all other ethical notions which presuppose life in a stable environment, could not even be formed. Consequently, such a world, however well it might promote pleasure, would be very ill adapted for the development of the moral qualities of human personality. In relation to this purpose it would be the worst of all possible worlds.

It would seem, then, that an environment intended to make possible the growth in free beings of the finest characteristics of personal life, must have a good deal in common with our present world. It must operate according to general and dependable laws: and it must involve real dangers, difficulties, problems, obstacles, and possibilities of pain, failure, sorrow, frustration, and defeat. If it did not contain the particular trials and perils which—subtracting man's own very considerable contribution—our world contains, it would have to contain others instead.

To realize this is not, by any means, to be in possession of a detailed theodicy. It is to understand that this world, with all its "heartaches and the thousand natural shocks that flesh is heir to," and environment so manifestly not designed for the maximization of human pleasure and the minimization of human pain, may be rather well adapted to the quite different purpose of "soul-making."

# CONTEMPORARY QUESTIONS IN
# THE PHILOSOPHY OF RELIGION

## *Alvin Plantinga on Christianity versus Secularism*

Among philosophers of religion today, Alvin Plantinga commands a great deal of attention not only from Christian thinkers, but also from agnostics and atheists. Plantinga, a prolific writer, is an outspoken defender of Christian belief. In the article we have selected for this chapter, he offers a diagnosis of the philosophy of religion based on past philosophical movements. He then speculates on what may be expected in the new millennium.

He begins his diagnosis by looking back almost a century to one of the first major philosophical movements that captured the imagination of early-twentieth-century philosophers—*logical positivism.* Positivists thought that all sorts of metaphysical and esoteric claims about the world had come to clutter up the domain of philosophy. With all these philosophies clamoring for attention, with little explanation given for why we should take any of them as true, logical positivists wanted to subject our claims about the world to rigorous analysis. They thought they could clear the philosophical barn of senseless old ideas, separating claims that had some justification, or meaning, from claims that were meaningless or nonsense.

Trying to set down clear rules or procedures for distinguishing meaningful claims from meaningless claims proved more difficult than they first expected. The first way the positivists thought they could determine meaningful from meaningless claims was by asking how a claim could be verified. They said that only claims that could be verified by the experience of our senses were meaningful, and those that couldn't were not.

For example, think of someone who says that each day while eating breakfast he sees a flock of crows in his backyard. If we doubted our friend's claim we could easily verify it: We could invite ourselves over for breakfast one day to see the crows. If our friend's claim were true, we would expect to see some crows flying around his backyard and squawking as we ate breakfast with him. If we didn't see or hear any crows, then his claim would be false. This sort of simple empirical verification of a claim is easy enough to describe and apply.

The positivists were extremely serious in their application of this "verifiability criterion," believing that it could be a universal principle for meaning. But when they applied the principle to itself, it fell apart. If only empirically verifiable claims are meaningful, how can we be sure this definition for determining meaning could *itself* be meaningful? In other words, to what experience can we refer in order to prove the claim "only sense experience counts" to be true? This conundrum disqualified it as a definition for distinguishing meaningful from meaningless statements.

The positivists' next choice for a criterion was *falsification.* Let's use a more serious claim this time. In the context of the philosophy of religion, the positivists asked how could the claim "God created the universe," even in theory, be shown to be false?

When an atheist says modern astronomy has shown that the Big Bang can account for the origin of the universe, the theist responds that God actually caused the Big Bang in the first place. Upon hearing this, the positivist then asks the theist: "What state of affairs today would have been different if your claim were false?" Or, putting the question a bit differently, "How could someone who didn't believe you show the claim 'God was behind the Big Bang' is false?" The difficulty for the theist is to then answer this question in a way that doesn't first of all merely assume that God caused the Big Bang. Positivists pointed out that since there was no way, even in theory, of showing how the belief that God created the universe could be false, the categories "true" and "false" simply don't apply to claims about God. These claims are just meaningless sentences.

This means of distinguishing between claims offered the positivists some hope for clearing away philosophical rubbish (as they saw it). Yet other philosophers were dissatisfied with how the criterion would deal with some important claims that failed the falsifiability test. This was not only the case with religious beliefs, but with moral claims as well. How, for example, can one falsify the claim "you should not lie to other people"?

Although this school of thought has long since fallen out of philosophical favor, Plantinga thinks theists should have learned a lesson. During the heyday of positivism, many theists either abandoned their religious beliefs entirely or at least pared down their beliefs to those they thought they could respectfully hold. Plantinga believes this only goes to show that theists should be careful about new and fashionable philosophies that are suspicious or hostile toward religious belief.

In our own time, Plantinga sees more hostile philosophies rearing their ugly heads against Christian belief. Positivism has retreated into history, but taking its place is a perennial "naturalism," the notion that physical science can explain all phenomena in the universe. The second head of the anti-theist hydra Plantinga calls "creative anti-realism." This is the idea that, without God's help, we human beings in some sense can create the world in our own image. Cows are cows and trees are trees because that's what human beings have decided they are. Offshoots of this second head are postmodernism and the relativism that usually goes along with it (see Chapter 9 for more on postmodernism). These philosophies, as Plantinga understands it, are wreaking havoc intellectually and morally, especially in the universities. He finds their potential destructiveness for Christians menacing, so he outlines four ways of responding to these attacks.

The first is through negative apologetics. Here Christians respond to the various challenges set before them, whether the problem of evil or the denigration from "masters of suspicion" such as Friedrich Nietzsche, Karl Marx, and Sigmund Freud. Plantinga is only mildly pleased with the fate of negative apologetics in the twentieth century, and is especially disappointed with the Christian response to the attacks of Nietzsche, Marx, and Freud.

The second way of responding to attacks from skeptics is through "positive apologetics." This activist approach to apologetics involves arguing for various proofs and evidences that support belief in God. An example of this is where theists argue belief in God is necessary in order to have objective moral standards.

Plantinga then discusses philosophical theology and Christian philosophical criticism. Those working in philosophical theology examine philosophical questions involved in theology, such as the relationship between soul and body, the resurrection of the body, and the nature of religious language. Christian philosophical criticism considers the need for Christian intellectuals to be engaged in philosophical reflection, sorting through the implications new philosophical movements have for Christian theism.

For Plantinga, developing a constructive Christian philosophy is the task Christian philosophers have in the new millennium. This involves engaging in philosophical work not in isolation from the secular world, but in close junction with non-Christian colleagues.

In evaluating professor Plantinga's article, it is important to keep in mind that he and the other Christians who share his vision do not make up the entire Christian community. Christianity covers the globe, and is made up of individuals as diverse as the Southern Baptists of the United States, the Anglicans of Canada, Presbyterians of South Korea, and the Eastern Orthodox Church of Russia. Moreover, not all Christians who study philosophy see the world as hostile to the Christian faith as Plantinga. Paul Ricoeur, a highly respected French philosopher and devout Protestant, has treated hostile critics of Christianity, such as Nietzsche, Marx, and Freud, as offering highly penetrating philosophical ideas. Nonetheless, the influence exerted on Christian thought by Plantinga and like-minded Evangelicals cannot be underrated. They represent a powerful voice in the contemporary philosophy of religion.

Plantinga offers insight into the way he and some other Christians see their task in the philosophy of religion. Perhaps the real value of this article is for more secular-minded individuals to see where today, in the philosophy of religion, some draw the battle line. As always, we hope this article will be a good basis for classroom discussion and debate.

# Christian Philosophy at the End of the Twentieth Century

## ALVIN PLANTINGA

MY ASSIGNMENT is to reflect on the condition and prospects of Christian philosophy at the end of the twentieth century. Now most philosophers don't even get to comment, prophetically, on the turn of a *century;* we get to comment on the turn of a *millennium!* . . . Of course I realize that my paper will be just one more in a flurry of speeches, papers, and declarations greeting the new millennium. We will no doubt hear much about how man (and woman) has finally come of age, or since we have already been hearing that for the last 60 years or so, *really* come of age. There will be strident claptrap about how third millennial men and women can no longer believe this or that, how various items of the Christian faith belong to an earlier and simpler time, and so on. . . . In American philosophy we have a technical term for all such declarations and calls: we call them "baloney."

I shall not take part in this man-has-now-come-of-ageism, or as-we-now-knowism, or other baloney. Still, one hopes we do learn

SOURCE: Alvin Plantinga, "Christian Philosophy at the End of the Twentieth Century," in *Christian Philosophy at the Close of the Twentieth Century,* ed. Sander Griffioen and Bert Balk (Kampen, Netherlands: Kok, 1995), pp. 329–353.

things as we go along; and we can sensibly ask how things stand with Christian philosophy now, on the threshold of a new century, and even a new millennium. I want to ask first what this century has brought for Christian philosophy; then I will propose a sort of typology for Christian philosophy, briefly evaluating our present condition with respect to each of the main areas of the typology; and along the way I shall issue an occasional *obiter dictum* as to what, as it seems to me, we Christian philosophers ought to do next.

## Christian Philosophy and the Twentieth Century

Well, how *has* the twentieth century treated Christian philosophy? As you may have noticed, the twentieth century includes many different temporal segments and has occurred at many different places; and things have gone differently in these different place-times.

. . . The main negative development during [the first half of the twentieth century], and in Anglo-American philosophy, would certainly be logical positivism and allied streams of thought. According to positivism, characteristically Christian utterances do not so much as have the grace to be false: they are "cognitively meaningless," sheer nonsense—*disguised* nonsense, to be sure, but nonsense nonetheless. The harrowing vicissitudes of positivism and its verifiability criterion of meaning are an instructive and oft-told story; I will not add another telling; but I am afraid it must be admitted that the response of Christian thinkers to it was not, on the whole, an edifying spectacle.

By now logical positivism has retreated into well-earned obscurity; but what has taken its place? Not one, but rather, in hydra fashion, two equally nasty phenomena. Out of the frying pan into the fire. First, note that logical positivism is just a special if specially noxious case of a broader positivism—a line of thought that elevates science and scientific knowledge at the expense of more important kinds of knowledge such as

knowledge of God and knowledge of how to live properly before him. But that broader positivism is itself a manifestation of a still broader perspective we can call "perennial naturalism." Christian philosophers since Augustine's great work *De Civitas Dei* have seen human history as a sort of arena for a contest or struggle: a struggle, says Augustine, between the *Civitas Dei* [City of God], on the one hand, and the *Civitas Mundi* [Earthly City] on the other. . . .

Naturalism is perhaps the dominant perspective or picture among contemporary Western intellectuals; its central tenet is that there is no God and nothing beyond nature. Human beings, therefore, must be understood, not in terms of their being image bearers of God, but in terms of their commonality with the rest of nature, i.e., nonhuman nature. The things we think distinctive about ourselves—religion, morality, love, scholarship, humor, adventure, politics—all must be understood in natural terms, which in our day means evolutionary terms.

. . . The naturalism that underlies and gives birth to these projects is quite as opposed to Christian ways of thinking as was logical positivism, and perhaps more dangerous because more plausible.

But the *Civitas Mundi* is divided into two precincts. The second head of that post-positivistic hydra is connected with the second precinct of the *Civitas Mundi:* I shall call it "creative anti-realism." Here the basic claim or idea is not that we human beings are just one more kind of animal with a rather unusual means of survival, but that we are actually responsible for the basic lineaments, the fundamental structure and framework of the world itself. Like perennial naturalism, creative anti-realism goes back to the ancient world, back at least to Protagoras's dictum "Man is the measure of all things, of the existence of things that are, and of the nonexistence of things that are not . . ." (*Theaetetus* 152 A). But, also, like perennial naturalism, creative anti-realism has received much more compelling formulation in the modern and contemporary world.

The story begins with Immanuel Kant. His basic idea, in his monumental first *Critique,* the *Critique of Pure Reason,* is that the fundamental categories that characterize the world in which we live are imposed upon that world by *our* noetic activity: they do not characterize that world as it is in itself. . . . According to an older way of thinking, *God's* knowledge is creative: according to this more recent Kantian way of thinking, it is *our* knowledge that is creative. I realize that it is extremely difficult to give a clear but accurate summary of Kant's thought here in three sentences. Indeed it is extremely difficult to give a clear but accurate summary of Kant's thought in three hundred sentences, or three hundred pages. That is because Kant's thought, in the first critique, does not lend itself to clear and accurate summary at *any* length; as far as I can see it contains deep ambiguities and confusions. Still, the understanding of Kant just outlined has been both historically influential, and intimately connected with the second precinct of the *Civitas Mundi.*

I believe that the thought of the first *Critique,* at least understood as above, is incompatible with Christianity. [Understood thusly, a horse], as well as the sun, owes its existence to *us:* it could not have existed apart from our noetic activity. From this perspective, then, it is not *God* who has created the heavens and the earth, but we ourselves — or at any rate God could not have done it without our help. We can reach the same conclusion by a much quicker route: *existence* is one of the categories of the understanding, a structure we human beings impose on things. But if so, then if it weren't for our noetic activity, there wouldn't be any things that exist. Indeed, since the things that exist are the only things there are, if it weren't for us and our conceptual activity, there wouldn't be or have been anything at all, no dinosaurs, stars, mountains, trees, or electrons. In fact, on this way of thinking, we owe our own existence to our categorizing activity, a thought that can easily induce a sort of intellectual vertigo. But then an implication of this way of thinking is that it is we who

have created the heavens and the earth, not God. As a matter of fact, taken strictly, this strand of Kant's thought would apply to God as well; if the category of existence is a merely human category we impose upon things, if things fall under or into this category only because of our noetic activity, then the same would be true of God himself. He, too, in a stunning reversal of roles, would owe his existence to us. . . .

It is then tempting to take the next step: that we live in different worlds, that there simply isn't any such thing as *the* way the world is, the same for each of us. Instead, there is my way of structuring reality (by choice or language, or whatever), your way, and in fact many different ways. There is no such thing as *the* way the world is, and no such thing as *truth,* objective truth, the same for each of us whether we know it or not. Instead, there is what is true from my perspective, in my version, in the world as I've structured it, what is true from *your* perspective, in *your* version, in the world as *you've* structured it, and so on. My beginning students at Calvin used to tell me, sometimes, after I proposed an absolutely conclusive and apodictically certain argument for some thesis or other, that while my thesis was certainly true *for me,* it wasn't true *for them.* At the time I thought that a peculiarly sophomoric confusion: the very idea of "truth for you" as opposed to "truth for me," I thought, if it is not just an inept way of speaking of what you believe as opposed to what I believe, makes no sense. But the fact is this confusion, as I then thought of it, is an expression of contemporary relativism, a way of thought as widespread as it is lamentable.

There is another and very contemporary way to arrive at this same relativism. As we are often told nowadays, we live in a postmodern era; and postmodernists pride themselves on rejecting the classical foundationalism that we all learned at our mother's knee. . . . According to classical foundationalism, well-founded belief is objective in this sense; at least in principle, any properly functioning human beings who think together about a disputed question with care and good will, can be expected to come to agreement. Well-founded belief is objective in another sense as well: it has to do with, is successfully aimed at, *objects,* things, things in themselves, to borrow a phrase. Well-founded belief is often or usually adequate to the thing; it has an *adequatio ad rem.* There are horses, in the world, and my thought of a given horse is indeed a thought of that horse. Furthermore, it is *adequate* to the horse, in the sense that the properties I take the horse to have are properties it really has. That it has those properties—the ones I take it to have—furthermore, does not depend upon me or upon how I think of it: the horse has those properties on its own account, independent of me or anyone else. My thought and belief is therefore objective in that it is centered upon an object independent of me; it is not directed to something I, as subject, have constructed or in some other way created.

Now what is characteristic of much postmodern thought is the rejection of objectivity in this second sense—often in the name of rejecting objectivity in the first sense. The typical argument for postmodern relativism leaps lightly from the claim that there is no objectivity of the first sort, to the claim that there is none of the second. As you have no doubt noticed, this is a whopping non sequitur; that hasn't curbed its popularity in the least. Classical foundationalism, so the argument runs, has failed: we now see that there is no rational procedure guaranteed to settle all disputes among people of good will; we do not necessarily share starting points for thought, together with forms of argument that are sufficient to settle all differences of opinion. That's the premise. The conclusion is that therefore we can't really think about objects independent of us, but only about something else, perhaps constructs we ourselves have brought into being. Put thus baldly, the argument does not inspire confidence; but even if we put it less baldly, is there really anything of substance here? In any event, by this route too we arrive at the thought that there isn't any such thing as a truth that is independent of us and our thoughts.

. . . However arrived at, it is this relativism that is the second head of the post-positivistic hydra. Clearly this head of the hydra is no more

receptive to Christian thought than the positivistic head it replaced. Contrary to what I used to think, it is vastly more than a mere confusion; it is instead a more or less willful rejection of something that lies very deep in Christian thought. Clearly one of the deepest impulses in Christian thought is the idea that there really is such a person as God, who has established the world a certain way: there really is a correct or right way of looking at things; this is the way God looks at things. Furthermore, things are the way God sees them for everyone, quite independently of what they might think, say, or wish. It is not the case that people can escape being desperately and irremediably wrong about God just by virtue of failing to believe the truth about him. . . .

So these are the hydra heads that have sprung up to replace logical positivism. The first, perennial naturalism, is particularly rampant in the sciences and among those who nail their banners to the mast of science. The second runs riot in the humanities, in literary studies, film studies, law, history, and to some degree in the human sciences. But both are dead opposed to Christian thought; both are wholly inimical to it; both are its sworn enemies. And one important task of the Christian philosopher—that is, of the Christian philosophical community—is consciousness-raising: pointing out that there is this conflict, and testing the spirits. There are a thousand intellectual projects that find their roots in these ways of thinking; we Christians and our children are often heavily influenced by these projects; they are unavoidable because of their widespread dominance; and they often corrupt and compromise the intellectual and spiritual life of the Christian community. It is our task as Christian philosophers to pay careful and determined attention to the way in which such projects are related to Christian thought.

## Christian Philosophy

But in waxing thus hortatory, I am getting a bit ahead of myself. I should like now to turn more directly to my assignment, which was to make some remarks about how I see the accomplishments and tasks of Christian philosophy at this point in our history; this will be connected with the above exhortation. The first thing to note, of course, is that there are several different parts, several different divisions to Christian philosophy. As I see it, there are essentially four different divisions: apologetics, both negative and positive, philosophical theology, Christian philosophical criticism, and constructive Christian philosophy. The philosophers of the Christian community have done better by some of these, during our century, than by others. Suppose we briefly take them each in turn.

## NEGATIVE APOLOGETICS

Roughly speaking, negative apologetics is the attempt to defend Christian belief against the various sorts of attacks that have been brought against it: the argument from evil, for example, or the claim that science has somehow shown Christian belief wanting. But . . . [i]f all thought has religious roots, then the thing to say about attacks on Christianity is just that they too have religious roots—non-Christian religious roots; thus they do not require an answer. Faith cannot reason with unbelief: it can only preach to it. . . .

Of course negative apologetics can also be useful for those who are not in the Christian community, but perhaps on its edges, perhaps thinking about joining it. And it can also be useful for those who are not on the edges but adamantly opposed to the Christian truth; perhaps once they really see just how weak their arguments really are, they will be moved closer to it.

Well, how has negative apologetics fared during our century? Reasonably well, I think, but not as well as one might hope. What sorts of considerations and objections really do trouble thoughtful Christians—students and others? No doubt several, but among the more important, during our century, I think, have been (1) the positivistic claim that Christianity really makes no sense; (2) the argument from evil, which is a sort of perennial concern of Christian apologetics; (3) the heady brew served up by Freud, Marx, Nietzsche, and other masters of suspicion; and (4) pluralistic considerations: given that there

are all these different religions in the world, isn't there something at least naïve and probably worse, in doggedly sticking with Christianity? Positivism, the first of these four, has by now crawled back into the woodwork; but I am sorry to say Christian apologetics cannot claim much of the credit. Far too many Christian philosophers were thoroughly intimidated by the positivistic onslaught, suspecting that there must be much truth to it, and suggesting various unlikely courses of action. Some thought we should just give up; others said, for example, that we should concede that Christianity is in fact nonsense, but insist that it is important nonsense; still others proposed that we continue to make characteristically Christian utterances, but mean something wholly different by them, something that would not attract the wrath of the positivists. This was not a proud chapter in our history, but since positivism is no longer with us, we shall avert our eyes from the unhappy spectacle and move on.

Turning to the second item on the list, there has been a good deal of work on the argument from evil, and in fact it is now, as opposed to forty years ago, rather rare for an atheologian to claim that there is a contradiction between the claim that there is a wholly good, all-powerful, all-knowing God, on the one hand, and the existence of evil on the other. This is due in large part to the efforts of Christian philosophers. Those atheologians who now press the argument from evil must resort to the *probabilistic* argument from evil: given all the evil the world contains, it is unlikely, improbable, that there is a wholly good, all-powerful, and all-knowing God. This argument is much messier, much more complicated, and much less satisfactory from the point of view of the objector. In other ways, however, this probabilistic argument is more realistic and perhaps more disturbing. Christian philosophers—William Alston and Peter van Inwagen, for example—have done good work here, but much remains to be done.[1]

[1] William Alston, "The Inductive Argument from Evil and the Human Cognitive Condition," and Peter van Inwagen, "The Problem of Evil, the Problem of Air, and the Problem of Silence," both in *Philosophical Perspectives #5: Philosophy of Religion, 1991.* Alston, pp. 29–67; van Inwagen,

Christian philosophers haven't done as well, I think, in defusing the sorts of objections offered by those masters of suspicion—Freud, with his claim that religious belief stems from a cognitive process aimed at psychological comfort rather than the truth, Marx and his claim that religious belief really results from cognitive malfunction consequent upon social malfunction, and Nietzsche with his shrilly strident claims to the effect that Christianity arises from and results in a sort of weak, sniveling, envious, and thoroughly disgusting sort of character. There are many who do not accept the details of what any of these three say, but nonetheless entertain the sneaking suspicion that there is something to these charges and that something like them might be true. Christian apologists must forthrightly and honestly address these doubts and these arguments, although in fact argument is hard to find in these thinkers.

Finally, pluralist objections too trouble many Christians, especially Christian academics and others who are acutely aware of some of the other major religions of the world. This is something of a new or revitalized worry for the Christian community; as a result we have just begun to work at it and think about it. But I venture to predict that these pluralist objections will loom large in the next segment of our adventure as Christians.

## POSITIVE APOLOGETICS

. . . First, theistic arguments can obviously be of value for those who don't already believe; they can move them closer to belief, and can bring it about that belief in God is at any rate among the live options for them. Only God bestows saving faith, of course, but his way of doing so can certainly involve cooperation with his children, as in preaching and even argumentation. But second,

pp. 135–65. [Editor's Note: These two papers have recently been reprinted, along with several other recent, significant works on the subject, in Daniel Howard-Snyder, ed., *The Evidential Argument from Evil* (Bloomington: Indiana University Press, 1996).]

theistic arguments can also be useful for *believers.* Calvin notes that believers struggle constantly with doubts; in this life, he says (as we saw above), "faith is always mixed with unbelief" and ". . . in the believing mind certainty is mixed with doubt . . ." (*Institutes,* III, ii, par. 18). At times the truth of the main lines of the gospel seems as certain and sure that there is such a country as the Netherlands; at other times you wake up in the middle of the night and find yourself wondering whether this whole wonderful Christian story is really anything more than just that: a wonderful story. Theistic arguments can be helpful here. Perhaps you accept (as I do) an argument to the effect that there could be no such thing as genuine moral obligation, if naturalism were true and there were no such person as God; perhaps it is also obvious to you that moral obligation is real and important; these thoughts can help dispel the doubt. Perhaps you think, as I do, that there could be no such thing as genuinely horrifying evil if there were no God; but you are also convinced that the world is full of horrifying evil; again, these thoughts can dispel the doubt. Perhaps, more abstractly, you think there could be no such thing as propositions, the things that are true or false, that stand in logical relations and that can be believed or disbelieved, if there were no such person as God; but you also find yourself convinced that there are such things as propositions; again, this thought can dispel the doubt, increase your confidence and repose.

How has positive apologetics (which I shall think of as just the effort to develop and provide theistic arguments) fared in the twentieth century? On the whole, I think, not well. Some Thomists have thought themselves committed to Thomas's view that the existence of God is provable, but they haven't for the most part thought that they could produce the arguments. . . .

But much more can and should be done. There are really a whole host of good theistic arguments, all patiently waiting to be developed in penetrating and profound detail. This is one area where contemporary Christian philosophers have a great deal of work to do. There are arguments from the existence of good and evil, right and wrong, moral obligation; there is an argument from the existence of horrifying evil, from intentionality and the nature of propositions and properties, from the nature of sets and numbers, from counterfactuals, and from the apparent fine-tuning of the universe. There is the ontological argument, but also the more convincing teleological argument, which can be developed in many ways. There is an argument from the existence of contingent beings, and even an argument from colors and flavors. There are arguments from simplicity, from induction, and from the falsehood of general skepticism. There is a general argument from the reliability of intuition, and also one from Kripke's Wittgenstein. There is an argument from the existence of *a priori* knowledge, and one from the causal requirement in knowledge. There are arguments from love, beauty, play and enjoyment, and from the perceived meaning of life. There are arguments from the confluence of justification and warrant, from the confluence of proper function and reliability, and from the existence, in nature, of organs and systems that function properly. (So far as I can see, there is no naturalistic account or analysis of proper function.) These arguments are not apodictic or certain; nevertheless they all deserve to be developed in loving detail; and each of them will be of value both as a theistic argument, and also as a way of thinking about the relation between God and the specific sort of phenomenon in question. I believe Christian philosophers of the next century (not to mention the remainder of this one) should pay a great deal more attention to theistic argument.

## PHILOSOPHICAL THEOLOGY

A second element of Christian philosophy: *philosophical theology.* This is a matter of thinking about the central doctrines of the Christian faith from a philosophical perspective; it is a matter of employing the resources of philosophy to deepen our grasp and understanding of them. Philosophical theology, of course, has been the stock-in-trade of Christian philosophers and theologians from the very beginning; think of Augustine's

great work on the Trinity, for example. At present, this enterprise is faring rather well, perhaps even flourishing; the last few years have seen a remarkable flurry of activity in philosophical theology as pursued by Christian philosophers. There is important work on the divine attributes: for example, the classic Stump-Kretzmann work on God's eternity and Nicholas Wolterstorff's work on God's everlastingness and his arguments against divine impassability. There is Brian Leftow's fine pair of books *Time and Eternity* and *Divine Ideas,* and Edward Wierenga's *The Nature of God.*[2] There has been excellent work on divine simplicity over the last 15 years—probably more work, in Anglo-American philosophy, at any rate, than there had been during the preceding 150 years—as well as on God's action in the world and the central doctrines of Original Sin, Incarnation, and Atonement. There has been fine work on freedom, foreknowledge, and middle knowledge. Of course not everyone is unreservedly enthusiastic about this work; some theologians seem to harbor the impression that philosophical theology as pursued by contemporary philosophers is often unduly ahistorical and uncontextual. Sometimes this arises from the thought that any concern with the above topics is ahistorical; those topics belong to another age and can't properly be discussed now. That seems to me historicism run amok; but no doubt some of this work could profit from closer contact with what theologians know. Still, the theologians don't seem to be doing the work in question. I therefore hope I will not be accused of interdisciplinary chauvinism if I point out that the best work in philosophical theology—in the English-speaking world and over the last quarter cen-

---

[2] Eleonore Stump and Norman Kretzmann, "Eternity," *Journal of Philosophy* 78 (1981): 429–58; Nicholas Wolterstorff, "God Everlasting," in C. Orlebeke and L. Smedes, editors, *God and the Good* (Grand Rapids: Eerdmans, 1975); Brian Leftow, *Time and Eternity* (Ithaca: Cornell University Press, 1991) and *Divine Ideas* (Ithaca: Cornell University Press, 1994); Edward Wierenga, *The Nature of God: An Inquiry into Divine Attributes* (Ithaca: Cornell University Press, 1989).

tury—has been done not by theologians but by philosophers.

## CHRISTIAN PHILOSOPHICAL CRITICISM

We come now to Augustinian Christian philosophy more precisely and narrowly so-called. This has two parts: Christian philosophical criticism, on the one hand, and, on the other, positive Christian philosophy. . . .

It is of the first importance that Christian philosophers engage in Christian philosophical and cultural criticism. This is true, of course, not just for philosophers, but for Christian intellectuals generally and especially for Christian intellectuals working in the humanities and the human sciences. But here we are concerned specifically with philosophy. We must take a careful look at the various projects and research programs we encounter: how are they related to Christianity? And we find, I think, that an astonishing proportion of them, when we examine them closely, spring out of the soil of perennial naturalism or creative anti-realism. I don't have the space here to give anything like a properly representative sample: let me just call your attention, then, to contemporary philosophy of mind. In the United States, philosophy of mind is really one part of a larger project that includes cognitive science, in particular certain parts of psychology, computer science, artificial intelligence, certain developments in epistemology, and more. It is thus an enormous project that involves several different disciplines and thousands of scholars. And it is fundamentally materialist in origin: its aim is to understand the basic phenomena of mind—intentionality or aboutness, consciousness, qualia, affect, and the like—in materialistic and naturalistic terms.

Now how should the Christian community think about this project? How does it fit in with the fact that God, who is not a material object, has knowledge (knows each of us), intentionality (he thinks about his creatures), affect (he loved the world so much that he sent his only begotten son to suffer and die, thereby redeeming us), and so on? Can Christian philosophers properly and in good conscience join these projects? What, if anything, can we learn from them? What stance should we take towards them?

. . . It is the job of the Christian philosophical community to carefully study these projects, claims, and positions, so that their relationship to Christian ways of thought is made evident. And this is not important just for Christian philosophers, but for the spiritual health and welfare of the Christian community.

## CONSTRUCTIVE CHRISTIAN PHILOSOPHY

I come finally to the fourth and last division of Christian philosophy, constructive Christian philosophy. This is, I think, clearly the most difficult of the four; it requires more creativity and intellectual suppleness, more insight and discernment than we can easily muster. But it is also in some ways the most important, and I'd like to emphasize that it is important to *do* this, not merely talk about how we ought to do it, how we might do it, what the best way of doing it might be, what will happen if we do it, what will happen if we don't, what the various theories of doing it are, and so on. An occupational hazard of academics is just that: *talking about* things, even things that themselves are essentially a matter of thinking and talking, instead of actually getting in there and doing them. That would be serious error: we must do it, and not merely talk about it. But what is it I say we must do? Here the aim is to consider the various questions philosophers ask and answer, and to answer these questions from an explicitly Christian or theistic perspective, taking advantage, in attempting to answer them, of all that we know, including what we know as Christians.

. . . There are questions that philosophers of all persuasions try to answer: how shall we understand morality, art, religion, humor, abstract objects, science? What is knowledge? What is meaning; how do terms get meaning, and what do they have when they have it? Do we think in terms of properties that we predicate of objects, or does thought and speech go on in some other way? How far does human freedom extend? What *is* freedom? These and a thousand other topics are among the topics the Christian philosophical community should address, and address from a distinctively and unabashedly Christian point of view. At one level, therefore, the Christian philosopher shares concerns, questions, and topics with his non-Christian colleagues. But he answers those questions differently, and, at another level, answers different questions. We might say (to borrow another phrase) that the Christian philosopher must be *in* the world, but not *of* the world. And this can be a cause of perplexity; it makes it hard to know just how to proceed; it gives us a hard row to hoe, or to change the metaphor, a faint trail to follow, with many opportunities for going wrong and winding up in a thicket. We are to be *in* the world: what this means, in this context, is that at certain levels we are engaged in the same philosophical projects as everyone else. We want to know how to understand ourselves and our world; this means we want to understand the topics just listed. But we are not to be *of* the world; this means that our way of understanding these things will inevitably differ from that of those who don't share our basic commitment to the Lord. These differences may sometimes be subtle, and of course may vary widely from area to area. . . .

So we contribute to the human philosophical conversation, but make our own distinctive contribution, a contribution that must be integral in the sense that it does not compromise basic Christian commitments, and does not compromise with ways of thinking that comport ill with Christian thought. But there is another way in which we are in but not of the world. A Christian epistemologist will of course give an account of the basic cognitive faculties with which the Lord has created us: perception, memory, moral knowledge, reason (the faculty of *a priori* knowledge and belief), sympathy or *Einfühlung* (whereby we understand the thoughts and feelings of another), testimony (whereby we learn

from others), induction (whereby we learn from experience), the ensemble of processes involved in scientific knowledge, and all the rest. So far, we might say, our account is in the world, in that the naturalist will want to give an account—perhaps a very different account—of all or some of the very same things. And, as I say, I think the resources of the Christian scheme of things provide the means for a good account of many departments of this capacious establishment for which satisfying accounts are not available in naturalistic ways of thinking.

But there is still more, and by virtue of this more a Christian epistemologist will not be of the world. For of course she will also want to think about *other* kinds of knowledge, kinds of knowledge that are of great, indeed maximal importance to us as Christians: knowledge of God, knowledge of the great truths of the gospel, as Jonathan Edwards calls them, knowledge of how we can have access to our only comfort in life and in death, and knowledge of how we can achieve our chief end of glorifying God and enjoying him forever. A Christian epistemologist will keep her eye on these things as she develops her epistemology. She will want to develop an epistemology that fits these things especially well; she won't be satisfied with an account onto which these things have to be grafted as ill-fitting afterthoughts. Here she may, once more, diverge from her unbelieving colleagues, who will see all of this as a manifestation not of knowledge but of superstition and error; here she is not of the world. . . .

But of course sin and its effects throw a monkey wrench into this machinery. We are inclined to gauge the rationality of a given belief relative to a given set of circumstances by thinking about what we or someone wiser than we would think in those circumstances; but if the operation of our faculties is compromised by sin, this procedure is at best tenuous and chancy. In this connection we circle back to an item of apologetics: the probabilistic argument from evil. According to the best versions of this argument, a properly functioning human being who is fully aware of the horrifying evils the world contains will be disinclined, or less inclined, to believe that the world is in fact under the control of a wholly good, all-powerful, and all-knowing person. It is therefore a defeater, and a powerful defeater, for theistic belief. But is this correct? What, in fact, would a wholly rational person, i.e., someone with a properly functioning Sensus Divinitatis, think, confronted with the evils our world contains? Presumably she would have an intimate, detailed, vivid, and explicit knowledge of God; she would have an intense awareness of his presence, glory, goodness, power, perfection; she would be as convinced of God's existence as of her own. She might therefore be *puzzled* by the existence of this evil in God's world, but the idea that perhaps there just *wasn't* any such person as God would no doubt not so much as cross her mind. Does it follow that the existence of horrifying evil is not for us a defeater, not even a defeated defeater, not even a defeater at all, of theistic belief? . . .

These are some of the questions: of course there are many more. My point has not been to catalog all the questions, but to illustrate a way in which the Christian philosopher is in but not of the world. The Christian epistemologist offers an account of knowledge, thus joining a human project with roots that antedate Christianity. But if she does things right, she will not automatically accept currently popular accounts; she will offer one of her own, one that arises naturally out of her Christian way of thinking about the world. This account should be superior to those offered by naturalists, and may also seem so to others, even to nontheists, thus serving as something like a theistic argument. Her account will of course be designed to fit and illuminate the kinds of knowledge we all have in common: perception, memory, reason, and the like; she is thus in the world. But it will also be designed and perhaps specially designed to fit and illuminate kinds of knowledge her unbelieving compatriot will dismiss: our knowledge of God, of the great truths of the gospel, and of how to appropriate the latter for our own lives; she is thus not of the world.

These are some of the ways in which the Christian philosopher will be in but not of the world. There is still another way, perhaps the most important way, one that a Christian philosopher neglects at great peril. For a Christian philosopher is first of all a Christian and only secondarily a philosopher. Her philosophy is her specific way of working out her vocation as a Christian; but then to be a proper Christian philosopher, she must be a proper Christian. This means that all of her thought and activity will be shaped and formed by the traditional ways in which we Christians try to make progress in the Christian life: prayer, Bible reading, taking part in the sacraments, associating with other Christians for fellowship and edification. Those who neglect these things are cutting off the source and root of their being as Christian philosophers.

## Conclusion

Christian philosophy at the end of the twentieth century is doing rather well along some dimensions, less well along others. And of course its work of properly relating to the Civitas Mundi is never done: as the latter constantly changes, so must the Christian response. . . . But the Christian philosophical community must also offer its own accounts of the main philosophical topics and concerns. . . . This task is challenging, formidable, difficult, frustrating; it is also fascinating, beguiling, fulfilling. Most of all, it is the service we Christian philosophers owe to the Lord and our community. I commend it to you.

## Study Questions

1. Do you think that arguments for the existence of God are contrary to the idea that our belief in God is based on faith and not reason? If not, what do you consider the relationship between faith and reason to be? Explain.

2. How does the ontological argument claim to prove the existence of God? Does the fact that it isn't based on experience of the world matter?

3. What are St. Thomas Aquinas's arguments for the existence of God? Some have argued that while one may doubt one or two of the arguments, taken together they seem highly compelling. Do you agree? Does the fact that he offers five distinct arguments indicate a lack of certainty on his part about the validity of any one of them taken individually? Or, do all five constitute a formidable case for the existence of God?

4. Philosophers and theologians developed arguments for the existence of God in a time when Christianity was widely practiced. In those days, publicly expressing doubt would likely to have led to one's imprisonment or execution. Therefore, these arguments were not exactly given to prove the existence of God; rather, they were assurances for what most people already accepted. Given our contemporary North American culture, where atheism is not a crime, should we think differently about the efficacy of these arguments?

5. Philosophers have argued that even if the arguments for the existence of God succeed, one still has not proved the Deity to be the God of Christianity (or Islam or Hinduism, for that matter). As a religious believer, how would you respond to this objection?

6. Philosophers have argued that the existence of God is somehow incompatible with the presence of evil in the world. Are the two mutually exclusive? If not, how do you reconcile the existence of God with evil in the world?

7. If, as an atheist or agnostic, you think that belief in an all-good, all-powerful God is incompatible with the presence of evil, how do you account for evil in the world? Is "evil" a word that, derived from religion, only makes sense within a religious context? An atheist or agnostic can call things terrible and wrong, but can he or she say it is "evil"?

8. *Case Study:* Suppose you're a devout believer. You pray every day for the well-being of your friends and family, and never miss a Sunday church service. One day while you and your girlfriend (or boyfriend), whom you love very much, are crossing the street, an inattentive driver talking on a cell phone roars around the corner and strikes your loved one, killing him (or her) instantly. How could a good God allow such a tragedy? Should the fact that you're a practicing theist allow you to expect special treatment from God, if he exists? Can the idea that God gave us freedom of will explain evils such as this? Is this a more reasonable a conclusion than atheism?

9. After reading Anselm, Aquinas, Hume, and Nietzsche, which philosopher do you think has a better understanding of the existence and nature of God? Can we say that their respective grounds for or against religious belief are a product of their personal styles or of different arguments?

10. What do you think of the expensive churches in our cities? Do you think that this is money well spent? Do these questions reflect at all on the truthfulness of the Christian message? Can one be rich and still be a good Christian?

11. Do you think that God as understood by Christianity is an ethical being? What do you think of the Russian novelist Dostoevsky's claim that "Without God, everything is permitted"?

12. Compare the design argument (as presented by Cleanthes in Hume's *Dialogues*) with the ontological argument (as seen in Anselm). Is it fair to say that the former is more solidly grounded in everyday experience, whereas the latter is too abstract? Why or why not?

13. What are some of Philo's arguments against Cleanthes' design argument in Hume's *Dialogues?* Is his skepticism concerning the presuppositions of religious belief well founded?

14. In the *Dialogues,* Philo says that on a planet of spiders God would be seen as a giant spider. What does this have to say about how contemporary religions view the Deity, for example, as an elderly man with a long white beard?

15. How does Philo present the problem of evil in the *Dialogues?* What is Cleanthes' reply to this problem? Is Philo right in thinking that the moral problems surrounding religious

belief are more difficult for theists to deal with than the metaphysical ones, for example, the design argument?

16. What is the main argument Hume gives against our believing in the reality of miracles? What four secondary reasons does he back this argument up with in Part 2 of the *Essay on Miracles?* Can you think of any way around Hume's argument?

17. When Nietzsche said that God was dead, what sense can you make of his claim?

18. What did Nietzsche mean when he said there was only one Christian and he died on the cross?

19. Is Nietzsche right to think that the "good" God of the Christians is a "descending type" in the history of the deities that human beings have worshipped, a sign of decadence?

20. Is Nietzsche right to think that it is more ennobling to create our own values in a god-less world, or are theists right to think that we need a good God to have a firm foundation for our moral codes?

21. Some philosophers have argued that since the Holocaust belief in God is impossible. Do you think that atrocities such as the Holocaust are incompatible with belief in God? Why or why not?

22. What are the main explanations of evil given by Christian philosophers according to Johnson? Does he effectively defeat these arguments?

23. What does Hick mean by "soul-making"? Does he adequately explain the presence of evil in the world? Do we really need evil in order to foster our moral development?

24. Can we really expect a good God to prevent all evil, whether natural or human? If a thief is about to steal money from you, does it make sense that a good God will intervene to stop him?

25. What two general forces does Plantinga see as opposing contemporary Christian thought? What is his advice to Christian philosophers to defend against them? Can you see any flaws in this advice?

# *Bibliography*

## GENERAL

Hick, John. *Philosophy of Religion.* 4th ed. Englewood Cliffs, NJ: Prentice-Hall, 1990. An excellent short introduction by a well-known philosopher of religion.

Stewart, David, ed. *Exploring the Philosophy of Religion.* 4th ed. Upper Saddle River, NJ: Prentice-Hall, 1998. A useful reader/textbook with selections from many classical and modern sources. Considerably thinner than Stump and Murray's volume.

Stump, Eleonore, and Michael J. Murray, eds. *The Philosophy of Religion: The Big Questions.* Oxford: Blackwell, 1999. A substantial reader containing fifty-three selections divided into seven sections based on questions to do with (1) God's nature, (2) whether we can rationally prove his existence, (3) the problem of evil, (4) the relationship between faith and reason, (5) the validity of religious doctrines and practices, (6) morality and religion, and (7) the relation of gender and ethnic diversity to religious thinking. A solid collection of essays and excerpts from longer works.

Yandell, Keith E. *Philosophy of Religion: A Contemporary Introduction.* London: Routledge, 1999. This text deals with not only Western monotheistic faiths such as Christianity and Judaism, but also Eastern religions such as Jainism and Buddhism. While it is intended to be an introductory study, his highly analytic approach will make it inaccessible to many students.

## ON ANSELM, AQUINAS, AND ARGUMENTS FOR THE EXISTENCE OF GOD

Hick, John. *Arguments for the Existence of God*. London: Macmillan, 1970.

Kretzmann, Norman, and Eleonore Stump, eds. *The Cambridge Companion to Aquinas*. Cambridge: Cambridge University Press, 1993. A fairly rigorous collection of essays on St. Thomas.

Plantinga, Alvin, ed. *The Ontological Argument, from St. Anselm to Contemporary Philosophers*. Garden City, NY: Anchor, 1965. A collection of essays for and against Anselm's argument.

Plantinga, Alvin. *God and Other Minds: A Study of the Rational Justification of Belief in God*. Ithaca, NY: Cornell University Press, 1990. A defense of arguments for the existence of God from a Christian evangelical.

## ON KIERKEGAARD, HUME, AND NIETZSCHE

Gaskin, J. C. A. *Hume's Philosophy of Religion*. 2nd ed. London: Macmillan, 1988.

Hume, David. *The Natural History of Religion*. In Anthony Flew, ed., *David Hume: Writings on Religion*. Chicago: Open Court, 1992. The third of Hume's important works on the philosophy of religion in which he lays out a philosophical history or "sociology" of religious belief as it moved from polytheism to monotheism. Hume is once again skeptical about the value of religion, but certainly seems to favor paganism over the belief in the one God. Flew's collection contains all of Hume's work on religion, including his essay on suicide. A must have for serious students of Hume.

Kierkegaard, Søren. *Fear and Trembling*. Trans. Alastair Hannay. Harmondsworth: Penguin, 1985. One of Kierkegaard's shorter and more accessible works in which he foregrounds the story of Abraham and Isaac as a parable of faith for the modern religious believer.

Nietzsche, Friedrich. *The Antichrist*. Trans. Walter Kaufmann. In *The Portable Nietzsche*. New York: Viking Press, 1977. Nietzsche's direct assault on Christianity and its psychology of pity.

Palmer, Donald D. *Kierkegaard for Beginners*. New York: Writers & Readers, 1996. A comics-and-text that introduces one to the great Dane's ideas in a highly palatable way.

Yandell, Keith E. *Hume's "Inexplicable Mystery": His Views on Religion*. Philadelphia : Temple University Press, 1990.

*Also see Chapters 3 and 4 for more on Hume, and Chapter 5 for more on Nietzsche.*

## THE CONTEMPORARY PHILOSOPHY OF RELIGION

Alston, William P. *Perceiving God: The Epistemology of Religious Experience*. Ithaca, NY: Cornell University Press, 1991. Alston is an analytic philosopher who believes that religious belief can be founded in ordinary experience of the world, and thus that we can "perceive" God.

Broad, C. D. *Religion, Philosophy and Psychical Research*. New York: Harcourt, Brace & Company, 1953. Broad is interested in the scientific evidence or lack thereof for paranormal and supernatural phenomena.

Buber, Martin. *I and Thou*. Trans. Ronald Gregor Smith. New York: Scribner's, 2000. Buber argues that we can build a mystical connection to God by first connecting intimately to others.

Flew, Anthony. *God: A Critical Inquiry.* La Salle, IL: Open Court, 1984. One of Flew's numerous books and collections of essays in defense of atheism.

Lewis, C. S. *Mere Christianity.* San Francisco: Harper, 2000. Radio talks given over the BBC during World War II by the author of *The Chronicles of Narnia.* Lewis calmly and simply defends Christianity as a living faith without denominational boundaries.

Murray, Michael J. *Reason for the Hope Within.* Grand Rapids, MI: Wm. B. Eerdmans Publishing, 1998. A collection of essays on philosophical theology and the philosophy of religion from a distinctly Christian perspective.

Russell, Bertrand. *Why I Am Not a Christian.* London: Allen & Unwin, 1985. Russell's famous attack on Christianity from the prime mover of analytic philosophy.

## SOME CLASSICS IN THE EASTERN PHILOSOPHY OF RELIGION

*Although our text doesn't include any work from Eastern philosophy, some of the texts from India, China, and other parts of Asia have been tremendously influential on Western spirituality. Here are some of these classics in modern translations and some reference works to get you started.*

*The Upanishads.* A collection of ancient Indian religious verse, some of which may date back to 1500 BC. Their central doctrine is "Brahman is Atman, and Atman is Brahman," or, in other words, our individual souls are part of the cosmos, and the cosmos is our soul writ large. Seek out the translation by Eknath Easwaran (Berkeley: Nilgiri Press, 1987).

*The Bhagavad Gita.* This ancient Indian epic poem featuring the god Krishna's sagely advice to Arjuna during a battle lays out some of the spiritual presuppositions of Hinduism. Geoffey Parrinder (Oxford: One World, 1996) offers a verse translation with a running commentary alongside the text.

Lao Tzu (or Tsu). *Tao Te Ching.* The founding document of Taoism, the philosophy of the way of inner peace and unity with nature from ancient China. The Gia-Fu Feng and Jane English edition (New York, Vintage Books, 1997), with English's striking black and white photographs, is a solid translation, along with being an excellent adornment to one's coffee table.

Confucius (K'ung Fu-Tzu). *Analects.* The very practical sayings of the ancient Chinese sage known to the West as Confucius. A complete and attractively printed version is edited by David Hinton (Washington: Counterpoint, 1998).

Rahula, Walpola. *What the Buddha Taught.* 2nd ed. New York: Grove Press, 1978. An introduction to Buddhism by a Theravada (traditional) Buddhist monk.

Thich Nhat Hann. *Being Peace.* Berkeley: Parallax Press, 1987. A modern classic written by a Vietnamese Zen Buddhist teacher written in a clear and simple language. A good first book for a budding student of Buddhism and for troubled souls of all stripes.

Powell, James. *Eastern Philosophy for Beginners.* New York: Writers and Readers, 2000. A fairly detailed comics-and-text treatment of the classical philosophies of India, China, Japan, and Tibet.

Osborne, Richard, and Borin Van Loon. *Introducing Eastern Philosophy.* Cambridge: Icon Books, 1996. Another comics-and-text introduction to Eastern thought, not quite as detailed as Powell's.

# Mind, Body, and Self

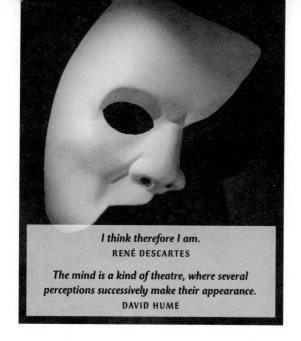

> *I think therefore I am.*
> RENÉ DESCARTES
>
> *The mind is a kind of theatre, where several perceptions successively make their appearance.*
> DAVID HUME

# PART I   THE MIND/BODY PROBLEM

## THE MYSTERIOUS CASE OF THE MIND AND THE BODY

### What Is Metaphysics?

Metaphysics, as you may recall from the Introduction and Chapter 1, means literally "that which is after or beyond physics," referring to the title given by Aristotle's ancient editor to the book he edited after putting together the *Physics*. It is that part of philosophy that deals with such fundamental questions as the nature of reality or being, the existence or nonexistence of God, the relationship between the mind and the body, the nature of the self, human freedom, and the meaning of life. We've already had a look at the philosophy of religion in Chapter 2. In this chapter we'll examine two more central metaphysical issues: the mind/body problem and the nature of the self. Along the way we'll also shed some light on a number of other metaphysical questions: What is truth? Are human beings free or determined? Do our lives have meaning?

### The Great Metaphysical Detective

The mind/body problem is a perplexing metaphysical conundrum, a case that might have baffled a Sherlock Holmes or a Hercule Poirot if they had taken up philosophical speculation. As you sit here reading this text, just what are you? A soul encased in a physical body? An animal that has developed self-consciousness after millions of years of evolution? A physical organism whose motions and behavior are regulated by a very complex supercomputer we call the human brain? Let's see what sort of questions a great detective might ask to solve this case. In our drama metaphysical you will be playing the role of Jennifer Smith, a young philosophy student who is taking the night off from her arduous studies to watch a romantic comedy on television.

Pretend that you—Jennifer—are sitting on your couch having a glass of wine, watching the classic romantic film *Tuckered out in Toledo.* Just when your favorite scene is about to start and your eyes are welling up with tears, your front door crashes open and an imposing man in a dark trench coat bursts in. "Who are you?" you demand.

"Don't be alarmed, young lady. I'm the Great Metaphysical Detective. But you can call me Meta."

"What do you want, Meta?"

"I want to know just one thing—what are you?"

"I'm Jennifer Smith," you reply.

"So you're Jennifer Smith. Does this entirely define your being?"

"Sure," you reply hesitatingly.

"I see. But what if your parents had decided to name you Tiffany instead of Jennifer? What if you got married and took your husband's last name? Would you be an entirely new person?"

"Of course not. I see what you're driving at. My *name* is Jennifer Smith, yet what I really am is much more. I'm the person sitting on a couch watching TV, drinking wine. I'm also the person who went to the doctor's yesterday because I have the flu. I'm the person with red hair, who's 21 years old, and who is 5′ 6″ tall. Does this answer your question?"

"Yes, in a manner of speaking. So what you're saying is that what you really are is a set of physical properties that change over time. So if I were to tell someone that Jennifer Smith has red hair, is in her early 20s, and is prone to illness, this would be a complete description of you? There would be nothing more to say in the matter? And further, if your physical properties changed—say you dyed your hair black—you would be a new person?"

You think for a while, then realize that you've overlooked something important. "Wait a minute," you reply, warming to your dialogue with the great detective, "there's something I missed. I'm also all the thoughts and feelings I've ever had, including those I'm having right now."

"Ah, I see. You're a collection of physical properties somehow connected to a series of thoughts and feelings. There's just one more thing I'd like to know: How are these physical properties related to your thoughts and feelings?"

"Elementary, my dear Meta. My physical properties are part of my body, while my thoughts and feelings exist in my mind. My mind is in my brain, but separate from it."

"In your brain? What does this mean?" queried Meta. "You mean you have a mind separate from your body? What happens when your body gets sick—doesn't it affect your thoughts, too? Maybe it makes you sad or depressed?"

"Well, I suppose it does . . . ," you reply, biting your lip in trepidation at the realization that metaphysics wasn't as easy as you first thought.

"Further, Ms. Smith," continued Meta, "How exactly does your mind plug into your body—through your brain? If so, how can a spiritual or mental thing connect to a physical thing? And what happens when you die—does your mind float away from your brain to some celestial realm? Is this a physical place, or a purely spiritual plane of being?"

"Hmmm . . . ," you think. "Maybe this isn't so elementary after all."

## Positions on the Mind/Body Problem

The mind/body problem, as featured in our little drama above, is indeed a difficult knot to unravel. There's been a number of serious attempts to solve it in modern Western philosophy, with Descartes' dualism being the first and probably most famous one.

Fortunately, we have some obvious facts to deal with. We can be pretty sure that we have physical bodies that have various properties or states: volume, mass, heat, cold, health, sickness, and so on. Further, we all have brains, extremely complex physical structures in our heads that seem to be the seat of thought. It's also quite clear that we are conscious, that we think and have feelings, and that these "mental states" are somehow connected to our physical state—for example, when we're sick or fatigued we can't think as clearly—yet at the same time are separate from them— I can imagine dinosaurs or rocket ships or the city of Paris without being anywhere near any of these. So how exactly how are these "physical states" connected to these "mental states"? That is the central question addressed in the mind/body problem.

The following chart outlines all the major theories of the relationship between the mind and the body discussed by modern Western thinkers. "Monist" theories argue there is basically only one thing or substance in us, and that it's either physical or mental or a combination of both. "Dualist" theories argue that there are two such substances. I've also included a prognosis of the health of each theory to indicate just how seriously each is taken by the living philosophical community.* The theories are listed in the rough order of the impact they've made on contemporary metaphysics.

| MIND/BODY THEORY | TYPE | PROGNOSIS | CENTRAL CLAIMS |
|---|---|---|---|
| 1. Materialism, or Physicalism | Monist | Alive & well | Only bodies and their brains exist. Mental states are somehow reducible to physical states. The "soul" or "mind" is just an illusion. Comes in many varieties. |
| *Major Types:* | | | |
| a. Identity Theory, or Reductive Materialism | Monist | Alive & well | Each type of mental state is identical to a type of brain state. One day neurological science will be able to precisely map out this identity (Armstrong, Smart). |
| b. Functionalism/ Anomalous Monism | Quasi-Monist | Alive & well | Functionalism: Mental states are functional states that might be realized in different ways in different organisms (Putnam). Anomalous Monism: Mental states "supervene" upon physical ones, |

* Note that each theory still has at least a few adherents among the living—for one thing, postmodernists are in a way "idealists" in that they emphasize the subjective nature of human experience, and thus throw into question the idea of an objective reality outside of our minds. See Chapters 4 and 9 for more on postmodern ideas about knowledge and reality.

| MIND/BODY THEORY | TYPE | PROGNOSIS | CENTRAL CLAIMS |
|---|---|---|---|
| | | | though they cannot be fully translated into physical descriptions. A "weak" form of materialism (Davidson). |
| c. Eliminative Materialism | Monist | Alive & well | Talk of mental states is folk psychology. As science progresses, we'll eliminate such talk (Churchland). |
| 2. Interactionism | Dualist | Alive & well | Mind and body are separate substances that interact causally. Sometimes referred to as "Cartesian dualism" or simply "dualism" (Descartes). |
| 3. Epiphenomenalism | Monist | Alive & well | The mind is a mere epiphenomenon, or by-product, of physical processes. It does not cause physical actions. |
| 4. Phenomenalism, or "Dual Aspect Theory" | Quasi-Dualist | Alive & well | All we really know are our mental phenomena (Hume). Though physical processes probably cause mental events, there is an irreducible subjective quality to an individual's thought and experience. We don't know what it's like to be a bat (Nagel). |
| 5. The New Mysterians | Unclear | Rare though healthy | Our limited human intellects cannot comprehend how a piece of meat—our brains—could be conscious. Yet we can be sure that strict materialism and dualism are both hopelessly flawed (McGinn). |
| 6. Double Aspect Theory, or Neutral Monism | Monist | Rare though healthy | Mind and body are two distinct aspects of a single neutral substance (Double Aspect: Spinoza; Neutral Monism: James and Russell). |
| 7. Idealism | Monist | Very ill | Only minds and their thoughts exist. Physical things exist only insofar as they are perceived (Berkeley). |
| 8. Parallelism, or Preestablished Harmony | Dualist | Deceased (largely) | Mind and body are separate things, but physical events parallel mental events, perhaps guaranteed by a preestablished harmony (Leibniz). |
| 9. Occasionalism | Dualist | Deceased (largely) | Physical events take place on the same occasion as their corresponding mental events, perhaps guaranteed by God's will (Malebranche). |

## MATERIALISM/PHYSICALISM

Materialists maintain that only bodies and their brains exist. They hold that mental states are somehow reducible to physical states, and the "soul" or "mind" is just an illusion. Materialists, sometimes called "physicalists," believe that the real world contains nothing but matter and energy and that objects only have physical properties, such as spatiotemporal position, mass, size, shape, motion, hardness, electrical charge, magnetism, and gravity. Materialism comes in many varieties.

### *Identity Theory/Reductive Materialism*

Identity theory, also known as reductive materialism, holds that types of mental states are identical to types of brain states. Neurological science will one day be able to precisely map out this identity, just as chemistry has charted the elements of nature in the periodic table found on the walls of university labs. An identity theorist might argue that "love" is a firing of neuron 3369 in our brain, "pain" is a signal sent by a nerve affected by some external stimulus to neuron 7892, and so on. Consciousness is just a name we give to our subjective experience of these physical events.

D. M. Armstrong (1926–) and J. J. C. Smart (1920–), members of the "Australian materialist" school, are the leading exponents of reductionism (although Armstrong is also connected with functionalism). This is the most basic and straightforward form of materialism, but has attracted its fair share of criticism. There are at least two troubling questions that reductionism doesn't seem able to adequately answer: (1) Will we ever be able to make the sort of direct identifications of types of mental and physical states that it predicts? (2) How does materialism take into account the fact that our subjective "qualia" might differ from person to person, for example, the taste of coffee, the look of the color yellow, or the smell of magnolias in the springtime?

### Functionalism/Anomalous Monism

Functionalism argues that mental states are functional states that should be looked at in terms of their causal links to the outside world, including human behavior. This is a new and improved version of Gilbert Ryle's behaviorism, which sees the mind not as a spiritual "ghost in the machine," as he characterizes Descartes' dualist view of the self, but as a collection of dispositions to behave in various ways. For the functionalist these functional states can be physically realized in a variety of ways, but cannot be mapped directly onto their equivalent brain states. For example, when I feel pain, the physical state that it's connected to in my body may be different from the physical state that supports pain in a nonhuman organism. Instead of nerves communicating electrical impulses to my brain, the state of consciousness felt as pain by an alien being might be caused by ripples in a green slimy fluid that fills the alien's body. The American Harvard-trained philosopher Hilary Putnam (1926–) founded functionalism, though of late has moved away from it.

Donald Davidson (1917–) has put forward a solution to the mind/body problem that is quite close to functionalism. His "anomalous monism" argues that mental events "supervene" upon physical ones, but that there are no general psychophysical laws or direct relationships of identity connecting these two types of events. Mental events are "supervenient" upon physical ones in the sense that if two organic beings have exactly the same set of physical properties, they *must* have the same set of mental states. There is no autonomous realm of mental states. However, it doesn't work the other way around: My belief that it's raining outside could be "realized" in my body by several different brain states. This is a "fuzzy" or "weak" form of materialism, basically monist, but with a dualist twist.

### Eliminative Materialism

Eliminative materialists argue that the other schools of materialism are too soft on believers in souls, spirits, and other types of mental substances. We no longer believe in witches, goblins, fairies, animal magnetism, or phlogiston, confining talk about such things to children's books or histories of science. Similarly, one day we'll realize that our talk of mental states such as beliefs, desires, and feelings is part of a folk psychology that has to be eliminated if science is to ever understand our cognitive processes.

Eliminative materialism got started when the American philosophers Paul Feyerabend and Richard Rorty criticized identity theorists for taking mental talk too seriously. Since these theorists argued that our mental states could be identified with our physical states, they gave legitimacy to the talk of mental states. Feyerabend and Rorty argued instead that such mental talk is scientifically sloppy and unsuited to describing the way the brain works. Paul Churchland and Patricia S. Churchland picked up their suggestion and developed eliminative materialism further. Eliminativists like the Churchlands argue that a more scientifically viable language with which to describe brain states will be provided by cognitive science, an amalgam of psychology, neurology, and computer science.

## INTERACTIONISM

This is Descartes' solution to the mind/body problem, which we'll study in detail in his work *The Meditations.* An interactionist is a dualist who believes that mind and body are separate substances that interact causally. There are physical things that operate according to physical laws, and mental things that operate according to their own laws, or are completely free. Sometimes the physical world influences the mental world, as when alcohol impairs our reasoning process, and sometimes the mental world influences physical things, as when I have a desire to go for a walk, which causes my legs to propel me outside and down the street. This position is sometimes referred to as "Cartesian dualism" or simply "dualism," although, strictly speaking, there are several types of dualism of which Descartes' position is only the most well known.

In most cases interactionists are also theists, believers in a supernatural supreme being, who see the mind as more or less the same thing as the soul. They hold that even though the body decays after death, the soul lives on in some sort of afterlife. In fact, it would be difficult to be a theist and *not* to be some sort of dualist: There must be some sort of spiritual substance separate from the physical world for theism to make sense.

This is the view that Gilbert Ryle criticizes in his book *The Concept of Mind.* He accuses Descartes of creating the myth of the "ghost in the machine" with his dualism. The major critique of interactionism has already been made by our great metaphysical detective: How can a physical substance—the body—cause mental events, or a mental thing—the mind—bring about changes in the physical world? Some sort of physical/mental interface seems to be required. Descartes proposed the pineal gland, while some other dualists (see the section on occasionalism, p. 201) proposed the will of God. The effectiveness of both these interfaces is viewed with skepticism by modern science, if not philosophy as a whole.

## EPIPHENOMENALISM

This theory sees the mind as a mere epiphenomenon, or by-product, of physical processes. It has no causal power over physical actions. T. H. Huxley (1825–1895), a proponent of Darwin's theory of evolution, argued that human consciousness was epiphenomenal, the product of mechanical interactions between physical systems in the body. One can understand this view by thinking of an old-fashioned train engine:

The human body (including the brain) is like the wheels, gears, pinions, boiler, and other mechanical parts of the locomotive; the mind is like the steam being emitted by the engine. The steam is real, but doesn't in any way "cause" the train to move forward.

The problem with epiphenomenalism is basically the same as that with interactionism, though cut in half: How can a physical system like the human body create a mental substance or thing like the mind? Materialists would say that the epiphenomenalists have it half right: Their view rightly eliminates the causal power of the mind as a spiritual substance, but wrongly leaves intact the mind as inhabiting a nonphysical realm separate from the body.

## PHENOMENALISM/"DUAL ASPECT THEORY"

Phenomenalism (a term that we've adapted for use here in a slightly different context than usually used by philosophers) can be traced back to David Hume's skepticism. Hume (1711–1776) claimed that all we ever really know are the phenomena in our minds. These are made up of various types of perceptions. We cannot ever know whether these perceptions match external reality, although in our everyday lives we choose to believe that they do out of custom or habit.

This basic suggestion was adapted by Thomas Nagel in his famous article "What Is It Like to Be a Bat?" into a view that he later christened, in his book *The View from Nowhere,* "dual aspect theory." Nagel's position is that the subjective nature of consciousness makes any philosophy of mind that explains mental events by reducing them to physical states inadequate, even though he admits that physical processes probably cause mental events. We only know what it's like to be us; we don't know what it's like to be a bat, or a member of any other species for that matter. We may be able to explain an "alien" perceptual capacity like bats' sonar in purely physical terms, but as human beings we'll never know what it's like to be conscious of a sensory apparatus that warns us of the approach of physical obstacles without being able to see them (as an experiment to prove Nagel's point, turn out all the lights and close all the blinds in your house or apartment after sunset, then run around—you'll be sure to smash into a few walls or pieces of furniture). In short, materialists can explain consciousness only by reducing it to something else, or by eliminating it altogether. Thus, materialism is at best an incomplete solution to the mind/body problem.

## THE NEW MYSTERIANS

This is not a pop group or a collection of crime-fighting superheroes, but a small group of metaphysicians who argue that we cannot solve the mind/body problem since it deals with matters beyond the cognitive powers of the human mind. Our limited human intellects cannot comprehend how a "piece of meat"—our brains—could be conscious. Yet we can be sure that strict materialism and dualism are both hopelessly flawed, for different reasons: the materialists because they have no idea how to map individual mental states onto their corresponding physical states, and the dualists because they can't explain how the mind, a mental system, interfaces with the body, a physical system. The British thinker Colin McGinn (1950–) is the best known of the New Mysterians. He believes that consciousness is a natural, not a supernatural, phenomenon, but we just don't know how it works.

This is an interesting take on the problem, though it, in essence, tells metaphysicians that it's time to close up shop and find another job, which they are unlikely to do. Yet the New Mysterians can appeal to the obvious fact that the mind/body problem remains unsolved after several centuries of work to support their conclusion that it is beyond our powers, at least at present, to solve it.

## DOUBLE ASPECT THEORY/NEUTRAL MONISM

Double aspect theory and neutral monism are really a collection of theories that say more or less the same thing: that mind and body are two aspects of a single underlying substance. Baruch Spinoza (1632–1677) argued that mind and body are two aspects of something that is neither mental nor physical. William James (1842–1919) was a neutral monist who argued that the basic stuff was "pure experience," and that mind and matter were just two different ways that this basic stuff gets organized. Bertrand Russell (1872–1970) followed James's lead, arguing that the basic stuff of the cosmos is neutral, but is organized in bodily form according to physical laws, and in mental form according to psychological laws. This solution of the mind/body problem sounds initially promising; but when we try to figure out just what this "neutral" substance is, and what we can say about it, things become vague and mysterious in a hurry.

## IDEALISM

Bishop George Berkeley (1685–1753), the most well known idealist, argued that only minds and their thoughts exist, and that physical things exist only insofar as they are perceived. Berkeley declared that *esse est percipi,* to exist is to be perceived. If something isn't a perception, an idea in someone's mind, then it doesn't exist. Does that mean that physical objects cease to exist when no one is observing them? Not at all, responded Berkeley: God perceives them (as well as everything else), so they continue to exist.

The obvious flaw in idealism is that the existence of the physical world seems so self-evident to us that it seems strange to claim that its reality depends on our perceiving it. Samuel Johnson, the eighteenth-century literary figure and writer of the first complete English dictionary, is reputed to have once kicked a rock in a fit of frustration and remarked, "I refute Berkeley thus!" Technically, he hadn't, since all Berkeley is claiming is that for something to exist, it must be a perception in someone's mind, so Johnson's rock was just as much an idea in his head as the definitions in his dictionary. Yet the idea that a tree falling in the forest makes a sound even if no one is there to hear it, or that the old gray couch in your living room continues to exist even while you're away on vacation, seems so self-evident that Berkeley's idealism seems a bit silly, at least to the modern mind. That's not to mention the fact that his whole idealist structure tends to collapse if one takes the supreme observer, God, out of the equation—without him, no one can guarantee that *your* perception of a given object will more or less correspond to *my* perception of it.

## PARALLELISM/PREESTABLISHED HARMONY

Parallelism is a form of dualism. Parallelism argues that mind and body are composed of separate substances, but the histories of these substances parallel each other like two railway tracks running alongside each other off into a dimly perceived horizon. So mental states parallel physical states, though they don't ever meet causally. So what guarantees that the histories of minds and bodies perfectly align with each other? G. W. Leibniz (1646–1716) suggested that God has created "a preestablished harmony" between mental and physical events. Naturally, the idea that God has established such a harmony for all time is a bit hard to swallow for at least the more scientifically inclined contemporary philosopher, not to mention the fact that it seems to rob we human beings of our free will.

## OCCASIONALISM

Occasionalism is a dualist theory that claims that physical events take place on the same occasion as their corresponding mental events. So when I think "move arm," my arm moves. How are these two events connected? By God's will. On each and every occasion that a mental event occurs, God intervenes to connect it to its corresponding physical event. Nicolas Malebranche (1638–1715) held this view. This view sounds a bit like the philosophical equivalent of a magician pulling a rabbit out of a hat, and is considered to be a mere historical oddity by modern philosophers of mind.

So the mysterious case of how our minds and bodies are related remains unsolved. We'll explore it in the readings that follow, starting with Descartes' famous defense of dualism in his *Meditations.*

# DESCARTES' DUALISM _____

René Descartes (1595–1650) was a philosopher, scientist, and mathematician. He is known as the "father of modern philosophy" because he launched a devastating attack on medieval scholasticism, with its reliance on the authority of texts, especially Aristotle's, rather than human reason alone. He is also known as the inventor of Cartesian coordinates, the two-dimensional grid system with $x$ and $y$ axes you probably remember from secondary-school math classes.

Descartes' general goal was to create a foundation for philosophical certainty. He was part of the Scientific Revolution of the seventeenth century in which Galileo, Hobbes, Kepler, and others introduced a mechanistic and materialistic view of the universe. Galileo announced confidently that the book of nature was written in the language of mathematics, and tried to read that book with a series of physical experiments. Kepler tried to establish the laws of planetary motion, while Hobbes believed he had created a political science based on the assumption that human beings were matter in motion who had selfish impulses that had to be curbed by the signing of a social contract.

Descartes was a follower of Galileo early on: His book *The World* (finished in 1634) presented a Galilean view of the cosmos. He didn't publish it in his lifetime out of fear of the Church's retribution. Yet his attempt to understand the universe in terms of the "new physics" of Galileo, Kepler, and Hobbes led him to his central metaphysical dilemma: How could this mechanistic and materialistic view of nature be reconciled with God's existence and the independence and freedom of the human soul?

Descartes was born at La Haye, France, and educated at the Jesuit college of La Flèche from 1606 to 1614. He was dubious of his education, which seemed to be full of contradictions, except in mathematics. He received a doctor of law from the University of Poitiers in 1616, but never practiced. In 1618 Descartes went to Holland to serve in the army of the Protestant Dutch Prince Maurice of Nassau, in 1619 moving on to serve in the army of Bavaria. On the night of November 10, 1619, he had a dream that he would create a universal foundation for the sciences. He committed his life to finding this foundation.

From 1619 to 1628 Descartes lived on and off again in Paris, traveling about in Western Europe in the 1620s. November 1628 found him in Paris, where he debated the prominent skeptic Chandoux. From there he quickly moved on to Holland, where he lived until 1649.

In 1638 Descartes published a collection of essays on geometry, optics, and meteors, which he introduced with his famous *Discourse on Method.* The *Discourse* introduced four basic methodological rules for Descartes' new philosophy: (1) Accept only clear and distinct ideas; (2) break up complex questions into a series of simpler ones; (3) begin with the simplest issues, and move on from there; (4) check everything over once finished. He also asserted "I think therefore I am," meaning that the one thing he could be sure of was that he existed as a mental thing, whether or not the physical world existed.

In 1641 *Meditations on First Philosophy* appeared in Latin. It drew much criticism, which Descartes responded to in his *Objections and Replies* in the same year. In it Descartes argued for a rationalist epistemology, a dualist metaphysics of mind and body, and for the existence of an all-powerful, all-good God. He hoped that this work could provide the foundation for the sciences he had dreamed about 22 years earlier.

*The Principles of Philosophy,* his most complete statement of his scientific and philosophical views, appeared in 1644. It discussed both physics and metaphysics, and gave descriptions of the universe and of various earthly phenomena. In it he argued that animals were soulless mechanisms that could be used as we human beings saw fit.

Descartes' last work was *The Passions of the Soul* (1649), which came out of his correspondence with Princess Elizabeth of Bohemia on the question of how the soul and the body, being separate substances, could interact. In this book Descartes proposed that the pineal gland acts as a sort of "interface" between our body's hardware and our mind's software. Bodily sensations travel along our nervous system and up our spinal column to this magical gland, which transforms these physical impulses into a spiritual energy that the mind can process. At death this interface is unplugged, and our soul or mind is free to journey to the hereafter.

In 1649 Descartes went to Sweden to act as Queen Christina's philosophy tutor. He died of pneumonia in February 1650 due to a combination of Sweden's chilly weather and Queen Christina's insistence that Descartes hold his lessons at five o'clock in the morning. At the time of his death, he was famous in France and elsewhere in Europe, even thought of as a sort of philosophical saint.

Descartes' philosophical method echoed that of geometry, moving from one deductively certain axiom or principle to another without relying on the evidence of his senses. Further, he rejected religious authority in favor of that provided by his reason, even though he was a committed Catholic.

The general goal of the *Meditations* is to provide a foundation for philosophy and the sciences that was free from all doubt. In Meditation 1, Descartes starts by doubting everything. He wonders whether everything he's presently thinking is just a dream, even going so far as to pretend that there's an "evil demon" who created the world and who is presently trying to trick him about all his beliefs. He puts himself in a sort of existential anguish to clear away the rubbish of received truths.

After thinking about it for a while, in Meditation 2, Descartes concludes that even if there's an evil demon who rules the world and who deceives him on every conceivable point, there's one thing that he can be sure of: that he exists as a thing that thinks, an *ego cogitans*. After all, what's doing the doubting if it isn't this thinking thing we call our mind? This is his "Archimedean point," the foundation of his temple of scientific certainty. Yet he can't help but feel that he knows the external world, too, so he does an experiment with a piece of wax to investigate the validity of sense-based knowledge. He first observes its properties in its solid state—it's white, smells like flowers, makes a sound if you rap it on the table, and so on. He then places it near the fire to melt it—it's now a gray blob, odorless, soft, and emits no sound if struck. He concludes that even though our senses tell us that the wax in its two different states are different objects, our mental introspection or reason tells us that it's the same wax. In other words, truth comes from the exercise of reason and not from sense experience.

Meditations 3–5 aren't included here because they don't bear directly on the mind/body problem. They focus on proving the existence of God, and thus on providing a foundation for believing that our senses' reports of the external world are more or less accurate. In Meditation 3, Descartes uses the famous (or infamous) ontological argument to prove the existence of God. We have an idea of an all-powerful and all-good being called God. Since we're imperfect, finite beings, this idea couldn't have originated in our minds. It must have come from something greater than us. This greater thing is God. And since to exist is better than not to exist, God must exist.

In Meditation 4, Descartes goes on to argue that since God must exist, and since he's all good, without a mean bone in his spiritual body, he wouldn't trick us about the validity of our reason, if not of the reports given to us by our senses. As long as our ideas are clear and distinct, we can take them to be true. Descartes traces human imperfections to three sources: (1) We can't understand all of God's mysterious ways; (2) if we looked at the structure of the whole universe, and not just our individual faults, imperfection would make more sense; (3) human beings have infinite free will (though not infinite power), so we occasionally get carried away and make mistakes.

In Meditation 5, Descartes concludes that God guarantees the validity of our knowledge of arithmetic and geometrical objects, and of material bodies insofar as they are reflections of geometrical objects. Further, just as we can't imagine a valley without a mountain, we can't imagine God without him actually existing: To his essence belongs existence. So once again, he must exist.

Finally, in Meditation 6, Descartes fleshes out his argument for mind/body dualism. We can know our minds as thinking, nonextended things with certainty, unlike our bodies, which are extended nonthinking things that we can't know with total certainty (though he is finally sure that "corporeal things exist" due to the fact that God is no deceiver). Further, I can clearly and distinctly understand my mind as distinct from my body, and my body is divisible, at least in theory—if I lose a leg or arm, I am still the same person, just minus an appendage. His conclusion is that the mind and the body are distinct things, even though they are closely intermingled. Descartes finishes by trying to account for the fact that our body sometimes gives us false sensory reports or urges us to desire something that's bad for us: The body is a complex machine like a clock that doesn't work as well when damaged (i.e., when we're ill) as when it's intact (i.e., when we're healthy). In addition, since it's so complex, its many connections can sometimes break down. Since we're a combination of *mind* and *body,* we're bound to be misled from time to time.

Descartes' dualism assumes that there are two substances in our universe: one mental, the other physical; the first consisting of thought, the second of extension in space. Each has its own set of properties: The mental substance can reason, feel, and will; the physical substance has shape, size, mass, temperature, and so on. These substances interact in various ways, yet have separate histories. Cartesian "interactionism" accounts nicely for the Christian hope that we have immortal souls that survive our bodily existence to live on in a purer spiritual realm.

There are some clear problems with Descartes' solution to the mind/body problem:

- How do we know that our "clear and distinct" reasoning is certain, especially with the threat of the evil demon hanging over us? Why does Descartes assume that mathematics is a reflection of a higher reality, rather than a conventional set of rules established by fallible human beings?
- Just how do mind and body interact? How does a mental substance affect a physical one and vice versa? After all, Descartes' description of the pineal gland as a sort of mind/body interface has no physiological evidence to support it.
- Can't physical changes in our bodies fundamentally alter our thinking processes? For example, physical fatigue, drugs, alcohol, illness, and brain damage due to an accident all seem to have a direct impact upon our minds, so the dualist claim for a separation of mind and body seems suspect.
- The Cartesian circle: Descartes needs an all-powerful, all-good God to exist to provide a guarantee of the certainty of his reason and, to a lesser degree, of his senses. Yet he uses his reason to prove the existence of God in the first place, principally by means of the ontological argument, which not all people agree is terribly rational in the first place. Isn't this a circle? Doesn't he use his reason to prove that God exists, then uses God to prove that his reason is valid?

Yet before you take these critiques too seriously, sit down by the fire with the father of modern philosophy for an hour or two and follow him on his tortuous journey from complete doubt to certainty about God, reason, mathematics, and his existence as a thinking thing.

# Meditations

## RENÉ DESCARTES

### *First Meditation*

#### WHAT CAN BE CALLED INTO DOUBT

Some years ago I was struck by the large number of falsehoods that I had accepted as true in my childhood, and by the highly doubtful nature of the whole edifice that I had subsequently based on them. I realized that it was necessary, once in the course of my life, to demolish everything completely and start again right from the foundations if I wanted to establish anything at all in the sciences that was stable and likely to last. But the task looked an enormous one, and I began to wait until I should reach a mature enough age to ensure that no subsequent time of life would be more suitable for tackling such inquiries. This led me to put the project off for so long that I would now be to blame if by pondering over it any further I wasted the time still left for carrying it out. So today I have expressly rid my mind of all worries and arranged for myself a clear stretch of free time. I am here quite alone, and at last I will devote myself sincerely and without reservation to the general demolition of my opinions.

But to accomplish this, it will not be necessary for me to show that all my opinions are false, which is something I could perhaps never manage. Reason now leads me to think that I should hold back my assent from opinions which are not completely certain and indubitable just as carefully as I do from those which are patently false. So, for the purpose of rejecting all my opinions, it will be enough if I find in each of them at least some reason for doubt. And to do this I will not need to run through them all individually, which would be an endless task. Once the foundations of a building are undermined, anything built on them collapses

of its own accord; so I will go straight for the basic principles on which all my former beliefs rested.

Whatever I have up till now accepted as most true I have acquired either from the senses or through the senses. But from time to time I have found that the senses deceive, and it is prudent never to trust completely those who have deceived us even once.

Yet although the senses occasionally deceive us with respect to objects which are very small or in the distance, there are many other beliefs about which doubt is quite impossible, even though they are derived from the senses—for example, that I am here, sitting by the fire, wearing a winter dressing-gown, holding this piece of paper in my hands, and so on. Again, how could it be denied that these hands or this whole body are mine? Unless perhaps I were to liken myself to madmen, whose brains are so damaged by the persistent vapours of melancholia that they firmly maintain they are kings when they are paupers, or say they are dressed in purple when they are naked, or that their heads are made of earthenware, or that they are pumpkins, or made of glass. But such people are insane, and I would be thought equally mad if I took anything from them as a model for myself.

A brilliant piece of reasoning! As if I were not a man who sleeps at night, and regularly has all the same experiences[1] while asleep as madmen do when awake—indeed sometimes even more improbable ones. How often, asleep at night, am I convinced of just such familiar events—that I am here in my dressing-gown, sitting by the fire—when in fact I am lying undressed in bed! Yet

---

[1] ". . . and in my dreams regularly represent to myself the same things" (French version).

SOURCE: René Descartes, *Meditations on First Philosophy* (1641), in *The Philosophical Writings of Descartes,* vol. 1, trans. John Cottingham, Robert Stoothoff, and Dugald Murdoch (Cambridge, UK: Cambridge University Press, 1984), pp. 12–23, 50–62. Reprinted with permission of Cambridge University Press.

at the moment my eyes are certainly wide awake when I look at this piece of paper; I shake my head and it is not asleep; as I stretch out and feel my hand I do so deliberately, and I know what I am doing. All this would not happen with such distinctness to someone asleep. Indeed! As if I did not remember other occasions when I have been tricked by exactly similar thoughts while asleep! As I think about this more carefully, I see plainly that there are never any sure signs by means of which being awake can be distinguished from being asleep. The result is that I begin to feel dazed, and this very feeling only reinforces the notion that I may be asleep.

Suppose then that I am dreaming, and that these particulars—that my eyes are open, that I am moving my head and stretching out my hands—are not true. Perhaps, indeed, I do not even have such hands or such a body at all. Nonetheless, it must surely be admitted that the visions which come in sleep are like paintings, which must have been fashioned in the likeness of things that are real, and hence that at least these general kinds of things—eyes, head, hands and the body as a whole—are things which are not imaginary but are real and exist. For even when painters try to create sirens and satyrs with the most extraordinary bodies, they cannot give them natures which are new in all respects; they simply jumble up the limbs of different animals. Or if perhaps they manage to think up something so new that nothing remotely similar has ever been seen before—something which is therefore completely fictitious and unreal—at least the colours used in the composition must be real. But similar reasoning, although these general kinds of things—eyes, head, hands and so on—could be imaginary, it must at least be admitted that certain other even simpler and more universal things are real. These are as it were the real colours from which we form all the images of things, whether true or false, that occur in our thought.

This class appears to include corporeal nature in general, and its extension; the shape of extended things; the quantity, or size and number of these things; the place in which they may ex-

ist, the time through which they may endure,[2] and so on.

So a reasonable conclusion from this might be that physics, astronomy, medicine, and all other disciplines which depend on the study of composite things, are doubtful; while arithmetic, geometry and other subjects of this kind, which deal only with the simplest and most general things, regardless of whether they really exist in nature or not, contain something certain and indubitable. For whether I am awake or asleep, two and three added together are five, and a square has no more than four sides. It seems impossible that such transparent truths should incur any suspicion of being false.

And yet firmly rooted in my mind is the long-standing opinion that there is an omnipotent God who made me the kind of creature that I am. How do I know that he has not brought it about that there is no earth, no sky, no extended thing, no shape, no size, no place, while at the same time ensuring that all these things appear to me to exist just as they do now? What is more, since I sometimes believe that others go astray in cases where they think they have the most perfect knowledge, may I not similarly go wrong every time I add two and three or count the sides of a square, or in some even simpler matter, if that is imaginable? But perhaps God would not have allowed me to be deceived in this way, since he is said to be supremely good. But if it were inconsistent with his goodness to have created me such that I am deceived all the time, it would seem equally foreign to his goodness to allow me to be deceived even occasionally; yet this last assertion cannot be made.[3]

Perhaps there may be some who would prefer to deny the existence of so powerful a God rather than believe that everything else is uncertain. Let us not argue with them, but grant them that everything said about God is a fiction. According to their supposition, then, I have arrived at my present state by fate or chance or a continuous

---

[2] ". . . the place where they are, the time which measures their duration" (French version).

[3] ". . . yet I cannot doubt that he does allow this" (French version).

chain of events, or by some other means; yet since deception and error seem to be imperfections, the less powerful they make my original cause, the more likely it is that I am so imperfect as to be deceived all the time. I have no answer to these arguments, but am finally compelled to admit that there is not one of my former beliefs about which a doubt may not properly be raised; and this is not a flippant or ill-considered conclusion, but is based on powerful and well thought-out reasons. So in future I must withhold my assent from these former beliefs just as carefully as I would from obvious falsehoods, if I want to discover any certainty.[4]

But it is not enough merely to have noticed this; I must make an effort to remember it. My habitual opinions keep coming back, and, despite my wishes, they capture my belief, which is as it were bound over to them as a result of long occupation and the law of custom. I shall never get out of the habit of confidently assenting to these opinions, so long as I suppose them to be what in fact they are, namely highly probable opinions—opinions which, despite the fact that they are in a sense doubtful, as has just been shown, it is still much more reasonable to believe than to deny. In view of this, I think it will be a good plan to turn my will in completely the opposite direction and deceive myself, by pretending for a time that these former opinions are utterly false and imaginary. I shall do this until the weight of preconceived opinion is counterbalanced and the distorting influence of habit no longer prevents my judgement from perceiving things correctly. In the meantime, I know that no danger or error will result from my plan, and that I cannot possibly go too far in my distrustful attitude. This is because the task now in hand does not involve action but merely the acquisition of knowledge.

I will suppose therefore that not God, who is supremely good and the source of truth, but rather some malicious demon of the utmost power and cunning has employed all his energies in order to deceive me. I shall think that the sky, the air, the earth, colours, shapes, sounds and all external things are merely the delusions of dreams which he has devised to ensnare my judgement. I shall consider myself as not having hands or eyes, or flesh, or blood or senses, but as falsely believing that I have all these things. I shall stubbornly and firmly persist in this meditation; and, even if it is not in my power to know any truth, I shall at least do what is in my power,[5] that is, resolutely guard against assenting to any falsehoods, so that the deceiver, however powerful and cunning he may be, will be unable to impose on me in the slightest degree. But this is an arduous undertaking, and a kind of laziness brings me back to normal life. I am like a prisoner who is enjoying an imaginary freedom while asleep; as he begins to suspect that he is asleep, he dreads being woken up, and goes along with the pleasant illusion as long as he can. In the same way, I happily slide back into my old opinions and dread being shaken out of them, for fear that my peaceful sleep may be followed by hard labour when I wake, and that I shall have to toil not in the light, but amid the inextricable darkness of the problems I have now raised.

## Second Meditation

### THE NATURE OF THE HUMAN MIND, AND HOW IT IS BETTER KNOWN THAN THE BODY

So serious are the doubts into which I have been thrown as a result of yesterday's meditation that I can neither put them out of my mind nor see any way of resolving them. It feels as if I have fallen unexpectedly into a deep whirlpool which tumbles me around so that I can neither stand on the bottom nor swim up to the top. Nevertheless I will make an effort and once more attempt the same path which I started on yesterday. Anything which admits of the slightest doubt I will set aside just as if I had found it to be wholly false; and I will proceed in this way until I recog-

---

[4] ". . . in the sciences" (added in French version).

[5] ". . . nevertheless it is in my power to suspend my judgement" (French version).

nize something certain, or, if nothing else, until I at least recognize for certain that there is no certainty. Archimedes used to demand just one firm and immovable point in order to shift the entire earth; so I too can hope for great things if I manage to find just one thing, however slight, that is certain and unshakeable.

I will suppose then, that everything I see is spurious. I will believe that my memory tells me lies, and that none of the things that it reports ever happened. I have no senses. Body, shape, extension, movement and place are chimeras. So what remains true? Perhaps just the one fact that nothing is certain.

Yet apart from everything I have just listed, how do I know that there is not something else which does not allow even the slightest occasion for doubt? Is there not a God, or whatever I may call him, who puts into me[6] the thoughts I am now having? But why do I think this, since I myself may perhaps be the author of these thoughts? In that case am not I, at least, something? But I have just said that I have no senses and no body. This is the sticking point: what follows from this? Am I not so bound up with a body and with senses that I cannot exist without them? But I have convinced myself that there is absolutely nothing in the world, no sky, no earth, no minds, no bodies. Does it now follow that I too do not exist? No: if I convinced myself of something[7] then I certainly existed. But there is a deceiver of supreme power and cunning who is deliberately and constantly deceiving me. In that case I too undoubtedly exist, if he is deceiving me; and let him deceive me as much as he can, he will never bring it about that I am nothing so long as I think that I am something. So after considering everything very thoroughly, I must finally conclude that this proposition, *I am, I exist,* is necessarily true whenever it is put forward by me or conceived in my mind.

But I do not yet have a sufficient understanding of what this "I" is, that now necessarily exists. So I must be on my guard against carelessly taking something else to be this "I," and so making a mistake in the very item of knowledge that I maintain is the most certain and evident of all. I will therefore go back and meditate on what I originally believed myself to be, before I embarked on this present train of thought. I will then subtract anything capable of being weakened, even minimally, by the arguments now introduced, so that what is left at the end may be exactly and only what is certain and unshakeable.

What then did I formerly think I was? A man. But what is a man? Shall I say "a rational animal"? No; for then I should have to inquire what an animal is, what rationality is, and in this way one question would lead me down the slope to other harder ones, and I do not now have the time to waste on subtleties of this kind. Instead I propose to concentrate on what came into my thoughts spontaneously and quite naturally whenever I used to consider what I was. Well, the first thought to come to mind was that I had a face, hands, arms and the whole mechanical structure of limbs which can be seen in a corpse, and which I called the body. The next thought was that I was nourished, that I moved about, and that I engaged in sense-perception and thinking; and these actions I attributed to the soul. But as to the nature of this soul, either I did not think about this or else I imagined it to be something tenuous, like a wind or fire or ether, which permeated my more solid parts. As to the body, however, I had no doubts about it, but thought I knew its nature distinctly. If I had tried to describe the mental conception I had of it, I would have expressed it as follows: by a body I understand whatever has a determinable shape and a definable location and can occupy a space in such a way as to exclude any other body; it can be perceived by touch, sight, hearing, taste or smell, and can be moved in various ways, not by itself but by whatever else comes into contact with it. For, according to my judgement, the power of self-movement, like the power of sensation or of thought, was quite foreign to the nature of a body; indeed, it was a source of wonder to me that certain bodies were found to contain faculties of this kind.

---

[6] ". . . puts into my mind" (French version).
[7] ". . . or thought anything at all" (French version).

But what shall I now say that I am, when I am supposing that there is some supremely powerful and, if it is permissible to say so, malicious deceiver, who is deliberately trying to trick me in every way he can? Can I now assert that I possess even the most insignificant of all the attributes which I have just said belong to the nature of a body? I scrutinize them, think about them, go over them again, but nothing suggests itself; it is tiresome and pointless to go through the list once more. But what about the attributes I assigned to the soul? Nutrition or movement? Since now I do not have a body, these are mere fabrications. Sense-perception? This surely does not occur without a body, and besides, when asleep I have appeared to perceive through the senses many things which I afterwards realized I did not perceive through the senses at all. Thinking? At last I have discovered it—thought; this alone is inseparable from me. I am, I exist—that is certain. But for how long? For as long as I am thinking. For it could be that were I totally to cease from thinking, I should totally cease to exist. At present I am not admitting anything except what is necessarily true. I am, then, in the strict sense only a thing that thinks[8]; that is, I am a mind, or intelligence, or intellect, or reason—words whose meaning I have been ignorant of until now. But for all that I am a thing which is real and which truly exists. But what kind of a thing? As I have just said—a thinking thing.

What else am I? I will use my imagination.[9] I am not that structure of limbs which is called a human body. I am not even some thin vapour which permeates the limbs—a wind, fire, air, breath, or whatever I depict in my imagination; for these are things which I have supposed to be nothing. Let this supposition stand;[10] for all that I am still something. And yet may it not perhaps be the case that these very things which I am supposing to be nothing, because they are unknown to me, are in reality identical with the "I" of which I am aware? I do not know, and for the moment I shall not argue the point, since I can make judgements only about things which are known to me. I know that I exist; the question is, what is this "I" that I know? If the "I" is understood strictly as we have been taking it, then it is quite certain that knowledge of it does not depend on things of whose existence I am as yet unaware; so it cannot depend on any of the things which I invent in my imagination. And this very word "invent" shows me my mistake. It would indeed be a case of fictitious invention if I used my imagination to establish that I was something or other; for imagining is simply contemplating the shape or image of a corporeal thing. Yet now I know for certain both that I exist and at the same time that all such images and, in general, everything relating to the nature of body, could be mere dreams and chimeras. Once this point has been grasped, to say "I will use my imagination to get to know more distinctly what I am" would seem to be as silly as saying "I am now awake, and see some truth; but since my vision is not yet clear enough, I will deliberately fall asleep so that my dreams may provide a truer and clearer representation." I thus realize that none of the things that the imagination enables me to grasp is at all relevant to this knowledge of myself which I possess, and that the mind must therefore be most carefully diverted from such things[11] if it is to perceive its own nature as distinctly as possible.

But what then am I? A thing that thinks. What is that? A thing that doubts, understands, affirms, denies, is willing, is unwilling, and also imagines and has sensory perceptions.

This is a considerable list, if everything on it

---

[8] The word "only" is most naturally taken as going with "a thing that thinks," and this interpretation is followed in the French version. When discussing this passage with Gassendi, however, Descartes suggests that he meant the "only" to govern "in the strict sense."

[9] ". . . to see if I am not something more" (added in French version).

[10] Lat. *maneat* ("let it stand"), first edition. The second edition has the indicative *manet:* "The proposition still stands, *viz.* that I am nonetheless something." The French version reads: "without **changing** this supposition, I find that I am still certain that I am something."

[11] ". . . from this manner of conceiving things" (French version).

belongs to me. But does it? Is it not one and the same "I" who is now doubting almost everything, who nonetheless understands some things, who affirms that this one thing is true, denies everything else, desires to know more, is unwilling to be deceived, imagines many things even involuntarily, and is aware of many things which apparently come from the senses? Are not all these things just as true as the fact that I exist, even if I am asleep all the time, and even if he who created me is doing all he can to deceive me? Which of all these activities is distinct from my thinking? Which of them can be said to be separate from myself? The fact that it is I who am doubting and understanding and willing is so evident that I see no way of making it any clearer. But it is also the case that the "I" who imagines is the same "I." For even if, as I have supposed, none of the objects of imagination are real, the power of imagination is something which really exists and is part of my thinking. Lastly, it is also the same "I" who has sensory perceptions, or is aware of bodily things as it were through the senses. For example, I am now seeing light, hearing a noise, feeling heat. But I am asleep, so all this is false. Yet I certainly *seem* to see, to hear, and to be warmed. This cannot be false; what is called "having a sensory perception" is strictly just this, and in this restricted sense of the term it is simply thinking.

From all this I am beginning to have a rather better understanding of what I am. But it still appears—and I cannot stop thinking this—that the corporeal things of which images are formed in my thought, and which the senses investigate, are known with much more distinctness than this puzzling "I" which cannot be pictured in the imagination. And yet it is surely surprising that I should have a more distinct grasp of things which I realize are doubtful, unknown and foreign to me, than I have of that which is true and known— my own self. But I see what it is: my mind enjoys wandering off and will not yet submit to being restrained within the bounds of truth. Very well then; just this once let us give it a completely free rein, so that after a while, when it is time to tighten the reins, it may more readily submit to being curbed.

Let us consider the things which people commonly think they understand most distinctly of all; that is, the bodies which we touch and see. I do not mean bodies in general—for general perceptions are apt to be somewhat more confused—but one particular body. Let us take, for example, this piece of wax. It has just been taken from the honeycomb; it has not yet quite lost the taste of the honey; it retains some of the scent of the flowers from which it was gathered; its colour, shape and size are plain to see; it is hard, cold and can be handled without difficulty; if you rap it with your knuckle it makes a sound. In short, it has everything which appears necessary to enable a body to be known as distinctly as possible. But even as I speak, I put the wax by the fire, and look: the residual taste is eliminated, the smell goes away, the colour changes, the shape is lost, the size increases; it becomes liquid and hot; you can hardly touch it, and if you strike it, it no longer makes a sound. But does the same wax remain? It must be admitted that it does; no one denies it, no one thinks otherwise. So what was it in the wax that I understood with such distinctness? Evidently none of the features which I arrived at by means of the senses; for whatever came under taste, smell, sight, touch or hearing has now altered—yet the wax remains.

Perhaps the answer lies in the thought which now comes to my mind; namely, the wax was not after all the sweetness of the honey, or the fragrance of the flowers, or the whiteness, or the shape, or the sound, but was rather a body which presented itself to me in these various forms a little while ago, but which now exhibits different ones. But what exactly is it that I am now imagining? Let us concentrate, take away everything which does not belong to the wax, and see what is left: merely something extended, flexible and changeable. But what is meant here by "flexible" and "changeable"? Is it what I picture in my imagination: that this piece of wax is capable of changing from a round shape to a square shape, or from a square shape to a triangular shape? Not at all; for I can grasp that the wax is capable of countless changes of this kind, yet I am unable to run through this immeasurable number of changes in my imagination, from which it follows that it is not the faculty of imagination that gives me my grasp of the wax as flexible and changeable. And what is meant by "extended"? Is the extension of the wax also unknown? For it increases if the wax melts, increases again if it boils, and is greater still if the heat is increased. I would not be making a correct judgement about the nature of wax unless I believed it capable of being extended in many more different ways than I will ever encompass in my imagination. I must therefore admit that the nature of this piece of wax is in no way revealed by my imagination, but is perceived by the mind alone. (I am speaking of this particular piece of wax; the point is even clearer with regard to wax in general.) But what is this wax which is perceived by the mind alone? [12] It is of course the same wax which I see, which I touch, which I picture in my imagination, in short the same wax which I thought it to be from the start. And yet, and here is the point, the perception I have of it [13] is a case not of vision or touch or imagination—nor has it ever been, despite previous appearances—but of purely mental scrutiny; and this can be imperfect and confused, as it was before, or clear and distinct as it is now, depending on how carefully I concentrate on what the wax consists in.

But as I reach this conclusion I am amazed at how weak and prone to error my mind is. For although I am thinking about these matters within myself, silently and without speaking, nonetheless the actual words bring me up short, and I am almost tricked by ordinary ways of talking. We say that we see the wax itself, if it is there before us, not that we judge it to be there from its colour or shape; and this might lead me to conclude without more ado that knowledge of the wax comes from what the eye sees, and not from the scrutiny of the mind alone. But then if I look out of the window and see men crossing the square, as I just happen to have done, I normally say that I see the men themselves, just as I say that I see the wax. Yet do I see any more than hats and coats which could conceal automatons? I *judge*

that they are men. And so something which I thought I was seeing with my eyes is in fact grasped solely by the faculty of judgement which is in my mind.

However, one who wants to achieve knowledge above the ordinary level should feel ashamed at having taken ordinary ways of talking as a basis for doubt. So let us proceed, and consider on which occasion my perception of the nature of the wax was more perfect and evident. Was it when I first looked at it, and believed I knew it by my external senses, or at least by what they call the "common" sense [14]—that is, the power of imagination? Or is my knowledge more perfect now, after a more careful investigation of the nature of the wax and of the means by which it is known? Any doubt on this issue would clearly be foolish; for what distinctness was there in my earlier perception? Was there anything in it which an animal could not possess? But when I distinguish the wax from its outward forms—take the clothes off, as it were, and consider it naked—then although my judgement may still contain errors, at least my perception now requires a human mind.

But what am I to say about this mind, or about myself? (So far, remember, I am not admitting that there is anything else in me except a mind.) What, I ask, is this "I" which seems to perceive the wax so distinctly? Surely my awareness of my own self is not merely much truer and more certain than my awareness of the wax, but also much more distinct and evident. For if I judge that the wax exists from the fact that I see it, clearly this same fact entails much more evidently that I myself also exist. It is possible that what I see is not really the wax; it is possible that I do not even have eyes with which to see anything. But when I see, or think I see (I am not here distinguishing the two), it is simply not possible that I who am now thinking am not something. By the same token, if I judge that the wax exists from the fact that I touch it, the same result follows, namely that I exist. If I judge that it exists from the fact that I imagine it, or for any other reason, exactly the same thing follows. And

[12] . . . which can only be conceived by the understanding or the mind" (French version).

[13] ". . . or rather the act whereby it is perceived" (added in French version).

[14] See note 27, p. 218 below.

the result that I have grasped in the case of the wax may be applied to everything else located outside me. Moreover, if my perception of the wax seemed more distinct[15] after it was established not just by sight or touch but by many other considerations, it must be admitted that I now know myself even more distinctly. This is because every consideration whatsoever which contributes to my perception of the wax, or of any other body, cannot but establish even more effectively the nature of my own mind. But besides this, there is so much else in the mind itself which can serve to make my knowledge of it more distinct, that it scarcely seems worth going through the contributions made by considering bodily things.

I see that without any effort I have now finally got back to where I wanted. I now know that even bodies are not strictly perceived by the senses or the faculty of imagination but by the intellect alone, and that this perception derives not from their being touched or seen but from their being understood; and in view of this I know plainly that I can achieve an easier and more evident perception of my own mind than of anything else. But since the habit of holding on to old opinions cannot be set aside so quickly, I should like to stop here and meditate for some time on this new knowledge I have gained, so as to fix it more deeply in my memory.

## Sixth Meditation

### THE EXISTENCE OF MATERIAL THINGS, AND THE REAL DISTINCTION BETWEEN MIND AND BODY

It remains for me to examine whether material things exist. And at least I now know they are capable of existing, in so far as they are the subject-matter of pure mathematics, since I perceive them clearly and distinctly. For there is no doubt that God is capable of creating everything that I am capable of perceiving in this manner; and I have never judged that something could not be made by him except on the grounds that there would be a contradiction in my perceiving it distinctly. The conclusion that material things exist is also suggested by the faculty of imagination, which I am aware of using when I turn my mind to material things. For when I give more attentive consideration to what imagination is, it seems to be nothing else but an application of the cognitive faculty to a body which is intimately present to it, and which therefore exists.

To make this clear, I will first examine the difference between imagination and pure understanding. When I imagine a triangle, for example, I do not merely understand that it is a figure bounded by three lines, but at the same time I also see the three lines with my mind's eye as if they were present before me; and this is what I call imagining. But if I want to think of a chiliagon, although I understand that it is a figure consisting of a thousand sides just as well as I understand the triangle to be a three-sided figure, I do not in the same way imagine the thousand sides or see them as if they were present before me. It is true that since I am in the habit of imagining something whenever I think of a corporeal thing, I may construct in my mind a confused representation of some figure; but it is clear that this is not a chiliagon. For it differs in no way from the representation I should form if I were thinking of a myriagon, or any figure with very many sides. Moreover, such a representation is useless for recognizing the properties which distinguish a chiliagon from other polygons. But suppose I am dealing with a pentagon: I can of course understand the figure of a pentagon, just as I can the figure of a chiliagon, without the help of the imagination; but I can also imagine a pentagon, by applying my mind's eye to its five sides and the area contained within them. And in doing this I notice quite clearly that imagination requires a peculiar effort of mind which is not required for understanding; this additional effort of mind clearly shows the difference between imagination and pure understanding.

---

[15] The French version has "more clear and distinct" and, at the end of this sentence, "more evidently, distinctly and clearly."

Besides this, I consider that this power of imagining which is in me, differing as it does from the power of understanding, is not a necessary constituent of my own essence, that is, of the essence of my mind. For if I lacked it, I should undoubtedly remain the same individual as I now am; from which it seems to follow that it depends on something distinct from myself. And I can easily understand that, if there does exist some body to which the mind is so joined that it can apply itself to contemplate it, as it were, whenever it pleases, then it may possibly be this very body that enables me to imagine corporeal things. So the difference between this mode of thinking and pure understanding may simply be this: when the mind understands, it in some way turns towards itself and inspects one of the ideas which are within it; but when it imagines, it turns towards the body and looks at something in the body which conforms to an idea understood by the mind or perceived by the senses. I can, as I say, easily understand that this is how imagination comes about, if the body exists; and since there is no other equally suitable way of explaining imagination that comes to mind, I can make a probable conjecture that the body exists. But this is only a probability; and despite a careful and comprehensive investigation, I do not yet see how the distinct idea of corporeal nature which I find in my imagination can provide any basis for a necessary inference that some body exists.

But besides that corporeal nature which is the subject-matter of pure mathematics, there is much else that I habitually imagine, such as colours, sounds, tastes, pain and so on—though not so distinctly. Now I perceive these things much better by means of the senses, which is how, with the assistance of memory, they appear to have reached the imagination. So in order to deal with them more fully, I must pay equal attention to the senses, and see whether the things which are perceived by means of that mode of thinking which I call "sensory perception" provide me with any sure argument for the existence of corporeal things.

To begin with, I will go back over all the things which I previously took to be perceived by the senses, and reckoned to be true; and I will go over my reasons for thinking this. Next, I will set out my reasons for subsequently calling these things into doubt. And finally I will consider what I should now believe about them.

First of all then, I perceived by my senses that I had a head, hands, feet and other limbs making up the body which I regarded as part of myself, or perhaps even as my whole self. I also perceived by my senses that this body was situated among many other bodies which could affect it in various favourable or unfavourable ways; and I gauged the favourable effects by a sensation of pleasure, and the unfavourable ones by a sensation of pain. In addition to pain and pleasure, I also had sensations within me of hunger, thirst, and other such appetites, and also of physical propensities towards cheerfulness, sadness, anger and similar emotions. And outside me, besides the extension, shapes and movements of bodies, I also had sensations of their hardness and heat, and of the other tactile qualities. In addition, I had sensations of light, colours, smells, tastes and sounds, the variety of which enabled me to distinguish the sky, the earth, the seas, and all other bodies, one from another. Considering the ideas of all these qualities which presented themselves to my thought, although the ideas were, strictly speaking, the only immediate objects of my sensory awareness, it was not unreasonable for me to think that the items which I was perceiving through the senses were things quite distinct from my thought, namely bodies which produced the ideas. For my experience was that these ideas came to me quite without my consent, so that I could not have sensory awareness of any object, even if I wanted to, unless it was present to my sense organs; and I could not avoid having sensory awareness of it when it was present. And since the ideas perceived by the senses were much more lively and vivid and even, in their own way, more distinct than any of those which I deliberately formed through meditating or which I found impressed on my memory, it seemed impossible that they should have come from within me; so the only alternative was that they came from other things. Since the sole source of my knowledge of these things was the ideas themselves, the supposition that the things resembled the ideas was bound to occur to me. In addition, I remembered that the use of my senses had come first, while the use of my reason came only later; and I saw that the ideas which I formed myself were less vivid than those which I perceived with the senses and were, for the most part, made up of elements of sensory ideas. In this way I easily convinced myself that I had nothing at all in the intellect which I had not previously had in sensation. As for the body which by some special right I called "mine," my belief that this body, more than any other, belonged to me had some justification. For I could never be separated from it, as I could from other bodies; and I felt all my appetites and emotions in, and on account of, this body; and finally, I was aware of pain and pleasurable ticklings in parts of this body, but not in other bodies external to it. But why should that curious sensation of pain give rise to a particular distress of mind; or why should a certain kind of delight follow on a tickling sensation? Again, why should that curious tugging in the stomach which I call hunger tell me that I should eat, or a dryness of the throat tell me to drink, and so on? I was not able to give any explanation of all this, except that nature taught me so. For there is absolutely no connection (at least that I can understand) between the tugging sensation and the decision to take food, or between the sensation of something causing pain and the mental apprehension of distress that arises from that sensation. These and other judgements that I made concerning sensory objects, I was apparently taught to make by nature; for I had already made up my mind that this was how things were, before working out any arguments to prove it.

Later on, however, I had many experiences which gradually undermined all the faith I had had in the senses. Sometimes towers which had looked round from a distance appeared square from close up; and enormous statues standing on their pediments did not seem large when observed from the ground. In these and countless other such cases, I found that the judgements of the external senses were mistaken. And this applied not just to the external senses but to the internal senses as well. For what can be more internal than pain? And yet I had heard that those who had had a leg or an arm amputated sometimes still seemed to feel pain intermittently in the missing part of the body. So even in my own case it was apparently not quite certain that a particular limb was hurting, even if I felt pain in it. To these reasons for doubting, I recently added two very general ones.[16] The first was that every sensory experience I have ever thought I was having while awake I can also think of myself as sometimes having while asleep; and since I do not believe that what I seem to perceive in sleep comes from things located outside me, I did not see why I should be any more inclined to believe this of what I think I perceive while awake. The second reason for doubt was that since I did not know the author of my being (or at least was pretending not to), I saw nothing to rule out the possibility that my natural constitution made me prone to error even in matters which seemed to me most true. As for the reasons for my previous confident belief in the truth of the things perceived by the senses, I had no trouble in refuting them. For since I apparently had natural impulses towards many things which reason told me to avoid, I reckoned that a great deal of confidence should not be placed in what I was taught by nature. And despite the fact that the perceptions of the senses were not dependent on my will, I did not think that I should on that account infer that they proceeded from things distinct from myself, since I might perhaps have a faculty not yet known to me which produced them.

But now, when I am beginning to achieve a better knowledge of myself and the author of my being, although I do not think I should heedlessly accept everything I seem to have acquired from the senses, neither do I think that everything should be called into doubt.

First, I know that everything which I clearly and distinctly understand is capable of being cre-

---

[16] Cf. Med. 1, above pp. 205–207.

ated by God so as to correspond exactly with my understanding of it. Hence the fact that I can clearly and distinctly understand one thing apart from another is enough to make me certain that the two things are distinct, since they are capable of being separated, at least by God. The question of what kind of power is required to bring about such a separation does not affect the judgement that the two things are distinct. Thus, simply by knowing that I exist and seeing at the same time that absolutely nothing else belongs to my nature or essence except that I am a thinking thing, I can infer correctly that my essence consists solely in the fact that I am a thinking thing. It is true that I may have (or, to anticipate, that I certainly have) a body that is very closely joined to me. But nevertheless, on the one hand I have a clear and distinct idea of myself, in so far as I am simply a thinking, non-extended thing; and on the other hand I have a distinct idea of body,[17] in so far as this is simply an extended, non-thinking thing. And accordingly, it is certain that I[18] am really distinct from my body, and can exist without it.

Besides this, I find in myself faculties for certain special modes of thinking,[19] namely imagination and sensory perception. Now I can clearly and distinctly understand myself as a whole without these faculties; but I cannot, conversely, understand these faculties without me, that is, without an intellectual substance to inhere in. This is because there is an intellectual act included in their essential definition; and hence I perceive that the distinction between them and myself corresponds to the distinction between the modes of a thing and the thing itself.[20] Of course I also recognize that there are other fac-

ulties (like those of changing position, of taking on various shapes, and so on) which, like sensory perception and imagination, cannot be understood apart from some substance for them to inhere in, and hence cannot exist without it. But it is clear that these other faculties, if they exist, must be in a corporeal or extended substance and not an intellectual one; for the clear and distinct conception of them includes extension, but does not include any intellectual act whatsoever. Now there is in me a passive faculty of sensory perception, that is, a faculty for receiving and recognizing the ideas of sensible objects; but I could not make use of it unless there was also an active faculty, either in me or in something else, which produced or brought about these ideas. But this faculty cannot be in me, since clearly it presupposes no intellectual act on my part,[21] and the ideas in question are produced without my co-operation and often even against my will. So the only alternative is that it is in another substance distinct from me—a substance which contains either formally or eminently all the reality which exists objectively in the ideas produced by this faculty (as I have just noted). This substance is either a body, that is, a corporeal nature, in which case it will contain formally and in fact everything which is to be found objectively or representatively in the ideas; or else it is God, or some creature more noble than a body, in which case it will contain eminently whatever is to be found in the ideas. But since God is not a deceiver, it is quite clear that he does not transmit the ideas to me either directly from himself, or indirectly, via some creature which contains the objective reality of the ideas not formally but only eminently. For God has given me no faculty at all for recognizing any such source for these ideas; on the contrary, he has given me a great propensity to believe that they are produced by corporeal things. So I do not see how God could be understood to be anything but a deceiver if the ideas were transmitted from a source other

---

[17] The Latin term *corpus* as used here by Descartes is ambiguous as between "body" (i.e., corporeal matter in general) and "the body" (i.e., this particular body of mine). The French version preserves the ambiguity.

[18] ". . . that is, my soul, by which I am what I am" (added in French version).

[19] ". . . certain modes of thinking which are quite special and distinct from me" (French version).

[20] ". . . between the shapes, movements and other modes or accidents of a body and the body which supports them" (French version).

[21] ". . . cannot be in me in so far as I am merely a thinking thing, since it does not presuppose any thought on my part" (French version).

than corporeal things. It follows that corporeal things exist. They may not all exist in a way that exactly corresponds with my sensory grasp of them, for in many cases the grasp of the senses is very obscure and confused. But at least they possess all the properties which I clearly and distinctly understand, that is, all those which, viewed in general terms, are comprised within the subject-matter of pure mathematics.

What of the other aspects of corporeal things which are either particular (for example that the sun is of such and such a size or shape), or less clearly understood, such as light or sound or pain, and so on? Despite the high degree of doubt and uncertainty involved here, the very fact that God is not a deceiver, and the consequent impossibility of there being any falsity in my opinions which cannot be corrected by some other faculty supplied by God, offers me a sure hope that I can attain the truth even in these matters. Indeed, there is no doubt that everything that I am taught by nature contains some truth. For if nature is considered in its general aspect, then I understand by the term nothing other than God himself, or the ordered system of created things established by God. And by my own nature in particular I understand nothing other than the totality of things bestowed on me by God.

There is nothing that my own nature teaches me more vividly than that I have a body, and that when I feel pain there is something wrong with the body, and that when I am hungry or thirsty the body needs food and drink, and so on. So I should not doubt that there is some truth in this.

Nature also teaches me, by these sensations of pain, hunger, thirst and so on, that I am not merely present in my body as a sailor is present in a ship,[22] but that I am very closely joined and, as it were, intermingled with it, so that I and the body form a unit. If this were not so, I, who am nothing but a thinking thing, would not feel pain when the body was hurt, but would perceive the damage purely by the intellect, just as a sailor perceives by sight if anything in his ship is broken. Similarly, when the body needed food or drink, I

should have an explicit understanding of the fact, instead of having confused sensations of hunger and thirst. For these sensations of hunger, thirst, pain and so on are nothing but confused modes of thinking which arise from the union and, as it were, intermingling of the mind with the body.

I am also taught by nature that various other bodies exist in the vicinity of my body, and that some of these are to be sought out and others avoided. And from the fact that I perceive by my senses a great variety of colours, sounds, smells and tastes, as well as differences in heat, hardness and the like, I am correct in inferring that the bodies which are the source of these various sensory perceptions possess differences corresponding to them, though perhaps not resembling them. Also, the fact that some of the perceptions are agreeable to me while others are disagreeable makes it quite certain that my body, or rather my whole self, in so far as I am a combination of body and mind, can be affected by the various beneficial or harmful bodies which surround it.

There are, however, many other things which I may appear to have been taught by nature, but which in reality I acquired not from nature but from a habit of making ill-considered judgements; and it is therefore quite possible that these are false. Cases in point are the belief that any space in which nothing is occurring to stimulate my senses must be empty; or that the heat in a body is something exactly resembling the idea of heat which is in me; or that when a body is white or green, the selfsame whiteness or greenness which I perceive through my senses is present in the body; or that in a body which is bitter or sweet there is the selfsame taste which I experience, and so on; or, finally, that stars and towers and other distant bodies have the same size and shape which they present to my senses, and other examples of this kind. But to make sure that my perceptions in this matter are sufficiently distinct, I must more accurately define exactly what I mean when I say that I am taught something by nature. In this context I am taking nature to be something more limited than the totality of things bestowed on me by God. For this includes many things that belong to the mind alone—for

---

[22] "... as a pilot in his ship" (French version).

example my perception that what is done cannot be undone, and all other things that are known by the natural light[23]; but at this stage I am not speaking of these matters. It also includes much that relates to the body alone, like the tendency to move in a downward direction, and so on; but I am not speaking of these matters either. My sole concern here is with what God has bestowed on me as a combination of mind and body. My nature, then, in this limited sense, does indeed teach me to avoid what induces a feeling of pain and to seek out what induces feelings of pleasure, and so on. But it does not appear to teach us to draw any conclusions from these sensory perceptions about things located outside us without waiting until the intellect has examined[24] the matter. For knowledge of the truth about such things seems to belong to the mind alone, not to the combination of mind and body. Hence, although a star has no greater effect on my eye than the flame of a small light, that does not mean that there is any real or positive inclination in me to believe that the star is no bigger than the light; I have simply made this judgement from childhood onwards without any rational basis. Similarly, although I feel heat when I go near a fire and feel pain when I go too near, there is no convincing argument for supposing that there is something in the fire which resembles the heat, any more than for supposing that there is something which resembles the pain. There is simply reason to suppose that there is something in the fire, whatever it may eventually turn out to be, which produces in us the feelings of heat or pain. And likewise, even though there is nothing in any given space that stimulates the senses, it does not follow that there is no body there. In these cases and many others I see that I have been in the habit of misusing the order of nature. For the proper purpose of the sensory perceptions given me by nature is simply to inform the mind of what is beneficial or harmful for the composite of which the mind is a part; and to this extent they are sufficiently clear and distinct. But I misuse them by treating them as reliable touchstones for immediate judgements about the essential nature of the bodies located outside us; yet this is an area where they provide only very obscure information.

I have already looked in sufficient detail at how, notwithstanding the goodness of God, it may happen that my judgements are false. But a further problem now comes to mind regarding those very things which nature presents to me as objects which I should seek out or avoid, and also regarding the internal sensations, where I seem to have detected errors[25]—e.g., when someone is tricked by the pleasant taste of some food into eating the poison concealed inside it. Yet in this case, what the man's nature urges him to go for is simply what is responsible for the pleasant taste, and not the poison, which his nature knows nothing about. The only inference that can be drawn from this is that his nature is not omniscient. And this is not surprising, since man is a limited thing, and so it is only fitting that his perfection should be limited.

And yet it is not unusual for us to go wrong even in cases where nature does urge us towards something. Those who are ill, for example, may desire food or drink that will shortly afterwards turn out to be bad for them. Perhaps it may be said that they go wrong because their nature is disordered, but this does not remove the difficulty. A sick man is no less one of God's creatures than a healthy one, and it seems no less a contradiction to suppose that he has received from God a nature which deceives him. Yet a clock constructed with wheels and weights observes all the laws of its nature just as closely when it is badly made and tells the wrong time as when it completely fulfils the wishes of the clockmaker. In the same way, I might consider the body of a man as a kind of machine equipped with and made up of bones, nerves, muscles, veins, blood and skin in such a way that, even if there were no mind in it, it would still perform all the same movements

---

[23] ". . . without any help from the body" (added in French version).
[24] ". . . carefully and maturely examined" (French version).

[25] ". . . and thus seem to have been directly deceived by my nature" (added in French version).

as it now does in those cases where movement is not under the control of the will or, consequently, of the mind.[26] I can easily see that if such a body suffers from dropsy, for example, and is affected by the dryness of the throat which normally produces in the mind the sensation of thirst, the resulting condition of the nerves and other parts will dispose the body to take a drink, with the result that the disease will be aggravated. Yet this is just as natural as the body's being stimulated by a similar dryness of the throat to take a drink when there is no such illness and the drink is beneficial. Admittedly, when I consider the purpose of the clock, I may say that it is departing from its nature when it does not tell the right time; and similarly when I consider the mechanism of the human body, I may think that, in relation to the movements which normally occur in it, it too is deviating from its nature if the throat is dry at a time when drinking is not beneficial to its continued health. But I am well aware that "nature" as I have just used it has a very different significance from "nature" in the other sense. As I have just used it, "nature" is simply a label which depends on my thought; it is quite extraneous to the things to which it is applied, and depends simply on my comparison between the idea of a sick man and a badly-made clock, and the idea of a healthy man and a well-made clock. But by "nature" in the other sense I understand something which is really to be found in the things themselves; in this sense, therefore, the term contains something of the truth.

When we say, then, with respect to the body suffering from dropsy, that it has a disordered nature because it has a dry throat and yet does not need drink, the term "nature" is here used merely as an extraneous label. However, with respect to the composite, that is, the mind united with this body, what is involved is not a mere label, but a true error of nature, namely that it is thirsty at a time when drink is going to cause it harm. It thus remains to inquire how it is that

the goodness of God does not prevent nature, in this sense, from deceiving us.

The first observation I make at this point is that there is a great difference between the mind and the body, inasmuch as the body is by its very nature always divisible, while the mind is utterly indivisible. For when I consider the mind, or myself in so far as I am merely a thinking thing, I am unable to distinguish any parts within myself; I understand myself to be something quite single and complete. Although the whole mind seems to be united to the whole body, I recognize that if a foot or arm or any other part of the body is cut off, nothing has thereby been taken away from the mind. As for the faculties of willing, of understanding, of sensory perception and so on, these cannot be termed parts of the mind, since it is one and the same mind that wills, and understands and has sensory perceptions. By contrast, there is no corporeal or extended thing that I can think of which in my thought I cannot easily divide into parts; and this very fact makes me understand that it is divisible. This one argument would be enough to show me that the mind is completely different from the body, even if I did not already know as much from other considerations.

My next observation is that the mind is not immediately affected by all parts of the body, but only by the brain, or perhaps just by one small part of the brain, namely the part which is said to contain the "common" sense.[27] Every time this part of the brain is in a given state, it presents the same signals to the mind, even though the other parts of the body may be in a different condition at the time. This is established by countless observations, which there is no need to review here.

I observe, in addition, that the nature of the body is such that whenever any part of it is moved

---

[26] ". . . but occurs merely as a result of the disposition of the organs" (French version).

[27] The supposed faculty which integrates the data from the five specialized senses (the notion goes back ultimately to Aristotle). "The seat of the common sense must be very mobile, to receive all the impressions coming from the senses, but must be moveable only by the spirits which transmit these impressions. Only the *conarion* [pineal gland] fits these conditions" (letter to Mersenne, 21 April 1641).

by another part which is some distance away, it can always be moved in the same fashion by any of the parts which lie in between, even if the more distant part does nothing. For example, in a cord *ABCD,* if one end *D* is pulled so that the other end *A* moves, the exact same movement could have been brought about if one of the intermediate points *B* or *C* had been pulled, and *D* had not moved at all. In similar fashion, when I feel a pain in my foot, physiology tells me that this happens by means of nerves distributed throughout the foot, and that these nerves are like cords which go from the foot right up to the brain. When the nerves are pulled in the foot, they in turn pull on inner parts of the brain to which they are attached, and produce a certain motion in them; and nature has laid it down that this motion should produce in the mind a sensation of pain, as occurring in the foot. But since these nerves, in passing from the foot to the brain, must pass through the calf, the thigh, the lumbar region, the back and the neck, it can happen that, even if it is not the part in the foot but one of the intermediate parts which is being pulled, the same motion will occur in the brain as occurs when the foot is hurt, and so it will necessarily come about that the mind feels the same sensation of pain. And we must suppose the same thing happens with regard to any other sensation.

My final observation is that any given movement occurring in the part of the brain that immediately affects the mind produces just one corresponding sensation; and hence the best system that could be devised is that it should produce the one sensation which, of all possible sensations, is most especially and most frequently conducive to the preservation of the healthy man. And experience shows that the sensations which nature has given us are all of this kind; and so there is absolutely nothing to be found in them that does not bear witness to the power and goodness of God. For example, when the nerves in the foot are set in motion in a violent and unusual manner, this motion, by way of the spinal cord, reaches the inner parts of the brain, and there gives the mind its signal for having a cer-

tain sensation, namely the sensation of a pain as occurring in the foot. This stimulates the mind to do its best to get rid of the cause of the pain, which it takes to be harmful to the foot. It is true that God could have made the nature of man such that this particular motion in the brain indicated something else to the mind; it might, for example, have made the mind aware of the actual motion occurring in the brain, or in the foot, or in any of the intermediate regions; or it might have indicated something else entirely. But there is nothing else which would have been so conducive to the continued well-being of the body. In the same way, when we need drink, there arises a certain dryness in the throat; this sets in motion the nerves of the throat, which in turn move the inner parts of the brain. This motion produces in the mind a sensation of thirst, because the most useful thing for us to know about the whole business is that we need drink in order to stay healthy. And so it is in the other cases.

It is quite clear from all this that, notwithstanding the immense goodness of God, the nature of man as a combination of mind and body is such that it is bound to mislead him from time to time. For there may be some occurrence, not in the foot but in one of the other areas through which the nerves travel in their route from the foot to the brain, or even in the brain itself; and if this cause produces the same motion which is generally produced by injury to the foot, then pain will be felt as if it were in the foot. This deception of the senses is natural, because a given motion in the brain must always produce the same sensation in the mind; and the origin of the motion in question is much more often going to be something which is hurting the foot, rather than something existing elsewhere. So it is reasonable that this motion should always indicate to the mind a pain in the foot rather than in any other part of the body. Again, dryness of the throat may sometimes arise not, as it normally does, from the fact that a drink is necessary to the health of the body, but from some quite opposite cause, as happens in the case of the man with dropsy. Yet it is much better that it should mislead on this occasion than that it should always mislead when the body is in good health. And the same goes for the other cases.

This consideration is the greatest help to me, not only for noticing all the errors to which my nature is liable, but also for enabling me to correct or avoid them without difficulty. For I know that in matters regarding the well-being of the body, all my senses report the truth much more frequently than not. Also, I can almost always make use of more than one sense to investigate the same thing; and in addition, I can use both my memory, which connects present experiences with preceding ones, and my intellect, which has by now examined all the causes of error. Accordingly, I should not have any further fears about the falsity of what my senses tell me every day; on the contrary, the exaggerated doubts of the last few days should be dismissed as laughable. This applies especially to the principal reason for doubt, namely my inability to distinguish between being asleep and being awake. For I now notice that there is a vast difference between the two, in that dreams are never linked by memory with all the other actions of life as waking experiences are. If, while I am awake, anyone were suddenly to appear to me and then disappear immediately, as happens in sleep, so that I could not see where he had come from or where he had gone to, it would not be unreasonable for me to judge that he was a ghost, or a vision created in my brain,[28] rather than a real man. But when I distinctly see where things come from and where and when they come to me, and when I can connect my perceptions of them with the whole of the rest of my life without a break, then I am quite certain that when I encounter these things I am not asleep but awake. And I ought not to have even the slightest doubt of their reality if, after calling upon all the senses as well as my memory and my intellect in order to check them, I receive no conflicting reports from any of these sources. For from the fact that God is not a deceiver it follows that in cases like these I am completely free from error. But since the pressure of things to be done does not always allow us to stop and make such a meticulous check, it must be admitted that in this human life we are often liable to make mistakes about particular things, and we must acknowledge the weakness of our nature.

[28] " . . . like those that are formed in the brain when I sleep" (added in French version).

# RYLE ON THE GHOST IN THE MACHINE _____

Gilbert Ryle (1900–1976) is the great critic of Cartesian dualism in the twentieth century. He studied at Oxford University, where he was later the Wayflete Professor of Metaphysical Philosophy from 1945 to 1968. He was also the editor of *Mind* from 1947 to 1971, and the author of *The Concept of Mind* (1954), *Dilemmas* (1954), and *Collected Papers* (1971).

Ryle was part of the "ordinary language" movement in philosophy pioneered by Ludwig Wittgenstein in the 1930s. This was based on the idea that a lot of classical philosophical problems were really misunderstandings of the way we ordinarily use language: They were really just confusions about vocabulary and grammar. If we could clarify the way we use ordinary language, many of these problems would disappear.

In his 1938 article "Categories," Ryle introduced his notion of a "category mistake" that would later act as the foundation of his critique of Cartesian dualism. A category mistake is describing something with terminology from a logical category that doesn't apply to it, or with terminology from two distinct logical categories in the same breath. Ryle gives a number of examples, his most striking being the case of the confused stranger who, after looking at the campus library, the arts building, the science labs, and a number of other buildings, asks, "Where is the university?" Is it a collection of all these buildings? Or of all the students who use them? Or of all the students and faculty and staff? Ryle answers that "university" is a way we group all these things together: It is a *concept* that unites them. It's a category mistake to think, like the stranger, that it's a specific building or a specific group of people.

Similarly, "mind" and "body" belong to separate logical categories, and we commit a category mistake when we ask how they relate to each other. "Body" is a physical thing, while "mind" is a concept we use to describe behavior.

Ryle calls Descartes' dualism the "official doctrine," which is based on the idea that the human mind is a "ghost in the machine" of the body. According to this doctrine, bodies exist in space and time, are subject to mechanical laws, and are publicly observable. Minds aren't in space, aren't subject to mechanical laws, and have a private career. We can introspect into our minds and know what's in them. But the minds of others are opaque to us. For all we know, they might be robots.

Our mental language, which consists of talk about beliefs, desires, pleasures, and pains, seems to describe an internal spiritual realm. Yet this is an illusion. Ryle believes that we can reduce such language to talk about externally observable behavior. If I "desire" some chocolate ice cream, I can become aware of this so-called desire only if someone observes me walking over to the ice cream parlor to buy a cone. Actually, Ryle makes it a bit more complicated than this: He says that our mental states are really *dispositions* to behave, whether or not we actually act on those dispositions. My desire for chocolate ice cream is not an internal mental state, but a disposition to go to the parlor to buy some. This disposition is connected to my actual behavior in a variety of ways.

There is an obvious critique of Ryle's "logical behaviorism": If mental states are really descriptions of behavior, or of dispositions to behave, how does this account for the situation where we mull over several courses of action in our mind, and reject all but one of these possibilities? Or the more obvious case of someone who knows something he or she is trying to hide from others, for example, a poker player with four aces trying to win a big pot? It would be odd to describe these as "dispositions to behave." Also, purely abstract thought, for example, Descartes sitting by his fire working through geometrical proofs, doesn't seem to be connected to observable behavior at all, unless you describe "behavior" to include thinking unconnected to physical actions, in which case Ryle's behaviorism becomes pretty wishy-washy stuff. It seems that the ghost in the machine isn't so easy to exorcise as Ryle thinks it is. Yet despite these shortcomings, Ryle does offer a powerful critique of Descartes' dualism.

The following reading is the first chapter from Ryle's classic work *The Concept of Mind.* In it he attacks Descartes and his ghostly ego, trying to show how Cartesian dualism is based on a major category mistake.

# The Ghost in the Machine

GILBERT RYLE

## *The Official Doctrine*

There is a doctrine about the nature and place of minds which is so prevalent among theorists and even among laymen that it deserves to be described as the official theory. Most philosophers, psychologists and religious teachers subscribe, with minor reservations, to its main articles and, although they admit certain theoretical difficulties in it, they tend to assume that these can be overcome without serious modifications being made to the architecture of the theory. It will be argued here that the central principles of the doctrine are unsound and conflict with the whole body of what we know about minds when we are not speculating about them.

The official doctrine, which hails chiefly from Descartes, is something like this. With the doubtful exceptions of idiots and infants in arms every human being has both a body and a mind. Some would prefer to say that every human being is both a body and a mind. His body and his mind are ordinarily harnessed together, but after the death of the body his mind may continue to exist and function.

Human bodies are in space and are subject to the mechanical laws which govern all other bodies in space. Bodily processes and states can be inspected by external observers. So a man's bodily life is as much a public affair as are the lives of animals and reptiles and even as the careers of trees, crystals and planets.

But minds are not in space, nor are their operations subject to mechanical laws. The workings of one mind are not witnessable by other observers; its career is private. Only I can take direct cognisance of the states and processes of my own mind. A person therefore lives through two collateral histories, one consisting of what happens in and to his body, the other consisting of what happens in and to his mind. The first is public, the second private. The events in the first history are events in the physical world, those in the second are events in the mental world.

It has been disputed whether a person does or can directly monitor all or only some of the episodes of his own private history; but, according to the official doctrine, of at least some of these episodes he has direct and unchallengeable cognisance. In consciousness, self-consciousness and introspection he is directly and authentically apprised of the present states and operations of his mind. He may have great or small uncertainties about concurrent and adjacent episodes in the physical world, but he can have none about at least part of what is momentarily occupying his mind.

It is customary to express this bifurcation of his two lives and of his two worlds by saying that the things and events which belong to the physical world, including his own body, are external, while the workings of his own mind are internal. This antithesis of outer and inner is of course meant to be construed as a metaphor, since minds, not being in space, could not be described as being spatially inside anything else, or as having things going on spatially inside themselves. But relapses from this good intention are common and theorists are found speculating how stimuli, the physical sources of which are yards or miles outside a person's skin, can generate mental responses inside his skull, or how decisions framed inside his cranium can set going movements of his extremities.

Even when "inner" and "outer" are construed as metaphors, the problem how a person's mind and body influence one another is notoriously

SOURCE: Gilbert Ryle, "Descartes' Myth," *The Concept of Mind* (London: Hutchinson, 1949), pp. 11–20, 22–23 (edited).

charged with theoretical difficulties. What the mind wills, the legs, arms and the tongue execute; what affects the ear and the eye has something to do with what the mind perceives; grimaces and smiles betray the mind's moods and bodily castigations lead, it is hoped, to moral improvement. But the actual transactions between the episodes of the private history and those of the public history remain mysterious, since by definition they can belong to neither series. They could not be reported among the happenings described in a person's autobiography of his inner life, but nor could they be reported among those described in some one else's biography of that person's overt career. They can be inspected neither by introspection nor by laboratory experiment. They are theoretical shuttlecocks which are forever being bandied from the physiologist back to the psychologist and from the psychologist back to the physiologist. . . .

There is thus a polar opposition between mind and matter, an opposition which is often brought out as follows. Material objects are situated in a common field, known as "space," and what happens to one body in one part of space is mechanically connected with what happens to other bodies in other parts of space. But mental happenings occur in insulated fields, known as "minds," and there is, apart maybe from telepathy, no direct causal connection between what happens in one mind and what happens in another. Only through the medium of the public physical world can the mind of one person make a difference to the mind of another. The mind is its own place and in his inner life each of us lives the life of a ghostly Robinson Crusoe. People can see, hear and jolt one another's bodies, but they are irremediably blind and deaf to the workings of one another's minds and inoperative upon them.

What sort of knowledge can be secured of the workings of a mind? On the one side, according to the official theory, a person has direct knowledge of the best imaginable kind of the workings of his own mind. Mental states and processes are (or are normally) conscious states and processes, and the consciousness which irradiates them can engender no illusions and leaves the door open for no doubts. A person's present thinkings, feelings and willings, his perceivings, rememberings and imaginings are intrinsically "phosphorescent"; their existence and their nature are inevitably betrayed to their owner. The inner life is a stream of consciousness of such a sort that it would be absurd to suggest that the mind whose life is that stream might be unaware of what is passing down it.

True, the evidence adduced recently by Freud seems to show that there exist channels tributary to this stream, which run hidden from their owner. People are actuated by impulses the existence of which they vigorously disavow; some of their thoughts differ from the thoughts which they acknowledge; and some of the actions which they think they will to perform they do not really will. They are thoroughly gulled by some of their own hypocrisies and they successfully ignore facts about their mental lives which on the official theory ought to be patent to them. Holders of the official theory tend, however, to maintain that anyhow in normal circumstances a person must be directly and authentically seized of the present state and workings of his own mind.

Besides being currently supplied with these alleged immediate data of consciousness, a person is also generally supposed to be able to exercise from time to time a special kind of perception, namely inner perception, or introspection. He can take a (non-optical) "look" at what is passing in his mind. Not only can he view and scrutinize a flower through his sense of sight and listen to and discriminate the notes of a bell through his sense of hearing; he can also reflectively or introspectively watch, without any bodily organ of sense, the current episodes of his inner life. This self-observation is also commonly supposed to be immune from illusion, confusion or doubt. A mind's reports of its own affairs have a certainty superior to the best that is possessed by its reports of matters in the physical world. Sense-perceptions can, but consciousness and introspection cannot, be mistaken or confused.

On the other side, one person has no direct access of any sort to the events of the inner life of another. He cannot do better than make problematic inferences from the observed behaviour of the other person's body to the states of mind which, by analogy from his own conduct, he supposes to be signalised by that behaviour. Direct access to the workings of a mind is the privilege of that mind itself; in default of such privileged access, the workings of one mind are inevitably occult to everyone else. For the supposed arguments from bodily movements similar to their own to mental workings similar to their own would lack any possibility of observational corroboration. Not unnaturally, therefore, an adherent of the official theory finds it difficult to resist this consequence of his premises, that he has no good reason to believe that there do exist minds other than his own. Even if he prefers to believe that to other human bodies there are harnessed minds not unlike his own, he cannot claim to be able to discover their individual characteristics, or the particular things that they undergo and do. Absolute solitude is on this showing the ineluctable destiny of the soul. Only our bodies can meet. . . .

## The Absurdity of the Official Doctrine

Such in outline is the official theory. I shall often speak of it, with deliberate abusiveness, as "the dogma of the Ghost in the Machine." I hope to prove that it is entirely false, and false not in detail but in principle. It is not merely an assemblage of particular mistakes. It is one big mistake and a mistake of a special kind. It is, namely, a category-mistake. It represents the facts of mental life as if they belonged to one logical type or category (or range of types or categories), when they actually belong to another. The dogma is therefore a philosopher's myth. In attempting to explode the myth I shall probably be taken to be denying well-known facts about the mental life of human beings, and my plea that I aim at doing nothing more than rectify the logic of mental-conduct concepts will probably be disallowed as mere subterfuge.

I must first indicate what is meant by the phrase "category-mistake." This I do in a series of illustrations.

A foreigner visiting Oxford or Cambridge for the first time is shown a number of colleges, libraries, playing fields, museums, scientific departments and administrative offices. He then asks "But where is the University? I have seen where the members of the Colleges live, where the Registrar works, where the scientists experiment and the rest. But I have not yet seen the University in which reside and work the members of your University." It has then to be explained to him that the University is not another collateral institution, some ulterior counterpart to the colleges, laboratories and offices which he has seen. The University is just the way in which all that he has already seen is organized. When they are seen and when their co-ordination is understood, the University has been seen. His mistake lay in his innocent assumption that it was correct to speak of Christ Church, the Bodleian Library, the Ashmolean Museum *and* the University, to speak, that is, as if "the University" stood for an extra member of the class of which these other units are members. He was mistakenly allocating the University to the same category as that to which the other institutions belong.

The same mistake would be made by a child witnessing the march-past of a division, who, having had pointed out to him such and such battalions, batteries, squadrons, etc., asked when the division was going to appear. He would be supposing that a division was a counterpart to the units already seen, partly similar to them and partly unlike them. He would be shown his mistake by being told that in watching the battalions, batteries and squadrons marching past he had been watching the division marching past. The march-past was not a parade of battalions, batteries, squadrons *and* a division; it was a parade of the battalions, batteries and squadrons *of* a division.

One more illustration. A foreigner watching his first game of cricket learns what are the functions of the bowlers, the batsmen, the fielders, the umpires and the scorers. He then says "But there is no one left on the field to contribute the famous element of team-spirit. I see who does the bowling, the batting and the wicket-keeping;

but I do not see whose role it is to exercise *esprit de corps.*" Once more, it would have to be explained that he was looking for the wrong type of thing. Team-spirit is not another cricketing-operation supplementary to all of the other special tasks. It is, roughly, the keenness with which each of the special tasks is performed, and performing a task keenly is not performing two tasks. Certainly exhibiting team-spirit is not the same thing as bowling or catching, but nor is it a third thing such that we can say that the bowler first bowls *and* then exhibits team-spirit or that a fielder is at a given moment *either* catching *or* displaying *esprit de corps.*

These illustrations of category-mistakes have a common feature which must be noticed. The mistakes were made by people who did not know how to wield the concepts *University, division* and *team-spirit.* Their puzzles arose from inability to use certain items in the English vocabulary. . . .

My destructive purpose is to show that a family of radical category-mistakes is the source of the double-life theory. The representation of a person as a ghost mysteriously ensconced in a machine derives from this argument. Because, as is true, a person's thinking, feeling and purposive doing cannot be described solely in the idioms of physics, chemistry and physiology, therefore they must be described in counterpart idioms. As the human body is a complex organised unit, so the human mind must be another complex organised unit, though one made of a different sort of stuff and with a different sort of structure. Or, again, as the human body, like any other parcel of matter, is a field of causes and effects, so the mind must be another field of causes and effects, though not (Heaven be praised) mechanical causes and effects.

## The Origin of the Category-Mistake

One of the chief intellectual origins of what I have yet to prove to be the Cartesian category-mistake seems to be this. When Galileo showed that his methods of scientific discovery were competent to provide a mechanical theory which

should cover every occupant of space, Descartes found in himself two conflicting motives. As a man of scientific genius he could not but endorse the claims of mechanics, yet as a religious and moral man he could not accept, as Hobbes accepted, the discouraging rider to those claims, namely that human nature differs only in degree of complexity from clockwork. The mental could not be just a variety of the mechanical.

He and subsequent philosophers naturally but erroneously availed themselves of the following escape-route. Since mental-conduct words are not to be construed as signifying the occurrence of mechanical processes, they must be construed as signifying the occurrence of non-mechanical processes; since mechanical laws explain movements in space as the effects of other movements in space, other laws must explain some of the non-spatial workings of minds as the effects of other non-spatial workings of minds. The difference between the human behaviours which we describe as intelligent and those which we describe as unintelligent must be a difference in their causation; so, while some movements of human tongues and limbs are the effects of mechanical causes, others must be the effects of non-mechanical causes, i.e., some issue from movements of particles of matter, others from workings of the mind.

The differences between the physical and the mental were thus represented as differences inside the common framework of the categories of "thing," "stuff," "attribute," "state," "process," "change," "cause," and "effect." Minds are things, but different sorts of things from bodies; mental processes are causes and effects, but different sorts of causes and effects from bodily movements. And so on. Somewhat as the foreigner expected the University to be an extra edifice, rather like a college but also considerably different, so the repudiators of mechanism represented minds as extra centres of causal processes, rather like machines but also considerably different from them. Their theory was a para-mechanical hypothesis.

That this assumption was at the heart of the doctrine is shown by the fact that there was from the beginning felt to be a major theoretical difficulty in explaining how minds can influence and be influenced by bodies. How can a mental process, such as willing, cause spatial movements like the movements of the tongue? How can a physical change in the optic nerve have among its effects a mind's perception of a flash of light? This notorious crux by itself shows the logical mould into which Descartes pressed his theory of the mind. It was the self-same mould into which he and Galileo set their mechanics. Still unwittingly adhering to the grammar of mechanics, he tried to avert disaster by describing minds in what was merely an obverse vocabulary. The workings of minds had to be described by the mere negatives of the specific descriptions given to bodies; they are not in space, they are not motions, they are not modifications of matter, they are not accessible to public observation. Minds are not bits of clockwork, they are just bits of not-clockwork.

As thus represented, minds are not merely ghosts harnessed to machines, they are themselves just spectral machines. Though the human body is an engine, it is not quite an ordinary engine, since some of its workings are governed by another engine inside it—this interior governor-engine being one of a very special sort. It is invisible, inaudible and it has no size or weight. It cannot be taken to bits and the laws it obeys are not those known to ordinary engineers. Nothing is known of how it governs the bodily engine. . . .

When two terms belong to the same category, it is proper to construct conjunctive propositions embodying them. Thus a purchaser may say that he bought a left-hand glove and a right-hand glove, but not that he bought a left-hand glove, a right-hand glove and a pair of gloves. "She came home in a flood of tears and a sedan-chair" is a well-known joke based on the absurdity of conjoining terms of different types. It would have been equally ridiculous to construct the disjunction "She came home either in a flood of tears or else in a sedan-chair." Now the dogma of the Ghost in the Machine does just this. It maintains that there exist both processes; that there are mechanical causes of corporeal movements and

mental causes of corporeal movements. I shall argue that these and other analogous conjunctions are absurd; but, it must be noticed, the argument will not show that either of the illegitimately conjoined propositions is absurd in itself. I am not, for example, denying that there occur mental processes. Doing long division is a mental process and so is making a joke. But I am saying that the phrase "there occur mental processes" does not mean the same sort of thing as "there occur physical processes," and, therefore, that it makes no sense to conjoin or disjoin the two.

If my argument is successful, there will follow some interesting consequences. First, the hallowed contrast between Mind and Matter will be dissipated, but dissipated not by either of the equally hallowed absorptions of Mind by Matter or of Matter by Mind, but in quite a different way. For the seeming contrast of the two will be shown to be as illegitimate as would be the contrast of "she came home in a flood of tears" and "she came home in sedan-chair." The belief that there is a polar opposition between Mind and Matter is the belief that they are terms of the same logical type.

It will also follow that both Idealism and Materialism are answers to an improper question. The "reduction" of the material world to mental states and processes, as well as the "reduction" of mental states and processes to physical states and processes, presuppose the legitimacy of the disjunction "Either there exist minds or there exist bodies (but not both)." It would be like saying, "Either she bought a left-hand and a right-hand glove or she bought a pair of gloves (but not both)."

It is perfectly proper to say, in one logical tone of voice, that there exist minds and to say, in another logical tone of voice, that there exist bodies. But these expressions do not indicate two different species of existence, for "existence" is not a generic word like "coloured" or "sexed." They indicate two different senses of "exist," somewhat as "rising" has different senses in "the tide is rising," "hopes are rising," and "the average age of death is rising." A man would be thought to be making a poor joke who said that three things are now rising, namely the tide, hopes and the average age of death. It would be just as good or bad a joke to say that there exist prime numbers and Wednesdays and public opinions and navies; or that there exist both minds and bodies. In the succeeding chapters I try to prove that the official theory does rest on a batch of category-mistakes by showing that logically absurd corollaries follow from it. The exhibition of these absurdities will have the constructive effect of bringing out part of the correct logic of mental-conduct concepts.

# THE PROBLEM OF CONSCIOUSNESS

## *Nagel's Bats*

Thomas Nagel (1937–) is an American philosopher who teaches at New York University and who has written on a wide variety of philosophical issues, including the mind/body problem. He is the author of *The Possibility of Altruism* (1970), *Mortal Questions* (1979), *The View from Nowhere* (1986), *The Last Word* (1996), and *What Does It All Mean? A Very Short Introduction to Philosophy* (1987), a "for beginners" sort of book often used in undergraduate philosophy courses.

In *The View from Nowhere,* Nagel tries to reconcile the subjective and personal elements of human experience with objective and impersonal truths about our knowledge, our values, and our lives. In *The Last Word,* Nagel attacks "subjectivism," which he takes to include relativism about knowledge, skepticism about ethics, and postmodernism, all of which he sees as the enemies of objective reason. Nagel argues that, to attack reason, we have to use a universal notion of reason or else engage in nonsense.

Yet he himself to a degree champions the value of subjective experience in his widely read article "What Is It Like to Be a Bat?" (1974). In it Nagel argues that materialist theories of the mind overlook a very important element of our human experience: the subjective nature of consciousness. All conscious beings have a subjective notion of what it's like to experience the world, know what it's like to *be* whomever or whatever they are. They have a point of view. This subjective experience might be quite similar among members of the same species, although not identical (even within the human species, our tastes and beliefs differ widely, and there's no reason to assume that my experience of a given phenomenon will be identical to yours).

Further, we certainly can't know what it's like to have the subjective experience of members of another species, for example, bats or Martians. To say that my subjective experience of the taste of chocolate ice cream is produced by the firing of neuron 2341 in some neurological map of my brain may explain that experience in purely physical terms; but it doesn't explain how I consciously experience that taste. It would be as though in response to my question, "Why do you find Bach's Brandenburg Concertos beautiful?" you answered by listing all the frequencies of the sounds produced by the orchestra playing these works. I might be impressed by your understanding of the physics of sound, but my question would stand.

Since materialism (in its simplest version) cannot describe consciousness other than by reducing it to something else, namely physical processes, or by eliminating it entirely, it doesn't really explain the nature of the mind at all.

We can term Nagel's position on the mind/body problem "phenomenalism" for a couple of reasons. First, he argues that even though our mental states might be produced by physical processes, we don't know how this connection between mental and physical states actually works. Further, our mental states are autonomous in that they have a subjective quality that *cannot* be reduced to any possible physical description of them. Our subjective mental phenomena have their own special status, a status that cannot be eliminated by reducing them to physical states of our body. A philosophy of mind must explain these mental phenomena in their own right if it's to be taken seriously, just as a music critic would have to say more about Bach's work than it consists of a serious of sounds with such and such frequencies and volume levels if we are to take them seriously.

# What Is It Like to Be a Bat?

## THOMAS NAGEL

CONSCIOUSNESS is what makes the mind-body problem really intractable. Perhaps that is why current discussions of the problem give it little attention or get it obviously wrong. The recent wave of reductionist euphoria has produced several analyses of mental phenomena and mental concepts designed to explain the possibility of some variesty of materialism, psychophysical identification, or reduction. But the problems dealt with are those common to this type of reduction and other types, and what makes the mind-body problem unique, and unlike the water-$H_2O$ problem or the Turing machine-IBM machine problem or the lightning-electrical discharge problem or the gene-DNA problem or the oak tree-hydrocarbon problem, is ignored.

Every reductionist has his favorite analogy from modern science. It is most unlikely that any of these unrelated examples of successful reduction will shed light on the relation of mind to brain. But philosophers share the general human weakness for explanations of what is incomprehensible in terms suited for what is familiar and well understood, though entirely different. This has led to the acceptance of implausible accounts of the mental largely because they would permit familiar kinds of reduction. I shall try to explain why the usual examples do not help us to understand the relation between mind and body— why, indeed, we have at present no conception of what an explanation of the physical nature of a mental phenomenon would be. Without consciousness the mind-body problem would be much less interesting. With consciousness it seems hopeless. The most important and characteristic feature of conscious mental phenomena is very poorly understood. Most reductionist theories do not even try to explain it. And careful examination will show that no currently available concept of reduction is applicable to it. Perhaps a new theoretical form can be devised for the purpose, but such a solution, if it exists, lies in the distant intellectual future.

Conscious experience is a widespread phenomenon. It occurs at many levels of animal life, though we cannot be sure of its presence in the simpler organisms, and it is very difficult to say in general what provides evidence of it. (Some

SOURCE: Thomas Nagel, "What Is It Like to Be a Bat?" *Philosophical Review* 83 (1974): 435–446 (last few pages and footnotes cut).

extremists have been prepared to deny it even of mammals other than man.) No doubt it occurs in countless forms totally unimaginable to us, on other planets in other solar systems throughout the universe. But no matter how the form may vary, the fact that an organism has conscious experience *at all* means, basically, that there is something it is like to *be* that organism. There may be further implications about the form of the experience; there may even (though I doubt it) be implications about the behavior of the organism. But fundamentally an organism has conscious mental states if and only if there is something that it is to *be* that organism—something it is like *for* the organism.

We may call this the subjective character of experience. It is not captured by any of the familiar, recently devised reductive analyses of the mental, for all of them are logically compatible with its absence. It is not analyzable in terms of any explanatory system of functional states, or intentional states, since these could be ascribed to robots or automata that behaved like people though they experienced nothing. It is not analyzable in terms of the causal role of experiences in relation to typical human behavior—for similar reasons. I do not deny that conscious mental states and events cause behavior, nor that they may be given functional characterizations. I deny only that this kind of thing exhausts their analysis. Any reductionist program has to be based on an analysis of what is to be reduced. If the analysis leaves something out, the problem will be falsely posed. It is useless to base the defense of materialism on any analysis of mental phenomena that fails to deal explicitly with their subjective character. For there is no reason to suppose that a reduction which seems plausible when no attempt is made to account for consciousness can be extended to include consciousness. Without some idea, therefore, of what the subjective character of experience is, we cannot know what is required of physicalist theory.

While an account of the physical basis of mind must explain many things, this appears to be the most difficult. It is impossible to exclude the phenomenological features of experience from a reduction in the same way that one excludes the phenomenal features of an ordinary substance from a physical or chemical reduction of it—namely, by explaining them as effects on the minds of human observers. If physicalism is to be defended, the phenomenological features must themselves be given a physical account. But when we examine their subjective character it seems that such a result is impossible. The reason is that every subjective phenomenon is essentially connected with a single point of view, and it seems inevitable that an objective, physical theory will abandon that point of view.

Let me first try to state the issue somewhat more fully than by referring to the relation between the subjective and the objective, or between the *pour-soi* and the *en-soi*.[1] This is far from easy. Facts about what it is like to be an *X* are very peculiar, so peculiar that some may be inclined to doubt their reality, or the significance of claims about them. To illustrate the connection between subjectivity and a point of view, and to make evident the importance of subjective features, it will help to explore the matter in relation to an example that brings out clearly the divergence between the two types of conception, subjective and objective.

I assume we all believe that bats have experience. After all, they are mammals, and there is no more doubt that they have experience than that mice or pigeons or whales have experience. I have chosen bats instead of wasps or flounders because if one travels too far down the phylogenetic tree, people gradually shed their faith that there is experience there at all. Bats, although more closely related to us than those other species, nevertheless present a range of activity and a sensory apparatus so different from ours that the problem I want to pose is exceptionally vivid (though it certainly could be raised with other species). Even without the benefit of philosophical reflection, anyone who has spent some time in an enclosed space with an excited bat knows

---

[1] Nagel refers to Sartre's terms for being-for-itself and being-in-itself, roughly free human consciousness and purely physical matter—ED.

what it is to encounter a fundamentally alien form of life.

I have said that the essence of the belief that bats have experience is that there is something that it is like to be a bat. Now we know that most bats (the microchiroptera, to be precise) perceive the external world primarily by sonar, or echolocation, detecting the reflections, from objects within range, of their own rapid, subtly modulated, high-frequency shrieks. Their brains are designed to correlate the outgoing impulses with the subsequent echoes, and the information thus acquired enables bats to make precise discriminations of distance, size, shape, motion, and texture comparable to those we make by vision. But bat sonar, though clearly a form of perception, is not similar in its operation to any sense that we possess, and there is no reason to suppose that it is subjectively like anything we can experience or imagine. This appears to create difficulties for the notion of what it is like to be a bat. We must consider whether any method will permit us to extrapolate to the inner life of the bat from our own case, and if not, what alternative methods there may be for understanding the notion.

Our own experience provides the basic material for our imagination, whose range is therefore limited. It will not help to try to imagine that one has webbing on one's arms, which enables one to fly around at dusk and dawn catching insects in one's mouth; that one has very poor vision, and perceives the surrounding world by a system of reflected high-frequency sound signals; and that one spends the day hanging upside down by one's feet in an attic. In so far as I can imagine this (which is not very far), it tells me only what it would be like for *me* to behave as a bat behaves. But that is not the question. I want to know what it is like for a bat to be a bat. Yet if I try to imagine this, I am restricted to the resources of my own mind, and those resources are inadequate to the task. I cannot perform it either by imagining additions to my present experience, or by imagining segments gradually subtracted from it, or by imagining some combination of additions, subtractions, and modifications.

To the extent that I could look and behave like a wasp or a bat without changing my funda-

mental structure, my experiences would not be anything like the experiences of those animals. On the other hand, it is doubtful that any meaning can be attached to the supposition that I should possess the internal neurophysiological constitution of a bat. Even if I could by gradual degrees be transformed into a bat, nothing in my present constitution enables me to imagine what the experiences of such a future stage of myself thus metamorphosed would be like. The best evidence would come from the experiences of bats, if we only knew what they were like.

So if extrapolation from our own case is involved in the idea of what it is like to be a bat, the extrapolation must be incompletable. We cannot form more than a schematic conception of what it is like. For example, we may ascribe general *types* of experience on the basis of the animal's structure and behavior. Thus we describe bat sonar as a form of three-dimensional forward perception; we believe that bats feel some versions of pain, fear, hunger, and lust, and that they have other, more familiar types of perception besides sonar. But we believe that these experiences also have in each case a specific subjective character, which it is beyond our ability to conceive. And if there's conscious life elsewhere in the universe, it is likely that some of it will not be describable even in the most general experiential terms available to us. (The problem is not confined to exotic cases, however, for it exists between one person and another. The subjective character of the experience of a person deaf and blind from birth is not accessible to me, for example, nor presumably is mine to him. This does not prevent us each from believing that the other's experience has such a subjective character.)

If anyone is inclined to deny that we can believe in the existence of facts like this whose exact nature we cannot possibly conceive, he should reflect that in contemplating the bats we are in much the same position that intelligent bats or Martians would occupy if they tried to form a conception of what it was like to be us. The structure of their own minds might make it impossible for them to succeed, but we know they would be wrong to conclude that there is not anything precise that it is like to be us: that only certain general types of mental state could be as-cribed to us (perhaps perception and appetite would be concepts common to us both; perhaps not). We know they would be wrong to draw such a skeptical conclusion because we know what it is like to be us. And we know that while it includes an enormous amount of variation and complexity, and while we do not possess the vo-cabulary to describe it adequately, its subjective character is highly specific, and in some respects describable in terms that can be understood only by creatures like us. The fact that we cannot ex-pect ever to accommodate in our language a detailed description of Martian or bat phenome-nology should not lead us to dismiss as mean-ingless the claim that bats and Martians have experiences fully comparable in richness of detail to our own. It would be fine if someone were to develop concepts and a theory that enabled us to think about those things; but such an under-standing may be permanently denied to us by the limits of our nature. And to deny the reality or logical significance of what we can never describe or understand is the crudest form of cognitive dissonance. This brings us to the edge of a topic that requires much more discussion than I can give it here: namely, the relation between facts on the one hand and conceptual schemes or sys-tems of representation on the other. My realism about the subjective domain in all its forms im-plies a belief in the existence of facts beyond the reach of human concepts. Certainly it is possible for a human being to believe that there are facts which humans never *will* possess the requisite concepts to represent or comprehend. Indeed, it would be foolish to doubt this, given the finite-ness of humanity's expectations. After all there would have been transfinite numbers even if everyone had been wiped out by the Black Death before Cantor discovered them. But one might also believe that there are facts which *could* not ever be represented or comprehended by human beings, even if the species lasted for ever—sim-ply because our structure does not permit us to operate with concepts of the requisite type. This impossibility might even be observed by other beings, but it is not clear that the existence of such beings, or the possibility of their existence,

is a precondition of the significance of the hy-pothesis that there are humanly inaccessible facts. (After all, the nature of beings with access to humanly inaccessible facts is presumably itself a humanly inaccessible fact.) Reflection on what it is like to be a bat seems to lead us, therefore, to the conclusion that there are facts that do not consist in the truth of propositions expressible in a human language. We can be compelled to rec-ognize the existence of such facts without being able to state or comprehend them.

I shall not pursue this subject, however. Its bearing on the topic before us (namely, the mind-body problem) is that it enables us to make a general observation about the subjective character of experience. Whatever may be the status of facts about what it is like to be a human being, or a bat, or a Martian, these appear to be facts that embody a particular point of view.

I am not adverting here to the alleged privacy of experience to its possessor. The point of view in question is not one accessible only to a single individual. Rather it is a *type*. It is often possible to take up a point of view other than one's own, so the comprehension of such facts is not limited to one's own case. There is a sense in which phe-nomenological facts are perfectly objective: one person can know or say of another what the qual-ity of the other's experience is. They are subjec-tive, however, in the sense that even this objec-tive ascription of experience is possible only for someone sufficiently similar to the object of as-cription to be able to adopt his point of view—to understand the ascription in the first person as well as in the third, so to speak. The more differ-ent from oneself the other experiencer is, the less success one can expect with this enterprise. In our own case we occupy the relevant point of view, but we will have as much difficulty understand-ing our own experience properly if we approach it from another point of view as we would if we tried to understand the experience of another species without taking up *its* point of view.

This bears directly on the mind-body prob-lem. For if the facts of experience—facts about what it is like for the experiencing organism—are accessible only from one point of view, then it is a mystery how the true character of experiences could be revealed in the physical operation of that organism. The latter is a domain of objective facts *par excellence*—the kind that can be observed and understood from many points of view and by individuals with differing perceptual systems. There are no comparable imaginative obstacles to the acquisition of knowledge about bat neurophysiology by human scientists, and intelligent bats or Martians might learn more about the human brain than we ever will.

This is not by itself an argument against reduction. A Martian scientist with no understanding of visual perception could understand the rainbow, or lightning, or clouds as physical phenomena, though he would never be able to understand the human concepts of rainbow, lightning, or cloud, or the place these things occupy in our phenomenal world. The objective nature of the things picked out by these concepts could be apprehended by him because, although the concepts themselves are connected with a particular point of view and a particular visual phenomenology, the things apprehended from that point of view are not: they are observable from the point of view but external to it; hence they can be comprehended from other points of view also, either by the same organisms or by others. Lightning has an objective character that is not exhausted by its visual appearance, and this can be investigated by a Martian without vision. To be precise, it has a more objective character than is revealed in its visual appearance. In speaking of the move from subjective to objective characterization, I wish to remain noncommittal about the existence of an end point, the completely objective intrinsic nature of the thing, which one might or might not be able to reach. It may be more accurate to think of objectivity as a direction in which the understanding can travel. And in understanding a phenomenon like lightning, it is legitimate to go as far away as one can from a strictly human viewpoint.

In the case of experience, on the other hand, the connection with a particular point of view seems much closer. It is difficult to understand what could be meant by the *objective* character of an experience, apart from the particular point of view from which its subject apprehends it. After all, what would be left of what it was like to be a bat if one removed the viewpoint of the bat? But if experience does not have, in addition to its subjective character, an objective nature that can be apprehended from many different points of view, then how can it be supposed that a Martian investigating my brain might be observing physical processes which were my mental processes (as he might observe physical processes which were bolts of lightning), only from a different point of view? How, for that matter, could a human physiologist observe them from another point of view?

We appear to be faced with a general difficulty about psychophysical reduction. In other areas the process of reduction is a move in the direction of greater objectivity, toward a more, accurate view of the real nature of things. This is accomplished by reducing our dependence on individual or species-specific points of view toward the object of investigation. We describe it not in terms of the impressions it makes on our senses, but in terms of its more general effects and of properties detectable by means other than the human senses. The less it depends on a specifically human viewpoint, the more objective is our description. It is possible to follow this path because although the concepts and ideas we employ in thinking about the external world are initially applied from a point of view that involves our perceptual apparatus, they are used by us to refer to things beyond themselves—toward which we *have* the phenomenal point of view. Therefore we can abandon it in favor of another, and still be thinking about the same things.

Experience itself, however, does not seem to fit the pattern. The idea of moving from appearance to reality seems to make no sense here. What is the analogue in this case to pursuing a more objective understanding of the same phenomena by abandoning the initial subjective viewpoint toward them in favor of another that is more objective but concerns the same thing? Certainly it *appears* unlikely that we will get closer to the real nature of human experience by leaving behind the particularity of our human point of view and striving for a description in terms accessible to beings that could not imagine what it was like to be us. If the subjective character of experience is fully comprehensible only from one point of view, then any shift to greater objectivity—that is, less attachment to a specific viewpoint—does not take us nearer to the real nature of the phenomenon: it takes us farther away from it.

In a sense, the seeds of this objection to the reducibility of experience are already detectable in successful cases of reduction; for in discovering sound to be, in reality, a wave phenomenon in air or other media, we leave behind one viewpoint to take up another, and the auditory, human or animal viewpoint that we leave behind remains unreduced. Members of radically different species may both understand the same physical events in objective terms, and this does not require that they understand the phenomenal forms in which those events appear to the senses of members of the other species. Thus it is a condition of their referring to a common reality that their more particular viewpoints are not part of the common reality that they both apprehend. The reduction can succeed only if the species-specific viewpoint is omitted from what is to be reduced.

But while we are right to leave this point of view aside in seeking a fuller understanding of the external world, we cannot ignore it permanently, since it is the essence of the internal world, and not merely a point of view on it. Most of the neobehaviorism of recent philosophical psychology results from the effort to substitute an objective concept of mind for the real thing, in order to have nothing left over which cannot be reduced. If we acknowledge that a physical theory of mind must account for the subjective character of experience, we must admit that no presently available conception gives us a clue how this could be done. The problem is unique. If mental processes are indeed physical processes, then there is something it is like, intrinsically, to undergo certain physical processes. What it is for such a thing to be the case remains a mystery.

## Eliminative Materialism

Paul Churchland (1942–) teaches at the University of California at San Diego and is the author of *Scientific Realism and the Plasticity of Mind* (1979), *Matter and Consciousness: A Contemporary Introduction to the Philosophy of Mind* (1984), and *The Engine of Reason, the Seat of the Soul: A Philosophical Journey into the Brain* (1995). He is known for his work in cognitive science and his defense of "eliminative materialism." He often writes with his wife, Patricia Smith Churchland, who shares similar views.

Churchland's eliminative materialism claims that when we talk about our mental states using terms such as "beliefs," "desires," "motives," or "intentions," we're engaging in folk psychology. This is a primitive, inaccurate way of speaking about our internal states. Yet, unlike the strongest form of materialism, identity theory, which claims that we can *reduce* mental states to physical states, eliminative materialism says that this takes our talk of mental states far too seriously: We won't be able match up our mental states on a one-to-one basis to our physical states because the language we use to describe our mental states is the product of a prescientific, confused way of thinking. It would be a miracle if these early descriptions of our mental life had been right in the first place, just as it would have been a miracle if medieval alchemy had attained the same understanding of the chemical elements as we have today.

Eliminative materialism claims instead that eventually we'll be able to eliminate the use of mental terminology all together, just as we no longer talk seriously about phlogiston, crystal spheres in the heavens, or witches. Neuroscience will be able to explain our so-called mental events more scientifically than our folk psychology will. So it's not a matter of our minds being identical with our bodies, but of our minds not existing at all.

Of course, Nagel's bats come flying in at this point. Even *if* Churchland's neuroscience can explain everything going on in our brains, we cannot escape the fact that we're conscious beings who *think,* however erroneously, we have subjective experiences or points of view. Eliminating "folk psychology" would eliminate, by definition, subjective consciousness from the mind/body problem.

Churchland has a quick response to this sort of critique: It begs the question. Human beings used to *really believe* that women who used their knowledge of herbal medicines to cure the sick were witches in league with the devil. This was an element of *their* subjective consciousness. We now know this belief is false. Similarly, we'll one day realize that our subjective notions of desires, motives, and beliefs are also inadequate representations of our brain states, which are better dealt with by a mature neuroscientific language.

Perhaps we can see the difference between Churchland and Nagel as the difference between biology and history. When studying a plague that affected a community a century ago, a biologist might obtain preserved tissue samples and look at them under a microscope. He or she probably wouldn't be interested in reading diaries describing the horrible suffering the plague inflicted on the community's members, unless they contained clear descriptions of the disease's symptoms. Yet the historian would be very interested in these diaries and in the effects of the plague on the social structure of the community.

Churchland's project is like that of the biologist: Folk concepts like "desires" just get in his way of advancing the cause of neuroscience. Nagel's goal is somewhat different: He's more like the historian who wants to explain not just the physical nature of the plague virus, but its effects on individuals' lives, which are, by their very nature, subjective. A history of the plague that consisted solely of a scientific description of the virus and statistics on the illnesses and deaths that the virus caused wouldn't really be a history at all. So each of their positions on the mind/body problem can be seen as useful given the nature of their respective projects. This, of course, leaves open the basic question of what's more valuable, a neuroscientific account of human thought, Churchland's aim, or a phenomenological account, Nagel's goal. That, it would seem, is an ethical or political question.

# Eliminative Materialism

## PAUL M. CHURCHLAND

THE IDENTITY THEORY was called into doubt not because the prospects for a materialist account of our mental capacities were thought to be poor, but because it seemed unlikely that the arrival of an adequate materialist theory would bring with it the nice one-to-one match-ups, between the concepts of folk psychology and the concepts of theoretical neuroscience, that inter-

SOURCE: Paul M. Churchland, *Matter and Consciousness* (Cambridge, MA: Bradford/MIT, 1984), pp. 43–49; reprinted in *Introduction to Philosophy*, ed. John Perry and Michael Bratman (Oxford: Oxford University Press, 1993), pp. 353–357.

theoretic reduction requires. The reason for that doubt was the great variety of quite different physical systems that could instantiate the required functional organization. *Eliminative materialism* also doubts that the correct neuroscientific account of human capacities will produce a neat reduction of our common-sense framework, but here the doubts arise from a quite different source.

As the eliminative materialists see it, the one-to-one match-ups will not be found, and our common-sense psychological framework is a false and radically misleading conception of the causes of human behavior and the nature of cognitive activity. On this view, folk psychology is not just an incomplete representation of our inner natures; it is an outright *mis*representation of our internal states and activities. Consequently, we cannot expect a truly adequate neuroscientific account of our inner lives to provide theoretical categories that match up nicely with the categories of our common-sense framework. Accordingly, we must expect that the older framework will simply be eliminated, rather than be reduced, by a matured neuroscience.

## Historical Parallels

As the identity theorist can point to historical cases of successful intertheoretic reduction, so the eliminative materialist can point to historical cases of the outright elimination of the ontology of an older theory in favor of the ontology of a new and superior theory. For most of the eighteenth and nineteenth centuries, learned people believed that heat was a subtle *fluid* held in bodies, much in the way water is held in a sponge. A fair body of moderately successful theory described the way this fluid substance—called "caloric"—flowed within a body, or from one body to another, and how it produced thermal expansion, melting, boiling, and so forth. But by the end of the last century it had become abundantly clear that the heat was not a substance at all, but just the energy of motion of the trillions of jostling molecules that make up the heated body itself. The new theory—the "corpuscular/

kinetic theory of matter and heat"—was much more successful than the old in explaining and predicting the thermal behavior of bodies. And since we were unable to *identify* caloric fluid with kinetic energy (according to the old theory, caloric is a material *substance:* according to the new theory, kinetic energy is a form of *motion*), it was finally agreed that there is *no such thing* as caloric. Caloric was simply eliminated from our accepted ontology.

A second example. It used to be thought that when a piece of wood burns, or a piece of metal rusts, a spiritlike substance called "phlogiston" was being released: briskly, in the former case, slowly in the latter. Once gone, that "noble" substance left only a base pile of ash or rust. It later came to be appreciated that both processes involve, not the loss of something, but the *gaining* of a substance taken from the atmosphere: oxygen. Phlogiston emerged, not as an incomplete description of what was going on, but as a radical misdescription. Phlogiston was therefore not suitable for reduction to or identification with some notion from within the new oxygen chemistry, and it was simply eliminated from science.

Admittedly, both of these examples concern the elimination of something nonobservable, but our history also includes the elimination of certain widely accepted "observables." Before Copernicus's views became available, almost any human who ventured out at night could look up at *the starry sphere of the heavens,* and if he stayed for more than a few minutes he could also see that it *turned,* around an axis through Polaris. What the sphere was made of (crystal?) and what made it turn (the gods?) were theoretical questions that exercised us for over two millennia. But hardly anyone doubted the existence of what everyone could observe with their own eyes. In the end, however, we learned to reinterpret our visual experience of the night sky within a very different conceptual framework, and the turning sphere evaporated.

Witches provide another example. Psychosis is a fairly common affliction among humans, and in earlier centuries its victims were standardly seen as cases of demonic possession, as instances of Satan's spirit itself, glaring malevolently out at us from behind the victims' eyes. That witches exist was not a matter of any controversy. One would occasionally see them, in any city or hamlet, engaged in incoherent, paranoid, or even murderous behavior. But observable or not, we eventually decided that witches simply do not exist. We concluded that the concept of a witch is an element in a conceptual framework that misrepresents so badly the phenomena to which it was standardly applied that literal application of the notion should be permanently withdrawn. Modern theories of mental dysfunction led to the elimination of witches from our serious ontology.

The concepts of folk psychology—belief, desire, fear, sensation, pain, joy, and so on—await a similar fate, according to the view at issue. And when neuroscience has matured to the point where the poverty of our current conceptions is apparent to everyone, and the superiority of the new framework is established, we shall then be able to set about *reconceiving* our internal states and activities, within a truly adequate conceptual framework at last. Our explanations of one another's behavior will appeal to such things as our neuropharmacological states, the neural activity in specialized anatomical areas, and whatever other states are deemed relevant by the new theory. Our private introspection will also be transformed, and may be profoundly enhanced by reason of the more accurate and penetrating framework it will have to work with—just as the astronomer's perception of the night sky is much enhanced by the detailed knowledge of modern astronomical theory that he or she possesses.

The magnitude of the conceptual revolution here suggested should not be minimized: it would be enormous. And the benefits to humanity might be equally great. If each of us possessed an accurate neuroscientific understanding of (what we now conceive dimly as) the varieties and causes of mental illness, the factors involved in learning, the neural basis of emotions, intelligence, and socialization, then the sum total of human misery might be much reduced. The simple increase in mutual understanding that the

new framework made possible could contribute substantially toward a more peaceful and humane society. Of course, there would be dangers as well: increased knowledge means increased power, and power can always be misused.

## Arguments for Eliminative Materialism

The arguments for eliminative materialism are diffuse and less than decisive, but they are stronger than is widely supposed. The distinguishing feature of this position is its denial that a smooth intertheoretic reduction is to be expected—even a species-specific reduction—of the framework of folk psychology to the framework of a matured neuroscience. The reason for this denial is the eliminative materialist's conviction that folk psychology is a hopelessly primitive and deeply confused conception of our internal activities. But why this low opinion of our common-sense conceptions?

There are at least three reasons. First, the eliminative materialist will point to the widespread explanatory, predictive, and manipulative failures of folk psychology. So much of what is central and familiar to us remains a complete mystery from within folk psychology. We do not know what *sleep* is, or why we have to have it, despite spending a full third of our lives in that condition. (The answer, "For rest." is mistaken. Even if people are allowed to rest continuously, their need for sleep is undiminished. Apparently, sleep serves some deeper functions, but we do not yet know what they are.) We do not understand how *learning* transforms each of us from a gaping infant to a cunning adult, or how differences in *intelligence* are grounded. We have not the slightest idea how *memory* works, or how we manage to retrieve relevant bits of information instantly from the awesome mass we have stored. We do not know what *mental illness* is, nor how to cure it.

In sum, the most central things about us remain almost entirely mysterious from within folk psychology. And the defects noted cannot be blamed on inadequate time allowed for their correction, for folk psychology has enjoyed no significant changes or advances in well over 2,000 years, despite its manifest failures. Truly successful theories may be expected to reduce, but significantly unsuccessful theories merit no such expectation.

This argument from explanatory poverty has a further aspect. So long as one sticks to normal brains, the poverty of folk psychology is perhaps not strikingly evident. But as soon as one examines the many perplexing behavioral and cognitive deficits suffered by people with *damaged* brains, one's descriptive and explanatory resources start to claw the air (see, for example chapter 7.3 [of *Matter and Consciousness* (Bradford/MIT, 1984)]). As with other humble theories asked to operate successfully in unexplored extensions of their old domain (for example, Newtonian mechanics in the domain of velocities close to the velocity of light, and the classical gas law in the domain of high pressures or temperatures), the descriptive and explanatory inadequacies of folk psychology become starkly evident.

The second argument tries to draw an inductive lesson from our conceptual history. Our early folk theories of motion were profoundly confused, and were eventually displaced entirely by more sophisticated theories. Our early folk theories of the structure and activity of the heavens were wildly off the mark, and survive only as historical lessons in how wrong we can be. Our folk theories of the nature of fire, and the nature of life, were similarly cockeyed. And one could go on, since the vast majority of our past folk conceptions have been similarly exploded. All except folk psychology, which survives to this day and has only recently begun to feel pressure. But the phenomenon of conscious intelligence is surely a more complex and difficult phenomenon than any of those just listed. So far as accurate understanding is concerned, it would be a *miracle* if we had got *that* one right the very first time, when we fell down so badly on all the other. Folk psychology has survived for so very long, presumably, not because it is basically correct in

its representations, but because the phenomena addressed are so surpassingly difficult that any useful handle on them, no matter how feeble, is unlikely to be displaced in a hurry.

A third argument attempts to find an a priori advantage for eliminative materialism over the identity theory and functionalism. It attempts to counter the common intuition that eliminative materialism is distantly possible, perhaps, but is much less probable than either the identity theory or functionalism. The focus again is on whether the concepts of folk psychology will find vindicating match-ups in a matured neuroscience. The eliminativist bets no: the other two bet yes. (Even the functionalist bets yes, but expects the match-ups to be only species-specific, or only person-specific. Functionalism, recall, denies the existence only of *universal* type/type identities.)

The eliminativist will point out that the requirements on a reduction are rather demanding. The new theory must entail a set of principles and embedded concepts that mirrors very closely the specific conceptual structure to be reduced. And the fact is, there are vastly many more ways of being an explanatorily successful neuroscience while *not* mirroring the structure of folk psychology. Accordingly, the a priori probability of eliminative materialism is not lower, but substantially *higher* than that of either of its competitors. One's initial intuitions here are simply mistaken.

Granted, this initial a priori advantage could be reduced if there were a very strong presumption in favor of the truth of folk psychology— true theories are better bets to win reduction. But according to the first two arguments, the presumptions on this point should run in precisely the opposite direction.

## Arguments against Eliminative Materialism

The initial plausibility of this rather radical view is low for almost everyone, since it denies deeply entrenched assumptions. That is at best a question-begging complaint, of course, since those assumptions are precisely what is at issue. But the following line of thought does attempt to mount a real argument.

Eliminative materialism is false, runs the argument, because one's introspection reveals directly the existence of pains, beliefs, desires, fears, and so forth. Their existence is as obvious as anything could be.

The eliminative materialist will reply that this argument makes the same mistake that an ancient or medieval person would be making if he insisted that he could just see with his own eyes that the heavens form a turning sphere, or that witches exist. The fact is, all observation occurs within some system of concepts, and our observation judgments are only as good as the conceptual framework in which they are expressed. In all three cases—the starry sphere, witches, and the familiar mental states—precisely what is challenged is the integrity of the background conceptual frameworks in which the observation judgments are expressed. To insist on the validity of one's experiences, *traditionally interpreted,* is therefore to beg the very question at issue. For in all three cases, the question is whether we should *re*conceive the nature of some familiar observational domain.

A second criticism attempts to find an incoherence in the eliminative materialist's position. The bald statement of eliminative materialism is that the familiar mental states do not really exist. But that statement is meaningful, runs the argument, only if it is the expression of a certain *belief,* and an *intention* to communicate, and a *knowledge* of the language, and so forth. But if the statement is true, then no such mental states exist, and the statement is therefore a meaningless string of marks or noises, and cannot be true. Evidently, the assumption that eliminative materialism is true entails that it cannot be true.

The hole in this argument is the premise concerning the conditions necessary for a statement to be meaningful. It begs the question. If eliminative materialism is true, then meaningfulness must have some different source. To insist on the "old" source is to insist on the validity of the very framework at issue. Again, an historical parallel

may be helpful here. Consider the medieval theory that being biologically *alive* is a matter of being ensouled by an immaterial *vital spirit.* And consider the following response to someone who has expressed disbelief in that theory.

> My learned friend has stated that there is no such thing as vital spirit. But this statement is incoherent. For if it is true, then my friend does not have vital spirit, and must therefore be *dead.* But if he is dead, then his statement is just a string of noises, devoid of meaning or truth. Evidently, the assumption that antivitalism is true entails that it cannot be true! Q.E.D.

This second argument is now a joke, but the first argument begs the question in exactly the same way.

A final criticism draws a much weaker conclusion, but makes a rather stronger case. Eliminative materialism, it has been said, is making mountains out of molehills. It exaggerates the defects in folk psychology, and underplays its real successes. Perhaps the arrival of a matured neuroscience will require the elimination of the occasional folk-psychological concept, continues the criticism, and a minor adjustment in certain folk-psychological principles may have to be endured. But the large-scale elimination forecast by the eliminative materialist is just an alarmist worry or a romantic enthusiasm.

Perhaps this complaint is correct. And perhaps it is merely complacent. Whichever, it does bring out the important point that we do not confront two simple and mutually exclusive possibilities here: pure reduction versus pure elimination. Rather, these are the end points of a smooth spectrum of possible outcomes, between which there are mixed cases of partial elimination and partial reduction. Only empirical research (see chapter 7 [of *Matter and Consciousness*]) can tell us where on that spectrum our own case will fall. Perhaps we should speak here, more liberally, of "revisionary materialism," instead of concentrating on the more radical possibility of an across-the-board elimination. Perhaps we should. But it has been my aim in this [selection] to make it at least intelligible to you that our collective conceptual destiny lies substantially toward the revolutionary end of the spectrum.

# PART II   THE SELF

## FIVE THEORIES OF THE SELF

### Prologue

A metaphysical question that is even more fundamental than the mind/body problem, one that informs not only philosophy, but also psychology, sociology, political science, economics, literature, religion, and popular culture, is "What is the self?" or, more generally, "What is human nature?" All the great thinkers, either inadvertently or deliberately, put forward some sort of theory of human nature. In this section we'll look at five theories of the self that have been of some significance in modern Western thought.

The five views of the self chosen for this chapter have some justification. They are all connected to important traditions in Western thought and literature, and although each tradition had its stars, none can be seen as the creation of just one great thinker. Second, they bear on some of the questions dealt with in the philosophy of mind. Third, these five theories of the self interact by answering the following questions in a unique set of ways:

- Where does valid knowledge come from? Can we know the external world?
- Is reason or passion more important in governing our lives?
- Do we have an authentic inner self separate from our empirical experiences or social life, or is the self defined by our interaction with the external world?
- Is morality individual or social? Are moral rules given to us by God, by nature, or by society? Or are they rational truths? Or are they purely self-chosen?
- What is the best life? Does it involve intellectual pursuits, fulfilling a creative impulse, a communion with nature, or vibrant social interactions?

As you go through the commentaries and readings that follow, try to sort out how each of the five theories of the self would answer the previous questions.

### The Rationalist Self

We will only briefly deal with the rationalist self, as you should already have a good sense of its fundamentals from the discussion of Descartes in Part I of this chapter. A rationalist is someone who believes that all reliable knowledge comes from our reason. Rationalism was the dominant movement in continental philosophy in the seventeenth and early eighteenth centuries in Western Europe. The holy trinity of rationalism consisted of the father of modern philosophy, Descartes, who we've already met in Part I; the Jewish-Dutch philosopher Baruch Spinoza (1632–1677), who believed that the universe was composed of a single neutral substance; and the German thinker Gottfried Wilhelm Leibniz (1646–1716), who believed that all things were made of tiny centers of force called "monads." The rationalist self can be outlined in four points, relying largely on Descartes' work:

## WE ARE ESSENTIALLY THINKING THINGS, *RES COGITANS*

The essential part of us is our mind or soul, not our body. Our mind is distinct from our body, and its essential nature is the fact that it thinks. So we are basically things that think, in Latin *res cogitans*. Other parts of our selves are secondary, for example, the body and its drives, which decays and disappears at death. The rationalists usually saw our imagination and passions as tied to the body and thus as obstacles in the search for true knowledge.

## ALL RELIABLE KNOWLEDGE COMES FROM REASON, USUALLY GUARANTEED BY A GOOD GOD

The rationalists believed that the only reliable source of knowledge is reason. This idea is usually justified by the argument that a good God wouldn't give us reason to distinguish truth from falsity if this reason were flawed, and by the related notion that since we are in essence thinking things, our reason is closer to this essence than our senses. We can entirely trust our clear and distinct ideas, but not ideas provided by our senses, which are bodily apparatuses, and thus distorted by their reliance on physical processes.

## WE HAVE INNATE IDEAS WITHIN US, NOT DEPENDENT ON EXPERIENCE

The rationalists generally believed that we have within us innate ideas, ideas that are "imprinted" on the mind at birth and not the product of experience. For example, Descartes believed that the "pure" ideas of mind and matter are used in our understanding of experience even before we have any experience, so they must be innate. He also believed that our idea of God is innate.

## LOGIC AND MATHEMATICS LEAD US TO TRUTH: ANALYSIS AND ATOMISM

Because of their emphasis on the value of reason and their distrust of the senses, the rationalists believed that logical analysis, including mathematics, was the best way of arriving at truth. This led them, as Descartes suggested in one of his rules of method, to believe that the best way to understand anything—whether it's the behavior of physical objects or of human beings—was to break down the object under study into smaller pieces, or atoms, and then to analyze these atoms. So rationalists tended to favor atomism and logical analysis as their basic methods. Spinoza's "geometric" way of writing, which consisted of definitions, axioms, and propositions tightly linked together, illustrated not only these two methods, but also his typically rationalist love of mathematics.

## *The Empiricist Self*

An empiricist is someone who thinks that all knowledge starts with the information given to us by our five senses. The heyday of empiricism was between approximately 1690 and 1780 in Britain, although empiricism continues to be a powerful force in both philosophy and science to this day. The empiricist hall of fame features three great thinkers: the Englishman John Locke (1632–1704), the founder of modern empiricism; the Irishman George Berkeley (1685–1753), a bishop in the Anglican Church; and the Scot David Hume (1711–1776), the most influential of the three.

## WE ARE A *TABULA RASA*, A BLANK SLATE WRITTEN ON BY EXPERIENCE

Locke believed that we start life as a *tabula rasa,* a blank slate on which experience (the data of our senses) writes information, just as a teacher writes information on a blackboard. We have no personal identity at birth: It develops as we experience life.

## ALL KNOWLEDGE AT LEAST STARTS FROM EXPERIENCE, IF NOT BEING GIVEN IN TOTALITY BY EXPERIENCE: THERE ARE NO INNATE IDEAS

Unlike the rationalists, the empiricists say that all valid knowledge at least starts with experience. Some moderate empiricists would say that things like logic and mathematics can't be found in experience (although we learn them from the senses, obviously!); other more radical empiricists say that everything we know we have learned or perceived at some point.

Berkeley went as far as to say that *esse est percipi,* to exist is to be perceived. He meant that the reason that things can be said to exist is because someone perceives them (he believed that our perceptions weren't arbitrary, and were guaranteed by God). This made him an idealist as well as an empiricist: Only our ideas are real, and physical objects exist only because we perceive them. So if a tree falls in an unpeopled forest, Berkeley would say there is no sound because there's no one to hear it.

The empiricists disagreed with Descartes on the question of innate ideas: No ideas are "carved" at birth into our minds by God or human nature. We are entirely the products of our upbringing, experiences, and education: We are unformed clay before our lives provide us with experiences that shape that clay.

## THE SELF, IN A NEGATIVE SENSE, IS A PASSIVE RECIPIENT OF SENSE DATA

The empiricists see the mind as a passive receptor for the data the five senses feed into it. It can compare new data to the data already in our memory, or use the imagination to construct new ideas out of the raw materials provided by old ones (e.g., by adding a horn to a white horse, we get a unicorn). Hume called these processes "the association of ideas," arguing that such associations were natural to the human mind. Yet the empiricists see the self as relatively passive: It cannot create something out of nothing. It must have already experienced its creations, at least in bits and pieces.

## THE SELF, IN A POSITIVE SENSE, IS A BUNDLE OF PERCEPTIONS HELD TOGETHER BY MEMORY

Hume put forward a radical empiricist picture of the self in its positive sense: The self is a heap or bundle of perceptions in perpetual flux held together by memory. Without our memory to hold our bundle of perceptions together, our sense of our individual self would collapse into a schizophrenic haze. Hume made two analogies that help us out here: The self is like a theater where our perceptions of the world pass by us like actors on a stage, and the self is like a republic whose laws and members constantly change, yet is held together by causal links between past, present, and future elements of this political body.

# The Romantic Self

Romanticism was a dominant force in European arts and letters from the 1790s until at least the mid-nineteenth century. It was very much a reaction against the Enlightenment, especially its empiricist philosophy, its mechanistic view of science, and its classical, emotionally restrained view of art and literature.

There are literally dozens of writers and thinkers who we could group under the romantic banner, but we'll mention only a few here. Romanticism got started with the "Storm and Stress" movement in German literature, in which the major figure was the poet, playwright, and novelist Johann Wolfgang Goethe (1749–1832). English romanticism first flowed from the pens of the poets William Blake (1757–1827), William Wordsworth (1770–1850), and Samuel Taylor Coleridge (1772–1834). The second generation of English romantic poets was led by John Keats (1795–1821), Lord Byron (1788–1824), and Percy Bysshe Shelley (1792–1822). Finally, comes the Irish poet William Butler Yeats (1865–1939), sometimes referred to as the "last romantic." We'll read Goethe and Shelley in this chapter, returning to romanticism in Chapter 8.

The romantic picture of the self involves a complex set of ideas expressed by many different writers, but can be boiled down into seven major themes.

## THE CREATIVE SELF, THE ARTIST AS GENIUS, AND THE SEARCH FOR DEPTH MEANING BY WAY OF THE UNCONSCIOUS MIND

Instead of the calm, rational self of the Enlightenment philosophers, which knew things because it was a *tabula rasa* (blank slate) upon which experience wrote information, the romantic self was active and creative, a soul with dark depths where fantasies and dreams were as real as mathematical equations. The romantic artist didn't *find,* but *created* truths. The romantic self was dynamic and creative, not just the passive recipient of sense data. It was an immensely active energy that subjected sense impressions to a metabolic process that turned them into original creations. Instead of reckoning truth by logic and analysis, the romantics (to use Coleridge's phrase) favored the "eliciting of truth at a flash." To modify Hume's analogy, the self is not a theater, but an actor performing on a stage.

Of course, the real geniuses were poets, who felt the Infinite Spirit of the world in them when they created. Their symbols of Nature probe deeper into her mysteries than experimental science or analytical reason. They use the unconscious mind to help understand the depth meaning of the natural world and of human actions. Shelley attacked the empiricist "theater" view of the self as a "curse" that enslaves us passively to our perceptions. He saw the creative mind as a fading coal, drawing on unconscious inspirations that flicker into life for a few brief moments. The point of creatively connecting to the unconscious is to search for the depth meaning of nature and human life, to strip the "veil of familiarity" from the world, and to seek out its hidden secrets.

## PASSION OVER REASON: THE CULT OF SENSIBILITY

The romantics rejected the rationalism and materialism of the Enlightenment by extolling passion over reason. The more direct and unmediated our passions and urges are, the more authentic and valuable they are. The abstract intellect, in Wordsworth's words, murders to dissect. It's not that reason had no role to play in experience; but that the romantics saw it as a cruel tyrant that prevented an intimate and direct experience of others and of nature. Perhaps the central passion for the romantics was the imagination, the power of creating new things and ideas by means of an inner vision.

At the start of the romantic period, there existed a strong "cult of sensibility," which we can see in Goethe's early romantic novel, *The Sorrows of Young Werther.* Its hero, Werther, is lovelorn and troubled, treating his heart like a "sick child," gratifying its every fancy. He is proud of his heart alone, for it is unique and individual, unlike knowledge, which is open to everyone. This is clearly an attack on both the rationalists and the empiricists and their desire to universalize our understanding of human nature.

## REBELLION AND FREEDOM: THE INDIVIDUAL IS EVERYTHING

The romantic artist threw down the gauntlet to society: The romantics celebrated the creative genius who broke the rules of society's game. The romantics saluted the rugged adventurer, the sublime saint or sage, the conqueror, the poet who dies a tragic death far from home (Byron and Shelley were cases in point, dying in Greece and Italy, respectively). This sense of the lonely genius cut off from society is still with us today.

The romantics yearned for freedom and self-expression, as least on the personal level. The individual, free self was the true creator of everything worthwhile. This led them to favor the particular over the universal. They treasured the single person, the solitary tree or brook, over rules and laws governing all people or natural things. This individualism and desire for freedom made them distrust rational, abstract systems of thought like Descartes', which they saw as confining and oppressive.

## COMMUNION WITH NATURE AS THE SOURCE OF WISDOM AND HAPPINESS

The romantics aimed at a mystical communion with nature as the highest state of being. Since rationalism and the Industrial Revolution had cut them off from "nature," the romantics felt that by reappropriating some sort of primal unity with the landscape, with the mountains, with the wild winds and the sea, with animals and birds, they could return to this earlier state.

William Wordsworth makes this clear in *The Tables Turned,* where he admonishes us to "Let Nature be your teacher":

> Sweet is the lore which nature brings;
> Our meddling intellect
> Mis-shapes the beauteous forms of things;
> —We murder to dissect.

Goethe echoes this enchantment with nature in the reading below, enumerating the beauties of a lovely valley teeming with mist, populated with trees, tall grass, flowers, a stream, and countless worms and insects.

The romantics' attachment to nature had a metaphysical foundation in a sort of mystical idealism. They had a vision of reality as a spiritual union of humanity and nature. A heightened energy of the soul, an overflow of feeling, led them to envisage a vivid, all-pervading sense of communion with nature as one great organism, full of spiritual energy.

## EVERYTHING IN FLUX: BECOMING OVER BEING

The romantics saw the world in flux, as becoming, rather than as static and changing, as being. They applied this philosophy to society, to history, and to nature. They saw the world as a process of dynamic change, evolving from one form to another in an endless movement. Thus, the most real thing in the universe was becoming, the fact that it was constantly changing.

Social communities were not static, unchanging sets of relationships, but mobile connections that changed over time. The romantics were thus keenly aware of how history changes our institutions, ideas, and values: how nothing lasts forever. They thus gave birth to historicism, the idea that all institutions, ideas, and values have to be understood in terms of the historical era where they existed and not as eternally valid things.

## ORGANICISM AND POETRY OVER MECHANISM AND ANALYSIS

The romantics rejected the view of nature as a world machine governed by static mathematical relationships in favor of the idea that it was like a constantly evolving organism. The world machine of the scientists of the seventeenth century was opposed by the romantic conception of a nature pervaded by one unified spirit.

Although reason and sense experience can give us barren bits of knowledge, they cannot enlarge our inner worlds or give us the generous impulse to take action. Shelley argues that science has allowed us to control nature, but circumscribed our inner world. Poetry is "the root and blossom" of all systems of thought, giving them their essential nourishment. What would virtue, love, patriotism, and friendship be "if poetry did not ascend to bring light and fire from those eternal regions where the owl-winged faculty of calculation dare not ever soar?" Reason or empirical knowledge by themselves cannot produce the good and noble things in life.

## THE WILD, THE EXOTIC, AND THE GOTHIC: EXTREME PSYCHIC STATES

The romantics liked wild, exotic images and places, disordered, overgrown gardens, Gothic architecture and stories, and extreme psychological states, sometimes brought on by drugs, for they felt these were the moments when they could be most creative.

Indeed, Samuel Taylor Coleridge and Thomas de Quincey both used opium to fuel their poetic reveries, with de Quincey chronicling his narcotic dreams in his book the *Confessions of an English Opium Eater* (1821). The literature of gothic horror flourished in the romantic era.

The romantics paid close attention to altered states of consciousness such as dreams, hallucinations, and suicidal depressions, and were open to the effects of narcotics, panics, and frenzies. They saw these altered states as bringing them closer to their inner selves and to nature, which had been closed off for them by the scientific rationalist view of the world. This preference pointed ahead to Freud's theory of the unconscious mind, the id, as the source of our instinctual drives, and to the link between creativity and chemically induced altered states of consciousness in the careers of contemporary artists, writers, and rock stars (witness William S. Burroughs, Jim Morrison, and Kurt Cobain).

## The Existentialist Self

Existentialism was a complex movement in Western European philosophy and literature during the nineteenth and twentieth centuries. The existentialists were a broad group of thinkers with related by but no means identical ideas. They shared the premise that *human existence* is a better starting point for philosophy than any *metaphysical essence* (e.g., Descartes' thinking thing). Freedom, the necessity of choice, and the absurdity of human existence were also common themes in existentialist works.

A parallel movement was phenomenology. Phenomenology is a difficult term to pin down: It involves the examination of the contents of human consciousness free from any moral or metaphysical assumptions. It looks at consciousness as a pure phenomenon, free from presuppositions about its character, including whether the objects that consciousness refers to really exist. Phenomenology is thus a "descriptive" discipline. The first important phenomenologist was Edmund Husserl (1859–1938), Martin Heidegger's teacher. Husserl was greatly opposed to the psychological reduction of human thought to instinctual drives: He believed that the logical content of thinking was more important than its connection to our physical being. Phenomenology helped to prepare the way for the existentialist notion that human consciousness is free, not determined by physical or psychological laws.

To understand the general shape of existentialism and phenomenology, imagine a central core of thinkers surrounded by two orbiting rings of more loosely associated figures. At the core of the existentialist solar system are Jean-Paul Sartre (1905–1980), the only thinker to explicitly claim that he was an existentialist; Søren Kierkegaard (1813–1855), the great Danish philosopher, who was the grandfather of the movement; and Martin Heidegger (1889–1976), the German thinker who systematized phenomenology in his book *Being and Time* (1927), but who rejected the label "existentialist." We might also include in this group Karl Jaspers (1883–1969), who wrote much in the same vein as Sartre and Heidegger, but who is not as highly regarded as his countryman Heidegger.

In the inner orbit surrounding this central core of thinkers, we find the Spanish philosopher José Ortega y Gasset (1883–1955), who later in life came to a view very similar to Sartre's; the French novelist and essayist Albert Camus (1913–1960), whose literature often spoke of the absurdity of life and of the need to revolt against this absurdity; Simone de Beauvoir (1908–1986), Sartre's close friend, who used existentialism, among other things, to point out the unequal status of the two sexes; and Maurice Merleau-Ponty (1908–1961), another friend of Sartre's, whose work centered on a phenomenology of experience.

At the outer rim of the existentialist solar system are writers more loosely associated with the movement. In it we find Fyodor Dostoevsky (1821–1881), the great Russian novelist, who often created an atmosphere of existential dread or anguish in his works, notably in *Notes from the Underground;* Franz Kafka (1883–1924), who wrote novels like *The Trial,* where the central character, Mr. K, is lost in an absurd, incomprehensible world; and Friedrich Nietzsche (1844–1900), one of the three or four great minds of the nineteenth century, who echoed the existentialist themes of human self-creation and a hatred of moral hypocrisy in his works.

## WE ARE THE SUM OF OUR ACTIONS:
## WE HAVE NO FIXED NATURE, ONLY A HISTORY

The existentialists believed that human beings have no fundamental unchanging reality: This is the "nothingness" in Sartre's book *Being and Nothingness.* As Sartre says, we are the sum of our actions, nothing more, nothing less. Ortega echoes Sartre when he says that we begin as something having no reality, neither corporeal (bodily) nor spiritual. We accumulate being as we go through life. We make ourselves through a dialectical series of experiments, carrying our experiences on our back like a vagabond carries his bundle of possessions. We have no nature, only a history, only the things we've done. Or as Sartre put it, our existence precedes our essence.

## FREE CONSCIOUS BEING VERSUS
## THE DETERMINED BEING OF THE PHYSICAL THING

Most existentialists propose the idea that there are two fundamentally different types of being: free conscious human being and determined physical being. As Ortega says, a stone is given its being, whereas man "has to make his own existence at every single moment." We're ontological centaurs, half physical, half nonphysical. Our true self is our nonphysical half, the free, transcendent part of us which projects into the future, which makes plans and attempts to carry them out. The existentialists were profoundly suspicious of people who make excuses for behaving in unfree ways based on the physical aspects of their being—their bodies and everything associated with them.

## THE FUNDAMENTAL FACT OF HUMAN LIFE IS THE NECESSITY OF CHOICE:
## OUR VALUES ARE SELF-CHOSEN AND NOT THE PRODUCT OF GOD, NATURE,
## OR SOCIETY (MORAL INDIVIDUALISM)

The twentieth-century phenomenologist Martin Heidegger, in his important book *Being and Time,* called human existence *Dasein,* or being-in-the-world. He believed that we are "thrown" into the world and that we are faced with the absolute necessity to make choices. If we avoid them or allow others to make them for us, we become "inauthentic." Ortega and Sartre agreed that choice is an inescapable part of our lives, present in every moment of our existence. Even *not* doing something is a sort of choice. Ortega says that we're free *by compulsion,* while Sartre says that human beings are "condemned to be free."

Further, given the fact that we're condemned to be free and have to make choices, our values are at their core self-chosen. We can pretend that the values we adopt are the product of our religion, of human nature, or of society; yet in choosing to follow them, we make them *our* values. Sartre put this even more strongly: He saw existentialism as the playing out of a consistently atheistic position. If God is dead, there is no cosmic guarantee of moral truth; therefore, all the values we choose are our own.

## LIFE IS FUNDAMENTALLY ABSURD AND FULL OF ANXIETY AND DREAD

The existentialists also believed that life is absurd and full of an amorphous sense of anxiety or dread, *angst* as Kierkegaard called it. Albert Camus used the myth of Sisyphus to show the absurdity of life. He says that human existence is like the ancient Greek story of Sisyphus, who was condemned by the gods to roll a rock up a hill every day, only to have it roll back down at night. His labors seem pointless and absurd. But our lives are like that: We have no cosmic guarantee that our projects are worthwhile (or worthless), yet our dignity comes in pursuing them anyway.

Some existentialists emphasized the anxiety or dread that we feel when thrown into a world that has no inherent meaning, a world where we are forced to make choices without any real guideposts (*if* we're being authentic, that is). Kierkegaard talked about the *angst* of trying to decide whether to take a leap of faith over the abyss of uncertainty into religious belief. Heidegger described the anxiety of our "being-towards-death," which he felt was a fundamental test of whether we lived our lives authentically. Sartre argued that we feel anguish at having to constantly exercise our fundamental freedom in the act of choice, which we are tempted to avoid by living in "bad faith" and blaming our failures on impersonal forces like physical shortcomings or religious and social rules.

## THE HUMAN CONDITION ALSO INVOLVES ALIENATION

A subsidiary theme tied to the idea that life is absurd is the idea that modern human beings are alienated in a number of ways. As conscious beings we're alienated from the world of physical objects, from things-in-themselves, as Sartre called them. The existentialists also saw human beings as alienated from social institutions such as the state and the church and from economic roles, though it's difficult to say whether they saw this type of alienation as fundamental to the human condition. We wear masks when we play social roles, like Pierre in Sartre's *Being and Nothingness,* who is only "pretending" to be a waiter as he whirls from table to table, his tray of drinks in hand. Sartre even believed that we can be alienated in our romantic relationships, as when we objectify the "Other" as a love object.

## BE AUTHENTIC! AVOID FALLING IN WITH THE CROWD/THE HERD/DAS MAN

Generally speaking, the existentialists demanded that people be authentic, true to themselves, and responsible for their actions as individuals. Kierkegaard said "the crowd is untruth" and that the highest truth is subjective; to mindlessly adopt the beliefs and values of others is to lose yourself to the group mind. Nietzsche put it even more strongly, ridiculing the "herd" for following the slave moralities of Christianity and democracy, while Heidegger said that to be authentic we must avoid following the commands of *Das Man,* "the they." Sartre also urged us to be authentic, to avoid bad faith, and to embrace human freedom. In short, to live authentically, we must live as freely choosing individuals.

# *The Performing Self*

Sociological ideas about personal identity and the self are too varied and diverse to discuss in detail here. Instead, we'll focus on just one school of thought in contemporary sociological theory here, symbolic interactionism, and on the model of the self described by one major figure in that school, Erving Goffman's dramaturgical model.

## THE SELF IS SOCIALLY CONSTRUCTED IN A PROCESS OF SYMBOLIC INTERACTION WITH OTHERS

For the symbolic interactionist school of sociological theory, we human beings act toward others on the basis of the meanings that symbolic social objects have for us, whether these objects are actually physical things like traffic signs, or concepts like friendship and obedience. We create these objects in social interactions with others. These meanings are maintained or modified in future interactions as social actors interpret and reinterpret these social objects.

Our self is socially constructed out of this process of interaction. There are two implications of this. First, the "self" is an entity of collaborative manufacture, and thus reliant on social interaction for it to come into existence (George Herbert Mead, an earlier interactionist, believed that even the mind itself developed to help the individual solve social problems). Second, and paradoxically, although we have to participate in interactions to build our selves, this interaction is already structured in terms of the social roles given to us by society, roles that we can adapt to our purposes only in part. There is no self independent of the external world, as Descartes thought, nor are we unambiguously free to make ourselves as we see fit, as Sartre and Ortega believed.

## WE CREATE OURSELVES BY MEANS OF A SERIES OF PUBLIC PERFORMANCES

The specific way that we interact, according to Goffman, is by means of a series of public performances, like actors on a stage. In our interactions with others, we try to maintain one or more idealized fronts that define who we are: teacher, student, police officer, mother, or bureaucrat. These fronts are like characters in a play or film. Goffman says that our public performances are part of a process of "impression management" whereby we express these fronts through a series of techniques and personal equipment such as the wearing of suitable clothing; the use of appropriate bodily gestures, facial expressions, and forms of speech; and so on.

We want both smoothness and authenticity in our performances: We want people to believe that we're "really" students, professors, doctors, lawyers, or bartenders. So we try to create a public persona that fits the role we're playing: A lawyer might wear a conservative suit and conduct business in a soberly furnished office, while a student might wear jeans and a baseball cap and spend a lot of time in the library or student union. Like actors, we want to perform well, to convince others of the reality of the front we are trying to maintain by managing their impressions of us. After all, as social actors we *need* the audience to accept our performance as valid, offering them a number of physical "cues" (like the police officer's uniform or the professor's leather briefcase) to convince them of this.

## THE DIVIDING LINE BETWEEN APPEARANCE AND REALITY IS FLUID

Fronts are fragile, and can break down easily if not carefully managed. Performers have to underplay or hide activities and facts that don't jibe with the idealized fronts they seek to inhabit. Also, they have to make their performances seem to be uncontrived or natural, like stage or film actors. The danger is always that the audience will see one as a "phony." There are any number of ways that the barrier between appearance and reality can break down: A professor forgets some basic information in an area in which she is supposedly an expert; a suave ladies' man has to admit that he still lives with his mother; or a much-idolized sports hero is caught using illegal drugs. Some audience tact is useful in surviving at least our minor gaffs: No performer likes a tough crowd. The dividing line between the appearance represented by the part we're playing and the reality that this part is merely a performance is fluid, and can dissolve quite quickly.

## WE ARE MERCHANTS OF MORALITY, USING AMORAL TECHNIQUES TO KEEP OUR PUBLIC SELF INTACT

As social performers, we are merchants of morality who use amoral techniques to try to maintain an expressive control over our public fronts. Our performances make moral claims and promises on our audience. We ask to be taken seriously as a parent, lawyer, friend, or student. Yet the techniques we use are amoral in the sense that, although their purpose is usually to uphold the "common official values" of society, they can be used in a moral or immoral way, depending on the attitude of the performer. Some performers might really believe in their performances, and be sincere in playing the role of a parent, lawyer, friend, or student. Others might play their role more cynically, aware that when they create a social front they're only "playing a part" that doesn't reflect their real or long-term goals. In the worst case, individuals can create social fronts that are deliberate deceptions aimed to trick people into believing something that isn't true, perhaps to gain some material advantage (Goffman is fascinated with the con man, who typifies this sort of deception).

Goffman even talks about our social theater being divided into the front of the stage, where we perform, and the back, where all the messy preparations are made (e.g., an office vs. the private space where we groom and dress ourselves). The public self is made up of the roles we play out on the front of the stage, where physical appearance, routines, and gestures are very important.

### THERE MAY BE NO AUTHENTIC INNER SELF

Since the division between appearance and reality is so fluid, there may be no authentic inner self lurking behind the curtain of the stage of everyday life. At times Goffman seems to hint that we're no more than the sum of our social roles, although, if this is true, it's hard to tell *who* is playing these roles. He concludes that the self is a *product* of a well-staged and performed scene, a "dramatic effect" arising from that scene. Our body is merely the "peg" on which we hang this dramatic effect for a while.

Indeed, the word "person" (from the Latin *persona*) originally meant "mask." There may well be no real person under the mask. We can see this possibility in exaggerated form when talking to drama students or watching actors being interviewed on television: To better express themselves, they sometimes slip into a variant of some role they've played in the past. Perhaps we're all just more restrained versions of these performers, relating to the world only through one or more fronts. This stands in stark contrast with the romantic view of the full reality of the inner self.

# EMPIRICISM: THE SELF AS A BUNDLE OF PERCEPTIONS _____

## *Hume on Personal Identity*

David Hume (1711–1776) is in many people's minds the greatest philosopher ever to write in the English language. He was born in Edinburgh to a middle-class family with a modest estate at Ninewells in southern Scotland. As the youngest male child, Hume wasn't entitled to much of an inheritance, so he had to make his own way in the world. He was educated in the Calvinist tradition in the Church of Scotland, and early in life occupied his mind with theological issues. Hume left for the University of Edinburgh at age 11, where he stayed until he was 15. He briefly considered a career in the law, but by his late teens was convinced that he was destined for the life of a philosopher.

From 1734 to 1737 Hume lived in France, most of this time in La Flèche, the small town where Descartes had studied a century earlier. There he wrote his most important work, *A Treatise of Human Nature* (published anonymously in three volumes in 1739 and 1740). It consisted of three books, one each on understanding, passion, and morality. The *Treatise* aimed to apply Isaac Newton's "experimental" method to human nature across a wide spectrum of philosophical issues: The *Treatise* is a mixture of epistemology, metaphysics, psychology, ethics, and political theory. Now considered among the greatest works in the Western philosophical canon, at the time it "fell *dead-born from the press,* without reaching such distinction as even to excite a murmur among the zealots" (to quote Hume's own assessment). In it Hume defended an empirical account of knowledge, linking him to the British empiricist tradition, which also includes John Locke (1632–1704) and George Berkeley (1685–1753).

Hume later recast Books 1 and 3 of the *Treatise* into two shorter works written in what he considered to be a more popular style. *An Enquiry Concerning Human Understanding* (1748) covers much the same material as Book 1 of the *Treatise* in an abbreviated fashion, adding his important "Essay on Miracles" and a discussion of human immortality. *An Enquiry Concerning the Principles of Morals* (1751) is a recasting of Book 3 of the *Treatise,* arguing for a morality based in utility and human sentiments. These two works achieved moderate fame at the time.

Hume was rejected for the Chair of Moral Philosophy at the University of Edinburgh in 1744–1745, despite the best efforts of friends like Adam Smith, in part due to a negative verdict from a committee of clergymen who thought they caught of whiff of atheism from the *Treatise.* Instead, Hume accepted the position of secretary to General St. Clair on his expedition to the French coast, and later as part of his embassy to the courts at Vienna and Turin.

Hume applied for a post at the University of Glasgow in 1751–1752, again failing. He did finally land a job in 1752 as librarian to the Advocates' Library in Edinburgh. This gave him a paltry income but a large collection of books to consult. His taste for saucy French books, however, got him fired in 1757. Yet he used his time there wisely, starting his six-volume *History of England* (1754–1762), which made him a household name among the literate classes more than his early philosophical works had done.

The other source of Hume's early literary fame was his *Essays, Moral and Political* (1741–1742), whose popular style was widely admired. They went through many ever-expanding editions. In 1757 he published his *Four Dissertations,* which included "The Natural History of Religion," "Of the Passions" (a truncated version of Book 2 of the *Treatise*), "Of Tragedy," and "Of the Standard of Taste." "The Natural History of Religion" offered a sort of sociology of the evolution of religious belief from ancient polytheism to modern monotheism. When the last two of these dissertations was added to the original batch of essays, and a number of other published and unpublished essays thrown into the mix (including Hume's notorious defense of suicide "Of Suicide"), we have what is known today as his *Essays, Moral, Political, and Literary.*

Hume went to France in1763, where he was already well known owing to his history and philosophy. He was toasted by the *crème de la crème* of French society, who loaded him with (in Hume's own words) their "excessive civilities." He took full advantage of this welcome, attending dances and *soirées,* hobnobbing with prominent *philosophes,* and having an affair with the Comtesse de Boufflers. His nickname "le bon David" reflected the personal warmth that the French felt for the witty Scot.

Hume returned to Britain in 1766. He lived with Jean Jacques Rousseau for a while in London, until he and Rousseau had a falling out due to the latter's paranoid delusion that Hume was out to ruin him. In 1769 Hume returned to his native Edinburgh, where he spent his last years revising his already published works. He died of a "disorder of the bowels" (maybe cancer) in the year of the American Revolution, 1776, refusing to embrace Christianity even on his deathbed. In 1779 his *Dialogues Concerning Natural Religion* was published. It expressed Hume's mature skepticism about the existence of God, and did indeed excite a murmur from the zealots.

In Book I of *A Treatise of Human Nature,* Hume defends an empiricist and skeptical view of the foundations of human knowledge. All knowledge starts with the impressions given us by our senses. Descartes was wrong to say that we have "innate" ideas in our mind at birth. Hume can further be characterized as a "phenomenalist" since he argued that all we can really know are the phenomena in our mind. The best we can say is that we have perceptions of various types and that our minds associate these perceptions together according to various relationships (e.g., space and time, resemblance, and cause and effect).

Hume argued that we embrace the fiction that nature is regular and that the future will resemble the past, but we can't ever know this as a fact. Our belief in causality is a habit or custom: We see one type of event constantly conjoined to another type of event, and our mind associates event A with event B, calling the prior event the "cause," the latter the "effect." For example, we see a fire, and associate the idea of heat with it, eventually concluding that fire is a *cause* of heat. Our belief in causality, and all other things for that matter, is the product of our "sensitive" or emotional natures, not our "cogitative" or logical faculties.

Our reading comes from Part 4 of Book 1 of the *Treatise.* Hume starts by asking us to point out a single unchanging perception that constitutes our self. Is it our image in a mirror? No, for that's only our body at a given moment in time. Is it the pain I feel in my shoulder as I type this sentence? Obviously not—this is a fleeting thing. Perhaps it's the collection of all sensations I presently feel? Yet these, too, will be succeeded by a new set of sensations by the same time tomorrow. Hume concludes that since all knowledge comes from empirical experience (he has already described thoughts and feelings as "internal" perceptions), and since there is no *single perception* of the self, the idea of a unified self is just a convenient fiction invented by our imaginations.

Instead, Hume sees the self as a bundle of perceptions that are in "perpetual flux and movement." It can be compared to a theater in that the perceptions that make up the self parade themselves before us, coming and going like actors on a stage, or to a republic in that even though the citizens that make up a state are constantly changing (due to births, deaths, immigration, and emigration), the republic retains its identity through these changes, being connected by "the relation of causation."

He concludes that if we have a perception of our "self," it's due to our memory gluing together all past perceptions into one whole (even though it really only *discovers* causal connections between them). Yet, as an aside, he muses that all these worries about the self and personal identity may be grammatical difficulties alone, going on in the final section of Book I of the *Treatise* to suggest that a walk by the river, a dinner with friends, or a game of backgammon might "obliterate all these chimeras." *

Hume's discussion of personal identity in this section offers us a radical empiricist view of the self: bereft of innate ideas or a solid rational core, constructed by the imagination out of the perceptual bricks provided by everyday empirical experience, forever in flux. As you read it, try to rise to Hume's challenge, and see if you can find a fixed "self" amid the flow of perceptions presently parading through the theater of your mind.

* *Treatise,* bk. 1, pt. 4, sec. 6, p. 269 in the Selby-Bigge edition.

# Of Personal Identity

## DAVID HUME

THERE ARE SOME PHILOSOPHERS, who imagine we are every moment intimately conscious of what we call our Self; that we feel its existence and its continuance in existence; and are certain, beyond the evidence of a demonstration, both of its perfect identity and simplicity.[1] The strongest sensation, the most violent passion, say they, instead of distracting us from this view, only fix it the more intensely, and make us consider their influence on *self* either by their pain or pleasure. To attempt a farther proof of this were to weaken its evidence; since no proof can be deriv'd from any fact, of which we are so intimately conscious; nor is there any thing, of which we can be certain, if we doubt of this.

Unluckily all these positive assertions are contrary to that very experience, which is pleaded for them, nor have we any idea of *self*, after the manner it is here explain'd. For from what impression cou'd this idea be deriv'd? This question 'tis impossible to answer without a manifest contradiction and absurdity; and yet 'tis a question, which must necessarily be answer'd, if we wou'd have the idea of self pass for clear and intelligible. It must be some one impression, that gives rise to every real idea. But self or person is not any one impression, but that to which our several impressions and ideas are suppos'd to have a reference. If any impression gives rise to the idea of self, that impression must continue invariably the same, thro' the whole course of our lives; since self is suppos'd to exist after that manner. But there is no impression constant and invariable. Pain and pleasure, grief and joy, passions and sensations succeed each other, and never all exist at the same time. It cannot, therefore, be from any

of these impressions, or from any other, that the idea of self is deriv'd; and consequently there is no such idea.

. . . For my part, when I enter most intimately into what I call *myself*, I always stumble on some particular perception or other, of heat or cold, light or shade, love or hatred, pain or pleasure. I never can catch *myself* at any time without a perception, and never can observe any thing but the perception. When my perceptions are remov'd for any time, as by sound sleep; so long am I insensible of *myself*, and may truly be said not to exist. And were all my perceptions remov'd by death, and cou'd I neither think, nor feel, nor see, nor love, nor hate after the dissolution of my body, I shou'd be entirely annihilated, nor do I conceive what is farther requisite to make me a perfect non-entity. If any one upon serious and unprejudic'd reflection, thinks he has a different notion of *himself*, I must confess I can reason no longer with him. All I can allow him is, that he may be in the right as well as I, and that we are essentially different in this particular. He may, perhaps, perceive something simple and continu'd, which he calls *himself*; tho' I am certain there is no such principle in me.

But setting aside some metaphysicians of this kind, I may venture to affirm of the rest of mankind, that they are nothing but a bundle or collection of different perceptions, which succeed each other with an inconceivable rapidity, and are in a perpetual flux and movement. Our eyes cannot turn in their sockets without varying our perceptions. Our thought is still more variable than our sight; and all our other senses and faculties contribute to this change; nor is there any single power of the soul, which remains unalterably the same, perhaps for one moment. The mind is a kind of theatre, where several percep-

---

[1] Hume seems to be referring to Descartes and other rationalists here—ED.

SOURCE: David Hume, *A Treatise of Human Nature*, ed. L. A. Selby-Bigge (Oxford: Oxford University Press, 1888), bk. 1, pt. 4, sec. 4, pp. 251–253, 256–262 (edited).

tions successively make their appearance; pass, re-pass, glide away, and mingle in an infinite variety of postures and situations. There is properly no *simplicity* in it at one time, nor *identity* in different; whatever natural propension we may have to imagine that simplicity and identity. The comparison of the theatre must not mislead us. They are the successive perceptions only, that constitute the mind; nor have we the most distant notion of the place, where these scenes are represented, or of the materials, of which it is compos'd.

. . . A change in any considerable part of a body destroys its identity; but 'tis remarkable, that where the change is produc'd *gradually* and *insensibly* we are less apt to ascribe to it the same effect. The reason can plainly be no other, than that the mind, in following the successive changes of the body, feels an easy passage from the surveying its condition in one moment to the viewing of it in another, and at no particular time perceives any interruption in its actions. From which continu'd perception, it ascribes a continu'd existence and identity to the object.

But whatever precaution we may use in introducing the changes gradually, and making them proportionable to the whole, 'tis certain, that where the changes are at last observ'd to become considerable, we make a scruple of ascribing identity to such different objects. There is, however, another artifice, by which we may induce the imagination to advance a step farther; and that is, by producing a reference of the parts to each other, and a combination to some *common end* or purpose. A ship, of which a considerable part has been chang'd by frequent reparations, is still consider'd as the same; nor does the difference of the materials hinder us from ascribing an identity to it. The common end, in which the parts conspire, is the same under all their variations, and affords an easy transition of the imagination from one situation of the body to another.

But this is still more remarkable, when we add a *sympathy* of parts to their *common end,* and suppose that they bear to each other, the reciprocal relation of cause and effect in all their actions and operations. This is the case with all animals and vegetables; where not only the several parts have a reference to some general purpose, but also a mutual dependance on, and connexion with each other. The effect of so strong a relation is, that tho' every one must allow, that in a very few years both vegetables and animals endure a *total* change, yet we still attribute identity to them, while their form, size, and substance are entirely alter'd. An oak, that grows from a small plant to a large tree, is still the same oak; tho' there be not one particle of matter, or figure of its parts the same. An infant becomes a man, and is sometimes fat, sometimes lean, without any change in his identity.

We may also consider the two following phaenomena, which are remarkable in their kind. The first is, that tho' we commonly be able to distinguish pretty exactly betwixt numerical and specific identity, yet it sometimes happens, that we confound them, and in our thinking and reasoning employ the one for the other. Thus a man, who hears a noise, that is frequently interrupted and renew'd, says, it is still the same noise; tho' 'tis evident the sounds have only a specific identity or resemblance, and there is nothing numerically the same, but the cause, which produc'd them. In like manner it may be said without breach of the propriety of language, that such a church, which was formerly of brick, fell to ruin, and that the parish rebuilt the same church of free-stone, and according to modern architecture. Here neither the form nor materials are the same, nor is there any thing common to the two objects, but their relation to the inhabitants of the parish; and yet this alone is sufficient to make us denominate them the same. But we must observe, that in these cases the first object is in a manner annihilated before the second comes into existence; by which means, we are never presented in any one point of time with the idea of difference and multiplicity; and for that reason are less scrupulous in calling them the same.

Secondly, we may remark, that tho' in a succession of related objects, it be in a manner requisite, that the change of parts be not sudden nor entire, in order to preserve the identity, yet where the objects are in their nature changeable and inconstant, we admit of a more sudden transition, than wou'd otherwise be consistent with that relation. Thus as the nature of a river consists in the motion and change of parts; tho' in less than four and twenty hours these be totally alter'd; this hinders not the river from continuing the same during several ages. What is natural and essential to any thing is, in a manner, expected; and what is expected makes less impression, and appears of less moment, than what is unusual and extraordinary. A considerable change of the former kind seems really less to the imagination, than the most trivial alteration of the latter; and by breaking less the continuity of the thought, has less influence in destroying the identity.

We now proceed to explain the nature of *personal identity,* which has become so great a question in philosophy, especially of late years in *England,* where all the abstruser sciences are study'd with a peculiar ardour and application. And here 'tis evident, the same method of reasoning must be continu'd, which has so successfully explain'd the identity of plants, and animals, and ships, and houses, and of all the compounded and changeable productions either of art or nature. The identity, which we ascribe to the mind of man, is only a fictitious one, and of a like kind with that which we ascribe to vegetables and animal bodies. It cannot, therefore, have a different origin, but must proceed from a like operation of the imagination upon like objects.

But lest this argument shou'd not convince the reader; tho' in my opinion perfectly decisive; let him weigh the following reasoning, which is still closer and more immediate. 'Tis evident, that the identity, which we attribute to the human mind, however perfect we may imagine it to be, is not able to run the several different perceptions into one, and make them lose their characters of distinction and difference, which are essential to them. 'Tis still true, that every distinct perception, which enters into the composition of the mind, is a distinct existence, and is different, and distinguishable, and separable from every other perception, either co-temporary or successive. But, as, notwithstanding this distinction and separability, we suppose the whole train of perceptions to be united by identity, a question naturally arises concerning this relation of identity; whether it be something that really binds our several perceptions together, or only asso-

ciates their ideas in the imagination. That is, in other words, whether in pronouncing concerning the identity of a person, we observe some real bond among his perceptions, or only feel one among the ideas we form of them. This question we might easily decide, if we wou'd recollect what has been already prov'd at large, that the understanding never observes any real connexion among objects, and that even the union of cause and effect, when strictly examin'd, resolves itself into a customary association of ideas. For from thence it evidently follows, that identity is nothing really belonging to these different perceptions, and uniting them together; but is merely a quality, which we attribute to them, because of the union of their ideas in the imagination, when we reflect upon them. Now the only qualities, which can give ideas an union in the imagination, are these three relations above-mention'd. These are the uniting principles in the ideal world, and without them every distinct object is separable by the mind, and may be separately consider'd, and appears not to have any more connexion with any other object, than if disjoin'd by the greatest difference and remoteness. 'Tis, therefore, on some of these three relations of resemblance, contiguity and causation, that identity depends; and as the very essence of these relations consists in their producing an easy transition of ideas; it follows, that our notions of personal identity, proceed entirely from the smooth and uninterrupted progress of the thought along a train of connected ideas, according to the principles above-explain'd.

The only question, therefore, which remains, is, by what relations this uninterrupted progress of our thought is produc'd, when we consider the successive existence of a mind or thinking person. And here 'tis evident we must confine ourselves to resemblance and causation, and must drop contiguity, which has little or no influence in the present case.

To begin with *resemblance;* suppose we cou'd see clearly into the breast of another, and observe that succession of perceptions, which constitutes his mind or thinking principle, and suppose that he always preserves the memory of a considerable part of past perceptions; 'tis evident that nothing cou'd more contribute to the bestowing a relation on this succession amidst all its variations. For what is the memory but a faculty, by which we raise up the images of past perceptions? And as an image necessarily resembles its object, must not the frequent placing of these resembling perceptions in the chain of thought, convey the imagination more easily from one link to another, and make the whole seem like the continuance of one object? In this particular, then, the memory not only discovers the identity, but also contributes to its production, by producing the relation of resemblance among the perceptions. The case is the same whether we consider ourselves or others.

As to *causation;* we may observe, that the true idea of the human mind, is to consider it as a system of different perceptions or different existences, which are link'd together by the relation of cause and effect, and mutually produce, destroy, influence, and modify each other. Our impressions give rise to their correspondent ideas; and these ideas in their turn produce other impressions. One thought chaces another, and draws after it a third, by which it is expell'd in its turn. In this respect, I cannot compare the soul more properly to any thing than to a republic or commonwealth, in which the several members are united by the reciprocal ties of government and subordination, and give rise to other persons, who propagate the same republic in the incessant changes of its parts. And as the same individual republic may not only change its members, but also its laws and constitutions; in like manner the same person may vary his character and disposition, as well as his impressions and ideas, without losing his identity. Whatever changes he endures, his several parts are still connected by the relation of causation. And in this view our identity with regard to the passions serves to corroborate that with regard to the imagination, by the making our distant perceptions influence each other, and by giving us a present concern for our past or future pains or pleasures.

As memory alone acquaints us with the continuance and extent of this succession of perceptions, 'tis to be consider'd, upon that account

chiefly, as the source of personal identity. Had we no memory, we never shou'd have any notion of causation, nor consequently of that chain of causes and effects, which constitute our self or person. But having once acquir'd this notion of causation from the memory, we can extend the same chain of causes, and consequently the identity of our persons beyond our memory, and can comprehend times, and circumstances, and actions, which we have entirely forgot, but suppose in general to have existed. For how few of our past actions are there, of which we have any memory? Who can tell me, for instance, what were his thoughts and actions on the first of *January* 1715, the 11th of *March* 1719, and the 3d of *August* 1733? Or will he affirm, because he has entirely forgot the incidents of these days, that the present self is not the same person with the self of that time; and by that means overturn all the most establish'd notions of personal identity? In this view, therefore, memory does not so much *produce* as *discover* personal identity, by shewing us the relation of cause and effect among our different perceptions. 'Twill be incumbent on those, who affirm that memory produces entirely our personal identity, to give a reason why we can thus extend our identity beyond our memory.

The whole of this doctrine leads us to a conclusion, which is of great importance in the present affair, *viz.* that all the nice and subtile questions concerning personal identity can never possibly be decided, and are to be regarded rather as grammatical than as philosophical difficulties. Identity depends on the relations of ideas; and these relations produce identity, by means of that easy transition they occasion. But as the relations, and the easiness of the transition may diminish by insensible degrees, we have no just standard, by which we can decide any dispute concerning the time, when they acquire or lose a title to the name of identity. All the disputes concerning the identity of connected objects are merely verbal, except so far as the relation of parts gives rise to some fiction or imaginary principle of union, as we have already observ'd. . . .

# ROMANTICISM: THE SELF AS AN ACTIVE, CREATIVE ENERGY

## *Goethe and the Romantic Attack on Rationalism and Empiricism*

Johann Wolfgang von Goethe (1749–1832) is considered the greatest of all German poets, although he was also a novelist, playwright, and scientist. He was born in Frankfurt on Main, and studied law from 1765 to 1768 at the University of Leipzig, then from 1770 to 1771 at Strasbourg, briefly practicing law in Frankfurt. During this time he became interested in literature, art, science, and the occult, and wrote love poems and a couple of plays. In Strasbourg he became friends with J. G. von Herder, who introduced Goethe to Shakespeare and German folk poetry, both large influences later in Goethe's career.

His early fame came from the play *Götz of Berlichingen* (1773), which was influenced by Shakespeare. It told the story of a German knight-outlaw, a sort of sixteenth-century Zorro or Robin Hood. This kicked off the *Sturm und Drang* (storm and stress) movement in German literature, which acted as an overture to romanticism.

After an unhappy affair with Charlotte Buff, he wrote *The Sorrows of Young Werther* (1774), a sentimental, deeply romantic novel, which we'll look at later. It consists of a collection of letters from the love-sick Werther to a friend who occasionally interrupts Werther's anguished prose with some third-person commentary. In the book Werther falls in love with Lotte, who is already betrothed to Albert. Much of the book consists of Werther's bemoaning his fate of loving a woman committed to another man. In the end, Lotte marries Albert, as a result of which Werther kills himself with a pistol, not being able to live in a world without Lotte's love. As you may have guessed, *The Sorrows of Young Werther* is the great grandfather of the modern romance novel.

Goethe was invited to Duke Karl Augustus's court at Weimar in 1775, where he lived off and on for the rest of his life. Weimar was, in part due to Goethe's influence, a center of German cultural life in the late eighteenth century. He served in a number of posts in the administration of Saxe-Weimar, the petty principality in central Germany that Duke Karl ruled. In his early Weimar days, Goethe became the intimate friend of the charming and sophisticated aristocrat Charlotte von Stein, who was married to a Weimar official. It's unclear whether Goethe's love of Charlotte was ever consummated. Yet she taught him the polished manners of court life, and widened his intellectual horizons.

Growing tired of Weimar, Goethe spent two years (1786–1788) in Italy. This sojourn brought him a new appreciation of classical art, architecture, and literature, and calmed in part the romantic longings and frenzies in his works. From then on his work was imbued with more of a classical spirit. When he returned to Weimar, his relationship with Charlotte had soured. He became the head of the duke's theater, and pursued scientific studies. He developed the idea of morphology in biology, which acted as forerunner of Darwin's theory of evolution. He published a book on optics in 1791, and the *Theory of Colours* in 1810.

Goethe's friendship and collaboration with Friedrich von Schiller between 1794 and 1805 (when Schiller died) was a high point of his literary endeavors. He wrote essays, poems, and the novel *Wilhelm Meister's Apprenticeship* (1796) during this period. Later in life he published the novels *Elective Affinities* (1809) and *Wilhelm Meister's Travels* (1821).

Yet Goethe's greatest work is undoubtedly the epic poem/play *Faust* (Volume I, 1808; Volume II, 1832). It tells the story of how Faust, a scientist and philosopher, sells his soul to the devil for worldly knowledge and the love of the beautiful Gretchen. It is considered a masterpiece of modern literature, with its grand allegorical theme of the modern individual seeking love and knowledge against the conventions of religion and morality.

Goethe moved from romanticism to classicism as he grew older. Yet early on his poems, plays, and novels portrayed the life of passionate longing in the bosom of both nature and one's true love as the only one worth living. In the selections below from *The Sorrows of Young Werther,* we see several aspects of the romantic image of the self. In the first selection, "Pride in the Heart," we find Werther communing with a spiritualized and enchanted nature and gratifying his heart's every fancy. He takes pride in his heart because unlike all the knowledge he's ever learned, which can be relearned by anyone else, his feelings are unique to him as a solitary being.

In the second selection, "Oh, You Rationalists!" we find Werther debating with Albert over the relative value of reason and the passions. Albert suggests that someone under the power of violent passions loses his reasoning power, and becomes as though drunk or insane. Werther responds in what would become a typically romantic fashion: All the great creators and innovators in history have been called drunk or insane at first; our passions motivate us to rebel against injustice, bear great physical burdens, or perform acts of courage. Reading between the lines a bit, Werther seems to think that a society motivated solely by reason might be very sensible and moral and sober, but it would accomplish nothing noble or great. Its deeds would look like the proverbial cats prowling about on a dark night: all equally gray.

# The Sorrows of Young Werther

## JOHANN WOLFGANG VON GOETHE

### Pride in the Heart

*May 10, 1771*

A wonderful serenity has taken possession of my entire soul, like these sweet spring mornings which I enjoy with all my heart. I am alone, and feel the enchantment of life in this spot, which was created for souls like mine. I am so happy, my dear friend, so absorbed in the exquisite sense of tranquil existence, that I neglect my art. I could not draw a single line at the present moment; and yet I feel that I was never a greater painter than I am now. When the lovely valley teems with mist

SOURCE: Johann Wolfgang von Goethe, *The Sorrows of Young Werther* (1774), trans. Victor Lange (New York: Rinehart, 1949); reprinted in *The Portable Romantic Reader,* ed. Howard E. Hugo (New York: Viking, 1960), pp. 77–81, 465–468.

around me, and the high sun strikes the impenetrable foliage of my trees, and but a few rays steel into the inner sanctuary, I lie in the tall grass by the trickling stream and notice a thousand familiar things: when I hear the humming of the little world among the stalks, and am near the countless indescribable forms of the worms and insects, then I feel the presence of the Almighty Who created us in His own image, and the breath of that universal love which sustains us, as we float in an eternity of bliss; and then, my friend, when the world grows dim before my eyes and earth and sky seem to dwell in my soul and absorb its power, like the form of a beloved—then I often think with longing, Oh, would I could express it, could impress upon paper all that is living so full and warm within me, that it might become the mirror of my soul, as my soul is the mirror of the infinite God! O my friend—but it will kill me—I shall perish under the splendor of these visions! . . .

*May 13*

You ask if you should send my books. My dear friend, for the love of God, keep them away from me! I no longer want to be guided, animated. My heart is sufficiently excited. I want strains to lull me, and I find them abundantly in my Homer. How often do I still the burning fever of my blood; you have never seen anything so unsteady, so restless, as my heart. But need I confess this to you, my dear friend, who have so often witnessed my sudden transitions from sorrow to joy, and from sweet melancholy to violent passions? I treat my heart like a sick child, and gratify its every fancy. Do not repeat this; there are people who would misunderstand it.

*May 9, 1772*

I have paid my visit to my native place with the devotion of a pilgrim, and have experienced many unexpected emotions. Near the great linden tree, a quarter of an hour from the town, I got out of the carriage and sent it on ahead so that I might enjoy the pleasure of recollection more vividly and to my heart's content. There I stood, under that same linden tree which used to

be the goal and end of my walks. How things have changed! Then, in happy ignorance, I sighed for a world I did not know, where I hoped to find the stimulus and enjoyment which my heart could desire; and now, on my return from that wide world, O my friend, how many disappointed hopes and unfulfilled plans have I brought back!

As I saw the mountains which lay stretched out before me, I thought how often they had been the object of my dearest desires. Here I used to sit for hours, wishing to be there, wishing that I might lose myself in the woods and valleys that now lay so enchanting and mysterious before me—and when I had to return to town at a definite time, how unwillingly did I leave this familiar place! I approached the town; and recognized all the well-known old summerhouses; I disliked the new ones, and all the changes which had taken place. I entered the gate, and all the old feelings returned. I cannot, dear friend, go into details, charming as they were; they would be dull reading. I had intended to lodge in the market place, near our old house. As I approached, I noticed that the school in which, as children, we had been taught by that good old lady, was converted into a shop. I called to mind the restlessness, the heaviness, the tears, and heartaches which I experienced in that confinement. Every step produced some particular impression. No pilgrim in the Holy Land could meet so many spots charged with pious memories, and his soul can hardly be moved with greater devotion. One incident will serve for illustration. I followed the stream down to a farm—it used to be a favorite walk of mine—and I paused where we boys used to amuse ourselves making ducks and drakes upon the water. I remember so well how I sometimes watched the course of that same stream, following it with strange feelings, and romantic ideas of the countries it was to pass through; but my imagination was soon exhausted. Yet I knew that the water continued flowing on and on . . . and I lost myself completely in the contemplation of the infinite distance. Exactly like this, my friend, so happy and so rich were the thoughts of the ancients. Their feelings and their poetry were fresh as childhood. And when Ulysses talks of the immeasurable sea and boundless earth, his words are true, natural, deeply felt, and mysterious. Of what use is it that I have learned, with every schoolboy, that the world is round? Man needs but little earth for his happiness, and still less for his final rest.

I am at present at the Prince's hunting lodge. He is a man with whom one can live quite well. He is honest and simple. There are, however, some curious characters about him whom I cannot quite understand. They are not dishonest, and yet they do not seem thoroughly honorable men. Sometimes I am disposed to trust them, and yet I cannot persuade myself to confide in them. It annoys me to hear the Prince talk of things which he has only read or heard of, and always from the point of view from which they have been represented by others.

He values my understanding and talents more highly than my heart, but I am proud of my heart alone. It is the sole source of everything—all our strength, happiness, and misery. All the knowledge I possess everyone else can acquire, but my heart is all my own.

## *"Oh, You Rationalists!"*

### *August 12, 1771*

. . . On this occasion Albert was deeply immersed in his subject; I finally ceased to listen to him, and became lost in reverie. With a sudden motion I pointed the mouth of the pistol to my forehead, over the right eye. "What are you doing?" cried Albert, turning the pistol away. "It is not loaded," said I. "Even so," he asked with impatience, "what is the meaning of this? I cannot imagine how a man can be so mad as to shoot himself; the very idea of it shocks me."

"Oh, you people!" I said, "why should you always have to label an action and call it mad or wise, good or bad? What does it all mean? Have you fathomed the motives of our actions? Can you explain the causes and make them inevitable? If you could, you would be less hasty with your 'labels.'"

"But you will admit," said Albert, "that some actions are vicious, let them spring from whatever

motives they may." I granted it, and shrugged my shoulders.

"Still," I continued, "there are some exceptions here too. Theft is a crime; but the man who commits it from extreme poverty to save his family from starvation, does he deserve pity or punishment? Who shall throw the first stone at a husband who in just resentment sacrifices his faithless wife and her perfidious seducer; or at the young girl who in an hour of rapture forgets herself in the overwhelming joys of love? Even our laws, cold and pedantic as they are, relent in such cases, and withhold their punishment."

"That is quite another thing," said Albert, "because a man under the influence of violent passion loses all reasoning power and is regarded as drunk or insane."

"Oh, you rationalists," I replied, smiling. "Passion! Drunkenness! Madness! You moral creatures, so calm and so righteous! You abhor the drunken man, and detest the eccentric; you pass by, like the Levite, and thank God, like the Pharisee, that you are not like one of them. I have been drunk more than once, my passions have always bordered on madness; I am not ashamed to confess it; I have learned in my own way that all extraordinary men who have done great and improbable things have ever been decried by the world as drunk or insane. And in ordinary life, too, is it not intolerable that no one can undertake anything noble or generous without having everybody shout, 'That fellow is drunk, he is mad'? Shame on you, ye sages!"

"Here you go again," said Albert; "you always exaggerate, and in this matter you are undoubtedly wrong; we were speaking of suicide, which you compare with great actions, when actually it is impossible to regard it as anything but weakness. It is much easier to die than to bear a life of misery with fortitude."

I was on the point of breaking off the conversation, for nothing puts me off so completely as when someone utters a wretched commonplace when I am talking from the depths of my heart. However, I controlled myself, for I had often heard the same observation with sufficient vexation; I answered him, therefore, with some heat,

"You call this a weakness—don't be led astray by appearances. When a nation which has long groaned under the intolerable yoke of a tyrant rises at last and throws off its chains, do you call that weakness? The man who, to save his house from the flames, finds his physical strength redoubled, so that he can lift burdens with ease which normally he could scarcely move; he who under the rage of an insult attacks and overwhelms half a dozen of his enemies—are these to be called weak? My friend, if a display of energy be strength, how can the highest exertion of it be a weakness?"

Albert looked at me and said, "Do forgive me, but I do not see that the examples you have produced bear any relation to the question." "That may be," I answered; "I have often been told that my method of argument borders a little on the absurd. But let us see if we cannot place the matter in another light by inquiring what may be a man's state of mind who resolves to free himself from the burden of life—a burden which often seems so pleasant to bear. Surely, we are justified in discussing a subject such as this only in so far as we can put ourselves in another man's situation."

"Human nature," I continued, "has its limits. It can endure a certain degree of joy, sorrow, and pain, but collapses as soon as this is exceeded. The question, therefore, is not whether a man is strong or weak, but whether he is able to endure the measure of his suffering, moral or physical; and in my opinion it is just as absurd to call a man a coward who kills himself as to call a man a coward who dies of a malignant fever."

## Shelley's Defense of Poetry

Percy Bysshe Shelley (1792–1822) was a rebel against religious, moral, and political authority, and one of the three great poets (along with Lord Byron and John Keats) of the second generation of romanticism in England.

Percy Shelley was born into a family of well-heeled aristocrats in Sussex in southern England. He attended Eton, a private boys' school, and then Oxford for less than a year starting in 1810, after which he was expelled for publishing the pamphlet *The Necessity of Atheism* (which he wrote along with Thomas Jefferson Hogg). After Shelley's father cut him off from his inheritance, he eloped with the sixteen-year-old Harriet Westbrook. He and Harriet traveled for two years in England and Ireland, writing political tracts and agitating for various radical causes. They lived for a time in Wales, where an enraged shepherd shot at him. In 1813 Shelley published the poem "Queen Mab," which had an atheistic theme.

Shelley's marriage fell apart during these travels, so in 1814 he took up with Mary Wollstonecraft Godwin, daughter of the pioneering feminist theorist Mary Wollstonecraft and the anarchist William Godwin, and traveled abroad. They were accompanied by Mary's stepsister Jane "Claire" Clairmont. Harriet drowned herself in a lake in a London park in 1816, and three weeks later Shelley and Wollstonecraft were married.

1816 found Shelley, Wollstonecraft, and Clairmont at Lake Geneva with Lord Byron, where Byron continued his affair with Claire (she was carrying his child). While there Shelley and Byron's lively conversations inspired Mary to write *Frankenstein* (1818), the classic gothic horror novel. Shelley wrote *The Revolt of Islam*, a paean to the revolutionary spirit, in 1817. From 1818 to 1822 the Shelleys and Clairmont lived in Italy, where Byron also lived. Shelley fell in love with Emilia Viviani and Jane Williams in 1821, his passions and rebellious spirit overruling any moral concerns for the sanctity of marriage. These were productive years for Shelley: During this time he wrote most of his better known works, including the drama in verse *Prometheus Unbound* (1820), and the poems "To a Skylark," "Ode to the West Wind," and "Ozymandias."

Shelley died before his thirtieth birthday. He drowned when his schooner capsized and sunk on July 8, 1822, on the way across the Bay of Lerici to visit his friend Leigh Hunt. When his fish-eaten body washed up on the shore ten days later, Byron and Leigh Hunt burned it on the beach, cutting out his heart first and giving it to Mary, who carried it with her for the rest of her life. His life, like his poetry, was a romantic tale full of passion and striking scenes.

Our reading comes from the last third of Shelley's important essay *A Defense of Poetry* (written in 1821; published in 1840). It was a reply to his friend Thomas Peacock's *The Four Ages of Poetry,* which argued that poetry was of little use in an age of scientific advance. In Peacock's words, "Poetry was the mental rattle that awakened the attention of intellect in the infancy of civil society; but for the maturity of mind to make a serious business of the playthings of its childhood, it is as absurd as for a full-grown man to . . . be charmed to sleep by the jingle of silver bells." Shelley rose to the defense of this mental rattle by writing a response to Peacock.

The first third of the essay occupies itself with defining poetry, then showing who are poets, and who are not. Shelley starts by defining *reason* as the principle of analysis that examines the way that individual things relate to each other, and *imagination* as the principle of synthesis that establishes the value of things and connects them to a universal nature. "Reason is to Imagination as the body to the spirit, as the shadow to the substance." Poetry is the exercise of the imagination.

He goes on to note how the dancing, singing, and highly metaphorical languages of primitive societies were all forms of poetry, and how in more settled societies artists, religious prophets, and legislators were also poets insofar as they used their imaginations to create new forms of things. All authors of "revolutions in opinion" are necessarily poets, Shelley declares.

In the middle part of *A Defense of Poetry,* Shelley gives historical examples of the beneficial effects of poetry on society. In the background of these examples is his argument that the "great instrument of moral good is the imagination," and thus that poetry "strengthens the faculty which is the organ of the moral nature in man." He starts with Homer's evocation of the perfect human character for preclassical Greece, moving on to show how the great dramatists of ancient Athens prospered alongside the other great artists and philosophers of the day.

Shelley then takes us to ancient Rome, whose poetry "lived in its institutions," on to the mythologies of Jesus Christ and the Celtic conquerors of the Roman Empire, which produced the institution of chivalry and the religion of love found in the songs of the medieval troubadours (which Shelley argues reduced inequality between the sexes). He then mentions the second and third great epic poets of Western history, Dante and John Milton, the authors of the *Divine Comedy* and *Paradise Lost.* These and other great works of poetry have contributed to social utility in its higher sense, not in providing for "the wants of our animal natures," but to the sort of utility that "strengthens and purifies the affections, enlarges the imagination, and adds spirit to sense."

In the following selection, the last third of the essay, Shelley gets down to actually defending the poetic imagination against rationalism and empiricism on metaphysical, moral, and aesthetic grounds. In this defense we find at least five elements of the romantic self (as outlined previously): the creative genius seeking depth meaning by way of the poetic insights produced by the unconscious mind; the superiority of passion and the imagination over reason; the need to commune with nature to find true wisdom; a glorification of the rebel and of political freedom; and a defense of organicism over mechanistic analysis. Shelley's *Defense* gives us a lively picture of the creative life as the best one, leaving the rationalists and empiricists to wallow in the mediocrity of their logical deductions or empirical facts.

# A Defense of Poetry

## PERCY BYSSHE SHELLEY

THE EXERTIONS of Locke, Hume, Gibbon, Voltaire, Rousseau,[1] and their disciples in favour of oppressed and deluded humanity are entitled to the gratitude of mankind. Yet it is easy to calculate the degree of moral and intellectual improvement which the world would have exhibited, had they never lived. A little more nonsense would have been talked for a century or two; and perhaps a few more men, women and children burnt as heretics. We might not at this moment have been congratulating each other on the abolition of the Inquisition in Spain.[2] But it exceeds all imagination to conceive what would have been the moral condition of the world if neither Dante, Petrarch, Boccaccio, Chaucer, Shakespeare, Calderon, Lord Bacon, nor Milton had ever existed; if Raphael and Michael Angelo had never been born; if the Hebrew poetry had never been translated; if a revival of the study of Greek Literature had never taken place; if no monuments of ancient sculpture had been handed down to us; and if the poetry of the religion of the ancient world had been extinguished together with its belief. The human mind could never, except by the intervention of these excitements, have been awakened to the invention of those grosser sciences, and that application of analytical reasoning to the aberrations of society, which it is now attempted to exalt over the direct expression of the inventive and creative faculty itself.

We have more moral, political and historical wisdom than we know how to reduce into practice: we have more scientific and economical knowledge than can be accommodated to the just distribution of the produce which it multiplies. The poetry, in these systems of thought, is concealed by the accumulation of facts and calculating processes. There is no want of knowledge respecting what is wisest and best in morals, government and political economy, or at least

[1] I follow the classification adopted by the author of The Four Ages of Poetry. Although Rousseau has been thus classed, he was essentially a poet. The others, even Voltaire, were mere reasoners. ["The Four Ages of Poetry" referred to by Shelley here was an essay by Thomas Peacock published in Ollier's *Literary Miscellany* which attacked the utility of poetry in the modern age. Shelley wrote *A Defense of Poetry* as an answer to it. The original draft of the *Defense* contained many allusions to the article and its author, which Shelley's editor later cut out. Locke, Hume, Voltaire, and Rousseau were all eighteenth-century philosophers; Edward Gibbon was a contemporary of these thinkers, famous for his massive history *The Decline and Fall of the Roman Empire*—ED.]
[2] This had just happened, in 1820—ED.

SOURCE: Percy Bysshe Shelley, *A Defense of Poetry* (1821), ed. Albert S. Cook (Boston: Ginn, 1891), pp. 36–44, 46. The reading represents the last third of Shelley's essay, with a few paragraphs from near the end cut. We have corrected or modernized Shelley's spelling in a few cases and added some footnotes.

what is wiser and better than what men now practise and endure. But we let *"I dare not* wait upon *I would,* like the poor cat i' the adage."[3] We want the creative faculty to imagine that which we know; we want the generous impulse to act that which we imagine; we want the poetry of life: our calculations have outrun conception; we have eaten more than we can digest. The cultivation of those sciences which have enlarged the limits of the empire of man over the external world has, for want of the poetical faculty, proportionally circumscribed those of the internal world, and man, having enslaved the elements, remains himself a slave. To what but a cultivation of the mechanical arts in a degree disproportioned to the presence of the creative faculty which is the basis of all knowledge is to be attributed the abuse of all invention for abridging and combining labour, to the exasperation of the inequality of mankind? From what other cause has it arisen that the discoveries which should have lightened, have added a weight to the curse imposed on Adam? Poetry, and the principle of Self, of which money is the visible incarnation, are the God and the Mammon of the world.

The functions of the poetical faculty are two fold: by one it creates new materials of knowledge, and power, and pleasure; by the other it engenders in the mind a desire to reproduce and arrange them according to a certain rhythm and order, which may be called the beautiful and the good. The cultivation of poetry is never more to be desired than at periods when from an excess of the selfish and calculating principle, the accumulation of the materials of external life exceed the quantity of the power of assimilating them to the internal laws of human nature. The body has then become too unwieldy for that which animates it.

Poetry is indeed something divine. It is at once the centre and circumference of knowledge; it is that which comprehends all science, and that to which all science must be referred. It is at the same time the root and the blossom of all other systems of thought: it is that from which all

spring, and that which adorns all; and that which if blighted denies the fruit and the seed, and withholds from the barren world the nourishment and the succession of the scions of the tree of life. It is the perfect and consummate surface and bloom of things; it is as the odour and the colour of the rose to the texture of the elements which compose it; as the form and splendour of unfaded beauty, to the secrets of anatomy and corruption. What were Virtue, Love, Patriotism, Friendship—what were the scenery of this beautiful universe which we inhabit—what were our consolations on this side the grave—and what were our aspirations beyond it—if Poetry did not ascend to bring light and fire from those eternal regions where the owl-winged faculty of calculation, dare not ever soar? Poetry is not like reasoning, a power to be exerted according to the determination of the will. A man cannot say, "I will compose poetry." The greatest poet even cannot say it: for the mind in creation is as a fading coal which some invisible influence, like an inconstant wind, awakens to transitory brightness; this power arises from within, like the colour of a flower which fades and changes as it is developed, and the conscious portions of our natures are unprophetic either of its approach or its departure. Could this influence be durable in its original purity and grace, it is impossible to predict the greatness of the results; but when composition begins inspiration is already on the decline, and the most glorious poetry that has ever been communicated to the world is probably a feeble shadow of the original conceptions of the poet. I appeal to the greatest Poets of the present day, whether it be not an error to assert that the greatest passages of poetry are produced by labour and study. . . .

Poetry is the record of the happiest and best moments of the happiest and best minds. We are aware of evanescent visitations of thought and feeling sometimes associated with place or person, sometimes regarding our own mind alone, and always arising unforseen and departing unbidden; but elevating and delightful beyond all expression: so that even in the desire and the regret they leave there cannot but be pleasure, par-

---

[3] William Shakespeare, *Macbeth* 1.7.44–45—ED.

ticipating as it does in the nature of its object. It is as it were the interpenetration of a diviner nature through our own, but its footsteps are like those of a wind over the sea, which the coming calm erases, and whose traces remain only as on the wrinkled sand which paves it. These and corresponding conditions of being are experienced principally by those of the most delicate sensibility and the most enlarged imagination. And the state of mind produced by them is at war with every base desire. The enthusiasm of virtue, love, patriotism, and friendship is essentially linked with such emotions; and whilst they last, self appears as what it is, an atom to an Universe. Poets are not only subject to these experiences as spirits of the most refined organization, but they can colour all that they combine with the evanescent hues of this ethereal world; a word, a trait in the representation of a scene or a passion will touch the enchanted chord, and reanimate in those who have ever experienced these emotions the sleeping, the cold, the buried image of the past. Poetry thus makes immortal all that is best and most beautiful in the world; it arrests the vanishing apparitions which haunt the interlunations of life; and veiling them, or in language or in form, sends them forth among mankind bearing sweet news of kindred joy to those with whom their sisters abide—abide because there is no portal of expression from the caverns of the spirit which they inhabit into the universe of things. Poetry redeems from decay the visitations of the divinity in man.

Poetry turns all things to loveliness: it exalts the beauty of that which is most beautiful, and it adds beauty to that which is most deformed: it marries exultation and horror; grief and pleasure, eternity and change; it subdues to union under its light yoke all irreconcilable things. It transmutes all that it touches, and every form moving within the radiance of its presence is changed by wondrous sympathy to an incarnation of the spirit which it breathes: its secret alchemy turns to potable gold the poisonous waters which flow from death through life; it strips the veil of familiarity from the world, and lays bare the naked and sleeping beauty which is the spirit of its forms.

All things exist as they are perceived; at least in relation to the percipient. "The mind is its own place, and of itself can make a Heaven of Hell, a Hell of Heaven."[4] But Poetry defeats the curse which binds us to be subjected to the accident of surrounding impressions. And whether it spreads its own figured curtain or withdraws life's dark veil from before the scene of things, it equally creates for us a being within our being. It makes us the inhabitants of a world to which the familiar world is a chaos. It reproduces the common Universe of which we are portions and percipients, and it urges from our inward sight the film of familiarity which obscures from us the wonder of our being. It compels us to feel that which we perceive, and to imagine that which we know. It creates anew the universe after it has been annihilated in our minds by the recurrence of impressions blunted by re-iteration. It justifies that bold and true word of Tasso: *Non merita nome di creatore, se non Iddio ed il Poeta.*[5]

. . . Poetry, as has been said, differs in this respect from logic that it is not subject to the control of the active powers of the mind, and that its birth and recurrence has no necessary connexion with consciousness or will. It is presumptuous to determine that these are the necessary conditions of all mental causation when mental effects are experienced insusceptible of being referred to them. The frequent recurrence of the poetical power, it is obvious to suppose, may produce in the mind an habit of order and harmony correlative with its own nature and with its effects upon other minds. But in the intervals of inspiration, and they may be frequent without being durable, a Poet becomes a man and is abandoned to the sudden reflux of the influences under which others habitually live. But as he is more delicately organized than other men and sensible to pain and pleasure both his own and that of others in a degree unknown to them: he will avoid the one and pursue the other with an ardour proportioned to this difference. And he renders him-

---

[4] John Milton, *Paradise Lost* 1.254 ff.—ED.
[5] "None merits the name of creator but God and the poet."
—ED.

self obnoxious to calumny, when he neglects to observe the circumstances under which these objects of universal pursuit and flight have disguised themselves in one another's garments.

But there is nothing necessarily evil in this error and thus cruelty, envy, revenge, avarice, and the passions purely evil, have never formed any portion of the popular imputations on the lives of poets. . . .

The most unfailing herald, companion and follower of the awakening of a great people to work a beneficial change in opinion or institution, is Poetry. At such periods there is an accumulation of the power of communicating and receiving intense and impassioned conceptions respecting man and nature. The persons in whom this power resides, may often as far as regards many portions of their nature have little apparent correspondence with that spirit of good of which they are the ministers. But even whilst they deny and ab-

jure, they are yet compelled to serve, the Power which is seated on the throne of their own soul. It is impossible to read the compositions of the most celebrated writers of the present day without being startled with the electric life which burns within their words. They measure the circumference and sound the depths of human nature with a comprehensive and all penetrating spirit, and they are themselves perhaps the most sincerely astonished at its manifestations, for it is less their spirit than the spirit of the age. Poets are the hierophants of an unapprehended inspiration, the mirrors of the gigantic shadows which futurity casts upon the present, the words which express what they understand not, the trumpets which sing to battle and feel not what they inspire: the influence which is moved not, but moves. Poets are the unacknowledged legislators of the World.

# EXISTENTIALISM: THE ABSURDLY FREE SELF

## *Ortega's Vagabond on the Road of Being*

José Ortega y Gasset (1883–1955) was a Spanish philosopher, journalist, and literary figure who went through several intellectual phases, but eventually embraced a view close to the existentialism of Martin Heidegger and Jean-Paul Sartre. Ortega was born in Madrid. He was educated at a Jesuit school, receiving his doctorate in philosophy from the University of Madrid in 1904. He studied in Germany from 1905 to 1907, and was a professor of metaphysics at the University of Madrid from 1910 to 1936. He was a charismatic teacher and a writer of colorful prose, so much so that his work has tended to be passed over by "serious" thinkers as more literature than philosophy.

In the 1920s and 1930s, Ortega was active in Spanish academic, literary, and political life. He edited *Revista de la Occidente* from 1923 to 1936, was a member of the Royal Academy of Moral and Political Sciences, opposed the dictatorship of Primo de Rivera in the late 1920s, and was a member of the Cortes (parliament) during the Second Republic between 1931 and 1932. He quit politics for good afterwards. When the Spanish Civil War broke out in 1936, he went into exile, living in Argentina and Portugal, refusing for a long time to teach in a country governed by Franco's fascists. He returned to Spain in 1948, and founded the Institute of Humanities in Madrid.

Ortega wrote many books in his lifetime, including *Meditations on Quixote* (1914), *Invertebrate Spain* (1922), *Mission of the University* (1930), *History as a Sys-*

tem (1939), *Man and People* (1957), and *What Is Philosophy?* (1958). He is best known for his 1929 book *The Revolt of the Masses,* which argued that twentieth-century society is characterized by the domination of masses of mediocre, interchangeable people. This domination operated without a guiding moral code, and resulted at minimum in a "tyranny of the majority" (to use John Stuart Mill's phrase), if not fascist and communist totalitarianism. Ironically, his very critique of mass culture added fuel to the fires of fascism in Spain.

In our reading from *History as a System,* we find Ortega laying out some of the central elements of the existentialist view of the self. First of all, he makes the basic distinction between free human consciousness and the determined being of physical things that Sartre would later call "being-for-itself" and "being-in-itself." He calls human beings "ontological centaurs," half physical, half transcendent.

This transcendent part gives itself projects, and then acts on them. To start with, we are nothing: We have no essential nature. We accumulate being as we walk along the path of life, just as a vagabond accumulates possessions in the bundle he slings over his back. We create our selves by a "dialectical series of experiments," by our history. What natural science is to the physical world, history is to the human world. For Ortega we *are* what we have *done.* In Sartre's language, our existence precedes our essence.

# Man Has No Nature

## JOSÉ ORTEGA Y GASSET

...THE STONE is given its existence; it need not fight for being what it is—a stone in the field. Man has to be himself in spite of unfavorable circumstances; that means he has to make his own existence at every single moment. He is given the abstract possibility of existing, but not the reality. This he has to conquer hour after hour. Man must earn his life, not only economically but metaphysically.

And all this for what reason? Obviously—but this is repeating the same thing in other words—because man's being and nature's being do not fully coincide. Because man's being is made of such strange stuff as to be partly akin to nature and partly not, at once natural and extranatural, a kind of ontological centaur, half immersed in nature, half transcending it. Dante would have likened him to a boat drawn up on the beach with one end of its keel in the water and the other in the sand. What is natural in him is realized by itself; it presents no problem. That is precisely why man does not consider it his true be-

SOURCE: José Ortega y Gasset, *History as a System and Other Essays Toward a Philosophy of History,* trans. Helene Weyl (New York: Norton, 1961), pp. 111–113, 201–203, 215–217. Copyright 1941, 1961 by W. W. Norton & Company, Inc. Used by permission of W. W. Norton & Company. Originally published in Spanish in 1939. Reprinted in *Existentialism from Dostoevsky to Sartre,* ed. Walter Kaufmann (New York: New American Library, 1975), pp. 153–157. Translations of Ortega's terminology: *Geist* is German for "spirit"; *causa sui* is Latin for "cause of itself," referring to the notion that God is the cause of his own being; *Realdialektik* is German for "real dialectic", i.e., a dialectic of actual historical events; *res gestae* is Latin for "things done," i.e., things human beings have done in the past.—ED.

ing. His extranatural part, on the other hand, is not there from the outset and of itself; it is but an aspiration, a project of life. And this we feel to be our true being; we call it our personality, our self. Our extra- and antinatural portion, however, must not be interpreted in terms of any of the older spiritual philosophies. I am not interested now in the so-called spirit (*Geist*), a pretty confused idea laden with speculative wizardry.

If the reader reflects a little upon the meaning of the entity he calls his life, he will find that it is the attempt to carry out a definite program or project of existence. And his self—each man's self—is nothing but this devised program. All we do we do in the service of this program. Thus man begins by being something that has no reality, neither corporeal nor spiritual; he is a project as such, something which is not yet but aspires to be. One may object that there can be no program without somebody having it, without an idea, a mind, a soul, or whatever it is called. I cannot discuss this thoroughly because it would mean embarking on a course of philosophy. But I will say this: although the project of being a great financier has to be conceived of in an idea, "being" the project is different from holding the idea. In fact, I find no difficulty in thinking this idea but I am very far from being this project.

Here we come upon the formidable and unparalleled character which makes man unique in the universe. We are dealing—and let the disquieting strangeness of the case be well noted—with an entity whose being consists not in what it is already, but in what it is not yet, a being that consists in not-yet-being. Everything else in the world is what it is. An entity whose mode of being consists in what it is already, whose potentiality coincides at once with his reality, we call a "thing." Things are given their being ready-made.

At every moment of my life there open before me divers possibilities: I can do this or that. If I do this, I shall be A the moment after; if I do that, I shall be B. At the present moment the reader may stop reading me or may go on. And, however slight the importance of this article, according as he does the one or the other the reader will be A or will be B, will have made of himself an A or a B. Man is the entity that makes itself, an entity which traditional ontology only stumbled upon precisely as its course was drawing to a close, and which it in consequence gave up the attempt to understand: the *causa sui*. With this difference, that the *causa sui* had only to "exert itself" in being the *cause* of itself and not in determining what *self* it was going to cause. It had, to begin with, a *self* previously determined and invariable, consistent, for example, to infinity.

But man must not only make himself: the weightiest thing he has to do is to determine *what* he is going to be. He is *causa sui* to the second power. By a coincidence that is not casual, the doctrine of the living being, when it seeks in tradition for concepts that are still more or less valid, finds only those which the doctrine of the divine being tried to formulate. If the reader has resolved now to go on reading into the next moment, it will be, in the last instance, because doing this is what is most in accordance with the general program he has mapped out for his life, and hence with the man of determination he has resolved to be. This vital program is the *ego* of each individual, his choice out of divers possibilities of being which at every instant open before him.

Concerning these possibilities of being the following remarks fall to be made:

1. That they likewise are not presented to me. I must find them for myself, either on my own or through the medium of those of my fellows with whom my life brings me in contact. I invent projects of being and of doing in the light of circumstance. This alone I come upon, this alone is given me: circumstance. It is too often forgotten that man is impossible without imagination, without the capacity to invent for himself a conception of life, to "ideate" the character he is going to be. Whether he be original or a plagiarist, man is the novelist of himself.

2. That among these possibilities I must choose. Hence, I am free. But, be it well understood, I am free *by compulsion*, whether I wish to be or not. Freedom is not an activity pursued by an entity that, apart from and previous to such pursuit, is already possessed of a fixed being. To be free means to be lacking in constitutive identity, not to have subscribed to a determined being, to be able to be other than what one was, to be unable to install oneself once and for all in any given being. The only attribute of the fixed, stable being in the free being is this constitutive instability.

In order to speak, then, of man's being we must first elaborate a non-Eleatic concept of being, as others have elaborated a non-Euclidean geometry. The time has come for the seed sown by Heraclitus to bring forth its mighty harvest. . . .

Man invents for himself a program of life, a static form of being, that gives a satisfactory answer to the difficulties posed for him by circumstance. He essays this form of life, attempts to realize this imaginary character he has resolved to be. He embarks on the essay full of illusions and prosecutes the experiment with thoroughness. This means that he comes to *believe* deeply that this character is his real being. But meanwhile the experience has made apparent the shortcomings and limitations of the said program of life. It does not solve all the difficulties, and it creates new ones of its own. When first seen it was full face, with the light shining upon it: hence the illusions, the enthusiasm, the delights believed in store. With the back view its inadequacy is straightway revealed. Man thinks out another program of life. But this second program is drawn up in the light, not only of circumstance, but also of the first. One aims at avoiding in the new project the drawbacks of the old. In the second, therefore, the first is still active; it is preserved in order to be avoided. Inexorably man shrinks from being what he was. On the second project of being, the second thorough experiment, there follows a third, forged in the light of the second and the first, and so on. Man "goes on being" and "unbeing"—living. He goes on accumulating being—the past; he goes on making for himself a being through his dialectical series of experiments. This is a dialectic not of logical but precisely of historical reason—the *Realdialektik* dreamt of somewhere in his papers by Dilthey, the writer to whom we owe more than to anyone else concerning the idea of life, and who is, to my mind, the most important thinker of the second half of the nineteenth century.

In what does this dialectic that will not tolerate the facile anticipations of logical dialectic consist? This is what we have to find out on the basis of facts. We must know what is this series, what are its stages, and of what nature is the link between one and the next. Such a discovery is what would be called history were history to make this its objective, were it, that is to say, to convert itself into historical reason.

Here, then, awaiting our study, lies man's authentic "being"—stretching the whole length of his past. Man is what has happened to him, what he has done. Other things might have happened to him or have been done by him, but what did in fact happen to him and was done by him, this constitutes a relentless trajectory of experiences that he carries on his back as the vagabond his bundle of all he possesses. Man is a substantial emigrant on a pilgrimage of being, and it is accordingly meaningless to set limits to what he is capable of being. In this initial illimitableness of possibilities that characterizes one who has no nature there stands out only one fixed, preestablished, and given line by which he may chart his course, only one limit: the past. The experiments already made with life narrow man's future. If we do not know what he is going to be, we know what he is not going to be. Man lives in view of the past.

*Man, in a word, has no nature; what he has is—history.* Expressed differently: what nature is to things, history, *res gestae*, is to man.

# Camus on the Absurdity of Life

Albert Camus (1913–1960) was a novelist, essayist, playwright, and journalist loosely connected with existentialism. He was born into a poor *pied-noir* (French colonial) family in Mondovi, Algeria. His father died in the Battle of the Marne in 1914 when Camus was a mere babe. His mother suffered a stroke that impaired her speech upon hearing of her husband's death. Camus was raised by his grandmother.

Camus studied at a *lycée* (an exclusive secondary school) in Algiers from 1924 to 1932, where he was an exceptional student. As a youth he loved sports, especially soccer, but this pursuit was cut short by the onset of tuberculosis. Camus studied philosophy on and off again at the University of Algiers starting in 1930, receiving a diploma in 1936.

In the early 1930s Camus held various menial jobs in Algeria. He joined the Communist Party in 1934 out of antifascist sentiments, but was thrown out as a "Trotskyite" two years later, although it was really due to Camus' coolness toward Algerian independence and his support for a humane socialism at odds with the Machiavellian politics of Stalin's Soviet Union. He was also active in the theater as a writer, director, and actor. In the late 1930s he wrote for the socialist newspaper *Alger-Republicain* and edited the *Soir-Republicain*. He also published a volume of essays on life in Algeria, the setting of most of his fictional works.

In 1940 Camus went to Paris to write for the *Paris-Soir,* but returned to Algeria after the paper's staff uprooted itself a couple of times as the Nazi armies surged through France. He married his second wife in 1940. Although information about this period of Camus' life is uncertain, he appears to have spent most of World War II in France, moving around a lot as he worked for the French resistance. He and Jean-Paul Sartre founded the leftist newspaper *Combat,* which Camus edited from 1943 to 1947. In it he argued for a moral resistance to fascism and for the intrinsic value of human life.

In these years of wandering, Camus carried around in his briefcase his three "absurds": the novel *The Stranger* (published in 1942), the philosophical essay *The Myth of Sisyphus* (1942), and the play *Caligula* (1945). These works all spoke of the absurdity of human existence, and of the need for people of integrity to face up to this absurdity by persevering with their lives and projects in the face of a meaningless cosmos.

*The Stranger* is considered one of the great novels of the twentieth century. It starts with a laconic report by Mersault, the book's central character, of his mother's death: "Mother died today. Or maybe yesterday, I don't know." We later learn of Mersault's empty relationship with his girlfriend Marie, who he's willing to marry simply because she asks him, and his indifference to his job and to the possibility of relocating to Paris. The turning point comes when Mersault shoots an Arab on the beach, in part in revenge for the Arab's cutting his friend Raymond with a knife, in part because the blazing sun beating down on his head made him unconcerned with the consequences of his actions. He's caught by the police, but shows no remorse over the immorality of his deed. He resists attempts by a priest to get him to confess his sins, not to mention attempts by his lawyer to save him from the guillotine. The novel ends on the night before his execution, when he looks out his prison window and gazes upon an indifferent cosmos, satisfied with his life and happy about his coming death. Mersault is a classic existentialist antihero, unwilling to compromise with conventional morality and religion, lucid in the face of the absurdity of life.

Camus' second important group of works centers on the theme of revolt. In the novel *The Plague* (1947), the city of Oran has been infected with a plague, and cordoned off from the outside world. The brave Dr. Rieux and his comrades fight against the disease, just as the French resistance fought against the disease of Nazism during the German occupation.

*The Rebel* (1951), in some ways Camus' most important work philosophically, gives the reader accounts of metaphysical, historical, and artistic rebellions. Camus defends the cause of the humane rebel committed to social justice over that of the nihilist revolutionary determined to remake the world in an ideological image, whatever the cost in human lives. This book, along with their disagreement over the policies of the Soviet Union, caused a falling out between Camus and Sartre in the early 1950s. His plays *The State of Siege* (1948) and *The Just Assassins* (1950) also deal with the theme of moral rebellion against unjust authority.

From 1954 on Camus was caught up in the politics surrounding the movement for Algerian independence. He had earlier shown his sympathy for the poverty of the Arabs in his newspaper articles, but as a *pied-noir* he couldn't support the independence movement or see Algeria as anything other than an integral part of France. He did, however, call for nonviolence from both the Arab rebels and the French authorities.

Camus' last complete novel was *The Fall* (1956). He received the Noble Prize for literature in 1957. Some of Camus' more interesting essays, including his anti–capital punishment "Reflections on the Guillotine," appeared in English as *Resistance, Rebellion, and Death* (1960). Camus died in a car accident on January 4, 1960, near Sens, France. The manuscript of his unfinished autobiographical novel *The Last Man* was found at the accident. It was published in 1994, bringing Camus yet more literary fame from beyond the grave.

Camus' work is important to an understanding of the existentialist view of the self on at least two fronts. First and foremost is his theme of the absurdity of life in a godless universe where death is inevitable and where meaning and morality are only human inventions. We find this theme at work in *The Myth of Sisyphus, The Stranger,* and elsewhere in his writings.

*The Myth of Sisyphus* starts with a striking claim: "There is but one truly serious philosophical problem, and that is suicide. Judging whether life is or is not worth living amounts to answering the fundamental problem of philosophy." Camus' answer to this fundamental question comes in the form of an allegory based on the story of the Greek hero Sisyphus. In the following selection, the conclusion of *The Myth of Sisyphus,* we hear Camus describe Sisyphus's fate. He is condemned by the gods to roll a rock up a hill every day, only to have it roll back down again every night. This is, naturally, Camus' allegory for human life in general: Each day we wake up, drink our coffee, go to school or work, return home, watch television, and then do it all over again the next day (unless it's a weekend, when we engage in other equally meaningless rituals). We each have our own absurd rock to roll up the hill of our lives.

The other major theme presented by Camus in *The Myth of Sisyphus* and elsewhere is that of the need to revolt against this absurdity. This is exactly what Sisyphus does: He realizes the pointlessness of what he's doing, but finds a joy in it all the same. He overcomes suffering by being lucid about his destiny. "He is stronger than his rock." For Camus there is no escape from the absurdity of life: We have to stare it straight in the face and accept it as the core of our lives. Only then can we be happy.

# The Myth of Sisyphus

## ALBERT CAMUS

THE GODS had condemned Sisyphus to ceaselessly rolling a rock to the top of a mountain, whence the stone would fall back of its own weight. They had thought with some reason that there is no more dreadful punishment than futile and hopeless labor.

If one believes Homer, Sisyphus was the wisest and most prudent of mortals. According to another tradition, however, he was disposed to practice the profession of highwayman. I see no contradiction in this. Opinions differ as to the reasons why he became the futile laborer of the underworld. To begin with, he is accused of a certain levity in regard to the gods. He stole their secrets. Aegina, the daughter of Aesopus, was carried off by Jupiter.[1] The father was shocked by that disappearance and complained to Sisyphus. He, who knew of the abduction, offered to tell about it on condition that Aesopus would give water to the citadel of Corinth. To the celestial thunderbolts he preferred the benediction of water. He was punished for this in the underworld. Homer tells us also that Sisyphus had put

Death in chains. Pluto could not endure the sight of his deserted, silent empire. He dispatched the god of war, who liberated Death from the hands of her conqueror.

It is said that Sisyphus, being near to death, rashly wanted to test his wife's love. He ordered her to cast his unburied body into the middle of the public square. Sisyphus woke up in the underworld. And there, annoyed by an obedience so contrary to human love, he obtained from Pluto permission to return to earth in order to chastise his wife. But when he had seen again the face of this world, enjoyed water and sun, warm stones and the sea, he no longer wanted to go back to the infernal darkness. Recalls, signs of anger, warnings were of no avail. Many years more he lived facing the curve of the gulf, the sparkling sea, and the smiles of earth. A decree of the gods was necessary. Mercury came and seized the impudent man by the collar and, snatching him from his joys, led him forcibly back to the underworld, where his rock was ready for him.

You have already grasped that Sisyphus is the absurd hero. He is, as much through his passions as through his torture. His scorn of the gods, his hatred of death, and his passion for life won him that unspeakable penalty in which the whole being is exerted toward accomplishing nothing. This is the price that must be paid for the passions of this earth. Nothing is told us about Sisy-

---

[1] Jupiter was the Latin name for the king of the Olympian Gods, known as Zeus to the Greeks. He hurled thunderbolts from his starry seat of power at those who disobeyed his commands. Aesopus was a minor river god whose daughter Aegina was one of the many divine and mortal women who Jupiter/Zeus had his way with. Pluto was the lord of the underworld, and Mercury the messenger of the gods—ED.

SOURCE: Albert Camus, *The Myth of Sisyphus and Other Essays,* trans. Justin O'Brien (New York: Vintage Books, 1983), pp. 119–123; originally published in French in 1942.

phus in the underworld. Myths are made for the imagination to breathe life into them. As for this myth, one sees merely the whole effort of a body straining to raise the huge stone, to roll it, and push it up a slope a hundred times over; one sees the face screwed up, the cheek tight against the stone, the shoulder bracing the clay-covered mass, the foot wedging it, the fresh start with arms outstretched, the wholly human security of two earth-clotted hands. At the very end of his long effort measured by skyless space and time without depth, the purpose is achieved. Then Sisyphus watches the stone rush down in a few moments toward that lower world whence he will have to push it up again toward the summit. He goes back down to the plain.

It is during that return, that pause, that Sisyphus interests me. A face that toils so close to stones is already stone itself! I see that man going back down with a heavy yet measured step toward the torment of which he will never know the end. That hour like a breathing-space which returns as surely as his suffering, that is the hour of consciousness. At each of those moments when he leaves the heights and gradually sinks toward the lairs of the gods, he is superior to his fate. He is stronger than his rock.

If this myth is tragic, that is because its hero is conscious. Where would his torture be, indeed, if at every step the hope of succeeding upheld him? The workman of today works everyday in his life at the same tasks, and his fate is no less absurd. But it is tragic only at the rare moments when it becomes conscious. Sisyphus, proletarian of the gods, powerless and rebellious, knows the whole extent of his wretched condition: it is what he thinks of during his descent. The lucidity that was to constitute his torture at the same time crowns his victory. There is no fate that cannot be surmounted by scorn.

If the descent is thus sometimes performed in sorrow, it can also take place in joy. This word is not too much. Again I fancy Sisyphus returning toward his rock, and the sorrow was in the beginning. When the images of earth cling too tightly to memory, when the call of happiness becomes too insistent, it happens that melancholy arises in

man's heart: this is the rock's victory, this is the rock itself. The boundless grief is too heavy to bear. These are our nights of Gethsemane. But crushing truths perish from being acknowledged. Thus, Oedipus at the outset obeys fate without knowing it. But from the moment he knows, his tragedy begins. Yet at the same moment, blind and desperate, he realizes that the only bond linking him to the world is the cool hand of a girl. Then a tremendous remark rings out: "Despite so many ordeals, my advanced age and the nobility of my soul make me conclude that all is well." Sophocles' Oedipus, like Dostoevsky's Kirilov, thus gives the recipe for the absurd victory. Ancient wisdom confirms modern heroism.[2]

One does not discover the absurd without being tempted to write a manual of happiness. "What!—by such narrow ways—?" There is but one world, however. Happiness and the absurd are two sons of the same earth. They are inseparable. It would be a mistake to say that happiness necessarily springs from the absurd discovery. It happens as well that the feeling of the absurd springs from happiness. "I conclude that all is well," says Oedipus, and that remark is sacred. It echoes in the wild and limited universe of man. It teaches that all is not, has not been, exhausted. It drives out of this world a god who had come into it with dissatisfaction and a preference for futile suffering. It makes of fate a human matter, which must be settled among men.

All Sisyphus' silent joy is contained therein. His fate belongs to him. His rock is a thing. Likewise, the absurd man, when he contemplates his torment, silences all the idols. In the universe suddenly restored to its silence, the myriad wondering little voices of the earth rise up. Unconscious, secret calls, invitations from all the faces, they are the necessary reverse and price of victory. There is no sun without shadow, and it is

---

[2] Gethsemane was the olive grove where Jesus met his disciples the night before his crucifixion. Oedipus was the mythical king of Thebes who, without knowing it, killed his father, married his mother, and much later gave his name to a psychological complex first described by Sigmund Freud. Kirilov is a nihilist in Fyodor Dostoevsky's novel *The Possessed* who wants to kill himself to become god—ED.

essential to know the night. The absurd man says yes and his efforts will henceforth be unceasing. If there is a personal fate, there is no higher destiny, or at least there is, but one which he concludes is inevitable and despicable. For the rest, he knows himself to be the master of his days. At that subtle moment when man glances backward over his life, Sisyphus returning toward his rock, in that slight pivoting he contemplates that series of unrelated actions which become his fate, created by him, combined under his memory's eye and soon sealed by his death. Thus, convinced of the wholly human origin of all that is human, a blind man eager to see who knows that the night has no end, he is still on the go. The rock is still rolling.

I leave Sisyphus at the foot of the mountain! One always finds one's burden again. But Sisyphus teaches the higher fidelity that negates the gods and raises rocks. He too concludes that all is well. This universe henceforth without a master seems to him neither sterile nor futile. Each atom of that stone, each mineral flake of that night filled mountain, in itself forms a world. The struggle itself toward the heights is enough to fill a man's heart. One must imagine Sisyphus happy.

## Sartre on Human Freedom

Jean-Paul Sartre (1905–1980) was born in Paris and was the only major literary or philosophical figure to openly admit to being an existentialist. His father was a naval officer who died in 1907. Young Jean-Paul was a brilliant self-taught student who read classic French literature at an early age, but who was ostracized and picked on by his classmates. He later said that he was an atheist from age 12 on. He studied philosophy at the prestigious *École Normale Supérieure* in 1924, receiving his *agrégation* (the next highest degree to a Ph.D. in the French system) in 1929 due in part to his cramming with Simone de Beauvoir, who would be his lifelong friend and sometimes lover. Sartre finished first, de Beauvoir second, perhaps indicative of things to come in their friendship.

In the early and mid-1930s, Sartre did a stint in the French army, studied phenomenology in Berlin, taught at a number of *lycées* (secondary schools), and wrote a number of essays and books that took a phenomenological approach to the imagination and the emotions. The most famous of these was *The Transcendence of the Ego* (1937), which criticized Freud's idea of a concrete ego as the center of human consciousness. His important philosophical novel *Nausea* appeared in 1938. The hero of the novel Roquentin is nauseated at the world around him, finding the physicality of things "too much." He realizes the absurdity of conscious life in a world of unconscious things while staring at the roots of an ancient chestnut tree. In the 1930s Sartre also started his on-again, off-again love affair with the Communist Party.

World War II found Sartre back in the French army. He was captured by the Germans in 1940, then released in 1941. He joined the French resistance in an intellectual capacity soon after, continuing to write and teach in his spare time. In 1943 he published *Being and Nothingness: An Essay in Phenomenological Ontology,* a long and difficult book that is one of the three imposing monuments of twentieth-century continental philosophy (along with Martin Heidegger's 1927 *Being and Time* and Maurice Merleau-Ponty's 1945 *The Phenomenology of Perception*). During the war he worked with and befriended Albert Camus, although they later had a falling out over Sartre's affiliation with communism.

In *Being and Nothingness* Sartre defends the idea that all human beings are radically free. He sees us as sharing *l'être pour-soi,* or being-for-itself: We are, at every moment, free to choose our actions and our destinies. Our consciousness is a nothingness. As such, we can make it whatever we want. Sartre concluded that we are always responsible for our actions: There is no God in the sky or unchanging human nature that we can appeal to as a source for moral rules.

Standing in opposition to being-for-itself was what Sartre called the being of physical things *l'être en-soi,* being-in-itself. Rocks and trees and telephone polls are solid, fixed things, unconscious, without any reason to be other than that given them by beings who exist for themselves. They have no purpose. They just *are.*

Now the obvious critique of this radical notion of freedom is that, as physical beings, our choices are limited in many ways. We cannot waltz across a busy street without risking being run over. We cannot fly without some sort of mechanism, or drink a deadly poison and survive. Psychologically speaking, we cannot go around insulting people without incurring their anger. Sartre's answer to this critique was quite clever: These limitations, which he called our "facticity," were real enough. Yet our transcendent being-for-itself is always in play: We can choose not to run across the street or to drink the poison. We can deny our facticity by an act of free choice. Ultimately, even if our lives our miserable and we feel trapped in them, we can always commit suicide. As Casca put it in an existential moment in Shakespeare's *Julius Caesar,* "So every bondman in his own hand bears/The power to cancel his captivity" (1.3).

His way of dealing with the obvious fact that others limit our freedom was clever, too: When others gaze upon us with "the look," they objectify us, turning us (in their own minds) into *en-soi* beings. We have to look back, to resist, to regain our *poir-soi* freedom. In the case of crossing the busy street, he might have said that we have to yell at the impatient drivers who treat us as physical obstacles to their forward progress, banging on their hoods to make them pay attention to us and to recognize us as *pour-soi* beings. To avoid being reduced to *en-soi* objects in the eyes of others, we have to demand that we not be reduced to physical things, to revolt against their objectifying look.

Sartre completes his idea of freedom with the concept of "bad faith." This is when free beings like us refuse to take responsibility for our decisions, attributing them to others, to our surrounding physical or social circumstances, or to abstract rules not of our own making. It's when we try to turn our free being-for-itself into a determined being-in-itself. We probably experience bad faith every day of our lives. It's when someone asks you to a party, and instead of telling them you don't like them and don't want to be around them, you get out of it by saying, "Sorry, I have to write an essay tonight." It's when you don't look for a job because you're "too tired," or the unemployment rate is too high. It's when you blame your parents or boyfriend or wife for being unhappy, even though you could change your relationship with them. We see these basic concepts at play in most of Sartre's philosophical and literary works, including the following essay.

After the war Sartre quit teaching for good, and founded the journal *Les Temps Modernes* (*Modern Times*) with de Beauvoir and Merleau-Ponty. He had became a permanent fixture at the Left Bank cafés in his native Paris, leading some foreign critics to observe that existentialism was a nihilist philosophy bred by long nights fueled by *café noirs* or bottles of Beaujolais. During the postwar period Sartre also tried to reconcile existentialism with Marxism, at first with some success in the succinct and clear *Search for a Method* (1960), and then more laboriously in the long and difficult two-volume *Critique of Dialectical Reason* (1960 and 1985), for which *Search for a Method* originally acted as an introduction. Sartre argued that Marxism was the only valid social philosophy of our time, just as existentialism is the only valid philosophy of individual existence.

This attempt brought him much criticism: After all, how can a philosophy of human freedom like existentialism be combined with a philosophy that emphasizes economic determinism like Marxism? Be that as it may, during the 1950s and 1960s Sartre was directly involved in many political struggles, including workers' strikes and student protests against the Vietnam War. He eventually broke with Soviet communism, criticizing the Soviet Union's invasions of Hungary in 1956 and of Czechoslovakia in 1968. He even turned down the 1964 Nobel Prize for Literature out of the fear that it would compromise his political integrity.

Sartre wrote a number of plays with political and philosophical themes. His classic existentialist drama *No Exit* (1944) features three dead characters trapped in a small room that turns out to be hell. They are condemned to this fate by their bad faith. Near the end one of the characters informs us that "hell is other people": We cannot escape their judgment of our faults and weaknesses as they objectify us with their gaze. He also wrote a trilogy of novels whose general title is *The Roads to Freedom* (1945 and 1949). It explores the themes of human freedom and authenticity in the lives of a group of friends living in France before and during World War II.

Our reading is Sartre's famous 1946 essay "Existentialism Is a Humanism." In general, it is a defense of existentialism as a positive, life-affirming philosophy against the cavils of Christian, Marxist, and other critics. This essay contains most of the major themes of existential thought:

1. As human beings, we "are condemned to be free"; there is no escaping our existential responsibility to make choices in our lives. It's true that these choices are subjective, but they have a wider significance than our individual lives. In deciding for ourselves, we decide for all humanity, our actions taken together creating an image of the ideal human person as we see it.
2. "Man is nothing else but that which he makes of himself. . . . he is nothing else but the sum of his actions." The projects we choose to pursue in our lives make up *who* we are. In other words, our existence precedes our essence: There is no fixed human nature that defines what we are. When we make ourselves, we start with nothing, just as the painter starts with a blank canvas when creating a work of art.
3. Our existential freedom takes place in an atmosphere of anguish: Our freedom of choice exists in a universe where there is no God or divine order to prove the validity of the values we guide our lives by. We are "abandoned" to a world of our own making.
4. This notion of freedom means that, if we are to live in "good faith," we cannot look for moral guidance anywhere but our conscious reason. Our instincts are no guide, for they can only be "ratified" or proven valid by action, and thus by choice, so relying on them is a vicious circle. Neither is the counsel of a priest or philosopher a good guide, for when we choose a counselor, we already have in mind the ad-

vice they are likely to give us. To ask others to make our moral decisions for us is to abdicate our freedom, to act in bad faith.

5. We must avoid this bad faith, and seek to live an authentic life. We should not take refuge in a naturalistic or materialistic explanation of character: There is no such thing as a "cowardly" temperament caused by thin blood or sensitive nerves. Similarly, we cannot blame our bad actions on our passions: We can choose to resist these, just as we can resist our physical shortcomings. To live authentically is to accept our freedom and to be the sole legislator of our own values and actions. This call for authenticity is the stern challenge that Sartre and the existentialists issue to us, a challenge that is not always easy to live up to.

# Existentialism Is a Humanism

## JEAN-PAUL SARTRE

MY PURPOSE HERE is to offer a defence of existentialism against several reproaches that have been laid against it.

First, it has been reproached as an invitation to people to dwell in quietism of despair. For if every way to a solution is barred, one would have to regard any action in this world as entirely ineffective, and one would arrive finally at a contemplative philosophy. . . .

From another quarter we are reproached for having underlined all that is ignominious in the human situation, for depicting what is mean, sordid or base to the neglect of certain things that possess charm and beauty and belong to the brighter side of human nature: for example, according to the Catholic critic, Mlle. Mercier, we forget how an infant smiles. . . .

From the Christian side, we are reproached as people who deny the reality and seriousness of human affairs. For since we ignore the commandments of God and all values prescribed as eternal, nothing remains but what is strictly voluntary. Everyone can do what he likes, and will be incapable, from such a point of view, of condemning either the point of view or the action of anyone else.

. . . The question is only complicated because there are two kinds of existentialists. There are, on the one hand, the Christians, amongst whom I shall name Jaspers and Gabriel Marcel, both professed Catholics; and on the other the existential atheists, amongst whom we must place Heidegger as well as the French existentialists and myself.[1] What they have in common is simply the fact that they believe that *existence* comes before *essence*—or, if you will, that we must begin from the subjective. What exactly do we mean by that?

If one considers an article of manufacture as, for example, a book or a paper-knife—one sees that it has been made by an artisan who had a conception of it; and he has paid attention, equally, to the conception of a paper-knife and

---

[1] Karl Jaspers (1883–1969) was a German existentialist who wrote voluminously on Sartre's favorite themes of freedom and authenticity. Gabriel Marcel (1889–1973) was a French thinker who tried to reconcile existentialism and Catholicism—ED.

SOURCE: Jean-Paul Sartre, *Existentialism and Humanism,* trans. Philip Mairet (1948; London: Methuen, 1974), pp. 23–24, 26–39, 41–52, 54–56. Originally published in French as *L'existentialisme est un humanisme.* Copyright 1948 by Editions Gallimard. Reprinted by permission of Georges Borchardt, Inc., for Editions Gallimard. Anthologized in *Existentialism from Dostoevsky to Sartre,* ed. Walter Kaufmann (New York: Meridian, 1975), pp. 345–369 (edited).

to the pre-existent technique of production which is a part of that conception and is, at bottom, a formula. Thus the paper-knife is at the same time an article producible in a certain manner and one which, on the other hand, serves a definite purpose, for one cannot suppose that a man would produce a paper-knife without knowing what it was for. Let us say, then, of the paper-knife that its essence—that is to say the sum of the formulae and the qualities which made its production and its definition possible—precedes its existence. The presence of such-and-such a paper-knife or book is thus determined before my eyes. Here, then, we are viewing the world from a technical standpoint, and we can say that production precedes existence.

When we think of God as the creator, we are thinking of him, most of the time, as a supernal artisan. . . . Thus, the conception of man in the mind of God is comparable to that of the paper-knife in the mind of the artisan: God makes man according to a procedure and a conception, exactly as the artisan manufactures a paper-knife, following a definition and a formula. Thus each individual man is the realisation of a certain conception which dwells in the divine understanding. In the philosophic atheism of the eighteenth century, the notion of God is suppressed, but not, for all that, the idea that essence is prior to existence; something of that idea we still find everywhere, in Diderot, in Voltaire and even in Kant. Man possesses a human nature; that "human nature," which is the conception of human being, is found in every man; which means that each man is a particular example of a universal conception, the conception of Man. In Kant, this universality goes so far that the wild man of the woods, man in the state of nature and the bourgeois are all contained in the same definition and have the same fundamental qualities. Here again, the essence of man precedes that historic existence which we confront in experience.

Atheistic existentialism, of which I am a representative, declares with greater consistency that if God does not exist there is at least one being whose existence comes before its essence, a being which exists before it can be defined by any conception of it. That being is man or, as Heidegger has it, the human reality. What do we mean by saying that existence precedes essence? We mean that man first of all exists, encounters himself, surges up in the world—and defines himself afterwards. If man as the existentialist sees him is not definable, it is because to begin with he is nothing. He will not be anything until later, and then he will be what he makes of himself. Thus, there is no human nature, because there is no God to have a conception of it. Man simply is. Not that he is simply what he conceives himself to be, but he is what he wills, and as he conceives himself after already existing—as he wills to be after that leap towards existence. Man is nothing else but that which he makes of himself. That is the first principle of existentialism. And this is what people call its "subjectivity," using the word as a reproach against us. But what do we mean to say by this, but that man is of a greater dignity than a stone or a table? For we mean to say that man primarily exists—that man is, before all else, something which propels itself towards a future and is aware that it is doing so. Man is, indeed, a project which possesses a subjective life, instead of being a kind of moss, or a fungus or a cauliflower. Before that projection of the self nothing exists; not even in the heaven of intelligence: man will only attain existence when he is what he purposes to be. Not, however, what he may wish to be. For what we usually understand by wishing or willing is a conscious decision taken—much more often than not—after we have made ourselves what we are. I may wish to join a party, to write a book or to marry—but in such a case what is usually called my will is probably a manifestation of a prior and more spontaneous decision. If, however, it is true that existence is prior to essence, man is responsible for what he is. Thus, the first effect of existentialism is that it puts every man in possession of himself as he is, and places the entire responsibility for his existence squarely upon his own shoulders. And, when we say that man is responsible for himself, we do not mean that he is responsible only for his own individuality, but that he is responsible for all men. . . . When we say that man chooses himself, we do mean that every one of us must choose himself; but by that we also mean that in choosing for himself he chooses for all men. For in effect, of all the actions a man may take in order to create himself as he wills to be, there is not one which is not creative, at the same time, of an image of man such as he believes he ought to be. To choose between this or that is at the same time to affirm the value of that which is chosen; for we are unable ever to choose the worse. What we choose is always the better; and nothing can be better for us unless it is better for all. If, moreover, existence precedes essence and we will to exist at the same time as we fashion our image, that image is valid for all and for the entire epoch in which we find ourselves. Our responsibility is thus much greater than we had supposed, for it concerns mankind as a whole. . . . I am thus responsible for myself and for all men, and I am creating a certain image of man as I would have him to be. In fashioning myself I fashion man.

This may enable us to understand what is meant by such terms—perhaps a little grandiloquent—as anguish, abandonment and despair. As you will soon see, it is very simple. First, what do we mean by anguish?—The existentialist frankly states that man is in anguish. His meaning is as follows—When a man commits himself to anything, fully realising that he is not only choosing what he will be, but is thereby at the same time a legislator deciding for the whole of mankind—in such a moment a man cannot escape from the sense of complete and profound responsibility. There are many, indeed, who show no such anxiety. But we affirm that they are merely disguising their anguish or are in flight from it. Certainly, many people think that in what they are doing they commit no one but themselves to anything: and if you ask them, "What would happen if everyone did so?" they shrug their shoulders and reply, "Everyone does not do so." But in truth, one ought always to ask oneself what would happen if everyone did as one is doing; nor can one escape from that disturbing thought except by a kind of self-deception. The man who lies in self-excuse, by saying "Everyone will not do it" must be ill at ease in his conscience, for the act of lying implies the universal value which it denies. By its very disguise his anguish reveals itself. . . .

. . . Clearly, the anguish with which we are concerned here is not one that could lead to quietism or inaction. It is anguish pure and simple, of the kind well known to all those who have borne responsibilities. When, for instance, a military leader takes upon himself the responsibility for an attack and sends a number of men to their death, he chooses to do it and at bottom he alone chooses. No doubt under a higher command, but its orders, which are more general, require interpretation by him and upon that interpretation depends the life of ten, fourteen or twenty men. In making the decision, he cannot but feel a certain anguish. All leaders know that anguish. It does not prevent their acting, on the contrary it is the very condition of their action, for the action presupposes that there is a plurality of possibilities, and in choosing one of these, they realize that it has value only because it is chosen. Now it is anguish of that kind which existentialism describes, and moreover, as we shall see, makes explicit through direct responsibility towards other men who are concerned. Far from being a screen which could separate us from action, it is a condition of action itself.

And when we speak of "abandonment"—a favorite word of Heidegger—we only mean to say that God does not exist, and that it is necessary to draw the consequences of his absence right to the end. The existentialist is strongly opposed to a certain type of secular moralism which seeks to suppress God at the least possible expense. . . . The existentialist, on the contrary, finds it extremely embarrassing that God does not exist, for there disappears with Him all possibility of finding values in an intelligible heaven. There can no longer be any good *a priori*, since there is no infinite and perfect consciousness to think it. It is nowhere written that "the good" exists, that one must be honest or must not lie, since we are now upon the plane where there are only men. Dostoevsky once wrote "If God did not exist, everything would be permitted"; and that, for existentialism, is the starting point. Everything is indeed permitted if God does not exist, and man is in consequence forlorn, for he cannot find anything to depend upon either within or outside himself. He discovers forthwith, that he is without excuse. For if indeed existence precedes essence, one will never be able to explain one's action by reference to a given and specific human nature; in other words, there is no determinism—man is free, man is freedom. Nor, on the other hand, if God does not exist, are we provided with any values or commands that could legitimise our behaviour. Thus we have neither behind us, nor before us in a luminous realm of values, any means of justification or excuse.—We are left alone, without excuse. That is what I mean when I say that man is condemned to be free. Condemned, because he did not create himself, yet is nevertheless at liberty, and from the moment that he is thrown into this world he is responsible for everything he does. The existentialist does not believe in the power of passion. He will never regard a grand passion as a destructive torrent upon which a man is swept into certain actions as by fate, and which, therefore, is an excuse for them. He thinks that man is responsible for his passion. Neither will an existentialist think that a man can find help through some sign being vouchsafed upon earth for his orientation: for he thinks that the man himself interprets the sign as he chooses. He thinks that every man, without any support or help whatever, is condemned at every instant to invent man. . . .

As an example by which you may the better understand this state of abandonment, I will refer to the case of a pupil of mine, who sought me out in the following circumstances. His father was quarrelling with his mother and was also inclined to be a "collaborator"; his elder brother had been killed in the German offensive of 1940 and this young man, with a sentiment somewhat primitive but generous, burned to avenge him. His mother was living alone with him, deeply afflicted by the semi-treason of his father and by the death of her eldest son, and her one consolation was in this young man. But he, at this mo-

ment, had the choice between going to England to join the Free French Forces or of staying near his mother and helping her to live. He fully realised that this woman lived only for him and that his disappearance—or perhaps his death—would plunge her into despair. He also realised that, concretely and in fact, every action he performed on his mother's behalf would be sure of effect in the sense of aiding her to live, whereas anything he did in order to go and fight would be an ambiguous action which might vanish like water into sand and serve no purpose. For instance, to set out for England he would have to wait indefinitely in a Spanish camp on the way through Spain; or, on arriving in England or in Algiers he might be put into an office to fill up forms. Consequently, he found himself confronted by two very different modes of action; the one concrete, immediate, but directed towards only one individual; and the other an action addressed to an end infinitely greater, a national collectivity, but for that very reason ambiguous—and it might be frustrated on the way. At the same time, he was hesitating between two kinds of morality; on the one side the morality of sympathy, of personal devotion and, on the other side, a morality of wider scope but of more debatable validity. He had to choose between those two. What could help him to choose? Could the Christian doctrine? No. Christian doctrine says: Act with charity, love your neighbour, deny yourself for others, choose the way which is hardest, and so forth. But which is the harder road? To whom does one owe the more brotherly love, the patriot or the mother? Which is the more useful aim, the general one of fighting in and for the whole community, or the precise aim of helping one particular person to live? Who can give an answer to that *a priori*? No one. Nor is it given in any ethical scripture. The Kantian ethic says, Never regard another as a means, but always as an end. Very well; if I remain with my mother, I shall be regarding her as the end and not as a means: but by the same token I am in danger of treating as means those who are fighting on my behalf; and the converse is also true, that if I go to the aid of the combatants I shall be treating them as the end at the risk of treating my mother as a means.

If values are uncertain, if they are still too abstract to determine the particular, concrete case under consideration, nothing remains but to trust in our instincts. That is what this young man tried to do; and when I saw him he said, "In the end, it is feeling that counts; the direction in which it is really pushing me is the one I ought to choose. If I feel that I love my mother enough to sacrifice everything else for her—my will to be avenged, all my longings for action and adventure then I stay with her. If, on the contrary, I feel that my love for her is not enough, I go." But how does one estimate the strength of a feeling? The value of his feeling for his mother was determined precisely by the fact that he was standing by her. I may say that I love a certain friend enough to sacrifice such or such a sum of money for him, but I cannot prove that unless I have done it. I may say, "I love my mother enough to remain with her," if actually I have remained with her. I can only estimate the strength of this affection if I have performed an action by which it is defined and ratified. But if I then appeal to this affection to justify my action, I find myself drawn into a vicious circle.

. . . In other words, feeling is formed by the deeds that one does; therefore I cannot consult it as a guide to action. And that is to say that I can neither seek within myself for an authentic impulse to action, nor can I expect, from some ethic, formulae that will enable me to act. You may say that the youth did, at least, go to a professor to ask for advice. But if you seek counsel—from a priest, for example you have selected that priest; and at bottom you already knew, more or less, what he would advise. In other words, to choose an adviser is nevertheless to commit oneself by that choice. If you are a Christian, you will say, Consult a priest; but there are collaborationists, priests who are resisters and priests who wait for the tide to turn: which will you choose? Had this young man chosen a priest of the resistance, or one of the collaboration, he would have decided beforehand the kind of advice he was to receive. Similarly, in coming to me, he knew

what advice I should give him, and I had but one reply to make. You are free, therefore choose that is to say, invent. No rule of general morality can show you what you ought to do: no signs are vouchsafed in this world. The Catholics will reply, "Oh, but they are!" Very well; still, it is I myself, in every case, who have to interpret the signs. . . .

As for "despair," the meaning of this expression is extremely simple. It merely means that we limit ourselves to a reliance upon that which is within our wills, or within the sum of the probabilities which render our action feasible. Whenever one wills anything, there are always these elements of probability. If I am counting upon a visit from a friend, who may be coming by train or by tram, I presuppose that the train will arrive at the appointed time, or that the tram will not be derailed. I remain in the realm of possibilities; but one does not rely upon any possibilities beyond those that are strictly concerned in one's action. Beyond the point at which the possibilities under consideration cease to affect my action, I ought to disinterest myself. For there is no God and no prevenient design, which can adapt the world and all its possibilities to my will. When Descartes said, "Conquer yourself rather than the world," what he meant was, at bottom, the same—that we should act without hope.

. . . Quietism is the attitude of people who say, "let others do what I cannot do." The doctrine I am presenting before you is precisely the opposite of this, since it declares that there is no reality except in action. It goes further, indeed, and adds, "Man is nothing else but what he purposes, he exists only in so far as he realises himself, he is therefore nothing else but the sum of his actions, nothing else but what his life is." Hence we can well understand why some people are horrified by our teaching. For many have but one resource to sustain them in their misery, and that is to think, "Circumstances have been against me, I was worthy to be something much better than I have been. I admit I have never had a great love or a great friendship; but that is because I never met a man or a woman who were worthy of it; if I have not written any very good books, it is because I had not the leisure to do so; or, if I have had no children to whom I could devote myself it is because I did not find the man I could have lived with. So there remains within me a wide range of abilities, inclinations and potentialities, unused but perfectly viable, which endow me with a worthiness that could never be inferred from the mere history of my actions." But in reality and for the existentialist, there is no love apart from the deeds of love; no potentiality of love other than that which is manifested in loving; there is no genius other than that which is expressed in works of art. The genius of Proust is the totality of the works of Proust; the genius of Racine is the series of his tragedies, outside of which there is nothing. Why should we attribute to Racine the capacity to write yet another tragedy when that is precisely what he—did not write? In life, a man commits himself, draws his own portrait and there is nothing but that portrait. No doubt this thought may seem comfortless to one who has not made a success of his life. On the other hand, it puts everyone in a position to understand that reality alone is reliable; that dreams, expectations and hopes serve to define a man only as deceptive dreams, abortive hopes, expectations unfulfilled; that is to say, they define him negatively, not positively. Nevertheless, when one says, "You are nothing else but what you live," it does not imply that an artist is to be judged solely by his works of art, for a thousand other things contribute no less to his definition as a man. What we mean to say is that a man is no other than a series of undertakings, that he is the sum, the organisation, the set of relations that constitute these undertakings.

In the light of all this, what people reproach us with is not, after all, our pessimism, but the sternness of our optimism. If people condemn our works of fiction, in which we describe characters that are base, weak, cowardly and sometimes even frankly evil, it is not only because those characters are base, weak, cowardly or evil. For suppose that, like Zola, we showed that the behaviour of these characters was caused by their heredity, or by the action of their environment upon them, or by determining factors, psychic or organic. People would be reassured, they would say, "You see, that is what we are like, no one can do anything about it." But the existentialist, when he portrays a coward, shows him as responsible for his cowardice. He is not like that on account of a cowardly heart or lungs or cerebrum, he has not become like that through his physiological organism; he is like that because he has made himself into a coward by his actions. There is no such thing as a cowardly temperament. There are nervous temperaments; there is what is called impoverished blood, and there are also rich temperaments. But the man whose blood is poor is not a coward for all that, for what produces cowardice is the act of giving up or giving way; and a temperament is not an action. A coward is defined by the deed that he has done. What people feel obscurely, and with horror, is that the coward as we present him is guilty of being a coward. What people would prefer would be to be born either a coward or a hero. One of the charges most often laid against the *Chemins de la Liberté* is something like this "But, after all, these people being so base, how can you make them into heroes?"[2] That objection is really rather comic, for it implies that people are born heroes: and that is, at bottom, what such people would like to think. If you are born cowards, you can be quite content, you can do nothing about it and you will be cowards all your lives whatever you do; and if you are born heroes you can again be quite content; you will be heroes all your lives eating and drinking heroically. Whereas the existentialist says that the coward makes himself cowardly, the hero makes himself heroic; and that there is always a possibility for the coward to give up cowardice and for the hero to stop being a hero. What counts is the total commitment, and it is not by a particular case or particular action that you are committed altogether.

We have now, I think, dealt with a certain number of the reproaches against existentialism. You have seen that it cannot be regarded as a philos-

---

[2] *Roads to Freedom,* Sartre's trilogy of novels set before and during World War II. The characters in these novels are pictured as flawed, ordinary people—ED.

ophy of quietism since it defines man by his action; nor as a pessimistic description of man, for no doctrine is more optimistic, the destiny of man is placed within himself. Nor is it an attempt to discourage man from action since it tells him that there is no hope except in his action, and that the one thing which permits him to have life is the deed. Upon this level therefore, what we are considering is an ethic of action and self-commitment. However, we are still reproached, upon these few data, for confining man within his individual subjectivity. There again people badly misunderstand us.

Our point of departure is, indeed, the subjectivity of the individual, and that for strictly philosophic reasons. It is not because we are bourgeois, but because we seek to base our teaching upon the truth, and not upon a collection of fine theories, full of hope but lacking real foundations. And at the point of departure there cannot be any other truth than this, *I think, therefore I am,* which is the absolute truth of consciousness as it attains to itself. Every theory which begins with man, outside of this moment of self-attainment, is a theory which thereby suppresses the truth, for outside of the Cartesian *cogito,* all objects are no more than probable, and any doctrine of probabilities which is not attached to a truth will crumble into nothing. In order to define the probable one must possess the true. Before there can be any truth whatever, then, there must be an absolute truth, and there is such a truth which is simple, easily attained and within the reach of everybody; it consists in one's immediate sense of one's self.

In the second place, this theory alone is compatible with the dignity of man, it is the only one which does not make man into an object. All kinds of materialism lead one to treat every man including oneself as an object—that is, as a set of pre-determined reactions, in no way different from the patterns of qualities and phenomena which constitute a table, or a chair or a stone. Our aim is precisely to establish the human kingdom as a pattern of values in distinction from the material world. But the subjectivity which we thus postulate as the standard of truth is no narrowly individual subjectivism, for as we have demonstrated, it is not only one's own self that one discovers in the *cogito,* but those of others too. Contrary to the philosophy of Descartes, contrary to that of Kant, when we say "I think" we are attaining to ourselves in the presence of the other, and we are just as certain of the other as we are of ourselves. Thus the man who discovers himself directly in the *cogito* also discovers all the others, and discovers them as the condition of his own existence. He recognises that he cannot be anything (in the sense in which one says one is spiritual, or that one is wicked or jealous) unless others recognise him as such. I cannot obtain any truth whatsoever about myself, except through the mediation of another. The other is indispensable to my existence, and equally so to any knowledge I can have of myself. Under these conditions, the intimate discovery of myself is at the same time the revelation of the other as a freedom which confronts mine, and which cannot think or will without doing so either for or against me. Thus, at once, we find ourselves in a world which is, let us say, that of "intersubjectivity." It is in this world that man has to decide what he is and what others are.

Furthermore, although it is impossible to find in each and every man a universal essence that can be called human nature, there is nevertheless a human universality of *condition.* It is not by chance that the thinkers of today are so much more ready to speak of the condition than of the nature of man. By his condition they understand, with more or less clarity, all the *limitations* which *a priori* define man's fundamental situation in the universe. His historical situations are variable: man may be born a slave in a pagan society or may be a feudal baron, or a proletarian. But what never vary are the necessities of being in the world, of having to labor and to die there. These limitations are neither subjective nor objective, or rather there is both a subjective and an objective aspect of them. Objective, because we meet with them everywhere and they are everywhere recognisable: and subjective because they are *lived* and are nothing if man does not live them—if, that is to say, he does not freely determine himself and his existence in relation to them. And, diverse though man's purpose may be, at least none of them is wholly foreign to me, since every human purpose presents itself as an attempt either to surpass these limitations, or to widen them, or else to deny or to accommodate oneself to them. Consequently every purpose, however individual it may be, is of universal value. . . .

This does not completely refute the charge of subjectivism. Indeed that objection appears in several other forms, of which the first is as follows. People say to us, "Then it does not matter what you do," and they say this in various ways. First they tax us with anarchy; then they say, "You cannot judge others, for there is no reason for preferring one purpose to another"; finally, they may say, "Everything being merely voluntary in this choice of yours, you give away with one hand what you pretend to gain with the other." These three are not very serious objections. As to the first, to say that it does not matter what you choose is not correct. In one sense choice is possible, but what is not possible is not to choose. I can always choose, but I must know that if I do not choose, that is still a choice. This, although it may appear merely formal, is of great importance as a limit to fantasy and caprice. For, when I confront a real situation—for example, that I am a sexual being, able to have relations with a being of the other sex and able to have children—I am obliged to choose my attitude to it, and in every respect I bear the responsibility of the choice which, in committing myself, also commits the whole of humanity. Even if my choice is determined by no *a priori* value whatever, it can have nothing to do with caprice. . . . In our view, on the contrary, man finds himself in an organised situation in which he is himself involved: his choice involves mankind in its entirety, and he cannot avoid choosing. Either he must remain single, or he must marry without having children, or he must marry and have children. In any case, and whichever—he may choose, it is impossible for him, in respect of this situation, not to take complete responsibility. Doubtless he chooses without reference to any

pre-established value, but it is unjust to tax him with caprice. Rather let us say that the moral choice is comparable to the construction of a work of art.

But here I must at once digress to make it quite clear that we are not propounding an aesthetic morality, for our adversaries are disingenuous enough to reproach us even with that. I mention the work of art only by way of comparison. That being understood, does anyone reproach an artist, when he paints a picture, for not following rules established *a priori*. Does one ever ask what is the picture that he ought to paint? As everyone knows, there is no pre-defined picture for him to make; the artist applies himself to the composition of a picture, and the picture that ought to be made is precisely that which he will have made. As everyone knows, there are no aesthetic values *a priori*, but there are values which will appear in due course in the coherence of the picture, in the relation between the will to create and the finished work. No one can tell what the painting of tomorrow will be like; one cannot judge a painting until it is done. What has that to do with morality? We are in the same creative situation. We never speak of a work of art as irresponsible; when we are discussing a canvas by Picasso, we understand very well that the composition became what it is at the time when he was painting it, and that his works are part and parcel of his entire life.

It is the same upon the plane of morality. There is this in common between art and morality, that in both we have to do with creation and invention. We cannot decide *a priori* what it is that should be done. I think it was made sufficiently clear to you in the case of that student who came to see me, that to whatever ethical system he might appeal, the Kantian or any other, he could find no sort of guidance whatever; he was obliged to invent the law for himself. Certainly we cannot say that this man, in choosing to remain with his mother—that is, in taking sentiment, personal devotion and concrete charity as his moral foundations—would be making an irresponsible choice, nor could we do so if he preferred the sacrifice of going away to England.

Man makes himself; he is not found ready-made; he makes himself by the choice of his morality, and he cannot but choose a morality, such is the pressure of circumstances upon him. We define man only in relation to his commitments; it is therefore absurd to reproach us for irresponsibility in our choice.

In the second place, people say to us, "You are unable to judge others." This is true in one sense and false in another. It is true in this sense, that whenever a man chooses his purpose and his commitment in all clearness and in all sincerity, whatever that purpose may be, it is impossible for him to prefer another. . . .

We can judge, nevertheless, for, as I have said, one chooses in view of others, and in view of others one chooses himself. One can judge, first— and perhaps this is not a judgment of value, but it is a logical judgment—that in certain cases choice is founded upon an error, and in others upon the truth. One can judge a man by saying that he deceives himself. Since we have defined the situation of man as one of free choice, without excuse and without help, any man who takes refuge behind the excuse of his passions, or by inventing some deterministic doctrine, is a self-deceiver. One may object: "But why should he not choose to deceive himself?" I reply that it is not for me to judge him morally, but I define his self-deception as an error. Here one cannot avoid pronouncing a judgment of truth. The self-deception is evidently a falsehood, because it is a dissimulation of man's complete liberty of commitment. Upon this same level, I say that it is also a self-deception if I choose to declare that certain values are incumbent upon me; I am in contradiction with myself if I will these values and at the same time say that they impose themselves upon me. If anyone says to me, "And what if I wish to deceive myself?" I answer, "There is no reason why you should not, but I declare that you are doing so, and that the attitude of strict consistency alone is that of good faith." Furthermore, I can pronounce a moral judgment. For I declare that freedom, in respect of concrete circumstances, can have no other end and aim but itself; and when once a man has seen that values

depend upon himself, in that state of forsakenness he can will only one thing, and that is freedom as the foundation of all values. That does not mean that he wills it in the abstract: it simply means that the actions of men of good faith have, as their ultimate significance, the quest of freedom itself as such. A man who belongs to some communist or revolutionary society wills certain concrete ends, which imply the will to freedom, but that freedom is willed in community. We will freedom for freedom's sake, in and through particular circumstances. And in thus willing freedom, we discover that it depends entirely upon the freedom of others and that the freedom of others depends upon our own. Obviously, freedom as the definition of a man does not depend upon others, but as soon as there is a commitment, I am obliged to will the liberty of others at the same time as my own. I cannot make liberty my aim unless I make that of others equally my aim. Consequently, when I recognise, as entirely authentic, that man is a being whose existence precedes his essence, and that he is a free being who cannot, in any circumstances, but will his freedom, at the same time I realize that I cannot not will the freedom of others. Thus, in the name of that will to freedom which is implied in freedom itself, I can form judgments upon those who seek to hide from themselves the wholly voluntary nature of their existence and its complete freedom. Those who hide from this total freedom, in a guise of solemnity or with deterministic excuses, I shall call cowards. Others, who try to show that their existence is necessary, when it is merely an accident of the appearance of the human race on earth—I shall call scum. But neither cowards nor scum can be identified except upon the plane of strict authenticity. Thus, although the content of morality is variable, a certain form of this morality is universal. . . .

The third objection, stated by saying, "You take with one hand what you give with the other," means, at bottom, "your values are not serious, since you choose them yourselves." To that I can only say that I am very sorry that it should be so; but if I have excluded God the Father, there must be somebody to invent values.

We have to take things as they are. And moreover, to say that we invent values means neither more nor less than this; that there is no sense in life *a priori*. Life is nothing until it is lived; but it is yours to make sense of, and the value of it is nothing else but the sense that you choose. Therefore, you can see that there is a possibility of creating a human community. I have been reproached for suggesting that existentialism is a form of humanism: people have said to me, "But you have written in your *Nausée* that the humanists are wrong, you have even ridiculed a certain type of humanism, why do you now go back upon that?" In reality, the word humanism has two very different meanings. One may understand by humanism a theory which upholds man as the end-in-itself and as the supreme value. . . . It is to assume that we can ascribe value to man according to the most distinguished deeds of certain men. . . . That kind of humanism is absurd, for only the dog or the horse would be in a position to pronounce a general judgment upon man and declare that he is magnificent, which they have never been such fools as to do—at least, not as far as I know. But neither is it admissible that a man should pronounce judgment upon Man. Existentialism dispenses with any judgment of this sort: an existentialist will never take man as the end, since man is still to be determined. And we have no right to believe that humanity is something to which we could set up a cult, after the manner of Auguste Comte.[3] The cult of humanity ends in Comtian humanism, shut-in upon itself, and—this must be said—in Fascism. We do not want a humanism like that.

But there is another sense of the word, of which the fundamental meaning is this: Man is all the time outside of himself: it is in projecting and losing himself beyond himself that he makes man to exist; and, on the other hand, it is by pursuing transcendent aims that he himself is able to exist. Since man is thus self-surpassing, and can grasp objects only in relation to his self-surpassing, he is himself the heart and center of his transcendence. There is no other universe except the human universe, the universe of human subjectivity. This relation of transcendence as constitutive of man (not in the sense that God is transcendent, but in the sense of self-surpassing) with subjectivity (in such a sense that man is not shut up in himself but forever present in a human universe)—it is this that we call existential humanism. This is humanism, because we remind man that there is no legislator but himself; that he himself, thus abandoned, must decide for himself; also because we show that it is not by turning back upon himself, but always by seeking, beyond himself, an aim which is one of liberation or of some particular realisation, that man can realize himself as truly human.

You can see from these few reflections that nothing could be more unjust than the objections people raise against us. Existentialism is nothing else but an attempt to draw the full conclusions from a consistently atheistic position. Its intention is not in the least that of plunging men into despair. And if by despair one means as the Christians do—any attitude of unbelief, the despair of the existentialists is something different. Existentialism is not atheist in the sense that it would exhaust itself in demonstrations of the non-existence of God. It declares, rather, that even if God existed that would make no difference from its point of view. Not that we believe God does exist, but we think that the real problem is not that of His existence; what man needs is to find himself again and to understand that nothing can save him from himself, not even a valid proof of the existence of God. In this sense existentialism is optimistic. It is a doctrine of action, and it is only by self-deception, by confining their own despair with ours that Christians can describe us as without hope.

---

[3] Auguste Comte (1798–1857) first used the term "sociology" as a science of society. He speculated that human civilization went through three historical stages, starting with a theological stage, where the gods are seen as the prime causal agents of natural events; followed by a metaphysical stage, where abstract forces take the gods' place; ending in a positive stage, where only facts well established by experience are used to explain nature. Later in his career he invented a religion of humanity to replace Christianity, somewhat at odds with his positivism—Ed.

# SOCIOLOGICAL THEORY:
# THE SOCIALLY CONSTRUCTED SELF

## *Goffman's Dramaturgical Model and the Performing Self*

Erving Goffman (1922–1982) was born in Manville, Alberta, Canada. He received his B.A. from the University of Toronto in 1945. He went on to study sociology and social anthropology at the University of Chicago, receiving his M.A. in 1949 and his Ph.D. in 1953. During his doctoral studies, he spent a year in the Shetland Islands off the northern coast of Scotland doing research for his thesis and for his first and most famous book *The Presentation of Self in Everyday Life* (1959). He taught at Berkeley from 1958 to 1968, then at the University of Pennsylvania from 1968 until his death.

Goffman's general project was the "microsociological" or small-scale analysis of the forms of talk, rituals, and habits found in everyday life, and how these helped to create our personal identities. His other works include *Asylums: Essays on the Social Situation of Mental Patients and Other Inmates* (1961), *Stigma: Notes on the Management of Spoiled Identity* (1963), *Interaction Ritual: Essays on Face-to-Face Behavior* (1967), *Frame Analysis: Essays on the Organization of Experience* (1974), *Gender Advertisements* (1979), and *Forms of Talk* (1981). In *Stigma*, Goffman looked at how stigmatized individuals must try to manage the impressions that others have of their stigma in order to be accepted by mainstream society, whereas in *Interaction Ritual*, he looked at such mundane experiences as how people interact when boarding a crowded elevator or bus.

Goffman is considered to be a member of the "symbolic interactionist" school of sociology that got its start with George Herbert Mead, but was given its clearest definition by Herbert Blumer in his book *Symbolic Interactionism*. Blumer argues that social interaction is defined by the meanings we attribute to symbols, and how these meanings are shared with others. We actively create our social selves through this symbolic interaction. The interactionists used qualitative rather than quantitative analyses of how people interact with each other to understand how our social identities are constructed.

In the following reading, from *The Presentation of Self in Everyday Life*, Goffman compares everyday life to a theater where we engage in dramatic performances and thereby construct our "self." The self is the product of an effectively staged and performed scene. This echoes Hume's idea of the self as a spectator in a theater of perceptions, or the gloomy view of life Shakespeare has Macbeth pronounce:

> Life's but a walking shadow, a poor player
> That struts and frets his hour upon the stage
> And then is heard no more: it is a tale
> Told by an idiot, full of sound and fury,
> Signifying nothing. (*Macbeth* 5.5)

Goffman calls his view the "dramaturgical" theory of the self. At its core is the idea that the way we present ourselves in this theater, whether it's a school, a workplace, a shopping mall, or a social event, is by means of impression management. We want to "look good," to be an effective worker, a good student (or in some cases a bad student!), the life of the party, attractive to potential romantic partners, and so forth. To do so, we have to manage the impressions that we give off to others.

The major way we do this is by means of the creation of a series of "fronts" associated with the various social roles that we perform for our audiences. It's a bit like putting on a mask to fit each situation we're in: Our front helps to define the situation for those observing our social performance. Through the fronts we assume we communicate to others the essential elements of the social role we're presently playing, just as actors use physical movements and different ways of delivering their lines to communicate the inner feelings and motivations of the characters they play. Of course, we don't want things to appear too contrived, too phony, so once in a while we inject an element of spontaneity into our performances.

One of the major issues raised by Goffman's and similar sociological analyses of the self is the question of whether there is an authentic, inner self underneath all those fronts or masks. Once we eliminate all the social roles we play—boyfriend, wife, mother, student, teacher, lawyer, doctor, coach, clerk—is there anything left over? This parallels Hume's skepticism about the self, except that Goffman sees the self not as a bundle of perceptions, but as social fronts. As you read Goffman, ask yourself a new question that parallels the one I asked at the end of the Hume commentary: Can you think of any part of what you call your "self" that isn't in some way connected to a social role you're performing in the theater of everyday life? Once all the masks have been removed, is there a face beneath them, or just empty space?

# The Presentation of Self in Everyday Life

## ERVING GOFFMAN

### *Performances*

#### BELIEF IN THE PART
#### ONE IS PLAYING

When an individual plays a part he implicitly requests his observers to take seriously the impression that is fostered before them. They are asked to believe that the character they see actually possesses the attributes he appears to possess, that the task he performs will have the consequences that are implicitly claimed for it, and that, in general, matters are what they appear to be. In line with this, there is the popular view that the individual offers his performance and puts on his show "for the benefit of other people." It will be convenient to begin a consideration of performances by turning the question around and looking at the individual's own belief in the impression of reality that he attempts to engender in those among whom he finds himself.

At one extreme, one finds that the performer can be fully taken in by his own act; he can be sincerely convinced that the impression of reality which he stages is the real reality. When his audience is also convinced in this way about the show he puts on—and this seems to be the typical

SOURCE: Erving Goffman, *The Presentation of Self in Everyday Life* (New York: Anchor Books, 1959), pp. 17–19, 22, 23–24, 27, 70–72, 252–253 (edited). Copyright 1959 by Erving Goffman. Used by permission of Doubleday, a division of Random House, Inc.

case—then for the moment at least, only the sociologist or the socially disgruntled will have any doubts about the "realness" of what is presented.

At the other extreme, we find that the performer may not be taken in at all by his own routine. This possibility is understandable, since no one is in quite as good an observational position to see through the act as the person who puts it on. Coupled with this, the performer may be moved to guide the conviction of his audience only as a means to other ends, having no ultimate concern in the conception that they have of him or of the situation. When the individual has no belief in his own act and no ultimate concern with the beliefs of his audience, we may call him cynical, reserving the term "sincere" for individuals who believe in the impression fostered by their own performance. It should be understood that the cynic, with all his professional disinvolvement, may obtain unprofessional pleasures from his masquerade, experiencing a kind of gleeful spiritual aggression from the fact that he can toy at will with something his audience must take seriously.[1] . . .

I have suggested two extremes: an individual may be taken in by his own act or be cynical about it. These extremes are something a little more than just the ends of a continuum. Each provides the individual with a position which has its own particular securities and defenses, so there will be a tendency for those who have traveled close to one of these poles to complete the voyage. Starting with lack of inward belief in one's role, the individual may follow the natural movement described by Park:

> It is probably no mere historical accident that the word person, in its first meaning, is a mask. It is rather a recognition of the fact that everyone is always and everywhere, more or less consciously, playing a role. . . . It is in these roles that we know each other; it is in these roles that we know ourselves.
>
> In a sense, and in so far as this mask represents the conception we have formed of ourselves—the role we are striving to live up to—this mask is our truer self, the self we would like to be.[2] . . .

## FRONT

I have been using the term "performance" to refer to all the activity of an individual which occurs during a period marked by his continuous presence before a particular set of observers and which has some influence on the observers. It will be convenient to label as "front" that part of the individual's performance which regularly functions in a general and fixed fashion to define the situation for those who observe the performance. Front, then, is the expressive equipment of a standard kind intentionally or unwittingly employed by the individual during his performance. For preliminary purposes, it will be convenient to distinguish and label what seem to be the standard parts of front.

First, there is the "setting," involving furniture, décor, physical layout, and other background items which supply the scenery and stage props for the spate of human action played out before, within, or upon it. A setting tends to stay put, geographically speaking, so that those who would use a particular setting as part of their performance cannot begin their act until they have brought themselves to the appropriate place and must terminate their performance when they leave it. It is only in exceptional circumstances that the setting follows along with the performers; we see this in the funeral cortège, the civic parade, and the dream-like processions that kings and queens are made of. In the main, these exceptions seem to offer some kind of extra protection for performers who are, or who have momentarily become, highly sacred. . . .

If we take the term "setting" to refer to the scenic parts of expressive equipment, one may take the term "personal front" to refer to the

---

[1] Perhaps the real crime of the confidence man is not that he takes money from his victims but that he robs all of us of the belief that middle-class manners and appearance can be sustained only by middle-class people. A disabused professional can be cynically hostile to the service relation his clients expect him to extend to them; the confidence man is in a position to hold the whole "legit" world in this contempt.

[2] Robert Ezra Park, *Race and Culture* (Glencoe, IL: Free Press, 1950), p. 249.

other items of expressive equipment, the items that we most intimately identify with the performer himself and that we naturally expect will follow the performer wherever he goes. As part of personal front we may include: insignia of office or rank; clothing; sex, age, and racial characteristics; size and looks; posture; speech patterns; facial expressions; bodily gestures; and the like. Some of these vehicles for conveying signs, such as racial characteristics, are relatively fixed and over a span of time do not vary for the individual from one situation to another. On the other hand, some of these sign vehicles are relatively mobile or transitory, such as facial expression, and can vary during a performance from one moment to the next.

It is sometimes convenient to divide the stimuli which make up personal front into "appearance" and "manner," according to the function performed by the information that these stimuli convey. "Appearance" may be taken to refer to those stimuli which function at the time to tell us of the performer's social statuses. These stimuli also tell us of the individual's temporary ritual state, that is, whether he is engaging in formal social activity, work, or informal recreation, whether or not he is celebrating a new phase in the season cycle or in his life-cycle. "Manner" may be taken to refer to those stimuli which function at the time to warn us of the interaction role the performer will expect to play in the oncoming situation. Thus a haughty, aggressive manner may give the impression that the performer expects to be the one who will initiate the verbal interaction and direct its course. A meek, apologetic manner may give the impression that the performer expects to follow the lead of others, or at least that he can be led to do so. . . .

In addition to the fact that different routines may employ the same front, it is to be noted that a given social front tends to become institutionalized in terms of the abstract stereotyped expectations to which it gives rise, and tends to take on a meaning and stability apart from the specific tasks which happen at the time to be performed in its name. The front becomes a "collective representation" and a fact in its own right.

When an actor takes on an established social role, usually he finds that a particular front has already been established for it. Whether his acquisition of the role was primarily motivated by a desire to perform the given task or by a desire to maintain the corresponding front, the actor will find that he must do both.

Further, if the individual takes on a task that is not only new to him but also unestablished in the society, or if he attempts to change the light in which his task is viewed, he is likely to find that there are already several well-established fronts among which he must choose. Thus, when a task is given a new front we seldom find that the front it is given is itself new. . . .

## REALITY AND CONTRIVANCE

In our own Anglo-American culture there seems to be two common-sense models according to which we formulate our conceptions of behavior: the real, sincere, or honest performance; and the false one that thorough fabricators assemble for us, whether meant to be taken unseriously, as in the work of stage actors, or seriously, as in the work of confidence men. We tend to see real performances as something not purposely put together at all, being an unintentional product of the individual's unself-conscious response to the facts in his situation. And contrived performances we tend to see as something painstakingly pasted together, one false item on another, since there is no reality to which the items of behavior could be a direct response. It will be necessary to see now that these dichotomous conceptions are by way of being the ideology of honest performers, providing strength to the show they put on, but a poor analysis of it.

First, let it be said that there are many individuals who sincerely believe that the definition of the situation they habitually project is the real reality. In this report I do not mean to question their proportion in the population but rather the structural relation of their sincerity to the performances they offer. If a performance is to come off, the witnesses by and large must be able to believe that the performers are sincere. This is the structural place of sincerity in the drama of events. Performers may be sincere—or be insincere but sincerely convinced of their own sincerity—but this kind of affection for one's part is not necessary for its convincing performance. There are not many French cooks who are really Russian spies, and perhaps there are not many women who play the part of wife to one man and mistress to another; but these duplicities do occur, often being sustained successfully for long periods of time. This suggests that while persons usually are what they appear to be, such appearances could still have been managed. There is, then, a statistical relation between appearances and reality, not an intrinsic or necessary one. In fact, given the unanticipated threats that play upon a performance, and given the need (later to be discussed) to maintain solidarity with one's fellow performers and some distance from the witnesses, we find that a rigid incapacity to depart from one's inward view of reality may at times endanger one's performance. Some performances are carried off successfully with complete dishonesty, others with complete honesty; but for performances in general neither of these extremes is essential and neither, perhaps, is dramaturgically advisable.

The implication here is that an honest, sincere, serious performance is less firmly connected with the solid world than one might first assume. And this implication will be strengthened if we look again at the distance usually placed between quite honest performances and quite contrived ones. In this connection take, for example, the remarkable phenomenon of stage acting. It does take deep skill, long training, and psychological capacity to become a good stage actor. But this fact should not blind us to another one: that almost anyone can quickly learn a script well enough to give a charitable audience some sense of realness in what is being contrived before them. And it seems this is so because ordinary social intercourse is itself put together as a scene is put together, by the exchange of dramatically inflated actions, counteractions, and terminating replies. Scripts even in the hands of unpracticed players can come to life because life itself is a dramatically enacted thing. All the world is not, of course, a stage, but the crucial ways in which it isn't are not easy to specify. . . .

## Conclusion

### STAGING AND THE SELF

The general notion that we make a presentation of ourselves to others is hardly novel; what ought to be stressed in conclusion is that the very structure of the self can be seen in terms of how we arrange for such performances in our Anglo-American society.

In this report, the individual was divided by implication into two basic parts: he was viewed as a *performer*, a harried fabricator of impressions involved in the all-too-human task of staging a performance; he was viewed as a *character*, a figure, typically a fine one, whose spirit, strength, and other sterling qualities the performance was designed to evoke. The attributes of a performer and the attributes of a character are of a different order, quite basically so, yet both sets have their meaning in terms of the show that must go on.

First, character. In our society the character one performs and one's self are somewhat equated, and this self-as-character is usually seen as something housed within the body of its possessor, especially the upper parts thereof, being a nodule, somehow, in the psychobiology of personality. I suggest that this view is an implied part of what we are all trying to present, but provides, just because of this, a bad analysis of the presentation. In this report the performed self was seen as some kind of image, usually creditable, which the individual on stage and in character effectively attempts to induce others to hold in regard to him. While this image is entertained *concerning* the individual, so that a self is imputed to him, this self itself does not derive from its possessor, but from the whole scene of his action, being generated by that attribute of local events which renders them interpretable by witnesses. A correctly staged and performed scene leads the audience to impute a self to a performed character, but this imputation—this self—is a *product* of a scene that comes off, and is not a *cause* of it. The self, then, as a performed character, is not an organic thing that has a specific location, whose fundamental fate is to be born, to mature, and to die; it is a dramatic effect arising diffusely from a scene that is presented, and the characteristic issue, the crucial concern, is whether it will be credited or discredited.

In analyzing the self then we are drawn from its possessor, from the person who will profit or lose most by it, for he and his body merely provide the peg on which something of collaborative manufacture will be hung for a time. And the means for producing and maintaining selves do not reside inside the peg; in fact these means are often bolted down in social establishments. There will be a back region with its tools for shaping the body, and a front region with its fixed props. There will be a team of persons whose activity on stage in conjunction with available props will constitute the scene from which the performed character's self will emerge, and another team, the audience, whose interpretive activity will be necessary for this emergence. The self is a product of all of these arrangements, and in all of its parts bears the marks of this genesis.

The whole machinery of self-production is cumbersome, of course, and sometimes breaks down, exposing its separate components: back region control; team collusion; audience tact; and so forth. But, well oiled, impressions will flow from it fast enough to put us in the grips of one of our types of reality—the performance will come off and the firm self accorded each performed character will appear to emanate intrinsically from its performer.

Let us turn now from the individual as character performed to the individual as performer. He has a capacity to learn, this being exercised in the task of training for a part. He is given to having fantasies and dreams, some that pleasurably unfold a triumphant performance, others full of anxiety and dread that nervously deal with vital discreditings in a public front region. He often manifests a gregarious desire for teammates and audiences, a tactful considerateness for their concerns; and he has a capacity for deeply felt shame, leading him to minimize the chances he takes of exposure.

These attributes of the individual *qua* performer are not merely a depicted effect of particular performances; they are psychobiological in nature, and yet they seem to arise out of intimate interaction with the contingencies of staging performances. . . .

## Study Questions

These questions can be used as either study aids, starting points for seminar discussions, or as topics for written assignments or essays.

1. What is a "monist" solution to the mind/body problem? a "dualist" solution? Give an example of each type of theory, and outline the strengths and weaknesses of each.
2. What are the three major materialist theories of the relationship between the mind and the body? How does each explain our subjective beliefs, desires, and intentions?
3. What is phenomenalism? Who are the "New Mysterians"? Compare and contrast these two approaches to the mind/body problem.
4. What are Descartes' basic arguments in favor of mind/body dualism? How does he account for the interaction of the mind and the body? Are his arguments successful?
5. What was Descartes' wax experiment? What does he think it proves? Is he right?
6. What is the "Cartesian circle"? Do we need to believe in a good God to believe in absolute truth?
7. What does Ryle mean by a "category mistake"? Give a couple of examples of category mistakes. How does he apply this idea to Cartesian dualism? Evaluate Ryle's critique of Descartes.
8. What is Ryle's "logical behaviorism"? How does it explain our subjective mental events? Are there any problems with this theory?

9. According to Nagel, why can't we know what it's like to be a bat? How does he think that this affects the mind/body problem? Is he right?

10. Can science explain human consciousness in physical terms? (Refer to Nagel.)

11. In his "eliminative materialism," what does Churchland think must be eliminated? Is this elimination likely to occur? Why or why not?

12. In what major ways do the rationalist and empiricist accounts of the self differ? Which, if either, better explains the nature of the self?

13. According to Hume, what, in essence, is the self? What two things does he compare it to? Is his skepticism about the self well grounded?

14. What arguments for a "romantic" approach to life does Werther offer in the selections from Goethe? Are they good arguments?

15. What three or four basic elements of the romantic view of the self stand in contrast to the rationalist and empiricist views of the self? How well does the romantic description of the self fare in relation to these other views?

16. How does Shelley define poetry? Why does he think that it has a positive moral and political effect on societies where it prospers? Does he exaggerate this effect?

17. In the last third of his *A Defense of Poetry,* how does Shelley defend the creative, intuitive self? Evaluate this defense.

18. What is Ortega's view of human nature? How does it compare to Sartre's?

19. What does Camus think is the only serious philosophical problem? How is this related to the myth of Sisyphus? Is Camus' diagnosis of human existence too pessimistic? Why or why not?

20. What is Sartre's view of human freedom? How is this related to his concept of "bad faith"? Does he think that we're responsible for our passions? Is his view reasonable?

21. What did Professor Sartre say to his young student who was trying to decide whether he should leave his mother and go to England to join the Free French army? What does this incident say about Sartre's view of existentialist ethics?

22. What does Goffman mean by a "front"? What does he mean by the setting, appearance, and manner of a front? How is the establishment of a front like a theatrical performance? Describe a couple of fronts you use in your everyday life.

23. Why does Goffman say that as social performers we're all "merchants of morality"? Why does he think that the techniques we use to support our various social fronts are "amoral"? Is his view of social life too cynical?

24. Does Goffman's dramaturgical view of the self as the product of a well-staged performance leave any room for an authentic inner self? What part of your self do you think is independent of all the social roles you play in everyday life, if any?

# *Bibliography*

## DESCARTES

Beck, Leslie. *The Metaphysics of Descartes: A Study of the Meditations.* Oxford: Clarendon Press, 1965.

Cottingham, John. *Descartes.* Oxford: Basil Blackwell, 1986. One of several books by Cottingham on Descartes and rationalism.

Cottingham, John, ed. *The Cambridge Companion to Descartes.* Cambridge, UK: Cambridge University Press, 1992. Another fine addition to the Cambridge Companion essay collections.

Curley, Edwin. *Descartes against the Skeptics.* Cambridge, MA: Harvard University Press, 1978.

Dicker, Georges. *Descartes: An Analytical and Historical Introduction.* Oxford: Oxford University Press, 1993. An overview of the basic arguments in the *Meditations.*

Doney, Willis. *Descartes: A Collection of Critical Essays.* Garden City, NY: Doubleday, 1967.

Frankfurt, Harry G. *Demons, Dreamers, and Madmen: The Defense of Reason in Descartes' Meditations.* Indianapolis: Bobbs-Merrill, 1970.

Rorty, A. O. *Essays on Descartes' Meditations.* Berkeley: University of California Press, 1986.

## THE CONTEMPORARY PHILOSOPHY OF MIND

Davidson, Donald. *Essays on Actions and Events.* Oxford: Oxford University Press, 1980. Contains the essay "Actions, Reasons, Causes," which attacks the behaviorist idea that all mental events can be redescribed as external behavior. Davidson argues that we have reasons for action that we don't always act on. Also contains a defense of his "anomalous monist" theory of the mind.

Dennett, Daniel C. *Consciousness Explained.* Boston: Little Brown and Co., 1991. In this much-read book, Dennett combines philosophy, psychology, and neuroscience to attack the "Cartesian theater" view of the mind. Dennett's solution is more or less materialism—consciousness comes from the firing of neurons in our brain. Our subjective "qualia" (e.g., the yummy taste of chocolate) are merely illusions produced by these firings.

Freud, Sigmund. *The Ego and the Id.* Trans. Joan Riviere. London: Hogarth Press, 1962. An extended essay where Freud defends his idea that the mind is composed of a conscious ego, an unconscious id, and a repressive superego.

Freud, Sigmund. *An Outline of Psychoanalysis.* Trans. James Strachey. New York: Norton, 1969. A clear exposition of Freud's mature view of the mind.

McGinn, Colin. *The Problem of Consciousness: Essays Toward a Resolution.* Oxford: Basil Blackwell, 1993.

McGinn, Colin. *The Character of Mind: An Introduction to the Philosophy of Mind.* Oxford: Oxford University Press, 1997. A good introductory overview of the subject.

McGinn, Colin. *The Mysterious Flame: Conscious Minds in a Material World.* New York: Basic Books, 2000. McGinn is one of the "New Mysterians" who maintain that metaphysical questions like the mind/body problem cannot be solved by our limited and contingent human intellects. Neither dualism nor strict materialism can explain how "a piece of meat" (i.e., our brains) could be conscious. An easier read than Dennett or Penrose.

Penrose, Roger. *The Emperor's New Mind: Concerning Computers, Minds, and the Laws of Physics.* New York: Penguin Books, 1989. A heavy-going book by a physicist who uses quantum theory to show that the "strong" view of artificial intelligence—that one day computers will be able to mimic human thinking and consciousness—is nonsense.

Searle, John R. *The Rediscovery of the Mind.* Cambridge MA: MIT Press, 1992. Searle discusses various theories of consciousness from Descartes to today, defending the autonomy of consciousness against materialist theories of the mind.

Williams, Bernard. *Problems of the Self.* Cambridge, UK: Cambridge University Press, 1973.

## HUME

Ayer, A. J. *Hume.* Oxford: Oxford University Press, 1980. A short introduction in the Past Masters Series by the great positivist, who is an admirer of Hume.

Baier, Annette C. *A Progress of Sentiments: Reflections on Hume's Treatise.* Cambridge, MA: Harvard University Press, 1991. A compelling interpretation of Hume's *Treatise* that sees its goal as the production of a positive moral and political philosophy.

Bricke, John. *Hume's Philosophy of Mind.* Princeton, NJ: Princeton University Press, 1980.

Chappell, V. C., ed. *Hume, A Collection of Critical Essays.* Garden City, NY: Anchor Books, 1966. A fine collection of essays on various aspects of Hume's thought.

Livingston, Donald W. *Hume's Philosophy of Common Life.* Chicago: University of Chicago Press, 1984.

Norton, David Fate. *David Hume, Common Sense Moralist, Sceptical Metaphysician.* Princeton, NJ: Princeton University Press, 1982. The author's thesis is contained in his title.

Norton, David Fate, ed. *The Cambridge Companion to Hume.* Cambridge, UK: Cambridge University Press, 1993. A collection of essays on Hume.

Passmore, John. *Hume's Intentions.* 3rd ed. London: Duckworth, 1980. Passmore tries to sort through Hume's various philosophical intentions.

Penelhum, Terence. *Hume.* London: Macmillan, 1975.

Popkin, Richard. *The High Road to Pyrrhonism.* San Diego: Austin Hill Press, 1980. Essays on skepticism, many of them on Hume.

Smith, Norman Kemp. *The Philosophy of David Hume.* London: Macmillan, 1941. A classic treatment of Hume's thought that interprets him as a "naturalist," as putting forward a view of morals grounded in a common human nature.

Stroud, Barry. *Hume.* London: Routledge, 1981. In "The Arguments of Philosophers" series.

## THE ROMANTICS

Abrams, M. H. *The Mirror and the Lamp: Romantic Theory and the Critical Tradition.* Oxford: Oxford University Press, 1973. In this famous study of romanticism, Abrams argues that the preromantic artist held up a mirror to reality, while the romantic artist sought to use his or her imagination and vision to light the lamp of illumination for humanity.

Barzun, Jacques. *Classic, Romantic, and Modern.* Rev. ed. Chicago: University of Chicago Press, 1975. A broad historical and cultural introduction.

Bowra, Maurice. *The Romantic Imagination.* Cambridge, MA: Harvard University Press, 1961.

Frye, Northrup, ed. *Romanticism Reconsidered.* New York: Columbia University Press, 1963. A collection of essays.

Frye, Northrup. *A Study of English Romanticism.* Chicago: University of Chicago Press, 1968. By the prominent literary critic.

Lovejoy, Arthur O. *Essays in the History of Ideas.* Baltimore: Johns Hopkins University Press, 1948. Contains Lovejoy's celebrated essay "The Meaning of Romanticism for the Historian of Ideas."

Roszak, Theodore. *Where the Wasteland Ends: Politics and Transcendence in Postindustrial Society.* Garden City, NY: Anchor Books, 1973. Roszak defends the "visionary power" of the romantics and their battle against the single vision of scientific rationalism. See Chapters 8 and 9 on Shelley, Blake, Wordsworth, and Goethe.

## EXISTENTIALISM

Barrett, William. *Irrational Man.* Garden City, NY: Anchor Books, 1962. A lively study which focuses on Kierkegaard, Nietzsche, Heidegger, and Sartre.

Grene, Marjorie. *Introduction to Existentialism.* Chicago: University of Chicago Press, 1976.

Howells, Christina, ed. *The Cambridge Companion to Sartre.* Cambridge, UK: Cambridge University Press, 1992. A collection of essays.

Kaufmann, Walter, ed. *Existentialism from Dostoevsky to Sartre.* Rev. ed. New York: Meridian, 1975. A widely used anthology of selections from the major existentialists, with a long introductory essay by Kaufmann.

Mora, J. Ferrater. *Ortega y Gasset: An Outline of His Philosophy.* London: Bowes & Bowes, 1956.

Murdoch, Iris. *Sartre: Romantic Rationalist.* New Haven, CT: Yale University Press, 1953. A study of Sartre's literature by the Irish novelist and philosopher.

O'Brien, Conor Cruise. *Albert Camus of Europe and Africa.* New York: Viking Press, 1970.

Solomon, Robert C. *From Rationalism to Existentialism: The Existentialists and Their Nineteenth-Century Backgrounds.* Lanham, MA: Littlefield Adams, 1972. Contains chapters on Kant, Hegel, Kierkegaard, Nietzsche, Husserl, Heidegger, and Sartre, with side glances at Camus, Merleau-Ponty, and other French existentialists. Clearly written, with lots of quotes.

Stevenson, Leslie. *Seven Theories of Human Nature.* London: Clarendon Press, 1974. A short work that looks at seven theories of human nature, those of Plato, Christianity, Marx, Freud, Sartre, B. F. Skinner, and Konrad Lorenz.

Tuttle, Howard. *The Crowd Is Untruth: The Existential Critique of Mass Society in the Thought of Kierkegaard, Nietzsche, Heidegger, and Ortega y Gasset.* New York: Peter Lang, 1996.

Warnock, Mary. *The Philosophy of Sartre.* London: Hutchinson, 1965.

Warnock, Mary. *Existentialism.* Oxford: Oxford University Press, 1970. A good starting point.

## SOCIOLOGICAL THEORY AND THE SELF

Berger, Peter, and Thomas Luckmann. *The Social Construction of Reality.* New York: Anchor Books, 1966. This book on the sociology of knowledge examines how we socially construct reality in our everyday lives.

Blumer, Herbert. *Symbolic Interactionism: Perspective and Method.* Berkeley: University of California Press, 1969. Blumer argues that social interaction is defined by the meaning we attribute to symbols, and how this meaning is shared with others. We actively create our social selves through this symbolic interaction. Blumer was a critic of functionalism, which saw social structure as a given that the self must accommodate itself to. Goffman was a symbolic interactionist.

Collins, Randall. *Four Sociological Traditions.* New York: Oxford University Press, 1994. Collins outlines four of the major sociological traditions, including the "conflict tradition" of Marx and Max Weber, and the interactionist tradition of Mead, Blumer, and Goffman.

Giddens, Anthony. *Central Problems in Social Theory.* London: Macmillan, 1979. Ruminations on the self and the interplay between human agency and structure in social theory.

Giddens, Anthony. "Action, Subjectivity, and the Constitution of Meaning." *Social Research* 53 (1986): 529–545. Giddens's "structuration theory" argues that to understand the social self, we have to take into account at the same time both our individual intentions and how social structures shape those intentions through our "practical consciousness" of how to do things.

Marx, Karl, and Friedrich Engels. *The German Ideology.* Available in many editions and collections. Marxism sees the self as a product of economic forces. This early work is perhaps less deterministic than Marx and Engels' later efforts. See Chapter 6 for more on Marxism.

Mead, George Herbert. *Mind, Self, and Society.* Chicago: University of Chicago Press, 1962. Mead's lectures written down by his students and edited by Charles W. Morris. Mead offers a "social behaviorist" position that emphasizes how we develop a concept of our self by putting ourselves in others' shoes and viewing ourselves from that external standpoint. His ideas contributed to the interactionist school of sociology, which included Blumer and Goffman.

Parsons, Talcott. *The Social System.* Glencoe, IL: The Free Press, 1951. In his mature work Parsons argues for a functionalist "systems theory" approach to social theory. The various parts of society each perform their own function, which together form a self-regulating, interdependent system. Individuals are part of this organic system.

Winch, Peter. *The Idea of a Social Science and Its Relation to Philosophy.* London: Routledge & Kegan Paul, 1958. Against much of the sociological tradition until the 1960s, Winch argues that we should look at people's reasons and motives for acting as they do instead of external causes to explain social behavior.

## Internet Resources

*A Dictionary of Philosophical Terms and Names* (see the general bibliography at the end of the Introduction for more details on this site): http://www.philosophypages.com/dy/index.htm.
Contains one-page articles on Descartes, Ryle, Hume, Kierkegaard, Nietzsche, Heidegger, and Sartre, along with many paragraph-length summaries of other thinkers.

*Internet Encyclopedia of Philosophy:* http://www.utm.edu/research/iep/.
Contains a substantial article on Descartes, and five separate articles on Hume.

*The Hume Archive:* http://www.utm.edu/research/hume/.
An excellent resource that contains about two-thirds of Hume's philosophical writings (including Book I of *A Treatise of Human Nature*) and a collection of eighteenth-century reviews and commentaries on Hume's work. By James Fieser of the University of Tennessee. Intermittently unavailable.

"Rene Descartes (1595–1650)": http://www.orst.edu/instruct/phl302/philosophers/descartes.html.
A short article and timeline on Descartes with links to a summary and complete text of the *Meditations* and to notes on contemporaries of Descartes such as Thomas Hobbes, Pierre Gassendi, and Princess Elizabeth. Part of course Web site for "Great Voyages: The History of Western Philosophy from 1492 to 1776," by Bill Uzgalis of Oregon State University.

*The Realm of Existentialism:* http://members.aol.com/KatharenaE./private/Philo/philo.html.
Stylish, intelligently designed site by Katharena Eiermann that summarizes the main themes of existentialism and features pages on a number of existentialist writers, including Kierkegaard, Nietzsche, Heidegger, Sartre, and Camus.

*Existentialism: An Introduction:* http://www.tameri.com/csw/exist/index.html
Christopher Scott Wyatt's detailed Web site covers all the major figures in existentialist

thought. A work in progress, Wyatt includes biographies, bibliographies, and summaries of major ideas for each thinker.

*Jean-Paul Sartre: Philosophy & Existentialism:* http://members.aol.com/DonJohnR/Philosophy/Sartre.html.
This site contains a list of Sartre's works, a chronology of his life, and links to e-texts of some of Sartre's works and to a few secondary sources.

"Erving Goffman," by B. Diane Blackwood: http://www.blackwood.org/Erving.htm.
A short overview of Goffman's life and work, with a bibliography.

*People are apt to be ticklish
in their absolute presuppositions.*
R. G. COLLINGWOOD

## CHAPTER FOUR

# Knowing Our World

## KNOWLEDGE AND THE HUMAN CONDITION

This chapter deals with what philosophers call *epistemology*. As with most of our words in philosophy, epistemology comes from two Greek words: *epistēmē,* meaning "knowledge"; and *logos,* "the study of." Epistemologists study knowledge, how we know things.

More precisely, the job of epistemologists is to ask how we should define words such as *knowledge, belief, truth,* and *certainty.* Although we often use these words synonymously in our day-to-day conversations, epistemologists think these words should be used quite carefully, as each has a particular meaning. For example, to describe some of our beliefs as "knowledge" would be a mistake. It would be the same as calling a circle a square.

Let's say there is a disagreement between friends over the date of a final exam. Wesley states, "I *know* the final exam is Tuesday." The rest of us say the date for the final is Monday. We think this because we were in class when the professor announced the date while Wesley slept in that morning. Despite our protestations, Wesley remains adamant. When he shows up to write the exam in the assigned classroom on Tuesday, nobody is there; he breaks into a sweat, realizing that the exam was written on Monday.

Ignoring for the moment that our friend is exceedingly stubborn, how do we reconcile his original claim that he "knew" the exam was supposed to be on Tuesday with the fact the exam was really on Monday?

Epistemologists point out that declarations about *knowing* something are quite different from claims about *believing* something. When we say we know something, a higher degree of certainty comes with this claim: We are saying it's very unlikely we are wrong. Beliefs, in comparison, carry a lesser degree of certainty than claims about knowledge (or "knowledge claims"). Therefore, we can speak of false beliefs but not of false knowledge. That belief could be wrong, but knowledge certain, goes back to Plato.

We describe something as a belief when we are not sure whether our claim is true. We could have misheard what someone said, or we can't remember exactly some item of information. Of course we can also be quite confident about our beliefs, but not to the extent we feel justified calling them knowledge. We acknowledge the possibility our beliefs could be mistaken. The admission that our beliefs might be false is called "fallibilism." In retrospect, Wesley would have been better off (at least epistemically) if he had said, "I *believe* the exam is on Tuesday."

Defining knowledge, belief, and certainty is a project linked to the concept of truth. Just how much certainty is required for us to say we know something to be true? To answer this question, we need to first review some other considerations.

Philosophers of language distinguish between ordinary sentences and sentences that are considered statements. Ordinary sentences could be imperatives or commands such as "Shut the door!" or performative sentences such as "I pronounce you man and wife." The latter is called a performative utterance. The philosopher John Austin (1911–1960) was the first to describe these statements as such because our pronouncement actually performs something—in this case, the moment the minister or justice of the peace says this sentence, the couple becomes legally married.

Statements, or propositions, are different. When we are talking about what we believe or what we know, we are asserting something that is either true or false. Statements are different from ordinary sentences, for example, in that we wouldn't consider it false to shut the door or true when a minister utters the phrase "I pronounce you man and wife."

A popular example used by philosophers of language is the proposition that "all bachelors are unmarried males." Not only is this a proposition but it is also self-evident or *necessarily true.* It is necessarily true because the predicate nominative "unmarried males" is contained within the subject "bachelor." A bachelor *is* an unmarried male—that's what the word *bachelor* means. Consequently, we don't have to go out and conduct a survey of the general male populace to find out whether it is true that all bachelors are unmarried males. This is an example of an a priori proposition (from the Greek for "prior to experience").

A priori propositions are made prior to empirical observations of the world. For this reason, these propositions are sometimes called "truths of reason." Knowing that there are such truths can be quite exciting for some people. Yet before we get too delighted, it is important to note that although we can say we "know" this claim about bachelors to be 100 percent certain and necessarily true, this piece of knowledge doesn't tell us anything particularly interesting about the real world.

If we were to say, in contrast to the previous proposition, "All bachelors are unhappy," we would be claiming something quite different. In order to decide whether this proposition is true, we would have to go out and do some empirical research. The truthfulness of this proposition would have to be determined not a priori, but rather a posteriori (from the Greek, meaning "after experience").

As part of our empirical investigation we would have to talk to as many bachelors as we could find, asking them how content they are. If after interviewing, say, 2,000 bachelors, we found them all to be extremely unhappy, we might feel justified affirming the truthfulness of the proposition that "all bachelors are unhappy." Propositions requiring empirical research to prove their truth or falsity are called "truths of fact."

There are problems with truths of fact too. It is one thing for the 2,000 bachelors we surveyed to be unhappy. But we can't go from this particular observation to the all-encompassing claim that *all* bachelors are unhappy. To establish the truthfulness of this claim, we would have to interview every single bachelor in the world. We would even have to somehow contact all the bachelors who have ever lived and all future bachelors if we wanted to be thorough!

Even if we were able to do such a worldwide survey and all bachelors responded they were unhappy, we would have to determine whether they were always unhappy or whether they were unhappy only once in a while. Even if we were able to determine that all these bachelors were always unhappy, we still wouldn't be able to say we've now established the truthfulness of our claim with 100 percent certainty. We could always have missed a bachelor somewhere, perhaps one who lived on a desert island full of palm trees and coconuts who was extremely content and happy with his life.

A very important consideration in this discussion is whether truths of reason are epistemically superior to truths of fact. Because truths of reason give us 100 percent certainty, shouldn't we try to have all our beliefs measure up to this degree of certainty? If we were to survey our friends and family, wouldn't they agree that absolutely certain beliefs are better than merely probable ones? The more certain our beliefs, the better!

Despite this first impression about our beliefs, we should recognize that the world in which we normally operate on a day-to-day basis is a world that can never give us this degree of certainty. The possibility will always exist that our various beliefs, whether about others or ourselves, may be wrong.

So what do we make of the lack of certainty inherent in truths of fact? Should we become skeptical about all empirical knowledge?

Philosophers have recently argued we just need to accept that we will never have absolute certainty regarding truths of fact—those beliefs about the everyday world. The reason is quite simple. Beliefs such as these are based on our experiences of the world. We see and hear things, and our brain then interprets our senses. Though we see and hear things correctly most of the time, our judgments are not infallible.

Though our day-to-day judgments and beliefs will never be absolutely certain, we shouldn't feel particularly troubled about this state of affairs. We are still able to accomplish a great deal, from building massive skyscrapers to flying jets across the world, from figuring out the human genome to landing rovers on Mars.

Having gone through the differences between belief, knowledge, and certainty, we can now return to the subject of truth. When we speak of truths of fact and truths of reason, is there a difference in what we mean by *truth* in each case?

Truths of reason, as we've noted, are guaranteed to be true due to the way they are worded. Truths of fact, in contrast, are less certain. So how do we measure this relative certainty? Because we don't have a "certainty meter" that can be held up to someone's head to measure the degree of certainty carried in each belief, some epistemologists speak about "justification" when it comes to truths of fact: Instead of talking about whether our beliefs are certain, they talk about *how much* they are justified.

The justification we have for a belief can be measured by the evidence we appeal to for believing it. For example, we can say the bus comes by our place every quarter hour because that's what is listed on the bus schedule. Because we take the bus on a regular basis, we know it keeps to a rigid schedule. To be sure, some of our beliefs will be more important than knowing a bus schedule. The beliefs we deem the most important are those that we'll want to, in the words of one philosopher, "justify to the hilt."

We next consider another important component in our discussion of terms central to epistemology: *theories of truth.* What makes a proposition true? Not surprisingly, philosophers have found many reasons for disagreement over this question.

To know whether it is true the bus will arrive at 10 AM, we can check the bus schedule at the bus stop with our watch. If the bus schedule is up to date, our watch is working properly, and the bus is running on time, when the bus arrives at 10 AM, we will be able to say our belief "the bus arrives at 10 AM" is true. We would then be right to say this claim constitutes knowledge on our part. In other words, our claim is a *justified true belief.*

Truths of this sort fit nicely into the *theory of truth as correspondence.* Epistemologists who think truth is a matter of correspondence say the task is to make sure our ideas or beliefs *correspond* to the objects out there in the real world. Aristotle put it this way:

> To say of what is that it is not, or of what is not that it is, is false, while to say of what is that it is, and of what is not that it is not, is true.

This is a rather complicated way of saying that if your claim corresponds to the way the world is, then the claim is true. If the world does not correspond to your claim, then your claim is false.

Truth as correspondence explains how we come to hold many of our beliefs. We have an idea about something; we then check the world to see if indeed our belief matches reality. We can check both ordinary and complex beliefs this way. And the checking we need to do is often of critical importance. Terrible accidents can occur because someone doesn't check things with enough care. If we try to cross the street thinking no cars are coming, but fail to see if our belief actually corresponds to the world of traffic, we could end up ceasing to think altogether. Just as seriously, scientists and engineers might believe that a rocket will be launched successfully; yet the *Challenger* tragedy illustrated how beliefs about the engineering of rocket science can fail to correspond to the actual operation of the rockets it produces.

Despite the effectiveness of the notion of truth as correspondence, and the fact it can be applied to a wide variety of beliefs, this view of truth has limitations. Think of our beliefs about politics and religion. How would we go about corresponding our belief in a given religion with the way the world really is? How do we, for example, find the objects in the world that correspond to our concepts of "God" or "salvation"? How would a Roman Catholic and a Baptist resolve doctrinal differences by referring to truth as correspondence? Is there something in the world we can measure these two views against to see which belief corresponds more accurately to reality?

This problem holds not only in the context of religion but also with our wide-ranging or global beliefs. Beliefs of this magnitude can be described as "worldviews" or "paradigms." When people describe themselves as being religious, liberals, feminists, musicians, or artists, we assume they see the world in a particular way; that they have a particular worldview. The religious person, for example, interprets what is going on around him or her through a specific frame of reference: that God is in control, there are forces of good and evil, and there is a specific objective moral code of behavior for us to follow.

This is the case with politics too. Compare a very conservative-minded with a very liberal-minded person. If we believe the truthfulness of their beliefs is based on how the world is, how do we go about showing who is right? Is there something out in the world with which we can compare our political beliefs? Because of the difficulty in establishing the truthfulness of a wide range of specific beliefs, a different view of truth is needed when it comes to more global beliefs.

This is the point where the *coherence theory of truth* steps in. Rather than having our beliefs correspond to the world, the task is to bring our beliefs about the world into a unified, structured, organized whole. Coherentists want to avoid having their beliefs contradict each other. They also want to avoid "epistemic danglers," beliefs that don't cohere with the overall structure. The epistemic responsibility is to have beliefs cohere.

The coherentist's position makes good sense. No matter how we describe ourselves, as Christian or Muslim, conservative or liberal, scientist or artist, we have to try to keep our beliefs fitting together and structured. A dangler for a conservative Christian could be holding to a literal reading of creation in the book of Genesis, at the same time believing the Darwinian account of human origins. Someone who is politically liberal may find herself staunchly against capital punishment yet extremely troubled by the rise in violent crime, tempting her to reconsider her view. Thoughtful people usually try to eliminate such inconsistencies as best as possible.

Truth as coherence, however, has some problems. Consider how a neo-Nazi could be wholly consistent in his racist views, with all his various beliefs neatly and compactly organized, cohering as a unified worldview. He hates all non-Aryans equally. Irrespective of this high degree of coherence and inner consistency, we would still say his worldview is terribly wrong.

This brings us to the third traditional theory of truth: *the pragmatist view.* We need to be careful here because there were some important differences between the three most well known pragmatists: Charles Sanders Peirce, John Dewey, and William James. Let's focus on James's view, keeping in mind that Peirce and Dewey might differ on certain points.

Though James's view of truth was somewhat different from that of his pragmatist colleagues, he was undoubtedly influenced by Peirce's belief that the main task of philosophy is not to deeply represent reality or to show how all our beliefs correspond to the world. Instead, it is to find ways of more effectively acting and negotiating our way through the world. The influence of Darwin on the pragmatists is apparent here. Having true beliefs, whatever that means, wasn't the goal of our primitive ancestors. They wanted instead to have beliefs that would help them survive in their daily struggle.

When it comes to simple beliefs—things like knowing sugar is sweet, our armchair is brown, or that mosquitoes bite human beings—James had little difficulty with the view that we should try to represent the world around us. One could hardly operate in the world without thinking like this. The pragmatist also agrees that our beliefs require some degree of coherence or agreement with each other.

What distinguishes the pragmatist's theory of truth from the other theories is the pragmatist's contention that truth should be *useful*. In a provocative passage from our reading James says "'it is useful because it is true' or that 'it is true because it is useful.' Both these phrases mean exactly the same thing. . . ."

A more recent pragmatist who also appears in this chapter's readings, Richard Rorty, puts the pragmatist view of truth slightly differently. He asks, "What would it mean for me if I believed X?" In the case of the neo-Nazi, it doesn't matter that his view is coherent. It wouldn't even matter if his beliefs corresponded to the world (which, incidentally, they don't). The pragmatist asks instead, "What would it mean for me if I believed the principles of Nazism were right?" Finding the implications of believing this view repugnant, the pragmatist rejects it.

The difficulty the pragmatist faces is how, philosophically, to justify this moral repugnance. Can the criterion of usefulness be used here? Bertrand Russell, the famous twentieth-century English philosopher, saw the pragmatist view of truth as morally troubling. He asked the following question: "If the Nazis had won the war, would we then say they had the 'truth' because their beliefs worked the best?" Russell's complaint here is that the pragmatists reduce truth to utility. In science this is an especially important matter. Even though scientists are able to do all sorts of useful things, we are still left with the question of whether all of these things *should* be done.

Philosophers will dispute the value of these three theories till the proverbial cows come home. Perhaps the best way of thinking about them can be through appeal to "timely use." It depends on what we are thinking about and what we are trying to do. We don't have to tenaciously stick to one theory of truth. Our basic or simple beliefs need to connect with the real world. We should try to make sure our higher-level beliefs are ordered and coherent. And whatever our beliefs are, they need to be useful in some way.

We need to now turn our attention to the question of where our knowledge comes from. Because we've already looked at the ancient Greeks on this issue, we will jump ahead to "modern philosophy," which is seen by most scholars as starting with René Descartes in the seventeenth century.

There was a major division between epistemologists at that time, a split between the "rationalists" and the "empiricists." Their differences have already been discussed in Chapter 3, "Mind, Body, and Self." Their main disagreement focused on the question, "How do we acquire ideas and knowledge about the world?"

Rationalists emphasized the powers of introspection, whereas empiricists thought we gained knowledge of our world through observation, through sensual experience of our surroundings. Broadly speaking, rationalism tended to draw the attention of more abstract thinkers, whereas empiricism appealed to the practically minded.

Rationalists contended that the human intellect is able to establish truths about the world a priori (independent of experience). They saw knowledge as secured by the powers of reason. They didn't go so far as to argue that our senses were of no use in proving our beliefs. This would have been a rather odd view to take, something along the lines of the ancient skeptics. Rather, they argued that in order for knowledge to be certain, we need to use the reasoning powers of the human intellect, for only it could understand the fundamental nature of the world.

The rationalists and the empiricists also differed on the concept of *innate ideas.* Innate ideas were ideas the mind had prior to all experience. The rationalists said we could have innate ideas; empiricists said we could not.

Modern philosophy begins with the French philosopher René Descartes. His work represented a decisive break with medieval scholasticism. He became one of the most important philosophers of the modern period partly because he reignited philosophical interest in epistemology. You were introduced to his famous claim, "Cogito ergo sum" (I am thinking, therefore I exist), in the previous chapter. Through his "methodological doubt" he showed how we could be skeptical about all sorts of things, but at the moment we think, we cannot doubt we exist. We should note, though, that Descartes went through the entire thought experiment contained in *The Meditations* in the comfort of his study, at no point venturing outside to check his conclusions with the empirical world. This was not surprising given the fact he believed that at least some of our basic ideas are not derived from experience and that reason is the font of all true knowledge.

It isn't unexpected as well, given their views of how knowledge is established, that the three most famous rationalists, Descartes, Spinoza, and Leibniz, were all able mathematicians. Their interest in mathematics, with its clarity and certainty, encouraged them to believe that general truths about the world could be established with the same certainty.

Descartes' view of how the mind acquired knowledge influenced both rationalists and empiricists. Descartes divided ideas of the mind into two sorts of "qualities," primary and secondary. Primary qualities were the more abstract of the two, including figure, magnitude, and motion. Some examples of secondary qualities are color, sound, and taste.

Descartes called primary ideas "clear and distinct": They had a quantifiable and measurable character. It is easy to see how Descartes' preference for primary qualities was due to his admiration for mathematics, which seemed to offer us confident knowledge about reality.

Descartes' view has been described as a "representational" view of knowledge. This position is quite basic: The mind can only have ideas or mental images of the world that exist outside the mind. The ideas the mind has of the world must be representative of the physical objects out there.

Yet, there is a problem with this view. Because Descartes believed all sense knowledge comes through ideas and is only representative of the external world, what assurance can we have that our ideas accurately correspond to the objects they represent? Moreover, this view implies there will always be a divide between the ideas in our mind and the world outside it. Interestingly, Descartes didn't resolve this issue with more philosophical reasoning. Instead, he assured us we could depend on our senses because God, who constructed them, is no deceiver. We can therefore have confidence in our ideas.

In contrast to rationalism stood empiricism, pioneered by John Locke and ably defended by David Hume. Empiricists were in agreement that our ideas, whether of the world or otherwise, are based on our experience. These ideas are a posteriori.

As an empiricist Locke approached the question of what we can know quite differently from Descartes. Whereas Descartes was a mathematician, John Locke was a physician. And just as Descartes' profession affected his philosophy, Locke's professional training also affected his philosophical outlook.

As a physician Locke knew it was well and good to rationally deliberate about disease, but little would get done if he did not closely examine his patient's body to determine the best course of treatment. Because Locke learned, as a physician, that he needed to base his diagnosis on what he saw actually taking place in the patient's body, he had a powerful incentive to believe our ideas could be gained only through observation, through our experience of the world.

Locke is well known for his claim that the human mind is born *tabula rasa,* a "blank slate." We are not born with ideas somehow imprinted on our minds. Our ideas rather come from our experience of the world, either through "sensation" or "reflection." Our senses impact directly upon the mind when we see, hear, smell, touch, or taste something. These simple ideas of our senses are the basis of our knowledge. Through the mind's ability to reflect, to think about those ideas, complex ideas are built up from simple ones.

Locke was careful to add that although our ideas ultimately derive from experience, not all knowledge comes directly through experience. Remember our distinction between truths of reason and truths of fact. Locke remained adamant (as did Kant afterward) that although we can know truths of reason apart from direct empirical observation, that doesn't mean we know them innately.

To take an example, through the use of reason we can know that "whatever is, is." But this doesn't show that this idea was in the mind *prior* to our thinking about it; that it was prior to experience. Geometry is another example. Although no one is born with the truths of geometry imprinted on his or her mind, the truths of geometry can be shown to be valid apart from sensual experience. A final example is our human capacity for intuition. Although not innate, it is a sort of knowledge not directly extracted from experience. Incidentally, J. S. Mill, who is discussed in our ethics chapter, came to disagree with Locke on the issue of truths of reason. Mill was a very strict empiricist, arguing that all knowledge, including truths of reason, comes from experience. This apparently held equally for both geometry and for unmarried bachelors.

David Hume described how the mind comes to acquire knowledge a little differently than Locke. Instead of using Locke's ideas of sensation and reflection, Hume wanted to sort all the contents of the human mind into either "impressions" or "ideas," both of which he saw as perceptions. Impressions include our basic sensations, passions, and emotions. They are our most immediate perceptions. Ideas have less impact on our minds than impressions. Hume describes ideas as "faint images" of impressions. Ideas are formed either in thought, reflection, or imagination and are of two sorts: simple and complex. Simple ideas are created by the mind as "copies of our impressions." Complex ideas come about through a combination of these simple ideas.

In the readings after Hume we shift gears somewhat, moving from questions of how we come to know the world to the more abstract issues surrounding notions of truth. We've already seen how William James's view of truth as usefulness represents a break from traditional notions of how we acquire knowledge of the world.

A. J. Ayer was one of the more colorful philosophers of his time. His promotion of logical positivism in the English-speaking world was a striking change of direction for philosophy in the early twentieth century. This philosophical movement was based in Vienna during the 1930s. Led by Moritz Schlick, its members included some of the sharpest minds of the twentieth century—Rudolf Carnap, Kurt Gödel, and Otto Neurath. After graduating from Oxford, A. J. Ayer, known to his friends as "Freddie," spent time at the University of Vienna where he was undoubtedly influenced by the positivist movement. The Viennese philosopher Ludwig Wittgenstein, though never an actual member of the group, greatly influenced both the positivists' outlook and Ayer's thought.

The relationship between Ayer and the positivists was reciprocal. Ayer's best-known contribution to both the positivist movement and to twentieth-century analytic philosophy was his book *Language, Truth and Logic,* published in 1936. Though Ayer would have vehemently denied the comparison, it came to be the positivists' statement of faith, a sort of ecclesiastical dogma for this school of thought. As a piece of astute philosophical reasoning, the book remains an important moment in the history of philosophy. Remarkably, Ayer wrote it at the tender age of twenty-six.

Ayer wanted to clean up the way we speak. He wasn't thinking about profanity but rather meaningless claims. He believed he could remove an enormous amount of the useless philosophical verbiage cluttering up our philosophical investigations.

Ayer's main targets of criticism were the religious believer and the metaphysician. Two examples of supposedly confused thinking in the history of philosophy are Anselm's ontological argument and Descartes' solution to the mind-body problem. Ayer wasn't trying to show that Anselm and Descartes were right or wrong; instead, Ayer was intent on showing that their respective claims were not *meaningful.* We'll see exactly how Ayer tried to distinguish between meaningful and meaningless statements in the commentary to follow.

R. G. Collingwood offers a nice contrast to those thinkers who approach subjects in the humanities and social sciences from a highly rationalistic point of view. For Collingwood, who was not only a philosopher but also an archeologist and a historian, the big question was "How can the mind represent past events?" Past events have the nasty habit of no longer being available for direct empirical observation. Unlike chemical reactions or biological experiments conducted in a laboratory, historical events cannot be repeated to test the validity of a theory or hypothesis.

Collingwood's approach to investigating historical events is rather straightforward: To understand them, we must reenact those events in our minds based on the evidence we have before us. Because we can no longer observe historical events, we have to think about how they might have transpired.

To aid in this effort, Collingwood makes an important distinction between the "outside" of an event, the physical movements associated with it, and the "inside," the thoughts of the historical actors. He concluded that historical thinking had to focus on the inside and thus all history is the history of thought. We reenact that thought in our present minds to understand the past. To this extent, Collingwood is in agreement with some of the other writers in this chapter, including Richard Rorty and the postmodernists. Collingwood thought, like them, that we have no direct contact with physical "reality." Such a claim, however, isn't too earth shattering. It is merely the recognition of our limitations as human observers of the world.

Epistemology, with its distinctions between belief and knowledge, certainty and truth, must invariably discuss science, because science has accomplished a number of great feats over the past couple of centuries, giving it an important epistemic and cultural status. Scientists have uncovered worlds, from microbiology to astrophysics. From uncovering the secrets of DNA to sending satellites deep into outer space, scientists continue to amaze the rest of us with their achievements.

These accomplishments have given scientists a certain eminence both with respect to their scientific work and issues dealing with culture in general. Carl Sagan, Stephen Jay Gould, and Stephen Hawking have spoken not only about their own fields of research but also about religion, popular culture, and politics. The question that naturally follows is "Why should being an astrophysicist, even a brilliant one such as Hawking, make us want to listen to his or her views on religion or culture?" We routinely think that an accomplished and successful scientist is able to talk authoritatively about everything. To this extent, the modern-day scientist has taken the place (and even the authority!) of the pastor or priest. Instead of looking to the clergy, many of us now turn to scientists for answers to human problems.

Science is connected to epistemological matters. Due to the success of scientific investigation, we've come to assume that scientists are more rational than the rest of us. Scientists are committed to truth, objectivity, and rational discussion. This commitment, along with being detached observers of the world, allows for discovery and scientific progress.

Historians of science have described scientific advancement as an incremental building upon past theories, like placing one brick on another in the wall of scientific Truth. To them, science advances piece by piece. In his book *The Structure of Scientific Revolutions* (originally published in 1962), Thomas Kuhn, a scientist trained in theoretical physics, seriously challenged this still-popular way of envisioning how science works. He argued that science doesn't progress in the way traditionally depicted.

Science does not advance so much by rational as by nonrational or irrational means. Kuhn maintained that science is not a teleological affair, where the end or goal is to get closer to the truth. Instead, he sees science as a process of evolutionary adaptation to the environment and problems of scientific researchers. For this reason, science becomes more and more specialized, as is evidenced in the increasing splintering of disciplines we see in academic life today.

A contemporary philosopher who has written on a variety of subjects, and has brought some of Kuhn's ideas into his philosophical outlook, is Richard Rorty. Rorty is as provocative in his writings on epistemology as he is on ethics and the philosophy of religion. For this reason, there are philosophers who consider him to be something of a pariah and so have little interest in his work. Others find him to be a refreshing change. What you think is up to you. Suffice to say Rorty wants us to put aside the traditional questions and issues of epistemology. He wants us to redefine, even discard, some of its key words, including *belief, knowledge,* and *truth.* In this sense he is an "antifoundationalist"—a skeptic about the capacity of epistemology to ground or ultimately justify knowledge claims.

Sandra Harding is the last writer whom we have included in this chapter. She confronts head-on the main thrust of work done by male epistemologists in the philosophical canon.

When epistemologists argue about what constitutes truth, objectivity, rationality, and knowledge, the fact that most of the philosophers participating in this discussion are men might go unnoticed. But noticing this fact raises some important considerations. Do men have a particular and quite different way of thinking about these matters than women do? For instance, do women and men have the same way of thinking about what constitutes "rationality"? Or do men give more credit to this human capacity than do women?

These are some of the questions feminist epistemologists ask. Their inquiry shouldn't be thought of as highly abstract deliberations that have nothing to do with real life. Feminists argue that these issues are radically connected to theories of human nature and the way research is carried out in the humanities and the sciences, usually to the detriment of the way women are represented by such research. Some feminist epistemologists, Susan Bordo for example, argue that philosophy and science have privileged a specifically masculine Cartesian reason that is disembodied and dispassionate in order to exclude women from these fields.

Epistemology covers a wide range of philosophical ideas and applications. It's the branch of philosophy that urges us to try to understand how we know our world. More and more challenges to the sort of epistemology practiced by the philosophical canon are coming forward every year.

Epistemologists of all sorts should welcome these challenges. They help to see how truth, knowledge, and objectivity can be described in a variety of ways. Even the most skeptical have something important to say about these words, even if this something contends there are some things we just cannot know.

# JOHN LOCKE'S BLANK SLATE

When it comes to theories of knowledge, John Locke (1632–1704) is the founder of modern empiricism. In the introduction to his *Essay,* he states his purpose: to "inquire into the original, certainty, and the extent of *human knowledge.*"

Human knowledge comprises all the ideas in our minds. Locke defines the term *ideas* as that which "serves best to stand for whatsoever is the *object* of the understanding when someone thinks . . . or *whatever it is which the mind can be employed about in thinking.*"

Locke likened the mind to a blank slate, like the board your professors write on during class. Like the chalk that gives content to the board, the various characters, words, and phrases written on the mind come from our experiences of the world.

One of the central elements of John Locke's epistemological position was his disavowal of *innate ideas,* ideas that were in, or imprinted on, our minds at birth. This denial wasn't merely for theoretical reasons. Locke thought that the belief in innate ideas could be played to the Church and the State's advantage, allowing authorities to argue that subservience is justified by appealing to particular innate ideas about God or the divine right of kings. Locke wanted to avoid all authoritarianism. Appeals to innate ideas could be turned against individual liberty because blind obedience to authority does not require investigation and critical thinking. Thus, for Locke, a thorough empiricism was a more stable foundation for knowledge. It was, as well, the best guarantee for individual freedom.

Our ideas are either ideas of "sensation" or of "reflection." By sensation Locke meant all those ideas acquired through our five senses. As understood by Locke, the great majority of our ideas are ideas of sensation. Reflection was the mind's capacity to reflect upon ideas acquired by sensation. From this reflection the mind is able to create a new set of ideas. This is the capacity of the human intellect not only to reflect on the ideas acquired through the senses but also to reflect on its own operations, whether through contemplation, reflection, or abstraction.

Locke also distinguished "simple" from "complex" ideas. Simple ideas come to the mind through one or more senses, through the mind's capacity for reflection, or through both sensation and reflection. The process is mostly passive. Once there, the mind has a capacity to think through these simple ideas (whether this process is described as introspection, reflection, doubting, or reasoning) and formulate more complex ones. The more abstract a complex idea, the further removed from simple ideas it becomes. A good example of a complex idea is a moral belief. When we have a moral belief, we no longer have an "idea" that can be directly reduced to a sensory experience. In each case, however, we can pull apart these complex ideas and discover the simple ideas of which they were originally composed.

In his writings Locke wanted to be as precise and definitive as possible in describing the operations of the mind. His view had a great impact on other empiricists to follow, including David Hume, laying the foundation for epistemology for at least a century to follow and for the modern philosophy of science to this day.

# An Essay concerning Human Understanding

## JOHN LOCKE

### *[Book 1]*

#### INTRODUCTION

1. *An Inquiry into the Understanding pleasant and useful.* Since it is the *understanding* that sets man above the rest of sensible beings, and gives him all the advantage and dominion which he has over them; it is certainly a subject even for its nobleness, worth our labour to inquire into. The understanding, like the eye, whilst it makes us see and perceive all other things, takes no notice of itself; and it requires art and pains to set it at a distance and make it its own object. But whatever be the difficulties that lie in the way of this inquiry; whatever it be that keeps us so much in the dark to ourselves; sure I am that all the light we can let in upon our minds, all the acquaintance we can make with our own understandings, will not only be very pleasant, but bring us great advantage, in directing our thoughts in the search of other things.

2. *Design.* This, therefore, being my purpose—to inquire into the original, certainty, and extent of *human knowledge*, together with the

SOURCE: John Locke, "An Essay concerning Human Understanding," abr. Richard Taylor (1690; Garden City, NY: Anchor Books, 1974), pp. 7–18, 31–33, 37–40 [bk. 1: introduction, secs. 1–4; chap. 1, secs. 1–9, 23, 24; chap. 2, secs. 1–3; chap. 3, secs. 1–2; bk. 2: chap. 9, secs. 1–4, 8, 15; chap. 12, secs. 1–7]; from abridged version in *The Empiricists* (Garden City, NY: Doubleday, 1961); abridgement copyright 1961, by Doubleday & Company, Inc.

grounds and degrees of *belief, opinion,* and as-sent;—I shall not at present meddle with the physical consideration of the mind; or trouble myself to examine wherein its essence consists; or by what motions of our spirit or alterations of our bodies we come to have any *sensation* by our organs, or any *ideas* in our understandings; and whether those ideas do in their formation, any or all of them, depend on matter or not. These are speculations which, however curious and enter-taining, I shall decline, as lying out of my way in the design I am now upon. It shall suffice to my present purpose, to consider the discerning fac-ulties of a man, as they are employed about the objects which they have to do with. And I shall imagine I have not wholly misemployed myself in the thoughts I shall have on this occasion, if, in this historical, plain method, I can give any ac-count of the ways whereby our understandings come to attain those notions of things we have; and can set down any measures of the certainty of our knowledge; or the grounds of those per-suasions which are to be found amongst men, so various, different, and wholly contradictory; and yet asserted somewhere or other with such assur-ance and confidence, that he that shall take a view of the opinions of mankind, observe their oppo-sition, and at the same time consider the fond-ness and devotion wherewith they are embraced, the resolution and eagerness wherewith they are maintained, may perhaps have reason to suspect, that either there is no such thing as truth at all, or that mankind hath no sufficient means to at-tain a certain knowledge of it.

3. *Method.* It is therefore worth while to search out the bounds between opinion and knowledge; and examine by what measures, in things whereof we have no certain knowledge, we ought to regulate our assent and moderate our persuasion. In order whereunto I shall pur-sue this following method:—

First, I shall inquire into the original of those *ideas,* notions, or whatever else you please to call them, which a man observes, and is conscious to himself he has in his mind; and the ways whereby the understanding comes to be furnished with them.

Secondly, I shall endeavour to show what *knowledge* the understanding hath by those ideas; and the certainty, evidence, and extent of it.

Thirdly, I shall make some inquiry into the nature and grounds of *faith* or *opinion:* whereby I mean that assent which we give to any propo-sition as true, of whose truth yet we have no cer-tain knowledge. And here we shall have occasion to examine the reasons and degrees of *assent.*

4. *What Idea stands for.* Before I proceed on to what I have thought on this subject, I must here in the entrance beg pardon of my reader for the frequent use of the word *idea* which he will find in the following treatise. It being that term which, I think, serves best to stand for whatso-ever is the *object* of the understanding when a man thinks, I have used it to express whatever is meant by *phantasm, notion, species,* or *whatever it is which the mind can be employed about thinking;* and I could not avoid frequently using it.

I presume it will be easily granted me, that there are such *ideas* in men's minds: every one is conscious of them in himself; and men's words and actions will satisfy him that they are in others.

## Book 2

### CHAPTER I. OF IDEAS IN GENERAL, AND THEIR ORIGINAL

1. *Idea is the Object of Thinking.* Every man be-ing conscious to himself that he thinks; and that which his mind is applied about whilst thinking being the *ideas* that are there, it is past doubt that men have in their minds several ideas,—such as are those expressed by the words *white-ness, hardness, sweetness, thinking, motion, man, elephant, army, drunkenness,* and others: it is in the first place then to be inquired, *How he comes by them?*

I know it is a received doctrine, that men have native ideas and original characters, stamped upon their minds in their very first being. This opinion I have at large examined already and, I suppose what I have said in the foregoing Book will be much more easily admitted, when I have shown whence the understanding may get all the ideas it has; and by what ways and degrees they may come into the mind;—for which I shall appeal to every one's own observation and experience.

2. *All Ideas come from Sensation or Reflection.* Let us then suppose the mind to be, as we say, white paper, void of all characters, without any ideas:—How comes it to be furnished? Whence comes it by that vast store which the busy and boundless fancy of man has painted on it with an almost endless variety? Whence has it all the *materials* of reason and knowledge? To this I answer, in one word, from EXPERIENCE. In that all our knowledge is founded; and from that it ultimately derives itself. Our observation employed either, about external sensible objects, or about the internal operations of our minds perceived and reflected on by ourselves, is that which supplies our understandings with all the *materials* of thinking. These two are the fountains of knowledge, from whence all the ideas we have, or can naturally have, do spring.

3. *The Objects of Sensation.* First, our Senses, conversant about particular sensible objects, do convey into the mind several distinct perceptions of things, according to those various ways wherein those objects do affect them. And thus we come by those *ideas* we have of *yellow, white, heat, cold, soft, hard, bitter, sweet,* and all those which we call sensible qualities; which when I say the senses convey into the mind, I mean, they from external objects convey into the mind what produces there those perceptions. This great source of most of the ideas we have, depending wholly upon our senses, and derived by them to the understanding, I call SENSATION.

4. *The Operations of our Minds, the other Source of them.* Secondly, the other fountain from which experience furnisheth the understanding with ideas is,—the perception of the operations of our own mind within us, as it is employed about the ideas it has got;—which operations, when the soul comes to reflect on and consider, do furnish the understanding with another set of ideas, which could not be had from things without. And such are *perception, thinking, doubting, believing, reasoning, knowing, willing,* and all the different actings of our own minds;—which we

being conscious of, and observing in ourselves, do from these receive into our understandings as distinct ideas as we do from bodies affecting our senses. This source of ideas every man has wholly in himself; and though it be not sense, as having nothing to do with external objects, yet it is very like it, and might properly enough be called *internal sense*. But as I call the other Sensation, so I call this REFLECTION, the ideas it affords being such only as the mind gets by reflecting on its own operations within itself. By reflection then, in the following part of this discourse, I would be understood to mean, that notice which the mind takes of its own operations, and the manner of them, by reason whereof there come to be ideas of these operations in the understanding. These two, I say, viz. external material things, as the objects of SENSATION, and the operations of our own minds within, as the objects of REFLECTION, are to me the only originals from whence all our ideas take their beginnings. The term *operations* here I use in a large sense, as comprehending not barely the actions of the mind about its ideas, but some sort of passions arising sometimes from them, such as is the satisfaction or uneasiness arising from any thought.

5. *All our Ideas are of the one or the other of these.* The understanding seems to me not to have the least glimmering of any ideas which it doth not receive from one of these two. *External objects* furnish the mind with the ideas of sensible qualities, which are all those different perceptions they produce in us; and *the mind* furnishes the understanding with ideas of its own operations.

These, when we have taken a full survey of them, and their several modes, combinations, and relations, we shall find to contain all our whole stock of ideas; and that we have nothing in our minds which did not come in one of these two ways. Let any one examine his own thoughts, and thoroughly search into his understanding; and then let him tell me, whether all the original ideas he has there, are any other than of the objects of his senses, or of the operations of his mind, considered as objects of his reflection. And how great a mass of knowledge soever he imagines to be lodged there, he will, upon taking a strict view, see that he has not any idea in his mind but what one of these two have imprinted;—though perhaps, with infinite variety compounded and enlarged by the understanding, as we shall see hereafter.

6. *Observable in Children.* He that attentively considers the state of a child, at his first coming into the world, will have little reason to think him stored with plenty of ideas, that are to be the matter of his future knowledge. It is *by degrees* he comes to be furnished with them. And though the ideas of obvious and familiar qualities imprint themselves before the memory begins to keep a register of time or order, yet it is often so late before some unusual qualities come in the way, that there are few men that cannot recollect the beginning of their acquaintance with them. And if it were worth while, no doubt a child might be so ordered as to have but a very few, even of the ordinary ideas, till he were grown up to a man. But all that are born into the world, being surrounded with bodies that perpetually and diversely affect them, variety of ideas, whether care be taken of it or not, are imprinted on the minds of children. Light and colours are busy at hand everywhere, when the eye is but open; sounds and some tangible qualities fail not to solicit their proper senses, and force an entrance to the mind;—but yet, I think, it will be granted easily, that if a child were kept in a place where he never saw any other but black and white till he were a man, he would have no more ideas of scarlet or green, than he that from his childhood never tasted an oyster, or a pineapple, has of those particular relishes.

7. *Men are differently furnished with these, according to the different Objects they converse with.* Men then come to be furnished with fewer or more simple ideas from without, according as the objects they converse with afford greater or less variety; and from the operations of their minds within, according as they more or less reflect on them. For, though he that contemplates the operations of his mind, cannot but have plain and clear ideas of them; yet, unless he turn his thoughts that way, and considers them *attentively,* he will no more have clear and distinct ideas of all the operations of his mind, and all that may

be observed therein, than he will have all the particular ideas of any landscape, or of the parts and motions of a clock, who will not turn his eyes to it, and with attention heed all the parts of it. The picture, or clock may be so placed, that they may come in his way every day; but yet he will have but a confused idea of all the parts they are made up of, till he applies himself with attention, to consider them each in particular.

8. *Ideas of Reflection later, because they need Attention.* And hence we see the reason why it is pretty late before most children get ideas of the operations of their own minds; and some have not any very clear or perfect ideas of the greatest part of them all their lives. Because, though they pass there continually, yet, like floating visions, they make not deep impressions enough to leave in their mind clear, distinct, lasting ideas, till the understanding turns inward upon itself, reflects on its own operations, and makes them the objects of its own contemplation. Children when they come first into it, are surrounded with a world of new things, which, by a constant solicitation of their senses, draw the mind constantly to them; forward to take notice of new, and apt to be delighted with the variety of changing objects. Thus the first years are usually employed and diverted in looking abroad. Men's business in them is to acquaint themselves with what is to be found without; and so growing up in a constant attention to outward sensations, seldom make any considerable reflection on what passes within them, till they come to be of riper years; and some scarce ever at all.

9. *The Soul begins to have Ideas when it begins to perceive.* To ask, at what *time* a man has first any ideas, is to ask, when he begins to perceive;— *having ideas,* and *perception,* being the same thing. I know it is an opinion, that the soul always thinks, and that it has the actual perception of ideas in itself constantly, as long as it exists; and that actual thinking is as inseparable from the soul as actual extension is from the body; which if true, to inquire after the beginning of a man's ideas is the same as to inquire after the beginning of his soul. For, by this account, soul and its ideas, as body and its extension, will begin to exist both at the same time. . . .

23. *A man begins to have ideas when he first has sensation. What sensation is.* If it shall be demanded then, *when* a man *begins* to have any ideas, I think the true answer is,—*when he first has any sensation.* For, since there appear not to be any ideas in the mind before the senses have conveyed any in, I conceive that ideas in the understanding are coeval with *sensation; which is such an impression or motion made in some part of the body, as produces some perception in the understanding.* It is about these impressions made on our senses by outward objects that the mind seems *first* to employ itself, in such operations as we call perception, remembering, consideration, reasoning, &c.

24. *The Original of all our Knowledge.* In time the mind comes to reflect on its own operations about the ideas got by sensation, and thereby stores itself with a new set of ideas, which I call ideas of reflection. These are the impressions that are made on our senses by outward objects that are extrinsical to the mind; and its own operations, proceeding from powers intrinsical and proper to itself, which, when reflected on by itself, become also objects of its contemplation— are, as I have said, the original of all knowledge. Thus the first capacity of human intellect is,— that the mind is fitted to receive the impressions made on it; either through the senses by outward objects, or by its own operations when it reflects on them. This is the first step a man makes towards the discovery of anything, and the groundwork whereon to build all those notions which ever he shall have naturally in this world. All those sublime thoughts which tower above the clouds, and reach as high as heaven itself, take their rise and footing here: in all that great extent wherein the mind wanders, in those remote speculations it may seem to be elevated with, it stirs not one jot beyond those ideas which *sense* or *reflection* have offered for its contemplation.

## CHAPTER 2. OF SIMPLE IDEAS

1. *Uncompounded Appearances.* The better to understand the nature, manner, and extent of our knowledge, one thing is carefully to be observed concerning the ideas we have; and that is that some of them are *simple* and some *complex.*

Though the qualities that affect our senses are, in the things themselves. So united and blended, that there is no separation, no distance between them: yet it is plain, the ideas they produce in the mind enter by the senses simple and unmixed. For, though the sight and touch often take in from the same object, at the same time, different ideas;—as a man sees at once motion and colour; the hand feels softness and warmth in the same piece of wax: yet the simple ideas thus united in the same subject, are as perfectly distinct as those that come in by different senses. The coldness and hardness which a man feels in a piece of ice being as distinct ideas in the mind as the smell and whiteness of a lily; or as the taste of sugar, and smell of a rose. And there is nothing can be plainer to a man than the clear and distinct perception he has of those simple ideas; which, being each in itself uncompounded, contains in it nothing but *one uniform appearance, or conception in the mind,* and is not distinguishable into different ideas.

2. *The Mind can neither make nor destroy them.* These simple ideas, the materials of all our knowledge, are suggested and furnished to the mind only by those two ways above mentioned, viz. sensation and reflection. When the understanding is once stored with these simple ideas, it has the power to repeat, compare, and unite them, even to an almost infinite variety, and so can make at pleasure new complex ideas. But it is not in the power of the most exalted wit, or enlarged understanding, by any quickness or variety of thought, to *invent* or *frame* one new simple idea in the mind, not taken in by the ways before mentioned: nor can any force of the understanding *destroy* those that are there. The dominion of man, in this little world of his own understanding being muchwhat the same as it is in the great world of visible things; wherein his power, however managed by art and skill, reaches no farther than to compound and divide the materials that are made to his hand; but can do nothing towards the making the least particle of new matter, or destroying one atom of what is

already in being. The same inability will every one find in himself, who shall go about to fashion in his understanding one simple idea, not received in by his senses from external objects, or by reflection from the operations of his own mind about them. I would have any one try to fancy any taste which had never affected his palate; or frame the idea of a scent he had never smelt: and when he can do this, I will also conclude that a blind man hath ideas of colours, and a deaf man true distinct notions of sounds.

3. *Only the qualities that affect the senses are imaginable.* This is the reason why—though we cannot believe it impossible to God to make a creature with other organs, and more ways to convey into the understanding the notice of corporeal things than those five, as they are usually counted, which he has given to man—yet I think it is not possible for any *man* to imagine any other qualities in bodies, howsoever constituted, whereby they can be taken notice of, besides sounds, tastes, smells, visible and tangible qualities. And had mankind been made but with four senses, the qualities then which are the objects of the fifth sense had been as far from our notice, imagination, and conception, as now any belonging to a sixth, seventh, or eighth sense can possibly be;—which, whether yet some other creatures, in some other parts of this vast and stupendous universe, may not have, will be a great presumption to deny. He that will not set himself proudly at the top of all things, but will consider the immensity of this fabric, and the great variety that is to be found in this little and inconsiderable part of it which he has to do with, may be apt to think that, in other mansions of it, there may be other and different intelligent beings, of whose faculties he has as little knowledge or apprehension as a worm shut up in one drawer of a cabinet hath of the senses or understanding of a man; such variety and excellency being suitable to the wisdom and power of the Maker. I have here followed the common opinion of man's having but five senses; though, perhaps, there may be justly counted more;—but either supposition serves equally to my present purpose.

# CHAPTER 3. OF SIMPLE IDEAS OF SENSE

1. *Division of simple Ideas.* The better to conceive the ideas we receive from sensation, it may not be amiss for us to consider them, in reference to the different ways whereby they make their approaches to our minds, and make themselves perceivable by us.

*First,* then, There are some which come into our minds *by one sense only.*

*Secondly,* There are others that convey themselves into the mind *by more senses than one.*

*Thirdly,* Others that are had from *reflection only.*

*Fourthly,* There are some that make themselves way, and are suggested to the mind *by all the ways of sensation and reflection.*

We shall consider them apart under these several heads.

*Ideas of one Sense.* There are some ideas which have admittance only through one sense, which is peculiarly adapted to receive them. Thus light and colours, as white, red, yellow, blue; with their several degrees or shades and mixtures, as green, scarlet, purple, sea-green, and the rest, come in only by the eyes. All kinds of noises, sounds, and tones, only by the ears. The several tastes and smells, by the nose and palate. And if these organs, or the nerves which are the conduits to convey them from without to their audience in the brain,—the mind's presence-room (as I may so call it)—are any of them so disordered as not to perform their functions, they have no postern to be admitted by; no other way to bring themselves into view, and be perceived by the understanding.

The most considerable of those belonging to the touch, are heat and cold, and solidity: all the rest, consisting almost wholly in the sensible configuration, as smooth and rough; or else, more or less firm adhesion of the parts, as hard and soft, tough and brittle, are obvious enough.

2. *Few simple Ideas have Names.* I think it will be needless to enumerate all the particular simple

ideas belonging to each sense. Nor indeed is it possible if we would; there being a great many more of them belonging to most of the senses than we have names for. The variety of smells, which are as many almost, if not more, than species of bodies in the world, do most of them want names. Sweet and stinking commonly serve our turn for these ideas, which in effect is little more than to call them pleasing or displeasing; though the smell of a rose and violet, both sweet, are certainly very distinct ideas. Nor are the different tastes, that by our palates we receive ideas of, much better provided with names. Sweet, bitter, sour, harsh, and salt are almost all the epithets we have to denominate that numberless variety of relishes, which are to be found distinct, not only in almost every sort of creatures, but in the different parts of the same plant, fruit, or animal. The same may be said of colours and sounds. I shall, therefore, in the account of simple ideas I am here giving, content myself to set down only such as are most material to our present purpose, or are in themselves less apt to be taken notice of though they are very frequently the ingredients of our complex ideas; amongst which, I think, I may well account solidity, which therefore I shall treat of in the next chapter. . . .

## CHAPTER 9. OF PERCEPTION

1. *Perception the first simple Idea of Reflection.* PERCEPTION, as it is the first faculty of the mind exercised about our ideas so it is the first and simplest idea we have from reflection, and is by some called thinking in general. Though thinking, in the propriety of the English tongue, signifies that sort of operation in the mind about its ideas, wherein the mind is active where it, with some degree of voluntary attention, considers anything. For in bare naked perception, the mind is, for the most part, only passive; and what it perceives, it cannot avoid perceiving.

2. *Reflection alone can give us the idea of what perception is.* What perception is, every one will know better by reflecting on what he does himself, when he sees, hears, feels, &c., or thinks than by any discourse of mine. Whoever reflects

on what passes in his own mind cannot miss it. And if he does not reflect, all the words in the world cannot make him have any notion of it.

3. *Arises in sensation only when the mind notices the organic impression.* This is certain, that whatever alterations are made in the body, if they reach not the mind; whatever impressions are made on the outward parts, if they are not taken notice of within, there is no perception. Fire may burn our bodies with no other effect than it does a billet, unless the motion be continued to the brain, and there the sense of heat, or idea of pain, be produced in the mind; wherein consists actual perception.

4. *Impulse on the organ insufficient.* How often may a man observe in himself, that whilst his mind is intently employed in the contemplation of some objects, and curiously surveying some ideas that are there, it takes no notice of impressions of sounding bodies made upon the organ of hearing, with the same alteration that uses to be for the producing the idea of sound? A sufficient impulse there may be on the organ: but it not reaching the observation of the mind, there follows no perception: and though the motion that uses to produce the idea of sound be made in the ear, yet no sound is heard. Want of sensation, in this case, is not through any defect in the organ, or that the man's ears are less affected than at other times when he does hear: but that which uses to produce the idea, though conveyed in by the usual organ, not being taken notice of in the understanding, and so imprinting no idea in the mind, there follows no sensation. So that wherever there is sense or perception, there some idea is actually produced, and present in the understanding.

8. *Sensations often changed by the Judgment.* We are further to consider concerning perception, that the ideas we receive by sensation are often, in grown people, altered by the judgment, without our taking notice of it. When we set before our eyes a round globe of any uniform colour, v.g. gold, alabaster, or jet, it is certain that the idea thereby imprinted on our mind is of a flat circle, variously shadowed, with several degrees of light and brightness coming to our eyes.

But we having, by use, been accustomed to perceive what kind of appearance convex bodies are wont to make in us; what alterations are made in the reflections of light by the difference of the sensible figures of bodies;—the judgment presently, by an habitual custom, alters the appearances into their causes. So that from that which is truly variety of shadow or colour, collecting the figure, it makes it pass for a mark of figure, and frames to itself the perception of a convex figure and an uniform colour; when the idea we receive from thence is only a plane variously coloured, as is evident in painting. To which purpose I shall here insert a problem of that very ingenious and studious promoter of real knowledge, the learned and worthy Mr. Molineux, which he was pleased to send me in a letter some months since; and it is this:—"Suppose a man *born* blind, and now adult, and taught by his *touch* to distinguish between a cube and a sphere of the same metal, and nighly of the same bigness, so as to tell, when he felt one and the other, which is the cube, which the sphere. Suppose then the cube and sphere placed on a table, and the blind man be made to see: *quaere,* whether *by his sight, before he touched them,* he could now distinguish and tell which is the globe, which the cube?" To which the acute and judicious proposer answers, "Not. For, though he has obtained the experience of how a globe, how a cube affects his touch, yet he has not yet obtained the experience, that what affects his touch so or so, must affect his sight so or so; or that a protuberant angle in the cube, that pressed his hand unequally, shall appear to his eye as it does in the cube."—I agree with this thinking gentleman, whom I am proud to call my friend, in his answer to this problem; and am of opinion that the blind man, at first sight, would not be able with certainty to say which was the globe, which the cube, whilst he only saw them; though he could unerringly name them by his touch, and certainly distinguish them by the difference of their figures felt. This I have set down, and leave with my reader, as an occasion for him to consider how much he may be beholden to experience, improvement, and acquired notions, where he thinks he had not the least use of, or help from them. And the rather, because this observing gentleman further adds, that "having, upon the occasion of my book, proposed this to divers very ingenious men, he hardly ever met with one that at first gave the answer to it which he thinks true, till by hearing his reasons they were convinced."

15. *Perception the Inlet of all materials of Knowledge.* Perception then being the *first* step and degree towards knowledge, and the inlet of all the materials of it; the fewer senses any man, as well as any other creature, hath; and the fewer and duller the impressions are that are made by them; and the duller the faculties are that are employed about them,—the more remote are they from that knowledge which is to be found in some men. But this being in great variety of degrees (as may be perceived amongst men) cannot certainly be discovered in the several species of animals, much less in their particular individuals. It suffices me only to have remarked here,—that perception is the first operation of all our intellectual faculties, and the inlet of all knowledge in our minds. And I am apt too to imagine, that it is perception, in the lowest degree of it, which puts the boundaries between animals and the inferior ranks of creatures. But this I mention only as my conjecture by the by; it being indifferent to the matter in hand which way the learned shall determine of it. . . .

## CHAPTER 12. OF COMPLEX IDEAS

1. *Made by the Mind out of simple Ones.* We have hitherto considered those ideas, in the reception whereof the mind is only passive, which are those simple ones received from sensation and reflection before mentioned, whereof the mind cannot make one to itself, nor have any idea which does not wholly consist of them. But as the mind is wholly passive in the reception of all its simple ideas, so it exerts several acts of its own, whereby out of its simple ideas, as the materials and foundations of the rest, the others are framed. The acts of the mind, wherein it exerts its power over its simple ideas, are chiefly these three: (1) Com-

bining several simple ideas into one compound one; and thus all *complex ideas* are made. (2) The second is bringing two ideas, whether simple or complex, together, and setting them by one another, so as to take a view of them at once, without uniting them into one; by which way it gets all its *ideas of relations.* (3) The third is separating them from all other ideas that accompany them in their real existence: this is called abstraction: and thus all its *general ideas* are made. This shows man's power, and its ways of operation, to be much the same in the material and intellectual world. For the materials in both being such as he has no power over, either to make or destroy, all that man can do is either to unite them together, or to set them by one another, or wholly separate them. I shall here begin with the first of these in the consideration of complex ideas, and come to the other two in their due places. As simple ideas are observed to exist in several combinations united together, so the mind has a power to consider several of them united together as one idea; and that not only as they are united in external objects, but as itself has joined them together. Ideas thus made up of several simple ones put together, I call *complex;*—such as are beauty, gratitude, a man, an army, the universe; which, though complicated of various simple ideas, or complex ideas made up of simple ones, yet are, when the mind pleases, considered each by itself, as one entire thing, and signified by one name.

2. *Made voluntarily.* In this faculty of repeating and joining together its ideas, the mind has great power in varying and multiplying the objects of its thoughts, infinitely beyond what sensation or reflection furnished it with: but all this still confined to those simple ideas which it received from those two sources, and which are the ultimate materials of all its compositions. For simple ideas are all from things themselves, and of these the mind *can* have no more, nor other than what are suggested to it. It can have no other ideas of sensible qualities than what come from without by the senses; nor any ideas of other kind of operations of a thinking substance, than what it finds in itself. But when it has once got these simple ideas, it is not confined barely to

observation, and what offers itself from without; it can, by its own power, put together those ideas it has, and make new complex ones, which it never received so united.

3. *Complex ideas are either of Modes, Substances, or Relations. Complex ideas,* however compounded and decompounded, though their number be infinite, and the variety endless, wherewith they fill and entertain the thoughts of men; yet I think they may be all reduced under these three heads:—

1. *Modes.*
2. *Substances.*
3. *Relations.*

4. *Ideas of Modes.* First, *Modes* I call such complex ideas which, however compounded, contain not in them the supposition of subsisting by themselves, but are considered as dependences on, or affections of substances;—such as are the ideas signified by the words triangle, gratitude, murder, &c. And if in this I use the word mode in somewhat a different sense from its ordinary signification, I beg pardon; it being unavoidable in discourses, differing from the ordinary received notions, either to make new words, or to use old words in somewhat a new signification; the later whereof, in our present case, is perhaps the more tolerable of the two.

5. *Simple and mixed Modes of simple ideas.* Of these *modes,* there are two sorts which deserve distinct consideration:—

First, there are some which are only variations, or different combinations of the same simple idea, without the mixture of any other;—as a dozen, or score; which are nothing but the ideas of so many distinct units added together, and these I call *simple modes* as being contained within the bounds of one simple idea.

Secondly, there are others compounded of simple ideas of several kinds, put together to make one complex one;—v.g. beauty, consisting of a certain composition of colour and figure, causing delight to the beholder; theft, which being the concealed change of the possession of anything, without the consent of the proprietor, contains, as is visible, a combination of several ideas of several kinds: and these I call *mixed modes.*

6. *Ideas of Substances, single or collective.* Secondly, the ideas of *substances* are such combinations of simple ideas as are taken to represent distinct *particular* things subsisting by themselves; in which the supposed or confused idea of substance, such as it is, is always the first and chief. Thus if to substance be joined the simple idea of a certain dull whitish colour, with certain degrees of weight, hardness, ductility, and fusibility, we have the idea of lead; and a combination of the ideas of a certain sort of figure, with the powers of motion, thought and reasoning, joined to substance, make the ordinary idea of a man. Now of substances also, there are two sorts of ideas:— one of *single* substances, as they exist separately, as of a man or a sheep; the other of several of those put together, as an army of men, or flock of sheep—which *collective* ideas of several substances thus put together are as much each of them one single idea as that of a man or an unit.

7. *Ideas of Relation.* Thirdly, the last sort of complex ideas is that we call *relation,* which consists in the consideration and comparing one idea with another. . . .

# DAVID HUME'S SKEPTICAL EMPIRICISM

David Hume (1711–1776) extended Locke's ideas by probing to their limits some of the skeptical implications of the notion that sense experience is the source of all knowledge.

Hume, like Locke, divided all the mind's perceptions into two classes. He distinguished them on the basis of their respective "force and vivacity." The more forcible perceptions he named "impressions," the less forcible "ideas." (In his *Enquiry concerning Human Understanding* he also uses the term *thoughts* for "ideas," though in what many take to be his more definitive *A Treatise of Human Nature,* he sticks more rigorously to the term *ideas* to describe our more faint perceptions.) Hume called impressions the more "lively" perceptions owing to the degree by which they impacted upon the mind. Impressions come about "when we hear, or see, or feel, or love, or hate, or desire, or will." In contrast to impressions, ideas come about through the mind's ability to reflect on our impressions. They are less intense, more pallid than our impressions.

Hume makes this important distinction at the beginning of section 2 of the *Enquiry concerning Human Understanding,* "Of the Origin of Ideas." Our remembrances, or to use Hume's term, our *ideas,* never compare in intensity or force with the pleasure or pain originally felt by our senses. Think, for example, of an accident such as dropping something on your foot, burning a finger, or crashing out while on your skateboard or in-line skates. The excruciating pain you felt at that moment isn't something you can replicate in its full intensity by thinking about it afterward (which, by the way, is probably a good thing).

What about Hume's view that all ideas are derived from original impressions garnered through the senses? At first blush this may not seem as evident as it was to Hume. The human capacity for imagination is quite wild and obscure (for example, think of some of the more exotic music videos of recent years). Doesn't it seem likely that at least some of the ideas popping up in our minds have nothing to do with the real world? How could Hume successfully argue that all of our ideas are derived, in some way, from our sense impressions?

Hume admitted that the mind, with its wonderful capacity for imagination, could come up with some incredible ideas—ideas of sea monsters and other sorts of bizarre creatures, for example. Moreover, we can think about worlds far removed from our own. Even though we seem to enjoy a broad liberty in the construction of ideas, Hume maintained that these ideas are actually quite restricted and limited compared to our immediate impressions.

In light of what our ideas are able to do, why would Hume unwaveringly assign them this secondary status?

Hume said that although the mind seemed to have the ability to create ideas quite independent of the world outside our minds, this power was no more than the mind's ability to reorganize what is gleaned by the senses and experience. In other words, our wild and crazy ideas are the result of our combining and abstracting various "lively impressions."

Hume asks us to think of a golden mountain. Though a golden mountain is quite removed from anything in the real world (though not as bizarre and incredible as it would have been in Hume's day), this idea comes from our combining two more lively impressions originally gained through the senses: that of a mountain and that of gold. Voilà! Nothing so incredible after all, it would seem.

If he could look at the special effects provided by modern technology, Hume would have more difficulty these days showing how all our ideas come from combinations of impressions derived from the senses. Think of Jim Henson's Muppets, or the characters in films such as *Dune, Star Wars,* and *Lord of the Rings.* To what impressions can we associate the characters Jabba the Hutt, Yoda, or Sauron? Perhaps a mutated frog or lizard, or a demon from mythology? More seriously, think of the Internet or theoretical work in quantum mechanics. What possible impressions could have given rise to these ideas? In such a scenario Hume's arrangement of impressions and ideas might have to be reversed: The idea comes first, with no impression contributing to its creation; the idea is then made into a physical object, which then becomes an impression.

Hume was quite skilled at answering questions such as this, even with the limited examples available in his own day. A case in point: What more abstract idea could one have than that of God? As we saw in our chapter on the philosophy of religion, God is by definition immutable and transcendent to this world. To what impression could this idea of God correspond? Put more exactly, how does this idea of God come about, given there is supposedly nothing in the world around us that corresponds to these attributes? Hume explains:

> The idea of God, as meaning an infinitely intelligent, wise, and good Being, arises from reflecting on the operations of our own mind, and augmenting, without limit, those qualities of goodness and wisdom.

Hume then sets out his challenge, which can be tried out on the counterexamples suggested above. He says:

> Those who would assert that this position is not universally true nor without exceptions, have only one, and that an easy method of refuting it; by producing that idea, which, in their opinion, is not derived from this source. It will then be incumbent on us, if we would maintain our doctrine, to produce the impression, or lively perception, which corresponds to it.

Do you think it is possible to have an idea that isn't first derived from an impression or set of impressions? If so, what is it?

Interestingly, Hume did allow for one exception to his view. This is the mind's ability, having seen a variety of shades of a given color, say blue, to form an idea of a shade that has never been seen. Though Hume grants this possibility, it "is so singular, that it is scarcely worth our observing, and does not merit that for it alone we should alter our general maxim."

To be sure, philosophers have the unpleasant habit of trying to see the cracks in another philosopher's view instead of seeing how that view can contribute to our understanding of a particular subject. We may want, therefore, to push Hume on this and say that if there can be one exception to his rule, then perhaps there could be more. However, given Hume's importance in the history of epistemology, perhaps we should focus on his insights rather than his shortcomings (especially because he admits some of these himself).

In section 4 of the *Enquiry*, Hume makes his famous distinction between "relations of ideas" and "matters of fact." Remember from the introduction that relations of ideas are propositions in fields of study such as geometry, algebra, and arithmetic. Consider a description of a triangle: a closed figure with three sides. Geometrical propositions are certain because their certainty is contained within their definitions. They are not empirical claims that have to be tested by experience. Yet as Hume notes, triangles don't exist in nature.

Our knowledge of matters of fact, in contrast, comes from our experience and observation of the world around us. We derive matters of fact from our impressions. Matters of fact can be wrong, unlike relations of ideas (or, at least, well-constructed relations of ideas). We can certainly make mistakes about our sense experience—we might see a glimpse of someone and think it is our friend, whereas it turns out to be just someone who looks like her. We might look at the clock and mistakenly think it is 11 AM when in fact it is noon. Nevertheless, matters of fact tell us about the world we live in. Contrary to what rationalists such as Descartes claimed, we cannot have true knowledge of the world without relying on sense experience.

Hume's best-known example of how knowledge of the world can come only through experience is the observation of the effect billiard balls have when striking each other. We cannot know a priori the way billiard balls will respond when struck. If we had been blind from birth, then suddenly had our sight restored in front of a billiard table, we would not be able to guess, without prior observation, that the billiard balls would scatter when the cue ball struck them.

This showed Hume that even a basic notion, such as our idea of cause and effect, is not something we are able to discover purely through reason, unassisted by experience. Instead, we learn the idea of causality from experience, from repeated observation of the relations between things. We know that a billiard ball striking another will cause the second one to move from "custom and habit." There is nothing inherent in the substance of billiard balls (or in any other object) that allows us to understand how they will interact with other objects in space. In short, we understand the nature of things only through our senses. Even scientific laws have no deeper basis than our observation of the customs and habits of physical bodies over time.

# An Enquiry concerning Human Understanding

## DAVID HUME

### Section 2. Of the Origin of Ideas

Every one will readily allow, that there is a considerable difference between the perceptions of the mind, when a man feels the pain of excessive heat, or the pleasure of moderate warmth, and when he afterwards recalls to his memory this sensation, or anticipates it by his imagination. These faculties may mimic or copy the perceptions of the senses; but they never can entirely reach the force and vivacity of the original sentiment. The utmost we say of them, even when they operate with greatest vigour, is, that they represent their object in so lively a manner, that we could *almost* say we feel or see it: But, except the mind be disordered by disease or madness, they never can arrive at such a pitch of vivacity, as to render these perceptions altogether undistinguishable. All the colours of poetry, however splendid, can never paint natural objects in such a manner as to make the description be taken for a real landscape. The most lively thought is still inferior to the dullest sensation.

We may observe a like distinction to run through all the other perceptions of the mind. A man, in a fit of anger, is actuated in a very different manner from one who only thinks of that emotion. If you tell me, that any person is in love, I easily understand your meaning, and form a just conception of his situation; but never can mistake that conception for the real disorders and agitations of the passion. When we reflect on our past sentiments and affections, our thought is a faithful mirror, and copies its objects truly; but the colours which it employs are faint and dull, in comparison of those in which our original perceptions were clothed. It requires no nice discernment or metaphysical head to mark the distinction between them.

Here therefore we may divide all the perceptions of the mind into two classes or species, which are distinguished by their different degrees of force and vivacity. The less forcible and lively are commonly denominated THOUGHTS or IDEAS. The other species want a name in our language, and in most others; I suppose, because it was not requisite for any, but philosophical purposes, to rank them under a general term or appellation. Let us, therefore, use a little freedom, and call them IMPRESSIONS; employing that word in a sense somewhat different from the usual. By the term *impression*, then, I mean all our more lively perceptions, when we hear, or see, or feel, or love, or hate, or desire, or will. And impressions are distinguished from ideas, which are the less lively perceptions, of which we are conscious, when we reflect on any of those sensations or movements above mentioned.

Nothing, at first view, may seem more unbounded than the thought of man, which not only escapes all human power and authority, but is not even restrained within the limits of nature and reality. To form monsters, and join incongruous shapes and appearances, costs the imagination no more trouble than to conceive the most natural and familiar objects. And while the body is confined to one planet, along which it creeps with pain and difficulty; the thought can in an instant transport us into the most distant regions of the universe; or even beyond the universe, into the unbounded chaos, where nature is supposed to lie in total confusion. What never was seen, or heard of, may yet be conceived; nor is any thing beyond the power of thought, except what implies an absolute contradiction.

But though our thought seems to possess this unbounded liberty, we shall find, upon a nearer

SOURCE: David Hume, *An Enquiry concerning Human Understanding* (1777; Indianapolis, IN: Hackett Publishing Company, 1977); from the 1777 edition, ed. Eric Steinberg, sec. 2, "Of the Origin of Ideas," and sec. 4, "Sceptical Doubts concerning the Operations of the Understanding," pp. 9–13, 15–25 (one paragraph from sec. 4 has been omitted).

examination, that it is really confined within very narrow limits, and that all this creative power of the mind amounts to no more than the faculty of compounding, transposing, augmenting, or diminishing the materials afforded us by the senses and experience. When we think of a golden mountain, we only join two consistent ideas, *gold,* and *mountain,* with which we were formerly acquainted. A virtuous horse we can conceive; because, from our own feeling, we can conceive virtue; and this we may unite to the figure and shape of a horse, which is an animal familiar to us. In short, all the materials of thinking are derived either from our outward or inward sentiment: The mixture and composition of these belongs alone to the mind and will. Or, to express myself in philosophical language, all our ideas or more feeble perceptions are copies of our impressions or more lively ones.

To prove this, the two following arguments will, I hope, be sufficient. First, when we analyse our thoughts or ideas, however compounded or sublime, we always find, that they resolve themselves into such simple ideas as were copied from a precedent feeling or sentiment. Even those ideas, which, at first view, seem the most wide of this origin, are found, upon a nearer scrutiny, to be derived from it. The idea of God, as meaning an infinitely intelligent, wise, and good Being, arises from reflecting on the operations of our own mind, and augmenting, without limit, those qualities of goodness and wisdom. We may prosecute this enquiry to what length we please; where we shall always find, that every idea which we examine is copied from a similar impression. Those who would assert, that this position is not universally true nor without exception, have only one, and that an easy method of refuting it; by producing that idea, which, in their opinion, is not derived from this source. It will then be incumbent on us, if we would maintain our doctrine, to produce the impression or lively perception, which corresponds to it.

Secondly. If it happens, from a defect of the organ, that a man is not susceptible of any species of sensation, we always find, that he is as little susceptible of the correspondent ideas. A blind man can form no notion of colours; a deaf man

of sounds. Restore either of them that sense, in which he is deficient; by opening this new inlet for his sensations, you also open an inlet for the ideas; and he finds no difficulty in conceiving these objects. The case is the same, if the object, proper for exciting any sensation, has never been applied to the organ. A LAPLANDER or NEGROE has no notion of the relish of wine. And though there are few or no instances of a like deficiency in the mind, where a person has never felt or is wholly incapable of a sentiment or passion, that belongs to his species; yet we find the same observation to take place in a less degree. A man of mild manners can form no idea of inveterate revenge or cruelty; nor can a selfish heart easily conceive the heights of friendship and generosity. It is readily allowed, that other beings may possess many senses, of which we can have no conception; because the ideas of them have never been introduced to us, in the only manner, by which an idea can have access to the mind, to wit, by the actual feeling and sensation.

There is, however, one contradictory phaenomenon, which may prove, that it is not absolutely impossible for ideas to arise, independent of their correspondent impressions. I believe it will readily be allowed, that the several distinct ideas of colour, which enter by the eye, or those of sound, which are conveyed by the ear, are really different from each other; though, at the same time, resembling. Now if this be true of different colours, it must be no less so of the different shades of the same colour; and each shade produces a distinct idea, independent of the rest. For if this should be denied, it is possible, by the continual gradation of shades, to run a colour insensibly into what is most remote from it; and if you will not allow any of the means to be different, you cannot, without absurdity, deny the extremes to be the same. Suppose, therefore, a person to have enjoyed his sight for thirty years, and to have become perfectly well acquainted with colours of all kinds, except one particular shade of blue, for instance, which it never has been his fortune to meet with. Let all the different shades of that colour, except that single one, be placed before him, descending gradually from the deepest to the lightest; it is plain, that he will perceive a blank, where that shade is wanting, and will be sensible, that there is a greater distance in that place between the contiguous colours than in any other. Now I ask, whether it be possible for him, from his own imagination, to supply this deficiency, and raise up to himself the idea of that particular shade, though it had never been conveyed to him by his senses? I believe there are few but will be of opinion that he can: And this may serve as a proof, that the simple ideas are not always, in every instance, derived from the correspondent impressions; though this instance is so singular, that it is scarcely worth our observing, and does not merit, that for it alone we should alter our general maxim.

Here, therefore, is a proposition, which not only seems, in itself, simple and intelligible; but, if a proper use were made of it, might render every dispute equally intelligible, and banish all that jargon, which has so long taken possession of metaphysical reasonings, and drawn such disgrace upon them. All ideas, especially abstract ones, are naturally faint and obscure: The mind has but a slender hold of them: They are apt to be confounded with other resembling ideas; and when we have often employed any term, though without a distinct meaning, we are apt to imagine it has a determinate idea, annexed to it. On the contrary, all impressions, that is, all sensations, either outward or inward, are strong and vivid: The limits between them are more exactly determined: Nor is it easy to fall into any error or mistake with regard to them. When we entertain, therefore, any suspicion, that a philosophical term is employed without any meaning or idea (as is but too frequent) we need but enquire, *from what impression is that supposed idea derived?* And if it be impossible to assign any, this will serve to confirm our suspicion. By bringing ideas into so clear a light, we may reasonably hope to remove all dispute, which may arise, concerning their nature and reality.[1]

---

[1] It is probable, that no more was meant by those, who denied innate ideas, than that all ideas were copies of our impressions; though it must be confessed, that the terms, which they employed, were not chosen with such caution, nor so exactly defined, as to prevent all mistakes about their doctrine.

## Section 4. Sceptical Doubts concerning the Operations of the Understanding

### PART I

All the objects of human reason or enquiry may naturally be divided into two kinds, *viz. Relations of Ideas* and *Matters of Fact.* Of the first kind are the sciences of Geometry, Algebra, and Arithmetic; and in short, every affirmation, which is either intuitively or demonstratively certain. *That the square of the hypotenuse is equal to the square of the two sides,* is a proposition, which expresses a relation between these figures. *That three times five is equal to the half of thirty,* expresses a relation between these numbers. Propositions of this kind are discoverable by the mere operation of thought, without dependence on what is any where existent in the universe. Though there never were a circle or triangle in nature, the truths, demonstrated by EUCLID, would for ever retain their certainty and evidence.

Matters of fact, which are the second objects

---

For what is meant by *innate?* If innate be equivalent to natural, then all the perceptions and ideas of the mind must be allowed to be innate or natural, in whatever sense we take the latter word, whether in opposition to what is uncommon, artificial, or miraculous. If by innate be meant, contemporary to our birth, the dispute seems to be frivolous; nor is it worth while to enquire at what time thinking begins, whether before, at, or after our birth. Again, the word *idea,* seems to be commonly taken in a very loose sense, by LOCKE and others; as standing for any of our perceptions, our sensations and passions, as well as thoughts. Now in this sense, I should desire to know, what can be meant by asserting, that self-love, or resentment of injuries, or the passion between the sexes is not innate?

But admitting these terms, *impressions* and *ideas,* in the sense above explained, and understanding by *innate,* what is original or copied from no precedent perception, then may we assert, that all our impressions are innate, and our ideas not innate.

To be ingenuous, I must own it to be my opinion, that LOCKE was betrayed into this question by the schoolmen, who, making use of undefined terms, draw out their disputes to a tedious length, without ever touching the point in question. A like ambiguity and circumlocution seem to run through that philosopher's reasonings on this as well as most other subjects.

of human reason, are not ascertained in the same manner; nor is our evidence of their truth, however great, of a like nature with the foregoing. The contrary of every matter of fact is still possible; because it can never imply a contradiction, and is conceived by the mind with the same facility and distinctness, as if ever so conformable to reality. *That the sun will not rise to-morrow* is no less intelligible a proposition, and implies no more contradiction, than the affirmation, *that it will rise*. We should in vain, therefore, attempt to demonstrate its falsehood. Were it demonstratively false, it would imply a contradiction, and could never be distinctly conceived by the mind.

It may, therefore, be a subject worthy of curiosity, to enquire what is the nature of that evidence, which assures us of any real existence and matter of fact, beyond the present testimony of our senses, or the records of our memory. This part of philosophy, it is observable, has been little cultivated, either by the ancients or moderns; and therefore our doubts and errors, in the prosecution of so important an enquiry, may be the more excusable; while we march through such difficult paths, without any guide or direction. They may even prove useful, by exciting curiosity, and destroying that implicit faith and security, which is the bane of all reasoning and free enquiry. The discovery of defects in the common philosophy, if any such there be, will not, I presume, be a discouragement, but rather an incitement, as is usual, to attempt something more full and satisfactory, than has yet been proposed to the public.

All reasonings concerning matter of fact seem to be founded on the relation of *Cause* and *Effect*. By means of that relation alone we can go beyond the evidence of our memory and senses. If you were to ask a man, why he believes any matter of fact, which is absent; for instance, that his friend is in the country, or in FRANCE; he would give you a reason; and this reason would be some other fact; as a letter received from him, or the knowledge of his former resolutions and promises. A man, finding a watch or any other machine in a desert island, would conclude, that there had once been men in that island. All our reasonings concerning fact are of the same nature. And here it is constantly supposed, that there is a connexion between the present fact and that which is inferred from it. Were there nothing to bind them together, the inference would be entirely precarious. The hearing of an articulate voice and rational discourse in the dark assures us of the presence of some person: Why? because these are the effects of the human make and fabric, and closely connected with it. If we anatomize all the other reasonings of this nature, we shall find, that they are founded on the relation of cause and effect, and that this relation is either near or remote, direct or collateral. Heat and light are collateral effects of fire, and the one effect may justly be inferred from the other.

If we would satisfy ourselves, therefore, concerning the nature of that evidence, which assures us of matters of fact, we must enquire how we arrive at the knowledge of cause and effect.

I shall venture to affirm, as a general proposition, which admits of no exception, that the knowledge of this relation is not, in any instance, attained by reasonings *a priori;* but arises entirely from experience, when we find, that any particular objects are constantly conjoined with each other. Let an object be presented to a man of ever so strong natural reason and abilities; if that object be entirely new to him, he will not be able, by the most accurate examination of its sensible qualities, to discover any of its causes or effects. ADAM, though his rational faculties be supposed, at the very first, entirely perfect, could not have inferred from the fluidity and transparency of water, that it would suffocate him, or from the light and warmth of fire, that it would consume him. No object ever discovers, by the qualities which appear to the senses, either the causes, which produced it, or the effects, which will arise from it; nor can our reason, unassisted by experience, ever draw any inference concerning real existence and matter of fact.

This proposition, *that causes and effects are discoverable, not by reason, but by experience,* will readily be admitted with regard to such objects, as we remember to have once been altogether unknown to us; since we must be conscious of the utter inability, which we then lay under, of foretelling, what would arise from them. Present two smooth pieces of marble to a man, who has no tincture of natural philosophy; he will never discover, that they will adhere together, in such a manner as to require great force to separate them in a direct line, while they make so small a resistance to a lateral pressure. Such events, as bear little analogy to the common course of nature, are also readily confessed to be known only by experience; nor does any man imagine that the explosion of gunpowder, or the attraction of a loadstone, could ever be discovered by arguments *a priori*. In like manner, when an effect is supposed to depend upon an intricate machinery or secret structure of parts, we make no difficulty in attributing all our knowledge of it to experience. Who will assert, that he can give the ultimate reason, why milk or bread is proper nourishment for a man, not for a lion or a tyger?

But the same truth may not appear, at first sight, to have the same evidence with regard to events, which have become familiar to us from our first appearance in the world, which bear a close analogy to the whole course of nature, and which are supposed to depend on the simple qualities of objects, without any secret structure of parts. We are apt to imagine, that we could discover these effects by the mere operation of our reason, without experience. We fancy, that were we brought, on a sudden, into this world, we could at first have inferred, that one Billiard-ball would communicate motion to another upon impulse; and that we needed not to have waited for the event, in order to pronounce with certainty concerning it. Such is the influence of custom, that, where it is strongest, it not only covers our natural ignorance, but even conceals itself, and seems not to take place, merely because it is found in the highest degree.

But to convince us, that all the laws of nature, and all the operations of bodies without exception, are known only by experience, the following reflections may, perhaps, suffice. Were any object presented to us, and were we required to pronounce concerning the effect, which will result from it, without consulting past observation; after what manner, I beseech you, must the mind

proceed in this operation? It must invent or imagine some event, which it ascribes to the object as its effect; and it is plain that this invention must be entirely arbitrary. The mind can never possibly find the effect in the supposed cause, by the most accurate scrutiny and examination. For the effect is totally different from the cause, and consequently can never be discovered in it. Motion in the second Billiard-ball is a quite distinct event from motion in the first; nor is there any thing in the one to suggest the smallest hint of the other. A stone or piece of metal raised into the air, and left without any support, immediately falls: But to consider the matter *a priori,* is there any thing we discover in this situation, which can beget the idea of a downward, rather than an upward, or any other motion, in the stone or metal?

And as the first imagination or invention of a particular effect, in all natural operations, is arbitrary, where we consult not experience; so must we also esteem the supposed tye or connexion between the cause and effect, which binds them together, and renders it impossible, that any other effect could result from the operation of that cause. When I see, for instance, a Billiard-ball moving in a straight line towards another; even suppose motion in the second ball should by accident be suggested to me, as the result of their contact or impulse; may I not conceive, that a hundred different events might as well follow from that cause? May not both these balls remain at absolute rest? May not the first ball return in a straight line, or leap off from the second in any line or direction? All these suppositions are consistent and conceivable. Why then should we give the preference to one, which is no more consistent or conceivable than the rest? All our reasonings *a priori* will never be able to shew us any foundation for this preference.

In a word, then, every effect is a distinct event from its cause. It could not, therefore, be discovered in the cause, and the first invention or conception of it, *a priori,* must be entirely arbitrary. And even after it is suggested, the conjunction of it with the cause must appear equally arbitrary; since there are always many other effects, which, to reason, must seem fully as consistent and natural. In vain, therefore, should we pretend to determine any single event, or infer any cause or effect, without the assistance of observation and experience.

Hence we may discover the reason, why no philosopher, who is rational and modest, has ever pretended to assign the ultimate cause of any natural operation, or to show distinctly the action of that power, which produces any single effect in the universe. It is confessed, that the utmost effort of human reason is, to reduce the principles, productive of natural phaenomena, to a greater simplicity, and to resolve the many particular effects into a few general causes, by means of reasonings from analogy, experience, and observation. But as to the causes of these general causes, we should in vain attempt their discovery; nor shall we ever be able to satisfy ourselves, by any particular explication of them. These ultimate springs and principles are totally shut up from human curiosity and enquiry. Elasticity, gravity, cohesion of parts, communication of motion by impulse; these are probably the ultimate causes and principles which we shall ever discover in nature; and we may esteem ourselves sufficiently happy, if, by accurate enquiry and reasoning, we can trace up the particular phaenomena to, or near to, these general principles. The most perfect philosophy of the natural kind only staves off our ignorance a little longer: As perhaps the most perfect philosophy of the moral or metaphysical kind serves only to discover larger portions of our ignorance. Thus the observation of human blindness and weakness is the result of all philosophy, and meets us, at every turn, in spite of our endeavours to elude or avoid it. . . .

## PART 2

But we have not, as yet, attained any tolerable satisfaction with regard to the question first proposed. Each solution still gives rise to a new question as difficult as the foregoing, and leads us on to farther enquiries. When it is asked, *What is the nature of all our reasonings concerning matter of fact?* the proper answer seems to be, that they are founded on the relation of cause and effect. When again it is asked, *What is the foundation of all our reasonings and conclusions concerning that relation?* it may be replied in one word, EXPERIENCE. But if we still carry on our sifting humour, and ask, *What is the foundation of all conclusions from experience?* this implies a new question, which may be of more difficult solution and explication. Philosophers, that give themselves airs of superior wisdom and sufficiency, have a hard task, when they encounter persons of inquisitive dispositions, who push them from every corner, to which they retreat, and who are sure at last to bring them to some dangerous dilemma. The best expedient to prevent this confusion, is to be modest in our pretensions; and even to discover the difficulty ourselves before it is objected to us. By this means, we may make a kind of merit of our very ignorance.

I shall content myself, in this section, with an easy task, and shall pretend only to give a negative answer to the question here proposed. I say then, that, even after we have experience of the operations of cause and effect, our conclusions from that experience are *not* founded on reasoning, or any process of the understanding. This answer we must endeavour, both to explain and to defend.

It must certainly be allowed, that nature has kept us at a great distance from all her secrets, and has afforded us only the knowledge of a few superficial qualities of objects; while she conceals from us those powers and principles, on which the influence of these objects entirely depends. Our senses inform us of the colour, weight, and consistence of bread; but neither sense nor reason can ever inform us of those qualities, which fit it for the nourishment and support of a human body. Sight or feeling conveys an idea of the actual motion of bodies; but as to that wonderful force or power, which would carry on a moving body for ever in a continued change of place, and which bodies never lose but by communicating it to others; of this we cannot form the most distant conception. But notwithstanding this ignorance of natural powers[2] and principles, we always presume, where we see like sensible

[2] The word, Power, is here used in a loose and popular sense. The more accurate explication of it would give additional evidence to this argument. . . .

qualities, that they have like secret powers, and expect, that effects, similar to those, which we have experienced, will follow from them. If a body of like colour and consistence with that of bread, which we have formerly eat, be presented to us, we make no scruple of repeating the experiment, and foresee, with certainty, like nourishment and support. Now this is a process of the mind or thought, of which I would willingly know the foundation. It is allowed on all hands, that there is no known connexion between the sensible qualities and the secret powers; and consequently, that the mind is not led to form such a conclusion concerning their constant and regular conjunction, by any thing which it knows of their nature. As to past *Experience,* it can be allowed to give *direct* and *certain* information of those precise objects only, and that precise period of time, which fell under its cognizance: But why this experience should be extended to future times, and to other objects, which, for aught we know, may be only in appearance similar; this is the main question on which I would insist. The bread, which I formerly eat, nourished me; that is, a body of such sensible qualities, was, at that time, endued with such secret powers: But does it follow, that other bread must also nourish me at another time, and that like sensible qualities must always be attended with like secret powers? The consequence seems nowise necessary. At least, it must be acknowledged, that there is here a consequence drawn by the mind; that there is a certain step taken; a process of thought, and an inference, which wants to be explained. These two propositions are far from being the same, *I have found that such an object has always been attended with such an effect,* and *I foresee, that other objects, which are, in appearance, similar, will be attended with similar effects.* I shall allow, if you please, that the one proposition may justly be inferred from the other: I know in fact, that it always is inferred. But if you insist, that the inference is made by a chain of reasoning, I desire you to produce that reasoning. The connexion between these propositions is not intuitive. There is required a medium, which may enable the mind to draw such an inference, if indeed it be drawn by reasoning and argument. What that medium is, I must confess, passes my comprehension; and it is incumbent on those to produce it, who assert, that it really exists, and is the origin of all our conclusions concerning matter of fact.

This negative argument must certainly, in process of time, become altogether convincing, if many penetrating and able philosophers shall turn their enquiries this way; and no one be ever able to discover any connecting proposition or intermediate step, which supports the understanding in this conclusion. But as the question is yet new, every reader may not trust so far to his own penetration, as to conclude, because an argument escapes his enquiry, that therefore it does not really exist. For this reason it may be requisite to venture upon a more difficult task; and enumerating all the branches of human knowledge, endeavour to shew, that none of them can afford such an argument.

All reasonings may be divided into two kinds, *viz.* demonstrative reasoning, or that concerning relations of ideas, and moral reasoning, or that concerning matter of fact and existence. That there are no demonstrative arguments in the case, seems evident; since it implies no contradiction, that the course of nature may change, and that an object, seemingly like those which we have experienced, may be attended with different or contrary effects. May I not clearly and distinctly conceive, that a body, falling from the clouds, and which, in all other respects, resembles snow, has yet the taste of salt or feeling of fire? Is there any more intelligible proposition than to affirm, that all the trees will flourish in DECEMBER and JANUARY, and decay in MAY and JUNE? Now whatever is intelligible, and can be distinctly conceived, implies no contradiction, and can never be proved false by any demonstrative argument or abstract reasoning *a priori.*

If we be, therefore, engaged by arguments to put trust in past experience, and make it the standard of our future judgment, these arguments must be probable only, or such as regard matter of fact and real existence, according to the division above mentioned. But that there is no argument of this kind, must appear, if our explication of that species of reasoning be admitted as solid and satisfactory. We have said, that all arguments concerning existence are founded on the relation of cause and effect; that our knowledge of that relation is derived entirely from experience; and that all our experimental conclusions proceed upon the supposition, that the future will be conformable to the past. To endeavour, therefore, the proof of this last supposition by probable arguments, or arguments regarding existence, must be evidently going in a circle, and taking that for granted, which is the very point in question.

In reality, all arguments from experience are founded on the similarity, which we discover among natural objects, and by which we are induced to expect effects similar to those, which we have found to follow from such objects. And though none but a fool or madman will ever pretend to dispute the authority of experience, or to reject that great guide of human life; it may surely be allowed a philosopher to have so much curiosity at least, as to examine the principle of human nature, which gives this mighty authority to experience, and makes us draw advantage from that similarity, which nature has placed among different objects. From causes, which appear *similar,* we expect similar effects. This is the sum of all our experimental conclusions. Now it seems evident, that if this conclusion were formed by reason, it would be as perfect at first, and upon one instance, as after ever so long a course of experience. But the case is far otherwise. Nothing so like as eggs; yet no one, on account of this appearing similarity, expects the same taste and relish in all of them. It is only after a long course of uniform experiments in any kind, that we attain a firm reliance and security with regard to a particular event. Now where is that process of reasoning, which, from one instance, draws a conclusion, so different from that which it infers from an hundred instances, that are nowise different from that single one? This question I propose as much for the sake of information, as with an intention of raising difficulties. I cannot find, I cannot imagine any such reasoning. But I keep my mind still open to instruction, if any one will vouchsafe to bestow it on me.

Should it be said, that, from a number of uniform experiments, we *infer* a connexion between the sensible qualities and the secret powers; this, I must confess, seems the same difficulty, couched in different terms. The question still recurs, On what process of argument this *inference* is founded? Where is the medium, the interposing ideas, which join propositions so very wide of each other? It is confessed, that the colour, consistence and other sensible qualities of bread appear not, of themselves, to have any connexion with the secret powers of nourishment and support. For otherwise we could infer these secret powers from the first appearance of these sensible qualities, without the aid of experience; contrary to the sentiment of all philosophers, and contrary to plain matter of fact. Here then is our natural state of ignorance with regard to the powers and influence of all objects. How is this remedied by experience? It only shews us a number of uniform effects, resulting from certain objects, and teaches us, that those particular objects, at that particular time, were endowed with such powers and forces. When a new object, endowed with similar sensible qualities, is produced, we expect similar powers and forces, and look for a like effect. From a body of like colour and consistence with bread, we expect like nourishment and support. But this surely is a step or progress of the mind, which wants to be explained. When a man says, *I have found, in all past instances, such sensible qualities conjoined with such secret powers:* And when he says, *similar sensible qualities will always be conjoined with similar secret powers;* he is not guilty of a tautology, nor are these propositions in any respect the same. You say that the one proposition is an inference from the other. But you must confess, that the inference is not intuitive; neither is it demonstrative: Of what nature is it then? To say it is experimental, is begging the question. For all inferences from experience suppose, as their foundation, that the future will resemble the past, and that similar powers will be conjoined with similar sensible qualities. If there be any suspicion, that the course of nature may change, and that the past may be no rule for the future, all experience becomes useless, and can give rise to no inference or conclusion. It is impossible, therefore, that any arguments from experience can prove this resemblance of the past to the future; since all these arguments are founded on the supposition of that resemblance. Let the course of things be allowed hitherto ever so regular; that alone, without some new argument or inference, proves not, that, for the future, it will continue so. In vain do you pretend to have learned the nature of bodies from your past experience. Their secret nature, and consequently, all their effects and influence, may change, without any change in their sensible qualities. This happens sometimes, and with regard to some objects: Why may it not happen always, and with regard to all objects? What logic, what process of argument secures you against this supposition? My practice, you say, refutes my doubts. But you mistake the purport of my question. As an agent, I am quite satisfied in the point; but as a philosopher, who has some share of curiosity, I will not say scepticism, I want to learn the foundation of this inference. No reading, no enquiry has yet been able to remove my difficulty, or give me satisfaction in a matter of such importance. Can I do better than propose the difficulty to the public, even though, perhaps, I have small hopes of obtaining a solution? We shall at least, by this means, be sensible of our ignorance, if we do not augment our knowledge.

It is certain, that the most ignorant and stupid peasants, nay infants, nay even brute beasts, improve by experience, and learn the qualities of natural objects, by observing the effects, which result from them. When a child has felt the sensation of pain from touching the flame of a candle, he will be careful not to put his hand near any candle; but will expect a similar effect from a cause, which is similar in its sensible qualities and appearance. If you assert, therefore, that the understanding of the child is led into this conclusion by any process of argument or ratiocination, I may justly require you to produce that argument; nor have you any pretence to refuse so equitable a demand. You cannot say, that the argument is abstruse, and may possibly escape your enquiry; since you confess, that it is obvious to the capacity of a mere infant. If you hesitate, therefore, a moment, or if, after reflection, you produce any intricate or profound argument, you, in a manner, give up the question, and confess, that it is not reasoning which engages us to suppose the past resembling the future, and to expect similar effects from causes, which are, to appearance, similar. This is the proposition which I intended to enforce in the present section. If I be right, I pretend not to have made any mighty discovery. And if I be wrong, I must acknowledge myself to be indeed a very backward scholar; since I cannot now discover an argument, which, it seems, was perfectly familiar to me, long before I was out of my cradle.

# WILLIAM JAMES'S PRAGMATIC VIEW OF TRUTH

We saw in the introduction to this chapter that pragmatists want to base the truth of a claim upon the claim's usefulness. William James (1842–1910), one of the founders of American pragmatism, said that these two sentences mean exactly the same thing:

> It is useful because it is true.
> It is true because it is useful.

Philosophers since James's time haven't been particularly impressed with this argument. It seems to deny the reality of the world on which we base truth claims. Nevertheless, his pragmatic view of truth has been quite influential on a number of other scholars.

At the beginning of our selection James starts out by at least tentatively agreeing with the correspondence view of truth. Yet, as James points out, this initial agreement doesn't go very far, because philosophers have continually disputed what actually constitutes "agreement" and "reality."

The so-called copy theory of truth maintains that the ideas obtained by our senses copy the world around us. The first difficulty James has with the copy view is that it isn't clear what exactly it is about an object that our ideas copy. Apparently, "a true idea must copy a real object." Does this mean the idea must copy the external aspect of the object? This is certainly part of the object's reality. Using James's own example, what in particular should our idea of a clock copy? Should it copy just the minute and second hands or its internal components too? For the copy theory to really work, James suggests that something more has to be copied than just an accurate image of the hands of the clock; after all, this isn't the "whole" clock.

Another difficulty for the pragmatist pertains to the "use" of truth. For those in the traditional epistemological camp, the whole point is to seek out true ideas. Having true beliefs is an end in itself. For James, this is a static view of truth. As an alternative the pragmatist asks, "Given that an idea is true, what real difference will this true idea make to the life of the person holding it?" By connecting usefulness to truth, James gives a new twist to the traditional view of truth. Instead of truth being a property somehow embedded in a belief or idea that makes it true, the pragmatist says, "Truth *happens* to an idea. It *becomes* true, is *made* true by events."

The pragmatist argues that truthfulness is connected with the practical outcome of a person believing something to be true. The relationship between truth and usefulness can be shown with how tools work. When we work on a car, we pick the particular tool that best allows us to do the operation we wish to perform. We call this the right tool, even though it would be the wrong tool in a different situation. For example, we wouldn't use an air pump to fix a crankshaft, yet it would be very useful in reinflating our tires. James put it this way:

> The pragmatic method . . . is to try to interpret each notion by tracing its respective practical consequences. What difference would it practically make to anyone if this notion rather than that notion were true? If no practical difference whatever can be traced, then the alternatives mean practically the same thing, and all dispute is idle.

James liked to use the example of science to illustrate his position. Scientists consider themselves successful when an experiment works as their hypothesis predicts. For James, this was an example of how a pragmatic conception of truth has practical use. But this view of truth also has a great deal of practical importance to ordinary life. We would not be able to get through our day-to-day lives, or even survive, unless we believe certain truths that help us to negotiate through the world, truths such as "cars cannot fly" or "things fall down, not up."

James talks about "verifying ideas." We should be careful of the language used here because it would be easy to mistake James's position for the positivist one (see the next section). James wasn't holding to the positivist definition of verification. His view was more basic. He said that even if we haven't visited a foreign country such as Japan, given all the circumstantial evidence we have for its existence, it is useful to believe that Japan exists. It is verified, or made true, by this utility.

In the last part of the reading James talks about how the traditional view of truth has us believing X or Y because we have some kind of obligation to believe true things. When we have a truth, it is our obligation to believe it. Yet James says that unless a belief has some kind of practical relevance or usefulness to us, we have no real obligation to recognize it as true or false.

James's view of truth certainly is very different from what has been maintained in the history of philosophical thinking on this subject. He makes us consider what difference it makes to our lives to believe something to be true. Should truth be useful? Or should truth be held for its own sake?

# Pragmatism's Conception of Truth

## WILLIAM JAMES

TRUTH, as any dictionary will tell you, is a property of certain of our ideas. It means their "agreement," as falsity means their "disagreement," with "reality." Pragmatists and intellectualists both accept this definition as a matter of course. They begin to quarrel only after the question is raised as to what may precisely be meant by the term "agreement," and what by the term "reality," when reality is taken as something for our ideas to agree with.

In answering these questions the pragmatists are more analytic and painstaking, the intellectualists more offhand and irreflective. The popular notion is that a true idea must copy its reality. Like other popular views, this one follows the analogy of the most usual experience. Our true ideas of sensible things do indeed copy them. Shut your eyes and think of yonder clock on the wall, and you get just such a true picture or copy of its dial. But your idea of its "works" (unless you are a clockmaker) is much less of a copy, yet it passes muster, for it in no way clashes with the reality. Even though it should shrink to the mere word "works," that word still serves you truly; and when you speak of the "time-keeping function" of the clock, or of its spring's "elasticity," it is hard to see exactly what your ideas can copy.

You perceive that there is a problem here. Where our ideas cannot copy definitely their object, what does agreement with that object mean? Some idealists seem to say that they are true whenever they are what God means that we ought to think about that subject. Others hold the copy-view all through, and speak as if our ideas possessed truth just in proportion as they approach to being copies of the Absolute's eternal way of thinking.

These views, you see, invite pragmatistic discussion. But the great assumption of the intellectualists is that truth means essentially an inert static relation. When you've got your true idea of anything, there's an end of the matter. You're in possession; you *know*; you have fulfilled your thinking destiny. You are where you ought to be mentally; you have obeyed your categorical imperative; and nothing more need follow on that climax of your rational destiny. Epistemologically you are in stable equilibrium.

Pragmatism, on the other hand, asks its usual question. "Grant an idea or belief to be true," it says, "what concrete difference will its being true make in any one's actual life? How will the truth be realized? What experiences will be different from those which would obtain if the belief were

SOURCE: William James, "Pragmatism's Conception of Truth," in *Pragmatism: A New Name for Some Old Ways of Thinking* (New York: Longmans, Green and Co., 1907), pp. 197–223.

false? What, in short, is the truth's cash-value in experiential terms?"

The moment pragmatism asks this question, it sees the answer: *True ideas are those that we can assimilate, validate, corroborate and verify. False ideas are those that we cannot.* That is the practical difference it makes to us to have true ideas; that, therefore, is the meaning of truth, for it is all that truth is known-as.

This thesis is what I have to defend. The truth of an idea is not a stagnant property inherent in it. Truth *happens* to an idea. It *becomes* true, is *made* true by events. Its verity *is* in fact an event, a process: the process namely of its verifying itself, its veri-*fication*. Its validity is the process of its valid-*ation*.

But what do the words verification and validation themselves pragmatically mean? They again signify certain practical consequences of the verified and validated idea. It is hard to find any one phrase that characterizes these consequences better than the ordinary agreement-formula—just such consequences being what we have in mind whenever we say that our ideas "agree" with reality. They lead us, namely, through the acts and other ideas which they instigate, into or up to, or towards, other parts of experience with which we feel all the while—such feeling being among our potentialities—that the original ideas remain in agreement. The connexions and transitions come to us from point to point as being progressive, harmonious, satisfactory. This function of agreeable leading is what we mean by an idea's verification. Such an account is vague and it sounds at first quite trivial, but it has results which it will take the rest of my hour to explain.

Let me begin by reminding you of the fact that the possession of true thoughts means everywhere the possession of invaluable instruments of action; and that our duty to gain truth, so far from being a blank command from out of the blue, or a "stunt" self-imposed by our intellect, can account for itself by excellent practical reasons.

The importance to human life of having true beliefs about matters of fact is a thing too notori-

ous. We live in a world of realities that can be infinitely useful or infinitely harmful. Ideas that tell us which of them to expect count as the true ideas in all this primary sphere of verification, and the pursuit of such ideas is a primary human duty. The possession of truth, so far from being here an end in itself, is only a preliminary means towards other vital satisfactions. If I am lost in the woods and starved, and find what looks like a cow-path, it is of the utmost importance that I should think of a human habitation at the end of it, for if I do so and follow it, I save myself. The true thought is useful here because the house which is its object is useful. The practical value of true ideas is thus primarily derived from the practical importance of their objects to us. Their objects are, indeed, not important at all times. I may on another occasion have no use for the house; and then my idea of it, however verifiable, will be practically irrelevant, and had better remain latent. Yet since almost any object may some day become temporarily important, the advantage of having a general stock of *extra* truths, of ideas that shall be true of merely possible situations, is obvious. We store such extra truths away in our memories, and with the overflow we fill our books of reference. Whenever such an extra truth becomes practically relevant to one of our emergencies, it passes from cold-storage to do work in the world and our belief in it grows active. You can say of it then either that "it is useful because it is true" or that "it is true because it is useful." Both these phrases mean exactly the same thing, namely that here is an idea that gets fulfilled and can be verified. True is the name for whatever idea starts the verification-process, useful is the name for its completed function in experience. True ideas would never have been singled out as such, would never have acquired a class-name, least of all a name suggesting value, unless they had been useful from the outset in this way.

From this simple cue pragmatism gets her general notion of truth as something essentially bound up with the way in which one moment in our experience may lead us towards other moments which it will be worth while to have been led to. Primarily, and on the common-sense level, the truth of a state of mind means this function of *a leading that is worth while.* When a moment in our experience, of any kind whatever, inspires us with a thought that is true, that means that sooner or later we dip by that thought's guidance into the particulars of experience again and make advantageous connexion with them. This is a vague enough statement, but I beg you to retain it, for it is essential.

Our experience meanwhile is all shot through with regularities. One bit of it can warn us to get ready for another bit, can "intend" or be "significant of" that remoter object. The object's advent is the significance's verification. Truth, in these cases, meaning nothing but eventual verification, is manifestly incompatible with waywardness on our part. Woe to him whose beliefs play fast and loose with the order which realities follow in his experience; they will lead him nowhere or else make false connexions.

By "realities" or "objects" here, we mean either things of common sense, sensibly present, or else common-sense relations, such as dates, places, distances, kinds, activities. Following our mental image of a house along the cow-path, we actually come to see the house; we get the image's full verification. *Such simply and fully verified leadings are certainly the originals and prototypes of the truth-process.* Experience offers indeed other forms of truth-process, but they are all conceivable as being primary verifications arrested, multiplied or substituted one for another.

Take, for instance, yonder object on the wall. You and I consider it to be a "clock," although no one of us has seen the hidden works that make it one. We let our notion pass for true without attempting to verify. If truths mean verification-process essentially, ought we then to call such unverified truths as this abortive? No, for they form the overwhelmingly large number of the truths we live by. Indirect as well as direct verifications pass muster. Where circumstantial evidence is sufficient, we can go without eye-witnessing. Just as we here assume Japan to exist without ever having been there, because it *works* to do so, everything we know conspiring with the belief, and nothing interfering, so we assume that thing to be a clock. We *use* it as a clock, regulating the length of our lecture by it. The verification of the assumption here means its leading to no frustration or contradiction. Verifi*ability* of wheels and weights and pendulum is as good as verification. For one truth-process completed there are a million in our lives that function in this state of nascency. They turn us *towards* direct verification; lead us into the *surroundings* of the objects they envisage; and then, if everything runs on harmoniously, we are so sure that verification is possible that we omit it, and are usually justified by all that happens.

Truth lives, in fact, for the most part on a credit system. Our thoughts and beliefs "pass," so long as nothing challenges them, just as banknotes pass so long as nobody refuses them. But this all points to direct face-to-face verifications somewhere, without which the fabric of truth collapses like a financial system with no cash-basis whatever. You accept my verification of one thing, I yours of another. We trade on each other's truth. But beliefs verified concretely by *somebody* are the posts of the whole superstructure.

Another great reason—beside economy of time—for waiving complete verification in the usual business of life is that all things exist in kinds and not singly. Our world is found once for all to have that peculiarity. So that when we have once directly verified our ideas about one specimen of a kind, we consider ourselves free to apply them to other specimens without verification. A mind that habitually discerns the kind of thing before it, and acts by the law of the kind immediately, without pausing to verify, will be a "true" mind in ninety-nine out of a hundred emergencies, proved so by its conduct fitting everything it meets, and getting no refutation.

*Indirectly or only potentially verifying processes may thus be true as well as full verification-processes.* They work as true processes would work, give us the same advantages, and claim our recognition for the same reasons. All this on the common-sense level of matters of fact, which we are alone considering.

But matters of fact are not only stock in trade. *Relations among purely mental ideas* form another sphere where true and false beliefs obtain, and here the beliefs are absolute, or unconditional. When they are true they bear the name either of definitions or of principles. It is either a principle or a definition that 1 and 1 make 2, that 2 and 1 make 3, and so on; that white differs less from gray than it does from black; that when the cause begins to act the effect also commences. Such propositions hold of all possible "ones," of all conceivable "whites" and "grays" and "causes." The objects here are mental objects. Their relations are perceptually obvious at a glance, and no sense-verification is necessary. Moreover, once true, always true, of those same mental objects. Truth here has an "eternal" character. If you can find a concrete thing anywhere that is "one" or "white" or "gray" or an "effect," then your principles will everlastingly apply to it. It is but a case of ascertaining the kind, and then applying the law of its kind to the particular object. You are sure to get truth if you can but name the kind rightly, for your mental relations hold good of everything of that kind without exception. If you then, nevertheless, failed to get truth concretely, you would say that you had classed your real objects wrongly.

In this realm of mental relations, truth again is an affair of leading. We relate one abstract idea with another, framing in the end great systems of logical and mathematical truth, under the respective terms of which the sensible facts of experience eventually arrange themselves, so that our eternal truths hold good of realities also. This marriage of fact and theory is endlessly fertile. What we say is here already true in advance of special verification, *if we have subsumed our objects rightly.* Our ready-made ideal framework for all sorts of possible objects follows from the very structure of our thinking. We can no more play fast and loose with these abstract relations than we can do so with our sense-experiences. They coerce us; we must treat them consistently, whether or not we like the results. The rules of addition apply to our debts as rigorously as to our assets. The hundredth decimal of $\pi$, the ratio of the circumference to its diameter, is predetermined ideally now, though no one may have computed it. If we should ever need the figure in our dealings with an actual circle we should need to have it given rightly, calculated by the usual rules; for it is the kind of truth that those rules elsewhere calculate.

Between the coercions of the sensible order and those of the ideal order, our mind is thus wedged tightly. Our ideas must agree with realities, be such realities concrete or abstract, be they facts or be they principles, under penalty of endless inconsistency and frustration.

So far, intellectualists can raise no protest. They can only say that we have barely touched the skin of the matter.

Realities mean, then, either concrete facts, or abstract kinds of thing and relations perceived intuitively between them. They furthermore and thirdly mean, as things that new ideas of ours must no less take account of, the whole body of other truths already in our possession. But what now does "agreement" with such three-fold realities mean?—to use again the definition that is current.

Here it is that pragmatism and intellectualism begin to part company. Primarily, no doubt, to agree means to copy, but we saw that the mere word "clock" would do instead of a mental picture of its works, and that of many realities our ideas can only be symbols and not copies. "Past time," "power," "spontaneity"—how can our mind copy such realities?

To "agree" in the widest sense with a reality *can only mean to be guided either straight up to it or into its surroundings, or to be put into such working touch with it as to handle either it or something connected with it better than if we disagreed.* Better either intellectually or practically! And often agreement will only mean the negative fact and nothing contradictory from the quarter of that reality comes to interfere with the way in which our ideas guide us elsewhere. To copy a reality is, indeed, one very important way of agreeing with it, but it is far from being essential. The essential thing is the process of being guided. Any idea that helps us to *deal*, whether practically or intellectually, with either the reality or its belongings, that doesn't entangle our progress in frustrations, that *fits*, in fact, and adapts our life to the reality's whole setting, will agree sufficiently to meet the requirement. It will hold true of that reality.

Thus, *names* are just as "true" or "false" as definite mental pictures are. They set up similar verification-processes, and lead to fully equivalent practical results.

All human thinking gets discursified; we exchange ideas; we lend and borrow verifications, get them from one another by means of social intercourse. All truth thus gets verbally built out, stored up, and made available for every one. Hence, we must *talk* consistently just as we must *think* consistently: for both in talk and thought we deal with kinds. Names are arbitrary, but once understood they must be kept to. We mustn't now call Abel "Cain" or Cain "Abel." If we do, we ungear ourselves from the whole book of Genesis, and from all its connexions with the universe of speech and fact down to the present time. We throw ourselves out of whatever truth that entire system of speech and fact may embody.

The overwhelming majority of our true ideas admit of no direct or fact-to-face verification—those of past history, for example, as of Cain and Abel. The stream of time can be remounted only verbally, or verified indirectly by the present prolongations or effects of what the past harbored. Yet if they agree with these verbalities and effects, we can know that our ideas of the past are true. *As true as past time itself was,* so true was Julius Caesar, so true were antediluvian monsters all in their proper dates and settings. That past time itself was, is guaranteed by its coherence with everything that's present. True as the present *is*, the past *was* also.

Agreement thus turns out to be essentially an affair of leading—leading that is useful because it is into quarters that contain objects that are important. True ideas lead us into useful verbal and conceptual quarters as well as directly up to useful sensible termini. They lead to consistency, stability and flowing human intercourse. They lead away from eccentricity and isolation, from foiled and barren thinking. The untrammelled

flowing of the leading-process, its general freedom from clash and contradiction, passes for its indirect verification; but all roads lead to Rome, and in the end and eventually, all true processes must lead to the face of directly verifying sensible experiences *somewhere,* which somebody's ideas have copied.

Such is the large loose way in which the pragmatist interprets the word agreement. He treats it altogether practically. He lets it cover any process of conduction from a present idea to a future terminus, provided only it run prosperously. It is only thus that "scientific" ideas, flying as they do beyond common sense, can be said to agree with their realities. It is, as I have already said, *as if* reality were made of ether, atoms or electrons, but we mustn't think so literally. The term "energy" doesn't even pretend to stand for anything "objective." It is only a way of measuring the surface of phenomena so as to string their changes on a simple formula.

Yet in the choice of these man-made formulas we cannot be capricious with impunity any more than we can be capricious on the common-sense practical level. We must find a theory that will *work;* and that means something extremely difficult; for our theory must mediate between all previous truths and certain new experiences. It must derange common sense and previous belief as little as possible, and it must lead to some sensible terminus or other that can be verified exactly. To "work" means both these things; and the squeeze is so tight that there is little loose play for any hypothesis. Our theories are wedged and controlled as nothing else is. Yet sometimes alternative theoretic formulas are equally compatible with all the truths we know, and then we choose between them for subjective reasons. We choose the kind of theory to which we are already partial; we follow "elegance" or "economy." Clerk-Maxwell somewhere says it would be "poor scientific taste" to choose the more complicated of two equally well-evidenced conceptions; and you will all agree with him. Truth in science is what gives us the maximum possible sum of satisfactions, taste included, but consistency both with previous truth and with novel fact is always the most imperious claimant.

I have led you through a very sandy desert. But now, if I may be allowed so vulgar an expression, we begin to taste the milk in the cocoanut. Our rationalist critics here discharge their batteries upon us, and to reply to them will take us out from all this dryness into full sight of a momentous philosophical alternative.

Our account of truth is an account of truths in the plural, of processes of leading, realized *in rebus,* and having only this quality in common, that they *pay.* They pay by guiding us into or towards some part of a system that dips at numerous points into sense-percepts, which we may copy mentally or not, but with which at any rate we are now in the kind of commerce vaguely designated as verification. Truth for us is simply a collective name for verification-processes, just as health, wealth, strength, etc., are names for other processes connected with life, and also pursued because it pays to pursue them. Truth is *made,* just as health, wealth and strength are made, in the course of experience. . . .

Truth makes no other kind of claim and imposes no other kind of ought than health and wealth do. All these claims are conditional; the concrete benefits we gain are what we mean by calling the pursuit a duty. In the case of truth, untrue beliefs work as perniciously in the long run as true beliefs work beneficially. Talking abstractly, the quality "true" may thus be said to grow absolutely precious and the quality "untrue" absolutely damnable: the one may be called good, the other bad, unconditionally. We ought to think the true, we ought to shun the false, imperatively. . . .

It is quite evident that our obligation to acknowledge truth, so far from being unconditional, is tremendously conditioned. Truth with a big T, and in the singular, claims abstractly to be recognized, of course; but concrete truths in the plural need be recognized only when their recognition is expedient. A truth must always be preferred to a falsehood when both relate to the situation; but when neither does, truth is as little of a duty as falsehood. . . .

With this admission that there are conditions that limit the application of the abstract imperative, *the pragmatistic treatment of truth sweeps back upon us in its fulness.* Our duty to agree with reality is seen to be grounded in a perfect jungle of concrete expediencies. . . .

Our critics certainly need more imagination of realities. I have honestly tried to stretch my own imagination and to read the best possible meaning into the rationalist conception, but I have to confess that it still completely baffles me. The notion of a reality calling on us to "agree" with it, and that for no reasons, but simply because its claim is "unconditional" or "transcendent," is one that I can make neither head nor tail of. I try to imagine myself as the sole reality in the world, and then to imagine what more I would "claim" if I were allowed to. If you suggest the possibility of my claiming that a mind should come into being from out of the void inane and stand and *copy* me, I can indeed imagine what the copying might mean, but I can conjure up no motive. What good it would do me to be copied, or what good it would do that mind to copy me, if further consequences are expressly and in principle ruled out as motives for the claim (as they are by our rationalist authorities) I cannot fathom. . . . Copying is one genuine mode of knowing (which for some strange reason our contemporary transcendentalists seem to be tumbling over each other to repudiate); but when we get beyond copying, and fall back on unnamed forms of agreeing that are expressly denied to be either copyings or leadings or fittings, or any other processes pragmatically definable, the *what* of the "agreement" claimed becomes as unintelligible as the why of it. Neither content nor motive can be imagined for it. It is an absolutely meaningless abstraction.

Surely in this field of truth it is the pragmatists and not the rationalists who are the more genuine defenders of the universe's rationality.

# A. J. AYER AND POSITIVISM

A. J. Ayer (1910–1989) was one of the key early figures in analytic philosophy in Britain. His positivism threatened to expunge from philosophy large areas of inquiry— theology, ethics, political theory, and aesthetics. What makes A. J. Ayer's book *Language, Truth and Logic* remarkable, and certainly provocative, is his contention that a significant portion of the things we say about reality, whether truths about the world or facts about our lives, are neither true nor false, but quite *meaningless.*

Ayer's critique was applicable to all language users, whether philosophers or not. He thought, however, the greatest offenders of those who utter meaningless claims were metaphysicians (those who distinguish what is really real—true reality—from the ordinary world we see around us), philosophers of religion, and theologians. Ayer also placed those who made ethical and aesthetic claims on his list of nonsense speakers.

How exactly does Ayer distinguish between meaningful and meaningless sentences? He argued that nonsense comes about when someone makes claims, either verbally or in writing, "which fail to conform to the conditions under which alone a sentence can be literally significant." The basis he used to determine whether a sentence is significant was his so-called criterion of verifiability:

> We say that a sentence is factually significant to any given person, if, and only if, he knows how to verify the proposition which it purports to express—that is, if he knows what observations would lead him, under certain conditions, to accept the proposition as being true, or reject it as being false.

What are some examples of meaningless sentences? Ayer quotes a metaphysical assertion made by the philosopher F. H. Bradley in *Appearance and Reality:* "[T]he Absolute enters into, but is itself incapable of, evolution and progress." Some more examples of meaningless metaphysical questions are arguments over whether humans have a soul, whether the mind is separate from the brain, whether humans have free will, and what the nature of God is. Perhaps you have heard of an infamous metaphysical debate from the Middle Ages: How many angels can dance on the head of a pin? Some examples of meaningless sentences in ethics and aesthetics include "Morality should strive toward the Good" or "True art captures what is intrinsic to the beautiful."

Let's test Ayer's criterion. What do you think of when you read these two examples taken from ethics and aesthetics? Do they make sense to you? How would we be able to determine if what they purport is true or not? Can you explain exactly what these claims are trying to say? What do they *mean?* Putting the problem a bit differently, if you think they make sense, but your friend Tracy doesn't, how would you resolve the disagreement? What items or objects in the real world would you check or point to in order to convince her you're right? Indeed, is there any way the dispute could be resolved by referring to facts independent of our assumptions?

Ayer said we are not able to explain what these assertions mean because there is nothing in the empirical world to which these sentences refer. Unless there is some empirical observation that can be used to determine whether or not these claims are true, we cannot consider them *genuine* statements. As we will see, the exception here could be a *tautology,* a statement that is true by definition, for example, "All red roses are red." However, the previous sentences are not tautologies.

If you still insist these sentences have meaning, Ayer says they only appear to have meaning because of their grammatical structure. It is possible for a sentence to give the impression that it refers to a real state of affairs, because we are tempted to assume language always speaks of something that *is.* Philosophers have called this the "bewitchment of language."

Was Ayer's test for the meaningfulness of claims correct? We'll see later that Ayer went too far in distinguishing between meaningful and meaningless claims; nevertheless, his position has some value. We only need to consider how people can be so easily swept up into a religious or political movement because of a gifted speaker or charismatic leader. Without actually considering how the words spoken can be verified, or shown to be true, people can be persuaded to perform extreme acts, even killing themselves or others. To this extent Ayer's verifiability criterion is a strong critique of propaganda and ideology.

Ayer had an interesting view of ethics, one out of step with the philosophical tradition. Despite the rigorous and tightly argued ethical positions of philosophers like Aristotle, Mill, and Kant, Ayer thought that how we reason in ethics is very different from how we normally reason in science.

Scientific investigation is a matter of empirical research and examination. The objects of scientific examination are out there in the real world. But what are the objects of morality? What kind of empirical state of affairs could be relevant to a claim such as "Adultery is wrong"? For Ayer, our ethical judgments are nothing more than expressions of our emotions. When you see someone stealing a bicycle, you say, "That's a terrible thing to do!" This reaction on your part means nothing more than someone who looks at a plate of cooked cow tongue and turnips and says, "Gross." The same thing occurs when you yell, "Yes!" when your favorite sports team scores. These are all just expressions of subjective emotions.

In the eighteenth century Francis Hutcheson and David Hume had already expressed a similar view about ethical claims (although mixed in with their view of ethics was the theory of moral sympathy, as we'll see in our ethics chapter). Despite Hutcheson's and Hume's pioneering work on an "emotivist" theory of ethics, it wasn't until Ayer's time that this position was extensively examined by philosophers.

With his criterion for determining meaningful claims, Ayer believed he could dispense with metaphysical and theological nonsense. Moreover, he thought he could show how ethical and aesthetic judgments are only affirmations of emotion, not of logical certainty or of fact.

Ayer's position was not without its critics. One of the more articulate was the Jesuit philosopher Father Frederick Copleston. Father Copleston is best known for his invaluable *History of Philosophy*—a commentary on the great minds and ideas in the history of philosophy. If you want more help understanding philosophy, these volumes are easy to find in most used-book stores (they should be cheap too!).

Father Copleston was also an able debater, having taken on both Ayer and the famous philosopher Bertrand Russell. Russell, like Ayer, was very skeptical about religious belief. The debates between Copleston, Ayer, and Russell are still included in some philosophy texts and are well worth reading. Regarding Ayer, Father Copleston had some pointed responses.

First, Copleston asked Ayer whether his criterion for determining the meaningfulness of a claim could survive its own test for meaningfulness. Let's repeat Ayer's position:

> We say that a sentence is factually significant to any given person, if, and only if, he knows how to verify the proposition which it purports to express—that is, if he knows what observations would lead him, under certain conditions, to accept the proposition as being true, or reject it as being false.

Father Copleston asked rhetorically, "Is this a tautology? true by definition?" Certainly not. There's nothing illogical about supposing it to be false. Can we point to some empirical fact that might at least in theory prove Ayer's criterion to be true or false? Again, the answer is no. Therefore the criterion fails by its own standards.

Father Copleston wasn't finished with his examination. He added that there are many things we say that remain meaningful although we may not be able to verify them. He gave the example that "the proliferation of the arms race may some day result in nuclear warfare and the total annihilation of humankind." Do you see the problem Copleston is raising?

Most of us would find this warning meaningful, and as a consequence, quite a frightening thought. The problem, for Ayer, is that a claim such as this can only be verified when everyone has been vaporized in a nuclear holocaust. But if everyone has been vaporized, no one would be left to verify the claim.

Although Ayer's position has some important difficulties, his view has a certain value, at least in its pared-down, more humble version. For example, when someone tells us something we find rather unbelievable, it's a smart thing to wonder under what conditions we would be able to determine the truthfulness of what is being claimed. This is the biggest problem with conspiracy theories or claims such as Elvis is still alive or aliens are controlling our thought patterns. There is good reason for supposing they are neither true nor false because there is no empirical state of affairs that could decisively disprove them. They are appeals to believe something justified not by reasons, reality, or facts but rather by unreflective emotions, psychological quirks, or warped personalities. Ayer was right to think we should consider such claims to be meaningless.

# The Elimination of Metaphysics

## A. J. AYER

### *Preface to First Edition*

The views which are put forward in this treatise derive from the doctrines of Bertrand Russell and Wittgenstein, which are themselves the logical outcome of the empiricism of Berkeley and David Hume. Like Hume, I divide all genuine propositions into two classes: those which, in his terminology, concern "relations of ideas," and those which concern "matters of fact." The former class comprises the *a priori* propositions of

SOURCE: A. J. Ayer, *Language, Truth and Logic* (New York: Dover Books, 1946), "Preface to First Edition" and chap. 1, "The Elimination of Metaphysics," pp. 31–32, 33–45. Reprinted by permission of Dover Publications, Inc.

logic and pure mathematics, and these I allow to be necessary and certain only because they are analytic. That is, I maintain that the reason why these propositions cannot be confuted in experience is that they do not make any assertion about the empirical world, but simply record our determination to use symbols in a certain fashion. Propositions concerning empirical matters of fact, on the other hand, I hold to be hypotheses, which can be probable but never certain. And in giving an account of the method of their validation I claim also to have explained the nature of truth.

To test whether a sentence expresses a genuine empirical hypothesis, I adopt what may be called a modified verification principle. For I require of an empirical hypothesis, not indeed that it should be conclusively verifiable, but that some possible sense-experience should be relevant to the determination of its truth or falsehood. If a putative proposition fails to satisfy this principle, and is not a tautology, then I hold that it is metaphysical, and that, being metaphysical, it is neither true nor false but literally senseless. It will be found that much of what ordinarily passes for philosophy is metaphysical according to this criterion, and, in particular, that it can not be significantly asserted that there is a non-empirical world of values, or that men have immortal souls, or that there is a transcendent God.

As for the propositions of philosophy themselves, they are held to be linguistically necessary, and so analytic. And with regard to the relationship of philosophy and empirical science . . . the philosopher is not in a position to furnish speculative truths, which would, as it were, compete with the hypotheses of science, nor yet to pass *a priori* judgements upon the validity of scientific theories, but that his function is to clarify the propositions of science by exhibiting their logical relationships, and by defining the symbols which occur in them. Consequently I maintain that there is nothing in the nature of philosophy to warrant the existence of conflicting philosophical "schools." And I attempt to substantiate this by providing a definitive solution of the problems which have been the chief sources of controversy between philosophers in the past.

The view that philosophizing is an activity of analysis is associated in England with the work of G. E. Moore and his disciples. But while I have learned a great deal from Professor Moore, I have reason to believe that he and his followers are not prepared to adopt such a thoroughgoing phenomenalism as I do, and that they take a rather different view of the nature of philosophical analysis. The philosophers with whom I am in the closest agreement are those who compose the "Viennese circle," under the leadership of Moritz Schlick, and are commonly known as logical positivists. And of these I owe most to Rudolf Carnap. Further, I wish to acknowledge my indebtedness to Gilbert Ryle, my original tutor in philosophy, and to Isaiah Berlin, who have discussed with me every point in the argument of this treatise, and made many valuable suggestions, although they both disagree with much of what I assert. . . .

A. J. Ayer
11 Foubert's Place, London
*July 1935*

## The Elimination of Metaphysics

The traditional disputes of philosophers are, for the most part, as unwarranted as they are unfruitful. The surest way to end them is to establish beyond question what should be the purpose and method of a philosophical enquiry. And this is by no means so difficult a task as the history of philosophy would lead one to suppose. For if there are any questions which science leaves it to philosophy to answer, a straightforward process of elimination must lead to their discovery.

We may begin by criticising the metaphysical thesis that philosophy affords us knowledge of a reality transcending the world of science and common sense. Later on, when we come to define metaphysics and account for its existence, we shall find that it is possible to be a metaphysician without believing in a transcendent reality; for we shall see that many metaphysical utterances are due to the commission of logical errors, rather than to a conscious desire on the part of their authors to go beyond the limits of experience. But it is convenient for us to take the case of those who believe that it is possible to have knowledge of a transcendent reality as a starting-point for our discussion. The arguments which we use to refute them will subsequently be found to apply to the whole of metaphysics.

One way of attacking a metaphysician who claimed to have knowledge of a reality which transcended the phenomenal world would be to enquire from what premises his propositions were deduced. Must he not begin, as other men do, with the evidence of his senses? And if so, what valid process of reasoning can possibly lead him to the conception of a transcendent reality? Surely from empirical premises nothing whatsoever concerning the properties, or even the existence, of anything super-empirical can legitimately be inferred. But this objection would be met by a denial on the part of the metaphysician that his assertions were ultimately based on the evidence of his senses. He would say that he was endowed with a faculty of intellectual intuition which enabled him to know facts that could not be known through sense-experience. And even if it could be shown that he was relying on empirical premises, and that his venture into a non-empirical world was therefore logically unjustified, it would not follow that the assertions which he made concerning this non-empirical world could not be true. For the fact that a conclusion does not follow from its putative premise is not sufficient to show that it is false. Consequently one cannot overthrow a system of transcendent metaphysics merely by criticising the way in which it comes into being. What is required is rather a criticism of the nature of the actual statements which comprise it. And this is the line of argument which we shall, in fact, pursue. For we shall maintain that no statement which refers to a "reality" transcending the limits of all possible sense-experience can possibly have any literal significance; from which it must follow that the labours of those who have striven to describe such a reality have all been devoted to the production of nonsense.

It may be suggested that this is a proposition which has already been proved by Kant. But although Kant also condemned transcendent metaphysics, he did so on different grounds. For he said that the human understanding was so constituted that it lost itself in contradictions when it ventured out beyond the limits of possible experience and attempted to deal with things in themselves. And thus he made the impossibility of a transcendent metaphysic not, as we do, a matter of logic, but a matter of fact. He asserted, not that our minds could not conceivably have had the power of penetrating beyond the phenomenal world, but merely that they were in fact devoid of it. And this leads the critic to ask how, if it is possible to know only what lies within the bounds of sense-experience, the author can be justified in asserting that real things do exist beyond, and how he can tell what are the boundaries beyond which the human understanding may not venture, unless he succeeds in passing them himself. As Wittgenstein says, "in order to draw a limit to thinking, we should have to think both sides of this limit," [1] a truth to which Bradley gives a special twist in maintaining that the man who is ready to prove that metaphysics is impossible is a brother metaphysician with a rival theory of his own. [2]

Whatever force these objections may have against the Kantian doctrine, they have none whatsoever against the thesis that I am about to set forth. It cannot here be said that the author is himself overstepping the barrier he maintains to be impassable. For the fruitlessness of attempting to transcend the limits of possible sense-experience will be deduced, not from a psychological hypothesis concerning the actual constitution of the human mind, but from the rule which determines the literal significance of language. Our charge against the metaphysician is not that he attempts to employ the understanding in a field where it cannot profitably venture, but that he produces sentences which fail to conform to the conditions under which alone a sentence can be literally significant. Nor are we ourselves obliged to talk nonsense in order to show that all sentences of a certain type are nec-

---

[1] *Tractatus Logico-Philosophicus*, Preface.
[2] Bradley, *Appearance and Reality*, 2nd ed., p. 1.

essarily devoid of literal significance. We need only formulate the criterion which enables us to test whether a sentence expresses a genuine proposition about a matter of fact, and then point out that the sentences under consideration fail to satisfy it. And this we shall now proceed to do. We shall first of all formulate the criterion in somewhat vague terms, and then give the explanations which are necessary to render it precise.

The criterion which we use to test the genuineness of apparent statements of fact is the criterion of verifiability. We say that a sentence is factually significant to any given person, if, and only if, he knows how to verify the proposition which it purports to express—that is, if he knows what observations would lead him, under certain conditions, to accept the proposition as being true, or reject it as being false. If, on the other hand, the putative proposition is of such a character that the assumption of its truth, or falsehood, is consistent with any assumption whatsoever concerning the nature of his future experience, then, as far as he is concerned, it is, if not a tautology, a mere pseudo-proposition. The sentence expressing it may be emotionally significant to him; but it is not literally significant. And with regard to questions the procedure is the same. We enquire in every case what observations would lead us to answer the question, one way or the other; and, if none can be discovered, we must conclude that the sentence under consideration does not, as far as we are concerned, express a genuine question, however strongly its grammatical appearance may suggest that it does.

As the adoption of this procedure is an essential factor in the argument of this book, it needs to be examined in detail.

In the first place, it is necessary to draw a distinction between practical verifiability, and verifiability in principle. Plainly we all understand, in many cases believe, propositions which we have not in fact taken steps to verify. Many of these are propositions which we could verify if we took enough trouble. But there remain a number of significant propositions, concerning matters of fact, which we could not verify even if we chose;

simply because we lack the practical means of placing ourselves in the situation where the relevant observations could be made. A simple and familiar example of such a proposition is the proposition that there are mountains on the farther side of the moon.[3] No rocket has yet been invented which would enable me to go and look at the farther side of the moon, so that I am unable to decide the matter by actual observation. But I do know what observations would decide it for me, if, as is theoretically conceivable, I were once in a position to make them. And therefore I say that the proposition is verifiable in principle, if not in practice, and is accordingly significant. On the other hand, such a metaphysical pseudo-proposition as "the Absolute enters into, but is itself incapable of, evolution and progress,"[4] is not even in principle verifiable. For one cannot conceive of an observation which would enable one to determine whether the Absolute did, or did not, enter into evolution and progress. Of course it is possible that the author of such a remark is using English words in a way in which they are not commonly used by English-speaking people, and that he does, in fact, intend to assert something which could be empirically verified. But until he makes us understand how the proposition that he wishes to express would be verified, he fails to communicate anything to us. And if he admits, as I think the author of the remark in question would have admitted, that his words were not intended to express either a tautology or a proposition which was capable, at least in principle, of being verified, then it follows that he has made an utterance which has no literal significance even for himself.

A further distinction which we must make is the distinction between the "strong" and the "weak" sense of the term "verifiable." A proposition is said to be verifiable, in the strong sense of the term, if, and only if, its truth could be conclusively established in experience. But it is verifiable, in the weak sense, if it is possible for

[3] This example has been used by Professor Schlick to illustrate the same point.

[4] A remark taken at random from *Appearance and Reality,* by F. H. Bradley.

experience to render it probable. In which sense are we using the term when we say that a putative proposition is genuine only if it is verifiable?

It seems to me that if we adopt conclusive verifiability as our criterion of significance, as some positivists have proposed,[5] our argument will prove too much. Consider, for example, the case of general propositions of law—such propositions, namely, as "arsenic is poisonous"; "all men are mortal"; "a body tends to expand when it is heated." It is of the very nature of these propositions that their truth cannot be established with certainty by any finite series of observations. But if it is recognised that such general propositions of law are designed to cover an infinite number of cases, then it must be admitted that they cannot, even in principle, be verified conclusively. And then, if we adopt conclusive verifiability as our criterion of significance, we are logically obliged to treat these general propositions of law in the same fashion as we treat the statements of the metaphysician.

In face of this difficulty, some positivists[6] have adopted the heroic course of saying that these general propositions are indeed pieces of nonsense, albeit an essentially important type of nonsense. But here the introduction of the term "important" is simply an attempt to hedge. It serves only to mark the authors' recognition that their view is somewhat too paradoxical, without in any way removing the paradox. Besides, the difficulty is not confined to the case of general propositions of law, though it is there revealed most plainly. It is hardly less obvious in the case of propositions about the remote past. For it must surely be admitted that, however strong the evidence in favour of historical statements may be, their truth can never become more than highly probable. And to maintain that they also constituted an important, or unimportant, type of nonsense would be unplausible, to say the very

least. Indeed, it will be our contention that no proposition, other than a tautology, can possibly be anything more than a probable hypothesis. And if this is correct, the principle that a sentence can be factually significant only if it expresses what is conclusively verifiable is self-stultifying as a criterion of significance. For it leads to the conclusion that it is impossible to make a significant statement of fact at all.

Nor can we accept the suggestion that a sentence should be allowed to be factually significant if, and only if, it expresses something which is definitely confutable by experience.[7] Those who adopt this course assume that, although no finite series of observations is ever sufficient to establish the truth of a hypothesis beyond all possibility of doubt, there are crucial cases in which a single observation, or series of observations, can definitely confute it. But, as we shall show later on, this assumption is false. A hypothesis cannot be conclusively confuted any more than it can be conclusively verified. For when we take the occurrence of certain observations as proof that a given hypothesis is false, we presuppose the existence of certain conditions. And though, in any given case, it may be extremely improbable that this assumption is false, it is not logically impossible. We shall see that there need be no self-contradiction in holding that some of the relevant circumstances are other than we have taken them to be, and consequently that the hypothesis has not really broken down. And if it is not the case that any hypothesis can be definitely confuted, we cannot hold that the genuineness of a proposition depends on the possibility of its definite confutation.

Accordingly, we fall back on the weaker sense of verification. We say that the question that must be asked about any putative statement of fact is not, "Would any observations make its truth or falsehood logically certain?" but simply, "Would any observations be relevant to the determination of its truth or falsehood?" And it is only if a

[5] E.g., M. Schlick, "Positivismus und Realismus," *Erkenntnis,* Vol. 1, 1930. F. Waismann, "Logische Analyse des Warscheinlichkeitsbegriffs," *Erkenntnis,* Vol. 1, 1930.
[6] E.g., M. Schlick, "Die Kausalität in der gegenwärtigen Physik," *Naturwissenschaft,* Vol. 19, 1931.

[7] This has been proposed by Karl Popper in his *Logik der Forschung.*

negative answer is given to this second question that we conclude that the statement under consideration is nonsensical.

To make our position clearer, we may formulate it in another way. Let us call a proposition which records an actual or possible observation an experiential proposition. Then we may say that it is the mark of a genuine factual proposition, not that it should be equivalent to an experiential proposition, or any finite number of experiential propositions, but simply that some experiential propositions can be deduced from it in conjunction with certain other premises without being deducible from those other premises alone.[8]

This criterion seems liberal enough. In contrast to the principle of conclusive verifiability, it clearly does not deny significance to general propositions or to propositions about the past. Let us see what kinds of assertion it rules out.

A good example of the kind of utterance that is condemned by our criterion as being not even false but nonsensical would be the assertion that the world of sense-experience was altogether unreal. It must, of course, be admitted that our senses do sometimes deceive us. We may, as the result of having certain sensations, expect certain other sensations to be obtainable which are, in fact, not obtainable. But, in all such cases, it is further sense-experience that informs us of the mistakes that arise out of sense-experience. We say that the senses sometimes deceive us, just because the expectations to which our sense-experiences give rise do not always accord with what we subsequently experience. That is, we rely on our senses to substantiate or confute the judgements which are based on our sensations. And therefore the fact that our perceptual judgements are sometimes found to be erroneous has not the slightest tendency to show that the world of sense-experience is unreal. And, indeed, it is plain that no conceivable observation, or se-

ries of observations, could have any tendency to show that the world revealed to us by sense-experience was unreal. Consequently, anyone who condemns the sensible world as a world of mere appearance, as opposed to reality, is saying something which, according to our criterion of significance, is literally nonsensical.

An example of a controversy which the application of our criterion obliges us to condemn as fictitious is provided by those who dispute concerning the number of substances that there are in the world. For it is admitted both by monists, who maintain that reality is one substance, and by pluralists, who maintain that reality is many, that it is impossible to imagine any empirical situation which would be relevant to the solution of their dispute. But if we are told that no possible observation could give any probability either to the assertion that reality was one substance or to the assertion that it was many, then we must conclude that neither assertion is significant. We shall see later on[9] that there are genuine logical and empirical questions involved in the dispute between monists and pluralists. But the metaphysical question concerning "substance" is ruled out by our criterion as spurious.

A similar treatment must be accorded to the controversy between realists and idealists, in its metaphysical aspect. A simple illustration, which I have made use of in a similar argument elsewhere,[10] will help to demonstrate this. Let us suppose that a picture is discovered and the suggestion made that it was painted by Goya. There is a definite procedure for dealing with such a question. The experts examine the picture to see in what way it resembles the accredited works of Goya, and to see if it bears any marks which are characteristic of a forgery; they look up contemporary records for evidence of the existence of such a picture, and so on. In the end, they may still disagree, but each one knows what empirical evidence would go to confirm or discredit

---

[8] This is an over-simplified statement, which is not literally correct. I give what I believe to be the correct formulation in the Introduction. . . .

[9] In Chapter 8.
[10] See "Demonstration of the Impossibility of Metaphysics," *Mind*, 1934, p. 339.

his opinion. Suppose, now, that these men have studied philosophy, and some of them proceed to maintain that this picture is a set of ideas in the perceiver's mind, or in God's mind, others that it is objectively real. What possible experience could any of them have which would be relevant to the solution of this dispute one way or the other? In the ordinary sense of the term "real," in which it is opposed to "illusory," the reality of the picture is not in doubt. The disputants have satisfied themselves that the picture is real, in this sense, by obtaining a correlated series of sensations of sight and sensations of touch. Is there any similar process by which they could discover whether the picture was real, in the sense in which the term "real" is opposed to "ideal"? Clearly there is none. But, if that is so, the problem is fictitious according to our criterion. This does not mean that the realist-idealist controversy may be dismissed without further ado. For it can legitimately be regarded as a dispute concerning the analysis of existential propositions, and so as involving a logical problem which, as we shall see, can be definitively solved.[11] What we have just shown is that the question at issue between idealists and realists becomes fictitious when, as is often the case, it is given a metaphysical interpretation.

There is no need for us to give further examples of the operation of our criterion of significance. For our object is merely to show that philosophy, as a genuine branch of knowledge, must be distinguished from metaphysics. We are not now concerned with the historical question how much of what has traditionally passed for philosophy is actually metaphysical. We shall, however, point out later on that the majority of the "great philosophers" of the past were not essentially metaphysicians, and thus reassure those who would otherwise be prevented from adopting our criterion by considerations of piety.

As to the validity of the verification principle, in the form in which we have stated it, a demonstration will be given in the course of this book. For it will be shown that all propositions which

have factual content are empirical hypotheses; and that the function of an empirical hypothesis is to provide a rule for the anticipation of experience.[12] And this means that every empirical hypothesis must be relevant to some actual, or possible, experience, so that a statement which is not relevant to any experience is not an empirical hypothesis, and accordingly has no factual content. But this is precisely what the principle of verifiability asserts.

It should be mentioned here that the fact that the utterances of the metaphysician are nonsensical does not follow simply from the fact that they are devoid of factual content. It follows from that fact, together with the fact that they are not *a priori* propositions. And in assuming that they are not *a priori* propositions, we are once again anticipating the conclusions of a later chapter in this book.[13] For it will be shown there that *a priori* propositions, which have always been attractive to philosophers on account of their certainty, owe this certainty to the fact that they are tautologies. We may accordingly define a metaphysical sentence as a sentence which purports to express a genuine proposition, but does, in fact, express neither a tautology nor an empirical hypothesis. And as tautologies and empirical hypotheses form the entire class of significant propositions, we are justified in concluding that all metaphysical assertions are nonsensical. Our next task is to show how they come to be made.

The use of the term "substance," to which we have already referred, provides us with a good example of the way in which metaphysics mostly comes to be written. It happens to be the case that we cannot, in our language, refer to the sensible properties of a thing without introducing a word or phrase which appears to stand for the thing itself as opposed to anything which may be said about it. And, as a result of this, those who are infected by the primitive superstition that to every name a single real entity must correspond assume that it is necessary to distinguish logically between the thing itself and any, or all, of its sen-

---

[11] See Chapter 8.

[12] See Chapter 6.
[13] Chapter 4.

sible properties. And so they employ the term "substance" to refer to the thing itself. But from the fact that we happen to employ a single word to refer to a thing, and make that word the grammatical subject of the sentences in which we refer to the sensible appearances of the thing, it does not by any means follow that the thing itself is a "simple entity," or that it cannot be defined in terms of the totality of its appearances. It is true that in talking of "its" appearances we appear to distinguish the thing from the appearances, but that is simply an accident of linguistic usage. Logical analysis shows that what makes these "appearances" the "appearances of" the same thing is not their relationship to an entity other than themselves, but their relationship to one another. The metaphysician fails to see this because he is misled by a superficial grammatical feature of his language.

A simpler and clearer instance of the way in which a consideration of grammar leads to metaphysics is the case of the metaphysical concept of Being. The origin of our temptation to raise questions about Being, which no conceivable experience would enable us to answer, lies in the fact that, in our language, sentences which express existential propositions and sentences which express attributive propositions may be of the same grammatical form. For instance, the sentences "Martyrs exist" and "Martyrs suffer" both consist of a noun followed by an intransitive verb, and the fact that they have grammatically the same appearance leads one to assume that they are of the same logical type. It is seen that in the proposition "Martyrs suffer," the members of a certain species are credited with a certain attribute, and it is sometimes assumed that the same thing is true of such a proposition as "Martyrs exist." If this were actually the case, it would, indeed, be as legitimate to speculate about the Being of martyrs as it is to speculate about their suffering. But, as Kant pointed out,[14] existence is not an attribute. For, when we ascribe an attribute to a thing, we covertly assert that it exists: so

that if existence were itself an attribute, it would follow that all positive existential propositions were tautologies, and all negative existential propositions self-contradictory; and this is not the case.[15] So that those who raise questions about Being which are based on the assumption that existence is an attribute are guilty of following grammar beyond the boundaries of sense.

A similar mistake has been made in connection with such propositions as "Unicorns are fictitious." Here again the fact that there is a superficial grammatical resemblance between the English sentences "Dogs are faithful" and "Unicorns are fictitious," and between the corresponding sentences in other languages, creates the assumption that they are of the same logical type. Dogs must exist in order to have the property of being faithful, and so it is held that unless unicorns in some way existed they could not have the property of being fictitious. But, as it is plainly self-contradictory to say that fictitious objects exist, the device is adopted of saying that they are real in some non-empirical sense—that they have a mode of real being which is different from the mode of being of existent things. But since there is no way of testing whether an object is real in this sense, as there is for testing whether it is real in the ordinary sense, the assertion that fictitious objects have a special non-empirical mode of real being is devoid of all literal significance. It comes to be made as a result of the assumption that being fictitious is an attribute. And this is a fallacy of the same order as the fallacy of supposing that existence is an attribute, and it can be exposed in the same way.

In general, the postulation of real non-existent entities results from the superstition, just now referred to, that, to every word or phrase that can be the grammatical subject of a sentence, there must somewhere be a real entity corresponding. For as there is no place in the empirical world for many of these "entities," a special non-empirical world is invoked to house them. To this error must be attributed, not only

[14] See *The Critique of Pure Reason,* "Transcendental Dialectic," Book 2, Chapter 3, section 4.

[15] This argument is well stated by John Wisdom, *Interpretation and Analysis,* pp. 62, 63.

the utterances of a Heidegger, who bases his metaphysics on the assumption that "Nothing" is a name which is used to denote something peculiarly mysterious,[16] but also the prevalence of such problems as those concerning the reality of propositions and universals whose senselessness, though less obvious, is no less complete.

These few examples afford a sufficient indication of the way in which most metaphysical assertions come to be formulated. They show how easy it is to write sentences which are literally nonsensical without seeing that they are nonsensical. And thus we see that the view that a number of the traditional "problems of philosophy" are metaphysical, and consequently fictitious, does not involve any incredible assumptions about the psychology of philosophers.

Among those who recognise that if philosophy is to be accounted a genuine branch of knowledge it must be defined in such a way as to distinguish it from metaphysics, it is fashionable to speak of the metaphysician as a kind of misplaced poet. As his statements have no literal meaning, they are not subject to any criteria of truth or falsehood: but they may still serve to express, or arouse, emotion, and thus be subject to ethical or aesthetic standards. And it is suggested that they may have considerable value, as means of moral inspiration, or even as works of art. In this way, an attempt is made to compensate the metaphysician for his extrusion from philosophy.[17]

I am afraid that this compensation is hardly in accordance with his deserts. The view that the metaphysician is to be reckoned among the poets appears to rest on the assumption that both talk nonsense. But this assumption is false. In the vast majority of cases the sentences which are produced by poets do have literal meaning. The difference between the man who uses language scientifically and the man who uses it emotively is not that the one produces sentences which are incapable of arousing emotion, and the other sentences which have no sense, but that the one is primarily concerned with the expression of true propositions, the other with the creation of a work of art. Thus, if a work of science contains true and important propositions, its value as a work of science will hardly be diminished by the fact that they are inelegantly expressed. And similarly, a work of art is not necessarily the worse for the fact that all the propositions comprising it are literally false. But to say that many literary works are largely composed of falsehoods, is not to say that they are composed of pseudo-propositions. It is, in fact, very rare for a literary artist to produce sentences which have no literal meaning. And where this does occur, the sentences are carefully chosen for their rhythm and balance. If the author writes nonsense, it is because he considers it most suitable for bringing about the effects for which his writing is designed.

The metaphysician, on the other hand, does not intend to write nonsense. He lapses into it through being deceived by grammar, or through committing errors of reasoning, such as that which leads to the view that the sensible world is unreal. But it is not the mark of a poet simply to make mistakes of this sort. There are some, indeed, who would see in the fact that the metaphysician's utterances are senseless a reason against the view that they have aesthetic value. And, without going so far as this, we may safely say that it does not constitute a reason for it.

It is true, however, that although the greater part of metaphysics is merely the embodiment of humdrum errors, there remain a number of metaphysical passages which are the work of genuine mystical feeling; and they may more plausibly be held to have moral or aesthetic value. But, as far as we are concerned, the distinction between the kind of metaphysics that is produced by a philosopher who has been duped by grammar, and the kind that is produced by a mystic

---

[16] See *Was ist Metaphysik,* by Heidegger: criticised by Rudolf Carnap in his "Überwindung der Metaphysik durch logische Analyse der Sprache," *Erkenntnis,* Vol. 2, 1932.

[17] For a discussion of this point, see also C. A. Mace, "Representation and Expression," *Analysis,* Vol. 1, No. 3; and "Metaphysics and Emotive Language," *Analysis,* Vol. 2, Nos. 1 and 2.

who is trying to express the inexpressible, is of no great importance: what is important to us is to realise that even the utterances of the metaphysician who is attempting to expound a vision are literally senseless; so that henceforth we may pursue our philosophical researches with as little regard for them as for the more inglorious kind of metaphysics which comes from a failure to understand the workings of our language.

# R. G. COLLINGWOOD'S IDEA OF HISTORY

Robin George Collingwood (1888–1943) actively explored and published on a diverse collection of questions. He was not only a philosopher but also a working archeologist and historian who was principally interested in the history of Britain under the Romans. He spent considerable time in the English countryside scraping and dusting ancient coins, monuments, and other relics from the ancient Roman occupation of the island. This time was well spent, for his work in archeology helped him to sort out a central epistemological question in the philosophy of history: How can we know the past?

Even within philosophy proper, Collingwood wrote on a wide variety of issues. *The Idea of History* (1945) is the most discussed book on the philosophy of history published in the last century. His youthful work *Speculum Mentis* (1924) argues there are five distinct forms of knowledge that have five distinct ways of knowing their objects—art, religion, science, history, and philosophy. *An Essay on Metaphysics* (1940) urges metaphysicians to give up their search for a "science of being" in exchange for seeing metaphysics as a historical endeavor; *The Principles of Art* (1938) sees art as the expression of our emotions; and *The New Leviathan* (1942), written in part during the Battle of Britain, is a defense of liberal civilization against fascism.

The background of Collingwood's epistemological dilemma with regard to history was his rejection of positivism. Remember that Ayer thought only those sentences that could be verified by sense experience counted as meaningful. Yet statements about the past are all about events finished and nonrepeatable, even if people stage tame reenactments of them (as Civil War reenactors do with battles such as Gettysburg and Bull Run). How would we be able to verify, by direct experience, a claim such as "in 1492 Columbus sailed the ocean blue"? We could try rounding up a bunch of our positivist friends, driving to strategically located points along the east coast of North America, and then spend some time staring across the Atlantic in the general direction of Spain. However, none of us will ever see Columbus's ships the *Niña,* the *Pinta,* and the *Santa María* plying their way through the waves to the New Land, no matter how intently we watch the eastern horizon.

The problem with knowing our historical past is pretty well the same as the problem a detective faces in investigating a crime. In neither case can we directly experience the phenomenon in question. Indeed, Collingwood makes this analogy explicit in *The Idea of History.*

Let's imagine there has been a murder at 19 Baker Street. Mary Graham's body was found in the kitchen cruelly stabbed with a large knife. No one saw anyone enter or leave the house that day or heard the murder taking place. A detective, who just happens to live next door, does some investigation and discovers that Mary has just broken up with her boyfriend, Jack Windsor, a professional boxer and part-time thug for a criminal gang. Jack denies having been in the area that day. The detective then examines the physical evidence and discovers that there is a large green smear of paint on Jack's coat and that the fence outside 19 Baker Street had just been painted an identical shade of green that morning. Further, although no one witnessed the murder, a neighbor heard the couple arguing violently several times over the last week and saw Mary stepping out with the suave and handsome James St. Clair the previous evening. Added to these facts is that Jack has been convicted twice of assault and has a large collection of Bowie knives in his apartment. Our detective puts two and two together and arrests Jack for the murder, despite the fact no one (other than Jack himself, who's not saying anything) can offer any direct sense experience that confirms he's guilty.

The point of the previous example is that in order to understand a past event, in this case a murder, we have to use current testimony and physical evidence to reconstruct it in our minds. Most important, the detective wants to know *why* the murder took place—in this case, because of jealousy. The detective wants to know what thoughts were in the murderer's head before he knows for sure who did the murder and how it was done. If he can figure this out, the details of the murder become clearer, and the physical evidence makes more sense. To do this he asks questions about the evidence and the crime: "Who would have a motive for killing Mary?"; "Who came and went from 19 Baker Street in the last few days?"; "Who were Mary's associates?"; and so on.

In the following selection, "Human Nature and Human History," taken from *The Idea of History,* Collingwood starts by arguing that the project conceived by Enlightenment thinkers such as Locke, Hume, and Kant to develop a "science of human nature" was hopelessly flawed. Their failure did not result because we can't know the human mind or because psychology was too primitive in their day to act as a basis for such a science, but because the analogy between understanding the human mind and the methods of the physical sciences was false. One cannot apply scientific laws to human thinking and human action.

For Collingwood we can know the human mind only through history, not physical science. Science can explain the way physical objects and processes interact and the physical causes of things, but not human reasons and intentions. It can answer the *what* question (e.g., "What chemical compounds make up a human hair?"), but not the *why* question (e.g., "Why did you get a haircut this morning?"). In natural processes the past dies, being replaced by the present—one dandelion in our front yard is plucked out by the gardener, but another grows to take its place, oblivious to the cruel fate of its flowery cousin. The dandelion has no understanding of the history of its species. But in historical processes the past survives in the present thanks to human thought. We can read Plato's *Republic* and try to understand what he was trying to say, even though he's been dead for over two millennia.

This led Collingwood to propose a distinction between the inside and the outside of a historical event. The inside of an event is the thoughts in the actors' minds; the outside of the event is the collection of all bodies and the movements associated with them. The events of nature are mere phenomena with no thought-side. They have causes. But human actions have an outside, our physical movements, as well as an inside, our reasons and intentions for acting the way we do. We can summarize Collingwood's distinction between natural and historical events with the following chart.

| EVENT TYPE | CONTENT OF EVENT | EXPLANATION OF EVENT | STATUS OF THE PAST |
|---|---|---|---|
| Natural | The outside—the physical side of the event—which we can call "phenomena" or "mere events" | Causes or laws | Dead |
| Historical | The outside + the inside—the physical *and* the thought-sides of the event—"actions" | The reenactment of past thought | Survives |

Collingwood argued that to know the past, the historian has to critically examine such evidence as literary texts, diaries, government documents, coins, pottery, art, architecture, gravesites, and so on to lead us to the thoughts that historical actors were thinking at the time. We have to *reenact* those thoughts in our own minds in order to understand the "insides" of historical events. Collingwood's whole philosophy of history can be summarized in his three principles:

1. All history is the history of thought.
2. The history of thought, and therefore of all history, is the re-enactment of past thought in the historian's own mind.
3. Re-enactment is not the passive surrender to the spell of another mind, but an active and critical thinking: the historian re-enacts past thought in the light of his or her own knowledge, judges its value, criticizes it, corrects errors, and so on.

In this sense Collingwood is a "methodological" idealist—he believed that only by reenacting the ideas in the heads of historical actors can we understand their actions. Historical knowledge is a knowledge of ideas, not of physical facts. In any case, they are no longer present for us to examine. Realism in history is misplaced because the objects of historical knowledge—historical events—are not *real,* but *ideal.* And like the detective, the historian must critically examine these ideas in order to understand them.

Collingwood has been criticized for his idealism on several points. First, he seems to emphasize too much the rational side of human action; second, his philosophy of history is good at explaining individual actions, but not group or mass action; third, there seems to be a mystical side to Collingwood's suggestion that we can reenact past thinking. Scholars sympathetic to Collingwood have dealt with all of these criticisms with varying degrees of success.* Nevertheless, Collingwood's insistence that historical knowledge is a rational knowledge of the human mind, and not the outcome of investigations by physical science or psychology, is an important antidote to the empiricism and positivism that dominated much of twentieth-century philosophy.

*See Douglas Mann, "Reconstructing the Past, A Structural Idealist View of History," *Clio* 27 (1998), pp. 221–249; and chapter 4 of Douglas Mann, *Structural Idealism* (Waterloo, Ontario: Wilfrid Laurier University Press, 2002) for a detailed discussion of criticisms of Collingwood.

# Human Nature and Human History

## R. G. COLLINGWOOD

### 1. *The Science of Human Nature*

Man, who desires to know everything, desires to know himself. Nor is he only one (even if, to himself, perhaps the most interesting) among the things he desires to know. Without some knowledge of himself, his knowledge of other things is imperfect: for to know something without knowing that one knows it is only a half-knowing, and to know that one knows is to know oneself. Self-knowledge is desirable and important to man, not only for its own sake, but as a condition without which no other knowledge can be critically justified and securely based.

Self-knowledge, here, means not knowledge of man's bodily nature, his anatomy and physiology; nor even a knowledge of his mind, so far as that consists of feeling, sensation, and emotion; but a knowledge of his knowing faculties, his thought or understanding or reason. How is such knowledge to be attained? It seems an easy matter until we think seriously about it; and then it seems so difficult that we are tempted to think it impossible. Some have even reinforced this temptation by argument, urging that the mind, whose business it is to know other things, has for that very reason no power of knowing itself. But this is open sophistry: first you say what the mind's nature is, and then you say that because it has this nature no one can know that it has it. Actually, the argument is a counsel of despair, based on recognizing that a certain attempted method of studying the mind has broken down, and on failure to envisage the possibility of any other.

It seems a fair enough proposal that, in setting out to understand the nature of our own mind, we should proceed in the same way as when we try to understand the world about us. In studying the world of nature, we begin by getting ac-quainted with the particular things and particular events that exist and go on there; then we proceed to understand them, by seeing how they fall into general types and how these general types are interrelated. These interrelations we call laws of nature; and it is by ascertaining such laws that we understand the things and events to which they apply. The same method, it might seem, is applicable to the problem of understanding mind. Let us begin by observing, as carefully as possible, the ways in which our own minds and those of others behave under given circumstances; then, having become acquainted with these facts of the mental world, let us try to establish the laws which govern them.

Here is a proposal for a "science of human nature" whose principles and methods are conceived on the analogy of those used in the natural sciences. It is an old proposal, put forward especially in the seventeenth and eighteenth centuries, when the principles and methods of natural science had been lately perfected and were being triumphantly applied to the investigation of the physical world. When Locke undertook his inquiry into that faculty of understanding which "sets Man above the rest of sensible Beings, and gives him all the Advantage and Dominion which he has over them," the novelty of his project lay not in his desire for a knowledge of the human mind, but in his attempt to gain it by methods analogous to those of natural science: the collection of observed facts and their arrangement in classificatory schemes. His own description of his method as an "historical, plain Method" is perhaps ambiguous; but his follower Hume was at pains to make it clear that the method to be followed by the science of human nature was identical with the method of physical science as he

SOURCE: R. G. Collingwood, *The Idea of History,* rev. ed., ed. Jan van der Dussen (1936; Oxford: Oxford University Press, 1993), pp. 205–209, 213–220, 224, 226–231 (edited). Reprinted by permission of Oxford University Press.

conceived it: its "only solid foundation," he wrote, "must be laid on experience and observation." Reid, in his *Inquiry into the Human Mind,* was if possible even more explicit. "All that we know of the body, is owing to anatomical dissection and observation, and it must be by an anatomy of the mind that we can discover its powers and principles." And from these pioneers the whole English and Scottish tradition of a "philosophy of the human mind" was derived. . . .

It is evident that such a science of human nature, if it could attain even a tolerable approximation to the truth, could hope for results of extreme importance. As applied to the problems of moral and political life, for example, its results would certainly be no less spectacular than were the results of seventeenth-century physics when applied to the mechanical arts in the eighteenth century. This was fully realized by its promoters. Locke thought that by its means he could "prevail with the busy Mind of Man, to be more cautious in meddling with things exceeding its Comprehension; to stop, when it is at the utmost of its Tether; and to sit down in a quiet Ignorance of those Things, which, upon Examination, are found to be beyond the reach of our Capacities." At the same time, he was convinced that the powers of our understanding are sufficient for our needs "in this state," and can give us all the knowledge we require for "the comfortable provision for this life, and the way that leads to a better." . . .

Hume is even bolder. "'Tis evident," he writes, "that all the sciences have a relation, more or less, to human nature . . . since they lie under the cognizance of men, and are judged of by their powers and faculties. 'Tis impossible to tell what changes and improvements we might make in these sciences were we thoroughly acquainted with the extent and force of human understanding." And in sciences directly concerned with human nature, like morals and politics, his hopes of a beneficent revolution are proportionately higher. "In pretending, therefore, to explain the principles of human nature, we in effect propose a complete system of the sciences, built on a foundation almost entirely new, and the only

one upon which they can stand with any security." Kant, for all his habitual caution, claimed no less when he said that his new science would put an end to all the debates of the philosophical schools, and make it possible to solve all the problems of metaphysics at once and for ever.

It need not imply any underestimate of what these men actually achieved if we admit that these hopes were in the main unfulfilled, and that the science of human nature, from Locke to the present day, has failed to solve the problem of understanding what understanding is, and thus giving the human mind knowledge of itself. It was not through any lack of sympathy with its objects that so judicious a critic as John Grote found himself obliged to treat the "philosophy of the human mind" as a blind alley out of which it was the duty of thought to escape.

What was the reason for this failure? Some might say that it was because the undertaking was in principle a mistake: mind cannot know itself. This objection we have already considered. Others, notably the representatives of psychology, would say that the science of these thinkers was not sufficiently scientific: psychology was still in its infancy. But if we ask these same men to produce here and now the practical results for which those early students hoped, they excuse themselves by saying that psychology is still in its infancy. Here I think they wrong themselves and their own science. Claiming for it a sphere which it cannot effectively occupy, they belittle the work it has done and is doing in its proper field. . . .

There remains a third explanation: that the "science of human nature" broke down because its method was distorted by the analogy of the natural sciences. This I believe to be the right one.

It was no doubt inevitable that in the seventeenth and eighteenth centuries, dominated as they were by the new birth of physical science, the eternal problem of self-knowledge should take shape as the problem of constructing a science of human nature. To any one reviewing the field of human research, it was evident that physics stood out as a type of inquiry which had discovered the right method of investigating its proper object, and it was right that the experiment should be made of extending this method to every kind of problem. But since then a great change has come over the intellectual atmosphere of our civilization. The dominant factor in this change has not been the development of other natural sciences like chemistry and biology, or the transformation of physics itself since more began to be known about electricity, or the progressive application of all these new ideas to manufacture and industry, important though these have been; for in principle they have done nothing that might not have been foreseen as implicit in seventeenth-century physics itself. The really new element in the thought of to-day as compared with that of three centuries ago is the rise of history. It is true that the same Cartesian spirit which did so much for physics was already laying the foundations of critical method in history before the seventeenth century was out;[1] but the modern conception of history as a study at once critical and constructive, whose field is the human past in its entirety, and whose method is the reconstruction of that past from documents written and unwritten, critically analysed and interpreted, was not established until the nineteenth, and is even yet not fully worked out in all its implications. Thus history occupies in the world of to-day a position analogous to that occupied by physics in the time of Locke: it is recognized as a special and autonomous form of thought, lately established, whose possibilities have not yet been completely explored. And just as in the seventeenth and eighteenth centuries there were materialists, who argued from the success of physics in its own sphere that all reality was physical, so among ourselves the success of history has led some people to suggest that its methods are applicable to all the problems of knowledge, in other words, that all reality is historical.

This I believe to be an error. I think that those who assert it are making a mistake of the same kind which the materialists made in the seventeenth century. But I believe, and in this essay I

[1] "Historical criticism was born in the seventeenth century from the same intellectual movement as the philosophy of Descartes." E. Bréhier, in *Philosophy and History: Essays presented to Ernst Cassirer* (Oxford, 1936), p. 160.

shall try to show, that there is at least one important element of truth in what they say. The thesis which I shall maintain is that the science of human nature was a false attempt—falsified by the analogy of natural science—to understand the mind itself, and that, whereas the right way of investigating nature is by the methods called scientific, the right way of investigating mind is by the methods of history. I shall contend that the work which was to be done by the science of human nature is actually done, and can only be done, by history: that history is what the science of human nature professed to be, and that Locke was right when he said (however little he understood what he was saying) that the right method for such an inquiry is the historical, plain method.

## 2. The Field of Historical Thought

. . . The historian, investigating any event in the past, makes a distinction between what may be called the outside and the inside of an event. By the outside of the event I mean everything belonging to it which can be described in terms of bodies and their movements: the passage of Caesar, accompanied by certain men, across a river called the Rubicon at one date, or the spilling of his blood on the floor of the senate-house at another. By the inside of the event I mean that in it which can only be described in terms of thought: Caesar's defiance of Republican law, or the clash of constitutional policy between himself and his assassins. The historian is never concerned with either of these to the exclusion of the other. He is investigating not mere events (where by a mere event I mean one which has only an outside and no inside) but actions, and an action is the unity of the outside and inside of an event. He is interested in the crossing of the Rubicon only in its relation to Republican law, and in the spilling of Caesar's blood only in its relation to a constitutional conflict. His work may begin by discovering the outside of an event, but it can never end there; he must always remember that the event was an action, and that his main task is to think himself into this action, to discern the thought of its agent.

In the case of nature, this distinction between the outside and the inside of an event does not arise. The events of nature are mere events, not the acts of agents whose thought the scientist endeavours to trace. It is true that the scientist, like the historian, has to go beyond the mere discovery of events; but the direction in which he moves is very different. Instead of conceiving the event as an action and attempting to rediscover the thought of its agent, penetrating from the outside of the event to its inside, the scientist goes beyond the event, observes its relation to others, and thus brings it under a general formula or law of nature. To the scientist, nature is always and merely a "phenomenon," not in the sense of being defective in reality, but in the sense of being a spectacle presented to his intelligent observation; whereas the events of history are never mere phenomena, never mere spectacles for contemplation, but things which the historian looks, not at, but through, to discern the thought within them.

In thus penetrating to the inside of events and detecting the thought which they express, the historian is doing something which the scientist need not and cannot do. In this way the task of the historian is more complex than that of the scientist. In another way it is simpler: the historian need not and cannot (without ceasing to be an historian) emulate the scientist in searching for the causes or laws of events. For science, the event is discovered by perceiving it, and the further search for its cause is conducted by assigning it to its class and determining the relation between that class and others. For history, the object to be discovered is not the mere event, but the thought expressed in it. To discover that thought is already to understand it. After the historian has ascertained the facts, there is no further process of inquiring into their causes. When he knows what happened, he already knows why it happened.

This does not mean that words like "cause" are necessarily out of place in reference to history; it only means that they are used there in a special sense. When a scientist asks "Why did that piece of litmus paper turn pink?" he means "On what kinds of occasions do pieces of litmus paper turn pink?" When an historian asks "Why did Brutus stab Caesar?" he means "What did Brutus think, which made him decide to stab Caesar?" The cause of the event, for him, means the thought in the mind of the person by whose agency the event came about: and this is not something other than the event, it is the inside of the event itself.

The processes of nature can therefore be properly described as sequences of mere events, but those of history cannot. They are not processes of mere events but processes of actions, which have an inner side, consisting of processes of thought; and what the historian is looking for is these processes of thought. All history is the history of thought.

But how does the historian discern the thoughts which he is trying to discover? There is only one way in which it can be done: by re-thinking them in his own mind. The historian of philosophy, reading Plato, is trying to know what Plato thought when he expressed himself in certain words. The only way in which he can do this is by thinking it for himself. This, in fact, is what we mean when we speak of "understanding" the words. So the historian of politics or warfare, presented with an account of certain actions done by Julius Caesar, tries to understand these actions, that is, to discover what thoughts in Caesar's mind determined him to do them. This implies envisaging for himself the situation in which Caesar stood, and thinking for himself what Caesar thought about the situation and the possible ways of dealing with it. The history of thought, and therefore all history, is the re-enactment of past thought in the historian's own mind.

This re-enactment is only accomplished, in the case of Plato and Caesar respectively, so far as the historian brings to bear on the problem all the powers of his own mind and all his knowledge of philosophy and politics. It is not a passive surrender to the spell of another's mind; it is a labour of active and therefore critical thinking. The historian not only re-enacts past thought, he re-enacts it in the context of his own knowledge and therefore, in re-enacting it, criticizes it, forms his own judgement of its value, corrects whatever errors he can discern in it. This criticism of the thought whose history he traces is not something secondary to tracing the history of it. It is an indispensable condition of the historical knowledge itself. Nothing could be a completer error concerning the history of thought than to suppose that the historian as such merely ascertains "what so-and-so thought," leaving it to some one else to decide "whether it was true." All thinking is critical thinking; the thought which re-enacts past thoughts, therefore, criticizes them in re-enacting them. . . .

It does not follow that all human actions are subject-matter for history; and indeed historians are agreed that they are not. But when they are asked how the distinction is to be made between historical and non-historical human actions, they are somewhat at a loss how to reply. From our present point of view we can offer an answer: so far as man's conduct is determined by what may be called his animal nature, his impulses and appetites, it is non-historical; the process of those activities is a natural process. Thus, the historian is not interested in the fact that men eat and sleep and make love and thus satisfy their natural appetites; but he is interested in the social customs which they create by their thought as a framework within which these appetites find satisfaction in ways sanctioned by convention and morality.

Consequently, although the conception of evolution has revolutionized our idea of nature by substituting for the old conception of natural process as a change within the limits of a fixed system of specific forms the new conception of that process as involving a change in these forms themselves, it has by no means identified the idea of natural process with that of historical process; and the fashion, current not long ago, of using the word "evolution" in an historical context, and talking of the evolution of parliament or the like, though natural in an age when the science of nature was regarded as the only true form of knowledge, and when other forms of knowledge, in order to justify their existence, felt bound to assimilate themselves to that model, was the re-

sult of confused thinking and a source of further confusions.

There is only one hypothesis on which natural processes could be regarded as ultimately historical in character: namely, that these processes are in reality processes of action determined by a thought which is their own inner side. This would imply that natural events are expressions of thoughts, whether the thoughts of God, or of angelic or demonic finite intelligences, or of minds somewhat like our own inhabiting the organic and inorganic bodies of nature as our minds inhabit our bodies. Setting aside mere flights of metaphysical fancy, such an hypothesis could claim our serious attention only if it led to a better understanding of the natural world. In fact, however, the scientist can reasonably say of it *"je n'ai pas eu besoin de cette hypothèse,"* and the theologian will recoil from any suggestion that God's action in the natural world resembles the action of a finite human mind under the conditions of historical life. This at least is certain: that, so far as our scientific and historical knowledge goes, the processes of events which constitute the world of nature are altogether different in kind from the processes of thought which constitute the world of history.

## 3. History as Knowledge of Mind

History, then, is not, as it has so often been misdescribed, a story of successive events or an account of change. Unlike the natural scientist, the historian is not concerned with events as such at all. He is only concerned with those events which are the outward expression of thoughts, and is only concerned with these in so far as they express thoughts. At bottom, he is concerned with thoughts alone; with their outward expression in events he is concerned only by the way, in so far as these reveal to him the thoughts of which he is in search.

In a sense, these thoughts are no doubt themselves events happening in time; but since the only way in which the historian can discern them is by re-thinking them for himself, there is another sense, and one very important to the historian, in which they are not in time at all. If the discovery of Pythagoras concerning the square on the hypotenuse is a thought which we to-day can think for ourselves, a thought that constitutes a permanent addition to mathematical knowledge, the discovery of Augustus, that a monarchy could be grafted upon the Republican constitution of Rome by developing the implications of *proconsulare imperium* and *tribunicia potestas,* is equally a thought which the student of Roman history can think for himself, a permanent addition to political ideas. If Mr. Whitehead is justified in calling the right-angled triangle an eternal object, the same phrase is applicable to the Roman constitution and the Augustan modification of it. This is an eternal object because it can be apprehended by historical thought at any time; time makes no difference to it in this respect, just as it makes no difference to the triangle. The peculiarity which makes it historical is not the fact of its happening in time, but the fact of its becoming known to us by our re-thinking the same thought which created the situation we are investigating, and thus coming to understand that situation.

Historical knowledge is the knowledge of what mind has done in the past, and at the same time it is the redoing of this, the perpetuation of past acts in the present. Its object is therefore not a mere object, something outside the mind which knows it; it is an activity of thought, which can be known only in so far as the knowing mind re-enacts it and knows itself as so doing. To the historian, the activities whose history he is studying are not spectacles to be watched, but experiences to be lived through in his own mind; they are objective, or known to him, only because they are also subjective, or activities of his own.

It may thus be said that historical inquiry reveals to the historian the powers of his own mind. Since all he can know historically is thoughts that he can re-think for himself, the fact of his coming to know them shows him that his mind is able (or by the very effort of studying them has become able) to think in these ways. And conversely, whenever he finds certain historical matters unintelligible, he has discovered a limitation of his own mind; he has discovered that there are certain ways in which he is not, or no longer, or not yet, able to think. Certain historians, sometimes whole generations of historians, find in certain periods of history nothing intelligible, and call them dark ages; but such phrases tell us nothing about those ages themselves, though they tell us a great deal about the persons who use them, namely that they are unable to re-think the thoughts which were fundamental to their life. It has been said that *die Weltgeschichte ist das Weltgericht;* and it is true, but in a sense not always recognized. It is the historian himself who stands at the bar of judgement, and there reveals his own mind in its strength and weakness, its virtues and its vices.

But historical knowledge is not concerned only with a remote past. If it is by historical thinking that we re-think and so rediscover the thought of Hammurabi or Solon, it is in the same way that we discover the thought of a friend who writes us a letter, or a stranger who crosses the street. Nor is it necessary that the historian should be one person and the subject of his inquiry another. It is only by historical thinking that I can discover what I thought ten years ago, by reading what I then wrote, or what I thought five minutes ago, by reflecting on an action that I then did, which surprised me when I realized what I had done. In this sense, all knowledge of mind is historical. The only way in which I can know my own mind is by performing some mental act or other and then considering what the act is that I have performed. If I want to know what I think about a certain subject, I try to put my ideas about it in order, on paper or otherwise; and then, having thus arranged and formulated them, I can study the result as an historical document and see what my ideas were when I did that piece of thinking: if I am dissatisfied with them, I can do it over again. If I want to know what powers my mind possesses as yet unexplored, for example, whether I can write poetry, I must try to write some, and see whether it strikes me and others as being the real thing. If I want to know whether I am as good a man as I hope, or as bad as I fear, I must examine acts that I have done, and understand what they really were: or else go and do some fresh acts and then examine those. All these inquiries are historical.

They proceed by studying accomplished facts, ideas that I have thought out and expressed, acts that I have done. On what I have only begun and am still doing, no judgement can as yet be passed.

The same historical method is the only one by which I can know the mind of another, or the corporate mind (whatever exactly that phrase means) of a community or an age. To study the mind of the Victorian age or the English political spirit is simply to study the history of Victorian thought or English political activity. Here we come back to Locke and his "historical, plain Method." Mind not only declares, but also enjoys or possesses, its nature, both as mind in general and as this particular sort of mind with these particular dispositions and faculties, by thinking and acting, doing individual actions which express individual thoughts. If historical thinking is the way in which these thoughts are detected as expressed in these actions, it would seem that Locke's phrase hits the truth, and that historical knowledge is the only knowledge that the human mind can have of itself. The so-called science of human nature or of the human mind resolves itself into history.

It will certainly be thought (if those who think in this way have had patience to follow me thus far) that in saying this I am claiming more for history than it can ever give. The false view of history as a story of successive events or a spectacle of changes has been so often and so authoritatively taught in late years, especially in this country, that the very meaning of the word has become debauched through the assimilation of historical process to natural process. Against misunderstandings arising from this source I am bound to protest, even if I protest in vain. But there is one sense in which I should agree that the resolution of a science of mind into history means renouncing part of what a science of mind commonly claims, and, I think, claims falsely. The mental scientist, believing in the universal and therefore unalterable truth of his conclusions, thinks that the account he gives of mind holds good of all future stages in mind's history: he thinks that his science shows what mind will always be, not only what it has been in the past and is now. The historian has no gift of proph-

ecy, and knows it; the historical study of mind, therefore, can neither foretell the future developments of human thought nor legislate for them, except so far as they must proceed—though in what direction we cannot tell—from the present as their starting-point. Not the least of the errors contained in the science of human nature is its claim to establish a framework to which all future history must conform, to close the gates of the future and bind posterity within limits due not to the nature of things (limits of that kind are real, and are easily accepted) but to the supposed laws of the mind itself. . . .

To regard such a positive mental science as rising above the sphere of history, and establishing the permanent and unchanging laws of human nature, is therefore possible only to a person who mistakes the transient conditions of a certain historical age for the permanent conditions of human life. It was easy for men of the eighteenth century to make this mistake, because their historical perspective was so short, and their knowledge of cultures other than their own so limited, that they could cheerfully identify the intellectual habits of a western European in their own day with the intellectual faculties bestowed by God upon Adam and all his progeny. Hume, in his account of human nature, never attempted to go beyond observing that in point of fact "we" think in certain ways, and left undiscussed the question what he meant by the word "we." Even Kant, in his attempt to go beyond the "question of fact" and settle the "question of right," only showed that we must think in these ways if we are to possess the kind of science which we actually possess. When he asks how experience is possible, he means by experience the kind of experience enjoyed by men of his own age and civilization. He was, of course, not aware of this. No one in his time had done enough work on the history of thought to know that both the science and the experience of an eighteenth-century European were highly peculiar historical facts, very different from those of other peoples and other times. Nor was it yet realized that, even apart from the evidence of history, men must have thought in very different ways when as yet they were hardly emerged from the ape. The idea of a science of human nature, as entertained in the eighteenth century, belonged to a time when it was still believed that the human species, like every other, was a special creation with unalterable characteristics. . . .

Man has been defined as an animal capable of profiting by the experience of others. Of his bodily life this would be wholly untrue: he is not nourished because another has eaten, or refreshed because another has slept. But as regards his mental life it is true; and the way in which this profit is realized is by historical knowledge. The body of human thought or mental activity is a corporate possession, and almost all the operations which our minds perform are operations which we learned to perform from others who have performed them already. Since mind is what it does, and human nature, if it is a name for anything real, is only a name for human activities, this acquisition of ability to perform determinate operations is the acquisition of a determinate human nature. Thus the historical process is a process in which man creates for himself this or that kind of human nature by re-creating in his own thought the past to which he is heir. . . .

The idea that man, apart from his self-conscious historical life, is different from the rest of creation in being a rational animal is a mere superstition. It is only by fits and starts, in a flickering and dubious manner, that human beings are rational at all. In quality, as well as in amount, their rationality is a matter of degree: some are oftener rational than others, some rational in a more intense way. But a flickering and dubious rationality can certainly not be denied to animals other than men. Their minds may be inferior in range and power to those of the lowest savages, but by the same standards the lowest savages are inferior to civilized men, and those whom we call civilized differ among themselves hardly less. There are even among non-human animals the beginnings of historical life: for example, among cats, which do not wash by instinct but are taught by their mothers. Such rudiments of education are something not essentially different from an historic culture.

Historicity, too, is a matter of degree. The historicity of very primitive societies is not easily distinguishable from the merely instinctive life of societies in which rationality is at vanishing-point. When the occasions on which thinking is done, and the kinds of things about which it is done, become more frequent and more essential to the life of society, the historic inheritance of thought, preserved by historical knowledge of what has been thought before, becomes more considerable, and with its development the development of a specifically rational life begins. . . .

## Conclusions

It remains to draw a few conclusions from the thesis I have tried to maintain.

First, as regards history itself. The methods of modern historical inquiry have grown up under the shadow of their elder sister, the method of natural science; in some ways helped by its example, in other ways hindered. Throughout this essay it has been necessary to engage in a running fight with what may be called a positivistic conception, or rather misconception, of history, as the study of successive events lying in a dead past, events to be understood as the scientist understands natural events; by classifying them and establishing relations between the classes thus defined. This misconception is not only an endemic error in modern philosophical thought about history, it is also a constant peril to historical thought itself. So far as historians yield to it, they neglect their proper task of penetrating to the thought of the agents whose acts they are studying, and content themselves with determining the externals of these acts, the kind of things about them which can be studied statistically. . . . At the present day, historical thought is almost everywhere disentangling itself from the toils of the positivistic fallacy, and recognizing that in itself history is nothing but the re-enactment of past thought in the historian's mind; but much still needs to be done if the full fruits of this recognition are to be reaped. . . .

Secondly, with regard to past attempts to construct such a science.

The positive function of so-called sciences of the human mind, whether total or partial (I refer to such studies as those on the theory of knowledge, of morals, of politics, of economics, and so forth), has always tended to be misconceived. Ideally, they are designed as accounts of one unchanging subject-matter, the mind of man as it always has been and always will be. Little acquaintance with them is demanded in order to see that they are nothing of the sort, but only inventories of the wealth achieved by the human mind at a certain stage in its history. The *Republic* of Plato is an account, not of the unchanging ideal of political life, but of the Greek ideal as Plato received it and re-interpreted it. The *Ethics* of Aristotle describes not an eternal morality but the morality of the Greek gentleman. Hobbes's *Leviathan* expounds the political ideas of seventeenth-century absolutism in their English form. Kant's ethical theory expresses the moral convictions of German pietism; his *Critique of Pure Reason* analyses the conceptions and principles of Newtonian science, in their relation to the philosophical problems of the day. These limitations are often taken for defects, as if a more powerful thinker than Plato would have lifted himself clean out of the atmosphere of Greek politics, or as if Aristotle ought to have anticipated the moral conceptions of Christianity or the modern world. So far from being a defect, they are a sign of merit; they are most clearly to be seen in those works whose quality is of the best. The reason is that in those works the authors are doing best the only thing that can be done when an attempt is made to construct a science of the human mind. They are expounding the position reached by the human mind in its historical development down to their own time.

When they try to justify that position, all they can do is to exhibit it as a logical one, a coherent whole of ideas. If, realizing that any such justification is circular, they try to make the whole depend on something outside itself, they fail, as indeed they must; for since the historical present includes in itself its own past, the real ground on which the whole rests, namely the past out of which it has grown, is not outside it but is included within it.

If these systems remain valuable to posterity, that is not in spite of their strictly historical character but because of it. To us, the ideas expressed

in them are ideas belonging to the past; but it is not a dead past; by understanding it historically we incorporate it into our present thought, and enable ourselves by developing and criticizing it to use that heritage for our own advancement.

. . . How can we ever satisfy ourselves that the principles on which we think are true, except by going on thinking according to those principles, and seeing whether unanswerable criticisms of them emerge as we work? To criticize the conceptions of science is the work of science itself as it proceeds; to demand that such criticism should be anticipated by the theory of knowledge is to demand that such a theory should anticipate the history of thought.

Finally, there is the question what function can be assigned to the science of psychology. At first sight its position appears equivocal. On the one hand, it claims to be a science of mind; but if so, its apparatus of scientific method is merely the fruit of a false analogy, and it must pass over into history and, as such, disappear. And this is certainly what ought to happen so far as psychology claims to deal with the functions of reason itself. To speak of the psychology of reasoning, or the psychology of the moral self (to quote the titles of two well-known books), is to misuse words and confuse issues, ascribing to a quasi-naturalistic science a subject-matter whose being and development are not natural but historical. But if psychology avoids this danger and renounces interference with what is properly the subject-matter of history, it is likely to fall back into a pure science of nature and to become a mere branch of physiology, dealing with muscular and nervous movements.

But there is a third alternative. In realizing its own rationality, mind also realizes the presence in itself of elements that are not rational. They are not body; they are mind, but not rational mind or thought. To use an old distinction, they are psyche or soul as distinct from spirit. These irrational elements are the subject-matter of psychology. They are the blind forces and activities in us which are part of human life as it consciously experiences itself, but are not parts of the historical process: sensation as distinct from thought, feelings as distinct from conceptions, appetite as distinct from will. Their importance to us consists in the fact that they form the proximate environment in which our reason lives, as our physiological organism is the proximate environment in which they live. They are the basis of our rational life, though no part of it. Our reason discovers them, but in studying them it is not studying itself. By learning to know them, it finds out how it can help them to live in health, so that they can feed and support it while it pursues its own proper task, the self-conscious creation of its own historical life.

# THOMAS KUHN ON THE STRUCTURE OF SCIENTIFIC REVOLUTIONS

Thomas Kuhn (1922–1996) was trained in theoretical physics while he was a student at Harvard. Largely because of his book *The Structure of Scientific Revolutions,* he is best known today for his work in the philosophy of science. First published in 1962, the book is highly regarded and influential in the philosophy of science and in the social sciences.

One of the important words Kuhn has brought into common usage is *paradigm.* We can think of paradigms as a particular way of thinking about something shared by a significant grouping of specialists in a field of research. A paradigm is similar to, though not synonymous with, a "model" or a "pattern." The word is now used in popular culture to refer to a way of thinking on the part of a wide community of people. Kuhn, however, on page x of his Preface, defines paradigms in the following way: "These I take to be universally recognized scientific achievements that for a time provide model problems and solutions to a community of practitioners."

Kuhn's interest is with "paradigm shifts" in science. Paradigm shifts occur during major scientific revolutions that change the way science is done. During such a shift a particular natural phenomenon or set of phenomena comes to be understood in a significantly different way. One example Kuhn uses is the "Copernican revolution" in astronomy. Copernicus played an important role in shifting the European paradigm that Earth is at the center of the solar system (the *geocentric* view of the ancient Greek philosopher Ptolemy, who lived ca. AD 100–170) to the view that the all planets of our solar system, including Earth, revolve around the sun (the *heliocentric* view).

What exactly happens when there is a significant leap in scientific thinking? How are major advancements made in science? How do scientists make major scientific discoveries, and how do they change the scientific thinking of the time? Kuhn argues that the big paradigm shifts in science come about neither because of purely rational factors nor because empirical evidence for a new theory is slowly and painstakingly uncovered by scientists. Science makes significant advances when scientists make imaginative leaps in their thinking, basic paradigm shifts, which are themselves dependent on a series of subjective factors.

Kuhn mentions Galileo (1564–1642) in the context of how scientific revolutions come about. Following Copernicus, Galileo also argued for the heliocentric view of the solar system. Historians of science have always been intrigued with how Galileo could have come to his conclusions and how he could have initiated such a radical change in the way we understand our place in our solar system.

Traditionally, historians of science have said that one key to finding out how Galileo (or other scientists, for that matter) came to see things differently is to compare and contrast his views with those of other scientists of his day. Kuhn, however, says we need to look rather at "the relationship between his views and those of his group," as well as his relation to his peers to better understand how Galileo influenced the revolution in cosmology.

*Incommensurability* is an important concept for Kuhn. To get a sense of what this word means, consider that people can have very different views on a given issue, for example, the differences between pro-life and pro-choice supporters in the abortion debate; advocates for gun control and members of the National Rifle Association; leaders of the PLO and Zionist Jews; and evolutionists and Christian creationists. No matter how much discussion and debate take place between these groups, it is difficult to see how they will be able to change each other's respective beliefs. The reason is that their views involve deep assumptions or presuppositions that make it difficult for the opposed groups to agree on particular facts. For example, watch a debate on television between pro-Israel and pro-Palestine advocates to get a sense of how people's political presuppositions color even their understanding of history. It is unlikely that these advocates will agree about the most basic historical facts, such as who started the 1948 or 1967 Arab-Israeli wars. Because their views are so different and seemingly incompatible, they are said to be "incommensurable."

Scientific theories compete with each other in a similar way. It is not that the standard tools of scientific investigation don't matter; observation, experimentation, and method remain relevant to science. There will certainly be much commonality between scientists in the way they observe and experience the world. What cannot be ignored in all this is that the scientist's personality and the spirit of the times in which he or she lives have a very important role in the way science changes and develops.

The way in which scientists are educated will also be a strong factor in how they do science. What universities did they attend? Who were their professors? Kuhn sees these various social and historical circumstances as all contributing to the way that scientists take their observations about the world and put them into "conceptual boxes." It's not that any two scientists investigating the same phenomenon empirically see the world differently. They just have very different ways of interpreting and categorizing what they see.

The various considerations Kuhn lists as the subjective factors contributing to scientific revolutions stand in contrast to what he calls "normal science." What he means by normal science can be found in any standard textbook description of the "scientific method." "Normal" scientists will certainly encounter problems from time to time but can usually solve them. Occasionally, however, a problem will resist solution, even when the best scientists in the field tackle it. If these "anomalies" become too difficult for the existing scientific model to manage and explain, eventually a scientific revolution takes place that allows the problem to be solved. Kuhn also calls these scientific revolutions "extraordinary episodes." "They are the tradition-shattering complements to the tradition-bound activity of normal science."

What makes Kuhn's book so interesting are the implications it has for the scientific method. The traditional model sees scientific investigation and progress as matters pursuing rational, transparent, and apolitical research. Kuhn wanted to show that progress and change in science take place in quite a different way than pictured by the traditional model. For example, change in the thinking of a scientific community may occur because the older group of scientists and researchers retire and leave the profession, thus allowing younger researchers the opportunity to advance their views. Just before the retirement of these older researchers, as they see their institutional power slipping away, many of them may become quite irrational and intolerant in their opposition to a new way of thinking, to a new paradigm. Yet once they're gone, the younger researchers are free to implement the new paradigm—not because they've finally convinced everyone of its validity but simply because the institutional opposition to it has disappeared.

This connects to another surprising claim made by Kuhn that "techniques of persuasive argumentation," rather than logic, play a more important role in changing the minds of scientists. The view that rhetoric sometimes trumps scientific data has made Kuhn something of a methodological hero to postmodernist thinkers, whom we'll discuss in the next section.

As you might imagine, many scientists have found Kuhn's views highly inflammatory. Certainly the many successes of modern science—from sending men to the moon to furthering knowledge in microbiology and genetics—fuel their sentiment that they are the most rational and objective researchers. As they see it, it wouldn't particularly matter if a poet isn't representing his or her object as accurately as the astrophysicist does. If a poet's description of love doesn't resonate with the rest of us, not much comes of it, except poor sales of the poet's books. But if an engineer miscalculates the structural integrity of an office tower, we face disaster and a loss of life.

Kuhn's critique of traditional science and description of scientific progress would have been less powerful, at least rhetorically, if it had been made by a theologian or English professor. The fact that Kuhn was trained in physics, and then in the history of science, makes his position all the more difficult to simply brush aside.

For those of you who go into the sciences, as you continue your university education it may serve you well to think about Kuhn's description of paradigms and scientific change while you learn physics, chemistry, biology, or astronomy from your science textbooks. See if you can discern the scientific revolutions lurking underneath the "normal" scientific methods and laws described by Kuhn.

# The Structure of Scientific Revolutions

## THOMAS S. KUHN

## 1. Introduction: A Role for History

History, if viewed as a repository for more than anecdote or chronology, could produce a decisive transformation in the image of science by which we are now possessed. That image has previously been drawn, even by scientists themselves, mainly from the study of finished scientific achievements as these are recorded in the classics and, more recently, in the textbooks from which each new scientific generation learns to practice its trade. Inevitably, however, the aim of such books is persuasive and pedagogic; a concept of science

SOURCE: Thomas S. Kuhn, *The Structure of Scientific Revolutions*, 3d ed. (Chicago: University of Chicago Press, 1996), pp. 1, 10, 18–19, 23–25, 36–38, 47–49, 64–65, 92–93, 110–112, 122–123, 158–159 (edited). Reprinted by permission of University of Chicago Press.

drawn from them is no more likely to fit the enterprise that produced them than an image of a national culture drawn from a tourist brochure or a language text. This essay attempts to show that we have been misled by them in fundamental ways. Its aim is a sketch of the quite different concept of science that can emerge from the historical record of the research activity itself. . . .

## 2. The Route to Normal Science

In this essay, "normal science" means research firmly based upon one or more past scientific achievements, achievements that some particular scientific community acknowledges for a time as supplying the foundation for its further practice. Today such achievements are recounted, though seldom in their original form, by science textbooks, elementary and advanced. These textbooks expound the body of accepted theory, illustrate many or all of its successful applications, and compare these applications with exemplary observations and experiments. Before such books became popular early in the nineteenth century (and until even more recently in the newly matured sciences), many of the famous classics of science fulfilled a similar function. Aristotle's *Physica,* Ptolemy's *Almagest,* Newton's *Principia* and *Opticks,* Franklin's *Electricity,* Lavoisier's *Chemistry,* and Lyell's *Geology*—these and many other works served for a time implicitly to define the legitimate problems and methods of a research field for succeeding generations of practitioners. They were able to do so because they shared two essential characteristics. Their achievement was sufficiently unprecedented to attract an enduring group of adherents away from competing modes of scientific activity. Simultaneously, it was sufficiently open-ended to leave all sorts of problems for the redefined group of practitioners to resolve.

Achievements that share these two characteristics I shall henceforth refer to as "paradigms," a term that relates closely to "normal science." . . . The study of paradigms, including many that are far more specialized than those named illustratively above, is what mainly prepares the student

for membership in the particular scientific community with which he will later practice. Because he there joins men who learned the bases of their field from the same concrete models, his subsequent practice will seldom evoke overt disagreement over fundamentals. Men whose research is based on shared paradigms are committed to the same rules and standards for scientific practice. That commitment and the apparent consensus it produces are prerequisites for normal science, i.e., for the genesis and continuation of a particular research tradition.

. . . Acquisition of a paradigm and of the more esoteric type of research it permits is a sign of maturity in the development of any given scientific field. . . .

We shall be examining the nature of this highly directed or paradigm-based research in the next section, but must first note briefly how the emergence of a paradigm affects the structure of the group that practices the field. When, in the development of a natural science, an individual or group first produces a synthesis able to attract most of the next generation's practitioners, the older schools gradually disappear. In part their disappearance is caused by their members' conversion to the new paradigm. But there are always some men who cling to one or another of the older views, and they are simply read out of the profession, which thereafter ignores their work. The new paradigm implies a new and more rigid definition of the field. Those unwilling or unable to accommodate their work to it must proceed in isolation or attach themselves to some other group.[1] Historically, they have often

[1] The history of electricity provides an excellent example which could be duplicated from the careers of Priestley, Kelvin, and others. Franklin reports that Nollet, who at mid-century was the most influential of the Continental electricians, "lived to see himself the last of his Sect, except Mr. B.—his Eleve and immediate Disciple" (Max Farrand [ed.], *Benjamin Franklin's Memoirs* [Berkeley, Calif., 1949], pp. 384–86). More interesting, however, is the endurance of whole schools in increasing isolation from professional science. Consider, for example, the case of astrology, which was once an integral part of astronomy. Or consider the continuation in the late eighteenth and early nineteenth centuries of a previously respected tradition of "romantic" chemistry. This

simply stayed in the departments of philosophy from which so many of the special sciences have been spawned. As these indications hint, it is sometimes just its reception of a paradigm that transforms a group previously interested merely in the study of nature into a profession or, at least, a discipline. In the sciences (though not in fields like medicine, technology, and law, of which the principal *raison d'être* is an external social need), the formation of specialized journals, the foundation of specialists' societies, and the claim for a special place in the curriculum have usually been associated with a group's first reception of a single paradigm. At least this was the case between the time, a century and a half ago, when the institutional pattern of scientific specialization first developed and the very recent time when the paraphernalia of specialization acquired a prestige of their own. . . .

## 3. *The Nature of Normal Science*

. . . Paradigms gain their status because they are more successful than their competitors in solving a few problems that the group of practitioners has come to recognize as acute. To be more successful is not, however, to be either completely successful with a single problem or notably successful with any large number. The success of a paradigm—whether Aristotle's analysis of motion, Ptolemy's computations of planetary position, Lavoisier's application of the balance, or Maxwell's mathematization of the electromagnetic field—is at the start largely a promise of success discoverable in selected and still incomplete examples. Normal science consists in the actualization of that promise, an actualization achieved by extending the knowledge of those facts that the paradigm displays as particularly

revealing, by increasing the extent of the match between those facts and the paradigm's predictions, and by further articulation of the paradigm itself.

Few people who are not actually practitioners of a mature science realize how much mop-up work of this sort a paradigm leaves to be done or quite how fascinating such work can prove in the execution. And these points need to be understood. Mopping-up operations are what engage most scientists throughout their careers. They constitute what I am here calling normal science. Closely examined, whether historically or in the contemporary laboratory, that enterprise seems an attempt to force nature into the preformed and relatively inflexible box that the paradigm supplies. No part of the aim of normal science is to call forth new sorts of phenomena; indeed those that will not fit the box are often not seen at all. Nor do scientists normally aim to invent new theories, and they are often intolerant of those invented by others.[2] Instead, normal-scientific research is directed to the articulation of those phenomena and theories that the paradigm already supplies.

Perhaps these are defects. The areas investigated by normal science are, of course, minuscule; the enterprise now under discussion has drastically restricted vision. But those restrictions, born from confidence in a paradigm, turn out to be essential to the development of science. By focusing attention upon a small range of relatively esoteric problems, the paradigm forces scientists to investigate some part of nature in a detail and depth that would otherwise be unimaginable. And normal science possesses a built-in mechanism that ensures the relaxation of the restrictions that bound research whenever the paradigm from which they derive ceases to function effectively. At that point scientists begin to behave differently, and the nature of their research problems changes. In the interim, however, during the period when the paradigm is successful, the profession will have solved problems

is the tradition discussed by Charles C. Gillispie in "The *Encyclopédie* and the Jacobin Philosophy of Science: A Study in Ideas and Consequences," *Critical Problems in the History of Science,* ed. Marshall Clagett (Madison, Wis., 1959), pp. 255–89; and "The Formation of Lamarck's Evolutionary Theory," *Archives internationales d'histoire des sciences,* 37 (1956), 323–38.

[2] Bernard Barber, "Resistance by Scientists to Scientific Discovery," *Science,* 134 (1961), 596–602.

that its members could scarcely have imagined and would never have undertaken without commitment to the paradigm. And at least part of that achievement always proves to be permanent. . . .

To scientists, at least, the results gained in normal research are significant because they add to the scope and precision with which the paradigm can be applied. That answer, however, cannot account for the enthusiasm and devotion that scientists display for the problems of normal research. No one devotes years to, say, the development of a better spectrometer or the production of an improved solution to the problem of vibrating strings simply because of the importance of the information that will be obtained. . . . Bringing a normal research problem to a conclusion is achieving the anticipated in a new way, and it requires the solution of all sorts of complex instrumental, conceptual, and mathematical puzzles. The man who succeeds proves himself an expert puzzle-solver, and the challenge of the puzzle is an important part of what usually drives him on.

The terms "puzzle" and "puzzle-solver" highlight several of the themes that have become increasingly prominent in the preceding pages. Puzzles are, in the entirely standard meaning here employed, that special category of problems that can serve to test ingenuity or skill in solution. Dictionary illustrations are "jigsaw puzzle" and "crossword puzzle," and it is the characteristics that these share with the problems of normal science that we now need to isolate. One of them has just been mentioned. It is no criterion of goodness in a puzzle that its outcome be intrinsically interesting or important. On the contrary, the really pressing problems, e.g., a cure for cancer or the design of a lasting peace, are often not puzzles at all, largely because they may not have any solution. Consider the jigsaw puzzle whose pieces are selected at random from each of two different puzzle boxes. Since that problem is likely to defy (though it may not) even the most ingenious of men, it cannot serve as a test of skill in solution. In any usual sense it is not a puzzle at all. Though intrinsic value is no criterion for a puzzle, the assured existence of a solution is.

We have already seen, however, that one of the things a scientific community acquires with a paradigm is a criterion for choosing problems that, while the paradigm is taken for granted, can be assumed to have solutions. To a great extent these are the only problems that the community will admit as scientific or encourage its members to undertake. Other problems, including many that had previously been standard, are rejected as metaphysical, as the concern of another discipline, or sometimes as just too problematic to be worth the time. A paradigm can, for that matter, even insulate the community from those socially important problems that are not reducible to the puzzle form, because they cannot be stated in terms of the conceptual and instrumental tools the paradigm supplies. Such problems can be a distraction, a lesson brilliantly illustrated by several facets of seventeenth-century Baconianism and by some of the contemporary social sciences. One of the reasons why normal science seems to progress so rapidly is that its practitioners concentrate on problems that only their own lack of ingenuity should keep them from solving.

If, however, the problems of normal science are puzzles in this sense, we need no longer ask why scientists attack them with such passion and devotion. A man may be attracted to science for all sorts of reasons. Among them are the desire to be useful, the excitement of exploring new territory, the hope of finding order, and the drive to test established knowledge. These motives and others besides also help to determine the particular problems that will later engage him. Furthermore, though the result is occasional frustration, there is good reason why motives like these should first attract him and then lead him on. The scientific enterprise as a whole does from time to time prove useful, open up new territory, display order, and test long-accepted belief. Nevertheless, *the individual* engaged on a normal research problem *is almost never doing any one of these things*. Once engaged, his motivation is of a rather different sort. What then challenges him is the conviction that, if only he is skilful enough, he will succeed in solving a puzzle that no one before has solved or solved so well. Many of the greatest scientific minds have devoted all of their professional attention to demanding puzzles of this sort. On most occasions any particular field of specialization offers nothing else to do, a fact that makes it no less fascinating to the proper sort of addict. . . .

. . . The pre-paradigm period, in particular, is regularly marked by frequent and deep debates over legitimate methods, problems, and standards of solution, though these serve rather to define schools than to produce agreement. . . . Furthermore, debates like these do not vanish once and for all with the appearance of a paradigm. Though almost non-existent during periods of normal science, they recur regularly just before and during scientific revolutions, the periods when paradigms are first under attack and then subject to change. The transition from Newtonian to quantum mechanics evoked many debates about both the nature and the standards of physics, some of which still continue. There are people alive today who can remember the similar arguments engendered by Maxwell's electromagnetic theory and by statistical mechanics. And earlier still, the assimilation of Galileo's and Newton's mechanics gave rise to a particularly famous series of debates with Aristotelians, Cartesians, and Leibnizians about the standards legitimate to science. When scientists disagree about whether the fundamental problems of their field have been solved, the search for rules gains a function that it does not ordinarily possess. While paradigms remain secure, however, they can function without agreement over rationalization or without any attempted rationalization at all. . . .

In the development of any science, the first received paradigm is usually felt to account quite successfully for most of the observations and experiments easily accessible to that science's practitioners. Further development, therefore, ordinarily calls for the construction of elaborate equipment, the development of an esoteric vocabulary and skills, and a refinement of concepts that increasingly lessens their resemblance to their usual common-sense prototypes. That professionalization leads, on the one hand, to an immense restriction of the scientist's vision and to

a considerable resistance to paradigm change. The science has become increasingly rigid. On the other hand, within those areas to which the paradigm directs the attention of the group, normal science leads to a detail of information and to a precision of the observation-theory match that could be achieved in no other way. Furthermore, that detail and precision-of-match have a value that transcends their not always very high intrinsic interest. Without the special apparatus that is constructed mainly for anticipated functions, the results that lead ultimately to novelty could not occur. And even when the apparatus exists, novelty ordinarily emerges only for the man who, knowing *with precision* what he should expect, is able to recognize that something has gone wrong. Anomaly appears only against the background provided by the paradigm. The more precise and far-reaching that paradigm is, the more sensitive an indicator it provides of anomaly and hence of an occasion for paradigm change. In the normal mode of discovery, even resistance to change has a use. . . . By ensuring that the paradigm will not be too easily surrendered, resistance guarantees that scientists will not be lightly distracted and that the anomalies that lead to paradigm change will penetrate existing knowledge to the core. The very fact that a significant scientific novelty so often emerges simultaneously from several laboratories is an index both to the strongly traditional nature of normal science and to the completeness with which that traditional pursuit prepares the way for its own change.

## 9. The Nature and Necessity of Scientific Revolutions

. . . Political revolutions are inaugurated by a growing sense, often restricted to a segment of the political community, that existing institutions have ceased adequately to meet the problems posed by an environment that they have in part created. In much the same way, scientific revolutions are inaugurated by a growing sense, again often restricted to a narrow subdivision of the scientific community, that an existing paradigm has ceased to function adequately in the exploration of an aspect of nature to which that paradigm itself had previously led the way. In both political and scientific development the sense of malfunction that can lead to crisis is prerequisite to revolution. . . .

This genetic aspect of the parallel between political and scientific development should no longer be open to doubt. The parallel has, however, a second and more profound aspect upon which the significance of the first depends. Political revolutions aim to change political institutions in ways that those institutions themselves prohibit. Their success therefore necessitates the partial relinquishment of one set of institutions in favor of another, and in the interim, society is not fully governed by institutions at all. Initially it is crisis alone that attenuates the role of political institutions as we have already seen it attenuate the role of paradigms. In increasing numbers individuals become increasingly estranged from political life and behave more and more eccentrically within it. Then, as the crisis deepens, many of these individuals commit themselves to some concrete proposal for the reconstruction of society in a new institutional framework. At that point the society is divided into competing camps or parties, one seeking to defend the old institutional constellation, the others seeking to institute some new one. And, once that polarization has occurred, *political recourse fails*. Because they differ about the institutional matrix within which political change is to be achieved and evaluated, because they acknowledge no suprainstitutional framework for the adjudication of revolutionary difference, the parties to a revolutionary conflict must finally resort to the techniques of mass persuasion, often including force. . . . There are other reasons, too, for the incompleteness of logical contact that consistently characterizes paradigm debates. For example, since no paradigm ever solves all the problems it defines and since no two paradigms leave all the same problems unsolved, paradigm debates always involve the question: Which problems is it more significant to have solved? Like

the issue of competing standards, that question of values can be answered only in terms of criteria that lie outside of normal science altogether, and it is that recourse to external criteria that most obviously makes paradigm debates revolutionary. Something even more fundamental than standards and values is, however, also at stake. I have so far argued only that paradigms are constitutive of science. . . .

## 10. Revolutions as Changes of World View

Examining the record of past research from the vantage of contemporary historiography, the historian of science may be tempted to exclaim that when paradigms change, the world itself changes with them. Led by a new paradigm, scientists adopt new instruments and look in new places. Even more important, during revolutions scientists see new and different things when looking with familiar instruments in places they have looked before. It is rather as if the professional community had been suddenly transported to another planet where familiar objects are seen in a different light and are joined by unfamiliar ones as well. Of course, nothing of quite that sort does occur: there is no geographical transplantation; outside the laboratory everyday affairs usually continue as before. Nevertheless, paradigm changes do cause scientists to see the world of their research-engagement differently. In so far as their only recourse to that world is through what they see and do, we may want to say that after a revolution scientists are responding to a different world.

It is as elementary prototypes for these transformations of the scientist's world that the familiar demonstrations of a switch in visual gestalt prove so suggestive. What were ducks in the scientist's world before the revolution are rabbits afterwards. The man who first saw the exterior of the box from above later sees its interior from below. Transformations like these, though usually more gradual and almost always irreversible, are common concomitants of scientific training.

Looking at a contour map, the student sees lines on paper, the cartographer a picture of a terrain. Looking at a bubble-chamber photograph, the student sees confused and broken lines, the physicist a record of familiar subnuclear events. Only after a number of such transformations of vision does the student become an inhabitant of the scientist's world, seeing what the scientist sees and responding as the scientist does. The world that the student then enters is not, however, fixed once and for all by the nature of the environment, on the one hand, and of science, on the other. Rather, it is determined jointly by the environment and the particular normal-scientific tradition that the student has been trained to pursue. Therefore, at times of revolution, when the normal-scientific tradition changes, the scientist's perception of his environment must be re-educated—in some familiar situations he must learn to see a new gestalt. After he has done so the world of his research will seem, here and there, incommensurable with the one he had inhabited before. That is another reason why schools guided by different paradigms are always slightly at cross-purposes. . . .

. . . Paradigms are not corrigible by normal science at all. Instead, as we have already seen, normal science ultimately leads only to the recognition of anomalies and to crises. And these are terminated, not by deliberation and interpretation, but by a relatively sudden and unstructured event like the gestalt switch. Scientists then often speak of the "scales falling from the eyes" or of the "lightning flash" that "inundates" a previously obscure puzzle, enabling its components to be seen in a new way that for the first time permits its solution. On other occasions the relevant illumination comes in sleep. No ordinary sense of the term "interpretation" fits these flashes of intuition through which a new paradigm is born. Though such intuitions depend upon the experience, both anomalous and congruent, gained with the old paradigm, they are not logically or piecemeal linked to particular items of that experience as an interpretation would be. Instead, they gather up large portions of that experience and transform them to the rather different bundle of experience that will thereafter be linked piecemeal to the new paradigm but not to the old. . . .

. . . The man who embraces a new paradigm at an early stage must often do so in defiance of the evidence provided by problem-solving. He must, that is, have faith that the new paradigm will succeed with the many large problems that confront it, knowing only that the older paradigm has failed with a few. A decision of that kind can only be made on faith.

That is one of the reasons why prior crisis proves so important. Scientists who have not experienced it will seldom renounce the hard evidence of problem-solving to follow what may easily prove and will be widely regarded as a will-o'-the-wisp. But crisis alone is not enough. There must also be a basis, though it need be neither rational nor ultimately correct, for faith in the particular candidate chosen. Something must make at least a few scientists feel that the new proposal is on the right track, and sometimes it is only personal and inarticulate aesthetic considerations that can do that. Men have been converted by them at times when most of the articulable technical arguments pointed the other way. When first introduced, neither Copernicus' astronomical theory nor De Broglie's theory of matter had many other significant grounds of appeal. Even today Einstein's general theory attracts men principally on aesthetic grounds, an appeal that few people outside of mathematics have been able to feel.

This is not to suggest that new paradigms triumph ultimately through some mystical aesthetic. On the contrary, very few men desert a tradition for these reasons alone. Often those who do turn out to have been misled. But if a paradigm is ever to triumph it must gain some first supporters, men who will develop it to the point where hardheaded arguments can be produced and multiplied. And even those arguments, when they come, are not individually decisive. Because scientists are reasonable men, one or another argument will ultimately persuade many of them. But there is no single argument that can or should persuade them all. Rather than a single group conversion, what occurs is an increasing shift in the distribution of professional allegiances.

At the start a new candidate for paradigm may have few supporters, and on occasions the supporters' motives may be suspect. Nevertheless, if they are competent, they will improve it, explore its possibilities, and show what it would be like to belong to the community guided by it. And as that goes on, if the paradigm is one destined to win its fight, the number and strength of the persuasive arguments in its favor will increase. More scientists will then be converted, and the exploration of the new paradigm will go on. Gradually the number of experiments, instruments, articles, and books based upon the paradigm will multiply. Still more men, convinced of the new view's fruitfulness, will adopt the new mode of practicing normal science, until at last only a few elderly hold-outs remain. And even they, we cannot say, are wrong. Though the historian can always find men—Priestley, for instance—who were unreasonable to resist for as long as they did, he will not find a point at which resistance becomes illogical or unscientific. At most he may wish to say that the man who continues to resist after his whole profession has been converted has *ipso facto* ceased to be a scientist.

# RICHARD RORTY ON TRUTH: DECONSTRUCTING KNOWLEDGE

Richard Rorty (1931–) doesn't try to be philosophical, at least in the traditional sense of the word. He believes the task of philosophy, first set out in a rigorous way by Plato, has shown itself to be a dead end. According to Rorty, we cannot definitively define the concepts basic to the philosophical project. This is an old problem—even Plato had difficulty in his own day with such common words as *good* and *justice*.

Rorty has discussed in depth two other important philosophical words, *knowledge* and *truth*. What do we mean when we say we know something or that something is true? In the introduction to this chapter we introduced you to some of the problems associated with these questions, including three traditional theories of truth: the correspondence, coherence, and pragmatist theories of truth.

Rorty is highly critical of attempts to make robust distinctions between philosophical terms such as *knowledge* and *opinion,* or *objectivity* and *subjectivity*. This view puts him at odds with those philosophers who call themselves "realists."

Realists maintain the task of philosophy is to be sure our beliefs correspond to the way the world is. Generally speaking, realists argue that the world, along with its objects, is independent of our thoughts and beliefs about it. For example, whether we believe it or not, our planet has an oval shape. The realist's goal here would be to make sure our belief about the shape of the earth matches the way the world is really shaped. If a realist encountered people who still believed the earth is flat, the realist would show clear evidence from the world itself that they were wrong about their beliefs. There are, the realist contends, facts about the world.

Rorty describes the realist's position as an attempt to see the world in a way impossible for the human investigator. He thinks the realist's desire to get at the facts about the world, as it *really* is, is like wishing all the objects in the world, animate and inanimate, could describe themselves to us as they really are. Some have described the realist's goal, somewhat tongue in cheek, as having "God's-eye view" of things.

In contrast to a realist, Rorty is an "anti-representationalist." True to his pragmatist roots, he thinks the main epistemological task is not to get reality right, but rather to *cope* with reality. Coping with reality, at least as Rorty sees it, is a matter of acquiring certain habits and behavior. Here Rorty comes closest to his pragmatist roots, especially to William James and John Dewey. For James, as discussed earlier, truth is "what is good for us to believe."

Rorty thinks many of the questions raised by the traditional philosophical canon are insoluble. He encourages philosophers to refocus their attention on the more concrete problems vexing society. After making a 2,500-year effort that dates back to Thales and Socrates, we are not any closer to precisely defining words such as *Good, Justice,* and *Truth.* Rorty concludes that *objectivity* should be redefined as meaning "the desire to enhance social *solidarity.*"

Rorty means by solidarity the idea that we need to see the similarities between us as much greater than our differences. Who does "us" and "our" refer to? Rorty says that this "us" is our immediate community. To be sure, we are members of a variety of communities, ranging from our own neighborhood to our country, from North America to the world. So exactly what community is Rorty thinking about here?

It doesn't matter that much, as long as we try to find new ways to include more and more people into it, or as he puts it, to promote "the desire to extend the reference of 'us' as far as we can." This practical impulse in Rorty's writings is a very powerful critique of the philosophical tradition, especially given the rather dismal failure of the latter to produce the clear and distinct truths it has promised for centuries. (To be fair, one could point out that Descartes proved that we exist as thinking things, though one is tempted to echo Shakespeare's Horatio speaking to Hamlet: "There needs no ghost my Lord, come from the grave, to tell us this.")

Many philosophers disagree with Rorty's take on the philosophical tradition with respect to truth and objectivity. Their main criticism has been that understanding truth as "what is good for us to believe" will lead to relativism.

Rorty doesn't disagree with the notion that we must justify our beliefs. He just thinks that after we have satisfactorily justified our beliefs, it doesn't add anything to then ask whether these beliefs are true or not. Saying our beliefs are "true" is just a compliment we give to well-justified beliefs, not a judgment that they have captured the essence of reality.

Many traditional philosophers think Rorty's "antiphilosophical" views are inaccurate and oversimplified. These philosophers don't want to give up on the grand philosophical project of trying to accurately represent the world through language and thought.

Despite the hostility in some quarters to his views, Rorty points out that the philosophical tradition is still worth studying as intellectual history. It is not necessary for you to decide at this point whether Rorty or the traditional philosophers are right about truth and objectivity. Philosophy has always had room for dissenters and kibitzers. Remember that the whole thing got rolling two and a half millennia ago because of another philosophical gadfly, Socrates.

# Science as Solidarity

## RICHARD RORTY

IN OUR CULTURE, the notions of "science," "rationality," "objectivity," and "truth" are bound up with one another. Science is thought of as offering "hard," "objective" truth: truth as correspondence to reality, the only sort of truth worthy of the name. Humanists—for example, philosophers, theologians, historians, and literary critics—have to worry about whether they are being "scientific," whether they are entitled to think of their conclusions, no matter how carefully argued, as worthy of the term "true." We tend to identify seeking "objective truth" with "using reason," and so we think of the natural sciences as paradigms of rationality. We also think of rationality as a matter of following procedures laid down in advance, of being "methodical." So we tend to use "methodical," "rational," "scientific," and "objective" as synonyms.

Worries about "cognitive status" and "objectivity" are characteristic of a secularized culture in which the scientist replaces the priest. The scientist is now seen as the person who keeps humanity in touch with something beyond itself. As the universe was depersonalized, beauty (and, in time, even moral goodness) came to be thought of as "subjective." So truth is now thought of as the only point at which human beings are responsible to something nonhuman. A commitment to "rationality" and to "method" is thought to be a recognition of this responsibility. The scientist becomes a moral exemplar, one who selflessly expresses himself again and again to the hardness of fact. . . .

These distinctions between hard facts and soft values, truth and pleasure, and objectivity and subjectivity are awkward and clumsy instruments. They are not suited to dividing up culture; they create more difficulties than they resolve. It

would be best to find another vocabulary, to start afresh. But in order to do so, we first have to find a new way of describing the natural sciences. It is not a question of debunking or downgrading the natural scientist, but simply of ceasing to see him as a priest. We need to stop thinking of science as the place where the human mind confronts the world, and of the scientist as exhibiting proper humility in the face of superhuman forces. We need a way of explaining why scientists are, and deserve to be, moral exemplars which does not depend on a distinction between objective fact and something softer, squishier, and more dubious.

To get such a way of thinking, we can start by distinguishing two senses of the term "rationality." In one sense . . . to be rational is to be methodical: that is, to have criteria for success laid down in advance. We think of poets and painters as using some faculty other than "reason" in their work because, by their own confession, they are not sure of what they want to do before they have done it. They make up new standards of achievements as they go along. By contrast, we think of judges as knowing in advance what criteria a brief will have to satisfy in order to invoke a favorable decision, and of business people as setting well-defined goals and being judged by their success in achieving them. Law and business are good examples of rationality, but the scientist, knowing in advance what would count as disconfirming his hypothesis and prepared to abandon that hypothesis as a result of the unfavorable outcome of a single experiment, seems a truly heroic example. Further, we seem to have a clear criterion for the success of a scientific theory—namely, its ability to predict, and thereby to enable us to control some portion

SOURCE: Richard Rorty, "Science as Solidarity," in *Objectivity, Relativism, and Truth* (Cambridge: Cambridge University Press, 1991), pp. 35–45 (edited). Reprinted with the permission of Cambridge University Press.

of the world. If to be rational means to be able to lay down criteria in advance, then it is plausible to take natural science as the paradigm of rationality.

The trouble is that in this sense of "rational" the humanities are never going to qualify as rational activities. If the humanities are concerned with ends rather than means, then there is no way to evaluate their success in terms of antecedently specified criteria. If we already knew what criteria we wanted to satisfy, we would not worry about whether we were pursuing the right ends. If we thought we knew the goals of culture and society in advance, we would have no use for the humanities—as totalitarian societies in fact do not. It is characteristic of democratic and pluralistic societies to continually redefine their goals. But if to be rational means to satisfy criteria, then this process of redefinition is bound to be nonrational. So if the humanities are to be viewed as rational activities, rationality will have to be thought of as something other than the satisfaction of criteria which are statable in advance.

Another meaning for "rational" is, in fact, available. In this sense, the word means something like "sane" or "reasonable" rather than "methodical." It names a set of moral virtues: tolerance, respect for the opinions of those around one, willingness to listen, reliance on persuasion rather than force. These are the virtues which members of a civilized society must possess if the society is to endure. In this sense of "rational," the word means something more like "civilized" than like "methodical." When so construed, the distinction between the rational and the irrational has nothing in particular to do with the difference between the arts and the sciences. On this construction, to be rational is simply to discuss any topic—religious, literary, or scientific—in a way which eschews dogmatism, defensiveness, and righteous indignation.

There is no problem about whether, in this latter, weaker, sense, the humanities are "rational disciplines." Usually humanists display the moral virtues in question. Sometimes they don't, but then sometimes scientists don't either. Yet these

moral virtues are felt to be not enough. Both humanists and the public hanker after rationality in the first, stronger sense of the term: a sense which is associated with objective truth, correspondence to reality, and method, and criteria.

We should not try to satisfy this hankering, but rather try to eradicate it. No matter what one's opinion of the secularization of culture, it was a mistake to try to make the natural scientist into a new sort of priest, a link between the human and the nonhuman. So was the idea that some sorts of truths are "objective" whereas others are merely "subjective" or "relative"—the attempt to divide up the set of true sentences into "genuine knowledge" and "mere opinion," or into the "factual" and "judgmental." So was the idea that the scientist has a special method which, if only the humanists would apply it to ultimate values, would give us the same kind of self-confidence about moral ends as we now have about technological means. I think that we should content ourselves with the second, "weaker" conception of rationality, and avoid the first, "stronger" conception. We should avoid the idea that there is some special virtue in knowing in advance what criteria you are going to satisfy, in having standards by which to measure progress.

One can make these issues somewhat more concrete by taking up the current controversy among philosophers about the "rationality of science." For some twenty years, ever since the publication of Thomas Kuhn's book *The Structure of Scientific Revolutions*, philosophers have been debating whether science is rational. Attacks on Kuhn for being an "irrationalist" have been as frequent and as urgent as were, in the thirties and forties, attacks on the logical positivists for saying that moral judgments were "meaningless." We are constantly being warned of the danger of "relativism," which will beset us if we give up our attachment to objectivity, and to the idea of rationality as obedience to criteria.

Whereas Kuhn's enemies routinely accuse him of reducing science to "mob psychology," and pride themselves on having (by a new theory of meaning, or reference, or verisimilitude) vindicated the "rationality of science," his pragmatist friends (such as myself) routinely congratulate him on having softened the distinction between science and nonscience. It is fairly easy for Kuhn to show that the enemies are attacking a straw man. But it is harder for him to save himself from his friends. For he has said that "there is no theory-independent way to reconstruct phrases like 'really there.'"[1] He has asked whether it really helps "to imagine that there is some one full, objective, true account of nature and that the proper measure of scientific achievement is the extent to which it brings us closer to that ultimate goal."[2] We pragmatists quote these passages incessantly in the course of our effort to enlist Kuhn in our campaign to drop the objective-subjective distinction altogether.

What I am calling "pragmatism" might also be called "left-wing Kuhnianism." It has been also rather endearingly called (by one of its critics, Clark Glymour) the "new fuzziness," because it is an attempt to blur just those distinctions between the objective and the subjective and between fact and value which the critical conception of rationality has developed. We fuzzies would like to substitute the idea of "unforced agreement" for that of "objectivity."

To say that unforced agreement is enough raises the specter of relativism. For those who say that a pragmatic view of rationality is unwholesomely relativistic ask: "Unforced agreement among whom? Us? The Nazis? Any arbitrary culture or group?" The answer, of course, is "us." This necessarily ethnocentric answer simply says that we must work by our own lights. Beliefs suggested by another culture must be tested by trying to weave them together with beliefs we already have. On the other hand, we can always enlarge the scope of "us" by regarding other people, or cultures, as members of the same community of inquiry as ourselves—by treating them as part of the group among whom unforced agreement is to be sought. What we cannot do is

to rise above all human communities, actual and possible. We cannot find a skyhook which lifts us out of mere coherence—mere agreement—to something like "correspondence with reality as it is in itself."

One reason why dropping this latter notion strikes many people as "relativistic" is that it denies the necessity that inquiry should someday converge to a single point—that Truth is "out there," up in front of us, waiting for us to reach it. This latter image seems to us pragmatists an unfortunate attempt to carry a religious view of the world over into an increasingly secular culture. All that is worth preserving of the claim that rational inquiry will converge to a single point is the claim that we must be able to explain why past false views were held in the past, and thus explain how to go about reeducating our benighted ancestors. To say that we think we are heading in the right direction is just to say, with Kuhn, that we can, by hindsight, tell the story of the past as a story of progress.

But the fact that we can trace such a direction and tell such a story does not mean that we have gotten closer to a goal which is out there waiting for us. We cannot, I think, imagine a moment at which the human race could settle back and say, "Well, now that we've finally arrived at the Truth we can relax." We should relish the thought that the sciences as well as the arts will *always* provide a spectacle of fierce competition between alternative theories, movements, and schools. The end of human activity is not rest, but rather richer and better human activity.

. . . Pragmatists would like to replace the desire for objectivity—the desire to be in touch with a reality which is more than some community with which we identify ourselves—with the desire for solidarity with that community. They think that the habits of relying on persuasion rather than force, of respect for the opinions of colleagues, of curiosity and eagerness for new data and ideas, are the *only* virtues which scientists have. They do not think that there is an intellectual virtue called "rationality" over and above these moral virtues.

On this view there is no reason to praise scientists for being more "objective" or "logical" or

---

[1] Thomas S. Kuhn, *The Structure of Scientific Revolutions*, 2d ed. (Chicago: University of Chicago Press, 1970), p. 206.
[2] Ibid., p. 171.

"methodical" or "devoted to truth" than other people. But there is plenty of reason to praise the institutions they have developed and within which they work, and to use these as models for the rest of culture. For these institutions give concreteness and detail to the idea of "unforced agreement." Reference to such institutions fleshes out the idea of "a free and open encounter"—the sort of encounter in which truth cannot fail to win. On this view, to say that truth will win in such an encounter is not to make a metaphysical claim about the connection between human reason and the nature of things. It is merely to say that the best way to find out what to believe is to listen to as many suggestions and arguments as you can.

My rejection of traditional notions of rationality can be summed up by saying that the only sense in which science is exemplary is that it is a model of human solidarity. We should think of the institutions and practices which make up various scientific communities as providing suggestions about the way in which the rest of culture might organize itself. . . . But, on this view, we shall not explain this better order by thinking of the scientists as having a "method" which the rest of us would do well to imitate, nor as benefiting from the desirable hardness of their subjects compared with the undesirable softness of other subjects.

. . . One consequence . . . is the suggestion that perhaps "the human sciences" *should* look quite different from the natural sciences. This suggestion is not based on epistemological or metaphysical considerations which show that inquiry into societies must be different from inquiry into things. Instead, it is based on the observation that natural scientists are interested primarily in predicting and controlling the behavior of things, and that prediction and control may not be what we want from our sociologists and our literary critics. . . .

Pragmatists think that one will suffer from Hume's itch only if one has been scratching oneself with what has sometimes been called "Hume's fork"—the distinction between "relations of ideas" and "matters of fact." This distinction survives in contemporary philosophy as the distinction between "questions of language" and "questions of fact." We pragmatists think that philosophers of language such as Wittgenstein, Quine, Goodman, Davidson, and others have shown us how to get along without these distinctions. Once one has lived without them for a while, one learns to live without those between knowledge and opinion, or between subjective and objective, as well. The purposes served by the latter distinctions come to be served by the unproblematic sociological distinction between areas in which unforced agreement is relatively infrequent and areas in which it is relatively frequent. So we do not itch for an explanation of the success of recent Western science any more than for the success of recent Western politics. That is why we fuzzies applaud Kuhn when he says that "one does not know what a person who denies the rationality of learning from experience is trying to say," but are aghast when he goes on to ask *why* "we have no rational alternatives to learning from experience."[3]

On the pragmatist view, the contrast between "relations of ideas" and "matters of fact" is a special case of the bad seventeenth-century contrasts between being "in us" and being "out there," between subject and object, between our beliefs and what those beliefs (moral, scientific, theological, etc.) are trying to get right. Pragmatists avoid this latter contrast by instead contrasting our beliefs with proposed alternative beliefs. They recommend that we worry only about the choice between two hypotheses, rather than about whether there is something which "makes" either true. To take this stance would rid us of questions about the objectivity of value, the rationality of science, and the causes of the viability of our language games. All such theoretical questions would be replaced with practical questions about whether we ought to keep our present values, theories, and practices or try to replace them with others. Given such a replacement, there would be nothing to be responsible to except ourselves.

. . . On this account, to be responsible is a

---

[3] Thomas S. Kuhn, "Rationality and Theory Choice," *Journal of Philosophy* 80 (1983): 569–70.

matter of what Peirce called "contrite fallibilism" rather than of respect for something beyond. The desire for "objectivity" boils down to a desire to acquire beliefs which will eventually receive unforced agreement in the course of a free and open encounter with people holding other beliefs.

Pragmatists interpret the goal of inquiry (in any sphere of culture) as the attainment of an appropriate mixture of unforced agreement with tolerant disagreement (where what counts as appropriate is determined, within that sphere, by trial and error). Such a reinterpretation of our sense of responsibility would, if carried through, gradually make unintelligible the subject-object model of inquiry, the child-parent model of moral obligation, and the correspondence theory of truth. A world in which those models, and that theory, no longer had any intuitive appeal would be a pragmatist's paradise.

When Dewey urged that we try to create such a paradise, he was said to be irresponsible. For, it was said, he left us bereft of weapons to use against our enemies; he gave us nothing with which to "answer the Nazis." When we new fuzzies try to revive Dewey's repudiation of criteriology, we are said to be "relativistic." We must, people say, believe that every coherent view is as good as every other, since we have no "outside" touchstone for choice among such views. We are said to leave the general public defenseless against the witch doctor, the defender of creationism, or anyone else who is clever and patient enough to deduce a consistent and wide-ranging set of theorems from his "alternative first principles."

Nobody is convinced when we fuzzies say that we can be just as morally indignant as the next philosopher. We are suspected of being contritely fallibilist when righteous fury is called for. Even when we actually display appropriate emotions we get nowhere, for we are told that we have no *right* to these emotions. When we suggest that one of the few things we know (or need to know) about truth is that it is what wins in a free and open encounter, we are told that we have defined "true" as "satisfies the standards of our community." But we pragmatists do not hold this relativist view. We do not infer from

"there is no way to step outside communities to a neutral standpoint" that "there is no rational way to justify liberal communities over totalitarian communities." For that inference involves just the notion of "rationality" as a set of ahistorical principles which pragmatists abjure. What we in fact infer is that there is no way to beat totalitarians in argument by appealing to shared common premises, and no point in pretending that a common human nature makes the totalitarians unconsciously hold such premises.

The claim that we fuzzies have no right to be furious at moral evil, no right to commend our views as true unless we simultaneously refute ourselves by claiming that there are objects out there which *make* those views true, begs all the theoretical questions. But it gets to the practical and moral heart of the matter. This is the question of whether notions like "unforced agreement" and "free and open encounter"—descriptions of social situations—can take the place in our moral lives of notions like "the world," "the will of God," "the moral law," "what our beliefs are trying to represent accurately," and "what makes our beliefs true." All the philosophical presuppositions which make Hume's fork seem inevitable are ways of suggesting that human communities must justify their existence by striving to attain a nonhuman goal. To suggest that we can forget about Hume's fork, forget about being responsible to what is "out there," is to suggest that human communities can only justify their existence by comparisons with other actual and possible human communities.

I can make this contrast a bit more concrete by asking whether free and open encounters, and the kind of community which permits and encourages such encounters, are for the sake of truth and goodness, or whether "the quest for truth and goodness" is simply the quest for that kind of community. Is the sort of community which is exemplified by groups of scientific inquirers and by democratic political institutions a means to an end, or is the formation of such communities the only goal we need? Dewey thought that it was the only goal we needed and I think he was right. But whether he was or not, this question is the one to which the debates about Kuhn's "irrationalism" and the new fuz-zies' "relativism" must eventually boil down.

Dewey was accused of blowing up the opti-mism and flexibility of a parochial and jejune way of life (the American) into a philosophical sys-tem. So he did, but his reply was that *any* philo-sophical system is going to be an attempt to ex-press the ideals of *some* community's way of life. He was quite ready to admit that the virtue of his philosophy was, indeed, nothing more than the virtue of the way of life which it commended. On his view, philosophy does not justify affilia-tion with a community in the light of something ahistorical called "reason" or "transcultural prin-ciples." It simply expatiates on the special advan-tages of that community over other communities.

What would it be like to be less fuzzy and parochial than this? I suggest that it would be to become less genial, tolerant, open-minded, and fallibilist than we are now. In the nontrivial, pe-jorative, sense of "ethnocentric," the sense in which we congratulate ourselves on being less ethnocentric now than our ancestors were three hundred years ago, the way to avoid ethnocen-trism is precisely to abandon the sort of thing we fuzzies are blamed for abandoning. It is to have only the most tenuous and cursory formulations of criteria for changing our beliefs, only the loos-est and most flexible standards. Suppose that for the last three hundred years we had been using an explicit algorithm for determining how just a society was and how good a physical theory was. Would we have developed either parliamentary democracy or relativity physics? Suppose that we had the sort of "weapons" against the fascists of which Dewey was said to deprive us—firm, un-revisable moral principles which were not merely "ours" but "universal" and "objective." How could we avoid having these weapons turn in our hands and bash all the genial tolerance out of our own heads?

Imagine, to use another example, that a few years from now you open your copy of the *New York Times* and read that the philosophers, in convention assembled, have unanimously agreed that values are objective, science rational, truth a matter of correspondence to reality, and so on. Recent breakthroughs in semantics and

meta-ethics, the report goes on, have caused the last remaining noncognitivists in ethics to recant. Similar breakthroughs in philosophy of science have led Kuhn formally to abjure his claim that there is no theory-independent way to recon-struct statements about what is "really there." All the new fuzzies have repudiated all their former views. By way of making amends for the intellectual confusion which the philosophical profession has recently caused, the philosophers have adopted a short, crisp set of standards of ra-tionality and morality. Next year the convention is expected to adopt the report of the committee charged with formulating a standard of aesthetic taste.

Surely the public reaction to this would not be "Saved!" but rather "Who on earth do these philosophers think they *are*?" It is one of the best things about the intellectual life we Western liberals lead that this *would* be our reaction. No matter how much we moan about the disorder and confusion of the current philosophical scene, about the treason of the clerks, we do not really want things any other way. What prevents us from relaxing and enjoying the new fuzziness is perhaps no more than cultural lag, the fact that the rhetoric of the Enlightenment praised the emerging natural sciences in a vocabulary which was left over from a less liberal and tolerant era. This rhetoric enshrined all the old philosophical oppositions between mind and world, appear-ance and reality, subject and object, truth and pleasure. Dewey thought that it was the contin-ued prevalence of such oppositions which pre-vented us from seeing that modern science was a new and promising invention, a way of life which had not existed before and which ought to be encouraged and imitated, something which re-quired a new rhetoric rather than justification by an old one.

Suppose that Dewey was right about this, and that eventually we learn to find the fuzziness which results from breaking down such opposi-tions spiritually comforting rather than morally offensive. What would the rhetoric of the cul-ture, and in particular of the humanities, sound like? Presumably it would be more Kuhnian, in the sense that it would mention particular concrete achievements—paradigms—more, and "method" less. There would be less talk about rigor and more about originality. The image of the great scientist would not be of somebody who got it right but of somebody who made it new. The new rhetoric would draw more on the vocabulary of Romantic poetry and socialist politics, and less on that of Greek metaphysics, religious morality, or Enlightenment scientism. A scientist would rely on a sense of solidarity with the rest of her profession, rather than a picture of herself as battling through the veils of illusion, guided by the light of reason.

If all this happened, the term "science," and thus the oppositions between the humanities, the arts, and the sciences, might gradually fade away. Once "science" was deprived of an honorific sense, we might not need it for taxonomy. We might feel no more need for a term which groups together paleontology, physics, anthropology, and psychology than we do for one which groups together engineering, law, social work, and medicine. The people now called "scientists" would no longer think of themselves as a member of a quasi-priestly order, nor would the public think of themselves as in the care of such an order.

In this situation, "the humanities" would no longer think of themselves as such, nor would they share a common rhetoric. Each of the disciplines which now fall under that rubric would worry as little about its method or cognitive status as do mathematics, civil engineering, and sculpture. It would worry as little about its philosophical foundations. For terms which denoted disciplines would not be thought to divide "subject-matters," chunks of the world which had "interface" with each other. Rather, they would be thought to denote communities whose boundaries were as fluid as the interests of their members. In this heyday of the fuzzy, there would be as little reason to be self-conscious about the nature and status of one's discipline as, in the ideal democratic community, about the nature and status of one's race or sex. For one's ultimate loyalty would be to the larger community which permitted and encouraged this kind of freedom and insouciance. This community would serve no higher end than its own preservation and self-improvement, the preservation and enhancement of civilization. It would identify rationality with that effort, rather than with the desire for objectivity. So it would feel no need for a foundation more solid than reciprocal loyalty.

# SANDRA HARDING AND THE CASE OF FEMINIST EPISTEMOLOGY: JUST WHOSE "KNOWLEDGE" ARE WE TALKING ABOUT?

When epistemologists argue about what constitutes truth, objectivity, rationality, and knowledge, the fact that most of the philosophers participating in the discussion are men usually goes unnoticed. What do we make of this historical fact? Do men and women really have distinct ways of thinking about these subjects? For instance, do women and men have the same way of thinking about what constitutes "rationality"? Or do men invest more philosophical capital in rationality than do women? Is there such a thing as gender-specific knowledge?

These are some of the questions feminist epistemologists ask. These questions shouldn't be thought of as highly abstract deliberations that have nothing to do with real life. Feminists would argue that these issues are connected to theories of human nature at a deep level and are connected to the way research is carried out in the humanities and social sciences. Most important, how we sort out these philosophical issues directly affects how we understand and treat women.

Male philosophers, since Plato, have argued that rationality is the epitome of human action. Unlike emotional behavior, rational behavior has been seen as the more virtuous activity, absolutely necessary for philosophical investigation. To be "objective" means to be emotionally detached from one's inquiry, whether philosophical or scientific. As we saw with the feminist critique of patriarchal health-care ethics, this emotional detachment is even prevalent in medical practice where the physician is detached from the patient. Operating this way is the epistemologist's methodology for turning up accurate facts and acquiring true knowledge.

The trouble with this way of thinking is that men are the ones making these claims, thus privileging what could be a male (or "androcentric") way of thinking. Privileging this way of thinking, or "discourse," will invariably have political consequences. It will give men positions of power in political, economic, religious, and cultural institutions. These powerful men then tell women that they should avoid emotion and irrationality. They ask, "How could we get things accomplished, accomplished the right way, if we don't do things rationally?"

Contrary to her description of how she sees the male-oriented (and highly idealized) way of favoring rationality, the feminist wants to question the assumption that research can indeed be value neutral. Can research really take place without the investigator imposing his own values and assumptions onto his research? The feminist epistemologist asserts that most male researchers, contrary to what they may believe, *do* infuse their research and theories with values, assumptions, and beliefs, thus privileging a male way of thinking.

If the feminist epistemologist is right, then the traditional way of doing epistemology will have some concrete social and political implications for women. Qualities seen as "feminine" will come to be valued as secondary to the more "masculine" qualities of rationality and scientific objectivity. This would include not only the values that women have but also their traits and occupations.

In her reading, Sandra Harding explores the possibility of a distinctive feminist methodology appropriate for use in the social sciences. She begins with an introductory review of how method, methodology, and epistemology are understood by feminists. In general, she is skeptical about the usefulness of a specifically "feminist" methodology.

Be that as it may, feminists face many difficulties in their attempt to eliminate sexism. She calls female researchers who are not yet recognized for their endeavors "lost women." So, as a start, the accomplishments by these "lost women" in the sciences and the humanities have to be acknowledged. But this is only the first step. Other instances of male dominance have to be uncovered. The uncovering will range from physical abuse to economic and political discrimination against women.

Harding then looks at how research has traditionally been done in the social sciences. She believes that the traditional way research has been conducted has been through a male-centered "logic of discovery." The central approach taken by the researchers, at least implicitly, was to "ask only those questions about nature and social life which (white, Western, bourgeois) men want answered." Of course, if this is the unconscious mentality behind most male social research, then women's concerns will never be seriously considered.

At the end of her reading, Harding considers whether men can participate in a feminist methodology. Can men, as men, uncover and address discriminatory practices against women? Or can only women conduct this research? If only women can make important contributions to feminist research, then feminists would be open to the charge of relativism. That is, feminists would have to stop making any truth claims about their findings—the best that they would be able to say is that their ideas are "true for us" but not for men or for nonfeminist women.

This sort of relativism is a real problem for doing science. Imagine saying only to blue-eyed people or people of Spanish descent that water is composed of two hydrogen atoms and one oxygen atom, but to others that it has a different chemical composition. All respectable chemists and physicists would ridicule such a claim.

This is complicated by the realization that if feminist inquiry must arise from women's experiences, then male inquirers will be shut out of feminist research. Harding mentions John Stuart Mill and Karl Marx as men who were able to make significant contributions to feminist thought, refuting in part this idea of epistemological "separatism." Harding also points out that men are not the only ones guilty of sexism and that women can also produce sexist literature. In the end, Harding believes that the term *feminist* can be applied to women and men alike. Being a feminist depends less on one's sex than on one's willingness to take into account women's experiences when doing research.

# Is There a Feminist Methodology?

## SANDRA HARDING

OVER THE LAST TWO decades feminist inquirers have raised fundamental challenges to the ways social science has analyzed women, men, and social life. Is there a distinctive feminist method of inquiry? How does feminist methodology challenge—or complement—traditional methodologies? On what grounds would one defend the assumptions and procedures of feminist researchers? Questions such as these have generated important controversies within feminist theory and politics, as well as curiosity and anticipation in the traditional discourses.

The most frequently asked question has been the first one: is there a distinctive feminist method of inquiry? However, it has been hard to get a clear focus on the kind of answer to this question that we should seek. My point here is to argue against the idea of a distinctive feminist method of research. . . .

## *Method, Methodology, Epistemology*

One reason it is difficult to find a satisfactory answer to questions about a distinctive feminist method is that discussions of method (techniques for gathering evidence) and methodology (a theory and analysis of how research should proceed) have been intertwined with each other and with epistemological issues (issues about an adequate theory of knowledge or justificatory strategy) in both the traditional and feminist discourses. This claim is a complex one and we shall sort out its components. But the point here is simply that "method" is often used to refer to all three as-

SOURCE: Sandra Harding, "Is There a Feminist Methodology?" introduction to *Feminism and Methodology: Social Science Issues,* ed. Sandra Harding (Bloomington: Indiana University Press, 1987), pp. 1–14 (edited; notes referring to other parts of the book have been omitted). Used by permission of Sandra Harding, Graduate School of Education and Information Studies, and Women's Studies, University of California, Los Angeles.

pects of research. Consequently, it is not at all clear what one is supposed to be looking for when trying to identify a distinctive "feminist method of research." This lack of clarity permits critics to avoid facing up to what *is* distinctive about the best feminist social inquiry. It also makes it difficult to recognize what one must do to advance feminist inquiry.

A research *method* is a technique for (or way of proceeding in) gathering evidence. One could reasonably argue that all evidence-gathering techniques fall into one of the following three categories: listening to (or interrogating) informants, observing behavior, or examining historical traces and records. In this sense, there are only three methods of social inquiry. Feminist researchers use just about any and all of the methods, in this concrete sense of the term, that traditional androcentric researchers have used. Of course, precisely how they carry out these methods of evidence gathering is often strikingly different. For example, they listen carefully to how women informants think about their lives and men's lives, and critically to how traditional social scientists conceptualize women's and men's lives. They observe behaviors of women and men that traditional social scientists have not thought significant. They seek examples of newly recognized patterns in historical data. . . .

A *methodology* is a theory and analysis of how research does or should proceed; it includes accounts of how "the general structure of theory finds its application in particular scientific disciplines."[1] Feminist researchers have argued that traditional theories have been applied in ways that make it difficult to understand women's participation in social life, or to understand men's activities as gendered (vs. as representing "the human").[2] They have produced feminist versions of traditional theories. Thus we can find examples of feminist methodologies in discussions of how phenomenological approaches can be used to begin to understand women's worlds, or of how Marxist political economy can be used to explain the causes of women's continuing exploitation in the household or in wage labor. But these sometimes heroic efforts raise questions about whether even feminist applications of these theories can succeed in producing complete and undistorted accounts of gender and of women's activities. And they also raise epistemological issues.

An *epistemology* is a theory of knowledge. It answers questions about who can be a "knower" (can women?); what tests beliefs must pass in order to be legitimated as knowledge (only tests against men's experiences and observations?); what kinds of things can be known (can "subjective truths" count as knowledge?), and so forth. Sociologists of knowledge characterize epistemologies as strategies for justifying beliefs: appeals to the authority of God, of custom and tradition, of "common sense," of observation, of reason, and of masculine authority are examples of familiar justificatory strategies. Feminists have argued that traditional epistemologies, whether intentionally or unintentionally, systematically exclude the possibility that women could be "knowers" or *agents of knowledge;* they claim that the voice of science is a masculine one; that history is written from only the point of view of men (of the dominant class and race); that the subject of a traditional sociological sentence is always assumed to be a man. They have proposed alternative theories of knowledge that legitimate women as knowers.[3] . . . These issues, too, are often referred to as issues about method. Epistemological issues certainly have crucial implications for how general theoretical structures can and should be applied in particular disciplines and for the choice of methods of research. But I

[1] Peter Caws, "Scientific Method," in *The Encyclopedia of Philosophy*, ed. Paul Edwards (New York: Macmillan, 1967), p. 339.
[2] Feminist methodologists have even achieved the heroic in showing that through ingenious applications of what have been widely regarded as hopelessly sexist theories—such as sociobiology—we can increase our understandings of women and gender. See Donna Haraway's discussion of this issue in "Animal Sociology and a Natural Economy of the Body

Politic," pt. 2, in *Signs: Journal of Women in Culture and Society* 4, no. 1 (1978).
[3] For further discussion of the feminist science and epistemology critiques see my *The Science Question in Feminism* (Ithaca, N.Y.: Cornell University Press, 1986) and Jean O'Barr and Sandra Harding, eds., *Sex and Scientific Inquiry* (Chicago: University of Chicago Press, 1987).

think that it is misleading and confusing to refer to these, too, as issues about method.

In summary, there are important connections between epistemologies, methodologies, and research methods. But I am arguing that it is *not* by looking at research methods that one will be able to identify the distinctive features of the best of feminist research. We shall next see that this distinctiveness is also not to be found in attempts to "add women" to traditional analyses.

## Problems with "Adding Women"

In order to grasp the depth and extent of the transformation of the social sciences required in order to understand gender and women's activities, one needs to recognize the limitations of the most obvious ways one could try to rectify the androcentrism of traditional analyses. Feminist researchers first tried to "add women" to these analyses. There were three kinds of women who appeared as obvious candidates for this process: women social scientists, women who contributed to the public life social scientists already were studying, and women who had been victims of the most egregious forms of male dominance.

In the first of these projects, scholars have begun to recover and to reappreciate the work of women researchers and theorists. Women's research and scholarship often has been ignored, trivialized, or appropriated without the credit which would have been given to a man's work. One of the notorious examples of this kind of sexist devaluation in the natural sciences is the treatment of Rosalind Franklin's work on DNA by her Nobel prizewinning colleagues.[4] How many other outstanding women social and natural scientists will we never have the chance to appreciate because they, unlike Franklin, had no close friend capable of setting the record straight?

However, there are severe problems with imagining that this is the only or most important way to eliminate sexism and androcentrism from social science. Obviously, one should not expect

to understand gender and women's roles in social life merely through learning about the work of women social scientists in the past. Insightful as these "lost women" were, their work could not benefit from the many feminist theoretical breakthroughs of the last two decades. Moreover, these women succeeded in entering a world which largely excluded women from the education and credentialling necessary to become social scientists. Thus their work was constrained by the immense pressures on them to make their research conform to what the men of their times thought about social life. Such pressures are still very great. Fortunately they often succeeded in resisting these pressures. Nevertheless, we should not expect their research projects to produce the kinds of powerful analyses that can emerge when women's and men's thinking is part of a broad social revolution such as the women's movement has created. What remains amazing is the intellectual courage and frequent flashes of brilliance exhibited in the thinking of these social scientists in spite of the social, professional, and political constraints they faced.[5]

A different concern of feminist social research has been to examine women's contributions to activities in the public world which were already the focus of social science analysis. We now can see that women, too, have been the originators of distinctively human culture, deviants, voters, revolutionaries, social reformers, high achievers, wage workers, and so forth. Important studies have expanded our understanding of women's roles in public life both historically and in other cultures today.

This focus still leaves some powerfully androcentric standards firmly in place, thereby insuring only partial and distorted analyses of gender and women's social activities. It falsely suggests that only those activities that men have found it important to study are the ones which constitute and shape social life. This leads us to ignore such crucial issues as how changes in the social

---

[4] See James Watson, *The Double Helix* (New York: New American Library, 1969), and Anne Sayre, *Rosalind Franklin and DNA* (New York: Norton, 1975).

[5] See Margaret Rossiter, *Women Scientists in America: Struggles and Strategies to 1940* (Baltimore: Johns Hopkins University Press, 1982), for documentation of the efforts by women natural and social scientists in the 19th and early 20th centuries.

practices of reproduction, sexuality, and mothering have shaped the state, the economy, and the other public institutions. Furthermore, this research focus does not encourage us to ask what have been the *meanings* of women's contributions to public life *for women*. For instance, Margaret Sanger's birth control movement played an important and unfortunate role in eugenics policy. But it also signified to women that they could plan their reproductive lives and in that sense systematically and effectively control the consequences of their sexual activities. This second meaning is not likely to be noticed when the focus is on only women's contributions to "men's world." To take another example, both white and black women worked courageously in the antislavery, black suffrage, and antilynching movements. But what did it mean for their lives *as women* to work in these movements? (They learned public speaking, political organizing, and the virulence of white men's hostility to women learning how to speak and organize, among other things!)[6]

A third kind of new focus of research on women can be found in the study of women as victims of male dominance. Male dominance takes many forms. Researchers have provided path-breaking studies of the "crimes against women"—especially rape, incest, pornography, and wife beating. They have examined the broader patterns of institutionalized economic exploitation and political discrimination against women. And they have looked at the forms of white male domination which have particularly victimized women of color in slavery, in state reproductive and welfare policies, in "protective" legislation, in union practices, and in other circumstances.[7] The emergence to public consciousness of this ugly underside of women's condition has made it impossible for serious thinkers to continue to believe in the reality of unmitigated social progress in this culture or most others. One might reasonably find contemporary cultures to be among the most barbaric from the perspective of the statistics on the victimization of women.

Victimologies have their limitations too. They tend to create the false impression that women have only been victims, that they have never successfully fought back, that women cannot be effective social agents on behalf of themselves or others. But the work of other feminist scholars and researchers tells us otherwise. Women have always resisted male domination.

I have pointed out problems with three basic approaches to the study of women and gender which initially looked promising. While each is valuable in its own right, the most widely acclaimed examples of the new feminist scholarship include analyses of these "kinds of women," but also move far beyond these projects.[8] Let us turn to look at just what it is that characterizes the best of this research, for these characteristics should offer more promising criteria than research methods for what is distinctive in feminist analyses.

## What's New in Feminist Analyses?

Let us ask about the history of feminist inquiry the kind of question Thomas Kuhn posed about the history of science.[9] He asked what the point would be of a philosophy of science for which the history of science failed to provide supporting evidence. We can ask what the point would be of elaborating a theory of the distinctive nature of feminist inquiry that excluded the best feminist social science research from satisfying its criteria. Some of the proposals for a feminist method have this unfortunate consequence. Formulating this question directs one to attempt to identify the characteristics that distinguish the most illuminating examples of feminist research.

[6] Bettina Aptheker, *Women's Legacy: Essays on Race, Sex and Class in American History* (Amherst: University of Massachusetts Press, 1982); and Angela Davis, *Women, Race and Class* (New York: Random House, 1983).
[7] It needs to be said that white women, too, have participated in oppressing women of color in a variety of ways.
[8] Peggy McIntosh provides an interestingly harsher judgment than I of these additive approaches to feminist scholarship in "Interactive Phases of Curricular Revision: A Feminist Perspective," working paper no. 124 (Wellesley, Mass.: Wellesley College Center for Research on Women, 1983).
[9] Thomas S. Kuhn, *The Structure of Scientific Revolutions*, 2d ed. (Chicago: University of Chicago Press, 1970).

## New Empirical and Theoretical Resources: Women's Experiences

Critics argue that traditional social science has begun its analyses only in men's experiences. That is, it has asked only the questions about social life that appear problematic from within the social experiences that are characteristic for men (white, Western, bourgeois men, that is). It has unconsciously followed a "logic of discovery" which we could formulate in the following way: Ask only those questions about nature and social life which (white, Western, bourgeois) men want answered. How can "we humans" achieve greater autonomy? What is the appropriate legal policy toward rapists and raped women which leaves intact the normal standards of masculine sexual behavior? On the one hand, many phenomena which appear problematic from the perspective of men's characteristic experiences do not appear problematic at all from the perspective of women's experiences. (The above two issues, for example, do not characteristically arise from women's experiences.) On the other hand, women experience many phenomena which they think do need explanation. Why do men find child care and housework so distasteful? Why do women's life opportunities tend to be constricted exactly at the moments traditional history marks as the most progressive? Why is it hard to detect black women's ideals of womanhood in studies of black families? Why is men's sexuality so "driven," so defined in terms of power? Why is risking death said to represent the distinctively human act but giving birth regarded as merely natural? Reflection on how social phenomena get defined as problems in need of explanation in the first place quickly reveals that there is no such thing as a problem without a person (or groups of them) who have this problem: a problem is always a problem *for* someone or other. Recognition of this fact, and its implications for the structure of the scientific enterprise, quickly brings feminist approaches to inquiry into conflict with traditional understandings in many ways.

The traditional philosophy of science argues that the origin of scientific problems or hypotheses is irrelevant to the "goodness" of the results of research. It doesn't matter where one's problems or hypotheses come from—from gazing into crystal balls, from sun worshipping, from observing the world around us, or from critical discussion with the most brilliant thinkers. There is no logic for these "contexts of discovery," though many have tried to find one. Instead, it is in the "context of justification," where hypotheses are tested, that we should seek the "logic of scientific inquiry." It is in this testing process that we should look for science's distinctive virtues (for its "method"). But the feminist challenges reveal that the questions that are asked—and, even more significantly, those that are not asked—are at least as determinative of the adequacy of our total picture as are any answers that we can discover. Defining what is in need of scientific explanation only from the perspective of bourgeois, white men's experiences leads to partial and even perverse understandings of social life. One distinctive feature of feminist research is that it generates its problematics from the perspective of women's experiences. It also uses these experiences as a significant indicator of the "reality" against which hypotheses are tested.

Recognition of the importance of using women's experiences as resources for social analysis obviously has implications for the social structures of education, laboratories, journals, learned societies, funding agencies—indeed, for social life in general. And it needs to be stressed that it is *women* who should be expected to be able to reveal *for the first time* what women's experiences are. Women should have an equal say in the design and administration of the institutions where knowledge is produced and distributed for reasons of social justice: it is not fair to exclude women from gaining the benefits of participating in these enterprises that men get. But they should also share in these projects because only partial and distorted understandings of ourselves and the world around us can be produced in a culture which systematically silences and devalues the voices of women.

Notice that it is "women's experiences" *in the*

*plural* which provide the new resources for research. This formulation stresses several ways in which the best feminist analyses differ from traditional ones. For one thing, once we realized that there is no universal *man,* but only culturally different men and women, then "man's" eternal companion—"woman"—also disappeared. That is, women come only in different classes, races, and cultures: there is no "woman" and no "woman's experience." Masculine and feminine are always categories within every class, race, and culture in the sense that women's and men's experiences, desires, and interests differ within every class, race, and culture. But so, too, are class, race, and culture always categories within gender, since women's and men's experiences, desires, and interests differ according to class, race, and culture. This leads some theorists to propose that we should talk about our "feminisms" only in the plural, since there is no one set of feminist principles or understandings beyond the very, very general ones to which feminists in every race, class, and culture will assent. Why should we have expected it to be any different? There are very few principles or understandings to which sexists in every race, class, and culture will assent!

Not only do our gender experiences vary across the cultural categories; they also are often in conflict in any one individual's experience. My experiences as a mother and a professor are often contradictory. Women scientists often talk about the contradictions in identity between what they experience as women and scientists. Dorothy Smith writes of the "fault line" between women sociologists' experience as sociologists and as women. The hyphenated state of many self-chosen labels of identity—black feminist, socialist feminist, Asian-American feminist, lesbian feminist—reflects this challenge to the "identity politics" which has grounded Western thought and public life. These fragmented identities are a rich source of feminist insight.

Finally, the questions an oppressed group wants answered are rarely requests for so-called pure truth. Instead, they are queries about how to change its conditions; how its world is shaped by forces beyond it; how to win over, defeat, or neutralize those forces arrayed against its emancipation, growth, or development; and so forth. Consequently, feminist research projects originate primarily not in any old "women's experiences," but in women's experiences in political struggles. (Kate Millett and others remind us that the bedroom and the kitchen are as much the site of political struggle as are the board room or the polling place.[10]) It may be that it is only through such struggles that one can come to understand oneself and the social world.

## New Purposes of Social Science: For Women

If one begins inquiry with what appears problematic from the perspective of women's experiences, one is led to design research *for* women. . . . That is, the goal of this inquiry is to provide for women explanations of social phenomena that they want and need, rather than providing for welfare departments, manufacturers, advertisers, psychiatrists, the medical establishment, or the judicial system answers to questions that they have. The questions about women that men have wanted answered have all too often arisen from desires to pacify, control, exploit, or manipulate women. Traditional social research has been *for men.* In the best of feminist research, the purposes of research and analysis are not separable from the origins of research problems.

## New Subject Matter of Inquiry: Locating the Researcher in the Same Critical Plane as the Overt Subject Matter

There are a number of ways we could characterize the distinctive subject matter of feminist social analysis. While studying women is not new, studying them from the perspective of their own experiences so that women can understand them-

[10] Kate Millett, *Sexual Politics* (New York: Doubleday & Co., 1969).

selves and the world can claim virtually no history at all. It is also novel to study gender. The idea of a systematic social construction of masculinity and femininity that is little, if at all, constrained by biology, is very recent. Moreover, feminist inquiry joins other "underclass" approaches in insisting on the importance of studying ourselves and "studying up," instead of "studying down." While employers have often commissioned studies of how to make workers happy with less power and pay, workers have rarely been in a position to undertake or commission studies of anything at all, let alone how to make employers happy with less power and profit. Similarly, psychiatrists have endlessly studied what they regard as women's peculiar mental and behavioral characteristics, but women have only recently begun to study the bizarre mental and behavioral characteristics of psychiatrists. If we want to understand how our daily experience arrives in the forms it does, it makes sense to examine critically the sources of social power.

The best feminist analysis goes beyond these innovations in subject matter in a crucial way: it insists that the inquirer her/himself be placed in the same critical plane as the overt subject matter, thereby recovering the entire research process for scrutiny in the results of research. That is, the class, race, culture, and gender assumptions, beliefs, and behaviors of the researcher her/himself must be placed within the frame of the picture that she/he attempts to paint. This does not mean that the first half of a research report should engage in soul searching (though a little soul searching by researchers now and then can't be all bad!). Instead, as we will see, we are often explicitly told by the researcher what her/his gender, race, class, culture is, and sometimes how she/he suspects this has shaped the research project—though of course we are free to arrive at contrary hypotheses about the influence of the researcher's presence on her/his analysis. Thus the researcher appears to us not as an invisible, anonymous voice of authority, but as a real, historical individual with concrete, specific desires and interests.

This requirement is no idle attempt to "do good" by the standards of imagined critics in classes, races, cultures (or of a gender) other than that of the researcher. Instead, it is a response to the recognition that the cultural beliefs and behaviors of feminist researchers shape the results of their analyses no less than do those of sexist and androcentric researchers. We need to avoid the "objectivist" stance that attempts to make the researcher's cultural beliefs and practices invisible while simultaneously skewering the research object's beliefs and practices to the display board. Only in this way can we hope to produce understandings and explanations which are free (or, at least, more free) of distortion from the unexamined beliefs and behaviors of social scientists themselves. Another way to put this point is that the beliefs and behaviors of the researcher are part of the empirical evidence for (or against) the claims advanced in the results of research. This evidence too must be open to critical scrutiny no less than what is traditionally defined as relevant evidence. Introducing this "subjective" element into the analysis in fact increases the objectivity of the research and decreases the "objectivism" which hides this kind of evidence from the public. This kind of relationship between the researcher and the object of research is usually discussed under the heading of the "reflexivity of social science." I refer to it here as a new subject matter of inquiry to emphasize the unusual strength of this form of the reflexivity recommendation. The reader will want to ask if and how this strong form of the reflexivity recommendation can be found in the following analyses. How is it implicitly directing inquiry? How might it have shaped some of these research projects yet more strongly?

To summarize my argument, it is features such as these three—not a "feminist method"—which are responsible for producing the best of the new feminist research and scholarship. They can be thought of as methodological features because they show us how to apply the general structure of scientific theory to research on women and gender. They can also be thought of as epistemological ones because they imply theories of knowledge different from the traditional ones. Clearly the extraordinary explanatory power of the results of feminist research in the social sciences . . . is due to feminist-inspired challenges to the grand theories and the background assumptions of traditional social inquiry.

## Two Final Issues

Before concluding this essay, I want to warn the reader against two inferences one should resist drawing from the analysis above. It is sometimes falsely supposed that in using women's experiences rather than men's as an empirical and theoretical resource, feminism espouses a kind of relativism. It is sometimes also falsely imagined that men cannot make important contributions to feminist research and scholarship. The two issues are related to each other.

First, we should note that on the account I gave above, women's and men's experiences are not equally reliable guides to the production of complete and undistorted social research. Feminist inquirers are never saying that sexist and antisexist claims are equally plausible—for example, that it's equally plausible to regard women as incapable of the highest kind of moral judgment (as men have claimed) and as exercising a different but equally "high" kind of moral judgment (as Carol Gilligan argues). Feminist researchers are arguing that women's and men's characteristic social experiences provide different but not equal grounds for reliable knowledge claims. Here I can only relativize relativism itself; that is, I can point to the limited social contexts in which it appears to be a reasonable position to advance . . .

The second faulty inference one might be tempted to make is that men cannot make important contributions to feminist research and scholarship. If the problems feminist inquiry addresses must arise from women's experiences, if feminist social science is to be for women, and if the inquirer is to be in the same critical plane as subject matters (which are often about women and gender), how could men do feminist social science? This vexing question has gained increasing attention as more and more men are, in fact, teaching in women's studies programs and producing analyses of women and gender.

On the one hand, there are clearly important contributions to the history of feminist thought which have been made by men. John Stuart Mill, Karl Marx, and Friedrich Engels are just the most obvious of these thinkers. Their writings are certainly controversial and, at best, imperfect; but so, too, are the writings of the most insightful women thinkers of these periods or, for that matter, in the present day. Moreover, there have always been women willing and able to produce sexist and misogynistic thought—Marabel Morgan and Phyllis Schlafly are just two of such recent writers. Obviously, neither the ability nor the willingness to contribute to feminist understanding is sex-linked . . . !

Moreover, significant contributions to *other* emancipation movements have been made by thinkers who were not themselves members of the group to be emancipated. Marx and Engels were not members of the proletariat. There are whites in our own nation as well as in South Africa and other racist regimes who have been willing and able to think in antiracist ways—indeed, they have been lynched, exiled, and banned for their antiracist writings. Gentiles in Europe and the United States have argued for and suffered because of their defenses of Jewish freedoms. So it would be historically unusual if the list of contributors to women's emancipation alone excluded by fiat all members of the "oppressor group" from its ranks.

On the other hand, surely women, like members of these other exploited groups, are wise to look especially critically at analyses produced by members of the oppressor group. Are women's experiences used as the test of adequacy of the problems, concepts, hypotheses, research design, collection, and interpretation of data? (Must the "women's experience" from which feminist problematics arise be the experience of the investigator her/himself?) Is the research project *for* women rather than for men and the institutions men control? Does the researcher or theorist place himself in the same class, race, culture, and gender-sensitive critical plane as his subjects of study? . . .

In addition to the scholarly or scientific benefits which could accrue from such studies, this kind of self-critical research by men makes a kind of political contribution to the emancipation of women which inquiries by *women* cannot achieve. Just as courageous whites can set an example for other whites, and can use for antiracist ends the great power institutional racism bestows on even the most antiracist of whites, so too can men make an important but different kind of contribution to women's emancipation. If men are trained by sexist institutions to value masculine authority more highly, then some courageous men can take advantage of that evil and use their masculine authority to resocialize men. . . .

My own preference is to argue that the designation "feminist" can apply to men who satisfy whatever standards women must satisfy to earn the label. The issue here is not so much one of the right to claim a label as it is of the prerequisites for producing less partial and distorted descriptions, explanations, and understandings.

## Study Questions

1. What is the difference between truths of reason and truths of fact? between belief and knowledge? Give some examples of each.

2. Outline the correspondence, coherence, and pragmatic theories of truth. Which theory is most likely to be used by modern science? Why?

3. What are "rationalism" and "empiricism" as theories of knowledge? What are the advantages and disadvantages of each?

4. In what sense was Descartes' view of knowledge a "representational" one? What is the main problem with such a view? How did Descartes solve this problem? Was this solution an effective one? Explain.

5. What does Locke mean by "ideas"? by "ideas of sensation" and "ideas of reflection"? by "simple" and "complex" ideas? Are his basic distinctions well justified?

6. What was Locke's objection to innate ideas? Is the mind in fact a blank slate at birth? Explain.

7. What did Hume mean by "impressions" and "ideas"? Give some examples of each.

8. Are all our ideas copies, or combinations, of our impressions? Do the fantastic creatures found in films such as *Star Wars* and *The Lord of the Rings* disprove Hume's theory in this regard?

9. What did Hume mean by "matters of fact" and "relations of ideas"? Does this distinction cover all the meaningful claims one could make? Explain.

10. What did Hume think was the basis for our idea of causality? Is this a sufficient basis for scientific laws, or do we need a more rigorous notion of causality to ground these laws? Explain.

11. What is James's criterion of truth? How does this vary from the "copy" theory of knowledge?

12. Is there any difference between believing something is true because it's useful to us and saying something is useful because it's true? Give some examples to illustrate your conclusion.

13. What is Ayer's "verification criterion"? What are the two classes of statements that Ayer thought were meaningful? Does this unfairly restrict the sorts of claims that philosophy can consider? Explain.

14. Why did Ayer think that ethics and metaphysics were "nonsense"? Evaluate his claim.

15. Would the claims "God exists because I feel Him in my heart" and "Theft is wrong because it hurts people" pass or fail Ayer's test of whether a sentence is meaningful? Explain.

16. What basic problem do positivists have with respect to historical knowledge? Why does Collingwood criticize the positivists' reliance on natural scientific techniques in explaining the past?

17. In what sense, according to Collingwood, is history like detective work? What is common to their methods? If Collingwood is right about their common nature, can there be such a thing as "objective" historical knowledge? Explain.

18. What is Collingwood's "inside-outside" distinction? What did he mean when he said that all history is the history of thought? Can you think of any exceptions to Collingwood's rule?

19. What does Kuhn mean by a "paradigm"? How does he explain scientific revolutions? Does his explanation make scientific truth too relativistic? Explain.

20. How does Kuhn distinguish between normal and revolutionary science? What are some of the examples he uses?

21. How can we apply Kuhn's notion of paradigm shifts in science to changes in our social or cultural values? Give some examples of fundamental paradigm shifts in Western values that have taken place over the last twenty or thirty years.

22. What is Rorty's anti-representationalist critique of traditional theories of truth? Why does he think the quest for truth is a hopeless one?

23. Why does Rorty want to replace the search for objectivity with one for solidarity? How would this shift to solidarity change the subject matter studied by philosophers?

24. What basic critique of the philosophical tradition do feminist epistemologists make? Is this critique valid? Does it lead to relativism? Explain.

25. Do women and men have different ways of knowing the world? What are some of the political effects of this difference, if it exists? If it doesn't, why have there been so few famous female philosophers?

# *Bibliography*

## GENERAL WORKS ON EPISTEMOLOGY

Ayer, A. J. *Philosophy in the Twentieth Century.* London: Phoenix, 1982. The story of philosophy in the twentieth century with a heavy focus on epistemology. See chapter 3 on pragmatism, chapter 7 on Collingwood, and chapter 9 on contemporary analytic philosophy.

Carr, Brian, and D. J. O'Connor. *Introduction to the Theory of Knowledge.* Minneapolis: University of Minnesota Press, 1982. An introduction to epistemological issues.

Dummett, Michael. *Truth and Other Enigmas.* Cambridge, MA: Harvard University Press, 1978. By an important analytic philosopher. Heavy going; not for the beginner.

Huxley, Aldous. *The Doors of Perception.* New York: Harper & Row, 1970. Huxley's account of his experiments with drugs and how they altered his perceptions. The rock band The Doors took their name from this book, having engaged in similar epistemological experiments.

Nagel, Thomas. *The View from Nowhere.* Oxford: Oxford University Press, 1986. Nagel discusses a variety of epistemological, metaphysical, and ethical issues with the intention of reconciling subjective and objective views of the world. Chapter 5 is on knowledge.

Recent films relevant to the theory of knowledge: *The Matrix* (Wachowski Brothers, 1999); *Memento* (Christopher Nolan, 2000); *Time Code* (Mike Figgis, 2000); *AI: Artificial Intelligence* (Stephen Spielberg, 2002); and *Minority Report* (Stephen Spielberg, 2002). *Memento* is especially interesting in its exploration of the nature of memory and causality. The main character in the film has a form of amnesia that has destroyed his short-term memory; the events in the film are shown to us backward, further confusing matters. *Time Code* divides the movie screen into four separate panels showing us events from the perspectives of four different characters.

Roszak, Theodore. *Where the Wasteland Ends: Politics and Transcendence in Postindustrial Society.* Garden City, NY: Anchor Books, 1973. A powerful counterargument to the view that epistemology must ape the methods of physical science in order to understand the nature of human knowledge. Roszak urges a return to the "transcendental" view of the Romantics.

Russell, Bertrand. *The Problems of Philosophy.* Oxford: Oxford University Press, 1912. This short book is supposedly an introduction to philosophy in general, but much of it is taken up with epistemological problems such as the nature of a priori knowledge and truth and falsity. Russell's book is a concise and clear blueprint for analytic philosophy in the twentieth century. The full text is available at http://www.ditext.com/russell/russell.html.

White, Alan R. *Truth.* Garden City, NY: Doubleday, 1970. White examines the three traditional and three modern views of truth.

Wittgenstein, Ludwig. *Philosophical Investigations.* Translated by G. E. M. Anscombe. Oxford: Basil Blackwell, 1974. The central work of one of the most important philosophers of language in the twentieth century, this book is famous for putting forward the idea that the meaning of words depends on how they are used in a variety of language games. For advanced students only.

## ON LOCKE

Chapell, Vere, ed. *The Cambridge Companion to Locke.* Cambridge: Cambridge University Press, 1994. A collection of articles by Locke scholars focusing on his epistemology and metaphysics.

Dunn, John. *Locke.* New York: Oxford University Press, 1984. Part of the Past Masters series, this short volume has been reprinted in *The British Empiricists: Locke, Berkeley, Hume.*

The Internet Encyclopedia of Philosophy: http://www.utm.edu/research/iep/
See article on Locke.

"John Locke (1632–1704)": http://www.orst.edu/instruct/ph1302/philosophers/locke.html
Another short article on Locke from the *Great Voyages: The History of Western Philosophy 1492–1776* Web page by Bill Uzgalis of Oregon State University. This one has a good timeline of Locke's life, a bibliography, and links to his major texts.

X-Refer: http://www.xrefer.com/
See article on Locke.

## ON HUME

Ayer, A. J. *Hume.* Oxford: Oxford University Press, 1980. A short introduction in the Past Masters series by the great positivist, who is an admirer of Hume.

Chappell, V. C., ed. *Hume, A Collection of Critical Essays.* Garden City, NY: Anchor, 1966. A fine collection of essays on various aspects of Hume's thought.

Passmore, John. *Hume's Intentions.* 3d ed. London: Duckworth, 1980. Passmore interprets Hume from a number of distinct perspectives, focusing on his epistemological views.

Quinton, Anthony. *Hume.* London: Routledge, 1999. A sixty-four-page introduction to Hume's philosophy from the Great Philosophers series by Lord Quinton, a prominent thinker in his own right.

Stroud, Barry. *Hume.* London: Routledge, 1981. In The Arguments of Philosophers series.

Ty's David Hume Home Page: http://www.geocities.com/Athens/3067/hume/h_index.html Contains a number of useful links, including those to electronic texts of Hume's works.


## ON JAMES AND AYER

Bird, Graham. *William James.* London: Routledge, 1986.

Hahn, Lewis Edwin, ed. *The Philosophy of A. J. Ayer.* Peru, IL: Open Court, 1992. A selection of Ayer's works.

Hanfling, Oswald. *Ayer.* London: Routledge, 1999. One of Routledge's The Great Philosophers series of short introductions (all of which have sixty-four or fewer pages). This one is peppered with quotes from Ayer's central works.

Myers, Gerald E. *William James: His Life and Thought.* New Haven, CT: Yale University Press, 1986. A hefty and comprehensive treatment of James's ideas. Chapter 10 is on knowledge.

William James: http://www.emory.edu/EDUCATION/mfp/james.html This site offers a comprehensive series of links to electronic texts of James's works, to a biography, and to other sites on James.


## ON COLLINGWOOD

Code, Lorraine. "Collingwood's Epistemological Individualism." *The Monist* 72 (1989): 543–567. Code criticizes Collingwood's "epistemological individualism," his focus on the knowing subject.

Dray, William H. *Philosophy of History.* Englewood Cliffs, NJ: Prentice-Hall, 1964. Dray discusses the key issues in the philosophy of history in this introductory book. See chapter 2 for an outline of Collingwood's position, along with some criticisms of it.

———. "R.G. Collingwood and the Understanding of Actions in History." In *Perspectives on History,* edited by William Dray. London: Routledge, 1980. One of several articles by Dray on Collingwood. In this one he reviews Collingwood's idea of reenactment and his inside-outside distinction.

Johnson, Peter. *R. G. Collingwood—an Introduction.* Bristol, UK: Thoemmes Press, 1998. A short introduction to Collingwood's complete thought.

Mink, Louis O. *Mind, History, and Dialectic: The Philosophy of R. G. Collingwood.* Bloomington: Indiana University Press, 1969. Mink treats Collingwood as a systematic dialectical philosopher. See Chapter 6 for his account of Collingwood's "grammar" of history.

Nielsen, Margit Hurup. "Re-enactment and Reconstruction in Collingwood's Philosophy of History." *History and Theory* 20 (1981): 1–31. Nielsen discusses Collingwood's idea that we can know the past only by reconstructing past thoughts in present minds.

van der Dussen, W. J. *History as a Science: The Philosophy of R. G. Collingwood.* The Hague: Martinus Nijhoff, 1981. A massive interpretation of Collingwood's philosophy of history that includes a detailed discussion of Collingwood's unpublished manuscripts on the subject.


## ON THE PHILOSOPHY OF SCIENCE AND SOCIAL SCIENCE

Feigl, Herbert, and May Broadbeck, eds. *Readings in the Philosophy of Science.* New York: Appleton-Century-Crofts, 1953. An older standard collection of articles.

Feyerabend, Paul. *Against Method.* 3d ed. London: Verso Books, 1993. Feyerabend is an "anarchist" philosopher of science who criticizes the pretensions of philosophy to legislate for science and the scientific method for its view that "anything goes."

Mann, Douglas. *Structural Idealism: A Theory of Social and Historical Explanation.* Waterloo, Ontario: Wilfrid Laurier University Press, 2002. This book discusses a wide variety of issues in the philosophy of social sciences and the philosophy of history. Chapter 4 reinterprets Collingwood's philosophy of history, specifically his idea that historians have to reenact the thoughts of historical actors to understand the past.

Meyerhoff, Hans, ed. *The Philosophy of History in Our Time.* Garden City, NY: Anchor Books, 1959. An older but still valuable collection of excerpts from a wide variety of philosophers of history.

Winch, Peter. *The Idea of a Social Science and Its Relation to Philosophy.* London: Routledge & Kegan Paul, 1958. Winch argues that social scientists must focus on human intentions instead of impersonal causes in understanding human life, seeing these intentions as expressed in language games, following Wittgenstein.

## ON POSTMODERNIST EPISTEMOLOGY

Calinescu, Matei. *Five Faces of Modernity.* Durham, NC: Duke University Press, 1987. The "five faces" are contemporary movements in art and literature: modernism, the avant-garde, decadence, kitsch, and postmodernism. The last chapter is on postmodernism.

Fish, Stanley. *Doing What Comes Naturally.* Durham, NC: Duke University Press, 1989. Fish, a prominent literary critic, focuses on the rhetoric inherent in literary, legal, and psychoanalytic studies in this book, arguing that all knowledge is tied to the historical context of its creation.

Latour, Bruno. *Science in Action: How to Follow Scientists and Engineers through Society.* Cambridge, MA: Harvard University Press, 1998. Latour studies the way that scientists "produce" truths through "trials of strength" in which power and money compete with experimental data as causal factors.

Lyotard, Jean-Francois. *The Postmodern Condition: A Report on Knowledge.* Translated by Geoff Bennington and Brian Massumi. Minneapolis: University of Minnesota Press, 1984. Lyotard argues that modern science will more and more reduce all knowledge to computer data and that scientific research must now be "performative," that is, pay off in cash terms, to be pursued. The postmodern condition is characterized by a general "incredulity toward meta-narratives" by our reluctance to believe in "big stories" such as Christian salvation, liberal human progress, or the coming of a communist utopia. We'll deal at greater length with this important work in Chapter 9.

Norris, Christopher. *Deconstruction: Theory and Practice.* London: Routledge, 1991. Norris gives an overview of deconstruction, an important movement in continental philosophy and North American literary theory that questions the objectivity of any given reading of a text, including philosophical ones. See our Chapter 9 for more on deconstruction.

## ON FEMINIST EPISTEMOLOGY

Bordo, Susan. *The Flight to Objectivity: Essays on Cartesianism and Culture.* Albany: State University of New York Press, 1987. In chapter 6 of her book Bordo argues that Descartes' cool, distant, mathematical form of reason represented a seventeenth-century flight from the feminine, a "Cartesian masculinization of thought" that was a cultural product of its times.

Code, Lorraine. "Is Sex of the Knower Epistemologically Significant?" *Metaphilosophy* 12 (July–October 1981): 267–276. Code concludes that "perhaps the admission of women to the kingdom of knowers, on an equal footing, will effect a shift in the standard evaluation of knowledge claims, granting greater respectability to the contribution made by the affective side of human nature."

Garry, Ann, and Marilyn Pearsall, eds. *Women, Knowledge, and Reality: Explorations in Feminist Philosophy.* Boston: Unwin Hyman, 1989. Essays on feminist epistemology and metaphysics.

Harding, Sandra, ed. *Feminism and Methodology.* Bloomington: Indiana University Press, 1987. Contains ten selections and essays on various feminist approaches to method in psychology, sociology, political science, and other fields. Harding's introduction and conclusion focus specifically on the question of whether feminism needs its own distinct epistemology.

Harding, Sandra, and Merrill Hintikka, eds. *Discovering Reality: Feminist Perspectives on Epistemology, Metaphysics, and Philosophy of Science.* Dordrecht, Holland: D. Reidel, 1983. Another good collection of articles on feminist epistemology and metaphysics.

Smith, Dorothy E. *The Everyday World as Problematic: A Feminist Sociology.* Boston: Northeastern Press, 1987. Smith is a central figure in "feminist standpoint theory," which argues that the social sciences should recognize the unique epistemological and social position of women.

## CHAPTER FIVE

# Ethics

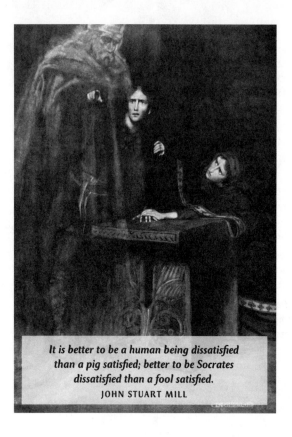

*It is better to be a human being dissatisfied than a pig satisfied; better to be Socrates dissatisfied than a fool satisfied.*
JOHN STUART MILL

## ETHICS: AN INTRODUCTION

At one time or another all of us have been told what we were doing was wrong. The misdeed could have merely been a fib we were trying to get past our mother or a verbal battle with a sibling. As we get older, we take on more responsibilities and obligations, so the ethical and moral issues we face become more difficult and complex, usually affecting a greater number of people.

Ethical theories attempt to provide a framework for making morally correct decisions. Part of the task is to resolve disputes over the rightness or wrongness of our actions and the actions of others. As with any other area of research, ethical theories have been developed in the attempt to order, explain, and understand the world around us.

Although philosophers disagree over the extent to which theories can successfully resolve our everyday moral decisions, most believe moral theories at least orient us to what is at stake when making our choices. Some philosophers even contend that ethical theories also help to develop our well-being, character, and moral intuitions.

Before going further, we need to spend a few moments clarifying our terminology, in particular the possible differences in meaning between the words *ethics* and *morals*. So far we have used the words interchangeably. But does talk about ethics differ from talk about morals?

At least in today's common usage, when referring to more private or personal beliefs about right and wrong, people usually talk about morals rather than ethics. We might say we are acting morally when we treat our family, friends, and acquaintances with common politeness and decency. We should tell the truth to our spouse, partner, girlfriend, or boyfriend. We would be courageous coming to their aid in an emergency, putting their welfare ahead of our own if need be. When we do this consistently, we are considered morally upright.

Ethics, in comparison, often refers to our behavior in the public domain, whether in the workplace or in a professional setting such as the university. As a consequence, many businesses and professions have developed "ethical codes of conduct" for their employees and members. These codes explain what sort of behavior employers expect of their employees and what a profession expects of its members. As a result, when a business manager treats her employees fairly, when she works diligently and is honest with office expenses, we consider her professional behavior to be highly ethical.

There is not, however, always a clear division between our private and public lives. Consider the room where you reside. It is your private space, your own personal domain. But if you are connected to the Internet and are downloading music files, your actions are probably contravening guidelines your university has for students (especially now that such downloading is considered illegal). In a case such as this, private moral conduct crosses the line into public ethics.

Despite the way these two words are now used, they share a similar origin. Etymology—the study of the origin and development of words—traces our English word *ethics* back to the Greek word *ethikos*. Used by Aristotle, *ethikos* implied a positive disposition or character on the part of the moral agent. Later, writing in Latin, Cicero used the word *moralis* as equivalent to the Greek term. Although these two words are often used differently in contemporary common usage, there is also good justification for using them synonymously.

Although philosophers have churned out some very complicated moral theories, many of the principles basic to the theories are reflected in our everyday moral decision-making processes. You may not be fully aware of it, but you most certainly argue for your moral beliefs using ethical principles formalized by these philosophers. Here are some basic moral values people commonly appeal to:

We should not treat a person like an object.

We need to think about the consequences of our decision.

We should care more about others.

The end justifies the means.

The end does not justify the means.

We have to do our duty.

Patience is a virtue.

We must maintain the rule of law.

The popularity of these appeals indicates the influence moral theories have had in contributing to our society's sense of fairness and justice. Acknowledging this importance, we should know in greater depth the ethical theories from which these sayings are derived, including their respective advantages and limitations. For example, when we argue that "the end justifies the means," we should be aware of the advantages and disadvantages of this way of explaining our action so we can avoid harming innocent parties.

In this chapter we address what exactly it is about the moral and ethical life we are trying to capture. Imagine sitting on a terrace at a café, watching a boy scout helping an elderly man cross a busy intersection. From our vantage point, judging the matter from the "outside," we would praise the boy's deed as ethically praiseworthy.

But is this an adequate judgment? What about the scout's intentions? What if we were able to read the scout's mind, discovering he didn't care at all about the elderly man? that he was doing this only to get his "goodwill" badge? How would we then judge the scout's actions?

For someone like John Stuart Mill, the most famous defender of utilitarianism, the central consideration for evaluating the ethics of an action is the amount of utility (i.e., pleasure or happiness) this action produces for all affected parties. Mill wouldn't be too concerned with the scout's inner motivations, as long as his action produces more happiness than unhappiness. As Mill noted, "He who saves a fellow creature from drowning does what is morally right, whether his motive be duty, or the hope of being paid for his trouble."

In contrast, other moral philosophers have given a central role to the intentions of the person acting (the "moral agent"). These philosophers have argued that the true gauge of morality must focus on the intentions of the moral agent. According to these philosophers, we can describe someone as morally praiseworthy only if he or she is acting with laudable motives.

It is possible to be mindful of our own intentions. But if right intentions determine the morality of an action, how will we be able to judge the moral quality of other people's intentions, given that we don't have access to their minds?

Even if we have seen someone do many good acts over several years and in a number of different situations, without access to the person's intentions we will never be able to say for sure whether that person is acting in a truly moral way or not. Because we seldom, if ever, have the opportunity to know someone's true intentions, we may be better off concerning ourselves only with how these actions affect others. If an old man is being helped across the street, perhaps we should be satisfied with the positive consequences of this outward behavior and regard it as morally praiseworthy.

As we'll see in the readings to follow, moral philosophers disagree about this matter of intentions. Mill and his utilitarian colleagues are not particularly concerned with the intentions of the moral agent. Instead, their interest lies in the results or consequences of our actions, which explains why utilitarians are part of a larger school of ethical thought called "consequentialism." Virtue ethics, however, is a moral theory that is very concerned with the intentions of the moral agent. As argued by Aristotle, who was introduced in Chapter 1, we are to cultivate moral virtues such as courage, generosity, and temperance in our daily actions in order to create a good character, one that naturally seeks to act and live well.

We'll get more into these matters later. In the meantime there is some other basic terminology important to ethical theory that we need to be familiar with.

When we talk about what *should* be done, we are making a *prescriptive claim.* Some synonyms for prescriptive claims are *norms* (short for *normative*), *ought* statements ("you ought or ought not to do X"), and *moral imperatives* (commands such as "Don't steal!").

Prescriptive statements can be compared to *descriptive claims.* Descriptive claims attempt to *describe* a given situation. An example would be saying, in a monotone voice, that the state of Oregon allows for physician-assisted suicide, or Canada doesn't have laws against performing abortions. In both cases, one is only stating what *is* the case—a descriptive assertion. However, saying "It is *right* for the state of Oregon to allow for physician-assisted suicide," or "Canadians *ought* to have laws against abortion" would be prescriptive claims. Here, the speaker is saying what *should* or *ought* to be the case.

Can a statement be both a descriptive and a prescriptive claim? It is possible, but it depends on the context. In the example of Oregon allowing for euthanasia, if the person's voice were quivering in anger while speaking, you would rightly assume that the person is not only telling you what *is* the case but is also quite angered by this state of affairs, thinking that it shouldn't be allowed. Put this way, the claim would be both descriptive and prescriptive.

Despite the difficulty of strictly separating the prescriptive from the descriptive, most moral theories fall into one or the other category. For example, the psychological egoists tell us that all our actions are secretly or overtly selfish. They are *describing* moral actions as self-interested, but not telling us what we should do. In contrast, the utilitarians are telling us how we ought to behave, and thus using prescriptive language—"always act to ensure the greatest happiness of the greatest number of people." They're not just *describing* our actions but also *prescribing* what we should do.

Having discussed these preliminary matters, we now move to the weightier ones. For example:

> From what basis do we argue for or against the ethical and moral issues that concern our society?
>
> From where do we get our notions of "right" and "wrong"?
>
> Is it possible to develop a theory that can be used to decide, in light of all moral challenges, what we should or shouldn't do?

The readings in this chapter each attempt to address these questions, albeit in very different ways.

The first selection, from Adam Smith, is devoid of the theoretical machinery often found in other moral theories. Smith's account, termed "moral sense theory," relies on what he describes as "human intuition." Smith's account thus has a strong emotional appeal. Like many philosophers, Smith developed his position from the writings of another philosopher. Smith based his moral theory on the ideas developed by the Scottish-Irish philosopher Francis Hutcheson (1694–1746).

Hutcheson was the first to use the concept of "moral sense." By this he meant that when we observe people or learn about their plight, we are able, through the human faculty of intuition, to recognize distinctions between right and wrong actions. For instance, when we see the misfortune of another, our moral sense makes it possible for us to identify with the pain and misery suffered by that person. Not only do we identify right behavior through intuition but through intuition we also receive our motivation for right behavior. When we see someone suffering pain, we identify with that pain and, as a result, seek to aid the person in distress.

Our motivation for action is, for Hutcheson, combined with another consideration, which came to be known as the "greatest happiness principle." This principle was later used by the utilitarian thinker Jeremy Bentham, and then John Stuart Mill. The basic idea of the principle is that when we act, we need to take into account how our actions will affect the happiness of those people implicated by our action, including ourselves. All things being equal, our moral decisions should aim at increasing the happiness of those affected by the decision taken.

Utilitarianism as well focuses on the consequences of our actions. As argued by John Stuart Mill, when we attempt to sort through the various options when making a moral choice, we should choose the course of action that maximizes *utility* (which can mean either "happiness" or "pleasure"). Mill's utilitarianism was part of a more general approach to ethics called "consequentialism," which we're already acquainted with from our discussion of the boy-scout example. As a consequentialist, we take into account either the consequences for ourselves only (called "ethical egoism," the notion that we *should* always pursue our self-interest) or the consequences for all those affected by our decision (as utilitarianism proper asks us to do). As a consequentialist, we figure out which course of action will result in the greater degree of utility, which is the action we should take.

In contrast to consequentialist theories, Immanuel Kant's deontological theory maintains that consequences play no part in the moral decision-making process. Kant's theory tries to describe duties (from the Greek *deon*) that follow from the "supreme principle of morality," the "categorical imperative."

According to deontology, when deciding whether or not to lie to somebody, instead of thinking about the consequences that will result from telling the truth as opposed to those of lying, we should instead uphold the moral principle "do not lie." No matter what the consequences of our truth telling, our duty is to follow this principle and not lie.

Though it is a broad generalization, it may very well be that in deciding matters of right and wrong, people tend to be either utilitarians or deontologists. An example is the political debate that surrounded the impeachment of President Bill Clinton as a result of his affair with Monica Lewinsky. The Democrats argued that even if Clinton did break the law, the consequences of removing him from office would be devastating for the American economy, political stability, and global peace. In other words, the negative consequences of removing a president from office should override the positive consequences of upholding the abstract moral principle of scrupulous honesty in political life.

In contrast to the Democrats, Republicans argued that because Clinton apparently lied under oath about his involvement with Monica Lewinsky, he had to be impeached and removed from office. They believed that the rule of law and the duty of political leaders to the American Constitution were clear. No exception could be made, even if such an exception would have good consequences.

After looking at Mill and Kant, we turn to the greatest critic of ethical theory in Western thought, Friedrich Nietzsche. We were introduced to Nietzsche's ideas in the chapter on the philosophy of religion. He never organized his thoughts, ethical or otherwise, into a philosophical theory as had Plato, Mill, and Kant. Nevertheless, he had a fairly concise philosophical outlook. To understand his position on ethics, we need to remember the general context of his views.

Proclaiming "the death of God," Nietzsche rightly saw the potentially devastating effect this pronouncement could have on a society that for centuries had defined itself as Christian. How would people react if their hopes for an afterlife were shattered? With what would we replace this way of seeing the world? What could be expected if the foundation for Christian values was removed?

For his part Nietzsche believed that rejection of the Christian worldview could lead to unbridled *nihilism*—that moral absolutes do not exist and that we cannot ever hope to absolutely justify our moral beliefs.

Who was to blame for this nihilism? Here Nietzsche turned the tables on his opponents. Nietzsche argued that because of its emphasis on "other-worldly" beliefs and values, its esteem for humility and pity, and its general disdain for the physical world given the superiority of the world to come, Christianity was to blame for nihilism.

According to Nietzsche, the Christians had it backward. They encouraged "slave morality": extolling humility, telling us to "turn the other cheek," while denigrating power and strength. Nietzsche generally preferred the opposite moral attitude—what he called "master morality." This morality embodied such virtues as courage, ruggedness, and a desire for power both over others and over one's own life. This reversal of values typified Nietzsche's concept of the "will to power," which he saw as dominant in all human life. This was the case even in the supposedly self-sacrificing life of the Christian priest or saint, a life that actually aimed at the control of others through the propagation of its slave morality.

Another important concept in Nietzsche's arsenal was that of the *Übermensch,* usually translated from the German as "Overman" (or "Superman," though this shouldn't be confused with the superhero from Krypton). The Overman was the person who overcame traditional moral restraints and created himself in his own image as a great thinker, artist, or political leader. This person went beyond good and evil, discarding the customary moral restraints of the society of the day.

Nietzsche was highly critical of slave morality because he believed it held back the human capacity for achieving a "higher humanity." Slave morality fed on what Nietzsche described as "*ressentiment.*" Although the word for resentment existed in German (*Empfindlichkeit*), Nietzsche preferred the French word. For Nietzsche *ressentiment* was an important part of the Christians' psychological makeup.

An example of *ressentiment* is the desire of the followers of slave morality to sacrifice all the fleshly pleasures of this world for a heavenly reward. Followers of slave morality also had indignation for those freethinkers who engross themselves in carnal activities.

Nietzsche wanted humankind to affirm this present world (the "world of life") and our mortal nature rather than wallow in this *ressentiment*—viewing humanity as tainted by original sin, as corrupted beings living in a fallen world. He urged us to build, with determination and strength, a world using all the human capacities at our disposal. This "higher type" of morality would lead humanity to "the enhancement of life."

Given his emphasis on the "will to power," the *Übermensch,* and master morality, Nietzsche has been maligned for promoting a brutal ethic. Even worse, the Nazis selectively used Nietzsche's view of life and morality as an underpinning for their racist and destructive ideologies. Some of this criticism is undoubtedly partly Nietzsche's fault. He wasn't always careful with what he thought and in one place rather cavalierly discusses how we should treat "the bungled and the botched."

Granting the seriousness of these statements, it should also be remembered that if people are selective enough, it is relatively easy to use almost any source as a basis for justifying immoral behavior. Even the Bible has been used to rationalize all sorts of wrongful acts, including wars, slavery, and the subjugation of women. As you read the passages from Nietzsche (and hopefully, some of the other books he wrote), you should ask whether he would have been horrified to have seen how twentieth-century fascism misappropriated his work and thought.

Although people generally think either about duties or consequences when making ethical decisions, these are not our only alternatives when making moral judgments. We saw in Chapter 1 that Plato spoke about the proper functioning (including the moral functioning) of a human being, this functioning being embodied in certain moral virtues. The result was "the good life." For his part Aristotle spoke of human teleology—the end of human activity as *eudaimonia,* the good life. This is achieved by following the *mean* (the balance between extremes) when making moral decisions. Both Plato and Aristotle appealed to the virtues in their ethics even though they explained how the virtues informed moral decisions in different ways.

Virtue ethics has recently found renewed popularity. Its approach to ethics is largely foreign to consequentialism and most duty-based methodologies. Instead of asking, "*What* should I *do?*" virtue ethics asks, "*Who* do I wish to *be?*" The focus is not particularly on principles, duties, or the consequences of our actions. Rather, the focus is on acting on those particular inner traits we as a society have found admirable and praiseworthy.

Some of the more traditional common virtues are honesty, courage, trustworthiness, and justice. For example, according to virtue ethics, when we are faced with the choice of whether or not to lie, instead of considering the consequences of our lying or our duty, we are motivated by an inner compunction or disposition to tell the truth. This compunction comes about over time with our habit of practicing this virtue. Just as a musician, over time, becomes skilled by practicing on the piano, so we become virtuous by practicing virtue. We do so as a free expression of the kind of people we are and who we wish to become.

Feminism, as you will see in Chapter 7, represents a radical break from the philosophical tradition. Feminists represent the tradition as being a highly rationalistic and predominantly male-oriented way of thinking. Though this is a highly provocative position, it also explains a lot about the history of ethical theory. When we read Plato, Aristotle, Mill, and Kant, we are taken by their seriousness and their emphasis on being rational and objective. They demand of us a distance from the very passions that so powerfully influence our everyday decisions. According to the traditional philosopher, we need to control our emotions and subjective beliefs. The heat of the moment is a poor basis from which to make our decisions.

Feminists have pointed out that just as our passions may lead to rash and careless choices, removing our emotions entirely from the decision-making process may be a strategy just as extreme. Our emotions—our empathy, sympathy, compassion, and kindness—are an integral component of our humanity, one that also needs to be taken into account when making ethical decisions.

This view of human nature has been developed by feminist moral philosophers into an approach called "care ethics." Its importance can especially be seen in the case of biomedical ethics.

The history of medicine has often neglected to see the patient as a living, breathing, feeling person. The patient's body has instead been treated as a machine the physician can fix with the tools of the medical profession. The patient plays a passive role, just as a motor does under the examination of a mechanic. This model has brought a great deal of harm to patients who need their physicians to listen to them speak about their ailment. Someone, say, dying of cancer may need his or her healthcare specialist to show compassion and empathy. The traditional model of healthcare ethics and the feminist model have been described as illustrating the difference between "the ethics of curing" and "the ethics of caring."

We add here an important note to this introduction on ethical theory. As you read and discuss the selections in this chapter, you will hopefully find them quite useful in addressing your own ethical questions. And though there are philosophers today who are fairly strict adherents of Mill, Kant, virtue ethics, or some other ethical theory, it would be well to keep in mind the relative weaknesses of each of these theories.

We should also be mindful of the extent to which a theory may be able to capture the essence of events and real-life moral problems faced on a daily level. In the cool, reflective hours in our study we may be able to consider dispassionately a moral issue. But in the heat of the moment, when real people are involved, including all the emotions and passions of life, we may see things a bit differently. For example, we may adamantly believe no one should have the right to commit euthanasia. But if one day we have to look into the eyes of someone who is terminally ill, in unremitting pain and pleading for death, we may rethink our tightly held principles. There is good reason to reflect on the gap between theory and life experience.

Another consideration, following from the previous discussion, is that ethical theory is not a sort of magical algorithm for solving moral problems. It is useful for sorting through many of the moral problems we face. But there will always be a gap, however fine, between theory and real life. We shouldn't see an ethical theory as a sort of magical box into which we insert a moral problem, turn a few handles, push a few buttons, and crank out a solution. Solutions derived using ethical theory in this aggressive and mechanistic way will only blindside us to real considerations, resulting in greater injustices. No matter how brilliant, simple, or complex the theory used, resolving ethical problems will always require reflective, careful, and balanced thought on our part.

# ADAM SMITH AND MORAL SENSE THEORY

Adam Smith (1723–1790) was one of the leading intellectual lights of the Scottish Enlightenment of the eighteenth century. He is most well known for his monumental treatise *The Wealth of Nations* (1776), published in the same year that the American Revolution started. It is a detailed examination of capitalist economics still used today by conservative thinkers to defend the free market against state interference. Smith argued that an "invisible hand" rules over such a market: If everyone pursues his or her individual economic self-interests, the market itself will regulate the prices of products and the wages paid workers, free from government control. In such a situation, everyone will be better off.

Despite his success with economic theory, Smith was prouder of his work in moral philosophy. He was especially pleased with his book *The Theory of Moral Sentiments* (1759), which espoused a moral sense approach to ethics.

Smith believed that when we see unfortunate things happen to people, we are drawn into feeling an empathy with the sufferer. This human ability to identify with another's misfortune is due to the human faculty of intuition. He put it this way: "It is the impressions of our own senses only, not those of his or hers, which our imaginations copy." What we see impacts upon our imagination, allowing us to identify with the pain of the person suffering. Thus, he referred to his moral theory as based on a "moral sense."

Suppose that we witness a terrible accident. We are struck by its horror partly because we can easily see ourselves in the same situation. Being able to know how we would feel in the same circumstances as the sufferer makes us feel sympathy and compassion for him or her. We can be drawn into someone else's unfortunate situation when we witness it firsthand, see it on television, or read about it in a newspaper, magazine, or book.

In *The Theory of Moral Sentiments,* Smith discusses this phenomenon in a clear and striking manner. While you read his description, you may well be drawn into his stories, thereby bringing out the very moral sense he is trying to explain.

Smith's discussion of how we judge another's actions may sound a bit like Aristotle's discussion of the "mean." In any action we perform, we need to choose between the two possible extremes. Smith talks a little like that himself, particularly where he says that when we see someone acting wrongly, we recognize its wrongness by its excess.

An important question arises from Smith's account of how moral sense works. What do we do in cases in which someone doesn't have this capacity for moral sense—when someone simply does not empathize with the plight of others? Smith doesn't specifically address this in great detail here. He does say, however, that it is impossible to spend time with such a person.

Why some lack this capacity for human empathy is an important issue. Moral philosophers have traditionally argued (certainly influenced by Plato) that people choose to do wrong out of ignorance. That is, no one willfully chooses to do wrong. It is the result of a mistake in reasoning. To correct wrong behavior, we need to educate the transgressor, bringing his or her thinking in line with reason and the good, with the truth.

More recent philosophers, undoubtedly using current neurological, genetic, sociological, and psychological research, have argued that the reasons why people act immorally or illegally are numerous and often extremely complex in nature. Wrong behavior will most likely *not* be corrected by teaching the offender Kant's categorical imperative or Mill's utilitarianism.

Smith's account of how we judge and make moral decisions has particular importance both for moral theory and for applied ethics. Some critics of Smith and moral sense theory argue that his account is too thin, too unphilosophical to be of much use. What is needed, they argue, is a more robust account of ethical theory.

In Smith's defense, some contemporary proponents of moral sense believe we can get too caught up in the mechanics of ethical theory. We can then lose sight of the fact that we typically operate by responding in a direct emotional manner to the various moral dilemmas in which we find ourselves. For instance, when we see someone injured and in need of help, we will try to rush to the person's aid. We do so without going through a complex process of moral reasoning, whether it's running all the variables through a hedonistic calculus or determining our duty under the categorical imperative. In fact, if someone actually claimed he or she *did* try to use such moral reasoning in pressing situations, most of us would think the person was completely missing the point.

Smith's moral theory has a distinct advantage over more complicated attempts to set out a model of the ethical decision-making process. It corresponds with the great outpouring of public sympathy we often see in times of disaster. Think, for example, of all those who donated money, blood, time, and other resources and services to aid those who were affected by the September 11, 2001, terrorists attacks in New York City, Washington, D.C., and Pennsylvania. Why did people do these selfless acts? Smith's explanation is quite uncomplicated and clear-cut—we can easily put ourselves in the place of the victims and their families. Without this sympathy, it's unlikely that selfless acts would happen.

# The Theory of Moral Sentiments

## ADAM SMITH

### Part 1. Of the Propriety of Action (Consisting of Three Sections)

#### SECTION I. OF THE SENSE OF PROPRIETY

#### Chapter 1. Of Sympathy

However selfish humans may be supposed, there are evidently some principles in their nature, which interest them in the fortune of others, and render their happiness necessary to them, though they derive nothing from it except the pleasure of seeing it. Of this kind is pity or compassion, the emotion that we feel for the misery of others, when we either see it, or are made to conceive it in a very lively manner. That we often derive sorrow from the sorrow of others is a matter of fact too obvious to require any instances to prove it; for this sentiment, like all the other original passions of human nature, is by no means confined to the virtuous and humane, though they perhaps may feel it with the most exquisite sensibility. The greatest ruffian, the most hardened violator of the laws of society, is not altogether without it.

As we have no immediate experience of what other men feel, we can form no idea of the manner in which they are affected except by conceiving what we ourselves should feel in the like sit-

SOURCE: Adam Smith, *The Theory of Moral Sentiments,* 6th ed. (1759; London: A. Millar, 1790), pt. 1, sec. 1, chaps. 1, 2, 4, 5 (edited); retrieved from Library of Economics and Liberty Web site: http://www.econlib.org/library/Smith/smMS1.html.

uation. Though our brother is upon the rack, as long as we ourselves are at our ease, our senses will never inform us of what he suffers. Our senses never did, and never can carry us beyond our own person. It is only by the imagination that we can form a conception of what are his sensations. Neither can that faculty help us to this any other way, than by representing to us what would be our own, if we were in his case. It is the impressions of our own senses only, not of his, which our imaginations copy.

By the imagination we place ourselves in his situation, we conceive ourselves enduring all the same torments, we enter as it were into his body, and become in some measure the same person with him, and thence form some idea of his sensations, and even feel something, though weaker in degree from the sufferer. His agonies, when they are thus brought home to ourselves, when we have thus adopted and made them our own, begin at last to affect us, and we then tremble and shudder at the thought of what he feels. For as to be in pain or distress of any kind excites the most excessive sorrow, so to conceive or to imagine that we are in it, excites some degree of the same emotion, in proportion to the vivacity or dullness of the conception.

That this is the source of our fellow-feeling for the misery of others, that it is by changing places in fancy with the sufferer, that we come either to conceive or to be affected by what he feels, may be demonstrated by many obvious observations, if it should not be thought sufficiently evident of itself. When we see a stroke aimed and just ready to fall upon the leg or arm of another person, we naturally shrink and draw back our own leg or our own arm; and when it does fall, we feel it in some measure, and are hurt by it as well as the sufferer. The mob, when they are gazing at a dancer on the slack rope, naturally writhe and twist and balance their own bodies, as they see him do, and as they feel that they themselves must do if in his situation. Persons of delicate and weak constitution of body complain, that in looking on the sores and ulcers of beggars in the streets, they are apt to feel an itching or uneasy sensation in the correspondent part of their own

bodies. The horror which they conceive at the misery of those wretches affects that particular part in themselves more than any other; because that horror arises from conceiving what they themselves would suffer, if they really were the wretches whom they are looking upon, and if that particular part in themselves was actually affected in the same miserable manner. The very force of this conception is sufficient, in their feeble frames, to produce that itching or uneasy sensation complained of. The most powerful men observe that in looking upon sore eyes they often feel a very sensible soreness in their own, which proceeds from the same reason; that organ being in the strongest man more delicate than any other part of the body is in the weakest.

Neither is it those circumstances only, which create pain or sorrow, which call forth our fellow-feeling. Whatever is the passion that arises from any object in the person principally concerned, an analogous emotion springs up, at the thought of his situation, in the breast of every attentive spectator. Our joy for the deliverance of those heroes of tragedy or romance who interest us is as sincere as our grief for their distress, and our fellow-feeling with their misery is not more real than that with their happiness. We enter into their gratitude towards those faithful friends who did not desert them in their difficulties; and we heartily go along with their resentment against those deceitful traitors who injured, abandoned, or deceived them. In every passion of which the mind of man is susceptible, the emotions of the by-stander always correspond by bringing the case home to himself, he imagines should be the sentiments of the sufferer.

Pity and compassion are words appropriated to signify our fellow-feeling with the sorrow of others. Sympathy, though its meaning was, perhaps, originally the same, may now, however, without much impropriety, be made use of to denote our fellow-feeling with any passion whatever.

Upon some occasions sympathy may seem to arise merely from the view of a certain emotion in another person. The passions, upon some occasions, may seem to be transfused from one person to another, instantaneously and antecedent to any knowledge of what excited them in the person principally concerned. Grief and joy, for example, strongly expressed in the look and gestures of any one, at once affect the spectator with some degree of a like painful or agreeable emotion. A smiling face is, to every body that sees it, a cheerful object; as a sorrowful countenance, on the other hand, is a melancholy one.

This, however, does not hold universally, or with regard to every passion. There are some passions of which the expressions excite no sort of sympathy, but before we are acquainted with what gave occasion to them, serve rather to disgust and provoke us against them. The furious behaviour of an angry man is more likely to exasperate us against himself than against his enemies. As we are unacquainted with his provocation, we cannot bring his case home to ourselves, nor conceive any thing like the passions it excites. But we plainly see what is the situation of those with whom he is angry, and to what violence they may be exposed from so enraged an adversary. We readily, therefore, sympathize with their fear or resentment, and are immediately disposed to take part against someone whom they appear to be in so much danger.

If the very appearances of grief and joy inspire us with some degree of the like emotions, it is because they suggest to us the general idea of some good or bad fortune that has befallen the person in whom we observe them: and in these passions this is sufficient to have some little influence upon us. The effects of grief and joy terminate in the person who feels those emotions, of which the expressions do not, like those of resentment, suggest to us the idea of any other person for whom we are concerned, and whose interests are opposite to his. The general idea of good or bad fortune, therefore, creates some concern for the person who has met with it, but the general idea of provocation excites no sympathy with the anger of the man who has received it. Nature, it seems, teaches us to be more averse to enter into this passion, and, till informed of its cause, to be disposed rather to take part against it.

Even our sympathy with the grief or joy of another, before we are informed of the cause of either, is always extremely imperfect. General lamentations, which express nothing but the anguish of the sufferer, create rather a curiosity to inquire into his situation, along with some disposition to sympathize with him, than any actual sympathy that is very sensible. The first question we ask is, "What has befallen you?" Until this question is answered, though we are uneasy both from the vague idea of his misfortune, and still more from torturing ourselves with conjectures about what it may be, yet our fellow-feeling is not very considerable.

Sympathy, therefore, does not arise so much from the view of the passion, as from that of the situation that excites it. We sometimes feel for another, a passion of which he himself seems to be altogether incapable; because, when we put ourselves in his case, that passion arises in our breast from the imagination, though it does not in him from the reality. We blush for the impudence and rudeness of another, though he himself appears to have no sense of the impropriety of his own behaviour; because we cannot help feeling with what confusion we ourselves should be covered, had we behaved in so absurd a manner.

Of all the calamities to which the condition of mortality exposes humankind, the loss of reason appears, to those who have the least spark of humanity, by far the most dreadful, and they behold that last stage of human wretchedness with deeper commiseration than any other. But the poor wretch, who is in it, laughs and sings perhaps, and is altogether insensible of her own misery. The anguish which humanity feels, therefore, at the sight of such an object, cannot be the reflection of any sentiment of the sufferer. The compassion of the spectator must arise altogether from the consideration of what she herself would feel if she were reduced to the same unhappy situation, and, what perhaps is impossible was at the same time able to regard it with his present reason and judgment.

What are the pangs of a mother, when she hears the moaning of her infant that during the agony of disease cannot express what the child feels? In her idea of what it suffers, she joins, to its real helplessness, her own consciousness of that helplessness, and her own terrors for the unknown consequences of its disorder; and out of all these, forms, for her own sorrow, the most complete image of misery and distress. The infant, however, feels only the uneasiness of the present instant, which can never be great. With regard to the future, it is perfectly secure, and in its thoughtlessness and want of foresight, possesses an antidote against fear and anxiety, the great tormentors of the human breast, from which reason and philosophy will, in vain, attempt to defend it, when it grows up to a man.

We sympathize even with the dead, and overlooking what is of real importance in their situation, that awful futurity which awaits them, we are chiefly affected by those circumstances, which strike our senses, but can have no influence upon their happiness. It is miserable, we think, to be deprived of the light of the sun; to be shut out from life and conversation; to be laid in the cold grave, a prey to corruption and the reptiles of the earth; to be no more thought of in this world, but to be obliterated, in a little time, from the affections, and almost from the memory, of their dearest friends and relations. Surely, we imagine, we can never feel too much for those who have suffered so dreadful a calamity. The tribute of our fellow-feeling seems doubly due to them now, when they are in danger of being forgot by every body; and, by the vain honours which we pay to their memory, we endeavour, for our own misery, artificially to keep alive our melancholy remembrance of their misfortune. That our sympathy can afford them no consolation seems to be an addition to their calamity; and to think that all we can do is unavailing, and that, what alleviates all other distress, the regret, the love, and the lamentations of their friends, can yield no comfort to them, serves only to exasperate our sense of their misery. The happiness of the dead, however, most assuredly, is affected by none of these circumstances; nor is it the thought of these things which can ever disturb the profound security of their repose. The idea of that dreary and endless melancholy, which the fancy naturally as-

cribes to their condition, arises altogether from our joining to the change which has been produced upon them, our own consciousness of that change, from our putting ourselves in their situation, and from our lodging, if I may be allowed to say so, our own living souls in their inanimated bodies, and thence conceiving what would be our emotions in this case. It is from this very illusion of the imagination, that the foresight of our own dissolution is so terrible to us, and that the idea of those circumstances, which undoubtedly can give us no pain when we are dead, makes us miserable while we are alive. And from thence arises one of the most important principles in human nature, the dread of death, the great poison to the happiness, but the great restraint upon the injustice of humankind, which, while it afflicts and mortifies the individual, guards and protects the society.

**Chapter 2. Of the Pleasure of Mutual Sympathy**

But whatever may be the cause of sympathy, or however it may be excited, nothing pleases us more than to observe in other people a fellow-feeling with all the emotions of our own breast; nor are we ever so much shocked as by the appearance of the contrary. Those who are fond of deducing all our sentiments from certain refinements of self-love, think themselves at no loss to account, according to their own principles, both for this pleasure and this pain. Man, say they, conscious of his own weakness, and of the need which he has for the assistance of others, rejoices whenever he observes that they adopt his own passions, because he is then assured of that assistance; and grieves whenever he observes the contrary, because he is then assured of their opposition. But both the pleasure and the pain are always felt so instantaneously, and often upon such frivolous occasions, that it seems evident that neither of them can be derived from any such self-interested consideration. A man is mortified when, after having endeavoured to divert the company, he looks round and sees that nobody laughs at his jests but himself. On the contrary, the mirth of the company is highly agreeable to him, and he regards this correspondence of their sentiments with his own as the greatest applause.

Neither does his pleasure seem to arise altogether from the additional vivacity which his mirth may receive from sympathy with theirs, nor his pain from the disappointment he meets with when he misses this pleasure; though both the one and the other, no doubt, do in some measure. When we have read a book or poem so often that we can no longer find any amusement in reading it by ourselves, we can still take pleasure in reading it to a companion. To him it has all the graces of novelty; we enter into the surprise and admiration which it naturally excites in him, but which it is no longer capable of exciting in us; we consider all the ideas which it presents rather in the light in which they appear to him, than in that in which they appear to ourselves, and we are amused by sympathy with his amusement which thus enlivens our own. On the contrary, we should be vexed if he did not seem to be entertained with it, and we could no longer take any pleasure in reading it to him. It is the same case here. The mirth of the company, no doubt, enlivens our own mirth, and their silence, no doubt, disappoints us. But though this may contribute both to the pleasure which we derive from the one, and to the pain which we feel from the other, it is by no means the sole cause of either; and this correspondence of the sentiments of others with our own appears to be a cause of pleasure, and the want of it a cause of pain, which cannot be accounted for in this manner. The sympathy, which my friends express with my joy, might, indeed, give me pleasure by enlivening that joy: but that which they express with my grief could give me none, if it served only to enliven that grief. Sympathy, however, enlivens joy and alleviates grief. It enlivens joy by presenting another source of satisfaction; and it alleviates grief by insinuating into the heart almost the only agreeable sensation that it is at that time capable of receiving.

It is to be observed accordingly, that we are still more anxious to communicate to our friends our disagreeable than our agreeable passions, that we derive still more satisfaction from their sympathy with the former than from that with the latter, and that we are still more shocked by the want of it.

How are the unfortunate relieved when they have found out a person to whom they can communicate the cause of their sorrow? Upon his sympathy they seem to disburden themselves of a part of their distress: he is not improperly said to share it with them. He not only feels a sorrow of the same kind with that which they feel, but as if he had derived a part of it to himself, what she feels seems to alleviate the weight of what they feel. Yet by relating their misfortunes they in some measure renew their grief. They awaken in their memory the remembrance of those circumstances that occasioned their affliction. Their tears accordingly flow faster than before, and they are apt to abandon themselves to all the weakness of sorrow. They take pleasure, however, in all this, and, it is evident, are sensibly relieved by it; because the sweetness of his sympathy more than compensates the bitterness of that sorrow, which, in order to excite this sympathy, they had thus enlivened and renewed. The cruellest insult, on the contrary, which can be offered to the unfortunate, is to appear to make light of their calamities. To seem not to be affected with the joy of our companions is but want of politeness; but not to wear a serious countenance when they tell us their afflictions, is real and gross inhumanity.

Love is an agreeable, resentment a disagreeable passion; and accordingly we are not half so anxious that our friends should adopt our friendships, as that they should enter into our resentments. We can forgive them though they seem to be little affected with the favours which we may have received, but lose all patience if they seem indifferent about the injuries which may have been done to us: nor are we half so angry with them for not entering into our gratitude, as for not sympathizing with our resentment. They can easily avoid being friends to our friends, but can hardly avoid being enemies to those with whom we are at variance. We seldom resent their being at enmity with the first, though upon that account we may sometimes affect to make an awkward quarrel with them; but we quarrel with them in good earnest if they live in friendship with the last. The agreeable passions of love and joy can satisfy and support the heart without any auxiliary pleasure. The bitter and painful emotions of grief and resentment more strongly require the healing consolation of sympathy.

As the person who is principally interested in any event is pleased with our sympathy, and hurt by the want of it, so we, too, seem to be pleased when we are able to sympathize with him, and to be hurt when we are unable to do so. We run not only to congratulate the successful, but also to console with the afflicted; and the pleasure which we find in the conversation of one whom in all the passions of his heart we can entirely sympathize with, seems to do more than compensate the painfulness of that sorrow with which the view of his situation affects us. On the contrary, it is always disagreeable to feel that we cannot sympathize with him, and instead of being pleased with this exemption from sympathetic pain, it hurts us to find that we cannot share his uneasiness. If we hear a person loudly lamenting his misfortunes, which, however, upon bringing the case home to ourselves, we feel, can produce no such violent effect upon us, we are shocked at his grief; and, because we cannot enter into it, call it pusillanimity and weakness. It disconcerts us, on the other hand, to see another too happy or too much elevated, as we call it, with any little piece of good fortune. We are disobliged even with his joy; and, because we cannot go along with it, call it levity and folly. We are even put out of humour if our companion laughs louder or longer at a joke than we think it deserves; that is, than we feel that we ourselves could laugh at it.

## Chapter 4. The Same Subject Continued [i.e. judging the propriety of the affections of others]

. . . In all such cases, that there may be some correspondence of sentiments between the spectator and the person principally concerned, the spectator must, first of all, endeavour, as much as he can, to put himself in the situation of the other, and to bring home to himself every little circumstance of distress which can possibly occur to the sufferer. He must adopt the whole case of her companion with all its minutest incidents; and strive to render as perfect as possible, that imaginary change of situation upon which his sympathy is founded.

Society and conversation, therefore, are the most powerful remedies for restoring the mind to its tranquility, if, at any time, it has unfortunately lost it; as well as the best preservatives of that equal and happy temper, which is so necessary to self-satisfaction and enjoyment. Men of retirement and speculation, who are apt to sit brooding at home over either grief or resentment, though they may often have more humanity, more generosity, and a nicer sense of honour, yet seldom possess that equality of temper which is so common among men of the world.

## Chapter 5. Of the Amiable and Respectable Virtues

Upon these two different efforts, upon that of the spectator to enter into the sentiments of the person principally concerned, and upon that of the person principally concerned, to bring down his emotions to what the spectator can go along with, are founded two different sets of virtues. The soft, the gentle, the amiable virtues, the virtues of candid condescension and indulgent humanity, are founded upon the one: the great, the awful and respectable, the virtues of self-denial, of self-government, of that command of the passions which subjects all the movements of our nature to what our own dignity and honour, and the propriety of our own conduct require, take their origin from the other.

. . . And hence it is, that to feel much for others and little for ourselves, that to restrain our selfish, and to indulge our benevolent affections, constitutes the perfection of human nature; and can alone produce among humankind that harmony of sentiments and passions in which consists their whole grace and propriety. As to love our neighbour as we love ourselves is the great law of Christianity, so it is the great precept of nature to love ourselves only as we love our neighbour, or what comes to the same thing, as our neighbour is capable of loving us.

# JOHN STUART MILL AND UTILITARIANISM

When we are faced with a difficult moral decision, we usually pay some attention to the consequences of our choices not only for ourselves but for all those we think will be affected by our decision. Unless we are egoists, by thinking about our actions in this way, we might try to make as many people happy and as few people unhappy with our decision as possible. This concern captures a basic intuition about ethics: We should try to maximize happiness or pleasure while minimizing unhappiness or pain.

The English philosopher Jeremy Bentham (1748–1832) developed a theory of ethics that emphasized this sense of *utility*. Although utility was traditionally understood as referring to the general welfare or good of people, Bentham gave it a narrower sense, defining *utility* as "happiness or pleasure." Unsurprisingly, this approach to ethics was called "utilitarianism."

Bentham actually thought one could mathematically measure pleasure and pain using a "hedonistic calculus." He thought if the net sum of the happiness of all concerned parties to an action was greater than any unhappiness it caused, it was a good action. If it turned out to produce more pain than pleasure, then it was a bad action. Bentham's account of utilitarianism was later called "act utilitarianism" because it focuses on the pleasure and pain produced by specific acts and not with the general moral rules embodied in these acts (theorists who focus on these rules are called "rule utilitarians").

Following Bentham's lead, John Stuart Mill (1806–1873) and Henry Sidgwick (1838–1900) went on to nuance the theory Bentham first laid out. The main improvement Mill made on Bentham's version of utilitarianism is the argument that we should be concerned both with the *quantity* of pleasure and pain arising from an action (as Bentham was) and with the *quality* of the pleasure we feel as a result. Naturally, this got Mill into all sorts of theoretical hot water, as people tend to disagree rather radically about the respective qualities of the diverse pleasures they pursue. (See Chapter 8 for more details on Mill's life and work.)

One of the differences between utilitarianism and other ethical theories lies in its emphasis on maximizing pleasure and happiness and minimizing pain. Another point of dissimilarity is that utilitarianism does not appeal to, or depend on, any sort of abstract moral principle or rule (other than the rule that one should promote happiness, which the utilitarians argue is more a natural principle of human psychology than a moral rule per se). This is quite a contrast to ethical approaches that appeal to absolute norms and standards such as the Ten Commandments or Kant's categorical imperative.

Utilitarianism works by having the moral agent conduct a sort of "moral calculus" before acting. When faced with a moral decision, we try to determine how our choice of action will affect others. We should act so as to produce the greatest amount of utility for all those affected by the decision. This was described as the "Utilitarian Maxim":

Act always in such a way as to produce the greatest net utility *for all affected parties*.

To illustrate how this works, consider the current semester at your university. You're very busy. You've taken on all sorts of obligations, but at the same time need to maintain a high grade-point average to get that job you've always dreamed about after graduating. The trouble is, various deadlines for assignments are coming up, and your paper for your philosophy course is due soon. Your friends have been talking about some Web sites where you can have someone write your paper for a fee. You know this is against academic regulations and that you could be suspended from the university if caught. Yet getting this paper out of the way, and getting a good mark on it, would be very nice. What should you do?

Using the Utilitarian Maxim, you first try to consider who will be affected by your decision ("all affected parties"). From your point of view, getting a good mark on your paper will certainly be advantageous. You will have more time to devote to other papers and exams. Your friends may be impressed you are willing to take such risks to succeed. Your family (who will not know about the cheating) will be pleased about the high marks you receive in school. So far, so good.

But here it gets tricky. To perform the calculus correctly, you also have to consider the "disutilities" that might result if things don't go as planned. What if you are discovered? The scope of those affected has to be enlarged. If you are caught cheating, your friends, parents, professor, and university will be affected. They will suffer disappointment because of your choice. Besides the embarrassment, there is the huge disutility connected with your being suspended from the university, thus losing the chance to go into the profession you dreamed of.

After imagining all those who could be affected by your choice, for or against, you then add up the utilities and subtract the disutilities for each possible course of action, taking the probability of being caught into account. There are certainly some positive utilities in favor of paying for the paper. There are even some utilities for those who offer the service—maybe they make a living from the fees they charge. But most of these utilities are outweighed by the subsequent disutilities if you are caught cheating. In this case, the overall well-being produced by writing your own paper outweighs the negative consequences of having it written by someone else and being caught. So in this case, the ethical decision would be to endure the short-term pain of writing the paper yourself.

There are some advantages to this way of doing ethics. First of all, the methodology is fairly straightforward and uncomplicated. This is an important characteristic of any moral theory. How can we expect a moral theory to be useful for the average person if one needs a Ph.D. in philosophy to understand it? Second, utilitarianism captures a basic intuition we have about ethics, the sense that when we make a moral decision, we should take into consideration the consequences of our decision and the overall benefit for all those involved.

Despite these advantages, some important disadvantages need to be pointed out. Notice in the previous example that there was neither any appeal to moral principles, such as "it is wrong to lie," nor any appeal to your duty as a student to do your own work. There also was no reference to the basic right of the university and the professor to demand that assignments submitted by students be their own work. When we focus only on the consequences and the general well-being produced by actions, concerns about principles, duties, and rights play no role in the decision-making process.

Critics of utilitarianism have pointed out that neglecting duties and rights, which are normally part of our moral decision-making process, places this theory on shaky ground. Consider a court case where you are under oath to tell the truth about a crime you witnessed. Let's suppose you know that the accused person is innocent of the crime he is being tried for but is a violent man who you are convinced will go on to assault and even murder others if let off. You might think that the general well-being would benefit if you lied and put him behind bars. Yet shouldn't there be an overriding duty to tell the truth no matter what consequences follow from your action? If you lied about the accused person's action, isn't this grossly unjust in that it denies the right to a fair trial?

The other problem utilitarianism faces is that we can never be sure about the consequences of our decisions. Can we always (if ever!) predict the future consequences of our actions? In the first example, if you decided to cheat, you might wind up receiving a high grade-point average, getting the dream job, succeeding in your career, and happily retiring to a life of leisure without anyone being the wiser. On the other hand, there remains the possibility you will be discovered. It is difficult to imagine what might follow from being exposed. Maybe once your little sister learns of your action, because of your bad example, she turns to a life of petty crime, and ends up in prison! This consequence, albeit unlikely, still illustrates the difficulty of trying to anticipate how our actions will affect others.

Utilitarianism, despite these criticisms, remains a powerful ethical theory. It certainly captures the basic intuition that we need to consider how others will be affected by our actions and that we should try to ensure the best consequences for all those involved. The methodology of utilitarianism is also quite easy to use, even if we can't always predict the consequences of specific actions.

# What Is Utilitarianism?

## JOHN STUART MILL

A PASSING REMARK is all that needs be given to the ignorant blunder of supposing that those who stand up for utility as the test of right and wrong use the term in that restricted and merely colloquial sense in which utility is opposed to pleasure. An apology is due to the philosophical opponents of utilitarianism for even the momentary appearance of confounding them with any one capable of so absurd a misconception; which is the more extraordinary, inasmuch as the contrary accusation, of referring everything to pleasure, and that, too, in its grossest form, is another of the common charges against utilitarianism:

and, as has been pointedly remarked by an able writer, the same sort of persons, and often the very same persons, denounce the theory "as impracticably dry when the word 'utility' precedes the word 'pleasure,' and as too practically voluptuous when the word 'pleasure' precedes the word 'utility.'" Those who know anything about the matter are aware that every writer, from Epicurus to Bentham, who maintained the theory of utility meant by it, not something to be contradistinguished from pleasure, but pleasure itself, together with exemption from pain; and instead of opposing the useful to the agreeable or the

SOURCE: John Stuart Mill, "What Utilitarianism Is," chap. 2 in *Utilitarianism* (1861), ed. George Sher (1861; Indianapolis, IN: Hackett, 1979), pp. 6–7, 11–14, 16–25 (edited).

ornamental, have always declared that the useful means these, among other things. Yet the common herd, including the herd of writers, not only in newspapers and periodicals, but in books of weight and pretension, are perpetually falling into this shallow mistake. Having caught up the word "utilitarian," while knowing nothing whatever about it but its sound, they habitually express by it the rejection or the neglect of pleasure in some of its forms; of beauty, of ornament, or of amusement. Nor is the term thus ignorantly misapplied solely in disparagement, but occasionally in compliment, as though it implied superiority to frivolity and the mere pleasures of the moment. And this perverted use is the only one in which the word is popularly known, and the one from which the new generation are acquiring their sole notion of its meaning. Those who introduced the word, but who had for many years discontinued it as a distinctive appellation, may well feel themselves called upon to resume it if by doing so they can hope to contribute anything towards rescuing it from this utter degradation.[1]

The creed which accepts as the foundation of morals, "utility" or the "greatest happiness principle," holds that actions are right in proportion as they tend to promote happiness; wrong as they tend to produce the reverse of happiness. By happiness is intended pleasure, and the absence of pain; by unhappiness, pain, and the privation of pleasure. To give a clear view of the moral standard set up by the theory, much more requires to be said; in particular, what things it includes in the ideas of pain and pleasure, and to what extent this is left an open question. But these sup-

plementary explanations do not affect the theory of life on which this theory of morality is grounded—namely, that pleasure and freedom from pain are the only things desirable as ends; and that all desirable things (which are as numerous in the utilitarian as in any other scheme) are desirable either for the pleasure inherent in themselves, or as means to the promotion of pleasure and the prevention of pain. . . .

I have dwelt on this point as being a necessary part of a perfectly just conception of utility or happiness considered as the directive rule of human conduct. But it is by no means an indispensable condition to the acceptance of the utilitarian standard; for that standard is not the agent's own greatest happiness, but the greatest amount of happiness altogether; and if it may possibly be doubted whether a noble character is always the happier for its nobleness, there can be no doubt that it makes other people happier, and that the world in general is immensely a gainer by it. Utilitarianism, therefore, could only attain its end by the general cultivation of nobleness of character, even if each individual were only benefited by the nobleness of others, and his own, so far as happiness is concerned, were a sheer deduction from the benefit. But the bare enunciation of such an absurdity as this last renders refutation superfluous.

According to the greatest happiness principle, as above explained, the ultimate end, with reference to and for the sake of which all other things are desirable—whether we are considering our own good or that of other people—is an existence exempt as far as possible from pain, and as rich as possible in enjoyments, both in point of quantity and quality; the test of quality and the rule for measuring it against quantity being the preference felt by those who, in their opportunities of experience, to which must be added their habits of self-consciousness and self-observation, are best furnished with the means of comparison. This, being according to the utilitarian opinion the end of human action, is necessarily also the standard of morality, which may accordingly be defined, "the rules and precepts for human conduct," by the observance of which an exis-

---

[1] The author of this essay has reason for believing himself to be the first person who brought the word "utilitarian" into use. He did not invent it, but adopted it from a passing expression in Mr. Galt's *Annals of the Parish*. After using it as a designation for several years, he and others abandoned it from a growing dislike to anything resembling a badge or watchword of sectarian distinction. But as a name for one single opinion, not a set of opinions—to denote the recognition of utility as a standard, not any particular way of applying it—the term supplies a want in the language, and offers, in many cases, a convenient mode of avoiding tiresome circumlocution.

tence such as has been described might be, to the greatest extent possible, secured to all mankind; and not to them only, but, so far as the nature of things admits, to the whole sentient creation.

Against this doctrine, however, arises another class of objectors who say that happiness, in any form, cannot be the rational purpose of human life and action; because, in the first place, it is unattainable; and they contemptuously ask, What right hast thou to be happy?—a question which Mr. Carlyle clenches by the addition, What right, a short time ago, hadst thou even *to be?* Next they say that men can do *without* happiness; that all noble human beings have felt this, and could not have become noble but by learning the lesson of *Entsagen,* or renunciation; which lesson, thoroughly learnt and submitted to, they affirm to be the beginning and necessary condition of all virtue.

The first of these objections would go to the root of the matter were it well founded; for if no happiness is to be had at all by human beings, the attainment of it cannot be the end of morality, or of any rational conduct. Though, even in that case, something might still be said for the utilitarian theory, since utility includes not solely the pursuit of happiness, but the prevention or mitigation of unhappiness; and if the former aim be chimerical, there will be all the greater scope and more imperative need for the latter, so long at least as mankind think fit to live and do not take refuge in the simultaneous act of suicide recommended under certain conditions by Novalis. When, however, it is thus positively asserted to be impossible that human life should be happy, the assertion, if not something like a verbal quibble, is at least an exaggeration. If by happiness be meant a continuity of highly pleasurable excitement, it is evident enough that this is impossible. A state of exalted pleasure lasts only moments or in some cases, and with some intermissions, hours or days, and is the occasional brilliant flash of enjoyment, not its permanent and steady flame. Of this the philosophers who have taught that happiness is the end of life were as fully aware as those who taunt them. The happiness

which they meant was not a life of rapture, but moments of such, in an existence made up of few and transitory pains, many and various pleasures, with a decided predominance of the active over the passive, and having as the foundation of the whole not to expect more from life than it is capable of bestowing. A life thus composed, to those who have been fortunate enough to obtain it, has always appeared worthy of the name of happiness. And such an existence is even now the lot of many during some considerable portion of their lives. The present wretched education and wretched social arrangements are the only real hindrance to its being attainable by almost all.

The objectors perhaps may doubt whether human beings, if taught to consider happiness as the end of life, would be satisfied with such a moderate share of it. But great numbers of mankind have been satisfied with much less. The main constituents of a satisfied life appear to be two, either of which by itself is often found sufficient for the purpose: tranquillity, and excitement. With much tranquillity, many find that they can be content with very little pleasure; with much excitement, many can reconcile themselves to a considerable quantity of pain. There is assuredly no inherent impossibility in enabling even the mass of mankind to unite both, since the two are so far from being incompatible that they are in natural alliance, the prolongation of either being a preparation for, and exciting a wish for, the other. It is only those in whom indolence amounts to a vice that do not desire excitement after an interval of repose; it is only those in whom the need of excitement is a disease that feel the tranquillity which follows excitement dull and insipid, instead of pleasurable in direct proportion to the excitement which preceded it. When people who are tolerably fortunate in their outward lot do not find in life sufficient enjoyment to make it valuable to them, the cause generally is caring for nobody but themselves. To those who have neither public nor private affections, the excitements of life are much curtailed, and in any case dwindle in value as the time approaches when all selfish interests must be terminated by death; while those who leave after them objects of personal affection, and especially those who have also cultivated a fellow-feeling with the collective interests of mankind, retain as lively an interest in life on the eve of death as in the vigour of youth and health. Next to selfishness, the principal cause which makes life unsatisfactory is want of mental cultivation. A cultivated mind—I do not mean that of a philosopher, but any mind to which the fountains of knowledge have been opened, and which has been taught, in any tolerable degree, to exercise its faculties—finds sources of inexhaustible interest in all that surrounds it: in the objects of nature, the achievements of art, the imaginations of poetry, the incidents of history, the ways of mankind, past and present, and their prospects in the future. It is possible, indeed, to become indifferent to all this, and that too without having exhausted a thousandth part of it, but only when one has had from the beginning no moral or human interest in these things, and has sought in them only the gratification of curiosity. . . .

The utilitarian morality does recognise in human beings the power of sacrificing their own greatest good for the good of others. It only refuses to admit that the sacrifice is itself a good. A sacrifice which does not increase or tend to increase the sum total of happiness, it considers as wasted. The only self-renunciation which it applauds is devotion to the happiness, or to some of the means of happiness, of others, either of mankind collectively or of individuals within the limits imposed by the collective interests of mankind.

I must again repeat, what the assailants of utilitarianism seldom have the justice to acknowledge, that the happiness which forms the utilitarian standard of what is right in conduct is not the agent's own happiness but that of all concerned. As between his own happiness and that of others, utilitarianism requires him to be as strictly impartial as a disinterested and benevolent spectator. In the golden rule of Jesus of Nazareth, we read the complete spirit of the ethics of utility. "To do as you would be done by," and "to love your neighbour as yourself," constitute the ideal perfection of utilitarian morality. As the means of making the nearest approach to this ideal, utility

would enjoin, first, that laws and social arrangements should place the happiness or (as speaking practically, it may be called) the interest of every individual as nearly as possible in harmony with the interest of the whole; and, secondly, that education and opinion, which have so vast a power over human character, should so use that power as to establish in the mind of every individual an indissoluble association between his own happiness and the good of the whole, especially between his own happiness and the practice of such modes of conduct, negative and positive, as regard for the universal happiness prescribes; so that not only he may be unable to conceive the possibility of happiness to himself, consistently with conduct opposed to the general good, but also that a direct impulse to promote the general good may be in every individual one of the habitual motives of action, and the sentiments connected therewith may fill a large and prominent place in every human being's sentient existence. If the impugners of the utilitarian morality represented it to their own minds in this its true character, I know not what recommendation possessed by any other morality they could possibly affirm to be wanting to it; what more beautiful or more exalted developments of human nature any other ethical system can be supposed to foster, or what springs of action, not accessible to the utilitarian, such systems rely on for giving effect to their mandates.

The objectors to utilitarianism cannot always be charged with representing it in a discreditable light. On the contrary, those among them who entertain anything like a just idea of its disinterested character sometimes find fault with its standard as being too high for humanity. They say it is exacting too much to require that people shall always act from the inducement of promoting the general interests of society. But this is to mistake the very meaning of a standard of morals and confound the rule of action with the motive of it. It is the business of ethics to tell us what are our duties, or by what test we may know them; but no system of ethics requires that the sole motive of all we do shall be a feeling of duty; on the contrary, ninety-nine hundredths of all our actions are done from other motives, and rightly so done if the rule of duty does not condemn them. It is the more unjust to utilitarianism that this particular misapprehension should be made a ground of objection to it, inasmuch as utilitarian moralists have gone beyond almost all others in affirming that the motive has nothing to do with the morality of the action, though much with the worth of the agent. He who saves a fellow creature from drowning does what is morally right, whether his motive be duty or the hope of being paid for his trouble; he who betrays the friend that trusts him is guilty of a crime, even if his object be to serve another friend to whom he is under greater obligation. But to speak only of actions done from the motive of duty, and in direct obedience to principle: it is a misapprehension of the utilitarian mode of thought to conceive it as implying that people should fix their minds upon so wide a generality as the world, or society at large. The great majority of good actions are intended not for the benefit of the world, but for that of individuals, of which the good of the world is made up; and the thoughts of the most virtuous man need not on these occasions travel beyond the particular persons concerned, except so far as is necessary to assure himself that in benefiting them he is not violating the rights, that is, the legitimate and authorised expectations, of any one else. The multiplication of happiness is, according to the utilitarian ethics, the object of virtue: the occasions on which any person (except one in a thousand) has it in his power to do this on an extended scale—in other words to be a public benefactor—are but exceptional; and on these occasions alone is he called on to consider public utility; in every other case, private utility, the interest or happiness of some few persons, is all he has to attend to. Those alone the influence of whose actions extends to society in general need concern themselves habitually about large an object. In the case of abstinences indeed—of things which people forbear to do from moral considerations, though the consequences in the particular case might be beneficial—it would be unworthy of an intelligent agent not to be consciously aware that the action is of a class which, if practised generally, would be generally injurious, and that this is the ground of the obligation to abstain from it. The amount of regard for the public interest implied in this recognition is no greater than is demanded by every system of morals, for they all enjoin to abstain from whatever is manifestly pernicious to society.

The same considerations dispose of another reproach against the doctrine of utility, founded on a still grosser misconception of the purpose of a standard of morality, and of the very meaning of the words "right" and "wrong." It is often affirmed that utilitarianism renders men cold and unsympathising; that it chills their moral feelings towards individuals; that it makes them regard only the dry and hard consideration of the consequences of actions, not taking into their moral estimate the qualities from which those actions emanate. If the assertion means that they do not allow their judgment respecting the rightness or wrongness of an action to be influenced by their opinion of the qualities of the person who does it, this is a complaint not against utilitarianism, but against having any standard of morality at all; for certainly no known ethical standard decides an action to be good or bad because it is done by a good or a bad man, still less because done by an amiable, a brave, or a benevolent man, or the contrary. These considerations are relevant, not to the estimation of actions, but of persons; and there is nothing in the utilitarian theory inconsistent with the fact that there are other things which interest us in persons besides the rightness and wrongness of their actions. The Stoics, indeed, with the paradoxical misuse of language which was part of their system, and by which they strove to raise themselves above all concern about anything but virtue, were fond of saying that he who has that has everything; that he, and only he, is rich, is beautiful, is a king. But no claim of this description is made for the virtuous man by the utilitarian doctrine. Utilitarians are quite aware that there are other desirable possessions and qualities besides virtue, and are perfectly willing to allow to all of them their full worth. They are also aware that a right action does not necessarily indicate a virtuous character, and that actions which are blamable often proceed from qualities entitled to praise. When this is apparent in any particular case, it modifies their estimation, not certainly of the act, but of the agent. I grant that they are, notwithstanding, of opinion that in the long run the best proof of a good character is good actions; and resolutely refuse to consider any mental disposition as good of which the predominant tendency is to produce bad conduct. This makes them unpopular with many people, but it is an unpopularity which they must share with every one who regards the distinction between right and wrong in a serious light; and the reproach is not one which a conscientious utilitarian need be anxious to repel.

If no more be meant by the objection than that many utilitarians look on the morality of actions, as measured by the utilitarian standards, with too exclusive a regard, and do not lay sufficient stress upon the other beauties of character which go toward making a human being lovable or admirable, this may be admitted. Utilitarians who have cultivated their moral feelings, but not their sympathies, nor their artistic perceptions, do fall into this mistake; and so do all other moralists under the same conditions. What can be said in excuse for other moralists is equally available for them, namely, that, if there is to be any error, it is better that it should be on that side. As a matter of fact, we may affirm that among utilitarians, as among adherents of other systems, there is every imaginable degree of rigidity and of laxity in the application of their standard; some are even puritanically rigorous, while others are as indulgent as can possibly be desired by sinner or by sentimentalist. But on the whole, a doctrine which brings prominently forward the interest that mankind have in the repression and prevention of conduct which violates the moral law is likely to be inferior to no other in turning the sanctions of opinion again such violations. It is true, the question "What does violate the moral law?" is one on which those who recognise different standards of morality are likely now and then to differ. But difference of opinion on moral questions was not first introduced into the world

by utilitarianism, while that doctrine does supply, if not always an easy, at all events a tangible and intelligible, mode of deciding such differences.

It may not be superfluous to notice a few more of the common misapprehensions of utilitarian ethics, even those which are so obvious and gross that it might appear impossible for any person of candour and intelligence to fall into them; since persons, even of considerable mental endowments, often give themselves so little trouble to understand the bearings of any opinion against which they entertain a prejudice, and men are in general so little conscious of this voluntary ignorance as a defect that the vulgarest misunderstandings of ethical doctrines are continually met with in the deliberate writings of persons of the greatest pretensions both to high principle and to philosophy. We not uncommonly hear the doctrine of utility inveighed against as a *godless* doctrine. If it be necessary to say anything at all against so mere an assumption, we may say that the question depends upon what idea we have formed of the moral character of the Deity. If it be a true belief that God desires, above all things, the happiness of his creatures, and that this was his purpose in their creation, utility is not only not a godless doctrine, but more profoundly religious than any other. If it be meant that utilitarianism does not recognise the revealed will of God as the supreme law of morals, I answer, that a utilitarian who believes in the perfect goodness and wisdom of *God* necessarily believes that whatever God has thought fit to reveal on the subject of morals must fulfil the requirements of utility in a supreme degree. But others besides utilitarians have been of opinion that the Christian revelation was intended, and is fitted, to inform the hearts and minds of mankind with a spirit which should enable them to find for themselves what is right, and incline them to do it when found, rather than to tell them, except in a very general way, what it is; and that we need a doctrine of ethics, carefully followed out, to *interpret* to us the will of God. Whether this opinion is correct or not, it is superfluous here to discuss; since whatever aid religion, either natural or revealed, can afford to ethical investigation, is as open to the utilitarian moralist as to any other. He can use it as the testimony of God to the usefulness or hurtfulness of any given course of action by as good a right as others can use it for the indication of a transcendental law having no connection with usefulness or with happiness.

Again, Utility is often summarily stigmatised as an immoral doctrine by giving it the name of Expediency, and taking advantage of the popular use of that term to contrast it with Principle. But the Expedient, in the sense in which it is opposed to the Right, generally means that which is expedient for the particular interest of the agent himself; as when a minister sacrifices the interests of his country to keep himself in place. When it means anything better than this, it means that which is expedient for some immediate object, some temporary purpose, but which violates a rule whose observance is expedient in a much higher degree. The Expedient, in this sense, instead of being the same thing with the useful, is a branch of the hurtful. Thus, it would often be expedient, for the purpose of getting over some momentary embarrassment, or attaining some object immediately useful to ourselves or others, to tell a lie. But inasmuch as the cultivation in ourselves of a sensitive feeling on the subject of veracity, is one of the most useful, and the enfeeblement of that feeling one of the most hurtful, things to which our conduct can be instrumental; and inasmuch as any, even unintentional, deviation from truth, does that much towards weakening the trustworthiness of human assertion, which is not only the principal support of all present social well-being, but the insufficiency of which does more than any one thing that can be named to keep back civilisation, virtue, everything on which human happiness on the largest scale depends; we feel that the violation, for a present advantage, of a rule of such transcendent expediency, is not expedient, and that he who, for the sake of a convenience to himself or to some other individual, does what depends on him to deprive mankind of the good, and inflict upon them the evil, involved in the greater or less reliance which they can place in each other's word, acts the part of one of their worst enemies.

Yet that even this rule, sacred as it is, admits of possible exceptions, is acknowledged by all moralists; the chief of which is when the withholding of some fact (as of information from a malefactor, or of bad news from a person dangerously ill) would save an individual (especially an individual other than oneself) from great and unmerited evil, and when the withholding can only be effected by denial. But in order that the exception may not extend itself beyond the need, and may have the least possible effect in weakening reliance on veracity, it ought to be recognised, and, if possible, its limits defined; and if the principle of utility is good for anything, it must be good for weighing these conflicting utilities against one another, and marking out the region within which one or the other preponderates.

Again, defenders of utility often find themselves called upon to reply to such objections as this—that there is not time, previous to action, for calculating and weighing the effects of any line of conduct on the general happiness. This is exactly as if anyone were to say that it is impossible to guide our conduct by Christianity because there is not time, on every occasion on which anything has to be done, to read through the Old and New Testaments. The answer to the objection is that there has been ample time, namely, the whole past duration of the human species. During all that time mankind have been learning by experience the tendencies of actions; on which experience all the prudence as well as all the morality of life are dependent. People talk as if the commencement of this course of experience had hitherto been put off, and as if, at the moment when some man feels tempted to meddle with the property or life of another, he had to begin considering for the first time whether murder and theft are injurious to human happiness. Even then I do not think that he would find the question very puzzling; but, at all events, the matter is now done to his hand. It is truly a whimsical supposition that, if mankind were agreed in considering utility to be the test of morality, they would remain without any agreement as to what *is* useful, and would take no measures for having their notions on the subject taught to the young and enforced by law and opinion. There is no difficulty in proving any ethical standard whatever to work ill if we suppose universal idiocy to be conjoined with it; but on any hypothesis short of that, mankind must by this time have acquired positive beliefs as to the effects of some actions on their happiness; and the beliefs which have thus come down are the rules of morality for the multitude, and for the philosopher until he has succeeded in finding better. That philosophers might easily do this, even now, on many subjects; that the received code of ethics is by no means of divine right; and that mankind have still much to learn as to the effects of actions on the general happiness, I admit or rather earnestly maintain. The corollaries from the principle of utility, like the precepts of every practical art, admit of indefinite improvement, and, in a progressive state of the human mind, their improvement is perpetually going on. But to consider the rules of morality as improvable is one thing; to pass over the intermediate generalisations entirely and endeavour to test each individual action directly by the first principle is another. It is a strange notion that the acknowledgment of a first principle is inconsistent with the admission of secondary ones. To inform a traveller respecting the place of his ultimate destination is not to forbid the use of landmarks and direction-posts on the way. The proposition that happiness is the end and aim of morality does not mean that no road ought to be laid down to that goal, or that persons going thither should not be advised to take one direction rather than another. Men really ought to leave off talking a kind of nonsense on this subject, which they would neither talk nor listen to on other matters of practical concernment. Nobody argues that the art of navigation is not founded on astronomy because sailors cannot wait to calculate the Nautical Almanac. Being rational creatures, they go to sea with it ready calculated; and all rational creatures go out upon the sea of life with their minds made up on the common questions of right and wrong, as well as on many of the far more difficult questions of wise and foolish. And this, as long as foresight is a human quality, it is to be presumed they will continue to do. Whatever we adopt as the fun-

damental principle of morality, we require subordinate principles to apply it by; the impossibility of doing without them, being common to all systems, can afford no argument against any one in particular; but gravely to argue as if no such secondary principles could be had, and as if mankind had remained till now, and always must remain, without drawing any general conclusions from the experience of human life is as high a pitch, I think, as absurdity has ever reached in philosophical controversy.

The remainder of the stock arguments against utilitarianism mostly consist in laying to its charge the common infirmities of human nature, and the general difficulties which embarrass conscientious persons in shaping their course through life. We are told that a utilitarian will be apt to make his own particular case an exception to moral rules, and, when under temptation, will see a utility in the breach of a rule, greater than he will see in its observance. But is utility the only creed which is able to furnish us with excuses for evil doing and means of cheating our own conscience? They are afforded in abundance by all doctrines which recognise as a fact in morals the existence of conflicting considerations, which all doctrines do that have been believed by sane persons. It is not the fault of any creed, but of the complicated nature of human affairs, that rules of conduct cannot be so framed as to require no exceptions, and that hardly any kind of action can safely be laid down as either always obligatory or always condemnable. There is no ethical creed which does not temper the rigidity of its laws by giving a certain latitude, under the moral responsibility of the agent, for accommodation to peculiarities of circumstances; and under every creed, at the opening thus made, self-deception and dishonest casuistry get in. There exists no moral system under which there do not arise unequivocal cases of conflicting obligation. These are the real difficulties, the knotty points both in the theory of ethics and in the conscientious guidance of personal conduct. They are overcome practically, with greater or with less success, according to the intellect and virtue of the individual; but it can hardly be pretended that any one will be the less qualified for dealing with them, from possessing an ultimate standard to which conflicting rights and duties can be referred. If utility is the ultimate source of moral obligations, utility may be invoked to decide between them when their demands are incompatible. Though the application of the standard may be difficult, it is better than none at all: while in other systems, the moral laws all claiming independent authority, there is no common umpire entitled to interfere between them; their claims to precedence one over another rest on little better than sophistry, and unless determined, as they generally are, by the unacknowledged influence of considerations of utility, afford a free scope for the action of personal desires and partialities. We must remember that only in these cases of conflict between secondary principles is it requisite that first principles should be appealed to. There is no case of moral obligation in which some secondary principle is not involved; and if only one, there can seldom be any real doubt which one it is, in the mind of any person by whom the principle itself is recognised.

# IMMANUEL KANT AND DEONTOLOGY

The German philosopher Immanuel Kant (1724–1804) is probably best known for his prodigiously difficult book *The Critique of Pure Reason* (1781). This work is a synthesis of empiricism and rationalism that attempts to solve most of the epistemological and metaphysical problems faced by eighteenth-century thought. Yet Kant's ethics have also been quite influential.

In contrast to the utilitarian focus on the consequences of our actions, Kant believed our "duties" should be foremost in the ethical decision-making process. These duties all flowed from a single moral principle, "the universal imperative of duty" or, put otherwise, the "categorical imperative." Even though there was a sole categorical imperative, Kant had two ways of formulating it. One way was in terms of universalization. Kant put it this way:

> Act only on that maxim through which you can, at the same time, will that it should become a universal law.

This roughly parallels the Golden Rule of Christianity that we should do unto others as we would have others do unto us. In other words, treat others as you would want to be treated.

The demand that we consider whether we can universalize our maxim has a basic intuitional appeal. We've all had moments, when faced with a moral problem, when we've said, "Well, it's just one time, and nobody will know, so doing something bad won't matter." But Kant doesn't want to make things so easy for us. He wants us to seriously consider whether what we are doing is ethical. So he asks us to consider what state of affairs would follow if our action were to be done by everyone in the same situation (this is the "universalizing" part of the imperative).

How would this work practically? Suppose we are late for a party. We are in a rush to get there, but our friend's apartment is across town. So we decide we need to speed to avoid being late. We have to drive only a bit over the speed limit and rush through a few yellow lights. We say to ourselves it's just this once—it's not as if we will do this every day. Just this one time we can be an exception.

Kant suddenly pulls up in his moral police cruiser and asks, "What would you think if everybody else acted this way? What would be the result? Would this be a rationally desirable situation?" By asking these questions, Kant is "universalizing" our moral decision. He wants us to see if we can make the principle behind our action, the maxim, even if we do it only once, valid for all other people in similar situations.

So we think about Officer Kant's questions for a moment. "Well, there are bound to be other people in my same situation each weekend in a city this size. If all were to speed and go through lights just because they were late for a party, even once, then there would be all sorts of accidents. Rules of the road, in fact, would cease to exist."

By considering that our actions would be impossible to universalize, we conclude that our actions are not ethically acceptable. We cannot make this action into a general maxim—a universal law of nature. In essence, Kant's theory makes it morally impossible to treat oneself, whether speeding or otherwise, as an exception.

Kant put forward a second formulation of his categorical imperative. It sounds quite different from his first, but he thought both formulations were equally descriptive of the categorical imperative:

> Act in such a way that you always treat humanity, whether in your own person or in the person of any other, never simply as a means, but always at the same time as an end.

This is the injunction not to treat oneself or others instrumentally. Our real value as human beings comes from the fact that our rational nature marks us out as ends in ourselves. This means we cannot treat the human person as an inanimate tool or object, something possessing no dignity, feelings, or personal concerns.

This way of fleshing out the imperative has important implications for how we are to understand human beings. For Kant, what sets us apart from the rest of nature is that we are rational beings.

Using a clear example to illustrate what Kant means, we certainly cannot make other human beings our slaves. This would be one of the most flagrant ways of treating others as a means rather than ends in themselves. Slaves are a means of supplying profit for their owners without their being paid for their work. We are not treating them as rational beings, allowing them to make their own decisions. Instead of recognizing their inherent value, we impose our own values on these people.

Another example of treating others as merely a means to an end would be asking a friend for a loan we have no intention of repaying. Besides the fact that we would not be able to universalize this maxim (because if all of us borrowed money without the intention of repaying the loan, the entire practice of loaning money would quickly cease as a practice), we would be using our friend just as a means to our selfish end.

An important consideration to Kant's admonition to avoid instrumentalization is that we also cannot treat ourselves as a mere means to some other end.

It is difficult to know what Kant would think about our current fascination with extreme sports. There is a good chance that he would regard it with mistrust because participants in these activities want a thrill or rush at the possible expense of harm to their bodies. Kant would consider using our bodies as a means for achieving this excitement to be morally unacceptable. Although this view of Kant's, at first blush, may seem a little strange, consider a person who, because of taking a dangerous risk, now is confined to a wheelchair and has limited use of his body. Thinking about Kant's criticism of how we may use our body may make a little more sense in this context.

Kant specifically discussed suicide in the context of using oneself instrumentally. Consider someone who wants to end her life because of psychological pain or depression or a case in which her life has become unbearable because of a debilitating disease. Kant opposed suicide because it treats a body as an object instead of an end in itself. That is, by killing ourselves, we use our bodies as a means of alleviating our suffering. Some of you may think, "Well, that's exactly the point! If I were dying of cancer, I may *want* to die before the disease finally kills me." Yet even in the case of extreme suffering, Kant would still say that the suicide is using his or her body merely as a means for some other end, instead of an end in itself.

What are we to make of Kant's approach to ethics?

One of the advantages of his view is that it takes seriously duties and principles. Unlike utilitarians, those who follow Kant's deontological methodology have a high respect for individual rights and justice. Despite whatever utilities or disutilities may be served in doing a particular action, Kant's foremost consideration is acting according to the categorical imperative. Even in cases in which a great weight of disutility results in our telling the truth, we are, nevertheless, bound to be honest. For Kant, the consequences of our actions have no part in the ethical decision-making process. First and foremost is our duty not to treat others or ourselves instrumentally, as means to an end.

Ironically, the categorical demand to always follow our duty, with no regard given to the consequences of our acts, has been the greatest criticism against Kant's "deontological monism." Think, for example, of a situation in which living under an authoritarian political regime, you are hiding some political dissidents in your apartment. The local authorities decide to gather up and get rid of all "troublemakers." A day after you hide these people in your home, the police come to your door to ask if you are harboring any political dissidents. Kant says that lying treats people as a means instead of ends and therefore that all dishonesty is wrong. This even applies to lying to people we find morally repugnant. So it would apply to cases such as this one, even when we have good reason to believe that if we tell the truth, the people we are hiding will be imprisoned and executed. Kant would maintain that if we lied to the police, wishing to avoid this consequence, no matter how terrible, we would not be acting ethically.

Kant's own example is even starker. Consider someone pursued by a murderer. We know where the fleeing person is, but the murderer confronts us in the street, demanding to know where his likely victim is hiding. For Kant, we cannot tell a lie. We must divulge the information. Again, we may be prone to think about the consequences of our actions, but Kant insists consequences play no role in the decision. Beyond all the other reasons he has given for us to follow the categorical imperative, he points out that figuring consequences into the decision-making process carries no certainty that good will always result. Although it is hard to imagine how lying to a murderer about the whereabouts of his next victim will bring worse consequences than a lie to a killer, this is a main criticism of utilitarianism, and Kant's point here merits consideration.

How does Kant's insistence that we must always follow the duty to tell the truth agree with your sense of right and wrong? In the previous scenario, does it seem we would be justified lying to a murderer when his intent is to kill an innocent person? Shouldn't lying to people bent on doing great harm to others be justifiable if it saves innocent lives? Shouldn't the anticipated consequences of our actions, in some fashion, figure into the decisions we make?

The answers to these questions depend on whom you ask. For utilitarians, the consequences of our actions should indeed figure into the decisions we make. For Kant, we must follow the categorical imperative. The consequences of our actions, good or bad, should play no role in making our moral choices. When evaluating Kant's position, keep in mind that he also denied the possibility of moral dilemmas.

Kant's approach to ethics remains a powerful theory. Even though you may have reservations about thoroughly embracing it, as a theory it does illuminate some important elements of the moral life by emphasizing our duties, not treating oneself or others instrumentally, not making oneself an exception to moral behavior, and not trying to anticipate and calculate future consequences.

# Groundwork of the Metaphysics of Morals

## IMMANUEL KANT

THERE IS THEREFORE only a single categorical imperative and it is this: *"Act only on that maxim through which you can at the same time will that it should become a universal law."*

Now if all imperatives of duty can be derived from this one imperative as their principle, then even although we leave it unsettled whether what we call duty may not be an empty concept, we shall still be able to show at least what we understand by it and what the concept means.

### The Formula of the Law of Nature

Since the universality of the law governing the production of effects constitutes what is properly called *nature* in its most general sense (nature as regards its form)—that is, the existence of things so far as determined by universal laws—the universal imperative of duty may also run as follows: *"Act as if the maxim of your action were to become through your will a universal law of nature."*

### Illustrations

We will now enumerate a few duties, following their customary division into duties towards self and duties towards others and into perfect and imperfect duties.[1]

1. A man feels sick of life as the result of a series of misfortunes that has mounted to the point of despair, but he is still so far in possession of his reason as to ask himself whether taking his own life may not be contrary to his duty to himself. He now applies the test "Can the maxim of my action really become a universal law of nature?" His maxim is "From self-love I make it my principle to shorten my life if its continuance threatens more evil than it promises pleasure." The only further question to ask is whether this principle of self-love can become a universal law of nature. It is then seen at once that a system of nature by whose law the very same feeling whose

[1] It should be noted that I reserve my division of duties entirely for a future *Metaphysic of Morals* and that my present division is therefore put forward as arbitrary (merely for the purpose of arranging my examples). Further, I understand here by a perfect duty one which allows no exception in the interests of inclination, and so I recognize among *perfect duties,* not only outer ones, but also inner. This is contrary to the accepted usage of the schools, but I do not intend to justify it here, since for my purpose it is all one whether this point is conceded or not.

SOURCE: Immanuel Kant, *Groundwork of the Metaphysics of Morals,* trans. H. J. Paton (New York: Harper & Row Torchbooks, 1948), pp. 88–91, 95–99.

function (*Bestimmung*) is to stimulate the furtherance of life should actually destroy life would contradict itself and consequently could not subsist as a system of nature. Hence this maxim cannot possibly hold as a universal law of nature and is therefore entirely opposed to the supreme principle of all duty.

2. Another finds himself driven to borrowing money because of need. He well knows that he will not be able to pay it back; but he sees too that he will get no loan unless he gives a firm promise to pay it back within a fixed time. He is inclined to make such a promise; but he has still enough conscience to ask "Is it not unlawful and contrary to duty to get out of difficulties in this way?" Supposing, however, he did resolve to do so, the maxim of his action would run thus: "Whenever I believe myself short of money, I will borrow money and promise to pay it back, though I know that this will never be done." Now this principle of self-love or personal advantage is perhaps quite compatible with my own entire future welfare; only there remains the question "Is it right?" I therefore transform the demand of self-love into a universal law and frame my question thus: "How would things stand if my maxim became a universal law?" I then see straight away that this maxim can never rank as a universal law of nature and be self-consistent, but must necessarily contradict itself. For the universality of a law that every one believing himself to be in need can make any promise he pleases with the intention not to keep it would make promising, and the very purpose of promising, itself impossible, since no one would believe he was being promised anything, but would laugh at utterances of this kind as empty shams.

3. A third finds in himself a talent whose cultivation would make him a useful man for all sorts of purposes. But he sees himself in comfortable circumstances, and he prefers to give himself up to pleasure rather than to bother about increasing and improving his fortunate natural aptitudes. Yet he asks himself further "Does my maxim of neglecting my natural gifts, besides agreeing in itself with my tendency to indulgence, agree also with what is called duty?" He then sees that a system of nature could indeed always subsist under such a universal law, although (like the South Sea Islanders) every man should let his talents rust and should be bent on devoting his life solely to idleness, indulgence, procreation, and, in a word, to enjoyment. Only he cannot possibly *will* that this should become a universal law of nature or should be implanted in us as such a law by a natural instinct. For as a rational being he necessarily wills that all his powers should be developed, since they serve him, and are given him, for all sorts of possible ends.

4. Yet a *fourth* is himself flourishing, but he sees others who have to struggle with great hardships (and whom he could easily help); and he thinks "What does it matter to me? Let every one be as happy as Heaven wills or as he can make himself; I won't deprive him of anything; I won't even envy him; only I have no wish to contribute anything to his well-being or to his support in distress!" Now admittedly if such an attitude were a universal law of nature, mankind could get on perfectly well—better no doubt than if everybody prates about sympathy and goodwill, and even takes pains, on occasion, to practise them, but on the other hand cheats where he can, traffics in human rights, or violates them in other ways. But although it is possible that a universal law of nature could subsist in harmony with this maxim, yet it is impossible to *will* that such a principle should hold everywhere as a law of nature. For a will which decided in this way would be in conflict with itself, since many a situation might arise in which the man needed love and sympathy from others, and in which, by such a law of nature sprung from his own will, he would rob himself of all hope of the help he wants for himself.

## The Canon of Moral Judgement

These are some of the many actual duties—or at least of what we take to be such—whose derivation from the single principle cited above leaps to the eye. We must *be able to will* that a maxim of our action should become a universal law—this is the general canon for all moral judgement of action. Some actions are so constituted that their maxim cannot even be *conceived* as a universal law of nature without contradiction, let alone be *willed* as what *ought* to become one. In the case of others we do not find this inner impossibility, but it is still impossible to *will* that their maxim should be raised to the universality of a law of nature, because such a will would contradict itself. It is easily seen that the first kind of action is opposed to strict or narrow (rigorous) duty, the second only to wider (meritorious) duty; and thus that by these examples all duties —so far as the type of obligation is concerned (not the object of dutiful action)—are fully set out in their dependence on our single principle.

If we now attend to ourselves whenever we transgress a duty, we find that we in fact do not will that our maxim should become a universal law—since this is impossible for us—but rather that its opposite should remain a law universally: we only take the liberty of making an *exception* to it for ourselves (or even just for this once) to the advantage of our inclination. Consequently if we weighed it all up from one and the same point of view—that of reason—we should find a contradiction in our own will, the contradiction that a certain principle should be objectively necessary as a universal law and yet subjectively should not hold universally but should admit of exceptions. Since, however, we first consider our action from the point of view of a will wholly in accord with reason, and then consider precisely the same action from the point of view of a will affected by inclination, there is here actually no contradiction, but rather an opposition of inclination to the precept of reason (*antagonismus*), whereby the universality of the principle (*universalitas*) is turned into a mere generality (*generalitas*) so that the practical principle of reason may meet our maxim half-way. This procedure, though in our own impartial judgement it cannot be justified, proves none the less that we in fact recognize the validity of the categorical imperative and (with all respect for it) merely permit ourselves a few exceptions which are, as we pretend, inconsiderable and apparently forced upon us.

We have thus at least shown this much—that if duty is a concept which is to have meaning and real legislative authority for our actions, this can be expressed only in categorical imperatives and by no means in hypothetical ones. At the same time—and this is already a great deal—we have set forth distinctly, and determinately for every type of application, the content of the categorical imperative, which must contain the principle of all duty (if there is to be such a thing at all). But we are still not so far advanced as to prove *a priori* that there actually is an imperative of this kind—that there is a practical law which by itself commands absolutely and without any further motives, and that the following of this law is duty. . . .

## The Formula of the End in Itself

. . . Suppose, however, there were something *whose existence* has *in itself* an absolute value, something which as *an end in itself* could be a ground of determinate laws; then in it, and in it alone, would there be the ground of a possible categorical imperative—that is, of a practical law.

Now I say that man, and in general every rational being, *exists* as an end in himself, *not merely as a means* for arbitrary use by this or that will: he must in all his actions, whether they are directed to himself or to other rational beings, always be viewed *at the same time as an end*. All the objects of inclination have only a conditioned value; for if there were not these inclinations and the needs grounded on them, their object would be valueless. Inclinations themselves, as sources of needs, are so far from having an absolute value to make them desirable for their own sake that it must rather be the universal wish of every rational being to be wholly free from them. Thus the value of all objects that can *be produced* by our action is always conditioned. Beings whose existence depends, not on our will, but on nature, have none the less, if they are non-rational beings, only a relative value as means and are consequently called *things*. Rational beings, on the other hand, are called *persons* because their nature already marks them out as ends in themselves—that is, as something which ought not to be used merely as a means—and consequently imposes to that extent a limit on all arbitrary treatment of them (and is an object of reverence). Persons, therefore, are not merely subjective ends whose existence as an object of our actions has a value *for us:* they are *objective ends*—that is, things whose existence is in itself an end, and indeed an end such that in its place we can put no other end to which they should serve *simply* as means; for unless this is so, nothing at all of *absolute* value would be found anywhere. But if all value were conditioned—that is, contingent—then no supreme principle could be found for reason at all.

If then there is to be a supreme practical principle and—so far as the human will is concerned—a categorical imperative, it must be such that from the idea of something which is necessarily an end for every one because it is an *end in itself* it forms an *objective* principle of the will and consequently can serve as a practical law. The ground of this principle is: *Rational nature exists as an end in itself.* This is the way in which a man necessarily conceives his own existence: it is therefore so far a *subjective* principle of human actions. But it is also the way in which every other rational being conceives his existence on the same rational ground which is valid also for me;[2] hence it is at the same time an *objective* principle, from which, as a supreme practical ground, it must be possible to derive all laws for the will. The practical imperative will therefore be as follows: *Act in such a way that you always treat humanity, whether in your own person or in the person of any other, never simply as a means, but always at the same time as an end.* We will now consider whether this can be carried out in practice.

## Illustrations

Let us keep to our previous examples.

*First,* as regards the concept of necessary duty to oneself, the man who contemplates suicide will ask "Can my action be compatible with the Idea of humanity *as an end in itself*?" If he does away with himself in order to escape from a painful situation, he is making use of a person merely as *a means* to maintain a tolerable state of affairs till the end of his life. But man is not a thing—not something to be used *merely* as a means: he must always in all his actions be regarded as an end in himself. Hence I cannot dispose of man in my person by maiming, spoiling, or killing. (A more precise determination of this principle in order to avoid all misunderstanding—for example, about having limbs amputated to save myself or about exposing my life to danger in order to preserve it, and so on—I must here forego: this question belongs to morals proper.)

*Secondly,* so far as necessary or strict duty to others is concerned, the man who has a mind to make a false promise to others will see at once that he is intending to make use of another man *merely as a means* to an end he does not share. For the man whom I seek to use for my own purposes by such a promise cannot possibly agree with my way of behaving to him, and so cannot himself share the end of the action. This incompatibility with the principle of duty to others leaps to the eye more obviously when we bring in examples of attempts on the freedom and property of others. For then it is manifest that a violator of the rights of man intends to use the person of others merely as a means without taking into consideration that, as rational beings, they ought always at the same time to be rated as ends—that is, only as beings who must themselves be able to share in the end of the very same action.[3]

*Thirdly,* in regard to contingent (meritorious) duty to oneself, it is not enough that an action should refrain from conflicting with humanity in our own person as an end in itself: it must also *harmonize with this end.* Now there are in hu-

---

[2] This proposition I put forward here as a postulate. . . .

[3] Let no one think that here the trivial *"quod tibi non vis fieri, etc."* can serve as a standard or principle. For it is merely derivative from our principle, although subject to various qualifications: it cannot be a universal law since it contains the ground neither of duties to oneself nor of duties of kindness to others (for many a man would readily agree that others should not help him if only he could be dispensed from affording help to them), nor finally of strict duties towards others; for on this basis the criminal would be able to dispute with the judges who punish him, and so on.

manity capacities for greater perfection which form part of nature's purpose for humanity in our person. To neglect these can admittedly be compatible with the *maintenance* of humanity as an end in itself, but not with the *promotion* of this end.

*Fourthly,* as regards meritorious duties to others, the natural end which all men seek is their own happiness. Now humanity could no doubt subsist if everybody contributed nothing to the happiness of others but at the same time refrained from deliberately impairing their happiness. This is, however, merely to agree negatively and not positively with *humanity as an end in itself* unless every one endeavours also, so far as in him lies, to further the ends of others. For the ends of a subject who is an end in himself must, if this conception is to have its *full* effect in me, be also, as far as possible, *my* ends.

## The Formula of Autonomy

This principle of humanity, and in general of every rational agent, *as an end in itself* (a principle which is the supreme limiting condition of every man's freedom of action) is not borrowed from experience; firstly, because it is universal, applying as it does to all rational beings as such, and no experience is adequate to determine universality; secondly, because in it humanity is conceived, not as an end of man (subjectively)—that is, as an object which, as a matter of fact, happens to be made an end—but as an objective end—one which, be our ends what they may, must, as a law, constitute the supreme limiting condition of all subjective ends and so must spring from pure reason. That is to say, the ground for every enactment of practical law lies *objectively in the rule* and in the form of universality which (according to our first principle) makes the rule capable of being a law (and indeed a law of nature); *subjectively,* however, it lies in the *end;* but (according to our second principle) the subject of all ends is to be found in every rational being as an end in himself. From this there now follows our third practical principle for the will—as the supreme condition of the will's conformity with universal practical reason—namely, the Idea *of the will of every rational being as a will which makes universal law.*

By this principle all maxims are repudiated which cannot accord with the will's own enactment of universal law. The will is therefore not merely subject to the law, but is so subject that it must be considered as also *making the law* for itself and precisely on this account as first of all subject to the law (of which it can regard itself as the author).

# FRIEDRICH NIETZSCHE: BEYOND GOD, GOOD, AND EVIL

Friedrich Nietzsche's approach to ethics, as noted in our introduction to this chapter, is quite different from the systematized, formulized views of Aristotle, Mill, and Kant. Yet Nietzsche used his own terminology, developed in part because of his criticisms of Christian values and morality.

We have looked at some of his terminology in the introduction, such as *Übermensch, ressentiment,* slave and master morality, nihilism, and the enhancement of life. We have also seen how these concepts contrast with the traditional values and doctrines of Christianity. Given this way of seeing the world, one might think Nietzsche is the kind of person others would try to avoid in day-to-day life.

Nietzsche indeed brings a sort of cynicism, a heavy philosophical doubt to our most firmly held beliefs and values. He tells us, without batting an eye, that "God is dead" and that religion actually oppresses, rather than lifts, the human spirit. He tells us the traditional virtues of humility, pity, and charity to others are just part of a "herd morality." Like religious beliefs, these values depress us physically and grind the human spirit into the ground. Nietzsche was also not enthusiastic about the worth of traditional moral theories. Consider his claim that our most firmly held beliefs are "nothing more than the twitching of our muscles."

Despite the unease we might feel from listening to Nietzsche's acerbic views of Christian values and traditional moral theory, a basic assumption of the philosophical method is that no matter how much discomfort our examination of things may evoke, we must press on with our inquiries.

Another assumption made by philosophers is that we can benefit from the criticisms of others. If criticism is seen in this way, the consequences of having our beliefs challenged can be quite positive. Either we will recognize that our belief is misguided and therefore in need of change, or we will see that our belief does in fact stand up to criticism, and we are therefore all the more justified holding it.

How, then, are we to assess Nietzsche's ethical views? Critical self-assessment is important, but not only for those who are the target of his critique. Even if you don't consider yourself religious, given that Christian values permeate society, the impact of his overall assessment of traditional morality will be of importance for you as well.

It is difficult to take the middle ground when it comes to Nietzsche. You will probably either love him or hate him. Not many people remain ambivalent to his ideas after studying him. Some of you may find Nietzsche to be a breath of fresh air. You may find his remarks and insights on the mark. He may be the first you have ever read who dares to speak against unquestioned assumptions. Others of you may find him too pessimistic, bordering on ranting. What are we to make, for example, of his praise for the "blond beasts" of prey rampaging through ancient and medieval Europe (*Genealogy* 1.11)? Or that the image of Jesus dying on the cross was a sublime seduction for centuries to come for the strong to humble themselves and adopt a slave morality (*Genealogy* 1.9)?

The selections chosen from his writings on ethics cover a wide range of matters: what morality, as commonly practiced, amounts to; why moral prohibitions come into being; how the terms "good," "bad," and "evil" came to be used in the modern sense; how Christianity elevated the values of the "herd" to a universal status; and what distinction he has made between "master" and "slave" moralities.

The first group of readings is an interesting account of why Nietzsche believes we attempt to be moral, along with his critique of utilitarianism, deontology, and moral sense theory. We normally take our efforts to be moral as a high-minded and noble undertaking. Nietzsche argues, however, that "being moral" is just a matter of following the custom of our day, passively accepting those rules or norms that are part of our social fabric of beliefs.

Nietzsche finds it interesting to study what factors lead from holding moral beliefs to the solidifying of those beliefs into tradition. When this solidification occurs, these moral values acquire a reverence. This results in people holding on to a tradition not because they have thoroughly examined the rightfulness of their norms but because there is an aura surrounding that tradition.

We all remember what it was like when, as children, we were not given reasons why our behavior, or the behavior of others, was called wrong or inappropriate. We became confused when we were told something was wrong without knowing the reasons *why* it was wrong. Over time people learn to live with this confusion by just accepting without question the principles they were told to keep. This removes all transparency in the moral climate.

There are two major reasons why there is silence on the part of moral authorities such as parents, the Church, and the State. It may be that the group forbidding the action never really considered the reasons behind the norm it is attempting to enforce. Parents, for example, may have uncritically accepted the moral injunction from their parents, thus making it difficult to later explain why it should be upheld. In these cases, the moral prohibition of an action (because it cannot be rationally justified) can be reduced purely and simply to the issue of respect for authority—we accept the prohibition due to a fear of punishment.

Nietzsche describes how we view those who challenge existing laws and norms, those who are uncomfortable with the uncritical acceptance of certain moral beliefs. When people challenge a particular moral belief, telling us, for example, that our commonly accepted attitudes are sexist or racist, they are initially labeled as outsiders, or "bad" people. But once the attitudes of our society change over time, once the law or norms are successfully changed or rejected, those previously regarded as "bad" people become "good" people. They may even come to be regarded as brave moral leaders.

An example of Nietzsche's critique of Christian values can be seen in his account of how we should regard pride and the morality of "selflessness." At first blush, we might think pride should always be shunned. We should do our best to get rid of it. Selflessness should always be encouraged and promoted. As Mill says, we should try to promote not only our own happiness but also that of all other people affected by our actions. Yet Nietzsche questions the denigration of pride and the elevation of selflessness as the highest virtue. He sees it as a relic of the Christian insistence that we turn the other cheek, that we humble ourselves before the powerful. Indeed, Nietzsche wants us to turn our system of values on its head—to invert our traditional hierarchy of values. Humility should be devalued and pride admired as more conducive to the well-being of the human species.

The second group of readings includes Nietzsche's more developed ideas on master and slave moralities, the origin of the value judgment "good," and the way the notion of *ressentiment* fits into Nietzsche's theory of values. We present two key sections from *Beyond Good and Evil,* along with substantial portions from Essay I of *On the Genealogy of Morals,* Nietzsche's most coherent and sustained critique of Christian morality.

In a nutshell, Nietzsche sees the history of Western civilization as a battleground between two conceptions of morality: master and slave morality. The former is the morality of warriors and aristocrats who call themselves "good" to distinguish themselves from the dirty, lowly, "bad" toiling masses. These masses, led by ascetic priests who channel their *ressentiment* against their noble masters into a religious and moral code that celebrates weakness and victimhood, cannot oppose their masters by direct physical force. Instead, they turn to this moral code of pity and humility, seducing their masters with the image of "God on the cross" (i.e., Jesus Christ) away from their master morality of courage, war, healthy physicality, and sex, away from "vigorous, free, joyful activity" (*Genealogy* 1.7). Now chastity and weakness are the preferred values. Slave morality has performed a "transvaluation of values": substituting for the dialectic of the "good" of the masters versus the "bad" of the toiling masses the opposition of the "good" of the meek and humble, who according to Jesus shall inherit the earth, to the "evil" of the splendid blond beasts of prey prowling about in search of fun. (Walter Kaufmann makes a very good case that the "blond beasts" of prey Nietzsche refers to are *not* the Aryan supermen of the Nazi myth but fierce lion-hearted individuals of all races.)

In his book *Genealogy* (1.13), Nietzsche gives us a pithy little parable of how this transvaluation of values works. Let's suppose you were a sheep capable of rational thought. Your herd is being attacked by ravenous eagles that periodically kill off some of your fellow sheep to feed themselves. What will you think about these eagles? Naturally, you and your sheepish comrades will be full of resentment against these eagles. You will call them "evil" (just as couples who go through difficult break-ups sometimes call each other "evil"). Yet what will the eagles think of the sheep? They'll merely think the sheep are tasty treats, a belief that certainly shouldn't define them as "evil." So the nature of good and evil depends on what moral perspective one occupies. This view is sometimes referred to as "moral perspectivism" and is one of Nietzsche's most lasting contributions to moral theory.

The following selections from Nietzsche are only a small fragment of his body of work. We hope that if these offerings tweak your interest, you will be encouraged to read more of this enigmatic and highly provocative philosopher.

# Nietzsche's Critique of Conventional Morality

## FRIEDRICH NIETZSCHE

### Daybreak

#### 97

*To become moral is not in itself moral.*—Subjection to morality can be slavish or vain or self-interested or resigned or gloomily enthusiastic or an act of despair, like subjection to a prince: in itself it is nothing moral.

#### 100

*Awakening from a dream.*—Wise and noble men once believed in the music of the spheres: wise and noble men still believe in the "moral significance of existence." But one day this music of the spheres too will no longer be audible to them! They will awaken and perceive that their ears had been dreaming.

#### 101

*Suspicious.*—To admit a belief merely because it is a custom—but that means to be dishonest, cowardly, lazy!—And so could dishonesty, cowardice and laziness be the preconditions of morality?

#### 131

*Fashions in morality.*—How the overall moral judgments have shifted! The great men of antique morality, Epictetus for instance, knew nothing of the now normal glorification of thinking of others, of living for others; in the light of our moral fashion they would have to be called downright immoral, for they strove with all their might *for* their *ego* and *against* feeling with oth-

SOURCE: Friedrich Nietzsche, *Daybreak*, trans. R. J. Hollingdale (1881; Cambridge: Cambridge University Press, 1997), pp. 59, 82–84, 105–106, 163 [secs. 97, 101, 131–132, 133 (edited), 174, 339].
Reprinted with the permission of Cambridge University Press.

ers (that is to say, with the sufferings and moral frailties of others). Perhaps they would reply to us: "If you are so boring or ugly an object to yourself, by all means think of others more than of yourself! It is right you should!"

## 132

*The echo of Christianity in morality.*—*"On n'est bon que par la pitié: il faut donc qu'il y ait quelque pitié dans tous nos sentiments"*—thus says morality today! And why is that?—That men today feel the sympathetic, disinterested, generally useful social actions to be the *moral* actions—this is perhaps the most general effect and conversion which Christianity has produced in Europe: although it was not its intention nor contained in its teaching. But it was the residuum of Christian states of mind left when the very much antithetical, strictly egoistic fundamental belief in the "one thing needful," in the absolute importance of eternal *personal* salvation, together with the dogmas upon which it rested, gradually retreated and the subsidiary belief in "love," in "love of one's neighbour," in concert with the tremendous practical effect of ecclesiastical charity, was thereby pushed into the foreground. The more one liberated oneself from the dogmas, the more one sought as it were a *justification* of this liberation in a cult of philanthropy: not to fall short of the Christian ideal in this, but where possible to outdo it, was a secret spur with all French freethinkers from Voltaire up to Auguste Comte: and the latter did in fact, with his moral formula *vivre pour autrui*, outchristian Christianity. In Germany it was Schopenhauer, in England John Stuart Mill who gave the widest currency to the teaching of the sympathetic affects and of pity or the advantage of others as the principle of behaviour: but they themselves were no more than an echo—those teachings have shot up with a mighty impetus everywhere and in the crudest and subtlest forms together from about the time of the French Revolution onwards, every socialist system has placed itself as if involuntarily on the common ground of these teachings. There is today perhaps no more firmly credited prejudice than this: that one *knows* what really consti-

tutes the moral. Today it seems *to do everyone good* when they hear that society is on the way to *adapting* the individual to general requirements, and that *the happiness and at the same time the sacrifice of the individual* lies in feeling himself to be a useful member and instrument of the whole: except that one is at present very uncertain as to where this whole is to be sought, whether in an existing state or one still to be created, or in the nation, or in a brotherhood of peoples, or in new little economic communalities. At present there is much reflection, doubt, controversy over this subject, and much excitement and passion; but there is also a wonderful and fair-sounding unanimity in the demand that the ego has to deny itself until, in the form of adaptation to the whole, it again acquires its firmly set circle of rights and duties—until it has become something quite novel and different. What is wanted—whether this is admitted or not—is nothing less than a fundamental remoulding, indeed weakening and abolition of the *individual:* one never tires of enumerating and indicting all that is evil and inimical, prodigal, costly, extravagant in the form individual existence has assumed hitherto, one hopes to manage more cheaply, more safely, more equitably, more uniformly if there exist only *large bodies and their members.* Everything that in any way corresponds to this body- and membership-building drive and its ancillary drives is felt to be *good,* this is the *moral undercurrent* of our age; individual empathy and social feeling here play into one another's hands. (Kant still stands outside this movement: he expressly teaches that we must be insensible towards the suffering of others if our beneficence is to possess moral value—which Schopenhauer, in a wrath easy to comprehend, calls *Kantian insipidity.*)

## 133

*"No longer to think of oneself."*—Let us reflect seriously upon this question: why do we leap after someone who has fallen into the water in front of us, even though we feel no kind of affection for him? Out of pity: at that moment we are thinking only of the other person—thus says thought-

lessness. Why do we feel pain and discomfort in common with someone spitting blood, though we may even be ill-disposed towards him? Out of pity: at that moment we are not thinking of ourself—thus says the same thoughtlessness. The truth is: in the feeling of pity—I mean in that which is usually and misleadingly called pity—we are, to be sure, not consciously thinking of ourself but are doing so *very strongly unconsciously;* as when, if our foot slips—an act of which we are not immediately conscious—we perform the most purposive counter-motions and in doing so plainly employ our whole reasoning faculty. An accident which happens to another offends us: it would make us aware of our impotence, and perhaps of our cowardice, if we did not go to assist him. Or it brings with it in itself a diminution of our honour in the eyes of others or in our own eyes. Or an accident and suffering incurred by another constitutes a signpost to some danger to us; and it can have a painful effect upon us simply as a token of human vulnerability and fragility in general. We repel this kind of pain and offence and requite it through an act of pity; it may contain a subtle self-defence or even a piece of revenge. That at bottom we are thinking very strongly of ourselves can be divined from the decision we arrive at in every case in which we *can* avoid the sight of the person suffering, perishing or complaining: we decide *not* to do so if we can present ourselves as the more powerful and as a helper, if we are certain of applause, if we want to feel how fortunate we are in contrast, or hope that the sight will relieve our boredom. . . .

## 174

*Moral fashion of a commercial society.*—Behind the basic principle of the current moral fashion: "moral actions are actions performed out of sympathy for others," I see the social effect of timidity hiding behind an intellectual mask: it desires, first and foremost, that *all the dangers* which life once held should be removed from it, and that *everyone* should assist in this with all his might: hence only those actions which tend towards the common security and society's sense of security

are to be accorded the predicate "good."—How little pleasure men must nowadays take in themselves when such a tyranny of timidity prescribes to them their supreme moral law, when they so uncontradictingly allow themselves to be ordered to look away from themselves but to have lynx-eyes for all the distress and suffering that exists elsewhere! Are we not, with this tremendous objective of obliterating all the sharp edges of life, well on the way to turning mankind into *sand?* Sand! Small, soft, round, unending sand! Is that your ideal, you heralds of the sympathetic affections?—In the meantime, the question itself remains unanswered whether one is of *more use* to another by immediately leaping to his side and *helping* him—which help can in any case be only superficial where it does not become a tyrannical seizing and transforming—or by *creating* something out of oneself that the other can behold with pleasure: a beautiful, restful, self-enclosed garden perhaps, with high walls against storms and the dust of the roadway but also a hospitable gate.

## 339

*Metamorphosis of duties.*—When duty ceases to be a burden but, after long practice, becomes a joyful inclination and a need, the rights of those others to whom our duties, now our inclinations, refer, become something different: namely occasions of pleasant sensations for us. From then onwards, the other becomes, by virtue of his rights, lovable (instead of feared and revered, as heretofore). We are now seeking *pleasure* when we recognise and sustain the sphere of his power. When the Quietists came to feel their Christianity no longer a burden and experienced only pleasure in God, they adopted as their motto "All for the honour of God": whatever they did under this banner was no longer a sacrifice; their motto came to the same thing as "all for our own pleasure!" To demand that duty must *always* be something of a burden—as Kant does—means to demand that it should never become habit and custom: in this demand there is concealed a remnant of ascetic cruelty.

## The Gay Science

### 4

*What preserves the species.*—The strongest and most evil spirits have so far done the most to advance humanity: again and again they relumed the passions that were going to sleep—all ordered society puts the passions to sleep—and they reawakened again and again the sense of comparison, of contradiction, of the pleasure in what is new, daring, untried; they compelled men to pit opinion against opinion, model against model. Usually by force of arms, by toppling boundary markers, by violating pieties— but also by means of new religions and moralities. In every teacher and preacher of what is *new* we encounter the same "wickedness" that makes conquerors notorious, even if its expression is subtler and it does not immediately set the muscles in motion, and therefore also does not make one that notorious. What is new, however, is always *evil,* being that which wants to conquer and overthrow the old boundary markers and the old pieties; and only what is old is good. The good men are in all ages those who dig the old thoughts, digging deep and getting them to bear fruit—the farmers of the spirit. But eventually all land is exploited, and the ploughshare of evil must come again and again.

Nowadays there is a profoundly erroneous moral doctrine that is celebrated especially in England: this holds that judgments of "good" and "evil" sum up experiences of what is "expedient" and "inexpedient." One holds that what is called good preserves the species, while what is called evil harms the species. In truth, however, the evil instincts are expedient, species-preserving, and indispensable to as high a degree as the good ones; their function is merely different.[1]

[1] This section illuminates Nietzsche's "immoralism" as well as his consistent opposition to utilitarianism. . . .

### 5

*Unconditional duties.*—All those who feel they need the strongest words and sounds, the most eloquent gestures and postures, in order to be effective *at all*—such as revolutionary politicians, socialists, preachers of repentance with or without Christianity, all of whom cannot tolerate semisuccesses—talk of "duties," and actually always of duties that are supposed to be unconditional. Without that they would lack the justification for their great pathos, and they understand this very well. Thus they reach for moral philosophies that preach some categorical imperative, or they ingest a goodly piece of religion, as Mazzini did,[2] for example. Because they desire the unconditional confidence of others, they need first of all to develop unconditional self-confidence on the basis of some ultimate and indisputable commandment that is inherently sublime, and they want to feel like, and be accepted as, its servants and instruments.

Here we have the most natural and usually very influential opponents of moral enlightenment and skepticism; but they are rare. Yet a very comprehensive class of such opponents is to be found wherever self-interest requires submission while reputation and honor seem to prohibit submission. Whoever feels that his dignity is incompatible with the thought of being the *instrument* of a prince or a party or sect or, even worse, of a financial power—say, because he is after all the descendant of an old and proud family—but who nevertheless wants to or must be such an instrument before himself and before the public,

[2] There is a large literature on Giuseppe Mazzini (1805–72), the Italian revolutionist. He hoped at one time to write a history of Italy "to enable the working class to apprehend . . . the 'mission' of Italy in God's providential ordering of the world." The work remained unwritten; "no one, however, can read even the briefest and most occasional writing of Mazzini without gaining some impression of the simple grandeur of the man, the lofty elevation of his moral tone, his unwavering faith in the living God, who is ever revealing Himself in the progressive development of humanity." (*Encyclopaedia Britannica,* 11th ed., vol. 17, p. 945).

SOURCE: Friedrich Nietzsche, *The Gay Science,* trans. Walter Kaufmann (1882; New York: Vintage Books, 1974), pp. 79–81, 91–93, 174–175 [secs. 4, 5, 19, 21 (edited), 116]. Copyright 1974 by Random House, Inc. Used by permission of Random House, Inc.

requires pompous principles that can be mouthed at any time; principles of some unconditional obligation to which one may submit without shame. Refined servility clings to the categorical imperative and is the mortal enemy of those who wish to deprive duty of its unconditional character; that is what decency demands of them, and not only decency.

## 19

*Evil.*—Examine the lives of the best and most fruitful people and peoples and ask yourselves whether a tree that is supposed to grow to a proud height can dispense with bad weather and storms; whether misfortune and external resistance, some kinds of hatred, jealousy, stubbornness, mistrust, hardness, avarice, and violence do not belong among the *favorable* conditions without which any great growth even of virtue is scarcely possible. The poison of which weaker natures perish strengthens the strong[3]—nor do they call it poison.

## 21

*To the teachers of selfishness.*—A man's virtues are called *good* depending on their probable consequences not for him but for us and society: the praise of virtues has always been far from "selfless," far from "unegoistic." Otherwise one would have had to notice that virtues (like industriousness, obedience, chastity, filial piety, and justice) are usually harmful for those who possess them, being instincts that dominate them too violently and covetously and resist the efforts of reason to keep them in balance with their other instincts. When you have a virtue, a real, whole virtue (and not merely a mini-instinct for some virtue), you are its *victim*. But your neighbor praises your virtue precisely on that account. One praises the industrious even though they harm their eyesight or the spontaneity and freshness of their spirit. One honors and feels sorry for the youth who has worked himself into the

ground because one thinks: "For society as a whole the loss of even the best individual is merely a small sacrifice. Too bad that such sacrifices are needed! But it would be far worse if the individual would think otherwise and considered his preservation and development more important than his work in the service of society." Thus one feels sorry for the youth not for his own sake but because a devoted *instrument*, ruthless against itself—a so-called "good man"—has been lost to society by his death.

Perhaps one gives some thought to the question whether it would have been more useful for society if he had been less ruthless against himself and had preserved himself longer. One admits that there would have been some advantage in that, but one considers the other advantage—that a sacrifice has been made and that the attitude of the sacrificial animal has once again been confirmed for all to see—greater and of more lasting significance.

Thus what is really praised when virtues are praised is, first, their instrumental nature and, secondly, the instinct in every virtue that refuses to be held in check by the over-all advantage for the individual himself—in sum, the unreason in virtue that leads the individual to allow himself to be transformed into a mere function of the whole. The praise of virtue is the praise of something that is privately harmful—the praise of instincts that deprive a human being of his noblest selfishness and the strength for the highest autonomy.

To be sure, for educational purposes and to lead men to incorporate virtuous habits one emphasizes effects of virtue that make it appear as if virtue and private advantage were sisters; and some such relationship actually exists. Blindly raging industriousness, for example—this typical virtue of an instrument—is represented as the way to wealth and honor and as the poison that best cures boredom and the passions, but one keeps silent about its dangers, its extreme dangerousness. That is how education always proceeds: one tries to condition an individual by various attractions and advantages to adopt a way of thinking and behaving that, once it has become a habit, instinct, and passion, will dom-

---

[3] Cf. *Twilight of the Idols,* Ch. 1, section 8 (VPN, 467). Also *Ecce Homo,* Ch. 1, section 2 (BWN, 680).

inate him *to his own ultimate disadvantage* but "for the general good."

## 116

*Herd instinct.*—Wherever we encounter a morality, we also encounter valuations and an order of rank of human impulses and actions. These valuations and orders of rank are always expressions of the needs of a community and herd: whatever benefits it most—and second most, and third most—that is also considered the first standard for the value of all individuals. Morality trains the individual to be a function of the herd and to ascribe value to himself only as a function. The conditions for the preservation of different communities were very different; hence there were very different moralities. Considering essential changes in the forms of future herds and communities, states and societies, we can proph-

esy that there will yet be very divergent moralities. Morality is herd instinct in the individual.

## *Beyond Good and Evil*

### 104

Not their love of men but the impotence of their love of men keeps the Christians of today from —burning us.

### 108

There are no moral phenomena at all, but only a moral interpretation of phenomena—

### 116

The great epochs of our life come when we gain the courage to rechristen our evil as what is best in us.

# The Genealogy of Master and Slave Morality

## FRIEDRICH NIETZSCHE

### *Beyond Good and Evil*

#### 199

Inasmuch as at all times, as long as there have been human beings, there have also been herds of men (clans, communities, tribes, peoples, states, churches) and always a great many people who obeyed, compared with the small number of those commanding—considering, then, that nothing has been exercised and cultivated better and longer among men so far than obedience— it may fairly be assumed that the need for it is now innate in the average man, as a kind of *formal conscience* that commands: "thou shalt un-

conditionally do something, unconditionally not do something else," in short, "thou shalt." This need seeks to satisfy itself and to fill its form with some content. According to its strength, impatience, and tension, it seizes upon things as a rude appetite, rather indiscriminately, and accepts whatever is shouted into its ears by someone who issues commands—parents, teachers, laws, class prejudices, public opinions.

The strange limits of human development, the way it hesitates, takes so long, often turns back, and moves in circles, is due to the fact that the herd instinct of obedience is inherited best, and at the expense of the art of commanding. If

SOURCE: Friedrich Nietzsche, *Beyond Good and Evil: Prelude to a Philosophy of the Future,* trans. Walter Kaufmann and R. J. Hollingdale (1886; New York: Vintage Books, 1989), pp. 84–86, 110–111, 204–208 [secs. 104, 108, 116, 199, 260]. Copyright 1966 by Random House, Inc. Reprinted by permission of Random House, Inc.

we imagine this instinct progressing for once to its ultimate excesses, then those who command and are independent would eventually be lacking altogether; or they would secretly suffer from a bad conscience and would find it necessary to deceive themselves before they could command —as if they, too, merely obeyed. This state is actually encountered in Europe today: I call it the moral hypocrisy of those commanding. They know no other way to protect themselves against their bad conscience than to pose as the executors of more ancient or higher commands (of ancestors, the constitution, of right, the laws, or even of God). Or they even borrow herd maxims from the herd's way of thinking, such as "first servants of their people" or "instruments of the common weal."

On the other side, the herd man in Europe today gives himself the appearance of being the only permissible kind of man, and glorifies his attributes, which make him tame, easy to get along with, and useful to the herd, as if they were the truly human virtues: namely, public spirit, benevolence, consideration, industriousness, moderation, modesty, indulgence, and pity. In those cases, however, where one considers leaders and bellwethers indispensable, people today make one attempt after another to add together clever herd men by way of replacing commanders: all parliamentary constitutions, for example, have this origin. Nevertheless, the appearance of one who commands unconditionally strikes these herd-animal Europeans as an immense comfort and salvation from a gradually intolerable pressure, as was last attested in a major way by the effect of Napoleon's appearance. The history of Napoleon's reception is almost the history of the higher happiness attained by this whole century in its most valuable human beings and moments.

## 260

Wandering through the many subtler and coarser moralities which have so far been prevalent on earth, or still are prevalent, I found that certain features recurred regularly together and were closely associated—until I finally discovered two basic types and one basic difference.

There are *master morality* and *slave morality*[1]—I add immediately that in all the higher and more mixed cultures there also appear attempts at mediation between these two moralities, and yet more often the interpenetration and mutual misunderstanding of both, and at times they occur directly alongside each other—even in the same human being, within a *single* soul.[2] The moral discrimination of values has originated either among a ruling group whose consciousness of its difference from the ruled group was accompanied by delight—or among the ruled, the slaves and dependents of every degree.

In the first case, when the ruling group determines what is "good," the exalted, proud states of the soul are experienced as conferring distinction and determining the order of rank. The noble human being separates from himself those in whom the opposite of such exalted, proud states finds expression: he despises them. It should be noted immediately that in this first type of morality the opposition of "good" and *"bad"* means approximately the same as "noble" and "contemptible." (The opposition of "good" and *"evil"* has a different origin.) One feels contempt for the cowardly, the anxious, the petty, those intent on narrow utility; also for the suspicious with their unfree glances, those who humble themselves, the doglike people who allow themselves to be maltreated, the begging flatterers, above all the liars: it is part of the fundamental faith of all aristocrats that the common people lie. "We truthful ones"—thus the nobility of ancient Greece referred to itself.

It is obvious that moral designations were everywhere first applied to *human beings* and only later, derivatively, to actions. Therefore it is a gross mistake when historians of morality start from such questions as: why was the compas-

---

[1] While the ideas developed here, and explicated at greater length a year later in the first part of the *Genealogy of Morals,* had been expressed by Nietzsche in 1878 in section 45 of *Human, All-Too-Human,* this is the passage in which his famous terms "master morality" and "slave morality" are introduced.

[2] These crucial qualifications, though added immediately, have often been overlooked. "Modern" moralities are clearly mixtures; hence their manifold tensions, hypocrisies, and contradictions.

sionate act praised? The noble type of man experiences *itself* as determining values; it does not need approval; it judges, "what is harmful to me is harmful in itself"; it knows itself to be that which first accords honor to things; it is *value-creating*. Everything it knows as part of itself it honors: such a morality is self-glorification. In the foreground there is the feeling of fullness, of power that seeks to overflow, the happiness of high tension, the consciousness of wealth that would give and bestow: the noble human being, too, helps the unfortunate, but not, or almost not, from pity, but prompted more by an urge begotten by excess of power. The noble human being honors himself as one who is powerful, also as one who has power over himself, who knows how to speak and be silent, who delights in being severe and hard with himself and respects all severity and hardness. "A hard heart Wotan put into my breast," says an old Scandinavian saga: a fitting poetic expression, seeing that it comes from the soul of a proud Viking. Such a type of man is actually proud of the fact that he is *not* made for pity, and the hero of the saga therefore adds as a warning: "If the heart is not hard in youth it will never harden." Noble and courageous human beings who think that way are furthest removed from that morality which finds the distinction of morality precisely in pity, or in acting for others, or in *désintéressement;* faith in oneself, pride in oneself, a fundamental hostility and irony against "selflessness" belong just as definitely to noble morality as does a slight disdain and caution regarding compassionate feelings and a "warm heart."

It is the powerful who *understand* how to honor; this is their art, their realm of invention. The profound reverence for age and tradition—all law rests on this double reverence—the faith and prejudice in favor of ancestors and disfavor of those yet to come are typical of the morality of the powerful; and when the men of "modern ideas," conversely, believe almost instinctively in "progress" and "the future" and more and more lack respect for age, this in itself would sufficiently betray the ignoble origin of these "ideas."

A morality of the ruling group, however, is most alien and embarrassing to the present taste in the severity of its principle that one has duties only to one's peers; that against beings of a lower rank, against everything alien, one may behave as one pleases or "as the heart desires," and in any case "beyond good and evil"—here pity and like feelings may find their place. The capacity for, and the duty of, long gratitude and long revenge—both only among one's peers—refinement in repaying, the sophisticated concept of friendship, a certain necessity for having enemies (as it were, as drainage ditches for the affects of envy, quarrelsomeness, exuberance—at bottom, in order to be capable of being good *friends*): all these are typical characteristics of noble morality which, as suggested, is not the morality of "modern ideas" and therefore is hard to empathize with today, also hard to dig up and uncover.

It is different with the second type of morality, *slave morality.* Suppose the violated, oppressed, suffering, unfree, who are uncertain of themselves and weary, moralize: what will their moral valuations have in common? Probably, a pessimistic suspicion about the whole condition of man will find expression, perhaps a condemnation of man along with his condition. The slave's eye is not favorable to the virtues of the powerful: he is skeptical and suspicious, *subtly* suspicious, of all the "good" that is honored there—he would like to persuade himself that even their happiness is not genuine. Conversely, those qualities are brought out and flooded with light which serve to ease existence for those who suffer: here pity, the complaisant and obliging hand, the warm heart, patience, industry, humility, and friendliness are honored—for here these are the most useful qualities and almost the only means for enduring the pressure of existence. Slave morality is essentially a morality of utility.

Here is the place for the origin of that famous opposition of "good" and "evil": into evil one's feelings project power and dangerousness, a certain terribleness, subtlety, and strength that does not permit contempt to develop. According to slave morality, those who are "evil" thus inspire fear; according to master morality it is precisely those who are "good" that inspire, and wish to inspire, fear, while the "bad" are felt to be contemptible.

The opposition reaches its climax when, as a logical consequence of slave morality, a touch of disdain is associated also with the "good" of this morality—this may be slight and benevolent—because the good human being has to be *undangerous* in the slaves' way of thinking: he is good-natured, easy to deceive, a little stupid perhaps, *un bonhomme.*[3] Wherever slave morality becomes preponderant, language tends to bring the words "good" and "stupid" closer together.

One last fundamental difference: the longing for *freedom*, the instinct for happiness and the subtleties of the feeling of freedom belong just as necessarily to slave morality and morals as artful and enthusiastic reverence and devotion are the regular symptom of an aristocratic way of thinking and evaluating.

This makes plain why love *as passion*—which is our European specialty—simply must be of noble origin: as is well known, its invention must be credited to the Provençal knight-poets, those magnificent and inventive human beings of the *"gai saber"*[4] to whom Europe owes so many things and almost owes itself.—

## On the Genealogy of Morals

### 4

The signpost to the *right* road was for me the question: what was the real etymological significance of the designations for "good" coined in the various languages? I found they all led back to the *same conceptual transformation*—that everywhere "noble," "aristocratic" in the social sense, is the basic concept from which "good" in the sense of "with aristocratic soul," "noble," "with a soul of a high order," "with a privileged soul" necessarily developed: a development which always runs parallel with that other in which "common," "plebeian," "low" are finally transformed into the concept "bad." The most convincing example of the latter is the German word *schlecht* [bad] itself: which is identical with *schlicht* [plain, simple]—compare *schlechtweg* [plainly], *schlechterdings* [simply]—and originally designated the plain, the common man, as yet with no inculpatory implication and simply in contradistinction to the nobility. About the time of the Thirty Years' War, late enough therefore, this meaning changed into the one now customary.

With regard to a moral genealogy this seems to me a *fundamental* insight; that it has been arrived at so late is the fault of the retarding influence exercised by the democratic prejudice in the modern world toward all questions of origin. And this is so even in the apparently quite objective domain of natural science and physiology, as I shall merely hint here. But what mischief this prejudice is capable of doing, especially to morality and history, once it has been unbridled to the point of hatred is shown by the notorious case of Buckle;[1] here the *plebeianism* of the modern spirit, which is of English origin, erupted once again on its native soil, as violently as a mud volcano and with that salty, noisy, vulgar eloquence with which all volcanos have spoken hitherto.—

### 7

One will have divined already how easily the priestly mode of valuation can branch off from the knightly-aristocratic and then develop into

---

[3] Literally "a good human being," the term is used for precisely the type described here.

[4] "Gay science": in the early fourteenth century the term was used to designate the art of the troubadours, codified in *Leys d'amors*. Nietzsche subtitled his own *Fröhliche Wissenschaft* (1882), *"la gaya scienza,"* placed a quatrain on the title page, began the book with a fifteen-page "Prelude in German Rhymes," and in the second edition (1887) added, besides a Preface and Book V, an "Appendix" of further verses.

[1] Henry Thomas Buckle (1821–1862), English historian, is known chiefly for his *History of Civilization* (1857ff.). The suggestion in the text is developed more fully in section 876 of *The Will to Power.*

its opposite; this is particularly likely when the priestly caste and the warrior caste are in jealous opposition to one another and are unwilling to come to terms. The knightly-aristocratic value judgments presupposed a powerful physicality, a flourishing, abundant, even overflowing health, together with that which serves to preserve it: war, adventure, hunting, dancing, war games, and in general all that involves vigorous, free, joyful activity. The priestly-noble mode of valuation presupposes, as we have seen, other things: it is disadvantageous for it when it comes to war! As is well known, the priests are the *most evil enemies*—but why? Because they are the most impotent. It is because of their impotence that in them hatred grows to monstrous and uncanny proportions, to the most spiritual and poisonous kind of hatred. The truly great haters in world history have always been priests; likewise the most ingenious haters: other kinds of spirit hardly come into consideration when compared with the spirit of priestly vengefulness. Human history would be altogether too stupid a thing without the spirit that the impotent have introduced into it—let us take at once the most notable example. All that has been done on earth against "the noble," "the powerful," "the masters," "the rulers," fades into nothing compared with what the *Jews* have done against them; the Jews, that priestly people, who in opposing their enemies and conquerors were ultimately satisfied with nothing less than a radical revaluation of their enemies' values, that is to say, an act of the *most spiritual revenge.* For this alone was appropriate to a priestly people, the people embodying the most deeply repressed priestly vengefulness. It was the Jews who, with awe-inspiring consistency, dared to invert the aristocratic value-equation (good = noble = powerful = beautiful = happy = beloved of God) and to hang on to this inversion with their teeth, the teeth of the most abysmal hatred (the hatred of impotence), saying "the wretched alone are the good; the poor, impotent, lowly alone are the good; the suffering, deprived, sick, ugly alone are pious, alone are blessed by God, blessedness is for them alone—and you, the powerful and noble, are on the contrary the evil, the cruel, the lustful, the insatiable, the godless to all eternity; and you shall be in all eternity the unblessed, accursed, and damned!" . . . One knows *who* inherited this Jewish revaluation. . . . In connection with the tremendous and immeasurably fateful initiative provided by the Jews through this most fundamental of all declarations of war, I recall the proposition I arrived at on a previous occasion (*Beyond Good and Evil,* section 195)—that with the Jews there begins *the slave revolt in morality:* that revolt which has a history of two thousand years behind it and which we no longer see because it—has been victorious.

## 8

But you do not comprehend this? You are incapable of seeing something that required two thousand years to achieve victory?—There is nothing to wonder at in that: all *protracted* things are hard to see, to see whole. *That,* however, is what has happened: from the trunk of that tree of vengefulness and hatred, Jewish hatred—the profoundest and sublimest kind of hatred, capable of creating ideals and reversing values, the like of which has never existed on earth before—there grew something equally incomparable, a *new love,* the profoundest and sublimest kind of love—and from what other trunk could it have grown?

One should not imagine it grew up as the denial of that thirst for revenge, as the opposite of Jewish hatred! No, the reverse is true! That love grew out of it as its crown, as its triumphant crown spreading itself farther and farther into the purest brightness and sunlight, driven as it were into the domain of light and the heights in pursuit of the goals of that hatred—victory, spoil, and seduction—by the same impulse that drove the roots of that hatred deeper and deeper and more and more covetously into all that was profound and evil. This Jesus of Nazareth, the incarnate gospel of love, this "Redeemer" who brought blessedness and victory to the poor, the sick, and the sinners—was he not this seduction in its most uncanny and irresistible form, a seduction and bypath to precisely those *Jewish* values and new ideals? Did Israel not attain the ultimate goal of its sublime vengefulness precisely through the bypath of this "Redeemer," this ostensible opponent and disintegrator of Israel? Was it not part of the secret black art of truly *grand* politics of revenge, of a farseeing, subterranean, slowly advancing, and premeditated revenge, that Israel must itself deny the real instrument of its revenge before all the world as a mortal enemy and nail it to the cross, so that "all the world," namely all the opponents of Israel, could unhesitatingly swallow just this bait? And could spiritual subtlety imagine any *more dangerous* bait than this? Anything to equal the enticing, intoxicating, overwhelming, and undermining power of that symbol of the "holy cross," that ghastly paradox of a "God on the cross," that mystery of an unimaginable ultimate cruelty and self-crucifixion of God *for the salvation of man?*

What is certain, at least, is that *sub hoc signo*[2] Israel, with its vengefulness and revaluation of all values, has hitherto triumphed again and again over all other ideals, over all *nobler* ideals.—

## II

This, then, is quite the contrary of what the noble man does, who conceives the basic concept "good" in advance and spontaneously out of himself and only then creates for himself an idea of "bad"! This "bad" of noble origin and that "evil" out of the cauldron of unsatisfied hatred —the former an after-production, a side issue, a contrasting shade, the latter on the contrary the original thing, the beginning, the distinctive *deed* in the conception of a slave morality—how different these words "bad" and "evil" are, although they are both apparently the opposite of the same concept "good." But it is *not* the same concept "good": one should ask rather precisely *who* is "evil" in the sense of the morality of *ressentiment*. The answer, in all strictness, is: *precisely* the "good man" of the other morality, precisely the noble, powerful man, the ruler, but dyed in another color, interpreted in another fashion, seen in another way by the venomous eye of *ressentiment*.

Here there is one thing we shall be the last to deny: he who knows these "good men" only as enemies knows only *evil enemies,* and the same men who are held so sternly in check *inter pares*[3] by custom, respect, usage, gratitude, and even more by mutual suspicion and jealousy, and who on the other hand in their relations with one another show themselves so resourceful in consideration, self-control, delicacy, loyalty, pride, and friendship—once they go outside, where the strange, the *stranger* is found, they are not much better than uncaged beasts of prey. There they savor a freedom from all social constraints, they compensate themselves in the wilderness for the tension engendered by protracted confinement and enclosure within the peace of society, they go *back* to the innocent conscience of the beast of prey, as triumphant monsters who perhaps emerge from a disgusting procession of murder, arson, rape, and torture, exhilarated and undisturbed of soul, as if it were no more than a students' prank, convinced they have provided the poets with a lot more material for song and praise. One cannot fail to see at the bottom of all these noble races the beast of prey, the splendid *blond beast*[4] prowling about avidly in search of spoil

---

[2] Under this sign.

[3] Among equals.

[4] This is the first appearance in Nietzsche's writings of the notorious "blond beast." It is encountered twice more in the present section; a variant appears in section 17 of the second essay; and then the *blonde Bestie* appears once more in *Twilight,* "The 'Improvers' of Mankind," section 2 (*Portable Nietzsche,* p. 502). That is all. For a detailed discussion of these passages see Kaufmann's *Nietzsche,* Chapter 7, section 3: ". . . The 'blond beast' is not a racial concept and does not refer to the 'Nordic race' of which the Nazis later made so much. Nietzsche specifically refers to Arabs and Japanese . . .—and the 'blondness' presumably refers to the beast, the lion."

Francis Golffing, in his free translation of the *Genealogy,* deletes the blond beast three times out of four; only where it appears the second time in the original text, he has "the blond Teutonic beast." This helps to corroborate the myth that the blondness refers to the Teutons. Without the image of the lion, however, we lose not only some of Nietzsche's

and victory; this hidden core needs to erupt from time to time, the animal has to get out again and go back to the wilderness: the Roman, Arabian, Germanic, Japanese nobility, the Homeric heroes, the Scandinavian Vikings—they all shared this need.

It is the noble races that have left behind them the concept "barbarian" wherever they have gone; even their highest culture betrays a consciousness of it and even a pride in it (for example, when Pericles says to his Athenians in his famous funeral oration "our boldness has gained access to every land and sea, everywhere raising imperishable monuments to its goodness *and wickedness*"). This "boldness" of noble races, mad, absurd, and sudden in its expression, the incalculability, even incredibility of their undertakings—Pericles specially commends the *rhathymia* of the Athenians—their indifference to and contempt for security, body, life, comfort, their hair-raising cheerfulness and profound joy in all destruction, in all the voluptuousness of victory and cruelty—all this came together, in the minds of those who suffered from it, in the image of the "barbarian," the "evil enemy," per-

---

poetry as well as any chance to understand one of his best known coinages; we also lose an echo of the crucial first chapter of *Zarathustra*, where the lion represents the second stage in "The Three Metamorphoses" of the spirit—above the obedient camel but below the creative child (*Portable Nietzsche*, pp. 138f.).

Arthur Danto has suggested that if lions were black and Nietzsche had written "Black Beast," the expression would "provide support for African instead of German nationalists" (*Nietzsche as Philosopher*, New York, Macmillan, 1965, p. 170). Panthers *are* black and magnificent animals, but anyone calling Negroes black beasts and associating them with "a disgusting procession of murder, arson, rape, and torture," adding that "the animal has to get out again and go back to the wilderness," and then going on to speak of "their hair-raising cheerfulness and profound joy in all destruction," would scarcely be taken to "provide support for . . . nationalists." On the contrary, he would be taken for a highly prejudiced critic of the Negro.

No other German writer of comparable stature has been a more extreme critic of German nationalism than Nietzsche. For all that, it is plain that in this section he sought to describe the behavior of the ancient Greeks and Romans, the Goths and the Vandals, not that of nineteenth-century Germans.

haps as the "Goths," the "Vandals." The deep and icy mistrust the German still arouses today whenever he gets into a position of power is an echo of that inextinguishable horror with which Europe observed for centuries that raging of the blond Germanic beast (although between the old Germanic tribes and us Germans there exists hardly a conceptual relationship, let alone one of blood).

I once drew attention to the dilemma in which Hesiod found himself when he concocted his succession of cultural epochs and sought to express them in terms of gold, silver, and bronze: he knew no way of handling the contradiction presented by the glorious but at the same time terrible and violent world of Homer except by dividing one epoch into two epochs, which he then placed one behind the other—first the epoch of the heroes and demigods of Troy and Thebes, the form in which that world had survived in the memory of the noble races who were those heroes' true descendants; then the bronze epoch, the form in which that same world appeared to the descendants of the downtrodden, pillaged, mistreated, abducted, enslaved: an epoch of bronze, as aforesaid, hard, cold, cruel, devoid of feeling or conscience, destructive and bloody.

Supposing that what is at any rate believed to be the "truth" really is true, and the *meaning of all culture* is the reduction of the beast of prey "man" to a tame and civilized animal, a *domestic animal,* then one would undoubtedly have to regard all those instincts of reaction and *ressentiment* through whose aid the noble races and their ideals were finally confounded and overthrown as the actual *instruments of culture;* which is not to say that the *bearers* of these instincts themselves represent culture. Rather is the reverse not merely probable—no! today it is *palpable!* These bearers of the oppressive instincts that thirst for reprisal, the descendants of every kind of European and non-European slavery, and especially of the entire pre-Aryan populace—they represent the *regression* of mankind! These "instruments of culture" are a disgrace to man and rather an accusation and counterargument against "culture" in general! One may be quite justified in continuing to fear the blond beast at the core of all noble races and in being on one's guard against it: but who would not a hundred times sooner fear where one can also admire than *not* fear but be permanently condemned to the repellent sight of the ill-constituted, dwarfed, atrophied, and poisoned?[5] And is that not *our* fate? What today constitutes *our* antipathy to "man"?—for we *suffer* from man, beyond doubt.

*Not* fear; rather that we no longer have anything left to fear in man; that the maggot[6] "man" is swarming in the foreground; that the "tame man," the hopelessly mediocre and insipid man, has already learned to feel himself as the goal and zenith, as the meaning of history, as "higher man"—that he has indeed a certain right to feel thus, insofar as he feels himself elevated above the surfeit of ill-constituted, sickly, weary and exhausted people of which Europe is beginning to stink today, as something at least relatively well-constituted, at least still capable of living, at least affirming life.

## 13

But let us return: the problem of the *other* origin of the "good," of the good as conceived by the man of *ressentiment,* demands its solution.

That lambs dislike great birds of prey does not seem strange: only it gives no ground for reproaching these birds of prey for bearing off little lambs. And if the lambs say among themselves: "these birds of prey are evil; and whoever is least like a bird of prey, but rather its opposite, a lamb —would he not be good?" there is no reason to

find fault with this institution of an ideal, except perhaps that the birds of prey might view it a little ironically and say: "*we* don't dislike them at all, these good little lambs; we even love them: nothing is more tasty than a tender lamb."

To demand of strength that it should *not* express itself as strength, that it should *not* be a desire to overcome, a desire to throw down, a desire to become master, a thirst for enemies and resistances and triumphs, is just as absurd as to demand of weakness that it should express itself as strength. A quantum of force is equivalent to a quantum of drive, will, effect—more, it is nothing other than precisely this very driving, willing, effecting, and only owing to the seduction of language (and of the fundamental errors of reason that are petrified in it) which conceives and misconceives all effects as conditioned by something that causes effects, by a "subject," can it appear otherwise. For just as the popular mind separates the lightning from its flash and takes the latter for an *action,* for the operation of a subject called lightning, so popular morality also separates strength from expressions of strength, as if there were a neutral substratum behind the strong man, which was *free* to express strength or not to do so. But there is no such substratum; there is no "being" behind doing, effecting, becoming; "the doer" is merely a fiction added to the deed—the deed is everything. The popular mind in fact doubles the deed; when it sees the lightning flash, it is the deed of a deed: it posits the same event first as cause and then a second time as its effect. Scientists do no better when they say "force moves," "force causes," and the like—all its coolness, its freedom from emotion notwithstanding, our entire science still lies under the misleading influence of language and has not disposed of that little changeling, the "subject" (the atom, for example, is such a changeling, as is the Kantian "thing-in-itself"); no wonder if the submerged, darkly glowering emotions of vengefulness and hatred exploit this belief for their own ends and in fact maintain no belief more ardently than the belief that *the strong man is free* to be weak and the bird of prey to be a lamb—for thus they gain the right to

---

[5] If the present section is not clear enough to any reader, he might turn to *Zarathustra*'s contrast of the *overman* and the *last man* (Prologue, sections 3–5) and, for good measure, read also the first chapter of two or part one. Then he will surely see how Aldous Huxley's *Brave New World* and George Orwell's *1984*—but especially the former—are developments of Nietzsche's theme. Huxley, in his novel, uses Shakespeare as a foil; Nietzsche, in the passage above, Homer.

[6] *Gewürm* suggests wormlike animals; *wimmelt* can mean swarm or crawl but is particularly associated with maggots—in a cheese, for example.

make the bird of prey *accountable* for being a bird of prey.

When the oppressed, downtrodden, outraged exhort one another with the vengeful cunning of impotence: "let us be different from the evil, namely good! And he is good who does not outrage, who harms nobody, who does not attack, who does not requite, who leaves revenge to God, who keeps himself hidden as we do, who avoids evil and desires little from life, like us, the patient, humble, and just"—this, listened to calmly and without previous bias, really amounts to no more than: "we weak ones are, after all, weak; it would be good if we did nothing *for which we are not strong enough*"; but this dry matter of fact, this prudence of the lowest order which even insects possess (posing as dead, when in great danger, so as not to do "too much"), has, thanks to the counterfeit and self-deception of impotence, clad itself in the ostentatious garb of the virtue of quiet, calm resignation, just as if the weakness of the weak—that is to say, their *essence,* their effects, their sole ineluctable, irremovable reality—were a voluntary achievement, willed, chosen, a *deed,* a *meritorious* act. This type of man *needs* to believe in a neutral independent "subject," prompted by an instinct for self-preservation and self-affirmation in which every lie is sanctified. The subject (or, to use a more popular expression, the *soul*) has perhaps been believed in hitherto more firmly than anything else on earth because it makes possible to the majority of mortals, the weak and oppressed of every kind, the sublime self-deception that interprets weakness as freedom, and their being thus-and-thus as a *merit.*

## 16

Let us conclude. The two *opposing* values "good and bad," "good and evil" have been engaged in a fearful struggle on earth for thousands of years; and though the latter value has certainly been on top for a long time, there are still places where the struggle is as yet undecided. One might even say that it has risen ever higher and thus become

more and more profound and spiritual: so that today there is perhaps no more decisive mark of a *"higher nature,"* a more spiritual nature, than that of being divided in this sense and a genuine battleground of these opposed values.[7]

The symbol of this struggle, inscribed in letters legible across all human history, is "Rome against Judea, Judea against Rome":—there has hitherto been no greater event than *this* struggle, *this* question, *this* deadly contradiction. Rome felt the Jew to be something like anti-nature itself, its antipodal monstrosity as it were: in Rome the Jew stood *"convicted* of hatred for the whole human race"; and rightly, provided one has a right to link the salvation and future of the human race with the unconditional dominance of aristocratic values, Roman values.

How, on the other hand, did the Jews feel about Rome? A thousand signs tell us; but it suffices to recall the Apocalypse of John, the most wanton of all literary outbursts that vengefulness has on its conscience. (One should not underestimate the profound consistency of the Christian instinct when it signed this book of hate with the name of the disciple of love, the same disciple to whom it attributed that amorous-enthusiastic Gospel: there is a piece of truth in this, however much literary counterfeiting might have been required to produce it.) For the Romans were the strong and noble, and nobody stronger and nobler has yet existed on earth or even been dreamed of: every remnant of them, every inscription gives delight, if only one divines *what* it was that was there at work. The Jews, on the contrary, were the priestly nation of *ressentiment par excellence,* in whom there dwelt an unequaled popular-moral genius: one only has to compare similarly gifted nations—the Chinese or the Ger-

---

[7] This remark which recalls *Beyond Good and Evil,* section 200, is entirely in keeping with the way in which the contrast of master and slave morality is introduced in *Beyond Good and Evil,* section 260; and it ought not to be overlooked. It sheds a good deal of light not only on this contrast but also on Nietzsche's *amor fati,* his love of fate. Those who ignore all this material are bound completely to misunderstand Nietzsche's moral philosophy.

mans, for instance—with the Jews, to sense which is of the first and which of the fifth rank.[8]

Which of them has won *for the present,* Rome or Judea? But there can be no doubt: consider to whom one bows down in Rome itself today, as if they were the epitome of all the highest values—and not only in Rome but over almost half the earth, everywhere that man has become tame or desires to become tame: *three Jews,* as is known, and *one Jewess* (Jesus of Nazareth, the fisherman Peter, the rug weaver Paul, and the mother of the aforementioned Jesus, named Mary). This is very remarkable: Rome has been defeated beyond all doubt.

There was, to be sure, in the Renaissance an uncanny and glittering reawakening of the classical ideal, of the noble mode of evaluating all things; Rome itself, oppressed by the new superimposed Judaized Rome that presented the aspect of an ecumenical synagogue and was called the "church," stirred like one awakened from seeming death: but Judea immediately triumphed again, thanks to that thoroughly plebeian (German and English) *ressentiment* movement called the Reformation, and to that which

[8] Having said things that can easily be misconstrued as grist to the mill of the German anti-Semites, Nietzsche goes out of his way, as usual, to express his admiration for the Jews and his disdain for the Germans.

was bound to arise from it, the restoration of the church—the restoration too of the ancient sepulchral repose of classical Rome.

With the French Revolution, Judea once again triumphed over the classical ideal, and this time in an even more profound and decisive sense: the last political noblesse in Europe, that of the *French* seventeenth and eighteenth century, collapsed beneath the popular instincts of *ressentiment*—greater rejoicing, more uproarious enthusiasm had never been heard on earth! To be sure, in the midst of it there occurred the most tremendous, the most unexpected thing: the ideal of antiquity itself stepped *incarnate* and in unheard-of splendor before the eyes and conscience of mankind—and once again, in opposition to the mendacious slogan of *ressentiment,* "supreme rights of the majority," in opposition to the will to the lowering, the abasement, the leveling and the decline and twilight of mankind, there sounded stronger, simpler, and more insistently than ever the terrible and rapturous counterslogan "supreme rights of the few"! Like a last signpost to the *other* path, Napoleon appeared, the most isolated and late-born man there has even been, and in him the problem of the *noble ideal as such* made flesh—one might well ponder *what* kind of problem it is: Napoleon, this synthesis of the *inhuman* and *superhuman.*

# JUSTIN OAKLEY: A VIRTUE ETHICS APPROACH _____

In order for an ethical theory to capture the interest of philosophers, and eventually that of people outside academic life, it needs to be relatively easy to understand and put into practice. If a moral philosopher devises a difficult and dense decision-making process for the moral agent to work through before arriving at the right choice, the moral theory will be of little practical help in solving moral issues.

Consider, for example, being in the position where we must decide, on the spot, whether we should tell a "white lie" in order to advance our career. Here, as in many cases where moral decisions are required, we will not have the time to go through a long process of deliberation, tracing a path through a system full of complex twists and turns. For his part, Mill says to assess the utilities for all affected parties, a process that may or may not require a great deal of time. Kant tells us that we cannot ever tell a lie, period.

Virtue ethics, too, involves a straightforward, decision-making process. Indeed, all these views have a certain appeal to our commonsense notion of what it means to be moral. This is not to say that virtue ethics has much in common with either Mill's view or Kant's. For both Mill and Kant, an approach to ethics focuses on the question, "What should I do?" Virtue ethics, in contrast, asks a very different question: "Who do I wish *to be?*"

The former way of putting the matter spotlights moral vocabulary such as "obligations," "rights," and "duties." With the latter, by asking what kind of person we wish to be, we put the emphasis for virtue ethics on the personal character of the moral agent, on *being,* as opposed to *doing.*

Simply put, the virtue-based approach to ethics believes all our actions, lying for example, will have an impact on who we are as persons. The act of lying will make us *be* a certain way. It is not merely a matter of lying and then getting on with our lives. The lie affects us in a profound way. Of course, the effect will depend on the severity of the lie and the frequency with which we abuse the truth. But a lie will have an impact upon our character, on the deepest sense of who we are.

Contrariwise, just as doing something wrong will harm our character, doing what is virtuous will develop our character. And just as a wrong action may not altogether corrupt our character, so we do not become instantaneously virtuous by doing something virtuous once. Instead, in order to become virtuous, we need to practice the virtues on a continual basis. Just as a good pianist or guitarist becomes good over time with practice, so we develop the habit of being virtuous by practicing, over time, virtuous behavior.

In contrast to using the typical language of other traditional moral theories, instead of talking about what we *should* do, we need to think about what character traits we want to exemplify. We might ask, "Who are our moral heroes, and what virtues do their lives embody?" For instance, people such as Mother Teresa, Desmond Tutu, Ghandi, and Martin Luther King Jr.? Once we identify the moral virtues in others, we can make a conscious choice to cultivate the same virtues in ourselves.

In the reading selection Justin Oakley describes this approach and how it also differs from mainstream views of moral theory such as utilitarianism and deontology. He then spends time in the last part of the reading reviewing some of the main criticisms philosophers have made of virtue ethics.

A virtue-based approach to ethics emphasizes moral character and the need for actually practicing virtuous acts. But does it give us a clear idea of exactly what the best virtues are? Can it sufficiently explain what right action is? Does this approach to ethics really have explanatory power, a capacity to distinguish a right act from a wrong one? Because not everyone will agree about which collection of virtues is the most desirable, even adherents to virtue ethics are likely to disagree about what to do in a given moral dilemma.

The other difficulty Oakley faces is the situation in which the moral agent may want to act in a virtuous manner, but in fact the act smacks of moral wrongness. The example Oakley uses is a doctor who withholds a diagnosis of cancer from a terminally ill patient. The patient's prognosis is dim, and death is imminent. To avoid bringing extremely upsetting news to a vulnerable patient, the physician tells only the family the devastating news. The charge that could be made here is that the physician acted according to virtue ethics, yet many of us would have objections to this behavior. Oakley discusses how a virtue theorist might respond to this charge.

This example from biomedical ethics is a nice conclusion to Oakley's reading because those who devise ethical theories have often been charged with offering theory quite divorced from real-life problems.

# A Virtue Ethics Approach

## JUSTIN OAKLEY

THE CLOSING DECADES of the twentieth century have seen a revitalization in ethics of the ancient notion of virtue. The origins of this renewed philosophical interest in the virtues can be traced back to Elizabeth Anscombe's article, "Modern Moral Philosophy," published in 1958,[1] but the bulk of work on virtue-based approaches to ethics did not begin to appear until the early 1980s, mainly in the writings of Philippa Foot, Bernard Williams and Alasdair MacIntyre.[2] Nowadays, a virtue-based approach to ethics has been developed to the point where it is widely recognized as offering a coherent and plausible alternative to the mainstream consequentialist and Kantian approaches. . . .

### The Rise of Virtue Ethics

While a virtue-based approach to ethics has its intrinsic merits, the turn towards virtue ethics has to a significant extent been motivated by dissatisfaction with certain aspects of mainstream ethical theories. One general complaint which advocates of virtue ethics have made about consequentialist and Kantian theories is that they place too much emphasis on questions about what we ought to *do,* at the expense of dealing with more basic questions about what sort of person we ought to be and what sort of life we ought to lead. Another general criticism which proponents of virtue ethics make of consequentialist and Kantian theories is that they are deficient even as ethics of action, for they are excessively abstract and thus say too little about what agents ought to do in concrete circumstances. A related charge is that these mainstream theories evaluate all acts in terms of "right," "wrong," "obligatory" or "permissible," and in doing so leave us with an impoverished moral vocabulary. A virtue ethics approach, by contrast, employs such evaluative terms as "courageous," "callous," "honest" and "just"— as well as the more familiar "right" and "wrong" —and thereby provides a much richer and more finely-grained range of evaluative possibilities. More specifically, many have argued that the impartiality characteristic of both consequentialist and Kantian approaches to ethics devalues the ethical importance of personal relationships such as friendship, and that the duty-based approaches of Kantianism and deontology lead to an objectionably minimalist conception of a good life. . . .

[1] E. Anscombe, "Modern Moral Philosophy," *Philosophy* 33 (1958).
[2] P. Foot, "Euthanasia," *Philosophy and Public Affairs* 6 (1977): 85–112. [Reprinted in *Virtues and Vices,* 1978.]; P. Foot, *Virtues and Vices* (Berkeley: University of California Press, 1978); B. Williams, "A Critique of Utilitarianism," in *Utilitarianism: For and Against,* ed. J. J. C. Smart and B. Williams (Cambridge: Cambridge University Press, 1973); A. MacIntyre, *After Virtue,* 2d ed. (Notre Dame, IN: University of Notre Dame Press, 1984).

SOURCE: Justin Oakley, "A Virtue Ethics Approach," in *A Companion to Bioethics,* ed. Helga Kuhse and Peter Singer (Oxford: Blackwell Publishers, 1998), pp. 86–97 (edited). Reprinted by permission of the publisher.

Some philosophers have regarded the . . . shortcomings of consequentialist and Kantian approaches as reasons to supplement or modify the accounts of moral motivation and deliberation usually given by those theories, while retaining a basically consequentialist or Kantian criterion of rightness. However, other philosophers have regarded those shortcomings as fatal defects of consequentialism and Kantianism, and have looked to virtue ethics as a thoroughly revisionary theory, capable of providing a criterion of rightness which will replace those given by the standard theories.

Many of virtue ethics' claims have often been put in a negative form, so the approach has become better known for what it is against rather than by what it is for. But focusing only on virtue theorists' critiques of standard ethical theories fails to distinguish the approach from those of others who have made similar criticisms. For example, advocates of feminist approaches to ethics . . . have also attacked mainstream impartialist ethical theories for their inadequate treatment of personal (and family) relationships, and proponents of particularism have also been critical of the excessive abstraction of conventional principle-based ethical theories. (Particularists argue that the search for general ethical principles leads us to overlook the multiplicity of features which can have moral relevance, and the variations in the moral relevance of those features across different contexts, and so urge us to focus primarily on examining the details of each case as closely as possible.) We therefore need a systematic account of the *positive* claims made by virtue ethics, in order to show what is essential to and distinctive about the approach. In the next section I will sketch a brief account of those positive claims.

## What Is Virtue Ethics?

There are *six* key claims which are essential to modern forms of virtue ethics. These claims are common to the different varieties of virtue ethics, and also help to distinguish the approach from utilitarianism and Kantianism. The first and per-

haps most fundamental claim made by virtue ethics states its criterion of rightness: [3]

> (a) An action is right if and only if it is what an agent with a virtuous character would do in the circumstances.

Thus, according to virtue ethics, reference to character is *essential* in the justification of right action. A right action is one that is in accordance with what a virtuous person would do in the circumstances, and what *makes* the action right is that it is what a person with a virtuous character would do here. For example, Philippa Foot argues that it is—other things being equal—right to save another's life, where continued life would still be a good to that person, because this is what a person with the virtue of benevolence would do.[4] Likewise, Rosalind Hursthouse argues that it is ordinarily right to keep a deathbed promise, even though living people would benefit from its being broken, because that is what a person with the virtue of justice would do here.[5]

The primacy given to character in (a) helps to distinguish virtue ethics from standard forms of Kantianism, utilitarianism and consequentialism, whereby actions are justified according to rules or outcomes. However, more recent advocates of Kantian, utilitarian and consequentialist theories have suggested that the relevant criterion of rightness can be understood as an internalized normative disposition in the character of the good agent. Such theories can therefore be put in terms of what a virtuous person would do, where such a person is one whose motivation to act is regulated by the correct rules, or is motivated to maximize utility.[6] How does (a) distinguish virtue ethics from those theories?

Unlike those forms of Kantianism, utilitarianism and consequentialism which tell us what sort

[3] R. Hursthouse, "Virtue Theory and Abortion," *Philosophy and Public Affairs* 20 (1991): 225; R. Hursthouse, "Normative Virtue Ethics," In *How Should One Live? Essays on the Virtues,* ed. R. Crisp (Oxford: Clarendon Press, 1996), p. 22.
[4] Foot, "Euthanasia," p. 106.
[5] Hursthouse, "Normative Virtue Ethics," p. 25.
[6] J. Oakley, "Varieties of Virtue Ethics," *Ratio* 9 (1996): 131–132.

of character is recommended by their respective theories, virtue ethics holds that reference to character is *essential* in a correct account of right action. By contrast, most forms of those other theories which tell us to develop a Kantian, utilitarian or consequentialist character allow that the rightness of an action can be determined independently of a reference to the character of a good Kantian, utilitarian or consequentialist agent. For example, act utilitarians hold that an act is right if and only if it results in the most utility of any act the agent could do. They then tell us that the best character to have is the one which would result in the most utility overall. But the sort of human character which can be relied upon to maximize utility overall may not allow the agent in every possible situation to perform the act with the best consequences. So, act utilitarians recognize that a person with the best character may act wrongly on certain occasions.

However, some recent versions of Kantianism, utilitarianism and consequentialism hold that right actions must necessarily be those which are guided by a certain sort of character, and so, like virtue ethics, these accounts give character an essential role in the justification of action. For example, recent revivals of rule utilitarianism have suggested that the aversions in an agent's character can play an analogous role in justifying actions to that played by rules in standard versions of rule utilitarianism. That is, rule utilitarianism standardly evaluates actions in a two-step process, by examining their conformity to a set of rules, and those rules in turn are justified if their being generally followed maximizes utility. Similarly, Richard Brandt has proposed a form of rule utilitarianism which

> orders the acceptable level of aversion to various act-types in accordance with the damage . . . that would likely be done if everyone felt free to indulge in the kind of behaviour in question. . . . The worse the effect if everyone felt free, the higher the acceptable level of aversion.[7]

On this sort of view then, the aversions in an agent's character are essential to a correct account of right action, just as rules in standard versions of rule utilitarianism are essential to justifications of right action. Thus, one must look beyond the primacy of character in (a) in order to distinguish virtue ethics from these other forms of character-based ethics.

The distinctiveness of virtue ethics compared to other theories is brought out more fully when we turn to the ways in which advocates of the approach ground the normative conceptions in the character of the virtuous agent. Modern virtue ethicists take one of two broad approaches to filling out the notion of a virtuous character. Many virtue ethicists take the Aristotelian view that the virtues are character traits which we need to live humanly flourishing lives. On this view, developed by Foot and Hursthouse,[8] benevolence and justice are virtues because they are part of an interlocking web of intrinsic goods—which includes friendship, integrity and knowledge—without which we cannot have *eudaimonia,* or a flourishing life for a human being. According to Aristotle, the characteristic activity of human beings is the exercise of our rational capacity, and only by living virtuously is our rational capacity to guide our lives expressed in an excellent way. There is a sense, then, in which someone lacking the virtues would not be living a *human* life. Another approach to grounding the virtues, developed principally by Michael Slote,[9] rejects the Aristotelian idea that the virtues are given by what humans need in order to flourish, and instead derives the virtues from our commonsense views about what character traits we typically find admirable—as exemplified in the lives of figures such as Albert Einstein and Mother Teresa—whether or not those traits help an individual to flourish.

A second claim made by virtue ethics is:

(b) Goodness is prior to rightness.

---

[7] R. Brandt, "Morality and Its Critics," *American Philosophical Quarterly* 26 (1989): 95; see also B. Hooker, "Rule-Consequentialism," *Mind* 99 (1990): 67–77.

[8] Foot, *Virtues and Vices;* R. Hursthouse, *Beginning Lives* (Oxford: Blackwell, 1987).
[9] M. Slote, *From Morality to Virtue* (New York: Oxford University Press, 1992).

Contrary to deontological theories and to traditional forms of Kantianism, virtue ethics holds that the notion of goodness is primary. Thus, no account can be given of what makes an action right without having first established what is valuable or good. This sort of priority of the good over the right is also found in utilitarian theories (and in consequentialist theories generally), and so claim (b) brings out a structural similarity between virtue ethics and those theories.

A third claim made by virtue ethics is:

(c) The virtues are irreducibly plural intrinsic goods.

The intrinsic goods embodied in the virtues cannot be reduced to a single underlying value, such as utility, but are plural. While this claim distinguishes virtue ethics from older, monistic forms of utilitarianism, it does not distinguish the approach from modern, pluralistic forms of preference utilitarianism. For preference utilitarians can allow that there is a plurality of things which have intrinsic value, at least in so far as people desire to have certain things (such as knowledge, autonomy and accomplishment) in themselves, and not merely for their good consequences.

Nevertheless, a further claim helps to distinguish virtue ethics from a preference utilitarian approach:

(d) The virtues are objectively good.

Virtue ethics sees the virtues as objectively good in the sense that they are good independent of any connections they may have with desire. The goodness of the virtues is based on their connections with essential human characteristics, or with what we consider admirable, and they remain good, whether or not the agent who has them desires (or would, if suitably informed, desire) to have them. By contrast, a preference utilitarian who accepts the plural value of the different virtues derives their value from the fact that the agent desires (or would, if suitably informed, desire) to have them.

However, some consequentialists allow that there can be plural intrinsic and objective values. On this view, it is valuable for agents (for example) to be autonomous, even if they do not (and would not, if suitably informed) desire to be autonomous. Two further claims help to distinguish virtue ethics from these forms of consequentialism:

(e) Some intrinsic goods are agent-relative.

Standard forms of consequentialism claim that all goods are *agent-neutral*. Roughly speaking, this means that a particular intrinsic good counts for the same in justification, whether it is *my* good or someone else's. So, for example, pluralistic consequentialists who accord intrinsic value to friendship and integrity tell me to maximize friendship and integrity *per se,* whether or not doing so is at the expense of my own friendships or integrity. By contrast, virtue ethics holds that certain goods, such as friendship, have *agent-relative* value. That is, the fact that a relationship is *my* friendship is itself a morally relevant feature, and carries additional moral weight in justifying what I do. Thus, if I find myself in circumstances where I must choose between performing a friendly act towards my friend and promoting friendships between others (for example, if my friend asks me to help him move house on the day I had been planning to throw a party to welcome new colleagues), virtue ethics would allow that I would be justified in acting for my friend.

Finally, unlike standard forms of consequentialism, which hold that we must maximize the good, virtue ethics claims that:

(f) Acting rightly does not require that we maximize the good.

Virtue ethics holds that acting rightly does not require agents to bring about the very best possible consequences they can. Rather, many virtue ethicists argue that we ought to aspire to a level of human *excellence*. For example, instead of being required to have the very best friendships we can have, virtue ethics tells us that we ought to have excellent friendships.

These six claims do not themselves add up to

a substantive ethical theory; they need to be filled out with some account of the virtues themselves before the theory can be applied to practical problems. . . .

## Criticisms of Virtue Ethics

A number of criticisms have been made of virtue-based approaches to ethics. I will describe two criticisms which I take to be particularly important, and outline how a virtue theorist might respond to them. Both of these objections centre on virtue ethics' appeal to "what the virtuous agent would do" as the determinant of right action (as in (a) above).

The first criticism raises doubts about whether the notion of virtue is clear or detailed enough to serve as the basis of a criterion of rightness. Many writers argue that this criterion of rightness is too *vague* to be an acceptable basis of justification in ethics. How do we determine what the basic virtues are, and so what a virtuous agent would be like? Is it possible to establish what a virtuous agent would be like without knowing what actions are right? And even if we could establish the character of a virtuous agent, the practical applications of such a model are unclear. What would a virtuous agent do in the great variety of situations in which people find themselves? Further, there is a plurality of virtuous character traits, and not all virtuous people seem to have these traits to the same degree, so virtuous people might not always respond to situations in the same way. For example, is the right action in a given a set of circumstances the action which would be done by an honest person, a kind person or a just person? And even if the range of possible virtuous characters is narrower than this suggests, how do we *know* what a virtuous person would do in a particular situation? As Robert Louden puts it:

> Due to the very nature of the moral virtues, there is . . . a very limited amount of advice on moral quandaries that one can reasonably expect from the virtue-oriented approach. We ought, of course, to do what the virtuous person would

do, but it is not always easy to fathom what the hypothetical moral exemplar would do were he in our shoes.[10]

Now, to the extent that the criticism here expresses a general worry about appeals to "what a certain person would do," it is worth remembering that such appeals are quite commonly and successfully used in justifications in a variety of areas. For example, novice doctors and lawyers being inducted into their professions sometimes justify their having acted in a certain way by pointing out that this is how their professional mentor would have acted here. Also, courts often rely significantly on claims about what a reasonable person would have foreseen, in determining a person's legal liability for negligent conduct. Moreover, any general worry about such appeals would also apply to many modern consequentialist theories, which hold that the rightness of an action is determined partly by appealing to what consequences would have been foreseen by a reasonable person in the agent's position.

However, those who accept reliance on such appeals in other areas might well have misgivings about the particular sort of appeal to such a standard which is made by virtue ethics. For establishing what counts as having reasonable foresight of the consequences of actions may be far easier than establishing what counts as having a virtuous character. And it may be considerably more difficult to determine which of the variety of virtuous character traits a virtuous person would act on in a given situation than it is to determine which consequences of a given action a reasonable person would actually foresee.[11]

Now, establishing the nature of a virtuous agent's character is indeed a complex matter, but it should be remembered that virtue ethics does not derive this from some prior account of right action. Rather, which character traits count as virtuous is determined by their involvement in

---

[10] R. Louden, "On Some Vices of Virtue Ethics," *American Philosophical Quarterly* 21 (1984): 229.

[11] J. Rachels, *The Elements of Moral Philosophy,* 2d ed. (Englewood Cliffs, NJ: Prentice-Hall, 1993), p. 178.

human flourishing or their admirability, as explained above. It is true to say that virtue ethics does not deliver an "algorithm" of right action (as Aristotle put it), and that a virtue ethics criterion of rightness is perhaps less precisely specifiable and less easily applicable than that given by consequentialist theories (although perhaps not compared to those given by Kantian theories). But it is perhaps an overreaction to argue that this undermines virtue ethics' claim to provide an acceptable approach to ethical justification. For virtue ethicists often given considerable detail about what virtuous agents have done and would do in certain situations, and these details can help us to identify what it is right to do in a particular situation. (We might not gain any more precision from the directives of contemporary Kantian and consequentialist theories which advise us to do what a good Kantian or consequentialist agent would do.) And further, virtue ethics need not claim that there is only one true account of what a virtuous person would be and do, for it can allow that, sometimes, whichever of two courses of action one chooses, one would be acting rightly. In some situations, that is, whether one does what a kind person would have done, or what an honest person would have done, one would still have acted rightly.[12]

The second major criticism of virtue ethics is more fundamental than the first, as it focuses on the plausibility of a purely character-based criterion of rightness, such as that given by virtue ethics in (a) above. That is, many have argued that reference to what an agent with a virtuous character would have done (no matter how precisely specifiable and unitary virtuous character traits are) is not sufficient to justify actions. In support of this criticism, many writers argue that people with very virtuous characters can sometimes be led by a virtuous character trait to act wrongly. For example, a benevolent doctor may be moved to withhold a diagnosis of terminal cancer from a patient, although the doctor reveals the news to the patient's family, and asks them to join in the deception. Or a compassionate father might

decide to donate most of the family's savings to a worthwhile charity, without sufficiently thinking through how his action is likely to result in severe impoverishment for his family in the long term. Likewise, a compassionate nurse caring for a convicted murderer in a prison hospital might be so moved by the story of the patient's deprived upbringing that the nurse may deliberately fail to raise the alarm when the patient makes a dash for freedom. As Robert Veatch puts the worry: "I am concerned about well-intentioned, bungling do-gooders. They seem to exist with unusual frequency in health care, law, and other professions with a strong history of stressing the virtue of benevolence with an elitist slant."[13] If we agree that thoroughly virtuous people can sometimes be led by their virtuous character traits to act wrongly, then this seems to cast strong doubt on the plausibility of virtue ethics' criterion of rightness in (a) above. Many critics have been led by such examples of moral ineptitude to claim that virtue ethics is incomplete, and must therefore be underwritten by a deontological or a utilitarian criterion of rightness.[14]

Now, some virtue theorists would question whether the agent does act wrongly in these sorts of cases.[15] However, suppose it is granted that the agent concerned does indeed act wrongly in some such cases. There is no reason to think that virtue ethics is committed to condoning such moral ineptitude. For most virtues are not simply a matter of having good motives or good dispositions, but have a practical component which

[13] R. Veatch, "The Danger of Virtue," *Journal of Medicine and Philosophy* 13 (1988): 445.

[14] W. Frankena, *Ethics,* 2d ed. (Englewood Cliffs, NJ: Prentice-Hall, 1973), pp. 63–71; E. D. Pellegrino and D. C. Thomasma, *The Virtues in Medical Practice* (New York: Oxford University Press, 1993); Rachels, *Elements of Moral Philosophy;* T. L. Beauchamp and J. F. Childress, eds., *Principles of Biomedical Ethics* (New York: Oxford University Press, 1994), pp. 62–69; R. M. Hare, "Methods of Bioethics: Some Defective Proposals," *Monash Bioethics Review* 1 (1994): 34–47; J. Driver, "Monkeying with Motives: Agent-Basing Virtue Ethics," *Utilitas* 7 (1995): 281–288.

[15] M. Slote, "Agent-Basing Virtue Ethics," in *Midwest Studies in Philosophy,* vol. 20: *Moral Concepts,* ed. P. French, T. E. Uehling, and H. K. Wettstein (Notre Dame, IN: University of Notre Dame Press, 1995).

[12] Hursthouse, "Normative Virtue Ethics," p. 34.

involves seeing to it that one's action succeeds in bringing about what the virtue dictates. Therefore, we might question the extent to which the agent really does have the virtuous character trait which we are assuming he does here. Is it really an act of benevolence to withhold a diagnosis of terminal cancer from a patient, leaving that patient to die in ignorance of his or her true condition? Alternatively, in cases where the action does not seem to call into question the degree to which the agent has the virtuous character trait under scrutiny, it might be that the agent was lacking in some other virtue which was appropriate here. Thus, the father seems to have an inadequate sense of loyalty towards his own family, and the nurse's sense of justice seems defective. However, in some cases, these sorts of responses may not be very plausible, and to that extent, the virtue ethics criterion of rightness in (a) may need to be re-examined. . . .

# RITA MANNING AND FEMINIST CARE ETHICS _____

"Care ethics" is, by definition, an engaged ethical theory. It is not an abstract, cool, cerebral, detached approach to ethical theory like Mill's or Kant's. It is a practical "hands-on" approach, quite similar in spirit to virtue ethics. After describing how the ethics of care is distinct from ethical models that focus more on the concept of justice, Rita Manning shows how this approach is an effective approach in health-care ethics.

She begins by addressing the five central motifs of an ethic of care. She then describes how a care ethic understands itself vis-à-vis a very important component of all serious ethical theories, namely *justice*. In this respect she discusses Lawrence Kohlberg's theory of how people develop their moral reasoning.

For Kohlberg, assuming Kant's description of ethical behavior, the ideal process of making moral decisions involves rational cognition. Much of Kohlberg's study was based on the work of Swiss psychologist Jean Piaget (1896–1980). Piaget, himself with Kantian inclinations, spent a great deal of time studying the moral development of children.

Kohlberg's investigation into the moral development of children saw them acting morally initially only out of fear of punishment. Slowly, children then develop their way through individual deal making and personal friendships. Kohlberg took this as the goal of all moral development, namely, the adherence to universal ethical principles.

The so-called Golden Rule can be seen as an example of this sort of reasoning. We reflect on how we feel once treated a certain way, for example, if something is stolen from us. When we feel bad as a result of having our property stolen, we realize we shouldn't treat another in a way we wouldn't want to be treated. We then move from this concrete realization to the belief that people in general shouldn't treat each other this way.

Although Kohlberg's description of the stages young people go through in their moral development was intriguing for researchers in various fields, including moral philosophy, what stood out from Kohlberg's experiments was the fact that all of his subjects were male. It was therefore quite reasonable that female theorists found this to be a severe limitation on the explanation of moral development for children of both genders.

Carol Gilligan is one of the most notable critics of Kohlberg's work. She was also the first to present a systematic description of care ethics. In response to Kohlberg's work, she decided to conduct similar experiments, but those that included both male and female subjects. She soon discovered that the female subjects had a distinct way of moral reasoning, combining rational and emotional modes of cognition. They spoke in a different voice, one that focused on care and relationships more than on impersonal principles of justice. This emotional capacity allowed for an empathy that, in turn, brought a unique engagement into the decision-making process.

How was this engagement unique? Instead of looking at a moral problem in an abstract, impartial manner, female subjects took into account the relationships and social contexts that bound the various participants in a dispute with each other. As a result, rather than seeing a moral problem as involving highly isolated moral agents, care ethics attempts to alleviate those fears most central to young women's ethical feelings: separation and abandonment. To mitigate these emotions, care ethics places emphasis on community and relationships.

After explaining what care ethics is and how it differs from other models of the moral decision-making process, Manning takes us into the applied side of care ethics. Manning, like other theorists in this chapter, shows how to apply the moral theory she defends, which is certainly to her credit.

# A Care Approach

## RITA MANNING

AN ETHIC OF CARE has emerged as a new way to conceptualize some deeply held moral intuitions. . . . In what follows, I shall briefly describe an ethic of care as I understand it. . . .

### Caring as an Ethical Perspective

An ethic of care is a way of understanding one's moral role, of looking at moral issues and coming to an accommodation in moral situations. There are five central ideas in an ethic of care: moral attention, sympathetic understanding, relationship awareness, accommodation and response. I will discuss each in turn.

#### MORAL ATTENTION

Moral attention is the attention to the situation in all its complexity. When I am morally attentive, I wish to become aware of all the details that

will allow me to respond to the situation with sympathetic understanding. In this case, I attend carefully to my patient in order to ascertain how she is feeling.

#### SYMPATHETIC UNDERSTANDING

When I sympathetically understand the situation, I am open to sympathizing and even identifying with the persons in the situation. I try to be aware of what the others in the situation would want me to do, what would most likely be in their best interests and how they would like me to carry out their wishes and interests. I call this attention to the best interests of others maternalism. It is done in the context of a special sensitivity to the wishes of the other and with an understanding of the other's interest that is shaped by a deep sympathy and understanding.

SOURCE: Rita Manning, "A Care Approach," in *A Companion to Bioethics,* ed. Helga Kuhse and Peter Singer (Oxford: Blackwell Publishers, 1998), pp. 98–105 (edited). Reprinted by permission of the publisher.

To return to my patient—I try to see her sympathetically. If I feel it hard to be sympathetic, I may try several strategies—perhaps imagining her as myself in an earlier medical crisis. As I adopt this sympathetic attitude I become aware of what she wants and needs from me. Finally, I look to satisfy her need in a way that will preserve her sense of competence (when the patient is relevantly competent) and increase her comfort.

## RELATIONSHIP AWARENESS

There is a special kind of relationship awareness that characterizes an ethic of care. I recognize that the other is in relationship with me. First there is the most basic relationship, that of fellow creatures. Second there is the immediate relationship of need and ability to fill the need. Finally, I may be in some role relationship with the other that calls for a particular response, such as health-care worker–patient. I am aware of all these relationships as I survey a situation from the perspective of an ethic of care. But there is another kind of relationship awareness that is involved as well. I am aware of the network of relationships that connects humans, and I care about preserving and nurturing these relationships. So I see my patient as a fellow fragile human. I recognize that she is in need of my help and that I am able to give it. I recognize my role as a health-care professional and the special obligation this implies. Next, I see her as a member of the appropriate health-care setting. Finally, I acknowledge the web of personal relationships that can either support or undermine her health and well-being. As I search for ways to help her, I do so with the desire to strengthen all these relationships.

## ACCOMMODATION

Related to the notion of relationship awareness is accommodation. Many times there are many persons involved and how best to help is not obvious. In this case, my desire to nurture networks of care requires that I try to accommodate the needs of all, including myself. It is not always possible, or wise, to do what everyone thinks they need, but it is often possible to do what you think is best while at the same time giving everyone concerned a sense of being involved and considered in the process.

## RESPONSE

Finally, an ethic of care requires a response on my part. It is not enough to stare at my patient and imagine her in a sympathetic way, to see our relationship as well as the myriad of relationships that connect her to others. I must make my caring concrete in the actions that I take to respond to her need.

## The Care Voice and the Justice Voice

Carol Gilligan's pioneering work, *In a Different Voice,* was the first systematic attempt to describe the voice of care and to distinguish it from what she called the voice of justice.[1] Since then, psychologists and philosophers have been busy elucidating the central concepts and testing for various aspects of the two voices. I begin with a brief history.

Lawrence Kohlberg developed a theory about how people reason and develop morally.[2] His theory of moral reasoning posited that people reason morally by applying principles to cases, thus yielding judgements about what they ought to do. Moral progress, on Kohlberg's account, is cognitive and proceeds to progressively more general principles, with ideal moral progress culminating in principles that are universal and binding on all persons.

Carol Gilligan noted that Kohlberg's subjects, though culturally diverse, were all male. She began to apply his tests to female subjects of various ages. Her conclusion was that some people, notably females, used a different reasoning strategy from that described by Kohlberg and that they progressed by moving through a different set of stages.

Gilligan theorized that some of her subjects

[1] Carol Gilligan, *In a Different Voice* (Cambridge, MA: Harvard University Press, 1982).
[2] Lawrence Kohlberg, *The Philosophy of Moral Development* (New York: Harper & Row, 1981).

appealed to an ethic of care. This involves a thorough understanding of the context, and a willingness to balance the needs of self and other in a way that preserves both. For Gilligan, moral progress was both cognitive and emotional—the growth in the ability to see the situation from the perspective of self and other and to care about one's self as well as others.

She illustrated the differences in moral reasoning with two 11-year-olds, Jake and Amy. Jake and Amy are both given Kohlberg's Heinz dilemma to solve. A druggist has invented a drug to combat cancer. Heinz's wife needs the drug but Heinz does not have the money to buy it and the druggist will not give it to him. The children are asked whether Heinz should steal the drug. Jake quickly answers affirmatively and defends his answer by appealing to the relative importance of life over property. Amy begins by saying that it depends. She points out all the things that could go wrong if Heinz steals the drug—perhaps he will get caught and go to jail and his wife will be worse off. She suggests instead that Heinz and the druggist should sit down and work it out to everyone's satisfaction.

Jake fits easily into Kohlberg's schemata: he imagines himself in Heinz's position and applies a principle that quickly yields an answer. He does not need any more information about Heinz, the druggist, Heinz's wife, etc. Amy, on the other hand, is virtually impossible to analyse on Kohlberg's scale because she never states or even implies a principle that will yield an answer. Instead, as she imagines herself in Heinz's shoes, she sees the complexity of the situation and realizes that its solution requires that Heinz and the druggist and Heinz's wife recognize their involvement in a relationship and that they honour this awareness by working out a solution that will enable them all to survive and, if possible, flourish.

For Jake the solution is cognitive: Heinz merely reasons about the situation and can take action on the basis of that reasoning. Amy sees a real solution as necessarily involving growth in moral sensitivity and commitment.

On the basis of such differences in her subjects' responses, Gilligan posited a moral orientation, which she calls the voice of care, in addition to the justice orientation of Kohlberg. I propose we sort out the differences by seeing how each voice answers two questions: What are moral agents like? What is the moral standing of persons and communities?

The justice voice says that moral agents are or should be isolated, abstract individuals who follow abstract rules in a cool and impartial manner. Moral agents are isolated in the sense that they are both independent of others and free to choose what relationships to have with others. The model of interaction is contractual—the moral agent chooses to whom she or he will be related and the conditions of the relationship. They are abstract in the sense that their moral obligations are specified independently of the particular facts about them and about the situations they find themselves in. Rather, their moral obligations are spelled out in abstract rules, rules that are general enough to bind all others similarly situated. In following these general rules, they must be cool and impartial. This requires unemotionally applying the rules in the same fashion, regardless of the ties of affection and/or enmity that call on them to be partial.

The voice of care, on the other hand, understands moral agents as embedded in particular social contexts, relationships and personal narratives, who direct their moral attention to real others and are open to sympathetic understanding and identification with those others.

In part because the justice voice conceives moral agency in the way it does, it gives the following answer to the question of the moral standing of persons and communities. All persons are equally valuable—hence there are no special obligations to particular others. Communities and relationships have no moral standing on their own account.

The care voice, on the other hand, agrees that though all persons are valuable, there are special obligations: those imposed by actual and potential relationships and those imposed by roles. Since it understands communities as more than mere aggregates of individuals, and relationships as more than properties of individual persons, it is committed to saying that communities and relationships have moral standing.

## CARE, JUSTICE AND SELF-UNDERSTANDING

There is an additional way to sort out the differences between the care and justice voice and that is in terms of self-understanding. This was suggested by Nona Lyons, who argued that a particular self-understanding, a "distinct way of seeing and being in relation to others" explains the moral agent's preference for a particular moral voice.[3] She identifies two different self-understandings: what she calls the separate/objective self and the connected self. Persons who fit the separate/objective self model describe themselves in terms of personal characteristics rather than connections to others. Connected selves, on the other hand, describe themselves in terms of connections to others: granddaughter of, friend of, etc. This suggests that the separate/objective self sees him- or herself as distinct from others in a more profound sense than does the connected self. The separate/objective self might, for example, see him- or herself as connected to others only through voluntary agreements. The separate/objective self might value autonomy more highly than good relationships with others.

Lyons describes further differences. Separate/objective selves recognize moral dilemmas as those which involve a conflict between their principles and someone else's desires, needs or demands. Connected selves, on the other hand, identify moral dilemmas as those which involve the breakdown of relationships with others. Separate/objective selves fear connection and dependence, and hence value autonomy and independence. Connected selves fear separation and abandonment, and hence value connection and responsiveness.

We can see then how these self-understandings support different moral orientations. Separate selves understand themselves as distinct from others. They conceive moral dilemmas as arising from the conflict between their moral principles and the needs, demands, desires and principles of others. As such, they must mediate their interaction with others in the voice of justice—in terms of ground rules and procedures that can be accepted by all. This is the only foundation for interaction at all, since ties of affection are not seen as strong enough to provide a basis for interaction, especially in persons who fear connection and dependence. This fear of dependence and attachment also explains why they value the objectivity and impartiality that can stand between them and intimates. At the same time, separate/objective selves recognize that interaction with others plays a role in one's satisfaction, so they value community and relationship in so far as these play a role in individual satisfaction.

Connected selves see themselves in terms of others, so relationship, rather than seen as voluntary and incidental to self-identity, is central. The problem of interaction is not then conceived of as how to get others to interact with oneself on terms that would be acceptable to all, but how to protect the ties of affection and connection which are central to one's very self-identity. Moral dilemmas arise over how to preserve these ties when they are threatened, and these dilemmas are mediated by the voice of care. Since the primary fear is of separation and abandonment, a strong value is placed on community and relationships.

## Some Implications of an Ethic of Care for Bioethics

An ethic of care has many implications for bioethics. First, the comments on self-understanding suggest that before we insist on one standard of moral practice for all practitioners and patients, we should be sensitive to the diverse self-understandings that we are bound to encounter. Second, the ethic of care can itself be applied to virtually every issue in bioethics. I will discuss just two—its implications for the organization

---

[3] Nona Lyons, "Two Perspectives on Self, Relationship, and Morality," *Harvard Educational Review* 53 (1983): 125–145.

of health-care practice, and its implications for the treatment of terminally ill patients.

## A CARING MODEL
## OF HEALTH-CARE PRACTICE

Recall the central features of an ethic of care: moral attention, sympathetic understanding, relationship awareness, accommodation and response. What implications might these features have for the organization of health-care practice? I shall focus on two features that have a special significance for the organization of health-care practice: moral attention and sympathetic understanding.

Moral attention would imply that practitioners have the time to attend to all the relevant details—in other words, to treat the whole patients and to do so in an unhurried manner. Sympathetic understanding is developed as information is gathered and understanding is developed about how the patient feels, what he or she desires, and what would be best for him or her. This also requires time with the patients.

Relationship awareness too takes time to develop. An ethic of care works best when the relationship is characterized by mutual trust. The other side of relationship awareness, the awareness of the other relationships that might sustain and nurture patients, must also be engaged. Here we must look to the effects on the patient's condition of the network of relationships that surround him or her. If such networks are too fragile or non-existent, we must do what we can to create them. Obviously policies that mandate that a patient be released from the hospital in a specific time, whether or not adequate aftercare is provided, would be incompatible with an ethic of care.

Medical practice in the West can be divided (though not neatly) into two tasks: the doctor/diagnostician/chief decision-makers diagnose the problem and provide instructions for responding to it. Other health-care professionals carry out the orders of the decision-maker (usually a doctor, hopefully in coordination with the patient). Practitioners in both groups are increasingly specialized and the increasing use of medical technology creates further distance between health-care provider and patient. This is surely not the most effective way to practice caring health care. The doctor does not have the time and often does not feel any obligation to get to know enough about patients to offer sensitive care. The increasing specialization of other health-care providers means that they too find it difficult to get to know their patients. In the United States, where medicine is by and large a profit-making industry, patients are paradoxically faced with less care and more caregivers. The nursing staff is often caught in the middle. Nurses, themselves overworked and economically insecure, become ever more important to the patients. Obviously, this is incompatible with an ethic of care. But, in the very real world in which we live, what are nurses to do? If they take an ethic of care seriously, they will feel continually inadequate. It will simply not be possible for them to care adequately for patients.

Some people see this as a criticism of an ethic of care: traditional caregivers (most often women) are faced with impossible demands to give care. I think there are two responses here. First, we must note that we all have an obligation to be caring persons, not in virtue of our gender or our job description, but because we are human beings. Nurses, then, do not have a special obligation to care, though health-care practice has often been organized in such a way that they were the ones most able to be genuinely caring. We all have an obligation to join the political fight for health care that is genuinely caring. Second, we all have obligations to care for ourselves. This obviously includes nurses.

## JUSTICE AND CARE

There will be times when a patients' rights model and a care model will be in tension (notably in the patients' rights conception of the autonomous, competent patient versus the care conception of the patient in need who may require maternal assistance). Still they can often work in tandem, and in my opinion they ought to be so wedded. Care and rights should be foundational values for medical institutions and the professionals working in these settings. I envision the marriage of justice and care in the following way. First, we must be sensitive to the self-understanding of those entrusted to our care. Some patients will feel more comfortable in some situations with one or another model of health-care practice. Second, respecting rights is a moral minimum below which we ought not to fall, but care is the moral ideal. Respecting patient rights, then, is a minimal moral requirement, but health-care professionals have not completely discharged their responsibilities until they treat their patients (and fellow professionals) in a genuinely caring way. There is a further amendment to the patients' rights model which must be made to make this a successful marriage. We should no longer assume that all patients are always capable of asserting and defending their rights in an autonomous way. Rather, we should recognize that they may be in need of care, and temporarily (and in some cases permanently) unable to assert and defend their rights. In this case, we care for them and see returning them to full autonomy as part of our obligation rather than as an assumption about their present status.

I want to anticipate one objection here—that my two reasons for insisting on a marriage of justice and care are incompatible. If some patients want to be treated in a justice way—merely having their rights respected—then, it will be said, we should not bring care in to the situation. My response is that treating these patients in this fashion can be either a caring or a non-caring act. One might recognize the personhood and uniqueness of patients and be content not to violate their rights without really caring about patients. I regard this as morally defective patient care. A caring response would involve respecting rights in a richer sense. It would require sympathetic moral attention, time spent with patients and their intimates and responses based on the insight thereby gained. But even if a health-care

professional cannot summon up the energy or find the time to care, not violating the patient's rights is still a moral minimum.

So much for the blending of justice and care. I now want to turn to an example of the implications of an ethic of care for treating patients. Though it has implications for every area of health-care practice, I will focus just on care for terminally ill patients.

## CARING PATIENT CARE

My grandfather's final months were spent between a nursing home and the hospital, both far from ideal environments for sensitive care. In both the hospital and the nursing home, rapid staff turnover and divided responsibilities for his care left him feeling uncared for, though he was kept physically comfortable. The fairly rigid visiting hours made it difficult for family members to spend as much time with him as we wished. But in some ways the most troubling lack for me was our inability to communicate honestly as his end neared. I visited him daily and we talked, though only about the most trivial things. When there were two or more visitors, we talked to each other as though he were not there. I suspect that this is a fairly common reaction to dying in our culture, but I think that the institutional settings reinforced it. The parade of attendants who interrupted us with their casual cheerfulness, and the denial that permeated the atmosphere, created a sense of unreality for us both.

I think that my experience was fairly typical. These particular institutional settings made it very hard to practice caring medicine for terminally ill patients. Hospice care, on the other hand, with its emphasis on treating the whole dying patient, might be the most caring way to deal with terminally ill patients. Of course, there are in reality hospices that are genuinely caring and those that are not. In addition, hospices are not immune from rapid turnover and distracted staff. But a hospice with a committed staff, working closely with patients and their families, without the wide range of responsibilities a hospital has and with an acceptance of the patient's imminent death, can provide a more caring atmosphere for dying patients. But in providing the care, it is important to help the patients and their intimates care for each other and for themselves.

## Conclusion

An ethic of care is a moral orientation that is sorely needed in our increasingly fractured society. Whether we are teachers or health-care providers, an ethic of care provides guidance about how to live our lives. But it is not just a moral philosophy; it has a political dimension as well. If we are to meet our fellow creatures as caring individuals, we must rethink and, when necessary, restructure our institutions to make this possible.

## Study Questions

1. What is the difference between a "descriptive" and a "prescriptive" moral theory? Can moral theory be prescriptive? Why or why not?

2. What would you do if you saw a person drowning in the middle of a lake? Would you dive in to try to save the person, go for help, or do nothing? Would it matter whether you were a good swimmer or not? What moral ideas would you use to solve this dilemma?

3. How do a utilitarian moral theory and a deontological moral theory decide between right and wrong? What general problems can be associated with each approach?

4. What is the basic claim made by Adam Smith and moral sense theory? Can it be either proven or refuted? Is there anything wrong with someone who doesn't feel a moral sympathy for the sufferings of others? What, if anything, should we do about such a person?

5. What are some of the situations in which sympathy for others arises, according to Smith? Which passions arouse our sympathies? Which ones do not?

6. How does John Stuart Mill want us to resolve moral problems? What sort of objections to his utilitarianism does he consider in the reading in this chapter? Does he deal with these successfully? Explain.

7. Is Mill right that the main goal of all human action is the promotion of happiness or pleasure and the avoidance of pain? Can you think of any important exceptions?

8. Can we really measure the quantity of pleasure and pain arising from a specific action? Can we designate certain actions as producing a greater quality of happiness than other actions? If watching mud wrestling makes me happy, and you prefer opera, can we argue rationally about which activity is qualitatively superior? Provide reasons for your answer.

9. Let's suppose there are two female candidates for a job. The first one, Jane, is exceptionally qualified for the position by her education and work experience. The second one, Lola, has average qualifications but is extremely attractive. The predominantly male hiring committee is composed entirely of utilitarians. They decide to hire Lola in order to provide for the greatest happiness of the greatest number of people (i.e., everyone but Jane). Is there anything wrong with their decision? Does this say anything about the weaknesses of utilitarianism? Explain.

10. You have a friend named Chris who is very kind to you in person. But as soon as you're gone, he spreads nasty rumors about you to whoever will listen. You never find out about his gossip and are quite happy to call Chris a friend. Is there anything wrong with his actions from a utilitarian point of view, assuming you have no chance of finding out his true nature?

11. Describe Kant's "categorical imperative." In what sense does Kant want us to universalize our moral decisions? Is he right to think that when I make a moral decision, I should ask myself, "What if everyone acted the same way in the same situation?" Explain.

12. Why does Kant think we shouldn't use people as means to our ends? Could we really follow such an ethic in our everyday lives? After all, aren't we constantly using people as means to our ends, whether they're bus drivers, waiters, teachers, or entertainers?

13. Let's suppose you made a promise a week ago to your friend Sally to meet her for lunch on Monday. But you've just met a very interesting man named Daniel who invites you to lunch the same day (he's busy the rest of the week), and besides, you're a bit tired of listening to Sally prattle on about her personal problems. Should you break your promise to Sally and go to lunch with Daniel? What would Kant say? Mill? a virtue ethicist?

14. Is Nietzsche right to think that if God is dead, we are faced with moral nihilism? Are Mill's concern for the happiness of as many people as possible and Kant's demand that we follow the categorical imperative both relics of Christian slave morality? Explain.

15. When Nietzsche says there are no moral phenomena at all, only moral interpretations of phenomena (*Beyond Good and Evil* 108), what did he mean? Was he right? Explain.

16. What is "moral perspectivism"? Give some examples introduced by Nietzsche, and evaluate them.

17. What did Nietzsche mean by "master" and "slave" morality? What are some of the historical examples he used to illustrate each type of morality? Is he right to admire master morality?

18. Are the virtue ethicists right in thinking that ethics is not about evaluating individual moral decisions but promoting certain moral virtues? Which virtues do you think are most valuable? Is it likely that the virtues *you* think are valuable are the same ones your classmates will value? Explain.

19. Can we really judge the character of other people? or just their actions? If only the latter, is virtue ethics then a hopelessly muddled project?

20. Can ethics be rationally grounded? Is there any problem in making moral decisions without having a clear idea of the nature of rightness or goodness?

21. Are the feminist care ethicists right to think that women have a greater ability to exercise care in concrete moral situations, whereas men tend to rely on abstract moral principles to solve moral problems? If there is such a difference, is it the product of our biology or of our culture?

22. Would the world be a better place if people in positions of power paid less attention to formal rights and notions of justice, and more to caring for those they rule over? Give some examples to illustrate your position.

# *Bibliography*
## GENERAL WORKS ON ETHICS

Campbell, Tom. *Adam Smith's Science of Morals.* London: Allen & Unwin, 1971.

*Encyclopedia of Ethics.* 2d ed. Edited by Lawrence C. Becker and Charlotte B. Becker. New York: Routledge, 2001. Features 581 articles on all the standard theories and theorists.

Ethics Updates: http://ethics.acusd.edu
The "meta" page for a series of subsidiary Web pages on many aspects of ethics. Contains pages on Kantian ethics, utilitarianism, virtue ethics, abortion, environmental ethics, gender,

and much more. The contents of each page vary, but most have links, lectures, and texts. Links to classic ethics texts on the Web can be found at http://ethics.acusd.edu/books.html.

Hume, David. *A Treatise of Human Nature.* Edited by David Fate Norton and Mary J. Norton. Oxford: Oxford University Press, 2000. Hume, a friend of Smith's, contributed to the development of moral sense theory in this three-volume classic of eighteenth-century thought originally published in 1739–1740. See bk. 2, pt. 1, sec. 1; pt. 2, secs. 5, 7, and 9; and bk. 3, pt. 3, secs. 2, and 6. The Selby-Bigge edition is also quite reliable.

Mackie, J. L. *Ethics: Inventing Right and Wrong.* Harmondsworth, UK: Penguin, 1977. Mackie argues for a subjectivist view of ethics: Moral ideas are just things human beings invent.

Norman, Richard. *The Moral Philosophers: An Introduction to Ethics.* 2d ed. Oxford: Oxford University Press, 1998. An overview divided into three parts, featuring discussions of the ancient Greeks; early modern thinkers such as Hume, Kant, and Mill; and twentieth-century thinkers. Norman covers all the major theories, with some criticism of each.

Rachels, James. *The Elements of Moral Philosophy.* 3d ed. New York: McGraw-Hill College, 2000. An invaluable short book that can act as a starting point for all budding students of ethical theory: Rachels covers all the main theories, from subjectivism and psychological egoism to utilitarianism and virtue ethics.

————. *Ethical Theory.* Oxford: Oxford University Press, 1998. A two-volume collection of articles on ethical theory.

Raphael, D. D. *Adam Smith.* Oxford: Oxford University Press, 1985. Part of Oxford's short and sweet Past Masters series.

Singer, Peter. *How Are We to Live? Ethics in an Age of Self-Interest.* Amherst, NY: Prometheus Press, 1995. A defense of the ethical life and an attack on selfishness by the prominent Australian moral philosopher.

————, ed. *A Companion to Ethics.* Oxford: Blackwell, 1993. A broad collection of articles on all important (and a few not so important) ethical theories. Have a look at Onora O'Neill on Kant, Will Kymlicka on social contract theory, Kurt Baier on egoism, and Gregory Pence on virtue ethics. Also contains articles on non-Western ethical systems such as Buddhism and ancient Chinese ethics and a section on applied ethics.

Warnock, G. J. *Contemporary Moral Philosophy.* London: Macmillan, 1967.

## ON MILL AND UTILITARIANISM

Bayles, Michael, ed. *Contemporary Utilitarianism.* Garden City, NY: Anchor Books, 1989. A collection of essays.

Ethics Updates—Utilitarianism: http://ethics.acusd.edu/theories/Utilitarianism/index.html Texts, lectures, links, and other resources on Bentham, Mill, and utilitarianism.

Hare, R. M. *Essays in Ethical Theory.* Oxford: Oxford University Press, 1989. A collection of essays by a contemporary utilitarian.

Plamenatz, John. *The English Utilitarians.* Oxford: Blackwell, 1949.

Ross, W. D. *The Right and the Good.* Oxford: Oxford University Press, 1930. A classic attack on utilitarianism by the prominent British "intuitionist."

Sen, Amartya, and Bernard Williams, eds. *Utilitarianism and Beyond.* Cambridge: Cambridge University Press, 1982. Another collection of essays on contemporary debates on utilitarianism.

Smart, J. J. C., and Bernard Williams. *Utilitarianism: For and Against.* Cambridge: Cambridge University Press, 1973. Smart explains and defends utilitarianism, whereas Williams attacks it.

Thomas, William. *Mill.* Oxford: Oxford University Press, 1985. An introduction to Mill's life and thought. In the Past Masters series.

Utilitarianism resources: http://www.utilitarianism.com
A list of links and other resources. The "Utilitarian Glossary" is quite valuable, offering excerpts from philosophy dictionaries defining key terms in utilitarian thought. Also see the "John Stuart Mill" link for a brief overview of his life and work. The full text of Mill's *Utilitarianism* is at http://www.utilitarianism.com/mill1.htm.


## ON KANT

Ethics Updates—Kant and Kantian Ethics: http://ethics.acusd.edu/theories/kant/
Some of Kant's texts, lectures on Kant, links, a biographical survey, and other relevant information.

Korsgaard, Christine. *Creating the Kingdom of Ends.* Cambridge: Cambridge University Press, 1996. Thirteen essays, seven on Kant himself, six comparing Kant to other theorists.

O'Neill, Onara. *Constructions of Reason: Explorations of Kant's Practical Philosophy.* Cambridge: Cambridge University Press, 1989. A collection of essays on the continued relevance of Kantianism.

Sullivan, Roger J. *Immanuel Kant's Moral Theory.* Cambridge: Cambridge University Press, 1989.

Wolff, Robert Paul, ed. *Kant: Foundations of the Metaphysics of Morals—Text and Critical Essays.* Indianapolis, IN: Bobbs-Merrill, 1969.


## ON NIETZSCHE

Danto, Arthur C. *Nietzsche as Philosopher: An Original Study.* New York: Columbia University Press, 1965. An attempt to figure out if Nietzsche's work expresses a systematic philosophy; written by an analytic philosopher somewhat skeptical about Nietzsche's general approach.

Kaufmann, Walter. *Nietzsche: Philosopher, Psychologist, Antichrist.* 4th ed. Princeton, NJ: Princeton University Press, 1975. Kaufmann's vigorous defense of his philosophical hero.

———, ed. and trans. *Basic Writings of Nietzsche.* New York: Modern Library, 2000. One of the best short collections of Nietzsche's works. Contains *The Birth of Tragedy, Beyond Good and Evil, On the Genealogy of Morals, Ecce Homo,* plus a few selections from other works.

———, ed. and trans. *The Portable Nietzsche.* New York: Viking, 1977. One of the best short collections of Nietzsche's works. Contains *Thus Spake Zarathustra, The Twilight of the Idols, The Antichrist,* along with a few other selections.

Magnus, Bernd, and Kathleen M. Higgins, eds. *The Cambridge Companion to Nietzsche.* Cambridge: Cambridge University Press, 1996. A collection of semispecialized essays by Nietzsche scholars such as Alexander Nehamas and Richard Schacht. Fairly advanced; for the more dedicated student of Nietzsche.

Nehamas, Alexander. *Nietzsche: Life as Literature.* Cambridge, MA: Harvard University Press, 1985. This is an excellent discussion of Nietzsche's perspectivism, as well as a good introduction to Nietzsche's philosophy.

Strong, Tracy B. *Friedrich Nietzsche and the Politics of Transfiguration.* Berkeley: University of California Press, 1975. Strong's focus is that underlying Nietzsche's works there exists a politics of transfiguration that challenges us to remake our lives in a radical way.

## ON VIRTUE ETHICS

Foot, Philippa. *Virtues and Vices and Other Essays in Moral Philosophy.* Berkeley: University of California Press, 1978.

MacIntyre, Alisdair. *After Virtue.* 2d ed. Notre Dame, IN: University of Notre Dame Press, 1997. The most celebrated modern defense of virtue ethics. MacIntyre urges us to return to Aristotle's notion that human beings have a *telos* grounded in the promotion of virtue and that modern systems of ethical theory lack substance because they fail to grasp this truth.

Slote, Michael, and Roger Crisp, eds. *Virtue Ethics.* Oxford: Oxford University Press, 1997. Features essays by Elizabeth Anscombe, Bernard Williams, Alisdair MacIntyre, Philippa Foot, Annette Baier, and six other ethicists.

## ON FEMINIST CARE ETHICS

Baier, Annette. *Moral Prejudices: Essays on Ethics.* Cambridge, MA: Harvard University Press, 1994. A collection of essays from a feminist ethicist who argues that moral relationships shouldn't be based on abstract ethical codes but on trust, a "moral prejudice."

"Feminist Ethics": http://plato.stanford.edu/entries/feminism-ethics/
Article by Rosemary Tong. An overview from the *Stanford Encyclopedia of Philosophy.*

Gilligan, Carol. *In a Different Voice: Psychological Theory and Women's Development.* Cambridge, MA: Harvard University Press, 1993. Gilligan provided the basic psychological foundation for the main claim of feminist care ethics that women speak in a different moral voice, favoring an ethics of care to the predominantly male ethic of justice and abstract rights. See our Chapter 7 for a more detailed treatment of Gilligan.

Noddings, Nel. *Caring: A Feminine Approach to Ethics and Moral Education.* Berkeley: University of California Press, 1984. Noddings systematizes Gilligan's insights, arguing that ethics always involves specific individuals in specific situations, and that for these specific individuals care is a better moral compass than the abstract principles favored by male thinkers.

*The history of all hitherto existing society is the history of class struggles.*
KARL MARX and FRIEDRICH ENGELS

# Political Theory

## INTRODUCTION: THE BASIC CONCEPTS AND HISTORY OF POLITICAL THEORY

Political theory has had a long and glorious tradition in Western philosophy, going back to Plato's *Republic* and Aristotle's *Politics* in ancient Greek thought. Since the dawn of literate civilization, human beings have speculated about the best means of governing themselves and about the nature of freedom, equality, and justice. Because debates about the rightness or wrongness of forms of political behavior and types of political institutions are at the core of political theory, it is seen by some contemporary philosophers as a subsidiary branch of ethics. Yet the key concepts that political theorists deal with are quite distinct, even if they occasionally parallel those found in ethics. Further, they are intimately bound up with the history of political life in the West, unlike most ethical concepts, which aspire to greater universality. Because this historical introduction will make liberal use of these key concepts, here are some quick definitions of each of them (these will be fleshed out in greater detail in the historical treatment of political theory that follows).

*Power*—The ability to exercise control over others, whether by brute force, force of personality, wealth, or the control of legal and political institutions.

*The State*—An organization claiming or actually exercising the sole use of legitimate power within a given geographical area. An elected democratic government can be said to be representing the state, whereas an organized crime family cannot, since it can't claim to be "legitimate."

*Freedom*—Having the capacity to act as one likes; *not* being under someone else's control or power. This is more or less equivalent to "liberty." Linked to this concept is that of "property," the legitimate control of land, material goods, corporate entities, or money. People with property usually claim the "freedom" to use it as they see fit, within certain legal limits.

Equality—One person or group having the same legal, social, political, or economic status as another. Linked to this concept is that of "class," a group of people who share a similar social or economic status (such as "workers" or "capitalists").

Justice—Although having many definitions in the history of political theory, this usually refers to "right" or "fair" treatment for an individual or group, or the best (most moral) structure for society and the state. Justice is often linked to equality in modern politics and is more generally related to the idea of "desert," that is, giving people what they deserve. A central issue in discussions of justice is how to most fairly distribute the economic resources of a society among its citizens.

Rights—Some thing or practice that an individual or group makes a very strong claim to or demands as a natural possession. This claim or demand is usually grounded in some notion of fairness, justice, or human nature, or in the divine order of things. For example, in democracies people usually claim a "right" to vote, whether or not they exercise it, but not a "right" to quality television programs, as no sane notion of justice or fairness supports this "right." Earlier in history, in an age when a king's fancy determined a person's guilt or innocence, people claimed a "right" to a speedy and fair trial, a right that is today recognized throughout the Western world. Socialists and left-wing liberals sometimes claim a right to work and a fair wage, although conservatives would dispute this right. Modern constitutions usually start with a list of the rights that its framers take to be self-evident for their country and era.

There are a number of basic questions asked by political theorists.* First, they might ask, as Plato did, "What is the just state?" Connected to this is a second, perhaps more practical, question: "How can the state best guarantee social peace and the personal security and property of its citizens?" This question much occupied social contract theorists such as Thomas Hobbes and John Locke. Third, theorists might see things from the ruler's point of view and ask, "How can a prince most effectively retain power?" This was Machiavelli's basic question. Fourth, they could ask, "How can the state guarantee individual rights, freedom, and justice for its citizens?" This is the basic question of liberal political theorists such as John Stuart Mill and John Rawls. Last, Marxists have asked, "How do economic inequalities in our society create an oppressive class system, and what can we do about it?" There have been, needless to say, many answers to these basic questions throughout the history of political thought. In order to help understand how these basic questions have been answered and how the concepts just outlined have been used by the great thinkers in the history of political theory, let's take a whirlwind tour through the history of Western political life.

In our chapter on the ancient Greeks, we saw how Plato answered the first question: Each group within the state should fulfill its "proper" function, the result being a harmony of the whole, and thus justice. Plato wasn't too concerned with individual rights—the philosopher kings, being the wise rulers he hoped they would be,

---

* Although philosophers tend to use the term "political philosophy" for this field of study, we've chosen to use the term "political theory," which is generally used in the social sciences, because it more clearly distinguishes this branch of philosophy from ethics, along with being more interdisciplinary.

would make sure that people were treated fairly, according to their class (perhaps less fairly if you had bronze mixed with your soul, and you were thus a lowly merchant or worker).

In a rough-and-ready sense, the Middle Ages, approximately AD 900–1450, witnessed the establishment of a parody of Plato's ideal republic across much of Europe and Asia. Everybody had a clear place in society, and woe be to those who tried to move up the ladder too quickly. At the bottom of society were the serfs, who worked the land and whose labor was the property of the middle class of the medieval pyramid, the feudal lords (the barons, earls, and dukes). In the towns artisans and merchants worked with some independence from these lords, though it would take the great democratic revolutions of the seventeenth and eighteenth centuries to give them real freedom. At the top of the medieval pyramid was the king, whose power was guaranteed, and could be taken away, by the Church, the representatives of God on earth. The medieval political system—"feudalism"—was a rigid hierarchy, a grand social pyramid. In most of Europe it provided little in the way of rights to those at the bottom and allowed those at the top to exercise power in any way they saw fit, as long as this exercise didn't anger the Church too much.

The medieval system came to an end slowly, over the period 1450–1800, for a whole series of reasons. One of the major reasons it declined was economic—the development of financial and industrial capitalism in the seventeenth and eighteenth centuries, respectively. But another major, early reason why the medieval social pyramid crumbled was the Renaissance (French for "rebirth") of the fifteenth and sixteenth centuries, a movement that started in Italy and soon spread throughout Western Europe. The Renaissance involved a great flowering of art (e.g., Leonardo da Vinci and Michelangelo), architecture, science (e.g., Copernicus and Galileo), technology (including the invention of the printing press), and literature. It involved the rebirth of classical ideals, a rereading of the great works of ancient Greece and Rome.

This rereading led to the development of "humanism," the idea that secular values, not religious ones, should be at the center of things. Thinkers no longer looked to the Christian heavens for solutions to their problems, but to science, reason, and history (although most of them remained Christians). Niccoló Machiavelli, for a long time a diplomat and bureaucrat within the government of Florence, was part of this humanist movement. Italy of the fifteenth and sixteenth centuries was chopped up into dozens of small states, dominated by five major ones—Milan, Venice, the Papal States, the Kingdom of Naples, and Florence. These states constantly spied and plotted against each other, fomented revolts in neighboring principalities, and invaded their neighbors largely with mercenaries who could rarely bring themselves to actually kill each other (it was bad for business). In this atmosphere of backstabbing petty potentates, Machiavelli wrote his classic short work *The Prince,* which defended "political realism"—the idea that the art of politics centered on the pursuit of power—by appealing to both human nature, of which he didn't have a high opinion, and the history of both the ancient world and of the Italy of his own lifetime, which he believed proved that the *end* of political power and civil peace justified the use of any *means,* fair or foul, to achieve that power and peace.

Yet we must travel to England to see the first stirring of the modern ideas of freedom, equality, and basic rights. In 1215 King John signed the Magna Carta, persuaded, no doubt, by the sharp swords of rebellious English barons. Along with guaranteeing a number of feudal rights to the barons, the Magna Carta gave all citizens the right not to be arrested, imprisoned, or have their property taken away except by the due process of law.

However, this victory over the arbitrary power of the king wasn't firmly established until the seventeenth century, more than four hundred years later. The Stuart kings of England and Scotland in this century, notably Charles I, claimed they ruled their lands by divine right, as a gift from God. Naturally, many people objected to this idea of the "divine right of kings," especially the English gentry (i.e., owners of small landholdings), who feared that the king would take away their property whenever he felt like it, and nonconforming (i.e., not part of the Anglican Church) Protestant sects such as the Puritans, who feared religious persecution from the Catholic-leaning Stuarts. The English Parliament, aided by these objectors, revolted against the monarchy, fighting a civil war with Charles's army from 1642 to 1646. Parliament won, tried Charles for treason, and cut off his head, thus perhaps proving that God did *not* favor the theory of the divine right of kings, at least in Charles's case.

Out of the chaos of the English Civil War came Thomas Hobbes's reflections on the state of nature and on the need for a social contract. Hobbes reasoned that in a natural state, one without law or government, human beings weren't very nice to each other. Life there was "solitary, poor, nasty, brutish and short," to quote a famous Hobbesianism. But more important, he suggested that, contrary to many of the thinkers of the Middle Ages, who believed in "natural rights" and basic principles of justice, there was no strong moral reason why we *should* be nice to each other before we sign a social contract. Justice was the product of social peace. As rational beings, we should agree to the rule of a legitimate sovereign, whether this be a king or a Parliament, to whom we should give up our individual rights to kill each other and to steal each other's property whenever we like in exchange for this social peace. Naturally, Hobbes's call for people in the state of nature to sign a social contract to guarantee the peace was a product of his fear of the lawlessness, violence, and political instability he saw close-up during the English Civil War. He recorded his reflections in *Leviathan* (1651), a work that inaugurated the "social contract" tradition in political theory.

In 1688 England witnessed a much more peaceful revolt, the "Glorious Revolution" (more a coup d'état, actually) of the English Parliament against the autocratic and openly Catholic King James II, which established once and for all Protestant rule and a constitutional parliamentary monarchy in the country. William and Mary of Orange came across the English Channel as the new king and queen, symbols of the end of the rule of the Stuart kings, with their contempt for Parliament. A year later a Bill of Rights followed, giving the citizen a broad set of basic liberties. Perhaps anticipating this series of events, John Locke took the social contract tradition in political theory a step forward in his *Second Treatise of Government,* which was published in 1690 but written several years before. In it he described a state of nature that was considerably less nasty than Hobbes's, but nasty enough to prevent us from being secure in our property, in the fruits of our labor. So once again we had to sign the social contract and agree to subordinate our individual freedom to the power of the state. Yet in Locke's case, the power of the state was strictly limited in scope. Locke thought that the whole point of government was to protect property, including the property we have in our own person—in other words, our lives. He went on to argue that if a government were acting tyrannically and unjustly threatened our personal security, or had lost the capacity to protect our property, we had a right to rebel against it, just as the English had just rebelled against James II in their Glorious Revolution.

The eighteenth century was a time of great revolutions. The first of these was in America in 1776, in which the British colonists in the thirteen colonies strung along the eastern seaboard of the continent took Locke at his word on the sanctity of personal property and on the right to rebel against tyranny, revolting against the British Crown on the grounds that the British State no longer fairly represented their political and economic interests. "No taxation without representation" was their battle cry. The American Congress declared its independence from Britain in a famous document that stated that "All men have the right to Life, Liberty, and the pursuit of Happiness," thus beginning the modern movement for equal political rights—though the authors of this document excluded women and black slaves from these rights, exclusions that would cause a lot of trouble in America in the nineteenth and twentieth centuries. Later, in 1791, the Americans enshrined these rights in their Constitution. The Bill of Rights recognized the rights to freedom of the press, speech, and peaceful assembly; the right to bear arms, and to a fair trial; and rights against unreasonable search and seizure.

A decade or so later, from 1789 to 1795, the French staged their own revolution against the monarchy, the remnants of their feudal system, and the political privileges of the aristocracy. The battle cry of the French revolutionaries was "Liberty, Equality and Fraternity," and they, like the English in the seventeenth century, cut off the head of their king, Louis XVI, to help bring about the reign of these new principles. They too made a list of the basic rights of the individual citizen to help ensure personal freedom and equality, the Declaration of the Rights of Man and Citizen of 1791. This list included the rights to legal equality, property, freedom of expression, political participation, and the presumption of innocence before the law.

The nineteenth century was the great age of liberalism, but also the great age of industrial capitalism. John Stuart Mill, in his work *On Liberty* (1859), delineated the need for modern societies to guarantee the basic liberal rights of freedom of thought, freedom of expression, freedom of action (as long as it didn't interfere with the actions of others), and religious toleration. Mill also worried that the "tyranny of the majority" and the excessive concern with equality in democracies might squash the right of individuals to think and act as they saw fit. These basic rights were slowly integrated into the structure of Western liberal democracies from Mill's day to our own.

Yet there were cracks in the liberal wall, cracks that Mill himself became more and more aware of as he grew older. One such crack was a great inequality between the sexes. Up to the Victorian age women were usually treated as little better than domestic servants, denied the right of free expression, the right to vote, and in some cases even the right to hold property, the whole point of the social contract, according to Locke. Mary Wollstonecraft pointed out in 1792 the injustice of the plight of women in her day in *A Vindication of the Rights of Woman,* a cause that Mill himself would later take up, urged on by his close confidante and later wife, Harriet Taylor, in his short work *The Subjection of Women* (1869). Wollstonecraft argued that if women were educated to employ their reason rather than the docile arts of seduction, they could be just as rational as men and thus deserving of equal political rights. In other words, the social inferiority of women was a product of cultural values instilled via education, not of natural female traits.

The second crack in the liberal wall was the result of the development of industrial capitalism in the West. The working conditions in the new factories were harsh, the new industrialism bringing about great economic inequalities. Young children were forced to work twelve- or fourteen-hour days, seven days a week, for paltry wages in the grimy mills of Manchester, Birmingham, and New York. The mill owners, whom Marx referred to as the "bourgeoisie," reaped huge profits. The injustice and inequality of this exploitation of the working class in Europe and America led to the rise of socialism, whose most famous exponent was Karl Marx. Marx and his confederate Friedrich Engels, himself the son of a wealthy Manchester factory owner, argued that the most basic reality in our lives was its economic aspect, the work we do and the class we belong to. They also argued that society was more and more being divided into two great classes—the bourgeoisie (or capitalists) and proletariat (or workers). Marx argued that these two classes would inevitably clash in a great revolution. Eventually, the proletariat would triumph, form a communist society, and abolish the exploitation and social inequalities produced by capitalism. Marx's ideas would have a huge impact on the politics of his own day, not to mention the world of the twentieth century.

In the twentieth century, liberal democracy faced three great challenges, one of them economic and the other two simultaneously ideological and military. The economic challenge was the Great Depression of the 1930s, kicked off by the crash of the stock market in America in 1929. Millions of people were put out of work. It seemed to many that capitalism was a dismal failure. The response of many Western governments to the Depression was the development of the liberal welfare state, with the institution of programs of employment insurance, welfare, greater state management of the economy (e.g., through central banks such as the Federal Reserve in the United States), and in some cases state-sponsored medical care. The problem now became how to balance the economic freedom promised by capitalism, which had disastrous consequences during the Great Depression, with the injustices and inequality of wealth produced by that system.

This problem is still with us today and is the central focus of John Rawls's magisterial 1971 work, *A Theory of Justice.* Rawls takes up the basic principles of the social contract position, arguing that justice is in essence fairness. If you didn't know what your lot in life was—if you were in the state of nature behind "a veil of ignorance"—you would indeed support Mill's principle of equal liberty for all, as long as that liberty didn't interfere with the liberty of other people. This is Rawls's first principle of justice. However, you would also want to make sure that whatever social and economic inequalities a society tolerated were for the good of the least advantaged and were attached to positions that anyone could aspire to. This is Rawls's second principle of justice. Rawls's work has sparked a healthy debate about how modern democracies can best balance the principles of freedom and equality in their institutions.

The second challenge to liberalism in the past century was the rise of fascism in Germany, Italy, Spain, and elsewhere in Europe in the 1920s and 1930s. At least in the

German case, this was in part caused by the economic disaster of the Great Depression. The Nazis openly advocated a program of military conquest based on a racist ideology of the innate superiority of the German people, the "master race," under the firm hand of a *Führer* (or leader)—none other than Adolf Hitler himself. Democracy, social equality, liberal freedoms, and Christianity were all signs of decadence to the Nazis. Germany and Italy were defeated in the Second World War (1939–1945), at the cost of millions of Russian, British, American, Canadian, Australian, French, and other Allied lives.

The third challenge to liberal democracy was the rise of communism in Russia, China, Eastern Europe, and the Third World, from the Russian Revolution of 1917 to the effective end of the Cold War in 1989 and the collapse of the Soviet Union in 1991. The Communists also attacked cherished liberal ideals, in this case the liberal ones of liberty and individual rights. They argued that under capitalism, the worker is exploited by the owners of the means of production—the classic Marxist position. The worker could never have true equality or political rights within a liberal democracy because he or she was a member of an exploited class. So a revolution against capitalism followed by the dictatorship of the proletariat under the guidance of the Communist Party was the only way to ensure the social equality and basic rights of the worker. This ideology dominated much of Asia for the best part of the last century, its battle with the capitalist West threatening to bring the world to nuclear Armageddon during the Cold War of the 1950s through 1980s. It still lingers on in a watered-down form in China to this day.

The apparent victory of liberal capitalism over fascism and communism led Francis Fukuyama to conclude in 1989, in an article in *The National Interest,* that we had arrived at the "end of history." He didn't mean that politics would end or that there would be no more competition between states in the world arena. Instead, he meant that given the defeat of fascism and the collapse of Soviet communism, there were no longer any major ideologies that could compete with liberal capitalism. Yet within the liberal framework, he admitted that quite a few problems remained to be ironed out.

To this day, modern Western constitutions attempt to enshrine the basic rights envisioned by liberalism. The problem is that these basic rights keep changing as various groups come forward to claim their just slice of the constitutional pie. Once, only all *men* were equal. Now Western democracies try to include women as full-fledged members of the social contract. In addition, over the last two generations, nonwhite minorities in the West have fought for political equality, an equality that seems to be promised them by such founding documents of the liberal state as the American Declaration of Independence and the French Declaration of the Rights of Man and Citizen. This was seen most spectacularly in the civil rights movement in the United States in the 1950s and 1960s, when American blacks and their white allies fought for fair treatment and for the implementation of their right to vote, a right largely denied them in the American South. Martin Luther King's dream of equality for all human beings can thus be traced back all the way to Hobbes's and Locke's delineation of the theory of the social contract: Why should racial minorities agree to such a contract if it didn't promise them equal treatment?

As a case in point of how our notion of basic rights changes, let's look at Canada's 1982 Constitution Act. Article 2 guarantees the "fundamental freedoms" of conscience, religion, thought, press (and other forms of communication), peaceful assembly, and association. So far, it sounds very much like the liberal constitutions and bills of rights of the eighteenth century. Article 7 guarantees the legal rights of life, liberty, and security of person, once again echoing the American and French founding political documents. But Article 15 guarantees the "equality rights" under the law "without discrimination based on race, national or ethnic origin, colour, religion, sex, age or mental or physical disability." These prohibitions against racial, sexual, and disability-based discriminations are very much the product of a late-twentieth-century notion of rights. The reign of the white male political elites has come to an end, as the full benefits of the liberal social contract are being slowly but surely constitutionally extended to more and more people.

However, don't imagine that this struggle to define and extend political rights has ended. Now gays are demanding some rights-based recognition of their sexuality in line with the equalities of sex, race, and religion promised by most modern constitutions. We can imagine a never-ending series of expansions of rights as new groups come forward to demand their slice of the aforementioned constitutional pie. Interesting questions for students to ask with regard to this evolution include "Where should this process of the extension of rights end?" and "To what degree can political constitutions guarantee equal treatment for groups that suffer from discrimination or some other lack of privilege?"

Rawls's rehabilitation of contract theory has inspired a new debate within liberalism over the last twenty-five years, that between contract theorists and "communitarians," who argue that political community rests on deeper foundations than the agreement of a group of rational proto-citizens in a hypothetical or real state of nature. One important contemporary segment of this debate is that between conservative contractarians or libertarians on the one hand, who argue for a minimal, "night watchman" type of state that arrests criminals and builds roads but doesn't play an active role in the economy, and left-wing communitarians on the other, who favor more state involvement in the economy to reduce inequalities and to promote general community interests. Is our individual happiness all that counts? Or do we owe our fellow citizens something more than just noninterference in their lives? This debate is the subject of the dialogue between Douglas Mann and Malcolm Murray included in this chapter.

The aftermath of the September 11, 2001, terrorist attacks on the World Trade Center and the Pentagon have certainly put into question Fukuyama's notion that history has ended and that fundamental debates over freedom, justice, and rights from now on will be at best mopping-up operations in a war already won by liberal democracy. Islamic fundamentalism offers the world a notion of justice very much at odds with Western liberal notions about the strict equality of all people, regardless of sex, religion, or ethnicity. Meanwhile, the U.S. government has taken measures in its war on terrorism that have put into question the civil rights both of its citizens at home and of foreign nationals. This "clash of civilizations" (to borrow Samuel Huntington's phrase) has certainly helped to reawaken basic debates over the great issues in political theory. The shades of Hobbes, Locke, Marx, and Mill cast long shadows not only over the history of political thought but over the coming century of real political conflict too.

# THE PROBLEM OF POWER 1: MACHIAVELLI'S PRINCE

Niccolò Machiavelli (1469–1527) was truly a Renaissance man—he wrote philosophy, history, and plays, along with acting as the second chancellor and secretary of the Republic of Florence from 1498 to 1512. As a practicing diplomat, Machiavelli was well aware of the political shenanigans that the princes of Renaissance Italy were up to, including the ruthless behavior of Cesare Borgia, son of Pope Alexander, toward his enemies both domestic and foreign (Borgia is widely assumed to be the inspiration for Machiavelli's picture of the ideal prince). After the fall of the republic, and the assumption of power by the infamous Medici family, Machiavelli was briefly thrown into jail and then released in 1513. He then went into exile for a number of years to a farm, where he wrote many of his greatest works, including *The Prince* in 1513, *The Art of War,* and *Discourses on the First Ten Books of Livy,* his most detailed analysis of history and politics.

Machiavelli's basic method in *The Prince* was what later became known as "political realism." He said in effect, "Let's look at how great political leaders in the past have actually behaved, and not at utopian political ideals, and draw some general conclusions from their histories about how a prince can get and keep power." In other words, we should look at the way that politics is *really* practiced in order to understand it.

He further assumed that human nature doesn't change all that much, so a study of ancient Greek or Roman politics was relevant to modern political life. In the following reading, we see some of the conclusions that Machiavelli drew from his study of history and contemporary politics on the essence of political power: that the prince must pay close attention to "the art of war"; that it is better to be feared than loved if one is to retain power; that the prince should emulate both the fierce lion (to scare his enemies) and sneaky fox (to avoid traps); that cruelty, if necessary, should be done all at once; and that the prince should appear religious, humble, and virtuous, but not be afraid to be what a conventional person might call "bad" to stay in power. In other words, the end justifies the means. We can perhaps summarize Machiavelli's advice to the prince by saying that morality and power are strange bedfellows: If you want to be good, you won't make an effective political leader.

Yet it's important to remember that Machiavelli isn't saying that he unequivocally admires the cunning and ruthless prince he's painting a picture of in this book. He generally favored a republican form of government over a monarchy, a preference that comes out from time to time even in *The Prince* and that he made even clearer in *The Discourses.* It's just that he was a realist about the power politics of his day, realizing that well-intentioned, peace-loving democrats would probably be all too easily squashed by the cunning foxes and voracious lions surrounding them. Unfortunately, many later writers assumed that he was championing the ruthless behavior he describes in *The Prince,* the term "Machiavellian" coming to mean someone who is sneaky, underhanded, and generally willing to do morally questionable things to keep and hold power. You can decide for yourself as you read the following selections whether Machiavelli himself was "Machiavellian."

# The Prince

## NICCOLÒ MACHIAVELLI

### Chapter 6. Of New Dominions Which Have Been Acquired by One's Own Arms and Ability

Let no one marvel if in speaking of new dominions both as to prince and state, I bring forward very exalted instances, for men walk almost always in the paths trodden by others, proceeding in their actions by imitation. Not being always able to follow others exactly, nor attain to the excellence of those he imitates, a prudent man should always follow in the path trodden by great men and imitate those who are most excellent, so that if he does not attain to their greatness, at any rate he will get some tinge of it. He will do as prudent archers, who when the place they wish to hit is too far off, knowing how far their bow will carry, aim at a spot much higher than the one they wish to hit, not in order to reach this height with their arrow, but by help of this high aim to hit the spot they wish to. . . .

. . . It must be considered that there is nothing more difficult to carry out, nor more doubtful of success, nor more dangerous to handle, than to initiate a new order of things. For the reformer has enemies in all those who profit by the old order, and only lukewarm defenders in all those who would profit by the new order, this lukewarmness arising partly from fear of their adversaries, who have the laws in their favour; and partly from the incredulity of mankind, who do not truly believe in anything new until they have had actual experience of it. Thus it arises that on every opportunity for attacking the reformer, his opponents do so with the zeal of partisans, the others only defend him half-heartedly, so that between them he runs great danger. It is necessary, however, in order to investigate thoroughly this question, to examine whether these innovators are independent, or whether they depend upon others, that is to say, whether in order to carry out their designs they have to entreat or are able to compel. In the first case they invariably succeed ill, and accomplish nothing; but when they can depend on their own strength and are able to use force, they rarely fail. Thus it comes about that all armed prophets have conquered and unarmed ones failed; for besides what has been already said, the character of peoples varies, and it is easy to persuade them of a thing, but difficult to keep them in that persuasion. And so it is necessary to order things so that when they no longer believe, they can be made to believe by force. Moses, Cyrus, Theseus, and Romulus would not have been able to keep their constitutions observed for so long had they been disarmed, as happened in our own time with Fra Girolamo Savonarola, who failed entirely in his new rules when the multitude began to disbelieve in him, and he had no means of holding fast those who had believed nor of compelling the unbelievers to believe. Therefore such men as these have great difficulty in making their way, and all their dangers are met on the road and must be overcome by their own abilities; but when once they have overcome them and have begun to be held in veneration, and have suppressed those who envied them, they remain powerful and secure, honoured and happy. . . .

### Chapter 8. Of Those Who Have Attained the Position of Prince by Villainy

. . . Agathocles the Sicilian rose not only from private life but from the lowest and most abject position to be King of Syracuse. The son of a pot-

SOURCE: Niccolò Machiavelli, *The Prince*, chaps. 6, 8, 14, 15, 17, 18, and 25, in *The Prince and the Discourses*, trans. Luigi Ricci (1515; New York: Random House, 1950), pp. 19–22, 31–32, 34–35, 53–56, 60–66, 91–93, 94 (edited).

ter, he led a life of the utmost wickedness through all the stages of his fortune. Nevertheless, his wickedness was accompanied by such vigour of mind and body that, having joined the militia, he rose through its ranks to be praetor of Syracuse. Having been appointed to this position, and having decided to become prince, and to hold with violence and without the support of others that which had been constitutionally granted him; and having imparted his design to Hamilcar the Carthaginian, who was fighting with his armies in Sicily, he called together one morning the people and senate of Syracuse, as if he had to deliberate on matters of importance to the republic, and at a given signal had all the senators and the richest men of the people killed by his soldiers. After their death he occupied and held rule over the city without any civil strife. And although he was twice beaten by the Carthaginians and ultimately besieged, he was able not only to defend the city, but leaving a portion of his forces for its defence, with the remainder he invaded Africa, and in a short time liberated Syracuse from the siege and brought the Carthaginians to great extremities, so that they were obliged to come to terms with him, and remain contented with the possession of Africa, leaving Sicily to Agathocles. Whoever considers, therefore, the actions and qualities of this man, will see few if any things which can be attributed to fortune; for, as above stated, it was not by the favour of any person, but through the grades of the militia, in which he had advanced with a thousand hardships and perils, that he arrived at the position of prince, which he afterwards maintained by so many courageous and perilous expedients. It cannot be called virtue to kill one's fellow-citizens, betray one's friends, be without faith, without pity, and without religion; by these methods one may indeed gain power, but not glory. For if the virtues of Agathocles in braving and overcoming perils, and his greatness of soul in supporting and surmounting obstacles be considered, one sees no reason for holding him inferior to any of the most renowned captains. Nevertheless his barbarous cruelty and inhumanity, together with his countless atrocities, do not permit of his being named among the

most famous men. We cannot attribute to fortune or virtue that which he achieved without either. . . .

Some may wonder how it came about that Agathocles, and others like him, could, after infinite treachery and cruelty, live secure for many years in their country and defend themselves from external enemies without being conspired against by their subjects; although many others have, owing to their cruelty, been unable to maintain their position in times of peace, not to speak of the uncertain times of war. I believe this arises from the cruelties being exploited well or badly. Well committed may be called those (if it is permissible to use the word well of evil) which are perpetuated once for the need of securing one's self, and which afterwards are not persisted in, but are exchanged for measures as useful to the subjects as possible. Cruelties ill committed are those which, although at first few, increase rather than diminish with time. Those who follow the former method may remedy in some measure their condition, both with God and man; as did Agathocles. As to the others, it is impossible for them to maintain themselves.

Whence it is to be noted, that in taking a state the conqueror must arrange to commit all his cruelties at once, so as not to have to recur to them every day, and so as to be able, by not making fresh changes, to reassure people and win them over by benefiting them. Whoever acts otherwise, either through timidity or bad counsels, is always obliged to stand with knife in hand, and can never depend on his subjects, because they, owing to continually fresh injuries, are unable to depend upon him. For injuries should be done all together, so that being less tasted, they will give less offence. Benefits should be granted little by little, so that they may be better enjoyed. And above all, a prince must live with his subjects in such a way that no accident of good or evil fortune can deflect him from his course; for necessity arising in adverse times, you are not in time with severity, and the good that you do does not profit, as it is judged to be forced upon you, and you will derive no benefit whatever from it.

## Chapter 14. The Duties of a Prince with Regard to the Militia

A prince should therefore have no other aim or thought, nor take up any other thing for his study, but war and its organisation and discipline, for that is the only art that is necessary to one who commands, and it is of such virtue that it not only maintains those who are born princes, but often enables men of private fortune to attain to that rank. And one sees, on the other hand, that when princes think more of luxury than of arms, they lose their state. The chief cause of the loss of states, is the contempt of this art, and the way to acquire them is to be well versed in the same.

Francesco Sforza, through being well armed, became, from private status, Duke of Milan; his sons, through wishing to avoid the fatigue and hardship of war, from dukes became private persons. For among other evils caused by being disarmed, it renders you contemptible; which is one of those disgraceful things which a prince must guard against, as will be explained later. Because there is no comparison whatever between an armed and a disarmed man; it is not reasonable to suppose that one who is armed will obey willingly one who is unarmed; or that any unarmed man will remain safe among armed servants. For one being disdainful and the other suspicious, it is not possible for them to act well together. And therefore a prince who is ignorant of military matters, besides the other misfortunes already mentioned, cannot be esteemed by his soldiers, nor have confidence in them.

He ought, therefore, never to let his thoughts stray from the exercise of war; and in peace he ought to practise it more than in war, which he can do in two ways: by action and by study. As to action, he must, besides keeping his men well disciplined and exercised, engage continually in hunting, and thus accustom his body to hardships; and meanwhile learn the nature of the land, how steep the mountains are, how the valleys debouch, where the plains lie, and understand the nature of rivers and swamps. To all this he should devote great attention. This knowledge is useful in two ways. In the first place, one learns to know one's country, and can the better see how to defend it. Then by means of the knowledge and experience gained in one locality, one can easily understand any other that it may be necessary to observe; for the hills and valleys, plains and rivers of Tuscany, for instance, have a certain resemblance to those of other provinces, so that from a knowledge of the country in one province one can easily arrive at a knowledge of others. And that prince who is lacking in this skill is wanting in the first essentials of a leader; for it is this which teaches how to find the enemy, take up quarters, lead armies, plan battles and lay siege to towns with advantage. . . .

But as to exercise for the mind, the prince ought to read history and study the actions of eminent men, see how they acted in warfare, examine the causes of their victories and defeats in order to imitate the former and avoid the latter, and above all, do as some men have done in the past, who have imitated some one, who has been much praised and glorified, and have always kept his deeds and actions before them, as they say Alexander the Great imitated Achilles, Caesar Alexander, and Scipio Cyrus. And whoever reads the life of Cyrus written by Xenophon, will perceive in the life of Scipio how gloriously he imitated the former, and how, in chastity, affability, humanity, and liberality Scipio conformed to those qualities of Cyrus as described by Xenophon.

A wise prince should follow similar methods and never remain idle in peaceful times, but industriously make good use of them, so that when fortune changes she may find him prepared to resist her blows, and to prevail in adversity.

## Chapter 15. Of the Things for Which Men, and Especially Princes, Are Praised or Blamed

It now remains to be seen what are the methods and rules for a prince as regards his subjects and friends. And as I know that many have written of this, I fear that my writing about it may be deemed presumptuous, differing as I do, especially in this matter, from the opinions of others. But my intention being to write something of use to those who understand, it appears to me more proper to go to the real truth of the matter than to its imagination; and many have imagined republics and principalities which have never been seen or known to exist in reality; for how we live is so far removed from how we ought to live, that he who abandons what is done for what ought to be done, will rather learn to bring about his own ruin than his preservation. A man who wishes to make a profession of goodness in everything must necessarily come to grief among so many who are not good. Therefore it is necessary for a prince, who wishes to maintain himself, to learn how not to be good, and to use this knowledge and not use it, according to the necessity of the case. . . .

## Chapter 17. Of Cruelty and Clemency, and Whether It Is Better to Be Loved or Feared

Proceeding to the other qualities before named, I say that every prince must desire to be considered merciful and not cruel. He must, however, take care not to misuse this mercifulness. Cesare Borgia was considered cruel, but his cruelty had brought order to the Romagna, united it, and reduced it to peace and fealty. If this is considered well, it will be seen that he was really much more merciful than the Florentine people, who, to avoid the name of cruelty, allowed Pistoia to be destroyed. A prince, therefore, must not mind incurring the charge of cruelty for the purpose of keeping his subjects united and faithful; for, with a very few examples, he will be more merciful than those who, from excess of tenderness, allow disorders to arise, from whence spring bloodshed and rapine; for these as a rule injure the whole community, while the executions carried out by the prince injure only individuals. And of all princes, it is impossible for a new prince to escape the reputation of cruelty, new states being

always full of dangers. Wherefore Virgil through the mouth of Dido says:

> Res dura, et regni novitas me talia cogunt
> Moliri, et late fines custode tueri.

Nevertheless, he must be cautious in believing and acting, and must not be afraid of his own shadow, and must proceed in a temperate manner with prudence and humanity, so that too much confidence does not render him incautious, and too much diffidence does not render him intolerant.

From this arises the question whether it is better to be loved more than feared, or feared more than loved. The reply is, that one ought to be both feared and loved, but as it is difficult for the two to go together, it is much safer to be feared than loved, if one of the two has to be wanting. For it may be said of men in general that they are ungrateful, voluble, dissemblers, anxious to avoid danger, and covetous of gain; as long as you benefit them, they are entirely yours; they offer you their blood, their goods, their life, and their children, as I have before said, when the necessity is remote; but when it approaches, they revolt. And the prince who has relied solely on their words, without making other preparations, is ruined; for the friendship which is gained by purchase and not through grandeur and nobility of spirit is bought but not secured, and at a pinch is not to be expended in your service. And men have less scruple in offending one who makes himself loved than one who makes himself feared; for love is held by a chain of obligation which, men being selfish, is broken whenever it serves their purpose; but fear is maintained by a dread of punishment which never fails.

Still, a prince should make himself feared in such a way that if he does not gain love, he at any rate avoids hatred: for fear and the absence of hatred may well go together, and will be always attained by one who abstains from interfering with the property of his citizens and subjects or with their women. And when he is obliged to take the life of any one, let him do so when there is a proper justification and manifest reason for it; but above all he must abstain from taking the property of others, for men forget more easily the death of their father than the loss of their patrimony. Then also pretexts for seizing property are never wanting, and one who begins to live by rapine will always find some reason for taking the goods of others, whereas causes for taking life are rarer and more fleeting.

But when the prince is with his army and has a large number of soldiers under his control, then it is extremely necessary that he should not mind being thought cruel; for without this reputation he could not keep an army united or disposed to any duty. Among the noteworthy actions of Hannibal is numbered this, that although he had an enormous army, composed of men of all nations and fighting in foreign countries, there never arose any dissension either among them or against the prince, either in good fortune or in bad. This could not be due to anything but his inhuman cruelty, which together with his infinite other virtues, made him always venerated and terrible in the sight of his soldiers, and without it his other virtues would not have sufficed to produce that effect. Thoughtless writers admire on the one hand his actions, and on the other blame the principal cause of them.

And that it is true that his other virtues would not have sufficed may be seen from the case of Scipio (famous not only in regard to his own times, but all times of which memory remains), whose armies rebelled against him in Spain, which arose from nothing but his excessive kindness, which allowed more licence to the soldiers than was consonant with military discipline. He was reproached with this in the senate by Fabius Maximus, who called him a corrupter of the Roman militia. Locri having been destroyed by one of Scipio's officers was not revenged by him, nor was the insolence of that officer punished, simply by reason of his easy nature; so much so, that some one wishing to excuse him in the senate, said that there were many men who knew rather how not to err, than how to correct the errors of others. This disposition would in time have tarnished the fame and glory of Scipio had

he persevered in it under the empire, but living under the rule of the senate this harmful quality was not only concealed but became a glory to him.

I conclude, therefore, with regard to being feared and loved, that men love at their own free will, but fear at the will of the prince, and that a wise prince must rely on what is in his power and not on what is in the power of others, and he must only contrive to avoid incurring hatred, as has been explained.

## Chapter 18. In What Way Princes Must Keep Faith

How laudable it is for a prince to keep good faith and live with integrity, and not with astuteness, every one knows. Still the experience of our times shows those princes to have done great things who have had little regard for good faith, and have been able by astuteness to confuse men's brains, and who have ultimately overcome those who have made loyalty their foundation.

You must know, then, that there are two methods of fighting, the one by law, the other by force: the first method is that of men, the second of beasts; but as the first method is often insufficient, one must have recourse to the second. It is therefore necessary for a prince to know well how to use both the beast and the man. This was covertly taught to rulers by ancient writers, who relate how Achilles and many others of those ancient princes were given to Chiron the centaur to be brought up and educated under his discipline. The parable of this semi-animal, semi-human teacher is meant to indicate that a prince must know how to use both natures, and that the one without the other is not durable.

A prince being thus obliged to know well how to act as a beast must imitate the fox and the lion, for the lion cannot protect himself from traps, and the fox cannot defend himself from wolves. One must therefore be a fox to recognise traps, and a lion to frighten wolves. Those that wish to be only lions do not understand this. Therefore, a prudent ruler ought not to keep faith when by so doing it would be against his interest, and when the reasons which made him bind himself no longer exist. If men were all good, this precept would not be a good one; but as they are bad, and would not observe their faith with you, so you are not bound to keep faith with them. Nor have legitimate grounds ever failed a prince who wished to show colourable excuse for the non-fulfilment of his promise. Of this one could furnish an infinite number of modern examples, and show how many times peace has been broken, and how many promises rendered worthless, by the faithlessness of princes, and those that have been best able to imitate the fox have succeeded best. But it is necessary to be able to disguise this character well, and to be a great feigner and dissembler; and men are so simple and so ready to obey present necessities, that one who deceives will always find those who allow themselves to be deceived.

I will only mention one modern instance. Alexander VI did nothing else but deceive men, he thought of nothing else, and found the occasion for it; no man was ever more able to give assurances, or affirmed things with stronger oaths, and no man observed them less; however, he always succeeded in his deceptions, as he well knew this aspect of things.

It is not, therefore, necessary for a prince to have all the above-named qualities, but it is very necessary to seem to have them. I would even be bold to say that to possess them and always to observe them is dangerous, but to appear to possess them is useful. Thus it is well to seem merciful, faithful, humane, sincere, religious, and also to be so; but you must have the mind so disposed that when it is needful to be otherwise you may be able to change to the opposite qualities. And it must be understood that a prince, and especially a new prince, cannot observe all those things which are considered good in men, being often obliged, in order to maintain the state, to act against faith, against charity, against humanity, and against religion. And, therefore,

he must have a mind disposed to adapt itself according to the wind, and as the variations of fortune dictate, and, as I said before, not deviate from what is good, if possible, but be able to do evil if constrained.

A prince must take great care that nothing goes out of his mouth which is not full of the above-named five qualities, and, to see and hear him, he should seem to be all mercy, faith, integrity, humanity, and religion. And nothing is more necessary than to seem to have this last quality, for men in general judge more by the eyes than by the hands, for every one can see, but very few have to feel. Everybody sees what you appear to be, few feel what you are, and those few will not dare to oppose themselves to the many, who have the majesty of the state to defend them; and in the actions of men, and especially of princes, from which there is no appeal, the end justifies the means. Let a prince therefore aim at conquering and maintaining the state, and the means will always be judged honourable and praised by every one, for the vulgar is always taken by appearances and the issue of the event; and the world consists only of the vulgar, and the few who are not vulgar are isolated when the many have a rallying point in the prince. A certain prince of the present time, whom it is well not to name, never does anything but preach peace and good faith, but he is really a great enemy to both, and either of them, had he observed them, would have lost him state or reputation on many occasions.

## Chapter 25. How Much Fortune Can Do in Human Affairs and How It May Be Opposed

It is not unknown to me how many have been and are of opinion that worldly events are so governed by fortune and by God, that men cannot by their prudence change them, and that on the contrary there is no remedy whatever, and for this they may judge it to be useless to toil much about them, but let things be ruled by chance. This opinion has been more held in our day, from the great changes that have been seen, and are daily seen, beyond every human conjecture. When I think about them, at times I am partly inclined to share this opinion. Nevertheless, that our free-will may not be altogether extinguished, I think it may be true that fortune is the ruler of half our actions, but that she allows the other half or thereabouts to be governed by us. I would compare her to an impetuous river that, when turbulent, inundates the plains, casts down trees and buildings, removes earth from this side and places it on the other; every one flees before it, and everything yields to its fury without being able to oppose it; and yet though it is of such a kind, still when it is quiet, men can make provision against it by dykes and banks, so that when it rises it will either go into a canal or its rush will not be so wild and dangerous. So it is with fortune, which shows her power where no measures have been taken to resist her, and directs her fury where she knows that no dykes or barriers have been made to hold her. And if you regard Italy, which has been the seat of these changes, and who has given the impulse to them, you will see her to be a country without dykes or banks of any kind. If she had been protected by proper measures, like Germany, Spain, and France, this inundation would not have caused the great changes that it has, or would not have happened at all.

This must suffice as regards opposition to fortune in general. But limiting myself more to particular cases, I would point out how one sees a certain prince to-day fortunate and to-morrow ruined, without seeing that he has changed in character or otherwise. I believe this arises in the first place from the causes that we have already discussed at length; that is to say, because the prince who bases himself entirely on fortune is ruined when fortune changes. I also believe that he is happy whose mode of procedure accords with the needs of the times, and similarly he is unfortunate whose mode of procedure is opposed to the times. For one sees that men in those things which lead them to the aim that

each one has in view, namely, glory and riches, proceed in various ways; one with circumspection, another with impetuosity, one by violence, another by cunning, one with patience, another with the reverse; and each by these diverse ways may arrive at his aim. One sees also two cautious men, one of whom succeeds in his designs, and the other not, and in the same way two men succeed equally by different methods, one being cautious, the other impetuous, which arises only from the nature of the times, which does or does not conform to their method of procedure. From this it results, as I have said, that two men, acting differently, attain the same effect, and of two others acting in the same way, one attains his goal and not the other. On this depend also the changes in prosperity, for if it happens that time and circumstances are favourable to one who acts with caution and prudence he will be successful, but if time and circumstances change he will be ruined, because he does not change his mode of procedure. No man is found so prudent as to be able to adapt himself to this, either because he cannot deviate from that to which his nature disposes him, or else because having always prospered by walking in one path, he cannot persuade himself that it is well to leave it; and therefore the cautious man, when it is time to act suddenly, does not know how to do so and is consequently ruined; for if one could change one's nature with time and circumstances, fortune would never change. . . .

I conclude then that fortune varying and men remaining fixed in their ways, they are successful so long as these ways conform to circumstances, but when they are opposed then they are unsuccessful. I certainly think that it is better to be impetuous than cautious, for fortune is a woman, and it is necessary, if you wish to master her, to conquer her by force; and it can be seen that she lets herself be overcome by the bold rather than by those who proceed coldly. And therefore, like a woman, she is always a friend to the young, because they are less cautious, fiercer, and master her with greater audacity.

# THE PROBLEM OF POWER 2: THE STATE OF NATURE AND THE SOCIAL CONTRACT

## *Thomas Hobbes and the War of Each against All*

Thomas Hobbes (1588–1679) was born in Westport, England, in the year of the Spanish Armada's abortive invasion of England—the English were saved by strong winds that may or may not have been the will of God, depending on which side you were on. Hobbes was very much influenced by the Scientific Revolution of the sixteenth and seventeenth centuries, which included such luminaries as the astronomer Nicolaus Copernicus (1473–1543), who put forward the "heliocentric" or sun-centered model of the solar system; the physicist and astronomer Galileo Galilei (1564–1642), who developed laws for the motion of bodies in space; and Hobbes's countryman Francis Bacon (1561–1626), whose slogan was "knowledge is power" and who insisted that this knowledge could be gained only through experiment and observation. Hobbes developed a materialist and mechanistic philosophy of both nature and the human world. He saw all bodies, including human bodies, as "matter in motion," as linked by causal laws, explaining both perception and emotions along these lines—the former as caused by moving particles entering our sense organs, the latter by the flow of blood into and out of the heart. He applied this mechanistic and materialist philosophy to his political theory. He saw the state as one large body, called the "sovereign," made up of many individual atoms—the subjects or citizens. Further, he saw these atom-citizens as regulated by laws of human nature, just as physical particles are regulated by laws of physical nature.

In 1640, just before the English Civil War started, Hobbes fled to the Continent, afraid that his sympathies for the Stuart line of kings would land him in trouble with the Puritan government under Oliver Cromwell. There he wrote his masterpiece, *Leviathan*. After it was published in 1651, he was forced to flee back to England, as his book attacked the papacy, which the Catholic authorities in France didn't appreciate, and seemed to root the authority of the king in popular will, which the exiled Stuarts didn't appreciate, being believers in the divine right of kings. *Leviathan* is by far his most famous work and the foundation of a whole school of political theory—"contractarianism." Hobbes argues in the following selections that without government or laws, our lives would be "solitary, poor, nasty, brutish, and short." Obviously, he was reflecting on England's experience during the bloody civil war that had ended just a few years earlier. In such a state all people were equal in the sense that they could each kill one another. The state of nature was a war of each against all: In it neither our property nor our lives are secure. There's no point engaging in large-scale agriculture, industry, or trade in such a state, because the fruits of our labors could be stolen from us at any moment by robbers unrestrained by law.

Something had to be done to avoid this sort of chaos. Hobbes's solution was the "social contract," an actual or hypothetical document (depending on how one interprets Hobbes's work) that acts as a peace treaty between the warring parties in the state of nature. This contract is regulated by a series of "laws of nature" that Hobbes believed to be the natural products of an unfettered human reason. The first three of these laws of nature, in a nutshell, are (1) seek peace if you can get it, (2) avoid political chaos by agreeing to lay aside as much natural freedom as do the other citizens signing the contract, and (3) keep your word. But to guarantee that the citizens keep their word toward each other, we need a strong ruler, a "sovereign" (which could be a king or a parliament), entrusted with enforcing the law and keeping the peace. And we can't really complain if this sovereign rules with a strong hand, unless the sovereign uses agents to try to kill us: Without the social contract and the power of the sovereign to protect us, there can be no personal security, no property, no economic life, no justice. In short, Hobbes is saying that individual political rights can be guaranteed only if a group of people get together and collectively give up some of their natural freedom to some overarching person or body with the power to enforce these rights.

# Leviathan

## THOMAS HOBBES

### *Part 1. Of Man*

#### CHAPTER 13. OF THE NATURAL CONDITION OF MANKIND AS CONCERNING THEIR FELICITY AND MISERY

**Men by Nature Equal**

Nature hath made men so equal in the faculties of body and mind as that, though there be found one man sometimes manifestly stronger in body or of quicker mind than another, yet when all is reckoned together the difference between man and man is not so considerable as that one man can thereupon claim to himself any benefit to which another may not pretend as well as he. For as to the strength of body, the weakest has strength enough to kill the strongest, either by secret machination or by confederacy with others that are in the same danger with himself.

And as to the faculties of the mind, setting aside the arts grounded upon words, and especially that skill of proceeding upon general and infallible rules, called science, which very few have and but in few things, as being not a native faculty born with us, nor attained, as prudence, while we look after somewhat else, I find yet a greater equality amongst men than that of strength. For prudence is but experience, which equal time equally bestows on all men in those things they equally apply themselves unto. That which may perhaps make such equality incredible is but a vain conceit of one's own wisdom, which almost all men think they have in a greater degree than the vulgar; that is, than all men but themselves, and a few others, whom by fame, or for concurring with themselves, they approve. For such is the nature of men that howsoever they may acknowledge many others to be more witty, or more eloquent or more learned, yet they will hardly believe there be many so wise as themselves; for they see their own wit at hand, and other men's at a distance. But this proveth

SOURCE: Thomas Hobbes, *Leviathan* (1651; Toronto and London: J. M. Dent & Sons [Everyman's Library], 1914), pp. 63–67, 68, 69, 70–71, 72, 74, 87, 89–90 (most spelling, punctuation, and capitalization have been modernized; subtitles added by the editors based on Hobbes's original marginal notations; notes by the editors).

rather that men are in that point equal, than unequal. For there is not ordinarily a greater sign of the equal distribution of anything than that every man is contented with his share.

### From Equality Proceeds Diffidence

From this equality of ability ariseth equality of hope in the attaining of our ends. And therefore if any two men desire the same thing, which nevertheless they cannot both enjoy, they become enemies; and in the way to their end (which is principally their own conservation, and sometimes their delectation only) endeavour to destroy or subdue one another. And from hence it comes to pass that where an invader hath no more to fear than another man's single power, if one plant, sow, build, or possess a convenient seat, others may probably be expected to come prepared with forces united to dispossess and deprive him, not only of the fruit of his labour, but also of his life or liberty. And the invader again is in the like danger of another.

### From Diffidence War

And from this diffidence of one another, there is no way for any man to secure himself so reasonable as anticipation; that is, by force, or wiles, to master the persons of all men he can so long till he see no other power great enough to endanger him: and this is no more than his own conservation requireth, and is generally allowed. Also, because there be some that, taking pleasure in contemplating their own power in the acts of conquest, which they pursue farther than their security requires, if others, that otherwise would be glad to be at ease within modest bounds, should not by invasion increase their power, they would not be able, long time, by standing only on their defence, to subsist. And by consequence, such augmentation of dominion over men being necessary to a man's conservation, it ought to be allowed him.

Again, men have no pleasure (but on the contrary a great deal of grief) in keeping company where there is no power able to overawe them all. For every man looketh that his companion should value him at the same rate he sets upon himself, and upon all signs of contempt or undervaluing naturally endeavours, as far as he dares (which amongst them that have no common power to keep them in quiet is far enough to make them destroy each other), to extort a greater value from his contemners, by damage; and from others, by the example.

So that in the nature of man, we find three principal causes of quarrel. First, competition; secondly, diffidence; thirdly, glory.

The first maketh men invade for gain; the second, for safety; and the third, for reputation. The first use violence, to make themselves masters of other men's persons, wives, children, and cattle; the second, to defend them; the third, for trifles, as a word, a smile, a different opinion, and any other sign of undervalue, either direct in their persons or by reflection in their kindred, their friends, their nation, their profession, or their name.

### Out of Civil States, There Is Always War of Every One against Every One

Hereby it is manifest that during the time men live without a common power to keep them all in awe, they are in that condition which is called war; and such a war as is of every man against every man. For WAR consisteth not in battle only, or the act of fighting, but in a tract of time, wherein the will to contend by battle is sufficiently known: and therefore the notion of *time* is to be considered in the nature of war, as it is in the nature of weather. For as the nature of foul weather lieth not in a shower or two of rain, but in an inclination thereto of many days together: so the nature of war consisteth not in actual fighting, but in the known disposition thereto during all the time there is no assurance to the contrary. All other time is PEACE.

### The Incommodities of Such a War

Whatsoever therefore is consequent to a time of war, where every man is enemy to every man, the same consequent to the time wherein men live without other security than what their own strength and their own invention shall furnish them withal. In such condition there is no place for industry, because the fruit thereof is uncertain: and consequently no culture of the earth; no navigation, nor use of the commodities that may be imported by sea; no commodious building; no instruments of moving and removing such things as require much force; no knowledge of the face of the earth; no account of time; no arts; no letters; no society; and which is worst of all, continual fear, and danger of violent death; and the life of man, solitary, poor, nasty, brutish, and short.

It may seem strange to some man that has not well weighed these things that Nature should thus dissociate and render men apt to invade and destroy one another: and he may therefore, not trusting to this inference, made from the passions, desire perhaps to have the same confirmed by experience. Let him therefore consider with himself: when taking a journey, he arms himself and seeks to go well accompanied; when going to sleep, he locks his doors; when even in his house he locks his chests; and this when he knows there be laws and public officers, armed, to revenge all injuries shall be done him; what opinion he has of his fellow-subjects, when he rides armed; of his fellow citizens, when he locks his doors; and of his children, and servants, when he locks his chests. Does he not there as much accuse mankind by his actions as I do by my words? But neither of us accuse man's nature in it. The desires, and other passions of man, are in themselves no sin. No more are the actions that proceed from those passions till they know a law that forbids them; which till laws be made they cannot know, nor can any law be made till they have agreed upon the person that shall make it.

It may peradventure be thought there was never such a time nor condition of war as this; and I believe it was never generally so, over all the world: but there are many places where they live so now. For the savage people in many places of America, except the government of small families, the concord whereof dependeth on natural lust, have no government at all, and live at this day in that brutish manner, as I said before. Howsoever, it may be perceived what manner of life there would be, where there were no common

power to fear, by the manner of life which men that have formerly lived under a peaceful government use to degenerate into a civil war.

But though there had never been any time wherein particular men were in a condition of war one against another, yet in all times kings and persons of sovereign authority, because of their independency, are in continual jealousies, and in the state and posture of gladiators, having their weapons pointing, and their eyes fixed on one another; that is, their forts, garrisons, and guns upon the frontiers of their kingdoms, and continual spies upon their neighbours, which is a posture of war. But because they uphold thereby the industry of their subjects, there does not follow from it that misery which accompanies the liberty of particular men.

### In Such a War Nothing Is Unjust
To this war of every man against every man, this also is consequent; that nothing can be unjust. The notions of right and wrong, justice and injustice, have there no place. Where there is no common power, there is no law; where no law, no injustice. Force and fraud are in war the two cardinal virtues. Justice and injustice are none of the faculties neither of the body nor mind. If they were, they might be in a man that were alone in the world, as well as his senses and passions. They are qualities that relate to men in society, not in solitude. It is consequent also to the same condition that there be no propriety,[1] no dominion, no *mine* and *thine* distinct; but only that to be every man's that he can get, and for so long as he can keep it. And thus much for the ill condition which man by mere nature is actually placed in; though with a possibility to come out of it, consisting partly in the passions, partly in his reason.

### The Passions That Incline Men to Peace
The passions that incline men to peace are: fear of death; desire of such things as are necessary to commodious living; and a hope by their industry to obtain them. And reason suggesteth con-

[1] Property.

venient articles of peace upon which men may be drawn to agreement. These articles are they which otherwise are called the laws of nature, whereof I shall speak more particularly in the two following chapters.

## CHAPTER 14. OF THE FIRST AND SECOND NATURAL LAWS, AND OF CONTRACTS

### Right of Nature What

The RIGHT OF NATURE, which writers commonly call *jus naturale,*[2] is the liberty each man hath to use his own power as he will himself for the preservation of his own nature; that is to say, of his own life; and consequently, of doing anything which, in his own judgement and reason, he shall conceive to be the aptest means thereunto.

### Liberty What

By LIBERTY is understood, according to the proper signification of the word, the absence of external impediments; which impediments may oft take away part of a man's power to do what he would, but cannot hinder him from using the power left him according as his judgement and reason shall dictate to him.

### A Law of Nature What

A LAW OF NATURE, *lex naturalis,* is a precept, or general rule, found out by reason, by which a man is forbidden to do that which is destructive of his life, or taketh away the means of preserving the same, and to omit that by which he thinketh it may be best preserved.

### Difference of Right and Law

For though they that speak of this subject use to confound *jus* and *lex, right* and *law,* yet they ought to be distinguished, because RIGHT consisteth in liberty to do, or to forbear; whereas LAW determineth and bindeth to one of them: so that law and right differ as much as obligation and liberty, which in one and the same matter are inconsistent.

[2] Natural right.

### Naturally Every Man Has Right to Every Thing

And because the condition of man (as hath been declared in the precedent chapter) is a condition of war of every one against every one, in which case every one is governed by his own reason, and there is nothing he can make use of that may not be a help unto him in preserving his life against his enemies; it followeth that in such a condition every man has a right to every thing, even to one another's body. And therefore, as long as this natural right of every man to every thing endureth, there can be no security to any man, how strong or wise soever he be, of living out the time which nature ordinarily alloweth men to live.

### The Fundamental Law of Nature

And consequently it is a precept, or general rule of reason: *that every man ought to endeavour peace, as far as he has hope of obtaining it; and when he cannot obtain it, that he may seek and use all helps and advantages of war.* The first branch of which rule containeth the first and fundamental law of nature, which is: *to seek peace and follow it.* The second, the sum of the right of nature, which is: *by all means we can to defend ourselves.*

### The Second Law of Nature

From this fundamental law of nature, by which men are commanded to endeavour peace, is derived this second law: *that a man be willing, when others are so too, as far-forth as for peace and defence of himself he shall think it necessary, to lay down this right to all things; and be contented with so much liberty against other men as he would allow other men against himself.* For as long as every man holdeth this right, of doing anything he liketh; so long are all men in the condition of war. But if other men will not lay down their right, as well as he, then there is no reason for anyone to divest himself of his: for that were to expose himself to prey, which no man is bound to, rather than to dispose himself to peace. This is that law of the gospel: *Whatsoever you require that others should do to you, that do ye to them. . . .*

### Contract What

The mutual transferring of right is that which men call CONTRACT. . . .

### Covenant What

Again, one of the contractors may deliver the thing contracted for on his part, and leave the other to perform his part at some determinate time after, and in the meantime be trusted; and then the contract on his part is called PACT, or COVENANT: or both parts may contract now to perform hereafter, in which cases he that is to perform in time to come, being trusted, his performance is called *keeping of promise,* or faith, and the failing of performance, if it be voluntary, *violation of faith.* . . .

### Signs of Contract Express

Signs of contract are either *express,* or *by inference.* Express are words spoken with understanding of what they signify: and such words are either of the time *present,* or *past;* as, *I give, I grant, I have given, I have granted, I will that this be yours:* or of the future; as, *I will give, I will grant,* which words of the future are called PROMISE. . . .

### Covenants of Mutual Trust, When Invalid

If a covenant be made wherein neither of the parties perform presently, but trust one another, in the condition of mere nature (which is a condition of war of every man against every man) upon any reasonable suspicion, it is void: but if there be a common power set over them both, with right and force sufficient to compel performance, it is not void. For he that performeth first has no assurance the other will perform after, because the bonds of words are too weak to bridle men's ambition, avarice, anger, and other passions, without the fear of some coercive power; which in the condition of mere nature, where all men are equal, and judges of the justness of their own fears, cannot possibly be supposed. And therefore he which performeth first does but betray himself to his enemy, contrary to the right he can never abandon of defending his life and means of living.

But in a civil estate, where there a power set up to constrain those that would otherwise violate their faith, that fear is no more reasonable;

and for that cause, he which by the covenant is to perform first is obliged so to do. . . .

### No Covenant with Beasts

To make covenants with brute beasts is impossible, because not understanding our speech, they understand not, nor accept of any translation of right, nor can translate any right to another: and without mutual acceptation, there is no covenant. . . .

### Covenants How Made Void

Men are freed of their covenants two ways; by performing, or by being forgiven. For performance is the natural end of obligation, and forgiveness the restitution of liberty, as being a retransferring of that right in which the obligation consisted.

### Covenants Extorted by Fear Are Valid

Covenants entered into by fear, in the condition of mere nature, are obligatory. For example, if I covenant to pay a ransom, or service for my life, to an enemy, I am bound by it. For it is a contract, wherein one receiveth the benefit of life; the other is to receive money, or service for it, and consequently, where no other law (as in the condition of mere nature) forbiddeth the performance, the covenant is valid. Therefore prisoners of war, if trusted with the payment of their ransom, are obliged to pay it: and if a weaker prince make a disadvantageous peace with a stronger, for fear, he is bound to keep it; unless (as hath been said before) there ariseth some new and just cause of fear to renew the war. And even in Commonwealths, if I be forced to redeem myself from a thief by promising him money, I am bound to pay it, till the civil law discharge me. For whatsoever I may lawfully do without obligation, the same I may lawfully covenant to do through fear: and what I lawfully covenant, I cannot lawfully break. . . .

### A Man's Covenant Not to Defend Himself Void

A covenant not to defend myself from force, by force, is always void. For (as I have shown before) no man can transfer or lay down his right to save himself from death, wounds, and imprisonment, the avoiding whereof is the only end of laying down any right; and therefore the promise of not resisting force, in no covenant transferreth any right, nor is obliging. For though a man may covenant thus, *unless I do so, or so, kill me;* he cannot covenant thus, *unless I do so, or so, I will not resist you when you come to kill me.* For man by nature chooseth the lesser evil, which is danger of death in resisting, rather than the greater, which is certain and present death in not resisting. And this is granted to be true by all men, in that they lead criminals to execution, and prison, with armed men, notwithstanding that such criminals have consented to the law by which they are condemned.

### No Man Obliged to Accuse Himself

A covenant to accuse oneself, without assurance of pardon, is likewise invalid. For in the condition of nature where every man is judge, there is no place for accusation: and in the civil state the accusation is followed with punishment, which, being force, a man is not obliged not to resist. The same is also true of the accusation of those by whose condemnation a man falls into misery; as of a father, wife, or benefactor. For the testimony of such an accuser, if it be not willingly given, is presumed to be corrupted by nature, and therefore not to be received: and where a man's testimony is not to be credited, he is not bound to give it. Also accusations upon torture are not to be reputed as testimonies. For torture is to be used but as means of conjecture, and light, in the further examination and search of truth: and what is in that case confessed tendeth to the ease of him that is tortured, not to the informing of the torturers, and therefore ought not to have the credit of a sufficient testimony: for whether he deliver himself by true or false accusation, he does it by the right of preserving his own life. . . .

## CHAPTER 15. OF OTHER LAWS OF NATURE

### The Third Law of Nature, Justice

From that law of nature by which we are obliged to transfer to another such rights as, being retained, hinder the peace of mankind, there fol-loweth a third; which is this: *that men perform their covenants made;* without which covenants are in vain, and but empty words; and the right of all men to all things remaining, we are still in the condition of war.

### Justice and Injustice What

And in this law of nature consisteth the fountain and original of JUSTICE. For where no covenant hath preceded, there hath no right been transferred, and every man has right to everything and consequently, no action can be unjust. But when a covenant is made, then to break it is *unjust:* and the definition of INJUSTICE, is no other than *the not performance of covenant.* And whatsoever is not unjust is *just.*

### Justice and Propriety Begin with the Constitution of Commonwealth

But because covenants of mutual trust, where there is a fear of not performance on either part (as hath been said in the former chapter), are invalid, though the original of justice be the making of covenants, yet injustice actually there can be none till the cause of such fear be taken away; which, while men are in the natural condition of war, cannot be done. Therefore before the names of just and unjust can have place, there must be some coercive power to compel men equally to the performance of their covenants, by the terror of some punishment greater than the benefit they expect by the breach of their covenant, and to make good that propriety which by mutual contract men acquire in recompense of the universal right they abandon: and such power there is none before the erection of a Commonwealth. And this is also to be gathered out of the ordinary definition of justice in the Schools,[3] for they say that *justice is the constant will of giving to every man his own.* And therefore where there is no *own,* that is, no propriety, there is no injustice; and where there is no coercive power erected, that is, where there is no Commonwealth, there is no propriety, all men having right to all things:

---

[3] Hobbes refers here to the Scholastic philosophers of the Middle Ages, monks and other churchmen who saw philosophy as the handmaiden of theology.

therefore where there is no Commonwealth, there nothing is unjust. So that the nature of justice consisteth in keeping of valid covenants, but the validity of covenants begins not but with the constitution of a civil power sufficient to compel men to keep them: and then it is also that propriety begins. . . .

## *Part 2. Of Commonwealth*

### CHAPTER 17. OF THE CAUSES, GENERATION, AND DEFINITION OF A COMMONWEALTH

**The End of Commonwealth, Particular Security**

The final cause, end, or design of men (who naturally love liberty, and dominion over others) in the introduction of that restraint upon themselves, in which we see them live in Commonwealths, is the foresight of their own preservation, and of a more contented life thereby; that is to say, of getting themselves out from that miserable condition of war which is necessarily consequent, as hath been shown, to the natural passions of men when there is no visible power to keep them in awe, and tie them by fear of punishment to the performance of their covenants, and observation of those laws of nature set down in the fourteenth and fifteenth chapters.

**Which Is Not to Be Had from the Law of Nature**

For the laws of nature, as *justice, equity, modesty, mercy,* and, in sum, *doing to others as we would be done to,* of themselves, without the terror of some power to cause them to be observed, are contrary to our natural passions, that carry us to partiality, pride, revenge, and the like. And covenants, without the sword, are but words and of no strength to secure a man at all. Therefore, notwithstanding the laws of nature (which every one hath then kept, when he has the will to keep them, when he can do it safely), if there be no power erected, or not great enough for our security, every man will and may lawfully rely on his own strength and art for caution against all other

men. And in all places, where men have lived by small families, to rob and spoil one another has been a trade, and so far from being reputed against the law of nature that the greater spoils they gained, the greater was their honour; and men observed no other laws therein but the laws of honour; that is, to abstain from cruelty, leaving to men their lives and instruments of husbandry. And as small families did then; so now do cities and kingdoms, which are but greater families (for their own security), enlarge their dominions upon all pretences of danger, and fear of invasion, or assistance that may be given to invaders; endeavour as much as they can to subdue or weaken their neighbours by open force, and secret arts, for want of other caution, justly; and are remembered for it in after ages with honour. . . .

**The Generation of a Commonwealth**

The only way to erect such a common power, as may be able to defend them from the invasion of foreigners, and the injuries of one another, and thereby to secure them in such sort as that by their own industry and by the fruits of the earth they may nourish themselves and live contentedly, is to confer all their power and strength upon one man, or upon one assembly of men, that may reduce all their wills, by plurality of voices, unto one will: which is as much as to say, to appoint one man, or assembly of men, to bear their person; and every one to own and acknowledge himself to be author of whatsoever he that so beareth their person shall act, or cause to be acted, in those things which concern the common peace and safety; and therein to submit their wills, every one to his will, and their judgements to his judgement. This is more than consent, or concord; it is a real unity of them all in one and the same person, made by covenant of every man with every man, in such manner as if every man should say to every man: *I authorize and give up my right of governing myself to this man, or to this assembly of men, on this condition, that thou give up, thy right to him, and authorize all his actions in like manner.* This done, the multitude so united in one person is called a COMMONWEALTH; in Latin, CIVITAS. This is the generation of that great LEVIATHAN,[4] or rather, to speak more reverently, of that *mortal god*, to which we owe, under the *immortal God*, our peace and defence. For by this authority, given him by every particular man in the Commonwealth, he hath the use of so much power and strength conferred on him that, by terror thereof, he is enabled to form the wills of them all, to peace at home, and mutual aid against their enemies abroad.

### The Definition of a Commonwealth
And in him consisteth the essence of the Commonwealth; which, to define it, is: *one person, of*

whose acts a great multitude, by mutual covenants one with another, have made themselves every one the author, to the end he may use the strength and means of them all as he shall think expedient for their peace and common defence.

### Sovereign, and Subject, What
And he that carryeth this person is called SOVEREIGN, and said to have *sovereign power;* and every one besides, his SUBJECT.

---

[4] The name of a great sea monster in the Bible.

## *John Locke and the Fruits of Our Labor*

John Locke (1632–1704) was not only the founder of modern empiricism in the realm of epistemology but also one of the founders of modern liberalism in political theory. He was born in the village of Wrington in Somerset, the son of a Puritan lawyer who fought with the parliamentary army against Charles I during the English Civil War (the same civil war that inspired Hobbes to write *Leviathan*). In 1652 Locke went to Christ Church College at Oxford University on a scholarship, graduating with his B.A. in 1656, receiving an M.A. in 1658. He studied medicine and the sciences, and while there met Robert Boyle, the prominent chemist.

He was a "Senior Student" at Oxford from 1659 to 1684. In 1662 he met Lord Ashley, later the Earl of Shaftesbury. The two became friends, with Locke serving as his secretary and personal physician. Ashley was a prominent "Whig," or liberal, and an opponent of the authoritarian Stuart kings. Locke finally received a medical degree in 1674.

Locke became part of Shaftesbury's entourage, which at the time was a dangerous place to be. Shaftesbury was tried for treason against the king in 1681 and fled to Holland in 1683, where he died. Locke went along with Shaftesbury to Holland and briefly advised William and Mary of Orange while there. King James II was deposed by the Glorious Revolution of 1688, with William and Mary being invited to become king and queen by the British Parliament. Locke returned to England after the revolution, now in favor with the powers that be. He held various minor government positions until he died in 1704.

Locke wrote widely on theology, economics, education, politics, and philosophy. The great moment in Locke's scholarly life, not to mention a defining moment in the history of modern Western thought, came in early 1690 when he published *An Essay concerning Human Understanding* and *Two Treatises of Government,* the foundations for the empiricist tradition in epistemology and the liberal tradition in political theory, respectively.

Locke's *Essay* was a defense of empiricism, the notion that all our knowledge comes from our senses. As we've seen in Chapter 4, Locke saw the human mind at birth as a tabula rasa, a blank slate on which experience writes its ideas. He rejected Descartes' argument that there are a number of innate ideas in our minds.

The first *Treatise* is an attack on the royal absolutism of Sir Robert Filmer's book *Patriarcha,* which argues that contemporary monarchs had a divine right to rule their people due to their direct descent from Adam, the first man. Filmer saw kings as fathers of their people. The people owed loyalty to their monarch just as obedient sons and daughters owe loyalty to their parents. Locke responded that because this descent from Adam could never be proven, Filmer's argument had no solid ground. Further, children grow up, and at a certain point in their lives are justified in throwing off the parental yoke.

The *Second Treatise of Government* is a presentation of Locke's own ideas. It starts with a picture of a state of nature where people are free and equal but are not engaged in a state of war with each other, as Hobbes thought they would be. Locke argued that one could make a distinction between a state of nature, a state that is without laws but not without reason and justice and that is fairly peaceful, and a state of war, in which each is the enemy of all (as in Hobbes's state of nature). He likens the state of nature to international politics: States are free to act toward other states as they see fit, but most of the time aren't actually at war with each other and are quite capable of treating each other fairly if they see fit.

Yet people couldn't ensure their property in such a state, as each person had the right to punish transgressions of their rights as they saw fit. They could act as judges in their own cases, which Locke thought wasn't a very happy situation, given our natural partiality for our own interests and our equally natural desire to punish our enemies. Locke thought that whatever objects we mix our labor with belong to us. Yet in the state of nature the fruits of our labor, our property, are not secure. This unhappy state of untrammeled freedom had to end. Locke thought a state had to be created, but not one with absolute power, such as Hobbes's Leviathan. Living under the power of an autocratic sovereign would be no better than living in the state of nature, for with such power the sovereign could act like a wolf among helpless sheep. Unlike Hobbes, Locke believed that the sheep had a perfect right to defend their rights against the depredations of autocratic wolves, even after the social contract is signed. For Locke the best government would be some sort of parliament that was able to defend the "life, liberty, and property" of the people it represented, although the English-style constitutional monarchy of the post-1688 period, with its sharing of power between the monarch, an aristocratic body such as the House of Lords, and a democratic body such as the House of Commons, was acceptable to him. Indeed, some interpreters have argued that the *Second Treatise* is in fact a defense of the Glorious Revolution against Stuart absolutism. This view cannot be supported, though, given the fact that Locke wrote the *Second Treatise* in the early 1680s while in hiding in Holland. We can simplify things even further by saying that Locke believed that the purpose of the state was to protect its citizens' property, keeping in mind the fact that he considered our lives and liberties to be types of property (very important types, in fact).

Popular consent was thus the foundation of the state's legitimacy. Locke even dealt with the most obvious objection to the idea of a social contract: the fact that few living people, if any, had actually agreed to it. Locke answered with the notion of "tacit consent": The fact that you go on living within the boundaries of a given country implies a tacit consent on your part to the legitimacy of its political institutions.

Yet he even provided a way out of this tacit consent in exceptional circumstances. Locke believed that if the king either dissolved parliament and ruled arbitrarily, ignoring preestablished laws; hindered parliament from meeting or being elected; delivered the country into the hands of a foreign power; or invaded the life, liberty, or property of his subjects, the government was in effect dissolved, and the people were free to create a new one. In other words, the people have a right to resist tyranny, even if this means rebellion. The thirteen colonies saw themselves as invoking this right to resist tyranny in the person of King George III when they rebelled in 1776, the leaders of the rebellion incorporating Lockean language into the American Declaration of Independence in the same year. Given this historical fact, Locke stands second only to Marx as being the most influential political philosopher in modern history. Our conception of the liberal democratic state owes much to the ideas laid out by him in his *Second Treatise.*

# The Second Treatise of Government

## JOHN LOCKE

### Chapter 2. Of the State of Nature

4. To understand political power aright, and derive it from its original, we must consider what estate all men are naturally in, and that is, a state of perfect freedom to order their actions, and dispose of their possessions and persons as they think fit, within the bounds of the law of Nature, without asking leave or depending upon the will of any other man.

A state also of equality, wherein all the power and jurisdiction is reciprocal, no one having more than another, there being nothing more evident than that creatures of the same species and rank, promiscuously born to all the same advantages of Nature, and the use of the same faculties, should also be equal one amongst another, without subordination or subjection, unless the lord and master of them all should, by any manifest declaration of his will, set one above another, and confer on him, by an evident and clear appointment, an undoubted right to dominion and sovereignty.

6. But though this be a state of liberty, yet it is not a state of licence; though man in that state have an uncontrollable liberty to dispose of his person or possessions, yet he has not liberty to destroy himself, or so much as any creature in his possession, but where some nobler use than its bare preservation calls for it. The state of Nature has a law of Nature to govern it, which obliges every one, and reason, which is that law, teaches all mankind who will but consult it, that being all equal and independent, no one ought to harm another in his life, health, liberty or possessions. . . .

7. And that all men may be restrained from invading others' rights, and from doing hurt to one another, and the law of Nature be observed,

SOURCE: John Locke, *An Essay concerning the True Original, Extent, and End of Civil Government* ["Second Treatise of Government"] (1690), chaps. 2–5, 7–9: paras. 4, 6–8, 13, 14, 16, 17, 19, 22, 27, 87–93, 95 (notes cut), 123, 124 (edited); retrieved from The Institute for American Liberty's Web site: http://www.liberty1.org/2dtreat.htm.

which willeth the peace and preservation of all mankind, the execution of the law of Nature is in that state put into every man's hands, whereby every one has a right to punish the transgressors of that law to such a degree as may hinder its violation. For the law of Nature would, as all other laws that concern men in this world, be in vain if there were nobody that in the state of Nature had a power to execute that law, and thereby preserve the innocent and restrain offenders; and if any one in the state of Nature may punish another for any evil he has done, every one may do so. For in that state of perfect equality, where naturally there is no superiority or jurisdiction of one over another, what any may do in prosecution of that law, every one must needs have a right to do.

8. And thus, in the state of Nature, one man comes by a power over another, but yet no absolute or arbitrary power to use a criminal, when he has got him in his hands, according to the passionate heats or boundless extravagancy of his own will, but only to retribute to him so far as calm reason and conscience dictate, what is proportionate to his transgression, which is so much as may serve for reparation and restraint. For these two are the only reasons why one man may lawfully do harm to another, which is that we call punishment. In transgressing the law of Nature, the offender declares himself to live by another rule than that of reason and common equity, which is that measure God has set to the actions of men for their mutual security, and so he becomes dangerous to mankind; the tie which is to secure them from injury and violence being slighted and broken by him, which being a trespass against the whole species, and the peace and safety of it, provided for by the law of Nature, every man upon this score, by the right he hath to preserve mankind in general, may restrain, or where it is necessary, destroy things noxious to them, and so may bring such evil on any one who hath transgressed that law, as may make him repent the doing of it, and thereby deter him, and, by his example, others from doing the like mischief. And in this case, and upon this ground, every man hath a right to punish the offender, and be executioner of the law of Nature.

13. To this strange doctrine, *viz.* That in the state of Nature every one has the executive power of the law of Nature—I doubt not but it will be objected that it is unreasonable for men to be judges in their own cases, that self-love will make men partial to themselves and their friends; and, on the other side, ill-nature, passion, and revenge will carry them too far in punishing others, and hence nothing but confusion and disorder will follow, and that therefore God hath certainly appointed government to restrain the partiality and violence of men. I easily grant that civil government is the proper remedy for the inconveniences of the state of Nature, which must certainly be great where men may be judges in their own case, since it is easy to be imagined that he who was so unjust as to do his brother an injury will scarce be so just as to condemn himself for it. . . .

14. It is often asked as a mighty objection, where are, or ever were, there any men in such a state of Nature? To which it may suffice as an answer at present, that since all princes and rulers of *independent* governments all through the world are in a state of Nature, it is plain the world never was, nor never will be, without numbers of men in that state. I have named all governors of *independent* communities, whether they are, or are not, in league with others; for it is not every compact that puts an end to the state of Nature between men, but only this one of agreeing together mutually to enter into one community, and make one body politic; other promises and compacts men may make one with another, and yet still be in the state of Nature. The promises and bargains for truck, etc., between the two men in the desert island, mentioned by Garcilasso de la Vega, in his history of Peru; or between a Swiss and an Indian, in the woods of America, are binding to them, though they are perfectly in a state of Nature in reference to one another for truth, and keeping of faith belongs to men as men, and not as members of society.

## Chapter 3. Of the State of War

16. The state of war is a state of enmity and destruction; and therefore declaring by word or action, not a passionate and hasty, but sedate, set-

tled design upon another man's life puts him in a state of war with him against whom he has declared such an intention, and so has exposed his life to the other's power to be taken away by him, or any one that joins with him in his defence, and espouses his quarrel; it being reasonable and just I should have a right to destroy that which threatens me with destruction; for by the fundamental law of Nature, man being to be preserved as much as possible, when all cannot be preserved, the safety of the innocent is to be preferred, and one may destroy a man who makes war upon him, or has discovered an enmity to his being, for the same reason that he may kill a wolf or a lion, because they are not under the ties of the common law of reason, have no other rule but that of force and violence, and so may be treated as a beast of prey, those dangerous and noxious creatures that will be sure to destroy him whenever he falls into their power.

17. And hence it is that he who attempts to get another man into his absolute power does thereby put himself into a state of war with him; it being to be understood as a declaration of a design upon his life. For I have reason to conclude that he who would get me into his power without my consent would use me as he pleased when he had got me there, and destroy me too when he had a fancy to it; for nobody can desire to have me in his absolute power unless it be to compel me by force to that which is against the right of my freedom—*i.e.* make me a slave. To be free from such force is the only security of my preservation, and reason bids me look on him as an enemy to my preservation who would take away that freedom which is the fence to it; so that he who makes an attempt to enslave me thereby puts himself into a state of war with me. He that in the state of Nature would take away the freedom that belongs to any one in that state must necessarily be supposed to have a design to take away everything else, that freedom being the foundation of all the rest; as he that in the state of society would take away the freedom belonging to those of that society or commonwealth must be supposed to design to take away from them everything else, and so be looked on as in a state of war.

19. And here we have the plain difference between the state of Nature and the state of war, which however some men have confounded, are as far distant as a state of peace, goodwill, mutual assistance, and preservation; and a state of enmity, malice, violence and mutual destruction are one from another. Men living together according to reason without a common superior on earth, with authority to judge between them, is properly the state of Nature. But force, or a declared design of force upon the person of another, where there is no common superior on earth to appeal to for relief, is the state of war; and it is the want of such an appeal gives a man the right of war even against an aggressor, though he be in society and a fellow-subject. Thus, a thief whom I cannot harm, but by appeal to the law, for having stolen all that I am worth, I may kill when he sets on me to rob me but of my horse or coat, because the law, which was made for my preservation, where it cannot interpose to secure my life from present force, which if lost is capable of no reparation, permits me my own defence and the right of war, a liberty to kill the aggressor, because the aggressor allows not time to appeal to our common judge, nor the decision of the law, for remedy in a case where the mischief may be irreparable. Want of a common judge with authority puts all men in a state of Nature; force without right upon a man's person makes a state of war both where there is, and is not, a common judge.

## Chapter 4. Of Slavery

22. The natural liberty of man is to be free from any superior power on earth, and not to be under the will or legislative authority of man, but to have only the law of Nature for his rule. The liberty of man in society is to be under no other legislative power but that established by consent in the commonwealth, nor under the dominion of any will, or restraint of any law, but what that legislative shall enact according to the trust put in it. Freedom, then, is not what Sir Robert Filmer tells us: *A liberty for every one to do what he lists, to live as he pleases, and not to be tied by any laws;* but freedom of men under government is

to have a standing rule to live by, common to every one of that society, and made by the legislative power erected in it. A liberty to follow my own will in all things where that rule prescribes not, not to be subject to the inconstant, uncertain, unknown, arbitrary will of another man, as freedom of nature is to be under no other restraint but the law of Nature.

## Chapter 5. Of Property

27. Though the earth and all inferior creatures be common to all men, yet every man has a *property* in his own *person*. This nobody has any right to but himself. The *labour* of his body and the *work* of his hands, we may say, are properly his. Whatsoever, then, he removes out of the state that Nature hath provided and left it in, he hath mixed his labour with it, and joined to it something that is his own, and thereby makes it his property. It being by him removed from the common state Nature placed it in, it hath by this labour something annexed to it that excludes the common right of other men. For this labour being the unquestionable property of the labourer, no man but he can have a right to what that is once joined to, at least where there is enough, and as good left in common for others.

## Chapter 7. Of Political or Civil Society

87. Man being born, as has been proved, with a title to perfect freedom and an uncontrolled enjoyment of all the rights and privileges of the law of Nature, equally with any other man, or number of men in the world, hath by nature a power not only to preserve his property—that is, his life, liberty, and estate, against the injuries and attempts of other men, but to judge of and punish the breaches of that law in others, as he is persuaded the offence deserves, even with death itself, in crimes where the heinousness of the fact, in his opinion, requires it. But because no political society can be, nor subsist, without having in itself the power to preserve the property, and in order thereunto punish the offences of all those

of that society, there, and there only, is political society where every one of the members hath quitted this natural power, resigned it up into the hands of the community in all cases that exclude him not from appealing for protection to the law established by it. And thus all private judgment of every particular member being excluded, the community comes to be umpire, and by understanding indifferent rules and men authorised by the community for their execution, decides all the differences that may happen between any members of that society concerning any matter of right, and punishes those offences which any member hath committed against the society with such penalties as the law has established; whereby it is easy to discern who are, and are not, in political society together. Those who are united into one body, and have a common established law and judicature to appeal to, with authority to decide controversies between them and punish offenders, are in civil society one with another; but those who have no such common appeal, I mean on earth, are still in the state of Nature, each being where there is no other, judge for himself and executioner; which is, as I have before showed it, the perfect state of Nature.

88. And thus the commonwealth comes by a power to set down what punishment shall belong to the several transgressions they think worthy of it, committed amongst the members of that society (which is the power of making laws), as well as it has the power to punish any injury done unto any of its members by any one that is not of it (which is the power of war and peace); and all this for the preservation of the property of all the members of that society, as far as is possible. But though every man entered into society has quitted his power to punish offences against the law of Nature in prosecution of his own private judgment, yet with the judgment of offences which he has given up to the legislative, in all cases where he can appeal to the magistrate, he has given up a right to the commonwealth to employ his force for the execution of the judgments of the commonwealth whenever he shall be called to it, which, indeed, are his own judgments, they being made by himself or his rep-

resentative. And herein we have the original of the legislative and executive power of civil society, which is to judge by standing laws how far offences are to be punished when committed within the commonwealth; and also by occasional judgments founded on the present circumstances of the fact, how far injuries from without are to be vindicated, and in both these to employ all the force of all the members when there shall be need.

89. Wherever, therefore, any number of men so unite into one society as to quit every one his executive power of the law of Nature, and to resign it to the public, there and there only is a political or civil society. And this is done wherever any number of men, in the state of Nature, enter into society to make one people one body politic under one supreme government: or else when any one joins himself to, and incorporates with any government already made. For hereby he authorises the society, or which is all one, the legislative thereof, to make laws for him as the public good of the society shall require, to the execution whereof his own assistance (as to his own decrees) is due. And this puts men out of a state of Nature into that of a commonwealth, by setting up a judge on earth with authority to determine all the controversies and redress the injuries that may happen to any member of the commonwealth, which judge is the legislative or magistrates appointed by it. And wherever there are any number of men, however associated, that have no such decisive power to appeal to, there they are still in the state of Nature.

90. And hence it is evident that absolute monarchy, which by some men is counted for the only government in the world, is indeed inconsistent with civil society, and so can be no form of civil government at all. For the end of civil society being to avoid and remedy those inconveniences of the state of Nature which necessarily follow from every man's being judge in his own case, by setting up a known authority to which every one of that society may appeal upon any injury received, or controversy that may arise, and which every one of the society ought to obey. Wherever any persons are who have not such an authority to appeal to, and de-

cide any difference between them there, those persons are still in the state of Nature. And so is every absolute prince in respect of those who are under his *dominion*.

91. For he being supposed to have all, both legislative and executive, power in himself alone, there is no judge to be found, no appeal lies open to any one, who may fairly and indifferently, and with authority decide, and from whence relief and redress may be expected of any injury or inconveniency that may be suffered from him, or by his order. So that such a man, however entitled, Czar, or Grand Signior, or how you please, is as much in the state of Nature, with all under his dominion, as he is with the rest of mankind. For wherever any two men are, who have no standing rule and common judge to appeal to on earth, for the determination of controversies of right betwixt them, there they are still in the state of Nature, and under all the inconveniencies of it, with only this woeful difference to the subject, or rather slave of an absolute prince. That whereas, in the ordinary state of Nature, he has a liberty to judge of his right, according to the best of his power to maintain it; but whenever his property is invaded by the will and order of his monarch, he has not only no appeal, as those in society ought to have, but, as if he were degraded from the common state of rational creatures, is denied a liberty to judge of, or defend his right, and so is exposed to all the misery and inconveniencies that a man can fear from one, who being in the unrestrained state of Nature, is yet corrupted with flattery and armed with power.

92. For he that thinks absolute power purifies men's blood, and corrects the baseness of human nature, need read but the history of this, or any other age, to be convinced to the contrary. He that would have been insolent and injurious in the woods of America would not probably be much better on a throne, where perhaps learning and religion shall be found out to justify all that he shall do to his subjects, and the sword presently silence all those that dare question it. . . .

93. In absolute monarchies, indeed, as well as other governments of the world, the subjects

have an appeal to the law, and judges to decide any controversies, and restrain any violence that may happen betwixt the subjects themselves, one amongst another. This every one thinks necessary, and believes; he deserves to be thought a declared enemy to society and mankind who should go about to take it away. But whether this be from a true love of mankind and society, and such a charity as we owe all one to another, there is reason to doubt. For this is no more than what every man, who loves his own power, profit, or greatness, may, and naturally must do, keep those animals from hurting or destroying one another who labour and drudge only for his pleasure and advantage; and so are taken care of, not out of any love the master has for them, but love of himself, and the profit they bring him. For if it be asked what security, what fence is there in such a state against the violence and oppression of this absolute ruler, the very question can scarce be borne. They are ready to tell you that it deserves death only to ask after safety. Betwixt subject and subject, they will grant, there must be measures, laws, and judges for their mutual peace and security. But as for the ruler, he ought to be absolute, and is above all such circumstances; because he has a power to do more hurt and wrong, it is right when he does it. To ask how you may be guarded from harm or injury on that side, where the strongest hand is to do it, is presently the voice of faction and rebellion. As if when men, quitting the state of Nature, entered into society, they agreed that all of them but one should be under the restraint of laws; but that he should still retain all the liberty of the state of Nature, increased with power, and made licentious by impunity. This is to think that men are so foolish that they take care to avoid what mischiefs may be done them by polecats or foxes, but are content, nay, think it safety, to be devoured by lions.

## Chapter 8. Of the Beginning of Political Societies

95. Men being, as has been said, by nature all free, equal, and independent, no one can be put

out of this estate and subjected to the political power of another without his own consent, which is done by agreeing with other men, to join and unite into a community for their comfortable, safe, and peaceable living, one amongst another, in a secure enjoyment of their properties, and a greater security against any that are not of it. This any number of men may do, because it injures not the freedom of the rest; they are left, as they were, in the liberty of the state of Nature. When any number of men have so consented to make one community or government, they are thereby presently incorporated, and make one body politic, wherein the majority have a right to act and conclude the rest.

## Chapter 9. Of the Ends of Political Society and Government

123. If man in the state of Nature be so free as has been said, if he be absolute lord of his own person and possessions, equal to the greatest and subject to nobody, why will he part with his freedom, this empire, and subject himself to the dominion and control of any other power? To which it is obvious to answer, that though in the state of Nature he hath such a right, yet the enjoyment of it is very uncertain and constantly exposed to the invasion of others; for all being kings as much as he, every man his equal, and the greater part no strict observers of equity and justice, the enjoyment of the property he has in this state is very unsafe, very insecure. This makes him willing to quit this condition which, however free, is full of fears and continual dangers; and it is not without reason that he seeks out and is willing to join in society with others who are already united, or have a mind to unite for the mutual preservation of their lives, liberties and estates, which I call by the general name — property.

124. The great and chief end, therefore, of men uniting into commonwealths, and putting themselves under government, is the preservation of their property; to which in the state of Nature there are many things wanting. . . .

# THE PROBLEM OF POWER 3: HISTORICAL MATERIALISM AND THE CLASS STRUGGLE _____

## *Karl Marx and Historical Materialism*

Karl Marx (1818–1883) was the father of modern socialism and communism, not to mention six children (three of whom died before reaching their teens) by his long-suffering wife, Jenny. He attended university first at Bonn, then at Berlin, then finally at Jena, where he completed his doctorate in 1841. During his days at the University of Berlin he came under the influence of the Young Hegelians, followers of the philosopher G. W. F. Hegel, who had died in 1831. Marx was the editor of the *Rheinische Zeitung* (*Rhineland Daily News*) in Cologne from 1842 to 1843, after which he moved to Paris to become editor of the short-lived *Deutsch-Französische Jahrbücher* (*German-French Yearbook*) in 1843. While in Paris he met his long-time collaborator Friedrich Engels (1820–1895), a son of a wealthy factory owner in Manchester, who cowrote some of Marx's works, along with bankrolling him during hard times. Marx spent much of the 1840s trying to stay one step ahead of various European police forces, moving from Germany to Brussels, Belgium, in 1845 (where he was connected with the Communist League); to Paris during the 1848 revolution; to Germany, where he barely escaped a charge of treason thanks to his oratorical skills in the courtroom; and finally to England in 1849. He took up residence in London, using the library of the British Museum to write his most famous work, *Das Kapital* (*Capital*), volume 1 of which finally appeared in 1867 (Engels edited Volumes II and III, which appeared after Marx's death). While in England he worked for the *New York Tribune* as a foreign correspondent, eking out a living from his journalism and from handouts from Engels.

Marx's early intellectual life focused on attacks against the leading lights of German philosophy of the time, notably Hegel's idealism and the "naive" materialism of thinkers such as Ludwig Feuerbach. Marx concluded that instead of shaping society, ideas were shaped *by* society: The economic system, or "mode of production," of a given society determines what sorts of values and principles that the society in question holds dear. Therefore, a feudal society will value things such as honor and loyalty, to keep rebellious lords and peasants in line, whereas a capitalist society will value freedom and equality, to keep the workforce as large and mobile as possible, thus keeping down wages. Political power, for Marx, was merely the expression of economic power, and the state, except during times of revolutionary change, merely the "organizing committee" for the ruling class.

Further, he saw the early capitalism of his own day as inherently exploitative. At the core of capitalist production was *surplus value:* the value left over after a factory owner paid for the fixed costs of production such as wages, raw materials, machinery, and rent. The remainder was kept as profit, a profit Marx saw as won from the sweat of the workers. Tied to his idea of surplus value was that of *alienation.* Marx argued in his *Economic and Philosophical Manuscripts of 1844* (not published until the twentieth century) that workers were alienated from (1) the objects of their labor, (2) their work and thus themselves (because they spent the whole day slaving away at a power loom or assembly line, rather than fishing or writing poetry), (3) their fellow workers (they competed for jobs and higher wages), and (4) their *species being*, or human nature, which Marx argued was to "externalize" oneself in labor, but not in labor owned by others.

Marx called his system "historical materialism." In the following selection he lays out with a minimum of digression the central tenets of this system. At the foundation of society is what Marx called the *substructure*. It consisted of

1. the *means of production:* raw materials, land, water, and sources of energy
2. the *forces of production,* which convert the means of production into finished products: factories, machines, technology, and so on
3. the *social relations of production:* the social relations between the classes—who works, for how much, for whom; the organization of the economy

Rising above the substructure of a society towered its *superstructure.* This consisted of

4. *law, politics, art, philosophy, and religion:* ideological reflections of the social relations of production and the mistaken focus of idealists such as Hegel (and later Fukuyama)

Marx's basic claim is that our philosophical, religious, and moral ideas are reflections of our material conditions, usually of our class interests. They are not independent motive forces in history, as Hegel and others claimed. When economic conditions in a society undergo a radical shift and a new class assumes a leading role, eventually a political revolution will follow, installing that leading class in power. Marx predicted that at the end of history a communist revolution would ensue, abolishing private property and the oppression of one class by another.

# Preface to A Contribution to a Critique of Political Economy

## KARL MARX

THE FIRST WORK which I undertook to dispel the doubts assailing me was a critical re-examination of the Hegelian philosophy of law; the introduction to this work being published in the *Deutsch-Französische Jahrbücher*[1] issued in Paris in 1844. My inquiry led me to the conclusion that

[1] *The German-French Yearbook,* which Marx published in Paris in 1844.

neither legal relations nor political forms could be comprehended whether by themselves or on the basis of a so-called general development of the human mind, but that on the contrary they originate in the material conditions of life, the totality of which Hegel, following the example of English and French thinkers of the eighteenth century, embraces within the term "civil society"; that the anatomy of this civil society, how-

SOURCE: Karl Marx, preface to *A Contribution to a Critique of Political Economy,* trans. S. W. Ryazanskaya (1859; Moscow: Progress Publishers, 1977); retrieved from http://www.southalabama.edu/philosophy/coker/phl_348/marx_preface_to_a_contribution_to_the_critique_of_political_economy.htm.

ever, has to be sought in political economy. The study of this, which I began in Paris, I continued in Brussels, where I moved owing to an expulsion order issued by M. Guizot.[2] The general conclusion at which I arrived and which, once reached, became the guiding principle of my studies can be summarised as follows. In the social production of their existence, men inevitably enter into definite relations, which are independent of their will, namely relations of production appropriate to a given stage in the development of their material forces of production. The totality of these relations of production constitutes the economic structure of society, the real foundation, on which arises a legal and political superstructure and to which correspond definite forms of social consciousness. The mode of production of material life conditions the general process of social, political and intellectual life. It is not the consciousness of men that determines their existence, but their social existence that determines their consciousness. At a certain stage of development, the material productive forces of society come into conflict with the existing relations of production or—this merely expresses the same thing in legal terms—with the property relations within the framework of which they have operated hitherto. From forms of development of the productive forces these relations turn into their fetters. Then begins an era of social revolution. The changes in the economic foundation lead sooner or later to the transformation of the whole immense superstructure. In studying such transformations it is always necessary to distinguish between the material transformation of the eco-

[2] The Premier of France from 1847 to 1848.

nomic conditions of production, which can be determined with the precision of natural science, and the legal, political, religious, artistic or philosophic—in short, ideological forms in which men become conscious of this conflict and fight it out. Just as one does not judge an individual by what he thinks about himself, so one cannot judge such a period of transformation by its consciousness, but, on the contrary, this consciousness must be explained from the contradictions of material life, from the conflict existing between the social forces of production and the relations of production. No social order is ever destroyed before all the productive forces for which it is sufficient have been developed, and new superior relations of production never replace older ones before the material conditions for their existence have matured within the framework of the old society. Mankind thus inevitably sets itself only such tasks as it is able to solve, since closer examination will always show that the problem itself arises only when the material conditions for its solution are already present or at least in the course of formation. In broad outline, the Asiatic, ancient, feudal and modern bourgeois modes of production may be designated as epochs marking progress in the economic development of society. The bourgeois mode of production is the last antagonistic form of the social process of production—antagonistic not in the sense of individual antagonism but of an antagonism that emanates from the individuals' social conditions of existence—but the productive forces developing within bourgeois society create also the material conditions for a solution of this antagonism. The prehistory of human society accordingly closes with this social formation.

## Theory, Praxis, and the Class Struggle

Marx wasn't satisfied just to propound his theory of historical materialism as an intellectual exercise. Theory by itself wasn't good enough: One had to act on that theory, put it into *practice*. This combination of theory and practice was termed "praxis" by later Marxists. We can see Marx's call for philosophers to act on their theories, to try to change the world, quite clearly in his unpublished (at the time) brief attack on his fellow materialist Ludwig Feuerbach, who in 1841 had published a widely read, psychologically based critique of Christianity entitled *The Essence of Christianity,* the focus of some of the theses not included in the following reading. The best that a non-revolutionary materialist such as Feuerbach could do was to "passively contemplate" the civil society (i.e., economic life) around him; only the activist materialism of a thinker such as Marx himself could envision the coming of a socialized humanity as a result of revolutionary praxis.

# Theses on Feuerbach

## KARL MARX

2. THE QUESTION whether objective truth can be attributed to human thinking is not a question of theory but is a *practical* question. Man must prove the truth—i.e. the reality and power, the this-sidedness of his thinking in practice. The dispute over the reality or non-reality of thinking that is isolated from practice is a purely *scholastic* question.

3. The materialist doctrine concerning the changing of circumstances and upbringing forgets that circumstances are changed by men and that it is essential to educate the educator himself. This doctrine must, therefore, divide society into two parts, one of which is superior to society.

The coincidence of the changing of circumstances and of human activity or self-changing can be conceived and rationally understood only as revolutionary practice.

8. All social life is essentially *practical.* All mysteries which lead theory to mysticism find their rational solution in human practice and in the comprehension of this practice.

9. The highest point reached by *contemplative* materialism, that is, materialism which does not comprehend sensuousness as practical activity, is contemplation of single individuals and of civil society.

10. The standpoint of the old materialism is civil society; the standpoint of the new is human society, or social humanity.

11. The philosophers have only *interpreted* the world, in various ways; the point is to *change* it.

SOURCE: *Marx/Engels Selected Works,* vol. 1 (1845; Moscow: Progress Publishers, 1969), pp. 13–15 (italics added); originally from Friedrich Engels, appendix in *Ludwig Feuerbach and the End of Classical German Philosophy,* trans. W. Lough (1886).

## *Marx and Engels on Revolution*

The most famous attempt at revolutionary praxis by Marx and his collaborator Engels came in 1848. Europe was engulfed in the fire of revolution: Angry mobs were marching in Paris, Berlin, Vienna, and other European capitals, demanding liberal or socialist reforms to the corrupt regimes in power in their native countries. The Parisian rebels even managed to evict their liberal king, Louis Philippe, from his throne and thus establish the Second Republic. Marx and Engels took up their pens to write what is probably the most famous political pamphlet in human history, *The Communist Manifesto,* to give theoretical structure to the struggle against the old regimes of Europe by the various parties of the Left, notably by the socialist parties of Germany. In it they saw all of human history as a struggle between classes, borrowing from the German philosopher G. W. F. Hegel the idea of the "dialectical" development of history, which Hegel applied to ideas and which Marx and Engels applied to economic classes and their struggle for political power. Thus, Marx's historical materialism is also sometimes called "dialectical materialism." Hegel believed that he could discern in the development of philosophical ideas a continual struggle between opposites, between a "thesis" and an "antithesis," which was eventually resolved by these opposites being combined into a "synthesis" that contained elements of both the thesis and the antithesis. And then the struggle starts over again as the old synthesis becomes a new thesis, opposed by a new antithesis. This idea can be expressed as follows:

THESIS 1 VS. ANTITHESIS 1 → SYNTHESIS 1 . . .
SYNTHESIS 1 becomes THESIS 2 VS. ANTITHESIS 2 → SYNTHESIS 2 . . .
and so on to the arrival of the Absolute Spirit (Hegel) or the End of History (Fukuyama)

Turning Hegel's ideas upside down, Marx saw in history a dialectical struggle not between ideas such as freedom and slavery but between economic classes. Instead of seeing "civil society" or economic life as determined by great ideas, as Hegel did, Marx saw our great ideas as determined by economic life, thereby reversing the causal relationship between the "base" and the "superstructure" of society. Using this new understanding of social relations as his guide, Marx divided history into five stages:

1. Primitive Communism: A society where hunting and gathering or basic agriculture dominates and most land and goods are held in common.
2. Ancient Slave Societies (Greece and Rome): Aristocrats and free men rule over an underclass of slaves, who do all the hard work.
3. Feudalism: The king and his lords oppress the peasants, who toil on the land.
4. Capitalism: The bourgeois (capitalist) factory owners and financiers control the means of production, oppressing the proletariat (workers).
5. Future Communism: Class differences and private property disappear, and everyone works for the good of society.

Marx and Engels hoped that the revolutions of 1848 heralded the coming of the last stage of history, that of communism, although the first major communist revolution didn't occur until 1917 in Russia, thirty-four years after Marx's death, led by Lenin, an important Marxist theorist in his own right. The end of history had to wait for another day, as across Europe the socialist rebels were crushed. But the document that heralded their hopes for a socialist utopia, *The Communist Manifesto,* still burns with the same revolutionary fervor it did a century and a half ago.

# Manifesto of the Communist Party

## KARL MARX AND FRIEDRICH ENGELS

A SPECTRE is haunting Europe—the spectre of communism. All the powers of old Europe have entered into a holy alliance to exorcise this spectre: Pope and Tsar, Metternich[1] and Guizot, French Radicals and German police-spies.

Where is the party in opposition that has not been decried as communistic by its opponents in power? Where is the opposition that has not hurled back the branding reproach of communism, against the more advanced opposition parties, as well as against its reactionary adversaries?

Two things result from this fact:

1. Communism is already acknowledged by all European powers to be itself a power.
2. It is high time that Communists should openly, in the face of the whole world, publish their views, their aims, their tendencies, and meet this nursery tale of the spectre of communism with a manifesto of the party itself.

To this end, Communists of various nationalities have assembled in London and sketched the following manifesto, to be published in the English, French, German, Italian, Flemish and Danish languages.

## 1. Bourgeois and Proletarians[2]

The history of all hitherto existing society is the history of class struggles. Freeman and slave, patrician and plebian, lord and serf, guild-master and journeyman, in a word, oppressor and oppressed, stood in constant opposition to one another, carried on an uninterrupted, now hidden, now open fight, a fight that each time ended, either in a revolutionary reconstitution of society at large, or in the common ruin of the contending classes.

In the earlier epochs of history, we find almost everywhere a complicated arrangement of society into various orders, a manifold gradation of social rank. In ancient Rome we have patricians, knights, plebians, slaves; in the Middle Ages, feudal lords, vassals, guild-masters, journeymen, apprentices, serfs; in almost all of these classes, again, subordinate gradations.

The modern bourgeois society that has sprouted from the ruins of feudal society has not done away with class antagonisms. It has but established new classes, new conditions of oppression, new forms of struggle in place of the old ones.

Our epoch, the epoch of the bourgeoisie, possesses, however, this distinct feature: it has simplified class antagonisms. Society as a whole is more and more splitting up into two great hostile camps, into two great classes directly facing each other—bourgeoisie and proletariat.

From the serfs of the Middle Ages sprang the chartered burghers of the earliest towns. From these burgesses the first elements of the bourgeoisie were developed.

The discovery of America, the rounding of the Cape, opened up fresh ground for the rising bourgeoisie. The East-Indian and Chinese markets, the colonisation of America, trade with the colonies, the increase in the means of exchange and in commodities generally, gave to commerce, to navigation, to industry, an impulse never be-

[1] A prominent Austrian statesman.

[2] By bourgeoisie is meant the class of modern capitalists, owners of the means of social production and employers of wage labor. By proletariat, the class of modern wage laborers who, having no means of production of their own, are reduced to selling their labor power in order to live. [*Note by Engels to 1888 English edition*]

SOURCE: Karl Marx and Friedrich Engels, *Manifesto of the Communist Party* (1888), trans. Samuel Moore, assisted by Friedrich Engels (several historical notes and pt. 3 deleted); retrieved from World History Archives: http://www.hartford-hwp.com/archives/26/176.html.

fore known, and thereby, to the revolutionary element in the tottering feudal society, a rapid development.

The feudal system of industry, in which industrial production was monopolized by closed guilds, now no longer suffices for the growing wants of the new markets. The manufacturing system took its place. The guild-masters were pushed aside by the manufacturing middle class; division of labor between the different corporate guilds vanished in the face of division of labor in each single workshop.

Meantime, the markets kept ever growing, the demand ever rising. Even manufacturers no longer sufficed. Thereupon, steam and machinery revolutionized industrial production. The place of manufacture was taken by the giant, MODERN INDUSTRY; the place of the industrial middle class by industrial millionaires, the leaders of the whole industrial armies, the modern bourgeois.

Modern industry has established the world market, for which the discovery of America paved the way. This market has given an immense development to commerce, to navigation, to communication by land. This development has, in turn, reacted on the extension of industry; and in proportion as industry, commerce, navigation, railways extended, in the same proportion the bourgeoisie developed, increased its capital, and pushed into the background every class handed down from the Middle Ages.

We see, therefore, how the modern bourgeoisie is itself the product of a long course of development, of a series of revolutions in the modes of production and of exchange.

Each step in the development of the bourgeoisie was accompanied by a corresponding political advance in that class. An oppressed class under the sway of the feudal nobility, an armed and self-governing association in the medieval commune:[3] here independent urban republic (as in Italy and Germany); there taxable "third estate" of the monarchy (as in France); afterward, in the period of manufacturing proper, serving either the semi-feudal or the absolute monarchy as a counterpoise against the nobility, and, in fact, cornerstone of the great monarchies in general—the bourgeoisie has at last, since the establishment of Modern Industry and of the world market, conquered for itself, in the modern representative state, exclusive political sway. The executive of the modern state is but a committee for managing the common affairs of the whole bourgeoisie.

The bourgeoisie, historically, has played a most revolutionary part.

The bourgeoisie, wherever it has got the upper hand, has put an end to all feudal, patriarchal, idyllic relations. It has pitilessly torn asunder the motley feudal ties that bound man to his "natural superiors," and has left no other nexus between man and man than naked self-interest, than callous "cash payment." It has drowned out the most heavenly ecstasies of religious fervor, of chivalrous enthusiasm, of philistine sentimentalism, in the icy water of egotistical calculation. It has resolved personal worth into exchange value, and in place of the numberless indefeasible chartered freedoms, has set up that single, unconscionable freedom—Free Trade. In one word, for exploitation, veiled by religious and political illusions, it has substituted naked, shameless, direct, brutal exploitation.

The bourgeoisie has stripped of its halo every occupation hitherto honored and looked up to with reverent awe. It has converted the physician, the lawyer, the priest, the poet, the man of science, into its paid wage laborers.

The bourgeoisie has torn away from the family its sentimental veil, and has reduced the family relation into a mere money relation.

---

[3] This was the name given their urban communities by the townsmen of Italy and France, after they had purchased or conquered their initial rights of self-government from their feudal lords. [*Engels: 1890 German edition*] "Commune" was the name taken in France by the nascent towns even before they had conquered from their feudal lords and masters local self-government and political rights as the "Third Estate." Generally speaking, for the economical development of the bourgeoisie, England is here taken as the typical country, for its political development, France. [*Engels: 1888 English edition*]

The bourgeoisie has disclosed how it came to pass that the brutal display of vigor in the Middle Ages, which reactionaries so much admire, found its fitting complement in the most slothful indolence. It has been the first to show what man's activity can bring about. It has accomplished wonders far surpassing Egyptian pyramids, Roman aqueducts, and Gothic cathedrals; it has conducted expeditions that put in the shade all former exoduses of nations and crusades.

The bourgeoisie cannot exist without constantly revolutionizing the instruments of production, and thereby the relations of production, and with them the whole relations of society. Conservation of the old modes of production in unaltered form, was, on the contrary, the first condition of existence for all earlier industrial classes. Constant revolutionizing of production, uninterrupted disturbance of all social conditions, everlasting uncertainty and agitation distinguish the bourgeois epoch from all earlier ones. All fixed, fast frozen relations, with their train of ancient and venerable prejudices and opinions, are swept away, all new-formed ones become antiquated before they can ossify. All that is solid melts into air, all that is holy is profaned, and man is at last compelled to face with sober senses his real condition of life and his relations with his kind.

The need of a constantly expanding market for its products chases the bourgeoisie over the entire surface of the globe. It must nestle everywhere, settle everywhere, establish connections everywhere.

The bourgeoisie has, through its exploitation of the world market, given a cosmopolitan character to production and consumption in every country. To the great chagrin of reactionaries, it has drawn from under the feet of industry the national ground on which it stood. All old-established national industries have been destroyed or are daily being destroyed. They are dislodged by new industries, whose introduction becomes a life and death question for all civilized nations, by industries that no longer work up indigenous raw material, but raw material drawn from the remotest zones; industries whose products are consumed, not only at home, but in every quarter of the globe. In place of the old wants, satisfied by the production of the country, we find new wants, requiring for their satisfaction the products of distant lands and climes. In place of the old local and national seclusion and self-sufficiency, we have intercourse in every direction, universal inter-dependence of nations. And as in material, so also in intellectual production. The intellectual creations of individual nations become common property. National one-sidedness and narrow-mindedness become more and more impossible, and from the numerous national and local literatures, there arises a world literature.

The bourgeoisie, by the rapid improvement of all instruments of production, by the immensely facilitated means of communication, draws all, even the most barbarian, nations into civilization. The cheap prices of commodities are the heavy artillery with which it forces the barbarians' intensely obstinate hatred of foreigners to capitulate. It compels all nations, on pain of extinction, to adopt the bourgeois mode of production; it compels them to introduce what it calls civilization into their midst, i.e., to become bourgeois themselves. In one word, it creates a world after its own image.

The bourgeoisie has subjected the country to the rule of the towns. It has created enormous cities, has greatly increased the urban population as compared with the rural, and has thus rescued a considerable part of the population from the idiocy of rural life. Just as it has made the country dependent on the towns, so it has made barbarian and semi-barbarian countries dependent on the civilized ones, nations of peasants on nations of bourgeois, the East on the West.

The bourgeoisie keeps more and more doing away with the scattered state of the population, of the means of production, and of property. It has agglomerated population, centralized the means of production, and has concentrated property in a few hands. The necessary consequence of this was political centralization. Independent, or but loosely connected provinces, with separate interests, laws, governments, and systems of taxation, became lumped together into one nation, with one government, one code of laws, one national class interest, one frontier, and one customs tariff.

The bourgeoisie, during its rule of scarce one hundred years, has created more massive and more colossal productive forces than have all preceding generations together. Subjection of nature's forces to man, machinery, application of chemistry to industry and agriculture, steam navigation, railways, electric telegraphs, clearing of whole continents for cultivation, canalization or rivers, whole populations conjured out of the ground—what earlier century had even a presentiment that such productive forces slumbered in the lap of social labor?

We see then: the means of production and of exchange, on whose foundation the bourgeoisie built itself up, were generated in feudal society. At a certain stage in the development of these means of production and of exchange, the conditions under which feudal society produced and exchanged, the feudal organization of agriculture and manufacturing industry, in one word, the feudal relations of property became no longer compatible with the already developed productive forces; they became so many fetters. They had to be burst asunder; they were burst asunder.

Into their place stepped free competition, accompanied by a social and political constitution adapted in it, and the economic and political sway of the bourgeois class.

A similar movement is going on before our own eyes. Modern bourgeois society, with its relations of production, of exchange and of property, a society that has conjured up such gigantic means of production and of exchange, is like the sorcerer who is no longer able to control the powers of the nether world whom he has called up by his spells. For many a decade past, the history of industry and commerce is but the history of the revolt of modern productive forces against

modern conditions of production, against the property relations that are the conditions for the existence of the bourgeois and of its rule. It is enough to mention the commercial crises that, by their periodical return, put the existence of the entire bourgeois society on its trial, each time more threateningly. In these crises, a great part not only of the existing products, but also of the previously created productive forces, are periodically destroyed. In these crises, there breaks out an epidemic that, in all earlier epochs, would have seemed an absurdity—the epidemic of over-production. Society suddenly finds itself put back into a state of momentary barbarism; it appears as if a famine, a universal war of devastation, had cut off the supply of every means of subsistence; industry and commerce seem to be destroyed. And why? Because there is too much civilization, too much means of subsistence, too much industry, too much commerce. The productive forces at the disposal of society no longer tend to further the development of the conditions of bourgeois property; on the contrary, they have become too powerful for these conditions, by which they are fettered, and so soon as they overcome these fetters, they bring disorder into the whole of bourgeois society, endanger the existence of bourgeois property. The conditions of bourgeois society are too narrow to comprise the wealth created by them. And how does the bourgeoisie get over these crises? On the one hand, by enforced destruction of a mass of productive forces; on the other, by the conquest of new markets, and by the more thorough exploitation of the old ones. That is to say, by paving the way for more extensive and more destructive crises, and by diminishing the means whereby crises are prevented.

The weapons with which the bourgeoisie felled feudalism to the ground are now turned against the bourgeoisie itself.

But not only has the bourgeoisie forged the weapons that bring death to itself; it has also called into existence the men who are to wield those weapons—the modern working class—the proletarians.

In proportion as the bourgeoisie, i.e., capital, is developed, in the same proportion is the proletariat, the modern working class, developed—a class of laborers, who live only so long as they find work, and who find work only so long as their labor increases capital. These laborers, who must sell themselves piecemeal, are a commodity, like every other article of commerce, and are consequently exposed to all the vicissitudes of competition, to all the fluctuations of the market.

Owing to the extensive use of machinery, and to the division of labor, the work of the proletarians has lost all individual character, and, consequently, all charm for the workman. He becomes an appendage of the machine, and it is only the most simple, most monotonous, and most easily acquired knack, that is required of him. Hence, the cost of production of a workman is restricted, almost entirely, to the means of subsistence that he requires for maintenance, and for the propagation of his race. But the price of a commodity, and therefore also of labor, is equal to its cost of production. In proportion, therefore, as the repulsiveness of the work increases, the wage decreases. What is more, in proportion as the use of machinery and division of labor increases, in the same proportion the burden of toil also increases, whether by prolongation of the working hours, by the increase of the work exacted in a given time, or by increased speed of machinery, etc.

Modern industry has converted the little workshop of the patriarchal master into the great factory of the industrial capitalist. Masses of laborers, crowded into the factory, are organized like soldiers. As privates of the industrial army, they are placed under the command of a perfect hierarchy of officers and sergeants. Not only are they slaves of the bourgeois class, and of the bourgeois state; they are daily and hourly enslaved by the machine, by the overlooker, and, above all, in the individual bourgeois manufacturer himself. The more openly this despotism proclaims gain to be its end and aim, the more petty, the more hateful and the more embittering it is.

The less the skill and exertion of strength implied in manual labor, in other words, the more modern industry becomes developed, the more is the labor of men superseded by that of women. Differences of age and sex have no longer any distinctive social validity for the working class. All are instruments of labor, more or less expensive to use, according to their age and sex.

No sooner is the exploitation of the laborer by the manufacturer, so far at an end, that he receives his wages in cash, than he is set upon by the other portion of the bourgeoisie, the landlord, the shopkeeper, the pawnbroker, etc.

The lower strata of the middle class—the small tradespeople, shopkeepers, and retired tradesmen generally, the handicraftsmen and peasants—all these sink gradually into the proletariat, partly because their diminutive capital does not suffice for the scale on which Modern Industry is carried on, and is swamped in the competition with the large capitalists, partly because their specialized skill is rendered worthless by new methods of production. Thus, the proletariat is recruited from all classes of the population.

The proletariat goes through various stages of development. With its birth begins its struggle with the bourgeoisie. At first, the contest is carried on by individual laborers, then by the work of people of a factory, then by the operative of one trade, in one locality, against the individual bourgeois who directly exploits them. They direct their attacks not against the bourgeois condition of production, but against the instruments of production themselves; they destroy imported wares that compete with their labor, they smash to pieces machinery, they set factories ablaze, they seek to restore by force the vanished status of the workman of the Middle Ages.

At this stage, the laborers still form an incoherent mass scattered over the whole country, and broken up by their mutual competition. If anywhere they unite to form more compact bodies, this is not yet the consequence of their own active union, but of the union of the bourgeoisie, which class, in order to attain its own political ends, is compelled to set the whole proletariat in motion, and is moreover yet, for a time, able to do so. At this stage, therefore, the proletarians do not fight their enemies, but the enemies of their enemies, the remnants of absolute monarchy, the landowners, the non-industrial bourgeois, the petty bourgeois. Thus, the whole historical movement is concentrated in the hands of the bourgeoisie; every victory so obtained is a victory for the bourgeoisie.

But with the development of industry, the proletariat not only increases in number; it becomes concentrated in greater masses, its strength grows, and it feels that strength more. The various interests and conditions of life within the ranks of the proletariat are more and more equalized, in proportion as machinery obliterates all distinctions of labor, and nearly everywhere reduces wages to the same low level. The growing competition among the bourgeois, and the resulting commercial crises, make the wages of the workers ever more fluctuating. The increasing improvement of machinery, ever more rapidly developing, makes their livelihood more and more precarious; the collisions between individual workmen and individual bourgeois take more and more the character of collisions between two classes. Thereupon, the workers begin to form combinations (trade unions) against the bourgeois; they club together in order to keep up the rate of wages; they found permanent associations in order to make provision beforehand for these occasional revolts. Here and there, the contest breaks out into riots.

Now and then the workers are victorious, but only for a time. The real fruit of their battles lie not in the immediate result, but in the ever expanding union of the workers. This union is helped on by the improved means of communication that are created by Modern Industry, and that place the workers of different localities in contact with one another. It was just this contact that was needed to centralize the numerous local struggles, all of the same character, into one national struggle between classes. But every class struggle is a political struggle. And that union, to attain which the burghers of the Middle Ages, with their miserable highways, required centuries, the modern proletarian, thanks to railways, achieve in a few years.

This organization of the proletarians into a class, and, consequently, into a political party, is continually being upset again by the competition between the workers themselves. But it ever rises up again, stronger, firmer, mightier. It compels legislative recognition of particular interests of the workers, by taking advantage of the divisions among the bourgeoisie itself. Thus, the Ten-Hours Bill in England was carried.

Altogether, collisions between the classes of the old society further in many ways the course of development of the proletariat. The bourgeoisie finds itself involved in a constant battle. At first with the aristocracy; later on, with those portions of the bourgeoisie itself, whose interests have become antagonistic to the progress of industry; at all times, with the bourgeoisie of foreign countries. In all these battles, it sees itself compelled to appeal to the proletariat, to ask for help, and thus to drag it into the political arena. The bourgeoisie itself, therefore, supplies the proletariat with its own elements of political and general education, in other words, it furnishes the proletariat with weapons for fighting the bourgeoisie.

Further, as we have already seen, entire sections of the ruling class are, by the advance of industry, precipitated into the proletariat, or are at least threatened in their conditions of existence. These also supply the proletariat with fresh elements of enlightenment and progress.

Finally, in times when the class struggle nears the decisive hour, the progress of dissolution going on within the ruling class, in fact within the whole range of old society, assumes such a violent, glaring character, that a small section of the ruling class cuts itself adrift, and joins the revolutionary class, the class that holds the future in its hands. Just as, therefore, at an earlier period, a section of the nobility went over to the bourgeoisie, so now a portion of the bourgeoisie goes over to the proletariat, and in particular, a portion of the bourgeois ideologists, who have raised themselves to the level of comprehending theoretically the historical movement as a whole.

Of all the classes that stand face to face with the bourgeoisie today, the proletariat alone is a genuinely revolutionary class. The other classes decay and finally disappear in the face of Modern Industry; the proletariat is its special and essential product.

The lower middle class, the small manufacturer, the shopkeeper, the artisan, the peasant, all these fight against the bourgeoisie, to save from extinction their existence as fractions of the middle class. They are therefore not revolutionary, but conservative. Nay, more, they are reactionary, for they try to roll back the wheel of history. If, by chance, they are revolutionary, they are only so in view of their impending transfer into the proletariat; they thus defend not their present, but their future interests; they desert their own standpoint to place themselves at that of the proletariat.

The "dangerous class," the social scum, that passively rotting mass thrown off by the lowest layers of the old society, may, here and there, be swept into the movement by a proletarian revolution; its conditions of life, however, prepare it far more for the part of a bribed tool of reactionary intrigue.

In the condition of the proletariat, those of old society at large are already virtually swamped. The proletarian is without property; his relation to his wife and children has no longer anything in common with the bourgeois family relations; modern industry labor, modern subjection to capital, the same in England as in France, in America as in Germany, has stripped him of every trace of national character. Law, morality, religion, are to him so many bourgeois prejudices, behind which lurk in ambush just as many bourgeois interests.

All the preceding classes that got the upper hand sought to fortify their already acquired status by subjecting society at large to their conditions of appropriation. The proletarians cannot become masters of the productive forces of society, except by abolishing their own previous mode of appropriation, and thereby also every other previous mode of appropriation. They have nothing of their own to secure and to fortify; their mission is to destroy all previous securities for, and insurances of, individual property.

All previous historical movements were movements of minorities, or in the interest of minorities. The proletarian movement is the self-conscious, independent movement of the immense majority, in the interest of the immense majority. The proletariat, the lowest stratum of our present society, cannot stir, cannot raise itself up, without the whole superincumbent strata of official society being sprung into the air.

Though not in substance, yet in form, the struggle of the proletariat with the bourgeoisie is at first a national struggle. The proletariat of each country must, of course, first of all settle matters with its own bourgeoisie.

In depicting the most general phases of the development of the proletariat, we traced the more or less veiled civil war, raging within existing society, up to the point where that war breaks out into open revolution, and where the violent overthrow of the bourgeoisie lays the foundation for the sway of the proletariat.

Hitherto, every form of society has been based, as we have already seen, on the antagonism of oppressing and oppressed classes. But in order to oppress a class, certain conditions must be assured to it under which it can, at least, continue its slavish existence. The serf, in the period of serfdom, raised himself to membership in the commune, just as the petty bourgeois, under the yoke of the feudal absolutism, managed to develop into a bourgeois. The modern laborer, on the contrary, instead of rising with the process of industry, sinks deeper and deeper below the conditions of existence of his own class. He becomes a pauper, and pauperism develops more rapidly than population and wealth. And here it becomes evident that the bourgeoisie is unfit any longer to be the ruling class in society, and to impose its conditions of existence upon society as an overriding law. It is unfit to rule because it is incompetent to assure an existence to its slave within his slavery, because it cannot help letting him sink into such a state, that it has to feed him, instead of being fed by him. Society can no longer live under this bourgeoisie, in other words, its existence is no longer compatible with society.

The essential conditions for the existence and for the sway of the bourgeois class is the formation and augmentation of capital; the condition for capital is wage labor. Wage labor rests exclusively on competition between the laborers. The advance of industry, whose involuntary promoter is the bourgeoisie, replaces the isolation of the laborers, due to competition, by the revolutionary combination, due to association. The development of Modern Industry, therefore, cuts from under its feet the very foundation on which the bourgeoisie produces and appropriates products. What the bourgeoisie therefore produces, above all, are its own grave-diggers. Its fall and the victory of the proletariat are equally inevitable.

## 2. Proletarians and Communists

In what relation do the Communists stand to the proletarians as a whole?

The Communists do not form a separate party opposed to the other working-class parties.

They have no interests separate and apart from those of the proletariat as a whole.

They do not set up any sectarian principles of their own, by which to shape and mold the proletarian movement.

The Communists are distinguished from the other working-class parties by this only:

(1) In the national struggles of the proletarians of the different countries, they point out and bring to the front the common interests of the entire proletariat, independently of all nationality.

(2) In the various stages of development which the struggle of the working class against the bourgeoisie has to pass through, they always and everywhere represent the interests of the movement as a whole.

The Communists, therefore, are on the one hand practically, the most advanced and resolute section of the working-class parties of every country, that section which pushes forward all others; on the other hand, theoretically, they have over the great mass of the proletariat the advantage of clearly understanding the lines of march, the conditions, and the ultimate general results of the proletarian movement.

The immediate aim of the Communists is the same as that of all other proletarian parties: Formation of the proletariat into a class, overthrow of the bourgeois supremacy, conquest of political power by the proletariat.

The theoretical conclusions of the Communists are in no way based on ideas or principles that have been invented, or discovered, by this or that would-be universal reformer.

They merely express, in general terms, actual relations springing from an existing class struggle, from a historical movement going on under our very eyes. The abolition of existing property relations is not at all a distinctive feature of communism.

All property relations in the past have continually been subject to historical change consequent upon the change in historical conditions.

The French Revolution, for example, abolished feudal property in favor of bourgeois property.

The distinguishing feature of communism is not the abolition of property generally, but the abolition of bourgeois property. But modern bourgeois private property is the final and most complete expression of the system of producing and appropriating products that is based on class antagonisms, on the exploitation of the many by the few.

In this sense, the theory of the Communists may be summed up in the single sentence: Abolition of private property.

We Communists have been reproached with the desire of abolishing the right of personally acquiring property as the fruit of a man's own labor, which property is alleged to be the groundwork of all personal freedom, activity and independence.

Hard-won, self-acquired, self-earned property! Do you mean the property of petty artisan and of the small peasant, a form of property that preceded the bourgeois form? There is no need to abolish that; the development of industry has to a great extent already destroyed it, and is still destroying it daily.

Or do you mean the modern bourgeois private property?

But does wage labor create any property for the laborer? Not a bit. It creates capital, i.e., that kind of property which exploits wage labor, and which cannot increase except upon conditions of begetting a new supply of wage labor for fresh exploitation. Property, in its present form, is based on the antagonism of capital and wage labor. Let us examine both sides of this antagonism.

To be a capitalist, is to have not only a purely personal, but a social STATUS in production. Capital is a collective product, and only by the united action of many members, nay, in the last resort, only by the united action of all members of society, can it be set in motion.

Capital is therefore not only personal; it is a social power.

When, therefore, capital is converted into common property, into the property of all members of society, personal property is not thereby transformed into social property. It is only the social character of the property that is changed. It loses its class character.

Let us now take wage labor.

The average price of wage labor is the minimum wage, i.e., that quantum of the means of subsistence which is absolutely requisite to keep the laborer in bare existence as a laborer. What, therefore, the wage laborer appropriates by means of his labor merely suffices to prolong and reproduce a bare existence. We by no means intend to abolish this personal appropriation of the products of labor, an appropriation that is made for the maintenance and reproduction of human life, and that leaves no surplus wherewith to command the labor of others. All that we want to do away with is the miserable character of this appropriation, under which the laborer lives merely to increase capital, and is allowed to live only in so far as the interest of the ruling class requires it.

In bourgeois society, living labor is but a means to increase accumulated labor. In com-munist society, accumulated labor is but a means to widen, to enrich, to promote the existence of the laborer.

In bourgeois society, therefore, the past dominates the present; in communist society, the present dominates the past. In bourgeois society, capital is independent and has individuality, while the living person is dependent and has no individuality.

And the abolition of this state of things is called by the bourgeois, abolition of individuality and freedom! And rightly so. The abolition of bourgeois individuality, bourgeois independence, and bourgeois freedom is undoubtedly aimed at.

By freedom is meant, under the present bourgeois conditions of production, free trade, free selling and buying.

But if selling and buying disappears, free selling and buying disappears also. This talk about free selling and buying, and all the other "brave words" of our bourgeois about freedom in general, have a meaning, if any, only in contrast with restricted selling and buying, with the fettered traders of the Middle Ages, but have no meaning when opposed to the communist abolition of buying and selling, or the bourgeois conditions of production, and of the bourgeoisie itself.

You are horrified at our intending to do away with private property. But in your existing society, private property is already done away with for nine-tenths of the population; its existence for the few is solely due to its non-existence in the hands of those nine-tenths. You reproach us, therefore, with intending to do away with a form of property, the necessary condition for whose existence is the non-existence of any property for the immense majority of society.

In one word, you reproach us with intending to do away with your property. Precisely so; that is just what we intend.

From the moment when labor can no longer be converted into capital, money, or rent, into a social power capable of being monopolized, i.e., from the moment when individual property can no longer be transformed into bourgeois property, into capital, from that moment, you say, individuality vanishes.

You must, therefore, confess that by "individual" you mean no other person than the bourgeois, than the middle-class owner of property. This person must, indeed, be swept out of the way, and made impossible.

Communism deprives no man of the power to appropriate the products of society; all that it does is to deprive him of the power to subjugate the labor of others by means of such appropriations.

It has been objected that upon the abolition of private property, all work will cease, and universal laziness will overtake us.

According to this, bourgeois society ought long ago to have gone to the dogs through sheer idleness; for those who acquire anything, do not work. The whole of this objection is but another expression of the tautology: There can no longer be any wage labor when there is no longer any capital.

All objections urged against the communistic mode of producing and appropriating material products, have, in the same way, been urged against the communistic mode of producing and appropriating intellectual products. Just as to the bourgeois, the disappearance of class property is the disappearance of production itself, so the disappearance of class culture is to him identical with the disappearance of all culture.

That culture, the loss of which he laments, is, for the enormous majority, a mere training to act as a machine.

But don't wrangle with us so long as you apply, to our intended abolition of bourgeois property, the standard of your bourgeois notions of freedom, culture, law, etc. Your very ideas are but the outgrowth of the conditions of your bourgeois production and bourgeois property, just as your jurisprudence is but the will of your class made into a law for all, a will whose essential character and direction are determined by the economical conditions of existence of your class.

The selfish misconception that induces you to transform into eternal laws of nature and of reason the social forms stringing from your present mode of production and form of property—historical relations that rise and disappear in the progress of production—this misconception you share with every ruling class that has preceded you. What you see clearly in the case of ancient property, what you admit in the case of feudal property, you are of course forbidden to admit in the case of your own bourgeois form of property.

Abolition of the family! Even the most radical flare up at this infamous proposal of the Communists.

On what foundation is the present family, the bourgeois family, based? On capital, on private gain. In its completely developed form, this family exists only among the bourgeoisie. But this state of things finds its complement in the practical absence of the family among proletarians, and in public prostitution.

The bourgeois family will vanish as a matter of course when its complement vanishes, and both will vanish with the vanishing of capital.

Do you charge us with wanting to stop the exploitation of children by their parents? To this crime we plead guilty.

But, you say, we destroy the most hallowed of relations, when we replace home education by social.

And your education! Is not that also social, and determined by the social conditions under which you educate, by the intervention direct or indirect, of society, by means of schools, etc.? The Communists have not intended the intervention of society in education; they do but seek to alter the character of that intervention, and to rescue education from the influence of the ruling class.

The bourgeois claptrap about the family and education, about the hallowed correlation of parents and child, becomes all the more disgusting, the more, by the action of Modern Industry, all the family ties among the proletarians are torn asunder, and their children transformed into simple articles of commerce and instruments of labor.

But you Communists would introduce community of women, screams the bourgeoisie in chorus.

The bourgeois sees his wife a mere instrument of production. He hears that the instruments of production are to be exploited in common, and, naturally, can come to no other conclusion that the lot of being common to all will likewise fall to the women.

He has not even a suspicion that the real point aimed at is to do away with the status of women as mere instruments of production.

For the rest, nothing is more ridiculous than the virtuous indignation of our bourgeois at the community of women which, they pretend, is to be openly and officially established by the Communists. The Communists have no need to introduce free love; it has existed almost from time immemorial.

Our bourgeois, not content with having wives and daughters of their proletarians at their disposal, not to speak of common prostitutes, take the greatest pleasure in seducing each other's wives.

Bourgeois marriage is, in reality, a system of wives in common and thus, at the most, what the Communists might possibly be reproached with is that they desire to introduce, in substitution for a hypocritically concealed, an openly legalized system of free love. For the rest, it is self-evident that the abolition of the present system of production must bring with it the abolition of free love springing from that system, i.e., of prostitution both public and private.

The Communists are further reproached with desiring to abolish countries and nationality.

The working men have no country. We cannot take from them what they have not got. Since the proletariat must first of all acquire political supremacy, must rise to be the leading class of the nation, must constitute itself *the* nation, it is, so far, itself national, though not in the bourgeois sense of the word.

National differences and antagonism between peoples are daily more and more vanishing, owing to the development of the bourgeoisie, to freedom of commerce, to the world market, to uniformity in the mode of production and in the conditions of life corresponding thereto.

The supremacy of the proletariat will cause them to vanish still faster. United action of the leading civilized countries at least is one of the first conditions for the emancipation of the proletariat.

In proportion as the exploitation of one individual by another will also be put an end to, the exploitation of one nation by another will also be put an end to. In proportion as the antagonism between classes within the nation vanishes, the hostility of one nation to another will come to an end.

The charges against communism made from a religious, a philosophical and, generally, from an ideological standpoint, are not deserving of serious examination.

Does it require deep intuition to comprehend that man's ideas, views, and conception, in one word, man's consciousness, changes with every change in the conditions of his material existence, in his social relations and in his social life?

What else does the history of ideas prove, than that intellectual production changes its character in proportion as material production is changed? The ruling ideas of each age have ever been the ideas of its ruling class.

When people speak of the ideas that revolutionize society, they do but express that fact that within the old society the elements of a new one have been created, and that the dissolution of the old ideas keeps even pace with the dissolution of the old conditions of existence.

When the ancient world was in its last throes, the ancient religions were overcome by Christianity. When Christian ideas succumbed in the eighteenth century to rationalist ideas, feudal society fought its death battle with the then revolutionary bourgeoisie. The ideas of religious liberty and freedom of conscience merely gave expression to the sway of free competition within the domain of knowledge.

"Undoubtedly," it will be said, "religious, moral, philosophical, and juridicial ideas have been modified in the course of historical development. But religion, morality, philosophy, political science, and law, constantly survived this change."

"There are, besides, eternal truths, such as Freedom, Justice, etc., that are common to all states of society. But communism abolishes eternal truths, it abolishes all religion, and all morality, instead of constituting them on a new basis; it therefore acts in contradiction to all past historical experience."

What does this accusation reduce itself to? The history of all past society has consisted in the development of class antagonisms, antagonisms that assumed different forms at different epochs.

But whatever form they may have taken, one fact is common to all past ages, viz., the exploitation of one part of society by the other. No wonder, then, that the social consciousness of past ages, despite all the multiplicity and variety it displays, moves within certain common forms, or general ideas, which cannot completely vanish except with the total disappearance of class antagonisms.

The communist revolution is the most radical rupture with traditional relations; no wonder that its development involved the most radical rupture with traditional ideas.

But let us have done with the bourgeois objections to communism. We have seen above that the first step in the revolution by the working class is to raise the proletariat to the position of ruling class to win the battle of democracy.

The proletariat will use its political supremacy to wrest, by degree, all capital from the bourgeoisie, to centralize all instruments of production in the hands of the state, i.e., of the proletariat organized as the ruling class; and to increase the total productive forces as rapidly as possible.

Of course, in the beginning, this cannot be effected except by means of despotic inroads on the rights of property, and on the conditions of bourgeois production; by means of measures, therefore, which appear economically insufficient and untenable, but which, in the course of the movement, outstrip themselves, necessitate further inroads upon the old social order, and are unavoidable as a means of entirely revolutionizing the mode of production.

These measures will, of course, be different in different countries.

Nevertheless, in most advanced countries, the following will be pretty generally applicable.

1. Abolition of property in land and application of all rents of land to public purposes.
2. A heavy progressive or graduated income tax.
3. Abolition of all rights of inheritance.
4. Confiscation of the property of all emigrants and rebels.
5. Centralization of credit in the banks of the state, by means of a national bank with state capital and an exclusive monopoly.
6. Centralization of the means of communication and transport in the hands of the state.
7. Extension of factories and instruments of production owned by the state; the bringing into cultivation of waste lands, and the improvement of the soil generally in accordance with a common plan.
8. Equal obligation of all to work. Establishment of industrial armies, especially for agriculture.
9. Combination of agriculture with manufacturing industries; gradual abolition of all the distinction between town and country by a more equable distribution of the populace over the country.
10. Free education for all children in public schools. Abolition of children's factory labor in its present form. Combination of education with industrial production, etc.

When, in the course of development, class distinctions have disappeared, and all production has been concentrated in the hands of a vast association of the whole nation, the public power will lose its political character. Political power, properly so called, is merely the organized power of one class for oppressing another. If the proletariat during its contest with the bourgeoisie is compelled, by the force of circumstances, to organize itself as a class; if, by means of a revolution, it makes itself the ruling class, and, as such, sweeps away by force the old conditions of production, then it will, along with these conditions, have swept away the conditions for the existence of class antagonisms and of classes generally, and will thereby have abolished its own supremacy as a class.

In place of the old bourgeois society, with its classes and class antagonisms, we shall have an association in which the free development of each is the condition for the free development of all.

[Section 3 consists of a series of polemical attacks on "reactionary," "bourgeois," and "utopian" socialism, and is omitted—ED.]

## 4. Position of the Communists in Relation to the Various Existing Opposition Parties

Section 2 has made clear the relations of the Communists to the existing working-class parties, such as the Chartists in England and the Agrarian Reformers in America.

The Communists fight for the attainment of the immediate aims, for the enforcement of the momentary interests of the working class; but in the movement of the present, they also represent and take care of the future of that movement. In France, the Communists ally with the Social Democrats[4] against the conservative and radical bourgeoisie, reserving, however, the right to take up a critical position in regard to phases and illusions traditionally handed down from the Great Revolution.

In Switzerland, they support the Radicals, without losing sight of the fact that this party consists of antagonistic elements, partly of Democratic Socialists, in the French sense, partly of radical bourgeois.

In Poland, they support the party that insists on an agrarian revolution as the prime condition

for national emancipation, that party which fomented the insurrection of Krakow in 1846.

In Germany, they fight with the bourgeoisie whenever it acts in a revolutionary way, against the absolute monarchy, the feudal squirearchy, and the petty-bourgeoisie.

But they never cease, for a single instant, to instill into the working class the clearest possible recognition of the hostile antagonism between bourgeoisie and proletariat, in order that the German workers may straightway use, as so many weapons against the bourgeoisie, the social and political conditions that the bourgeoisie must necessarily introduce along with its supremacy, and in order that, after the fall of the reactionary classes in Germany, the fight against the bourgeoisie itself may immediately begin.

The Communists turn their attention chiefly to Germany, because that country is on the eve of a bourgeois revolution that is bound to be carried out under more advanced conditions of European civilization and with a much more developed proletariat than that of England was in the seventeenth, and France in the eighteenth century, and because the bourgeois revolution in Germany will be but the prelude to an immediately following proletarian revolution.

In short, the Communists everywhere support every revolutionary movement against the existing social and political order of things.

In all these movements, they bring to the front, as the leading question in each, the property question, no matter what its degree of development at the time.

Finally, they labor everywhere for the union and agreement of the democratic parties of all countries.

The Communists disdain to conceal their views and aims. They openly declare that their ends can be attained only by the forcible overthrow of all existing social conditions. Let the ruling classes tremble at a communist revolution. The proletarians have nothing to lose but their chains. They have a world to win.

Working men of all countries, unite!

---

[4] [*NOTE by Engels to 1888 English edition:* The party then represented in Parliament by Ledru-Rollin, in literature by Louis Blanc (1811–82), in the daily press by the *Réforme.* The name of Social-Democracy signifies, with these its inventors, a section of the Democratic or Republican Party more or less tinged with socialism.]

# THE LIBERAL DEBATE ON FREEDOM AND JUSTICE _____

## *Mill on Liberty of Thought and Action*

John Stuart Mill (1806–1873) was the son of the Scottish utilitarian philosopher James Mill, a close associate of Jeremy Bentham, the English founder of radical utilitarianism. Educated by his father in the utilitarian philosophy of Bentham from a young age, James Mill seemed to have used an early version of B. F. Skinner's behaviorism to give his son an early education. Little John Stuart was learning Greek by the age of three, Latin by eight, and by fourteen had had his head crammed full with a rigorous education in history, politics, philosophy, languages, and the Greek and Roman classics. Mill was a sensitive youth who was never allowed to go out and play with his chums, but brilliant all the same.

Mill started to work for the East India Company at the age of seventeen and had a nervous breakdown at twenty, perhaps due to the intellectual force-feeding of his early education, as some scholars have suggested. For this and other reasons, he turned away from Bentham's radical utilitarianism, with its pleasure-pain calculus, to a wider view of human motivations, gaining insights from British Romantic poets and essayists such as Samuel Taylor Coleridge (one of the two seminal minds of the age, along with Bentham, according to Mill) and Thomas Carlyle. The young Mill befriended Mrs. Harriet Taylor, the friendship being both a source of much gossip to the wagging tongues of the day and of intellectual inspiration for Mill's later liberalism, notably his feminist views. He married Harriet after her husband died in 1851. He was also briefly a member of Parliament, from 1865 to 1868.

Epistemologically, he was an empiricist who believed that knowledge came from the senses, and, as we've already seen in the ethics chapter, a moderate utilitarian, who believed that the point of life was to pursue qualitatively refined pleasures (i.e., going to the opera is better than attending a mud-wrestling match). Happiness was the sole human goal worthy of consideration. Yet not all forms of happiness were equal—it's better to be an unhappy Socrates than a happy pig, as Mill himself noted.

His principal works in the field of political theory were *Principles of Political Economy* (1848), *On Liberty* (1859), *Representative Government* (1861), and *The Subjection of Women* (1869). In *On Liberty* (excerpts of which follow), Mill argues against the tyranny of the majority, which he feared would overcome minority opinion in liberal democracies, and for a maximum of liberty of thought and expression, up to the point where that liberty *concretely* harmed the freedom of others, which Mill thought wasn't a common occurrence (merely hurting someone's feelings didn't count; whereas yelling "fire" in a crowded theater when there was no fire would).

Mill argued for the freedom of expression on a wide scale in order to encourage what he saw as a quickly disappearing individuality in modern societies. When we hear someone express an opinion, there are three possible relations between that opinion and the truth. Yet in each case Mill thinks our reaction to it should be the same. We should obviously tolerate new ideas that are true—it would be shear stubbornness on our part to stick to false ideas. Second, a new idea might be only *partially* right, in which case we should admit our fallibility and try to reduce our ignorance by listening to it. Yet Mill even argued that we should tolerate opinions that are clearly "wrong," for these have the virtue of forcing the "right" people to defend their view and thereby sharpen their wits. In the current context, how do we know that Nazism and fascism are morally bankrupt? We can listen to living fascists expound their ideas, and then we can point out their inconsistencies or foolishness.

Mill thought we should allow "experiments of living" to give free scope to the development of the human character. Further, he was suspicious of the state acting in a paternalistic way—he gave the examples of the Russia and China of his own day, which he took to be backward societies in which the government absorbed pretty well all the best minds of the nation into government bureaucracies, thereby stifling individual initiative and enterprise.

His work is still used today by both the Left and Right to defend freedom of thought. He was used in the twentieth century by right-wing libertarians to attack government "interference" in the economy, and by countercultural groups, such as the hippies of the 1960s, to defend their alternative lifestyles. His basic idea—that we should have as much freedom as is compatible with the freedom of others—has become a founding principle of modern liberal democracies. What this principle actually means in practice is another question. Yet, all in all, *On Liberty* represents a vigorous defense of freedom of thought, independence of character, and personal eccentricity against the dull tyranny of the conformist majority we find in all societies.

# On Liberty

## JOHN STUART MILL

### Chapter 1. Introductory

The subject of this Essay is not the so-called Liberty of the Will, so unfortunately opposed to the misnamed doctrine of Philosophical Necessity; but Civil, or Social Liberty: the nature and limits of the power which can be legitimately exercised by society over the individual. . . .

The struggle between Liberty and Authority is the most conspicuous feature in the portions of history with which we are earliest familiar, particularly in that of Greece, Rome, and England. But in old times this contest was between subjects, or some classes of subjects, and the government. By liberty, was meant protection against the tyranny

of the political rulers. The rulers were conceived (except in some of the popular governments of Greece) as in a necessarily antagonistic position to the people whom they ruled. They consisted of a governing One, or a governing tribe or caste, who derived their authority from inheritance or conquest; who, at all events, did not hold it at the pleasure of the governed, and whose supremacy men did not venture, perhaps did not desire, to contest, whatever precautions might be taken against its oppressive exercise. Their power was regarded as necessary, but also as highly dangerous; as a weapon which they would attempt to use against their subjects, no less than against ex-

SOURCE: John Stuart Mill, *On Liberty* (1859), chaps. 1–3; retrieved from Serendipity Web site: http://www.serendipity.li/jsmill/on_lib.htm, based on Internet Wiretap online edition scanned from Harvard Classics, vol. 25 (P.F. Collier & Son, 1909).

ternal enemies. To prevent the weaker members of the community from being preyed upon by innumerable vultures, it was needful that there should be an animal of prey stronger than the rest, commissioned to keep them down. But as the king of the vultures would be no less bent upon preying upon the flock than any of the minor harpies, it was indispensable to be in a perpetual attitude of defence against his beak and claws. The aim, therefore, of patriots, was to set limits to the power which the ruler should be suffered to exercise over the community; and this limitation was what they meant by liberty. . . .

A time, however, came in the progress of human affairs, when men ceased to think it a necessity of nature that their governors should be an independent power, opposed in interest to themselves. It appeared to them much better that the various magistrates of the State should be their tenants or delegates, revocable at their pleasure. In that way alone, it seemed, could they have complete security that the powers of government would never be abused to their disadvantage. By degrees, this new demand for elective and temporary rulers became the prominent object of the exertions of the popular party, wherever any such party existed; and superseded, to a considerable extent, the previous efforts to limit the power of rulers. As the struggle proceeded for making the ruling power emanate from the periodical choice of the ruled, some persons began to think that too much importance had been attached to the limitation of the power itself. *That* (it might seem) was a resource against rulers whose interests were habitually opposed to those of the people. What was now wanted was, that the rulers should be identified with the people; that their interest and will should be the interest and will of the nation. The nation did not need to be protected against its own will. There was no fear of its tyrannizing over itself. Let the rulers be effectually responsible to it, promptly removable by it, and it could afford to trust them with power of which it could itself dictate the use to be made. Their power was but the nation's own power, concentrated, and in a form

convenient for exercise. This mode of thought, or rather perhaps of feeling, was common among the last generation of European liberalism, in the Continental section of which, it still apparently predominates. . . .

But, in political and philosophical theories, as well as in persons, success discloses faults and infirmities which failure might have concealed from observation. The notion, that the people have no need to limit their power over themselves, might seem axiomatic, when popular government was a thing only dreamed about, or read of as having existed at some distant period of the past. Neither was that notion necessarily disturbed by such temporary aberrations as those of the French Revolution, the worst of which were the work of an usurping few, and which, in any case, belonged, not to the permanent working of popular institutions, but to a sudden and convulsive outbreak against monarchical and aristocratic despotism. In time, however, a democratic republic came to occupy a large portion of the earth's surface, and made itself felt as one of the most powerful members of the community of nations; and elective and responsible government became subject to the observations and criticisms which wait upon a great existing fact. It was now perceived that such phrases as "self-government," and "the power of the people over themselves," do not express the true state of the case. The "people" who exercise the power, are not always the same people with those over whom it is exercised, and the "self-government" spoken of, is not the government of each by himself, but of each by all the rest. The will of the people, moreover, practically means, the will of the most numerous or the most active *part* of the people; the majority, or those who succeed in making themselves accepted as the majority; the people, consequently, *may* desire to oppress a part of their number; and precautions are as much needed against this, as against any other abuse of power. The limitation, therefore, of the power of government over individuals, loses none of its importance when the holders of power are regularly accountable to the community, that is, to the strongest party therein. This view of things, recommending itself equally to the intelligence of thinkers and to the inclination of those important classes in European society to whose real or supposed interests democracy is adverse, has had no difficulty in establishing itself; and in political speculations "the tyranny of the majority" is now generally included among the evils against which society requires to be on its guard.

Like other tyrannies, the tyranny of the majority was at first, and is still vulgarly, held in dread, chiefly as operating through the acts of the public authorities. But reflecting persons perceived that when society is itself the tyrant— society collectively, over the separate individuals who compose it—its means of tyrannizing are not restricted to the acts which it may do by the hands of its political functionaries. Society can and does execute its own mandates: and if it issues wrong mandates instead of right, or any mandates at all in things with which it ought not to meddle, it practises a social tyranny more formidable than many kinds of political oppression, since, though not usually upheld by such extreme penalties, it leaves fewer means of escape, penetrating much more deeply into the details of life, and enslaving the soul itself. Protection, therefore, against the tyranny of the magistrate is not enough; there needs protection also against the tyranny of the prevailing opinion and feeling; against the tendency of society to impose, by other means than civil penalties, its own ideas and practices as rules of conduct on those who dissent from them; to fetter the development, and, if possible, prevent the formation, of any individuality not in harmony with its ways, and compel all characters to fashion themselves upon the model of its own. There is a limit to the legitimate interference of collective opinion with individual independence; and to find that limit, and maintain it against encroachment, is as indispensable to a good condition of human affairs, as protection against political despotism. . . .

The object of this Essay is to assert one very simple principle, as entitled to govern absolutely the dealings of society with the individual in the way of compulsion and control, whether the means used be physical force in the form of legal penalties, or the moral coercion of public opinion. That principle is, that the sole end for which mankind are warranted, individually or collectively in interfering with the liberty of action of any of their number, is self-protection. That the only purpose for which power can be rightfully exercised over any member of a civilized community, against his will, is to prevent harm to others. His own good, either physical or moral, is not a sufficient warrant. He cannot rightfully be compelled to do or forbear because it will be better for him to do so, because it will make him happier, because, in the opinions of others, to do so would be wise, or even right. These are good reasons for remonstrating with him, or reasoning with him, or persuading him, or entreating him, but not for compelling him, or visiting him with any evil, in case he do otherwise. To justify that, the conduct from which it is desired to deter him must be calculated to produce evil to some one else. The only part of the conduct of any one, for which he is amenable to society, is that which concerns others. In the part which merely concerns himself, his independence is, of right, absolute. Over himself, over his own body and mind, the individual is sovereign. . . .

. . . There is a sphere of action in which society, as distinguished from the individual, has, if any, only an indirect interest; comprehending all that portion of a person's life and conduct which affects only himself, or, if it also affects others, only with their free, voluntary, and undeceived consent and participation. When I say only himself, I mean directly, and in the first instance: for whatever affects himself, may affect others through himself; and the objection which may be grounded on this contingency, will receive consideration in the sequel. This, then, is the appropriate region of human liberty. It comprises, first, the inward domain of consciousness; demanding liberty of conscience, in the most comprehensive sense; liberty of thought and feeling; absolute freedom of opinion and sentiment on all subjects, practical or speculative, scientific, moral, or theological. The liberty of expressing and publishing opinions may seem to fall under a different principle, since it belongs to that part of the conduct of an individual which concerns other people; but, being almost of as much importance as the liberty of thought itself, and resting in great part on the same reasons, is practically inseparable from it. Secondly, the principle requires liberty of tastes and pursuits; of framing the plan of our life to suit our own character; of doing as we like, subject to such consequences as may follow; without impediment from our fellow-creatures, so long as what we do does not harm them even though they should think our conduct foolish, perverse, or wrong. Thirdly, from this liberty of each individual, follows the liberty, within the same limits, of combination among individuals; freedom to unite, for any purpose not involving harm to others: the persons combining being supposed to be of full age, and not forced or deceived.

No society in which these liberties are not, on the whole, respected, is free, whatever may be its form of government; and none is completely free in which they do not exist absolute and unqualified. The only freedom which deserves the name, is that of pursuing our own good in our own way, so long as we do not attempt to deprive others of theirs, or impede their efforts to obtain it. Each is the proper guardian of his own health, whether bodily, *or* mental and spiritual. Mankind are greater gainers by suffering each other to live as seems good to themselves, than by compelling each to live as seems good to the rest. . . .

## Chapter 2. Of the Liberty of Thought and Discussion

. . . If all mankind minus one, were of one opinion, and only one person were of the contrary opinion, mankind would be no more justified in silencing that one person, than he, if he had the power, would be justified in silencing mankind. Were an opinion a personal possession of no value except to the owner; if to be obstructed in the enjoyment of it were simply a private injury, it would make some difference whether the injury was inflicted only on a few persons or on many. But the peculiar evil of silencing the expression of an opinion is, that it is robbing the human race; posterity as well as the existing generation; those who dissent from the opinion, still more than those who hold it. If the opinion is right, they are deprived of the opportunity of exchanging error for truth: if wrong, they lose, what is almost as great a benefit, the clearer perception and livelier impression of truth, produced by its collision with error.

It is necessary to consider separately these two hypotheses, each of which has a distinct branch of the argument corresponding to it. We can never be sure that the opinion we are endeavouring to stifle is a false opinion; and if we were sure, stifling it would be an evil still.

First: the opinion which it is attempted to suppress by authority may possibly be true. Those who desire to suppress it, of course deny its truth; but they are not infallible. They have no authority to decide the question for all mankind, and exclude every other person from the means of judging. To refuse a hearing to an opinion, because they are sure that it is false, is to assume that *their* certainty is the same thing as *absolute* certainty. All silencing of discussion is an assumption of infallibility . . . it is as evident in itself as any amount of argument can make it, that ages are no more infallible than individuals; every age having held many opinions which subsequent ages have deemed not only false but absurd; and it is as certain that many opinions, now general, will be rejected by future ages, as it is that many, once general, are rejected by the present. . . .

A theory which maintains that truth may justifiably be persecuted because persecution cannot possibly do it any harm, cannot be charged with being intentionally hostile to the reception of new truth. . . . But, indeed, the dictum that truth always triumphs over persecution, is one of those pleasant falsehoods which men repeat after one another till they pass into commonplaces, but which all experience refutes. History teems with instances of truth put down by persecution.

If not suppressed forever, it may be thrown back for centuries. . . . It is a piece of idle sentimentality that truth, merely as truth, has any inherent power denied to error, of prevailing against the dungeon and the stake. Men are not more zealous for truth than they often are for error, and a sufficient application of legal or even of social penalties will generally succeed in stopping the propagation of either. The real advantage which truth has, consists in this, that when an opinion is true, it may be extinguished once, twice, or many times, but in the course of ages there will generally be found persons to rediscover it, until some one of its reappearances falls on a time when from favourable circumstances it escapes persecution until it has made such head as to withstand all subsequent attempts to suppress it. . . .

. . . Who can compute what the world loses in the multitude of promising intellects combined with timid characters, who dare not follow out any bold, vigorous, independent train of thought, lest it should land them in something which would admit of being considered irreligious or immoral? . . . No one can be a great thinker who does not recognize, that as a thinker it is his first duty to follow his intellect to whatever conclusions it may lead. Truth gains more even by the errors of one who, with due study and preparation, thinks for himself, than by the true opinions of those who only hold them because they do not suffer themselves to think. . . .

Let us now pass to the second division of the argument, and dismissing the supposition that any of the received opinions may be false, let us assume them to be true, and examine into the worth of the manner in which they are likely to be held, when their truth is not freely and openly canvassed. However unwillingly a person who has a strong opinion may admit the possibility that his opinion may be false, he ought to be moved by the consideration that however true it may be, if it is not fully, frequently, and fearlessly discussed, it will be held as a dead dogma, not a living truth.

There is a class of persons (happily not quite so numerous as formerly) who think it enough if a person assents undoubtingly to what they think true, though he has no knowledge whatever of the grounds of the opinion, and could not make a tenable defence of it against the most superficial objections. Such persons, if they can once get their creed taught from authority, naturally think that no good, and some harm, comes of its being allowed to be questioned. Where their influence prevails, they make it nearly impossible for the received opinion to be rejected wisely and considerately, though it may still be rejected rashly and ignorantly; for to shut out discussion entirely is seldom possible, and when it once gets in, beliefs not grounded on conviction are apt to give way before the slightest semblance of an argument. Waiving, however, this possibility—assuming that the true opinion abides in the mind, but abides as a prejudice, a belief independent of, and proof against, argument—this is not the way in which truth ought to be held by a rational being. This is not knowing the truth. Truth, thus held, is but one superstition the more, accidentally clinging to the words which enunciate a truth. . . .

It still remains to speak of one of the principal causes which make diversity of opinion advantageous, and will continue to do so until mankind shall have entered a stage of intellectual advancement which at present seems at an incalculable distance. We have hitherto considered only two possibilities: that the received opinion may be false, and some other opinion, consequently, true; or that, the received opinion being true, a conflict with the opposite error is essential to a clear apprehension and deep feeling of its truth. But there is a commoner case than either of these; when the conflicting doctrines, instead of being one true and the other false, share the truth between them; and the nonconforming opinion is needed to supply the remainder of the truth, of which the received doctrine embodies only a part. . . .

Truth, in the great practical concerns of life, is so much a question of the reconciling and combining of opposites, that very few have minds sufficiently capacious and impartial to make the adjustment with an approach to correctness, and it has to be made by the rough process of a struggle between combatants fighting under hostile banners. On any of the great open questions just enumerated, if either of the two opinions has a better claim than the other, not merely to be tolerated, but to be encouraged and countenanced, it is the one which happens at the particular time and place to be in a minority. . . .

We have now recognized the necessity to the mental well-being of mankind (on which all their other well-being depends) of freedom of opinion, and freedom of the expression of opinion, on four distinct grounds; which we will now briefly recapitulate.

First, if any opinion is compelled to silence, that opinion may, for aught we can certainly know, be true. To deny this is to assume our own infallibility.

Secondly, though the silenced opinion be an error, it may, and very commonly does, contain a portion of truth; and since the general or prevailing opinion on any object is rarely or never the whole truth, it is only by the collision of adverse opinions that the remainder of the truth has any chance of being supplied.

Thirdly, even if the received opinion be not only true, but the whole truth; unless it is suffered to be, and actually is, vigorously and earnestly contested, it will, by most of those who receive it, be held in the manner of a prejudice, with little comprehension or feeling of its rational grounds. And not only this, but, fourthly, the meaning of the doctrine itself will be in danger of being lost, or enfeebled, and deprived of its vital effect on the character and conduct: the dogma becoming a mere formal profession, inefficacious for good, but cumbering the ground, and preventing the growth of any real and heartfelt conviction, from reason or personal experience. . . .

## Chapter 3. On Individuality, as One of the Elements of Well Being

Such being the reasons which make it imperative that human beings should be free to form opinions, and to express their opinions without re-

serve; and such the baneful consequences to the intellectual, and through that to the moral nature of man, unless this liberty is either conceded, or asserted in spite of prohibition; let us next examine whether the same reasons do not require that men should be free to act upon their opinions— to carry these out in their lives, without hindrance, either physical or moral, from their fellow-men, so long as it is at their own risk and peril. . . . Acts of whatever kind, which, without justifiable cause, do harm to others, may be, and in the more important cases absolutely require to be, controlled by the unfavorable sentiments, and, when needful, by the active interference of mankind. The liberty of the individual must be thus far limited; he must not make himself a nuisance to other people. But if he refrains from molesting others in what concerns them, and merely acts according to his own inclination and judgment in things which concern himself, the same reasons which show that opinion should be free, prove also that he should be allowed, without molestation, to carry his opinions into practice at his own cost. . . . As it is useful that while mankind are imperfect there should be different opinions, so is it that there should be different experiments of living; that free scope should be given to varieties of character, short of injury to others; and that the worth of different modes of life should be proved practically, when any one thinks fit to try them. It is desirable, in short, that in things which do not primarily concern others, individuality should assert itself. Where, not the person's own character, but the traditions of customs of other people are the rule of conduct, there is wanting one of the principal ingredients of human happiness, and quite the chief ingredient of individual and social progress. . . .

It is not by wearing down into uniformity all that is individual in themselves, but by cultivating it and calling it forth, within the limits imposed by the rights and interests of others, that human beings become a noble and beautiful object of contemplation; and as the works partake the character of those who do them, by the same process human life also becomes rich, diversified, and animating, furnishing more abundant aliment to high thoughts and elevating feelings, and strengthening the tie which binds every individual to the race, by making the race infinitely better worth belonging to. In proportion to the development of his individuality, each person becomes more valuable to himself, and is therefore capable of being more valuable to others. There is a greater fullness of life about his own existence, and when there is more life in the units there is more in the mass which is composed of them. . . .

There is only too great a tendency in the best beliefs and practices to degenerate into the mechanical; and unless there were a succession of persons whose ever-recurring originality prevents the grounds of those beliefs and practices from becoming merely traditional, such dead matter would not resist the smallest shock from anything really alive, and there would be no reason why civilization should not die out, as in the Byzantine Empire. Persons of genius, it is true, are, and are always likely to be, a small minority; but in order to have them, it is necessary to preserve the soil in which they grow. Genius can only breathe freely in an *atmosphere* of freedom. . . .

In this age the mere example of nonconformity, the mere refusal to bend the knee to custom, is itself a service. Precisely because the tyranny of opinion is such as to make eccentricity a reproach, it is desirable, in order to break through that tyranny, that people should be eccentric. Eccentricity has always abounded when and where strength of character has abounded; and the amount of eccentricity in a society has generally been proportional to the amount of genius, mental vigor, and moral courage which it contained. That so few now dare to be eccentric, marks the chief danger of the time. . . .

The combination of all these causes forms so great a mass of influences hostile to Individuality, that it is not easy to see how it can stand its ground. It will do so with increasing difficulty, unless the intelligent part of the public can be made to feel its value—to see that it is good there should be differences, even though not for the better, even though, as it may appear to them, some should be for the worse. If the claims of Individuality are ever to be asserted, the time is now, while much is still wanting to complete the enforced assimilation. It is only in the earlier stages that any stand can be successfully made against the encroachment. The demand that all other people shall resemble ourselves, grows by what it feeds on. If resistance waits till life is reduced *nearly* to one uniform type, all deviations from that type will come to be considered impious, immoral, even monstrous and contrary to nature. Mankind speedily become unable to conceive diversity, when they have been for some time unaccustomed to see it.

## Wollstonecraft on the Equality of the Sexes

Mary Wollstonecraft (1759–1797), perhaps the first real feminist author, was born in London in humble circumstances but was determined to make her own way in the world, contrary to social norms of the day for her sex. In the 1780s she worked as a teacher and governess in both England and Ireland, her *Thoughts on the Education of Daughters* (1787) summarizing her conclusions on how to educate young women. Wollstonecraft thought that the traditional early education of young women in England handicapped their reason, thus preventing the full development of their personalities. In 1788 she moved to London, where she published her novel *Mary, a Fiction* that year. She also worked as a translator (she was self-taught in French and German) and did book reviews for a radical publisher. While in London, she met the anarchist William Godwin, the radical pamphleteer Tom Paine, and the poets William Blake and William Wordsworth, along with other leading thinkers and artists of the day.

Like many British writers of the age, she became wrapped up in the debate over the French Revolution that had been going on just across the English Channel since 1789. The conservative Anglo-Irish politician and thinker Edmund Burke said in his book *Reflections on the Revolution in France* (1790) that violent political changes such as the one going on in France were dangerous disruptions of the political community of the "the living, the dead, and the yet to be born." Wollstonecraft responded with her book *A Vindication of the Rights of Man* (1791), a defense of the French Revolution as a struggle for human rights. In fact, she was so enthusiastic about the revolution that she went to Paris in December 1792 to observe it from close up. Before leaving for Paris, she wrote *A Vindication of the Rights of Woman* (1792) in only six weeks. In it she extends the liberal position put forward in her *Vindication* of the previous year to argue for the rights of women, focusing once again on changing their early education as the best path to their social and political liberation.

In France she met and had a torrid affair with the American adventurer Gilbert Imlay. The affair ended in 1795 after Mary had given birth to their daughter, Fanny, and Imlay lost interest in Wollstonecraft. She had returned to England in 1795, where she twice attempted suicide because of Imlay's philandering. However, things improved for Wollstonecraft when her renewed friendship with William Godwin turned to love, and then marriage in 1797. Sadly, she died in the same year shortly after giving birth to their daughter, Mary, later to become the author of *Frankenstein* and wife of the English poet Percy Bysshe Shelley.

A major problem existed for early liberals: If we all have an equal right to basic liberties based on our status as rational beings with the power to communicate and make agreements with each other, why, at least until the early twentieth century, have women been excluded from some of these liberties? Wollstonecraft argues that women are, or can be, as rational as men but are prevented from being so by an education that keeps them in a perpetually immature state. Women of her own day were taught to dance, sing, play musical instruments, make pleasant chitchat, and look pretty in order to attract a husband, and not how to be good mothers, educators, or even self-sufficient beings (as Wollstonecraft thought they should be). Change the education of women, she said, and one will see women become just as rational as men and assume a more active role in the public world.

Overall, Wollstonecraft agreed with the general Enlightenment belief in the rational progress of the human race, although she also embodied some of the new Romantic vogue for the importance of sentiments and strong emotions in literature and life. She was also very much concerned with the need for women to attach themselves to fairly conventional notions of sexual morality, perhaps learning lessons from her own unhappy love life. Her *Vindication* is perhaps the founding document of liberal feminism, a movement we'll hear more about in the next chapter. She is very much the patron saint of the modern feminist movement.

# A Vindication of the Rights of Woman

MARY WOLLSTONECRAFT

## To M. Talleyrand-Perigord, Late Bishop of Autun[1]

. . . Contending for the rights of woman, my main argument is built on this simple principle, that if she be not prepared by education to become the companion of man, she will stop the progress of knowledge and virtue; for truth must be common to all, or it will be inefficacious with respect to its influence on general practice. And how can woman be expected to co-operate unless she knows why she ought to be virtuous? unless freedom strengthens her reason till she comprehends her duty, and see in what manner it is connected with her real good? If children are to be educated to understand the true principle of patriotism, their mother must be a patriot; and the love of mankind, from which an orderly train of virtues spring, can only be produced by considering the moral and civil interest of mankind; but the education and situation of woman at present shuts her out from such investigations. . . .

Consider—I address you as a legislator—whether, when men contend for their freedom, and to be allowed to judge for themselves respecting their own happiness, it be not inconsistent and unjust to subjugate women, even though you firmly believe that you are acting in the manner best calculated to promote their happiness? Who made man the exclusive judge, if woman partake with him of the gift of reason?

In this style argue tyrants of every denomination, from the weak king to the weak father of a family; they are all eager to crush reason, yet always assert that they usurp its throne only to be useful. Do you not act a similar part when you force all women, by denying them civil and political rights, to remain immured in their families groping in the dark? for surely, sir, you will not assert that a duty can be binding which is not founded on reason? If, indeed, this be their destination, arguments may be drawn from reason; and thus augustly supported, the more understanding women acquire, the more they will be attached to their duty—comprehending it—for unless they comprehend it, unless their morals be fixed on the same immutable principle as those of man, no authority can make them discharge it in a virtuous manner. They may be convenient slaves, but slavery will have its constant effect, degrading the master and the abject dependent. . . .

## Introduction

After considering the historic page, and viewing the living world with anxious solicitude, the most melancholy emotions of sorrowful indignation have depressed my spirits, and I have sighed when obliged to confess that either Nature has made a great difference between man and man, or that the civilisation which has hitherto taken place in the world has been very partial. I have turned over various books written on the subject of education, and patiently observed the conduct of parents and the management of schools; but what has been the result?—a profound conviction that the neglected education of my fellow-creatures is the grand source of the misery I de-

---

[1] Talleyrand (1754–1838) was the leading French diplomat during the early period of the French Revolution (1789–1792) and in the Napoleonic Wars (1799–1815). Originally the Bishop of Autun, he became active in politics once the Revolution broke out, and resigned his post in 1791. In the same year he wrote an important report on public education for the French National Assembly.

SOURCE: Mary Wollstonecraft, *A Vindication of the Rights of Woman* (1792), dedication, introduction, chaps. 1–3; retrieved from http://oregonstate.edu/instruct/phl302/texts/wollstonecraft/woman-contents.html.

plore, and that women, in particular, are rendered weak and wretched by a variety of concurring causes, originating from one hasty conclusion. The conduct and manners of women, in fact, evidently prove that their minds are not in a healthy state; for, like the flowers which are planted in too rich a soil, strength and usefulness are sacrificed to beauty; and the flaunting leaves, after having pleased a fastidious eye, fade, disregarded on the stalk, long before the season when they ought to have arrived at maturity. One cause of this barren blooming I attribute to a false system of education, gathered from the books written on this subject by men who, considering females rather as women than human creatures, have been more anxious to make them alluring mistresses than affectionate wives and rational mothers; and the understanding of the sex has been so bubbled by this specious homage, that the civilised women of the present century, with a few exceptions, are only anxious to inspire love, when they ought to cherish a nobler ambition, and by their abilities and virtues exact respect.

. . . In the government of the physical world it is observable that the female in point of strength is, in general, inferior to the male. This is the law of Nature; and it does not appear to be suspended or abrogated in favour of woman. A degree of physical superiority cannot, therefore, be denied, and it is a noble prerogative! But not content with this natural preeminence, men endeavour to sink us still lower, merely to render us alluring objects for a moment; and women, intoxicated by the adoration which men, under the influence of their senses, pay them, do not seek to obtain a durable interest in their hearts, or to become the friends of the fellow-creatures who find amusement in their society. . . .

My own sex, I hope, will excuse me, if I treat them like rational creatures, instead of flattering their *fascinating* graces, and viewing them as if they were in a state of perpetual childhood, unable to stand alone. I earnestly wish to point out in what true dignity . . . human happiness consists. I wish to persuade women to endeavour to acquire strength, both of mind and body, and to convince them that the soft phrases, susceptibil-

ity of heart, delicacy of sentiment, and refinement of taste, are almost synonymous with epithets of weakness, and that those beings who are only the objects of pity, and that kind of love which has been termed its sister, will soon become objects of contempt.

Dismissing, then, those pretty feminine phrases, which the men condescendingly use to soften our slavish dependence, and despising that weak elegancy of mind, exquisite sensibility, and sweet docility of manners, supposed to be the sexual characteristics of the weaker vessel, I wish to show that elegance is inferior to virtue, that the first object of laudable ambition is to obtain a character as a human being, regardless of the distinction of sex, and that secondary views should be brought to this simple touchstone. . . .

## Chapter 1. The Rights and Involved Duties of Mankind Considered

. . . In what does man's pre-eminence over the brute creation consist? The answer is as clear as that a half is less than the whole, in Reason.

What acquirement exalts one being above another? Virtue, we spontaneously reply.

For what purpose were the passions implanted? That man by struggling with them might attain a degree of knowledge denied to the brutes, whispers Experience.

Consequently the perfection of our nature and capability of happiness must be estimated by the degree of reason, virtue, and knowledge, that distinguish the individual, and direct the laws which bind society: and that from the exercise of reason, knowledge and virtue naturally flow, is equally undeniable, if mankind be viewed collectively. . . .

## Chapter 2. The Prevailing Opinion of a Sexual Character Discussed

To account for, and excuse the tyranny of man, many ingenious arguments have been brought forward to prove, that the two sexes, in the acquirement of virtue, ought to aim at attaining a very different character; or, to speak explicitly, women are not allowed to have sufficient strength of mind to acquire what really deserves the name of virtue. Yet it should seem, allowing them to have souls, that there is but one way appointed by Providence to lead *mankind* to either virtue or happiness.

If then women are not a swarm of ephemeron triflers, why should they be kept in ignorance under the specious name of innocence? Men complain, and with reason, of the follies and caprices of our sex, when they do not keenly satirise our headstrong passions and grovelling vices. Behold, I should answer, the natural effect of ignorance! The mind will ever be unstable that has only prejudices to rest on, and the current will run with destructive fury when there are no barriers to break its force. Women are told from their infancy, and taught by the example of their mothers, that a little knowledge of human weakness, justly termed cunning, softness of temper, *outward* obedience, and a scrupulous attention to a puerile kind of propriety, will obtain for them the protection of man; and should they be beautiful, everything else is needless, for at least twenty years of their lives. . . .

Women ought to endeavour to purify their heart; but can they do so when their uncultivated understandings make them entirely dependent on their senses for employment and amusement, when no noble pursuits set them above the little vanities of the day, or enables them to curb the wild emotions that agitate a reed, over which every passing breeze has power? To gain the affections of a virtuous man, is affectation necessary? Nature has given woman a weaker frame than man; but, to ensure her husband's affections, must a wife, who, by the exercise of her mind and body whilst she was discharging the duties of a daughter, wife, and mother, has allowed her constitution to retain its natural strength, and her nerves a healthy tone,—is she, I say, to condescend to use art, and feign a sickly delicacy, in order to secure her husband's affection? Weakness may excite tenderness, and gratify the arrogant pride of man; but the lordly caresses of a protector will not gratify a noble mind that pants for and deserves to be respected. Fondness is a poor substitute for friendship!

In a seraglio [harem], I grant, that all these arts are necessary; the epicure must have his palate tickled, or he will sink into apathy; but have women so little ambition as to be satisfied with such a condition? Can they supinely dream life away in the lap of pleasure, or the languor of weariness, rather than assert their claim to pursue reasonable pleasures, and render themselves conspicuous by practising the virtues which dignify mankind? Surely she has not an immortal soul who can loiter life away merely employed to adorn her person, that she may amuse the languid hours, and soften the cares of a fellow-creature who is willing to be enlivened by her smiles and tricks, when the serious business of life is over.

Besides, the woman who strengthens her body and exercises her mind will, by managing her family and practising various virtues, become the friend, and not the humble dependent of her husband; and if she, by possessing such substantial qualities, merit his regard, she will not find it necessary to conceal her affection, nor to pretend to an unnatural coldness of constitution to excite her husband's passions. In fact, if we revert to history, we shall find that the women who have distinguished themselves have neither been the most beautiful nor the most gentle of their sex. . . .

Noble morality! and consistent with the cautious prudence of a little soul that cannot extend its views beyond the present minute division of existence. If all the faculties of woman's mind are only to be cultivated as they respect her dependence on man; if, when a husband be obtained, she have arrived at her goal, and meanly proud rests satisfied with such a paltry crown, let her grovel contentedly, scarcely raised by her employments above the animal kingdom; but, if struggling for the prize of her high calling, she look beyond the present scene, let her cultivate her understanding without stopping to consider what character the husband may have whom she is destined to marry. Let her only determine, without being too anxious about present happiness, to acquire the qualities that ennoble a rational being, and a rough inelegant husband may shock her taste without destroying her peace of mind. She will not model her soul to suit the frailties of her companion, but to bear with them; his character may be a trial, but not an impediment to virtue. . . .

I love man as my fellow; but his sceptre, real or usurped, extends not to me, unless the reason of an individual demands my homage; and even then the submission is to reason, and not to man. In fact, the conduct of an accountable being must be regulated by the operations of its own reason; or on what foundation rests the throne of God?

It appears to me necessary to dwell on these obvious truths, because females have been insulated, as it were; and while they have been stripped of the virtues that should clothe humanity, they have been decked with artificial graces that enable them to exercise a short-lived tyranny. Love, in their bosoms, taking place of every nobler passion, their sole ambition is to be fair, to raise emotion instead of inspiring respect; and this ignoble desire, like the servility in absolute monarchies, destroys all strength of character. Liberty is the mother of virtue, and if women be, by their very constitution, slaves, and not allowed to breathe the sharp invigorating air of freedom, they must ever languish like exotics, and be reckoned beautiful flaws in nature. . . .

## Chapter 3. The Same Subject Continued

. . . I am aware that this argument would carry me further than it may be supposed I wish to go; but I follow truth, and still adhering to my first position, I will allow that bodily strength seems to give man a natural superiority over woman; and this is the only solid basis on which the superiority of the sex can be built. But I still insist that not only the virtue but the *knowledge* of the two sexes should be the same in nature, if not in degree, and that women, considered not only as moral but rational creatures, ought to endeavour to acquire human virtues (or perfections) by the same means as men, instead of being educated like a fanciful kind of *half* being—one of Rousseau's wild chimeras. . . .

Women, as well as despots, have now perhaps more power than they would have if the world, divided and subdivided into kingdoms and families, were governed by laws deduced from the exercise of reason; but in obtaining it, to carry on the comparison, their character is degraded, and licentiousness spread through the whole aggregate of society. The many become pedestal to the few. I, therefore, will venture to assert that till women are more rationally educated, the progress of human virtue and improvement in knowledge must receive continual checks. And if it be granted that woman was not created merely to gratify the appetite of man, or to be the upper servant who provides his meals and takes care of his linen, it must follow that the first care of those mothers or fathers who really attend to the education of females should be, if not to strengthen the body, at least not to destroy the constitution by mistaken notions of beauty and female excellence; nor should girls ever be allowed to imbibe the pernicious notion that a defect can, by any chemical process of reasoning, become an excellence. . . .

But should it be proved that woman is naturally weaker than man, whence does it follow that it is natural for her to labour to become still weaker than nature intended her to be? Arguments of this cast are an insult to common sense, and savour of passion. The divine right of husbands, like the divine right of kings, may, it is to be hoped, in this enlightened age, be contested without danger; and though conviction may not silence many boisterous disputants, yet, when any prevailing prejudice is attacked, the wise will consider, and leave the narrow minded to rail with thoughtless vehemence at innovation. . . .

To preserve personal beauty, woman's glory! the limbs and faculties are cramped with worse than Chinese bands, and the sedentary life which they are condemned to live, whilst boys frolic in the open air, weakens the muscles and relaxes the nerves.—As for Rousseau's[2] remarks, which have

---

[2] Jean-Jacques Rousseau (1712–1778), Wollstonecraft's principal foil in her *Vindication*, was a key *philosophe* of the French Enlightenment who championed "sensibility" over bare reason and primitive simplicity over the corrupting influences of civilized society. In his book on education, *Émile*, he argues that women should be educated in questions of taste alone, and not in rational pursuits, since they are incapable of becoming scientists or philosophers by their very nature as beings of passion.

since been echoed by several writers, that they have naturally, that is, from their birth, independent of education, a fondness for dolls, dressing, and talking—they are so puerile as not to merit a serious refutation. That a girl, condemned to sit for hours together listening to the idle chat of weak nurses, or to attend at her mother's toilet, will endeavour to join the conversation, is, indeed, very natural; and that she will imitate her mother or aunts, and amuse herself by adorning her lifeless doll, as they do in dressing her, poor innocent babe! is undoubtedly a most natural consequence. For men of the greatest abilities have seldom had sufficient strength to rise above the surrounding atmosphere; and if the pages of genius have always been blurred by the prejudices of the age, some allowance should be made for a sex, who, like kings, always see things through a false medium. . . .

Women are everywhere in this deplorable state; for, in order to preserve their innocence, as ignorance is courteously termed, truth is hidden from them, and they are made to assume an artificial character before their faculties have acquired any strength. Taught from their infancy that beauty is woman's sceptre, the mind shapes itself to the body, and roaming round its gilt cage, only seeks to adore its prison. Men have various employments and pursuits which engage their attention, and give a character to the opening mind; but women, confined to one, and having their thoughts constantly directed to the most insignificant part of themselves, seldom extend their views beyond the triumph of the hour. But were their understanding once emancipated from the slavery to which the pride and sensuality of man and their short-sighted desire, like that of dominion in tyrants, of present sway, has subjected them, we should probably read of their weaknesses with surprise. . . .

## *Rawls on the Principles of Justice*

The work with the greatest impact on political theory in the second half of the twentieth century was undoubtedly John Rawls's imposing 1971 tome, *A Theory of Justice,* the source of our reading. Rawls (1921–2002) was born in Baltimore, Maryland, and received his Ph.D. from Princeton in 1950. He taught at Harvard from 1962 until his retirement in 1991.

Rawls works within the social contract theory tradition of Hobbes, Locke, Rousseau, and Kant. But he adds a major twist to this tradition, the notion of the "veil of ignorance." Let's suppose as you're sitting around the campfire and chatting about political theory with your rational comrades in the state of nature, which Hobbes has already told us is a nasty and brutish place to be, you decide you want to sign a social contract and form a peaceful, law-governed society. Rawls says that people in such a position, to be just, are obligated to cloak their individual interests and capabilities under a "veil of ignorance": They should pretend that they don't know how rich, how beautiful, how smart, or how well connected they are, or even what sex or race they belong to. He concludes that if you put yourself in such an "original position," you have no choice but to opt for "justice as fairness," to set your society up so that it doesn't favor any one group—neither the rich, nor the beautiful, nor white people, nor men—in its political, social, and economic institutions.

Of course, for Rawls, this state of nature is only a hypothetical place—it exists only in the mind of the theorist. But it's useful all the same. From this original position and the basic concept of justice as fairness, Rawls derives two principles, which can be summarized as follows:

1. Liberty Principle: Give people as much freedom as you can, as long as it doesn't interfere with other people's freedoms. This is very similar to Mill's basic notion of liberty.
2. Equality Principle: Try to guarantee that people are treated as equally as possible. If your society is going to introduce inequalities, make sure that they are for the good of the worst off (e.g., an incentive system that rewards hard work) and that these unequal positions are open to everyone (e.g., no hereditary aristocracies based on race).

From these two basic principles Rawls lays out the theoretical groundwork for the modern liberal welfare state, one that guarantees basic rights, such as freedom of speech and the right to vote, to its citizens and that tries to take care of its least advantaged members economically through programs of public assistance, such as employment insurance and welfare.

In his second book, *Political Liberalism* (1993), Rawls takes up the question of how to deal with "cultural pluralism"—the diversity of cultures within the modern democratic societies—in a just state. *Political Liberalism* is in part a response to the critics of *A Theory of Justice*. Rawls argues that cultural pluralism in a just state requires that the state be neutral to "theories of the good," to ideas of what life is best for the citizens of that state. This "neutralist liberalism" has three basic requirements: (1) *reasonableness* in that people from different cultural backgrounds agree to work together; (2) an *overlapping consensus* of the value of the political community in question between different cultural groups (which is missing from some societies, for example, Yugoslavia in the early 1990s); (3) assurance of the citizens' *autonomy* by encouraging their use of "public reason," that is, by their actively participating in that society's political institutions.

# A Theory of Justice

## JOHN RAWLS

### 3. The Main Idea of the Theory of Justice

My aim is to present a conception of justice which generalizes and carries to a higher level of abstraction the familiar theory of the social contract as found, say, in Locke, Rousseau, and Kant.[1] In order to do this we are not to think of the original contract as one to enter a particular society or to set up a particular form of government. Rather,

---

[1] As the text suggests, I shall regard Locke's *Second Treatise of Government*, Rousseau's *The Social Contract*, and Kant's ethical works beginning with *The Foundations of the Metaphysics of Morals* as definitive of the contract tradition. For all of its greatness, Hobbes's *Leviathan* raises special problems. A general historical survey is provided by J. W. Gough, *The Social Contract*, 2nd ed. (Oxford, The Clarendon Press, 1957), and Otto Gierke, *Natural Law and the Theory of Society*, trans. with an introduction by Ernest Barker (Cambridge, The University Press, 1934). A presentation of the contract view as primarily an ethical theory is to be found in G. R. Grice,

SOURCE: John Rawls, *A Theory of Justice* (Cambridge, MA: Belknap Press, 1971), pp. 11–13, 60–62.

the guiding idea is that the principles of justice for the basic structure of society are the object of the original agreement. They are the principles that free and rational persons concerned to further their own interests would accept in an initial position of equality as defining the fundamental terms of their association. These principles are to regulate all further agreements; they specify the kinds of social cooperation that can be entered into and the forms of government that can be established. This way of regarding the principles of justice I shall call justice as fairness.

Thus we are to imagine that those who engage in social cooperation choose together, in one joint act, the principles which are to assign basic rights and duties and to determine the division of social benefits. Men are to decide in advance how they are to regulate their claims against one another and what is to be the foundation charter of their society. Just as each person must decide by rational reflection what constitutes his good, that is, the system of ends which it is rational for him to pursue, so a group of persons must decide once and for all what is to count among them as just and unjust. The choice which rational men would make in this hypothetical situation of equal liberty, assuming for the present that this choice problem has a solution, determines the principles of justice.

In justice as fairness the original position of equality corresponds to the state of nature in the traditional theory of the social contract. This original position is not, of course, thought of as an actual historical state of affairs, much less as a primitive condition of culture. It is understood as a purely hypothetical situation characterized so as to lead to a certain conception of justice.[2]

Among the essential features of this situation is that no one knows his place in society, his class position or social status, nor does any one know his fortune in the distribution of natural assets and abilities, his intelligence, strength, and the like. I shall even assume that the parties do not know their conceptions of the good or their special psychological propensities. The principles of justice are chosen behind a veil of ignorance. This ensures that no one is advantaged or disadvantaged in the choice of principles by the outcome of natural chance or the contingency of social circumstances. Since all are similarly situated and no one is able to design principles to favor his particular condition, the principles of justice are the result of a fair agreement or bargain. For given the circumstances of the original position, the symmetry of everyone's relations to each other, this initial situation is fair between individuals as moral persons, that is, as rational beings with their own ends and capable, I shall assume, of a sense of justice. The original position is, one might say, the appropriate initial status quo, and thus the fundamental agreements reached in it are fair. This explains the propriety of the name "justice as fairness": it conveys the idea that the principles of justice are agreed to in an initial situation that is fair. The name does not mean that the concepts of justice and fairness are the same, any more than the phrase "poetry as metaphor" means that the concepts of poetry and metaphor are the same.

Justice as fairness begins, as I have said, with one of the most general of all choices which persons might make together, namely, with the choice of the first principles of a conception of justice which is to regulate all subsequent criticism and reform of institutions. Then, having chosen a conception of justice, we can suppose that they are to choose a constitution and a legislature to enact laws, and so on, all in accordance with the principles of justice initially agreed upon. Our social situation is just if it is such that by this

*The Grounds of Moral Judgment* (Cambridge, The University Press, 1967). See also §19, note 30.

[2] Kant is clear that the original agreement is hypothetical. See *The Metaphysics of Morals*, pt. 1 (*Rechtslehre*), especially §§47, 52; and pt. 2 of the essay "Concerning the Common Saying: This May Be True in Theory but It Does Not Apply in Practice," in *Kant's Political Writings*, ed. Hans Reiss and trans. by H. B. Nisbet (Cambridge, The University Press, 1970), pp. 73–87. See Georges Vlachos, *La Pensée politique de Kant* (Paris, Presses Universitaires de France, 1962), pp. 326–

335; and J. G. Murphy, *Kant: The Philosophy of Right* (London, Macmillan, 1970), pp. 109–112, 133–136, for a further discussion.

sequence of hypothetical agreements we would have contracted into the general system of rules which defines it. Moreover, assuming that the original position does determine a set of principles (that is, that a particular conception of justice would be chosen), it will then be true that whenever social institutions satisfy these principles those engaged in them can say to one another that they are cooperating on terms to which they would agree if they were free and equal persons whose relations with respect to one another were fair. They could all view their arrangements as meeting the stipulations which they would acknowledge in an initial situation that embodies widely accepted and reasonable constraints on the choice of principles. The general recognition of this fact would provide the basis for a public acceptance of the corresponding principles of justice. No society can, of course, be a scheme of cooperation which men enter voluntarily in a literal sense; each person finds himself placed at birth in some particular position in some particular society, and the nature of this position materially affects his life prospects. Yet a society satisfying the principles of justice as fairness comes as close as a society can to being a voluntary scheme, for it meets the principles which free and equal persons would assent to under circumstances that are fair. In this sense its members are autonomous and the obligations they recognize self-imposed.

One feature of justice as fairness is to think of the parties in the initial situation as rational and mutually disinterested. This does not mean that the parties are egoists, that is, individuals with only certain kinds of interests, say in wealth, prestige, and domination. But they are conceived as not taking an interest in one another's interests.

## 11. Two Principles of Justice

I shall now state in a provisional form the two principles of justice that I believe would be chosen in the original position. In this section I wish to make only the most general comments, and therefore the first formulation of these principles is tentative. As we go on I shall run through several formulations and approximate step by step the final statement to be given much later. I believe that doing this allows the exposition to proceed in a natural way.

The first statement of the two principles reads as follows.

> First: each person is to have an equal right to the most extensive basic liberty compatible with a similar liberty for others.
>
> Second: social and economic inequalities are to be arranged so that they are both (a) reasonably expected to be to everyone's advantage, and (b) attached to positions and offices open to all. . . .

By way of general comment, these principles primarily apply, as I have said, to the basic structure of society. They are to govern the assignment of rights and duties and to regulate the distribution of social and economic advantages. As their formulation suggests, these principles presuppose that the social structure can be divided into two more or less distinct parts, the first principle applying to the one, the second to the other. They distinguish between those aspects of the social system that define and secure the equal liberties of citizenship and those that specify and establish social and economic inequalities. The basic liberties of citizens are, roughly speaking, political liberty (the right to vote and to be eligible for public office) together with freedom of speech and assembly; liberty of conscience and freedom of thought; freedom of the person along with the right to hold (personal) property; and freedom from arbitrary arrest and seizure as defined by the concept of the rule of law. These liberties are all required to be equal by the first principle, since citizens of a just society are to have the same basic rights.

The second principle applies, in the first approximation, to the distribution of income and wealth and to the design of organizations that make use of differences in authority and responsibility, or chains of command. While the distribution of wealth and income need not be equal, it must be to everyone's advantage, and at the same time, positions of authority and offices of command must be accessible to all. One applies the second principle by holding positions open, and then, subject to this constraint, arranges social and economic inequalities so that everyone benefits.

These principles are to be arranged in a serial order with the first principle prior to the second. This ordering means that a departure from the institutions of equal liberty required by the first principle cannot be justified by, or compensated for, by greater social and economic advantages. The distribution of wealth and income, and the hierarchies of authority, must be consistent with both the liberties of equal citizenship and equality of opportunity.

It is clear that these principles are rather specific in their content, and their acceptance rests on certain assumptions that I must eventually try to explain and justify. A theory of justice depends upon a theory of society in ways that will become evident as we proceed. For the present, it should be observed that the two principles (and this holds for all formulations) are a special case of a more general conception of justice that can be expressed as follows.

> All social values—liberty and opportunity, income and wealth, and the bases of self-respect —are to be distributed equally unless an un-

equal distribution of any, or all, of these values is to everyone's advantage.

Injustice, then, is simply inequalities that are not to the benefit of all. Of course, this conception is extremely vague and requires interpretation.

As a first step, suppose that the basic structure of society distributes certain primary goods, that is, things that every rational man is presumed to want. These goods normally have a use whatever a person's rational plan of life. For simplicity, assume that the chief primary goods at the disposition of society are rights and liberties, powers and opportunities, income and wealth. . . . These are the social primary goods. Other primary goods such as health and vigor, intelligence and imagination, are natural goods; although their possession is influenced by the basic structure, they are not so directly under its control. Imagine, then, a hypothetical initial arrangement in which all the social primary goods are equally distributed: everyone has similar rights and duties, and income and wealth are evenly shared. This state of affairs provides a benchmark for judging improvements. If certain inequalities of wealth and organizational powers would make everyone better off than in this hypothetical starting situation, then they accord with the general conception. . . .

## The Libertarian-Communitarian Debate

Lately, there's been a lively debate within democratic political theory between two more or less "liberal" camps. First are those who believe that the social contract approach to political theory is still valid and that rational actors in a state of nature would opt for minimal state interference in their lives when signing a hypothetical social contract. We can call this group "libertarian" because of their focus on liberty as the basic political good. Second is what has come to be called the "communitarian" approach, one that puts forward the idea that political association is a natural thing and that the state should play an active role in fostering the well-being of its citizens. In the reading, Malcolm Murray and Douglas Mann return to Plato's time and method by having out their political differences in the form of a dialogue between two fictitious characters, Philopolis and Eleutheria. Mann takes up the communitarian position, putting it forward through Philopolis. Murray (1960–), who teaches at the University of Prince Edward Island and works within the social contract tradition, takes up a libertarian position through the persona of Eleutheria. The dialogue might serve as a useful model for students who wish to write on controversial philosophical issues. Sometimes it's more interesting to listen to a person's point of view if a worthy opponent is heard challenging it. As Hume said at the start of his own *Dialogues concerning Natural Religion,* philosophical questions that can't be easily settled seem "to lead us naturally into the style of dialogue and conversation," and opposite sentiments, "even without any decision, afford an agreeable amusement."

# A Dialogue concerning Liberty and Community

## DOUGLAS MANN AND MALCOLM MURRAY

[*Two friends, Philopolis and Eleutheria, are wandering through the marketplace sampling the wares at the various stalls they visit.*[1] *They find themselves, oblivious to each other's presence, at a bookseller's stall, each absorbed in scanning, turning over, and reading several of the learned tomes they find on display there. Philopolis looks at, and recognizes his old friend. They return the books they were perusing to their proper places and shake hands.*]

**P:** Eleutheria! It's been a long time. But I see that you haven't lost your interest in augmenting your library.

**E:** Hello Philopolis! No, my interest remains high, though my pocket book is low. Perhaps that is just as well; I find the likelihood of reading a particular book diminishes once I put it on my shelf.

**P:** Say, I was just the other day speaking to our old colleague Nomosius about certain matters political, and he mentioned that he had run into you lately, and that you had been discussing his work on ethics and the state. Would you like

[1] The temporal and geographic location of this dialogue should not be confused with any actual time or place. Furthermore, its characters should not be mistaken for any real persons, either living or dead.

to discuss these issues over a glass of wine in the café across the square?

**E:** Delighted.

[*They cross the square to the café that Philopolis has suggested. They sit down and order two glasses of wine. Philopolis looks back across the square at the merchants talking to their customers, singing the praises of their merchandise, and exchanging their goods for money. After a moment of thought, he begins.*]

**P:** Eleutheria, look at our friend the bookseller. Look at the care he takes in arranging his books, cleaning them, explaining their merits to his customers. He's probably thinking of the declining quality of book-binding, or the orders from the publishers he has to make, or satisfying the needs of his favourite customers. And when he considers politics, maybe he thinks of the odious book tax that the government has placed on his wares, and how this affects his sales.

Look, next door to him is a lady selling shirts: she might be thinking of how cheap foreign imports have cut into her sales, of the consequent need for higher tariffs on clothing, or on how government labour regulations have caused wages to increase, and so on. Each of them re-

SOURCE: Douglas Mann and Malcolm Murray, "A Dialogue concerning Liberty and Community," *Dialogue* 40, no. 2 (spring 2001), pp. 255–277. The dialogue was edited by the authors for this volume.

gards political questions that reflect on their self-interest, and spend little time meditating on the question of the general good of the state. But don't you think that there's a need for a group of people who *do* contemplate this good, and are willing and able to act upon it? After all, isn't the community more than the sum of its parts, a rag-tag collection of individual self-interests?

**E:** Well, Philopolis, I have nothing against people who contemplate such questions as what is the Good. I certainly wouldn't want to forbid such a pursuit. Nevertheless, I am reluctant to surmise that any good can come of it. After all, what is good for one individual may be a loathsome nuisance to another. And if we want to say only one of these individuals has the right concept of the good, I would be curious to see on what basis such an argument can be made. Perhaps you can convince me otherwise, but I would suspect the appeal can be to nothing else than who thumps his chest loudest.

**P:** I shall leave the chest-thumping to the lawyers, petty politicians, and sophists in the city (for there are more than enough of *them*). But I admit that my sense of the public good may be elusive and slippery, especially to sceptics like yourself.

How can I begin? How can I give the spirit that animates the polis flesh? [*P muses for a moment, then notices a new figure walking jig-jag through the market.*] Ah . . . observe the ragged beggar across the square. He asks the bookseller for a few coins, then the shirt lady, then all the other merchants. Some give a small pittance, mainly to get rid of him, no doubt, or to make themselves feel proud as they display their charitable natures to the crowd. But they probably say to themselves, "we pity this poor fellow, but he's not OUR responsibility. We didn't make him poor. Let someone else take care of him." And in this limited sense, they're right, they're not *personally* responsible for his poverty.

But should the community simply ignore him? Refuse to dedicate some small amount of the taxes it collects to a simple shelter for him and his ilk? Maybe a few dollars to a public kitchen to save him from starvation? At minimum, *these*

*things* are part of what I mean by the public good, a good that transcends the narrowly-defined interests of the individuals who make up the community.

**E:** I apologize, Philopolis, for you have confused me. You say two things that do not appear to go together. On the one hand, helping that poor beggar is an example of a public good. On the other, you say that public goods are things that transcend the interests of the individuals who make up the community. Which is it, pray tell? Does the good the beggar receives have nothing to do with *him*, but rather something beyond him? To me this is like talk of psychic power and hocus-pocus.

Listen, if I give alms to that beggar, surely that is a good *to that beggar*. That sense of good I understand. What is this other good that I am furthering in your eyes, that transcends the individuals' conceptions of good? I have no comprehension of that sense of good.

**P:** Ah Eleutheria, you have eyes but you cannot see. I agree that your "generous" gift of alms to the beggar does *indeed* result in a "good" for that beggar, in the form of a shiny coin or two glittering in his poor benighted palm. But this sense of private good is indeed "transcended" when the community makes an effort to provide some measure of support to the beggar. Tell me Eleutheria, do you love your wife and children?

**E:** Yes, presuming we understand that "love" is a generic word for many things insufficiently catalogued.

**P:** I shall disregard the excessive care with which you've answered my question, and take it as a simple "yes." Can you say that this feeling is promoted by some sense of self-interest, or a good private to yourself? Or do you instead have a feeling that your family as a *whole* has value, and that your self-interests are somehow subsumed within this greater value? And isn't this feeling or value the same sort of feeling or value that public-spirited citizens have for their community, writ small?

**E:** I would be a fool to suggest that my love for my family is wholly self-interested, but neither is it something that subsumes my self-interest.

No marriage lasts long in which self-interest is always suppressed for the interest of the family. (I am terribly sorry to hear about your divorce, by the way, but I digress.) Being self-interested is not to be equated with selfishness. My interests may extend to my family. These are still *my* interests, though. So, first off, it is not clear that I do supplant my self-interest for something higher, such as love.

Secondly, even if I did supplant my self-interest for the interests of something beyond me, such as my family, there is little to support the conclusion that I ought to thereby supplant my self-interest for the interests of my community. My wife's telling me to buy new shoes for my children is something I will do, however grudgingly, precisely because she is my wife and they are my children. But for a community member to tell me to buy some shoes for that beggar is not something to which I feel equally committed. Either I am an unfeeling cad not to treat this neighbour in my community on equal footing with my wife (or for that matter to treat the beggar on equal terms with my children), or, as I believe, any theory that suggests I do is psychologically unsound.

Lastly, if you were to insist that I am a cad, I would still maintain that the good I am to further in my community can only be understood in terms relative to persons; not to an abstract entity devoid of any mental states. It is my wife and children that I further by buying them shoes, not the family. To see my point, try to imagine an act that harms the individual members of a family, yet furthers the interests of that family. It is inconceivable, I say. Likewise, it is incoherent to think of the greater good of the community independently of the good of the individual members of that community.

**P:** Well, you've said quite a mouthful, but at least three points strike me as flaws in your argument. Firstly, your feelings toward your wife and your neighbour don't have to be *either* equally strong *or* separated by a chasm of difference. I see the feeling of a community as a hierarchical scale, with one's family feelings being strongest, then one's feelings for one's neighbours as less

strong, and then for the community as a whole, including all the strangers contained therein, as the least strong. But that's not to say that one's communal feelings are at odds with one's feelings for one's family: ideally, they are an *extension* of those feelings.

Secondly, I certainly didn't mean to imply that the community is an abstract metaphysical entity with its own mental states. That would be patently absurd. To speak in such language is to speak purely *metaphorically*. Even the great atomist Hobbes, whom you no doubt admire, prefaced his *Leviathan* with a picture of the body of the sovereign made up of dozens of tiny individual faces, to illustrate the way that the body politic consists of some sort of communal will.

Lastly, I take your point about collective harm being no more than a sum of individual harms. But "harm" is a difficult notion to define in a consistent manner. Think of the case of a child who wants to play with his friends instead of doing his school work: if you force him to do the latter, it might seem to be a harm *to him*, yet in another sense, it might turn out to be a long-term good. So isn't this a "harm" to one member of your family, that could turn out to be a "good" to your family, at least in the future sense?

**E:** I can see that we shall be here for a while longer. Our meager glasses of this barely palatable house wine are insufficient for our task. Here comes the waiter now. Let me order a bottle.

**P:** Yes, a good idea. Maybe a nice dry white, to match your dry wit.

**E:** [*Eleutheria calls a passing waiter and makes the order.*] Let me see, then, where were we? Ah, yes . . . you have suggested that my concern for strangers in my community is an extension of the concerns I have for my close kin. These original concerns I have toward my kin, presumably, are naturally inherent in our species, or have evolved over time so that for all intents and purposes they are natural, notwithstanding child and spousal abuse—which by the way is certainly not a rare event. To model the state after the traditional family is to fashion a brow-beating hierarchical state, one which modern thinkers ought to resist. Leaving that sobering thought aside, perhaps there is no harm in conceding your point: the point, that is, that my concern for strangers is an extension of my concern for my family. That is to say, there is no harm so long as you recognize, as you have admitted, that as one proceeds further from one's family and friends, the less concern one has; especially if to act on that weakened concern is at the expense of doing good for one's family or friends. Can we agree on that?

**P:** Yes, we can. Pray continue your argument —I will let you lead me by the nose for a while, but with the hopes that you lead me somewhere worth the trip.

**E:** Very well. I am glad you are so obliging, Philopolis, although I hear that being led by the nose to water is no guarantee that one will drink. In this case, we are at the water already. You say my interests in my family and my interests in the community are of the same kind. I say, whether this is so or not hardly matters. Community spirit is such a watered down sort of kin spirit, that the appeal to the "sameness" is as idle as remarking that fat and thin people are really the same, since there is an imperceptible progression, ounce by ounce, between weighing one hundred and three hundred pounds.

Notwithstanding this point, there is a further philosophical problem. Although some people might equate their interests with the interests of the community, nothing from this observation could show that we all ought to do so.

[*The waiter arrives with a chilled bottle of char-donnay. Eleutheria samples it and gives his assent. The waiter pours the two glasses, and places the bottle in a bucket of ice. He picks something up from the floor and hands it to Eleutheria. The waiter remarks, "Sir, I beg your pardon, but is this your wallet?"*]

**E:** Yes, it is, Thank you. [*The waiter leaves.*]

**P:** You see, Eleutheria, how the waiter gives palpable evidence of the very community spirit that you so recently were inveighing against. But in any case, there are two senses of the word "should" here: "should" in the sense of a universal moral imperative, and in the sense of bringing about the best consequences. My sense of should is primarily the latter: we *should* behave towards others with some sort of community spirit, at least until they betray that spirit by behaving self-ishly, *because* it will bring about a better communal life for everybody. It's a pragmatic, not a metaphysical, "should."

I'll give you a simple example: it may be easier for me just to throw my trash over my neighbour's fence and forget about it. Of course, he'll probably start doing the same. So we might sign an implicit "contract" to toss it into the street instead, on neither of our properties. But what sort of a community would that sort of thinking leave us with? The sort of community we see in squalid urban jungles, where it's everyone for themselves. It's not a great leap to go from a simple case like trash to messier ones like pollution, crime, poverty, and the decaying physical structure of our cities, all important communal issues, issues that can't be adequately dealt with on the model of the isolated contract signer.

**E:** Ironically enough, the tragedy of the commons, or in this case the debacle of the public street, is used as an argument for privatization; not a commune. The logic is simply this: we know people will take care of things if they have a self-interest in doing so. One way of doing this is through privatization.

Don't choke, Philopolis! Personally, I do not advocate privatization—especially for things like streets and garbage pick-up. The point, though, is the recognition that we can not abandon self-interest when we create public rules. Implicitly you and your ilk recognize this when you make such convoluted efforts to convince me my self-interest really includes strangers on the street.

Let me return to one of my so-called "errors." Recall your example of the child. Have I "harmed" him by forcing him to do his home-work against his will? Or have I acted rightly, though he does not appreciate that fact? I think the latter. This in no way reveals an error in my thinking, however, since I deny the analogy that how I ought to treat my child is how society ought to treat me. If anything, your example helps my side, not works against it.

Consider the analogy closely. A parent can do things to their children because they purportedly know what is best for them. But at some point the child grows up. My parents used to change my diaper and wipe my nose, but they certainly don't do that anymore. And why is that? Because I have grown up enough to make my own decisions. I have taken on my own identity. I am no longer merely an extension of them.

So, Philopolis, to follow the analogy of paternalism, the state ought to back off when I become an autonomous adult; not continue to intercede with their notions of my good—even if they're right!

**P:** Slow down there Eleutheria. By no means do I want to suggest that we abandon self-interest when making public rules, just that we rein in self-interest with some sense of communal or public interest. This can and often does conflict with individual, private interests, as you can see in my parable of the Hobbesian system of garbage disposal.

Be that as it may, I would be very interested in your account of how a group of purely self-interested individuals could provide a series of government services for a community, especially when these services don't benefit all people equally. For example: some people might use a given park or library frequently, others not at all.

Further, I reject your equation of communalism and paternalism: not all communities, or families for that matter, need to be run on the model of a stern Pater informing his household from on high how he wants them to behave. Further, although I agree in general that adult human beings no longer need their noses wiped for them by the state, citizens who "fall through the cracks" of our society revert to a sort of "second childhood," one of dependence upon others for their well-being. Think of the unemployed, those on welfare, the crippled, the insane: wouldn't expelling these people from the bonds of community be like throwing a child of six months out of the cradle, expecting it to walk and to take care of itself?

**E:** Well, your second point is very clever indeed. As you were speaking I couldn't help thinking how glad I am to have run in to you, Philopolis, for you always entertain me with your keen insight. Some people, alas, do have wretched lives and would want our help. But you are unfair to surmise that I would wish to eject them from the bonds of the community. The question is not "Ought we help them?" for there is something sinister about even posing such a question. Nor is the question, as some suggest, "How best ought we to help them?" as if their best interests may be furthered by offering them no help whatsoever—maybe to spur them out of their sloth, fix their mental derangement, help them become well. No, the question we are interested in is: "Should we force others to help?" You'll notice, my friend, something odd here. We don't normally agree to be forced to do something we wouldn't otherwise want to do. And if we would agree, presumably it's because we desire to do it anyway—but then why agree to be forced to do it? Still, despite our wanting to help others in need, we may worry about whether our generosity will disadvantage us relative to others and worry about whether our generosity will in fact do the trick of relieving suffering. Both worries could be circumvented by imposing a rule on others to force us to be generous. Of course, we would not agree to a *carte blanche* rule since that would be too binding on us. Our desire to help others is not so strong it should supplant our desire to protect our own family—as you have already noted, Philopolis.

Similarly, it seems to me, you have misrepresented the theory of the isolated contract signer if you think individuals care nothing about garbage and crime. People can do to others anything at all so long as those others consent. This includes taxing those others to pay people to remove garbage from their streets. Would they consent? Sure they would, so long as privatized services were not more efficient, cheaper, or offered better assurance of clean streets—which I doubt. And my theory certainly justifies condemning crime, since crime is doing to others without the appropriate consent. It is clearly wrong. The prevention of crime requires a police force to help punish wrongdoers and perhaps dissuade others. Why would we give some of our tax money to help this cause, you may ask? Because it is in my interest to lessen crime. It is that simple.

Libraries and parks, unfortunately, fare less well. But I prefer, as you know, to augment my own library.

**P:** But Eleutheria, do you really claim that political philosophy must be grounded in the reasoning of an abstract, individual decision-maker? Or perhaps in terms of some sort of "ideal" decision-maker, divorced from all flesh-and-blood individuals? Which is it?

**E:** Yes and no. The matter isn't quite as cut and dried as that. Individuals are keen on satisfying their interests and they want, therefore, a political structure that best accommodates their particular interests. Unfortunately, the interests of the various individuals or groups inevitably conflict and a theory that tries to accommodate all interests is therefore a mishmash and doomed to failure. Your and my interests, for example, would be well met by a political structure that supplied free books and wine. This would hardly satisfy the interests of book and wine merchants. The solution is to back away from grounding political theory on a subjective conception of the good that any individual or group happens to hold and, instead, adopt a political structure that is as neutral as possible to these competing interests. So yes, I believe political structures must be grounded on the interests of an abstract individual rather than any particular person or group. And no, I resist that this abstract concept of an individual must be entirely alien from any actual person's interest.

**P:** If you ground all your fine notions in this "abstract individual," then what is the necessity of consulting the goals and desires of any specific concrete individual? What if that specific individual disagrees with the political arrangements that you, the grand contractarian theorist, claims he would want in his "best" or most "rational" state? Aren't you trying to have your cake and eat it?

**E:** If a political institution claims that it satisfies the interests of the people yet defines "people" in a sense entirely removed from any individual, we have a right to complain. I would be

the last person to disagree with you on that point. Does the contractarian political state that I envision succumb to such a grievous indiscretion? I wish very much, Philopolis, to disabuse you of believing the answer is yes. The question is how . . . [*While Eleutheria ruminates, Philopolis refills their wine glasses. Eleutheria hits upon his strategy and begins again . . .*] Earlier, I claimed that we need a conception of justified politics that is neutral to any one conception of the good. In order to do so, we must nevertheless appeal to something to which every reasonable person would consent. Your concern, I take it, is how we are to define "reasonable"? Instead of redirecting our otherwise profitable discussion concerning whether liberty corrupts the community to a discussion on theories of rationality, let me present to you another way of looking at the issue that will be independent of theories of rationality.

There are certain necessary conditions that any political structure must meet in order for actual individuals to pursue their various, individualized conceptions of the good. The preservation of liberty is not considered itself a good that I and my ilk are trying to ram down others' throats like stale cake. Rather, I see liberty as a necessary precondition of a social institution that best enables a heterogenous population to pursue their individual desires, their subjective renderings of the good. Although it is frightfully evident that many would wish to deny others the liberty to pursue their notion of the good (think of homophobes and anti-abortionists, for example), it seems ludicrous to suppose anyone would reject their own liberty to pursue their own notions of the good!

**P:** But sometimes what is liberty to one person is to another a restriction on their own freedom, on quite good grounds. This is especially true in a competitive society with limited resources. Everyone can't be rich. Everyone can't have political power. There will be winners and losers within all competitive schemes, and, leaving aside whether a given scheme determines winners and losers in a "fair" manner, the winners will demand the "freedom" to enjoy the spoils of their victories, while the losers will bewail the restrictions on their freedom caused by their condition of poverty or powerlessness.

**E:** My dear friend, Philopolis, you are confusing liberty with freedom. In one sense, "liberty" refers to a particular sort of basic right. In another sense, it refers to freedom, to being free, or having the pure freedom of doing what you want. And this sense of being free to do what you want may include the absence of both external and internal constraints. And should we see being free as merely having no external constraints, we may even incorporate some further notions of autonomy. The freedom to do whatever you want, however, is not a basic right. The inhabitants of a land where everyone has pure freedom, but no liberty rights, is a land where lives are brutish and short.

**P:** By no means do I wish to defend the anarchic freedom you so rightly deny. But your distinction between liberty and freedom seems at best to be a scholastic point: when we say in ordinary language "I have the liberty to do X," we are, in essence, saying "I have the freedom to do X." But no sane person imagines that political liberty means "everything is permitted." Your distinction is grammatical, not real. But the problem gets back to that one little word "reasonable" you mentioned earlier but seemed to slough off as unimportant: empires can rise and fall on the meaning of little words like this one. The reasonableness (or, dare I say it, the "rationality") of one's defence of a given definition of liberty is not based on abstract considerations of right, but on the concrete reality of your present social and economic situation. If that situation changed to a less advantageous one, or you were operating, theoretically speaking, in ignorance of your personal situation, then you would be far more likely to favour a more egalitarian set of political arrangements. Otherwise, the rich and the powerful are those most likely to favour libertarian political schemes, and to use rhetoric to seduce the poor and the powerless into joining their libertarian laments.

**E:** Beautifully put, my friend. You claim that an individual's adoption of a moral theory depends on the social-psychological circumstances in which she finds herself. I agree! Simply, I ask,

so what? That we are socially situated is really quite irrelevant, since that wouldn't alone show that we have homogenous interests. The term "social" is a catch-all phrase for a multiplicity of factors. Although there is some plausibility that any one factor will have an influence on many people, it goes against probability that many individuals will be equally affected by all the same variables together. Having heterogenous interests matters to me for two reasons. It shows there is no political community if community is defined as a group of individuals with homogenous goals, notwithstanding our common social influences. Further, it shows that a political institution that governs this heterogenous bunch must be as neutral as possible precisely because the biases you're pointing out exist. These two observations support, not damage, liberal theory.

**P:** But the individual is always situated, both in a trivial and in a more meaningful sense. In the trivial sense, my dear Eleutheria, as you sit here sipping a glass of wine, chatting about political theory with me, you are quite a different individual from the person who plays at home with his children, or who fills out forms in the workplace. But more meaningfully, you are situated in a given social and economic way, as an educated white male roughly in the middle classes. These circumstances, I claim, make it *easier* for you to adhere to a liberal contractarian position, a position that places the burden for most of what we call "public spending" on groups of freely contracting individuals, and not on the state.

**E:** It would indeed be a complaint against a liberal political structure that was biased to only one group—white males, typically. But saying a political structure predicated on liberty preservation biases the rich, white male property owners' liberty at the expense of any other group's liberty is an out and out misunderstanding. Everyone's liberty is treated equally. What you want to point out is that everyone's freedom under such a system is unequal. This is not merely a grammatical point, since the liberal structure promises only to be neutral with regards to liberty.

**P:** Let's say that I agree that there is a real distinction to be made between liberty and freedom, as you describe them. Then we would have to posit the individual's basic liberty as an *a priori* condition for the realization of freedom taken in the more positive sense. So far I agree. But here's the rub: I believe that in any decent society, liberty (i.e., the absence of impediments to my self-expression and self-development) *requires,* even on liberal grounds, some degree of positive freedom, at least in terms of a reasonable guarantee of the ground conditions of my economic well being. In your distinction between negative liberties and positive freedoms you've unearthed what is perhaps the core of our disagreement.

**E:** Well, we disagree, then, on whether negative liberty *requires* positive freedom. Perhaps we can lay this discord aside without harm.

**P:** Maybe our two basic presuppositions are irreconcilable. Let me ask you a question: why do philosophers rarely if ever change their minds concerning their basic positions, even if confronted by solid arguments? How many times has each of us encountered a professor of philos-

ophy in a public forum doggedly defending his or her point of view against all comers? It seems that even philosophers, the supposed pinnacles of rational clarity of thought, hold on to their foundational beliefs like the mangiest mutt holds on to an old bone.

**E:** Yes, I am familiar with dogged debaters, but that hardly shows the debate is a hopeless task in principle—depending merely on one's preconceived, perhaps involuntary, biases. I am afraid, however, you will think my resisting your clever argument is proof enough for your side. My only strategy left is to remain silent. Besides, our bottle is empty.

[*The two friends agree to defer the discussion for a later date. They equally share the bill and pay a handsome tip to the helpful waiter. After they leave the café, they shake hands and continue on their separate ways, idly browsing the wares of the marketplace. The waiter gathers the money from the table and remarks, "Ah, my kindness paid!"*]

## Liberalism Triumphant? Fukuyama on the End of History

Francis Fukuyama (1952–) was born in Chicago and received his Ph.D. in political science from Harvard. He did three stints as analyst at the Rand Corporation think tank between 1979 and 1996, worked briefly as a diplomat, and is presently a professor of public policy at George Mason University.

Fukuyama was a conservative foreign policy analyst and planner for the State Department when his 1989 *National Interest* article, "The End of History?" (most of which appears in the following reading), caused quite a furor in political and philosophical circles. His basic message is the "good news" that liberal capitalism won the Cold War, even though pockets of communism, the largest of which was China, remained throughout the world. The march of ideas throughout history has finally reached its end point, that of liberal democracy as the final form of human government. Humanity tried a number of alternatives to liberal democracy, the two most important ones in the twentieth century being fascism and communism. But the former was defeated in the Second World War, and the latter crumbled in the late 1980s. Even China was liberalizing by the 1980s, whereas the old Soviet leadership had finally realized the need to give up on Marxism as the basic ideology of their society (two years later the Soviet Union dissolved itself, its Eastern European allies turning away from Russian-imposed Marxism during the same period).

Fukuyama's method is pure Hegelianism (see the comments on Hegel in the introduction to Marx earlier in this chapter): What really counted in history, including intellectual history, were the "great ideas," with political and economic events being at best a reflection of these ideas. He wanted to turn Marx on his head, just as Marx had already done to Hegel. Great political-economic events such as the fall of communism were not the products of economic hardship. After all, the Soviet Union suffered from this for decades but stuck to Marxism right from Lenin's day to the early 1980s. Instead, they were caused by a great loss of faith by both the elite and the masses in the Marxist ideology that supported the Soviet state, a loss of faith reflected in this elite's acceptance of Mikhail Gorbachev's *glasnost* and *perestroika* reforms in the 1980s. Fukuyama's idealism had two major flaws, according to his critics: He ignored messy real-world counterexamples to his "end of history" hypothesis, such as the civil war in Yugoslavia in the early 1990s; and his impersonal Hegelian dialectic, such as the Marxist view of history, tended to drain individual actions of their moral significance.

Due to the fame gained from the furor surrounding this article, he received a generous grant to turn the article into a book, *The End of History and the Last Man* (1992). He expanded on his ideas in the article by connecting this period of time to the triumph of Friedrich Nietzsche's "last man," a dull and impotent creature who feels no strong drives or spiritual energies, instead satisfied to sit around and twiddle his thumbs (or engage in globalized world trade and get rich, as the case may be). The end of history, as Fukuyama makes quite clear, will be "a very sad time," even if none of us is hungry.

He continued to address the big questions in his later books, *Trust: The Social Virtues and the Creation of Prosperity* (1995), *The Great Disruption: Human Nature and the Reconstitution of the Social Order* (1999), and *Our Posthuman Future: Consequences of the Biotechnology Revolution* (2003). His interests range from international political economy to the foundations of democracy and the interconnection of history and ideas, more specifically, how our notion of human nature is connected to our political ideals.

# The End of History

## FRANCIS FUKUYAMA

IN WATCHING the flow of events over the past decade or so, it is hard to avoid the feeling that something very fundamental has happened in world history. The past year has seen a flood of articles commemorating the end of the Cold War, and the fact that "peace" seems to be breaking out in many regions of the world. Most of these analyses lack any larger conceptual framework for distinguishing between what is essential and what is contingent or accidental in world history, and are predictably superficial. If Mr. Gorbachev were ousted from the Kremlin or a new Ayatollah proclaimed the millennium from a desolate Middle Eastern capital, these same commentators would scramble to announce the rebirth of a new era of conflict.

SOURCE: Francis Fukuyama, "The End of History?" *The National Interest* 16 (summer 1989): 3–10, 14–18 (edited). Reprinted by permission of the author.

And yet, all of these people sense dimly that there is some larger process at work, a process that gives coherence and order to the daily headlines. The twentieth century saw the developed world descend into a paroxysm of ideological violence, as liberalism contended first with the remnants of absolutism, then bolshevism and fascism, and finally an updated Marxism that threatened to lead to the ultimate apocalypse of nuclear war. But the century that began full of self-confidence in the ultimate triumph of Western liberal democracy seems at its close to be returning full circle to where it started: not to an "end of ideology" or a convergence between capitalism and socialism, as earlier predicted, but to an unabashed victory of economic and political liberalism.

The triumph of the West, of the Western *idea,* is evident first of all in the total exhaustion of viable systematic alternatives to Western liberalism. In the past decade, there have been unmistakable changes in the intellectual climate of the world's two largest communist countries, and the beginnings of significant reform movements in both. But this phenomenon extends beyond high politics and it can be seen also in the ineluctable spread of consumerist Western culture in such diverse contexts as the peasants' markets and color television sets now omnipresent throughout China, the cooperative restaurants and clothing stores opened in the past year in Moscow, the Beethoven piped into Japanese department stores, and the rock music enjoyed alike in Prague, Rangoon, and Tehran.

What we may be witnessing is not just the end of the Cold War, or the passing of a particular period of postwar history, but the end of history as such: that is, the end point of mankind's ideological evolution and the universalization of Western liberal democracy as the final form of human government. This is not to say that there will no longer be events to fill the pages of *Foreign Affairs'* yearly summaries of international relations, for the victory of liberalism has occurred primarily in the realm of ideas or consciousness and is as yet incomplete in the real or material world. But there are powerful reasons for believing that it is the ideal that will govern the material world *in the long run.* To understand how this is so, we must first consider some theoretical issues concerning the nature of historical change.

## 1

The notion of the end of history is not an original one. Its best known propagator was Karl Marx, who believed that the direction of historical development was a purposeful one determined by the interplay of material forces, and would come to an end only with the achievement of a communist utopia that would finally resolve all prior contradictions. But the concept of history as a dialectical process with a beginning, a middle, and an end was borrowed by Marx from his great German predecessor, Georg Wilhelm Friedrich Hegel.

For better or worse, much of Hegel's historicism has become part of our contemporary intellectual baggage. The notion that mankind has progressed through a series of primitive stages of consciousness on his path to the present, and that these stages corresponded to concrete forms of social organization, such as tribal, slave-owning, theocratic, and finally democratic-egalitarian societies, has become inseparable from the modern understanding of man. Hegel was the first philosopher to speak the language of modern social science, insofar as man for him was the product of his concrete historical and social environment and not, as earlier natural right theorists would have it, a collection of more or less fixed "natural" attributes. The mastery and transformation of man's natural environment through the application of science and technology was originally not a Marxist concept, but a Hegelian one. Unlike later historicists whose historical relativism degenerated into relativism *tout court,* however, Hegel believed that history culminated in an absolute moment—a moment in which a final, rational form of society and state became victorious. . . .

. . . Hegel saw in Napoleon's defeat of the Prussian monarchy at the Battle of Jena [1806] the victory of the ideals of the French Revolution, and the imminent universalization of the state incorporating the principles of liberty and equality. . . . The Battle of Jena marked the end of history because it was at that point that the *vanguard* of humanity (a term quite familiar to Marxists) actualized the principles of the French Revolution. While there was considerable work to be done after 1806—abolishing slavery and the slave trade, extending the franchise to workers, women, blacks, and other racial minorities, etc.—the basic *principles* of the liberal democratic state could not be improved upon. The two world wars in this century and their attendant revolutions and upheavals simply had the effect of extending those principles spatially, such that the various provinces of human civilization were brought up to the level of its most advanced outposts, and of forcing those societies in Europe and North America at the vanguard of civilization to implement their liberalism more fully.

The state that emerges at the end of history is liberal insofar as it recognizes and protects through a system of law man's universal right to freedom, and democratic insofar as it exists only with the consent of the governed. . . .

## 2

For Hegel, the contradictions that drive history exist first of all in the realm of human consciousness, i.e. on the level of ideas[1]—not the trivial election year proposals of American politicians, but ideas in the sense of large unifying world views that might best be understood under the rubric of ideology. Ideology in this sense is not restricted to the secular and explicit political doctrines we usually associate with the term, but can include religion, culture, and the complex of moral values underlying any society as well.

Hegel's view of the relationship between the ideal and the real or material worlds was an extremely complicated one, beginning with the fact that for him the distinction between the two was only apparent.[2] He did not believe that the real world conformed or could be made to conform to ideological preconceptions of philosophy professors in any simpleminded way, or that the "material" world could not impinge on the ideal. Indeed, Hegel the professor was temporarily thrown out of work as a result of a very material event, the Battle of Jena. But while Hegel's writing and thinking could be stopped by a bullet from the material world, the hand on the trigger of the gun was motivated in turn by the ideas of liberty and equality that had driven the French Revolution.

For Hegel, all human behavior in the material world, and hence all human history, is rooted in a prior state of consciousness—an idea similar to the one expressed by John Maynard Keynes when he said that the views of men of affairs were usually derived from defunct economists and academic scribblers of earlier generations. This consciousness may not be explicit and self-aware, as are modern political doctrines, but may rather take the form of religion or simple cultural or moral habits. And yet this realm of consciousness *in the long run* necessarily becomes manifest in the material world, indeed creates the material world in its own image. Consciousness is cause and not effect, and can develop autonomously from the material world; hence the real subtext underlying the apparent jumble of current events is the history of ideology.

Hegel's idealism has fared poorly at the hands of later thinkers. Marx reversed the priority of the real and the ideal completely, relegating the entire realm of consciousness—religion, art, culture, philosophy itself—to a "superstructure" that was determined entirely by the prevailing material mode of production. Yet another unfortunate legacy of Marxism is our tendency to retreat into materialist or utilitarian explanations of political or historical phenomena, and our dis-

---

[1] This notion was expressed in the famous aphorism from the preface to the *Philosophy of History* to the effect that "everything that is rational is real, and everything that is real is rational."

[2] Indeed, for Hegel the very dichotomy between the ideal and material worlds was itself only an apparent one that was ultimately overcome by the self-conscious subject; in his system, the material world is itself only an aspect of mind.

inclination to believe in the autonomous power of ideas. . . .

The materialist bias of modern thought is characteristic not only of people on the Left who may be sympathetic to Marxism, but of many passionate anti-Marxists as well. Indeed, there is on the Right what one might label the *Wall Street Journal* school of deterministic materialism that discounts the importance of ideology and culture and sees man as essentially a rational, profit-maximizing individual. It is precisely this kind of individual and his pursuit of material incentives that is posited as the basis for economic life as such in economic textbooks.[3] . . .

As we look around the contemporary world, the poverty of materialist theories of economic development is all too apparent. The *Wall Street Journal* school of deterministic materialism habitually points to the stunning economic success of Asia in the past few decades as evidence of the viability of free market economics, with the implication that all societies would see similar development were they simply to allow their populations to pursue their material self-interest freely. Surely free markets and stable political systems are a necessary precondition to capitalist economic growth. But just as surely the cultural heritage of those Far Eastern societies, the ethic of work and saving and family, a religious heritage that does not, like Islam, place restrictions on certain forms of economic behavior, and other deeply ingrained moral qualities, are equally important in explaining their economic performance.[4] And yet the intellectual weight of materialism is such that not a single respectable contemporary theory of economic development addresses consciousness and culture seriously as

the matrix within which economic behavior is formed.

Failure to understand that the roots of economic behavior lie in the realm of consciousness and culture leads to the common mistake of attributing material causes to phenomena that are essentially ideal in nature. For example, it is commonplace in the West to interpret the reform movements first in China and most recently in the Soviet Union as the victory of the material over the ideal—that is, a recognition that ideological incentives could not replace material ones in stimulating a highly productive modern economy, and that if one wanted to prosper one had to appeal to baser forms of self-interest. But the deep defects of socialist economies were evident thirty or forty years ago to anyone who chose to look. Why was it that these countries moved away from central planning only in the 1980s? The answer must be found in the consciousness of the elites and leaders ruling them, who decided to opt for the "Protestant" life of wealth and risk over the "Catholic" path of poverty and security.[5] That change was in no way made inevitable by the material conditions in which either country found itself on the eve of the reform, but instead came about as the result of the victory of one idea over another.[6] . . .

But while man's very perception of the material world is shaped by his historical consciousness of it, the material world can clearly affect in return the viability of a particular state of consciousness. In particular, the spectacular abundance of advanced liberal economies and the infinitely diverse consumer culture made possible by them seem to both foster and preserve liberalism in the political sphere. I want to avoid the materialist determinism that says that liberal eco-

---

[3] In fact, modern economists, recognizing that man does not always behave as a *profit*-maximizer, posit a "utility" function, utility being either income or some other good that can be maximized: leisure, sexual satisfaction, or the pleasure of philosophizing. That profit must be replaced with a value like utility indicates the cogency of the idealist perspective.

[4] One need look no further than the recent performance of Vietnamese immigrants in the U.S. school system when compared to their black or Hispanic classmates to realize that culture and consciousness are absolutely crucial to explain not only economic behavior but virtually every other important aspect of life as well.

[5] I understand that a full explanation of the origins of the reform movements in China and Russia is a good deal more complicated than this simple formula would suggest. The Soviet reform, for example, was motivated in good measure by Moscow's sense of *insecurity* in the technological-military realm. Nonetheless, neither country on the eve of its reforms was in such a state of *material* crisis that one could have predicted the surprising reform paths ultimately taken.

[6] It is still not clear whether the Soviet peoples are as "Protestant" as Gorbachev and will follow him down that path.

nomics inevitably produces liberal politics, because I believe that both economics and politics presuppose an autonomous prior state of consciousness that makes them possible. But that state of consciousness that permits the growth of liberalism seems to stabilize in the way one would expect at the end of history if it is underwritten by the abundance of a modern free market economy. We might summarize the content of the universal homogenous state as liberal democracy in the political sphere combined with easy access to VCRs and stereos in the economic.

## 3

Have we in fact reached the end of history? Are there, in other words, any fundamental "contradictions" in human life that cannot be resolved in the context of modern liberalism, that would be resolvable by an alternative political-economic structure? If we accept the idealist premises laid out above, we must seek an answer to this question in the realm of ideology and consciousness. Our task is not to answer exhaustively the challenges to liberalism promoted by every crackpot messiah around the world, but only those that are embodied in important social or political forces and movements, and which are therefore part of world history. For our purposes, it matters very little what strange thoughts occur to people in Albania or Burkina Faso, for we are interested in what one could in some sense call the common ideological heritage of mankind.

In the past century, there have been two major challenges to liberalism, those of fascism and of communism. The former[7] saw the political

[7] I am not using the term "fascism" here in its most precise sense, fully aware of the frequent misuse of this term to denounce anyone to the right of the user. "Fascism" here denotes any organized ultra-nationalist movement with universalistic pretensions—not universalistic with regard to its nationalism, of course, since the latter is exclusive by definition, but with regard to the movement's belief in its right to rule other people. Hence Imperial Japan would qualify as fascist while former strongman Stoessner's Paraguay or Pinochet's Chile would not. Obviously fascist ideologies cannot be universalistic in the sense of Marxism or liberalism, but the structure of the doctrine can be transferred from country to country.

weakness, materialism, anomie, and lack of community of the West as fundamental contradictions in liberal societies that could only be resolved by a strong state that forged a new "people" on the basis of national exclusiveness. Fascism was destroyed as a living ideology by World War II. This was a defeat, of course, on a very material level, but it amounted to a defeat of the idea as well. What destroyed fascism as an idea was not universal moral revulsion against it, since plenty of people were willing to endorse the idea as long as it seemed the wave of the future, but its lack of success. After the war, it seemed to most people that German fascism as well as its other European and Asian variants were bound to self-destruct. There was no material reason why new fascist movements could not have sprung up again after the war in other locales, but for the fact that expansionist ultranationalism, with its promise of unending conflict leading to disastrous military defeat, had completely lost its appeal. The ruins of the Reich chancellory as well as the atomic bombs dropped on Hiroshima and Nagasaki killed this ideology on the level of consciousness as well as materially, and all of the proto-fascist movements spawned by the German and Japanese examples like the Peronist movement in Argentina or Subhas Chandra Bose's Indian National Army withered after the war.

The ideological challenge mounted by the other great alternative to liberalism, communism, was far more serious. Marx, speaking Hegel's language, asserted that liberal society contained a fundamental contradiction that could not be resolved within its context, that between capital and labor, and this contradiction has constituted the chief accusation against liberalism ever since. But surely, the class issue has actually been successfully resolved in the West. As Kojève (among others) noted, the egalitarianism of modern America represents the essential achievement of the classless society envisioned by Marx. This is not to say that there are not rich people and poor people in the United States, or that the gap between them has not grown in recent years. But the root causes of economic inequality do not have to do with the underlying legal and social structure of our society, which remains fundamentally egalitarian and moderately redistributionist, so much as with the cultural and social characteristics of the groups that make it up, which are in turn the historical legacy of premodern conditions. Thus black poverty in the United States is not the inherent product of liberalism, but is rather the "legacy of slavery and racism" which persisted long after the formal abolition of slavery.

As a result of the receding of the class issue, the appeal of communism in the developed Western world, it is safe to say, is lower today than any time since the end of the First World War. This can be measured in any number of ways: in the declining membership and electoral pull of the major European communist parties, and their overtly revisionist programs; in the corresponding electoral success of conservative parties from Britain and Germany to the United States and Japan, which are unabashedly pro-market and anti-statist; and in an intellectual climate whose most "advanced" members no longer believe that bourgeois society is something that ultimately needs to be overcome. This is not to say that the opinions of progressive intellectuals in Western countries are not deeply pathological in any number of ways. But those who believe that the future must inevitably be socialist tend to be very old, or very marginal to the real political discourse of their societies. . . .

If we admit for the moment that the fascist and communist challenges to liberalism are dead, are there any other ideological competitors left? Or put another way, are there contradictions in liberal society beyond that of class that are not resolvable? Two possibilities suggest themselves, those of religion and nationalism.

The rise of religious fundamentalism in recent years within the Christian, Jewish, and Muslim traditions has been widely noted. One is inclined to say that the revival of religion in some way attests to a broad unhappiness with the impersonality and spiritual vacuity of liberal consumerist societies. Yet while the emptiness at the core of liberalism is most certainly a defect in the ideology—indeed, a flaw that one does not need the

perspective of religion to recognize[8]—it is not at all clear that it is remediable through politics. Modern liberalism itself was historically a consequence of the weakness of religiously-based societies which, failing to agree on the nature of the good life, could not provide even the minimal preconditions of peace and stability. In the contemporary world only Islam has offered a theocratic state as a political alternative to both liberalism and communism. But the doctrine has little appeal for non-Muslims, and it is hard to believe that the movement will take on any universal significance. Other less organized religious impulses have been successfully satisfied within the sphere of personal life that is permitted in liberal societies.

The other major "contradiction" potentially unresolvable by liberalism is the one posed by nationalism and other forms of racial and ethnic consciousness. It is certainly true that a very large degree of conflict since the Battle of Jena has had its roots in nationalism. Two cataclysmic world wars in this century have been spawned by the nationalism of the developed world in various guises, and if those passions have been muted to a certain extent in postwar Europe, they are still extremely powerful in the Third World. Nationalism has been a threat to liberalism historically in Germany, and continues to be one in isolated parts of "post-historical" Europe like Northern Ireland.

But it is not clear that nationalism represents an irreconcilable contradiction in the heart of liberalism. In the first place, nationalism is not one single phenomenon but several, ranging from mild cultural nostalgia to the highly organized and elaborately articulated doctrine of National Socialism. Only systematic nationalisms of the latter sort can qualify as a formal ideology on the level of liberalism or communism. The vast majority of the world's nationalist movements do not have a political program beyond the negative

[8] I am thinking particularly of Rousseau and the Western philosophical tradition that flows from him that was highly critical of Lockean or Hobbesian liberalism, though one could criticize liberalism from the standpoint of classical political philosophy as well.

desire of independence *from* some other group or people, and do not offer anything like a comprehensive agenda for socio-economic organization. As such, they are compatible with doctrines and ideologies that do offer such agendas. While they may constitute a source of conflict for liberal societies, this conflict does not arise from liberalism itself so much as from the fact that the liberalism in question is incomplete. Certainly a great deal of the world's ethnic and nationalist tension can be explained in terms of peoples who are forced to live in unrepresentative political systems that they have not chosen.

While it is impossible to rule out the sudden appearance of new ideologies or previously unrecognized contradictions in liberal societies, then, the present world seems to confirm that the fundamental principles of socio-political organization have not advanced terribly far since 1806. Many of the wars and revolutions fought since that time have been undertaken in the name of ideologies which claimed to be more advanced than liberalism, but whose pretensions were ultimately unmasked by history. In the meantime, they have helped to spread the universal homogenous state to the point where it could have a significant effect on the overall character of international relations.

## 4

What are the implications of the end of history for international relations? Clearly, the vast bulk of the Third World remains very much mired in history, and will be a terrain of conflict for many years to come. But let us focus for the time being on the larger and more developed states of the world who after all account for the greater part of world politics. Russia and China are not likely to join the developed nations of the West as liberal societies any time in the foreseeable future, but suppose for a moment that Marxism-Leninism ceases to be a factor driving the foreign policies of these states—a prospect which, if not yet here, the last few years have made a real possibility. How will the overall characteristics of a de-ideologized world differ from those of the one

with which we are familiar at such a hypothetical juncture?

The most common answer is—not very much. For there is a very widespread belief among many observers of international relations that underneath the skin of ideology is a hard core of great power national interest that guarantees a fairly high level of competition and conflict between nations. . . .

. . . Since the Second World War, European nationalism has been defanged and shorn of any real relevance to foreign policy, with the consequence that the nineteenth-century model of great power behavior has become a serious anachronism. The most extreme form of nationalism that any Western European state has mustered since 1945 has been Gaullism, whose self-assertion has been confined largely to the realm of nuisance politics and culture. International life for the part of the world that has reached the end of history is far more preoccupied with economics than with politics or strategy. . . .

The automatic assumption that Russia shorn of its expansionist communist ideology should pick up where the czars left off just prior to the Bolshevik Revolution is therefore a curious one. It assumes that the evolution of human consciousness has stood still in the meantime, and that the Soviets, while picking up currently fashionable ideas in the realm of economics, will return to foreign policy views a century out of date in the rest of Europe. This is certainly not what happened to China after it began its reform process. . . .

The real question for the future, however, is the degree to which Soviet elites have assimilated the consciousness of the universal homogenous state that is post-Hitler Europe. From their writings and from my own personal contacts with them, there is no question in my mind that the liberal Soviet intelligentsia rallying around Gorbachev have arrived at the end-of-history view in a remarkably short time, due in no small measure to the contacts they have had since the Brezhnev era with the larger European civilization around them. "New political thinking," the general rubric for their views, describes a world dominated by economic concerns, in which there are no ideological grounds for major conflict between nations, and in which, consequently, the use of military force becomes less legitimate. . . .

The post-historical consciousness represented by "new thinking" is only one possible future for the Soviet Union, however. There has always been a very strong current of great Russian chauvinism in the Soviet Union, which has found freer expression since the advent of *glasnost*. It may be possible to return to traditional Marxism-Leninism for a while as a simple rallying point for those who want to restore the authority that Gorbachev has dissipated. But as in Poland, Marxism-Leninism is dead as a mobilizing ideology: under its banner people cannot be made to work harder, and its adherents have lost confidence in themselves. Unlike the propagators of traditional Marxism-Leninism, however, ultranationalists in the USSR believe in their Slavophile cause passionately, and one gets the sense that the fascist alternative is not one that has played itself out entirely there.

The Soviet Union, then, is at a fork in the road: it can start down the path that was staked out by Western Europe forty-five years ago, a path that most of Asia has followed, or it can realize its own uniqueness and remain stuck in history. The choice it makes will be highly important for us, given the Soviet Union's size and military strength, for that power will continue to preoccupy us and slow our realization that we have already emerged on the other side of history.

## 5

The passing of Marxism-Leninism first from China and then from the Soviet Union will mean its death as a living ideology of world historical significance. For while there may be some isolated true believers left in places like Managua, Pyongyang, or Cambridge, Massachusetts, the fact that there is not a single large state in which it is a going concern undermines completely its pretensions to being in the vanguard of human history. And the death of this ideology means the growing "Common Marketization" of international relations, and the diminution of the likelihood of large-scale conflict between states.

This does not by any means imply the end of international conflict *per se*. For the world at that point would be divided between a part that was historical and a part that was post-historical. Conflict between states still in history, and between those states and those at the end of history, would still be possible. There would still be a high and perhaps rising level of ethnic and nationalist violence, since those are impulses incompletely played out, even in parts of the post-historical world. Palestinians and Kurds, Sikhs and Tamils, Irish Catholics and Walloons, Armenians and Azeris, will continue to have their unresolved grievances. This implies that terrorism and wars of national liberation will continue to be an important item on the international agenda. But large-scale conflict must involve large states still caught in the grip of history, and they are what appear to be passing from the scene.

The end of history will be a very sad time. The struggle for recognition, the willingness to risk one's life for a purely abstract goal, the worldwide ideological struggle that called forth daring, courage, imagination, and idealism, will be replaced by economic calculation, the endless solving of technical problems, environmental concerns, and the satisfaction of sophisticated consumer demands. In the post-historical period there will be neither art nor philosophy, just the perpetual caretaking of the museum of human history. I can feel in myself, and see in others around me, a powerful nostalgia for the time when history existed. Such nostalgia, in fact, will continue to fuel competition and conflict even in the post-historical world for some time to come. Even though I recognize its inevitability, I have the most ambivalent feelings for the civilization that has been created in Europe since 1945, with its north Atlantic and Asian offshoots. Perhaps this very prospect of centuries of boredom at the end of history will serve to get history started once again.

# Study Questions

1. Machiavelli says that the wise prince must sometimes act like a lion, at other times like a fox. What does he mean by this? Can we apply this prescription to modern political leadership?

2. How did Machiavelli want his prince to behave toward his own subjects? toward other princes? Do modern leaders still behave as the prince did? Justify your answer.

3. Is it better for a leader to be loved or feared? What did Machiavelli think? Why?

4. How did the turmoil of the English Civil War affect Hobbes's approach to politics?

5. How did Hobbes see the state of nature? What did he think that people in such a state should do? How do his ideas help us understand contemporary democracy?

6. Do you think that Hobbes believed that his state of nature was a real time and place, one before the founding of all governments, or mostly a convenient fiction invented to help us understand the foundations of political power? If the latter, does this take away from the validity of Hobbes's call for a strong sovereign to avoid political anarchy? Explain.

7. Why does Hobbes think that we're all equal in the state of nature? Should this basic equality matter to the political philosopher? Explain.

8. How was Locke's state of nature different from Hobbes's? How does Locke's distinction between a "state of nature" and a "state of war" play into this difference? Which thinker offers a more accurate picture of life in a state where there is no police, laws, or government?

9. What did Locke think was the point of government? Under what sort of conditions did he believe that we have a right to revolt against an existing government? Is his description of the rationale and limits of government power reasonable? Explain.

10. How did Marx relate the "substructure" and "superstructure" of capitalist societies? What does this have to say about our religious, political, and philosophical ideas? Is he right? Explain.

11. Is analyzing modern society (and social change) in terms of a "class struggle" useful or illuminating? Why or why not?

12. Is Marx right in saying that capitalism exploits the working class? Is work under capitalism "alienating"? Explain.

13. Are capitalist societies unjust? Is there a better alternative? Explain.

14. Is Mill correct in saying that the state has no right to interfere with our fellow citizens' opinions and with their public expression of them, as long as these opinions don't cause immediate harm to others? Would you extend this right of free expression to those advocating sexism? or racism? Explain your answers.

15. Is it healthy for a society to tolerate opinions that are clearly "wrong"? If so, why?

16. Is Mill's warning that we should beware "the tyranny of the majority" in liberal democracies still relevant today? In what ways does this tyranny affect our everyday lives, if at all?

17. Can a liberal political theory deal with the injustices done to women, as Wollstonecraft seemed to think it could? Could a liberal philosophy such as Mill's really support the equality of the sexes? Explain.

18. Are women still, as in Wollstonecraft's day, taught to depend on their personal beauty and emotions rather than on their rational faculties to get through life (e.g., in their early peer-group interactions, by their parents, by advertising, by films and television)? Is this the inevitable result of differences between the sexes, or the product of an oppressive sexist society?

19. If you were operating behind Rawls's veil of ignorance, what idea of justice would you propose? Would it be "justice as fairness"? Why or why not?

20. Do Rawls's two principles of justice adequately balance the ideals of freedom and equality that liberals have long held dear? Do his principles serve to buttress the welfare state? How?

21. What are the relative advantages of the libertarian and communitarian positions with regard to government intervention into the economy? Can we say that one approach is more just than the other? Do we owe our fellow citizens anything more than noninterference in their lives? Explain your answers.

22. Would a group of rational signers of a hypothetical social contract agree to anything more than a minimal public sector, that is, to funding a police force, garbage disposal, and road building, but not libraries and parks? Explain.

23. Why does Fukuyama think that we've arrived at the end of history? Is he right? Is this a good thing? Explain.

24. What are the advantages and disadvantages in seeing history as directed by ideas, as Hegel and Fukuyama suggest?

# *Bibliography*

## GENERAL

Skinner, Quentin. *The Foundations of Modern Political Thought.* Cambridge: Cambridge University Press, 1978.

## ON MACHIAVELLI

DeGrazia, Sebastian. *Machiavelli in Hell.* Princeton, NJ: Princeton University Press, 1989.

Mansfield, Harvey C. *Machiavelli's Virtue.* Chicago: University of Chicago Press, 1996.

Pitkin, Hanna Fenichel. *Fortune Is a Woman: Gender and Politics in the Thought of Niccolo Machiavelli.* Berkeley: University of California Press, 1984.

Skinner, Quentin. *Machiavelli.* Oxford: Oxford University Press, 1981. A short introduction.

## ON HOBBES AND LOCKE

Chapell, Vere, ed. *The Cambridge Companion to Locke.* Cambridge: Cambridge University Press, 1994.

Dunn, John. *Locke.* New York: Oxford University Press, 1984. Part of the Past Masters series, this short volume has been reprinted in John Dunn, J. O. Urmson, and A. J. Ayer, *The British Empiricists: Locke, Berkeley, Hume* (Oxford: Oxford University Press, 1992).

———. *The Political Thought of John Locke.* Cambridge: Cambridge University Press, 1984.

Gauthier, David. *The Logic of Leviathan: The Moral and Political Theory of Thomas Hobbes.* Oxford: Clarendon Press, 1969. By an important modern contract theorist.

Harris, Ian. *The Mind of John Locke: A Study of Political Theory in Its Intellectual Setting.* Cambridge: Cambridge University Press, 1998.

Locke, John. *Two Treatises of Government.* Edited by Peter Laslett. Cambridge: Cambridge University Press, 1967. A definitive scholarly edition.

MacPherson, C. B. *The Political Theory of Possessive Individualism: Hobbes to Locke.* Oxford: Oxford University Press, 1962. A classic study of contract theory.

Strauss, Leo. *Natural Right and History.* Chicago: University of Chicago Press, 1953. See chap. 5 for a unique interpretation of Hobbes's and Locke's political ideas.

————. *The Political Theory of Thomas Hobbes: Its Basis and Genesis.* Chicago: University of Chicago Press, 1962.

The Internet Encyclopedia of Philosophy: http://www.utm.edu/research/iep/
Contains an article on Locke.

John Locke (1632–1704): http://www.philosophypages.com/ph/lock.htm
A short article on Locke from *A Dictionary of Philosophical Terms and Names.*

John Locke (1632–1704): http://www.orst.edu/instruct/phl302/philosophers/locke.html
A short article on Locke from the *Great Voyages: The History of Western Philosophy 1492–1776* Web page by Bill Uzgalis of Oregon State University. This one has a good timeline of Locke's life, a bibliography, and links to his major texts, including *The Second Treatise of Government.*

## ON MARX

Eagleton, Terry. *Marx.* London: Routledge, 1999. A very short introduction in Routledge's Great Philosophers series by a prominent Marxist literary critic and cultural theorist.

Fromm, Erich. *Marx's Concept of Man.* New York: Ungar, 1961. A leading light of the Frankfurt School of Critical Theory (which married Marx and Freud) gives his take on the master.

McLellan, David. *Karl Marx: His Life and Thought.* New York: Harper & Row, 1973. McLellan has written and edited several other reliable books on Marx.

McMurtry, John. *The Structure of Marx's World-View.* Princeton, NJ: Princeton University Press, 1978.

Singer, Peter. *Karl Marx.* Oxford: Oxford University Press, 1980. A short introduction.

Tucker, Robert, ed. *The Marx-Engels Reader.* 2d ed. New York: Norton, 1978. The standard short collection of Marx and Engels's writings.

Marx & Engels Internet Archive: www.marxists.org/archive/marx/index.htm
A great resource for works by Marx and Engels, this site also includes biographies, images, and an encyclopedia.

The McMaster University Archive of Economic Thought: http://socserv.mcmaster.ca/econ/ugcm/3ll3/
A large archive of texts on economics, political theory, and related subjects. Includes texts by Hobbes, Hume, Locke, Marx, Mill, and many others.

The Value of Knowledge—a Miniature Library of Philosophy: http://www.marxists.org/reference/subject/philosophy/index.htm
This collection of texts from 120 thinkers traces the development of the relationship between matter and consciousness from Galileo to postmodernism. The focus is on Marxism, but there are also texts on classical epistemology, the philosophy of science, psychology, existentialism, and feminism.

## ON MILL, WOLLSTONECRAFT, AND RAWLS

Bryon, Valerie. *Feminist Political Theory: An Introduction.* London: Macmillan, 1992. Good on the development of feminist thought up until the radical feminism of the 1960s and 1970s.

Kelly, Gary. *Revolutionary Feminism: The Life and Career of Mary Wollstonecraft.* New York: St. Martin's, 1992.

Nozick, Robert. *Anarchy, State, and Utopia.* New York: Basic Books, 1974. Nozick, a political theorist in his own right, attacks Rawls from a libertarian perspective.

Plamenatz, John. *The English Utilitarians.* Oxford: Blackwell, 1949. On Mill and friends.

Robson, John M. *The Improvement of Mankind: The Social and Political Thought of John Stuart Mill.* Toronto: University of Toronto Press, 1968.

Todd, Janet. *Mary Wollstonecraft: A Revolutionary Life.* New York: Columbia University Press, 2000.

## ON CONTEMPORARY DEBATES IN LIBERAL POLITICAL THEORY

Avineri, Shlomo, and Avner de-Shalit, eds. *Communitarianism and Individualism.* Oxford: Oxford University Press, 1992. A good collection of essays by the leading lights in the communitarianism versus contractarianism debate.

Gauthier, David. *Morals by Agreement.* Oxford: Oxford University Press, 1986. A modern contractarian.

Kymlicka, Will. *Liberalism, Community and Culture.* Oxford: Clarendon Press, 1989.

Sandel, Michael. *Liberalism and the Limits of Justice.* Cambridge: Cambridge University Press, 1982. A communitarian perspective.

## ON FUKUYAMA

Kimball, Roger. "Francis Fukuyama and the End of History," *The New Criterion On Line,* February 1992. Available at http://www.newcriterion.com/archive/10/feb92/fukuyama.htm

## CHAPTER SEVEN

# Feminist Theory

> *Women must be freed from the tyranny*
> *of their biology by any means available.*
> SHULAMITH FIRESTONE
>
> *Women are not in control of their bodies; nature is.*
> CAMILLE PAGLIA

## SEX, GENDER, AND THE HISTORY OF FEMINIST THEORY

### What Is Feminism?

A number of key issues carry over from political theory in general to feminist theory in particular. The major issue for feminists is, of course, the inequality of the sexes and the injustice of political, social, and economic arrangements that support this inequality. Tied to this central issue is the question of whether liberal political theory can deal with women's issues: Can Mill's defense of liberty or Rawls's theory of justice be used to argue for equal rights and opportunities for women? Radical and socialist feminists have seen liberalism as a failure in this regard. In addition, there is the issue of how early education shapes our view of relations between the sexes, the main focus of Mary Wollstonecraft's work. Are the gender roles we play out in our lives entirely a product of this early education, or is there something natural about them? Feminist theory has given various answers to this question.

In one of the readings in this chapter, Marilyn Frye gives us the clearest definition of feminism we could reasonably hope for: A feminist is someone who believes that women are oppressed (and, one presumes, wants to do something about it). Frye's definition expresses the negative side of feminism. The positive side is the women's movement's call to reform the family, the workplace, the legal system, politics, and perhaps culture to allow for a greater equality of the sexes.

Yet to go beyond Frye's simple definition here would be to perform the labors of Sisyphus: Just when we think we've rolled the rock up the hill of meaning and arrived at a complete definition of the term, someone will come along to inform us there's something we've forgotten. Instead of trying to add an endless series of footnotes to Frye's admirably concise definition, let's look at the history of the women's movement for a fuller view of just what feminism is.

## The Three Waves of Feminism

### THE FIRST WAVE

Women as a mass first took an active role in politics during the French Revolution of 1789–1795. On October 5, 1789, a mob of Parisian women marched first on the Hôtel de Ville to demand cheaper bread prices, arming themselves with a hodgepodge of garden implements and pistols, then moved on to the royal palace of Versailles to parley with King Louis on the matter. Women were also influential behind the scenes. Madame Roland's salon was a gathering point for the moderate republican "Girondin" party. Charlotte Corday murdered Marat, a prominent radical Jacobin, in his bath in revenge for the Jacobin reign of terror in her home province of Normandy. A handful of radicals in the Revolution argued for the rights of women and slaves, modeling their arguments on the Declaration of the Rights of Man and of the Citizen passed by the National Assembly in 1789. Olympe de Gouge (1748–1793), a Girondin activist, published her "Declaration of the Rights of Women" in 1791. It called for equal legal and political rights for women. She was rewarded for her efforts on behalf of sexual equality with a visit to Madame Guillotine in 1793 after being convicted of treason by the National Convention (the revolutionary parliament).

British radicalism was inspired by the Revolution, even though the government tried to stifle it during the revolutionary and Napoleonic Wars (1792–1815). Wollstonecraft's *A Vindication of the Rights of Woman* of 1792, the founding document of feminist theory in the West, is very much the product of a new awareness of equality and human rights caused by revolutionary events in France. Paralleling these political events came the Romantic movement in literature, with its emphasis on sensibility over reason. This heralded the entrance of women such as Jane Austen and the Brontë sisters into the world of literature and thus a partial opening of Western culture to women's voices.

Despite these bare beginnings in the French Revolution, it wasn't until the middle of the nineteenth century that the women's movement assumed a concrete form. The 1830s and 1840s were times of great social upheaval in Europe. Men of liberal principles battled it out with conservative defenders of privilege. France saw two revolutions, in 1830 and 1848, while Britain saw mass Chartist demonstrations demanding greater democracy in the kingdom. Small numbers of American women began to publicly advocate sexual equality in the 1830s. This movement was tied to the larger movement to abolish slavery, at least until the victory by Union forces in the Civil War (1861–1865).

Early feminists such as Elizabeth Cady Stanton (1815–1902) and Lucretia Mott (1793–1880) fought for equal rights for both women and black people at the same time. In fact, when Mott and Stanton tried to attend the World Anti-Slavery Conference in 1840 in London, but were told that as women they could only watch from the galleries, they became convinced that they had to take more direct political action to improve women's status. In 1848, the year of revolution in Paris, Berlin, and other European capitals, they organized the Seneca Falls Convention in New York state. The delegates voted narrowly in favor of the pursuit of the right to vote as a central goal of the movement and issued a "Declaration of Sentiments" that starts by paralleling the U.S. Declaration of Independence: "We hold these truths to be self-evident: that all men and women are created equal."

Stanton, Mott, and their new comrade Susan B. Anthony (1820–1906) fought throughout the nineteenth century for women's rights. They split from the Abolitionists after the Fifteenth Amendment was passed in 1870, which gave black men, at least in theory, the right to vote. When Anthony registered and voted in the 1872 presidential elections on the grounds that the Fifteenth Amendment implied that women had the right to vote too, she was arrested and fined one hundred dollars, which she refused to pay.

Early First Wave feminism in America and Britain set the following goals:

- The right to vote—"women's suffrage"
- The right of a wife to own property separate from her husband and to keep her own wages, which in the early nineteenth century were paid directly to her husband
- The right to an education—most colleges would accept only male students until around the turn of the century—and the opportunity to pursue independent careers
- The right to a fair divorce and protection against marital violence

In Britain "suffragettes" fought for the vote too, getting started a few years later than their American cousins. At first they campaigned politely. A few liberal men such as John Stuart Mill supported women's suffrage from the 1860s on, both in and out of Parliament, but to no effect. When Emmeline Pankhurst (1858–1928) grew tired of the ineffectiveness of these early efforts, she formed a splinter group called the Women's Social and Political Union in 1903. Pankhurst and her daughters Christabel and Sylvia fought tirelessly for the right to vote, using such tactics as burning empty buildings, smashing windows, marching, picketing, and going on hunger strikes to make male politicians sit up and take notice.

In 1918 these British suffragettes won the right to vote for propertied and university-educated women over the age of thirty (the age qualification dropped to twenty-one in 1928, giving women and men equal voting rights). America soon followed suit and extended the vote to women in 1920, when the Nineteenth Amendment to the Constitution was ratified. Women won the right to vote in Australia as early as 1909, in Canada in 1918, in Germany and Sweden in 1919, and in most other Western democracies by the 1920s.

Slowly, in the late nineteenth and early twentieth centuries, state governments in the United States and national governments in most other Western democracies passed laws that gave women basic property rights and the right to a fair divorce, while institutions of higher education opened their doors to both sexes. By the 1920s the First Wave had largely achieved its goal of the formal legal and political equality of the sexes.

An odd sidelight in the history of feminism was the Social Purity movement, which started in America in the 1870s. These feminists argued that women are morally purer than men and not as much in the grip of their base desires. They used the examples of prostitution, rape, domestic violence, and drunkenness to show how men were more the prisoners of their sexual and aggressive urges than were women. In fact, they argued that sex, violence, and alcohol were linked together, fighting for the prohibition of alcohol as a way of curbing excessive sexual desire and violence in men. The notorious Carrie Nation (1846–1911) toured America with bricks and bats in hand, breaking up bars in her drive to purify American men of the demon of alcohol. In 1919 the temperance movement got its way, as the U.S. Congress passed the Eighteenth Amendment, which enacted Prohibition. The result was the Roaring Twenties, bathtub gin, speakeasies, and a vast expansion of organized crime. Beer kegs and whiskey bottles were legally dry until 1934, when America's disastrous experiment with legally enforced temperance finally ended.

Another tributary stream within the First Wave was socialist feminism. Its central argument was that capitalism and private property were to blame for women's oppression. Friedrich Engels argued in *The Origins of the Family, Private Property and the State* that in primitive hunter-gatherer societies, men and women lived together in rough equality and that it was only the institution of private property in ancient societies that made wives the property of their husbands. Earlier, in *The Communist Manifesto,* Marx and Engels had ridiculed the bourgeoisie for using their wives as "mere instruments of production" and for fretting over the Communist call to abolish the family. After the Russian Revolution of 1917 Soviet feminists won such rights as legal equality, the vote, the rights to divorce and abortion, and even maternity leaves, only to have them largely disappear under Stalin in the 1930s. Socialist feminism would resurface as a major element of the Second Wave in the 1960s, as seen in Shulamith Firestone's *The Dialectic of Sex.*

During World War II (1939–1945) the battle against fascism occupied both women and men in America, Britain, and their democratic allies. Women in North America, Britain, and Russia turned in their oven mitts and aprons to build planes, tanks, and guns or to work as nurses and clerical staff in the armed forces while their men fought the Nazis and Japanese. "Rosie the Riveter" became the model for American womanhood, a tough working woman never without her trademark kerchief wrapped around her head. When the war ended, though, Rosie and her female coworkers were pressured to hand over their jobs to the returning soldiers, sailors, and airmen, exchanging them for the domestic bliss of married life in the newly built suburbs. The baby boom soon followed.

The 1950s were a time of great social conformity. The only female dissenting voice of note was that of Simone de Beauvoir (1908–1986), French existentialist, whose important work *The Second Sex* (1949 in French) shows how women were defined as the "Other" in philosophy, literature, history, and biology. De Beauvoir, though not claiming to be a feminist, tried to show that men such as her sometimes beau Jean-Paul Sartre simply assumed that women, as wives, mothers, and prostitutes, would always be around to provide for their physical needs. She argued that women epitomized, to use Sartre's own terminology, physically determined "in-itself" being, as opposed to the transcendentally free male sex, who exemplified "for-itself" being (see Chapter 3 for the details of Sartre's philosophy).

De Beauvoir is a transitional figure, a connecting bridge between the First Wave, with its concern for basic rights such as the right to vote, to property, and to education, and the Second Wave, whose critique of male-dominated society was to call for much more far-reaching social changes.

## THE SECOND WAVE

The Second Wave can be said to start with Betty Friedan's publication of *The Feminine Mystique* in 1963, with its critique of the sleepy social conformity of the post-war housewife living out the American dream amid dishwashers and diapers. Friedan initiated liberal feminism's critique of the male-dominated nuclear family, a central theme of the Second Wave. Friedan also formed the National Organization for Women in 1966, whose initial goal was to open up more careers to women. Because most of this chapter deals with the ideas of the Second Wave, this introduction will focus on just the highlights.

The Second Wave of feminism moved the fight for equality from the realm of politics and the law to that of social and economic relationships. In a nutshell, Second Wave theorists argued that the formal legal and political equality won by the First Wave wasn't good enough, for it didn't address the deeper inequalities suffered by women in their family and sex lives, in the workplace, and in intellectual and popular culture.

The mid- and late 1960s saw the hippie counterculture flourishing in America alongside the civil rights and antiwar movements. Many women, Shulamith Firestone included, joined these mass protests, often becoming radicalized as a result of their experiences. The women's liberation movement came out of this ferment. "Women's libbers," as they were derogatorily called, burned their bras as symbols of their oppression as sexual objects, demonstrated against beauty pageants, rejected monogamy and the traditional male-dominated family as part of a sexual revolution, and demanded concrete social changes such as readily available birth control, the right to an abortion, funding for day care and rape crisis centers, equal pay for equal work, and affirmative action programs to increase the number of women entering professional careers.

Although early Second Wave feminism was dominated by liberal reformers such as Betty Friedan, by the 1970s the women's movement became more and more associated with radical feminism. These Second Wave radicals argued that we live in a patriarchy, where male power is expressed in pretty well all facets of society: in our political institutions, the law, the media, the economy, family life, and popular culture.

Kate Millett and Shulamith Firestone sketched out distinct theories of patriarchy in their 1970 books *Sexual Politics* and *The Dialectic of Sex* (although Firestone also used traditional Marxist language in her book). This idea of patriarchy became a theoretical assumption for radical feminists. Even now, two decades or more after many of the social and economic changes demanded by the Second Wave have already been enacted, latter-day radicals such as Susan Faludi insist that patriarchy is still very much in place and that mainstream women's rejection of radicalism is part of an anti-feminist backlash.

In the 1970s Susan Brownmiller, Adrienne Rich, Andrea Dworkin, and Catharine MacKinnon turned the light of radical feminist theory on our sexual behavior. They argued that patriarchy tried to enforce male power over women through pornography, sexual harassment, homophobia against lesbians, and rape. They saw sexual violence as widespread in our society, but as largely swept under the carpet by mainstream power structures and the media. Brownmiller argued that rape is about power, not sexual desire, and that all men are potential or real rapists. MacKinnon and others campaigned to have sexual harassment condemned by the law (which she succeeded in doing) and fought alongside Dworkin to enact municipal ordinances banning pornography as a violation of women's civil rights, which they briefly succeeded in doing in Minneapolis in 1983 and 1984 (the Supreme Court later overturned these ordinances as unconstitutional). They offered a loaded definition of pornography as sexually explicit pictures or words that dehumanized women, showing them to be mere sexual objects who enjoyed humiliation, mutilation, and rape. They argued that pornography eroticized male power and promoted female civic inequality.

Adrienne Rich, Marilyn Frye, and others argued that lesbianism was just as natural as heterosexuality and that social pressure is the only reason many women choose a straight sexual orientation. In fact, some radicals argued that heterosexual women were "sleeping with the enemy," so politically motivated lesbianism became common among Second Wave radical feminists.

A new model of manhood also came out of the radical feminist critique of patriarchy: the sensitive male in touch with his emotions, a man who shares the housework and other burdens of family life and who willingly gives up his role as family patriarch in exchange for a more egalitarian set of arrangements where his "partner" (i.e., his wife, whether by cohabitation or law) can pursue an independent career. Despite the ridicule this model has attracted from both comedians and media pundits, it remains to this day a powerful influence on white middle-class, North American men.

The 1970s were the high point of Second Wave activism, when radical feminism was in its heyday. In 1973 the *Roe v. Wade* Supreme Court decision in the United States gave women the right to abortion during the first two trimesters of a pregnancy, before the fetus was viable. Yet perhaps the most dramatic moment in Second Wave feminism came in 1972, when the U.S. Congress finally passed the Equal Rights Amendment (ERA) outlawing all forms of discrimination based on sex (it was first introduced in 1923). The ERA turned out to be the Second Wave's Waterloo: Even though Congress extended the deadline for the required ratification by thirty-eight states from seven to ten years, by 1982 only thirty-five states had done so, leaving it dead in the water. Yet despite the ERA's defeat in the United States, other countries have entrenched sexual equality into their constitutions. For example, Canada's 1982 Charter of Rights and Freedoms guarantees equality before and under the law without discrimination based on race, ethnic origin, religion, sex, or disability.

Second Wave feminism did effect some very positive social changes. Yet its radical form, which came to dominate the Second Wave in the 1970s, created a number of real theoretical and practical problems. It was seen by its various critics as dogmatic, inflexible, intolerant of dissent, antimale, antisex (or at least anti–heterosexual sex), a front for lesbianism, a sophisticated interest group to advance the economic interests of white middle-class women in corporate and academic life, or a throwback to Social Purity feminism (with its "women good, men bad" position).

Perhaps the most significant weakness of Second Wave radicalism was its tendency to picture women as the passive victims of male oppression. This tied into the theory of patriarchy, which some critics saw as a massive conspiracy theory. The idea that patriarchy was an unchanging monolith implied (1) that men are the implacable enemies of women's rights and can't be trusted, regardless of empirical evidence to the contrary; (2) that women have no power over their lives, so resistance to patriarchy is futile; and (3) that it's better to take refuge in a sentimental notion of sisterly solidarity or to form an entirely separate women's culture than to take the bull by its horns and force social and economic changes in a male-dominated society.

Another important problem, at least with the radicals in the Second Wave, was their puritanical attitude toward sexuality, especially heterosexuality. Theorists such as Brownmiller and Dworkin painted a very dark picture of male sexual desire, tying it on the deepest level to violence, power, and the oppression of women. Many radicals came to believe that all men were, at least in their heart, rapists, and that women who slept with men and enjoyed it were somehow deluding themselves about the authenticity of their desires. This also led radicals to attack pornography and prostitution and to call for a strict censorship of text and images of women that pictured them as sexual objects or otherwise degraded them.

Naturally, heterosexual women committed to feminism sometimes felt torn. On the one hand, they were told that men were the cause of their misfortunes and that male sexual desire was oppressive, if not violent; on the other, they had boyfriends and husbands whom they cared for, and who, in most cases, neither raped nor beat them. To use a Marxist metaphor, there seemed to be a gap between theory and practice in their lives.

Further, some of the feminist-inspired economic reforms to come out of the 1970s and 1980s had a dubious moral foundation. A case in point is affirmative action programs. Second Wave feminists argued that because gender inequalities were structural and tied to a patriarchal ideology that not only oppressed women directly but blocked their drive to succeed, equality of opportunity wasn't good enough. Women would still be discriminated against in the hiring process. They argued for (and in many cases got) programs that aimed to redress gender imbalances in professional life by compelling corporations, the public-service sector, and universities to hire a preestablished quota of women, even if their qualifications were inferior to those of male candidates.

The "sins of the father" argument could be used against affirmative action. Men seeking work in the 1980s and later could legitimately ask why they had to suffer for the metaphorical sins of their fathers, who were the ones actually responsible for gender imbalances in the workplace. Even if affirmative action programs weren't meant to punish innocent bystanders for the crimes of others, they sometimes seemed to do so by those whom they disadvantaged. This continues to be a burning problem in practical ethics: Should women or racial minorities be given special treatment in hiring processes to redress gender and racial imbalances in a workforce, or should the law merely guarantee the equality of opportunity and let the best woman or man win?

Second Wave feminism must be credited with reforming our attitudes toward the male-dominated nuclear family, with creating a workplace where it's more likely that women will be fairly compensated and can work without being sexually harassed, with giving women reproductive rights, and in general with pointing out the continuing ways in which women's lives are limited by our society. Yet some of the demons of the Second Wave couldn't be exorcised. This gave birth to a small group of theoretical critics of radical feminism and a wider turning away from feminism among young women in the West. We can characterize these developments as the birth of a Third Wave.

## THE THIRD WAVE

By the 1980s women of all classes started to ask themselves some serious questions about the value of the feminist movement. Had feminism itself become oppressive toward its followers in its intolerance to dissent, isolated from the lives of ordinary women, and immune to criticism? Has the political correctness movement sponsored by feminism, and its call to censor certain forms of sexual expression, damaged freedom of speech? Has the Second Wave alienated young women from the movement in its puritanical attitude toward sex, its antimale rhetoric, and its condescending attitude toward poor and minority women? The radical feminists of the Second Wave had no easy answers to these questions, other than to insist that those asking them were operating under a "false consciousness" generated by patriarchy.

The Third Wave can be defined in a negative sense by its turning away from sexual repression and the idea that women were the passive victims of patriarchal oppression. In a positive sense, it can be defined by its demand that women assume responsibility for their lives, fight oppression both without *and* within traditional power structures, and create cultural icons who are more than simple rejections of mainstream male society. Not surprisingly, Third Wave feminism wasn't, at least at first, a product of academia and theory but of the cultural practices of women such as the pop singer Madonna and the television talk-show host Oprah Winfrey, who became one of the richest people in America by dint of her own efforts. Unlike radical feminism, which was defined to a large degree by writers such as Millett and Firestone, Third Wave feminism rode to international attention aboard such pop cultural vessels as the Venetian gondola in Madonna's 1984 music video "Like a Virgin." Feminist theory took a while to catch up to that gondola.

We can find a historical parallel to the shift from Second to Third Wave feminism in mid-seventeenth-century England. During the rule of the Puritan-led Parliament in Oliver Cromwell's Republic (1653–1660), strict moral rules governed both art and life. However, in the Restoration period (from 1660 on), when the Stuart kings returned to power, these moral strictures were moderated or disappeared, and the arts sprang to life again. The music of Henry Purcell enchanted palace and theater audiences, while John Dryden provided the literate classes with drama and comedy. In addition, sexual mores loosened up, with King Charles II notorious for his fondness for mistresses. Feminism, and to a lesser degree our society as a whole, may be now going through such a shift from Puritanism to the Restoration attitude of being more forgiving toward freedom of expression and sexuality for women.

Camille Paglia acted as the gadfly and scourge of radical and academic feminism in the 1990s. She came to fame with her 1990 book, *Sexual Personae,* which celebrated pagan beauty and the power of demonic natural forces in the history of Western art and literature. It starts by informing us that "in the beginning was nature. . . . We cannot hope to understand sex and gender until we clarify our attitude toward nature." Paglia went on to attack not only the idea of sexual difference as purely a social construction but also the notion that women were not responsible for using their common sense to avoid sexual violence, Dworkin and MacKinnon's hostility toward pornography, the "Stalinist" attitude of Gloria Steinem and other prominent radical feminists toward dissent, the intrusion of dense and obscure French theorists such as Foucault and Derrida into American academic life, and the very idea of patriarchy itself. She celebrated decadence of all types, from Oscar Wilde to Madonna, from classic Hollywood films to rock and roll.

Christina Hoff Sommers, a sober academic philosopher, added fuel to Paglia's fire with her 1994 book, *Who Stole Feminism?* Hoff Sommers claimed that prominent feminists such as Gloria Steinem, Catharine MacKinnon, and Naomi Wolf in her early days deliberately distorted or lied about research on the status of women in America in order to support the notion that patriarchy was alive and well and that women had to band together and accept the orthodox views of the leadership of the feminist movement in order to maintain what few rights they had already won. She starts her book by quoting Steinem to the effect that 150,000 women die every year in America due to anorexia nervosa, a claim that Wolf repeated in her much-read 1991 book, *The Beauty Myth.* After a bit of checking, Hoff Sommers discovered that the real figure varied from a high of 101 deaths in 1983 to a low of 54 in 1991, vastly different from the figure quoted by Steinem and Wolf. Hoff Sommers goes on to show how Second Wave "gender" feminists—that is, those feminists who believe that patriarchy still rules supreme and that women are engaged in a "gender war" with men—have used these distortions of the facts to stir up fear among women in order to maintain an ideological hegemony over the women's movement, to "steal" feminism from equity feminists such as Betty Friedan, Susan Sontag, and Hoff Sommers herself.

Due in part to such critiques, even Wolf herself recanted somewhat her earlier allegiance to Second Wave feminism in her 1993 book, *Fire with Fire.* The book is largely an attempt to understand why young American women in the early 1990s had turned their back on feminism. Much of it is a muted attack on the intolerance and puritanism of Second Wave radicalism and a celebration of women's ability to use existing power structures to effect change, not to mention Wolf's firmly heterosexual romantic life.

The Third Wave is in no way questioning the legal, political, and social achievements of liberal feminism, including full equality before the law, the right to day care and abortion, women's active participation in democratic politics, and women's entry en masse into the workforce on an increasingly equal footing. Instead, it calls on women to stop playing the role of the passive victims of patriarchy and to take control over their own fate as sexual, economic, and political beings. It also asks women to acknowledge that even if biology is not destiny, we are not entirely free from its directives, so feminists shouldn't endlessly blame men for being heterosexual or for having politically incorrect desires. In short, the Third Wave calls for greater pragmatism and realism in feminist theory.

## Sex and Gender: Is Difference Natural or Cultural?

Feminist theory raises a number of philosophically interesting and vexing questions. Perhaps the most basic is "Are men and women essentially different, or is this difference constructed entirely by culture?" Early feminists tended to argue that men and women *were* different in some respects, but that this was a positive thing, because women were more virtuous and sensitive and could soften and expand men's less moral characters. Besides, as Wollstonecraft herself argues, men and women were more or less equal in the key area of intelligence or capacity for abstract thought, women's perceived inadequacies being the product of a shoddy education. This idea that men and women are different thanks to their biologies is called "essentialism." Carol Gilligan gave this view some credibility thanks to her psychological studies, which aimed to prove that young women spoke in a different moral voice than young men, preferring an ethics of care to the male-dominant ethics of justice.

By the 1980s, though, feminist theorists started to move to the other extreme, arguing that there was nothing that naturally distinguished men from women. Many stopped using the term "sex" to describe men and women, preferring the term "gender" (the use of the term becoming a political badge of loyalty to feminism). These "social constructionists" argued that both psychological traits, such as women's supposed emotional nature and need to nurture, *and* social roles, such as being a wife and mother, were programmed into women by patriarchal society. Theorists such as Susan Moller Okin and Donna Haraway, the author of a manifesto championing gender-bending cyborgs, saw the differences between men and women as cultural, not natural.

As budding philosophers, we should always be aware of the terminology we use. When we look at how Second Wave feminists use the term "gender" with regard to concrete political policies, we find that it most often refers to the male and female biological sexes. For example, affirmative action programs target the hiring of women as a biological sex, not people who consider themselves to be playing "female" gender roles. Also, men are often excluded from joining women's rights organizations, from attending "take-back-the-night" rallies, or from teaching feminist theory, even if they are sympathetic to feminist goals. Naomi Wolf tells the story in *Fire with Fire* of her profeminist boyfriend's exclusion from a meeting of a feminist group because he was a man. So when push comes to shove, the Second Wave's use of the term "gender" to describe difference often dissolves into simple biology.

We consider the above distinction important because the term "sex" should be used to describe differences between men and women as beings with distinct bodily structures, including sex-specific genitalia, the ability to give birth in the case of women, greater physical strength in the case of men, and some minor psychological differences caused by genetic predispositions to behave in certain ways. The political goal of feminism is to advance the cause of women as a *sex*. We can reserve the term "gender" to describe differences between men and women that are the product of nurture or culture, for example, gender roles such as women staying at home to cook, clean, and perform child care, or men's once total domination of political life.

Strictly speaking, the difference between sex and gender can be seen as lying on a continuum, with essential differences, such as that between men's and women's physical bodies, at one end; deeply entrenched psychological characteristics, such as male aggressiveness and female nurturing, somewhere in the middle; and cultural artifacts, such as the former domination of the professions of medicine, the law, and higher education by men, at the other. At the first extreme, we can use the term "sex" to describe the differences between men and women; at the other, "gender." It really comes down to what we're talking about: If the differences between men and women are fluid and constructed by society, then the term "gender" seems appropriate to describe these differences; if not, then the older and more concrete term "sex" would seem more useful.

## Patriarchy, Sexism, and Sexual Expression

The last part of this introduction will lay out for debate a number of key issues in feminist theory. When we look at radical feminism later in this chapter, we'll see that its central claim is that modern societies are all patriarchies where men oppress women on all levels: in family life, the economy, politics, and cultural life. Whether or not this was ever a conscious conspiracy on the part of men, it's hard to deny that up until the early twentieth century women were oppressed in a number of fundamental ways. Even after the reforms of the First Wave had been passed into law, the limited educational and economic horizons for women left them as second-class citizens at least until the late 1960s.

The question that has to be addressed here is whether, given the great gains made by the women's movement over the last generation, we can no longer meaningfully claim that we live in a totally male-dominated society. Indeed, in some fields affirmative action programs have given profeminist women a slightly advantaged status—in academic life, for example (although female professors, despite having good jobs, often complain about the "chilly climate" they feel surrounds women in academic life, notably in disciplines long dominated by men, such as philosophy).

So the first issue to be opened up for debate is based on a simple question: Do we currently live in a patriarchy in which women are systematically and structurally oppressed by men? Further we can ask, If the answer to this question is "yes," what is the nature of that oppression? If the causes of this oppression could be eliminated, would patriarchy itself end, and along with it the need for a feminist movement, just as the antislavery movement in America lost its reason to exist with Lincoln's Emancipation Proclamation? Admittedly, sexism is a more complex issue than slavery, which was abolished with the stroke of a pen. Yet the question remains: In what ways are women oppressed, and if this oppression could be more or less eliminated, would the need for feminist theory, and for a women's movement, end?

The next set of questions revolve around what used to be called "male chauvinism," now called "sexism." Sexism is the illegitimate discrimination against a person due solely to his or her sex. As with the previous question concerning the existence of patriarchy, we can ask in what ways modern society treats women in a sexist way. Are women barred from certain types of employment due to their sex? Are public or private institutions morally obliged to hire a certain percentage of women to overcome sexism in the workplace? Do certain aspects of popular culture—rap music, *Playboy* centerfolds, or Hollywood films—treat women in a sexist way?

Last, we should address the question of whether certain aspects of men's sexuality oppress women. Is heterosexuality felt to be compulsory and oppressive by women in our culture? Do women committed to their own liberation have to sever emotional and sexual ties with men? Does male sexuality objectify women? Are pornography, prostitution, stripping, and rape forms of male domination? How do fashion, beauty magazines, makeup, and women's concern with their body images contribute to women's fight for social and economic equality?

As you move through this chapter, think about all of these questions, and debate them with your classmates—hopefully in a reasonable and calm atmosphere!

# THE ORIGINS OF MODERN LIBERAL FEMINISM

## *Betty Friedan on the Empty Lives of Postwar Housewives*

Betty Friedan (1921–) is the major figure in early Second Wave liberal feminism in America. She founded NOW (the National Organization for Women) in 1966, serving as president of the organization until 1970. She was active in the early 1970s in organizing the women's movement and has taught off and on at various universities. In addition to *The Feminine Mystique* (1963), she wrote *The Second Stage* (1981), more reflections on feminism, and *The Fountain of Age* (1993), her meditations on growing old.

Liberal feminism agrees with feminism in general that the central problem of contemporary society is an inequality between the sexes. Liberal feminists, however, call for legal, political, and social reforms to correct this problem, and not radical separatism, cultural revolution, or the end of capitalism. They ask democratic societies to take more seriously their own founding documents and principles—for example, the U.S. Declaration of Independence, which declares that all *men* are created equal—and to extend the promise of liberty and equality to women. This would involve reforms to the state, the legal system, the family, and the workplace. In short, liberal feminists believe that they can use the legal and political tools already available in liberal democracies to solve the problem of sexual inequality.

Friedan's groundbreaking book *The Feminine Mystique,* from which the following selection comes, challenges the suffocating male idealization of women as wives and mothers, an idealization to which the title refers. Friedan argues that male culture in the America of the 1950s and early 1960s suppressed women's natural desire to become full human beings by trapping them in the gilded cages of suburban bungalows and in their limited social roles. The "problem that has no name" is the empty lives of these postwar housewives who lived out their "Ozzie and Harriet" existence as good housekeepers, mothers, cookers, and cleaners, yet felt all the same that their lives were empty, unfulfilled.

Friedan interviewed some of these housewives in the course of writing various magazine articles. After World War II, a baby boom went hand in hand with the post-war economic boom. Women were forgoing educations to get married and raise a family in the newly built suburbs, their husbands working at nine-to-five jobs. Birth rates in America skyrocketed, approaching Third-World proportions.

Friedan's interviews with these women resulted in the same message from most of them: They were strangely dissatisfied with their lives. Yet the problem lay deeply buried within the minds of these American women. "Is this all there is?" they asked. They were told by psychologists, moralists, and other experts that really feminine women don't want education, careers, or political rights, just a good husband and children. They were reminded that the American suburban housewife was the envy of the world, freed by science and technology from drudgery and disease and free to buy cars, clothes, appliances, and other consumer goods.

Yet why didn't they get any deep spiritual satisfaction from waxing floors? The problem wasn't with their husbands or children or homes. Psychologists had no name for it. It resulted in chronic depressions, in unexplained crying, in women running out into the street in desperation. Neither was it a function of these women's level of education: Many met their husbands while attending college. In fact, some journalists even blamed increased female education for this discontent. "Don't women know that their men aren't always happy either?" they asked. "They have to go to work five or six days a week to bring home the bacon that pays for the easy lifestyle of their wives and children."

Friedan didn't accept the idea that there was no answer to these women's dilemma. She noted the strange newness of a problem not related to poverty, hunger, sickness, or cold. Women who spend their whole lives in pursuit of the ideal of feminine fulfillment found a disturbing inner voice stirring. The problem was not sexual; in fact, women were made into sexual creatures, living for orgasms as the bright spot of their humdrum daily existences. The chains that bound were those of mind and spirit.

So the problem wasn't too much education, too little sex, a loss of femininity, or the excessive demands of housework. These women wanted something more than a husband, children, and a home. Over the next twenty or so years, Second Wave feminism tried to define exactly what this "something" missing was. Its various answers included sexual freedom, birth control, the destruction of the traditional nuclear family, independent careers, economic equality, political participation, and a distinct and separate female culture.

*The Feminine Mystique* points ahead to Marilyn Frye's caged-bird scenario: The suburban housewife, with a shiny new car in the driveway, the fanciest technological gadgets in the kitchen, enough money for good food, medicines, and toys for her children, is still miserable in the midst of plenty because she's trapped by the narrowness of her social and economic role of being a nurturer, cleaner, and cook. She is like a bird in a gilded cage, well fed and cared for, yet unequal, trapped, not free. Admittedly, the bars in Friedan's cage are perhaps easier to see than the ones that Frye describes. Yet they were just as limiting for the postwar housewife as those that later feminists talked about as barriers for women in general. Friedan effectively describes the feeling of being trapped felt by women of her generation, leaving to others in Second Wave feminism the task of explaining how this cage came to be and how its door could be opened.

# The Problem That Has No Name

## BETTY FRIEDAN

THE PROBLEM LAY BURIED, unspoken, for many years in the minds of American women. It was a strange stirring, a sense of dissatisfaction, a yearning that women suffered in the middle of the twentieth century in the United States. Each suburban wife struggled with it alone. As she made the beds, shopped for groceries, matched slipcover material, ate peanut butter sandwiches with her children, chauffeured Cub Scouts and Brownies, lay beside her husband at night—she was afraid to ask even of herself the silent question—"Is this all?"

For over fifteen years there was no word of this yearning in the millions of words written about women, for women, in all the columns, books and articles by experts telling women their role was to seek fulfillment as wives and mothers. Over and over women heard in voices of tradition and of Freudian sophistication that they could desire no greater destiny than to glory in their own femininity. Experts told them how to catch a man and keep him, how to breastfeed children and handle their toilet training, how to cope with sibling rivalry and adolescent rebellion; how to buy a dishwasher, bake bread, cook gourmet snails, and build a swimming pool with their own hands; how to dress, look, and act more feminine and make marriage more exciting; how to keep their husbands from dying young and their sons from growing into delinquents. They

were taught to pity the neurotic, unfeminine, unhappy women who wanted to be poets or physicists or presidents. They learned that truly feminine women do not want careers, higher education, political rights—the independence and the opportunities that the old-fashioned feminists fought for. Some women, in their forties and fifties, still remembered painfully giving up those dreams, but most of the younger women no longer even thought about them. A thousand expert voices applauded their femininity, their adjustment, their new maturity. All they had to do was devote their lives from earliest girlhood to finding a husband and bearing children. . . .

By the end of the fifties, the United States birthrate was overtaking India's. The birth-control movement, renamed Planned Parenthood, was asked to find a method whereby women who had been advised that a third or fourth baby would be born dead or defective might have it anyhow. Statisticians were especially astounded at the fantastic increase in the number of babies among college women. Where once they had two children, now they had four, five, six. Women who had once wanted careers were now making careers out of having babies. So rejoiced *Life* magazine in a 1956 paean to the movement of American women back to the home.

In a New York hospital, a woman had a ner-

SOURCE: Betty Friedan, "The Problem That Has No Name," chap. 1 in *The Feminine Mystique* (1963; New York: Norton, 1983), pp. 15–32 (edited significantly). Copyright 1983, 1974, 1973, 1963 by Betty Friedan. Used by permission of W. W. Norton & Company, Inc.

vous breakdown when she found she could not breastfeed her baby. In other hospitals, women dying of cancer refused a drug which research had proved might save their lives: its side effects were said to be unfeminine. "If I have only one life, let me live it as a blonde," a larger-than-life-sized picture of a pretty, vacuous woman proclaimed from newspaper, magazine, and drugstore ads. And across America, three out of every ten women dyed their hair blonde. They ate a chalk called Metrecal, instead of food, to shrink to the size of the thin young models. Department-store buyers reported that American women, since 1939, had become three and four sizes smaller. "Women are out to fit the clothes, instead of vice-versa," one buyer said.

Interior decorators were designing kitchens with mosaic murals and original paintings, for kitchens were once again the center of women's lives. Home sewing became a million-dollar industry. Many women no longer left their homes, except to shop, chauffeur their children, or attend a social engagement with their husbands. Girls were growing up in America without ever having jobs outside the home. In the late fifties, a sociological phenomenon was suddenly remarked: a third of American women now worked, but most were no longer young and very few were pursuing careers. They were married women who held part-time jobs, selling or secretarial, to put their husbands through school, their sons through college, or to help pay the mortgage. Or they were widows supporting families. Fewer and fewer women were entering professional work. The shortages in the nursing, social work, and teaching professions caused crises in almost every American city. Concerned over the Soviet Union's lead in the space race, scientists noted that America's greatest source of unused brain-power was women. But girls would not study physics: it was "unfeminine." A girl refused a science fellowship at Johns Hopkins to take a job in a real-estate office. All she wanted, she said, was what every other American girl wanted—to get married, have four children and live in a nice house in a nice suburb.

The suburban housewife—she was the dream image of the young American women and the envy, it was said, of women all over the world. The American housewife—freed by science and labor-saving appliances from the drudgery, the dangers of childbirth and the illnesses of her grandmother. She was healthy, beautiful, educated, concerned only about her husband, her children, her home. She had found true feminine fulfillment. As a housewife and mother, she was respected as a full and equal partner to man in his world. She was free to choose automobiles, clothes, appliances, supermarkets; she had everything that women ever dreamed of.

In the fifteen years after World War II, this mystique of feminine fulfillment became the cherished and self-perpetuating core of contemporary American culture. Millions of women lived their lives in the image of those pretty pictures of the American suburban housewife, kissing their husbands goodbye in front of the picture window, depositing their stationwagonsful of children at school, and smiling as they ran the new electric waxer over the spotless kitchen floor. They baked their own bread, sewed their own and their children's clothes, kept their new washing machines and dryers running all day. They changed the sheets on the beds twice a week instead of once, took the rug-hooking class in adult education, and pitied their poor frustrated mothers, who had dreamed of having a career. Their only dream was to be perfect wives and mothers; their highest ambition to have five children and a beautiful house, their only fight to get and keep their husbands. They had no thought for the unfeminine problems of the world outside the home; they wanted the men to make the major decisions. They gloried in their role as women, and wrote proudly on the census blank: "Occupation: housewife."

For over fifteen years, the words written for women, and the words women used when they talked to each other, while their husbands sat on the other side of the room and talked shop or politics or septic tanks, were about problems with their children, or how to keep their husbands happy, or improve their children's school, or cook chicken or make slipcovers. Nobody argued whether women were inferior or superior to men; they were simply different. Words like "emancipation" and "career" sounded strange and embarrassing; no one had used them for years. When a Frenchwoman named Simone de Beauvoir wrote a book called *The Second Sex,* an American critic commented that she obviously "didn't know what life was all about," and besides, she was talking about French women. The "woman problem" in America no longer existed.

If a woman had a problem in the 1950's and 1960's, she knew that something must be wrong with her marriage, or with herself. Other women were satisfied with their lives, she thought. What kind of a woman was she if she did not feel this mysterious fulfillment waxing the kitchen floor? She was so ashamed to admit her dissatisfaction that she never knew how many other women shared it. If she tried to tell her husband, he didn't understand what she was talking about. She did not really understand it herself. For over fifteen years women in America found it harder to talk about this problem than about sex. Even the psychoanalysts had no name for it. When a woman went to a psychiatrist for help, as many women did, she would say, "I'm so ashamed," or "I must be hopelessly neurotic." "I don't know what's wrong with women today," a suburban psychiatrist said uneasily. "I only know something is wrong because most of my patients happen to be women. And their problem isn't sexual." Most women with this problem did not go to see a psychoanalyst, however. "There's nothing wrong really," they kept telling themselves. "There isn't any problem."

But on an April morning in 1959, I heard a mother of four, having coffee with four other mothers in a suburban development fifteen miles from New York, say in a tone of quiet desperation, "the problem." And the others knew, without words, that she was not talking about a problem with her husband, or her children, or her home. Suddenly they realized they all shared the same problem, the problem that has no name. They began, hesitantly, to talk about it. Later, after they had picked up their children at nursery school and taken them home to nap, two of the women cried, in sheer relief, just to know they were not alone. . . .

Just what was this problem that has no name? What were the words women used when they tried to express it? Sometimes a woman would say "I feel empty somehow . . . incomplete." Or she would say, "I feel as if I don't exist." Sometimes she blotted out the feeling with a tranquilizer. Sometimes she thought the problem was with her husband, or her children, or that what she really needed was to redecorate her house, or move to a better neighborhood, or have an affair, or another baby. Sometimes, she went to a doctor with symptoms she could hardly describe: "A tired feeling . . . I get so angry with the children it scares me . . . I feel like crying without any reason." (A Cleveland doctor called it "the housewife's syndrome.") A number of women told me about great bleeding blisters that break out on their hands and arms. "I call it the housewife's blight," said a family doctor in Pennsylvania. "I see it so often lately in these young women with four, five and six children who bury themselves in their dishpans. But it isn't caused by detergent and it isn't cured by cortisone."

Sometimes a woman would tell me that the feeling gets so strong she runs out of the house and walks through the streets. Or she stays inside her house and cries. Or her children tell her a joke, and she doesn't laugh because she doesn't hear it. I talked to women who had spent years on the analyst's couch, working out their "adjustment to the feminine role," their blocks to "fulfillment as a wife and mother." But the desperate tone in these women's voices, and the look in their eyes, was the same as the tone and the look of other women, who were sure they had no problem, even though they did have a strange feeling of desperation. . . .

In 1960, the problem that has no name burst like a boil through the image of the happy American housewife. . . . Some said it was the old problem—education: more and more women had education, which naturally made them unhappy in their role as housewives. "The road from Freud to Frigidaire, from Sophocles to Spock, has turned out to be a bumpy one," reported the

*New York Times* (June 28, 1960). "Many young women—certainly not all—whose education plunged them into a world of ideas feel stifled in their homes. They find their routine lives out of joint with their training. Like shut-ins, they feel left out. In the last year, the problem of the educated housewife has provided the meat of dozens of speeches made by troubled presidents of women's colleges who maintain, in the face of complaints, that sixteen years of academic training is realistic preparation for wifehood and motherhood." . . .

Home economists suggested more realistic preparation for housewives, such as high-school workshops in home appliances. College educators suggested more discussion groups on home management and the family, to prepare women for the adjustment to domestic life. A spate of articles appeared in the mass magazines offering "Fifty-eight Ways to Make Your Marriage More Exciting." No month went by without a new book by a psychiatrist or sexologist offering technical advice on finding greater fulfillment through sex. . . .

A number of educators suggested seriously that women no longer be admitted to the four-year colleges and universities: in the growing college crisis, the education which girls could not use as housewives was more urgently needed than ever by boys to do the work of the atomic age.

The problem was also dismissed with drastic solutions no one could take seriously. (A woman writer proposed in *Harper's* that women be drafted for compulsory service as nurses' aides and baby-sitters.) And it was smoothed over with the age-old panaceas: "love is their answer," "the only answer is inner help," "the secret of completeness—children," "a private means of intellectual fulfillment," "to cure this toothache of the spirit—the simple formula of handing one's self and one's will over to God."

The problem was dismissed by telling the housewife she doesn't realize how lucky she is—her own boss, no time clock, no junior executive gunning for her job. What if she isn't happy—does she think men are happy in this world? Does she really, secretly, still want to be a man?

Doesn't she know yet how lucky she is to be a woman? . . .

Of the growing thousands of women currently getting private psychiatric help in the United States, the married ones were reported dissatisfied with their marriages, the unmarried ones suffering from anxiety and, finally, depression. Strangely, a number of psychiatrists stated that, in their experience, unmarried women patients were happier than married ones. So the door of all those pretty suburban houses opened a crack to permit a glimpse of uncounted thousands of American housewives who suffered alone from a problem that suddenly everyone was talking about, and beginning to take for granted, as one of those unreal problems in American life that can never be solved—like the hydrogen bomb. . . .

Even so, most men, and some women, still did not know that this problem was real. But those who had faced it honestly knew that all the superficial remedies, the sympathetic advice, the scolding words and the cheering words were somehow drowning the problem in unreality. A bitter laugh was beginning to be heard from American women. They were admired, envied, pitied, theorized over until they were sick of it, offered drastic solutions or silly choices that no one could take seriously. They got all kinds of advice from the growing armies of marriage and child-guidance counselors, psychotherapists, and armchair psychologists, on how to adjust to their role as housewives. No other road to fulfillment was offered to American women in the middle of the twentieth century. Most adjusted to their role and suffered or ignored the problem that has no name. It can be less painful, for a woman, not to hear the strange, dissatisfied voice stirring within her.

It is no longer possible to ignore that voice, to dismiss the desperation of so many American women. This is not what being a woman means, no matter what the experts say. For human suffering there is a reason; perhaps the reason has not been found because the right questions have not been asked, or pressed far enough. I do not accept the answer that there is no problem because American women have luxuries that women in other times and lands never dreamed of; part of the strange newness of the problem is that it cannot be understood in terms of the age-old material problems of man: poverty, sickness, hunger, cold. The women who suffer this problem have a hunger that food cannot fill. It persists in women whose husbands are struggling interns and law clerks, or prosperous doctors and lawyers; in wives of workers and executives who make $5,000 a year or $50,000. It is not caused by lack of material advantages; it may not even be felt by women preoccupied with desperate problems of hunger, poverty or illness. And women who think it will be solved by more money, a bigger house, a second car, moving to a better suburb, often discover it gets worse.

It is no longer possible today to blame the problem on loss of femininity: to say that education and independence and equality with men have made American women unfeminine. I have heard so many women try to deny this dissatisfied voice within themselves because it does not fit the pretty picture of femininity the experts have given them. I think, in fact, that this is the first clue to the mystery: the problem cannot be understood in the generally accepted terms by which scientists have studied women, doctors have treated them, counselors have advised them, and writers have written about them. Women who suffer this problem, in whom this voice is stirring, have lived their whole lives in the pursuit of feminine fulfillment. They are not career women (although career women may have other problems); they are women whose greatest ambition has been marriage and children. For the oldest of these women, these daughters of the American middle class, no other dream was possible. The ones in their forties and fifties who once had other dreams gave them up and threw themselves joyously into life as housewives. For the youngest, the new wives and mothers, this was the only dream. They are the ones who quit high school and college to marry, or marked time in some job in which they had no real interest until they married. These women are very "feminine" in the usual sense, and yet they still suffer the problem. . . .

If the secret of feminine fulfillment is having children, never have so many women, with the freedom to choose, had so many children, in so few years, so willingly. If the answer is love, never have women searched for love with such determination. And yet there is a growing suspicion that the problem may not be sexual, though it must somehow be related to sex. I have heard from many doctors evidence of new sexual problems between man and wife—sexual hunger in wives so great their husbands cannot satisfy it. "We have made woman a sex creature," said a psychiatrist at the Margaret Sanger marriage counseling clinic. "She has no identity except as a wife and mother. She does not know who she is herself. She waits all day for her husband to come home at night to make her feel alive. And now it is the husband who is not interested. It is terrible for the women, to lie there, night after night, waiting for her husband to make her feel alive." Why is there such a market for books and articles offering sexual advice? The kind of sexual orgasm which Kinsey found in statistical plenitude in the recent generations of American women does not seem to make this problem go away. . . .

Can the problem that has no name be somehow related to the domestic routine of the housewife? When a woman tries to put the problem into words, she often merely describes the daily life she leads. What is there in this recital of comfortable domestic detail that could possibly cause such a feeling of desperation? Is she trapped simply by the enormous demands of her role as modern housewife: wife, mistress, mother, nurse, consumer, cook, chauffeur; expert on interior decoration, child care, appliance repair, furniture refinishing, nutrition, and education? Her day is fragmented as she rushes from dishwasher to washing machine to telephone to dryer to station wagon to supermarket, and delivers Johnny to the Little League field, takes Janey to dancing class, gets the lawnmower fixed and meets the 6:45. She can never spend more than 15 minutes on any one thing; she has no time to read books, only magazines; even if she had time, she has lost the power to concentrate. At the end of the day, she is so terribly tired that sometimes her husband has to take over and put the children to bed.

This terrible tiredness took so many women to doctors in the 1950's that one decided to investigate it. He found, surprisingly, that his patients suffering from "housewife's fatigue" slept more than an adult needed to sleep—as much as ten hours a day—and that the actual energy they expended on housework did not tax their capacity. The real problem must be something else, he decided—perhaps boredom. Some doctors told their women patients they must get out of the house for a day, treat themselves to a movie in town. Others prescribed tranquilizers. Many suburban housewives were taking tranquilizers like cough drops. "You wake up in the morning, and you feel as if there's no point in going on another day like this. So you take a tranquilizer because it makes you not care so much that it's pointless."

It is easy to see the concrete details that trap the suburban housewife, the continual demands on her time. But the chains that bind her in her trap are chains in her own mind and spirit. They are chains made up of mistaken ideas and misinterpreted facts, of incomplete truths and unreal choices. They are not easily seen and not easily shaken off.

How can any woman see the whole truth within the bounds of her own life? How can she believe that voice inside herself, when it denies the conventional, accepted truths by which she has been living? And yet the women I have talked to, who are finally listening to that inner voice, seem in some incredible way to be groping through to a truth that has defied the experts.

I think the experts in a great many fields have been holding pieces of that truth under their microscopes for a long time without realizing it. I found pieces of it in certain new research and theoretical developments in psychological, social and biological science whose implications for women seem never to have been examined. I found many clues by talking to suburban doctors, gynecologists, obstetricians, child-guidance clinicians, pediatricians, high-school guidance counselors, college professors, marriage counselors, psychiatrists and ministers—questioning them not on their theories, but on their actual experience in treating American women. I became aware of a growing body of evidence, much of which has not been reported publicly because it does not fit current modes of thought about women—evidence which throws into question the standards of feminine normality, feminine adjustment, feminine fulfillment, and feminine maturity by which most women are still trying to live.

I began to see in a strange new light the American return to early marriage and the large families that are causing the population explosion; the recent movement to natural childbirth and breastfeeding; suburban conformity, and the new neuroses, character pathologies and sexual problems being reported by the doctors. I began to see new dimensions to old problems that have long been taken for granted among women: menstrual difficulties, sexual frigidity, promiscuity, pregnancy fears, childbirth depression, the high incidence of emotional breakdown and suicide among women in their twenties and thirties, the menopause crises, the so-called passivity and immaturity of American men, the discrepancy between women's tested intellectual abilities in childhood and their adult achievement, the changing incidence of adult sexual orgasm in American women, and persistent problems in psychotherapy and in women's education.

If I am right, the problem that has no name stirring in the minds of so many American women today is not a matter of loss of femininity or too much education, or the demands of domesticity. It is far more important than anyone recognizes. It is the key to these other new and old problems which have been torturing women and their husbands and children, and puzzling their doctors and educators for years. It may well be the key to our future as a nation and a culture. We can no longer ignore that voice within women that says: "I want something more than my husband and my children and my home."

# RADICAL AND SOCIALIST FEMINISM

## Shulamith Firestone on the Dialectic of Sex

Shulamith Firestone (1945–) was born in Ottawa, Canada. She attended the Art Institute of Chicago in the 1960s, becoming involved in the civil rights and anti–Vietnam War movements as a student. She turned to women's liberation in part out of her exasperation with the lack of concern of her male revolutionary comrades with women's problems. She also edited the journals *Redstockings* and *Notes from the Second Year* and was a member of the New York Radical Feminists. She is remembered primarily because of her manifesto of radical and socialist feminism, *The Dialectic of Sex* (1970). She faded from the feminist limelight after the heyday of radical feminism in the late 1960s and early 1970s, though *The Dialectic of Sex* remained highly influential in the Second Wave for years after. Her 1998 book, *Airless Spaces,* is a series of short stories about people's lives in mental hospitals.

Radical feminism is grounded in the notion that our society is a "patriarchy" in all significant ways—in terms of family life, economic and political structures, cultural practices, and ideological self-justifications. *Patriarchy* is an old word that means "the rule of the father," or the rule of men in general. But radical feminists have given it a new twist, arguing that not only is the state run by men but that women's submissive status has been deeply embedded in the organization of the family, our romantic relationships, our economy, and our culture. This widened notion of patriarchy was first argued for in detail by Kate Millett in her 1970 book, *Sexual Politics,* which was for a while the theoretical bible of Second Wave radical feminism.

Radical feminists believe that only a revolution against the whole patriarchal structure will bring it down and allow for women's equality. Piecemeal reform won't work. Some radical feminists, such as Adrienne Rich, argued for sexual separatism: the creation of a separate women's culture that would exist parallel to patriarchy. Rich argues that there is nothing "natural" about heterosexuality: Without the oppressive economic and political relations between men and women characteristic of patriarchy, more women would be drawn toward lesbianism. She goes on to argue that all intimate relationships between women exist on a "lesbian continuum," whether or not these are explicitly sexual. Many prominent Second Wave feminists (including Kate Millett, Andrea Dworkin, and Marilyn Frye) agreed with Rich, turning their backs on heterosexuality in their personal lives.

Others turned to socialist feminism, shifting Marx's class struggle into the sexual arena. Socialist feminists see the cause of women's oppression as economic. They argue that capitalist societies are unique in creating patriarchal oppression by promoting male domination in the family and the economy through a division of labor in which women are confined in the home as mothers and housewives, and in the workforce at low-paying and low-status jobs. Firestone combines elements of radical and socialist feminism in the selections from *The Dialectic of Sex* that follow.

She argues that radical feminists are talking about a revolution based on changing women's fundamental biological condition through technology. Just as Marx suggested that the proletariat seize the means of production from the capitalists, Firestone suggests that women should seize the means of reproduction from male-dominated society. Further, Firestone believes that because sexual difference pervades our entire culture, feminists have to question not only the organization of culture as a whole but the organization of nature itself by controlling the reproductive process.

Marx and Engels's dialectical materialism was of some use, she suggested. Marx's materialist method, which sought the ultimate cause for historical events in economic struggles, avoided the stagnant "metaphysical" view of history. However, Marx and Engels's "economic filter" prevented them from seeing that underlying their cherished class struggle there existed the sexual substratum of the dialectic, a dialectic of sexual difference. So Firestone suggests that we draw a theoretical circle around economics and develop a new, but still materialist, view of history based on sex as its primary category. She goes on in the core of her book to lay out how this dialectic has historically affected romance, the family, culture, and economics.

Firestone's utopian speculations on how to end the dialectic of sex are contained in her conclusion, much of which follows in the reading. In it she makes four general demands: (1) the freeing of women from the tyranny of their reproductive biology and the diffusing of child care throughout the community; (2) the full self-determination, including economic, of women and children; (3) the total integration of women and children into society; and (4) sexual freedom for women and children to do what they want when they want with whom they want.

One of the major social barriers to the fulfillment of these demands is the continued allure of marriage for women, despite steadily increasing divorce rates. Firestone bemoans the fact that the institution of marriage is buttressed by pious sermons, guidance manuals, and psychological counseling. Oddly, she says, everyone debunks marriage, yet winds up married anyway. When a marriage fails, people blame themselves, not the institution. At the altar they're convinced "it can't happen to me!" and say "I do" with the conviction that they'll beat the house odds, even though many of their friends have failed to do so. This is no doubt in part due to the obvious benefits of marriage, which Firestone freely admits: physical security, psychological integration into a couple-oriented society, and a steady supply of sex. In the end, though, marriage is organized around a fundamental, biologically based oppression that must be corrected by a feminist revolution.

Firestone offers some alternatives to then-current social institutions that she felt would allow for greater sexual equality in modern society in a section of her Conclusion not included in our readings:

- Increase women's taking up of professions where there is no stigma attached to being single: sailors, firefighters, detectives, pilots, and so on. One could argue that this has happened to some degree already, as more and more women every year become doctors, lawyers, engineers, and university professors, if not sailors or pilots.
- Encourage couples to live together in uncommitted relationships instead of compelling them to marry. Firestone wonders whether women's desire for children is genuine, instead of a displacement of other needs. In any case, artificial reproduction will make these uncommitted relationships a more realistic possibility.
- Create households of ten or so people living together for a limited amount of time determined by a social contract. They would be expected to spread the

responsibility for early child care throughout the household and to rotate chores fairly. By stripping away sexual and class inequalities, human relations could be based on love alone, not feelings of possessiveness for things or people. Children would have full rights within such households. People could leave the household after the contract ended, say in seven to ten years. Instead of existing under the patriarchal rule of submissive children and wives, such households, Firestone hoped, would encourage equal treatment for all.

- Create, with the aid of modern machinery, a "cybernetic socialist" economy that would at first redistribute drudgery more fairly and provide a guaranteed annual income for all. Eventually, it would eliminate labor by means of robotic and cybernetic technologies, allowing everyone to wile away their days in play.
- Abolish the public school system, replacing it with noncompulsory "learning centers." How would children gain basic skills? She argues that the rote learning of facts will become outdated, being replaced by computer storage devices (much as the calculator has made the learning of basic arithmetic more or less obsolete). Modern technology can teach us the basic skills we need, when we need them. Machines will eliminate all work that has no personal value for the worker.

Given these social changes, and other similar developments, Firestone argues that her four demands can be fulfilled. Specifically, (1) the demand for reproductive freedom can be accomplished by technology, with no more need for the repressive socialization process of the traditional family; (2) women's economic self-determination will be provided by a cybernetic socialism, where work is divorced from wages, and everyone chooses his or her own lifestyle, all without inconveniencing others; (3) the concept of childhood would be abolished, as children would gain full legal, economic, and sexual rights, mingling in society at will; and (4) the incest taboo and monogamy would end, as all relations could be become sexual, fundamentally restructuring our psychosexuality.

Firestone concludes that there would no longer be any need to guarantee the passing on of power and property from patriarch to patriarch, so blood ties would lose their significance. Women would become pregnant only as a tongue-in-cheek archaism in the wake of artificial means of reproduction. Love and sex would be reintegrated, and we would have the means to create a paradise on earth.

Many criticisms of Firestone's views come to mind. First and foremost, she probably overstates the power of technology to bring about social change or to end the need to work. She also overestimates the role of nurture over nature with respect to family life and childbearing. It doesn't seem likely, even thirty years after *The Dialectic of Sex,* that women are prepared to give up the rearing of their children to communal households. Further, the socialist movement has largely collapsed in America, as the drive for general equality has been engulfed by capitalist prosperity. So her cybernetic socialism may be a dead issue (at least for the time being). Last, her call for children's legal and sexual freedom would probably be met with as much horror today as it was no doubt met with in 1970.

Despite this, Firestone's *The Dialectic of Sex* gives us a picture of Second Wave radical feminism at its most bold and daring. Her predictions of women entering en masse into single professions and of the collapse of the patriarchal family have started to come true. She gives us a vivid picture of how the struggle of sexual classes throughout history has created the male-dominated society of her day (and perhaps ours).

# The Dialectic of Sex

## SHULAMITH FIRESTONE

SEX CLASS IS SO DEEP as to be invisible. Or it may appear as a superficial inequality, one that can be solved by merely a few reforms, or perhaps by the full integration of women into the labor force. But the reaction of the common man, woman, and child—"*That?* Why you can't change *that!* You must be out of your mind!"—is the closest to the truth. We are talking about something every bit as deep as that. This gut reaction—the assumption that, even when they don't know it, feminists are talking about changing a fundamental biological condition—is an honest one. That so profound a change cannot be easily fit into traditional categories of thought, e.g., "political," is not because these categories do not apply but because they are not big enough: radical feminism bursts through them. If there were another word more all-embracing than *revolution* we would use it.

Until a certain level of evolution had been reached and technology had achieved its present sophistication, to question fundamental biological conditions was insanity. Why should a woman give up her precious seat in the cattle car for a bloody struggle she could not hope to win? But, for the first time in some countries, the preconditions for feminist revolution exist—indeed, the situation is beginning to *demand* such a revolution.

The first women are fleeing the massacre, and, shaking and tottering, are beginning to find each other. Their first move is a careful joint observation, to resensitize a fractured consciousness. This is painful: No matter how many levels of consciousness one reaches, the problem always goes deeper. It is everywhere. The division yin and yang pervades all culture, history, economics, nature itself; modern Western versions of sex discrimination are only the most recent layer. To so heighten one's sensitivity to sexism presents problems far worse than the black militant's new awareness of racism: Feminists have to question, not just all of *Western* culture, but the organization of culture itself, and further, even the very organization of nature. Many women give up in despair: if *that's* how deep it goes they don't want to know. Others continue strengthening and enlarging the movement, their painful sensitivity to female oppression existing for a purpose: eventually to eliminate it.

Before we can act to change a situation, however, we must know how it has arisen and evolved, and through what institutions it now operates. Engels' "[We must] examine the historic succession of events from which the antagonism has sprung in order to discover in the conditions thus created the means of ending the conflict." For feminist revolution we shall need an analysis of the dynamics of sex war as comprehensive as the Marx-Engels analysis of class antagonism was for the economic revolution. More comprehensive. For we are dealing with a larger problem, with an

SOURCE: Shulamith Firestone, "The Dialectic of Sex," chap. 1 in *The Dialectic of Sex: The Case for Feminist Revolution* (New York: Bantam Books, 1971), pp. 1–5 (edited).

oppression that goes back beyond recorded history to the animal kingdom itself.

In creating such an analysis we can learn a lot from Marx and Engels: Not their literal opinions about women—about the condition of women as an oppressed class they know next to nothing, recognizing it only where it overlaps with economics—but rather their analytic *method*.

Marx and Engels outdid their socialist forerunners in that they developed a method of analysis which was both *dialectical* and *materialist*. The first in centuries to view history dialectically, they saw the world as process, a natural flux of action and reaction, of opposites yet inseparable and interpenetrating. Because they were able to perceive history as movie rather than as snapshot, they attempted to avoid falling into the stagnant "metaphysical" view that had trapped so many other great minds. (This sort of analysis itself may be a product of the sex division, as discussed in Chapter 9.) They combined this view of the dynamic interplay of historical forces with a materialist one, that is, they attempted for the first time to put historical and cultural change on a real basis, to trace the development of economic classes to organic causes. By understanding thoroughly the mechanics of history, they hoped to show men how to master it.

Socialist thinkers prior to Marx and Engels, such as Fourier, Owen and Bebel, had been able to do no more than moralize about existing social inequalities, positing an ideal world where class privilege and exploitation should not exist—in the same way that early feminist thinkers posited a world where male privilege and exploitation should not exist—by mere virtue of good will. In both cases, because the early thinkers did not really understand how the social injustice had evolved, maintained itself, or could be eliminated, their ideas existed in a cultural vacuum, utopian. Marx and Engels, on the other hand, attempted a scientific approach to history. They traced the class conflict to its real economic origins, projecting an economic solution based on objective preconditions already present: the seizure by the proletariat of the means of production would lead to a communism in which government had withered away, no longer needed to repress the lower class for the sake of the higher. In the classless society the interests of every individual would be synonymous with those of the larger society.

But the doctrine of historical materialism, much as it was a brilliant advance over previous historical analysis, was not the complete answer, as later events bore out. For though Marx and Engels grounded their theory in reality, it was only a *partial* reality. Here is Engels' strictly economic definition of historical materialism from *Socialism: Utopian or Scientific:*

> Historical materialism is that view of the course of history which seeks the *ultimate* cause and the great moving power of all historical events in the economic development of society, in the changes of the modes of production and exchange, in the consequent division of society into distinct classes, and in the struggles of these classes against one another. (Italics mine)

Further, he claims:

> . . . that all past history with the exception of the primitive stages was the history of class struggles; that these warring classes of society are always the products of the modes of production and exchange—in a word, of the economic conditions of their time; that the *economic* structure of society always furnishes the real basis, starting from which we can alone work out the *ultimate* explanation of the whole superstructure of juridical and political institutions as well as of the religious, philosophical, and other ideas of a given historical period. (Italics mine)

It would be a mistake to attempt to explain the oppression of women according to this strictly economic interpretation. The class analysis is a beautiful piece of work, but limited: although correct in a linear sense, it does not go deep enough. There is a whole sexual substratum of the historical dialectic that Engels at times dimly perceives, but because he can see sexuality only through an economic filter, reducing everything to that, he is unable to evaluate [it] in its own right.

Engels did observe that the original division of labor was between man and woman for the purposes of childbreeding; that within the family the husband was the owner, the wife the means of production, the children the labor; and that reproduction of the human species was an important economic system distinct from the means of production.

But Engels has been given too much credit for these scattered recognitions of the oppression of women as a class. In fact he acknowledged the sexual class system only where it overlapped and illuminated his economic construct. Engels didn't do so well even in this respect. But Marx was worse: There is a growing recognition of Marx's bias against women (a cultural bias shared by Freud as well as all men of culture), dangerous if one attempts to squeeze feminism into an orthodox Marxist framework—freezing what were only incidental insights of Marx and Engels about sex class into dogma. Instead, we must enlarge historical materialism to *include* the strictly Marxian, in the same way that the physics of relativity did not invalidate Newtonian physics so much as it drew a circle around it, limiting its application—but only through comparison—to a smaller sphere. For an economic diagnosis traced to ownership of the means of production, even of the means of *re*production, does not explain everything. There is a level of reality that does not stem directly from economics.

The assumption that, beneath economics, reality is psychosexual is often rejected as ahistorical by those who accept a dialectical materialist view of history because it seems to land us back where Marx began: groping through a fog of utopian hypotheses, philosophical systems that might be right, that might be wrong (there is no way to tell), systems that explain concrete historical developments by *a priori* categories of thought; historical materialism, however, attempted to explain "knowing" by "being" and not vice versa.

But there is still an untried third alternative: We can attempt to develop a materialist view of history based on sex itself.

# The Ultimate Revolution

## SHULAMITH FIRESTONE

### Structural Imperatives

Before we talk about revolutionary alternatives, let's summarize—to determine the specifics that must be carefully excluded from any new structures. Then we can go on to "utopian speculation" directed by at least negative guidelines.

We have seen how women, biologically distinguished from men, are culturally distinguished from "human." Nature produced the fundamental inequality—half the human race must bear and rear the children of all of them—which was later consolidated, institutionalized, in the interests of men. Reproduction of the species cost women dearly, not only emotionally, psychologically, culturally but even in strictly material (physical) terms: before recent methods of contraception, continuous childbirth led to constant "female trouble," early aging, and death. Women were the slave class that maintained the species in order to free the other half for the business of the world—admittedly often its drudge aspects, but certainly all its creative aspects as well.

This natural division of labor was continued only at great cultural sacrifice: men and women developed only half of themselves, at the expense of the other half. The division of the psyche into

SOURCE: Shulamith Firestone, "The Ultimate Revolution," conclusion of *The Dialectic of Sex: The Case for Feminist Revolution* (New York: Bantam Books, 1971), pp. 203–209, 221–224, 238–242 (edited).

male and female to better reinforce the reproductive division was tragic: the hypertrophy in men of rationalism, aggressive drive, the atrophy of their emotional sensitivity was a physical (war) as well as a cultural disaster. The emotionalism and passivity of women increased their suffering (we cannot speak of them in a symmetrical way, since they were victimized as a class by the division). Sexually men and women were channeled into a highly ordered—time, place, procedure, even dialogue—heterosexuality restricted to the genitals, rather than diffused over the entire physical being. . . .

## The Slow Death of the Family

The increasing erosion of the functions of the family by modern technology should, by now, have caused some signs of its weakening. However, this is not absolutely the case. Though the institution is archaic, artificial cultural reinforcements have been imported to bolster it: Sentimental sermons, manuals of guidance, daily columns in newspapers and magazines, special courses, services, and institutions for (professional) couples, parents, and child educators, nostalgia, warnings to individuals who question or evade it, and finally, if the number of dropouts becomes a serious threat, a real backlash, including outright persecution of nonconformists. The last has not happened only because it is not yet necessary.

Marriage is in the same state as the Church: Both are becoming functionally defunct, as their preachers go about heralding a revival, eagerly chalking up converts in a day of dread. And just as God has been pronounced dead quite often but has this sneaky way of resurrecting himself, so everyone debunks marriage, yet ends up married.*

What is keeping marriage so alive? I have pointed out some of the cultural bulwarks of

* Ninety-five percent of all American women still marry and 90 percent bear children, most often more than two. Families with children in the medium range (two to four) are as predominant as ever, no longer attributable to the postwar baby boom.

marriage in the twentieth century. We have seen how the romantic tradition of nonmarital love, the hetairism that was the necessary adjunct to monogamic marriage, has been purposely confused with that most pragmatic of institutions, making it more appealing—thus restraining people from experimenting with other social forms that could satisfy their emotional needs as well or better.

Under increasing pressure, with the pragmatic bases of the marriage institution blurred, sex roles relaxed to a degree that would have disgraced a Victorian. *He* had no crippling doubts about his role, nor about the function and value of marriage. To him it was simply an economic arrangement of some selfish benefit, one that would most easily satisfy his physical needs and reproduce his heirs. His wife, too, was clear about her duties and rewards: ownership of herself and of her full sexual, psychological, and housekeeping services for a lifetime, in return for long-term patronage and protection by a member of the ruling class, and—in her turn—limited control over a household and over her children until they reached a certain age. Today this contract based on divided roles has been so disguised by sentiment that it goes completely unrecognized by millions of newlyweds, and even most older married couples.

But this blurring of the economic contract, and the resulting confusion of sex roles, has not significantly eased woman's oppression. In many cases it has put her in only a more vulnerable position. With the clear-cut arrangement of matches by parents all but abolished, a woman, still part of an underclass, must now, in order to gain the indispensable male patronage and protection, play a desperate game, hunting down bored males while yet appearing cool. And even once she is married, any overlap of roles generally takes place on the wife's side, not on the husband's: the "cherish and protect" clause is the first thing forgotten—while the wife has gained the privilege of going to work to "help out," even of putting her husband through school. More than ever she shoulders the brunt of the marriage, not only emotionally, but now also in its more practical aspects. She has simply added his job to hers.

A second cultural prop to the outmoded institution is the privatization of the marriage experience: each partner enters marriage convinced that what happened to his parents, what happened to his friends can never happen to him. Though Wrecked Marriage has become a national hobby, a universal obsession—as witnessed by the booming business of guidebooks to marriage and divorce, the women's magazine industry, an affluent class of marriage counselors and shrinks, whole repertoires of Ball-and-Chain jokes and gimmicks, and cultural products such as soap opera, the marriage-and-family genre on TV, e.g., *I Love Lucy* or *Father Knows Best,* films and plays like Cassavetes' Faces and Albee's *Who's Afraid of Virginia Woolf?*—still one encounters everywhere a defiant "We're different" brand of optimism in which the one good (outwardly exemplary, anyway) marriage in the community is habitually cited to prove that *it* is possible.

The privatization process is typified by comments like, "Well, I know I'd make a great mother." It is useless to point out that *everyone* says that, that the very parents or friends now dismissed as "bad" parents and "poor" marital partners all began marriage and parenthood in exactly the same spirit. After all, does anyone *choose* to have a "bad" marriage? Does anyone *choose* to be a "bad" mother? And even if it were a question of "good" vs. "bad" marital partners or parents, there will always be as many of the latter as the former; under the present system of universal marriage and parenthood just as many spouses and children must pull a bad lot as a good one; in fact any classes of "good" and "bad" are bound to recreate themselves in identical proportions.* Thus the privatization process func-

tions to keep people blaming themselves, rather than the institution, for its failure: Though the institution consistently proves itself unsatisfactory, even rotten, it encourages them to believe that somehow their own case will be different. . . .

Warnings can have no effect, because logic has nothing to do with why people get married. Everyone has eyes of his own, parents of his own. If he chooses to block all evidence, it is because he must. In a world out of control, the only institutions that grant him an *illusion* of control, that seem to offer any safety, shelter or warmth, are the "private" institutions: religion, marriage/family, and, most recently, psychoanalytic therapy. But, as we have seen, the family is neither private nor a refuge, but is directly connected to—is even the cause of—the ills of the larger society which the individual is no longer able to confront.

## Alternatives

Thus, in the larger context of a cybernetic socialism, the establishment of the household as the alternative to the family for reproduction of children, combined with every imaginable life style for those who chose to live singly or in nonreproductive units, would resolve all the basic dilemmas that now arise from the family to obstruct human happiness. Let us go over our four minimal demands to see how our imaginary construction would fare.

1. *The freeing of women from the tyranny of their biology by any means available, and the diffusion of the childbearing and childrearing role to the society as a whole, to men and other children as well as women.* This has been corrected. *Childbearing* could be taken over by technology, and if this proved too much against our past tradition and psychic structure (which it certainly would at first) then ad-

---

*But what does this dichotomy of good/bad really mean? Perhaps after all, it is only a euphemistic class distinction: sensitive and educated, as opposed to uneducated, underprivileged, harassed, and therefore indifferent. But even though a child born to educated or upper-class parents is luckier in every respect, and is apt to receive a fair number of privileges by virtue of his class, name, and the property he is due to

inherit, the distribution of children is equal among all classes—if indeed children born to the unfortunate do not outnumber all others—in this way reproducing in identical proportion the original inequality.

equate incentives and compensations would have to be developed—other than the ego rewards of possessing the child—to reward women for their special social contribution of pregnancy and childbirth. Most of *childrearing,* as we have seen, has to do with the maintaining of power relations, forced internalization of family values, and many other ego concerns that war with the happiness of the individual child. This repressive socialization process would now be unnecessary in a society in which the interests of the individual coincided with those of the larger society. Any childrearing responsibility left would be diffused to include men and other children equally with women. In addition, new methods of instant communication would lessen the child's reliance on even this egalitarian primary unit.

2. *The economic independence and self-determination of all.* Under socialism, even if still a money economy, work would be divorced from wages, the ownership of the means of production in the hands of all the people, and wealth distributed on the basis of need, independent of the social value of the individual's contribution to society. We would aim to eliminate the dependence of women and children on the labor of men, as well as all other types of labor exploitation. Each person could choose his life style at will, changing it to suit his tastes without seriously inconveniencing anyone else; no one would be bound into any social structure against his will, for each person would be totally self-governing as soon as he was physically able.

3. *The total integration of women and children into the larger society.* This has been fulfilled: The concept of childhood has been abolished, children having full legal, sexual, and economic rights, their educational/work activities no different from those of adults. During the few years of their infancy we have replaced the psychologically destructive genetic "parenthood" of one or two arbitrary adults with a diffusion of the responsibility for physical welfare over a larger number of people. The child would still form intimate love relationships, but instead of developing close ties with a decreed "mother" and "father," the child might now form those ties with people of his own choosing, of whatever age or sex. Thus all adult-child relationships will have been mutually chosen—equal, intimate relationships free of material dependencies. Correspondingly, though children would be fewer, they would not be monopolized, but would mingle freely throughout the society to the benefit of all, thus satisfying that legitimate desire to be around the young which is often called the reproductive "instinct."

4. *Sexual freedom, love, etc.* So far we have not said much of love and sexual freedom because there is no reason for it to present a problem: there would be nothing obstructing it. With full liberty human relationships eventually would be redefined for the better. If a child does not know his own mother, or at least does not attach a special value to her over others, it is unlikely that he would choose her as his first love object, only to have to develop inhibitions on this love. It is possible that the child might form his first close physical relationships with people his own size out of sheer physical convenience, just as men and women, all else being equal, might prefer each other over those of the same sex for sheer physical fit. But if not, if he should choose to relate sexually to adults, even if he should happen to pick his own genetic mother, there would be no *a priori* reasons for her to reject his sexual advances, because the incest taboo would have lost its function. The "household," a transient social form, would not be subject to the dangers of inbreeding.

Thus, without the incest taboo, adults might return within a few generations to a more natural polymorphous sexuality, the concentration on genital sex and orgasmic pleasure giving way to total physical/emotional relationships that *included* that. Relations with children would include as much genital sex as the child was capable of—probably considerably more than we now believe—but because genital sex would no longer be the central focus of the relationship, lack of orgasm would not present a serious problem. Adult/child and homosexual sex taboos would disappear, as well as nonsexual friendship (Freud's "aim-inhibited" love). All close relationships would include the physical, our concept of exclusive physical partnerships (monogamy) disappearing from our psychic structure, as well as the construct of a Partner Ideal. But how long it would take for these changes to occur, and in what forms they would appear, remains conjecture. The specifics need not concern us here. We need only set up the preconditions for a free sexuality: whatever forms it took would be assuredly an improvement on what we have now, "natural" in the truest sense.

In the transitional phase, adult genital sex and the exclusiveness of couples within the household might have to be maintained in order for the unit to be able to function smoothly, with a minimum of internal tension caused by sexual frictions. It is unrealistic to impose theories of what *ought* to be on a psyche already fundamentally organized around specific emotional needs. And this is why individual attempts to eliminate sexual possessiveness are now always inauthentic. We would do much better to concentrate on overthrowing the social structures that have produced this psychical organization, allowing for the eventual—if not in our lifetime—fundamental restructuring (or should I say destructuring?) of our psychosexuality.

Above, I have drawn up only a very rough plan in order to make the general direction of a feminist revolution more vivid: Production and reproduction of the species would both be, simultaneously, reorganized in a nonrepressive way. The birth of children to a unit which disbanded or recomposed as soon as children were physically able to be independent, one that was meant to serve immediate needs rather than to pass on power and privilege (the basis of patriarchy is the inheritance of property gained through labor) would eliminate the power psychology, sexual repression, and cultural sublimation. Family chauvinism, class privilege based on birth, would be eliminated. The blood tie of the mother to the child would eventually be severed—if male jealousy of "creative" childbirth actually exists, we will soon have the means to create life independently of sex—so that pregnancy, now freely acknowledged as clumsy, inefficient, and painful, would be indulged in, if at all, only as a tongue-in-cheek archaism, just as already women today wear virginal white to their weddings. A cybernetic socialism would abolish economic classes, and all forms of labor exploitation, by granting all people a livelihood based only on material needs. Eventually drudge work (jobs) would be eliminated in favor of (complex) play, activity done for its own sake, by both adults and children. Love and sexuality would be reintegrated, flowing unimpeded.

The revolt against the biological family could bring on the first successful revolution, or what was thought of by the ancients as the Messianic Age. Humanity's double curse when it ate the Apple of Knowledge (the growing knowledge of the laws of the environment creating repressive civilization), that man would toil by the sweat of his brow in order to live, and woman would bear children in pain and travail, can now be undone through man's very efforts in toil. We now have the knowledge to create a paradise on earth anew. The alternative is our own suicide through that knowledge, the creation of a hell on earth, followed by oblivion.

# Marilyn Frye on Oppression

Marilyn Frye (1941–) was born in Tulsa, Oklahoma, and has lived in various places in the United States and western Canada. She has helped run a bookstore, a lesbian center, and a small press, and now teaches philosophy and feminist theory at Michigan State University. She graduated from Stanford in 1966 and went on to receive a Ph.D. in philosophy from Cornell University in 1969.

In the following selection from her book *The Politics of Reality* (1983), Frye puts forth the radical feminist case that women, as a distinct sex, are oppressed. Frye is a radical, lesbian feminist who takes on not only heterosexual men as the founders and sustainers of patriarchy but gay men too as participating in male supremacy. She also blasts privileged, heterosexual white women as oppressing women of color. So she takes Firestone's politics of sexual difference and adds to it a politics of sexual orientation and race.

Frye argues that the fundamental claim of feminism is that all women are oppressed. She says that women are forced to smile and be cheerful at work, or they will be seen as difficult to work with and fired, if not raped, beaten, and murdered. Further, women suffer from a Catch-22 regarding their sexuality: If they give in too easily to male advances, they're seen as "easy"; but if they resist too long, they're seen as frigid man haters. Both are used as justifications for rape. Last, Frye lists a number of social conditions that contribute to women's oppression: sexual harassment; sexual discrimination in hiring; the despotism of husbands and parents; and the conflicting expectations of being simultaneously a woman, a wife, and a mother.

Some people say, she notes, that men suffer from stress from being stuck in their own gender roles and are "oppressed" by their act of oppressing women. However, for Frye this is nonsense that leeches all meaning out of the term *oppression:* People can be unhappy, even miserable, without being "oppressed." Merely feeling bad due to the actions of others proves nothing about one's potential status as an oppressed group. So Frye wants to sharpen the concept, which she proceeds to do in the following chapter from her book.

Women in our society, she argues, suffer from networks of forces and barriers that chain them in. Frye uses the metaphor of a "birdcage" to describe the fate of women under patriarchy. She argues that women are like birds in a cage. Microscopically, the caged bird isn't constrained by any single wire in the cage; any given wire could be evaded. Yet macroscopically, it's held in by the whole network of wires.

Frye illustrates this metaphor with examples from everyday life. A case in point is her objection to a man opening a door for a woman: The gallant door-opening prince, like men in general, are helpful when it's not important but are nowhere to be found when their help is really needed. Frye feels that this symbolic ritual merely signals a contempt for women as dependent and incapable creatures. For this and a whole host of other (not entirely clear) reasons, women are like the bird, macroscopically and systematically oppressed by a network of barriers to its free flight.

Frye goes on to note that it's no good to say that social structure oppresses everyone: We have to look at the context of the limitation in question. Frye gives the examples of a rich playboy breaking his leg in a skiing accident, of drivers having to drive on only one side of the road, and of white people incurring dangers going for a stroll in a black American ghetto as examples of limitations or hardships that are insignificant and nonoppressive to those who suffer them. To distinguish true oppression from mere inconvenience, one must look at who makes and maintains social barriers, at whose interests it serves to keep them in place, and at whether or not these barriers are structural, systematically hemming in a whole group of people.

Frye concludes that to be a woman *is* to be part of a group that is systematically limited, hemmed in, and kept down, economically, politically, and in terms of physical safety. Women are oppressed, as women; but men are *not* oppressed, as men (though they might be oppressed as black men, Jewish men, etc.). Further, because wherever there's an oppressed group, there must be an oppressor, we can safely assume that Frye is saying that women, as a sexual class, are oppressed structurally and systematically by men, again as a sexual class. Thus, Frye is setting up a clear social dualism in her work, a dualism that calls on women to challenge this oppression on a structural level.

Given that this oppression is structural, Frye argues that radical social changes must take place before women can live their lives as full human beings. However, unlike Firestone, she is less than clear as to what these changes are. In any case, her metaphor of the bird in a gilded cage is a striking one. An interesting question to ponder as you read this chapter is whether at least some of the birds have managed to escape their cages in the time since Frye first described their plight.

# Oppression

## MARILYN FRYE

IT IS A FUNDAMENTAL CLAIM of feminism that women are oppressed. The word "oppression" is a strong word. It repels and attracts. It is dangerous and dangerously fashionable and endangered. It is much misused, and sometimes not innocently.

The statement that women are oppressed is frequently met with the claim that men are oppressed too. We hear that oppressing is oppressive to those who oppress as well as to those they oppress. Some men cite as evidence of their oppression their much-advertised inability to cry. It is tough, we are told, to be masculine. When the stresses and frustrations of being a man are cited as evidence that oppressors are oppressed by their oppressing, the word "oppression" is being stretched to meaninglessness; it is treated as though its scope includes any and all human experience of limitation or suffering, no matter the cause, degree, or consequence. Once such usage has been put over on us, then if ever we deny that any person or group is oppressed, we seem to imply that we think they never suffer and have no feelings. We are accused of insensitivity; even of bigotry. For women, such accusation is particularly intimidating, since sensitivity is one of the few virtues that has been assigned to us. If we are found insensitive, we may fear we have no re-

SOURCE: Marilyn Frye, "Oppression," in *The Politics of Reality: Essays in Feminist Theory* (Trumansburg, NY: The Crossing Press, 1983), pp. 1–16. Selections from abridged version in *Gender Basics,* ed. Anne Minas (Belmont, CA: Wadsworth Press, 2000), pp. 10–16.

deeming traits at all and perhaps are not real women. Thus are we silenced before we begin: the name of our situation drained of meaning and our guilt mechanisms tripped.

But this is nonsense. Human beings can be miserable without being oppressed, and it is perfectly consistent to deny that a person or group is oppressed without denying that they have feelings or that they suffer.

We need to think clearly about oppression, and there is much that mitigates against this. I do not want to undertake to prove that women are oppressed (or that men are not), but I want to make clear what is being said when we say it. We need this word, this concept, and we need it to be sharp and sure.

## 1

The root of the word "oppression" is the element "press." *The press of the crowd; pressed into military service; to press a pair of pants; printing press; press the button.* Presses are used to mold things or flatten them or reduce them in bulk, sometimes to reduce them by squeezing out the gasses or liquids in them. Something pressed is something caught between or among forces and barriers which are so related to each other that jointly they restrain, restrict, or prevent the thing's motion or mobility. Mold. Immobilize. Reduce.

The mundane experience of the oppressed provides another clue. One of the most characteristic and ubiquitous features of the world as experienced by oppressed people is the double bind—situations in which options are reduced to a very few, and all of them expose one to penalty, censure, or deprivation. For example, it is often a requirement upon oppressed people that we smile and be cheerful. If we comply, we signal our docility and our acquiescence in our situation. We need not, then, be taken note of. We acquiesce in being made invisible, in our occupying no space. We participate in our own erasure. On the other hand, anything but the sunniest countenance exposes us to being perceived as mean, bitter, angry, or dangerous. This means,

at the least, that we may be found "difficult" or unpleasant to work with, which is enough to cost one one's livelihood; at worst, being seen as mean, bitter, angry or dangerous has been known to result in rape, arrest, beating, and murder. One can only choose to risk one's preferred form and rate of annihilation.

Another example: It is common in the United States that women, especially younger women, are in a bind where neither sexual activity nor sexual inactivity is all right. If she is heterosexually active, a woman is open to censure and punishment for being loose, unprincipled, or a whore. The "punishment" comes in the form of criticism, snide and embarrassing remarks, being treated as an easy lay by men, scorn from her more restrained female friends. She may have to lie and hide her behavior from her parents. She must juggle the risks of unwanted pregnancy and dangerous contraceptives. On the other hand, if she refrains from heterosexual activity, she is fairly constantly harassed by men who try to persuade her into it and pressure her to "relax" and "let her hair down"; she is threatened with labels like "frigid," "uptight," "man-hater," "bitch," and "cocktease." The same parents who would be disapproving of her sexual activity may be worried by her inactivity because it suggests she is not or will not be popular, or is not sexually normal. She may be charged with lesbianism. If a woman is raped, then if she has been heterosexually active she is subject to the presumption that she liked it (since her activity is presumed to show that she likes sex), and if she has not been heterosexually active, she is subject to the presumption that she liked it (since she is supposedly "repressed and frustrated"). Both heterosexual activity and heterosexual nonactivity are likely to be taken as proof that you wanted to be raped, and hence, of course, weren't *really* raped at all. You can't win. You are caught in a bind, caught between systematically related pressures.

Women are caught like this, too, by networks of forces and barriers that expose one to penalty, loss, or contempt whether one works outside the home or not, is on welfare or not, bears children or not, raises children or not, marries or not, stays married or not, is heterosexual, lesbian, both, or neither. Economic necessity; confinement to racial and/or sexual job ghettos; sexual harassment; sex discrimination; pressures of competing expectations and judgments about *women, wives,* and *mothers* (in the society at large, in racial and ethnic subcultures and in one's own mind); dependence (full or partial) on husbands, parents, or the state; commitment to political ideas; loyalties to racial or ethnic or other "minority" groups; the demands of self-respect and responsibilities to others. Each of these factors exists in complex tension with every other, penalizing or prohibiting all of the apparently available options. And nipping at one's heels, always, is the endless pack of little things. If one dresses one way, one is subject to the assumption that one is advertising one's sexual availability; if one dresses another way, one appears to "not care about oneself" or to be "unfeminine." If one uses "strong language," one invites categorization as a whore or slut; if one does not, one invites categorization as a "lady"—one too delicately constituted to cope with robust speech or the realities to which it presumably refers.

The experience of oppressed people is that the living of one's life is confined and shaped by forces and barriers which are not accidental or occasional and hence avoidable, but are systematically related to each other in such a way as to catch one between and among them and restrict or penalize motion in any direction. It is the experience of being caged in: All avenues, in every direction, are blocked or booby trapped.

Cages. Consider a birdcage. If you look very closely at just one wire in the cage, you cannot see the other wires. If your conception of what is before you is determined by this myopic focus, you could look at that one wire, up and down the length of it, and be unable to see why a bird would not just fly around the wire any time it wanted to go somewhere. Furthermore, even if, one day at a time, you myopically inspected each wire, you still could not see why a bird would have trouble going past the wires to get anywhere. There is no physical property of any one wire, *nothing* that the closest scrutiny could dis-

cover, that will reveal how a bird could be inhibited or harmed by it except in the most accidental way. It is only when you step back, stop looking at the wires one by one, microscopically, and take a macroscopic view of the whole cage, that you can see why the bird does not go anywhere; and then you will see it in a moment. It will require no great subtlety of mental powers. It is perfectly *obvious* that the bird is surrounded by a network of systematically related barriers, no one of which would be the least hindrance to its flight, but which, by their relations to each other, are as confining as the solid walls of a dungeon.

It is now possible to grasp one of the reasons why oppression can be hard to see and recognize: one can study the elements of an oppressive structure with great care and some good will without seeing the structure as a whole, and hence without seeing or being able to understand that one is looking at a cage and that there are people there who are caged, whose motion and mobility are restricted, whose lives are shaped and reduced.

The arresting of vision at a microscopic level yields such common confusion as that about the male door-opening ritual. This ritual, which is remarkably widespread across classes and races, puzzles many people, some of whom do and some of whom do not find it offensive. Look at the scene of the two people approaching a door. The male steps slightly ahead and opens the door. The male holds the door open while the female glides through. Then the male goes through. The door closes after them. "Now how," one innocently asks, "can those crazy women's libbers say that is oppressive? The guy *removed* a barrier to the lady's smooth and unruffled progress." But each repetition of this ritual has a place in a pattern, in fact in several patterns. One has to shift the level of one's perception in order to see the whole picture.

The door-opening pretends to be a helpful service, but the helpfulness is false. This can be seen by noting that it will be done whether or not it makes any practical sense. Infirm men and men burdened with packages will open doors for able-bodied women who are free of physical burdens. Men will impose themselves awkwardly and jostle everyone in order to get to the door first. The act is not determined by convenience or grace. Furthermore, these very numerous acts of unneeded or even noisome "help" occur in counterpoint to a pattern of men not being helpful in many practical ways in which women might welcome help. What *women* experience is a world in which gallant princes charming commonly make a fuss about being helpful and providing small services when help and services are of little or no use, but in which there are rarely ingenious and adroit princes at hand when substantial assistance is really wanted either in mundane affairs or in situations of threat, assault, or terror. There is no help with the (his) laundry; no help typing a report at 4:00 A.M.; no help in mediating disputes among relatives or children. There is nothing but advice that women should stay indoors after dark, be chaperoned by a man, or when it comes down to it, "lie back and enjoy it."

The gallant gestures have no practical meaning. Their meaning is symbolic. The door-opening and similar services provided are services which really are needed by people who are for one reason or another incapacitated—unwell, burdened with parcels, etc. So the message is that women are incapable. The detachment of the acts from the concrete realities of what women need and do not need is a vehicle for the message that women's actual needs and interests are unimportant or irrelevant. Finally, these gestures imitate the behavior of servants toward masters and thus mock women, who are in most respects the servants and caretakers of men. The message of the false helpfulness of male gallantry is female dependence, the invisibility or insignificance of women, and contempt for women.

One cannot see the meanings of these rituals if one's focus is riveted upon the individual event in all its particularity, including the particularity of the individual man's present conscious intentions and motives and the individual woman's conscious perception of the event in the moment. It seems sometimes that people take a deliberately myopic view and fill their eyes with things seen microscopically in order not to see macroscopically. At any rate, whether it is de-

liberate or not, people can and do fail to see the oppression of women because they fail to see macroscopically and hence fail to see the various elements of the situation as systematically related in larger schemes.

As the cageness of the birdcage is a macroscopic phenomenon, the oppressiveness of the situations in which women live our various and different lives is a macroscopic phenomenon. Neither can be *seen* from a microscopic perspective. But when you look macroscopically you can see it—a network of forces and barriers which are systematically related and which conspire to the immobilization, reduction, and molding of women and the lives we live. . . .

### 3

It seems to be the human condition that in one degree or another we all suffer frustration and limitation, all encounter unwelcome barriers, and all are damaged and hurt in various ways. Since we are a social species, almost all of our behavior and activities are structured by more than individual inclination and the conditions of the planet and its atmosphere. No human is free of social structures, nor (perhaps) would happiness consist in such freedom. Structure consists of boundaries, limits, and barriers; in a structured whole, some motions and changes are possible, and others are not. If one is looking for an excuse to dilute the word "oppression," one can use the fact of social structure as an excuse and say that everyone is oppressed. But if one would rather get clear about what oppression is and is not, one needs to sort out the sufferings, harms, and limitations and figure out which are elements of oppression and which are not.

From what I have already said here, it is clear that if one wants to determine whether a particular suffering, harm, or limitation is part of someone's being oppressed, one has to look at it *in context* in order to tell whether it is an element in an oppressive structure: one has to see if it is part of an enclosing structure of forces and barriers which tends to the immobilization and reduction of a group or category of people. One has to look at how the barrier or force fits with others and to whose benefit or detriment it works. As soon as one looks at examples, it becomes obvious that not everything which frustrates or limits a person is oppressive, and not every harm or damage is due to or contributes to oppression.

If a rich white playboy who lives off income from his investments in South African diamond mines should break a leg in a skiing accident at Aspen and wait in pain in a blizzard for hours before he is rescued, we may assume that in that period he suffers. But the suffering comes to an end; his leg is repaired by the best surgeon money can buy and he is soon recuperating in a lavish suite, sipping Chivas Regal. Nothing in this picture suggests a structure of barriers and forces. He is a member of several oppressor groups and does not suddenly become oppressed because he is injured and in pain. Even if the accident was caused by someone's malicious negligence, and hence someone can be blamed for it and morally faulted, that person still has not been an agent of oppression.

Consider also the restriction of having to drive one's vehicle on a certain side of the road. There is no doubt that this restriction is almost unbearably frustrating at times, when one's lane is not moving and the other lane is clear. There are surely times, even, when abiding by this regulation would have harmful consequences. But the restriction is obviously wholesome for most of us most of the time. The restraint is imposed for our benefit, and does benefit us; its operation tends to encourage our *continued* motion, not to immobilize us. The limits imposed by traffic regulations are limits most of us would cheerfully impose on ourselves given that we knew others would follow them too. They are part of a structure which shapes our behavior, not to our reduction and immobilization, but rather to the protection of our continued ability to move and act as we will.

Another example: The boundaries of a racial ghetto in an American city serve to some extent to keep white people from going in, as well as to keep ghetto dwellers from going out. A particular white citizen may be frustrated or feel deprived because s/he cannot stroll around there and enjoy the "exotic" aura of a "foreign" culture, or shop for bargains in the ghetto swap shops. In fact, the existence of the ghetto, of racial segregation, does deprive the white person of knowledge and harm her/his character by nurturing unwarranted feelings of superiority. But this does not make the white person in this situation a member of an oppressed race or a person oppressed because of her/his race. One must look at the barrier. It limits the activities and the access of those on both sides of it (though to different degrees). But it is a product of the intention, planning, and action of whites for the benefit of whites, to secure and maintain privileges that are available to whites generally, as members of the dominant and privileged group. Though the existence of the barrier has some bad consequences for whites, the barrier does not exist in systematic relationship with other barriers and forces forming a structure oppressive to whites; quite the contrary. It is part of a structure which oppresses the ghetto dwellers and thereby (and by white intention) protects and furthers white interests as dominant white culture understands them. This barrier is not oppressive to whites, even though it is a barrier to whites.

Barriers have different meanings to those on opposite sides of them, even though they are barriers to both. The physical walls of a prison no more dissolve to let an outsider in than to let an insider out, but for the insider they are confining and limiting while to the outsider they may mean protection from what s/he takes to be threats posed by insiders—freedom from harm or anxiety. A set of social and economic barriers and forces separating two groups may be felt, even painfully, by members of both groups and yet may mean confinement to one and liberty and enlargement of opportunity to the other.

The service sector of the wives/mommas/assistants/girls is almost exclusively a woman-only sector; its boundaries not only enclose women but to a very great extent keep men out. Some men sometimes encounter this barrier and experience it as a restriction on their movements, their activities, their control or their choices of "life-style." Thinking they might like the simple nurturant life (which they may imagine to be quite free of stress, alienation, and hard work), and feeling deprived since it seems closed to them, they thereupon announce the discovery that they are oppressed, too, by "sex roles." But that barrier is erected and maintained by men, for the benefit of men. It consists of cultural and economic forces and pressures in a culture and economy controlled by men in which, at every economic level and in all racial and ethnic subcultures, economy, tradition—and even ideologies of liberation—work to keep at least local culture and economy in male control.[1]

The boundary that sets apart women's sphere is maintained and promoted by men generally for the benefit of men generally, and men generally do benefit from this existence, even the man who bumps into it and complains of the inconvenience. That barrier is protecting his classification and status as a male, as superior, as having a right to sexual access to a female or females. It protects a kind of citizenship which is superior to that of females of his class and race, his access to a wider range of better paying and higher status work, and his right to prefer unemployment to the degradation of doing lower status or "women's" work.

If a person's life or activity is affected by some force or barrier that person encounters, one may not conclude that the person is oppressed simply because the person encounters that barrier or force; nor simply because the encounter is unpleasant, frustrating, or painful to that person at that time; nor simply because the existence of the barrier or force, or the processes which maintain or apply it, serve to deprive that person of something of value. One must look at the barrier or force and answer certain questions about it. Who constructs and maintains it? Whose interests are served by its existence? Is it part of a structure which tends to confine, reduce, and immobilize some group? Is the individual a member of the confined group? Various forces, barriers, and limitations a person may encounter or live with may be part of an oppressive structure or not, and if they are, that person may be on either the oppressed or the oppressor side of it. One cannot tell which by how loudly or how little the person complains. . . .

## 5

One is marked for application of oppressive pressures by one's membership in some group or category. Much of one's suffering and frustration befalls one partly or largely because one is a member of that category. In the case at hand, it is the category, *woman*. Being a woman is a major factor in my not having a better job than I do; being a woman selects me as a likely victim of sexual assault or harassment; it is my being a woman that reduces the power of my anger to a proof of my insanity. If a woman has little or no economic or political power, or achieves little of what she wants to achieve, a major causal factor in this is that she is a woman. For any woman of any race or economic class, being a woman is significantly attached to whatever disadvantages and deprivations she suffers, be they great or small.

None of this is the case with respect to a person's being a man. Simply being a man is not what stands between him and a better job; whatever assaults and harassments he is subject to, being male is not what selects him for victimization; being male is not a factor which would make his anger impotent—quite the opposite. If a man has little or no material or political power, or achieves little of what he wants to achieve, his being male is no part of the explanation. Being male is something he has going *for* him, even if race or class or age or disability is going against him.

Women are oppressed, *as women*. Members of certain racial and/or economic groups and classes, both the males and the females, are oppressed *as* members of those races and/or classes. But men are not oppressed *as men*.

. . . and isn't it strange that any of us should have been confused and mystified about such a simple thing?

[1] Of course this is complicated by race and class. Machismo and "Black manhood" politics seem to help keep Latin or Black men in control of more cash than Latin or Black women control; but these politics seem to me also to ultimately help keep the larger economy in *white* male control.

# SEXUAL DIFFERENCE AND THE SOCIAL CONSTRUCTION OF GENDER

## *Carol Gilligan on the Different Voice of Women*

Carol Gilligan (1936–) has a Ph.D. in education from Harvard and teaches at the Harvard Graduate School of Education. Her research focuses on young women's psychological development, particularly their development as moral beings. Gilligan wanted to challenge the prevailing dogma on the psychological growth of children established by Freud, Jean Piaget, and Lawrence Kohlberg that young women are stuck in the lower levels of moral development, with only young men being capable of attaining the abstract, impersonal considerations of justice and rights seen by these theorists as the goal of this development.

Her mentor at Harvard was Kohlberg, for whom she worked as a research assistant in the early 1970s. Kohlberg studied the moral development of boys, speculating that they went through six stages of moral development. When he applied his theory of moral development to young women, he concluded that they tended to come up short, rarely making it beyond stage 3, where goodness is seen as helping and pleasing others. They seldom reached the three higher stages, where morality is tied to rules (stage 4) and then universal moral principles (stages 5 and 6). Gilligan points out that the problem with Kohlberg's research was that it excluded female subjects and was thus biased against the "different voice" that young women used to deal with moral dilemmas.

In her book *In a Different Voice,* originally published in 1982, she uses a number of empirical studies to try to show that young women spoke in a different moral voice, one that valued care and relationships over abstract rules and moral principles. Nancy Chodorow's studies showed that young girls develop a greater sense of empathy with others. She found that because masculine identity is shaped by separation, men fear intimacy; because feminine identity is grounded in attachment, women feel threatened by separation. Janet Lever's studies examined how boys and girls play children's games. If disputes break out during play, boys usually attempt to resolve them by "sticking to the rules" in order to continue the game, whereas girls usually quit the game to keep their relationships intact. Gilligan used these studies, along with a few of her own, to show that two fairly distinct "voices" can be heard in the moral discourse of young men and women.

Gilligan found that the young women she studied often felt a sense of detachment from mainstream Western culture because they had to stifle their relationship-centered inner voices to avoid a conflict with the ethics of male-dominated culture. She argues that this culture has sought to impose its own moral voice on both sexes, both in the schoolyard and in the academy.

The *male voice* speaks with an "ethics of justice," which focuses on rules and a respect for individual rights. Tied to this emphasis on individual rights is a fear of attachment and commitment, and a valuing of separation. The male voice, with its focus on justice and rights, sees inequality and oppression as its enemies. Boys learn independence, fair play, and organizational behavior in the competitive games of their youth, turning these into hierarchies of rules and principles in their adult lives. The male voice views the self in individual terms but puts a "universal" notion of the self at the center of moral decision making: Moral rules must apply to everyone, everywhere, independent of context. The central image that comes out of the ethics of justice is that of a hierarchy.

The *female voice* is governed by an "ethics of care." This moral voice values relationships, connectedness, intimacy, and nurture; it fears detachment and being abandoned. Its central focus is on maintaining peace and caring for those in need. The feminine voice sees morality as contextual, as tied to individual narratives, and not to abstract and inflexible moral principles. Young girls tend to define themselves in relation to others around them, so responsibilities to others are what count the most. Moral dilemmas should be solved within relationships, not by tossing them aside. Gilligan argues that women's reluctance to judge according to a strict hierarchy of rules is not just weak-kneed moral relativism, as some male developmental theorists have suggested, but an attempt to take into account the intricacies of individuals' lives and experiences in moral decision making. We can see a web as the central metaphor of the ethics of care.

The middle chapters of *In a Different Voice* deal with three case studies done by Gilligan herself that illustrate the existence of these distinct moral voices. In the key one, Gilligan asked young men and women to imagine a man who is contemplating stealing a drug that he can't afford to buy to cure his ailing wife. Young men and women were asked how they would resolve this dilemma. The young men studied tended to weigh the right to life of the sick woman with the property rights of the druggist in attempting to resolve it. The young women in the study tended to think that the theft was morally acceptable because caring for one's family is far more important than the druggist's abstract property rights.

Overall, Gilligan says that women care for others by taking a variety of voices into account. Men assume that care in their private lives, devaluing it in their public lives. An unbalanced concept of moral adulthood results. Yet neither voice is superior: Both have to be integrated to produce a full-fledged view of moral life and to allow each voice to speak freely. In other words, rights and responsibilities have to be integrated.

Gilligan's work raises the important issue in feminist theory of whether the psychological traits traditionally associated with each sex, such as men's greater abstract rationality and aggressiveness, or women's greater empathy and need to nurture, are determined by biology or by culture. Those who argue for the former position are called "essentialists" or "biological determinists," whereas those who argue for the latter view are called "social constructionists."

An essentialist argues that there are at least some psychological differences between men and women that transcend cultural differences and gendered social roles. These differences are deeply entrenched, being based on real psychological and physiological differences that cannot be easily erased by changes in our cultural values or in our socialization process. A social constructionist, on the other hand, argues that all psychological gender traits are "constructed" by the society in which we live: There's no such thing as a "natural" male or female psychological characteristic.

Gilligan waffles on the degree to which she believes that differences between male and female moral voices are grounded in essential sexual differences, noting that the link between the two moral voices she describes in her book and men and women as distinct sexes is merely "an empirical observation," and that this association wasn't meant "to represent a generalization about either sex" (p. 2). She also claims that this distinction between male and female voices may not hold in different cultures at different times.

The "Letter to Readers" that Gilligan added to the 1993 edition of her book doesn't clarify matters much. In it she argues that psychological differences between the sexes are the result of body differences, family relationships, and the social and cultural position of the sexes (p. xi); in other words, they are both biological *and* cultural. Later, she says that women have a hard time distinguishing between their own distinct voice and the socially constructed feminine voice, often confusing the two (p. xvii).

The closest she comes to resolving this dilemma is when she says that she finds the question of whether gender characteristics are biologically determined or socially constructed "to be deeply disturbing," because this implies that people are either genetically determined or the products of socialization. This robs women of their distinctive voice and thus the possibility of resistance, creativity, and change (p. xix). In short, to say that our gender traits are either essentially tied to our biological sex *or* are socially constructed by our culture destroys our freedom of thought and action.

Be that as it may, some of Gilligan's critics have branded her an essentialist, purely and simply. Because she bases her idea of the two "voices" on considerable empirical research, we can be fairly sure that she believed that these two voices were realities at the time that *In a Different Voice* was published, whether or not this could ever change. Further, she gives us a fairly lively picture of the distinctiveness of the female voice in her book. At minimum we can say that Gilligan's work has *contributed* to an essentialist view of gender traits, even if these characteristics are valid only for late-twentieth-century Americans.

Other than her lack of clarity on her own position in the essentialist-constructionist debate, there is another obvious critique of Gilligan's work—that her findings are merely a snapshot of the distorted gender roles under patriarchy and that her picture of relationship-friendly, nurturing, caring young women is merely a reproduction of the old image of women as wives, mothers, and homemakers, an image that feminists want to erase from Western culture. This critique is not without merit, as her "ethics of care," with its focus on a web of relationships, seems to push aside questions of rights and justice, key moral weapons in women's fight for equality. In any case, Gilligan's work is important to feminist theory in its argument that male-dominated culture produces a narrow, one-sided view of moral life, a view that could be enriched by an ethics of care.

# In a Different Voice

## CAROL GILLIGAN

### Introduction

Over the past ten years, I have been listening to people talking about morality and about themselves. Halfway through that time, I began to hear a distinction in these voices, two ways of speaking about moral problems, two modes of describing the relationship between other and self. Differences represented in the psychological literature as steps in a developmental progression suddenly appeared instead as a contrapuntal theme, woven into the cycle of life and recurring in varying forms in people's judgments, fantasies, and thoughts. The occasion for this observation was the selection of a sample of women for a study of the relation between judgment and action in a situation of moral conflict and choice. Against the background of the psychological descriptions of identity and moral development which I had read and taught for a number of years, the women's voices sounded distinct. It was then that I began to notice the recurrent problems in interpreting women's development and to connect these problems to the repeated exclusion of women from the critical theory-building studies of psychological research.

This book records different modes of thinking about relationships and the association of these modes with male and female voices in psychological and literary texts and in the data of my research. The disparity between women's experience and the representation of human development, noted throughout the psychological literature, has generally been seen to signify a problem in women's development. Instead, the failure of women to fit existing models of human growth may point to a problem in the rep-

resentation, a limitation in the conception of human condition, an omission of certain truths about life. . . .

### Woman's Place in Man's Life Cycle

. . . At a time when efforts are being made to eradicate discrimination between the sexes in the search for social equality and justice, the differences between the sexes are being rediscovered in the social sciences. This discovery occurs when theories formerly considered to be sexually neutral in their scientific objectivity are found instead to reflect a consistent observational and evaluative bias. Then the presumed neutrality of science, like that of language itself, gives way to the recognition that the categories of knowledge are human constructions. The fascination with point of view that has informed the fiction of the twentieth century and the corresponding recognition of the relativity of judgment infuse our scientific understanding as well when we begin to notice how accustomed we have become to seeing life through men's eyes.

A recent discovery of this sort pertains to the apparently innocent classic *The Elements of Style* by William Strunk and E. B. White. The Supreme Court ruling on the subject of discrimination in classroom texts led one teacher of English to notice that the elementary rules of English usage were being taught through examples which counterposed the birth of Napoleon, the writings of Coleridge, and statements such as "He was an interesting talker. A man who had traveled all over the world and lived in half a dozen countries," with "Well, Susan, this is a fine mess you are in" or, less drastically, "He saw a woman, accompanied by two children, walking slowly down the road."

Psychological theorists have fallen as innocently as Strunk and White into the same observational bias. Implicitly adopting the male life as the norm, they have tried to fashion women out of a masculine cloth. It all goes back, of course, to Adam and Eve—a story which shows, among other things, that if you make a woman out of a man, you are bound to get into trouble. In the life cycle, as in the Garden of Eden, the woman has been the deviant.

The penchant of developmental theorists to project a masculine image, and one that appears frightening to women, goes back at least to Freud, who built his theory of psychosexual development around the experiences of the male child that culminate in the Oedipus complex.[1] In the 1920s, Freud struggled to resolve the contradictions posed for his theory by the differences in female anatomy and the different configuration of the young girl's early family relationships. After trying to fit women into his masculine conception, seeing them as envying that which they missed, he came instead to acknowledge, in the strength and persistence of women's pre-Oedipal attachments to their mothers, a developmental difference. He considered this difference in women's development to be responsible for what he saw as women's developmental failure.

Having tied the formation of the superego or conscience to castration anxiety, Freud considered women to be deprived by nature of the impetus for a clear-cut Oedipal resolution. Consequently, women's superego—the heir to the Oedipus complex—was compromised: it was never "so inexorable, so impersonal, so independent of its emotional origins as we require it to be in men." From this observation of difference, that "for women the level of what is ethically normal is different from what it is in men," Freud concluded that women "show less sense of justice than men, that they are less ready to submit to the great exigencies of life, that they are more often influenced in their judgements by feelings of affection or hostility."[2]

Thus a problem in theory became cast as a problem in women's development, and the problem in women's development was located in their experience of relationships. Nancy Chodorow, attempting to account for "the reproduction within each generation of certain general and nearly universal differences that characterize masculine and feminine personality and roles," attributes these differences between the sexes not to anatomy but rather to "the fact that women, universally, are largely responsible for early child care." Because this early social environment differs for and is experienced differently by male and female children, basic sex differences recur in personality development. As a result, "in any given society, feminine personality comes to define itself in relation and connection to other people more than masculine personality does."[3]

In her analysis, Chodorow relies primarily on Robert Stoller's studies which indicate that gender identity, the unchanging core of personality formation, is "with rare exception firmly and irreversibly established for both sexes by the time a child is around three." Given that for both sexes the primary caretaker in the first three years of life is typically female, the interpersonal dynamics of gender identity formation are different for boys and girls. Female identity formation takes place in a context of ongoing relationship since "mothers tend to experience their daughters as more like, and continuous with, themselves."

[1] Sigmund Freud, *Three Essays on the Theory of Sexuality,* vol. 7, *The Standard Edition of the Complete Psychological Works of Sigmund Freud,* trans. and ed. James Strachey (1905; reprinted by London: Hogarth Press, 1961).

[2] Sigmund Freud, "Some Psychical Consequences of the Anatomical Distinction between the Sexes" (1925), vol. 19, *The Standard Edition of the Complete Psychological Works of Sigmund Freud,* trans. and ed. James Strachey (London: The Hogarth Press, 1961), pp. 257–258.

[3] Nancy Chodorow, "Family Structure and Feminine Personality" in *Woman, Culture and Society,* ed. M. A. Rosaldo and L. Lamphere (Stanford, CA: Stanford University Press, 1974), pp. 43–44.

Correspondingly, girls, in identifying themselves as female, experience themselves as like their mothers, thus fusing the experience of attachment with the process of identity formation. In contrast, "mothers experience their sons as a male opposite," and boys, in defining themselves as masculine, separate their mothers from themselves, thus curtailing "their primary love and sense of empathic tie." Consequently, male development entails a "more emphatic individuation and a more defensive firming of experienced ego boundaries." For boys, but not girls, "issues of differentiation have become intertwined with sexual issues."[4]

Writing against the masculine bias of psychoanalytic theory, Chodorow argues that the existence of sex differences in the early experiences of individuation and relationship "does not mean that women have 'weaker' ego boundaries than men or are more prone to psychosis." It means instead that "girls emerge from this period with a basis for 'empathy' built into their primary definition of self in a way that boys do not." Chodorow thus replaces Freud's negative and derivative description of female psychology with a positive and direct account of her own: "Girls emerge with a stronger basis for experiencing another's needs or feelings as one's own (or of thinking that one is so experiencing another's needs and feelings). Furthermore, girls do not define themselves in terms of the denial of preoedipal relational modes to the same extent as do boys. Therefore, regression to these modes tends not to feel as much a basic threat to their ego. From very early, then, because they are parented by a person of the same gender . . . girls come to experience themselves as less differentiated than boys, as more continuous with and related to the external object-world, and as differently oriented to their inner object-world as well."[5]

Consequently, relationships, and particularly issues of dependency, are experienced differently by women and men. For boys and men, separation and individuation are critically tied to gender identity since separation from the mother is essential for the development of masculinity. For girls and women, issues of femininity or feminine identity do not depend on the achievement of separation from the mother or on the progress of individuation. Since masculinity is defined through separation while femininity is defined through attachment, male gender identity is threatened by intimacy while female gender identity is threatened by separation. Thus males tend to have difficulty with relationships, while females tend to have problems with individuation. The quality of embeddedness in social interaction and personal relationships that characterizes women's lives in contrast to men's, however, becomes not only a descriptive difference but also a developmental liability when the milestones of childhood and adolescent development in the psychological literature are markers of increasing separation. Women's failure to separate then becomes by definition a failure to develop.

The sex differences in personality formation that Chodorow describes in early childhood appear during the middle childhood years in studies of children's games. Children's games are considered by George Herbert Mead and Jean Piaget as the crucible of social development during the school years.[6] In games, children learn to take the role of the other and come to see themselves through another's eyes. In games, they learn respect for rules and come to understand the ways rules can be made and changed.

Janet Lever, considering the peer group to be the agent of socialization during the elementary school years and play to be a major activity of socialization at that time, set out to discover whether there are sex differences in the games that children play.[7] Studying 181 fifth-grade, white, middle-class children, ages ten and eleven, she observed the organization and structure of their playtime activities. She watched the children

---

[4] Nancy Chodorow, *The Reproduction of Mothering* (Berkeley: University of California Press, 1978), pp. 150, 166–167.
[5] Chodorow, "Family Structure," p. 167.

[6] George Herbert Mead, *Mind, Self and Society* (Chicago: University of Chicago Press, 1934); Jean Piaget, *The Moral Development of the Child* (New York: Free Press, 1932).
[7] Janet Lever, "Sex Differences in the Games Children Play," *Social Problems* 23 (1976): 478–487.

as they played at school during recess and in physical education class, and in addition kept diaries of their accounts as to how they spent their out-of-school time. From this study, Lever reports sex differences: boys play out of doors more often than girls do; boys play more often in large and age-heterogeneous groups; they play competitive games more often, and their games last longer than girls' games. The last is in some ways the most interesting finding. Boys' games appeared to last longer not only because they required a higher level of skill and were thus less likely to become boring, but also because, when disputes arose in the course of a game, boys were able to resolve the disputes more effectively than girls: "During the course of this study, boys were seen quarrelling all the time, but not once was a game terminated because of a quarrel and no game was interrupted for more than seven minutes. In the gravest debates, the final word was always, to 'repeat the play,' generally followed by a chorus of 'cheater's proof.'[8] In fact, it seemed that the boys enjoyed the legal debates as much as they did the game itself, and even marginal players of lesser size or skill participated equally in these recurrent squabbles. In contrast, the eruption of disputes among girls tended to end the game.

Thus Lever extends and corroborates the observations of Piaget in his study of the rules of the game, where he finds boys becoming through childhood increasingly fascinated with the legal elaboration of rules and the development of fair procedures for adjudicating conflicts, a fascination that, he notes, does not hold for girls. Girls, Piaget observes, have a more "pragmatic" attitude toward rules, "regarding a rule as good as long as the game repaid it."[9] Girls are more tolerant in their attitudes toward rules, more willing to make exceptions, and more easily reconciled to innovations. As a result, the legal sense, which Piaget considers essential to moral development, "is far less developed in little girls than in boys."[10]

The bias that leads Piaget to equate male development with child development also colors Lever's work. The assumption that shapes her discussion of results is that the male model is the better one since it fits the requirements for modern corporate success. In contrast, the sensitivity and care for the feelings of others that girls develop through their play have little market value and can even impede professional success. Lever implies that, given the realities of adult life, if a girl does not want to be left dependent on men, she will have to learn to play like a boy.

To Piaget's argument that children learn the respect for rules necessary for moral development by playing rule-bound games, Lawrence Kohlberg adds that these lessons are most effectively learned through the opportunities for role-taking that arise in the course of resolving disputes.[11] Consequently, the moral lessons inherent in girls' play appear to be fewer than in boys'. Traditional girls' games like jump rope and hopscotch are turn-taking games, where competition is indirect since one person's success does not necessarily signify another's failure. Consequently, disputes requiring adjudication are less likely to occur. In fact, most of the girls whom Lever interviewed claimed that when a quarrel broke out, they ended the game. Rather than elaborating a system of rules for resolving disputes, girls subordinated the continuation of the game to the continuation of relationships.

Lever concludes that from the games they play, boys learn both the independence and the organizational skills necessary for coordinating the activities of large and diverse groups of people. By participating in controlled and socially approved competitive situations, they learn to deal with competition in a relatively forthright manner—to play with their enemies and to compete with their friends—all in accordance with the rules of the game. In contrast, girls' play tends to occur in smaller, more intimate groups, often the

[8] Lever, "Sex Differences," p. 482.
[9] Piaget, *Moral Development,* p. 83.
[10] Piaget, *Moral Development,* p. 77.

[11] Lawrence Kohlberg, "Stage and Sequence: The Cognitive-Development Approach to Socialization," in *Handbook of Socialization Theory and Research,* ed. D. A. Goslin (Chicago: Rand McNally, 1969).

best-friend dyad, and in private places. This play replicates the social pattern of primary human relationships in that its organization is more cooperative. Thus, it points less, in Mead's terms, toward learning to take the role of "the generalized other," less toward the abstraction of human relationships. But it fosters the development of the empathy and sensitivity necessary for taking the role of "the particular other" and points more toward knowing the other as different from the self.

The sex differences in personality formation in early childhood that Chodorow derives from her analysis of the mother-child relationship are thus extended by Lever's observations of sex differences in the play activities of middle childhood. Together these accounts suggest that boys and girls arrive at puberty with a different interpersonal orientation and a different range of social experiences. Yet, since adolescence is considered a crucial time for separation, the period of "the second individuation process,"[12] female development has appeared most divergent and thus most problematic at this time. . . .

"It is obvious," Virginia Woolf says, "that the values of women differ very often from the values which have been made by the other sex."[13] Yet, she adds, "it is the masculine values that prevail." As a result, women come to question the normality of their feelings and to alter their judgments in deference to the opinion of others. In the nineteenth century novels written by women, Woolf sees at work "a mind which was slightly pulled from the straight and made to alter its clear vision in deference to external authority." The same deference to the values and opinions of others can be seen in the judgments of twentieth century women. The difficulty women experience in finding or speaking publicly in their own voices emerges repeatedly in the form of qualification and self-doubt, but also in intimations of a divided judgment, a public assessment and private assessment which are fundamentally at odds.

Yet the deference and confusion that Woolf criticizes in women derive from the values she sees as their strength. Women's deference is rooted not only in their social subordination but also in the substance of their moral concern. Sensitivity to the needs of others and the assumption of responsibility for taking care lead women to attend to voices other than their own and to include in their judgment other points of view. Women's moral weakness, manifest in an apparent diffusion and confusion of judgment, is thus inseparable from women's moral strength, an overriding concern with relationships and responsibilities. The reluctance to judge may itself be indicative of the care and concern for others that infuse the psychology of women's development and are responsible for what is generally seen as problematic in its nature.

Thus women not only define themselves in a context of human relationship but also judge themselves in terms of their ability to care. Women's place in man's life cycle has been that of nurturer, caretaker, and helpmate, the weaver of those networks of relationships on which she in turn relies. But while women have thus taken care of men, men have, in their theories of psychological development, as in their economic arrangements, tended to assume or devalue that care. When the focus on individuation and individual achievement extends into adulthood and maturity is equated with personal autonomy, concern with relationships appears as a weakness of women rather than as a human strength.[14]

The discrepancy between womanhood and adulthood is nowhere more evident than in the studies on sex-role stereotypes reported by Broverman, Vogel, Broverman, Clarkson, and Rosenkrantz.[15] The repeated finding of these studies is that the qualities deemed necessary for adulthood—the capacity for autonomous thinking, clear decision-making, and responsible action—are those associated with masculinity and considered undesirable as attributes of the feminine

---

[12] Peter Blos, "The Second Individuation Process of Adolescence," in *The Psychoanalytic Study of the Child*, vol. 22, ed. A. Freud (New York: International Universities Press, 1967).

[13] Virginia Woolf, *A Room of One's Own* (New York: Harcourt, Brace and World, 1929), p. 76.

[14] Jean Baker Miller, *Toward a New Psychology of Women* (Boston: Beacon Press, 1976).

[15] I. Broverman, S. Vogel, D. Broverman, F. Clarkson, and P. Rosenkrantz, "Sex-Role Stereotypes: A Current Appraisal," *Journal of Social Issues* 28 (1972): 59–78.

self. The stereotypes suggest a splitting of love and work that relegates expressive capacities to women while placing instrumental abilities in the masculine domain. Yet looked at from a different perspective, these stereotypes reflect a conception of adulthood that is itself out of balance, favoring the separateness of the individual self over connection to others, and leaning more toward an autonomous life of work than toward the interdependence of love and care.

The discovery now being celebrated by men in mid-life of the importance of intimacy, relationships, and care is something that women have known from the beginning. However, because that knowledge in women has been considered "intuitive" or "instinctive," a function of anatomy coupled with destiny, psychologists have neglected to describe its development. In my research, I have found that women's moral development centers on the elaboration of that knowledge and thus delineates a critical line of psychological development in the lives of both of the sexes. The subject of moral development not only provides the final illustration of the reiterative pattern in the observation and assessment of sex differences in the literature on human development, but also indicates more particularly why the nature and significance of women's development has been for so long obscured and shrouded in mystery.

The criticism that Freud makes of women's sense of justice, seeing it as compromised in its refusal of blind impartiality, reappears not only in the work of Piaget but also in that of Kohlberg. While in Piaget's account of the moral judgment of the child, girls are an aside, a curiosity to whom he devotes four brief entries in an index that omits "boys" altogether because "the child" is assumed to be male,[16] in the research from which Kohlberg derives his theory, females simply do not exist. Kohlberg's six stages that describe the development of moral judgment from childhood to adulthood are based empirically on a study of eighty-four boys whose development Kohlberg has followed for a period of over twenty years.[17] Although Kohlberg claims universality for his stage sequence, those groups not included in his original sample rarely reach his higher stages.[18] Prominent among those who thus appear to be deficient in moral development when measured by Kohlberg's scale are women, whose judgments seem to exemplify the third stage of his six-stage sequence. At this stage morality is conceived in interpersonal terms and goodness is equated with helping and pleasing others. This conception of goodness is considered by Kohlberg and Kramer to be functional in the lives of mature women insofar as their lives take place in the home.[19] Kohlberg and Kramer imply that only if women enter the traditional arena of male activity will they recognize the inadequacy of this moral perspective and progress like men toward higher stages where relationships are subordinated to rules (stage four) and rules to universal principles of justice (stages five and six).

Yet herein lies a paradox, for the very traits that traditionally have defined the "goodness" of women, their care for and sensitivity to the needs of others, are those that mark them as deficient in moral development. In this version of moral development, however, the conception of maturity is derived from the study of men's lives and reflects the importance of individuation in their development. Piaget, challenging the common impression that a developmental theory is built like a pyramid from its base in infancy, points out that a conception of development instead hangs from its vertex of maturity, the point toward which progress is traced.[20] Thus, a change in the

[16] Jean Piaget, *The Moral Judgment of the Child* (New York: Free Press, 1932).

[17] Lawrence Kohlberg, *The Development of Modes of Thinking and Choices in Years 10 to 16* (Ph.D. diss., University of Chicago, 1958); Lawrence Kohlberg, *The Philosophy of Moral Development* (San Francisco: Harper and Row, 1981).

[18] Carolyn P. Edwards, "Societal Complexity and Moral Development: A Kenyan Study," *Ethos* (1975): 505–527; Constance Holstein, "Development of Moral Judgment: A Longitudinal Study of Males and Females," *Child Development* 47 (1976): 51–61; Elizabeth L. Simpson, "Moral Development Research: A Case Study of Scientific Cultural Bias," *Human Development* 17 (1974): 81–106.

[19] L. Kohlberg and R. Kramer, "Continuities and Discontinuities in Child and Adult Moral Development," *Human Development* 12 (1969): 934–120.

[20] Jean Piaget, *Structuralism* (New York: Basic Books, 1970).

definition of maturity does not simply alter the description of the highest stage but recasts the understanding of development, changing the entire account.

When one begins with the study of women and derives developmental constructs from their lives, the outline of a moral conception different from that described by Freud, Piaget, or Kohlberg begins to emerge and informs a different description of development. In this conception, the moral problem arises from conflicting responsibilities rather than from competing rights and requires for its resolution a mode of thinking that is contextual and narrative rather than formal and abstract. This conception of morality as concerned with the activity of care centers moral development around the understanding of responsibility and relationships, just as the conception of morality as fairness ties moral development to the understanding of rights and rules. . . .

Thus it becomes clear why a morality of rights and noninterference may appear frightening to women in its potential justification of indifference and unconcern. At the same time, it becomes clear why, from a male perspective, a morality of responsibility appears inconclusive and diffuse, given its insistent contextual relativism. Women's moral judgments thus elucidate the pattern observed in the description of the developmental differences between the sexes, but they also provide an alternative conception of maturity by which these differences can be assessed and their implications traced. The psychology of women that has consistently been described as distinctive in its greater orientation toward relationships and interdependence implies a more contextual mode of judgment and a different moral understanding. Given the differences in women's conceptions of self and morality, women bring to the life cycle a different point of view and order human experience in terms of different priorities.

The myth of Demeter and Persephone, which McClelland cites as exemplifying the feminine attitude toward power,[21] was associated with the Eleusinian Mysteries celebrated in ancient Greece for over two thousand years. As told in the Homeric *Hymn to Demeter,* the story of Persephone indicates the strengths of interdependence, building up resources and giving, that McClelland found in his research on power motivation to characterize the mature feminine style. Although, McClelland says, "it is fashionable to conclude that no one knows what went on in the Mysteries, it is known that they were probably the most important religious ceremonies, even partly on the historical record, which were organized by and for women, especially at the onset before men by means of the cult of Dionysos began to take them over." Thus McClelland regards the myth as "a special presentation of feminine psychology."[22] It is, as well, a life-cycle story par excellence.

Persephone, the daughter of Demeter, while playing in a meadow with her girlfriends, sees a beautiful narcissus which she runs to pick. As she does so, the earth opens and she is snatched away by Hades, who takes her to his underworld kingdom. Demeter, goddess of the earth, so mourns the loss of her daughter that she refuses to allow anything to grow. The crops that sustain life on earth shrivel up, killing men and animals alike, until Zeus takes pity on man's suffering and persuades his brother to return Persephone to her mother. But before she leaves, Persephone eats some pomegranate seeds, which ensures that she will spend part of every year with Hades in the underworld.

The elusive mystery of women's development lies in its recognition of the continuing importance of attachment in the human life cycle. Woman's place in man's life cycle is to protect this recognition while the developmental litany intones the celebration of separation, autonomy, individuation, and natural rights. The myth of Persephone speaks directly to the distortion in this view by reminding us that narcissism leads to death, that the fertility of the earth is in some mysterious way tied to the continuation of the mother-daughter relationship, and that the life cycle itself arises from an alternation between the

[21] David McClelland, *Power: The Inner Experience* (New York: Irvington, 1975).

[22] McClelland, *Power,* p. 96.

world of women and that of men. Only when life-cycle theorists divide their attention and begin to live with women as they have lived with men will their vision encompass the experience of both sexes and their theories become correspondingly more fertile.

## IMAGES OF RELATIONSHIP

. . . While the truths of psychological theory have blinded psychologists to the truth of women's experience, that experience illuminates a world which psychologists have found hard to trace, a territory where violence is rare and relationships appear safe. The reason women's experience has been so difficult to decipher or even discern is that a shift in the imagery of relationships gives rise to a problem of interpretation. The images of hierarchy and web, drawn from the texts of men's and women's fantasies and thoughts, convey different ways of structuring relationships and are associated with different views of morality and self. But these images create a problem in understanding because each distorts the other's representation. As the top of the hierarchy becomes the edge of the web and as the center of a network of connection becomes the middle of a hierarchical progression, each image marks as dangerous the place which the other defines as safe. Thus the images of hierarchy and web inform different modes of assertion and response: the wish to be alone at the top and the consequent fear that others will get too close; the wish to be at the center of connection and the consequent fear of being too far out on the edge. These disparate fears of being stranded and being caught give rise to different portrayals of achievement and affiliation, leading to different modes of action and different ways of assessing the consequences of choice.

The reinterpretation of women's experience in terms of their own imagery of relationships thus clarifies that experience and also provides a nonhierarchical vision of human connection. Since relationships, when cast in the image of hierarchy, appear inherently unstable and morally problematic, their transposition into the image of web changes an order of inequality into a structure of interconnection. But the power of the images of hierarchy and web, their evocation of feelings and their recurrence in thought, signifies the embeddedness of both of these images in the cycle of human life. The experiences of inequality and interconnection, inherent in the relation of parent and child, then give rise to the ethics of justice and care, the ideals of human relationship—the vision that self and other will be treated as of equal worth, that despite differences in power, things will be fair; the vision that everyone will be responded to and included, that no one will be left alone or hurt. These disparate visions in their tension reflect the paradoxical truths of human experience—that we know ourselves as separate only insofar as we live in connection with others, and that we experience relationship only insofar as we differentiate other from self.

## VISIONS OF MATURITY

. . . As we have listened for centuries to the voices of men and the theories of development that their experience informs, so we have come more recently to notice not only the silence of women but the difficulty in hearing what they say when they speak. Yet in the different voice of women lies the truth of an ethic of care, the tie between relationship and responsibility, and the origins of aggression in the failure of connection. The failure to see the different reality of women's lives and to hear the differences in their voices stems in part from the assumption that there is a single mode of social experience and interpretation. By positing instead two different modes, we arrive at a more complex rendition of human experience which sees the truth of separation and attachment in the lives of women and men and recognizes how these truths are carried by different modes of language and thought.

To understand how the tension between responsibilities and rights sustains the dialectic of human development is to see the integrity of two disparate modes of experience that are in the end connected. While an ethic of justice proceeds from the premise of equality—that everyone should be treated the same—an ethic of care rests on the premise of nonviolence—that no one should be hurt. In the representation of maturity, both perspectives converge in the realization that just as inequality adversely affects both parties in an unequal relationship, so too violence is destructive for everyone involved. This dialogue between fairness and care not only provides a better understanding of relations between the sexes but also gives rise to a more comprehensive portrayal of adult work and family relationships.

As Freud and Piaget call our attention to the differences in children's feelings and thought,

enabling us to respond to children with greater care and respect, so a recognition of the differences in women's experience and understanding expands our vision of maturity and points to the contextual nature of developmental truths. Through this expansion in perspective, we can begin to envision how a marriage between adult development as it is currently portrayed and women's development as it begins to be seen could lead to a changed understanding of human development and a more generative view of human life.

# FEMINISM AND RACE

## *bell hooks Talks Back*

bell hooks (1952–) is a poet, social critic, feminist theorist, and black activist. She was born in Kentucky and adopted her nom de plume from her outspoken great-grandmother (her real name is Gloria Watkins). She has taught women's studies at Oberlin College and, from 1993, at City College in New York.

hooks (she doesn't capitalize her name) is a prolific writer. Her many books include *Ain't I a Woman: Black Women and Feminism* (1981), *Feminist Theory: From Margin to Center* (1984), *Yearning: Race, Gender and Cultural Politics* (1990), *Killing Rage: Ending Racism* (1995), and *Feminism Is for Everybody: Passionate Politics* (2000).

hooks has championed the right of nonwhite, working-class, and poor women to "talk back," to speak not only against sexist oppression but against racism and class-based biases. She's the bad conscience of American feminism, reminding it of its predominantly white middle-class character, and of the biases that go along with this character.

It's difficult to situate hooks in terms of the three waves discussed in the introduction to this chapter. Historically speaking, she rode the late fringe of the Second Wave, coming to public attention with her early 1980s work. However, she can also be seen as part of the Third Wave in that she's not afraid of expressing herself sexually, advocating an eroticized classroom (anathema to puritans such as Dworkin and MacKinnon), showing off her own sexuality by publishing nude photos. Perhaps she's a wave unto herself.

In any case, in the reading that follows, hooks reminisces. In her youth, "talking back" meant speaking as an equal to an authority figure. Black men preached in their churches, while black women preached in their own church, the home. So the silencing of women wasn't the problem, as it is for women from a WASP background. Instead, the problem was to create a black woman's speech that would compel people to listen.

Young bell was punished when a child for talking back to adults, so she began recording her thoughts in diaries and poems. Writing was a way for her to capture lost speech. She was told that if she were too chatty, her punishment would be to be carted off to an insane asylum. So she avoided any guilt or punishment associated with her work by taking the name of her acid-tongued great-grandmother as a writer-identity, thus avoiding giving way to the impulse to silence herself and to give up writing.

hooks goes on to complain of the lack of material written by black women on feminist bookshelves, and of their middle-class biases. This charge that feminism in America is a predominantly white middle-class phenomenon continues to haunt the women's movement to this day.

To "talk back" is to express yourself in a liberated voice, as the subject of speech. hooks's resistance to being shut up by the adults around her taught hooks the value of resistance in general to the forces of domination that seek to oppress free speech and free thought everywhere. For hooks, talking back was a double-edged sword: It cut through the domination of women by men and of black women by their white dominators.

# Talking Back

## BELL HOOKS

IN THE WORLD of the southern black community I grew up in, "back talk" and "talking back" meant speaking as an equal to an authority figure. It meant daring to disagree and sometimes it just meant having an opinion. In the "old school," children were meant to be seen and not heard. My great-grandparents, grandparents, and parents were all from the old school. To make yourself heard if you were a child was to invite punishment, the back-hand lick, the slap across the face that would catch you unaware, or the feel of switches stinging your arms and legs.

To speak then when one was not spoken to was a courageous act—an act of risk and daring. And yet it was hard not to speak in warm rooms where heated discussions began at the crack of dawn, women's voices filling the air, giving orders, making threats, fussing. Black men may have excelled in the art of poetic preaching in the male-dominated church, but in the church of the home, where the everyday rules of how to live and how to act were established, it was black women who preached. There, black women spoke in a language so rich, so poetic, that it felt to me like being shut off from life, smothered to death if one were not allowed to participate.

It was in that world of woman talk (the men were often silent, often absent) that was born in me the craving to speak, to have a voice, and not just any voice but one that could be identified as belonging to me. To make my voice, I had to speak, to hear myself talk—and talk I did—darting in and out of grown folks' conversations and dialogues, answering questions that were not di-

SOURCE: bell hooks, *Talking Back: Thinking Feminist, Thinking Black* (Boston: South End Press, 1989), pp. 5–9. Selection from abridged version in *Gender Basics,* ed. Anne Minas (Belmont, CA: Wadsworth, 2000), pp. 78–81. Reprinted by permission of South End Press.

rected at me, endlessly asking questions, making speeches. Needless to say, the punishments for these acts of speech seemed endless. They were intended to silence me—the child—and more particularly the girl child. Had I been a boy, they might have encouraged me to speak believing that I might someday be called to preach. There was no "calling" for talking girls, no legitimized rewarded speech. The punishments I received for "talking back" were intended to suppress all possibility that I would create my own speech. That speech was to be suppressed so that the "right speech of womanhood" would emerge.

Within feminist circles, silence is often seen as the sexist "right speech of womanhood"— the sign of woman's submission to patriarchal authority. This emphasis on woman's silence may be an accurate remembering of what has taken place in the households of women from WASP backgrounds in the United States, but in black communities (and diverse ethnic communities), women have not been silent. Their voices can be heard. Certainly for black women, our struggle has not been to emerge from silence into speech but to change the nature and direction of our speech, to make a speech that compels listeners, one that is heard.

Our speech, "the right speech of womanhood," was often the soliloquy, the talking into thin air, the talking to ears that do not hear you—the talk that is simply not listened to. Unlike the black male preacher whose speech was to be heard, who was to be listened to, whose words were to be remembered, the voices of black women—giving orders, making threats, fussing—could be tuned out, could become a kind of background music, audible but not acknowledged as significant speech. Dialogue— the sharing of speech and recognition—took place not between mother and child or mother and male authority figure but among black women. I can remember watching fascinated as our mother talked with her mother, sisters, and women friends. The intimacy and intensity of their speech—the satisfaction they received from talking to one another, the pleasure, the joy. It was in this world of woman speech, loud talk,

angry words, women with tongues quick and sharp, tender sweet tongues, touching our world with their words, that I made speech my birthright—and the right to voice, to authorship, a privilege I would not be denied. It was in that world and because of it that I came to dream of writing, to write.

Writing was a way to capture speech, to hold onto it, keep it close. And so I wrote down bits and pieces of conversations, confessing in cheap diaries that soon fell apart from too much handling, expressing the intensity of my sorrow, the anguish of speech—for I was always saying the wrong thing, asking the wrong questions. I could not confine my speech to the necessary corners and concerns of life. I hid these writings under my bed, in pillow stuffings, among faded underwear. When my sisters found and read them, they ridiculed and mocked me—poking fun. I felt violated, ashamed, as if the secret parts of my self had been exposed, brought into the open, and hung like newly clean laundry, out in the air for everyone to see. The fear of exposure, the fear that one's deepest emotions and innermost thoughts will be dismissed as mere nonsense, felt by so many young girls keeping diaries, holding and hiding speech, seems to me now one of the barriers that women have always needed and still need to destroy so that we are no longer pushed into secrecy or silence.

Despite my feelings of violation, of exposure, I continued to speak and write, choosing my hiding places well, learning to destroy work when no safe place could be found. I was never taught absolute silence; I was taught that it was important to speak but to talk a talk that was in itself a silence. Taught to speak and yet beware of the betrayal of too much heard speech, I experienced intense confusion and deep anxiety in my efforts to speak and write. Reciting poems at Sunday afternoon church service might be rewarded. Writing a poem (when one's time could be "better" spent sweeping, ironing, learning to cook) was luxurious activity, indulged in at the expense of others. Questioning authority, raising issues that were not deemed appropriate subjects brought pain, punishments—like telling mama I wanted to die before her because I could not live without her—that was crazy talk, crazy speech, the kind that would lead you to end up in a mental institution. "Little girl," I would be told, "if you don't stop all this crazy talk and crazy acting you are going to end up right out there at Western State."

Madness, not just physical abuse, was the punishment for too much talk if you were female. Yet even as this fear of madness haunted me, hanging over my writing like a monstrous shadow, I could not stop the words, making thought, writing speech. For this terrible madness which I feared, which I was sure was the destiny of daring women born to intense speech (after all, the authorities emphasized this point daily), was not as threatening as imposed silence, as suppressed speech.

Safety and sanity were to be sacrificed if I was to experience defiant speech. Though I risked them both, deep-seated fears and anxieties characterized my childhood days. I would speak but I would not ride a bike, play hardball, or hold the gray kitten. Writing about the ways we are traumatized in our growing-up years, psychoanalyst Alice Miller makes the point in *For Your Own Good* that it is not clear why childhood wounds become for some folk an opportunity to grow, to move forward rather than backward in the process of self-realization. Certainly, when I reflect on the trials of my growing-up years, the many punishments, I can see now that in resistance I learned to be vigilant in the nourishment of my spirit, to be tough, to courageously protect that spirit from forces that would break it.

While punishing me, my parents often spoke about the necessity of breaking my spirit. Now when I ponder the silences, the voices that are not heard, the voices of those wounded and/or oppressed individuals who do not speak or write, I contemplate the acts of persecution, torture—the terrorism that breaks spirits, that makes creativity impossible. I write these words to bear witness to the primacy of resistance struggle in any situation of domination (even within family life); to the strength and power that emerges from sustained resistance and the profound conviction that these forces can be healing, can protect us from dehumanization and despair. . . .

. . . For us, true speaking is not solely an expression of creative power; it is an act of resistance, a political gesture that challenges politics of domination that would render us nameless and voiceless. As such, it is a courageous act—as such, it represents a threat. To those who wield oppressive power, that which is threatening must necessarily be wiped out, annihilated, silenced.

Recently, efforts by black women writers to call attention to our work serve to highlight both our presence and absence. Whenever I peruse women's bookstores, I am struck not by the rapidly growing body of feminist writing by black women, but by the paucity of available published material. Those of us who write and are published remain few in number. The context of silence is varied and multi-dimensional. Most obvious are the ways racism, sexism, and class exploitation act to suppress and silence. Less obvious are the inner struggles, the efforts made to gain the necessary confidence to write, to rewrite, to fully develop craft and skill—and the extent to which such efforts fail.

Although I have wanted writing to be my life-work since childhood, it has been difficult for me to claim "writer" as part of that which identifies and shapes my everyday reality. Even after publishing books, I would often speak of wanting to be a writer as though these works did not exist. And though I would be told, "you are a writer," I was not yet ready to fully affirm this truth. Part of myself was still held captive by domineering forces of history, of familial life that had charted a map of silence, of right speech. I had not completely let go of the fear of saying the wrong thing, of being punished. Somewhere in the deep recesses of my mind, I believed I could avoid both responsibility and punishment if I did not declare myself a writer.

One of the many reasons I chose to write using the pseudonym bell hooks, a family name (mother to Sarah Oldham, grandmother to Rosa Bell Oldham, great-grandmother to me), was to construct a writer-identity that would challenge and subdue all impulses leading me away from speech into silence. I was a young girl buying bubble gum at the corner store when I first really heard the full name bell hooks. I had just "talked back" to a grown person. Even now I can recall the surprised look, the mocking tones that informed me I must be kin to bell hooks—a sharp-tongued woman, a woman who spoke her mind, a woman who was not afraid to talk back. I claimed this legacy of defiance, of will, of courage, affirming my link to female ancestors who were bold and daring in their speech. Unlike my bold and daring mother and grandmother, who were not supportive of talking back, even though they were assertive and powerful in their speech, bell hooks as I discovered, claimed, and invented her was my ally, my support.

That initial act of talking back outside the

home was empowering. It was the first of many acts of defiant speech that would make it possible for me to emerge as an independent thinker and writer. In retrospect, "talking back" became for me a rite of initiation, testing my courage, strengthening my commitment, preparing me for the days ahead—the days when writing, rejection notices, periods of silence, publication, ongoing development seem impossible but necessary.

Moving from silence into speech is for the oppressed, the colonized, the exploited, and those who stand and struggle side by side a gesture of defiance that heals, that makes new life and new growth possible. It is that act of speech, of "talking back," that is no mere gesture of empty words, that is the expression of our movement from object to subject—the liberated voice.

# THE REVOLT AGAINST THE SECOND WAVE

## *Naomi Wolf on Victim Feminism and Power Feminism*

Naomi Wolf (1962–) was born in San Francisco. She graduated from Yale in 1984 and two years later was a Rhodes Scholar at Oxford University. She is a poet, journalist, critic, and lecturer and the author of *The Beauty Myth: How Images of Beauty Are Used against Women* (1990); *Fire with Fire: The New Female Power and How to Use It* (1994), the source of our selections; *Promiscuities: The Secret Struggle for Womanhood* (1997); and *Misconceptions: Truth, Lies, and the Unexpected on the Journey to Motherhood* (2001).

In 1993 she married *New Republic* editor David Shipley, giving birth to their child Rosa in 1995. She also worked as an adviser on welfare and family issues to the Clinton administration. Naturally, Wolf's gravitation into traditional male power structures has caused many radical feminists to look on her with suspicion. This suspicion was further aggravated when, after the birth of her daughter, Wolf asked the pro-choice movement to accept the guilt that comes from the realization that abortion is the taking of a life.

Wolf made her name with her best seller *The Beauty Myth* (1990), which argued that the pressure of male-dominated contemporary culture on women to be beautiful is a form of social control over women. She argues that when women entered the workforce en masse, men felt threatened, so they struck back by subtly compelling women to spend time, money, and emotional energy on selecting and buying clothes, cosmetics, dieting, plastic surgery, and other aesthetic enhancements. Her idea of working women being victims of a "beauty myth" seemed to destine Wolf for a career as a young representative of Second Wave feminism.

*Fire with Fire,* however, gives us a somewhat different picture of sexual politics. Wolf is now interested in including women within the feminist movement who would reject much of the politics of Second Wave radicalism. The key question she asks in the book is why is it that in the early 1990s most American women no longer called themselves "feminists," even though they were happy to reap the benefits of the women's movement? Her answer to this question takes up about half of her book. Here is her list of what she takes to be the causes of this alienation of women from the feminist movement:

1. The movement's bad habits left over from the revolutionary Left of the 1960s, especially the Marxist celebration of subversive, marginal culture and its fear of using mainstream power structures to effect change
2. Dyke-baiting—the antifamily, pro-lesbian perception of the movement
3. Economic silencing—women on the job are expected to distance themselves from feminism in order to have a successful career
4. The distorted media coverage of feminism
5. Feminists' hostility toward the media
6. A clubhouse mentality of preaching only to the converted
7. The publication of theories that sound extreme and absurd to mainstream women
8. A fear of debate within the feminist community
9. The shift of feminist debate to university academics, with their use of arcane and obscure language borrowed from French postmodern theorists
10. The perception that the movement was white, middle class, and elitist

Wolf downplays many of these critiques, yet takes them seriously as challenges to feminism. In our selections we'll first focus on Wolf's treatment of the "bad intellectual habits" of the feminist movement, including its inflexibility of thought, consensus thinking, drive toward ideological purity, and tendency to put forward theories that, if interpreted literally, look absurd. On this last issue one can feel the tug-of-war between Second and Third Wave feminism going on in Wolf's mind. She tries to show the kernel of truth in such extreme claims as Susan Brownmiller's implication that all men are rapists, or Andrea Dworkin's even more extreme suggestion that because women cannot possibly give "real" consent to sex with a man in a patriarchal society, all sexual intercourse is de facto rape, even though she is fully aware that such radical views have damaged the credibility of the feminist movement.

*Fire with Fire* is also interesting for its division of feminist theory into two broad tendencies. "Victim feminism" sees women as the passive victims of patriarchy, as naturally noncompetitive in the face of male aggressiveness. It is antisexual, self-sacrificing, resentful of money and power, and self-righteous. "Power feminism" is "unapologetically sexual," against sexism but *not* men, and tolerant of other women's choices about their opinions, body images, and personal lives. Most important, power feminism aims to see women as moral adults, as responsible power seekers in an egalitarian world. Naturally, Wolf urges women to embrace power feminism.

Further, Wolf gushily embraces heterosexual desire (and practice) in the later chapters of *Fire with Fire.* Her sexual fantasies of being dominated by virile men are strictly taboo to most of the old warriors of Second Wave feminism. She speaks of the "absolute delight" that the male sexual response instills in her, for male sexual attention "is the sun in which I bloom." This "return to the body" (my phrase) is very characteristic of the Third Wave, moving Wolf closer to Camille Paglia, away from the sometimes puritanical radical feminists of the Second Wave.

Wolf speaks of the need to frankly acknowledge the fact that women, like men, have an animal nature that needs to be satisfied. She also moves herself away from the strictly constructionist view of gender, arguing that from time to time hetero-sexual women have to shut down the "critical mind" and return to that primal place of purely physical desire.

She also argues for a greater tolerance toward dissent within feminism. Women should be free to express themselves as they see fit, without fear of censure from other women. Feminism shouldn't be about forcing "conversion" on those with dif-fering views.

Wolf's basically liberal feminist foundation comes out clearly when she con-cludes that feminism is a humanistic movement for social justice that aims at giving equal power to each sex. She argues that although women are frequently victimized by men, they should all the same avoid turning themselves into *natural* victims by parading their status as victims on a public stage. Instead, they should use the power of personal and national politics to take control of women's fate in America.

# Fire with Fire

## NAOMI WOLF

### *Oxygen Deprivation: Bad Intellectual Habits*

#### INFLEXIBILITY OF THOUGHT

> Do I contradict myself?
> Very well I contradict myself,
> (I am large, I contain multitudes.)
> —Walt Whitman

Once a movement feels it has been pushed out of the great stream of American life, it will tend to treasure—and hold on for dear life to—the iden-tity it has. The normal push and tug of main-stream life, which polishes ideas as the ocean pol-ishes glass, feels threatening. The degradation of

debate about women's issues has led some aspects of feminism into intellectually destructive habits.

These habits involve either/or thinking. You are either victim or oppressor; you are either for us or against us; you are either a nonsexist woman or a sexist man. Either/or thinking is the natural mental reaction to a perception of scarcity. When people feel they have no options, they cling to the assurances of polarized certainties. It is only when people feel rich in confidence and space that they dare to pursue the subtleties of what Gloria Steinem calls both/and thinking. Femi-nism must embrace this psychology of plenty. . . .

But women do have a uniquely legitimate fear of too-free play with ideas. Since women lack

SOURCE: Naomi Wolf, *Fire with Fire: The New Female Power and How It Will Change the 21st Century* (New York: Random House, 1993), from chap. 8, "Oxygen Deprivation: Bad Intellectual Habits"; chap. 9, "Two Traditions"; and chap. 13, "Victim Feminism's Recent Impasses," pp. 107–112, 120–123, 135–142, 184–189 (edited). Copyright 1993 by Naomi Wolf. Used by permission of Random House, Inc.

legislative power, words about women too often, and too quickly, become statutes about women. The legal treatment of women depends not on verifiable facts or on rules of conduct that can be universalized, but rather on gut feelings and fuzzy impressions about what sort of behavior toward or by women is appropriate. Attitudes about rape, for instance, and about who "deserves" it, become the real legal circumstances in which one finds oneself trying to establish the guilt of one's rapist and one's own innocence. If enough voices say that abortion is murder, real abortion rights are at stake. Every gain we have made in the raising of legal consciousness around rape and domestic violence has been the result of years of painstaking persuasion on the part of feminists. In this climate, a research study, an editorial in a major newspaper, even a TV movie about date rape or domestic violence is likely to affect courts and legislatures.

Critics of feminism misunderstand this tendency to retreat into an intellectual huddle about certain contested issues. Often feminists don't dread the ideas themselves, but the concrete legislation that may result. When some feminists resist Camille Paglia's wide opinion that women who go to a man's room are asking for date rape, or a Katie Roiphe's view that the "rape crisis" is imaginary, it is because such language can elicit not only a fun debate, but also an actual rollback of women's legal rights.

The opposition understands and makes use of the quick pairing of speech and legislation when it comes to women: A woman cannot voice anxiety about pornography, for instance, without the cry of censorship being let loose to harry her mental investigation into the ground. But for us to fear dissent and become guarded in our opinions, because legal consequences might follow too closely and uncontrollably behind them, is a price too high to pay.

## CONSENSUS THINKING

Consensus thinking is some feminists' reaction to this sense that a free play of ideas is a luxury we don't have. "We confirm our reality by shar-

ing," reads a T-shirt produced by a women's group. But today this love of consensus is just the problem. These distortions led to some habits of thought unworthy of feminism. We should never "confirm" our reality prematurely by "sharing" at the expense of challenging and testing our reality through honest dissent and debate. The legacy of the consciousness-raising movement gives great weight to the act of having other women confirm one's own life experiences, thus breaking down isolation and putting individual struggles into a social context. While that "confirmation of reality by sharing" worked magnificently for the Second Wave, it has left a tendency in some feminist subcultures to value consensus thinking in a way that can promote the tyranny of the group perspective over the creation of community from distinct, individual visions. . . .

Recently, I was invited to debate Susie Bright, a lesbian feminist who is propornography and pro-sadomasochism, and who wrote a column for the lesbian S&M journal called, enragingly to some, *On Our Backs*. A reader of mine called my office. "How," asked this reader, "can Naomi *speak* to that woman?" "That woman"—how many Victorian housewives have mouthed those words to one another as a scarlet courtesan passed them on the promenade, showing off her too-bright plumage? I haven't read Susie Bright's books, I found myself answering the woman silently; I haven't even been to the debate yet and heard what she has to say. How can anyone else assume she knows what I think if *I* don't know yet? The woman's response depressed me, because of the volumes it spoke about why people turn away from some kinds of feminism.

Bright's biography presents a set of thorny, tantalizing contradictions; I was eager to experience the rush of clashing perspectives merging into new thought patterns. The trousseau reflex of censure and ostracism, of "not speaking to" someone who has offended us (usually a woman friend) would have preempted an energizing disruption.

At the end of her book *Feminism Without Illusions*, Elizabeth Fox-Genovese writes: "Recognizing the danger that many other feminists, whose views differ from mine, may consider my criticisms disloyal, I can only hope that the scope of the movement permits the acceptance of divergent viewpoints as part of a continuing effort to make sense of what women need."

I understand Fox-Genovese's caution; I feel her sense of unease myself as I criticize aspects of a movement I champion. But what a depressing sentence to read from the pen of a college professor. If criticism of a movement amounts to disloyalty, that movement has set up the conditions of its own fossilization.

Few will tune in to the saga of feminism if they already know how it will end. Why cough up fifteen dollars and give up a great episode of *Cheers* for a seat at a debate, for a previously approved test pattern? If we cling to a party line, we bore ourselves and disconnect our listeners, who reasonably sense that they'll have heard it all before.

## IDEOLOGICAL PURITY

The dynamic behind the question was the theme of contamination that so haunts women in general and victim feminism in particular. Feminist discourse is studded with warnings about the dangers of behaving impurely. Money, fame, and nasty opinions are the usual culprits. Women risk being "co-opted," "assimilated," and "tokenized." They have "sold out" or "crossed the line." Victim feminism speaks about ideological corruption in the same language eighteenth-century ballads used to warn virginal milkmaids to beware the wily procuresses who wanted to lure them, with gold and finery, from a life of rural innocence into one of urban sin.

Indeed, we cannot understand victim feminism's fear of corruption without understanding women's millennia-old relationship to prostitution. All women suffer a hangover from our long understanding of the relationship between wives, nuns, and virgins, on the one hand, and prostitutes and courtesans, on the other. For centuries, in almost every Western culture, virtually every woman who was not an aristocrat had to uphold an ideology of respectability and chastity

that distinguished her from a prostitute. While she was given the benefit of her "decent" status—protection, shelter, a position in society—this came at a heavy price: sexual self-abnegation and dependency. In contrast to that double-edged respectability, the prostitute's life had a double-edged lack of respectability. Though streetwalkers led the most diseased and unprotected of lives, courtesans lived well, often in the center of glittering society and intellectual life. By the nineteenth century, everyone knew that even the poorest of prostitutes had the chance to make more money more quickly than the working-class factory girls and shopgirls who made up the largest category of working women since the start of the Industrial Revolution.

And every "respectable" woman knew how fine was the line that separated her status from that of the prostitute. Merely by acting on a sexual impulse, getting pregnant outside marriage, or losing a husband, a "nice" woman could be propelled into the whore's life. Consequently, such a woman would have to believe in and maintain a stigma on "bad women" and bad behavior so that she would never give in to her own temptation to "cross the line." And since she had forsaken so much pleasure, she had to inflate the value of chastity and perfect a hatred of seduction, or "selling out," in order to compensate herself.

The conditions that put so much weight on the difference between "good women" and "whores" are mostly gone, but the centuries of acculturation handed down from mother to daughter remain. This mentality's legacy keeps some feminists supersensitive to staying on the "correct" side of any given issue, even at the expense of a fruitful embrace of intellectual ambiguity or worldly power.

## LITERALIZED THEORY

This tendency toward rigidity led to a too-literal translation of influential theories. From the 1970s to the present, a number of theories emerged that freed the way we could think about gender, but that translated poorly into popular conversation. These were then circulated in catchphrases that ranged from the preposterous to the threatening, further alienating many from the movement.

The press does something with feminists that it does not do with other political movements: It regularly interviews feminist theorists and philosophers as if they were the leaders of organizations. This is the equivalent of *Time* interviewing Martin Heidegger, a German philosopher who questioned the nature of objective reality, on his views on the German government. If he responded by saying "You refer to the European Community but that organization is a phenomenological illusion," the readers might well harbor worries about the soundness of the political viewpoint he is portrayed as representing.

Why might this mass confusion be so commonplace? The simple reason is that most of the heads of women's organizations are busy with an agenda that is palatable, commonsensical, and unscary to the majority of Americans: health care, family leave, pay equity, and voters' rights, to name a few. If the average American saw feminist organization's literature, she or he would find very little to object to, and quite a lot to sign up in support of. But rather than receiving that literature, our average American is likelier to hear a theorist, quoted way out of context, saying something to the effect that "all sex is rape." This media sleight-of-hand creates the impression that the two kinds of work are really part of one sinister organization, and that NOW is lobbying Congress to legislate lesbian separatism, or censorship of nude images, or castration of male house pets.

These are some of the theories that came to be perceived as political road maps rather than as intellectual provocations:

### All Men Are Rapists

Susan Brownmiller's study *Against Our Will: Men, Women and Rape* explained that some men's rape of women keeps all women subjected to men. She pointed out that rape is institutionalized as part of warfare, and she located men's ability to rape in their biological construction. "By anatomical fiat . . . the human male was a natural predator and the human female served as its natural prey." Thus, her work trickled down as, "All men are rapists." This sentence has helped close down discussion between men and women, clouded feminist thinking about men and sexuality, and done men as a whole a grave injustice.

### All Heterosexual Sex Is Rape

In her book *Toward a Feminist Theory of the State,* Catharine MacKinnon argued that rape, sexual harassment, and pornography are used to enforce female inequality. Her argument was important in changing the way sexual abuse was seen. Rather than being an isolated matter between individuals, it became a civil rights issue. But her insight—that sex occurs in a context of social inequality—is often misrepresented as "All Heterosexual Sex Is Rape."

### All Intercourse Is Rape

Andrea Dworkin's troubling and groundbreaking book *Intercourse* also questioned—sometimes too sweepingly—the issue of whether women can really consent to intercourse in an unequal world. "Intercourse in reality is a use and abuse simultaneously . . . consent in this world of fear is so passive that the woman consenting could be dead and sometimes is." The book was reviewed widely and derisively in the mainstream press; the reviews led readers to believe that a guiding light of feminist thinking was also telling them flatly, "All heterosexual intercourse is rape" for they did not dwell on Dworkin's theoretical focus, the issue of consent.

These important theories marked a turning point at which many otherwise supportive women signed off in disgust: As a mainstream columnist put it, "By the Seventies an astonishing rhetoric had developed about the wicked penis and the male as rapist. . . . This is when ordinary feminists started to preface everything by saying, 'I'm not a feminist, but . . .' and to follow a separate path, or rather many different paths."

### All Women Are Lesbians

The poet Adrienne Rich published an essay, "Compulsory Heterosexuality and Lesbian Existence," which suggested that since women's and men's first erotic bond is with the mother, lesbianism is in fact the "natural" state for women. She suggested that those who become heterosexual are forced into that orientation by socialization and by economic dependence. She doubted whether, given "profound emotional impulses and complementarities drawing women toward women, there is a mystical/biological heterosexual inclination, a 'preference' or 'choice' that draws women toward men." And she suggested that all woman-to-woman intimacies, from a mother suckling a child to a dying woman tended by nurses, "exist on a lesbian continuum."

While Rich's main theory—that we can't know if our sexuality is chosen until we account for everything coercing us toward it—is perfectly sound, her arguments trickled down into, "All men get love from women only through coercion"; "All female closeness is lesbian"; and, not to put too fine a point on it, "Straight women are deluding themselves."

As the influence of these theories spread, it became noticeably démodé for a feminist to admit out loud to wanting intercourse, let alone to wanting a good steady supply of high-quality intercourse.

**Feminists Want Men and Women to Be the Same**

Much feminist writing took apart the assumption that sex differences are "opposite" and innate and sex differences were called "the social fiction of gender." But this idea entered popular conversation as "feminists want women to be like men," an idea that many women and men would find unattractive. It even surfaced as the idea that "Feminists want men and women to be the same." Phyllis Schlafly and other anti-ERA activists exploited this particular anxiety throughout the seventies, creating such myths as the feminist dream of "unisex bathrooms." This left people with the impression that feminists want to eradicate sex differences, a thought that, understandably, disturbed many. For one does not have to be deluded or sexist to appreciate sexual differentiation, whether it is artificially exaggerated or not, just as one can appreciate racial diversity without being racist.

As journalists transmitted these theories to readers who were unfamiliar with the original sources, mainstream audiences' picture of what one had to believe in order to be a feminist grew ever more bizarre and distorted.

## Two Traditions

While feminism was having trouble getting its message out, some of the problem had to do with the message itself. Over the last twenty years, the old belief in a tolerant assertiveness, a claim to human participation and human rights —power feminism—was embattled by the rise of a set of beliefs that cast women as beleaguered, fragile, intuitive angels: victim feminism.

Victim feminism is when a woman seeks power through an identity of powerlessness. . . .

This feminism has slowed women's progress, impeded their self-knowledge, and been responsible for most of the inconsistent, negative, even chauvinistic spots of regressive thinking that are alienating many women and men. Victim feminism is by no means confined to the women's movement; it is what all of us do whenever we retreat into appealing for status on the basis of feminine specialness instead of human worth, and fight underhandedly rather than honorably.

One of the features of this feminism is its misuse of the reality of women's victimization. Right now, critics of feminism such as Katie Roiphe in *The Morning After*, and Camille Paglia just about anywhere, are doing something slick and dangerous with the notion of victimization. They are taking the occasional excesses of the rape crisis movement and using them to ridicule the entire push to raise consciousness about sexual violence. Roiphe, for instance, paints an impressionistic picture of hysterical "date-rape victims" who have made it all up, but she never looks squarely at the epidemic of sex crimes that has been all too indelibly documented by the Justice Department and the FBI. In her definition, victim feminism includes the acts of fearing rape, and of confronting the real scars that rape inflicts. In her eagerness to do away with the Dworkin/ MacKinnon picture of systematic male brutality, she washes away the real differences in power that do exist between men and women—such as physical strength. In her world of Princeton eating clubs, when a man grabs a woman's breast, the woman dumps a glass of milk on his head. End of story. In real life, where the provosts might not be drinking sherry nearby, the spunky lass might find herself dragged into an alley and peremptorily sodomized.

Though these critics' view of how often rape is imaginary belongs in another solar system, we do need to talk about the victim problem in current victim feminism, but we need to define it in a completely different way. There *is* something wrong with the way some feminist attitudes approach the persona of the victim. But documenting or protesting a very real rape epidemic is not the problem.

No, there is nothing wrong with identifying one's victimization. That act is critical. There is a lot wrong with molding it into an identity. Here is a highly subjective comparison of the two different ways by which women can approach power.

*Victim feminism:*

Charges women to identify with powerlessness even at the expense of taking responsibility for the power they do possess.

Is sexually judgmental, even antisexual.

Idealizes women's childrearing capacity as proof that women are better than men.

Depends on influence or persuasion rather than on seeking clout in a straightforward way.

Believes women to be naturally noncompetitive, cooperative, and peace loving.

Sees women as closer to nature than men are.

Exalts intuition, "women's speech," and "women's ways of knowing," not as complements to, but at the expense of, logic, reason, and the public voice.

Denigrates leadership and values anonymity.

Is self-sacrificing, and thus fosters resentment of others' recognition and pleasures.

Sees money as contaminating.

Puts community first and self later, hence tends toward groupthink, as well as toward hostility toward individual achievement.

Is judgmental of other women's sexuality and appearance.

Believes it is possessed of "the truth," which must be spread with missionary zeal.

Projects aggression, competitiveness, and violence onto "men" or "patriarchy," while its devotees are blind to those qualities in themselves.

Is obsessed with purity and perfection, hence is self-righteous.

Casts women *themselves* as good and attacks men *themselves* as wrong.

Has a psychology of scarcity: There is only so much to go around, so one woman's gain is another's loss. If there is inequity, wants women to "equalize downward"—e.g., to give up "heterosexual privilege" by not marrying, instead of extending civil rights; to give up beauty, instead of expanding the definition.

Wants all other women to share its opinions.

Thinks dire: believes sensuality cannot coincide with seriousness; fears that to have too much fun poses a threat to the revolution.

*Power feminism:*

Examines closely the forces arrayed against a woman so she can exert her power more effectively.

Knows that a woman's choices affect many people around her and can change the world.

Encourages a woman to claim her individual voice rather than merging her voice in a collective identity, for only strong individuals can create a just community.

Is unapologetically sexual; understands that good pleasures make good politics.

Seeks power and uses it responsibly, both for women as individuals and to make the world more fair to others.

Knows that poverty is not glamorous; wants women to acquire money, both for their own dreams, independence, and security, and for social change.

Acknowledges women's interest in "signature," recognition, and fame, so that women can take credit for themselves and give generously to others.

Asks a woman to give to herself and seek what she needs, so she can give to others freely, without resentment.

Is tolerant of other women's choices about sexuality and appearance; believes that what every woman does with her body and in her bed is her own business.

Acknowledges that aggression, competitiveness, the wish for autonomy and separation, even the danger of selfish and violent behavior, are as much a part of female identity as are nurturant behaviors; understands that women, like men, must learn to harness these impulses; sees women as moral adults.

Seeks "bilingualism"—the joining together of what is best about women's traditional knowledge and commitments with traditionally male resources.

Has strong convictions, but is always skeptical and open, and questions all authority, including its own.

Hates sexism without hating men.

Sees that neither women nor men have a monopoly on character flaws; does not attack men as a gender, but sees disproportionate male power, and the social valuation of maleness over femaleness, as being wrong.

Has a psychology of abundance; wants all women to "equalize upward" and get more; believes women deserve to feel that the qualities of stars and queens, of sensuality and beauty, can be theirs.

Wants all women to express their own opinions.

Knows that making social change does not contradict the principle that girls just want to have fun. Motto: "If I can't dance, it's not my revolution."

Power feminism has little heavy base ideology beyond the overarching premise "More for women." The ideology it does uphold is flexible and inclusive. Its core tenets are these:

1. Women matter as much as men do.
2. Women have the right to determine their lives.
3. Women's experiences matter.
4. Women have the right to tell the truth about their experiences.
5. Women deserve more of whatever it is they are not getting enough of because they are women: respect, self-respect, education, safety, health, representation, money.

Those are the basics. No overdetermined agendas, no loyalty oaths, just the commitment to get those unmarked "power units"—health, education, the vote—to women, for women to use as adult individuals, with conflicting visions and wills. What women do with those units of potential is up to them.

My beliefs about what you should do with that power may contradict yours. Let us claim full representation, and fight our beliefs out in the public arena, as men who cannot be reduced to a group identity do. On this level of the definition of power feminism, the statement "I am a feminist" means only "I am a sentient, strong individual who objects to being held back—or having other women held back—on the basis of gender." It is the very beginning of the conversation about what a given woman believes, not the endpoint.

But doesn't opening up the definition risk making the term meaningless? I think we can lay that fear to rest. When women engage fully in the political process, they tend, as we are starting to see, to vote their interests. And we are safer in a country in which women feel empowered to promote a myriad of beliefs than in one in which all women share my views of what is best for the gender, or yours.

On one level all women should be able to own the word "feminism" as describing a theory of self-worth, and the worth of other women. On this level, saying "I am a feminist" should be like saying "I am a human being." It is on this level that we can press for women who believe anything they want to to enter public life; this level wants the world thrown open to all women regardless of their goodness: On this level women should be free to exploit or save, give or take, destroy or build, to exactly the same extent that men are. This is the level of simple realization of women's will, whether we like the result or not. On this level Camille Paglia is certainly a feminist; Indira Gandhi was a feminist; Mother Teresa [was] a feminist. On this level "feminist" is a word that belongs to every woman who is operating at her full speed; ideally, it includes wanting other women to operate at their full speed, but it recognizes that women have many opinions about the best ways to empower women, and Mother Teresa's are not going to be mine.

On another level, of course, feminism should be broadly understood as a humanistic movement for social justice. This definition excludes more people than the former one does, but it draws in far more people than the popular current image of feminism does. On this level, "I am a feminist" means "No one should stand in my way because of my gender, and no one should stand in anyone's way because of this race, gender, orientation." As a humanistic movement its parameters are these: no hate. It is illogical to claim one's rights as a woman yet deny them to others on the basis of their skin color or sexual orientation. It also sets a narrower focus than does "humanism": On this level, it is okay to work on behalf of women because female humans are oppressed in ways unique to their gender. But working on behalf of women does not allow one *ever* to deify them as better than, or cosmically separate from, their male counterparts. The "no hate" plank of the definition includes not hating on the basis of gender, including when it comes to men.

Before we go on to compare power and victim feminism, let us be clear what "the victim problem" in victim feminism is *not*. The idea of female victimization is tremendously muddled right now.

Feminists are currently under siege for allegedly creating a "cult of the victim." This wave of "it's all in your head" theory was inevitable, given the recent success of the victim's-rights movement in drawing attention to the widespread nature of sex crimes. Critics who charge this pursue a scorched-earth policy: if there are some unrepresentative excesses in the fight against sexual violence, demolish the whole, in spite of the fact of the suffering of millions. I too will be talking about some mistakes victim feminism has made in framing the theme of female victimization. But my intent is very different. I am calling for a recognition of female victimization that does not leave out autonomy and sexual freedom; I am calling on us to look clearly at the epidemic of crimes against women without building a too-schematic world view upon it. . . .

The problem in victim feminism that I object to is *not* the act of protesting harm. There is no way around it: Women are not natural victims, but they sure *are* victimized. Domestic violence is the number-one reason women seek medical attention; one third of all female murder victims are killed by husbands or boyfriends; up to 45 percent of abused women are battered during pregnancy; 60 percent of battered women are beaten when pregnant; half of all homeless women and children are fleeing domestic violence. Women are victims of violent intimates at a rate three times that of men. These are raw facts. And facing them is the first step toward changing them.

But it is not "blaming the victim" to issue the warning that people worn out with fighting are tempted to redefine victim status itself as a source of strength and identity. . . .

The focus of some feminists, like Andrea Dworkin, Catharine MacKinnon, and Adrienne Rich, on female victimization foreshadowed over female agency, derives from conditions that were once truer than they are now. During the early seventies women were indeed overwhelmingly silenced and negated; and during the Reagan-Bush administrations, the structures of power were indeed basically immovable. But the gender-quake means that the core rationale of this kind of foreshadowing is becoming obsolete.

For power, we learned in the genderquake, is hardly unshakably male; we can make it female with ease: with votes, with voices, and with a little money from a lot of wallets. These writers should be read and understood. But grieving for the real victimization that women suffer must be a feminism that also teaches women how to see and use their enormous power so as never to be helpless victims again.

Virtually every women's political organization, and most grassroots groups, seek power feminist goals. But the language of victim feminism often dominates discussion of the movement in the mass media. Critics of feminism often cast feminists as extremists who are going too far and must temper or dilute their message for the mainstream. I am arguing the opposite—that women in the mainstream have gone much further in articulating an embrace of power than has this brand of feminism; and that victim feminism is not going remotely far enough to keep up with them. The unidentified power feminism of mainstream women has far outstripped the victim feminism of many insiders. But the power-feminist images and icons we have—from Roseanne Arnold to Queen Latifah to Janet Reno—are seldom "owned" by organized feminism. So mainstream women identify intensely with the power feminism that these women represent, but do not identify that vision with the movement.

## Victim Feminism's Recent Impasses

. . . Victim-feminist anxiety over robust female heterosexuality has led to a situation in which there is an elaborate vocabulary with which to describe sexual harm done by men, but almost no vocabulary in which a woman can celebrate sex with men. Indeed, there is almost no feminist culture in which I can recognize my own sexual life. . . .

The next phase of feminism must be about saying a sexual yes as well as a sexual no, and women are going to have to start telling their truths about their sexual lives. I'll come clean with my subjective truth.

I am sick of the opposition trying to make me choose between being sexual and serious; and I am sick of being split the same way by victim feminism. I want to be a serious thinker and not have to hide the fact that I have breasts; I want female sexuality to accompany, rather than undermine, female political power. I want to be able to talk, without fear of political repercussions, about things that are among the most important in my life. I know that the experiences of degradation that millions of women undergo are all too real; and I know I may be a statistical anomaly; but the Dworkinite description of coercion, invasion, and one-sided objectification as a *norm* of male sexuality just does not match my own experience. I have unquestionably felt sexual threat and hatred from men on the street, seen it often in the mass media, and witnessed the terrible evidence in my work with rape survivors. But that tragic side of women's experience of some men's sexual violence is not the whole truth, nor should it stand in for the whole truth. Millions of men rape and sexually abuse; many, many more millions do not. Instead of looking solely at the damage done and defining all men and all male sexuality by those violent acts, we must also begin to study and celebrate whatever choices and conditions lead so many more men to be unable to include rape, coercion, or abuse within the scope of their actions.

Why should the sentence "I want to make love," when spoken to a man, subordinate a woman? Or even "I want to go down on you" or "Fuck me"? Why shouldn't I talk about the absolute delight that male sexual global response instills in me? When I hear an unqualified narrative of male sexual destructiveness, and do not interrupt it, I feel that I betray my body's deepest friendships. Where is the story that I recognize? The story of how male sexuality has comforted me when I was sad, energized me when I was listless, grounded me when I was feeling tentative, and been to me the source of creativity?

The armored monsters attacked by critics of masculinity and sexual violence absolutely exist. But I have had the good luck not to have slept with them. I do not recognize them in my knowledge of how the male body needs kindness as well as tension. I've seen men delirious with affection; I have seen the word "love" trigger an erection. Give me room for my knowledge too; it is no less important than that of a woman who has experienced nothing but abuse. Don't tell me that the best friends of my body and heart are undifferentiated predators, who think of their genitals as if they were guns. My joyful life experiences with men are neither politically invalid nor so aberrant. Let us give the love of men, too, its legitimate feminist weight.

I want men, male care, male sexual attention. This desire doesn't necessarily make a woman a slave or an addict; I am a human organism with a dominant orientation: What can be intrinsically wrong with that? Male sexual attention is the sun in which I bloom. The male body is ground and shelter to me, my lifelong destination. When it is maligned categorically, I feel as if my homeland is maligned.

There has got to be room in feminism for these loyalties too; for a radical heterosexuality, an eros between men and women that does not diminish female power, but affirms it. . . .

We should lighten up on ourselves. It is scary for a feminist woman to acknowledge that she is also an animal, because it is just our animal nature that a sexist society wants to use to constrain us. But we are beasts of the field, with all of those impulses. Let's be less afraid of our animal nature —even when it leads those of us who are heterosexual to feel the greater knowledge of self in the arms of a man. . . .

We can reclaim that primal and animal nature with its voluptuous ebbing and flowing of who does what to whom; this does not make us traitors to consciousness. At times, the critical mind has got to shut down; we have to become simply breasts, simply mouths, simply sex, even as men are known sometimes to want to be just sex. Let us make room for that need without being made to feel that we are abdicating evolution—or revolution. When a woman sleeps with a man, she is not "collaborating" by taking the "enemy" within; she is saying yes to one of many ways of being female in three dimensions—mind, spirit, and hungry flesh. . . .

## Camille Paglia's Critique of the Second Wave

Camille Paglia (1947–) is a teacher, historian of art and literature, essayist, commentator, media pundit, and rebel feminist. She received her B.A. in 1968 from the State University of New York and her Ph.D. in 1974 from Yale, where she studied literature. Her mentor at Yale was the celebrated critic, scholar, and defender of Romantic poetry, Harold Bloom. She has taught at Bennington College (1972–1979) in Vermont, at Wesleyan University (1980), at Yale (1981–1984), and since 1984 at the University of Arts in Philadelphia. She is now University Professor of Humanities and Media Studies. She is the author of *Sexual Personae: Art and Decadence from Nefertiti to Emily Dickinson* (1991); *Sex, Art, and American Culture* (1992); *Vamps and Tramps: New Essays* (1994); and *The Birds* (2004).

Paglia is a self-proclaimed bisexual and Italian American, in-your-face motormouth who celebrates decadent writers such as de Sade and Oscar Wilde, not to mention equally decadent rock and pop stars such as the late Jimi Hendrix and Madonna. In fact, her December 1990 article in the *New York Times* defending Madonna as the future of feminism catapulted her into public attention. She is also a fan of film, especially Hollywood epics such as *Ben-Hur,* and an enemy of political correctness. Paglia argues that alongside the long-dominant Judeo-Christian element of Western culture, a partially buried pagan element has had a vital effect on Western art and literature. In fact, the popular culture of the last four decades represents the third great revival of paganism in the West, after the Renaissance and the Romantic movement of approximately 1790–1830.

In her masterwork *Sexual Personae* Paglia looks at the history of art and literature in the West. She sees it as driven by a sexual dialectic composed of a masculine "Apollonian" element and a feminine "Dionysian" element. These were named after the Greek gods Apollo, who rode about the heavens on a chariot of fire, and Dionysus, the god of wine and wild women. The Apollonian element is rational, using its power to impose an order and structure on the world, whereas the Dionysian element is bound to the earth, the passions, and nature, to the unconscious mind and its drives. Tied to this is her claim that sexuality is not entirely a social construction, as feminists such as Donna Haraway and Susan Moller Okin seem to claim, but is tied to deeply entrenched natural drives.

Culture is the product of this dialectic between the Apollonian and the Dionysian. Without the male impulse toward order and structure, the murky earthbound Dionysian impulse would have left us tied to primitive tribal cultures. Indeed, Paglia argues that if "civilization had been left in female hands, we would still be living in grass huts," a comment not designed to endear her to the feminist establishment. By this she means that civilization is all about building structures that last—stone buildings, political hierarchies, intellectual systems—and that the permanence of these structures is to a great degree a *male* achievement.* What radical feminists call "patriarchy," notes Paglia, is really just civilization.

Paglia's central claim to fame is as a critic of this very Second Wave feminist establishment, which she sees as puritanical about sex, Stalinist in its attempt to rein in potential dissenters, and blatantly ignorant of the history of art and literature. She has reserved her most venomous attacks for such Second Wave icons as Catharine MacKinnon, Andrea Dworkin, and Gloria Steinem, although she has also taken potshots at Naomi Wolf and other younger feminists. Indeed, in *Fire with Fire* Wolf grudgingly admits having to deal with the force of Paglia's attack. Paglia is also critical of the Second Wave's picture of women as passive victims of male domination. Paglia takes as her heroes strong women such as Madonna and Amelia Earhart, not to mention flamboyant gay male artists such as Robert Mapplethorpe. She is very much an admirer of First Wave feminism, having read Simone de Beauvoir's *The Second Sex* at the age of 16, not to mention spending three of her high school years pouring through fading newspapers and magazines in the Syracuse Public Library for information about Earhart.

Paglia is a social libertarian. She favors the decriminalization of drugs and prostitution, is pro-choice on the abortion issue, and is a vehement opponent of the Dworkin-MacKinnon push to ban pornography as the product of an antisexual puritanism that has disgraced the feminist movement. Paglia has also argued for a broad-based education in the humanities—the classics, history, art, literature, and philosophy—instead of the carving up of the university into smaller and smaller departmental units. In *Sex, Art and American Culture,* she is especially scornful of politically inspired subdisciplines, such as women's studies, which have "puffed up clunky, mundane contemporary women authors into Oz-like skywriting dirigibles" (p. 243).

Our selection comes from Paglia's essay "No Law in the Arena" in her book *Vamps and Tramps.* In it she argues that sex is the product of an interplay between culture and nature. The first part of her essay is primarily concerned with the issue of sexual consent. Paglia has been accused by radical feminists of condoning rape.

---

*Thanks to Professor Paglia herself for bringing this point to my attention and for several other helpful suggestions regarding this commentary.—Ed.

In response to this charge, she says that although rape is without doubt a heinous crime, its importance has been blown out of proportion by Second Wave feminism to the point where it eclipses in moral significance all the wars, massacres, and natural disasters in human history. The Second Wave obsession with rape has helped to create an unhealthy mass psychosis among women.

Paglia wants women to take responsibility for their sexual lives and to learn the rules of the game of sex. The overarching thing that they must learn, she says, is that "there is no law in the arena" (as an Arab sheik tells Ben-Hur in the Hollywood epic). Paglia thinks that women should learn to defend themselves and to avoid innocently straying into dangerous situations—such as going to a drunken frat boy's bedroom at 2 AM—then crying rape after the fact. She argues against excessively protective legislation of sexual conduct from higher political powers, as long as such conduct stops short of physical violence.

Academic feminists want to cushion middle-class kids from discomfort and fear by enforcing a genteel Victorian code of manners. Yet this produces only sheltered, coddled, infantile personalities, Daddy's little girls alienated from their own bodies. But "women are not in control of their bodies," declares Paglia; "nature is." For example, nature, not patriarchy, makes motherhood and career clash. The desire to propagate the species isn't a cultural construction but a primal natural urge.

Paglia argues that women have never been powerless. Even under "patriarchy," women were always in control of the sexual and emotional spheres of life, and still are. She argues that rape is not an act of political oppression but one of desperation, a ritual enactment of the natural aggression inherent in male sexuality. When we look at the mating behavior of other animal species, we clearly see the female of the species choosing her mate. Human beings are no different. Women size men up, see what they're made of, and men will do anything to win women's favor. Paglia calls middle-class feminists who ignore this fact and who want "rational" love lives "imbeciles" for ignoring the wild Dionysian forces at work in sexuality.

Paglia agrees that all people have an absolute right to consent to sex but notes that this consent may be nonverbal (e.g., going to man's apartment after a first date). She wants to deconstruct the bourgeois code of "niceness," to give white middle-class girls a crash course in common sense. Working-class women are not as naive about sex as middle-class ones and know how to defend themselves better. Later in the essay Paglia discusses pornography. She laments the fact that many "pro-sex" feminists were more or less hidden from public view in the 1970s and 1980s, the field of battle being conceded to puritanical feminists such as Dworkin and MacKinnon. Paglia argues that women of the Sixties rock n' roll generation were silenced or driven out of the women's movement by its puritanical wing, regaining some lost ground only in the 1990s, when young women became sceptical of the anti-sex views of Dworkin, MacKinnon, and their allies. For Paglia, "Pornography degrades women" is an idiotic statement uttered only by women who have never looked at it. Porn actresses are rarely coerced, most of them enjoying their work. Further, the puritans ignore the huge gay male porn industry as an inconvenient fact that disproves their claim that all pornography is hate speech (or hate visuals) against women.

Paglia says that the antisex feminists are forever softening, censoring, and politicizing sex. Pornography strips sexuality of its romantic veneer, leaving our crude animality, a rude violation of bourgeois notions of decorum. Paglia champions gay men for recognizing the power of beauty, pitying middle-class professional women who can't stand the thought of being ignored by male colleagues for a flash of leg from a sexy young woman.

Paglia's conclusion in the essay is that bisexuality is a great pagan ideal that should be revived and that a pagan education would sharpen the mind, steel the will, and seduce our senses.

Paglia effectively demolishes the general dogma held by most Second Wave feminists that all gender differences are socially constructed, reminding them that art and literature have for over three millennia shown us how nature defines us as sexual beings. She also saws off the edges of a few other theoretical points made by radical feminism, notably its unflinching critique of patriarchy and its castigation of male heterosexuality as a source of great evil. And, like Wolf, she asks women to accept responsibility for their own fate and to avoid slipping into a rhetoric of victimhood to explain away personal or political failures.

The big question here is simple enough: Even if Paglia's critiques are largely valid, does she go too far? Is her brand of confrontational feminism, or "Amazon" feminism (to use her own phrase), really applicable to all women, whether or not they have forceful personalities? Could it really work with meeker women caught in intimidating or dangerous situations at school or in the workplace? Shouldn't we hold men responsible for their actions in *all* instances? Is she playing with fire by arguing that nonverbal body language and entering drunken frat boys' bedrooms can stand in for verbal consent to sex? These and many other questions are raised by her work. However we answer them, Paglia has without doubt forced Second Wave feminists to question some of their most cherished ideological certainties.

# No Law in the Arena

## CAMILLE PAGLIA

### Introduction: The Horses of Passion

At the end of the Christian millennium and the century of Freud, sex is still shrouded in mystery. A question mark hangs over every important sexual issue. Despite bitter public controversy and heated private debate, we have no answers. Indeed, we have barely begun to formulate the questions accurately.

Sex, I have argued in my prior books, is animality and artifice, a dynamic interplay of nature and culture. To study it, one must weigh the testimony of art and draw on all the scholarly resources of the social and natural sciences. In my opinion, the many schools of modern psychol-ogy, whose roots were in the late nineteenth century, reached their height in the eclectic 1960s, which fused widely diverse theories and practices, from Freudian verbal analysis to Reichian body manipulation. In that decade in America, Western science and Asian Hinduism momentarily came together, but the brilliant insights gained from this encounter were experienced by isolated individuals and dissipated into the general culture. The psychedelic Sixties left their imprint in images and music more than in books.

For the last twenty-five years, sex theory has been in a state of chaos. Single-issue activism turned into fanaticism, on both the left and right.

SOURCE: Camille Paglia, "No Law in the Arena: A Pagan Theory of Sexuality," in *Vamps and Tramps: New Essays* (New York: Vintage, 1994), pp. 19–38, 63–67, 92–94 (edited). Copyright 1994 by Camille Paglia. Used by permission of Vintage Books, a division of Random House, Inc.

Understanding of eroticism has actually regressed, as ideology has become paramount. The major conceptual breakthrough of the Sixties was its Romantic movement back toward nature, the awesome, star-studded panorama dwarfing social conventions and forms. The Sixties flower-power view of nature had too much Rousseauist benevolence, but it was more right than wrong. Organicism is the true deconstruction. With the failure or reluctance of Sixties visionaries to enter the professions or mainstream politics, the Seventies suffered from an intellectual vacuum, which was filled by a narrow, blinkered social constructionism—the simplistic behaviorist belief that nature does not exist, that everything we are comes from social conditioning.

Social constructionism was a crude distortion of the vast Sixties cosmic vision. It was promulgated for sectarian political purposes by three groups. First, the new Seventies breed of Stalinist feminist tried, in the abortion crusade, to wipe out all reference to nature or religion—a misconceived strategy that backfired and simply strengthened the pro-life opposition. Second, ambitious literature academics, ignorant of science, used esoteric, language-based, social constructionist French theory to advance their careers after the collapse of the academic job market in the Seventies recession. Third, gay activists, after the identification of AIDS in the early Eighties, used fascist tactics to stop public discussion of it in anything but political terms—as if disease occurred in people's prejudices rather than in the suffering body.

But what AIDS shows us is nature itself, risen up with terrible force to mock our delusions of knowledge and control. AIDS, above all, forces nature back onto the agenda of sex theory. Unfortunately for the shallow ideology of current feminism and gay liberation, whose ultimate aims I support, this means that procreation must be dealt with much more fully and honestly than has yet been done. The avoidance of that issue by the left has simply ceded it to and helped the rise of the right, which frames the argument in moral or rather Judeo-Christian terms.

For me, the ultimate power in the universe is nature, not God, whose existence I can understand only as depersonalized vital energy. But as I have repeatedly said, merely because nature is supreme does not mean we must yield to it. I take the Late Romantic view that everything great in human history has been achieved in defiance of nature. Law, art, and technology are defense mechanisms, Apollonian lines drawn against the Dionysian turbulence of nature. Melville's Captain Ahab, crippled and scarred, shaking his fist at the stormy heavens, symbolizes the rebellion of imagination against fate. . . .

The Greeks invented not only the major genres of literature and the disciplines of philosophy but organized athletics, in their mathematics-based track and field form. Dramatic competition is built into the agonistic plot structure of Greek tragedy as well as the oratorical Western mode of legal argumentation. I want to transfer that rhythmic choreography of opposition into sex theory. Late-twentieth-century America has more in common with imperial Rome than with classical Athens, and so it is to the Hellenized Roman world that I would look for pagan models. We need new living myths.

The current discourse about sex is too genteel. Freud's severe, conflict-based system has lost popularity to a casual, sentimental style of user-friendly psychological counseling that I find typically Protestant, in the glad-handing Chamber of Commerce way. The operatic perversions of Krafft-Ebing and the unsettling daemonism of Ferenczi are completely gone. Yet sex war remains, and is likely to be our permanent condition. Competition and conflict are operating at every level of even our cooperative ventures, at work or at home. Our dream life itself, as Freud has shown, is both power play and passion play.

In war there can also be honor, the code of aristocratic chivalry, applied by medieval knights (*chevaliers*, "horsemen") to battlefield, court, and bedchamber. If women want freedom and equality, they must learn the rules of the game. The title of this essay comes from *Ben-Hur* (1959), the Hollywood epic that depicts the explosive tension in Judaea under Roman occupation. An Arab sheik persuades the vengeful prince Judah Ben-Hur (Charlton Heston) to race his exquisite white horses at Jerusalem by promising a head-to-head showdown with the evil Roman tribune, Messala (Stephen Boyd). The sheik says, "There is no law in the arena."

Sex today occurs in the dust and clamor of the imperial circus. Private grievances are dragged into the glare of day and become meat for the masses. Plato's lofty metaphor of the charioteer, the soul subduing by cool rationality the horses of bestial passion, was brutally revised by Rome, with its grandiose gladiatorial spectacles. The chaste elegance of the contemplative Delphic Charioteer was inconceivable in the hurly-burly hippodromes of the Hellenistic Mediterranean. Under the empire, as we see from the sober writings of Marcus Aurelius, the philosophic ideal of Stoic detachment became a way to survive cultural instability. Then as now, there is no going back. Conservative paradigms deserve our respect but also our recognition that they are nostalgic longings for a simpler and irretrievable past.

Sex in our age has become gladiatorial, with male and female, gay and straight whipping and goading each other for position. This is our lot. We must accept it and devise a simple new rule book and training regime that puts the combatants on equal footing. Neither women nor gays should plead for special protections or preferential treatment. The arena is the social realm, marked off from nature but ritually formalizing nature's aggressions. My libertarian position is that, in the absence of physical violence, sexual conduct cannot and must not be legislated from above, that all intrusion by authority figures into sex is totalitarian.

The ultimate law of the sexual arena is personal responsibility and self-defense. We must be prepared to go it alone, without the infantilizing assurances of external supports like trauma counselors, grievance committees, and law courts. I say to women: get down in the dirt, in the realm of the senses. Fight for your territory, hour by hour. Take your blows like men. I exalt the pagan personae of athlete and warrior, who belong to shame rather than guilt culture and whose ethic is candor, disciplines, vigilance, and valor.

## Sex Crime: Rape

The area where contemporary feminism has suffered the most self-inflicted damage is rape. What began as a useful sensitization of police officers, prosecutors, and judges to the claims of authentic rape victims turned into a hallucinatory over-extension of the definition of rape to cover every unpleasant or embarrassing sexual encounter. Rape became the crime of crimes, overshadowing all the wars, massacres, and disasters of world history. The feminist obsession with rape as a symbol of male-female relations is irrational and delusional. From the perspective of the future, this period in America will look like a reign of mass psychosis, like that of the Salem witch trials. . . .

The philistinism of feminist discourse on rape in the Eighties and Nineties has been astonishing. My generation was well-educated in the Sixties in major literary texts that have since been marginalized by blundering women's studies: our sense of criminality and the mystery of motivation came principally from Dostoyevsky's *Crime and Punishment,* Camus's *The Stranger,* and Genet's *The Maids.* There was also Poe's "The Tell-Tale Heart" and "The Cask of Amontillado," as well as eerie films like Fritz Lang's *M,* Alfred Hitchcock's *Psycho,* and Richard Fleischer's *Compulsion* (on the Leopold and Loeb case). The shrill feminist melodrama of male oppressor/female victim came straight out of nickelodeon strips of mustache-twirling villains and squealing maidens tied to train tracks. Those who revere and live with great art recognize Clytemnestra, Medea, Lady Macbeth, and Hedda Gabler—conspirators and death-dealers of implacable will —as equally the forebears of modern woman.

Rape should more economically be defined as either stranger rape or the forcible intrusion of sex into a nonsexual context, such as a professional situation. However, even the latter is excusable if a sexual overture is welcomed, as can be the case in both gay and straight life. There *is* such a thing as seduction, and it needs encouragement rather than discouragement in our puritanical Anglo-American world. The fantastic fetishism of rape by mainstream and anti-porn feminists has in the end trivialized rape, impugned women's credibility, and reduced the sympathy we should feel for legitimate victims of violent sexual assault.

What I call Betty Crocker feminism—a naively optimistic Pollyannaish or Panglossian view of reality—is behind much of this. Even the most morbid of the rape ranters have a childlike faith in the perfectibility of the universe, which they see as blighted solely by nasty men. They simplistically project outward onto a mythical "patriarchy" their own inner conflicts and moral ambiguities. In *Sexual Personae,* I critiqued the sunny Rousseauism running through the last two hundred years of liberal thinking and offered the dark tradition of Sade, Darwin, Nietzsche, and Freud as more truthful about human perversity. It is more accurate to see primitive egotism and animality ever-simmering behind social controls—cruel energies contained and redirected for the greater good—than to predicate purity and innocence ravaged by corrupt society. Nor does the Foucault view of numb, shapeless sensoriums tyrannically impinged on by faceless systems of language-based power make any more sense, in view of daily news reports of concretely applied and concretely suffered random beatings, mutilations, murders, arson, massacres, and ethnic exterminations around the world.

Rape will not be understood until we revive the old concept of the barbaric, the uncivilized. The grotesque cliché "patriarchy" must go, or rather be returned to its proper original application to periods like Republican Rome or Victorian England. What feminists call patriarchy is simply *civilization,* an abstract system designed by men but augmented and now co-owned by women. Like a great temple, civilization is a gender-neutral structure that all should respect. Feminists who prate of patriarchy are self-exiled in grass huts.

Ideas of civilization and barbarism have become unfashionable because of their political misuse in the nineteenth century. The West has neither a monopoly on civilization nor the right or obligation to impose its culture on others. Nor, as *Sexual Personae* argues, are any of us as individuals ever completely civilized. However, it is equally wrong to dismiss all progressive theories of history, which is not just scattered bits of data upon which we impose wishful narratives. Societies do in fact evolve in economic and political complexity.

Even though we no longer wish to call one society "higher" or "more advanced" than another, it is unwise to equate tribal experience, with its regimentation by tradition and its suppression of the individual by the group, with life under industrial capitalism, which has produced liberalism and feminism. Law and order, which protect women, children, and the ill and elderly, are a function of hierarchy, another of the big bad words of feminism. Law and order were achieved only a century ago in the American West, which still lives in our national mythology. Disintegration into banditry is always near at hand, as was shown in 1989 in the notorious case of the Central Park woman jogger—a savage attack significantly called "wilding" by its schoolboy perpetrators. Sex crime means back to nature.

When feminism rejected Freud twenty-five years ago, it edited out of its mental life the barbarities of the homicidal Oedipal psychodrama, which the annals of crime show is more than a metaphor. The irony is that Freud's master paradigm of "family romance," which structures our adult relationships in love and at work, has a special appropriateness to the current feminist debate. Too much of the date-rape and sexual harassment crisis claimed by white middle-class women is caused partly by their own mixed signals, which I have observed with increasing distress as a teacher for over two decades. . . .

The sex education of white middle-class girls is clearly deficient, since it produces young women unable to foresee trouble or to survive sexual misadventure or even raunchy language without crying to authority figures for help. A sense of privilege and entitlement, as well as ignorance of the dangers of life, has been institutionalized by American academe, with its summer-resort, give-the-paying-customers-what-they-want mentality. Europe has thus far been relatively impervious to the date-rape hysteria, since its tortured political history makes sugary social fantasies of the American kind less possible. Fun-and-fabulous teenage dating is not high on the list of priorities for nations which, in the lifetime of half their population, had firsthand knowledge of war, devastation, and economic collapse. The media-fueled disproportion and distortion of the date-rape debate are partially attributable to American arrogance and parochialism.

White middle-class girls at the elite colleges and universities seem to want the world handed to them on a platter. They have been sheltered, coddled, and flattered. Having taught at a wide variety of institutions over my ill-starred career, I have observed that working-class or lower-middle-class girls, who are from financially struggling families and who must take a patchwork of menial off-campus jobs to stay in school, are usually the least hospitable to feminist rhetoric. They see life as it is and have fewer illusions about sex. It is affluent, upper-middle-class students who most spout the party line—as if the grisly hyper-emotionalism of feminist jargon satisfies their hunger for meaningful experience outside their eventless upbringing. In the absence of war, invent one.

The real turmoil is going on inside the nuclear family, which, with its caged quarters and cheerful ethic of "togetherness," must generate invisible barriers to the threat of incest. Here is the real source of the epidemic eating disorders, blamed by incompetent feminist analysts on the media. Anorexia, for example, remains primarily a white middle-class phenomenon. The daughter stops her disturbing sexual maturation by stripping off her female contours, the hormone-triggered fleshiness of breasts, hips, and buttocks. She wants to remain a child, when her innocent erotic stratagems had no consequence. Again and again, among students as well as the date-rape heroines canonized on television talk shows, I have seen the flagrant hair-tossing and eye-batting mannerisms of Daddy's little girl, who since childhood has used flirtation and seductiveness to win attention within the family. . . .

Modern society is now structured so as to put a crippling impediment between women's physical development and their career ambitions. Feminist ideology began by claiming to give women freedom, enlightenment, and self-determination, but it has ended by alienating professional women from their own bodies. Every signal from the body—like the sudden quiet inwardness and psychological reorientation of girls at puberty, when they mysteriously recede in classroom assertiveness—is automatically interpreted in terms of social oppression. Teachers are supposedly "discouraging" the girls; adjusting your behavior to attract a mate is dismissed as a voluntary or legitimate choice. Girls are taught the mechanics of reproduction and sexual intercourse as clinically as if they were learning to operate a car or computer. The repressed, sanitized style of the WASP managerial class now governs public discussion of sex. Anything dark or ambiguous is blamed on "ignorance," "superstition," or "lack of education."

It was after my tumultuous lecture at Brown University in March 1992 that I saw this process of cultural repression most clearly. Taking questions at the reception, I sat with an African-American security guard as several hundred students seethed around me. Those who doubt the existence of political correctness have never seen the ruthless Red Guards in action, as I have done on campus after campus. For twenty years, meaningful debate of controversial issues of sex or race was silenced by overt or covert intimidation.

As I watched a half-dozen pampered, white middle-class girls, their smooth, plump cheeks contorted with rage, shriek at me about rape, I had two thoughts. First, America is failing its young women; these are infantile personalities, emotionally and intellectually undeveloped. Second, it's not rape they're screaming about. Rape is simply a symbol of the horrors and mysteries of the body, which their education never deals with or even acknowledges. It was a Blakean epiphany: I suddenly saw the fear and despair of the lost, stripped of old beliefs but with nothing solid to replace them. Feminism had constructed a spectral sexual hell that these girls inhabited; it was their entire cultural world, a godless new religion of fury and fanaticism. Two months later, as I sat in London, discoursing at length with poised, literate, witty Cambridge University women of the same age as those at Brown, I became even more indignant at the travesty of Ivy League education.

Women are not in control of their bodies; nature is. Ancient mythology, with its sinister archetypes of vampire and Gorgon, is more accurate than feminism about the power and terror of female sexuality. Science is far from untangling women's intricate hormonal system, which is dauntingly intertwined with the emotions. Women live with unpredictability. Reproduction remains a monumental challenge to our understanding. The Eleusinian Mysteries, with their secret, torch-lit night rituals, represented woman's grandeur on the scale that she deserves. We must return to pagan truths.

The elite schools, defining women students only as "future leaders," masters of the social realm, limit and stunt them. The mission of feminism is to seek the full political and legal equality of women with men. There should be no impediments to women's social advance. But it is the first lesson of Buddhism, Hinduism, and Judeo-Christianity that we are much greater than our social selves. I envision two spheres: one is social, the other sexual and emotional. Perhaps one-third of each sphere overlaps the other; this is the area where feminism has correctly said, "The personal is political." But there is vastly more to the human story. Man has traditionally ruled the social sphere; feminism tells him to move over and share his power. But woman rules the sexual and emotional sphere, and there she has no rival. Victim ideology, a caricature of social history, blocks women from recognition of their dominance in the deepest, most important realm.

Ambitious young women today are taught to ignore or suppress every natural instinct, if it conflicts with the feminist agenda imposed on them. All literary and artistic works, no matter how great, that document the ambivalence of female sexuality they are trained to dismiss as "misogynous." In other words, their minds are being programmed to secede from their bodies — exactly the opposite of what the Sixties sexual and cultural revolution was all about. There is a huge gap between feminist rhetoric and women's actual sex lives, where feminism is of little help except with a certain stratum of deferential, malleable, white middle-class men. In contrast, Hollywood actresses, used to expressing emotional truths, are always reappearing after pregnancy to proclaim, "I'm not important. My child is important." The most recent was Kelly McGillis, who said, "Motherhood has changed me. I'm not as ambitious as I used to be." It is nature, not patriarchal society, that puts motherhood and career on a collision course. . . .

Rape is an act of desperation, a confession of envy and exclusion. All men—even, I have written, Jesus himself—began as flecks of tissue inside a woman's womb. Every boy must stagger out of the shadow of a mother goddess, whom he never fully escapes. Because of my history of wavering gender and sexual orientation, I feel I have a special insight into these matters: I see with the eyes of the rapist. Hence I realize how dangerously misleading the feminist rape discourse is. Rape is a breaking and entering; but so is the bloody act of defloration. Sex is inherently problematic.

Women have it. Men want it. What is *it*? The secret of life, symbolized in heroic sagas by the golden fleece sought by Jason, or by the Gorgon's head brandished as a sexual trophy by Cellini's Perseus. The rapist is sickened by the conflict between his humiliating neediness and his masculine rage for autonomy. He feels suffocated by woman and yet entranced and allured by her. He is betrayed into dependency by his own impulses, the leaping urges of the body. Stalking women like prey returns him to prehistoric freedom, when the wiliest, swiftest, and strongest survived. Rape-murder is a primitive theft of energy, a cannibalistic drinking of life force. . . .

Rape-murder comes from the brutish region of pure animal appetite. Feminist confidence that the whole human race can be "reeducated" to totally eliminate the possibility of rape is pure folly. Even if, very optimistically, 80 percent of all men could be reprogrammed, 20 percent would remain, toward whom women would still have to remain vigilant. Even if 99 percent were neutralized—absurdly unlikely—that would leave 1 percent, against whom women's level of self-defense would need to be just as high as against 90 percent. Wave after wave of boys hit puberty every year. Do feminists, with their multicultural pretensions, really envision a massive export of white bourgeois good manners all around the world? Speak of imperialism! When Balthasar, one of the Magi, advises Ben-Hur to leave vengeance to God, the sheik murmurs, "Balthasar is a good man. But until all men are like him, we must keep our swords bright." . . .

Until feminism permits the return of the ancient identification of woman and nature in its full disturbing power, rape will remain an enigma. Rape is an invasion of territory, a despoilment of virgin ground. The radically different sexual geography of men's and women's bodies has led to feminist inability to understand male psychology. "She made me do it": this strange assertion by rapists expresses man's sense of subservience to woman's sexual allure. The rapist feels enslaved, insignificant: women seem enclosed, impervious. From the outside, female sexuality glows like the full moon. The stormy complexity of the rapist's inner life has been obscured by the therapeutic jargon he is soon speaking in prison, once he has been brainwashed by the social-welfare workers. Until women grasp the blood-sport aspect of rape, they will be unable to protect themselves.

Films of the mating behavior of most other species—a staple of public television in America—demonstrate that the female *chooses*. Males pursue, show off, brawl, scuffle, and make general fools of themselves for love. A major failing of most feminist ideology is its dumb, ungenerous stereotyping of men as tyrants and abusers, when in fact—as I know full well, from my own mortifying lesbian experience—men are tormented by women's flirtatiousness and hemming and hawing, their manipulations and changeableness, their humiliating rejections. Cock teasing is a universal reality. It is part of women's merciless testing and cold-eyed comparison shopping for potential mates. Men will do anything to win the favor of women. Women literally *size up* men—"What can you show me?" —in bed and out. If middle-class feminists think they conduct their love lives perfectly rationally, without any instinctual influences from biology, they are imbeciles.

Following the sexual revolution of the Sixties, dating has become a form of Russian roulette. Some girls have traditional religious values and mean to remain virgin until marriage. Others are leery of AIDS, unsure of what they want, but can be convinced. For others, anything goes: they'll jump into bed on the first date. What's a guy to do? Surely, for the good of the human species, we want to keep men virile and vigorous. They should feel free to seek sex and to persuade reluctant women. As a libertarian, I believe that we have absolute right to our own body and that no one may lay a hand on us without our consent. But consent may be nonverbal, expressed by language or behavior—such as going to a stranger's apartment on the first date, which I think should correctly be interpreted as consent to sex. "Verbal coercion" is a ridiculous concept: I agree with Ovid that every trick of rhetoric should be used in the slippery art of love.

Sexual personae are the key to this new age of uncertainty. I follow the gay male model in defining every date as a potential sexual encounter. Given that the rules are in flux, the issue of sexual availability must be negotiated, implicitly or explicitly, from the first moment on. Women must take responsibility for their share in this exchange, which means they must scrupulously critique their own mannerisms and clothing choices and not allow themselves to drift willy-nilly into compromising situations. As a teacher, I have seen time and again a certain kind of American middle-class girl who projects winsome malleability, a soft, unfocused, help-me-please persona that, in adult life, is a recipe for disaster. These are the ones who end up with the string of abusive boyfriends or in sticky situations with overfamiliar male authority figures who call them "honey."

Deconstruction of the bourgeois code of "niceness" is a priority here. My generation tried it but seems mostly to have failed. Second, white girls need a crash course in common sense. You get back what you put out. Or as I say about girls wearing Madonna's harlot outfits, if you advertise, you'd better be ready to sell! Suburban girls don't realize that they were raised in an artificially pacified zone and that the world at large, including the college campus, is a far riskier place. I call my feminism "streetwise" or "street-smart" feminism. Women from working-class families usually agree with my view of the fool-hardiness of feminist rhetoric, which encourages girls to throbbingly proclaim, "We can dress just as we want and go anywhere we want at any time!" This is true only to the point that women are willing to remain in a state of wary alertness and to fight their own fights. Men are in danger too. In America, one sees overprotected white girls bopping obliviously down the city street, lost in their headphones, or jogging conspicuously and bouncingly braless, a sight guaranteed to invite unwanted attention. . . .

## Sex War: Abortion, Battering, Sexual Harassment

The principle controversies of recent feminism have usually in some way involved a failure to deal with the issue of aggression. In the hundred-year-old nature versus nurture debate, contemporary feminists have taken the Rousseauist position that we are born good and society makes us bad. Extreme forms of sexual expression can only be understood through a sympathetic study of pornography, one of the most controversial issues in feminism. For more than fifteen years, the syllabi and reserve reading shelves of women's studies courses have been dominated by two sex-killing styles, the anti-art puritanism of the Catharine MacKinnon school and the word-obsessed, labyrinthine abstraction of Lacanian analysis. The pro-sex wing of feminism was virtually invisible until very recently, for two reasons. First, its adherents outside academe wrote fiction or journalism and never produced major theoretical statements anywhere near MacKinnon's level of argument. Second, its adherents inside academe shut themselves off in jargon-spouting conferences, which had no cultural impact or purpose beyond personal careerism. Free-speech feminists mobilized to defeat MacKinnon-inspired anti-porn statutes in Minneapolis and Indianapolis but then fell back into torpor, abandoning academe to the virulent ideologues, who seized administrative power in campus-life issues. . . .

A major problem with pro-sex feminism has been its failure to embrace the men's magazines, without which no theory of sexuality will ever be complete. I have gone out of my way to publish in and endorse *Playboy* and *Penthouse,* which have been vilified by both mainstream and anti-porn feminists, as well as by mainstream members of NOW. I love the irony of bringing contemporary feminism full circle, back to where Gloria Steinem made her name by infiltrating a Playboy Club. In the Eighties, feminists and religious conservatives pressured convenience stores and drugstore chains to ban the men's magazines. This has led to a massive cultural ignorance on the part of feminists, inside and outside academe, about what is actually *in* those magazines.

Idiotic statements like "Pornography degrades women" or "Pornography is the subordination of women" are only credible if you never look at pornography. Preachers, senators, and feminist zealots carry on about materials they have no direct contact with. They usually rely on a few selectively culled inflammatory examples that bear little resemblance to the porn market as a whole. Most pornography shows women in as many dominant as subordinate postures, with the latter usually steamily consensual. Specialty mail services can provide nonconsensual sadomasochistic scenarios, but they are difficult to find, except in the vast underground of cartoon art, so subversively individualistic that it has thus far escaped the feminist thought police. Cartoons in R. Crumb's fabled Sixties style show the comic, raging id uncensored. Despite hundreds of studies, the cause-and-effect relationship between pornography and violence has never been satisfactorily proved. Pornography is a self-enclosed world of pure imagination. Feminist claims that porn actresses are coerced and abused are wildly exaggerated and usually based on one or two atypical tales.

Feminist anti-porn discourse virtually always ignores the gigantic gay male porn industry, since any mention of the latter would bring crashing to the ground the absurd argument that pornography is by definition the subordination of women. I have learned an enormous amount from gay porn, which a few lesbians have commendably tried to imitate but not with sterling success. The greatest erotic images of women remain those created by male artists and photographers, from Botticelli, Titian, Ingres, and Courbet to Richard Avedon and Helmut Newton. The advertising pages of gay newspapers are adorned with stunning icons of gorgeous male nudes, for which I have yet to see an impressive lesbian equivalent. Men, gay or straight, can get beauty and lewdness into one image. Women are forever softening, censoring, politicizing. . . .

Far from poisoning the mind, pornography shows the deepest truth about sexuality, stripped of romantic veneer. No one can claim to be an expert in gender studies who is uncomfortable with pornography, which focuses on our primal identity, our rude and crude animality. Porn dreams of eternal fires of desire, without fatigue, incapacity, aging, or death. What feminists denounce as woman's humiliating total accessibility in porn is actually her elevation to high priestess of a pagan paradise garden, where the body has become a bountiful fruit tree and where growth and harvest are simultaneous. "Dirt" is contamination to the Christian but fertile loam to the pagan. The most squalid images in porn are shock devices to break down bourgeois norms of decorum, reserve, and tidiness. The Dionysian body fluids, fully released to coat every gleaming surface, return us to the full-body sensuality of the infant condition. In crowded orgy tableaux, like those on Hindu temples, matter and energy melt. In the cave spaces of porn, camera lights are torches of the Eleusinian Mysteries, giving us flashes of nature's secrets.

Gay men appreciate pornography as I do because they accept the Hellenic principle that some people are born more beautiful than others. Generic granola feminists are likely to call this "lookism"—an offense against equality. I take the Wildean view that equality is a moral imperative in politics but that the arts will always be governed by the elitism of talent and the tyranny of appearance. Pornography's total exposure of ripe flesh, its dynamic of vigor and vitality, is animated by the cruel pre-Christian idolatry of beauty and strength.

Pornography *is* art, sometimes harmonious,

sometimes dissonant. Its glut and glitter are a Babylonian excess. Modern middle-class women cannot bear the thought that their hard-won professional achievements can be outweighed in an instant by a young hussy flashing a little tits and ass. But the gods have given her power, and we must welcome it. Pornography forces a radical reassessment of sexual value, nature's bequest and our tarnished treasure.

## Conclusion: Citizens of the Empire

As America's pagan popular culture expands around the world, and as multicultural influences flow back and are absorbed by us in turn, we have re-created the polyglot complexity of the Roman empire at its height. We should accept the imperial model of moral dichotomy, the state of perpetual tension between the sober virtues of the republican past and the luxury and decadence of the present. Opposition, rather than approval, produces the sculptural carving out of selfhood.

Creative duality is my master principle. We must belong simultaneously to the mainstream culture and to our ever-receding ethnic origins. Imperialism may begin as a system of unilateral domination, but it ends as artistic and intellectual cosmopolitanism, revolutionary in its own right. In today's global existence, the alternative to imperialism is not unconditional freedom but tribalism, fractious and fragmented. . . .

I see the dynamic of history as an oscillation between Apollonian and Dionysian principles, order and energy, which become, at their extremes, fascism or chaos. In sexual terms, this promises eternal conflict between repression and debauchery. We must learn how to make tiny corrections to avoid the uncontrolled swing of the pendulum that, over a generation, swept us from Fifties conformism to Sixties rebellion to Seventies excess and the cataclysm of AIDS. We now live with the smell of funeral pyres. . . .

My model of dualism is the drag queen, who negotiates between sexual personae, day by day. I sometimes call my system "drag queen feminism." Queens are "fierce," in every sense. Masters of aggressive, bawdy speech, they know the street and its dangers and fight it out without running to authority figures, who would hardly be sympathetic. Queens, unlike feminists, know that woman is dominatrix of the universe. They take on supernatural energy when ritualistically donning their opulent costume, the historical regalia of woman's power. Prostitute and drag queen are sexual warriors who offer a pagan challenge to bourgeois gentility, now stultifying modern life from corporate boardrooms to academia to suburban shopping malls.

Bisexuality is our best hope of escape from the animosities and false polarities of the current sex wars. Whether or not we can put it into practice, bisexuality is a great pagan ideal. Perhaps bisexual *responsiveness* is all we can hope for. Indeed, that is the lesson of art history, which exposes us to the many ravishing forms of human beauty. The homosexual Botticelli produced, in *The Birth of Venus,* one of the most sublime images of the power of woman. And Michelangelo, adorning the Sistine Chapel with twenty homoerotic *ignudi* (nude Greek youths), made the most radical statement yet of the enduring duality of pagan and Christian in our culture.

A pagan education would sharpen the mind, steel the will, and seduce the senses. Our philosophy should be both contemplative and pugilistic, admitting aggression (as Christianity does not) as central to our mythology. The beasts of passion must be confronted, and the laws of nature understood. Conflict cannot be avoided, but perhaps it can be confined to a mental theater. In the imperial arena, there is no law but imagination.

## Study Questions

1. What, according to Friedan, was the "problem that has no name" suffered by postwar American housewives? Have changes in the status of women since the 1950s largely eliminated this problem, or does it remain a social reality?

2. Is the suburban housewife a "caged bird," trapped in oppressive gender roles? Or can her work be seen as part of a rational division of labor between husband and wife?

3. What are the main differences between liberal, radical, and socialist feminism? Which school of thought offers the most effective solution to the problem of sexual inequality in our society?

4. What is a "patriarchy"? Do we currently live in a patriarchal society? Explain your reasoning either way.

5. Is heterosexuality the natural human condition or merely a sexual orientation arbitrarily imposed upon women by patriarchal society?

6. Why does Firestone believe that marriage is a hopelessly unreformable institution? Is she right?

7. What social changes does Firestone propose to help women achieve equal status in modern society? Are the changes she proposes realistic?

8. According to Firestone, how can modern technology be used by women to seize control of the means of reproduction? Does this new technology really free women from the dialectic of sex? Explain why or why not.

9. What is Frye's "birdcage" metaphor? In what ways does she think that women are oppressed? Is her birdcage metaphor still valid?

10. According to Frye, in what way is the man who holds the door for a passing woman "oppressing" her? Is she right that such chivalrous rituals should be eliminated?

11. Is Catharine MacKinnon right that pornography is a form of sexual politics that helps to institutionalize male power? Is it a violation of women's civil rights? Should it be banned? If we banned porn, would this have a negative slippery-slope effect on sexually explicit forms of art? Explain why or why not.

12. What are the main characteristics of the two moral voices that Gilligan describes in her book *In a Different Voice*? Can you hear these two voices speaking in distinct ways in the women and men around you today?

13. How would you solve the moral dilemma mentioned in the introduction to Gilligan's selection—would you support the poor man's decision to steal the drug he cannot afford to pay for to cure his wife, or the property rights of the druggist to sell his products at whatever price he sees fit to charge? What moral principles would you employ to solve this problem? What moral voice do these principles come closest to sounding like?

14. With respect to differences in men and women's psychological traits, what is essentialism? social constructionism? Which position do you think is more accurate? Why?

15. Is Gilligan's picture of the ethics of care, which she associates with women, merely a snapshot of the distorted gender roles existing under patriarchy? Explain your reasoning.

16. Are the women's movement and feminism in general dominated by white middle-class women? If so, does this matter?

17. Is talking back to authority figures a good way to help create a more egalitarian society, as bell hooks suggests it is?

18. Of the ten reasons that Wolf lists for young women's reluctance to call themselves "feminists," which ones (if any) are the most valid? Why?

19. What are the "literalized theories" put forward by Brownmiller, Dworkin, MacKinnon, and Rich that Wolf identifies as turning mainstream women and men away from feminism? Are any of them defendable? If so, how?

20. According to Wolf, what are the basic characteristics of victim feminism? of power feminism? Does this distinction oversimplify the differences in feminist theory? Does power feminism represent the future of the women's movement?

21. Does Wolf's admission that male sexual attention "is the sun in which I bloom" discredit her as a feminist? Why or why not?

22. Is Paglia right that if civilization had been left in female hands, we'd still be living in grass huts? Are the radical feminists wrong to condemn Western culture as a "patriarchy" that has done little if anything for women?

23. Is Paglia right to attack Second Wave feminism for picturing women as the passive victims of male domination? If women are oppressed, shouldn't we see them as the victims of this oppression?

24. How does Paglia attack Second Wave feminists on the issue of sexual consent? Is she right that strict academic codes of conduct and sexual harassment rules produce only "sheltered, coddled, infantile personalities" unable to handle themselves in the rough-and-tumble sexual arena?

25. Is Paglia right that women have always been in control of the sexual and emotional spheres of life, and that the female of the species almost always chooses which males to mate with? Explain your reasoning.

26. What is the Third Wave's critique of Second Wave feminism on one or more of the following issues: (a) the social construction of gender, (b) women's status as oppressed victims, (c) sexuality, or (d) pornography and censorship? Is this critique valid?

## Bibliography

This list focuses on feminist writers in the Second and Third Waves and excludes the works excerpted in this chapter, along with other works by the same authors listed in the previous commentaries. For readings and Web sites on the history of political theory and women's place in it, refer to the bibliography in the previous chapter.

Bordo, Susan. *The Flight to Objectivity: Essays on Cartesianism and Culture.* Albany: State University of New York Press, 1987. Bordo argues that Descartes' rationalism, an integral part of the Western philosophical canon, is a distinctly masculine phenomenon.

Brownmiller, Susan. *Against Our Will: Men, Women and Rape.* New York: Simon & Schuster, 1975. This early study helped to open up the debate on rape in feminist theory but is now seen as highly suspect due to its questionable empirical research and its assumption that because the point of rape is to maintain men's power over women, all men are potential or real rapists.

Butler, Judith P. *Gender Trouble: Feminism and the Subversion of Identity.* New York: Routledge, 1990. Butler is a highly influential "queer theorist" who tries to deconstruct fixed gender identities by means of her "performative" view of sexual difference, that the difference between men and women is only a matter of the way that we "perform" our gender roles. All the rage in certain academic circles, Butler's dense and murky prose is difficult to navigate. Not for the faint of intellect.

Butler, Judith, and Joan W. Scott, eds. *Feminists Theorize the Political.* New York: Routledge, 1992. This collection of twenty-two essays examines the effect of poststructuralist or postmodernist thought on feminism as a political movement. Includes Judith Butler, "Contingent Foundations: Feminism and the Question of 'Postmodernism,'" pp. 3–21; Joan W. Scott, "Experience," pp. 24–40; Drucilla L. Cornell, "Gender, Sex, and Equivalent Rights," pp. 280–296; Jane Flax, "The End of Innocence," pp. 445–463.

Chodorow, Nancy. *Feminism and Psychoanalytic Theory.* New Haven, CT: Yale University Press, 1990.

Code, Lorraine. "Is Sex of the Knower Epistemologically Significant?" *Metaphilosophy* 12 (1981): 267–276.

De Beauvoir, Simone. *The Second Sex.* Translated by H. M. Parshley. New York: Vintage, 1952. Although not claiming to be a feminist, de Beauvoir kept the light of feminist theory burning in the immediate postwar period with this melange of biology, existential philosophy, Freudian psychology, literary criticism, economics, and history. Her central claim is that men have always constructed women as the "Other," objectifying women as bodies filling social roles such as wife, mother, or prostitute.

Dworkin, Andrea. *Women Hating.* New York: Dutton, 1974.

Faludi, Susan. *Backlash: The Undeclared War against American Women.* New York: Crown, 1991. Faludi argues that there was a "backlash" against feminism in the 1980s and 1990s that tried to scare women away from the fight for sexual equality by associating their unhappiness with feminism itself. The real problem, says Faludi, is that feminism hasn't gone far enough.

———. *Stiffed: The Betrayal of the American Man.* New York: Perennial, 1999.

Foucault, Michel. *The History of Sexuality.* Vol. I, *An Introduction.* Translated by Robert Hurley. New York: Random House, 1980. Foucault's reading of the history of sexuality and his idea of power/knowledge were very influential on academic feminism in the 1980s and later.

Garry, Ann, and Marilyn Pearsall, eds. *Women, Knowledge, and Reality: Explorations in Feminist Philosophy.* 2d ed. New York: Routledge, 1996.

Gilligan, Carol. *The Birth of Pleasure.* New York: Knopf, 2002. Gilligan's reflections on romantic love and pleasure in a male-dominated culture.

Greer, Germaine. *The Female Eunuch.* New York: McGraw-Hill, 1970. A pioneering Australian feminist theorist who argues with great verve that women have been oppressed into accepting their status (up until the 1960s at least) as metaphorical eunuchs, as delicate, inoffensive, eroticized, and passive beings.

Griffin, Susan. *Women and Nature: The Roaring inside Her.* New York: Harper & Row, 1978. One of a number of "ecofeminists" to appear in the 1970s who argued that women are closer to nature and that women's oppression by men parallels nature's oppression by the human race.

Haraway, Donna. "A Manifesto for Cyborgs: Science, Technology, and Socialist Feminism in the 1980s." *Socialist Review* 80 (1985): 65–107. Important essay by a socialist-postmodernist feminist on blurring sexual boundaries by embracing the science-fiction image of the genderless cyborg.

Harding, Sandra. *The Science Question in Feminism.* Ithaca, NY: Cornell University Press, 1986. One of several books and edited collections by Harding that explores feminist epistemology—the idea that philosophy and the social and natural sciences have distinctive "male" and "female" ways of doing research and of knowing the world.

———, ed. *Feminism and Methodology: Social Science Issues.* Bloomington: Indiana University Press, 1987. Another of Harding's works on feminist epistemology and methodology, this time focusing on the social sciences. The introduction provides a good overview. Includes Sandra Harding, "Introduction: Is There a Feminist Methodology?" pp. 1–14; Dorothy E. Smith, "Women's Perspective as a Radical Critique of Sociology," pp. 84–96; Catharine MacKinnon, "Feminism, Marxism and the State: Toward a Feminist Jurisprudence," pp. 135–156; Nancy Harstock, "The Feminist Standpoint: Developing the Ground for a Specifically Feminist Materialism," pp. 157–180.

Harding, Sandra, and Merrill P. Hintikka, eds. *Discovering Reality: Feminist Perspectives on Epistemology, Metaphysics, and Philosophy of Science.* Dordrect, Holland: D. Reidel, 1983.

Hite, Shere. *The Hite Report: A Nationwide Study on Female Sexuality.* New York: Macmillan, 1976. Hite interviewed women from around the country on their sexual lives, publishing the results in this report, which exploded many myths surrounding women's sexuality.

Irigaray, Luce. *The Irigaray Reader.* Edited by Margaret Whitford. Cambridge, MA: Basil Blackwell, 1991. A representative sampling of the writings of a controversial French feminist.

Laqueur, Thomas. *Making Sex: Body and Gender from the Greeks to Freud.* Cambridge, MA: Harvard University Press, 1990. Laqueur shows how differences between the sexes were portrayed in early scientific speculation, in medical texts, and in psychological literature up until the nineteenth century.

MacKinnon, Catharine. "Francis Biddle's Sister: Pornography, Civil Rights, and Speech." In *Feminism Unmodified: Discourses on Life and Law,* edited by Catharine MacKinnon. Cambridge, MA: Harvard University Press, 1987. MacKinnon's attack on pornography and call for its censorship. She can be critiqued for offering a static, loaded definition of porn and for opening up the possibility of the slide down a slippery slope from the censorship of violent antifemale pornography to the banning of sexually explicit works of art of a more legitimate nature.

Marks, Elaine, and Isabelle de Courtivron, eds. *New French Feminisms.* New York: Schocken Books, 1981. A collection of translated selections from the major French feminists. Includes Hélène Cixous' important postmodern feminist essay "The Laugh of the Medusa."

Millett, Kate. *Sexual Politics.* Garden City, NY: Doubleday, 1970. The theory of patriarchy is born.

Moi, Toril. *Sexual/Textual Politics: Feminist Literary Theory.* New York: Methuen, 1985. An introduction to feminist literary theory that is especially good on the French theorists.

Nicholson, Linda J., ed. *Feminism/Postmodernism*. London: Routledge, 1990. An interesting collection of essays on the interplay between feminist theory and postmodernism. Includes Nancy Fraser and Linda Nicholson, "Social Criticism without Philosophy: An Encounter between Feminism and Postmodernism," pp. 19–38 (a survey of trends); Jane Flax, "Postmodernism and Gender Relations in Feminist Theory," pp. 39–62; Susan Bordo, "Feminism, Postmodernism, and Gender-Skepticism," pp. 133–156; Judith Butler, "Gender Trouble, Feminist Theory, and Psychoanalytic Discourse," pp. 324–340.

————, ed. *The Second Wave*. London: Routledge, 1996. A reader that includes selections from de Beauvoir, Fraser, Butler, Chodorow, Gilligan, MacKinnon, Haraway, and others.

Okin, Susan Moller. *Justice, Gender, and the Family*. New York: Basic Books, 1990. Okin takes issue with modern male political theorists such as John Rawls for failing to include gender as a key factor in their discussion of social equality as a basic principle in liberal societies.

Paglia, Camille. *Sex, Art and American Culture*. New York: Vintage, 1992. A mixture of newspaper articles, reviews, longer essays, and cartoons chronicling Paglia's critique of Second Wave feminism and its allies in contemporary America.

Pateman, Carole. "Women and Consent." *Political Theory* 8 (1980): 149–168.

Rich, Adrienne. "Compulsory Heterosexuality and Lesbian Existence." *Signs* (1980): 631–660. Rich argues here against the assumption that heterosexuality is a "natural" state for women.

Sandilands, Catriona. "Political Animals: The Paradox of Ecofeminist Politics." *Trumpeter* 11, no. 4 (fall 1994): 167–172. An incisive critique of ecofeminism.

Smith, Dorothy E . *The Conceptual Practises of Power: A Feminist Sociology of Knowledge*. Toronto: University of Toronto Press, 1990.

————. *The Everyday World as Problematic: A Feminist Sociology*. Boston: Northeastern Press, 1987. Smith is a sociologist of knowledge who helped to introduce "standpoint theory," the notion that sociological investigations are always colored by the standpoint of the investigator, which is usually that of white middle-class men. She argues that adopting women's perspective would produce quite different results, because our interests always shape the way we see the social world, and the interests of female investigators are different from those of males.

Solanis, Valerie. *The Scum Manifesto*. New York: Olympia Press, 1970. A radical feminist man-hating rant by the woman who shot Andy Warhol. SCUM stands for "The Society for Cutting Up Men." Not to be taken too seriously, one would hope, but interesting as a historical document.

Sommers, Christina Hoff. *The War against Boys: How Misguided Feminism Is Harming Our Young Men*. New York: Simon & Schuster, 2000.

————. *Who Stole Feminism? How Women Have Betrayed Women*. New York: Simon & Schuster, 1994. Sommers is an "equity" feminist and philosophy professor who argues that "gender" feminists such as MacKinnon, Steinem, and Faludi have deliberately distorted or lied about empirical research on eating disorders, male sexual violence, and women's psychological and economic status to make their case for the continued existence of patriarchy, with the media and university administrators uncritically accepting these distortions out of fear of the wrath of these women. She accuses them of being totalitarian as teachers, indoctrinating their students with propaganda.

Spivak, Gayatri Chakrovorty. *In Other Worlds: Essays in Cultural Politics*. New York: Methuen, 1987. See especially "Can the Subaltern Speak?"

Thomson, Judith Jarvis. "A Defense of Abortion." *Philosophy and Public Affairs* (1971): 47–66. A widely read and much-attacked philosophical defense of abortion.

Vetterling-Braggin, Mary, Frederick Elliston, and Jane English, eds. *Feminism and Philosophy.* Totowa, NJ: Littlefield Adams, 1977. An older collection that gives a good picture of the relation of feminism and philosophy in the late 1970s. Includes Alison Jaggar, "Political Philosophies of Women's Liberation," pp. 5–21 (Jaggar categorizes feminism into six political philosophies: conservative, liberal, Marxist, radical, lesbian separatist, and socialist); Ann Ferguson, "Androgyny as an Ideal for Human Development," pp. 45–69; Janice Moulton, "The Myth of the Neutral 'Man,'" pp. 124–137; Susan Griffin, "Rape: The All-American Crime," pp. 313–332; Marilyn Frye and Carolyn Shafer, "Rape and Respect," pp. 333–346.

Warren, Karen. "The Power and Promise of Ecological Feminism." In *Environmental Ethics: Divergence and Convergence,* edited by Susan J. Armstrong and Richard G. Botzler, pp. 434–444. New York: McGraw Hill, 1993. A clear statement of the central ecofeminist position. Also available in Warren's book *Ecological Feminist Philosophies.*

Wilson, Edward O. *On Human Nature.* Cambridge, MA: Harvard University Press, 1978. Though not explicitly about feminism, this book by the famed sociobiologist offers a picture of sexual differences as grounded in evolutionary genetics. Wilson argues that because 99 percent of human development took place in primitive hunter-gatherer societies, it would be very strange if we didn't inherit some sex-specific traits from this long period of evolution.

Woolf, Virginia. *A Room of One's Own.* London: Grafton Books, 1977. Woolf, a feminist novelist from the early twentieth century, based this book on two talks she gave to literary societies in 1928. In them she argues that women need a "room of their own," that is, personal space, as well as financial and emotional independence, to fully develop as human beings.

Young, Iris Marion. *Justice and the Politics of Difference.* Princeton, NJ: Princeton University Press, 1990.

## Internet Resources

The Cyborg Manifesto: http://www.stanford.edu/dept/HPS/Haraway/CyborgManifesto.html Donna Haraway's Cyborg Manifesto, from her book *Simians, Cyborgs and Women: The Reinvention of Nature* (New York: Routledge, 1991).

"The Dialectic of Sex: Shulamith Firestone Revisited": http://www.comp.lancs.ac.uk/sociology/soc050sf.html
A short article by Sara Franklin, a sociologist from Lancaster University, revisiting the *Dialectic of Sex,* questioning Firestone's excessive faith in technology to effect social change.

Feminist Theory: http://www.cddc.vt.edu/feminism/index.html
Created by Kristan Switala and others, hosted by Virginia Tech University. It's divided into fields of feminism, national groups, and individual feminists. The individual feminists' listings usually consist of brief biographies and comprehensive bibliographies. The site focuses on academic feminists, with a number of significant theorists missing (e.g., Dworkin, Firestone, Paglia).

Judith Butler: http://www.theory.org.uk/ctr-butl.htm
A few remarks by David Gauntlett on Butler's take on gender.

## CHAPTER EIGHT

# Aesthetics

*Whither is fled the visionary gleam?*
*Where is it now, the glory and the dream?*
WILLIAM WORDSWORTH

*Things fall apart; the centre cannot hold;*
*Mere anarchy is loosed upon the world.*
WILLIAM BUTLER YEATS

## THE PHILOSOPHY OF ART AND BEAUTY

### In the Beginning

When the first flickers of abstract thought came to our primitive cave-dwelling ancestors, they took up whatever natural colors they had at hand and drew pictures on their stone canvases of the antelopes, bulls, and horses they hunted. At Lascaux in France we can still see some of these 20,000-year-old drawings of the local wildlife on cave walls (to see these paintings and the other works of art mentioned in this chapter, see the list of Web sites at the end of the Bibliography). It was in art, including singing and dancing, and not in morality or metaphysics or politics, that the human mind first dimly expressed itself. What their sense of beauty or artistic creativity was we could only guess at, though it seems likely that their drawings had a magical value. But we can be sure that even though aesthetics as a separate division within philosophy came relatively late onto the scene, at the end of the eighteenth century to be precise, the actual practice it refers to, the artistic representation of the world, came first in the history of human thought. This representation was some sort of direct response to the mysteries of nature, an attempt to capture its wild essence in picture form.

Our word *aesthetic* comes from the ancient Greek word *aisthetikos,* the root of which is the term for sense perception. The term was first introduced into philosophy by German thinkers in the eighteenth century, who used it to refer to the study of both our sense perceptions *and* our instincts and emotions. It was the study of our *Sinnlichkeit,* a German word that refers to both our sensory and our sensual (including our erotic) natures. By the early nineteenth century the meaning of the term had narrowed to refer to the philosophy of art and beauty. The study of our sense perceptions became part of epistemology, whereas the province of human instincts was largely ceded to psychology. Another wrinkle in the history of aesthetics is that British philosophers such as Lord Shaftesbury, David Hume, Edmund Burke, and Hugh

Blair were already speculating about the nature of art and beauty in the eighteenth century without using the word *aesthetics* at all.

In modern philosophy aesthetics is a part of value theory, the study of what we value and why we value it. The most obvious part of value theory, ethics, asks, "What is right?" Closely associated with this question are those posed by political theory: "What is justice?" "What is equality?" "What is freedom?" Aesthetics completes the circle of value theory by asking, "What is beauty?" and "What is art?" Some philosophers also claim that truth has its own value, and thus considerations about truth are part of value theory, although it seems more likely that the value we assign to truth over falsity is moral in nature: We think of a liar as an immoral person and attribute moral virtue to an honest politician or businessperson.

Although aesthetics, as a discipline, didn't become a major philosophical field of research until the eighteenth century, long before then a number of philosophers explored its key concepts. The first-century AD Greek philosopher Longinus wrote about the aesthetic experience and its relationship to literature. Longinus added a crucial component to aesthetic theory: the concept of the *sublime.* Although this concept helped to deepen aesthetics as a philosophical inquiry, the meaning given it by Longinus probably helped to keep aesthetics from being taken more seriously by philosophers for a long time afterward.

The sublime, according to Longinus, was literature's capacity to lift us to another level of being, to take us beyond our merely human experience. He believed that this was not a rational process of engagement with the world, yet was a very real activity all the same. The sublime allows us as mortal beings to transcend our earthly state, to bring us closer to the gods. Longinus's emphasis on the nonrational, coupled to the idea that we can transcend our mortality, didn't put his views in particularly good stead with more traditionally minded philosophers.

Contrast this idea of the sublime with what you know of the view of human reason found in thinkers such as Plato, Anselm, Aquinas, and Descartes. Given the fact that our aesthetic experience of the world seems to require some understanding of human irrationality, it is no surprise that philosophy has been cool toward this field of inquiry throughout most of Western history. This suspicion remains to some degree today.

The core of this introduction to aesthetics will be organized into three sections, each of which attempts to answer a key question in aesthetics: What is beauty?; What is art?; and Should art have a moral, political, or spiritual function? Needless to say, these three questions are related to each other.

## What Is Beauty?

Our first question is perhaps the hardest to answer: What is beauty? Many have seen beauty as in the eye of the beholder and thus as hopelessly subjective (and perhaps beyond the purview of philosophical speculation). I might like classical music, whereas you like rap; I might like classical art by painters such as Raphael and Rembrandt, but you like modern artists such as Jackson Pollock and Andy Warhol. How can we judge differences between individual tastes such as these? Shouldn't the understanding of beauty be left to our individual judgments?

Yet we often agree about which things are beautiful and which ones are not: A handsome actor or beautiful actress might be admired by millions; an enchanting mountain landscape might take the breath away of all but the most jaded tourist; and a great work of art might keep its reputation for hundreds of years. So a reasonable person might suppose that these things share some quality that our senses or our intellect can appreciate as contributing toward their beauty. For this reason, the effort to understand the nature of beauty should be made.

As just hinted, we can imagine two extremes, two opposite poles, when it comes to establishing the nature of beauty. The first pole sees beauty as an objective reality—as some very real property in beautiful objects that all rational or healthy people can appreciate. This is the "objectivist" or "realist" view of beauty. At the other pole we find the subjectivists—those who claim that the appreciation of beauty is a purely individual feeling or choice and that there's nothing in the nature of reality that compels us to find the same things beautiful.

The earliest substantial contribution to the theory of aesthetics came from Plato. Recall from the chapter on ancient philosophy his famous theory of the Forms. Plato saw the realm of the Forms as necessary to explain how we can see a collection of things with both similarities and differences as making up a species or class. For example, even though there are many types of trees—elms, spruce, maples, weeping willows, and birches—despite all their differences, we can recognize and categorize them all as "trees." But how is this possible? How are we able to know that pines and maples and willows all come under the classification of "treehood"?

For Plato, our ability to recognize and classify all trees *as* trees is due to there being a Form of Treeness, an eternal archetype of all specific trees. In fact, each class of thing had its own Form associated with it. He believed that by contemplating the eternal Forms of things, the objects of this temporal world could be rationally known and understood, albeit as mere shadowy representations of these Forms.

Given that the objects of this world are mere shadowy imitations (in Greek, *mimesis*) of the true Forms, any work of art that depicts the finite and unstable objects of this world will be only a copy of an already existing copy.

As one might guess, Plato thought little of art. It was a useless representation of an already dull copy. Further, it needlessly inflamed the emotions. He saw beauty as intellectual in nature, as discovered in the rational contemplation of the realm of the Forms. For him a perfect geometrical object, such as a triangle or square, had more real beauty than attractive people, landscapes, or works of art (although he didn't deny that these had their own sensual charms). For Plato beauty was objective and rational, but not the product of our sense perceptions.

In his 1757 book, *A Philosophical Enquiry into the Sublime and the Beautiful,* Edmund Burke offered a psychological account of beauty, contrasting it to the sublime. He claimed that each was evoked by a fairly specific set of empirical qualities we could perceive through the senses. Beauty wasn't the product of our perceiving proportion, fitness, utility, or perfection in an object. Ladders and chairs and morally perfect people are rarely seen as beautiful. Instead, beautiful things tended to be small, smooth, delicate, made up of parts that gradually melted into each other, and with clean and bright colors that weren't too gaudy. Think of peacocks and flowers. Sublime things were, by contrast, dark and obscure, powerful, vast, rugged, magnificent, suggestive of difficulty, and lit with somber colors. Sudden changes from darkness to light and from quiet to noise are also sublime, as are the powerful sounds of waterfalls and cannonades. In all these cases, beauty and sublimity are not the product of our rational reflection on the world, as with Plato. Rather, they are the way physical objects affect our senses. Burke's elevation of the sublime to an equal footing with that of beauty had a powerful effect on Kant's aesthetics.

The German philosopher Immanuel Kant (1724–1804) was a prolific writer on all sorts of philosophical subjects. Because Kant's writings are often dense and difficult to understand, we'll just briefly outline his views on aesthetics here. This outline is important because his philosophy of aesthetics was extremely influential on thinkers who discussed aesthetics for at least a century after his lifetime.

For Kant the human spirit has three basic faculties or powers: its capacities for knowledge, desires, and feelings. These correspond to three cognitive or mental faculties: our Understanding, our Reason (or in another sense, the Will), and our Imagination. In his *Critique of Pure Reason* Kant deals mostly with the way our Understanding processes sense data into knowledge with the help of a priori concepts such as space, time, and causality; whereas in his *Critique of Practical Reason* he outlines how our free Reason chooses to regulate our desires with moral laws. He deals with the power of judgment in general in his *Critique of Judgement* (1790), especially with how we make aesthetic judgments, judgments of taste.

Kant sees these judgments as a distinct type of cognitive activity, separate from the structured empirical knowledge provided by the Understanding and the moral imperatives our Reason forms. He argues that the aesthetic experience of beauty involves a free play between the Imagination and the Understanding, one where they are in harmony and the former isn't constrained by the attempt by the latter to interpret sense experience conceptually, as it does in scientific knowledge. This free play allows us to appreciate the pure form of a work of art—in this sense, Kant is a "formalist." Art gives us a sense of disinterested pleasure in its pure form, which the Imagination sees as a unity even though the Understanding cannot reduce it under a concept. We look at a great painting such as the *Mona Lisa* and imagine it as artistic unity quite apart from any scientific analysis we might make of the paint used to create it, its physical measurements, the frequency of light striking its surface, or any other empirical concepts we might apply to it. This experience is subjective in the sense that each of us feels that pleasure as individuals. Yet Kant thinks that our individual experiences are also universal in that our human constitutions are enough alike that we can share a roughly equivalent awareness of the beauty of things. As in his epistemology, Kant attempts in his aesthetics to unify subjective and objective accounts of human experience.

In 1764, early in his philosophical career, Kant argued that whereas beauty charms, the sublime moves. He came back to this distinction in his *Critique of Judgement.* For Kant the sublime is either having our senses overwhelmed by the size or complexity of something or experiencing nature as a powerful and mighty force—as in thunderstorms, volcanoes, and tidal waves. A sublime experience builds up sense data in our Imagination, causing it to short-circuit our Understanding, the faculty of knowledge. We are overwhelmed by the sublime—our experience of it is accompanied by a feeling of awe or wonder and momentary pain, followed by pleasure. Just as beauty connects our Imagination to our Understanding, the sublime, which evokes an absence of limits and a sense of infinity, connects our Imagination to our Reason, which Kant saw as the faculty of human freedom.

Shortly after Kant wrote his three critiques, the Romantic movement burst out in European art, literature, and music. The Romantics' sense of beauty was based on the pleasure we get from communing with nature. Yet the Romantics' picture of nature wasn't the lawful and mathematically structured nature of the Enlightenment, but one that alternated between the peaceful tranquillity of a field of flowers on a summer day and the sublime dread of mighty waterfalls, perilous crevices, and fearsome beasts. William Blake's tyger was a sublime predator that showed the mark of the Creator; his English meadows were a green and pleasant land threatened with dark satanic mills. Samuel Taylor Coleridge's Kubla Khan built a stately pleasure dome beside a sacred river that ran through measureless caverns of ice; Mary Shelley's Frankenstein created a misshapen gothic horror who roamed the world causing terror. The other Romantic poets praised the gentle beauties of daffodils, nightingales, and, of course, of the young women of the neighborhood (Robbie Burns was especially notorious in this regard). This beauty was subjectively felt by the individual imagination yet was transcendental in that it emanated from a common nature. We are able to connect to nature through our strong feelings and our unconscious minds.

Up to now we have seen that some thinkers—Plato being the best example—see beauty as an objective reality that we appreciate through our reason. Others, such as the Romantics, see beauty in a more subjective light, as the product of individual sensibilities. In the next section we'll trace a second debate that parallels that about beauty—the debate about the nature of art and of artistic creativity.

## What Is Art?

When we ask, "What is art?" we open up a Pandora's box of further questions that are not any easier to answer. Here are the most important ones:

- How do we know if a given object is a work of art? Does the artist's signing it make it art? Or does it have to be validated by a gallery owner or museum curator? or by the public in general?
- Does art have to be beautiful? or sublime? Does its viewing or hearing have to give us pleasure?
- Does art have to objectively represent nature? or merely the artist's subjective feelings or ideas?
- Must art seek a popular audience? or just the approval of an aesthetic elite?
- What is the source of artistic creativity? our reason? our imagination? the unconscious mind? random events and actions?

In this section we will see that in the history of Western art, there have been not one but at least four major answers to the question "What is art?" Each of these answers deals with the secondary questions just listed in its own, distinct way (for an account of the attempts made by analytic philosophers to define the general properties of all art, see the commentary in the section on Arthur Danto).

Before we move to these answers, we should summarize the forms in which the artistic impulse has been expressed throughout history. The following chart categorizes these forms according the basic medium used by each to express its aesthetic message or impulse.

| VISUAL MEDIA | AUDITORY MEDIA | AUDIOVISUAL MEDIA | NARRATIVE MEDIA |
|---|---|---|---|
| Painting | Orchestral music | Dance | Literature, poetry |
| Sculpture | Popular music (nonnarrative) | Performance art | Theater, opera |
| Architecture | | | Film |
| Graphic arts (posters, engraving) | | | Television |

One might point out the obvious fact that narrative media such as literature and film have visual or auditory components: We read a book or watch and listen to a movie. Yet their essence lies in the fact that they tell a story that takes place over time, unlike orchestral music, which can appeal to us purely in terms of its harmonies and melodies, or a painting, which can capture at best a single moment in a story. Visual art forms such as paintings and sculpture cannot "tell" a story over time. In addition, a narrative medium can transfer its narrative from one medium to another, so novels and stories can be made into films, and films into television shows, and so on. By contrast, one cannot make a movie about a piece of sculpture, though one can make a film about the sculptor's life or about how the sculpture was produced, both of which are narratives.

Here is a brief summary of the four most important views of art in Western history in chart form. We'll deal with each movement in some detail, giving a few examples of each to show how actual art forms relate to the aesthetic theories of the ages that created them. Needless to say, these distinctions are very broadly drawn. Each aesthetic age influenced the one that followed it—for example, the Romantics took something from the cult of sensibility of the Enlightenment, and modernist painters were heavily influenced by impressionism. Even so, these four "paradigms" of art represent four distinct ways of looking at aesthetics.

| | PSYCHOLOGICAL TONE | SOURCE OF INSPIRATION | RELATION TO ENVIRONMENT |
|---|---|---|---|
| Classical art is . . . | rational | objective | artificial (nature is idealized or improved) |
| Romantic art is . . . | imaginative | subjective | natural (nature as wild and sublime) |
| Modernist art is . . . | fragmented, unsettling, or shocking | experimental | abstract or surreal (with an elitist orientation) |
| Postmodern art is . . . | playful | allusive (it alludes to other traditions) | popular (a commodity that the masses like) |

Classicism is a recurring phenomenon in Western artistic history. The first classicism is obviously the art and architecture of the ancient classical world, notably of classical Greece in the fifth and fourth centuries BC. More broadly, we can speak of the classical art of Greece, Rome, and the cities and nations they influenced as dominating Europe and the Middle East from 600 BC to AD 500.

The second classicism was the revival of classical learning and artistic styles in the Renaissance, roughly AD 1450–1600, centered in Italy but extended throughout Western Europe. This produced the art of Raphael, Leonardo, and Michelangelo. The third classicism is the neoclassical vogue in painting and architecture in the eighteenth century, the Enlightenment. Needless to say, the classical impulse is still alive and well in the modern world: We can see it in the shape of all those copies of Greek and Roman temples that house our banks and government offices, and in the heroic statues of military and political leaders that populate our parks.

Classical art has three basic elements: It is *rational* in that it attempts to appeal to our reason, not our passions; it is *objective* in that it follows Plato's notion that art should be a representation of reality, and not just of the artist's inner vision; and it is *artificial,* in that the nature it pictures is idealized and ordered—it is an artificial construction of human reason. Classical art pays a lot of attention to form, to proper proportions, to order, to balance, to gravity. We can see this sense of geometrical form and proper proportion admirably displayed in the fifth-century BC Parthenon, the temple built by the citizens of Athens to their goddess Athena. Its Doric columns are symmetrical and solid and taper slightly downward, creating an atmosphere of solidity and gravity. This is only the most famous of a large number of classical temples that survive as ruins in various states of repair today, bearing mute witness to the ideals of order and harmony favored by classical architects.

Classical art survives mostly in statues, the most famous of which is arguably the Venus de Milo (or Aphrodite of Melos to the Greeks). It dates back to around 100 BC and is a typical product of the Hellenistic Age. Even though the goddess is half naked, a toga draped around her waist, her sexuality is muted, almost rational. Here we see the ordered, idealized nature of classicism in human form. Not surprisingly, the pagan gods often served as ideals of beauty for classical sculptors—unlike the Christian god, they were seen as both human and more than human at the same time.

The Renaissance was a rebirth of classical literary, philosophical ideas and artistic ideas. Michelangelo's *David* (1500–1504) shows an idealized young male body that almost could have come through a time warp from classical Athens or Rome. Once again we see the calmness and the sense of decorum and restraint characteristic of ancient classical art as seen in the Venus de Milo. David represents the perfect male body—all leanness and muscle, yet strangely asexual, as with Venus. Not wild nature, but nature tamed by reason.

Yet the real glories of Renaissance art came in painting, not sculpture. There are literally dozens of mostly Italian masterpieces in this category to choose as an example. The one that is most associated with the history of philosophy is Raphael's *The School of Athens* (1510–1511), which pictures Plato and Aristotle striding down the steps of an idealized Academy surrounded by all the great scientists and philosophers of ancient Greece (who were in reality Raphael's friends). We're immediately struck by the wonderful symmetry of the composition, framed by an arch and frescoes in the upper corners of the picture. Classical statues frame the central promenade. Some of the thinkers are engaged in intense debates; others lost in deep speculations or reading. Raphael turns ancient Greek philosophy into a heroic series of endeavors pursued in the spirit of restraint and reason. This is no real school, being wildly anachronistic—the thinkers pictured were active in at least three different centuries; even so, it evokes the classical spirit of rationality and objectivity.

In the eighteenth century, classicism received yet another revival in neoclassical art and architecture. Tiny Greek temples dotted the landscapes on the estates of French and British aristocrats, and classical scenes featuring pagan gods and Greek and Roman heroes worked out with gravity and restraint were used by a number of painters. The most striking examples of neoclassicism in painting came from the brush of the French painter Jacques-Louis David, for example, in *The Death of Socrates* (1787). Socrates is shown striking the pose of a classical hero making some grand philosophical point as he accepts the hemlock and thus his death; his friends gather around him grieving for the demise of their teacher. All is calm, order, and discipline. David took an active role in the French Revolution, becoming the semi-official painter of the Jacobin party. *The Death of Marat* applies classical lessons about heroic gravitas to a contemporary subject, turning the scurrilous revolutionary pamphleteer Marat into a classical hero.

Romantic art started around the time of the French Revolution, the 1790s, and dominated European literature, music, and art until at least around 1850 (though it dominated music for another few decades and found echoes in allied schools of art until the end of the nineteenth century). Romantic art has three elements. It is *imaginative.* As we'll see in the section on Romanticism, the Romantic poets saw literature as based on strong feelings and on the imagination, not on reason. Our imagination transmutes the data given to it by the senses by a creative process into a work of art. Love became a sublime passion instead of a feeling of gentle warmth, thus giving birth to the romance novel.

It is *subjective.* Art is the product of creative genius that reaches deep into the unconscious mind and thus into our primal nature to produce something new. This dive into the unconscious sometimes employed dreams, hallucinations, and drug-induced reveries to achieve its effect. The Romantics' visionary gleam opposed the objective representation of nature aimed at by classical and neoclassical artists.

It is *natural,* tied to nature in its wild and pristine state. Nature was simultaneously beautiful and sublime, sweet and dangerous. The Romantics sought a direct communion to nature in their work, nature taken in an organic, not a mechanistic, sense. Romantic literature was natural in another sense: It attempted to approximate the language of common folk, not the artificial language of the courts and high culture. Romantic art followed suit in picturing our natural passions instead of the artificial feelings of posing heroes.

The principal focus of Romanticism was literature, especially poetry. William Wordsworth and Percy Bysshe Shelley were the most articulate voices in describing the Romantic aesthetic. Wordsworth spoke of the need to include strong feelings and use a simple, natural language in writing poetry, whereas Shelley made a sharp distinction between reason, which merely analyzes things that are already there, and the imagination, which is the truly creative faculty in our souls. All the Romantic writers were very much aware of themselves as outcasts or lonely geniuses (Lord Byron being perhaps the most extreme version of this), and all of them wrote long elegies to the beauties and inspirations provided by nature. We'll revisit the literary theory of Romanticism later in this chapter.

As for other forms of art, the Romantics made their second biggest splash in music. Beethoven, Schubert, Brahms, Berlioz, Wagner, and Tchaikovsky are only some of the leading lights of a large group of nineteenth-century Romantic composers. Their swelling melodies attempted to tug at our heartstrings much more directly than the baroque counterpoint of Bach or the cheerful classicism of Mozart, while their sense of drama tried to evoke the sublime—consider the first four notes of Beethoven's Fifth Symphony or the cannon blasts in Tchaikovsky's *1812 Overture.*

In Romantic art and sculpture we find themes similar to those outlined previously. Have a look at Théodore Géricault's *The Raft of the Medusa* (1818–1819), one of the best examples of Romantic art's attempt to evoke the sublime. The original painting is mammoth in size. It portrays Géricault's vision of a real tragedy of the time. The sea is indeed dark and stormy, as is only fitting. Nature is pictured as wild, uncontrollable, and merciless—we can almost hear the wind howling. The darkness of the picture and the artist's use of browns, blacks, and deep reds follow Burke's prescription for a sublime color scheme perfectly. The fear obvious in the sailors' postures and faces is not our fear, yet a careful viewing evokes it all the same. Géricault follows Burke's notion of the sublime once again—the distant terror the painting makes us feel causes delight.

In Auguste Rodin's *The Kiss* (1886) we see the passion of Romantic art in marble. The lovers' bodies are wrapped up into each other, seeming to form one organic mass. Even though this piece has almost become a cliché image of romantic love in our day, Rodin shows us the unrestrained sexuality of two ordinary lovers in a much more direct fashion than any classical artist would dare. Rodin's *The Thinker* has given us yet another Romantic cliché—that of deep thought as a passionate quest.

A late echo of Romanticism in painting came in the form of the Pre-Raphaelite movement in England, its most illustrious members being Edward Burne-Jones, Dante Gabriel Rossetti, William Holman Hunt, and John William Waterhouse. They formed a formal brotherhood in 1848 that lasted only five years. Yet for over half a century the Pre-Raphaelite movement produced a volley of paintings on a diversity of subjects that defied the academic classicism of the day. Their works dealt with a mixture of classical myths such as those connected to Ulysses, Circe, and Pandora; medieval tales such as the Arthur legends; and stories from the Bible. They painted with a sense of moral and religious seriousness, mystical vision, richness of color, and subtle sexuality. Their name refers to their intention to return to the spirit of medieval and early Renaissance art before Raphael. An example is Waterhouse's *Circe Offering the Cup to Ulysses* (1891), depicting a scene from the *Odyssey* in which the sorceress Circe offers Ulysses a magical potion to turn him into her love slave. Here we see the magical flavor, historical aura, depth of color, and thinly submerged sexuality typical of the Pre-Raphaelites. Though, strictly speaking, not Romantic, the movement produced art that shared the main aesthetic elements of Romanticism—its imaginative quality, its subjectivity, its desire to return to nature.

The impressionists acted as a vital link between Romantic and modernist art, though they didn't really fit into either category. They shared the love of color and movement and the passionate energy of the Romantics, yet began to experiment with the effects of light on objects and often painted very ordinary scenes from everyday life, in the modernist spirit. Renoir's *Dance at Bougival* (1883) is full of lively energy, the dancers sashaying, oblivious to the picnickers in the background. Renoir's impressionism represents the lighter side of the movement—he used bright colors, and his subjects were usually common folk, healthy-looking people having fun. The impressionists sought to give their viewers an *impression* of reality, not reality itself. Their art was subjective in spirit and experimented with nature, especially with the effects of light and movement on the human eye.

Modernism was a movement in art, architecture, literature, and music that started in the 1890s and dominated Europe and North America at least until the

1960s (with strong echoes to the present). Modernist works had three basic qualities. They were *fragmented, unsettling,* or *shocking.* Modernists attempt to shock their audiences with pictures, music, and literature where (to quote William Butler Yeats) "Things fall apart; the centre cannot hold." Their works were highly *experimental*—art no longer concerned itself with accurately representing the surface structures of things, as classical and most Romantic art did. Instead, it reworked reality, trying out various techniques to create unique aesthetic experiences. Because of this experimentalism, modernist art tended to be *abstract* or *surreal,* and thus no longer tried to appeal to broad or even educated tastes but to the taste of an aesthetic avant-garde isolated in the great metropoles of Paris, London, New York, Vienna, and Berlin.

Because of these developments, the ritual and public exhibition value of a piece of art waned, while the aura of the artist triumphed. An object or work became art because the artist signed it. It was then validated by the art dealer or museum creator who exhibited it, who then tried to convince rich patrons of its value. Whether or not it evoked beauty or gave pleasure was largely beside the point. Modernist art was largely intellectual in nature. It aroused our emotions insofar as it could unsettle us and make us think in new ways.

Fragmentation and experimentation are the central themes of T. S. Eliot's 1922 poem *The Wasteland,* which is a patchwork of classical allegories, London street scenes, quotations from sacred scriptures, and mystical references to tarot cards and the Arthur legends. In the same year Luigi Pirandello published his play *Six Characters in Search of an Author.* Its unfinished characters flail about as mere names, in search of the author who had failed to flesh out their full natures. They are unstable, lost, without fixed standards.

Modernist composers such as Igor Stravinksy and Arnold Schoenberg continued this theme of fragmentation and experimentation in their works. Their compositions are dissonant and jarring, in some cases totally lacking anything like melody. Schoenberg even invented a new twelve-tone scale, writing unlistenable music with it.

But the most striking developments in modernism were in fine art. If we can pinpoint a moment when modernism began, it was in 1893 when the Norwegian artist Edvard Munch painted *The Scream.* In the foreground a man with a distorted face screams, full of existential dread. Behind him a sinewy river winds away into the distance; above him a sky with swirling colors seems to highlight his anxiety. We're not sure why he's upset—he is fearful of things in general. The painting unsettles us, jars us from our complacency. The Age of Fragmentation had begun.

The first full-fledged movement in modernist art was cubism, developed and most fully explored by Pablo Picasso and Georges Braque beginning in 1907. The cubists broke up the human figure and physical objects into flattened geometrical fragments, showing us three dimensions on a two-dimensional plane. They also distorted these fragments, superimposing masks on human faces, making eyes and mouths grotesquely large, or indicating movement by showing the same fragment in several positions simultaneously. Marcel Duchamp's *Nude Descending a Staircase No. 2* (1912) is a good example of the cubist technique. The painting is not beautiful in the conventional sense, or even sublime—it is an avant-garde experiment with shapes, colors, and movement.

Cubism began to challenge the old relationship between the artist and popular taste, as more and more modernist artists had to appeal either to their own personalities or to the goodwill of gallery owners and wealthy patrons to validate their work. Duchamp's *Nude* was greeted with derision by the press in New York, where it was first shown. This explicit appeal to the avant-garde by modern artists made it seem elitist to many people.

Salvador Dali was the master of surrealism. His melting clocks, burning giraffes, and morphing human bodies were distinctly modernist not only in their fragmentation of reality, their shock value (at least at the time), their experimentalism, and their obvious surrealism, but in their evocation of the Freudian unconscious with its meaning-charged dreamscape. In *The Persistence of Memory* (1931), Dali meditates on the passage of time by showing three melting stopwatches in a barren environment featuring a withered tree and a distant ocean. There are meticulously crafted elements of reality here, but a reality transformed according to the surreal logic of the unconscious mind. Dali's paintings don't represent nature directly but give us unsettling unconscious images. Not surprisingly, Dali also produced surrealist films full of fragmented dreamlike images. The most famous of these is *An Andalusian Dog,* which he made in 1929 with Luis Buñuel. It can still shock the viewer today.

For some artists, painting became entirely nonrepresentational—it no longer pictured real-world objects. The pure geometry of the Dutch artist Piet Mondrian's *Composition in Red, Yellow and Blue* of 1926 abandons representation totally. The picture is a series of red, yellow, blue, and white rectangles. This was abstraction and the experimental spirit at its most extreme. It's difficult to think of this painting as unsettling or shocking, though the notion that it expresses any sort of beauty is indeed unsettling. Art in this case had become a mental exercise.

Jackson Pollock brought abstract expressionism to the world in his drip paintings done in the 1940s and 1950s. His canvases, often massive, were streaks and blobs of colors that intertwined and were layered on top of each other, created by dripping and splattering paint from soaked brushes. His *Convergence* of 1952 typifies his technique. His works were obviously fragmented and experimental and defied traditional notions of beauty. Nature had disappeared entirely; even the intentions of the artist were partly swallowed by the quasi-random technique used, even if his emotions were expressed in them. Once again, the gallery owner or museum curator, and more generally the art-appreciating elite, needed to validate these as art before they were treated as such by the general public.

Probably the most outrageous and experimental artistic movement in the modernist period was Dada, which started in 1916 in Zurich, Switzerland. The Dadaists created nonsense art that aimed to tear up artistic tradition entirely, to "make it new," in the words of the poet Ezra Pound. Tristan Tzara, the movement's founder, created Dada poetry by cutting up words from newspapers, mixing them together in a bag, then randomly selecting out a few and assembling them into a poem. Dada artists created collages by gluing together on a board buttons, train tickets, pieces of wood, and other detritus of everyday life. Probably the most notoriously shocking and experimental of the various Dada forays into art were the ready-mades, pioneered by Marcel Duchamp. Duchamp took ordinary objects, arranged them in an art space, and then signed them. His *Fountain* (1917) was an ordinary urinal signed "R. Mutt." The art object was now defined by the artist's signature, his or her act of creation involving merely *seeing* an object in a new way. Whether Duchamp's urinal is either beautiful or natural we leave to the reader's judgment. Yet the idea that this is *art* still unsettles us.

One of the offshoots of Dadaism was performance art. In 1961 the Italian artist Piero Manzoni signed human bodies and called them "Living Sculptures." In the same year he also canned his own feces, calling it "Artist Shit." In 1960 Yves Klein performed his Monotone Symphony in Paris. Ten musicians played a single note on their instruments while three naked women covered themselves in blue paint and rubbed up against canvases mounted on the walls. Klein presided over the event in a black dinner jacket, at the end of the performance exclaiming, "The myth is in the art." Here the artist had become comic maestro, challenging us to redefine our notion of the aesthetic. For both Manzoni and Klein, art was whatever the artist said it was.

One of the readings in this chapter comes from the heyday of modernism. Walter Benjamin argues that modern means of mechanical reproduction, such as photography and printing, had robbed artistic masterpieces of their magical aura, their cult value. *Anyone* can own a copy of Raphael's *The School of Athens* or a recording of Beethoven's Fifth Symphony. Taking the place of these masterpieces were modern art forms such as photography and film, which were progressive in that they could appeal directly to the aesthetic sensibilities of the masses and not just to those of a social elite. Although Benjamin wrote during the heyday of modernism, he looked forward to a popularization of art as part of a social revolution by the working class.

Finally, from the 1960s on we see the start of a new movement in art, postmodernism. We'll deal with the theory and practice of postmodernism in greater detail in the following chapter, so we'll only outline it here. Postmodern art is *playful,* eschewing the stern experimentalism of the modernists for a sense of humor. It is *allusive* in that it alludes to the artistic tradition, borrowing from and recycling the past. This borrowing is sometimes accomplished through a parody of the past rather than a neoclassical copying of it. Postmodern art is also *popular,* at least in intent, in the sense that it produces commodities that the mass publics of Western societies can understand and appreciate. There's nothing mysterious about Andy Warhol's silk-screened colored images of Marilyn Monroe, Elvis Presley, and Campbell's soup cans, as banal as these might be.

Postmodern art tries to return to the need for some sense of validation by the masses, though it also seeks validation from fellow artists and from its ironic or playful connection to the history of art. The use of columns, statues, and ornamentation in postmodern architecture urges the viewer to think of how postmodern buildings are related to classical and Gothic architecture. Admittedly, postmodern literature is something of a different kettle of fish, retaining a lot of the fragmentation and experimentation of modernism.

A good example of postmodern architecture is Michael Graves's 1985 Portland Building in Portland, Oregon. It combines modernist materials such as steel and glass with ancient motifs such as the pseudo-Egyptian brown columns on its front façade and the postmodern playfulness of ornamental garlands along its side. Over its entrance stands a huge hammered copper statue of the goddess Portlandia executed by the artist Raymond Kaskey, who based it not on a real classical goddess but on a picture of a woman on Portland's city seal. She parodies classical statues, holding a menacing trident in her left hand as she beckons Portlanders into the building with her right. Unlike the head-scratching reaction of most people to modernist statuary, such as Henry Moore's work, people "get" Portlandia right away. As she was transported to the building on a large truck, crowds gathered to watch, later pushing forward to touch the goddess before she was elevated to her permanent place of honor. She is the people's goddess, not a deity understood only by an alienated New York, Paris, or Berlin artistic avant-garde.

Our tour of the history of art and of aesthetic ideals leaves open an important question: Is art purely a social or historical product? Historicists of various types see art as a function of the historical location or interpretive community it comes from. G. W. F. Hegel initiated the view that art traditions dialectically evolve over time, acting as moments in the development of the Absolute Spirit. Picking up from Hegel, Marxist aesthetics argues that works of art are the products of specific economic classes. We can thus call art "decadent" or "progressive" depending on whether it reflects the interests of the current ruling class or of the revolutionary class they are oppressing. Feminists and postcolonial critics have made similar distinctions between progressive and regressive forms of art. This question leads us straight into our last section, on the question of whether art has a moral, political, or spiritual function beyond the aesthetic pleasure it gives us.

## Should Art Have a Moral, Political, or Spiritual Function?

As seen in the various illustrations in the previous section, the philosophy of how art should be done has widely varied over time. You've seen how some artists have wanted to represent as realistically as possible things in the world, whether human-made or natural objects or the human form. This "representational" view of art measured the ability of the artist by the capacity to mirror what is being observed. Explaining the artist's work this way carries some deep philosophical assumptions. What is represented must be done so accurately and truthfully, without distortion or deception. The artist must make the finished product as true to the original object or person being depicted as possible.

Yet not everyone agreed with this representational view of art. As previously mentioned, Plato believed that the artist was not doing humanity any favor by further replicating already shadowy images. The objects of this world, dim objects of the True Forms, should not be further replicated and dimmed by painting or sculpting them and then showing them to an impressionable public. Here is where we see one of the most important questions of aesthetics arising, that of the proper relationship between art and morality.

Plato believed that our goal as philosophically inclined human beings was, through a rational contemplation of the Eternal Forms, to come to true knowledge. If we are truly dedicated to this contemplation, when we die, we will remain in the realm of the Forms, instead of being reincarnated back into this world, perhaps as a dog or rat. For the artist to divert our attention from contemplating the Forms not just an earthly object but, even worse, to a representation of an earthly object, is to sidetrack us from our real goal as human beings and as philosophers. Hence the artist's work isn't just an idle and harmless amusement but actually immoral, a corruption of our rational natures by objects intended to inflame our passions. Plato's objection to the artist's work is an early example of the very uneasy tension between morality and art.

Given the thoroughly metaphysical nature of Plato's theory of the Forms and the strangeness of his ideas about reincarnation and remembering knowledge from past lives, Plato's criticism of the artist's trade probably doesn't strike us moderns as a particularly good basis for believing that art is immoral. Yet we don't need to accept Plato's metaphysics in order to contemplate the relationship between art and morality.

So the question remains: Can we evaluate art morally, distinguish between good and bad art on moral grounds? Do we say to ourselves, "Good art equals moral enrichment" and "Bad art equals moral depravity"? One obvious example from everyday life involves the sexual content of contemporary painting, films, and music. Some people think that sexually explicit art is bad art because it leads to sexual promiscuity.

From the other end of the spectrum you may think that judging the goodness or badness of art is not a moral issue at all. Harkening back to the realists, we may think a piece of art is good because it superbly represents its object, say, a person or landscape. When we think of good art, we may think of the famous *Mona Lisa* or of paintings by Rembrandt such as *The Night Watch.* Picasso's *Don Quixote,* though it isn't representational art, may nevertheless also be judged to be good art because it is a powerful picture of Quixote's character.

If good art is understood this way, bad art, we might think, is produced by amateurs, by painters without skill who used little effort and cheap paint and paper to create their work, or by composers who write music to be played in elevators or in jingles featured in radio and television commercials. In such cases, we are using aesthetic criteria to judge the work of art. We are seeing art as produced for art's sake.

This view of the independence of art from any moral, political, or religious function can be called "aestheticism." This was an important view in the late nineteenth and early twentieth centuries among British and Irish writers and critics such as Oscar Wilde, Clive Bell, and Walter Pater, all of whom had little patience for attempts to inject moral and political lessons into art and literature. For such writers beauty and pleasure alone justified the creation of art and literature. Their motto was *ars gratia artis,* "art for art's sake." Wilde went so far as to say that instead of art contributing to a good life, the point of life was to furnish materials for great art. This aestheticism is a recurrent phenomenon throughout the history of Western art and philosophy and acts as a powerful counterpoint to the notion that art must serve some useful function, whether moral, political, or religious.

One of the main reasons for linking art and morality is that art plays a very important part in challenging our beliefs and values about other aspects of our lives. Because art is housed in museums and viewed by thousands each day, it becomes an inseparable part of our culture. In many respects it forms a story or commentary about our culture—it helps to define it for us.

By looking at the art made and collected by a given society, we can tell a great deal about the values, norms, and intellectual beliefs of that particular society. We have seen in the section "What Is Art?" that nineteenth-century Western societies favored Romantic and impressionistic art. This art was representational, imaginative, and passionate, with a definite vision of the world. In contrast, the early-twentieth-century art of the modernists was more fragmented, abstract, and discordant. This attitude reflected both the chaos and destruction of the First and Second World Wars and the moral and religious disruptions caused by the march of modern science and technology.

Art can certainly motivate or challenge our political views. We can imagine a work that depicts the oppression of peoples—a film of noble peasants toiling in the fields to make their masters rich, or a sculpture of a ragged, slouched old woman laboring under her load, eking out a meager existence. Such art should have a real impact upon us, making us take seriously the plight of someone living under an oppressive regime.

Aristotle viewed art a bit like this. Although disagreeing with Plato's critique of art, Aristotle nevertheless thought that tragedy worked only if the story had a moral component. To show otherwise, for instance, by showing an evil character ending up with good luck, would be quite wrong. The goal of a good tragedy is to produce a *catharsis* in the audience. Certainly this cathartic effect of the theater was moral in nature, for it had the general well-being of the audience in mind. Ideally, they would leave the theater and go back to their homes scattered throughout the *polis* purged of their negative emotions by the catharsis they had just experienced.

Besides the moral and political nature of art, its appeal can also be spiritual in nature. We can look at art depicting a religious scene such as a Renaissance painting of Christ's crucifixion and be quite moved by otherworldly thoughts—by the contemplation of God, our salvation, and of a life beyond this one.

Of course, art can sometimes be simultaneously moral, political, and spiritual. A sculpture of a victorious ancient king decked out in the full regalia of his office is an example of art serving such a tripartite function—he could be shown as a moral leader, as a military conqueror, and with divine sanction all at the same time. Here art serves the sort of ritual function that Walter Benjamin saw as extinguished by modern techniques of mechanical reproduction.

In distinguishing between good and bad art on the basis of a moral standard, the Russian novelist Leo Tolstoy is an important figure. He had a moral view of art. Artists who impart to their audience harmful and destructive moral feelings produce bad art, whereas those who impart the opposite produce good art.

So far he was in agreement with the likes of Aristotle. Tolstoy, however, then took quite a different tack by maintaining that religious art most clearly shows our love for both God and other human beings. Moral goodness is defined by the teachings of Christ in the Bible, most particularly the stories and verses that Tolstoy selected himself.

To respond to Tolstoy's position, we could simply reject the belief that good art enhances the moral quality of the audience—if art is truly a representation of beauty, then it belongs to an entirely different category of values. We might derive real pleasure from a comedic film in which the actors make fools of themselves, from a rock song with an explosive guitar riff, or from a painting of a splendid landscape. In each case, we can explain this pleasure aesthetically but not learn any moral lessons at all from this pleasure.

In addition, there is the very real fear that judging art in moral terms could open up a Pandora's box of political interference in the production of art by self-righteous special-interest groups. This has happened a number of times in Western history, as when the Catholic Church banned dozens of works of literature they found offensive in the early modern period, and in the 1930s and 1940s when the Nazis burned books by Jewish authors and ridiculed and banned modernist paintings and sculpture as decadent. Given that most works of art will probably offend someone somewhere, at the end of the day there might be precious little art and literature left for us to enjoy if we take this approach too far.

A different response to Tolstoy is to agree that art serves a moral function, but instead of seeing art as enhancing the spiritual bonds between humanity, seeing it as a way to challenge our moral and aesthetic assumptions, thereby opening up the possibility of social and political liberation. As Herbert Marcuse has argued, the value of art may very well lie in its ability to challenge the moral and political beliefs of its viewers and not just to reinforce the viewers' assumed values. Marcuse is a provocative example here, because he thought that art that is especially sensual and graphic in its sexuality gets at the root of our unexamined prejudices. He generally agreed with Sigmund Freud that our two most basic instincts are Eros and Thanatos, the sex and death instincts. Civilization must repress both of these to survive. Yet the odd twist that Marcuse added to Freud's theory is the notion of *surplus repression.* This was the "extra" repression of our instincts, especially our sexuality, that society imposes upon us beyond what is strictly necessary to maintain civilized social relations. It does this by making us work long hours to buy things we don't need, even though modern technology has made shorter work weeks possible and thus opened up the possibility of more and more people joining the realm of freedom, the realm where we play instead of work. Of course, play isn't good for business, so industrial societies use advertising and other techniques to convince us that we need to buy new clothes, televisions, computers, and SUVs in order to enjoy our lives. But to afford these things, we have to work harder and repress the very possibility of play that seems to be promised by our advanced system of production and consumption.

So part of Marcuse's message was that art was a form of play and was thus a negation of the surplus repression and the system of production and consumption found in most modern societies. It was an affirmation of what Freud called the Pleasure Principle, which wanted to play, to follow Eros, as opposed to the Reality Principle, which tells us to restrain our instincts in favor of long-term goals. For Marcuse, good art breaks through this Reality Principle, nourishing our erotic natures. For instance, when we look at a sexually explicit photograph, painting, or sculpture, we may become very uncomfortable, defensive, even outraged. Good art is erotic and challenges the repressive forces that limit our thinking and our action. Marcuse would say to us that art has fulfilled its purpose by breaking through social repression.

Yet before we climb aboard Marcuse's freedom train and embrace the potential of art for erotic liberation, we have to consider a powerful counterargument to Marcuse's view of art. Feminists such as Naomi Wolf argue that any depiction of women, sexually or not, could involve their "objectification." In addition, Wolf argues that patriarchy—our still male-dominated society—uses various insidious techniques to compel women to try to measure up to an artificial standard of beauty through dieting, plastic surgery, the use of cosmetics, and the wearing of sexually suggestive clothes. Wolf calls this the "beauty myth."

What Wolf means by objectification is that in drawings, paintings, sculpture, films, and photographs, women are reduced to being mere objects for the male gaze. No advanced mental activity, feelings, or personality is attributed to the woman being depicted. Quite the opposite: All these attributes are negated, leaving only the active gaze of the presumably male observer and the passive posture of the female object. Moreover, because women are often depicted in a sexual manner, as lounging half naked on a couch, or lying in bed seemingly waiting for their lover, the gaze is obviously sexual. The woman is shown as merely an object for the male onlooker's use.

Wolf, along with many of the Second Wave feminist theorists who influenced her early in her career, have called into question the very nature of feminine beauty and of the artist's aesthetic or moral right to depict it. If all representational art that features the female form has at least potentially a political connotation, a moral meaning, then the question of censorship raises its ugly head. Should we censor art whose aim is to objectify women, to turn images of women into sexual objects whose purpose is to titillate men? What's the difference between legitimate art and pornography? If a piece of art offends one group of people but is seen as sexually liberating for another, which group should we listen to?

Arthur Danto takes on the twin questions of the morality of censoring and subsidizing the arts head-on in his essay later in this chapter. He argues that art isn't a frivolous entertainment but an essential part of what it means to be human, and therefore should be seen as an essential component of democratic societies. He takes what he defines as the "liberal" position, arguing that the state should subsidize even art that is morally questionable but should not censor that art in any way, disagreeing with both the libertarians, who oppose censorship but don't want to subsidize the arts, and the fundamentalists, who favor censorship but think that money given to the arts would be better spent elsewhere. He uses the example of Robert Mapplethorpe's homoerotic photographs to show how art can challenge our sensibilities in a meaningful way.

This leads us to the last issue we have to deal with in this introduction. Feminists, multiculturalists, and others have acted on their belief that art and literature cannot be judged by aesthetic criteria alone but should be subject to moral support or condemnation. They have attacked the Western Canon, the notion that certain books and poems are great works of literature of enduring value. The problem with the Canon, they note, is that it is almost entirely the product of white men, most of whom are dead. So when teaching university literature courses, they replace some of the better-known classic works of literature with those written by less well known female and nonwhite authors, arguing that this will help eliminate sexism, racism, and imperialism in their students.

Harold Bloom has taken on the feminists, multiculturalists, and Marxists who want to politicize literature by picking which books are worth reading not on their aesthetic merits but according to the sex, race, or class of the writer. Bloom argues that this politicization represents a flight from the aesthetic by the "school of resentment," which harbors ill will toward strong poets such as Dante and Shakespeare, who cannot be lumped into simplistic moral categories or explained away as the products of limited historical circumstances. Bloom considers this politicization of literature disastrous, seeing writing and reading as solitary acts that cannot be judged according to what he calls "Platonic moralism" or "Aristotelian social science." He shares the aestheticism of Wilde and Pater, though not the need for social change found in Marcuse's work. He bemoans the threat to the Canon by all those who see in it bad morals and bad politics.

So, as we've seen, aesthetic issues have become political issues in modern academia. Whether or not they *should* be is another question.

# EDMUND BURKE ON THE SUBLIME AND THE BEAUTIFUL

Edmund Burke (1729–1797) was born in Dublin; his father was a Protestant lawyer and his mother, a Roman Catholic. Burke went to London in 1750 to study the law but soon turned his attentions toward literature instead, associating with such luminaries of the English Enlightenment as the writer Dr. Johnson (of the very-first-dictionary fame) and the painter Joshua Reynolds.

Burke is known more as a political writer and active politician than a philosopher, although it was much more common to move back and forth between literary endeavors and public life in the eighteenth century than it is today. He published his most important philosophical works early in life: *A Vindication of Natural Society* (1756) and the first edition of *A Philosophical Enquiry into the Sublime and the Beautiful* (1757). Most of his other books were political essays and speeches.

Politically, Burke was a Whig or liberal. He was elected as a member of Parliament (MP) for Wendover in 1765 and became a fierce opponent of the Tory government of the day. In 1774 he was elected in Bristol and then in 1781 became MP for Malton, his pursuit of various political causes forcing him to keep changing his constituency. His speeches were masterpieces of eloquence. Yet given that they could last up to eight hours, they had a tendency to empty the House of Commons. He also held a number of other political posts.

Burke championed a number of causes in his political life. He opposed domestic political corruption and George III's attempt to win back power from Parliament; he supported a more moderate policy toward the American colonies in the period leading up to the American Revolution, free trade with Ireland, full civil rights for British Catholics, and later in life the abolition of slavery. He is perhaps most famous for his 1790 book, *Reflections on the Revolution in France,* in which he opposed the radical changes of the French Revolution as disruptive of the time-honored French constitution. This work made him the preeminent conservative thinker of the day and alienated many of his old liberal friends such as Thomas Paine and Jeremy Bentham. Burke opposed the idea of abstract political rights, preferring instead the idea of a social contract between the living, the dead, and the yet to be born. He cloaked this contract in a divine sanction, although he clearly did not believe in the divine right of kings to do whatever they wanted—their power was a trust that could be abused. Instead, he believed in a hierarchical society ruled by a constitutional monarchy where king and Parliament shared power. The psychological foundation of the state was an instinct of political loyalty, not a rational perception of natural law or natural rights.

Burke stands as a bridge between empiricist thinkers such as Locke and Hume, who tried to link all ideas to our sensory perceptions, and nineteenth-century idealism and Romanticism. Burke's psychological account of aesthetics appealed very much to both Kant and the Romantics. He tried to explain the nature and source of what he considered to be our two principal aesthetic feelings: those of beauty and of the sublime. Although the sublime was referred to even in ancient discussions of art, Burke elevated it to a new position of importance in aesthetics. The language of Romantic art and literature benefited from this elevation, for it explained our sense of wonder at dangerous precipices, fearsome beasts, dark and stormy nights, cheering crowds, and sudden cannon blasts. He said, in short, that the feelings associated with these phenomena are of a very different sort than those associated with our affection for beautiful landscapes, people, or pieces of art.

He saw the beautiful as connected to love and similar feelings of affection. The appearance of an object of beauty gives us pleasure. Yet this pleasure is not based on the object's specific proportions, which vary from beautiful object to beautiful object; nor on its utility—we don't think of hammers and saws as beautiful, as useful as they sometimes are; nor on its perfection—we don't love a beautiful man or woman because of his or her fine moral qualities or intellectual brilliance. On the positive side, beautiful objects share a number of sensory qualities:

- Small things are more beautiful than big ones.
- Their surface is smooth, and not rugged.
- There is a variety in the direction that their parts move; yet these parts melt into each other, as in the way a bird's neck slowly tapers into its body.
- They are delicate, like a small flower, but not sickly.
- They have "clean and bright" colors that are not strong or glaring, such as light greens and blues, pink, or violet; if they have stronger colors, these are mixed up with each other and with softer colors so as not to startle us, as in a peacock.

In contrast, the sublime is produced by an idea of fear or terror that doesn't directly threaten our lives yet awakens in us a sense of awe or wonder. We retreat from our own deaths yet find some delight in the idea of danger and death, as we see in mountain climbing, skiing, car racing, and watching horror films. This sublime delight is awakened in us by a number of allied sensory phenomena (some of the examples are mine, not Burke's):

- Obscurity and darkness are sublime because they are voids that we people with the objects of our imaginary fears: ghosts, demons, pagan gods, hidden attackers.
- The feeling of power or strength in something is sublime: The tiger is more sublime than the dog, the bull than the ox. Powerful things can hurt us; impotent things cannot.
- The vastness or magnitude of something is sublime: The pyramids of Egypt are much more sublime than an English country cottage. Rugged surfaces, such as those found in mountain ranges, are more sublime than smooth ones found on the prairies. Infinity is also sublime, even if it's an illusion: Think of gazing across a seemingly endless desert or straight up along the edge of a very tall building.
- A magnificent thing—something that contains a vast profusion of elements, such as a starry sky on a clear night—is sublime.
- An object that suggests great difficulty, such as the massive standing blocks and lintels of stone at Stonehenge, is sublime.

- As for light, sudden changes from darkness to light, and vice versa, are sublime. An overwhelmingly powerful light such as that of the sun is also sublime.
- Somber colors—browns, blacks, or deep purples—are more sublime than gaudy or light colors: Compare a Gothic cathedral to a modern government building.
- Loud sounds from a thunderclap, a waterfall, a cannon blast, or the cheer of a crowd are sublime. In addition, a sudden sound is more sublime than a gradually building one: Think once again of thunder or of a big gun firing. Low, intermittent sounds against a background of silence (e.g., creaking doors and animal moans) are also sublime, as they too evoke in us a sense of uncertainty and thus terror.

Burke gives us a good start in our investigation of the aesthetic—he makes a real attempt to tell us exactly what beauty and sublimity are made up of on an empirical or psychological level. His concept of the sublime explains a range of feelings with which we approach the natural and human worlds that cannot be explained by the feelings of pleasure we get from objects of beauty. For Burke, our aesthetic experience of the world involves a combination of terror and pleasure, of the sublime and the beautiful.

# A Philosophical Enquiry into the Origin of Our Ideas of the Sublime and the Beautiful

EDMUND BURKE

## Part 1 [Preliminary Remarks]

### SECTION 7. OF THE SUBLIME

Whatever is fitted in any sort to excite the ideas of pain, and danger, that is to say, whatever is in any sort terrible, or is conversant about terrible objects, or operates in a manner analogous to terror, is a source of the *sublime;* that is, it is productive of the strongest emotion which the mind is capable of feeling. I say the strongest emotion, because I am satisfied the ideas of pain are much more powerful than those which enter on the part of pleasure. Without all doubt, the torments which we may be made to suffer, are much greater in their effect on the body and mind, than any pleasures which the most learned voluptuary could suggest, or than the liveliest imagination, and the most sound and exquisitely sensible body could enjoy. . . . When danger or pain press too nearly, they are incapable of giving any delight, and are simply, terrible; but at certain distances, and with certain modifications, they may be, and they are delightful, as we every day experience. The cause of this I shall endeavour to investigate hereafter.

SOURCE: Edmund Burke, *A Philosophical Enquiry into the Origin of Our Ideas of the Sublime and the Beautiful.* Selections from *The Works of the Right Honourable Edmund Burke,* vol. 1, *The World's Classics* (1759; London: Humprey Milford/Oxford University Press, 1925), pp. 91–92, 94–95, 103, 108–110, 115–116, 122–124, 127–133, 138–139, 156–157, 160–165, 172. The original footnotes and editorial apparatus have been deleted, some spelling modernized, and an explanatory footnote and bracketed titles added.

## SECTION 10: OF BEAUTY

The passion which belongs to generation, merely as such, is lust only; this is evident in brutes, whose passions are more unmixed, and which pursue their purposes more directly than ours. The only distinction they observe with regard to their mates, is that of sex. . . . But man, who is a creature adapted to a greater variety and intricacy of relation, connects with the general passion, the idea of some *social* qualities, which direct and heighten the appetite which he has in common with all other animals; and as he is not designed like them to live at large, it is fit that he should have something to create a preference, and fix his choice; and this in general should be some sensible quality; as no other can so quickly, so powerfully, or so surely produce its effect. The object therefore of this mixed passion which we call love, is the *beauty* of the *sex*. Men are carried to the sex in general, as it is the sex, and by the common law of nature; but they are attached to particulars by personal *beauty*. I call beauty a social quality; for where women and men, and not only they, but when other animals give us a sense of joy and pleasure in beholding them, (and there are many that do so) they inspire us with sentiments of tenderness and affection towards their persons; we like to have them near us, and we enter willingly into a kind of relation with them, unless we should have strong reasons to the contrary. But to what end, in many cases, this was designed, I am unable to discover. . . .

## SECTION 18: THE RECAPITULATION

To draw the whole of what has been said into a few distinct points. The passions which belong to self-preservation, turn on pain and danger; they are simply painful when their causes immediately affect us; they are delightful when we have an idea of pain and danger, without being actually in such circumstances; this delight I have not called pleasure, because it turns on pain, and because it is different enough from any idea of positive pleasure. Whatever excites this delight, I call *sublime*. The passions belonging to self-preservation are the strongest of all the passions.

The second head to which the passions are referred with relation to their final cause, is society. There are two sorts of societies. The first is, the society of sex. The passion belonging to this is called love, and it contains a mixture of lust; its object is the beauty of women. The other is the great society with man and all other animals. The passion subservient to this is called likewise love, but it has no mixture of lust, and its object is beauty; which is a name I shall apply to all such qualities in things as induce in us a sense of affection and tenderness, or some other passion the most nearly resembling these. . . .

## Part 2 [On the Sublime]

### SECTION I. OF THE PASSION CAUSED BY THE SUBLIME

The passion caused by the great and sublime in *nature*, when those causes operate most powerfully, is astonishment; and astonishment is that state of the soul, in which all its motions are suspended, with some degree of horror. In this case the mind is so entirely filled with its object, that it cannot entertain any other, nor by consequence reason on that object which employs it. Hence arises the great power of the sublime, that far from being produced by them, it anticipates our reasonings, and hurries us on by an irresistible force. Astonishment, as I have said, is the effect of the sublime in its highest degree; the inferior effects are admiration, reverence and respect.

### SECTION 2. TERROR

No passion so effectually robs the mind of all its powers of acting and reasoning as fear. For fear being an apprehension of pain or death, it operates in a manner that resembles actual pain. Whatever therefore is terrible, with regard to sight, is sublime too, whether this cause of terror, be endued with greatness of dimensions or not; for it is impossible to look on any thing as trifling, or contemptible, that may be dangerous. There are many animals, who though far from being large, are yet capable of raising ideas of the sublime, because they are considered as objects of terror.

As serpents and poisonous animals of almost all kinds. And to things of great dimensions, if we annex an adventitious idea of terror, they become without comparison greater. A level plain of a vast extent on land, is certainly no mean idea; the prospect of such a plain may be as extensive as a prospect of the ocean; but can it ever fill the mind with any thing so great as the ocean itself? This is owing to several causes, but it is owing to none more than this, that the ocean is an object of no small terror. Indeed terror is in all cases whatsoever, either more openly or latently the ruling principle of the sublime. . . .

## SECTION 3. OBSCURITY

To make any thing very terrible, obscurity seems in general to be necessary. When we know the full extent of any danger, when we can accustom our eyes to it, a great deal of the apprehension vanishes. Every one will be sensible of this, who considers how greatly night adds to our dread, in all cases of danger, and how much the notions of ghosts and goblins, of which none can form clear ideas, affect minds, which give credit to the popular tales concerning such sorts of beings. Those despotic governments, which are founded on the passions of men, and principally upon the passion of fear, keep their chief as much as may be from the public eye. The policy has been the same in many cases of religion. Almost all the heathen temples were dark. Even in the barbarous temples of the Americans at this day, they keep their idol in a dark part of the hut, which is consecrated to his worship. For this purpose too the Druids performed all their ceremonies in the bosom of the darkest woods, and in the shade of the oldest and most spreading oaks. . . .

## SECTION 5. POWER

Besides these things which *directly* suggest the idea of danger, and those which produce a similar effect from a mechanical cause, I know of nothing sublime which is not some modification of power. And this branch rises as naturally as the other two branches, from terror, the common stock of every thing that is sublime. The idea of power at first view, seems of the class of these in-different ones, which may equally belong to pain or to pleasure. But in reality, the affection arising from the idea of vast power, is extremely remote from that neutral character. For first, we must remember, that the idea of pain, in its highest degree, is much stronger than the highest degree of pleasure; and that it preserves the same superiority through all the subordinate gradations. From hence it is, that where the chances for equal degrees of suffering or enjoyment are in any sort equal, the idea of the suffering must always be prevalent. And indeed the ideas of pain, and above all of death, are so very affecting, that whilst we remain in the presence of whatever is supposed to have the power of inflicting either, it is impossible to be perfectly free from terror. Again, we know by experience, that for the enjoyment of pleasure, no great efforts of power are at all necessary; nay we know, that such efforts would go a great way towards destroying our satisfaction: for pleasure must be stolen, and not forced upon us; pleasure follows the will; and therefore we are generally affected with it by many things of a force greatly inferior to our own. But pain is always inflicted by a power in some way superior, because we never submit to pain willingly. So that strength, violence, pain and terror, are ideas that rush in upon the mind together. Look at a man, or any other animal of prodigious strength, and what is your idea before reflection? Is it that this strength will be subservient to you, to your ease, to your pleasure, to your interest in any sense? No; the emotion you feel is, lest this enormous strength should be employed to the purposes of rapine and destruction. That power derives all its sublimity from the terror with which it is, generally accompanied, will appear evidently from its effect in the very few cases, in which it may be possible to strip a considerable degree of strength of its ability to hurt. When you do this, you spoil it of every thing sublime, and it immediately becomes contemptible. An ox is a creature of vast strength; but he is an innocent creature, extremely serviceable, and not at all dangerous; for which reason the idea of an ox is by no means grand. A bull is strong too; but his strength is of another kind; often very destructive, seldom (at least amongst us) of any use in our business; the idea of a bull is therefore great, and it has frequently a place in sublime descriptions, and elevating comparisons. . . .

## SECTION 7. VASTNESS

Greatness of dimension, is a powerful cause of the sublime. . . . Extension is either in length, height, or depth. Of these the length strikes least; an hundred yards of even ground will never work such an effect as a tower an hundred yards high, or a rock or mountain of that altitude. I am apt to imagine likewise, that height is less grand than depth; and that we are more struck at looking down from a precipice, than at looking up at an object of equal height, but of that I am not very positive. A perpendicular has more force in forming the sublime, than an inclined plane; and the effects of a rugged and broken surface seem stronger than where it is smooth and polished. It would carry us out of our way to enter in this place into the cause of these appearances; but certain it is they afford a large and fruitful field of speculation. However, it may not be amiss to add to these remarks upon magnitude; that, as the great extreme of dimension is sublime, so the last extreme of littleness is in some measure sublime likewise; when we attend to the infinite divisibility of matter, when we pursue animal life into these excessively small, and yet organized beings, that escape the nicest inquisition of the sense, when we push our discoveries yet downward, and consider those creatures so many degrees yet smaller, and the still diminishing scale of existence, in tracing which the imagination is lost as well as the sense, we become amazed and confounded at the wonders of minuteness; nor can we distinguish in its effect this extreme of littleness from the vast itself. . . .

## SECTION 8. INFINITY

Another source of the sublime, is *Infinity;* if it does not rather belong to the last. Infinity has a tendency to fill the mind with that sort of delightful horror, which is the most genuine effect, and truest test of the sublime. There are scarce any things which can become the objects of our senses that are really, and in their own nature infinite. But the eye not being able to perceive the bounds of many things, they seem to be infinite, and they produce the same effects as if they were really so. We are deceived in the like manner, if the parts of some large object are so continued to any indefinite number, that the imagination meets no check which may hinder its extending them at pleasure.

Whenever we repeat any idea frequently, the mind by a sort of mechanism repeats it long after the first cause has ceased to operate. After whirling about; when we sit down, the objects about us still seem to whirl. After a long succession of noises, as the fall of waters, or the beating of forge hammers, the hammers beat and the water roars in the imagination long after the first sounds have ceased to affect it; and they die away at last by gradations which are scarcely perceptible. If you hold up a straight pole, with your eye to one end, it will seem extended to a length almost incredible. Place a number of uniform and equidistant marks on this pole, they will cause the same deception, and seem multiplied without end. The senses strongly affected in some one manner, cannot quickly change their tenor, or adapt themselves to other things; but they continue in their old channel until the strength of the first mover decays. This is the reason of an appearance very frequent in madmen; that they remain whole days and nights, sometimes whole years, in the constant repetition of some remark, some complaint, or song; which having struck powerfully on their disordered imagination, in the beginning of their frenzy, every repetition reinforces it with new strength; and the hurry of their spirits, unrestrained by the curb of reason, continues it to the end of their lives.

## SECTION II. INFINITY
## IN PLEASING OBJECTS

Infinity, though of another kind, causes much of our pleasure in agreeable, as well as of our delight in sublime images. The spring is the pleasantest of the seasons; and the young of most animals, though far from being completely fashioned, afford a more agreeable sensation than the full grown; because the imagination is entertained with the promise of something more, and does not acquiesce in the present object of the sense. In unfinished sketches of drawing, I have often seen something which pleased me beyond the best finishing; and this I believe proceeds from the cause I have just now assigned.

## SECTION 12. DIFFICULTY

Another source of greatness is *Difficulty*. When any work seems to have required immense force and labour to effect it, the idea is grand. Stonehenge, neither for disposition nor ornament, has any thing admirable; but those huge rude masses of stone, set on end, and piled each on other, turn the mind on the immense force necessary for such a work. Nay the rudeness of the work increases this cause of grandeur, as it excludes the idea of art, and contrivance; for dexterity produces another sort of effect which is different enough from this.

## SECTION 13. MAGNIFICENCE

*Magnificence* is likewise a source of the sublime. A great profusion of things which are splendid or valuable in themselves, is *magnificent*. The starry heaven, though it occurs so very frequently to our view, never fails to excite an idea of grandeur. This cannot be owing to any thing in the stars themselves, separately considered. The number is certainly the cause. The apparent disorder augments the grandeur, for the appearance of care is highly contrary to our ideas of magnificence. Besides, the stars lie in such apparent confusion as makes it impossible on ordinary occasions to reckon them. This gives them the advantage of a sort of infinity. In works of art, this kind of grandeur, which consists in multitude, is to be very cautiously admitted. . . . There are, however, a sort of fireworks, and some other things, that in this way succeed well, and are truly grand. There are also many descriptions in the poets and orators which owe their sublimity to a richness and profusion of images, in which the mind is so dazzled as to make it impossible to attend to that exact coherence and agreement of the allusions, which we should require on every other occasion. . . .

## SECTION 14. LIGHT

Having considered extension, so far as it is capable of raising ideas of greatness; *colour* comes next under consideration. All colours depend on *light*. Light therefore ought previously to be examined, and with it, its opposite, darkness. With regard to light; to make it a cause capable of producing the sublime, it must be attended with some circumstances, besides its bare faculty of shewing other objects. Mere light is too common a thing to make a strong impression on the mind, and without a strong impression nothing can be sublime. But such a light as that of the sun, immediately exerted on the eye, as it overpowers the sense, is a very great idea. Light of an inferior strength to this, if it moves with great celerity, has the same power; for lightning is certainly productive of grandeur, which it owes chiefly to the extreme velocity of its motion. A quick transition from light to darkness, or from darkness to light, has yet a greater effect. But darkness is more productive of sublime ideas than light.

## SECTION 16. COLOUR CONSIDERED AS PRODUCTIVE OF THE SUBLIME

Among colours, such as are soft, or cheerful, (except perhaps a strong red which is cheerful) are unfit to produce grand images. An immense mountain covered with a shining green turf, is nothing in this respect, to one dark and gloomy; the cloudy sky is more grand than the blue; and night more sublime and solemn than day. Therefore in historical painting, a gay or gaudy drapery, can never have a happy effect: and in buildings, when the highest degree of the sublime is intended, the materials and ornaments ought neither to be white, nor green, nor yellow, nor blue, nor of a pale red, nor violet, nor spotted, but of sad and fuscous colours, as black, or brown, or deep purple, and the like. . . .

## SECTION 17. SOUND AND LOUDNESS

The eye is not the only organ of sensation, by which a sublime passion may be produced. Sounds have a great power in these as in most other passions. I do not mean words, because words do not affect simply by their sounds, but by means altogether different. Excessive loudness alone is sufficient to overpower the soul, to suspend its action, and to fill it with terror. The noise of vast cataracts, raging storms, thunder, or artillery, awakes a great and aweful sensation in the mind, though we can observe no nicety or artifice in those sorts of music. The shouting of multitudes has a similar effect; and by the sole strength of the sound, so amazes and confounds the imagination, that in this staggering, and hurry of the mind, the best established tempers can scarcely forbear being borne down, and joining in the common cry, and common resolution of the crowd.

## SECTION 18. SUDDENNESS

A sudden beginning, or sudden cessation of sound of any considerable force, has the same power. The attention is roused by this; and the faculties driven forward, as it were, on their guard. Whatever either in sights or sounds makes the transition from one extreme to the other easy, causes no terror, and consequently can be no cause of greatness. In every thing sudden and unexpected, we are apt to start; that is, we have a perception of danger, and our nature rouses us to guard against it. It may be observed, that a single sound of some strength, though but of short duration, if repeated after intervals, has a grand effect. Few things are more aweful than the striking of a great clock, when the silence of the night prevents the attention from being too much dissipated. The same may be said of a single stroke on a drum, repeated with pauses; and of the successive firing of cannon at a distance; all the effects mentioned in this section have causes very nearly alike.

## Part 3 [On Beauty]

### SECTION I. OF BEAUTY

It is my design to consider beauty as distinguished from the sublime; and in the course of the enquiry, to examine how far it is consistent with it. But previous to this, we must take a short review of the opinions already entertained of this quality; which I think are hardly to be reduced to any fixed principles; because men are used to talk of beauty in a figurative manner, that is to say, in a manner extremely uncertain, and indeterminate. By beauty I mean, that quality or those qualities in bodies by which they cause love, or some passion similar to it. I confine this definition to the merely sensible qualities of things, for the sake of preserving the utmost simplicity in a subject which must always distract us, whenever we take in those various causes of sympathy which attach us to any persons or things from secondary considerations, and not from the direct force which they have merely on being viewed. I likewise distinguish love, by which I mean that satisfaction which arises to the mind upon contemplating any thing beautiful, of whatsoever nature it may be, from desire or lust; which is an energy of the mind, that hurries us on to the possession of certain objects, that do not affect us as they are beautiful, but by means altogether different. We shall have a strong desire for a woman of no remarkable beauty; whilst the greatest beauty in men, or in other animals, though it causes love, yet excites nothing at all of desire. Which shews that beauty, and the passion caused by beauty, which I call love, is different from desire, though desire may sometimes operate along with it; but it is to this latter that we must attribute those violent and tempestuous passions, and the consequent emotions of the body which attend what is called love in some of its ordinary acceptations, and not to the effects of beauty merely as it is such.

## SECTION 2. PROPORTION NOT THE CAUSE OF BEAUTY IN VEGETABLES

Beauty hath usually been said to consist in certain proportions of parts. On considering the matter, I have great reason to doubt, whether beauty be at all an idea belonging to proportion. Proportion relates almost wholly to convenience, as every idea of order seems to do; and it must therefore be considered as a creature of the understanding, rather than a primary cause acting on the senses and imagination. It is not by the force of long attention and enquiry that we find any object to be beautiful; beauty demands no assistance from our reasoning; even the will is unconcerned; the appearance of beauty as effectually causes some degree of love in us, as the application of ice or fire produces the ideas of heat or cold. . . .

## SECTION 8. THE RECAPITULATION

On the whole; if such parts in human bodies as are found proportioned, were likewise constantly found beautiful, as they certainly are not; or if they were so situated, as that a pleasure might flow from the comparison, which they seldom are; or if any assignable proportions were found, either in plants or animals, which were always attended with beauty, which never was the case; or if, where parts were well adapted to their purposes, they were constantly beautiful, and when no use appeared, there was no beauty, which is contrary to all experience; we might conclude, that beauty consisted in proportion or utility. But since, in all respects, the case is quite otherwise; we may be satisfied, that beauty does not depend on these, let it owe its origin to what else it will.

## SECTION 9. PERFECTION NOT THE CAUSE OF BEAUTY

There is another notion current, pretty closely allied to the former; that *Perfection* is the constituent cause of beauty. This, opinion has been made to extend much further than to sensible objects. But in these, so far is perfection, considered as such, from being the cause of beauty; that this quality, where it is highest in the female sex, almost always carries with it an idea of weakness and imperfection. Women are very sensible of this; for which reason, they learn to lisp, to totter in their walk, to counterfeit weakness, and even sickness. In all this, they are guided by nature. Beauty in distress is much the most affecting beauty. Blushing has little less power; and modesty in general, which is a tacit allowance of imperfection, is itself considered as an amiable quality, and certainly heightens every other that

is so. I know, it is in every body's mouth, that we ought to love perfection. This is to me a sufficient proof, that it is not the proper object of love. Who ever said, we *ought* to love a fine woman, or even any of these beautiful animals, which please us? Here to be affected, there is no need of the concurrence of our will.

## SECTION 12. THE REAL CAUSE OF BEAUTY

Having endeavoured to show what beauty is not, it remains that we should examine, at least with equal attention, in what it really consists. Beauty is a thing much too affecting not to depend upon some positive qualities. And, since it is no creature of our reason, since it strikes us without any reference to use, and even where no use at all can be discerned, since the order and method of nature is generally very different from our measures and proportions, we must conclude that beauty is, for the greater part, some quality in bodies, acting mechanically upon the human mind by the intervention of the senses. We ought therefore to consider attentively in what manner those sensible qualities are disposed, in such things as by experience we find beautiful, or which excite in us the passion of love, or some correspondent affection.

## SECTION 13. BEAUTIFUL OBJECTS SMALL

The most obvious point that presents itself to us in examining any object, is its extent or quantity. And what degree of extent prevails in bodies, that are held beautiful, may be gathered from the usual manner of expression concerning it. I am told that in most languages, the objects of love are spoken of under diminutive epithets. It is so in all the languages of which I have any knowledge. . . . Anciently in the English language the diminishing *ling* was added to the names of persons and things that were the objects of love. Some we retain still, as *darling* (or little dear) and a few others. But to this day in ordinary conversation, it is usual to add the endearing name of *little* to every thing we love; the French and Italians make use of these affectionate diminutives even more than we. In the animal creation, out of our own species, it is the small we are inclined to be fond of; little birds, and some of the smaller kinds of beasts. A great beautiful thing, is a manner of expression scarcely ever used; but that of a great ugly thing, is very common. There is a wide difference between admiration and love. The sublime, which is the cause of the former, always dwells on great objects, and terrible; the latter on small ones, and pleasing; we submit to what we admire, but we love what submits to us; in one case we are forced, in the other we are flattered into compliance. In short, the ideas of the sublime and the beautiful stand on foundations so different, that it is hard, I had almost said impossible, to think of reconciling them in the same subject, without considerably lessening the effect of the one or the other upon the passions. So that attending to their quantity, beautiful objects are comparatively small.

## SECTION 14. SMOOTHNESS

The next property constantly observable in such objects is *Smoothness:* a quality so essential to beauty, that I do not now recollect any thing beautiful that is not smooth. In trees and flowers, smooth leaves are beautiful; smooth slopes of earth in gardens; smooth streams in the landscape; smooth coats of birds and beasts in animal beauties; in fine women, smooth skins; and in several sorts of ornamental furniture, smooth and polished surfaces. A very considerable part of the effect of beauty is owing to this quality; indeed the most considerable. For take any beautiful object, and give it a broken and rugged surface, and however well formed it may be in other respects, it pleases no longer. Whereas let it want ever so many of the other constituents, if it wants not this, it becomes more pleasing than almost all the others without it. This seems to me so evident, that I am a good deal surprised, that none who have handled the subject have made any mention of the quality of smoothness in the enumeration of those that go to the forming of

beauty. For indeed any ruggedness, any sudden projection, any sharp angle, is in the highest degree contrary to that idea.

## SECTION 15. GRADUAL VARIATION

But as perfectly beautiful bodies are not composed of angular parts, so their parts never continue long in the same right line. They vary their direction every moment, and they change under the eye by a deviation continually carrying on, but for whose beginning or end you will find it difficult to ascertain a point. The view of a beautiful bird will illustrate this observation. Here we see the head increasing insensibly to the middle, from whence it lessens gradually until it mixes with the neck; the neck loses itself in a larger swell, which continues to the middle of the body, when the whole decreases again to the tail; the tail takes a new direction; but it soon varies its new course; it blends again with the other parts; and the line is perpetually changing, above, below, upon every side. In this description I have before me the idea of a dove; it agrees very well with most of the conditions of beauty. It is smooth and downy; its parts are (to use that expression) melted into one another; you are presented with no sudden protuberance through the whole, and yet the whole is continually changing. Observe that part of a beautiful woman where she is perhaps the most beautiful, about the neck and breasts; the smoothness; the softness; the easy and insensible swell; the variety of the surface, which is never for the smallest space the same; the deceitful maze, through which the unsteady eye slides giddily, without knowing where to fix, or whither it is carried. Is not this a demonstration of that change of surface continual and yet hardly perceptible at any point which forms one of the great constituents of beauty? . . .

## SECTION 16. DELICACY

An air of robustness and strength is very prejudicial to beauty. An appearance of *delicacy,* and even of fragility, is almost essential to it. Whoever examines the vegetable or animal creation, will find this observation to be founded in nature. It is not the oak, the ash, or the elm, or any of the robust trees of the forest, which we consider as beautiful; they are awful and majestic; they inspire a sort of reverence. It is the delicate myrtle, it is the orange, it is the almond, it is the jessamine, it is the vine, which we look on as vegetable beauties.[1] It is the flowery species, so remarkable for its weakness and momentary duration, that gives us the liveliest idea of beauty, and elegance . . . I need here say little of the fair sex, where I believe the point will be easily allowed me. The beauty of women is considerably owing to their weakness, or delicacy, and is even enhanced by their timidity, a quality of mind analogous to it. . . .

### SECTION 17. BEAUTY IN COLOUR

As to the colours usually found in beautiful bodies; it may be somewhat difficult to ascertain them, because in the several parts of nature, there is an infinite variety. However, even in this variety, we may mark out something on which to settle. First, the colours of beautiful bodies must not be dusky or muddy, but clean and fair. Secondly, they must not be of the strongest kind. Those which seem most appropriated to beauty, are the milder of every sort; light greens; soft blues; weak whites; pink reds; and violets. Thirdly, if the colours be strong and vivid, they are always diversified, and the object is never of one strong colour; there are almost always such a number of them (as in variegated flowers) that the strength and glare of each is considerably abated. In a fine complexion, there is not only some variety in the colouring, but the colours, neither the red nor the white are strong and glaring. Besides, they are mixed in such a manner, and with such gradations, that it is impossible to fix the bounds. On the same principle it is, that the dubious colour in the necks and tails of peacocks, and about the heads of drakes, is so very agreeable. In reality, the beauty both of shape

and colouring are as nearly related, as we can well suppose it possible for things of such different natures to be.

### SECTION 18. RECAPITULATION

On the whole, the qualities of beauty, as they are merely sensible qualities, are the following. First, to be comparatively small. Secondly, to be smooth. Thirdly, to have a variety in the direction of the parts; but fourthly, to have those parts not angular, but melted as it were into each other. Fifthly, to be of a delicate frame, without any remarkable appearance of strength. Sixthly, to have its colours clear and bright; but not very strong and glaring. Seventhly, or if it should have any glaring colour, to have it diversified with others. These are, I believe, the properties on which beauty depends; properties that operate by nature, and are less liable to be altered by caprice, or confounded by a diversity of tastes, than any other.

### SECTION 27. THE SUBLIME AND BEAUTIFUL COMPARED

On closing this general view of beauty, it naturally occurs, that we should compare it with the sublime; and in this comparison there appears a remarkable contrast. For sublime objects are vast in their dimensions, beautiful ones comparatively small; beauty should be smooth, and polished; the great, rugged arid, negligent; beauty should shun the right line, yet deviate from it insensibly; the great in many cases loves the right line, arid when it deviates, it often makes a strong deviation; beauty should not be obscure; the great ought to be dark and gloomy; beauty should be light and delicate; the great ought to be solid, and even massive. They are indeed ideas of a very different nature, one being founded on pain, the other on pleasure; and however they may vary afterwards from the direct nature of their causes, yet these causes keep up an eternal distinction between them, a distinction never to be forgotten by any whose business it is to affect the passions. . . .

---

[1] "Jessamine" is an old name for jasmine, a shrub with fragrant flowers.

# THE ROMANTIC VIEW OF ART

Romanticism was the dominant movement in literature, music, painting, and sculpture in the Western world from the 1790s until roughly the 1850s, although its presence lingered on long afterward in a variety of fields. Its earliest manifestations were in Britain in the works of writers such as William Blake, Robert Burns, William Wordsworth, and Samuel Taylor Coleridge, and in Germany in the youthful work of Johann Wolfgang Goethe and Friedrich Schiller. Romanticism was more popular in literature and music than in painting and other visual media, though it found representatives in all fields of art.

As we've seen in the introduction to this chapter, the Romantics saw art as having three characteristics:

- It is imaginative. They saw it as based on strong feelings and the imagination, not on reason. Artists are not fact-grubbing scientists or calculating mathematicians and logicians: They are spontaneous creatures of passion.
- It is subjective. Art is the product of creative genius that reaches deep into the unconscious mind and thus into our primal nature to produce something new. This dive into the unconscious sometimes employed dreams, hallucinations, and drug-induced reveries to achieve its effect. This was opposed to the objective representation of nature aimed at by classical and neoclassical artists.
- It is natural. The Romantics sought a direct communion with nature in their work, nature seen in a rich, organic sense, not in the cold mechanistic way that Galileo, Bacon, and Newton saw it. Romantic literature was natural in another sense: It attempted to approximate the language of common folk, not the artificial language of the courts and of high culture.

Romantic literature illustrates this triple view of art in a variety of ways.

William Blake (1757–1827), William Wordsworth (1770–1850), and Samuel Taylor Coleridge (1772–1834) were the first generation of English Romantic poets. Blake was known not only for his poetry, which was highly allegorical (he invented his own collection of mythological characters), but also for his work as a printer, engraver, and visionary painter. His most famous collection of poetry was his early *Songs of Innocence* (1789). His poem *The Tyger* connects the great striped beast to its divine maker, thus sanctifying its wildness. It illustrates the notion of the sublime that we've already discussed in the section on Edmund Burke. Blake's cat is a fearsome beast that no mortal hand or mortal eye could frame or produce, inspiring awe and terror. Blake's poem pictures nature as an unruly cauldron that the poetic imagination uses to forge its products.

His *Jerusalem,* later to become a working-class anthem in England, evokes the divine imprint on England's "green and pleasant lands." It is full of lively images from the war between the principles of calculation and nature—these lands under threat from dark satanic mills (which could refer to either the new factories being built in England or to the mills of the Enlightenment mind, churning out mathematical calculations); the holy Lamb of God; arrows of desire; chariots of fire. Blake sees the face of God in the appearances of nature, deifying it through his subjective poetic imagination.

Our major author in this section is William Wordsworth. He was born in Cockermouth, in Cumbria. He attended St. John's College at Cambridge, receiving his degree in 1791. As a youth Wordsworth had a love of nature and wandering. He went on a walking tour of France and Switzerland in the summer of 1790, an auspicious time to choose to go on such a trip, for he encountered the tumults of the early phase of the French Revolution up close. He supported the revolutionaries at first, though in middle age came to recant his radical politics.

While in France he had a love affair with Annette Vallon. The couple had a daughter, Caroline, in 1792, though they never married. From 1795 on Wordsworth lived with his sister, Dorothy, in various places in rural England. Dorothy was Wordsworth's helpmate and confidante. In 1795 he met Coleridge, and three years later they published the groundbreaking *Lyrical Ballads,* a collection of Wordsworth's shorter poems combined with Coleridge's longer piece *The Rime of the Ancyent Marinere.* This collection heralded the beginning of Romantic poetry in England.

In 1798 and 1799 Wordsworth, Coleridge, and Dorothy Wordsworth visited Germany, returning to England to settle for a few years in Dove Cottage at Grasmere, Westmorland. Wordsworth, Coleridge, and Robert Southey all lived in the Lake District at this time, so they became known as the Lake Poets. In 1802 Wordsworth married Mary Hutchinson.

The years between 1793 and 1807 were his most vital period poetically. During this time Wordsworth led the charge of the English Romantic poets against their classicist predecessors. At the end of this period he published *Poems in Two Volumes,* which collected his best work from the 1798 to 1807 period. He worked on his book-length autobiographical poem, *The Prelude,* throughout his life, which was published by his wife three months after he died in 1850.

In *The Tables Turned* from *Lyrical Ballads,* Wordsworth insists that we let nature be our teacher and turn off our rational faculties to hear the sweet music of woodland birds. His argument is simple enough: Our intellect murders the beauty of nature by imposing rational forms on it. This is the polar opposite of Plato's view of the connection between art, nature, and the human spirit.

In *Ode: Intimations of Immortality from Recollections of Childhood* (1807) Wordsworth expands on this notion with a picture of the simple piety we feel for the earth in its youth, as seen by a child whose vision of nature has not yet been clouded by cold reason. Wordsworth gives us snapshots of the many splendors of nature—the shimmering moon, lambs grazing, fragrant flowers, a roaring waterfall. He asks his modern urban reader, "Whither is fled the visionary gleam? / Where is it now, the glory and the dream?" The disappearance of the visionary dream of nature is no doubt a poke at classical artists and poets, who tried to rationalize and sanitize nature. For Wordsworth nature is eternally young, whereas the gray truths of reason are favored by those handicapped by "palsied Age."

Wordsworth's most important statement of the aesthetics of Romanticism came in the 1800 Preface to the *Lyrical Ballads.* This Preface was in effect Romanticism's marching orders in the century that followed. First of all, Wordsworth wanted to restore poetry to a simpler language, to speak in "language really used by men," to defeat the artificiality of classicism. He featured "incidents and situations from common life" in his poems, scenes with peddlers, peasants, and village girls, not epic tales of Greek gods and goddesses prancing through the woods, or of Christian saints struggling with Satan and his devilish minions. His art was natural, not artificial.

Poetry was to involve a direct sensory experience of life. Good poetry is a "spontaneous overflow of powerful feelings," where we bring together ideas in "a state of excitement." Poetry is about strong feelings, passions, and the imagination, not reason or order. Yet he also saw it as "emotion recollected in tranquillity," when we look back at our powerful feelings and transform these into verse. And the poet was just an ordinary person who happened to have a more lively sensibility than his fellows.

We've already encountered Percy Bysshe Shelley in Chapter 3 regarding the Romantic theory of the self. We return to his 1821 essay *A Defense of Poetry* here, reading a somewhat different section than featured in Chapter 3. Shelley sharply distinguishes Reason, the faculty that analyzes things and discerns their differences, from the Imagination, the faculty of synthesis, which gives things color, discovering their value and their similarities. The former is the shadow, the latter the substance of our lives. Poetry is the expression of the Imagination and is the foundation of all systems of thought. It is to be especially valued in ages that are full of selfishness and calculation, as Shelley saw his own age.

Shelley was also quite explicit about the nature of the creative act. The creative mind is like a fading coal, anxious to get the last dregs of unconscious insights onto paper before they cool and expire from consciousness. He agreed with Wordsworth that the poet was someone with a delicate sensibility and an enlarged imagination, yet he was more inclined to assign the status of genius to the greatest poets than his predecessor had been.

The poet makes beautiful things immortal and adds beauty to deformed things. For Shelley, art is alchemical—it has the power to transmute the humdrum world of sense into something transcendental. Poetry "redeems from decay the visitations of divinity in man," stripping the veil of familiarity from the world, laying bare the "naked and sleeping beauty" of things. Art is a form of sorcery, not the ordered rational calculation of the classical artist. It is a transformation of nature and human beings by the creative Imagination.

Last, we turn to Thomas de Quincey (1785–1859) for a brief look at the dark side of Romanticism. De Quincey became addicted to opium while at school in Oxford in 1804 and became a daily user of the drug in its liquid form by 1813. He used it at first to enhance his imaginative powers and to inspire his writing, later to relieve the pains of various illnesses.

He befriended Coleridge, Wordsworth, and Southey in 1807, living with them in the Lake District in 1809. De Quincey made his living by writing reviews, stories, and articles for various periodicals, including the *Westmorland Gazette, London Magazine,* and *Blackwood's.* He married Margaret Simpson, with whom he had eight children. From 1828 on he lived in Edinburgh and Glasgow, on the run from creditors during the early 1840s.

De Quincey was a prolific writer but published few books, his career as a journalist getting in the way of his more extended literary efforts. The reading selection includes a brief passage from his most famous work, the autobiographical *Confessions of an English Opium-Eater* (1820). In this passage de Quincey relates an opium dream in which he envisions all sorts of tropical beasts and birds and the gods of ancient Egypt and India dogging his heels. Such imaginative bursts as the crocodiles with cancerous kisses and slimy things slithering through the mud of the Nile riverbank are good examples of how the Romantic artistic vision could descend to sublime excesses, especially when under the influence of hallucinatory narcotics. These excesses are still with us today in the lives of the high priests of popular culture, Hollywood stars and rock musicians, for which we have the Romantics to thank.

# The Tyger

## WILLIAM BLAKE

Tyger! Tyger! burning bright
In the forests of the night,
What immortal hand or eye
Could frame thy fearful symmetry?

In what distant deeps or skies
Burnt the fire of thine eyes?
On what wings dare he aspire?
What the hand dare seize the fire?

And what shoulder, & what art,
Could twist the sinews of thy heart?
And when thy heart began to beat,
What dread hand? & what dread feet?

What the hammer? what the chain?
In what furnace was thy brain?
What the anvil? what dread grasp
Dare its deadly terrors clasp?

When the stars threw down their spears,
And water'd heaven with their tears,
Did he smile his work to see?
Did he who made the Lamb make thee?

Tyger! Tyger! burning bright
In the forests of the night,
What immortal hand or eye,
Could frame thy fearful symmetry?

SOURCE: William Blake, *Songs of Innocence and of Experience* (London, 1794).

# And Did Those Feet in Ancient Time (Jerusalem)

## WILLIAM BLAKE

And did those feet in ancient time
Walk upon England's mountains green?
And was the holy Lamb of God
On England's pleasant pastures seen?

And did the Countenance Divine
Shine forth upon our clouded hills?
And was Jerusalem builded here
Among these dark Satanic Mills?

Bring me my Bow of burning gold:
Bring me my Arrows of desire:
Bring me my Spear: O clouds unfold!
Bring me my Chariot of fire.
I will not cease from Mental Fight,
Nor shall my Sword sleep in my hand
Till we have built Jerusalem
In England's green & pleasant Land.

SOURCE: William Blake, Preface to *Milton* (1808).

# The Tables Turned

## WILLIAM WORDSWORTH

Up! Up! my friend, and clear your looks,
Why all this toil and trouble?
Up! up! my friend, and quit your books,
Or surely you'll grow double.

The sun above the mountain's head,
A freshening lustre mellow,
Through all the long green fields has spread,
His first sweet evening yellow.

Books! 'tis a dull and endless strife,
Come, hear the woodland linnet,
How sweet his music; on my life
There's more of wisdom in it.

And hark! how blithe the throstle sings!
And he is no mean preacher;
Come forth into the light of things,
Let Nature be your teacher.

She has a world of ready wealth,
Our hearts and minds to bless—
Spontaneous wisdom breathed by health,
Truth breathed by chearfulness.

One impulse from a vernal wood
May teach you more of man;
Of moral evil and of good,
Than all the sages can.

Sweet is the lore which nature brings;
Our meddling intellect
Mis-shapes the beauteous forms of things;
—We murder to dissect.

Enough of science and of art;
Close up these barren leaves;
Come forth, and bring with you a heart
That watches and receives.

SOURCE: William Wordsworth, *Lyrical Ballads* (London, 1798).

# Ode: Intimations of Immortality from Recollections of Early Childhood

## WILLIAM WORDSWORTH

The Child is the Father of the Man;
And I could wish my days to be
Bound each to each by natural piety.

### 1

There was a time when meadow, grove, and
    stream,
The earth, and every common sight,
        To me did seem
        Apparelled in celestial light,
The glory and the freshness of a dream.

SOURCE: William Wordsworth, *Poems in Two Volumes* (1807).

It is not now as it hath been of yore;—
        Turn whereso'er I may,
            By night or day,
The things which I have seen I now can see
    no more.

### 2

        The Rainbow comes and goes,
        And lovely is the Rose,
        The Moon doth with delight
Look round her when the heavens are bare,

Waters on a starry night
Are beautiful and fair;
The sunshine is a glorious birth;
But yet I know, where'er I go,
That there hath past away a glory from the
earth.

### 3

Now, while the birds thus sing a joyous song,
And while the young lambs bound
As to the tabor's sound,
To me alone there came a thought of grief:
A timely utterance gave that thought relief,
And I again am strong:
The cataracts blow their trumpets from the
steep;
No more shall grief of mine the season wrong;
I hear the Echoes through the mountains
throng,
The Winds come to me from the fields of
sleep,
And all the earth is gay;
Land and sea
Give themselves up to jollity,
And with the heart of May
Doth every Beast keep holiday;—
Thou Child of Joy,
Shout round me, let me hear thy shouts,
thou happy Shepherd-boy!

### 4

Ye blessèd Creatures, I have heard the call
Ye to each other make; I see
The heavens laugh with you in jubilee;
My heart is at your festival,
My head hath its coronal,
The fulness of your bliss, I feel—I feel it all.
O evil day! if I were sullen
While Earth herself is adorning,
This sweet May-morning,
And the Children are culling
On every side,
In a thousand valleys far and wide,
Fresh flowers; while the sun shines
warm,
And the Babe leaps up on his Mother's
arm:—

I hear, I hear, with joy I hear!
—But there's a Tree, of many, one,
A single Field which I have looked upon,
Both of them speak of something that is
gone:
The Pansy at my feet
Doth the same tale repeat:
Whither is fled the visionary gleam?
Where is it now, the glory and the dream?

### 5

Our birth is but a sleep and a forgetting:
The Soul that rises with us, our life's Star,
Hath had elsewhere its setting,
And cometh from afar:
Not in entire forgetfulness,
And not in utter nakedness,
But trailing clouds of glory do we come
From God, who is our home:
Heaven lies about us in our infancy!
Shades of the prison-house begin to close
Upon the growing Boy,
But He beholds the light, and whence it
flows,
He sees it in his joy;
The Youth, who daily farther from the east
Must travel, still is Nature's Priest,
And by the vision splendid
Is on his way attended;
At length the Man perceives it die away,
And fade into the light of the common day.

### 6

Earth fills her lap with pleasures of her own;
Yearnings she hath in her own natural kind,
And, even with something of a Mother's
mind,
And no unworthy aim,
The homely Nurse doth all she can
To make her Foster-child, her Inmate Man,
Forget the glories he hath known,
And that imperial palace whence he came.

### 7

Behold the Child among his new-born
blisses,
A six year's Darling of a pigmy size!

See, where 'mid work of his own hand he lies,
Fretted by sallies of his mother's kisses,
With light upon him from his father's eyes!
See, at his feet, some little plan of chart,
Some fragment from his dream of human life,
Shaped by himself with newly-learned art;
    A wedding or a festival,
    A mourning or a funeral;
      And this hath now his heart,
    And unto this he frames his song.
      Then will he fit his tongue
To dialogues of business, love, or strife;
    But it will not be long
    Ere this be thrown aside,
    And with new joy and pride
The little Actor cons another part;
Filling from time to time his "humorous
    stage"
With all the persons, down to palsied Age,
That Life brings with her in her equipage;
    As if his whole vocation
    Were endless imitation.

### 8

Thou, whose exterior semblance doth belie
    Thy Soul's immensity;
Thou best Philosopher, who yet dost keep
Thy heritage, thou Eye among the blind,
That, deaf and silent, read'st the eternal
    deep,
Haunted for ever by the eternal mind,—
    Mighty Prophet! Seer blest!
    On whom those truths do rest,
Which we are toiling all our lives to find,
In darkness lost, the darkness of the grave,
Thou, over whom thy Immortality
Broods like the Day, a Master o'er a Slave,
A Presence which is not to be put by;
Thou little Child, yet glorious in the might
Of heaven-born freedom on thy being's
    height,
Why with such earnest pains dost thou
    provoke
The years to bring the inevitable yoke,
Thus blindly with thy blessedness at strife?
Full soon thy Soul shall have her earthly
    freight,

And custom lie upon thee with a weight,
Heavy as frost, and deep almost as life!

### 9

    O joy! that in our embers
    Is something that doth live,
    That nature yet remembers
    What was so fugitive!
The thought of our past years in me doth
    breed
Perpetual benediction: not indeed
For that which is most worthy to be blest;
Delight and liberty, the simple creed
Of Childhood, whether busy or at rest,
With new-fledged hope still fluttering in his
    breast:—
    Not for these I raise
    The song of thanks and praise;
    But for those obstinate questionings
    Of sense and outward things,
    Failings from us, vanishings;
    Blank misgivings of a Creature
Moving about in worlds not realised,
High instincts before which our mortal
    Nature
Did tremble like a guilty Thing surprised:
    But for those first affections,
    Those shadowy recollections,
    Which, be they what they may,
Are yet the fountain-light of all our day,
Are yet a master-light of all our seeing;
    Uphold us, cherish, and have power to
    make
Our noisy years seem moments in the being
Of the eternal Silence: truths that wake,
    To perish never:
Which neither listlessness, nor mad
    endeavour,
    Nor Man nor Boy,
Nor all that is at enmity with joy,
Can utterly abolish or destroy!
    Hence in a season of calm weather
    Though inland far we be,
Our Souls have sight of that immortal sea
    Which brought us hither,
    Can in a moment travel thither,
And see the Children sport upon the shore,

And hear the mighty waters rolling
   evermore.

### 10

Then sing, ye Birds, sing, sing a joyous song!
      And let the young Lambs bound
      As to the tabor's sound!
We in thought will join your throng,
      Ye that pipe and ye that play,
      Ye that through your hearts today
      Feel the gladness of May!
What though the radiance which was once
   so bright
Be now for ever taken from my sight,
   Though nothing can bring back the hour
Of splendour in the grass, of glory, in the
   flower;
      We will grieve not, rather find
      Strength in what remains behind;
      In the primal sympathy
      Which having been must ever be;
      In the soothing thoughts that spring
      Out of human suffering;
      In the faith that looks through death,
In years that bring the philosophic mind.

### 11

And O, ye Fountains, Meadows, Hill, and
   Groves,
Forebode not any severing of our loves!
Yet in my heart of hearts I feel your might;
I only have relinquished one delight
To live beneath your more habitual sway.
I love the Brooks which down their chan-
   nels fret,
Even more than when I tripped as they;
The innocent brightness of a new-born Day
      Is lovely yet;
The Clouds that gather round the set-
   ting sun
Do take a sober colouring from an eye
That hath kept watch o'er man's mortality;
Another race hath been, and other palms
   are won.
Thanks to the human heart by which we live,
Thanks to its tenderness, its joys, and fears,
To me the meanest flower that blows
   can give
Thoughts that do often lie too deep for
   tears.

# Preface to the Second Edition of *Lyrical Ballads*

## WILLIAM WORDSWORTH

THE PRINCIPAL OBJECT, then, proposed in these Poems was to choose incidents and situations from common life, and to relate or describe them, throughout, as far as was possible in a selection of language really used by men, and, at the same time, to throw over them a certain colouring of imagination, whereby ordinary things should be presented to the mind in an unusual aspect; and, further, and above all, to make these incidents and situations interesting by tracing in them, truly though not ostentatiously, the pri-mary laws of our nature: chiefly, as far as regards the manner in which we associate ideas in a state of excitement. Humble and rustic life was generally chosen, because, in that condition, the essential passions of the heart find a better soil in which they can attain their maturity, are less under restraint, and speak a plainer and more emphatic language; because in that condition of life our elementary feelings co-exist in a state of greater simplicity, and, consequently, may be more accurately contemplated, and more forcibly commu-

SOURCE: William Wordsworth, *Lyrical Ballads,* 2nd ed. (1800) (edited).

nicated; because the manners of rural life germinate from those elementary feelings, and, from the necessary character of rural occupations, are more easily comprehended, and are more durable; and, lastly, because in that condition the passions of men are incorporated with the beautiful and permanent forms of nature. The language, too, of these men has been adopted (purified indeed from what appear to be its real defects, from all lasting and rational causes of dislike or disgust) because such men hourly communicate with the best objects from which the best part of language is originally derived; and because, from their rank in society and the sameness and narrow circle of their intercourse, being less under the influence of social vanity, they convey their feelings and notions in simple and unelaborated expressions. Accordingly, such a language, arising out of repeated experience and regular feelings, is a more permanent, and a far more philosophical language, than that which is frequently substituted for it by Poets, who think that they are conferring honour upon themselves and their art, in proportion as they separate themselves from the sympathies of men, and indulge in arbitrary and capricious habits of expression, in order to furnish food for fickle tastes, and fickle appetites, of their own creation.

I cannot, however, be insensible to the present outcry against the triviality and meanness, both of thought and language, which some of my contemporaries have occasionally introduced into their metrical compositions; and I acknowledge that this defect, where it exists, is more dishonourable to the Writer's own character than false refinement or arbitrary innovation, though I should contend at the same time, that it is far less pernicious in the sum of its consequences. From such verses the Poems in these volumes will be found distinguished at least by one mark of difference, that each of them has a worthy *purpose*. Not that I always began to write with a distinct purpose formally conceived; but habits of meditation have, I trust, so prompted and regulated my feelings, that my descriptions of such objects as strongly excite those feelings, will be found to carry along with them a *purpose*. If this

opinion be erroneous, I can have little right to the name of a Poet. For all good poetry is the spontaneous overflow of powerful feelings: and though this be true, Poems to which any value can be attached were never produced on any variety of subjects but by a man who, being possessed of more than usual organic sensibility, had also thought long and deeply. For our continued influxes of feeling are modified and directed by our thoughts, which are indeed the representatives of all our past feelings; and, as by contemplating the relation of these general representatives to each other, we discover what is really important to men, so, by the repetition and continuance of this act, our feelings will be connected with important subjects, till at length, if we be originally possessed of much sensibility, such habits of mind will be produced, that, by obeying blindly and mechanically the impulses of those habits, we shall describe objects, and utter sentiments, of such a nature, and in such connexion with each other, that the understanding of the Reader must necessarily be in some degree enlightened, and his affections strengthened and purified.

Having dwelt thus long on the subjects and aim of these Poems, I shall request the Reader's permission to apprise him of a few circumstances relating to their *style*, in order, among other reasons, that he may not censure me for not having performed what I never attempted. The Reader will find that personifications of abstract ideas rarely occur in these volumes; and are utterly rejected, as an ordinary device to elevate the style, and raise it above prose. My purpose was to imitate, and, as far as possible, to adopt the very language of men; and assuredly such personifications do not make any natural or regular part of that language. They are, indeed, a figure of speech occasionally prompted by passion, and I have made use of them as such; but have endeavoured utterly to reject them as a mechanical device of style, or as a family language which Writers in metre seem to lay claim to by prescription. I have wished to keep the Reader in the company of flesh and blood, persuaded that by so doing I shall interest him. Others who pursue a different track will interest him likewise; I do not interfere with their claim, but wish to prefer a claim of my own. There will also be found in these volumes little of what is usually called poetic diction; as much pains has been taken to avoid it as is ordinarily taken to produce it; this has been done for the reason already alleged, to bring my language near to the language of men; and further, because the pleasure which I have proposed to myself to impart, is of a kind very different from that which is supposed by many persons to be the proper object of poetry. Without being culpably particular, I do not know how to give my Reader a more exact notion of the style in which it was my wish and intention to write, than by informing him that I have at all times endeavoured to look steadily at my subject; consequently, there is I hope in these Poems little falsehood of description, and my ideas are expressed in language fitted to their respective importance. Something must have been gained by this practice, as it is friendly to one property of all good poetry, namely, good sense: but it has necessarily cut me off from a large portion of phrases and figures of speech which from father to son have long been regarded as the common inheritance of Poets. I have also thought it expedient to restrict myself still further, having abstained from the use of many expressions, in themselves proper and beautiful, but which have been foolishly repeated by bad Poets, till such feelings of disgust are connected with them as it is scarcely possible by any art of association to overpower. . . .

I have said that poetry is the spontaneous overflow of powerful feelings: it takes its origin from emotion recollected in tranquility: the emotion is contemplated 'till, by a species of reaction, the tranquility gradually disappears, and an emotion, kindred to that which was before the subject of contemplation, is gradually produced, and does itself actually exist in the mind. In this mood successful composition generally begins, and in a mood similar to this it is carried on; but the emotion, of whatever kind, and in whatever degree, from various causes, is qualified by various pleasures, so that in describing, any passions whatsoever, which are voluntarily described, the mind will, upon the whole, be in a state of enjoyment. If Nature be thus cautious to preserve in a state of enjoyment a being so employed, the Poet ought to profit by the lesson held forth to him, and ought especially to take care, that, whatever passions he communicates to his Reader, those passions, if his Reader's mind be sound and vigorous, should always be accompanied with an overbalance of pleasure. . . .

# A Defense of Poetry

## PERCY BYSSHE SHELLEY

ACCORDING TO ONE MODE of regarding those two classes of mental action which are called Reason and Imagination, the former may be considered as mind contemplating the relations borne by one thought to another, however produced; and the latter as mind, acting upon those thoughts so as to colour them with its own light, and composing from them as from elements, other thoughts, each containing within itself the principle of its own integrity. The one is the *to poiein*, or the principle of synthesis and has for its objects those forms which are common to

SOURCE: Percy Bysshe Shelley, *A Defense of Poetry,* ed. Albert S. Cook (1821; Boston: Ginn, 1891), pp. 1–2, 28-42 (edited).

universal nature and existence itself; the other is the *to logizein* or principle of analysis and its action regards the relations of things, simply as relations; considering thoughts, not in their integral unity but as the algebraical representations which conduct to certain general results. Reason is the enumeration of quantities already known; Imagination is the perception of the value of those quantities, both separately and as a whole. Reason respects the differences, and Imagination the similitudes of things. Reason is to Imagination as the instrument to the agent, as the body to the spirit, as the shadow to the substance.

Poetry, in a general sense, may be defined to be "the expression of the Imagination": and Poetry is connate with the origin of man. . . .

The functions of the poetical faculty are two fold: by one it creates new materials of knowledge, and power, and pleasure; by the other it engenders in the mind a desire to reproduce and arrange them according to a certain rhythm and order, which may be called the beautiful and the good. The cultivation of poetry is never more to be desired than at periods when from an excess of the selfish and calculating principle, the accumulation of the materials of external life exceed the quantity of the power of assimilating them to the internal laws of human nature. The body has then become too unwieldy for that which animates it.

Poetry is indeed something divine. It is at once the centre and circumference of knowledge; it is that which comprehends all science, and that to which all science must be referred. It is at the same time the root and the blossom of all other systems of thought: it is that from which all spring, and that which adorns all; and that which if blighted denies the fruit and the seed, and withholds from the barren world the nourishment and the succession of the scions of the tree of life. It is the perfect and consummate surface and bloom of things; it is as the odour and the colour of the rose to the texture of the elements which compose it; as the form and splendour of unfaded beauty, to the secrets of anatomy and corruption. What were Virtue, Love, Patriotism, Friendship—What were the scenery of this beau-

tiful universe which we inhabit—what were our consolations on this side the grave—and what were our aspirations beyond it—if Poetry did not ascend to bring light and fire from those eternal regions where the owl-winged faculty of calculation, dare not ever soar? Poetry is not like reasoning, a power to be exerted according to the determination of the will. A man cannot say, "I will compose poetry." The greatest poet even cannot say it: for the mind in creation is as a fading coal which some invisible influence, like an inconstant wind, awakens to transitory brightness; this power arises from within, like the colour of a flower which fades and changes as it is developed, and the conscious portions of our natures are unprophetic either of its approach or its departure. . . .

Poetry is the record of the happiest and best moments of the happiest and best minds. We are aware of evanescent visitations of thought and feeling sometimes associated with place or person, sometimes regarding our own mind alone, and always arising unforseen and departing unbidden; but elevating and delightful beyond all expression: so that even in the desire and the regret they leave there cannot but be pleasure, participating as it does in the nature of its object. It is as it were the interpenetration of a diviner nature through our own, but its footsteps are like those of a wind over the sea, which the coming calm erases, and whose traces remain only as on the wrinkled sand which paves it. These and corresponding conditions of being are experienced principally by those of the most delicate sensibility and the most enlarged imagination. And the state of mind produced by them is at war with every base desire. The enthusiasm of virtue, love, patriotism, and friendship is essentially linked with such emotions; and whilst they last, self appears as what it is, an atom to an Universe. Poets are not only subject to these experiences as spirits of the most refined organization, but they can colour all that they combine with the evanescent hues of this etherial world; a word, a trait in the representation of a scene or a passion will touch the enchanted chord, and reanimate in those who have ever experienced these emotions the sleeping, the cold, the buried image of the past. Poetry thus makes immortal all that is best and most beautiful in the world; it arrests the vanishing apparitions which haunt the interlunations of life; and veiling them, or in language or in form, sends them forth among mankind bearing sweet news of kindred joy to those with whom their sisters abide—abide because there is no portal of expression from the caverns of the spirit which they inhabit into the universe of things. Poetry redeems from decay the visitations of the divinity in man.

Poetry turns all things to loveliness: it exalts the beauty of that which is most beautiful, and it adds beauty to that which is most deformed: it marries exultation and horror; grief and pleasure, eternity and change; it subdues to union under its light yoke all irreconcilable things. It transmutes all that it touches, and every form moving within the radiance of its presence is changed by wondrous sympathy to an incarnation of the spirit which it breathes: its secret alchemy turns to potable gold the poisonous waters which flow from death through life; it strips the veil of familiarity from the world, and lays bare the naked and sleeping beauty which is the spirit of its forms.

# Opium Dream

## THOMAS DE QUINCEY

UNDER THE CONNECTING FEELING of tropical heat and vertical sun-lights, I brought together all creatures, birds, beasts, reptiles, all trees and plants, usages and appearances, that are found in all tropical regions, and assembled them together in China or Indostan. From kindred feelings, I soon brought Egypt and all her gods under the same law. I was stared at, hooted at, grinned at, chattered at, by monkeys, by paroquets, by cockatoos. I ran into pagodas: and was fixed, for centuries, at the summit, or in secret rooms; I was the idol; I was the priest; I was worshipped; I was sacrificed. I fled from the wrath of Brama through all the forests of Asia: Vishnu bated me: Seeva laid in wait for me. I came suddenly upon Isis and Osiris: I had done a deed, they said, which the ibis and the crocodile trembled at. I was buried, for a thousand years, in stone coffins, with mummies and sphynxes, in narrow chambers at the heart of the eternal pyramids. I was kissed, with cancerous kisses, by crocodiles; and laid, confounded with all unutterable slimy things, amongst reeds and Nilotic mud.

SOURCE: Thomas de Quincey, *Confessions of an English Opium-Eater* (1821).

# TOLSTOY ON THE RELIGIOUS FUNCTION OF ART

The Russian novelist Leo Tolstoy (1828–1910) is better known for his literature than his philosophy. His most famous novel, *War and Peace* (1869), an epic story set in Russia during Napoleon's invasion of the country in 1812, was certainly influenced by his own experiences as a soldier in the Crimean War. *Anna Karenina* (1877) and *The Death of Ivan Ilich* (1886) are among his other well-known novels. They are wonderfully written, rich stories. In 1884, in light of his religious experience, Tolstoy wrote *A Confession*. The reading selection that follows comes from his 1898 book, *What Is Art?*

Tolstoy's various writings are often understood as representing different stages in his personal development. His novels, written in the earlier period of his life, stand in contrast to his later work, a phase dominated by religious themes and the implications they held for day-to-day living. Although his adult life spanned the latter half of the nineteenth century, in many respects his ideas from this period were quite ahead of their time. He was a vegetarian, and his views on the wrongness of war and the value of passive resistance came to influence no less a luminary than Mahatma Gandhi.

Along with holding these progressive views, Tolstoy made his own alterations to the Bible. The Gospels, the first four books of the New Testament, record the life and sayings of Christ. Believing he could distinguish between passages that were the core of the teachings of Christ and those that were later added by the Church, he abridged the Gospels. Though this wasn't the first time another edition of the Gospels was attempted, given the still strongly conservative Christian feelings that dominated his day and age, it was certainly a bold undertaking on his part. Given his wide-ranging views, it comes as no surprise that he was a man who wasn't afraid of controversy. This sense of controversy isn't absent from his views on aesthetics, our primary interest in this chapter.

It is obvious that people disagree over what is and what is not good art. We therefore feel compelled to try to show how our judgment of what makes good art is justified, to define just what "good art" is. There are two basic approaches we can take in this regard. Our first is to find out what most people accept as good art and to then come up with a general definition that would include all these pieces of art. Our second option works the other way around: We first come up with a definition of what constitutes good art in general, then use it to determine which individual pieces of art are good and which are not.

Tolstoy mentions these two ways of proceeding, clearly choosing the second option. The first option, he believes, is too elitist. The upper class, having the time and leisure to enjoy the arts, is not necessarily in the best position to decide what is good art. Moreover, this approach would be self-defeating, because even the artistic preferences of the upper classes frequently change. Good art becomes bad art, and vice versa, every time cultural leaders change their tastes.

So what is Tolstoy's definition? Tolstoy teases it out by using an analogy to food. "What," he asks, "is the aim and purpose of food?" Though some would say its purpose is the pleasure we get from eating, Tolstoy considers this view to be quite superficial and ignoble. The primary importance of eating is nourishment rather than pleasure. We eat food to nourish our body.

The same goes for art. It is wrong to think the aim of art is the pleasure we feel in contemplating beautiful things. In both cases, Tolstoy believes, the *pleasure* we receive from the particular activity cannot be its true aim or purpose. The primary importance of art lies in the ability of artists to communicate their higher feelings to their audience, to join them together in a moral and spiritual communion. It places artists into a radical relationship with those who receive their artistic impressions.

Tolstoy goes on to talk about "infectiousness." If artists are able to infect their audience with "the condition of the author's soul" through their work, then this is a sure sign they have produced good art. In fact, as Tolstoy himself says, "The stronger the infection the better is the art." The indispensable condition going along with this infectiousness is the artist's *sincerity.* The deeper the sincerity on the part of the artist, Tolstoy believes, the more profoundly the art will affect the audience. And the more the audience is affected, the greater the art is.

But here's the clincher. Tolstoy believes the art that best inculcates human connectedness and compassion between people is Christian art: "The flowing from love of God and man." In other words, good art promotes the sort of religious and moral feelings that give our lives a deeper meaning. Thus, for him aesthetic values are mixed up with religious truths, which he saw as the highest truths human beings could know.

Tolstoy was certainly thorough in his discussion of aesthetics. He wanted to propose a general definition of good art before going out into the world and finding such art. It won't work to define what good art is *after the fact*—after we have grouped together all works of art we have decided to be good.

The one point that may appear his weakest, however, is his belief that Christian art is the highest form of art. For most of us today, religion doesn't have the same impact as it would have had on people in Tolstoy's day. Yet given your own religious beliefs, you may think that this is the very strength of Tolstoy's position.

# What Is Art?

## LEO TOLSTOY

### *Chapter 4*

All the existing aesthetic standards are built on this plan. Instead of giving a definition of true art and then deciding what is and what is not good art by judging whether a work conforms or does not conform to this definition, a certain class of works which for some reason pleases a certain circle of people is accepted as being art, and a definition of art is then devised to cover all these productions. . . . No matter what insanities appear in art, when once they find acceptance among the upper classes of our society a theory is quickly invented to explain and sanction them; just as if there had never been periods in history when certain special circles of people recognized and approved false, deformed, and insensate, art which subsequently left no trace and has been utterly forgotten. And to what lengths the insanity and deformity of art may go, especially when as in our days it knows that it is considered infallible, may be seen by what is being done in the art of our circle today.

So that the theory of art founded on beauty, expounded by aesthetics and in dim outline professed by the public, is nothing but the setting up as good of that which has pleased and pleases us, i.e., pleases a certain class of people.

In order to define any human activity, it is necessary to understand its sense and importance; and in order to do this it is primarily necessary to examine that activity in itself, in its dependence on its causes and in connection with its effects, and not merely in relation to the pleasure we can get from it.

SOURCE: Leo Tolstoy, *What Is Art? An Essay on Art*, trans. Aylmer Maude (1899; New York: Oxford University Press, 1963), pp. 115–118, 120–123, 227–230, and 238–242 (edited, with some spelling and punctuation modernized). By permission of Oxford University Press.

If we say that the aim of any activity is merely our pleasure and define it solely by that pleasure, our definition will evidently be a false one. But this is precisely what has occurred in the efforts to define art. Now if we consider the food question it will not occur to anyone to affirm that the importance of food consists in the pleasure we receive when eating it. Everybody understands that the satisfaction of our taste cannot serve as a basis for our definition of the merits of food, and that we have therefore no right to presuppose that dinners with cayenne pepper, Limburg cheese, alcohol, and so on, to which we are accustomed and which please us, form the very best human food.

In the same way beauty, or that which pleases us, can in no sense serve as a basis for the definition of art; nor can a series of objects which afford us pleasure serve as the model of what art should be.

To see the aim and purpose of art in the pleasure we get from it is like assuming (as is done by people of the lowest moral development, e.g., by savages) that the purpose and aim of food is the pleasure derived when consuming it.

Just as people who conceive the aim and purpose of food to be pleasure cannot recognize the real meaning of eating, so people who consider the aim of art to be pleasure cannot realize its true meaning and purpose, because they attribute to an activity the meaning of which lies in its connection with the other phenomena of life, the false and exceptional aim of pleasure. People come to understand that the meaning of eating lies in the nourishment of the body, only when they cease to consider that the object of that activity is pleasure. And it is the same with regard to art. People will come to understand the meaning of art only when they cease to consider that the aim of that activity is beauty, i.e., pleasure. The acknowledgment of beauty (i.e., of a certain kind of pleasure received from art) as being the aim of art, not only fails to assist us in finding a definition of what art is, but on the contrary by transferring the question into a region quite foreign to art (into metaphysical, psychological, physiological, and even historical, discussions as to why such a production pleases one person and such another displeases or pleases some one else), it renders such definition impossible. And since discussions as to why one man likes pears and another prefers meat do not help towards finding a definition of what is essential in nourishment, so the solution of questions of taste in art (to which the discussions on art involuntarily come) not only does not help to make clear in what this particular human activity which we call art really consists, but renders such elucidation quite impossible until we rid ourselves of a conception which justifies every kind of art at the cost of confusing the whole matter.

To the question, What is this art to which is offered up the labour of millions, the very lives of men, and even morality itself? we have extracted replies from the existing aesthetics which all amount to this: that the aim of art is beauty, that beauty is recognized by the enjoyment it gives, and that artistic enjoyment is a good and important thing, because it *is* enjoyment. In a word, that enjoyment is good because it is enjoyment. Thus what is considered the definition of art is no definition at all, but only a shuffle to justify existing art. Therefore, however strange it may seem to say so, in spite of the mountains of books written about art, no exact definition of art has been constructed. And the reason of this is that the conception of art has been based on the conception of beauty.

## Chapter 5

. . . In order to correctly define art, it is necessary, first of all, to cease to consider it as a means to pleasure, and to consider it as one of the conditions of human life. Viewing it in this way we cannot fail to observe that art is one of the means of intercourse between man and man.

Every work of art causes the receiver to enter into a certain kind of relationship both with him who produced or is producing the art, and with all those who, simultaneously, previously, or subsequently, receive the same artistic impression.

Speech, transmitting the thoughts and experiences of men, serves as a means of union among them, and art serves a similar purpose. The peculiarity of this latter means of intercourse, distinguishing it from intercourse by means of words, consists in this, that whereas by words a man transmits his thoughts to another, by art he transmits his feelings.

The activity of art is based on the fact that a man receiving through his sense of hearing or sight another man's expression of feeling, is capable of experiencing the emotion which moved the man who expressed it. To take the simplest example: one man laughs, and another who hears becomes merry, or a man weeps, and another who hears feels sorrow. A man is excited or irritated, and another man seeing him is brought to a similar state of mind. By his movements or by the sounds of his voice a man expresses courage and determination or sadness and calmness, and this state of mind passes on to others. A man suffers, manifesting his sufferings by groans and spasms, and this suffering transmits itself to other people; a man expresses his feelings of admiration, devotion, fear, respect, or love, to certain objects, persons, or phenomena, and others are infected by the same feelings of admiration, devotion, fear, respect, or love, to the same objects, persons, or phenomena.

And it is on this capacity of man to receive another man's expression of feeling and to experience those feelings himself, that the activity of art is based.

If a man infects another or others directly, immediately, by his appearance or by the sounds he gives vent to at the very time he experiences the feeling; if he causes another man to yawn when he himself cannot help yawning, or to laugh or cry when he himself is obliged to laugh or cry, or to suffer when he himself is suffering—that does not amount to art.

Art begins when one person with the object of joining another or others to himself in one and the same feeling, expresses that feeling by certain external indications. To take the simplest example: a boy, having experienced, let us say, fear on encountering a wolf, relates that encounter; and, in order to evoke in others the feeling he has experienced, describes himself, his condition before the encounter, the surroundings, the wood, his own lightheartedness, and then the wolf's appearance, its movements, the distance between himself and the wolf, etc. All this, if only the boy when telling the story again experiences the feelings he had lived through, and infects the hearers and compels them to feel what he had experienced, is art. If even the boy had not seen a wolf but had frequently been afraid of one, and if wishing to evoke in others the fear he had felt, he invented an encounter with a wolf and recounted it so as to make his hearers share the feelings he experienced when he feared the wolf, that also would be art. And just in the same way it is art if a man, having experienced either the fear of suffering or the attraction of enjoyment (whether in reality or in imagination), expresses these feelings on canvas or in marble so that others are infected by them. And it is also art if a man feels, or imagines to himself, feelings of delight, gladness, sorrow, despair, courage, or despondency, and the transition from one to another of these feelings, and expresses them by sounds so that the hearers are infected by them and experience them as they were experienced by the composer.

The feelings with which the artist infects others may be most various—very strong or very weak, very important or very insignificant, very bad or very good: feelings of love of one's county, self-devotion and submission to fate or to God expressed in a drama, raptures of lovers described in a novel, feelings of voluptuousness expressed in a picture, courage expressed in a triumphal march, merriment evoked by a dance, humour evoked by a funny story, the feeling of quietness transmitted by an evening landscape or by a lullaby, or the feeling of admiration evoked by a beautiful arabesque—it is all art.

If only the spectators or auditors are infected by the feelings which the author has felt, it is art.

*To evoke in oneself a feeling one has once experienced and having evoked it in oneself then by means of movements, lines, colours, sounds, or forms expressed in words, so to transmit that feeling that others experience the same feelings—this is the activity of art.*

*Art is a human activity consisting in this, that one man consciously by means of certain ex-*

*ternal signs, hands on to others feelings he has lived through, and that others are infected by these feelings and also experience them. . . .*

## Chapter 15

Art, in our society, has become so perverted that not only has bad art come to be considered good, but even the very perception of what art really is has been lost. In order to be able to speak about the art of our society it is, therefore, first of all necessary to distinguish art from counterfeit art.

There is one indubitable sign distinguishing real art from its counterfeit, namely, the infectiousness of art. If a man without exercising effort and without altering his standpoint, on reading, hearing, or seeing another man's work, experiences a mental condition which unites him with that man and with others who are also affected by that work, then the object evoking that condition is a work of art. And however poetic, realistic, striking, or interesting, a work may be, it is not a work of art if it does not evoke that feeling (quite distinct from all other feelings) of joy and of spiritual union with another (the author) and with others (those who are also infected by it). . . .

If a man is infected by the author's condition of soul, if he feels this emotion and this union with others, then the object which has effected this is art; but if there be no such infection, if there be not this union with the author and with others who are moved by the same work—then it is not art. And not only is infection a sure sign of art, but the degree of infectiousness is also the sole measure of excellence in art.

*The stronger the infection the better is the art, as art,* speaking of it now apart from its subject-matter, i.e., not considering the value of the feelings it transmits.

And the degree of the infectiousness of art depends on three conditions:

(1) On the greater or lesser individuality of the feeling transmitted; (2) on the greater or lesser clearness with which the feeling is transmitted; (3) on the sincerity of the artist, i.e. on the greater or lesser force with which the artist himself feels the emotion he transmits. . . .

But most of all is the degree of infectiousness of art increased by the degree of sincerity in the artist. As soon as the spectator, hearer, or reader, feels that the artist is infected by his own production and writes, sings, or plays, for himself, and not merely to act on others, this mental condition of the artist infects the recipient; and, on the contrary, as soon as the spectator, reader, or hearer, feels that the author is not writing, singing, or playing, for his own satisfaction—does not himself feel what he wishes to express—but is doing it for him, the receiver, a resistance immediately springs up, and the most individual and the newest feelings and the cleverest technique not only fail to produce any infection but actually repel.

I have mentioned three condition of contagiousness in art, but they may all be summed up into one, the last, sincerity, i.e., that the artist should be impelled by an inner need to express his feeling. That condition includes the first; for if the artist is sincere he will express the feeling as he experienced it. And as each man is different from every one else, his feeling will be individual for every one else; and the more individual it is—the more the artist has drawn it from the depths of his nature—the more sympathetic and sincere will it be. And this same sincerity will impel the artist to find clear expression for the feeling which he wishes to transmit.

Therefore this third condition—sincerity—is the most important of the three. It is always complied with in peasant art, and this explains why such art always acts so powerfully; but it is a condition almost entirely absent from our upper-class art, which is continually produced by artists actuated by personal aims of covetousness or vanity.

Such are the three conditions which divide art from its counterfeits, and which also decide the quality of every work of art considered apart from its subject-matter. . . .

## Chapter 16

Christian art, i.e., the art of our time, should be catholic in the original meaning of the word, i.e., universal, and therefore it should unite all men. And only two kinds of feeling unite all men: first, feelings flowing from a perception of our sonship to God and of the brotherhood of man; and next, the simple feelings of common life accessible to every one without exception—such as feelings of merriment, of pity, of cheerfulness, of tranquility, etc. Only these two kinds of feelings can now supply material for art good in its subject-matter.

And the action of these two kinds of art apparently so dissimilar, is one and the same. The feelings flowing from the perception of our sonship to God and the brotherhood of man—such as a feeling of sureness in truth, devotion to the will of God, self-sacrifice, respect for and love of man—evoked by Christian religious perception; and the simplest feelings, such as a softened or a merry mood caused by a song or an amusing jest intelligible to everyone, or by a touching story, or a drawing, or a little doll: both alike produce one and the same effect—the loving union of man with man. Sometimes people who are together, if not hostile to one another, are at least estranged in mood and feeling, till perchance a story, a performance, a picture, or even a building, but oftenest of all music, unites them all as by an electric flash, and in place of their former isolation or even enmity they are conscious of union and mutual love. Each is glad that another feels what he feels; glad of the communion established not only between him and all present, but also with all now living who will yet share the same impression; and, more than that, he feels the mysterious gladness of a communion which, reaching beyond the grave, unites us with all men of the past who have been moved by the same feelings and with all men of the future who will yet be touched by them. And effect is produced both by religious art which transmits feelings of love of God and one's neighbour by universal art transmitting the very simplest feelings common to all men. . . .

Christian art either evokes in men feelings which, through love of God and of one's neighbour, draw them to closer and ever closer union and make them ready for and capable of such union; or evokes in them feelings which show them that they are already united in the joys and sorrows of life. And therefore the Christian art of our time can be and is of two kinds: (1) art transmitting feelings flowing from a religious perception of man's position in the world in relation to God and to his neighbour—religious art in the limited meaning of the term; and (2) art transmitting the simplest feelings of common life, but such always as are accessible to all men in the whole world—the art of common life—the art of the people—universal art. Only these two kinds of art can be considered good art in our time.

The first, religious art, transmitting both positive feelings of love of God and one's neighbour and negative feelings of indignation and horror at the violation of love, manifests itself chiefly in the form of words, and to some extent also in painting and sculpture: the second kind (universal art) transmitting feelings accessible to all, manifests itself in words, in painting, in sculpture, in dances, in architecture and most of all in music.

# WALTER BENJAMIN ON THE WORK OF ART IN THE MECHANICAL AGE

Walter Benjamin (1892–1940) was loosely associated with, but never formally joined, the Institute for Social Research formed at the University of Frankfurt in 1923, popularly known as the Frankfurt School. It numbered among its members at various times Herbert Marcuse, Theodor Adorno, Max Horkheimer, and Erich Fromm. They aimed to update Marx for the modern age and in many cases turned to the insights of psychoanalysis, especially Freud's ideas, to do so. They were critical of the role of art, popular culture, and consumerism in contemporary capitalist societies and thus are sometimes referred to as "critical theorists." Popular culture, like all culture, had an economic basis—movies and popular music were produced by a "culture industry" whose basic aim, according to Adorno and Horkheimer at least, was to stupefy the masses with endless variations of the same sort of product and thus blunt their will to revolt. Marcuse later picked up the theme of criticizing the role of consumer goods and popular culture under capitalism, arguing that modern industrial societies seek to manufacture false needs in order to build up "surplus repression" in the masses— to make people work long and hard hours to buy things they don't need. He borrowed the idea of repression—our tendency as "civilized" people to mentally block the expression of our basic drives, sex and aggression—from Freud. We'll hear more from Marcuse in the following section.

After Hitler came to power in Germany in 1933, the Frankfurt School slowly broke up, most of its members fleeing the country. Benjamin was Jewish, like a number of his other comrades at Frankfurt, and thus under constant threat of persecution from the Nazis. He moved to Paris after the Nazis assumed power. When Hitler's armies invaded France in 1940, Benjamin fled to the south of the country, seeking entry into Spain. When the Spanish authorities denied him this, he committed suicide.

His work is a combination of Marxism, literary criticism, and mysticism inspired by the Kabbala, the arcane Jewish religious tradition. He was interested in the way that literature, art, popular culture, and the philosophy of history intersected. His important essay "The Work of Art in the Age of Mechanical Reproduction" took seriously the effect of new technologies on traditional art forms, notably painting. Original works of art have a unique presence in time and space. The *Mona Lisa* exists in only one place at a given time—presently, in the Louvre Museum—and if you want to see the original, you must travel to Paris to do so. The "authentic" *Mona Lisa* is inseparable from this presence. Authentic works of art are unique, whereas copies and forgeries are inauthentic, phony. There is only one *real* painting but any number of *fake* ones. Benjamin observed that the arts of mechanical reproduction—photography, lithography, and printing—allowed everyone to have a Leonardo or a Rembrandt in their photo album or on their living room wall. Yet by doing so, they had robbed these masterpieces of their "aura" as unique pieces of art.

Works of art once had a cult or ritual value: A statue of Venus or the Madonna would lie hidden in the inner recesses of the temple where it was worshipped. Art lived in holy places and emanated a religious aura. This aura was largely the product of the work of art's distance from the lives of the masses, just as a mountain range that is distant in a literal sense has an aura to someone looking upon it from afar. But as art became secular, it relied more and more on its exhibition value. It was now the object of mass viewings and mass admiration. It became "closer" to the common folk. As this happened, art lost its ritual value, its magic, its aura.

However, this wasn't necessarily bad. Benjamin championed photography and film for politicizing art and thus aesthetics insofar as they stripped traditional art forms of their aura. By contrast, Adorno defended modern "high" art by artists such as Picasso and Dali as critical and was suspicious of popular art forms such as cinema. Benjamin was especially interested in the effects of film, which he saw as narrowing the distance between audience and critic. Film penetrates directly into reality. So everyone can be an expert on the cinema, or at least on the films he or she has seen.

The mechanical reproduction of images in films proletarianizes art by its very nature—it makes it the province of the common man and woman. *Everyone* can go to see a film. Further, films are public events: They are seen by *groups* of people in public halls, as opposed to paintings, which until recently were usually viewed in exclusive private salons.

Mind you, Benjamin was critical of the capitalist exploitation of film by Hollywood and the European film industry. He criticized the cult of the movie star, which turns the image and personality of the star into a commodity. He also noted that the mechanical techniques used by filmmakers—editing, slow motion, close-ups, and out-of-sequence shooting—all contributed to the death of the aura of the actor, an aura that couldn't survive the transition from the stage to the film studio. In film the camera substitutes for the live audience in a theater, with the actor becoming little better than a prop in the hands of the filmmaker.

In summary, Benjamin believed that the mechanical reproduction of art by means of printing, photography, and film ripped the fabric of tradition away from the aesthetic experience of the masses. The aura of the masterpiece had vanished. In this sense he subscribed to the first two elements of the aesthetics of modernism: Art is fragmented (consider the use of collage in film) and experimental. Yet his Marxist politics prevented him from subscribing fully to the third element of modernism: the idea that art should be abstract or surreal and thus the province of an aesthetic avant-garde elite. Art should appeal to the masses, and the best art to do this wasn't the experiments of Dada and the surrealists (as interesting as these might be), but photography and film.

# The Work of Art in the Age of Mechanical Reproduction

## WALTER BENJAMIN

### 1

In principle a work of art has always been reproducible. Man-made artifacts could always be imitated by men. Replicas were made by pupils in practice of their craft, by masters for diffusing their works, and, finally, by third parties in the pursuit of gain. Mechanical reproduction of a work of art, however, represents something new. Historically, it advanced intermittently and in leaps at long intervals, but with accelerated intensity. The Greeks knew only two procedures of technically reproducing works of art: founding and stamping. Bronzes, terra cottas, and coins were the only art works which they could produce in quantity. All others were unique and could not be mechanically reproduced. With the woodcut graphic art became mechanically reproducible for the first time, long before script became reproducible by print. The enormous changes which printing, the mechanical reproduction of writing, has brought about in literature are a familiar story. However, within the phenomenon

SOURCE: Walter Benjamin, "The Work of Art in the Age of Mechanical Reproduction," in *Illuminations*, ed. Hannah Arendt, trans. Harry Zohn (1936; New York: Harcourt, Brace & World, 1968), pp. 220–227, 236–237 (edited; most of Benjamin's notes omitted). Copyright 1955 by Suhrkamp Verlag, Frankfurt a. M. English translation by Harry Zohn copyright 1968 and renewed 1996 by Harcourt, Inc. Reprinted by permission of Harcourt, Inc.

which we are here examining from the perspective of world history, print is merely a special, though particularly important, case. During the Middle Ages engraving and etching were added to the woodcut; at the beginning of the nineteenth century lithography made its appearance.

With lithography the technique of reproduction reached an essentially new stage. This much more direct process was distinguished by the tracing of the design on a stone rather than its incision on a block of wood or its etching on a copperplate and permitted graphic art for the first time to put its products on the market, not only in large numbers as hitherto, but also in daily changing forms. Lithography enabled graphic art to illustrate everyday life, and it began to keep pace with printing. But only a few decades after its invention, lithography was surpassed by photography. For the first time in the process of pictorial reproduction, photography freed the hand of the most important artistic functions which henceforth devolved only upon the eye looking into a lens. Since the eye perceives more swiftly than the hand can draw, the process of pictorial reproduction was accelerated so enormously that it could keep pace with speech. A film operator shooting a scene in the studio captures the images at the speed of an actor's speech. Just as lithography virtually implied the illustrated newspaper, so did photography foreshadow the sound film. The technical reproduction of sound was tackled at the end of the last century. These convergent endeavors made predictable a situation which Paul Valéry pointed up in this sentence: "Just as water, gas, and electricity are brought into our houses from far off to satisfy our needs in response to a minimal effort, so we shall be supplied with visual or auditory images, which will appear and disappear at a simple movement of the hand, hardly more than a sign."[1] Around 1900 technical reproduction had reached a standard that not only permitted it to reproduce transmitted works of art and thus to cause the

most profound change in their impact upon the public; it also had captured a place of its own among the artistic processes. For the study of this standard nothing is more revealing than the nature of the repercussions that these two different manifestations—the reproduction of works of art and the art of the film—have had on art in its traditional form.

## 2

Even the most perfect reproduction of a work of art is lacking in one element: its presence in time and space, its existence at the place where it happens to be. This unique existence of the work of art determined the history to which it was subject throughout the time of its existence. This includes the changes which it may have suffered in physical condition over the years as well as the various changes in its ownership. The traces of the first can be revealed only by chemical or physical analyses which it is impossible to perform on a reproduction; changes of ownership are subject to a tradition which must be traced from the situation of the original.

The presence of the original is the prerequisite to the concept of authenticity. Chemical analyses of the patina of a bronze can help to establish this, as does the proof that a given script of the Middle Ages stems from an archive of the fifteenth century. The whole sphere of authenticity is outside technical—and, of course, not only technical—reproducibility. Confronted with its manual reproduction, which was usually branded as a forgery, the original preserved all its authority; not so *vis-à-vis* technical reproduction. The reason is twofold. First, process reproduction is more independent of the original than manual reproduction. For example, in photography, process reproduction can bring out those aspects of the original that are unattainable to the naked eye yet accessible to the lens, which is adjustable and chooses its angle at will. And photographic reproduction, with the aid of certain processes, such as enlargement or slow motion, can capture images which escape natural vision. Secondly, technical reproduction can put the copy of the

[1] Paul Valéry, *Aesthetics,* "The Conquest of Ubiquity," translated by Ralph Manheim, New York: Pantheon Books, 1964, p. 226.

original into situations which would be out of reach for the original itself. Above all, it enables the original to meet the beholder halfway, be it in the form of a photograph or a phonograph record. The cathedral leaves its locale to be received in the studio of a lover of art; the choral production, performed in an auditorium or in open air, resounds in the drawing room.

The situations into which the product of mechanical reproduction can be brought may not touch the actual work of art, yet the quality of its presence is always depreciated. This holds not only for the art work but also, for instance, for a landscape which passes in review before the spectator in a movie. In the case of the art object, a most sensitive nucleus—namely, its authenticity—is interfered with whereas no natural object is vulnerable on that score. The authenticity of a thing is the essence of all that is transmissible from its beginning, ranging from its substantive duration to its testimony to the history which it has experienced. Since the historical testimony rests on the authenticity, the former, too, is jeopardized by reproduction when substantive duration ceases to matter. And what is really jeopardized when the historical testimony is affected is the authority of the object.

One might subsume the eliminated element in the term "aura" and go on to say: that which withers in the age of mechanical reproduction is the aura of the work of art. This is a symptomatic process whose significance points beyond the realm of art. One might generalize by saying: the technique of reproduction, detaches the reproduced object from the domain of tradition. By making many reproductions it substitutes a plurality of copies for a unique existence. And in permitting the reproduction to meet the beholder or listener in his own particular situation, it reactivates the object reproduced. These two processes lead to a tremendous shattering of tradition which is the obverse of the contemporary crisis and renewal of mankind. Both processes are intimately connected with the contemporary mass movements. Their most powerful agent is the film. Its social significance, particularly in its most positive form, is inconceivable without its

destructive, cathartic aspect, that is, the liquidation of the traditional value of the cultural heritage. This phenomenon is most palpable in the great historical films. It extends to ever new positions. In 1927 Abel Gance exclaimed enthusiastically: "Shakespeare, Rembrandt, Beethoven will make films . . . all legends, all mythologies and all myths, all founders of religion, and the very religions . . . await their exposed resurrection, and the heroes crowd each other at the gate."[2] Presumably without intending it, he issued an invitation to a far-reaching liquidation.

## 3

During long periods of history, the mode of human sense perception changes with humanity's entire mode of existence. The manner in which human sense perception is organized, the medium in which it is accomplished, is determined not only by nature but by historical circumstances as well . . . if changes in the medium of contemporary perception can be comprehended as decay of the aura, it is possible to show its social causes.

The concept of aura which was proposed above with reference to historical objects may usefully be illustrated with reference to the aura of natural ones. We define the aura of the latter as the unique phenomenon of a distance, however close it may be. If, while resting on a summer afternoon, you follow with your eyes a mountain range on the horizon or a branch which casts its shadow over you, you experience the aura of those mountains, of that branch. This image makes it easy to comprehend the social bases of the contemporary decay of the aura. It rests on two circumstances, both of which are related to the increasing significance of the masses in contemporary life. Namely, the desire of contemporary masses to bring things "closer" spatially and humanly, which is just as ardent as their

---

[2] Abel Gance, "Le Temps de l'image est venu," *L'Art cinématographique,* vol. 2, pp. 94 f, Paris, 1927. [Gance was a pioneer director in silent films in France, perhaps most famous for his epic film *Napoléon* (1927). The title translates as "The Time of the Image has Come"—ED.]

bent toward overcoming the uniqueness of every reality by accepting its reproduction. . . . Every day the urge grows stronger to get hold of an object at very close range by way of its likeness, its reproduction. Unmistakably, reproduction as offered by picture magazines and newsreels differs from the image seen by the unarmed eye. Uniqueness and permanence are as closely linked in the latter as are transitoriness and reproducibility in the former. To pry an object from its shell, to destroy its aura, is the mark of a perception whose "sense of the universal equality of things" has increased to such a degree that it extracts it even from a unique object by means of reproduction. Thus is manifested in the field of perception what in the theoretical sphere is noticeable in the increasing importance of statistics. The adjustment of reality to the masses and of the masses to reality is a process of unlimited scope, as much for thinking as for perception.

## 4

The uniqueness of a work of art is inseparable from its being imbedded in the fabric of tradition. This tradition itself is thoroughly alive and extremely changeable. An ancient statue of Venus, for example, stood in a different traditional context with the Greeks, who made it an object of veneration, than with the clerics of the Middle Ages, who viewed it as an ominous idol. Both of them, however, were equally confronted with its uniqueness, that is, its aura. Originally the contextual integration of art in tradition found its expression in the cult. We know that the earliest art works originated in the service of a ritual—first the magical, then the religious kind. It is significant that the existence of the work of art with reference to its aura is never entirely separated from its ritual function. In other words, the unique value of the "authentic" work of art has its basis in ritual, the location of its original use value. This ritualistic basis, however remote, is still recognizable as secularized ritual even in the most profane forms of the cult of beauty. The secular cult of beauty, developed during the Renaissance and prevailing for three centuries,

clearly showed that ritualistic basis in its decline and the first deep crisis which befell it. With the advent of the first revolutionary means of reproduction, photography, simultaneously with the rise of socialism, art sensed the approaching crisis which has become evident a century later. At the time, art reacted with the doctrine of *l'art pour l'art,* that is, with a theology of art. This gave rise to what might be called a negative theology in the form of the idea of "pure" art, which not only denied any social function of art but also any categorizing by subject matter. . . .

An analysis of art in the age of mechanical reproduction must justice to these relationships, for they lead us to an all-important insight: for the first time in world history, mechanical reproduction emancipates the work of art from its parasitical dependence on ritual. To an ever greater degree the work of art reproduced becomes the work of art designed for reproduction.[3] From a photographic negative, for example, one can make any number of prints; to ask for the "authentic" print makes no sense. But the instant the criterion of authenticity ceases to be applicable to artistic production, the total function of art is reversed. Instead of being based on ritual, it begins to be based on another practice—politics.

## 5

Works of art are received and valued on different planes. Two polar types stand out: with one, the accent is on the cult value; with the other, on the exhibition value of the work. Artistic production begins with ceremonial objects destined to serve in a cult. One may assume that what mattered was their existence, not their being on view. The elk portrayed by the man of the Stone Age on

---

[3] In the case of films, mechanical reproduction is not, as with literature and painting, an external condition for mass distribution. Mechanical reproduction is inherent in the very technique of film production. This technique not only permits in the most direct way but virtually causes mass distribution. It enforces distribution because the production of a film is so expensive that an individual who, for instance, might afford to buy a painting no longer can afford to buy a film. In 1927 it was calculated that a major film, in order to pay its way, had to reach an audience of nine million. . . .

the walls of his cave was an instrument of magic. He did expose it to his fellow men, but in the main it was meant for the spirits. Today the cult value would seem to demand that the work of art remain hidden. Certain statues of gods are accessible only to the priest in the cella; certain Madonnas remain covered nearly all year round; certain sculptures on medieval cathedrals are invisible to the spectator on ground level. With the emancipation of the various art practices from ritual go increasing opportunities for the exhibition of their products. It is easier to exhibit a portrait bust that can be sent here and there than to exhibit the statue of a divinity that has its fixed place in the interior of a temple. The same holds for the painting as against the mosaic or fresco that preceded it. And even though the public presentability of a mass originally may have been just as great as that of a symphony, the latter originated at the moment when its public presentability promised to surpass that of the mass.

With the different methods of technical reproduction of a work of art, its fitness for exhibition increased to such an extent that the quantitative shift between its two poles turned into a qualitative transformation of its nature. This is comparable to the situation of the work of art in prehistoric times when, by the absolute emphasis on its cult value, it was, first and foremost, an instrument of magic. Only later did it come to be recognized as a work of art. In the same way today, by the absolute emphasis on its exhibition value the work of art becomes a creation with entirely new functions, among which the one we are conscious of, the artistic function, later may be recognized as incidental. This much is certain: today photography and the film are the most serviceable exemplifications of this new function.

## 12

Mechanical reproduction of art changes the reaction of the masses toward art. The reactionary attitude toward a Picasso painting change into the progressive reaction toward a Chaplin movie. The progressive reaction is characterized by the direct, intimate fusion of visual and emotional enjoyment with the orientation of the expert. Such fusion is of great social significance. The greater the decrease in the social significance of an art form, the sharper the distinction between criticism and enjoyment by the public. The conventional is uncritically enjoyed, and the new is criticized with aversion. With regard to the screen, the critical and the receptive attitudes of the public coincide. The decisive reason for this is that individual reactions are predetermined by the mass audience response they are about to produce, and this is nowhere more pronounced than in the film. The moment these responses become manifest they control each other. Again, the comparison with painting is fruitful. A painting has always had an excellent chance to be viewed by one person or by a few. The simultaneous contemplation of paintings by a large public, such as developed in the nineteenth century, is an early symptom of the crisis of painting, a crisis which was by no means occasioned exclusively by photography but rather in a relatively independent manner by the appeal of art works to the masses.

Painting simply is in no position to present an object for simultaneous collective experience, as it was possible for architecture at all times, for the epic poem in the past, and for the movie today. Although this circumstance in itself should not lead one to conclusions about the social role of painting, it does constitute a serious threat as soon as painting, under special conditions and, as it were, against its nature, is confronted directly by the masses. In the churches and monasteries of the Middle Ages and at the princely courts up to the end of the eighteenth century, a collective reception of paintings did not occur simultaneously, but by graduated and hierarchized mediation. The change that has come about is an expression of the particular conflict in which painting was implicated by the mechanical reproducibility of paintings. Although paintings began to be publicly exhibited in galleries and salons, there was no way for the masses to organize and control themselves in their reception. Thus the same public which responds in a progressive manner toward a grotesque film is bound to respond in a reactionary manner to surrealism.

# HERBERT MARCUSE ON ART AS NEGATION

Herbert Marcuse (1898–1979) was born in Berlin. He received his doctorate in literature in 1922 from the University of Freiburg, afterward returning to Berlin to sell books. He came back to Freiburg in 1928 to study for several years with the famous existentialist philosopher Martin Heidegger. In 1933 Marcuse briefly became a member of the Institute for Social Research at the University of Frankfurt. From this point on his name was linked to the critical theory of the Frankfurt School. Being a Jewish radical, he fled Nazi-inspired anti-Semitism for America in 1934 and joined his Frankfurt comrades in New York at the New School for Social Research. He lived in America for the rest of his life, continuing the Frankfurt School's critical reworking of Marxism in the light of psychoanalytic research and political and economic developments in modern capitalist societies, notably consumerism.

Marcuse's first claim to fame was his 1941 book, *Reason and Revolution,* in which he showed that Marx was more influenced by the dialectical thinking of his great predecessor G. W. F. Hegel than had previously been supposed. During World War II Marcuse worked for the OSS (the forerunner of the CIA) and for the U.S. State Department.

In the 1950s he published two important books—*Eros and Civilization* (1955) and *Soviet Marxism* (1958). In the former he attempted to reconcile Marx and Freud, arguing that under capitalism our basic instincts are excessively frustrated. He looked forward to a nonrepressive civilization where work would become play and where our sexuality could be freely expressed. In the latter book he analyzed the post-Stalinist Soviet Union, criticizing the top-heavy Soviet bureaucracy, yet suggesting that liberalizing trends would eventually take a permanent hold in Russia (he was right about this, by the way).

The peak of Marcuse's fame came in the 1960s, when he became the theoretical hero of the student revolutionaries of the New Left. In 1964 he published his most well known work, *One Dimensional Man;* in 1969, at the end of this tumultuous decade, *An Essay on Liberation* appeared. In these and other writings he defended radical movements of all stripes, from the hippies to Third-World liberation movements, as part of a general revolt against repressive societies around the world. This defense of radicalism didn't earn him many points with the academic establishment—Brandeis University rewarded his efforts by giving him the boot in 1965, one year after he published one of the greatest works in the twentieth century on social theory. He spent the rest of his teaching career at the University of California.

In *Eros and Civilization* Marcuse says that modern civilization imposes upon us a "surplus repression" of our instincts in order to maintain social control and high levels of productivity in the masses. This surplus repression exceeds the normal sort of repression of our sexual and aggressive instincts that Freud argued, in *Civilization and Its Discontents,* was necessary for all civilizations. Freud's social philosophy was a major influence on Marcuse. In Chapter 9 of *Eros and Civilization,* Marcuse deals with aesthetics, showing that in its original meaning the word *aesthetic* mixed together pleasure, sensuousness, beauty, truth, art, and freedom. He argues that art is in essence sensual and erotic, a servant of Freud's Pleasure Principle. Insofar as this is true, it is also an ally in the struggle against the surplus repression imposed on us by contemporary industrial societies:

Art challenges the prevailing principle of reason: it represents the order of sensuousness, it invokes a tabooed logic—the logic of gratification as against that of repression. Behind the sublimated aesthetic form, the unsublimated content shows forth: the commitment of art to the pleasure principle. (p. 168)

In *One Dimensional Man,* Marcuse extends this defense of art as simultaneously sensual and politically critical as part of a wider analysis of the "technological logic of domination" found in all modern industrial societies (both East and West). In his opening chapter he argues that these societies have discovered new forms of social control, mainly by manipulating us into thinking that the false needs promoted by consumerism are in fact our true needs. These false needs are superimposed on us to repress us, to perpetuate toil, misery, and social injustice. They compel us to consume, relax, and have fun, but all in accordance with the ways that everyone else consumes, relaxes, and has fun. Advertising helps to clarify these matters for the consumer.

This breeds in us a one-dimensional way of thinking, a technological logic of mass production and consumption. This way of thinking is both wasteful of natural raw materials and destructive of our moral and aesthetic integrity. It even threatens our sense of alienation from our work, as the objects we produce and purchase become part of our very being. People define themselves in terms of the commodities they own—their cars, their houses, their kitchen gadgets, their stereos and televisions.

Real freedom would be freedom from the economy, from the daily struggle to make a living. Marcuse suggests that the way out of this dilemma is not to satisfy more false needs but to use modern technology to reduce our labor time to the minimum needed to fulfill our vital needs, and thereby to move work from what Marx called the realm of necessity to the realm of freedom. In fact, Marcuse thought that the technology already exists that would allow us to do this and that it was only the promotion of false needs by the techno-industrial system that chains us to forty-hour-plus work weeks.

Later in *One Dimensional Man,* Marcuse argues that the art of high culture up until the early twentieth century was two-dimensional, sublimated, a thorn in the saddle of the culture that surrounded it. It was "the unhappy consciousness of a divided world, the defeated possibilities, the hopes unfulfilled, and the promises betrayed" (p. 61). High culture was traditionally part of a "Great Refusal" of the status quo, part of a refusal to behave. It transcended everyday experience. Now this Great Refusal has been absorbed by our technological society, by social reality. Works of alienation and images from high culture become TV commercials used to comfort and excite us and to sell us things.

Marcuse even had an answer for those who pointed out that in modern culture we can more freely express our sexuality and have therefore escaped some of the old repressions. Marcuse sees the freer sexuality of the modern age as part of a "repressive desublimation." Now the Pleasure Principle has absorbed the Reality Principle, and sexuality is channeled by mechanisms of social control into "socially constructive forms." He argues that traditional societies had wider universes of libidinal (i.e., erotic) pleasures—their members derived pleasure from handicrafts, from making and eating homemade bread, from direct contact with wild nature, and so on. Now our erotic experience has been reduced to sexual satisfaction, images of which bombard us in ads, television shows, and films. Sex has been desublimated. But in the process it becomes a new form of social control, a new way of hooking us into the system of production and consumption.

In the reading below, Chapter 1 of his last book, *The Aesthetic Dimension* (1978), Marcuse returns to many of the themes previously outlined in the course of criticizing Marxist aesthetics: art as erotic, as opening up tabooed zones of experience; high culture as part of a Great Refusal of social reality; the value of rebellious subjectivity and of anything that can break the stranglehold of everyday reality on the too-socialized individual. The best art is a negation of the status quo. Whether it comes from the oppressors or the oppressed is largely irrelevant. In this sense the slogan "art for art's sake" is right. When art shatters our Reality Principle by showing us the decadent and the taboo, it will have more power to liberate people than art that self-consciously tries to give us explicit political messages. As socialist realism showed, most of the latter art winds up being trash.

The following reading has more contemporary relevance than might be immediately evident. It's true that the sort of Marxist approach to art criticized by Marcuse—the idea that only the art of the revolutionary class, the proletariat, is progressive, whereas the art of the ruling capitalist class is decadent—has largely retreated from the scene. Yet the structure of the Marxist argument has reappeared in new forms in feminist aesthetics and in multiculturalist criticisms of the Western artistic and literary canons. Feminists and multiculturalists modify the Marxist argument by substituting sex or race for class as the litmus test for the goodness or badness of a piece of art. Many feminists argue that Western art and literature are decadent in that they have been produced mostly by men in order to objectify and oppress women. Multiculturalists claim that the most progressive art and literature are produced by nonwhites and by the citizens of the former colonies of the great European empires (hence "postcolonial" art and literature), whereas much of the fine art, poetry, and novels of the European and American canons, from Shakespeare and Milton to Thomas de Quincey and Jane Austen, has hidden imperialist motifs. In both cases the history of Western art and literature is seen as a series of moral and political crimes against oppressed groups. This is precisely the ideological view of art that Marcuse is opposed to in the reading, in which he argues that even the most decadent, apolitical art can be liberating if it frees us from one-dimensional thinking and acting.

# The Aesthetic Dimension

## HERBERT MARCUSE

IN A SITUATION where the miserable reality can be changed only through radical political praxis, the concern with aesthetics demands justification. It would be senseless to deny the element of despair inherent in this concern: the retreat into a world of fiction where existing conditions are changed and overcome only in the realm of the imagination. However, this purely ideological conception of art is being questioned with increasing intensity. It seems that art as art expresses a truth, an experience, a necessity which, although not in the domain of radical praxis, are

SOURCE: Herbert Marcuse, chap. 1 in *The Aesthetic Dimension: Toward a Critique of Marxist Aesthetics*, trans. Erica Sherover and Herbert Marcuse (Boston: Beacon Press, 1978), pp. 1–11, 13, 15–21 (edited; original notes omitted). Copyright 1978. Reprinted by permission of Beacon Press.

nevertheless essential components of revolution. With this insight, the basic conception of Marxist aesthetics, that is its treatment of art as ideology, and the emphasis on the class character of art, become again the topic of critical reexamination.

This discussion is directed to the following theses of Marxist aesthetics:

1. There is a definite connection between art and the material base, between art and the totality of the relations of production. With the change in production relations, art itself is transformed as part of the superstructure, although, like other ideologies, it can lag behind or anticipate social change.
2. There is a definite connection between art and social class. The only authentic, true, progressive art is the art of an ascending class. It expresses the consciousness of this class.
3. Consequently, the political and the aesthetic, the revolutionary content and the artistic quality tend to coincide.
4. The writer has an obligation to articulate and express the interests and needs of the ascending class. (In capitalism, this would be the proletariat.)
5. A declining class or its representatives are unable to produce anything but "decadent" art.
6. Realism (in various senses) is considered as the art form which corresponds most adequately to the social relationships, and thus is the "correct" art form.

. . . Ideology becomes mere ideology, in spite of Engels's emphatic qualifications, and a devaluation of the entire realm of subjectivity takes place, a devaluation not only of the subject as *ego cogito,* the rational subject, but also of inwardness, emotions, and imagination. The subjectivity of individuals, their own consciousness and unconscious tends to be dissolved into class consciousness. Thereby, a major prerequisite of revolution is minimized, namely, the fact that the need for radical change must be rooted in the subjectivity of individuals themselves, in their intelligence and their passions, their drives and their goals. Marxist theory succumbed to that very reification which it had exposed and combated in

society as a whole. Subjectivity became an atom of objectivity; even in its rebellious form it was surrendered to a collective consciousness. The deterministic component of Marxist theory does not lie in its concept of the relationship between social existence and consciousness, but in the reductionistic concept of consciousness which brackets the particular content of individual consciousness and, with it, the subjective potential for revolution. . . .

Liberating subjectivity constitutes itself in the inner history of the individuals—their own history, which is not identical with their social existence. It is the particular history of their encounters, their passions, joys, and sorrows—experiences which are not necessarily grounded in their class situation, and which are not even comprehensible from this perspective. To be sure, the actual manifestations of their history are determined by their class situation, but this situation is not the ground of their fate—of that which happens to them. Especially in its nonmaterial aspects it explodes the class framework. It is all too easy to relegate love and hate, joy and sorrow, hope and despair to the domain of psychology, thereby removing them from the concerns of radical praxis. Indeed, in terms of political economy they may not be "forces of production," but for every human being they are decisive, they constitute reality. . . .

I shall submit the following thesis: the radical qualities of art, that is to say, its indictment of the established reality and its invocation of the beautiful image *(schöner Schein)* of liberation are grounded precisely in the dimensions where art *transcends* its social determination and emancipates itself from the given universe of discourse and behavior while preserving its overwhelming presence. Thereby art creates the realm in which the subversion of experience proper to art becomes possible: the world formed by art is recognized as a reality which is suppressed and distorted in the given reality. This experience culminates in extreme situations (of love and death, guilt and failure, but also joy, happiness, and fulfillment) which explode the given reality in the name of a truth normally denied or even unheard. The inner logic of the work of art terminates in the emergence of another reason, another sensibility, which defy the rationality and sensibility incorporated in the dominant social institutions.

Under the law of the aesthetic form, the given reality is necessarily *sublimated:* the immediate content is stylized, the "data" are reshaped and reordered in accordance with the demands of the art form, which requires that even the representation of death and destruction invoke the need for hope—a need rooted in the new consciousness embodied in the work of art.

Aesthetic sublimation makes for the affirmative, reconciling component of art, though it is at the same time a vehicle for the critical, negating function of art. The transcendence of immediate reality shatters the reified objectivity of established social relations and opens a new dimension of experience: rebirth of the rebellious subjectivity. Thus, on the basis of aesthetic sublimation, a *desublimation* takes place in the perception of individuals—in their feelings, judgments, thoughts; an invalidation of dominant norms, needs, and values. With all its affirmative-ideological features, art remains a dissenting force.

We can tentatively define "aesthetic form" as the result of the transformation of a given content (actual or historical, personal or social fact) into a self-contained whole: a poem, play, novel, etc. The work is thus "taken out" of the constant process of reality and assumes a significance and truth of its own. The aesthetic transformation is achieved through a reshaping of language, perception, and understanding so that they reveal the essence of reality in its appearance: the repressed potentialities of man and nature. The work of art thus re-presents reality while accusing it. . . .

Aesthetic form, autonomy, and truth are interrelated. Each is a socio-historical phenomenon, and each *transcends* the socio-historical arena. While the latter limits the autonomy of art it does so without invalidating the *trans*historical truths expressed in the work. The truth of art lies in its power to break the monopoly of established reality (i.e., of those who established it) to *define* what is *real*. In this rupture, which is the achievement of the aesthetic form, the fictitious world of art appears as true reality.

Art is committed to that perception of the world which alienates individuals from their functional existence and performance in society—it is committed to an emancipation of sensibility, imagination, and reason in all spheres of subjectivity and objectivity. The aesthetic transformation becomes a vehicle of recognition and indictment. But this achievement presupposes a degree of autonomy which withdraws art from the mystifying power of the given and frees it for the expression of its own truth. Inasmuch as man and nature are constituted by an unfree society, their repressed and distorted potentialities can be represented only in an *estranging* form. The world of art is that of another *Reality Principle,* of estrangement—and only as estrangement does art fulfill a *cognitive* function: it communicates truths not communicable in any other language; *it contradicts.*

However, the strong affirmative tendencies toward reconciliation with the established reality coexist with the rebellious ones. I shall try to show that they are not due to the specific class determination of art but rather to the redeeming character of the *catharsis.* The catharsis itself is grounded in the power of aesthetic form to call fate by its name, to demystify its force, to give the word to the victims—the power of recognition which gives the individual a modicum of freedom and fulfillment in the realm of unfreedom. The interplay between the affirmation and the indictment of that which is, between ideology and truth, pertains to the very structure of art. But in the authentic works, the affirmation does not cancel the indictment: reconciliation and hope still preserve the memory of things past.

The affirmative character of art has yet another source: it is in the commitment of art to Eros, the deep affirmation of the Life Instincts in their fight against instinctual and social oppression. The permanence of art, its historical immortality throughout the millennia of destruction, bears witness to this commitment.

. . . Ideology is not always *mere* ideology, false consciousness. The consciousness and the representation of truths which appear as abstract in relation to the established process of production are also ideological functions. Art presents one of these truths. As ideology, it opposes the given society. The autonomy of art contains the categorical imperative: "things must change." If the liberation of human beings and nature is to be possible at all, then the social nexus of destruction and submission must be broken. . . .

Compared with the often one-dimensional optimism of propaganda, art is permeated with pessimism, not seldom intertwined with comedy. Its "liberating laughter" recalls the danger and the evil that have passed—this time! But the pessimism of art is not counterrevolutionary. It serves to warn against the "happy consciousness" of radical praxis: as if all of that which art invokes and indicts could be settled through the class struggle. . . .

However correctly one has analyzed a poem, play, or novel in terms of its social content, the questions as to whether the particular work is good, beautiful, and true are still unanswered. But the answers to these questions cannot again be given in terms of the specific relations of production which constitute the historical context of the respective work. The circularity of this method is obvious. In addition it falls victim to an easy relativism which is contradicted clearly enough by the permanence of certain qualities of art through all changes of style and historical periods (transcendence, estrangement, aesthetic order, manifestations of the beautiful).

The fact that a work truly represents the interests or the outlook of the proletariat or of the bourgeoisie does not yet make it an authentic work of art. This "material" quality may facilitate its reception, may lend it greater concreteness, but it is in no way constitutive. The universality of art cannot be grounded in the world and world outlook of a particular class, for art envisions a concrete universal, humanity *(Menschlichkeit)*, which no particular class can incorporate, not even the proletariat, Marx's "universal class." The inexorable entanglement of joy and sorrow,

celebration and despair, Eros and Thanatos[1] cannot be dissolved into problems of class struggle. History is also grounded in nature. And Marxist theory has the least justification to ignore the metabolism between the human being and nature, and to denounce the insistence on this natural soil of society as a regressive ideological conception.

The emergence of human beings as "species beings"[2]—men and women capable of living in that community of freedom which is the potential of the species—this is the subjective basis of a classless society. Its realization presupposes a radical transformation of the drives and needs of the individuals: an organic development within the socio-historical. Solidarity would be on weak grounds were it not rooted in the instinctual structure of individuals. In this dimension, men and women are confronted with psycho-physical forces which they have to make their own without being able to overcome the naturalness of these forces. This is the domain of the primary drives: of libidinal and destructive energy. Solidarity and community have their basis in the subordination of destructive and aggressive energy to the social emancipation of the life instincts.

. . . The fact that the artist belongs to a privileged group negates neither the truth nor the aesthetic quality of his work. What is true of "the classics of socialism" is true also of the great artists: they break through the class limitations of their family, background, environment. Marxist theory is not family research. The progressive character of art, its contribution to the struggle for liberation cannot be measured by the artists' origins nor by the ideological horizon of their class. Neither can it be determined by the presence (or absence) of the oppressed class in their works. The criteria for the progressive character of art are given only in the work itself as a whole: in what it says and how it says it.

In this sense art is "art for art's sake" inas-

---

[1] [These two basic instincts—the drives toward sex and death—Freud saw as the core of our psychic lives—ED.]
[2] [Marcuse refers to Marx's vision of a nonalienated human existence outlined in his *Economic and Philosophical Manuscripts of 1844*—ED.]

much as the aesthetic form reveals tabooed and repressed dimensions of reality: aspects of liberation. The poetry of Mallarmé is an extreme example; his poems conjure up modes of perception, imagination, gestures—a feast of sensuousness which shatters everyday experience and anticipates a different reality principle.[3]

The degree to which the distance and estrangement from praxis constitute the emancipatory value of art becomes particularly clear in those works of literature which seem to close themselves rigidly against such praxis. Walter Benjamin has traced this in the works of Poe, Baudelaire, Proust, and Valéry. They express a "consciousness of crisis" *(Krisenbewusstsein):* a

[3] [Stéphane Mallarmé (1842–1898) was a French symbolist poet whose work was known for its musical and elusive quality—ED.]

pleasure in decay, in destruction, in the beauty of evil; a celebration of the asocial, of the anomic— the secret rebellion of the bourgeois against his own class. . . .

The "secret" protest of this esoteric literature lies in the ingression of the primary erotic-destructive forces which explode the normal universe of communication and behavior. They are asocial in their very nature, a subterranean rebellion against the social order. Inasmuch as this literature reveals the dominion of Eros and Thanatos beyond all social control, it invokes needs and gratifications which are essentially destructive. In terms of political praxis, this literature remains elitist and decadent. It does nothing in the struggle for liberation—except to open the tabooed zones of nature and society in which even death and the devil are enlisted as allies in the refusal to abide by the law and order of repression. . . .

# NAOMI WOLF ON THE BEAUTY MYTH

Discussions about the nature of beauty can take some fairly esoteric and abstract turns, especially when they come from a Plato or Kant. Yet one way of making this discussion more relevant to everyday life is to look at how beauty, especially female beauty, is represented in popular culture, mass media, and the workplace. Some thinkers have been very critical of such popular portrayals of feminine beauty.

Even though the feminist movement, revitalized in the 1970s, did much to further the legal, political, and economic rights of women, Naomi Wolf (1962–) believes that in some respects the conditions of life for many women have not improved all that much. Recall from Chapter 7 that between publishing *The Beauty Myth* in 1990 and *Fire with Fire* in 1994, Wolf recanted some of her Second Wave radical feminist views. In this section we are revisiting an earlier period in her career as a feminist theorist. In *The Beauty Myth,* she asks the question, "Do women today *feel* free?" Her answer is very clearly, "No."

Wolf is willing to admit that the women's movement has done much to advance the interests, legal and material, of women. But women have other, seemingly insurmountable problems that have slowed down or halted any liberation gained through the previous efforts of the women's rights movement. According to Wolf, working women today suffer from all sorts of physical and psychological ailments, such as neurosess about their body image and eating disorders, due to the social pressures exerted upon them in their newly "liberated" positions in the economy and in public life.

The main culprit at work, Wolf believes, is the so-called beauty myth. As she puts it, this amounts to a concerted, violent backlash against feminist concerns and struggles. At the heart of this attack on feminism is the media's portrayal of women as limited to certain social roles and aesthetic ideals. This portrayal forces unrealistic and fabricated expectations on women that they can never fulfill. These expectations center around what it means to a woman to be beautiful. But as Wolf illustrates through many examples, trying to fulfill this media-driven image of feminine beauty results in great physical and psychological harm to the women who feel trapped in the iron maidens created by these false ideals.

Wolf points out very poignantly that the depiction of female beauty in art and the media today does not reflect some eternal aesthetic truth, some standard that is binding for all women, both past and present. It is a construction imposed upon women by our culture, brought about by many nonaesthetic factors, mostly economic and political in nature.

An interesting fact that Wolf uses to back her claim that the current standard of beauty is far from universal is how women have been portrayed in paintings and sculpture over the centuries in different cultures. Her most famous example is the so-called Rubenesque images of women found in early modern paintings such as those of the Flemish artist Peter Paul Rubens (1577–1640), who painted images of robustly rounded, substantial women. This is the opposite of the current look of the runway model, who is so drawn and gaunt that one could mistake her for a heroin addict.

Considering how beauty has been constructed very differently in various societies over the centuries, coupled to how it is portrayed today, it's not surprising that Wolf says that the beauty myth is not about women at all. Instead, "It is about men's institutions and institutional power." In other words, the beauty myth is promoted by a concerted male effort to keep women in their place by making them feel anxious about their physical beauty in the workplace and in public life. This is accomplished by socializing women into trying to conform to an ideal of beauty that is impossible for most of them to achieve.

Though this may not seem evident at first, think for a moment about how the beauty myth is conveyed in today's society. Its clearest and most forceful portrayal comes in advertising, which bombards us with images of cute teenage models to sell women shampoo, hair dye, lipstick, and clothes. Wolf gives the telling example of the $20 billion spent by American women each year on cosmetics to improve their appearance as a case in point of how the beauty myth penetrates into women's everyday consciousness.

The larger context of Wolf's critique of the beauty myth is the profound suspicion of most Second Wave feminists—especially the radical feminists of the 1970s and 1980s who came to dominate academic debates in those years—of images of female beauty found both in high art and in popular culture. They have tended to see all such images as objectifications of women's bodies by the male gaze, a gaze that is explicitly sexual.

Chapter 7 mentioned Andrea Dworkin and Catharine MacKinnon's critique of pornography as a violation of the civil rights of women. They believe in essence that pictures of naked women should be unavailable for purchase and banned from public view. Yet the radicals didn't object only to pornography. In a significant number of cases, radical feminists and their intellectual allies have argued that the depiction of female beauty, especially naked female beauty, in the fine art of the last several centuries shares pornography's desire to objectify women. Indeed, in his much-read 1972 book on the history of art, *Ways of Seeing,* John Berger argued that in art from the Renaissance to the twentieth century, women were pictured as being aware of the gaze of a male spectator. This awareness was tied to the submission of women to "the owner of both woman and painting"—the artist's male patron. Paintings of nude women were designed to flatter the egos of their male viewers and to remind women of their passive social role.

Yet there are two sides to this story. Third Wave feminists such as Camille Paglia and Christina Hoff Sommers have heavily criticized radicals such as Dworkin and MacKinnon for their anti-aesthetic attitude and their puritanical misunderstanding of the erotic nature of art, literature, and music. Hoff Sommers discusses a famous case in her book *Who Stole Feminism?* A feminist English professor at Pennsylvania State University considered a reproduction of Francisco Goya's tasteful nude *The Naked Maja* on display at the back of her classroom offensive and demanded that the harassment officer remove it for the "chilling atmosphere" it created (pp. 11–12). She won her case, and the Goya was removed. She also mentions the case of Chris Robison, a graduate student at the University of Nebraska, who was forced to remove a small photo of his wife wearing a bikini at the beach because it offended two of his female office mates. These and other cases are testament to the strong drive for the censorship of art in radical feminist aesthetics. In her book Hoff Sommers questions Wolf's empirical claims too, for instance, her claim that 150,000 American women die of anorexia every year. After a few phone calls, she discovered that the true number of deaths per year is at most around 100, which Hoff Sommers takes as typical of the exaggerated statistics found in accounts of the "backlash" against women described by gender feminists such as Wolf and Susan Faludi (pp. 270–271).

Be that as it may, Wolf's description of the beauty myth does match the gut instincts of many women in modern society who feel compelled to beautify themselves in order to live up to male expectations about their physical appearance. As the philosopher Ludwig Wittgenstein once said, we often are not able to notice what needs to be noticed because it's too obvious.

# The Beauty Myth

## NAOMI WOLF

*AT LAST,* after a long silence, women took to the streets. In the two decades of radical action that followed the rebirth of feminism in the early 1970s, Western women gained legal and reproductive rights, pursued higher education, entered the trades and the professions, and overturned ancient and revered beliefs about their social role. A generation on, do women feel free?

The affluent, educated, liberated women of the First World, who can enjoy freedoms unavailable to any women ever before, do not feel as free as they want to. And they can no longer restrict to the subconscious their sense that this lack of freedom has something to do with—with apparently frivolous issues, things that really should not matter. Many are ashamed to admit that such trivial concerns—to do with physical appearance, bodies, faces, hair, clothes—matter

SOURCE: Naomi Wolf, *The Beauty Myth: How Images of Beauty Are Used against Women* (New York: William Morrow, 1991), pp. 9–10, 12–19.

so much. But in spite of shame, guilt, and denial, more and more women are wondering if it isn't that they are entirely neurotic and alone but rather that something important is indeed at stake that has to do with the relationship between female liberation and female beauty.

The more legal and material hindrances women have broken through, the more strictly and heavily and cruelly images of female beauty have come to weigh upon us. Many women sense that women's collective progress has stalled; compared with the heady momentum of earlier days, there is a dispiriting climate of confusion, division, cynicism, and above all, exhaustion. After years of much struggle and little recognition, many older women feel burned out; after years of taking its light for granted, many younger women show little interest in touching new fire to the torch.

During the past decade, women breached the power structure; meanwhile, eating disorders rose exponentially and cosmetic surgery became the fastest-growing medical specialty. During the past five years, consumer spending doubled, pornography became the main media category, ahead of legitimate films and records combined, and thirty-three thousand American women told researchers that they would rather lose ten to fifteen pounds than achieve any other goal. More women have more money and power and scope and legal recognition than we have ever had before; but in terms of how we feel about ourselves *physically,* we may actually be worse off than our unliberated grandmothers. Recent research consistently shows that inside the majority of the West's controlled, attractive, successful working women, there is a secret "underlife" poisoning our freedom; infused with notions of beauty, it is a dark vein of self-hatred, physical obsessions, terror of aging, and dread of lost control.

It is no accident that so many potentially powerful women feel this way. We are in the midst of a violent backlash against feminism that uses images of female beauty as a political weapon against women's advancement: the beauty myth. It is the modern version of a social reflex that has been in force since the Industrial Revolution. As women released themselves from the feminine

mystique of domesticity, the beauty myth took over its lost ground, expanding as it waned to carry on its work of social control. . . .

The beauty myth tells a story: The quality called "beauty" objectively and universally exists. Women must want to embody it and men must want to possess women who embody it. This embodiment is an imperative for women and not for men, which situation is necessary and natural because it is biological, sexual, and evolutionary: Strong men battle for beautiful women, and beautiful women are more reproductively successful. Women's beauty must correlate to their fertility, and since this system is based on sexual selection, it is inevitable and changeless.

None of this is true. "Beauty" is a currency system like the gold standard. Like any economy, it is determined by politics, and in the modern age in the West it is the last, best belief system that keeps male dominance intact. In assigning value to women in a vertical hierarchy according to a culturally imposed physical standard, it is an expression of power relations in which women must unnaturally compete for resources that men have appropriated for themselves.

"Beauty" is not universal or changeless, though the West pretends that all ideals of female beauty stem from one Platonic Ideal Woman; the Maori admire a fat vulva, and the Padung, droopy breasts. Nor is "beauty" a function of evolution: Its ideals change at a pace far more rapid than that of the evolution of species, and Charles Darwin was himself unconvinced by his own explanation that "beauty" resulted from a "sexual selection" that deviated from the rule of natural selection; for women to compete with women through "beauty" is a reversal of the way in which natural selection affects all other mammals. . . .

Nor has the beauty myth always been this way. Though the pairing of the older rich men with young, "beautiful" women is taken to be somehow inevitable, in the matriarchal Goddess religions that dominated the Mediterranean from about 25,000 B.C.E. to about 700 B.C.E., the situation was reversed: "In every culture, the Goddess has many lovers. . . . The clear pattern is of an older woman with a beautiful but expendable youth—Ishtar and Tammuz, Venus and Adonis, Cybele and Attis, Isis and Osiris . . . their only function the service of the divine 'womb.'" Nor is it something only women do and only men watch: Among the Nigerian Wodaabes, the women hold economic power and the tribe is obsessed with male beauty; Wodaabe men spend hours together in elaborate makeup sessions, and compete—provocatively painted and dressed, with swaying hips and seductive expressions— in beauty contests judged by women. There is no legitimate historical or biological justification for the beauty myth; what it is doing to women today is a result of nothing more exalted than the need of today's power structure, economy, and culture to mount a counteroffensive against women.

If the beauty myth is not based on evolution, sex, gender, aesthetics, or God, on what is it based? It claims to be about intimacy and sex and life, a celebration of women. It is actually composed of emotional distance, politics, finance, and sexual repression. The beauty myth is not about women at all. It is about men's institutions and institutional power.

The qualities that a given period calls beautiful in women are merely symbols of the female behavior that that period considers desirable: *The beauty myth is always actually prescribing behavior and not appearance.* Competition between women has been made part of the myth so that women will be divided from one another. Youth and (until recently) virginity have been "beautiful" in women since they stand for experiential and sexual ignorance. Aging in women is "unbeautiful" since women grow more powerful with time, and since the links between generations of women must always be newly broken: Older women fear young ones; young women fear old; and the beauty myth truncates for all the female life span. Most urgently, women's identity must be premised upon our "beauty" so that we will remain vulnerable to outside approval, carrying the vital sensitive organ of self-esteem exposed to the air.

Though there has, of course, been a beauty myth in some form for as long as there has been patriarchy, the beauty myth in its modern form is a fairly recent invention. The myth flourishes when material constraints on women are dangerously loosened. . . . The beauty myth in its modern form gained ground after the upheavals of industrialization, as the work unit of the family was destroyed, and urbanization and the emerging factory system demanded what social engineers of the time termed the "separate sphere" of domesticity, which supported the new labor category of the "breadwinner" who left home for the workplace during the day. The middle class expanded, the standards of living and of literacy rose, the size of families shrank; a new class of literate, idle women developed, on whose submission to enforced domesticity the evolving system of industrial capitalism depended. Most of our assumptions about the way women have always thought about "beauty" date from no earlier than the 1830s, when the cult of domesticity was first consolidated and the beauty index invented.

For the first time new technologies could reproduce—in fashion plates, daguerreotypes, tintypes, and rotogravures—images of how women should look. In the 1840s the first nude photographs of prostitutes were taken; advertisements using images of "beautiful" women first appeared in mid-century. Copies of classical artworks, postcards of society beauties and royal mistresses, Currier and Ives prints, and porcelain figurines flooded the separate sphere to which middle-class women were confined.

Since the Industrial Revolution, middle-class Western women have been controlled by ideals and stereotypes as much as by material constraints. This situation, unique to this group, means that analyses that trace "cultural conspiracies" are uniquely plausible in relation to them. The rise of the beauty myth was just one of several emerging social fictions that masqueraded as natural components of the feminine sphere, the better to enclose those women inside it. . . .

So the fictions simply transformed themselves once more: Since the women's movement had successfully taken apart most other necessary fictions of femininity, all the work of social control once spread out over the whole network of these fictions had to be reassigned to the only strand left intact, which action consequently strengthened it a hundredfold. This reimposed onto liberated women's faces and bodies all the limitations, taboos, and punishments of the repressive laws, religious injunctions and reproductive enslavement that no longer carried sufficient force. Inexhaustible but ephemeral beauty work took over from inexhaustible but ephemeral housework. As the economy, law, religion, sexual mores, education, and culture were forcibly opened up to include women more fairly, a private reality colonized female consciousness. By using ideas about "beauty," it reconstructed an alternative female world with its own laws, economy, religion, sexuality, education, and culture, each element as repressive as any that had gone before.

Since middle-class Western women can best be weakened psychologically now that we are stronger materially, the beauty myth, as it has resurfaced in the last generation, has had to draw on more technological sophistication and reactionary fervor than ever before. The modern arsenal of the myth is a dissemination of millions of images of the current ideal; although this barrage is generally seen as a collective sexual fantasy, there is in fact little that is sexual about it. It is summoned out of political fear on the part of male-dominated institutions threatened by women's freedom, and it exploits female guilt and apprehension about our own liberation-latent fears that we might be going too far. This frantic aggregation of imagery is a collective reactionary hallucination willed into being by both men and women stunned and disoriented by the rapidity with which gender relations have been transformed: a bulwark of reassurance against the flood of change. The mass depiction of the modern woman as a "beauty" is a contradiction: Where modern women are growing, moving, and expressing their individuality, as the myth has it, "beauty" is by definition inert, timeless, and generic. That this hallucination is necessary and deliberate is evident in the way "beauty" so directly contradicts women's real situation.

And the unconscious hallucination grows ever more influential and pervasive because of what is now conscious market manipulation: powerful industries—the $33-billion-a-year diet industry, the $20-billion cosmetics industry, the $300-million cosmetic surgery industry, and the $7-billion pornography industry—have arisen from the capital made out of unconscious anxieties, and are in turn able, through their influence on mass culture, to use, stimulate, and reinforce the hallucination in a rising economic spiral.

This is not a conspiracy theory; it doesn't have to be. Societies tell themselves necessary fictions in the same way that individuals and families do. . . . Possibilities for women have become so open-ended that they threaten to destabilize the institutions on which a male-dominated culture has depended, and a collective panic reaction on the part of both sexes has forced a demand for counterimages.

The resulting hallucination materializes, for women, as something all too real. No longer just an idea, it becomes three-dimensional, incorporating within itself how women live and how they do not live: It becomes the Iron Maiden. The original Iron Maiden was a medieval German instrument of torture, a body-shaped casket painted with the limbs and features of a lovely, smiling young woman. The unlucky victim was slowly enclosed inside her; the lid fell shut to immobilize the victim, who died either of starvation or, less cruelly, of the metal spikes embedded in her interior. The modern hallucination in which women are trapped or trap themselves is similarly rigid, cruel, and euphemistically painted. Contemporary culture directs attention to imagery of the Iron Maiden, while censoring real women's faces and bodies.

Why does the social order feel the need to defend itself by evading the fact of real women, our faces and voices and bodies, and reducing the meaning of women to these formulaic and endlessly reproduced "beautiful" images? Though unconscious personal anxieties can be a powerful force in the creation of a vital lie, economic necessity practically guarantees it. An economy that depends on slavery needs to promote images of slaves that "justify" the institution of slavery. Western economies are absolutely dependent now on the continued underpayment of women.

An ideology that makes women feel "worth less" was urgently needed to counteract the way feminism had begun to make us feel worth more. This does not require a conspiracy; merely an atmosphere. The contemporary economy depends right now on the representation of women within the beauty myth. . . . As soon as a woman's primary social value could no longer be defined as the attainment of virtuous domesticity, the beauty myth redefined it as the attainment of virtuous beauty. It did so to substitute both a new consumer imperative and a new justification for economic unfairness in the workplace where the old ones had lost their hold over newly liberated women. . . .

The beauty myth of the present is more insidious than any mystique of femininity yet: A century ago, Nora slammed the door of the doll's house; a generation ago, women turned their backs on the consumer heaven of the isolated multiapplianced home; but where women are trapped today, there is no door to slam. The contemporary ravages of the beauty backlash are destroying women physically and depleting us psychologically. If we are to free ourselves from the dead weight that has once again been made out of femaleness, it is not ballots or lobbyists or placards that women will need first; it is a new way to see.

# ARTHUR DANTO ON CENSORING AND SUBSIDIZING THE ARTS

Arthur Danto (1924–) is an American philosopher of art, history, science, and knowledge who teaches at Columbia University. He is the author of many books, including *The Transfiguration of the Commonplace: A Philosophy of Art* (1981), *The Philosophical Disenfranchisement of Art* (1986), *Connections to the World: The Basic Concepts of Philosophy* (1989), *After the End of Art: Contemporary Art and the Pale of History* (1997), and *The Abuse of Beauty: Aesthetics and the Concept of Art* (2003). Danto is part of a group of analytic philosophers who have attempted to sort out such aesthetic problems as the vexing question "What is art?" We will therefore briefly look at these philosophers' efforts in this regard before focusing on Danto's views on censorship and subsidy in the arts.

Since the mid-1950s, analytic philosophers have searched for an adequate definition of art, preferably one that describes a set of properties that all art objects share but that non-art objects have only in part, if at all. There have been, speaking broadly, four general answers from analytic thinkers to the question "What is art?"

The skeptical view is the position that there is no one property or set of properties that defines all art objects. The creativity of artists—their ability to come up with entirely new definitions of what constitutes an object of art (think about Duchamp's *Fountain*)—frustrates and will frustrate all attempts to come up with such a definition. The best we can do is to sketch out the way that art objects resemble each other.

The functionalist view, pioneered by Monroe Beardsley in his book *Aesthetics* (1958) and in later works, argues that all art objects perform the function of giving their audience an "aesthetic experience." So the world of art objects has a functional unity not shared with objects outside that world. Two problems with functionalism are that (1) the concept of what an "aesthetic experience" is changes over time (what would Rembrandt have thought of Duchamp's works?) and (2) it has a hard time dealing with things such as *Fountain,* which many reasonable people would argue don't give them an aesthetic experience at all. Indeed, a common joke about modern art galleries is that one cannot tell the difference between "real" water fountains, fire extinguishers, and toilets and installation pieces that merely "look like" these things.

The institutional view of art was argued for by Danto himself in his 1964 article "The Artworld." He states that an object becomes a piece of art insofar as it is approved of by some element of the *art world,* the collection of museum and gallery curators, journalists, critics, performers, and other aficionados who at present concern themselves with art. George Dickie picked up this idea in his book *Art and the Aesthetic* (1974) and expanded on it in later works. He argues that for an object to become art, it must be created by an artist who understands what he or she is doing, who intends to present it to an art world public, and which is subsequently sanctioned in some way by an artistic institution. To use one of Danto's examples, Andy Warhol's *Brillo Box* differs from everyday Brillo boxes primarily because it is presented by the artist to a museum or gallery as being "about something," whereas the Brillo boxes sitting in your kitchen cupboard are just Brillo boxes, untouched by any institutional justification. The problem with the institutional definition is obvious: How do we know that institution X is part of the art world? Because it produces or sanctions pieces of art? The definition may indeed be circular.

The historicist view argues that objects become art when they are related to a cultural or historical tradition, with the stipulation that these traditions could radically differ from one time and place to another. In the context of the radical experimentation of modern art, Warhol's *Brillo Box* might be a work of art, but if it were transported back to the seventeenth century, the notion that it was art would be laughed at by both the artists of the day and their patrons. The problems with this definition are that (1) some works of art help to inaugurate entirely new traditions, such as Duchamp's *Nude Descending a Staircase No. 2,* and (2) it opens itself up to an extreme relativism—culture X might value an old shoe as a great work of art, whereas culture Y finds the notion ridiculous.

The reason that these analytic attempts to define art are relevant here, besides the part that Danto played in them, is that the debate over whether to censor or subsidize the arts depends very much on just *what counts as a work of art.* Danto introduces a few controversial examples of works that may or may not be objects of art: Andres Serrano's *Piss Christ* (1989), a photo of a plastic Jesus floating in a vial of urine; and at greater length the explicitly erotic, perhaps obscene, photographs of Robert Mapplethorpe. Are such things works of art simply because they're displayed in galleries? Should the state subsidize, or even allow the exhibition of, the frankly homosexual images produced by Mapplethorpe or Serrano's affront to Christian values? Danto argues that there are four general answers to the second question:

1. The libertarian answer argues that because freedom is the key value in a democracy, the state should neither support nor interfere with the arts in any way.
2. The fundamentalist (or feminist) answer is really a collection of related views that say, in essence, that there are more important moral problems than those connected with art, so the state shouldn't subsidize a relatively trivial activity; yet at the same time some so-called works of art offend community standards and

therefore should be censored. Alternatively, some feminists argue for the censorship of erotic images and films they see as pornographic because they denigrate women or deny them their civil rights.
3. The liberal answer argues that art should not be censored but should be subsidized by the state as a valuable part of human life.
4. The official "National Endowment for the Arts" answer argues that art should be subsidized but can also be censored if seen as obscene. Danto takes this to be a sign of the "politically correct" (though he doesn't use this term) times we live in.

Danto is a liberal. He interprets the "life, liberty, and pursuit of happiness" description of the purpose of the American state found in the U.S. Constitution as not just the requirement that we don't interfere with each other's lives but the positive requirement that the state enhance our life, liberty, and happiness through art, which is for him closer to a religious experience than to mere entertainment. Therefore the notion that the state uses tax money to support the arts makes perfect sense to him. In addition, it should not censor those arts, because part of the way that art makes our lives more meaningful is that it can challenge our aesthetic and moral sensibilities. *You* may not like the *Piss Christ* or Mapplethorpe's male nudes pictured in homoerotic activities. In fact, you might think that these things aren't even works of art at all, even if displayed in galleries. Yet these works serve to celebrate our freedom, regardless of their content. For Danto, censorship and freedom are incompatible. We might grimace at a photo of a nude man urinating in another's mouth—but if we ban it, we deny a part of that liberty that is at the core of the way we define our democratic culture. Naturally, many would disagree with Danto's generous liberalism.

# Censorship and Subsidy in the Arts

## ARTHUR DANTO

IT COULD NEVER have been foreseen, when the National Endowment for the Arts was established in 1965, that when the time came for renewal of its franchise, a quarter of a century later, art would no longer be perceived as an unqualified spiritual good. No one foresaw either the sexual revolution to come, or the liberationist demands which were to politicize it, or that there would be an increasingly explicit homosexual consciousness which was to seek to express itself in art, or that forms of artistic expression, marginal or underground in 1965, would become aesthetically mainstream by 1990. And possibly some of the acrimony with which the question of subsidy was debated can be traced to a kind of disenchantment, a sense even of betrayal by art, of all things secular the most exalted, so that a tension would have grown up between forms of art admired by the art world and forms of expression found repugnant to the moral sen-

SOURCE: Arthur Danto, "Censorship and Subsidy in the Arts," in *Beyond the Brillo Box: The Visual Arts in Post-historical Perspective* (New York: Farrar Straus Giroux, 1992), pp. 163–165, 168–177 (edited).

sibilities of the electorate, which was inconceivable in 1965. The uneasy extension of the Endowment's life for another three years from 1990 left unresolved the political and moral questions to which the tensions gave rise, nor can the issue of censorship any longer be discussed in abstraction from the complex of issues concerning the needs, rights, and interests of a diversified electorate in a political democracy, though it would have been assumed in 1965 that the question could not arise in a democracy, and that censorship in its nature belonged to the more repressive forms of the state.

As we have two concepts to consider together, then, subsidy (or endowment) and censorship, it will be valuable to identify the four possible combinations these generate, each of which, it goes without saying, has its partisans. This means that we cannot responsibly take a stand, either on censorship or on subsidy, without meeting the objections the other three positions will raise.

1. Art should be neither subsidized nor should it be censored. This is the libertarian view, which countenances a very restricted set of things governments can rightfully support, but holds in any case that government violates its legitimate limits by interfering in any way with the exercise of freedom.

2. Art should not be subsidized, but it should be censored even so. This may well be the position of religious fundamentalists, who will argue, on the one hand, that there cannot be anything with a lower claim to support than art, given the terrible human needs to which a morally responsible government must be sensitive. But these very moral responsibilities mean that a government might actively intervene in censoring art which is morally objectionable, even if it has not subsidized it. A weaker version of this position is that a government has a right to censor art, even if it has not subsidized it. . . . A still weaker version gives groups a right to demand that certain forms of artistic expression be censored whether or not the art has been subsidized, though if it is censorable, it was wrong to have subsidized it. This captures some of the feminist position on pornography, if we grant that it can be pornography and remain art, something not everyone

will accept. (Censoring pornography which is not art falls outside my purview.)

3. Art should be subsidized and not be censored. This is the liberal position, and it is my own. My argument with the libertarian, then, will differ from my argument with the fundamentalist, since the latter has a scale of allowable subsidies and can imagine, there being no greater priority, that art might be subsidized.

4. Art should both be subsidized and be subject to censorship. This is the actual view of the Endowment, which sought to enforce an antiobscenity requirement which a great many in the Congress found sympathetic. They were, on the other hand, more anxious not to be thought of as philistines than to be thought of as defenders of freedom under the First Amendment, which reflects, almost precisely, the temper of these times.

The conflict is further complicated by the fact that a different order of relationship holds between citizens and freedom of expression than holds between citizens and art, which is less a right they have than perhaps a need. Freedom may or may not be a need, but it is categorically a right. Our relationship to freedom defines us as a nation. Our relationship to art instead defines us as a culture. So quite different styles of argument apply when, from the position we mean to defend, we turn from one to another of the remaining positions. There is no straight course through this difficult terrain.

[*Danto goes on to discuss the proliferation of museums in America in the late 1950s and early 1960s, and how this was related to the importation of popular culture into the world of high art via the Pop Art of Roy Lichtenstein and others, which featured such common images as those of Campbell's soup cans, Dick Tracy, and the American flag. He then argues that going to a museum today is like the pilgrimage of religious believers to a cathedral containing sacred relics, and not just another form of entertainment.*]

Aesthetic pleasure is altogether an eighteenth-century concept. The term "aesthetic" was, so far as I know, first used then, though its connection with art was not immediate. The first division of Kant's *Critique of Pure Reason* is entitled "Transcendental Aesthetic," and it has largely to do with sense-experience in contrast with reason. That was 1781, but the term must fairly soon after have become connected with what we now think of as aesthetics, since in 1790 Kant published his *Critique of Aesthetic Judgement,* which treats of beauty and sublimity. It does not, however, especially treat art other than in terms of what it has in common with physical beauty. Kant thinks of aesthetics in terms of disinterested contemplation, where the paradigm aesthetic moment might be gazing at sunsets, as in the acutely romantic images of Caspar David Friedrich. But perhaps disinterested contemplation was an available attitude only when art was no longer seen as something with condensed power and magical presence. It would be very difficult, in reading Kant, to understand art as something people want to possess, or to collect, or in whose possession they sense their national identity, or in which they take pride. Kant seems to have taken a view of art as the occasion for aesthetic gratification and almost nothing else.

The disinterested aesthetic attitude distances art as something deep or dangerous or difficult or dark, and connects it with the faculty of taste, rather than passion or fear or feeling or hope. And I make mention of this fact in part because as an eighteenth-century concept—and a late one at that—it is not surprising that aesthetic considerations should have played no role to speak of in the great political documents of the eighteenth century, and hence no role in the American Constitution. The Constitution neither forbids nor does it oblige any governmental role in regard to art, and my sense is that an issue would probably never have arisen when art was thought of in the language of taste, pleasure, and gratification, and hence as almost quintessentially frivolous, or at least subjective and personal. The aesthetic attitude was revived in the 1950s and made almost official through the influence of the largely formalistic theories of the critic Clement Greenberg, who not incidentally regarded Kant's third critique, which in fact says almost nothing about art, as the greatest philosophical work on art ever written.

When it comes, then, to constitutional authority in the matter of subsidy of art, there is an understandable silence. The only enabling text might be found in the pursuit of happiness clause in our famous triad of basic rights. But the eighteenth century understood rights as side constraints—on governments, and the most it could assure would be that the state should not interfere with the individual's pursuit of happiness, nor with his involvement with art as maker or enjoyer of it, if this indeed should be compassed by the pursuit of happiness as a right. The government's obligation is only to protect us in the exercise of these rights, but beyond this constabulary function it has no license to do more. It is this very narrow view of the limits of the government simply to assure us our life, our liberty, and our freedom to work out our individual happiness which underlies the libertarian position on artistic subsidy and, needless to say, its position on censorship as violating both freedom and the pursuit of happiness. But in recent times a more strenuous view of the responsibility of the state has grown up, according to which we have rights we cannot enjoy without positive governmental support in matters of health and welfare. And advocates of this more strenuous schedule of rights transform "life," which in eighteenth-century discourse took "death" as its antonym, and instead advanced a normative view of life as something *worth* living. They would not consider that to be life which is barren, poor, squalid, brutalized, or unfulfilled. It would only be against this reformulation of basic rights that art might be a candidate for subsidy. The argument would have to be made that a life without art would be unacceptable, and that governmental subsidy is required to assure the exercise of this right. And that certainly cannot have been an eighteenth-century idea. My sense is—that it came forward at the time of the "BLAM!" era, when art began to be thought of as something which defines a form of meaningfulness which the museum expresses and to which the Endowment was a response and an acknowledgment.

This widened notion of rights is tacitly accepted by those who hold the fundamentalist position, inasmuch as they counter the demand for artistic subsidy on grounds not of principle but of priority. Their question is whether it is really moral to give money for art when there are so many needs conspicuously more desperate than a supposed need for art could be. This is a difficult position to counter, for though it accepts a twentieth-century conception of needs and rights, it seems to hold an eighteenth-century conception of art as pretty pleasures for the well-off. The tacit principle is that public funds should be allocated to no need when there are other needs more pressing, and hence that the maximally disadvantaged have highest priority, which then turns out be the only moral priority inasmuch as, as Christ acknowledged, the poor ye shall always have with you. In a society racked with crime, disease, ignorance, and poverty, is it morally acceptable to allocate funds for the enhancement of lives already tolerably well-off? On the other hand, it is a somewhat dangerous position in that anyone likely to be using it must, by its criteria, already be leading a morally unacceptable life. If the only morally acceptable life consists in helping those worse off than oneself, is it morally acceptable to use money for anything else? And are we not all in fact leading morally unacceptable lives if the schedule holds?

What is sometimes called "overridingness" has become a topic of intense investigation in contemporary moral philosophy. It was Aristotle's deep perception that morality is made for human beings rather than the other way around, and there is something decidedly wrong in then supposing the only morally acceptable life is that of the saint, in which the concerns of the worst off override all other concerns. The very moment, however, that we relax the requirement of sainthood, on ourselves as on our governments, and at the same time adhere to the widened notion of rights, there is room for the right to a meaningful life—and with this room for government support of art, just because access to art has come increasingly to be regarded as part of a meaningful form of life for modern persons. The issue, then, is how much support should be given, not whether any should be given at all.

And though this cannot be settled a priori, it is clear that constraints are going to be raised by those who retreat from the posture of sainthood, such as that the art should at least not offend the moral values of those whose lives it is to enhance. Surely if support of art is morally acceptable, this must mean that the art itself must be morally acceptable? Art may be life-enhancing—but only if it is life-enhancing art?

I shall return to those dubious inferences, but for now I mean only to express agreement that the right way to defend subsidy is to ground the claims in art being pivotal in meaningful lives, even if no one has a clear view of why this should be true or how the view should be justified. The tacit common view, it seems to me, is that art provides the highest values which secular existence acknowledges, except perhaps for love. Nobody is especially able to explain why this is so. Not long ago I spent part of my visit to an exhibition of Monet's so-called Serial Paintings of the 1890s at the Boston Museum of Fine Arts studying my fellow visitors. This was a very popular show, and it required significant effort to see it. One had to buy special tickets in advance, stand in line, and put up with being jostled by others seeking to get a better view of a particular facade of the Cathedral of Rouen, or poplar trees at Giverny, or the valley of the Creuse, or fields of grain stacks. What could they have been getting out of all this? I was going to have to deal with these paintings as a critical problem, but that was not their reason for being there. Nor could most of them be having much by way of visual pleasure, since the paintings were difficult and in some cases actually ugly. They were not aesthetes. The viewers seemed to feel, however, that they were in the presence of things of great moment, worth a sacrifice for the sake of being in their presence. And they wore their green or lavender metal badges the way pilgrims to Santiago de Compostela wore cockle shells, signs of having participated in an endeavor of great meaning.

No philosophy of art known to me especially accounts for this, certainly not that of Kant, with its emphasis on disinterested pleasure. The only exception might be the spectacular vision of Hegel, who contends that art, philosophy, and religion are the three moments, as he calls them, of Absolute Spirit, for it suggests that the defining attributes of any of the three must have some place in the other two. Hegel's view takes on a surprising confirmation when we reflect on one of the most familiar facts of all in connection with art, though one whose significance has been rarely remarked. Were art the unqualified good the consensus of the sixties implied, one would think that those who spend the bulk of their time with art should be the best and happiest of people. But the truth is altogether different: art people have terrifying egos, and are filled with intolerance and condescension, and spend their time in fierce bickers as to what is art and what is not. This is not true merely in the so-called fine arts but in literature and literary studies as well, departments of which are swept with the most acrimonious exchange of charge and countercharge. This could be explained if art really were religion in another form, for religion is the locus of dissent and heresy and imposed orthodoxy and bitter strife and deep and total intolerance. Philosophy at its deepest level is defined by irresoluble oppositions and paradoxes, and though there are no known cases of Phenomenologists burning Positivists at the stake, there is no solution to the issues which divide them. It follows, then, for deep reasons, that art should generate disharmony and division and plurality. It follows further that art cannot be integral to meaningful lives without the shadow of dissent, difference, offense. If there is a basic right to a meaningful life in which art is an integral part, there is no escaping the possibility of bruising moral sensibilities. Art could not have the seriousness it has without the implication of danger and of disagreement. When aesthetics was defined through taste, it was conceded that tastes differ. The differences I speak of are deeper than the divisions of taste because it is impossible, on the basis of taste alone, to explain why people would want to destroy, exclude, condemn, abuse, ridicule, riot, and censor. The in-

temperate critical response to Pop in the sixties might have been seen as a sign that in endowing art we were endowing strife!

Occasionally, though I characteristically enter art shows, as I did the Monet exhibition, as a critic who views art from the perspective of questions to be answered and explanations to be discovered, I am touched in the same deep and inchoate way in which I am supposing the pilgrims to the Monet show were. Oddly, this happened to me with the exhibition of Robert Mapplethorpe's photographs, held at the Whitney Museum of American Art in the summer of 1988, before Mapplethorpe became a household word in America. I had not thought to write the show up, but at a party someone spoke of the gay sensibility that suffused the exhibition and thought it ought to be dealt with, critically, by someone. It was then common knowledge in the art world that Mapplethorpe was dying of AIDS.

To the right of the entrance were three images: a portrait of Louise Nevelson, recently dead but in her portrait already looking like death under the heavy white cosmetic she characteristically used and the black circles under her eyes; a male nude, shown seated from behind; and then a male nipple, greatly enlarged in the photograph, with the pores and cracks of the surrounding skin, with hairs growing out of it, which conveyed a particularly desolate feeling: it looked like the skin Swift described with loathing as seen by the diminished Gulliver on the breasts of gigantic ladies, seductive in the eyes of those on their scale. It is a lesson in erotic optics. The dead artist, the vulnerable buttocks, the leathery button of sensitive flesh formed, I thought, a kind of rebus, a moral puzzle to be solved. The show was brilliantly installed. One worked one's way past portraits, nudes, and still lifes, some in shaped and classy frames, until one came to a room, diagonally across from the threshold, of difficult images: it was like entering a dark circle of hell. These were the famous images of leathered male eroticists engaged in the rituals of bondage and humiliation, among them a self-portrait in which the artist, a bullwhip coming out of his anus like an immense rat's tail, looks defiance over his shoulder at the viewer. These were men living out fantasies any of us might have had in fierce dreams. I found myself pretty shaken by them, perhaps because a boundary between fantasy and enactment had been crossed. But there one was, trapped in the farthest corner of the exhibition. One remembered now the images one had seen as more threatening than one had conceded, and one feared what lay ahead. The final image of the show was again a self-portrait, in which Mapplethorpe showed himself as a kind of dandy, with a look of philosophical interrogation on his brow. He expressed on our behalf, as it were, a general questioning with which everyone should have left the show. The question was posed through the initial triad of images, and it concerned the connections between art, death, sex, and the moral scene of the flesh.

Mapplethorpe's impending death could not be erased from consciousness, and I was told by many of how he had turned up at the opening in a wheelchair, but struggled through the show and then sent a gesture of gratitude to the Whitney in the form of a photograph he had done of a classical head in profile. What I want to stress is that he did not disown the images at what he and everyone else knew was the end of his life. If anything, he was grateful that they were being seen. And though they were special in a way, it was clear enough that the sensibility perspicuous in them was in everything, even the most seemingly innocuous of still lifes and flower studies. Richard Howard has said that Mapplethorpe aestheticized the phallus, but those phalluses were heavy, brutal, sullen prongs of flesh, and the truth was the inverse of Howard's claim: he had phallusized the aesthetic, transforming everything with the sexually energized archetype of male power. Sex drives the Mapplethorpe world, the way blind will drives the world in the philosophy of Schopenhauer. The entire exhibition was coded by the images that have since caused so great a stir, so those images are the key to the code, and his last artistic testament. The dying have a special authority. Mapplethorpe wanted us to respond to what gave meaning to his life and to what, even facing death as a consequence of having

pursued that meaning, it is difficult to believe he regretted.

I found and find it difficult to forget that show. It was a hot bright day in August when I saw it, and it was sparsely attended. There were no lines, but there was an absolutely appropriate reverential silence. There were no snorts of outrage, no stifled giggles, simply murmurs. It is a matter of some sadness to me that no one, ever again, will be able to see Mapplethorpe's work in that way. People will be jostled in crowds as they file past the images, or be directed to some special room where the explicit images are segregated, and asked to make their minds up whether they are obscene. They are in fact terrifyingly obscene and at the same time beautiful, if Rilke is right in saying that "Beauty's nothing / but beginning of Terror we're just able to bear, / and why we adore it so is because it serenely disdains to destroy us." The moral distance between beauty and prettiness must be measured in light-years of spiritual displacement.

When the prosecution was held against The Contemporary Art Institute in Cincinnati, for exhibiting Mapplethorpe's photographs, I found that I hated the experts. They were arrogant Kantians who treated these extraordinary images as formal exercises. One of them described a finger inserted in a penis as "a central image, very symmetrical, a very ordered classical composition." Images of men with objects stuck in their anuses were merely acknowledged to be "figure studies." The notorious image of one man urinating in another man's mouth was characterized as a classical composition. This demoralized the jurors, who in effect were compelled to say that they did not trust their eyes, that they really would never understand art. It was testimony of a kind that inserted a gap between the populace and works of art which the Endowment was instead established to close. There really would be no reason for an Endowment if the perception of experts and of the ordinary viewer are as radically untranslatable as the expert testimony in the case implied. Bob Colacello's recent biography of Warhol tells the same story: Warhol had left some photograph hairy arm stuffed up a hairy anus" and several other "more predictable penetrations." When Colacello demurred that the girls who worked in the office would find these objectionable, Warhol was despicably hypocritical: "Just tell them it's *art,* Bob. They're landscapes." Of the first-anus image he exclaimed, "I mean. it so, so . . . abstraaaact." In Warhol's vocabulary, "abstraaaact" applied to non-abstract contents he knew would offend. And that was the stance of the experts at the Cincinnati trial, in the event a successful strategy.

Of course, the trial was misconceived. On the same April 24, 1990, page on which *The New York Times* reported the trial of Dennis Barrie, against whom one of the charges was "pandering," which meant, among other things, "showing a child in a state of nudity," the newspaper ran an article on Barbara Piasecka Johnson's collection of religious art, which was being circulated in Poland. The picture the *Times* reproduced is Giovanni Bellini's *Madonna and Child with Donor,* and there the baby Jesus is, as naked as a radish. It is a proof, as Leo Steinberg would say, of God's fun enfleshment as human. Of course, you could describe it in as compromising a way as you chose, e.g.: "This woman is showing her kid to some joker down on his knees and staring at his little thing sticking out—and he's wearing his hair sort of long, like it was a woman's hairdo." The trick is to find a description adequate to its status as art. I would find equally poor a description which saw Bellini's work only as a composition in diagonals. Under neither description could I answer a question about the "redeeming social value" of Bellini's image. At a minimum I would want an acknowledgment that the man who paid for the painting has himself shown in a posture of adoration of the incarnate redeemer. There are many reasons, almost all of them metaphorical, why we fall to our knees.

When Andreas Serrano's work was punitively singled out by the Endowment, I heard many say that had he only refrained from the aggressive title *Piss Christ,* his photograph would have been acceptable, since, judged on aesthetic grounds alone, it was even quite beautiful. But I don't think Serrano meant to draw our attention to the handsome yellowness of otherwise anonymous pee: it was central to his intention that it be recognized for what it was really a photograph of— a plastic Jesus immersed in real urine. After all, Christ was spat upon and humiliated, mocked and sullied in some of the great religious images, and urine is a standing symbol for contempt or it would not play so great a role in S-M ritual degradations. Like all the body's fluids, it carries powerful meanings. Once, when the Helms amendment was under hot debate, I found myself defending *Piss Christ* against a man who upheld what he called morality in the media and who was clearly a pious person. We were guests on a show called the *McLaughlin Report,* concerning the redeeming social value of which I am not in the least certain, and we were riding back to Manhattan together in a limousine. I reminded him of Yeats's line "Love has pitched his mansion in the place of excrement." "I wouldn't call that Yeats's finest line," he responded, and I asked him to quote me a finer. We finished our trip in uneasy, almost symbolic silence. People talk about Christ's perfect body, but truly bodies are messy, smelly things. I have read of a thirteenth-century treatise in which is written: "Man is nought but fetid sperm, a bag of excrement, and food for worms. . . . In life he produces dung and vomit, in death he will produce stench and decay." Still, Christ was man under an aspect, even if God under another, and flesh had to be flesh if there were to be the instrumental sufferings of redemption. I believe Serrano when he describes himself as a religious artist. There may be a question of why the Endowment should, given the separation of Church and state, sponsor art like Serrano's, but that question aside, there can be no grounds for rejecting his difficult images.

A senator who appeared that day on the program made the point that artists must be accountable if supported, as anyone else must be, and my question then was how we distinguish censorship from accountability. The question could not arise save against an acknowledgment of artistic content—if we addressed art simply as Kantian formalists, the truth is that artists would be judged on abstract criteria, like symmetry and proportion and classical composition, and there would be little difference between bringing artillery before ballistics experts and artworks before aesthetic ones, and we would not speak of rejection as censorship, any more than when we finally terminate the production of a Stealth bomber. But if we acknowledge content, and suppose formalist considerations subservient to it, then accountability really is censorship. The senator truly posed a paradox: we are, in the case of art, giving subsidy to something we cannot, without forfeiting a deep freedom, call to account. We can then stop subsidy, but there is something willful in a government pledged to defend a freedom it is unprepared to tolerate in art.

Some will be offended, beyond question, but to defer to sensitive minorities is analogous to deferring to the least advantaged members of society in determining disbursement. I can imagine people outraged that someone should paint bowls of peonies at taxpayer expense when there are terrible demands from a suffering population. I can imagine someone calling vases of tulips painted at taxpayer expense obscene while AIDS ravages the nation. If we have an obligation to support art in the interests of meaningful lives for our citizens we have an obligation to allow that things which define human meaning can, when we think about them, or are made to feel them as through works of art, be pretty scary

things. We will have to accept this cost, even if no one imagined in 1965 that we would.

Imagine a work of public sculpture meant to be a monument to freedom. Freedom is to be its content, and the artist then seeks suitable symbols to convey this meaning. There is a contract between the artist and the commissioning agency, however, and in virtue of this the artist is not free: he is accountable, even if his subject is freedom. Freedom is celebrated when we allow or even support works whatever their content, even if it be bondage, as in some of the rank images from the leather world of Mapplethorpe. I would like, then, to think that every work of art supported by the government is a celebration of freedom, no matter what its content. Our system expresses itself through the National Endowment by forfeiting accountability while responding to the demand for meaningful lives.

Against this difficult imperative, it is astonishing how exactly right the Endowment was in sponsoring the mooted exhibitions of Robert Mapplethorpe and Andreas Serrano. Their values were not of course "ours," but no values are except those which define us as a nation, which means primarily the value of free expression. In that sense the values are exactly ours in subsidizing exhibitions which express values which are not ours at all.

# HAROLD BLOOM ON THE WESTERN CANON ─────────────

Harold Bloom (1930–) was born in New York and studied at Cornell and Yale Universities. He is one of the preeminent literary critics in America today, having taught since 1955 at Yale University. Yet he is an outcast from the tribe of critics, for he has almost single-handedly taken on most of the dominant schools of criticism of the last forty years. He is an agonist (from the ancient Greek word *agon,* meaning "contest" or "game"), a fighter who sees the writing of poetry and other literature as aesthetic competitions with fairly clear winners and losers.

Earlier in his career Bloom set out to defend Romantic poetry as a vital part of the Western Canon against modernist critics such as T. S. Eliot, who saw it as immature rambling about nature. He did so in *Shelley's Mythmaking* (1959), *The Visionary Company: A Reading of English Romantic Poetry* (1961), *Blake's Apocalypse* (1963), and *Yeats* (1970). Romantic poetry became academically respectable once again thanks to Bloom and like-minded critics.

In the middle part of his career Bloom turned from making close analyses of the Romantic masters to putting forward a general theory of poetry and literature. In the central books from this period, *The Anxiety of Influence* (1973), *A Map of Misreading* (1975), and *Poetry and Repression* (1976), he argues that great poets operate under an anxiety of the influence by those who came before them. To overcome this anxiety, this fear, they deliberately misread their predecessors and thereby repress their predecessors' influence upon them.

Of late Bloom has spent some considerable energy defending the Western Canon of literature, the set of literary works that has traditionally been seen as having outstanding and permanent aesthetic merit. The idea of a "canon" has been borrowed from Christianity, in which it refers to the list of writings accepted as genuine histories of Christ's life or as valid statements of Christian doctrines. Bloom's list of the literary Canon, appended to the end of his book *The Western Canon* (1994), consists of hundreds of authors and books. Yet the main players are clear enough: the Bible, the Torah, Homer, Plato, Dante, Chaucer, Milton, the Romantic poets (Blake, Wordsworth, Coleridge, Shelley, Yeats, and a few others), Whitman, Tolstoy, Nietzsche, Freud, and most of all, Shakespeare. Shakespeare is the king of the Canon for Bloom. Shakespeare cannot be deconstructed, historicized, or feminized—he towers over all attempts to trivialize him, to explain away his genius as the product of this or that set of social and economic circumstances.

The true test of the canonicity of the works written by these authors is the fact that we can read them over and over again and derive new insights and new meaning from them generation after generation (as opposed to the majority of explicitly political literature, which we can read usefully only once, and even then painfully). Whether or not they provide us with valuable moral, political, or religious lessons, according to Bloom, is entirely beside the point. In short, Oscar Wilde was right: Art must always be produced for art's sake.

Most contemporary literary critics have attacked the traditional idea that the Western Canon speaks for itself, that its works have an inherent aesthetic value that justifies their reading. Bloom calls all those who seek to take apart the Western Canon for moral or political reasons the "School of Resentment," an obvious reference to Friedrich Nietzsche's idea that the ignoble slave morality of the herd is nourished by their *ressentiment* of the strong and powerful. Bloom argues that the great works of the Western Canon have an "aesthetic dignity" quite apart from their power to morally or politically educate us. His list of enemies features most of the major schools of literary criticism today:

- The Marxists, who believe that good literature comes from the revolutionary class alone. We've already dealt with Marxist aesthetics in the Marcuse section. The Marxists provide Bloom with the central metaphor of the School of Resentment—the idea of art and literature as part of a class struggle.
- Deconstructionists (also called poststructuralists) such as Jacques Derrida and Bloom's former colleague at Yale Paul de Man, who argue that the meaning of a text is always deferred and unstable and that we can endlessly play with

textual criticism because there is no objective reality outside the text on which aesthetic judgments can be based. Deconstructionists tend to be relativist about the value of a piece of literature, arguing that any attempt to prefer one to another is an arbitrary act of egoism or power. See Chapter 9 for more on deconstruction.

- The "New Historicists," who largely follow the work of Michel Foucault. They argue with the Marxists that all pieces of art and literature are the product of a given historical location, going even further than Marx would have by adding the notion that all philosophical, political, and aesthetic ideals have at their core a power/knowledge equation. To *know* something is to exercise *power* over someone. They agree with the deconstructionists that purely aesthetic judgments are arbitrary, given the fact that all critics are tied to specific ideological ways of thinking.
- The multiculturalists, who argue that the Western Canon has been dominated too long by dead, white, European males and that most of these authors should be replaced by non-European, nonwhite authors (whether alive or dead).
- Feminists, who argue that the male-dominated Western literary Canon is tied to patriarchy and the oppression of women, so it has to be replaced with a counter-canon consisting of a large number of hitherto-ignored female authors, along with a handful of profeminist male authors.

What all five branches of the School of Resentment share is the belief that the value of a literary work is relative to something nonaesthetic—whether class, history, race, or sex—and that good literature should serve a political or moral function. Bloom attacks all five of these approaches to criticism in the reading selection that follows, the opening essay to his 1994 book, *The Western Canon.* He argues that great literature is a solitary thing, something we read and write for ourselves and for strangers. That it comes from some sort of social struggle is irrelevant. He sees the School of Resentment as yet another rebirth of Plato's moralism—his idea that we should ban poetry and certain types of music from the state for their corruptive influences. Such moralism may give us psychological comfort, but it produces and champions bad literature.

Good writing doesn't provide us with useful moral lessons—we certainly wouldn't want to live our lives according to the warrior code of Homer's bloodthirsty heroes, follow the backstabbing ethic of Shakespeare's Richard III, or rent the apartment upstairs to Dostoevsky's Raskolnikov (even if he gives us a rent deposit and promises to be quiet). Literature is not the story of conventional moral behavior—at least good literature, that is.

Bloom adds a pragmatic twist to his argument about the need to delineate and defend the Western Canon—critics have to distinguish good from bad literature because human beings are mortal and don't have the time to read all the books ever written (by Bloom's account the Canon consists of 3,000 works, by the way). Critics and readers must choose, and this choice is best done in terms of the aesthetic power of the works being chosen and not whatever moral or political lessons they might teach us.

As you may have guessed, his attack on the schools of criticism just mentioned has caused quite a furor in academic circles. Bloom has thrown down the gauntlet to all those who see literature, and by extension art as a whole, as having a moral, political, or spiritual function. He argues that great art is done for purely aesthetic reasons. We should value it as such and not judge it according to whatever ideology is presently fashionable.

# An Elegy for the Canon

## HAROLD BLOOM

ORIGINALLY THE CANON meant the choice of books in our teaching institutions, and despite the recent politics of multiculturalism, the Canon's true question remains: What shall the individual who still desires to read attempt to read, this late in history? The Biblical threescore years and ten no longer suffice to read more than a selection of the great writers in what can be called the Western tradition, let alone in all the world's traditions. Who reads must choose, since there is literally not enough time to read everything, even if one does nothing but read. Mallarmé's grand line—"the flesh is sad, alas, and I have read all the books"—has become a hyperbole. Overpopulation, Malthusian repletion, is the authentic context for canonical anxieties. Not a moment passes these days without fresh rushes of academic lemmings off the cliffs[;] they proclaim the political responsibilities of the critic, but eventually all this moralizing will subside. Every teaching institution will have its department of cultural studies, an ox not to be gored, and an aesthetic underground will flourish, restoring something of the romance of reading.

Reviewing bad books, W. H. Auden once remarked, is bad for the character. Like all gifted moralists, Auden idealized despite himself, and he should have survived into the present age, wherein the new commissars tell us that reading good books is bad for the character, which I think is probably true. Reading the very best writers—let us say Homer, Dante, Shakespeare, Tolstoy—is not going to make us better citizens. Art is perfectly useless, according to the sublime Oscar Wilde, who was right about everything. He also told us that all bad poetry is sincere. Had I the power to do so, I would command that these words be engraved above every gate at every university, so that each student might ponder the splendor of the insight.

President Clinton's inaugural poem, by Maya Angelou, was praised in a *New York Times* editorial as a work of Whitmanian magnitude, and its sincerity is indeed overwhelming; it joins all the other instantly canonical achievements that flood our academies. The unhappy truth is that we cannot help ourselves; we can resist, up to a point, but past that point even our own universities would feet compelled to indict us as racists and sexists. I recall one of us, doubtless with irony, telling a *New York Times* interviewer that "We are all feminist critics." That is the rhetoric suitable for an occupied country, one that expects no liberation from liberation. Institutions may hope to follow the advice of the prince in Lampedusa's *The Leopard,* who counsels his peers, "Change everything just a little so as to keep everything exactly the same." . . .

This [approach] reduces the aesthetic to ideology, or at best to metaphysics. A poem cannot be read *as a poem,* because it is primarily a social document or, rarely yet possibly, an attempt

SOURCE: Harold Bloom, "An Elegy for the Canon," in *The Western Canon: The Books and School of the Ages* (New York: Riverhead Books, 1994) pp. 15–20, 22–24, 28–30, 34–39 (edited). Copyright 1994 by Harold Bloom. Reprinted by permission of Harcourt, Inc.

to overcome philosophy. Against this approach I urge a stubborn resistance whose single aim is to preserve poetry as fully and purely as possible. Our legions who have deserted represent a strand in our traditions that has always been in flight from the aesthetic: Platonic moralism and Aristotelian social science. The attack on poetry either exiles it for being destructive of social well-being or allows it sufferance if it will assume the work of social catharsis under the banners of the new multiculturalism. Beneath the surfaces of academic Marxism, Feminism, and New Historicism, the ancient polemic of Platonism and the equally archaic Aristotelian social medicine continue to course on. I suppose that the conflict between these strains and the always beleaguered supporters of the aesthetic can never end. We are losing now, and doubtless we will go on losing, and there is a sorrow in that, because many of the best students will abandon us for other disciplines and professions, an abandonment already well under way. They are justified in doing so, because we could not protect them against our profession's loss of intellectual and aesthetic standards of accomplishment and value. All that we can do now is maintain some continuity with the aesthetic and not yield to the lie that what we oppose is adventure and new interpretations. . . .

The Canon, a word religious in its origins, has become a choice among texts struggling with one another for survival, whether you interpret the choice as being made by dominant social groups, institutions of education, traditions of criticism, or, as I do, by late-coming authors who feel themselves chosen by particular ancestral figures. Some recent partisans of what regards itself as academic radicalism go so far as to suggest that works join the Canon because of successful advertising and propaganda campaigns. The compeers of these skeptics sometimes go farther and question even Shakespeare, whose eminence seems to them something of an imposition. If you worship the composite god of historical process, you are fated to deny Shakespeare his palpable aesthetic supremacy, the really scandalous originality of his plays. Originality becomes a literary equivalent of such terms as individual enterprise, self-reliance, and competition, which

do not gladden the hearts of Feminists, Afrocentrists, Marxists, Foucault-inspired New Historicists, or Deconstructors—of all those whom I have described as members of the School of Resentment. . . .

The flight from or repression of the aesthetic is endemic in our institutions of what still purport to be higher education. Shakespeare, whose aesthetic supremacy has been confirmed by the universal judgment of four centuries, is now "historicized" into pragmatic diminishment, precisely because his uncanny aesthetic power is a scandal to any ideologue. The cardinal principle of the current School of Resentment can be stated with singular bluntness: what is called aesthetic value emanates from class struggle. This principle is so broad that it cannot be wholly refuted. I myself insist that the individual self is the only method and the whole standard for apprehending aesthetic value. But "the individual self," I unhappily grant, is defined only against society, and part of its agon with the communal inevitably partakes of the conflict between social and economic classes. Myself the son of a garment worker, I have been granted endless time to read and meditate upon my reading. The institution that sustained me, Yale University, is ineluctably part of an American Establishment, and my sustained meditation upon literature is therefore vulnerable to the most traditional Marxist analyses of class interest. All my passionate proclamations of the isolate selfhood's aesthetic value are necessarily qualified by the reminder that the leisure for meditation must be purchased from the community.

No critic, not even this one, is a hermetic Prospero working white magic upon an enchanted island. Criticism, like poetry, is (in the hermetic sense) a kind of theft from the common stock. And if the governing class, in the days of my youth, freed one to be a priest of the aesthetic, it doubtless had its own interest in such a priesthood. Yet to grant this is to grant very little. The freedom to apprehend aesthetic value may rise from class conflict, but the value is not identical with the freedom, even if it cannot be achieved without that apprehension. Aesthetic value is by definition engendered by an interaction between artists, an influencing that is always an interpretation. The freedom to be an artist, or a critic, necessarily rises out of social conflict. But the source or origin of the freedom to perceive, while hardly irrelevant to aesthetic value, is not identical with it. There is always guilt in achieved individuality; it is a version of the guilt of being a survivor and is not productive of aesthetic value. . . .

. . . Shakespeare *is* the secular canon, or even the secular scripture; forerunners and legatees alike are defined by him alone for canonical purposes. This is the dilemma that confronts partisans of resentment: either they must deny Shakespeare's unique eminence (a painful and difficult matter) or they must show why and how history and class struggle produced just those aspects of his plays that have generated his centrality in the Western Canon.

Here they confront insurmountable difficulty in Shakespeare's most idiosyncratic strength: he is always ahead of you, conceptually and imagistically, whoever and whenever you are. He renders you anachronistic because he contains you; you cannot subsume him. You cannot illuminate him with a new doctrine, be it Marxism or Freudianism or Demanian linguistic skepticism. Instead, he will illuminate the doctrine, not by prefiguration but by postfiguration as it were: all of Freud that matters most is there in Shakespeare already, with a persuasive critique of Freud besides. The Freudian map of the mind is Shakespeare's; Freud seems only to have prosified it. Or, to vary my point, a Shakespearean reading of Freud illuminates and overwhelms the text of Freud; a Freudian reading of Shakespeare reduces Shakespeare, or would if we could bear a reduction that crosses the line into absurdities of loss. *Coriolanus* is a far more powerful reading of Marx's *Eighteenth Brumaire of Louis Napoleon* than any Marxist reading of *Coriolanus* could hope to be.

Shakespeare's eminence is, I am certain, the rock upon which the School of Resentment must at last founder. How can they have it both ways? If it is arbitrary that Shakespeare centers the Canon, then they need to show why the dominant social class selected him rather than, say, Ben Jonson, for that arbitrary role. Or if history

and not the ruling circles exalted Shakespeare, what was it in Shakespeare that so captivated the mighty Demiurge, economic and social history? Clearly this line of inquiry begins to border on the fantastic; how much simpler to admit that there is a *qualitative* difference, a difference in kind, between Shakespeare and every other writer, even Chaucer, even Tolstoy, or whoever. Originality is the great scandal that resentment cannot accommodate, and Shakespeare remains the most original writer we will ever know. . . .

The silliest way to defend the Western Canon is to insist that it incarnates all of the seven deadly moral virtues that make up our supposed range of normative values and democratic principles. This is palpably untrue. The *Iliad* teaches the surpassing glory of armed victory, while Dante rejoices in the eternal torments he visits upon his very personal enemies. Tolstoy's private version of Christianity throws aside nearly everything that anyone among us retains, and Dostoevsky preaches anti-Semitism, obscurantism, and the necessity of human bondage. Shakespeare's politics, insofar as we can pin them down, do not appear to be very different from those of his Coriolanus, and Milton's ideas of free speech and free press do not preclude the imposition of all manner of societal restraints. Spenser rejoices in the massacre of Irish rebels, while the egomania of Wordsworth exalts his own poetic mind over any other source of splendor.

The West's greatest writers are subversive of all values, both ours and their own. Scholars who urge us to find the source of our morality and our politics in Plato, or in Isaiah, are out of touch with the social reality in which we live. If we read the Western Canon in order to form our social, political, or personal moral values, I firmly believe we will become monsters of selfishness and exploitation. To read in the service of any ideology is not, in my judgment, to read at all. The reception of aesthetic power enables us to learn how to talk to ourselves and how to endure ourselves. The true use of Shakespeare or of Cervantes, of Homer or of Dante, of Chaucer or of Rabelais, is to augment one's own growing inner self. Reading deeply in the Canon will not make one a better or a worse person, a more useful or more harmful citizen. The mind's dialogue with itself is not primarily a social reality. All that the Western Canon can bring one is the proper use of one's own solitude, that solitude whose final form is one's confrontation with one's own mortality.

We possess the Canon because we are mortal and also rather belated. There is only so much time, and time must have a stop, while there is more to read than there ever was before. From the Yahwist and Homer to Freud, Kafka, and Beckett is a journey of nearly three millennia. Since that voyage goes past harbors as infinite as Dante, Chaucer, Montaigne, Shakespeare, and Tolstoy, all of whom amply compensate a lifetime's rereadings, we are in the pragmatic dilemma of excluding something else each time we read or reread extensively. One ancient test for the canonical remains fiercely valid: unless it demands rereading, the work does not qualify. The inevitable analogue is the erotic one. If you are Don Giovanni and Leporello keeps the list, one brief encounter will suffice.

Contra certain Parisians, the text is there to give not pleasure but the high unpleasure or more difficult pleasure that a lesser text will not provide. I am not prepared to dispute admirers of Alice Walker's *Meridian,* a novel I have compelled myself to read twice, but the second reading was one of my most remarkable literary experiences. It produced an epiphany in which I saw clearly the new principle implicit in the slogans of those who proclaim the opening-up of the Canon. The correct test for the new canonicity is simple, clear, and wonderfully conducive to social change: it must not and cannot be reread, because its contribution to societal progress is its generosity in offering itself up for rapid ingestion and discarding. From Pindar through Hölderlin to Yeats, the self-canonizing greater ode has proclaimed its agonistic immortality. The socially acceptable ode of the future will doubtless spare us such pretensions and instead address itself to the proper humility of shared sisterhood, the new sublimity of quilt making that is now the preferred trope of Feminist criticism.

Yet we must choose: As there is only so much time, do we reread Elizabeth Bishop or Adrienne Rich? Do I again go in search of lost time with Marcel Proust, or am I to attempt yet another rereading of Alice Walker's stirring denunciation of all males, black and white? My former students, many of them now stars of the School of Resentment, proclaim that they teach social selflessness, which begins in learning how to read selflessly. The author has no self, the literary character has no self, and the reader has no self. Shall we gather at the river with these generous ghosts, free of the guilt of past self-assertions, and be baptized in the waters of Lethe? What shall we do to be saved?

The study of literature, however it is conducted, will not save any individual, any more than it will improve any society. Shakespeare will not make us better, and he will not make us worse, but he may teach us how to overhear ourselves when we talk to ourselves. Subsequently, he may teach us how to accept change, in ourselves as in others, and perhaps even the final form of change. Hamlet is death's ambassador to us, perhaps one of the few ambassadors ever sent out by death who does not lie to us about our inevitable relationship with that undiscovered country. The relationship is altogether solitary, despite all of tradition's obscene attempts to socialize it. . . .

If we were literally immortal, or even if our span were doubled to seven score of years, say, we could give up all argument about canons. But we have an interval only, and then our place knows us no more, and stuffing that interval with bad writing, in the name of whatever social justice, does not seem to me to be the responsibility of the literary critic. . . .

The terms "power" and "authority" have pragmatically opposed meanings in the realms of politics and what we still ought to call "imaginative literature." If we have difficulty in seeing the opposition, it may be because of the intermediate realm that calls itself "spiritual." Spiritual power and spiritual authority notoriously shade over into both politics and poetry. Thus we must distinguish the aesthetic power and authority of the Western Canon from whatever spiritual, political, or even moral consequences it may have fostered. Although reading, writing, and teaching are necessarily social acts, even teaching has its solitary aspect, a solitude only the two could share, in Wallace Stevens's language. Gertrude Stein maintained that one wrote for oneself and for strangers, a superb recognition that I would extend into a parallel apothegm: one reads for oneself and for strangers. The Western Canon does not exist in order to augment preexisting societal elites. It is there to be read by you and by strangers, so that you and those you will never meet can encounter authentic aesthetic power and the authority of what Baudelaire (and Erich Auerbach after him) called "aesthetic dignity." One of the ineluctable stigmata of the canonical is aesthetic dignity, which is not to be hired. . . .

All canons, including our currently fashionable counter-canons, are elitist, and as no secular canon is ever closed, what is now acclaimed as "opening up the canon" is a strictly redundant operation. Although canons, like all lists and catalogs, have a tendency to be inclusive rather than exclusive, we have now reached the point at which a lifetime's reading and rereading can scarcely take one through the Western Canon. Indeed, it is now virtually impossible to master the Western Canon. Not only would it mean absorbing well over three thousand books, many, if not most, marked by authentic cognitive and imaginative difficulties, but the relations between these books grow more rather than less vexed as our perspectives lengthen. There are also the vast complexities and contradictions that constitute the essence of the Western Canon, which is anything but a unity or stable structure. No one has the authority to tell us what the Western Canon is, certainly not from about 1800 to the present day. It is not, cannot be, precisely the list I give, or that anyone else might give. If it were, that would make such a list a mere fetish, just another commodity. But I am not prepared to agree with the Marxists that the Western Canon is another instance of what they call "cultural capital." It is not clear to me that a nation as contradictory as the United States of America could ever be the context for "cultural capital," except for those slivers of high culture that contribute to mass culture. We have not had an official high culture

in this country since about 1800, a generation after the American Revolution. Cultural unity is a French phenomenon, and to some degree a German matter, but hardly an American reality in either the nineteenth century or the twentieth. In our context and from our perspective, the Western Canon is a kind of survivor's list. . . .

The issue is the mortality or immortality of literary works. Where they have become canonical, they have survived an immense struggle in social relations, but those relations have very little to do with class struggle. Aesthetic value emanates from the struggle between texts: in the reader, in language, in the classroom, in arguments within a society. Very few working-class readers ever matter in determining the survival of texts, and left-wing critics cannot do the working class's reading for it. Aesthetic value rises out of memory, and so (as Nietzsche saw) out of pain, the pain of surrendering easier pleasures in favor of much more difficult ones. Workers have anxieties enough and turn to religion as one mode of relief. Their sure sense that the aesthetic is, for them, only another anxiety helps to teach us that successful literary works are achieved anxieties, not releases from anxieties. Canons, too, are achieved anxieties, not unified props of morality, Western or Eastern. If we could conceive of a universal canon, multicultural and multivalent, its one essential book would not be a scripture, whether Bible, Koran, or Eastern text, but rather Shakespeare, who is acted and read everywhere, in every language and circumstance. Whatever the convictions of our current New Historicists, for whom Shakespeare is only a signifier for the social energies of the English Renaissance, Shakespeare for hundreds of millions who are not white Europeans is a signifier for their own pathos, their own sense of identity with the characters that Shakespeare fleshed out by his language. For them his universality is not historical but fundamental; he puts their lives upon his stage. In his characters they behold and confront their own anguish and their own fantasies, not the manifested social energies of early mercantile London. . . .

The death of the author, proclaimed by Foucault, Barthes, and many clones after them, is another anticanonical myth, similar to the battle cry of resentment that would dismiss "all of the dead, white European males"—that is to say, for a baker's dozen, Homer, Virgil, Dante, Chaucer, Shakespeare, Cervantes, Montaigne, Milton, Goethe, Tolstoy, Ibsen, Kafka, and Proust. Livelier than you are, whoever you are, these authors were indubitably male, and I suppose "white." But they are not dead, compared to any living author whomsoever. Among us now are Garcia Marquez, Pynchon, Ashbery, and others who are likely to become as canonical as Borges and Beckett among the recently deceased, but Cervantes and Shakespeare are of another order of vitality. The Canon is indeed a gauge of vitality, a measurement that attempts to map the incommensurate. The ancient metaphor of the writer's immortality is relevant here and renews the power of the Canon for us. Curtius has an excursus on "Poetry as Perpetuation" where he cites Burckhardt's reverie on "Fame in Literature" as equating fame and immortality. But Burckhardt and Curtius lived and died before the Age of Warhol, when so many are famous for fifteen minutes each. Immortality for a quarter of an hour is now freely conferred and can be regarded as one of the more hilarious consequences of "opening up the Canon."

The defense of the Western Canon is in no way a defense of the West or a nationalist enterprise. If multiculturalism meant Cervantes, who could quarrel with it? The greatest enemies of aesthetic and cognitive standards are purported defenders who blather to us about moral and political values in literature. We do not live by the ethics of the *Iliad,* or by the politics of Plato. Those who teach interpretation have more in common with the Sophists than with Socrates. What can we expect Shakespeare to do for our semiruined society, since the function of Shakespearean drama has so little to do with civic virtue or social justice? Our current New Historicists, with their odd blend of Foucault and Marx, are only a very minor episode in the endless history of Platonism. Plato hoped that by banishing the poet, he would also banish the tyrant. Banishing Shakespeare, or rather reducing him to his contexts, will not rid us of our tyrants. In any case, we cannot rid ourselves of Shakespeare, or of the Canon that he centers. Shakespeare, as we like to forget, largely invented us; if you add the rest of the Canon, then Shakespeare and the Canon wholly invented us. Emerson, in *Representative Men,* got this exactly right: "Shakespeare is as much out of the category of eminent authors, as he is out of the crowd. He is inconceivably wise; the others, conceivably. A good reader can, in a sort, nestle into Plato's brain, and think from thence; but not into Shakespeare's. We are still out of doors. For executive faculty, for creation, Shakespeare is unique."

Nothing that we could say about Shakespeare now is nearly as important as Emerson's realization. Without Shakespeare, no canon, because without Shakespeare, no recognizable selves in us, whoever we are. We owe to Shakespeare not only our representation of cognition but much of our capacity for cognition. The difference between Shakespeare and his nearest rivals is one of both kind and degree, and that double difference defines the reality and necessity of the Canon. Without the Canon, we cease to think. You may idealize endlessly about replacing aesthetic standards with ethnocentric and gender considerations, and your social aims may indeed be admirable. Yet only strength can join itself to strength, as Nietzsche perpetually testified.

## Study Questions

1. What are the basic characteristics of classical art? Give a few examples of such art, discussing what makes them uniquely classical.
2. What view of nature do we see in Romantic art? Discuss a few examples.
3. How did modernist art break from both classicism and Romanticism? How would a modernist define art and the role of the artist? Give a few examples, discussing each.

4. Go to an art gallery, choose a couple of your favorite paintings, sculptures, or installation pieces, and see how the theories of art outlined in the introduction apply to them. Are they classical, Romantic, modernist, or postmodernist? How can you be sure?

5. Does art have a moral, political, or social function? What would Plato and Aristotle say? Should art be created purely for its own sake? Justify your answer either way.

6. What psychological characteristics did Burke associate with the sublime? with the beautiful? Was his distinction well founded?

7. Using Burke's definition of the sublime, describe a few things you have encountered in your life that could be classified as sublime. Did they evoke the sense of fear and terror that Burke associated with the sublime?

8. How did the Romantics view the act of artistic creation? How was this connected to their view of nature?

9. What was the role of the imagination and of strong feelings in the aesthetics of Wordsworth and Shelley? How does the Romantic poetry you've read give evidence of this role?

10. What did Tolstoy see as the function of art and as the role of the artist? Can we still take his view of the function of art seriously?

11. What did Adorno and most of the Frankfurt School think about popular music? Were they right?

12. What did Benjamin think happened to high art in the age of mechanical reproduction? What did it lose? What did he think of this loss? Why did he defend film as an art form?

13. Should good art have a unique aura surrounding it, or should we treat it as a commodity like clothes, cosmetics, and compact discs, something we buy at the corner store or a shopping mall?

14. What did Marcuse mean by "surplus repression"? Do we really suffer from this in consumer capitalist societies? Is there anything we can do about it?

15. What did Marcuse mean when he said that art was a form of negation, a Great Refusal of social reality? How did he connect this to the erotic nature of art? Does art really play this role? Give a couple of examples that fit Marcuse's theory.

16. What are the basic principles of Marxist aesthetics according to Marcuse in *The Aesthetic Dimension?* How does he attack these principles?

17. What does Wolf mean by the "beauty myth"? Does it really exist? Can we blame male power structures for imposing standards of beauty on women? Should women refuse to abide by these standards, even if it harms their professional careers?

18. Why in general are feminists suspicious of or hostile to images of female beauty, especially of the naked female body? Do such images objectify women? Is this objectification intentional on the artist's part, or is it something that feminists have projected onto such images for political reasons?

19. Case Study: Suppose that for years a nineteenth-century neoclassical painting entitled *Diana Triumphant,* depicting a naked woman holding a spear has hung at the back of your philosophy lecture hall. One day a group of militant feminists burst into the class and demand to have it removed because they find it offensive, and they think that most people will agree with them. Your professor does a quick poll and discovers that Diana has in fact offended only 5 percent of the male students and 30 percent of the female students—the rest of them prefer that she stay just where she is. The militants refuse to change their minds. How should we decide Diana's fate? Should we use majority rule and let Diana stay? Or should we prohibit art that offends even a minority of people if they are sufficiently adamant in their views? How small a minority should we have to please in this regard? What if only one student had objected to Diana's presence?

20. Is the institutional definition of art adequate? If I place a pair of my old shoes under a clear plastic box in an art gallery and affix the title *The Running Man* to the base of this

box, have I in fact created a work of art? Does it matter whether or not I call myself an "artist" or whether a patron of the gallery buys my work?

21. Have a look at *Piss Christ* and at Robert Mapplethorpe's photographs on the Internet. Do they fit the functionalist or historicist definitions of art? Can we make a case for censoring them? Does such art really celebrate our freedom, as Danto claims?

22. What is Danto's basic position on government subsidies for the arts? Is Danto's position on subsidies a reasonable one? If you pay $1,000 a year in taxes, is it fair that $2 of this amount subsidizes works of art you find to be morally offensive?

23. Should literature be judged according to the moral and political messages it gives? Should we refuse to read books with sexist, racist, or imperialist themes? Should university professors not teach such books? Explain your answers.

24. Why does Bloom defend the Western Canon? Which schools of literary criticism does he attack, and why? Will great authors such as Homer, Dante, and Shakespeare always be admired, or is this admiration based on specifically Western values and politics?

25. Is it a good idea for literature departments in colleges and universities to make their students read books by female and nonwhite authors for political reasons if this means passing up more widely acclaimed books by white males? Why or why not?

# *Bibliography*

## GENERAL WORKS ON AESTHETICS

Art Renewal Center: http://www.artrenewal.org/
A large online museum of art, especially good on the nineteenth and early twentieth centuries, with short biographical and interpretive essays on a number of artists. To quote the home page: "We are providing a forum for artists, scholars, collectors and the public to appreciate great art, and to recognize that they're not alone in their suspicions about the emptiness of modern and postmodern art. These suspicions are fully justified by the overwhelming body of evidence and historical facts." Searchable by name, movement, nationality, and birth and death dates.

Berger, John. *Ways of Seeing.* New York: Vintage Books, 1972. A short book, much used in undergraduate fine arts courses. Berger was a real cultural iconoclast in his day. He critically discusses the way we "see" works of art, with chapters on Walter Benjamin, on nudes as an expression of patriarchal domination, and on the way oil painting served to buttress social inequality.

CFGA: http://cgfa.sunsite.dk
Extensive gallery of fine art from the Middle Ages to the start of the twentieth century. Indexed by name, country, and time period. Excellent on the Renaissance and Romanticism.

Collingwood, R. G. *The Principles of Art.* Oxford: Oxford University Press, 1958. An important work that argues for the idea of art as an expression of the imagination.

Cooper, David, Crispin Sartwell, and Joseph Margolis, eds. *A Companion to Aesthetics.* Oxford: Blackwell, 1995. A reference work with 130 articles, mostly short, on all key issues.

Graham, Gordon. *Philosophy of the Arts: An Introduction to Aesthetics.* 2d ed. London: Routledge, 2000. Focuses on the issue of the value of the arts, with chapters on art and pleasure, emotion, and understanding, along with other chapters specifically on music, painting, film, poetry, architecture, and the aesthetic appreciation of nature.

Maynard, Patrick, and Susan Feagin, eds. *Aesthetics.* Oxford: Oxford University Press, 1998. A reader containing fifty-seven articles and selections with a multicultural focus.

Features pieces by Oscar Wilde, Clive Bell, John Dewey, Nietzsche, Aristotle, Hume, Kant, Collingwood, Burke, Arthur Danto, Roland Barthes, and John Berger, among many others. Comprehensive.

Sheppard, Anne D. R. *Aesthetics: An Introduction to the Philosophy of Art.* Oxford: Oxford University Press, 1987. A short introduction divided into two parts. In the first part, Sheppard explores definitions of art such as imitation, expression, and formalism; in the second part, she looks at literature in terms of issues such as the correctness of interpretation and literature's moral effect on its audience.

Townsend, Dabney. *An Introduction to Aesthetics.* Oxford: Blackwell, 2002. Contains chapters on defining art, aesthetic analysis, the artist, the audience, and the relation between them.

## ON BURKE AND THE ROMANTICS

Abrams, M. H. *The Mirror and the Lamp: Romantic Theory and the Critical Tradition.* Oxford: Oxford University Press, 1973. In this famous study of Romanticism, Abrams argues that the pre-Romantic artist held up a mirror to reality, whereas the Romantic artist sought to use imagination and vision to light the lamp of illumination for humanity.

Brown, David Blayney. *Romanticism.* London: Phaidon, 2001. Focuses on Romantic painting.

Day, Aidan. *Romanticism.* London: Routledge, 1996. An overview of Blake, Wordsworth, Coleridge, Shelley, and other Romantic writers that takes into account recent historicist, postmodern, and feminist readings of these authors.

Ferguson, Frances. *Solitude and the Sublime: Romanticism and the Aesthetics of Individuation.* New York: Routledge, 1992. Includes discussions of Burke, Kant, Wordsworth, the gothic novel, and the natural sublime.

Heath, Duncan. *Introducing Romanticism.* Illustrated by Judy Boreham. New York: Totem Books, 2000. A comics-and-text introduction.

Hobson, Anthony. *J. W. Waterhouse.* London: Phaidon, 1993. A survey of the important Pre-Raphaelite painter by a sympathetic author, with reproductions.

John William Waterhouse: http://www.jwwaterhouse.com/index.cfm
An attractive and comprehensive Web site by a fan of Waterhouse and the Pre-Raphaelites.

McGann, Jerome. *The Romantic Ideology.* Chicago: University of Chicago Press, 1991. McGann is critical of the "Romantic ideology" of Coleridge, Wordsworth, Shelley, and others, arguing that Romantic literature was produced in a specific historical context and embodied certain ideologies characteristic of that context.

Romantic links, electronic texts, and home pages: http://dept.english.upenn.edu/~mgamer/Romantic/
An extensive series of links.

See also the bibliographies appended to Chapter 3 and the section on Bloom in this bibliography.

## ON KANT AND TOLSTOY

Berlin, Isaiah. *The Hedgehog and the Fox: An Essay on Tolstoy's View of History.* New York: Simon & Schuster, 1970. Hedgehogs believe in one big truth, such as God, whereas foxes are empirically minded people who believe in a lot of things. Berlin sees Tolstoy as a fox who wanted to be a hedgehog, using *War and Peace* as his major evidence for this claim.

Gifford, Henry, ed. *Leo Tolstoy: A Critical Anthology.* Harmondsworth, UK: Penguin, 1971.

Kant, Immanuel. *Critique of Judgement.* Translated by J. C. Meredith. Oxford: Oxford University Press, 1997. One of several modern editions of Kant's seminal work.


## ON THE FRANKFURT SCHOOL

Arato, Andrew, and Eike Gebhardt, eds. *The Essential Frankfurt School Reader.* New York: Continuum, 1978.

Jay, Martin. *The Dialectical Imagination: A History of the Frankfurt School and the Institute of Social Research 1923–1950.* Boston: Little, Brown, 1973. The authoritative intellectual history of the school in its heyday.

Kellner, Douglas. *Herbert Marcuse and the Crisis of Marxism.* Berkeley: University of California Press, 1984.

MacIntyre, Alasdair. *Marcuse.* London: Fontana, 1970. A short introduction by the noted virtue ethicist.

Marcuse, Herbert. *Eros and Civilization.* Boston: Beacon Press, 1955. Marcuse's attempt to marry Marx and Freud that critiques our civilization for engaging in surplus repression.

———. *One Dimensional Man.* 2d ed. Boston: Beacon Press, 1991. First published in 1964 by Beacon Press. Marcuse's most important foray into cultural theory in which he criticizes the technological logic of domination of modern industrial societies and the one-dimensional thinking it promotes.


## FEMINISM ON ART AND BEAUTY

Broude, Norma, and Mary D. Garrard, eds. *The Expanding Discourse: Feminism and Art History.* New York: Icon Editions, 1992. Twenty-nine articles on various issues in the history of art from a feminist perspective, including pieces on the painting of nudes in the Renaissance, sexual violence in Rubens, Berthe Morisot, Gaugin, Frida Kahlo, Georgia O'Keeffe, and Judy Chicago.

Chadwick, Whitney. *Women, Art, and Society.* 2d ed. Rev. and exp. London: Thames & Hudson, 1996. A look at why the work of female artists has often been marginalized.

Hoff Sommers, Christina. *Who Stole Feminism? How Women Have Betrayed Women.* New York: Simon & Schuster, 1994. Hoff Sommers offers a detailed critique of Second Wave radical feminism, which she calls "gender feminism." Good on critiquing Wolf's notion of a beauty myth and on the feminist politicization of art (see her Chapter 12, "Gender Wardens," on this issue).

Paglia, Camille. *Sex, Art and American Politics.* New York: Vintage Books, 1992. A series of short and medium-length essays on modern culture that is heavily critical of both old-school feminists such as Andrea Dworkin and Catharine MacKinnon and French-inspired postmodern thought. Paglia defends rock music, drag queens, gay artists such as Robert Mapplethorpe, epic films, and the work of her mentor Harold Bloom, among other things.

———. *Sexual Personae: Art and Decadence from Nefertiti to Emily Dickinson.* New York: Vintage Books, 1991. Paglia's sweeping treatment of Western art and literature, which she sees as a dialectical struggle between Dionysus and Apollo, or nature and culture. In it she traces the cult of beauty back to ancient Egypt and Greece, and defends the "aestheticism" of Walter Pater and Oscar Wilde against the notion that art should have a moral or political purpose.

Pollock, Griselda. *Differencing the Canon: Feminist Desire and the Writing of Art's Histories.* London: Routledge, 1999. Pollock returns to the much-debated question in feminist aesthetics of whether the old masters should all be chucked from the artistic canon as patriarchal, being replaced by the works from underappreciated female artists such as Artimesia Gentileschi and Mary Cassatt.

Reckitt, Helena, ed. *Art and Feminism.* Survey by Peggy Phelan. London: Phaidon, 2001. A survey of works of art informed by feminism produced from the 1960s to the present. Illustrated.

## ANALYTIC AESTHETICS AND THE DEFINITION OF ART

Beardsley, Monroe C. *The Aesthetic Point of View: Selected Essays.* Edited by Michael J. Wreen and Donald M. Callen. Ithaca, NY: Cornell University Press, 1982. A defense of functionalism by its main proponent.

Davies, Stephen. *Definitions of Art.* Ithaca, NY: Cornell University Press, 1991.

Dickie, George. *The Art Circle: A Theory of Art.* New York: Haven, 1984. Dickie's revised version of his institutional theory.

————. *An Introduction to Aesthetics: An Analytic Approach.* New York: Oxford University Press, 1997. A short, analytically inclined introduction to all the big issues in the field.

Lamarque, Peter, and Stein Olsen, eds. *Aesthetics and the Philosophy of Art: The Analytic Tradition: An Anthology.* Oxford: Blackwell, 2003.

Weitz, Morris. "The Role of Theory in Aesthetics." *Journal of Aesthetics and Art Criticism* 15: 27–35. Weitz takes a skeptical view of our ability to find some core property in all objects of art.

## BLOOM AND THE WESTERN CANON

Allen, Graham. *Harold Bloom: A Poetics of Conflict.* New York: Prentice-Hall, 1994. An overview of Bloom's work. Each chapter contains a representative sample of Bloom's literary criticism.

Bloom, Harold. *The Anxiety of Influence: A Theory of Poetry.* 2d ed. New York: Oxford University Press, 1997. First published 1973 by Oxford University Press. Here Bloom argues that great poets systematically misread their literary tradition in order to overcome their "anxiety of influence," to establish themselves as the rebellious children of overbearing metaphorical fathers. Ironically influential in postmodernist circles, given Bloom's later attacks on post-structuralist deconstructions of the literary Canon.

————. *The Visionary Company: A Reading of English Romantic Poetry.* Rev. and exp. ed. Ithaca, NY: Cornell University Press, 1971. First published 1961 by Doubleday. Bloom's defense of the Romantics against the "New Criticism" of T. S. Eliot and others.

Fite, David. *Harold Bloom: The Rhetoric of Romantic Vision.* Amherst: University of Massachusetts Press, 1985.

O'Hara, Daniel T. *The Romance of Interpretation: Visionary Criticism from Pater to de Man.* New York: Columbia University Press, 1985.

Sauerberg, Lars Ole. *Versions of the Past—Visions of the Future: The Canonical in the Criticism of T. S. Eliot, F. R. Leavis, Northrop Frye, and Harold Bloom.* London: Macmillan, 1997.

Schultz, William R. *Genetic Codes of Culture? The Deconstruction of Tradition by Kuhn, Bloom, and Derrida.* New York: Garland, 1994. Focuses on how these three thinkers deconstruct tradition in science, poetry, and philosophy.

## WEB REFERENCE PAGES FOR ARTWORK

Follow these Web links to see the works of art mentioned in this chapter. You can also follow the links listed on Wadsworth's companion Web site for this book at http://www.wadsworth.com/cgi-wadsworth/course_products_wp.pl?fid= M81i&discipline_number=5.

Alternatively, you can go to a search engine such as Google, click on "Images," and then input the title of the work of art; or you can try the CFGA or the Art Renewal Center, listed in the Bibliography.

1. Lascaux cave paintings: http://www.historyguide.org/ancient/lecture1b.html

2. The Parthenon: http://www.timelessmyths.com/classical/mainland.html

3. Venus de Milo/Aphrodite of Melos: http://www.seakayakgreece.com/aphrodite.htm

4. Michelangelo's *David*: http://cgfa.sunsite.dk/michelan/p-michela2.htm

5. Raphael's *The School of Athens*: http://cgfa.sunsite.dk/raphael/p-raphae39.htm

6. David's *The Death of Socrates*: http://cgfa.sunsite.dk/jdavid/p-jdavid30.htm

7. David's *The Death of Marat*: http://cgfa.sunsite.dk/jdavid/p-jdavid26.htm

8. Géricault's *The Raft of the Medusa*: http://cgfa.sunsite.dk/gericaul/p-gericau7.htm

9. Rodin's *The Kiss*: http://cgfa.sunsite.dk/r/p-rodin2.htm

10. Waterhouse's *Circe Offering the Cup to Ulysses*: http://cgfa.sunsite.dk/waterhou/p-waterho6.htm

11. Renoir's *Dance at Bougival*: http://cgfa.sunsite.dk/renoir/p-renoir33.htm

12. Munch's *The Scream*: http://www.ouc.bc.ca/fiar/images/FINA131/munch_sc.jpg

13. Duchamp's *Nude Descending a Staircase No. 2*: http://www.uncg.edu/rom/courses/dafein/civ/nude_no2.jpg

14. Dali's *The Persistence of Memory*: http://www.mystudios.com/treasure/dali/persistence.jpg

15. Mondrian's *Composition in Red, Yellow and Blue* (1926): http://www.sospeso.com/contents/articles/boulez_p1.html

16. Pollock's *Convergence*: http://www.dawnsartroom.com/pollock_-_convergence.jpg

17. Duchamp's *Fountain*: http://www.thespoon.com/art/about/images/duchamp-fountain.jpg

18. For Manzoni: http://home.sprynet.com/~mindweb/page21.htm; for Klein: http://members.aol.com/mindwebart3/page30.htm

19. Graves's Portland Building and Portlandia: http://www.skyscrapers.com/re/en/wm/bu/122646/ or http://www.vocalgentry.org/portland/photos/portlandia.jpg

20. Serrano's *Piss Christ*: http://www.usc.edu/schools/annenberg/asc/projects/comm544/library/images/502.html

21. For Mapplethorpe: http://www.masters-of-photography.com/M/mapplethorpe/mapplethorpe.html or http://www.mapplethorpe.org/

22. Bellini's *Madonna and Child with Donor*: http://www.initaly.com/regions/veneto/pix/bell/donor.jpg

The Medium is the Message
MARSHALL MCLUHAN

CHAPTER NINE

# The Philosophy of Culture

## INTRODUCTION: WHAT IS CULTURE?
## CAN WE PHILOSOPHIZE ABOUT IT?

When we attend an opera, read a romance novel, watch a science-fiction show on television, or listen to popular music, we are engaging with culture. We swim like fish in the omnipresent waters of culture. Connecting with it is unavoidable, unlike some of the moral and political issues dealt with in previous chapters. But can we philosophize about it? Some philosophers have tended to be hesitant to do so both because the term is so difficult to define and because any arguments that could be made about it, unlike in logic, are very difficult to prove. And leaving aside problems associated with defining the term, culture is a slippery thing to get a handle on. It's always in flux, always flowing forward, like Heraclitus's river. It's always "becoming" something else.

However, some of the most interesting philosophical writing over the last generation or so fits into the broad category of "the philosophy of culture," and scholars who work in the relatively new disciplines of communications and cultural studies have written at great lengths about the nature of our culture. So it behooves us to spend some time looking at the shape of modern culture as part of our attempt to expand the canon of philosophy. In this chapter we'll look at some of the more important and interesting ideas about modern culture put forward over the last forty or so years by focusing on three central themes: (1) cultural critique, (2) technology, and (3) postmodernism.

Before we can talk about a "philosophy of culture," we'd better sort out just what "culture" is. Raymond Williams, in his book *Culture and Society 1780–1950,* says that "culture" originally meant "tending to natural growth" and a process of human train-ing—it had an organic sense to it. Later, in the eighteenth and early nineteenth cen-turies, it came to have four more meanings:

1. A general state or habit of the mind
2. The general state of intellectual development in a society as a whole
3. The general body of the arts
4. A whole way of life: material, intellectual, and spiritual (a meaning it came to have later in the nineteenth century)

If we condense Williams's four definitions into one, we can loosely define culture as the body of social and historical practices of a people or civilization as expressed in intellectual life, the arts (both high and popular), daily habits, and the material objects and economic structures that make these possible.

How do we philosophically approach the phenomenon of culture? One way is by doing cultural critique. In his pioneering work *Culture and Anarchy* (1875), Mat-thew Arnold leaned toward the fourth of Williams's definitions of culture, defining it as "a pursuit of our total perfection by means of getting to know, on all matters which concern us, the best which has been thought and said in the world . . ." Two pages later he defines perfection as "a harmonious expansion of *all* the powers which make the bounty and worth of human nature." In his central chapter "Sweetness and Light," he divided up the British society of his day into three classes: the Philistines (the mid-dle classes), who gave their lives and thoughts to becoming rich, that is, to business; the Barbarians (the aristocrats), who had a staunch individualism, who cared for their bodies and exercised chivalry, but whose accomplishments were chiefly exterior and lacked "light" (i.e., intellectual depth); and the Populace (the working class), whose upper elements were chiefly concerned with industrial machinery and allied to the Philistines, but whose main body was barely removed from poverty and squalor.

All three classes—the Populace in their beer-swilling squalor, the Philistines in their greed, and even the Barbarians in their obsession with appearances—lacked the "sweetness and light" that went into culture's pursuit of perfection. Thus Arnold offers us a picture of culture as a moral force, as a striving for perfection. Underlying this im-age of culture as a search for perfection was a class-based critique of his own society as one that *lacked* this very perfection or even any serious attempt to strive for it.

A second cultural analyst, Oswald Spengler, in his massive two-volume study of the rise and fall of civilizations, *The Decline of the West* (1917 and 1922), treated cul-tures as organic things that grew in the springtime of their lives, reached fruition in their summers, then slowly declined in their falls and winters, the whole cycle taking as long as a 1,000 years. He used the original definition of "culture" mentioned pre-viously: something tending toward a natural growth and decay. The eight cultures he found in world history—the Egyptian, Chinese, ancient Semitic (Babylonian), Indian, Mexican (Mayan-Aztec), Magian (Arabian), Apollonion (Graeco-Roman), and Faustian (modern Western)—each went through "morphological stages." They planted their seeds in myth and primitive religious thoughts in their springs, shooting up the buds of rational/mystical cosmological considerations in their summers, achieving rational Enlightenment and sprouting forth great philosophical systems in their falls, finally declining from cultures to skeptical, megalopolitan civilizations in their winters. The element of cultural critique in all of this was Spengler's classification of Western civilization as one in its last wintry gasps, no doubt partly under the influence of Germany's defeat in the First World War. He saw the cults of science, utility, and personal happiness; the decline of religion; Nietzsche's skepticism; the decline of philosophy from a calling to a professional occupation; the rise of socialism; and a mass of other things as clear evidence that we are now living in the winter of our culture. Though now largely discredited, Spengler's account of the decline of the West exercised a powerful influence on early-twentieth-century culture.

Turning to the authors included in this chapter, Christopher Lasch, Charles Taylor, and the Unabomber all have distinct reasons for why they believe that our current culture is rotten to the core. Lasch, based on his analysis of American culture in the 1960s and 1970s, concluded in his book *The Culture of Narcissism* that Spengler wasn't too far off the mark: We now live in a culture where psychological therapy has largely replaced religion, where people narcissistically pursue narrow personal goals, endlessly searching for a happiness that will always elude them, thanks in part to consumerism and its need to program into us an insatiable need to consume more and more products. Taylor is less pessimistic: He suggests that the very individualism that Lasch mocks is an important element in our cultural self-definition, although it is under attack from three malaises: Lasch's narcissism, the reign of instrumental rationality, and decline of democracy in a culture that worships specialization and expertise. Theodore Kaczynski, the notorious Unabomber, takes a Luddite position that focuses on the deprival of freedom resulting from our excessive dependence on technology: Our culture has created a race of mindless drones who live only to serve the industrial-technological system, a system that he feels we'd be better off just trashing to revive the freedoms we've lost.*

A second important issue for the philosophy of culture, not unrelated to the first, is the role of technology. Has modern technology alienated us from nature, as the Romantic poets suggest? Or should we embrace it as the early-twentieth-century Italian writer F. T. Marinetti and his futurist colleagues suggest, seeing all its manifestations—modern communications, modern means of transportation, modern art, modern literature, modern warfare—as uniquely human things of beauty?

As part of this attempt to understand the role of technology in our culture, we can look at how modern media and technologies of communication change our ways of perceiving our world, change our physical and moral natures. The dean of philosophers of media and communications is Marshall McLuhan. His ideas were nurtured in the 1950s when he wrote about advertising. But he achieved fame in the psychedelic 1960s, when his cryptic claims about technology and media were taken to heart by the so-called flower-power generation. His books *The Gutenberg Galaxy* (1962) and *Understanding Media* (1964) were (and still are) groundbreaking attempts at understanding contemporary culture. McLuhan thought that every new communications technology extends the human body in either space or time. Simultaneously, this new technology or media amputates, or cuts off, some other human physical

*The Luddites were early-nineteenth-century English handicrafts workers who deliberately destroyed the new weaving machines and the factories that housed them to protect their traditional livelihoods. Metaphorically, a Luddite is anyone who advocates the aggressive rejection of new technology for moral or political reasons. See the commentary on the Unabomber for details on the Luddites.

power. He also thought that each new media alters the relationship or "ratio" between our senses, emphasizing one and reducing the power of another.

Here's an example: When you buy a car, you can "extend" your body through much more space than you can by walking or using a bicycle. Driving to a town one hundred miles away takes less than two hours, whereas for our horse-driven ancestors it would have been a major journey, taking several days. Yet at the same time you lose the benefits of exercise, gain weight, and have to react to your fellow drivers' decisions in a split second, causing stress and road rage. Also, you can no longer run into friends walking down the street and have a chat with them, or pause to pet a neighborhood cat. So buying a car changes both your body and the relationship between your senses.

Another example is connecting to the Internet from a home computer (because McLuhan died in 1980, he obviously wasn't aware of the Internet, though it's easy enough to extend his style of analysis to this case). On the one hand, we can connect almost instantaneously to anyone else on the Internet with e-mail, do academic research on the World Wide Web, or have some fun surfing through Web sites on our favorite musicians, movie stars, or Eastern philosophies. We can extend our minds, our audiovisual awareness, through space. On the other hand, we're stuck at our desks or in crowded public computer rooms while we're doing this, deprived of the sounds, smells, touch, and taste of the world around us—of both other people and our natural environment. The extension through time and space that the Internet gives us comes at the price of deadening our sensory awareness of our immediate worlds.

A burning issue for many cultural theorists is how the power of computers and their associated "virtual realities" shape or distort our lives. William Gibson, the author of a number of "cyberpunk" novels that depict a dark future where high-tech corporations rule the day, coined the term "cyberspace" in his 1984 novel *Neuromancer.* His character Bobby Case defined it as "mankind's consensual illusion"—in the novel, a virtual space full of representations of computer programs and data that Bobby and his hacker friends could mentally maneuver through after "jacking in" by means of specially designed computer decks (modems that link their user's brain directly into this cyberspace). In essence, Gibson anticipated the Internet, the global communications network that today, at least potentially, links together all personal and institutional computers.

Some thinkers, such as Mark Kingwell, don't approve of all these and similar developments: He thinks that our technological culture has sped up our lives to the detriment of happiness and philosophical reflection. It's as though we feel we are all on this big bus called modern culture, and if we try to slow down, a specially designed bomb will explode, killing us all. We need the fastest computers, the quickest means of transportation, the snappiest commentaries on television, the visually thickest films. Opposed to this, Kingwell hints at a subversive movement for slowness, for using and abusing the technology of speed against itself. Others, such as Heidi Hochenedel, think that these advances in modern means of communications have more mixed effects and that we shouldn't be too quick to condemn the clarity, speed, and expanded scope for communication that e-mail and the Internet bring us—we can now connect to people on the other side of the world at the speed of light, and this is no mean feat.

Connected to the analysis of our technological culture is the question of whether we now live in a different era—no longer "modern times" but a postmodern epoch, the third theme of this chapter. We will try to define the term "postmodernism" and to answer this question at greater length in the section on postmodern culture. Suffice it to say that many contemporary philosophers of culture answer this question in the affirmative: We do in fact live in a "postmodern" era, and therefore modernity—the era of mass industrial production, the belief in moral and political progress, and the search for truth in philosophy and literature—is over. Postmodernity is supposedly a postindustrial era dominated by mass media and computer simulations, one in which most of us reject grand truths, including the notion that philosophical language can "represent" reality.

The French thinker J. F. Lyotard in his 1979 book, *The Postmodern Condition,* says that our postmodern era is defined by the fact that we no longer believe in metanarratives, "big stories" such as the march of liberal progress, the reality and benevolence of the Christian God, the emancipation of the working class through a Communist revolution, or the power of Reason to give us Truth. It's not that large numbers of people here and there don't believe in these stories; instead, he argues that our culture is no longer *defined* by these ideas (as it was up until the middle of the twentieth century).

The other thinker we'll look at in this section, Jean Baudrillard, is the *enfant terrible* of French postmodern philosophers. He believes (extending McLuhan's analysis) that postmodern culture's love of film, television, computers, virtual reality games, and technological means of communication in general has resulted in a "death of the real" and the coming of a "hyperreal" culture. Now, instead of the mass-produced copies of some general model characteristic of the Industrial Age, we have simulations of reality in television shows, computer games, and Web pages as our central cultural preoccupations.

Both Lyotard and Baudrillard are part of a philosophical movement usually termed "post-structuralism." Evidently, this movement came *after* structuralism. What is "structuralism"? In general, any thinker who sees in phenomena such as language, mythology, politics, history, and popular culture underlying *structures* that help us to understand and explain those phenomena are "structuralists." More specifically, modern structuralism got its kick start from Ferdinand de Saussure (1857–1913), a turn-of-the-century linguist who saw language as a system of signs, a sort of "code." He called the science of this code "semiology." Saussure broke down each word in a language into two elements: (1) a *signifier,* the marks on paper or sounds representing the word (e.g., *cat*), and (2) a *signified,* the concept or meaning connected to this representation (e.g., "a furry beast with whiskers who purrs and likes to prowl around at night"):

*Signifier*                                                    *Signified*

*cat*

*le chat* (French)

*die Katze* (German)

. . . and so on through all human languages

Saussure argued, against a large part of the philosophical tradition, that the relation between signifier and signified (which together make up the "sign") is arbitrary: After all, in French the furry beast becomes *le chat,* in German *die Katze.* The meaning of words isn't guaranteed by reality—it is purely the product of human conventions and structures. Later, analysts of cultural phenomena such as fashion, every-day dress, music, magazine ads, music videos, and films adopted a semiological approach to their subject matter, interpreting these things as codes or forms of language (e.g., the closely cropped hair, heavy black boots, and aggressive behavior of the British skinhead subculture has been read semiologically as a desperate attempt to retrieve lost working-class masculine values). Semiology—the reading of the practices of everyday life as systems of signs—has had a tremendous impact on the new discipline of cultural studies, for it allows scholars to "decode" what might seem to be random or unplanned choices (such as musical tastes or clothes) as culturally meaningful events.

The structuralists thought that we know the world through conceptual or linguistic structures, not as pure data. The post-structuralists take the structuralist position on language one step further. Post-structuralists agree with the structuralists that we can't get outside of language to find the "true" meanings of words, but find structuralism too formal and restricting. Under the inspiration of Jacques Derrida, they conclude that all human phenomena can be read as languages and that "there is nothing outside the text." In simple terms, all things that attempt to convey meaning—from Plato's *Republic* to low-budget horror films, from the Bible to shopping malls—are texts. Further, these post-structuralist thinkers see signifier and signified as collapsing into each other—the mark or sound of a linguistic sign is seen as entering an intimate relationship with its real-world referent, just as the "real" world simultaneously collapses into a world of ideas and concepts constructed by human culture.

The post-structuralists believe that the signs used by a given language don't have fixed meanings—texts can be read in many different ways. There is no one "true" reading of a text, because there is no extratextual reality to guarantee its truth. It would be like trying to anchor a ship in a bottomless sea. Because everything is a text, the post-structuralists generally argue that we live in an "intertextual" universe: The only way we can check our interpretation of one text is by comparing it to another. Naturally, this has led many more traditionally minded thinkers to attack the post-structuralists as relativists—if we can't pin the meaning of even *simple* words down by seeing how they correspond to some nonlinguistic reality, then how can we do philosophy? If we give up on truth, doesn't this turn all philosophy into literature, or even worse, rhetoric? However odd this might seem, this is precisely what some radical post-structuralist thinkers seem to be saying.

Whether or not their critique is valid, post-structuralist thought has been very influential in the philosophy of culture. Under the influence of Derrida, many followers of the movement took up the method of deconstruction (see Chapter 4) to attack what they saw as oppressive intellectual power structures based on binary opposites such as "male/female," "white/black," "colonialism/tribalism," "reason/emotion," and "Christian/pagan." These pairs, they argue, underlie Western systems of value, justifying the oppression of those defined by the second term in the pair (e.g., women, blacks) by those defined by the first (e.g., men, whites). By deconstructively tearing these and other binary pairs apart, post-structuralists have given us feminist, black, postcolonialist, queer, and other readings of the central "texts" of our culture that differ markedly from the canonical readings provided by the previously dominant white male cultural elites. Literature, art, science, popular culture, and even philosophy itself, after put under the scalpel of deconstruction, no longer seem to be the innocent pursuits of truth or pleasure that they may have once seemed to the cultural elites prior to the 1960s (although, as any good Marxist or Freudian will tell you, their false innocence had been exposed long before the coming of post-structuralism).

We finish this reader with a selection from the Canadian thinker John Ralston Saul that nicely ties in the philosophy of culture to the Greek foundations of Western thought. Saul presents us with a fundamental challenge: the idea that we live in an "unconscious" civilization, one in which we have abandoned the traditional Western notion of individualism in favor of corporatism, a state of affairs in which our primary allegiances are to the corporate bodies that we work within, not to our individual sense of reason or to any notion of the public good. This has led us to a blind acceptance of modern ideologies such as economic determinism and the worship of the marketplace.

We've come full circle with Saul. He appeals to Socrates' idea that the job of the philosopher is to go out into the world and question people about what they think they know, to question their moral and political presuppositions, to act as a gadfly. Only by taking up once again the Socratic project of questioning the ideologies that dominate our culture can we free that culture from the corporatism that has turned us from reasonable citizens into slaves of corporate ideology. We thus end where we started (not unusual for philosophers, by the way): with the idea of philosophy as a fundamental questioning of the beliefs and values of our culture, with Socrates' claim that the unexamined life is not worth living. This was the first reason explicitly given by Western thinkers to be a philosopher, and is probably still the best one.

# ROTTEN AT THE CORE: NARCISSISM AND MALAISE

## *Christopher Lasch and the Culture of Narcissism*

Christopher Lasch (1932–1994) was a leading American critic of both liberalism and consumer capitalism. He was the author of a number of works that interwove history, psychology, and politics, the most famous ones being *The Culture of Narcissism* (1979), *The Minimal Self* (1984), and *The True and Only Heaven: Progress and Its Critics* (1991). A conservative dinosaur to some, to others he was a late representative of the Frankfurt School of critical theory, which combined Marxism with the psychological insights into the unconscious mind of Freud and psychoanalysis. Lasch was mainly interested in applying his own brand of critical theory to American culture. His early works explicitly appeal to Marx and Freud, as does his 1965 book, *The New Radicalism in America*, which offered a radical critique of American culture based on bringing Marxism and Freudian psychoanalysis together into one theoretical model. Later, he turned away to some degree from his formative influences toward a renewal of religious faith as the best road to a revival of the democratic spirit in American life. His last major book, *The True and Only Heaven*, opposed a heroic conception of life to the humdrum banality of the liberal capitalist view of the citizen as a happy consumer, spending weekends looking for bargains in suburban shopping malls.

His basic claim, at least in his writings in the 1970s and 1980s (and around which he wobbles a fair bit), is that consumer capitalism has eroded older, more durable ideas of the self, especially the "rugged individualism" of the economic or historical man of the nineteenth century, and replaced this with a culture that celebrates the self-loving narcissistic "psychological self." This self is constantly insecure and in search of admiration and quick pleasures, fleeing from commitment to others and to long-term projects of labor or spirit. This new "minimal" self finds its solace not in religion or family life but in therapy, self-help books, and short-term working and sexual relationships. Perhaps ironically (given his distrust of psychotherapy), Lasch sees his attack on this narcissistic self as underpinned by the extension of the insights gained from individual cases of therapy done on extremely narcissistic patients into a social criticism of the whole culture. For Lasch in his heyday, American culture as a whole was his patient, and he was the psychoanalyst offering a pessimistic diagnosis of its sorry state.

The following selections are taken from Lasch's lively best seller *The Culture of Narcissism.* In them we hear Lasch give us his rather biting definition of the narcissistic personality, elements of which we can all too easily recognize in our friends and neighbors. He explains that this is largely a product of advertising, the "propaganda of commodities," which instills in us an endless alienation from the products we consume (to sell more of them, naturally); that this culture has led to an escalation of cynicism and self-consciousness, as more and more people are forced to do work they see as beneath them; and that we have experienced in the last generation or two an erosion of family life and of romantic love, which are replaced with an uncommitted, anxious promiscuity and a "sex war" between unhappy feminists and their confused male lovers. Lasch's way out is ambiguous: He speaks at the end of the book about struggling against both bureaucracy and capitalism and of the creation of "communities of competence." But even if Doctor Lasch is unsure about the cure, he *is* sure about the disease: the culture of narcissism.

# The Culture of Narcissism

## CHRISTOPHER LASCH

### The Narcissistic Personality of Our Time

#### NARCISSISM IN RECENT CLINICAL LITERATURE

. . . On the principle that pathology represents a heightened version of normality, the "pathological narcissism" found in character disorders of this type should tell us something about narcissism as a social phenomenon. Studies of personality disorders that occupy the border line between neurosis and psychosis, though written for clinicians and making no claims to shed light on social or cultural issues, depict a type of personality that ought to be immediately recognizable, in a more subdued form, to observers of the

SOURCE: Christopher Lasch, *The Culture of Narcissism: American Life in an Age of Diminishing Expectations* (New York: Norton, 1978). Selections from preface, chaps. 2, 4, and 8, pp. 38, 39–40, 71–74, 90–96, 187–198 (edited). Copyright 1991 by Christopher Lasch. Used by permission of W. W. Norton & Company, Inc.

contemporary cultural scene: facile at managing the impressions he gives to others, ravenous for admiration but contemptuous of those he manipulates into providing it; unappeasably hungry for emotional experiences with which to fill an inner void; terrified of aging and death. . . .

Because the intrapsychic world of these patients is so thinly populated—consisting only of the "grandiose self," in Kernberg's words, "the devalued, shadowy images of self and others, and potential persecutors"—they experience intense feelings of emptiness and inauthenticity. Although the narcissist can function in the everyday world and often charms other people (not least with his "pseudo-insight into his personality"), his devaluation of others, together with his lack of curiosity about them, impoverishes his personal life and reinforces the "subjective experience of emptiness." Lacking any real intellectual engagement with the world—notwithstanding a frequently inflated estimate of his own intellectual abilities—he has little capacity for sublimation. He therefore depends on others for constant infusions of approval and admiration. He "must attach [himself] to someone, living an almost parasitic" existence. At the same time, his fear of emotional dependence, together with his manipulative, exploitive approach to personal relations, makes these relations bland, superficial, and deeply unsatisfying. "The ideal relationship to me would be a two month relationship," said a borderline patient. "That way there'd be no commitment. At the end of the two months I'd just break it off."

Chronically bored, restlessly in search of instantaneous intimacy—of emotional titillation without involvement and dependence—the narcissist is promiscuous and often pansexual as well, since the fusion of pregenital and Oedipal impulses in the service of aggression encourages polymorphous perversity. The bad images he has internalized also make him chronically uneasy about his health, and hypochondria in turn gives him a special affinity for therapy and for therapeutic groups and movements. . . .

# The Banality of Pseudo-Self-Awareness: Theatrics of Politics and Everyday Existence

The death of conscience is not the death of self-consciousness.

HARRY CROSBY

## THE PROPAGANDA OF COMMODITIES

In the early days of industrial capitalism, employers saw the workingman as no more than a beast of burden—"a man of the type of the ox," in the words of the efficiency expert Frederick W. Taylor. Capitalists considered the worker purely as a producer; they cared nothing for the worker's activities in his leisure time—the little leisure that was left to him after twelve or fourteen hours in the factory. Employers attempted to supervise the worker's life on the job, but their control ended when the worker left the factory at closing time. Even when Henry Ford established a Sociological Department at the Ford Motor Works in 1914, he regarded the supervision of the workers' private lives merely as a means of making the men sober, thrifty, industrious producers. Ford's sociologists attempted to impose an old-fashioned Protestant morality on the labor force; they inveighed against tobacco, liquor, and dissipation.

Only a handful of employers at this time understood that the worker might be useful to the capitalist as a consumer; that he needed to be imbued with a taste for higher things; that an economy based on mass production required not only the capitalistic organization of production but the organization of consumption and leisure as well. "Mass production," said the Boston department store magnate Edward A. Filene in 1919, "demands the education of the masses; the masses must learn to behave like human beings in a mass production world. . . . They must achieve, not mere literacy, but culture." In other words, the modern manufacturer has to "educate" the masses in the culture of consumption. The mass production of commodities in ever-increasing abundance demands a mass market to absorb them.

The American economy, having reached the point where its technology was capable of satisfying basic material needs, now relied on the creation of new consumer demands—on convincing people to buy goods for which they are unaware of any need until the "need" is forcibly brought to their attention by the mass media. Advertising, said Calvin Coolidge, "is the method by which the desire is created for better things." The attempt to "civilize" the masses has now given rise to a society dominated by appearances—the society of the spectacle. In the period of primitive accumulation, capitalism subordinated being to having, the use value of commodities to their exchange value. Now it subordinates possession itself to appearance and measures exchange value as a commodity's capacity to confer prestige—the illusion of prosperity and well-being. "When economic necessity yields to the necessity for limitless economic development," writes Guy Debord, "the satisfaction of basic and generally recognized human needs gives way to an uninterrupted fabrication of pseudo-needs."

In a simpler time, advertising merely called attention to the product and extolled its advantages. Now it manufactures a product of its own: the consumer, perpetually unsatisfied, restless, anxious, and bored. Advertising serves not so much to advertise products as to promote consumption as a way of life. It "educates" the masses into an unappeasable appetite not only for goods but for new experiences and personal fulfillment. It upholds consumption as the answer to the age-old discontents of loneliness, sickness, weariness, lack of sexual satisfaction; at the same time it creates new forms of discontent peculiar to the modern age. It plays seductively on the malaise of industrial civilization. Is your job boring and meaningless? Does it leave you with feelings of futility and fatigue? Is your life empty? Consumption promises to fill the aching void; hence the attempt to surround commodities with an aura of romance; with allusions to exotic places and vivid experiences; and with images of female breasts from which all blessings flow.

The propaganda of commodities serves a double function. First, it upholds consumption as an alternative to protest or rebellion. Paul Nystrom, an early student of modern marketing, once noted that industrial civilization gives rise to a "philosophy of futility," a pervasive fatigue, a "disappointment with achievements" that finds an outlet in changing the "more superficial things in which fashion reigns." The tired worker, instead of attempting to change the conditions of his work, seeks renewal in brightening his immediate surroundings with new goods and services.

In the second place, the propaganda of consumption turns alienation itself into a commodity. It addresses itself to the spiritual desolation of modern life and proposes consumption as the cure. It not only promises to palliate all the old unhappiness to which flesh is heir; it creates or exacerbates new forms of unhappiness—personal insecurity, status anxiety, anxiety in parents about their ability to satisfy the needs of the young. Do you look dowdy next to your neighbors? Do you own a car inferior to theirs? Are your children as healthy? as popular? doing as well in school? Advertising institutionalizes envy and its attendant anxieties.

The servant of the status quo, advertising has nevertheless identified itself with a sweeping change in values, a "revolution in manners and morals" that began in the early years of the twentieth century and has continued until the present. The demands of the mass-consumption economy have made the work ethic obsolete even for workers. Formerly the guardians of public health and morality urged the worker to labor as a moral obligation; now they teach him to labor so that he can partake of the fruits of consumption. In the nineteenth century, elites alone obeyed the laws of fashion, exchanging old possessions for new ones for no other reason than that they had gone out of style. Economic orthodoxy condemned the rest of society to a life of drudgery and mere subsistence. The mass production of luxury items now extends aristocratic habits to the masses. The apparatus of mass promotion attacks ideologies based on the postponement of gratification; it allies itself with sexual "revolution"; it sides or seems to side with women against male oppression and with the young against the authority of their elders. The logic of demand creation requires that women smoke and drink in public, move about freely, and assert their right to happiness instead of living for others. The advertising industry thus encourages the pseudo-emancipation of women, flattering them with its insinuating reminder, "You've come a long way, baby," and disguising the freedom to consume as genuine autonomy. Similarly it flatters and glorifies youth in the hope of elevating young people to the status of full-fledged consumers in their own right, each with a telephone, a television set, and a hi-fi in his own room. The "education" of the masses has altered the balance of forces within the family, weakening the authority of the husband in relation to the wife and parents in relation to their children. It emancipates women and children from patriarchal authority, however, only to subject them to the new paternalism of the advertising industry, the industrial corporation, and the state. . . .

## THE THEATER OF EVERYDAY LIFE

A number of historical currents have converged in our time to produce not merely in artists but in ordinary men and women an escalating cycle of self-consciousness—a sense of the self as a performer under the constant scrutiny of friends and strangers. Erving Goffman, the sociologist of the performing self, writes in a characteristic passage: "As human beings we are presumably creatures of variable impulse with moods and energies that change from one moment to the next. As characters put on for an audience, however, we must not be subject to ups and downs. . . . A certain bureaucratization of the spirit is expected so that we can be relied upon to give a perfectly homogeneous performance at every appointed time." This "bureaucratization of the spirit" has become more and more oppressive and is now widely recognized, thanks to Goffman, as an important element in the contemporary malaise.

The self-consciousness that mocks all attempts at spontaneous action or enjoyment derives in the last analysis from the waning belief in the reality of the external world, which has lost its immediacy in a society pervaded by "symbolically mediated information." The more man objectifies himself in his work, the more reality takes on the appearance of illusion. As the workings of the modern economy and the modern social order become increasingly inaccessible to everyday intelligence, art and philosophy abdicate the task of explaining them to the allegedly objective sciences of society, which themselves have retreated from the effort to master reality into the classification of trivia. Reality thus presents itself, to laymen and "scientists" alike, as an impenetrable network of social relations—as "role playing," the "presentation of self in everyday life." To the performing self, the only reality is the identity he can construct out of materials furnished by advertising and mass culture, themes of popular film and fiction, and fragments torn from a vast range of cultural traditions, all of them equally contemporaneous to the contemporary mind. In order to polish and perfect the part he has devised for himself, the new Narcissus gazes at his own reflection, not so much in admiration as in unremitting search of flaws, signs of fatigue, decay. Life becomes a work of art, while "the first art work in an artist," in Norman Mailer's pronouncement, "is the shaping of his own personality." The second of these principles has now been adopted not only by those who write "advertisements for myself" for publication but by the everyday artist in the street.

All of us, actors and spectators alike, live surrounded by mirrors. In them, we seek reassurance of our capacity to captivate or impress others, anxiously searching out blemishes that might detract from the appearance we intend to project. The advertising industry deliberately encourages this preoccupation with appearances. In the twenties, "the women in ads were constantly observing themselves, ever self-critical. . . . A noticeable proportion of magazine ads directed at women depicted them looking into mirrors. . . . Ads of the 1920s were quite explicit about this narcissistic imperative. They unabashedly used pictures of veiled nudes, and women in auto-erotic stances to encourage self-comparison and to remind women of the primacy of their sexuality." A booklet advertising beauty aids depicted on its cover a nude with the caption: "Your Masterpiece—Yourself."

Today the treatment of such themes is more explicit than ever; moreover, advertising encourages men as well as women to see the creation of the self as the highest form of creativity. In an earlier stage of capitalist development, industrialization reduced the artisan or peasant to a proletarian, stripped him of his land and tools, and stranded him in the marketplace with nothing to sell but his labor power. In our time, the elimination of skills not only from manual work but from white-collar jobs as well has created conditions in which labor power takes the form of personality rather than strength or intelligence. Men and women alike have to project an attractive image and to become simultaneously role players and connoisseurs of their own performance.

Changes in the social relations of production, which have given society the appearance of something opaque and impenetrable, have also given rise to the new idea of personality described by Richard Sennett in *The Fall of Public Man*. Whereas the eighteenth-century concept of character stressed the elements common to human nature, the nineteenth century began to see personality as the unique and idiosyncratic expression of individual traits. Outward appearances, in this view, involuntarily expressed the inner man. People soon became obsessed, according to Sennett, with the fear of inadvertently giving themselves away through their actions, facial expressions, and details of dress. In the same century, as Edgar Wind has shown, the art critic Giovanni Morelli propounded the theory that original paintings could be distinguished from forgeries by close examination of insignificant details—the characteristic rendering of an ear or an eye—that betrayed the hand of the master. "Every painter," Morelli insisted, "has his own peculiarities which escape him without his being aware of them."

Naturally these discoveries about personality and its involuntary expression had the effect, not only on artists and critics but on laymen as well, of encouraging self-conscious self-scrutiny. Artists could never again become unconscious of details; indeed the new attention to detail, as one critic has pointed out, obliterated the very notion of detail. Similarly, in everyday life the average man became a connoisseur of his own performance and that of others, bringing the skills of a novelist to the task of "decoding isolated details of appearance," as Sennett writes of Balzac, "magnifying the detail into an emblem of the whole man." But the mastery of these new social skills, while increasing esthetic satisfaction, has created new forms of uneasiness and anxiety. Imprisoned in his self-awareness, modern man longs for the lost innocence of spontaneous feeling. Unable to express emotion without calculating its effects on others, he doubts the authenticity of its expression in others and therefore derives little comfort from audience reactions to his own performance, even when the audience claims to be deeply moved. Andy Warhol complains:

> Day after day I look in the mirror and I still see something—a new pimple. . . . I dunk a Johnson and Johnson cotton ball into Johnson and Johnson rubbing alcohol and rub the cotton ball against the pimple. . . . And while the alcohol is drying I think about nothing. How it's always in style. Always in good taste. . . . When the alcohol is dry, I'm ready to apply the flesh-colored acne-pimple medication. . . . So now the pimple's covered. But am I covered? I have to look into the mirror for some more clues. Nothing is missing. It's all there. The affectless gaze. . . . The bored languor, the wasted pallor. . . . The graying lips. The shaggy silver-white hair, soft and metallic. . . . Nothing is missing. I'm everything my scrapbook says I am.

The sense of security provided by the mirror proves fleeting. Each new confrontation with the mirror brings new risks. Warhol confesses that he is "still obsessed with the idea of looking into the mirror and seeing no one, nothing."

The analysis of interpersonal relations in the theater of everyday life—an analysis which deliberately sticks to the surface of social intercourse and makes no attempt to uncover its psychological depths—leads to conclusions similar to those of psychoanalysis. The psychoanalytic description of the pathological narcissist, whose sense of selfhood depends on the validation of others whom he nevertheless degrades, coincides in many particulars with the description of the performing self in literary criticism and in the sociology of everyday life. The developments that have created a new awareness of motive and involuntary expression—not least among which is the popularization of psychiatric modes of thought—cannot be disentangled from the historical changes that have produced not merely a new concept of personality, but a new form of personality organization. The pathological narcissist reveals, at a deeper level, the same anxieties which in milder form have become so common in everyday intercourse. The prevailing forms of social life, as we have seen, encourage many forms of narcissistic behavior. Moreover, they have altered the process of socialization . . . in ways that give further encouragement to narcissistic patterns by rooting them in the individual's earliest experience.

## IRONIC DETACHMENT
## AS AN ESCAPE FROM ROUTINE

We have not yet exhausted, however, what can be learned from role theory alone. In our society, anxious self-scrutiny (not to be confused with critical self-examination) not only serves to regulate information signaled to others and to interpret signals received; it also establishes an ironic distance from the deadly routine of daily life. On the one hand, the degradation of work makes skill and competence increasingly irrelevant to material success and thus encourages the presentation of the self as a commodity; on the other hand, it discourages commitment to the job and drives people, as the only alternative to boredom and despair, to view work with self-critical detachment. When jobs consist of little more than meaningless motions, and when social routines, formerly dignified as ritual, degenerate into role playing, the worker—whether he toils on an assembly line or holds down a high-paying job in a large bureaucracy—seeks to escape from the resulting sense of inauthenticity by creating an

ironic distance from his daily routine. He attempts to transform role playing into a symbolic elevation of daily life. He takes refuge in jokes, mockery, and cynicism. If he is asked to perform a disagreeable task, he makes it clear that he doesn't believe in the organization's objectives of increased efficiency and greater output. If he goes to a party, he shows by his actions that it's all a game—false, artificial, insincere; a grotesque travesty of sociability. In this way he attempts to make himself invulnerable to the pressures of the situation. By refusing to take seriously the routines he has to perform, he denies their capacity to injure him. Although he assumes that it is impossible to alter the iron limits imposed on him by society, a detached awareness of those limits seems to make them matter less. By demystifying daily life, he conveys to himself and others the impression that he has risen beyond it, even as he goes through the motions and does what is expected of him.

As more and more people find themselves working at jobs that are in fact beneath their abilities, as leisure and sociability themselves take on the qualities of work, the posture of cynical detachment becomes the dominant style of everyday intercourse. Many forms of popular art appeal to this sense of knowingness and thereby reinforce it. They parody familiar roles and themes, inviting the audience to consider itself superior to its surroundings. Popular forms begin to parody themselves: Westerns take off on Westerns; soap operas like *Fernwood, Soap,* and *Mary Hartman, Mary Hartman* assure the viewer of his own sophistication by mocking the conventions of soap opera. Yet much popular art remains romantic and escapist, eschews this theater of the absurd, and promises escape from routine instead of ironic detachment from it. Advertising and popular romance dazzle their audience with visions of rich experience and adventure. They promise not cynical detachment but a piece of the action, a part in the drama instead of cynical spectatorship. Emma Bovary, prototypical consumer of mass culture, still dreams; and her dreams, shared by millions, intensify dissatisfaction with jobs and social routine.

Unreflective accommodation to routine becomes progressively more difficult to achieve. While modern industry condemns people to jobs that insult their intelligence, the mass culture of romantic escape fills their heads with visions of experience beyond their means—beyond their emotional and imaginative capacities as well—and thus contributes to a further devaluation of routine. The disparity between romance and reality, the world of the beautiful people and the workaday world, gives rise to an ironic detachment that dulls pain but also cripples the will to change social conditions, to make even modest improvements in work and play, and to restore meaning and dignity to everyday life. . . .

## The Flight from Feeling: Sociopsychology of the Sex War

> Suddenly she wished she was with some other man and not with Edward. . . . Pia looked at Edward. She looked at his red beard, his immense spectacles. I don't like him, she thought. That red beard, those immense spectacles. . . .
>
> Pia said to Edward that he was the only person she had ever loved for this long. "How long is it?" Edward asked. It was seven months.
>
> DONALD BARTHELME

> I think more and more . . . that there is no such thing as rationality in relationships. I think you just have to say okay that's what you feel right now and what are we going to do about it. . . . I believe everybody should really be able to basically do what they want to do as long as it's not hurting anybody else.
>
> LIBERATED BRIDEGROOM

### THE TRIVIALIZATION OF PERSONAL RELATIONS

Bertrand Russell once predicted that the socialization of reproduction—the supersession of the family by the state—would "make sex love itself more trivial," encourage "a certain triviality in all personal relations," and "make it far more difficult to take an interest in anything after one's own death." At first glance, recent developments appear to have refuted the first part of this prediction. Americans today invest personal rela-

tions, particularly the relations between men and women, with undiminished emotional importance. The decline of childrearing as a major preoccupation has freed sex from its bondage to procreation and made it possible for people to value erotic life for its own sake. As the family shrinks to the marital unit, it can be argued that men and women respond more readily to each other's emotional needs, instead of living vicariously through their offspring. The marriage contract having lost its binding character, couples now find it possible, according to many observers, to ground sexual relations in something more solid than legal compulsion. In short, the growing determination to live for the moment, whatever it may have done to the relations between parents and children, appears to have established the preconditions of a new intimacy between men and women.

This appearance is an illusion. The cult of intimacy conceals a growing despair of finding it. Personal relations crumble under the emotional weight with which they are burdened. The inability "to take an interest in anything after one's own death," which gives such urgency to the pursuit of close personal encounters in the present, makes intimacy more elusive than ever. The same developments that have weakened the tie between parents and children have also undermined relations between men and women. Indeed the deterioration of marriage contributes in its own right to the deterioration of care for the young.

This last point is so obvious that only a strenuous propaganda on behalf of "open marriage" and "creative divorce" prevents us from grasping it. It is clear, for example, that the growing incidence of divorce, together with the ever-present possibility that any given marriage will end in collapse, adds to the instability of family life and deprives the child of a measure of emotional security. Enlightened opinion diverts attention from this general fact by insisting that in specific cases, parents may do more harm to their children by holding a marriage together than by dissolving it. It is true that many couples preserve their marriage, in one form or another, at the expense of the child. Sometimes they embark on a life full of distractions that shield them against daily emotional involvements with their off-spring. Sometimes one parent acquiesces in the neurosis of the other (as in the family configuration that produces so many schizophrenic patients) for fear of disturbing the precarious peace of the household. More often the husband abandons his children to the wife whose company he finds unbearable, and the wife smothers the children with incessant yet perfunctory attentions. This particular solution to the problem of marital strain has become so common that the absence of the father impresses many observers as the most striking fact about the contemporary family. Under these conditions, a divorce in which the mother retains custody of her children merely ratifies the existing state of affairs—the effective emotional desertion of his family by the father. But the reflection that divorce often does no more damage to children than marriage itself hardly inspires rejoicing.

## THE BATTLE OF THE SEXES: ITS SOCIAL HISTORY

While the escalating war between men and women has psychological roots in the disintegration of the marital relation, and more broadly in the changing patterns of socialization . . . , much of this tension can be explained without reference to psychology. The battle of the sexes also constitutes a social phenomenon with a history of its own. The reasons for the recent intensification of sexual combat lie in the transformation of capitalism from its paternalistic and familial form to a managerial, corporate, bureaucratic system of almost total control: more specifically, in the collapse of "chivalry"; the liberation of sex from many of its former constraints; the pursuit of sexual pleasure as an end in itself; the emotional overloading of personal relations; and most important of all, the irrational male response to the emergence of the liberated woman.

It has been clear for some time that "chivalry is dead." The tradition of gallantry formerly masked and to some degree mitigated the organized oppression of women. While males monopolized political and economic power, they made their domination of women more palatable by surrounding it with an elaborate ritual of deference and *politesse*. They set themselves up as protectors of the weaker sex, and this cloying but useful fiction set limits to their capacity to exploit women through sheer physical force. The counterconvention of *droit de seigneur,* which justified the predatory exploits of the privileged classes against women socially inferior to themselves, nevertheless showed that the male sex at no time ceased to regard most women as fair game. The long history of rape and seduction, moreover, served as a reminder that animal strength remained the basis of masculine ascendancy, manifested here in its most direct and brutal form. Yet polite conventions, even when they were no more than a façade, provided women with ideological leverage in their struggle to domesticate the wildness and savagery of men. They surrounded essentially exploitive relationships with a network of reciprocal obligations, which if nothing else made exploitation easier to bear.

The symbiotic interdependence of exploiters and exploited, so characteristic of paternalism in all ages, survived in male-female relations long after the collapse of patriarchal authority in other areas. Because the convention of deference to the fair sex was so closely bound up with paternalism, however, it lived on borrowed time once the democratic revolutions of the eighteenth and nineteenth centuries had destroyed the last foundations of feudalism. The decline of paternalism, and of the rich public ceremonial formerly associated with it, spelled the end of gallantry. Women themselves began to perceive the connection between their debasement and their sentimental exaltation, rejected their confining position on the pedestal of masculine adoration, and demanded the demystification of female sexuality.

Democracy and feminism have now stripped the veil of courtly convention from the subordination of women, revealing the sexual antagonisms formerly concealed by the "feminine mystique." Denied illusions of comity, men and women find it more difficult than before to confront each other as friends and lovers, let alone as equals. As male supremacy becomes ideologically untenable, incapable of justifying itself as protection, men assert their domination more directly, in fantasies and occasionally in acts of raw violence. Thus the treatment of women in movies, according to one study, has shifted "from reverence to rape."

Women who abandon the security of well-defined though restrictive social roles have always exposed themselves to sexual exploitation, having surrendered the usual claims of respectability. Mary Wollstonecraft, attempting to live as a free woman, found herself brutally deserted by Gilbert Imlay. Later feminists forfeited the privileges of sex and middle-class origin when they campaigned for women's rights. Men reviled them publicly as sexless "she-men" and approached them privately as loose women. A Cincinnati brewer, expecting to be admitted to Emma Goldman's hotel room when he found her alone, became alarmed when she threatened to wake the whole establishment. He protested, "I thought you believed in free love." Ingrid Bengis reports that when she hitchhiked across the country, men expected her to pay for rides with sexual favors. Her refusal elicited the predictable reply: "Well, girls shouldn't hitchhike in the first place."

What distinguishes the present time from the past is that defiance of sexual conventions less and less presents itself as a matter of individual choice, as it was for the pioneers of feminism. Since most of those conventions have already collapsed, even a woman who lays no claim to her rights nevertheless finds it difficult to claim the traditional privileges of her sex. All women find themselves identified with "women's lib" merely by virtue of their sex, unless by strenuous disavowals they identify themselves with its enemies. All women share in the burdens as well as the benefits of "liberation," both of which can be summarized by saying that men no longer treat women as ladies.

## THE SEXUAL "REVOLUTION"

The demystification of womanhood goes hand in hand with the desublimation of sexuality. The "repeal of reticence" has dispelled the aura of mystery surrounding sex and removed most of the obstacles to its public display. Institutionalized sexual segregation has given way to arrangements that promote the intermingling of the sexes at every stage of life. Efficient contraceptives, legalized abortion, and a "realistic" and "healthy" acceptance of the body have weakened the links that once tied sex to love, marriage, and procreation. Men and women now pursue sexual pleasure as an end in itself, unmediated even by the conventional trappings of romance.

Sex valued purely for its own sake loses all reference to the future and brings no hope of permanent relationships. Sexual liaisons, including marriage, can be terminated at pleasure. This means, as Willard Waller demonstrated a long time ago, that lovers forfeit the right to be jealous or to insist on fidelity as a condition of erotic union. In his sociological satire of the recently divorced, Waller pointed out that the bohemians of the 1920s attempted to avoid emotional commitments while eliciting them from others. Since the bohemian was "not ready to answer with his whole personality for the consequences of the affair, nor to give any assurance of its continuance," he lost the right to demand such an assurance from others. "To show jealousy," under these conditions, became "nothing short of a crime. . . . So if one falls in love in Bohemia, he conceals it from his friends as best he can." In similar studies of the "rating and dating complex" on college campuses, Waller found that students who fell in love invited the ridicule of their peers. Exclusive attachments gave way to an easygoing promiscuity as the normal pattern of sexual relations. Popularity replaced purity as the measure of a woman's social value; the sentimental cult of virginity gave way to "playful woman-sharing," which had "no negative effect," as Wolfenstein and Leites pointed out in their study of movies, "on the friendly relations between the men."[1] In the thirties and forties, the cinematic fantasy in which a beautiful girl dances

---

[1] The transition in American movies from the vamp to the "good-bad girl," according to Wolfenstein and Leites, illustrates the decline of jealousy and the displacement of sexual passion by sexiness. "The dangerousness of the vamp was

with a chorus of men, favoring one no more than the others, expressed an ideal to which reality more and more closely conformed. In *Elmtown's Youth,* August Hollingshead described a freshman girl who violated conventional taboos against drinking, smoking, and "fast" behavior and still retained her standing in the school's most prominent clique, partly because of her family's wealth but largely by means of her carefully calibrated promiscuity. "To be seen with her adds to a boy's prestige in the elite peer group. . . . She pets with her dates discreetly— never goes too far, just far enough to make them come back again." In high school as in college, the peer group attempts through conventional ridicule and vituperation to prevent its members from falling in love with the wrong people, indeed from falling in love at all; for as Hollingshead noted, lovers "are lost to the adolescent world with its quixotic enthusiasms and varied group activities."

These studies show that the main features of the contemporary sexual scene had already established themselves well before the celebrated "sexual revolution" of the sixties and seventies: casual promiscuity, a wary avoidance of emotional commitments, an attack on jealousy and possessiveness. Recent developments, however, have introduced a new source of tension: the modern woman's increasingly insistent demand for sexual fulfillment. In the 1920s and 1930s, many women still approached sexual encounters with a hesitance that combined prudery and a realistic fear of consequences. Superficially seductive, they took little pleasure in sex even when they spoke the jargon of sexual liberation and professed to live for pleasure and thrills. Doctors worried about female frigidity, and psychiatrists had no trouble in recognizing among their fe-

male patients the classic patterns of hysteria described by Freud, in which a coquettish display of sexuality often coexists with powerful repression and a rigid, puritanical morality.

Today women have dropped much of their sexual reserve. In the eyes of men, this makes them more accessible as sexual partners but also more threatening. Formerly men complained about women's lack of sexual response; now they find this response intimidating and agonize about their capacity to satisfy it. "I'm sorry they ever found out they could have orgasms too," Heller's Bob Slocum says. The famous Masters-Johnson report on female sexuality added to these anxieties by depicting women as sexually insatiable, inexhaustible in their capacity to experience orgasm after orgasm. Some feminists have used the Masters report to attack the "myth of the vaginal orgasm," to assert women's independence of men, or to taunt men with their sexual inferiority. "Theoretically, a woman could go on having orgasms indefinitely if physical exhaustion did not intervene," writes Mary Jane Sherfey. According to Kate Millett, "While the male's sexual potential is limited, the female's appears to be biologically nearly inexhaustible." Sexual "performance" thus becomes another weapon in the war between men and women; social inhibitions no longer prevent women from exploiting the tactical advantage which the current obsession with sexual measurement has given them. Whereas the hysterical woman, even when she fell in love and longed to let herself go, seldom conquered her underlying aversion to sex, the pseudoliberated woman of *Cosmopolitan* exploits her sexuality in a more deliberate and calculating way, not only because she has fewer reservations about sex but because she manages more successfully to avoid emotional entanglements. "Women with narcissistic personalities," writes Otto Kernberg, "may appear quite 'hysterical' on the surface, with their extreme coquettishness and exhibitionism, but the cold, shrewdly calculating quality of their seductiveness is in marked contrast to the much warmer, emotionally involved quality of hysterical pseudo-hypersexuality."

---

associated with the man's intolerance for sharing her with other men. Her seductive appearance and readiness for love carried a strong suggestion that there had been and might be other men in her life. . . . The good-bad girl is associated with a greater tolerance for sharing the woman. . . . In effect, the woman's attraction is enhanced by her association with other men. All that is needed to eliminate unpleasantness is the assurance that these relations were not serious."

## TOGETHERNESS

Both men and women have come to approach personal relations with a heightened appreciation of their emotional risks. Determined to manipulate the emotions of others while protecting themselves against emotional injury, both sexes cultivate a protective shallowness, a cynical detachment they do not altogether feel but which soon becomes habitual and in any case embitters personal relations merely through its repeated profession. At the same time, people demand from personal relations the richness and intensity of a religious experience. Although in some ways men and women have had to modify their demands on each other, especially in their inability to exact commitments of lifelong sexual fidelity, in other ways they demand more than ever. In the American middle class, moreover, men and women see too much of each other and find it hard to put their relations in proper perspective. The degradation of work and the impoverishment of communal life force people to turn to sexual excitement to satisfy all their emotional needs. Formerly sexual antagonism was tempered not only by chivalric, paternalistic conventions but by a more relaxed acceptance of the limitations of the other sex. Men and women acknowledged each other's shortcomings without making them the basis of a comprehensive indictment. Partly because they found more satisfaction than is currently available in casual relations with their own sex, they did not have to raise friendship itself into a political program, an ideological alternative to love. An easygoing, everyday contempt for the weaknesses of the other sex, institutionalized as folk wisdom concerning the emotional incompetence of men or the brainlessness of women, kept sexual enmity within bounds and prevented it from becoming an obsession.

Feminism and the ideology of intimacy have discredited the sexual stereotypes which kept women in their place but which also made it possible to acknowledge sexual antagonism without raising it to the level of all-out warfare. Today the folklore of sexual differences and the acceptance of sexual friction survive only in the working class. Middle-class feminists envy the ability of working-class women to acknowledge that men get in their way without becoming man-haters. "These women are less angry at their men because they don't spend that much time with them," according to one observer. "Middle-class women are the ones who were told men had to be their companions."[2]

## FEMINISM AND THE INTENSIFICATION OF SEXUAL WARFARE

Not merely the cult of sexual companionship and "togetherness" but feminism itself has caused women to make new demands on men and to hate men when they fail to meet those demands. Feminist consciousness-raising, moreover, has had irreversible effects. Once women begin to question the inevitability of their subordination and to reject the conventions formerly associated with it, they can no longer retreat to

[2] Psychiatric and sociological studies of working-class life confirm these observations. "An American middle-class wife tends to expect her husband to treat her as an equal," wrote a psychiatrist in 1957. ". . . She expects cooperation, sharing of responsibility, and individual consideration. . . . In the lower-class family of Italians, . . . the wife . . . does not expect to be treated as an equal. Rather she expects him to make the chief decisions, relieving her of the responsibility so that she can tend to the needs of the large brood of children." Rainwater, Coleman, and Handel reported in their study of working-class wives: "Middle class wives tend to see a greater interchangeability between the marriage partners in handling the work that must be done. There is much more interest in doing things together, whether it be the dishes or painting the walls; 'togetherness' is largely a middle class value."

In the twenty years since these descriptions were written, the ideology of marital companionship has made headway in working-class as well as middle-class families, while feminism, penetrating finally into the consciousness of working-class women, has made conventional sexual stereotyping suspect and has thus made it hard for people to indulge in routine depreciation of the opposite sex without self-consciousness. As working-class women begin to assert their rights or at least to listen to feminist ideas, their husbands see in this turn of events another blow to their own self-respect, the crowning indignity heaped on the workingman by a middle-class liberalism that has already destroyed his savings, bused his children to distant schools, undermined his authority over them, and now threatens to turn even his wife against him.

the safety of those conventions. The woman who rejects the stereotype of feminine weakness and dependence can no longer find much comfort in the cliché that all men are beasts. She has no choice except to believe, on the contrary, that men are human beings, and she finds it hard to forgive them when they act like animals. Although her own actions, which violate the conventions of female passivity and thus appear to men as a form of aggression, help to call up animal-like actions in males, even her understanding of this dynamic does not make it any easier to make allowances for her adversary. "You want too much," an older woman says to a younger one. "You aren't willing to compromise. Men will never be as sensitive or aware as women are. It's just not in their nature. So you have to get used to that, and be satisfied with . . . either sexual satisfaction or theoretical intelligence or being loved and *not* understood or else being left alone to do the things you want to do."

A woman who takes feminism seriously, as a program that aims to put the relations between men and women on a new footing, can no longer accept such a definition of available alternatives without recognizing it as a form of surrender. The younger woman rightly replies that no one should settle for less than a combination of sex, compassion, and intelligent understanding. The attempt to implement these demands, however, exposes her to repeated disappointments, especially since men appear to find the demand for tenderness as threatening to their emotional security as the demand for sexual satisfaction. Thwarted passion in turn gives rise in women to the powerful rage against men so unforgettably expressed, for example, in the poems of Sylvia Plath.

> No day is safe from news of you,
> Walking about in Africa maybe, but thinking
> of me.

Women's rage against men originates not only in erotic disappointments or the consciousness of oppression but in a perception of marriage as the ultimate trap, the ultimate routine in a routinized society, the ultimate expression of the banality that pervades and suffocates modern life. For the heroine of *The Bell Jar,* marriage represents the apotheosis of the everyday: "It would mean getting up at seven and cooking him eggs and bacon and toast and coffee and dawdling about in my nightgown and curlers after he'd left for work to wash up the dirty plates and make the bed, and then when he came home after a lively, fascinating day he'd expect a big dinner, and I'd spend the evening washing up, even more dirty plates till I fell into bed, utterly exhausted." If the man protests that he is exhausted too, and that his "fascinating day" consists of drudgery and humiliation, his wife suspects that he wishes merely to give her domestic prison the appearance of a rose-covered cottage.

In theory, it should be possible for feminists to advance beyond the present stage of sexual recrimination by regarding men simply as a class enemy, involuntarily caught up in the defense of masculine privilege and therefore exempt from personal blame. The symbiotic interdependence of men and women, however, makes it hard to attain such intellectual detachment in everyday life. The "class enemy" presents himself in ordinary existence as a lover, husband, or father, on whom women proceed to make demands that men usually fail to meet. According to the feminists' own analysis of the way in which the subjection of women damages women and impoverishes the emotional life of men, men cannot possibly meet the full erotic demands of women under the existing sexual arrangements; yet feminism itself gives those demands the strongest ideological support. It therefore intensifies the problem to which it simultaneously offers the solution. On the one hand, feminism aspires to change the relations between men and women so that women will no longer be forced into the role of "victim and shrew," in the words of Simone de Beauvoir. On the other hand, it often makes women more shrewish than ever in their daily encounters with men. This contradiction remains unavoidable so long as feminism insists that men oppress women and that this oppression is intolerable, at the same time urging women to approach men not simply as oppressors but as friends and lovers. . . .

# Charles Taylor and the Malaises of Modernity

With Charles Taylor (1931–), we turn from narcissism to malaise. Taylor, a Canadian political scientist and philosopher who teaches at McGill University in Montréal, Québec, and was educated at McGill and Oxford, is the author of a substantial study on Hegel (1973) and many articles on philosophical issues, collected in *Philosophical Papers,* Volumes 1 and 2 (1981) and in *Philosophical Arguments* (1995). His heftiest tome is *Sources of the Self: The Making of Modern Identity* (1992), which offers a rich, historically complex account of the making of the modern notion of the self, traced through Aristotle, St. Augustine, Locke, the Romantics, and others. Here Taylor attacks postmodern skepticism about the self, preferring to see it as the product of a deep philosophical and religious evolution toward an everyday sense of the Good not based on hierarchies of birth or wealth. Indeed, the formation of human identity has been a central theme of Taylor's thought from the beginning.

His 1991 Massey Lectures for the Canadian Broadcasting Corporation's radio service, entitled *The Malaise of Modernity* (published in the United States a year later as *The Ethics of Authenticity*), takes on the issue of how much the pursuit of self-fulfillment and authenticity has led to what Lasch called "the culture of narcissism." The first of the three malaises that he outlines in the following reading is that of *individualism,* the coming of a flattened, narcissistic self without a "heroic dimension" to its existence, a self that suffers from a "disenchantment of the world." Second, he looks at how the pursuit of *instrumental reason*—the type of reason that says we should use the most efficient or economical means to achieve the goals we set, without worrying about the greater moral or aesthetic consequences of that pursuit—has led both to greater individual liberty *and* to the dominance of technological solutions, which he connects to a loss of resonance and depth in our lives. Third, he says that we must be concerned with the *political effects* of individualism and the ethic of instrumental rationality, how our industrial-technological society has led to the "soft despotism" of experts and an alienation from and loss of control over the public sphere.

Taylor summarizes the tripartite malaise of modernity as a (1) a loss of meaning, (2) an eclipse of ends, and (3) a loss of freedom. But Taylor suggests that we have to see both sides of the modern search for authenticity and build a model of the self that contains the best elements of this search, dispensing with the rest. So he's much less pessimistic about our culture than Lasch is: The search for modern identity in terms of authenticity is a worthy path to tread upon. But we have to be careful about the land mines planted on it by the three malaises of modernity.

Of late, Taylor, like Rawls, has been interested in the problems associated with multiculturalism. In his important paper "The Politics of Recognition," which can be found in *Multiculturalism: Examining the Politics of Recognition* (1994), Taylor argues that we should respect the vital need for recognition felt by all cultural groups and not try to sacrifice that need to a "neutralist" liberalism, with its idea of a self unencumbered by cultural, moral, or political traditions. He can thus be seen as part of the communitarian camp, as unsympathetic to the narrow account given by contract theorists of the ground of political association in instrumental reason alone, in our fear of other selfish, potentially violent, but ultimately rational denizens of Hobbes's state of nature.

# The Malaise of Modernity

## CHARLES TAYLOR

I WANT TO WRITE HERE about some of the malaises of modernity. I mean by this features of our contemporary culture and society that people experience as a loss or a decline, even as our civilization "develops." Sometimes people feel that some important decline has occurred during the last years or decades—since the Second World War, or the 1950s, for instance. And sometimes the loss is felt over a much longer historical period: the whole modern era from the seventeenth century is frequently seen as the time frame of decline. Yet although the time scale can vary greatly, there is certain convergence on the themes of decline. They are often variations around a few central melodies. I want to pick out two such central themes here, and then throw in a third that largely derives from these two. These three by no means exhaust the topic, but they do get at a great deal of what troubles and perplexes us about modern society.

The worries I will be talking about are very familiar. No one needs to be reminded of them; they are discussed, bemoaned, challenged, and argued against all the time in all sorts of media. That sounds like a reason not to talk about them further. But I believe that this great familiarity hides bewilderment, that we don't really understand these changes that worry us, that the usual run of debate about them in fact misrepresents them—and thus makes us misconceive what we can do about them. The changes defining modernity are both well-known and very perplexing, and that is why it's worth talking still more about them.

(1) The first source of worry is individualism. Of course, individualism also names what many people consider the finest achievement of modern civilization. We live in a world where people have a right to choose for themselves their own pattern of life, to decide in conscience what convictions to espouse, to determine the shape of their lives in a whole host of ways that their ancestors couldn't control. And these rights are generally defended by our legal systems. In principle, people are no longer sacrificed to the demands of supposedly sacred orders that transcend them.

Very few people want to go back on this achievement. Indeed, many think that it is still incomplete, that economic arrangements, or patterns of family life, or traditional notions of hierarchy still restrict too much our freedom to be ourselves. But many of us are also ambivalent. Modern freedom was won by our breaking loose from older moral horizons. People used to see themselves as part of a larger order. In some cases, this was a cosmic order, a "great chain of Being," in which humans figured in their proper place along with angels, heavenly bodies, and our fellow earthly creatures. This hierarchical order in the universe was reflected in the hierarchies of human society. People were often locked into a given place, a role and station that was properly theirs and from which it was almost unthinkable to deviate. Modern freedom came about through the discrediting of such orders.

But at the same time as they restricted us, these orders gave meaning to the world and to the activities of social life. The things that surround us were not just potential raw materials or instruments for our projects, but they had the significance given them by their place in the chain of being. The eagle was not just another bird, but the king of a whole domain of animal life. By the same token, the rituals and norms of society had more than merely instrumental significance. The discrediting of these orders has been called the

SOURCE: Charles Taylor, "Three Malaises," chap. 1 in *Malaise of Modernity* (Cambridge, Mass.: Harvard University Press, 1991), pp. 1–12.

"disenchantment" of the world. With it, things lost some of their magic.

A vigorous debate has been going on for a couple of centuries as to whether this was an unambiguously good thing. But this is not what I want to focus on here. I want to look rather at what some have seen to be the consequences for human life and meaning.

The worry has been repeatedly expressed that the individual lost something important along with the larger social and cosmic horizons of action. Some have written of this as the loss of a heroic dimension to life. People no longer have a sense of a higher purpose, of something worth dying for. Alexis de Tocqueville sometimes talked like this in the last century, referring to the "petits et vulgaires plaisirs" that people tend to seek in the democratic age.[1] In another articulation, we suffer from a lack of passion. Kierkegaard saw "the present age" in these terms. And Nietzsche's "last men" are at the final nadir of this decline; they have no aspiration left in life but to a "pitiable comfort."[2]

This loss of purpose was linked to a narrowing. People lost the broader vision because they focussed on their individual lives. Democratic equality, says Tocqueville, draws the individual towards himself, "et menace de le renfermer enfin tout entier dans la solitude de son propre coeur."[3] In other words, the dark side of individualism is a centring on the self, which both flattens and narrows our lives, makes them poorer in meaning, and less concerned with others or society.

This worry has recently surfaced again in concern at the fruits of a "permissive society," the doings of the "me generation," or the prevalence of "narcissism," to take just three of the best-known contemporary formulations. The sense that lives have been flattened and narrowed, and that this is connected to an abnormal and regret-

table self-absorption, has returned in forms specific to contemporary culture. This defines the first theme I want to deal with.

(2) The disenchantment of the world is connected to another massively important phenomenon of the modern age, which also greatly troubles many people. We might call this the primacy of instrumental reason. By "instrumental reason" I mean the kind of rationality we draw on when we calculate the most economical application of means to a given end. Maximum efficiency, the best cost-output ratio, is its measure of success.

No doubt sweeping away the old orders has immensely widened the scope of instrumental reason. Once society no longer has a sacred structure, once social arrangements and modes of action are no longer grounded in the order of things or the will of God, they are in a sense up for grabs. They can be redesigned with their consequences for the happiness and well-being of individuals as our goal. The yardstick that henceforth applies is that of instrumental reason. Similarly, once the creatures that surround us lose the significance that accrued to their place in the chain of being, they are open to being treated as raw materials or instruments for our projects.

In one way this change has been liberating. But there is also a widespread unease that instrumental reason not only has enlarged its scope but also threatens to take over our lives. The fear is that things that ought to be determined by other criteria will be decided in terms of efficiency or "cost-benefit" analysis, that the independent ends that ought to be guiding our lives will be eclipsed by the demand to maximize output. There are lots of things one can point to that give substance to this worry: for instance, the ways the demands of economic growth are used to justify very unequal distributions of wealth and income, or the way these same demands make us insensitive to the needs of the environment, even to the point of potential disaster. Or else, we can think of the way much of our social planning, in crucial areas like risk assessment, is dominated by forms of cost-benefit analysis that involve grotesque calculations, putting dollar as-

---

[1] Alexis de Tocqueville, *De la Démocratie in Amérique,* vol. 2 (Paris: Garnier-Flammarion, 1981), p. 385.

[2] "Erbärmliches Behagen"; *Also Sprach Zarathustra,* Zarathustra's Preface, sect. 3.

[3] Tocqueville, *De la Démocratie,* p. 127.

sessments on human lives.[4] The primacy of instrumental reason is also evident in the prestige and aura that surround technology, and makes us believe that we should seek technological solutions even when something very different is called for. We see this often enough in the realm of politics, as Bellah and his colleagues forcefully argue in their new book.[5] But it also invades other domains, such as medicine. Patricia Benner has argued in a number of important works that the technological approach in medicine has often sidelined the kind of care that involves treating the patient as a whole person with a life story, and not as the locus of a technical problem. Society and the medical establishment frequently undervalue the contribution of nurses, who more often than not provide this humanly sensitive caring, as against that of specialists with high-tech knowledge.[6]

The dominant place of technology is also thought to have contributed to the narrowing and flattening of our lives that I have just been discussing in connection with the first theme. People have spoken of a loss of resonance, depth, or richness in our human surroundings. Almost 150 years ago, Marx, in the *Communist Manifesto,* remarked that one of the results of capitalist development was that "all that is solid melts in air." The claim is that the solid, lasting, often expressive objects that served us in the past are being set aside for the quick, shoddy, replaceable commodities with which we now surround ourselves. Albert Borgman speaks of the "device paradigm," whereby we withdraw more and more from "manifold engagement" with our environment and instead request and get products designed to deliver some circumscribed benefit. He contrasts what is involved in heating our homes,

with the contemporary central heating furnace, with what this same function entailed in pioneer times, when the whole family had to be involved in cutting and stacking the wood and feeding the stove or fireplace.[7] Hannah Arendt focussed on the more and more ephemeral quality of modern objects of use and argued that "the reality and reliability of the human world rest primarily on the fact that we are surrounded by things more permanent than the activity by which they are produced."[8] This permanence comes under threat in a world of modern commodities.

This sense of threat is increased by the knowledge that this primacy is not just a matter of a perhaps unconscious orientation, which we are prodded and tempted into by the modern age. As such it would be hard enough to combat, but at least it might yield to persuasion. But it is also clear that powerful mechanisms of social life press us in this direction. A manager in spite of her own orientation may be forced by the conditions of the market to adopt a maximizing strategy she feels is destructive. A bureaucrat, in spite of his personal insight, may be forced by the rules under which he operates to make a decision he knows to be against humanity and good sense.

Marx and Weber and other great theorists have explored these impersonal mechanisms, which Weber has designated by the evocative term of "the iron cage." And some people have wanted to draw from these analyses the conclusion that we are utterly helpless in the face of such forces, or at least helpless unless we totally dismantle the institutional structures under which we have been operating for the last centuries—that is, the market and the state. This aspiration seems so unrealizable today that it amounts to declaring us helpless.

[4] For the absurdities of these calculations, see R. Bellah et al., *The Good Society* (Berkeley: University of California Press, 1991), pp. 114–19.

[5] Bellah et al., *The Good Society,* chapter 4.

[6] See especially Patricia Benner and Judith Wrubel, *The Primacy of Caring: Stress and Coping in Health and Illness* (Menlo Park, CA: Addison-Wesley, 1989).

[7] Albert Borgman, *Technology and the Character of Contemporary Life* (Chicago: University of Chicago Press, 1984), pp. 41–42. Borgman even seems to echo Nietzsche's picture of the "last men" when he argues that the original liberating promise of technology can degenerate into "the procurement of frivolous comfort" (p. 39).

[8] Hannah Arendt, *The Human Condition* (Garden City, NJ: Doubleday Anchor Edition, 1959), p. 83.

I want to return to this below, but I believe that these strong theories of fatality are abstract and wrong. Our degrees of freedom are not zero. There is a point to deliberating what ought to be our ends, and whether instrumental reason ought to have a lesser role in our lives than it does. But the truth in these analyses is that it is not just a matter of changing the outlook of individuals, it is not just a battle of "hearts and minds," important as this is. Change in this domain will have to be institutional as well, even though it cannot be as sweeping and total as the great theorists of revolution proposed.

(3) This brings us to the political level, and to the feared consequences for political life of individualism and instrumental reason. One I have already introduced. It is that the institutions and structures of industrial-technological society severely restrict our choices, that they force societies as well as individuals to give a weight to instrumental reason that in serious moral deliberation we would never do, and which may even be highly destructive. A case in point is our great difficulties in tackling even vital threats to our lives from environmental disasters, like the thinning ozone layer. The society structured around instrumental reason can be seen as imposing a great loss of freedom, on both individuals and the group—because it is not just our social decisions that are shaped by these forces. An individual lifestyle is also hard to sustain against the grain. For instance, the whole design of some modern cities makes it hard to function without a car, particularly where public transport has been eroded in favour of the private automobile.

But there is another kind of loss of freedom, which has also been widely discussed, most memorably by Alexis de Tocqueville. A society in which people end up as the kind of individuals who are "enclosed in their own hearts" is one where few will want to participate actively in self-government. They will prefer to stay at home and enjoy the satisfactions of private life, as long as the government of the day produces the means to these satisfactions and distributes them widely.

This opens the danger of a new, specifically modern form of despotism, which Tocqueville calls "soft" despotism. It will not be a tyranny of terror and oppression as in the old days. The government will be mild and paternalistic. It may even keep democratic forms, with periodic elections. But in fact, everything will be run by an "immense tutelary power,"[9] over which people will have little control. The only defence against this, Tocqueville thinks, is a vigorous political culture in which participation is valued, at several levels of government and in voluntary associations as well. But the atomism of the self-absorbed individual militates against this. Once participation declines, once the lateral associations that were its vehicles wither away, the individual citizen is left alone in the face of the vast bureaucratic state and feels, correctly, powerless. This demotivates the citizen even further, and the vicious cycle of soft despotism is joined.

Perhaps something like this alienation from the public sphere and consequent loss of political control is happening in our highly centralized and bureaucratic political world. Many contemporary thinkers have seen Tocqueville's work as prophetic.[10] If this is so, what we are in danger of losing is political control over our destiny, something we could exercise in common as citizens. This is what Tocqueville called "political liberty." What is threatened here is our dignity as citizens. The impersonal mechanisms mentioned above may reduce our degrees of freedom as a society, but the loss of political liberty would mean that even the choices left would no longer be made by ourselves as citizens, but by irresponsible tutelary power.

These, then, are the three malaises about modernity that I want to deal with in this book. The first fear is about what we might call a loss of meaning, the fading of moral horizons. The second concerns the eclipse of ends, in face of rampant instrumental reason. And the third is about a loss of freedom.

Of course, these are not uncontroversial. I have spoken about worries that are widespread

[9] Tocqueville, *De la Démocratie*, p. 385.
[10] See for instance R. Bellah et al., *Habits of the Heart* (Berkeley: University of California Press, 1985).

and mentioned influential authors, but nothing here is agreed. Even those who share some form of these worries dispute vigorously how they should be formulated. And there are lots of people who want to dismiss them out of hand. Those who are deeply into what the critics call the "culture of narcissism" think of the objectors as hankering for an earlier, more oppressive age. Adepts of modern technological reason think the critics of the primacy of the instrumental are reactionary and obscurantist, scheming to deny the world the benefits of science. And there are proponents of mere negative freedom who believe that the value of political liberty is overblown, and that a society in which scientific management combines with maximum independence for each individual is what we ought to aim at. Modernity has its boosters as well as its knockers.

Nothing is agreed here, and the debate continues. But in the course of this debate, the essential nature of the developments, which are here being decried, there being praised, is often misunderstood. And as a result, the real nature of the moral choices to be made is obscured. In particular, I will claim that the right path to take is neither that recommended by straight boosters nor that favoured by outright knockers. Nor will a simple trade-off between the advantages and costs of, say, individualism, technology, and bureaucratic management provide the answer. The nature of modern culture is more subtle and complex than this. I want to claim that both boosters and knockers are right, but in a way that can't be done justice to by a simple trade-off between advantages and costs. There is in fact both much that is admirable and much that is debased and frightening in all the developments I have been describing, but to understand the relation between the two is to see that the issue is not how much of a price in bad consequences you have to pay for the positive fruits, but rather how to steer these developments towards their greatest promise and avoid the slide into the debased forms. . . .

## The Luddites Attack: The Strange Case of the Unabomber

Our third cultural critic is Theodore Kaczynski, also known as the Unabomber. Kaczynski was a brilliant mathematician who obtained his Ph.D. at the University of Michigan and taught briefly at Berkeley in the late 1960s before retreating to a cabin in rural Montana in 1971, where he lived intermittently for the next twenty-four years. He lived in primitive conditions, growing his own food, riding into town on a rickety old bike to pick up essential supplies. He didn't even have a computer or an Internet connection!

For obscure reasons Kaczynski decided to declare war on industrial-technological society from his rural fortress of solitude. From 1977 to 1995, he sent sixteen mail bombs to various people, including an airline executive, university researchers in technical fields, a computer store owner, and a public relations executive, killing three of them and injuring another twenty-three. His bombs were homemade, aided by trips to the junkyard and the local hardware store. The FBI named him the "Una-bomber" because his early attacks seemed to indicate that his principal targets were universities and airlines.

For years he eluded the authorities, making sure not to include identifying elements in his bombs and taking buses to mail them from remote locales. The only evidence available was a police sketch made from a witness's report of a man in a hood and dark glasses mailing a parcel in Salt Lake City. His moment of glory came in 1995, when he promised to end his bombing campaign if his 35,000-word manifesto *Industrial Society and Its Future* (typed in his cabin on an old typewriter) was published by a major newspaper or magazine. Hoping against hope that he would keep his word, the FBI and attorney general recommended that it be published by the *Washington Post* and the *New York Times,* as it was in September 1995 (for his complete manifesto, go to www.thecourier.com/manifest.htm).

He was caught very soon afterward. Kaczynski's brother, David, noticed similarities between the manifesto and some of his brother's old writings and tipped off the FBI with his suspicions. The FBI raided the cabin, finding the offending typewriter and a collection of bomb-making materials, including an unaddressed but sealed package, thus suggesting that the Unabomber's campaign of terror wasn't over. He plea-bargained a life sentence in 1998.

In his manifesto, excerpted in the reading, the Unabomber advocates an attack on the whole industrial-technological system, calling it a "disaster" for the human race. He is clearly in the Luddite tradition of seeing violence as the only way of slowing the progress of technology. The original Luddites struck from 1811 to 1816 in the industrial towns and cities of central and southern England, destroying the steam-powered looms and factories that they felt were taking away their traditional handicraft jobs. Their pretended leader was "Ned Ludd," a fictional character invented to confuse the authorities. The British army eventually rounded them up, but not before they had created a legend that would fuel anti-industrial and technological speculation and politics for the next couple of centuries. Those who sympathize with slowing down or stopping the advance of technology today are called "neo-Luddites," being the distant descendants of the original crew of machine breakers.

Kaczynski argues that industrial society has taken away our freedom by removing us from "the power process," which consists of having a challenging but realistic goal, making an effort to attain that goal, attaining the goal, and thus achieving autonomy. Instead, our lives consist largely of the pursuit of surrogate activities (under the banner of which Kaczynski includes most careers), activities geared to fulfilling not our basic needs but artificial ones such as climbing the corporate hierarchy or playing the latest computer game (paragraphs 33–41). The entertainment industry and media feed these artificial needs and thus support the whole system, also offering a means of escape through the "large amounts of sex and violence" they dish out (paragraph 147).

There can be no compromise between technology and freedom, he says, because technology is too strong a social force, stripping away our freedom by the many little compromises that it compels us to make (paragraph 125). When a new technology is introduced—for example, the telephone or automobile—we seem to be free to either use it or reject it. But after a while we become dependent on it and feel a strong sense of psychological deprivation if we have to go without it for too long (think about those days when your e-mail system goes down). We become *prisoners* of our technologies—we can't live without them.

Kaczynski's sketch of the future is a dark one, where machines we can't afford to turn off run our economies and lives for us and where people are genetically engineered to "suit the needs of the system." His solution is a breakdown of all industrial society and the return to small-scale communities dependent only on locally manufactured technologies.

Many media pundits have suggested that we can't take seriously the philosophical ideas of a killer, a man who was obviously somewhat deranged. Yet Kaczynski argues, with some merit, that if he had never killed anyone, his ideas would have been "swamped by the vast volume of material put out by the media," thus having no real effect (paragraph 196). The more serious question here is the ethical one of publishing the work of a murderer. We should certainly sympathize with Kaczynski's victims and refuse to condone violence as the political tactic of choice. What he did was wrong. Yet keep in mind that almost all of the great revolutionaries throughout history—including Washington, Robespierre, and Lenin—have been willing to kill their enemies for political ideals such as freedom and equality, and all heads of state who fight wars in the name of national security—or for more dubious reasons such as honor or revenge—engage in mass killing for reasons that may seem to future generations highly questionable (World War I and Vietnam being cases in point). So condemning the Unabomber on this point may be slightly hypocritical, unless this condemnation comes from confirmed pacifists such as the Quakers or Mennonites.

Students will probably find in the following excerpts that the Unabomber's attack on our industrial society has a certain force to it, suffering little from the fact that it was written in a cabin in Montana, far from the corridors of higher learning. He opposes (among other things) the noise and ceaseless expansion of modern cities, genetic engineering, environmental degradation, and the distortions of reality practiced by the media, positions shared by many more respectable critics of science and technology. Whether these critiques justify his mail-bomb campaign, or a general revolt against industrial civilization, is an open question.

# Industrial Society and Its Future

## THE UNABOMBER AKA THEODORE KACZYNSKI

### Introduction

1. The Industrial Revolution and its consequences have been a disaster for the human race. They have greatly increased the life-expectancy of those of us who live in "advanced" countries, but they have destabilized society, have made life unfulfilling, have subjected human beings to indignities, have led to widespread psychological suffering (in the Third World to physical suffering as well) and have inflicted severe damage on the natural world. The continued development of technology will worsen the situation. It will certainly subject human beings to greater indignities and inflict greater damage on the natural world, it will probably lead to greater social disruption and psychological suffering, and it may lead to increased physical suffering even in "advanced" countries.

2. The industrial-technological system may survive or it may break down. If it survives, it MAY eventually achieve a low level of physical and psychological suffering, but only after passing through a long and very painful period of adjustment and only at the cost of permanently reducing human beings and many other living organisms to engineered products and mere cogs in the social machine. Furthermore, if the system survives, the consequences will be inevitable: There is no way of reforming or modifying the system so as to prevent it from depriving people of dignity and autonomy.

3. If the system breaks down the consequences

SOURCE: The Unabomber, "Industrial Society and Its Future," manifesto published in the *Washington Post* and *New York Times* (September 1995). Reprinted on various sites on the Internet.

will still be very painful. But the bigger the system grows the more disastrous the results of its breakdown will be, so if it is to break down it had best break down sooner rather than later.

4. We therefore advocate a revolution against the industrial system. This revolution may or may not make use of violence: it may be sudden or it may be a relatively gradual process spanning a few decades. We can't predict any of that. But we do outline in a very general way the measures that those who hate the industrial system should take in order to prepare the way for a revolution against that form of society. This is not to be a POLITICAL revolution. Its object will be to overthrow not governments but the economic and technological basis of the present society.

## The Power Process

33. Human beings have a need (probably based in biology) for something that we will call the "power process." This is closely related to the need for power (which is widely recognized) but is not quite the same thing. The power process has four elements. The three most clear-cut of these we call goal, effort and attainment of goal. (Everyone needs to have goals whose attainment requires effort, and needs to succeed in attaining at least some of his goals.) The fourth element is more difficult to define and may not be necessary for everyone. We call it autonomy. . . .

36. Nonattainment of important goals results in death if the goals are physical necessities, and in frustration if nonattainment of the goals is compatible with survival. Consistent failure to attain goals throughout life results in defeatism, low self-esteem or depression.

37. Thus, in order to avoid serious psychological problems, a human being needs goals whose attainment requires effort, and he must have a reasonable rate of success in attaining his goals.

## Surrogate Activities

39. We use the term "surrogate activity" to designate an activity that is directed toward an artificial goal that people set up for themselves merely in order to have some goal to work toward, or let us say, merely for the sake of the "fulfilment" that they get from pursuing the goal. Here is a rule of thumb for the identification of surrogate activities. Given a person who devotes much time and energy to the pursuit of goal X, ask yourself this: If he had to devote most of his time and energy to satisfying his biological needs, and if that effort required him to use his physical and mental facilities in a varied and interesting way, would he feel seriously deprived because he did not attain goal X? If the answer is no, then the person's pursuit of a goal X is a surrogate activity. . . .

40. In modern industrial society only minimal effort is necessary to satisfy one's physical needs. It is enough to go through a training program to acquire some petty technical skill, then come to work on time and exert very modest effort needed to hold a job. The only requirements are a moderate amount of intelligence, and most of all, simple OBEDIENCE. If one has those, society takes care of one from cradle to grave. (Yes, there is an underclass that cannot take physical necessities for granted, but we are speaking here of mainstream society.) Thus it is not surprising that modern society is full of surrogate activities. These include scientific work, athletic achievement, humanitarian work, artistic and literary creation, climbing the corporate ladder, acquisition of money and material goods far beyond the point at which they cease to give any additional physical satisfaction, and social activism when it addresses issues that are not important for the activist personally, as in the case of white activists who work for the rights of nonwhite minorities. These are not always pure surrogate activities, since for many people they may be motivated in part by needs other than the need to have some goal to pursue. . . . But for most people who pursue them, these activities are in large part surrogate activities. . . .

41. . . . In our society people do not satisfy their biological needs AUTONOMOUSLY. but by functioning as parts of an immense social machine. In contrast, people generally have a great deal of autonomy in pursuing their surrogate activities.

## Sources of Social Problems

45. . . . We aren't the first to mention that the world today seems to be going crazy. This sort of thing is not normal for human societies. There is good reason to believe that primitive man suffered from less stress and frustration and was better satisfied with his way of life than modern man is. It is true that not all was sweetness and light in primitive societies. . . . But it does appear that GENERALLY SPEAKING the kinds of problems that we have listed [previously] . . . were far less common among primitive peoples than they are in modern society.

46. We attribute the social and psychological problems of modern society to the fact that that society requires people to live under conditions radically different from those under which the human race evolved and to behave in ways that conflict with the patterns of behavior that the human race developed while living under the earlier conditions. It is clear from what we have already written that we consider lack of opportunity to properly experience the power process as the most important of the abnormal conditions to which modern society subjects people. But it is not the only one. Before dealing with disruption of the power process as a source of social problems we will discuss some of the other sources.

47. Among the abnormal conditions present in modern industrial society are excessive density of population, isolation of man from nature, excessive rapidity of social change and the breakdown of natural small-scale communities such as the extended family, the village or the tribe.

48. It is well known that crowding increases stress and aggression. The degree of crowding that exists today and the isolation of man from nature are consequences of technological progress. All pre-industrial societies were predominantly rural. The Industrial Revolution vastly increased the size of cities and the proportion of the population that lives in them, and modern agricultural technology has made it possible for the Earth to support a far denser population than it ever did before. . . .

49. For primitive societies the natural world (which usually changes only slowly) provided a stable framework and therefore a sense of security. In the modern world it is human society that dominates nature rather than the other way around, and modern society changes very rapidly owing to technological change. Thus there is no stable framework.

51. The breakdown of traditional values to some extent implies the breakdown of the bonds that hold together traditional small-scale social groups. The disintegration of small-scale social groups is also promoted by the fact that modern conditions often require or tempt individuals to move to new locations, separating themselves from their communities. Beyond that, a technological society HAS TO weaken family ties and local communities if it is to function efficiently. In modern society an individual's loyalty must be first to the system and only secondarily to a small-scale community, because if the internal loyalties of small-scale communities were stronger than loyalty to the system, such communities would pursue their own advantage at the expense of the system.

## The Nature of Freedom

94. By "freedom" we mean the opportunity to go through the power process, with real goals not the artificial goals of surrogate activities, and without interference, manipulation or supervision from anyone, especially from any large organization. Freedom means being in control (either as an individual or as a member of SMALL group) of the life-and-death issues of one's existence; food, clothing, shelter and defense against whatever threats there may be in one's environment. Freedom means having power; not the power to control other people but the power to control the circumstances of one's own life. One does not have freedom if anyone else (especially a large organization) has power over one, no matter how benevolently, tolerantly and permissively that power may be exercised. It is important not to confuse freedom with mere permissiveness. . . .

96. As for our constitutional rights, consider for example that of freedom of the press. We certainly don't mean to knock that right: it is a very important tool for limiting concentration of po-

litical power and for keeping those who do have political power in line by publicly exposing any misbehavior on their part. But freedom of the press is of very little use to the average citizen as an individual. The mass media are mostly under the control of large organizations that are integrated into the system. Anyone who has a little money can have something printed, or can distribute it on the Internet or in some such way, but what he has to say will be swamped by the vast volume of material put out by the media, hence it will have no practical effect. To make an impression on society with words is therefore almost impossible for most individuals and small groups. Take us (FC) for example. If we had never done anything violent and had submitted the present writings to a publisher, they probably would not have been accepted. If they had been accepted and published, they probably would not have attracted many readers, because it's more fun to watch the entertainment put out by the media than to read a sober essay. Even if these writings had had many readers, most of these readers would soon have forgotten what they had read as their minds were flooded by the mass of material to which the media expose them. In order to get our message before the public with some chance of making a lasting impression, we've had to kill people.

## Technology Is a More Powerful Social Force Than the Aspiration for Freedom

125. It is not possible to make a LASTING compromise between technology and freedom, because technology is by far the more powerful social force and continually encroaches on freedom through REPEATED compromises. . . .

127. A technological advance that appears not to threaten freedom often turns out to threaten freedom very seriously later on. For example, consider motorized transport. A walking man formerly could go where he pleased, go at his own pace without observing any traffic regulations, and was independent of technological support

systems. When motor vehicles were introduced they appeared to increase man's freedom. They took no freedom away from the walking man, no one had to have an automobile if he didn't want one, and anyone who did choose to buy an automobile could travel much faster than the walking man. But the introduction of motorized transport soon changed society in such a way as to restrict greatly man's freedom of locomotion. When automobiles became numerous, it became necessary to regulate their use extensively. In a car, especially in densely populated areas, one cannot just go where one likes at one's own pace: one's movement is governed by the flow of traffic and by various traffic laws. One is tied down by various obligations: license requirements, driver test, renewing registration, insurance, maintenance required for safety, monthly payments on purchase price. Moreover, the use of motorized transport is no longer optional. Since the introduction of motorized transport the arrangement of our cities has changed in such a way that the majority of people no longer live within walking distance of their place of employment, shopping areas and recreational opportunities, so that they HAVE TO depend on the automobile for transportation. Or else they must use public transportation, in which case they have even less control over their own movement than when driving a car. Even the walker's freedom is now greatly restricted. In the city he continually has to stop and wait for traffic lights that are designed mainly to serve auto traffic. In the country, motor traffic makes it dangerous and unpleasant to walk along the highway. (Note the important point we have illustrated with the case of motorized transport: When a new item of technology is introduced as an option that an individual can accept or not as he chooses, it does not necessarily REMAIN optional. In many cases the new technology changes society in such a way that people eventually find themselves FORCED to use it.)

128. While technological progress AS A WHOLE continually narrows our sphere of freedom, each new technical advance CONSIDERED BY ITSELF appears to be desirable. Electricity, in-

door plumbing, rapid long-distance communications . . . how could one argue against any of these things, or against any other of the innumerable technical advances that have made modern society? It would have been absurd to resist the introduction of the telephone, for example. It offered many advantages and no disadvantages. Yet . . . all these technical advances taken together have created a world in which the average man's fate is no longer in his own hands or in the hands of his neighbors and friends, but in those of politicians, corporation executives and remote, anonymous technicians and bureaucrats whom he as an individual has no power to influence. The same process will continue in the future. . . .

129. Another reason why technology is such a powerful social force is that, within the context of a given society, technological progress marches in only one direction; it can never be reversed. Once a technical innovation has been introduced, people usually become dependent on it, unless it is replaced by some still more advanced innovation. Not only do people become dependent as individuals on a new item of technology, but, even more, the system as a whole becomes dependent on it. (Imagine what would happen to the system today if computers, for example, were eliminated.) Thus the system can move in only one direction, toward greater technologization. Technology repeatedly forces freedom to take a step back—short of the overthrow of the whole technological system.

130. Technology advances with great rapidity and threatens freedom at many different points at the same time (crowding, rules and regulations, increasing dependence of individuals on large organizations, propaganda and other psychological techniques, genetic engineering, invasion of privacy through surveillance devices and computers, etc.). . . . To fight each of the threats separately would be futile. Success can be hoped for only by fighting the technological system as a whole; but that is revolution not reform.

133. No social arrangements, whether laws, institutions, customs or ethical codes, can provide permanent protection against technology.

History shows that all social arrangements are transitory; they all change or break down eventually. But technological advances are permanent within the context of a given civilization. . . .

134. For all of the foregoing reasons, technology is a more powerful social force than the aspiration for freedom. . . .

## Control of Human Behavior

147. To start with, there are the techniques of surveillance. Hidden video cameras are now used in most stores and in many other places, computers are used to collect and process vast amounts of information about individuals. Information so obtained greatly increases the effectiveness of physical coercion (i.e., law enforcement).[1] Then there are the methods of propaganda, for which the mass communication media provide effective vehicles. Efficient techniques have been developed for winning elections, selling products, influencing public opinion. The entertainment industry serves as an important psychological tool of the system, possibly even when it is dishing out large amounts of sex and violence. Entertainment provides modern man with an essential means of escape. While absorbed in television, videos, etc., he can forget stress, anxiety, frustration, dissatisfaction. Many primitive peoples, when they don't have work to do, are quite content to sit for hours at a time doing nothing at all, because they are at peace with themselves and their world.

---

[1] If you think that more effective law enforcement is unequivocally good because it suppresses crime, then remember that crime as defined by the system is not necessarily what YOU would call crime. Today, smoking marijuana is a "crime," and, in some places in the U.S., . . . possession of ANY firearm, registered or not, may be made a crime, and the same thing may happen with disapproved methods of child-rearing, such as spanking. In some countries, expression of dissident political opinions is a crime, and there is no certainty that this will never happen in the U.S., since no constitution or political system lasts forever.

If a society needs a large, powerful law enforcement establishment, then there is something gravely wrong with that society; it must be subjecting people to severe pressures if so many refuse to follow the rules, or follow them only because forced. Many societies in the past have gotten by with little or no formal law-enforcement.

But most modern people must be constantly occupied or entertained, otherwise they get "bored," i.e., they get fidgety, uneasy, irritable.

151. . . . Whereas formerly the limits of human endurance have imposed limits on the development of societies, . . . industrial-technological society will be able to pass those limits by modifying human beings, whether by psychological methods or biological methods or both. In the future, social systems will not be adjusted to suit the needs of human beings. Instead, human beings will be adjusted to suit the needs of the system.[2]

156. In paragraph 127 we pointed out that if the use of a new item of technology is INITIALLY optional, it does not necessarily REMAIN optional, because the new technology tends to change society in such a way that it becomes difficult or impossible for an individual to function without using that technology. This applies also to the technology of human behavior. In a world in which most children are put through a program to make them enthusiastic about studying, a parent will almost be forced to put his kid through such a program, because if he does not, then the kid will grow up to be, comparatively speaking, an ignoramus and therefore unemployable. Or suppose a biological treatment is discovered that, without undesirable side-effects, will greatly reduce the psychological stress from which so many people suffer in our society. If large numbers of people choose to undergo the treatment, then the general level of stress in society will be reduced, so that it will be possible for the system to increase the stress-producing pressures. In fact, something like this seems to have happened already with one of our society's most important psychological tools for enabling people to reduce (or at least temporarily escape from) stress, namely, mass entertainment (see paragraph 147). Our use of mass entertainment is "optional": No law requires us to watch television, listen to the radio, read magazines. Yet mass entertainment is a means of escape and stress-reduction on which most of us have be-

come dependent. Everyone complains about the trashiness of television, but almost everyone watches it. A few have kicked the TV habit, but it would be a rare person who could get along today without using ANY form of mass entertainment. (Yet until quite recently in human history most people got along very nicely with no other entertainment than that which each local community created for itself.) Without the entertainment industry the system probably would not have been able to get away with putting as much stress-producing pressure on us as it does.

158. It presumably would be impractical for all people to have electrodes inserted in their heads so that they could be controlled by the authorities. But the fact that human thoughts and feelings are so open to biological intervention shows that the problem of controlling human behavior is mainly a technical problem; a problem of neurons, hormones and complex molecules; the kind of problem that is accessible to scientific attack. Given the outstanding record of our society in solving technical problems, it is overwhelmingly probable that great advances will be made in the control of human behavior.

## Human Suffering

170. "Oh!" say the technophiles, "Science is going to fix all that! We will conquer famine, eliminate psychological suffering, make everybody healthy and happy!" Yeah, sure. That's what they said 200 years ago. The Industrial Revolution was supposed to eliminate poverty, make everybody happy, etc. The actual result has been quite different. The technophiles are hopelessly naive (or self-deceiving) in their understanding of social problems. They are unaware of (or choose to ignore) the fact that when large changes, even seemingly beneficial ones, are introduced into a society, they lead to a long sequence of other changes, most of which are impossible to predict. . . . The result is disruption of the society. So it is very probable that in their attempt to end poverty and disease, engineer docile, happy personalities and so forth, the technophiles will create social systems that are terribly troubled, even more so than the present

---

[2] To be sure, past societies have had means of influencing behavior, but these have been primitive and of low effectiveness compared with the technological means that are now being developed.

one . . . it is not all clear that the survival of industrial society would involve less suffering than the breakdown of that society would. Technology has gotten the human race into a fix from which there is not likely to be any easy escape.

## The Escape

173. . . . It might be argued that the human race would never be foolish enough to hand over all the power to the machines. But we are suggesting neither that the human race would voluntarily turn power over to the machines nor that the machines would willfully seize power. What we do suggest is that the human race might easily permit itself to drift into a position of such dependence on the machines that it would have no practical choice but to accept all of the machines' decisions. As society and the problems that face it become more and more complex and machines become more and more intelligent, people will let machines make more of their decisions for them, simply because machine-made decisions will bring better results than man-made ones. Eventually a stage may be reached at which the decisions necessary to keep the system running will be so complex that human beings will be incapable of making them intelligently. At that stage the machines will be in effective control. People won't be able to just turn the machines off, because they will be so dependent on them that turning them off would amount to suicide.

174. On the other hand it is possible that human control over the machines may be retained. In that case the average man may have control over certain private machines of his own, such as his car or his personal computer, but control over large systems of machines will be in the hands of a tiny elite—just as it is today, but with two differences. Due to improved techniques the elite will have greater control over the masses; and because human work will no longer be necessary the masses will be superfluous, a useless burden on the system. If the elite is ruthless they may simply decide to exterminate the mass of humanity. If they are humane they may use propaganda or other psychological or biological techniques to reduce the birth rate until the mass of human-

ity becomes extinct, leaving the world to the elite. Or, if the elite consist of soft-hearted liberals, they may decide to play the role of good shepherds to the rest of the human race. They will see to it that everyone's physical needs are satisfied, that all children are raised under psychologically hygienic conditions, that everyone has a wholesome hobby to keep him busy, and that anyone who may become dissatisfied undergoes "treatment" to cure his "problem." Of course, life will be so purposeless that people will have to be biologically or psychologically engineered either to remove their need for the power process or to make them "sublimate" their drive for power into some harmless hobby. These engineered human beings may be happy in such a society, but they most certainly will not be free. They will have been reduced to the status of domestic animals.

175. But suppose now that the computer scientists do not succeed in developing artificial intelligence, so that human work remains necessary. Even so, machines will take care of more and more of the simpler tasks so that there will be an increasing surplus of human workers at the lower levels of ability. (We see this happening already. There are many people who find it difficult or impossible to get work, because for intellectual or psychological reasons they cannot acquire the level of training necessary to make themselves useful in the present system.) On those who are employed, ever-increasing demands will be placed; they will need more and more training, more and more ability, and will have to be ever more reliable, conforming and docile, because they will be more and more like cells of a giant organism. Their tasks will be increasingly specialized so that their work will be, in a sense, out of touch with the real world, being concentrated on one tiny slice of reality. The system will have to use any means that it can, whether psychological or biological, to engineer people to be docile, to have the abilities that the system requires and to "sublimate" their drive for power into some specialized task. But the statement that the people of such a society will have to be docile may require qualification. The society may find competitiveness useful, provided that ways are found

of directing competitiveness into channels that serve the needs of the system. We can imagine a future society in which there is endless competition for positions of prestige and power. But no more than a very few people will ever reach the top, where the only real power is. . . .

178. Whatever else may be the case, it is certain that technology is creating for human beings a new physical and social environment radically different from the spectrum of environments to which natural selection has adapted the human race physically and psychologically. If man is not adjusted to this new environment by being artificially re-engineered, then he will be adapted to it through a long and painful process of natural selection. The former is far more likely than the latter.

## Strategy

181. . . . the two main tasks for the present are to promote social stress and instability in industrial society and to develop and propagate an ideology that opposes technology and the industrial system. When the system becomes sufficiently stressed and unstable, a revolution against technology may be possible.

183. But an ideology, in order to gain enthusiastic support, must have a positive ideal as well as a negative one; it must be FOR something as well as AGAINST something. The positive ideal that we propose is Nature. That is, WILD nature; those aspects of the functioning of the Earth and its living things that are independent of human management and free of human interference and control. And with wild nature we include human nature, by which we mean those aspects of the functioning of the human individual that are not subject to regulation by organized society but are products of chance, or free will, or God (depending on your religious or philosophical opinions).

197. Some people take the line that modern man has too much power, too much control over nature; they argue for a more passive attitude on the part of the human race. At best these people are expressing themselves unclearly, because they fail to distinguish between power for LARGE ORGANIZATIONS and power for INDIVIDUALS and

SMALL GROUPS. It is a mistake to argue for powerlessness and passivity, because people NEED power. Modern man as a collective entity—that is, the industrial system—has immense power over nature, and we (FC)[3] regard this as evil. But modern INDIVIDUALS and SMALL GROUPS OF INDIVIDUALS have far less power than primitive man ever did. Generally speaking, the vast power of "modern man" over nature is exercised not by individuals or small groups but by large organizations. To the extent that the average modern INDIVIDUAL can wield the power of technology, he is permitted to do so only within narrow limits and only under the supervision and control of the system. . . . The individual has only those technological powers with which the system chooses to provide him. His PERSONAL power over nature is slight.

198. Primitive INDIVIDUALS and SMALL GROUPS actually had considerable power over nature; or maybe it would be better to say power WITHIN nature. When primitive man needed food he knew how to find and prepare edible roots, how to track game and take it with homemade weapons. He knew how to protect himself from heat, cold, rain, dangerous animals, etc. But primitive man did relatively little damage to nature because the COLLECTIVE power of primitive society was negligible compared to the COLLECTIVE power of industrial society.

199. Instead of arguing for powerlessness and passivity, one should argue that the power of the INDUSTRIAL SYSTEM should be broken, and that this will greatly INCREASE the power and freedom of INDIVIDUALS and SMALL GROUPS.

203. Imagine an alcoholic sitting with a barrel of wine in front of him. Suppose he starts saying to himself, "Wine isn't bad for you if used in moderation. Why, they say small amounts of wine are even good for you! It won't do me any harm if I take just one little drink. . . ." Well you know what is going to happen. Never forget that the human race with technology is just like an alcoholic with a barrel of wine.

---

[3] "Freedom Club," the fictitious group that the Unabomber claimed membership of. As far as anyone knows, the Freedom Club consisted of Kaczynski alone.

# OUR TECHNOLOGICAL CULTURE _____

## *The Futurists*

We live in a culture that depends to a tremendous degree on technology. In this we'll look at four different perspectives on the value and effects of technology in our culture. First is the *Manifesto* of the futurists, who were early-twentieth-century writers and artists who took a very different stance on the value of technology than did the Unabomber at the end of the century.

Futurism was a wide artistic movement centered in Italy and Russia that was unique because the ideological goals of the movement predated its artistic products. Emilio Filippo Tommaso Marinetti (1876–1944) was an Italian poet, essayist, and novelist who moved to Paris to study in 1893, producing a paean to modern machinery, speed, and warfare in his *Futurist Manifesto,* which was published in the Paris newspaper *Le Figaro* on September 20, 1909. This and other manifestos provided the futurist movement with its protechnology marching orders.

The Italian futurist movement that Marinetti was largely responsible for sparking into flames wanted to create a new art for Italy based on a glorification of the modern: modern technology, modern speed, modern means of warfare, modern literature. They saw an appreciation of the beauty of technology, the "machine aesthetic," as a natural extension of the human beings who created those technologies, not as something alien to human life. The Italian futurists, under the banner of Marinetti's *Manifesto,* wanted to throw all those crusty old Renaissance paintings into the canals, creating in their place an art and architecture suitable for the modern machine age: sleek, aerodynamic, functional, without unnecessary ornamentation. They wanted to do so with courage, audacity, and revolt, creating their art as part of a great struggle against liberalism, conventional morality, and democracy. If fact, the futurists were tied to fascism in Italy from the early 1920s on, with Benito Mussolini making Marinetti a member of the Italian Academy in 1929. The fascists found in the futurists natural allies, each seeking to champion modern machines, mass warfare, and the end of the liberal state. Needless to say, the downfall of fascism more or less ended the movement's credibility.

Futurism was linked to other movements in modern art, such as cubism and Dada. Like the Dadaists, futurist artists glued together scraps of paper such as train tickets, pieces of wood, and other detritus of our technological civilization onto a board or piece of canvas and called it art (or collage, to be precise). They also composed sound collages and "aero poems" meant to be read over the radio of an airplane in flight; they held poetry readings that trashed civilized conventions and sometimes erupted into riots. Their motto was "down with the past, up with the now!"—this "now" being very much tied up with modern technology. But this new technology wasn't just functional—it was beautiful, sensual, even erotic. It was a short path from Marinetti stroking his "beautiful shark," his mud-splattered car as it was hauled out of a ditch, to J. G. Ballard's 1973 novel, *Crash* (made into a controversial film by David Cronenberg in 1996), in which the central characters derive pleasure from an erotic attachment to their automobiles, exploring with sexual abandon each other's car-crash-caused scars and gashes.

Are we in love with our cars, our computers, our home entertainment systems?

Has technology become what Marx earlier called a "fetish" for our culture? Marinetti's answer was an enthusiastic "yes," with a "so what?" added as a muttered and angry footnote.

# The Futurist Manifesto

## EMILIO FILIPPO TOMMASO MARINETTI

WE HAD STAYED UP all night, my friends and I, under hanging mosque lamps with domes of filigreed brass, domes starred like our spirits, shining like them with the prisoned radiance of electric hearts. For hours we had trampled our native sloth into rich Persian rugs, arguing up to the last confines of logic and blackening many reams of paper with our frenzied scribbling.

An immense pride was buoying us up, because we felt ourselves alone at that hour, alone, awake, and on our feet, like proud beacons or forward sentries against an army of hostile stars glaring down at us from their celestial encampments. Alone with stokers feeding the hellish fires of great ships, alone with the black spectres who grope in the red-hot bellies of locomotives launched on their crazy courses, alone with drunkards reeling like wounded birds along the city walls.

Suddenly we jumped, hearing the mighty noise of the huge double-decker trams that rumbled by outside, ablaze with colored lights, like villages on holiday suddenly struck and uprooted by the flooding Po and dragged over falls and through gorges to the sea.

Then the silence deepened. But, as we listened to the old canal muttering its feeble prayers and the creaking bones of sickly palaces above their damp green beards, under the windows we suddenly heard the famished roar of automobiles.

"Let's go!" I said. "Friends, away! Let's go! Mythology and the Mystic Ideal are defeated at last. We're about to see the Centaur's birth and, soon after, the first flight of Angels! . . . We must shake at the gates of life, test the bolts and hinges. Let's go! Look there, on the earth, the very first dawn! There's nothing to match the splendor of the sun's red sword, slashing for the first time through our millennial gloom!"

We went up to the three snorting beasts, to lay amorous hands on their torrid breasts. I stretched out on my car like a corpse on its bier, but revived at once under the steering wheel, a guillotine blade that threatened my stomach.

The raging broom of madness swept us out of ourselves and drove us through streets as rough and deep as the beds of torrents. Here and there, sick lamplight through window glass taught us to distrust the deceitful mathematics of our perishing eyes.

I cried, "The scent, the scent alone is enough for our beasts."

And like young lions we ran after Death, its dark pelt blotched with pale crosses as it escaped down the vast violet living and throbbing sky.

But we had no ideal Mistress raising her divine form to the clouds, nor any cruel Queen to whom to offer our bodies, twisted like Byzantine rings! There was nothing to make us wish for death, unless the wish to be free at last from the weight of our courage!

And on we raced, hurling watchdogs against doorsteps, curling them under our burning tires like collars under a flatiron. Death, domesticated, met me at every turn, gracefully holding out a paw, or once in a while hunkering down, making velvety caressing eyes at me from every puddle.

"Let's break out of the horrible shell of wis-

SOURCE: F. T. Marinetti, "The Futurist Manifesto," *Le Figaro* (Paris), February 20, 1909 (complete).

dom and throw ourselves like pride-ripened fruit into the wide, contorted mouth of the wind! Let's give ourselves utterly to the Unknown, not in desperation but only to replenish the deep wells of the Absurd!"

The words were scarcely out of my mouth when I spun my car around with the frenzy of a dog trying to bite its tail, and there, suddenly, were two cyclists coming towards me, shaking their fists, wobbling like two equally convincing but nevertheless contradictory arguments. Their stupid dilemma was blocking my way— Damn! Ouch! . . . I stopped short and to my disgust rolled over into a ditch with my wheels in the air. . . .

O maternal ditch, almost full of muddy water! Fair factory drain! I gulped down your nourishing sludge; and I remembered the blessed black breast of my Sudanese nurse. . . . When I came up—torn, filthy, and stinking—from under the capsized car, I felt the white-hot iron of joy deliciously pass through my heart!

A crowd of fishermen with handlines and gouty naturalists were already swarming around the prodigy. With patient, loving care those people rigged a tall derrick and iron grapnels to fish out my car, like a big beached shark. Up it came from the ditch, slowly, leaving in the bottom, like scales, its heavy framework of good sense and its soft upholstery of comfort.

They thought it was dead, my beautiful shark, but a caress from me was enough to revive it; and there it was, alive again, running on its powerful fins!

And so, faces smeared with good factory muck—plastered with metallic waste, with senseless sweat, with celestial soot—we, bruised, our arms in slings, but unafraid, declared our high intentions to all the living of the earth:

## Manifesto of Futurism

1. We intend to sing the love of danger, the habit of energy and fearlessness.
2. Courage, audacity, and revolt will be essential elements of our poetry.
3. Up to now literature has exalted a pensive immobility, ecstasy, and sleep. We intend to exalt aggressive action, a feverish insomnia, the racer's stride, the mortal leap, the punch and the slap.
4. We affirm that the world's magnificence has been enriched by a new beauty: the beauty of speed. A racing car whose hood is adorned with great pipes, like serpents of explosive breath—a roaring car that seems to ride on grapeshot is more beautiful than the Victory of Samothrace.
5. We want to hymn the man at the wheel, who hurls the lance of his spirit across the Earth, along the circle of its orbit.
6. The poet must spend himself with ardor, splendor, and generosity, to swell the enthusiastic fervor of the primordial elements.
7. Except in struggle, there is no more beauty. No work without an aggressive character can be a masterpiece. Poetry must be conceived as a violent attack on unknown forces, to reduce and prostrate them before man.
8. We stand on the last promontory of the centuries! . . . Why should we look back, when what we want is to break down the mysterious doors of the Impossible? Time and Space died yesterday. We already live in the absolute, because we have created eternal, omnipresent speed.
9. We will glorify war—the world's only hygiene—militarism, patriotism, the destructive gesture of freedom-bringers, beautiful ideas worth dying for, and scorn for woman.
10. We will destroy the museums, libraries, academies of every kind, will fight moralism, feminism, every opportunistic or utilitarian cowardice.
11. We will sing of great crowds excited by work, by pleasure, and by riot; we will sing of the multicolored, polyphonic tides of revolution in the modern capitals; we will sing of the vibrant nightly fervor of arsenals and shipyards blazing with violent electric moons; greedy railway stations that devour smoke-plumed serpents; factories hung on clouds by the crooked lines of their smoke; bridges that stride the rivers like giant gymnasts, flashing in the sun with a glitter of knives; adventurous steamers that sniff the horizon;

deep-chested locomotives whose wheels paw the tracks like the hooves of enormous steel horses bridled by tubing; and the sleek flight of planes whose propellers chatter in the wind like banners and seem to cheer like an enthusiastic crowd.

It is from Italy that we launch through the world this violently upsetting incendiary manifesto of ours. With it, today, we establish *Futurism,* because we want to free this land from its smelly gangrene of professors, archaeologists, *ciceroni*[1] and antiquarians. For too long has Italy been a dealer in second-hand clothes. We mean to free her from the numberless museums that cover her like so many graveyards.

Museums: cemeteries! . . . Identical, surely, in the sinister promiscuity of so many bodies unknown to one another. Museums: public dormitories where one lies forever beside hated or unknown beings. Museums: absurd abattoirs of painters and sculptors ferociously slaughtering each other with color-blows and line-blows, the length of the fought-over walls!

That one should make an annual pilgrimage, just as one goes to the graveyard on All Souls' Day; that I grant. That once a year one should leave a floral tribute beneath the Gioconda,[2] I grant you that. . . . But I don't admit that our sorrows, our fragile courage, our morbid restlessness should be given a daily conducted tour through the museums. Why poison ourselves? Why rot?

And what is there to see in an old picture except the laborious contortions of an artist throwing himself against the barriers that thwart his desire to express his dream completely? . . . Admiring an old picture is the same as pouring our sensibility into a funerary urn instead of hurtling it far off, in violent spasms of action and creation.

Do you, then, wish to waste all your best powers in this eternal and futile worship of the past, from which you emerge fatally exhausted, shrunken, beaten down?

In truth I tell you that daily visits to museums, libraries, and academies (cemeteries of empty exertion, Calvaries of crucified dreams, registries of aborted beginnings!) are, for artists, as damaging as the prolonged supervision by parents of certain young people drunk with their talent and their ambitious wills. When the future is barred to them, the admirable past may be a solace for the ills of the moribund, the sickly, the prisoner. . . . But we want no part of it, the past, we the young and strong *Futurists!*

So let them come, the gay incendiaries with charred fingers! Here they are! Here they are! . . . Come on! set fire to the library shelves! Turn aside the canals to flood the museums! . . . Oh, the joy of seeing the glorious old canvases bobbing adrift on those waters, discolored and shredded! . . . Take up your pickaxes, your axes and hammers and wreck, wreck the venerable cities, pitilessly!

The oldest of us is thirty: so we have at least a decade for finishing our work. When we are forty, other younger and stronger men will probably throw us in the wastebasket like useless manuscripts—we want it to happen!

They will come against us, our successors, will come from far away, from every quarter, dancing to the winged cadence of their first songs, flexing the hooked claws of predators, sniffing doglike at the academy doors the strong odor of our decaying minds, which will have already been promised to the literary catacombs.

But we won't be there. . . . At last they'll find us—one winter's night—in open country, beneath a sad roof drummed by a monotonous rain. They'll see us crouched beside our trembling aeroplanes in the act of warming our hands at the poor little blaze that our books of today will give out when they take fire from the flight of our images.

They'll storm around us, panting with scorn and anguish, and all of them, exasperated by our proud daring, will hurtle to kill us, driven by a hatred the more implacable the more their hearts will be drunk with love and admiration for us.

Injustice, strong and sane, will break out radiantly in their eyes.

[1] Tour guides.
[2] Leonardo's *Mona Lisa.*

Art, in fact, can be nothing but violence, cruelty, and injustice.

The oldest of us is thirty: even so we have already scattered treasures, a thousand treasures of force, love, courage, astuteness, and raw willpower; have thrown them impatiently away, with fury, carelessly, unhesitatingly, breathless, and unresting. . . . Look at us! We are still untired! Our hearts know no weariness because they are fed with fire, hatred, and speed! . . . Does that amaze you? It should, because you can never remember having lived! Erect on the summit of the world, once again we hurl our defiance at the stars!

You have objections?—Enough! Enough! We know them. . . . We've understood! . . . Our fine deceitful intelligence tells us that we are the revival and extension of our ancestors—Perhaps! . . . If only it were so!—But who cares? We don't want to understand! . . . Woe to anyone who says those infamous words to us again!

Lift up your heads!

Erect on the summit of the world, once again we hurl defiance to the stars!

## The Medium Is the Message: Marshall McLuhan

Herbert Marshall McLuhan (1911–1980) was born in Edmonton, Alberta, ahead of his time. He was the most important philosopher of media and communications in the twentieth century. He studied at the University of Manitoba in the early 1930s, from which he received his B.A. and M.A., spending the late 1930s teaching English at the Universities of Wisconsin and St. Louis. In 1937 McLuhan embraced Roman Catholicism, which some scholars find odd, given the celebration of modern technology and means of communication that can be read into his work. Between 1939 and 1943 he studied at Cambridge University, receiving his second M.A. and his Ph.D. in literature. He taught for two years at Assumption College in Windsor, Ontario, then received an appointment from St. Michael's College (the University of Toronto) in 1946, where he taught until his retirement in 1979.

McLuhan's star rose to giddy heights in the 1960s, propelled by his books *The Gutenberg Galaxy: The Making of Typographic Man* (1962) and *Understanding Media: The Extensions of Man* (1964), his masterworks on how media have shaped human culture. But we have to go back to the 1950s to get a glimpse of McLuhan's first forays into the field of communications theory. His greatest influence was Harold Innis, a colleague at the University of Toronto, who in books such as *Empire and Communications* (1950) discussed the political consequences of communications technologies. McLuhan's first book, *The Mechanical Bride: Folklore of Industrial Man* (1951), was a satirical look at advertising, foreshadowing more rambunctious theories to come. It juxtaposed ads, comics, and text, its supposed theme being how the "death of sex" brought about by advertising sought to turn human beings into dreaming robots. From this time on, McLuhan wrote in such a fashion that the order you read the chapters in his book didn't matter—he was making a point about the nonlinearity of modern electronic culture.

In *The Gutenberg Galaxy,* McLuhan tells the story of the central place of the printing press in Western culture. In this book McLuhan delineates the "three ages of man," each determined by the form of communication that dominated it:

1. A preliterate tribal age, where speech ruled supreme
2. The Gutenberg Age, where print and thus the visual sense dominated

3. Our own Electronic Age of Retribalization, which brings with it a full sensory involvement, including touch

The acoustic space of tribal cultures gave way to the linear, bounded space of the print age, with nationalism and industrialism as its driving political and economic forces. This age showed us the "linear" physics of Descartes and Newton, where motion could be graphically displayed as a series of straight lines through three-dimensional space; the linear, perspective-based art of the old masters; and straight-line, linear narrative in literature (the classic nineteenth-century novel starts at the beginning and ends at the end). This gave way to the curved, multifaceted space of the electronic age, a space that engages all our senses at once. Notably, it revived our lost senses of hearing and touch.

In the 1960s, McLuhan taught out of the "Coach House," the home of his Centre for Culture and Technology at the University of Toronto, now headed by Derrick de Kerckhove, who continues McLuhan's work. He made the cover of *Time* magazine, was a regular visitor to television studios across North America, and even did an interview for *Playboy* (in the March 1969 issue, pp.53–74, 158) that is well worth flipping through the pictures to get to (this interview is a nice summary of his basic ideas by the way). He was for a few years the prince of the philosophy of popular culture. In his books *The Medium Is the Massage* (1967) and *War and Peace in the Global Village* (1968) he worked with Quentin Fiore to produce collages of photos, ads, quotations from admired authors, pithy McLuhanisms, and groovy graphics that very much reflected the experimental feeling of artistic adventure that dominated the late 1960s.

At the end of the decade he published another enigmatic work, *Culture Is Our Business* (1970), which mixed contemporary ads, headline-style text, quotations from authors such as James Joyce and T. S. Eliot, and the odd comment from McLuhan. The book is very much in the style of *The Mechanical Bride,* except that television advertising is included. His thesis can be found by reversing the title: In the electronic age, *business* is our culture. All of these cut-and-paste works make use of McLuhan's favorite technique of "thought probes," where he throws out a provocative question or one-liner (in the case of the three books just mentioned, illustrated with a graphic or quote) to get his audience thinking about media effects.

McLuhan's star dimmed in the 1970s and 1980s, despite the efforts of his son Eric to finish his father's work on his "laws of media." He registered briefly on the pop cultural radar screens in 1977 when Woody Allen gave him a cameo appearance in his film *Annie Hall,* reminding his audience of McLuhan's dry wit. But McLuhan's star shot up once again with the coming of the Internet and other means of global communications from the late 1980s on. He became the patron saint of a whole generation of technophiles, *Wired* magazine formally assigning him that title in its masthead.

Much of McLuhan's philosophy of communications and media can be found in his most influential work, *Understanding Media,* the source of the reading selections. In a nutshell, McLuhan believes that technology generally, and communications media specifically, radically affect the form and scale of social organization, a thesis he borrowed from Innis but refashioned in his own image. McLuhan defined a "medium" as any extension of our bodies or minds, or more specifically, of the human central nervous system (he seemed to mean this quite literally). For example, an automobile extends the power of the human foot, whereas a computer extends the power of the human mind. The messages put out by our media are important not for their content but for the change in pace, scale, or patterns of life that they cause. McLuhan's famous mantra "the medium is the message" means simply that the effects of a medium on our perception of the world is far more important than any concrete messages being relayed by the medium in question.

New media bring with them new ratios between our senses—for example, with the advent of print, our eyes became more important than our ears. McLuhan didn't separate the psychological from the physiological effects of media: He speculated that new technologies selectively amputate our limbs or senses—for example, the automobile amputates our legs; a book amputates our sense of hearing—and that our central nervous system naturally blocks out communication overloads—for example, when a person blocks out a series of conversations at a noisy party to concentrate on the person with whom they're speaking.

Further, McLuhan classified all media as either hot or cool. Hot media were "high definition," providing lots of information, requiring little "filling in"; cool media were low definition, requiring more perceptual work to fill in the gaps they provide. Radio, print, photographs, films, and lectures are all "hot" in the sense that they involve one or more of our senses in depth; whereas the telephone, speech, cartoons, television, and seminars are all "cool," requiring our active involvement to complete the patterns of communication they offer us. He didn't live long enough to classify the World Wide Web and e-mail as media of communication, though Heidi Hochenedel does this for us later in this chapter—she sees the Internet as "tepid," as sharing the qualities of both hot and cool media.

In the modern culture, electronic communications have created a new world of instant awareness, a global village, where constraints of space and time are irrelevant. A war in Africa becomes an element of suppertime's television entertainment to a suburban couple in North America; a speech by a national political leader a thousand miles away is transmitted with less than a second's delay over the radio or Internet. The global village is a community that worships speed, as we'll see when we turn to Mark Kingwell's article.

McLuhan's major contribution to the philosophy of culture can be seen in his notion that the nature of our culture is determined by the media we use to communicate with others. Our current culture is dominated by electronic technologies, so we shouldn't be surprised if our dominant modes of expression—our literature, our politics, and our entertainments—are shaped by these technologies. Consider how different the political campaigns must have been before the age of radio and television or how virtual reality and computer games have affected films such as *Run Lola Run* and *The Matrix* over the last decade or so. McLuhan has been accused of being an apologist for the banality of the messages relayed to us by the new electronic media. His reply to his critics was simple: To save ourselves from the abusive power of the media, we must first understand them.

# Understanding Media

MARSHALL MCLUHAN

## Introduction

James Reston wrote in *The New York Times* (July 7, 1957):

> A health director . . . reported this week that a small mouse, which presumably had been watching television, attacked a little girl and her full-grown cat. . . . Both mouse and cat survived, and the incident is recorded here as a reminder that things seem to be changing.

After three thousand years of explosion, by means of fragmentary and mechanical technologies, the Western world is imploding. During the mechanical ages we had extended our bodies in space. Today, after more than a century of electric technology, we have extended our central nervous system itself in a global embrace, abolishing both space and time as far as our planet is concerned. Rapidly, we approach the final phase of the extensions of man—the technological simulation of consciousness, when the creative process of knowing will be collectively and corporately extended to the whole of human society, much as we have already extended our senses and our nerves by the various media. Whether the extension of consciousness, so long sought by advertisers for specific products, will be "a good thing" is a question that admits of a wide solution. There is little possibility of answering such questions about the extensions of man without considering all of them together. Any extension, whether of skin, hand, or foot, affects the whole psychic and social complex.

Some of the principal extensions, together with some of their psychic and social consequences, are studied in this book. Just how little consideration has been given to such matters in the past can be gathered from the consternation of one of the editors of this book. He noted in dismay that "seventy-five per cent of your material is new. A successful book cannot venture to be more than ten per cent new." Such a risk seems quite worth taking at the present time when the stakes are very high, and the need to understand the effects of the extensions of man becomes more urgent by the hour.

In the mechanical age now receding, many actions could be taken without too much concern. Slow movement insured that the reactions were delayed for considerable periods of time. Today the action and the reaction occur almost at the same time. We actually live mythically and integrally, as it were, but we continue to think in the old, fragmented space and time patterns of the pre-electric age.

Western man acquired from the technology of literacy the power to act without reacting. The advantages of fragmenting himself in this way are seen in the case of the surgeon who would be quite helpless if he were to become humanly involved in his operation. We acquired the art of carrying out the most dangerous social operations with complete detachment. But our detachment was a posture of noninvolvement. In the electric age, when our central nervous system is technologically extended to involve us in the whole of mankind and to incorporate the whole of mankind in us, we necessarily participate, in depth, in the consequences of our every action. It is no longer possible to adopt the aloof and dissociated role of the literate Westerner.

The Theater of the Absurd dramatizes this recent dilemma of Western man, the man of action who appears not to be involved in the action. Such is the origin and appeal of Samuel Beckett's clowns. After three thousand years of specialist

SOURCE: Marshall McLuhan, *Understanding Media* (New York: McGraw-Hill, 1964), pp. 3–9, 11–21, 22–25, 26–27, 27–28, 29, 30–31 (edited).

explosion and of increasing specialism and alienation in the technological extensions of our bodies, our world has become compressional by dramatic reversal. As electrically contracted, the globe is no more than a village. Electric speed in bringing all social and political functions together in a sudden implosion has heightened human awareness of responsibility to an intense degree. It is this implosive factor that alters the position of the Negro, the teen-ager, and some other groups. They can no longer be *contained,* in the political sense of limited association. They are now *involved* in our lives, as we in theirs, thanks to the electric media.

This is the Age of Anxiety for the reason of the electric implosion that compels commitment and participation, quite regardless of any "point of view." The partial and specialized character of the viewpoint, however noble, will not serve at all in the electric age. At the information level the same upset has occurred with the substitution of the inclusive image for the mere viewpoint. If the nineteenth century was the age of the editorial chair, ours is the century of the psychiatrist's couch. As extension of man the chair is a specialist ablation of the posterior, a sort of ablative absolute of backside, whereas the couch extends the integral being. The psychiatrist employs the couch, since it removes the temptation to express private points of view and obviates the need to rationalize events.

The aspiration of our time for wholeness, empathy and depth of awareness is a natural adjunct of electric technology. The age of mechanical industry that preceded us found vehement assertion of private outlook the natural mode of expression. Every culture and every age has its favorite model of perception and knowledge that it is inclined to prescribe for everybody and everything. The mark of our time is its revulsion against imposed patterns. We are suddenly eager to have things and people declare their beings totally. There is a deep faith to be found in this new attitude—a faith that concerns the ultimate harmony of all being. Such is the faith in which this book has been written. It explores the contours of our own extended beings in our technologies, seeking the principle of intelligibility in each of them. In the full confidence that it is possible to win an understanding of these forms that will bring them into orderly service, I have looked at them anew, accepting very little of the conventional wisdom concerning them. One can say of media as Robert Theobald has said of economic depressions: "There is one additional factor that has helped to control depressions, and that is a better understanding of their development." Examination of the origin and development of the individual extensions of man should be preceded by a look at some general aspects of the media, or extensions of man, beginning with the never-explained numbness that each extension brings about in the individual and society.

## The Medium Is the Message

In a culture like ours, long accustomed to splitting and dividing all things as a means of control, it is sometimes a bit of a shock to be reminded that, in operational and practical fact, the medium is the message. This is merely to say that the personal and social consequences of any medium—that is, of any extension of ourselves—result from the new scale that is introduced into our affairs by each extension of ourselves, or by any new technology. Thus, with automation, for example, the new patterns of human association tend to eliminate jobs, it is true. That is the negative result. Positively, automation creates roles for people, which is to say depth of involvement in their work and human association that our preceding mechanical technology had destroyed. Many people would be disposed to say that it was not the machine, but what one did with the machine, that was its meaning or message. In terms of the ways in which the machine altered our relations to one another and to ourselves, it mattered not in the least whether it turned out cornflakes or Cadillacs. The restructuring of human work and association was shaped by the technique of fragmentation that is the essence of machine technology. The essence of automation technology is the opposite. It is integral and decentralist in depth, just as the machine was fragmentary, centralist, and superficial in its patterning of human relationships.

The instance of the electric light may prove illuminating in this connection. The electric light is pure information. It is a medium without a message, as it were, unless it is used to spell out some verbal ad or name. This fact, characteristic of all media, means that the "content" of any medium is always another medium. The content of writing is speech, just as the written word is the content of print, and print is the content of the telegraph. If it is asked, "What is the content of speech?," it is necessary to say, "It is an actual process of thought, which is in itself nonverbal." An abstract painting represents direct manifestation of creative thought processes as they might appear in computer designs. What we are considering here, however, are the psychic and social consequences of the designs or patterns as they amplify or accelerate existing processes. For the "message" of any medium or technology is the change of scale or pace or pattern that it introduces into human affairs. The railway did not introduce movement or transportation or wheel or road into human society, but it accelerated and enlarged the scale of previous human functions, creating totally new kinds of cities and new kinds of work and leisure. This happened whether the railway functioned in a tropical or a northern environment, and is quite independent of the freight or content of the railway medium. The airplane, on the other hand, by accelerating the rate of transportation, tends to dissolve the railway form of city, politics, and association, quite independently of what the airplane is used for.

Let us return to the electric light. Whether the light is being used for brain surgery or night baseball is a matter of indifference. It could be argued that these activities are in some way the "content" of the electric light, since they could not exist without the electric light. This fact merely underlines the point that "the medium is the message" because it is the medium that shapes and controls the scale and form of human association and action. The content or uses of such media are as diverse as they are ineffectual in shaping the form of human association. Indeed, it is only too typical that the "content" of any medium blinds us to the character of the medium. It is only today that industries have become aware of the various kinds of business in which they are engaged. When IBM discovered that it was not in the business of making office equipment or business machines, but that it was in the business of processing information, then it began to navigate with clear vision. The General Electric Company makes a considerable portion of its profits from electric light bulbs and lighting systems. It has not yet discovered that, quite as much as A.T.& T., it is in the business of moving information.

The electric light escapes attention as a communication medium just because it has no "content." And this makes it an invaluable instance of how people fail to study media at all. For it is not till the electric light is used to spell out some brand name that it is noticed as a medium. Then it is not the light but the "content" (or what is really another medium) that is noticed. The message of the electric light is like the message of electric power in industry, totally radical, pervasive, and decentralized. For electric light and power are separate from their uses, yet they eliminate time and space factors in human association exactly as do radio, telegraph, telephone, and TV, creating involvement in depth. . . .

In accepting an honorary degree from the University of Notre Dame a few years ago, General David Sarnoff made this statement: "We are too prone to make technological instruments the scapegoats for the sins of those who wield them. The products of modern science are not in themselves good or bad; it is the way they are used that determines their value." That is the voice of the current somnambulism. Suppose we were to say, "Apple pie is in itself neither good nor bad; it is the way it is used that determines its value." Or, "The smallpox virus is in itself neither good nor bad; it is the way it is used that determines its value." Again, "Firearms are in themselves neither good nor bad; it is the way they are used that determines their value." That is, if the slugs reach the right people firearms are good. If the TV tube fires the right ammunition at the right people it is good. I am not being perverse. There is simply nothing in the Sarnoff statement that will bear scrutiny, for it ignores the nature of the medium, of any and all media, in the true Narcissus style of one hypnotized by the amputation and extension of his own being in a new technical form. General Sarnoff went on to explain his attitude to the technology of print, saying that it was true that print caused much trash to circulate, but it had also disseminated the Bible and the thoughts of seers and philosophers. It has never occurred to General Sarnoff that any technology could do anything but *add* itself on to what we already are.

Such economists as Robert Theobald, W. W. Rostow, and John Kenneth Galbraith have been explaining for years how it is that "classical economics" cannot explain change or growth. And the paradox of mechanization is that although it is itself the cause of maximal growth and change, the principle of mechanization excludes the very possibility of growth or the understanding of change. For mechanization is achieved by fragmentation of any process and by putting the fragmented parts in a series. Yet, as David Hume showed in the eighteenth century, there is no principle of causality in a mere sequence. That one thing follows another accounts for nothing. Nothing follows from following, except change. So the greatest of all reversals occurred with electricity, that ended sequence by making things instant. With instant speed the causes of things began to emerge to awareness again, as they had not done with things in sequence and in concatenation accordingly. Instead of asking which came first, the chicken or the egg, it suddenly seemed that a chicken was an egg's idea for getting more eggs.

Just before an airplane breaks the sound barrier, sound waves become visible on the wings of the plane. The sudden visibility of sound just as sound ends is an apt instance of that great pattern of being that reveals new and opposite forms just as the earlier forms reach their peak performance. Mechanization was never so vividly fragmented or sequential as in the birth of the movies, the moment that translated us beyond mechanism into the world of growth and organic interrelation. The movie, by sheer speeding up the mechanical, carried us from the world of sequence and connections into the world of creative configuration and structure. The message of the movie medium is that of transition from lineal connections to configurations. It is the transition that produced the now quite correct observation: "If it works, it's obsolete." When electric speed further takes over from mechanical movie sequences, then the lines of force in structures and in media become loud and clear. We return to the inclusive form of the icon.

To a highly literate and mechanized culture the movie appeared as a world of triumphant illusions and dreams that money could buy. It was at this moment of the movie that cubism occurred, and it has been described by E. H. Gombrich (*Art and Illusion*) as "the most radical attempt to stamp out ambiguity and to enforce one reading of the picture—that of a man-made construction, a colored canvas." For cubism substitutes all facets of an object simultaneously for the "point of view" or facet of perspective illusion. Instead of the specialized illusion of the third dimension on canvas, cubism sets up an interplay of planes and contradiction or dramatic conflict of patterns, lights, textures that "drives home the message" by involvement. This is held by many to be an exercise in painting, not in illusion.

In other words, cubism, by giving the inside and outside, the top, bottom, back, and front and the rest, in two dimensions, drops the illusion of perspective in favor of instant sensory awareness of the whole. Cubism, by seizing on instant total awareness, suddenly announced that *the medium is the message*. Is it not evident that the moment that sequence yields to the simultaneous, one is in the world of the structure and of configuration? Is that not what has happened in physics as in painting, poetry, and in communication? Specialized segments of attention have shifted to total field, and we can now say, "The medium is the message" quite naturally. Before the electric speed and total field, it was not obvious that the medium is the message. The message, it seemed, was the "content," as people used to ask what a painting was *about*. Yet they never thought to ask what a melody was about, nor what a house or a dress was about. In such matters, people retained some sense of the whole pattern, of form and function as a unity. But in the electric age this integral idea of structure and configuration has become so prevalent that educational theory has taken up the matter. Instead of working with specialized "problems" in arithmetic, the structural approach now follows the lines of force in the field of numbers and has small children meditating about number theory and "sets."

Cardinal Newman said of Napoleon, "He understood the grammar of gunpowder." Napoleon had paid some attention to other media as well, especially the semaphore telegraph that gave him a great advantage over his enemies. He is on record for saying that "Three hostile newspapers are more to be feared than a thousand bayonets."

Alexis de Tocqueville was the first to master the grammar of print and typography. He was thus able to read off the message of coming change in France and America as if he were reading aloud from a text that had been handed to him. In fact, the nineteenth century in France and in America was just such an open book to de Tocqueville because he had learned the grammar of print. So he, also, knew when that grammar did not apply. He was asked why he did not write a book on England, since he knew and admired England. He replied:

> One would have to have an unusual degree of philosophical folly to believe oneself able to judge England in six months. A year always seemed to me too short a time in which to appreciate the United States properly, and it is much easier to acquire clear and precise notions about the American Union than about Great Britain. In America all laws derive in a sense from the same line of thought. The whole of society, so to speak, is founded upon a single fact; everything springs from a simple principle. One could compare America to a forest pierced by a multitude of straight roads all converging on the same point. One has only to find the center and

everything is revealed at a glance. But in England the paths run criss-cross, and it is only by travelling down each one of them that one can build up a picture of the whole.

De Tocqueville, in earlier work on the French Revolution, had explained how it was the printed word that, achieving cultural saturation in the eighteenth century, had homogenized the French nation. Frenchmen were the same kind of people from north to south. The typographic principles of uniformity, continuity, and lineality had overlaid the complexities of ancient feudal and oral society. The Revolution was carried out by the new literati and lawyers.

In England, however, such was the power of the ancient oral traditions of common law, backed by the medieval institution of Parliament, that no uniformity or continuity of the new visual print culture could take complete hold. The result was that the most important event in English history has never taken place; namely, the English Revolution on the lines of the French Revolution. The American Revolution had no medieval legal institutions to discard or to root out, apart from monarchy. And many have held that the American Presidency has become very much more personal and monarchical than any European monarch ever could be.

De Tocqueville's contrast between England and America is clearly based on the fact of typography and of print culture creating uniformity and continuity. England, he says, has rejected this principle and clung to the dynamic or oral common-law tradition. Hence the discontinuity and unpredictable quality of English culture. The grammar of print cannot help to construe the message of oral and nonwritten culture and institutions. The English aristocracy was properly classified as barbarian by Matthew Arnold because its power and status had nothing to do with literacy or with the cultural forms of typography. Said the Duke of Gloucester to Edward Gibbon upon the publication of his *Decline and Fall:* "Another damned fat book, eh, Mr. Gibbon? Scribble, scribble, scribble, eh, Mr. Gibbon?" De Tocqueville was a highly literate aristocrat who was quite able to be detached from the values and assumptions of typography. That is why he alone understood the grammar of typography. And it is only on those terms, standing aside from any structure or medium, that its principles and lines of force can be discerned. For any medium has the power of imposing its own assumption on the unwary. Prediction and control consist in avoiding this subliminal state of Narcissus trance. But the greatest aid to this end is simply in knowing that the spell can occur immediately upon contact, as in the first bars of a melody.

*A Passage to India* by E. M. Forster is a dramatic study of the inability of oral and intuitive oriental culture to meet with the rational, visual European patterns of experience. "Rational," of course, has for the West long meant "uniform and continuous and sequential." In other words, we have confused reason with literacy, and rationalism with a single technology. Thus in the electric age man seems to the conventional West to become irrational. In Forster's novel the moment of truth and dislocation from the typographic trance of the West comes in the Marabar Caves. Adela Quested's reasoning powers cannot cope with the total inclusive field of resonance that is India. After the Caves: "Life went on as usual, but had no consequences, that is to say, sounds did not echo nor thought develop. Everything seemed cut off at its root and therefore infected with illusion."

*A Passage to India* (the phrase is from Whitman, who saw America headed Eastward) is a parable of Western man in the electric age, and is only incidentally related to Europe or the Orient. The ultimate conflict between sight and sound, between written and oral kinds of perception and organization of existence is upon us. Since understanding stops action, as Nietzsche observed, we can moderate the fierceness of this conflict by understanding the media that extend us and raise these wars within and without us.

Detribalization by literacy and its traumatic effects on tribal man is the theme of a book by the psychiatrist J. C. Carothers, *The African Mind in Health and Disease* (World Health Or-

ganization, Geneva, 1953). Much of his material appeared in an article in *Psychiatry* magazine, November, 1959: "The Culture, Psychiatry, and the Written Word." Again, it is electric speed that has revealed the lines of force operating from Western technology in the remotest areas of bush, savannah, and desert. One example is the Bedouin with his battery radio on board the camel. Submerging natives with floods of concepts for which nothing has prepared them is the normal action of all of our technology. But with electric media Western man himself experiences exactly the same inundation as the remote native. We are no more prepared to encounter radio and TV in our literate milieu than the native of Ghana is able to cope with the literacy that takes him out of his collective tribal world and beaches him in individual isolation. We are as numb in our new electric world as the native involved in our literate and mechanical culture.

Electric speed mingles the cultures of prehistory with the dregs of industrial marketeers, the nonliterate with the semiliterate and the postliterate. Mental breakdown of varying degrees is the very common result of uprooting and inundation with new information and endless new patterns of information. Wyndham Lewis made this a theme of his group of novels called *The Human Age*. The first of these, *The Childermass,* is concerned precisely with accelerated media change as a kind of massacre of the innocents. In our own world as we become more aware of the effects of technology on psychic formation and manifestation, we are losing all confidence in our right to assign guilt. Ancient prehistoric societies regard violent crime as pathetic. The killer is regarded as we do a cancer victim. "How terrible it must be to feel like that," they say. J. M. Synge took up this idea very effectively in his *Playboy of the Western World*.

If the criminal appears as a nonconformist who is unable to meet the demand of technology that we behave in uniform and continuous patterns, literate man is quite inclined to see others who cannot conform as somewhat pathetic. Especially the child, the cripple, the woman, and the colored person appear in a world of visual and typographic technology as victims of injustice. On the other hand, in a culture that assigns roles instead of jobs to people—the dwarf, the skew, the child create their own spaces. They are not expected to fit into some uniform and repeatable niche that is not their size anyway. Consider the phrase "It's a man's world." As a quantitative observation endlessly repeated from within a homogenized culture, this phrase refers to the men in such a culture who have to be homogenized Dagwoods in order to belong at all. It is in our I.Q. testing that we have produced the greatest flood of misbegotten standards. Unaware of our typographic cultural bias, our testers assume that uniform and continuous habits are a sign of intelligence, thus eliminating the ear man and the tactile man.

C. P. Snow, reviewing a book of A. L. Rowse (*The New York Times Book Review,* December 24, 1961) on *Appeasement* and the road to Munich, describes the top level of British brains and experience in the 1930s. "Their I.Q.'s were much higher than usual among political bosses. Why were they such a disaster?" The view of Rowse, Snow approves: "They would not listen to warnings because they did not wish to hear." Being anti-Red made it impossible for them to read the message of Hitler. But their failure was as nothing compared to our present one. The American stake in literacy as a technology or uniformity applied to every level of education, government, industry, and social life is totally threatened by the electric technology. The threat of Stalin or Hitler was external. The electric technology is within the gates, and we are numb, deaf, blind, and mute about its encounter with the Gutenberg technology, on and through which the American way of life was formed. It is, however, no time to suggest strategies when the threat has not even been acknowledged to exist. I am in the position of Louis Pasteur telling doctors that their greatest enemy was quite invisible, and quite unrecognized by them. Our conventional response to all media, namely that it is how they are used that counts, is the numb stance of the technological idiot. For the "content" of a medium is like the juicy piece of meat carried by the burglar to distract the watchdog of the mind. The effect of the medium is made strong and intense just because it is given another medium as "content." The content of a movie is a novel or a play or an opera. The effect of the movie form is not related to its program content. The "content" of writing or print is speech, but the reader is almost entirely unaware either of print or of speech.

Arnold Toynbee is innocent of any understanding of media as they have shaped history, but he is full of examples that the student of media can use. At one moment he can seriously suggest that adult education, such as the Workers Educational Association in Britain, is a useful counterforce to the popular press. Toynbee considers that although all of the oriental societies have in our time accepted the industrial technology and its political consequences: "On the cultural plane, however, there is no uniform corresponding tendency." (Somervell, I. 267) This is like the voice of the literate man, floundering in a milieu of ads, who boasts, "Personally, I pay no attention to ads." The spiritual and cultural reservations that the oriental peoples may have toward our technology will avail them not at all. The effects of technology do not occur at the level of opinions or concepts, but alter sense ratios or patterns of perception steadily and without any resistance. The serious artist is the only person able to encounter technology with impunity, just because he is an expert aware of the changes in sense perception.

The operation of the money medium in seventeenth-century Japan had effects not unlike the operation of typography in the West. The penetration of the money economy, wrote G. B. Sansom (in *Japan,* Cresset Press, London, 1931) "caused a slow but irresistible revolution, culminating in the breakdown of feudal government and the resumption of intercourse with foreign countries after more than two hundred years of seclusion." Money has reorganized the sense life of peoples just because it is an *extension* of our sense lives. This change does not depend upon approval or disapproval of those living in the society.

Arnold Toynbee made one approach to the transforming power of media in his concept of "etherialization," which he holds to be the principle of progressive simplification and efficiency in any organization or technology. Typically, he is ignoring the *effect* of the challenge of these forms upon the response of our senses. He imagines that it is the response of our opinions that is relevant to the effect of media and technology in society, a "point of view" that is plainly the result of the typographic spell. For the man in a literate and homogenized society ceases to be sensitive to the diverse and discontinuous life of forms. He acquires the illusion of the third dimension and the "private point of view" as part of his Narcissus fixation, and is quite shut off from Blake's awareness or that of the Psalmist, that we become what we behold.

Today when we want to get our bearings in our own culture, and have need to stand aside from the bias and pressure exerted by any technical form of human expression, we have only to visit a society where that particular form has not been felt, or a historical period in which it was unknown. Professor Wilbur Schramm made such a tactical move in studying *Television in the Lives of Our Children.* He found areas where TV had not penetrated at all and ran some tests. Since he had made no study of the peculiar nature of the TV image, his tests were of "content" preferences, viewing time, and vocabulary counts. In a word, his approach to the problem was a literary one, albeit unconsciously so. Consequently, he had nothing to report. Had his methods been employed in 1500 A.D. to discover the effects of the printed book in the lives of children or adults, he could have found out nothing of the changes in human and social psychology resulting from typography. Print created individualism and nationalism in the sixteenth century. Program and "content" analysis offer no clues to the magic of these media or to their subliminal charge.

Leonard Doob, in his report *Communication in Africa,* tells of one African who took great pains to listen each evening to the BBC news, even though he could understand nothing of it.

Just to be in the presence of those sounds at 7 P.M. each day was important for him. His attitude to speech was like ours to melody—the resonant intonation was meaning enough. In the seventeenth century our ancestors still shared this native's attitude to the forms of media, as is plain in the following sentiment of the Frenchman Bernard Lam expressed in *The Art of Speaking* (London, 1696):

> 'Tis an effect of the Wisdom of God, who created Man to be happy, that whatever is useful to his conversation (way of life) is agreeable to him . . . because all victual that conduces to nourishment is relishable, whereas other things that cannot be assimilated and be turned into our substance are insipid. A Discourse cannot be pleasant to the Hearer that is not easie to the Speaker; nor can it be easily pronounced unless it be heard with delight.

Here is an equilibrium theory of human diet and expression such as even now we are only striving to work out again for media after centuries of fragmentation and specialism.

Pope Pius XII was deeply concerned that there be serious study of the media today. On February 17, 1950, he said:

> It is not an exaggeration to say that the future of modern society and the stability of its inner life depend in large part on the maintenance of an equilibrium between the strength of the techniques of communication and the capacity of the individual's own reaction.

Failure in this respect has for centuries been typical and total for mankind. Subliminal and docile acceptance of media impact has made them prisons without walls for their human users. As A. J. Liebling remarked in his book *The Press,* a man is not free if he cannot see where he is going, even if he has a gun to help him get there. For each of the media is also a powerful weapon with which to clobber other media and other groups. The result is that the present age has been one of multiple civil wars that are not limited to the world of art and entertainment. In *War and Human Progress,* Professor J. U. Nef declared: "The total wars of our time have been the result of a series of intellectual mistakes. . . ."

If the formative power in the media are the media themselves, that raises a host of large matters that can only be mentioned here, although they deserve volumes. Namely, that technological media are staples or natural resources, exactly as are coal and cotton and oil. Anybody will concede that society whose economy is dependent upon one or two major staples like cotton, or grain, or lumber, or fish, or cattle is going to have some obvious social patterns of organization as a result. Stress on a few major staples creates extreme instability in the economy but great endurance in the population. The pathos and humor of the American South are embedded in such an economy of limited staples. For a society configured by reliance on a few commodities accepts them as a social bond quite as much as the metropolis does the press. Cotton and oil, like radio and TV, become "fixed charges" on the entire psychic life of the community. And this pervasive fact creates the unique cultural flavor of any society. It pays through the nose and all its other senses for each staple that shapes its life.

That our human senses, of which all media are extensions, are also fixed charges on our personal energies, and that they also configure the awareness and experience of each one of us, may be perceived in another connection mentioned by the psychologist C. G. Jung:

> Every Roman was surrounded by slaves. The slave and his psychology flooded ancient Italy, and every Roman became inwardly, and of course unwittingly, a slave. Because living constantly in the atmosphere of slaves, he became infected through the unconscious with their psychology. No one can shield himself from such an influence (*Contributions to Analytical Psychology*, London, 1928).

## Media Hot and Cold

"The rise of the waltz," explained Curt Sachs in the *World History of the Dance*, "was a result of that longing for truth, simplicity, closeness to nature, and primitivism, which the last two-thirds of the eighteenth century fulfilled." In the century of jazz we are likely to overlook the emergence of the waltz as a hot and explosive human expression that broke through the formal feudal barriers of courtly and choral dance styles.

There is a basic principle that distinguishes a hot medium like radio from a cool one like the telephone, or a hot medium like the movie from a cool one like TV. A hot medium is one that extends one single sense in "high definition." High definition is the state of being well filled with data. A photograph is, visually, "high definition." A cartoon is "low definition," simply because very little visual information is provided. Telephone is a cool medium, or one of low definition, because the ear is given a meager amount of information. And speech is a cool medium of low definition, because so little is given and so much has to be filled in by the listener. On the other hand, hot media do not leave so much to be filled in or completed by the audience. Hot media are, therefore, low in participation, and cool media are high in participation or completion by the audience. Naturally, therefore, a hot medium like radio has very different effects on the user from a cool medium like the telephone.

A cool medium like hieroglyphic or ideogrammic written characters has very different effects from the hot and explosive medium of the phonetic alphabet. The alphabet, when pushed to a high degree of abstract visual intensity, became typography. The printed word with its specialist intensity burst the bonds of medieval corporate guilds and monasteries, creating extreme individualist patterns of enterprise and monopoly. But the typical reversal occurred when extremes of monopoly brought back the corporation, with its impersonal empire over many lives. The hotting-up of the medium of writing to repeatable print intensity led to nationalism and the religious wars of the sixteenth century. The heavy and unwieldy media, such as stone, are time binders. Used for writing, they are very cool indeed, and serve to unify the ages; whereas paper is a hot medium that serves to unify spaces horizontally, both in political and entertainment empires.

Any hot medium allows of less participation than a cool one, as a lecture makes for less participation than a seminar, and a book for less than dialogue. With print many earlier forms were excluded from life and art, and many were given strange new intensity. But our own time is crowded with examples of the principle that the hot form excludes, and the cool one includes. When ballerinas began to dance on their toes a century ago, it was felt that the art of the ballet had acquired a new "spirituality." With this new intensity, male figures were excluded from ballet. The role of women had also become fragmented with the advent of industrial specialism and the explosion of home functions into laundries, bakeries, and hospitals on the periphery of the community. Intensity or high definition engenders specialism and fragmentation in living as in entertainment, which explains why any intense experience must be "forgotten," "censored," and reduced to a very cool state before it can be "learned" or assimilated. The Freudian "censor" is less of a moral function than an indispensable condition of learning. Were we to accept fully and directly every shock to our various structures of awareness, we would soon be nervous wrecks, doing double-takes and pressing panic buttons every minute. The "censor" protects our central system of values, as it does our physical nervous system by simply cooling off the onset of experience a great deal. For many people, this cooling system brings on a lifelong state of psychic *rigor mortis,* or of somnambulism, particularly observable in periods of new technology.

An example of the disruptive impact of a hot technology succeeding a cool one is given by Robert Theobald in *The Rich and the Poor.* When Australian natives were given steel axes by the missionaries, their culture, based on the stone axe, collapsed. The stone axe had not only been scarce but had always been a basic status symbol of male importance. The missionaries provided quantities of sharp steel axes and gave them to women and children. The men had even to borrow these from the women, causing a collapse of male dignity. A tribal and feudal hierarchy of traditional kind collapses quickly when it meets any hot medium of the mechanical, uniform, and repetitive kind. The medium of money or wheel or writing, or any other form of specialist speed-up of exchange and information, will serve to fragment a tribal structure. Similarly, a very much greater speed-up, such as occurs with electricity, may serve to restore a tribal pattern of intense involvement such as took place with the introduction of radio in Europe, and is now tending to happen as a result of TV in America. Specialist technologies detribalize. The nonspecialist electric technology retribalizes. The process of upset resulting from a new distribution of skills is accompanied by much culture lag in which people feel compelled to look at new situations as if they were old ones, and come up with ideas of "population explosion" in an age of implosion. Newton, in an age of clocks, managed to present the physical universe in the image of a clock. But poets like Blake were far ahead of Newton in their response to the challenge of the clock. Blake spoke of the need to be delivered "from single vision and Newton's sleep," knowing very well that Newton's response to the challenge of the new mechanism was itself merely a mechanical repetition of the challenge. Blake saw Newton and Locke and others as hypnotized Narcissus types quite unable to meet the challenge of mechanism. W. B. Yeats gave the full Blakean version of Newton and Locke in a famous epigram:

> Locke sank into a swoon;
> The garden died;
> God took the spinning jenny
> Out of his side.

Yeats presents Locke, the philosopher of mechanical and lineal associationism, as hypnotized by his own image. The "garden," or unified consciousness, ended. Eighteenth-century man got an extension of himself in the form of the spinning machine that Yeats endows with its full sexual significance. Woman, herself, is thus seen as a technological extension of man's being.

Blake's counterstrategy for his age was to meet mechanism with organic myth. Today, deep in the electric age, organic myth is itself a simple and automatic response capable of mathematical formulation and expression, without any of the imaginative perception of Blake about it. Had he encountered the electric age, Blake would not have met its challenge with a mere repetition of electric form. For myth *is* the instant vision of a complex process that ordinarily extends over a long period. Myth is contraction or implosion of any process, and the instant speed of electricity confers the mythic dimension on ordinary industrial and social action today. We *live* mythically but continue to think fragmentarily and on single planes. . . .

The new electric structuring and configuring of life more and more encounters the old lineal and fragmentary procedures and tools of analysis from the mechanical age. More and more we turn from the content of messages to study total effect. Kenneth Boulding put this matter in *The Image* by saying, "The meaning of a message is the change which it produces in the image." Concern with *effect* rather than *meaning* is a basic change of our electric time, for effect involves the total situation, and not a single level of information movement. Strangely, there is recognition of this matter of effect rather than information in the British idea of libel: "The greater the truth, the greater the libel."

The effect of electric technology had at first been anxiety. Now it appears to create boredom. We have been through the three stages of alarm, resistance, and exhaustion that occur in every disease or stress of life, whether individual or collective. At least, our exhausted slump after the first encounter with the electric has inclined us to expect new problems. However, backward countries that have experienced little permeation with our own mechanical and specialist culture are much better able to confront and to understand electric technology. Not only have backward and nonindustrial cultures no specialist habits to overcome in their encounter with electromagnetism, but they have still much of their traditional oral culture that has the total, unified "field" character of our new electromagnetism. Our old industrialized areas, having eroded their oral traditions automatically, are in the position of having to rediscover them in order to cope with the electric age.

In terms of the theme of media hot and cold, backward countries are cool, and we are hot. The "city slicker" is hot, and the rustic is cool. But in terms of the reversal of procedures and values in the electric age, the past mechanical time was hot, and we of the TV age are cool. The waltz was a hot, fast mechanical dance suited to the industrial time in its moods of pomp and circumstance. In contrast, the Twist is a cool, involved and chatty form of improvised gesture. The jazz of the period of the hot new media of movie and radio was hot jazz. Yet jazz of itself tends to be a casual dialogue form of dance quite lacking in the repetitive and mechanical forms of the waltz. Cool jazz came in quite naturally after the first impact of radio and movie had been absorbed. . . .

The "hard" sell and the "hot" line become mere comedy in the TV age, and the death of all the salesmen at one stroke of the TV axe has turned the hot American culture into a cool one that is quite unacquainted with itself. America, in fact, would seem to be living through the reverse process that Margaret Mead described in *Time* magazine (September 4, 1954): "There are too many complaints about society having to move too fast to keep up with the machine. There is great advantage in moving fast if you move completely, if social, educational, and recreational changes keep pace. You must change the whole pattern at once and the whole group together—and the people themselves must decide to move."

Margaret Mead is thinking here of change as uniform speed-up of motion or a uniform hotting-up of temperatures in backward societies. We are certainly coming within conceivable range of a world automatically controlled to the point where we could say, "Six hours less radio in Indonesia next week or there will be a great falling off in literary attention." Or, "We can program twenty more hours of TV in South Africa next week to cool down the tribal temperature raised by radio last week. Whole cultures could now be programmed to keep their emotional climate stable in the same way that we have begun to know something about maintaining equilibrium in the commercial economies of the world. . . .

Throughout *The City in History,* Lewis Mumford favors the cool or casually structured towns over the hot and intensely filled-in cities. The great period of Athens, he feels, was one during which most of the democratic habits of village life and participation still obtained. Then burst forth the full variety of human expression and exploration such as was later impossible in highly developed urban centers. For the highly developed situation is, by definition, low in opportunities of participation, and rigorous in its demands of specialist fragmentation from those who would control it. For example, what is known as "job enlargement" today in business and in management consists in allowing the employee more freedom to discover and define his function. Likewise, in reading a detective story the reader participates as co-author simply because so much has been left out of the narrative. The open-mesh silk stocking is far more sensuous than the smooth nylon, just because the eye must act as hand in filling in and completing the image, exactly as in the mosaic of the TV image. . . .

Nevertheless, it makes all the difference whether a hot medium is used in a hot or a cool culture. The hot radio medium used in cool or nonliterate cultures has a violent effect, quite unlike its effect, say in England or America, where radio is felt as entertainment. A cool or low literacy culture cannot accept hot media like movies or radio as entertainment. They are, at least, as radically upsetting for them as the cool TV medium has proved to be for our high literacy world.

And as for the cool war and the hot bomb scare, the cultural strategy that is desperately needed is humor and play. It is play that cools off the hot situations of actual life by miming them.

Competitive sports between Russia and the West will hardly serve that purpose of relaxation. Such sports are inflammatory, it is plain. And what we consider entertainment or fun in our media inevitably appears as violent political agitation to a cool culture.

One way to spot the basic difference between hot and cold media uses is to compare and contrast a broadcast of a symphony performance with a broadcast of a symphony rehearsal. Two of the finest shows ever released by the CBC were of Glenn Gould's procedure in recording piano recitals, and Igor Stravinsky's rehearsing the Toronto symphony in some of his new work. A cool medium like TV, when really used, demands this involvement in process. The neat tight package is suited to hot media, like radio and gramophone. Francis Bacon never tired of contrasting hot and cool prose. Writing in "methods" or complete packages, he contrasted with writing in aphorisms, or single observations such as "Revenge is a kind of wild justice." The passive consumer wants packages, but those, he suggested, who are concerned in pursuing knowledge and in seeking causes will resort to aphorisms, just because they are incomplete and require participation in depth.

The principle that distinguishes hot and cold media is perfectly embodied in the folk wisdom: "Men seldom make passes at girls who wear glasses." Glasses intensify the outward-going vision, and fill in the feminine image exceedingly, Marion the Librarian notwithstanding. Dark glasses, on the other hand, create the inscrutable and inaccessible image that invites a great deal of participation and completion.

## The Drug Called Speed

Mark Kingwell (1963– ) is a very productive (he's written seven books so far) young philosopher who teaches at the University of Toronto. He was educated at the Universities of Toronto and Edinburgh and at Yale, where he obtained his Ph.D. His main interests are political theory and philosophical reflections on popular culture. The latter has made him something of a media darling in Canada thanks to his frequent appearances on television and in magazines and newspapers (he writes for the Toronto *Globe and Mail, Harper's, The Utne Reader,* and a number of other magazines and newspapers), where he comments on such diverse matters as modern citizen-ship, happiness, UFOs, and pop music.

Kingwell has written two substantial meditations on popular culture. In the first, *Dreams of Millennium: Report from a Culture on the Brink* (1996), he offers often pithy observations on everything from body piercing to the Borg of *Star Trek,* from urban poverty to neo-Luddism, from prophecies of environmental collapse to the conspiracy mongering of the television show *The X-Files,* linking all of these to the turning of the millennium and the hopes and fears that this great millennial shift brought with it.

In *Better Living: In Pursuit of Happiness from Plato to Prozac* (1998), Kingwell explores various philosophical and popular ideas about happiness. Much of both books is taken up with first-person narratives of Kingwell's own experiences of the various phenomena of popular culture he decides to explore, from popping Prozac to see just how happy he could be, to staring at his naked body in a mirror, musing on the contemporary obsession with working out and "reclaiming the body." In these books Kingwell takes on the role of a philosophical reporter on our culture, his re-ports usually tinged with a wry skepticism (if not cynicism).

He has also written two books on political theory. *A Civil Tongue: Justice, Dia-logue, and the Politics of Pluralism* (1995) argues that civility is an essential ingre-dient in the soup of modern pluralist, democratic politics. In *The World We Want: Virtue, Vice, and the Good Citizen* (2000), Kingwell suggests that in the era of a glob-alized consumer economy we need a new model of citizenship based on greater in-dividual participation in democratic processes to prevent us from forgetting about politics altogether as we drive to the local shopping mall in our brand new sports utility vehicles.

In the following 1998 article from *Harper's Magazine,* "Fast Forward: Our High-Speed Chase to Nowhere," Kingwell suggests that speed has become a drug for us and that technological progress in our means of transportation and information pro-cessing hasn't improved our ability to think or make wise decisions, or our general quality of life. It has just made everything move faster, making our current technolo-gies out of date at an ever-increasing rate. Consider Moore's Law of computer de-sign: Eighteen months after you buy your shiny new computer, it will be obsolete, a new model with a blazingly fast processor chip appearing that makes working with your old clunker seem like watching snails race. Interestingly, Kingwell says that the truly privileged in our culture are those with the greatest access to this speed, those who can do what they want to do, to get where they want to go, as quickly as pos-sible, and then be able to take a time-out from our speed-driven culture. *Speed* is the new luxury good in our culture. Against this speed is the underground movement for *slowness,* people who actually think before they speak and write, who turn off their cell phones at movies, who sit under a tree and read a good book. *They* are the new subversives.

Kingwell's dialectic of speed and slowness underlying our culture is a dia-lectic that tears at us every day of our lives as we race to work, classes, dinners, par-ties, or airports, wondering what the rush is all about. The question Kingwell is asking here is not that different from that asked by the more moderate among neo-Luddites: Wouldn't it be a good idea to turn off some of our technology and slow down a bit?

# Fast Forward: Our High-Speed Chase to Nowhere

## MARK KINGWELL

SPEED, ACCORDING TO the physics textbooks we all read in high school, is a function of distance over time: $V = d/t$. Space divided by time, the three dimensions of extension dissolved into the fourth, mysterious vector of duration. Miles per hour. Feet per second. Bodies rushing through time, into the future. But the indisputable fact that speed measures ground covered during periods of time fails to communicate why we yearn for acceleration, for the sudden enlarging of sensory volume that makes for the *feeling* of speed. This is a neurophysiological condition, familiar to most of us, that we might agree to call velocitization: the adrenal throb of neurons that accompanies large increases in velocity, the electrochemical, brain-fluid high we miss only when it's gone.

That's why coming down a freeway off-ramp finds us an overexcited traffic hazard, a portrait of unwilling deceleration still craving those now impossible seventy miles an hour. Or makes for the night of white-line fever following a day-long drive, the inside of our eyelids relentlessly patterned with oncoming dashes, one after the other, in an insomniac fugue of speed-jockey withdrawal. It is this *sensation* of speed that we desire, the impressionable meat inside our skulls lit up by that increase in sensory information. *We want to be velocitized.*

Speed is a drug, and not just in the old-time hepcat high of Dexedrine or bennies, those ingested, on-the-road amphetamines, or even in the newer, hi-tech crystal meth to be found, probably, in some corner of a schoolyard near you. The experience of speed itself releases into the electrochemical soup of our heads a cascade of naturally occurring drugs, not the least of which are epinephrine and norepinephrine, the hormones that course through the brain in the bone-melting, stomach-clenching high of sexual attraction.

I have flown perhaps five or six hundred miles an hour while travelling in a commercial airliner. But the now banal insight about this now banal experience is that . . . there is no speed here. A slight pressing into my seat on takeoff, insulated from the engine's roar and cloaked in the unreality of carpeting and suit bags and laptops; a brief, fierce application of brakes and a reversal of engines on landing, especially if the airport is old and the runways are short. But otherwise, obviously, nothing. A sense of floating—music in my ears, a drink in my hand, peanut salt on my fingers, and not much in my head. A toboggan ride is faster, and more thrilling.

. . . I start to read Milan Kundera's novel *Slowness* one snowy Sunday afternoon. I do it with the television on, a Bulls-Rockets game bouncing away in the background. "A picture-perfect fast break," Isiah Thomas says to Bob. Like many people, I often read while watching television. I'm not especially proud of this habit, but somehow I'm not appropriately ashamed of it either. Like most of us, I am also capable of simultaneously listening to music, carrying on a conversation, and eating—all while driving fifteen miles above the speed limit, scanning the horizon for signs of authority. Am I the proud owner of a parallel-processing new brain? Could I go even faster with smart drugs? [1]

I have my laptop open to take notes, so I

[1] Smart drugs have been with us for thousands of years, in the form of caffeine and nicotine, stimulants we use to push our consciousness everyday. Who among us is unaware at any given moment, of exactly where he lies on the curve of his daily caffeine regimen? Americans spend well over $10 billion on coffee, tea, and their accoutrements every year.

won't have to mark up Kundera's text. The laptop is a PowerBook 5300/100; it runs a 100-megahertz PowerPC 603e chip. This machine was considered pretty fast when I bought it eighteen months ago—not scary fast, just high-end quick. But now it feels slow, because I know there are so many faster machines out there, working at speeds closer to parallel. In fact, my 5300 has been placed in the "discontinued archive" by the Macintosh product developers, destined for quick-time oblivion in the big boneyard of machine death.

"Speed is the form of ecstasy the technical revolution has bestowed on man," writes Kundera on his book's second page. He is decrying the false "ecstatic" speed of the man in a machine—the artificial annihilation of time—as compared with the bodily speed of the runner. The man behind the wheel feels nothing but a mindless, futureless impatience, a desire to go faster that exists only in the present, obliterating all other modalities of temporality in a literal *ek-stasis*. The running man, by contrast, feels the many past, present, and future costs of speed, the burn in his lungs, the fatigue in his legs. Unlike the driver, the runner must resist the constant urge to quit, to slow down and rest. He must play mind games with himself, set intermediate goals, and then set new ones, knowing that eventually he will reach a point where the pain slips away, a fragile, short-lived euphoria of pure *human* speed.

. . . In an essay called "*Sur la télévision,*" the sociologist Pierre Bourdieu lambasted the media-age creature he called "le fast-thinker": the person who grinds out what appears to be intellectual discourse under the glare of the klieg lights. *Le fast-thinker* is not an intellectual, only the simulation of one; he is adept at the snappy phrase, the blustery and authoritative opinion, and, of course, the unanswerable statistical put-down. In the hurly-burly of talk television, on programs as disparate as *Meet the Press* and *Jenny Jones,* the most successful performer is not the person with the truth but the one with the sharpest tongue and the handiest numbers.

Meanwhile, we sit at home and click nervously from one image to another, gazing at the disembodied heads of our televisual oracles as they flash across the screen. The medium, here, is the message, and the rapid-fire jump cuts seem to define not only our politics but our experience as well.

Alexander the Great and Napoleon moved through their respective worlds of overweening ambition and conquest at precisely the same speed. Top velocity for them, or anyone, was the gallop of a horse.

Machines change everything. Between December 18, 1898, when Comte Gaston de Chasseloup-Laubat set the first land-speed record in an automobile, his 36-horsepower Jean-taud achieving a top speed of 39.24 miles per hour on an open road near Acheres, France, and October 15, 1997, when Richard Noble's ThrustSSC jet car broke the sound barrier in a car travelling 763.035 miles per hour (Mach 1.01) in the Nevada desert, the arc of human speed has bent its curve more and more steeply. Millennia of steady-state velocity have passed, and now in this crazy century of upthrust records limits are set and shattered in days, hours, even minutes. Chasseloup-Laubat held his record for less than two months, his Belgian archrival Camille Jenatzy taking it from him in January of 1899 by hitting 49.92 miles per hour. The Frenchman managed, with some elementary streamlining, to respond by getting his car up to a respectable 57.6 miles per hour. But Jenatzy was more obsessed. He designed a new streamlined electric car, the first expressly built to break records, and shot to 65.79 miles per hour that April.

The name of this new car? *La Jamais Contente.* "Never happy." Here we have modernity in a nutshell, the same joyful fascination with speed—the same celebration of the sleek beauty of the machine age and its ceaseless imperatives—to be found a decade later in Emilio Filippo Tommaso Marinetti's original Futurist manifesto, published in *Le Figaro* in 1909. "Hoorah!" Marinetti wrote of the speedy machines he loved so much, the race cars and biplanes and swift war machines. "No more contact with the vile earth!"

But Marinetti's happy paean to "dynamism," his love of machine speed, reached its apotheosis, its own terminal velocity, only when he declared himself a fascist another decade later, in 1919. The speed of modern life had found its perfect political complement. Faster things for faster living. *Get with the program! Right now!*

The movement of our century can be plotted on a parabolic curve, a violent calculus of progress and quickness and neuronal excitement that is never, finally, happy, because it still has not achieved the pure limit-speed of infinity over zero. The upgrade imperative of the parabola is buried deep in the logic of speed, where machines not only go faster with each generation but also move from generation to generation at a brisker pace. The speed of personal computers, dutifully conforming to Moore's Law, now doubles in eighteen months or less. Technology's genius is that it plots its upgrade ambition on this striving curve, carrying us ever and ever more sharply upward. When it comes to our machines, nobody has to plan obsolescence. There is no military-industrial conspiracy to keep the eternal light bulb out of your hands, as suggested in a famous riff in the middle of *Gravity's Rainbow*. Obsolescence just happens.

Why? Well, consider gravity's rainbow itself. It is the other parabola dominating our era's span, the ballistic curve first plotted in the sixteenth century, when mathematicians brought forth the scribbles that could help them deliver cannon payloads more accurately. The two curves of speed and ballistics, the true golden arches, have never been far from the heart of war, our miserable keynote.

Speed, said Sun Tzu, is the essence of war. "History progresses at the speed of its weapons systems," adds the French philosopher Paul Virilio. "War has always been a worksite of movement, a speed-factory." It took ancient Greek warriors over a decade to reach, and then destroy, a targeted city; we can now do so, from anywhere, in a few minutes. A single nuclear submarine can quickly reduce dozens of distant cities to molten glass and twisted metal. In the 1940s,

the speed of naval "strike power," still the dominant form of military might, was measured in knots: in nautical miles per hour. By the 1960s, when the astronauts of *Apollo 10* achieved a record speed of 24,791 miles per hour, it was measured in Machs: thousands of miles per hour. Now operational velocity inches ever closer to light speed itself. Speed's annihilation of time and place means, finally, speedy annihilation of places—and times.

. . . Everyone says: go faster. Everyone says: upgrade. Everyone says: be more efficient. We all hang on the curve, afraid to fall off. But the curve itself is not just a parabola; it is a paradox. It can never reach its ultimate goal, can only ever approach it more nearly by minute increments, because the end point of this insistent arch does not really exist. We know that Achilles must catch the tortoise in Zeno's famous riddle, but when we try to think about it logically he seems always thwarted, this famously fleet warrior, getting closer to the lumbering tortoise but never reaching him, no matter how quickly he runs.

In 1995, the science-fiction writer Bruce Sterling, whose body resides most of the time in Austin, Texas, posted a message on the Web inviting people to write what he called "The Handbook of Dead Media," an exercise in "media forensics" or (varying the metaphor) "a naturalist's field guide for the communications paleontologist." The idea was to track the history of the once-vibrant but now forgotten, the junk store of silenced communications along the road of obsolescence: the phenakistoscope, the teleharmonium, the stereopticon, the Telefon Hirmondo, the Antikythera Device, and a thousand more gadgets and extensions of human experience that once lived and do so no more.

The point of the Dead Media Project, beyond its surface technoanthropology, is to counter the hype of Net gurus, their tendency to champion nonexistent "vaporware" in terms otherwise reserved for the Second Coming and to load all technological change into the operating system we might call Progress 2.0. This "Whig version of technological history," as Sterling calls it, not only generates unspeakable hype but spins off into aggressive, upgrade-or-die evolutionary imperatives—as if we're going somewhere in particular, as if technology really is teleology. Aging techies and watered-down McLuhanites can make a lot of money packaging and selling that brand of fear to the rest of us, but this is a phantom economy.

"We live in the Golden Age of Dead Media," Sterling writes on his Web site. "Our entire culture has been sucked into the black hole of computation, an utterly frenetic process of virtual planned obsolescence. But you know—that process needn't be unexamined or frenetic. We can examine that process whenever we like, and the frantic pace is entirely our own fault. What's our big hurry anyway?"

The Dead Media Project has a deeper lesson than historical awareness, though. It doesn't simply unsettle the fallacies embedded in techno-rhetoric; it doesn't just hint that the speed of technological "progress" has far more to do with money, power, markets, and politics than with simple technical efficiency. It also, more importantly, undermines the *essentialism* of speed, the dangerous and false idea that media themselves have an internal desire to go faster.

Media don't crave speed. We do.

Extreme speeds are not available to most of us. They are the preserve of the elite who get to rise above the slow yet frenetic plodding of the urban lifescape. Sitting in traffic these days, watching the dollars count themselves off in the red numerals of the taxi's meter as helicopters take off from distant office buildings, I realize that speed is the ultimate luxury good. Our cities' momentous flow of corpuscular traffic, pumping and squeezing in the arteries (physical and virtual) of our movement, our progress, is more and more sclerotic, slowing with the sludge of its own success. More than 700,000 cars enter Manhattan every day, joining the estimated 176,000 that are already there, along with the delivery trucks that block narrow streets and nearly 12,000 yellow cabs. Traffic crawls along in midtown at seven miles per hour. Mad cabbies honk and speed through the gaps and help maintain the average pedestrian injury rate at about 250 per day. The bicycle couriers are the ones on speed.

The traffic stops, again. The meter in the taxi doesn't. I think: I can run a mile in seven minutes, but I have only a 14.4 modem and operating system 7.5 in my laptop. Am I fast? At what point, I wonder, do I get out and walk?

"Reading," says Virilio, "implies time for reflection, a slowing-down that destroys the mass's dynamic efficiency." Like Kundera, we feel we should resist speed by engaging in activities, like reading or gardening or ambling, that are perforce slower. We feel we should make ourselves slow down. Indeed, there is an underground of this resistance in the culture, a theme of sundial slowness set against the overarching digital quickness of life—a theme that grows more obvious, and somehow more oddly frenzied, as we near the socially constructed limit of the millennium.[2]

But notice the paradox. Time for reflection, the indispensable precondition of reading or any other "slow" activity, is possible only with the prior benefit of speed. Leisure time is a luxury good, too, the flip side of being able to move fast when you want to. Those idyllic gardens, so conducive to rest and restoration, are mostly found in rooftop condos or in the leafy confines behind million-dollar brownstones. For most of us, precious moments at the golf course or at a tropical island resort are purchased only at the cost of long, harried hours on the expressway or waiting for connecting flights in Dallas, Texas.

Anyone who believes that the current young generation thinks and works faster than people in some notional, low-tech past hasn't been paying attention. And those who accuse kids today of a generalized attention deficit disorder, a compulsion to whip their heads around like distracted cats at the profusion of jump-cut images in our world, are also missing something crucial.

[2] The urgent apocalypticism of neo-Luddites, members of food co-ops, deep ecologists, quasi-unabombers, and other denizens of the environmental fringe is matched only by the ingenuity with which they design their ever-proliferating Web sites.

Certainly there are more images and information now, more advertisements in our lives—three thousand "marketing messages" a day, according to some estimates—and kids seem to grow up faster, to *be* faster, than ever before. But it has yet to be proved that our enormous investment in computer technology in recent years has resulted in increased productivity, or that the ability to "process" hundreds of images and millions of bits of information has anything to do with *thinking*—with constructing or analyzing an argument, with making good decisions—much less knowledge in the strong sense. And the sum total effect of this explosion of velocity is not a feeling of speed but one of boredom; the frustrating truth about the World Wide Web is that it is slow.[3] Worse, it's often slow to no purpose, the seconds and minutes ticking away only to reveal that there is after all nothing of interest on the downloaded page. We are here approaching the metaphysical limits of speed, where the fast becomes the slow, and vice versa. In such moments, the newspaper as delivery system is state of the art.

. . . Faster and faster can only mean, in the end, stasis. The logical outcome of efficiency is uselessness: solving problems has no point but the ultimate elimination of problem-solving itself. What is the point of being able to read a page every three seconds? To read every book ever written? Then what? Meanwhile, the vehicles of our speed ruin the planet as fast as we move around it.

Speed, we might admit, is our preeminent trope of control and domination. But even as speed excites us, we are drugged into a narcolepsy of cheap contentment whose danger we don't

even recognize. The Canadian political scientist and performance artist Arthur Kroker labels ours "a crash culture," one in which we are always speeding up to a standstill, a spasm of useless speed that masks the coercion of "contemporary society as it undergoes a simultaneous acceleration and terminal shutdown." Not Marinetti's pure modern speed worship anymore but rather a curious post-modern double movement of velocity and lethargy.

For the citizens of a decadent techno-utopia, boredom, not failure, is the great enemy of human happiness. And fear of boredom is the heart of the gentle domination of our new speed driven regime. Yet there is no simple equation here, and the calculus of boredom's vectors and variables is more complex than we know. It is possible, even easy, to be bored at five hundred miles an hour. It is also possible for an instant to expand to fill the available space of consciousness, to watch a household accident or botched layup decelerate into the brain-jamming significance of heroic narrative, a real-time slow-motion sequence à la John Woo. We experience both hasty leisure and deliberate speed, moments that never end and decades that pass in a blink. How fast you move is not the same as how fast you are going.

Where, then, are we going in our fast-forward drive toward the future? Whence this urge, this speedy imperative? Is "technology" to blame? We might derive some solace from distancing ourselves from the principle of our rapidity, from blaming our machines and repeating the mantra that the medium is the message—but this would be too easy. And it would be a lie. Our machines do not make us forget. Our quick vehicles do not cause our panic, our wretched drivenness. The motor of speed, the transcendental impulse, lies buried not in the engine or the microprocessor but within each one of us, in our mortality. Speed was born of death, of both the desire to inflict it with weapons and the desire to transcend it. We are forever dividing more and more space by less and less time, yet we cannot escape time except in the liminal ecstasy of death. We love speed, because it means we can leave our un-

[3] Those who can pay for the privilege, of course, benefit from T1 lines, cable modems, and high-speed fiber-optic connections. And even in the world envisioned by companies such as Lucent Technologies, which recently announced a new fiber-optic cable that will transmit 10 million calls over a single fiber, it is probable that our data needs (for video, audio, and as yet unheralded marvels) will simply expand to fill the available bandwidth, in much the same way that the volume of traffic quickly grows to exceed the capacities of newly constructed freeways.

happy consciousness in the dust—can for an instant pull apart the Cartesian mind-body confection with these superb machines. That's what the overload of sensory volume and pulsing adrenaline achieves: a minute and thrilling breach in the mostly impregnable union of mind and matter. We don't just risk death in speed; we press the limits of our mortality.

The final irony of our speed mania is that death, when we finally get there, may not be a kind of escape velocity at all but instead something like what was imagined by the ancient Greeks, a dull impatient wishing to be elsewhere. Hitting the wall, crashing into the ground, we may dissolve, not into sweet unconsciousness but rather into a bleak waiting room of forever thwarted speed, a shadowy endgame in which nothing ever happens. And even when it arrives after a long, painful illness or years of institutional dullness, death almost always comes too soon. It takes us from the hurly-burly of this quick life and seizes us, suddenly.

The Bastard in Shakespeare's *King John* says, "The spirit of the time shall teach me speed." But while the velocities go up, our mortality remains unchanged. No matter how quickly you move, death drives the fastest car on the highway. In the end, death always does the overtaking. Our desire to escape the vile earth necessarily ends with us buried in it.

## *Love and War on the Net*

As an antidote to Kingwell's skepticism about the utility of the wonderful new technologies of our day, Heidi Hochenedel is all in favor of the intoxicating speed they bring. Hochenedel (1967–), another young scholar interested in the philosophy of technology and cultural studies who teaches in and around Portland, Oregon, claims that although such new forms of communication as e-mail, chat rooms, and video-conferencing *do* have their problems, by and large they have *improved* the quality of human relationships in the global village, not degraded them as "techno-skeptics" such as Mark Kingwell and Arthur Kroker have suggested.

Hochenedel puts forward the idea that in terms of McLuhan's hot/cool division of media types, the Internet is a warm, or "tepid," medium in that it shares some of the qualities of hot media, such as the printed word, and those of cool media, such as television. Further, she strongly asserts that many of the claims of the techno-skeptics, for example, the notion that e-mail and other forms of computer-mediated communication discourage coherent thought, or that sitting in front of a computer screen for hours creates a "disembodied" effect, are "myths" cooked up by them to create a bit of intellectual drama.

Overall, she suggests that we adopt a "techno-pragmatic" attitude to new communication media, accepting both their bad and good effects. She asks us to walk down a middle path, one midway between the Unabomber's dark pessimism about technology and the giddy optimism of people such as Microsoft cofounder Bill Gates and Kingwell's "watered-down McLuhanites" trying to stampede us into buying the cutting-edge computer system of the moment. She sees this middle path down the information superhighway as the safest one to take, one that avoids the irrational fearmongering of the skeptics while not failing to recognize the definite but manageable negative effects of modern electronic communications.

# Love and War in the Global Village:
# A Techno-Pragmatic Perspective

## HEIDI NELSON HOCHENEDEL

### Techno-Pragmatism

At the dawn of the twenty-first century, attitudes toward the information superhighway and computer-mediated communication have tended to be either techno-utopian or techno-skeptical. Techno-utopians like Bill Gates (in his book *The Road Ahead*) idealize technology, virtual reality, and computer-mediated communication, arguing that they serve only to enhance human experience, bringing people closer together. These people believe that the new media promote freedom and democracy, but blithely ignore any unwelcome consequences caused by the new techno-environment. Techno-skeptics like Mark Kingwell, Arthur Kroker, and David Shenk focus instead on unforeseen techno-pollution, arguing that any benefits that result from technological innovations are far outweighed by the presence of data smog and data trash. The techno-skeptics focus on the road kill lain waste by virtual road rage along the information superhighway, while the techno-utopians describe the highway as a crowded sidewalk of the global village where people gather to beat drums, chant, and groove to a McLuhanesque tribal rhythm. The under-represented alternative to techno-utopia and techno-skepticism is what I shall term "techno-pragmatism," a middle-of-the-road view that describes life on the Internet as somewhere between a pleasant sidewalk and a twenty-five lane mega-freeway. The purpose of this essay is to explore the effects of computer-mediated communication on human relationships from a techno-pragmatic perspective. I shall argue that computer-mediated communication is quite dif-

ferent from any medium we have ever used before, and that it is not entirely classifiable in traditional McLuhanesque terms—it's neither hot nor cool, but both. I shall go on to sketch some of the unanticipated psychological effects of this new medium and conclude that we must deconstruct the categories of virtual and real relationships.

Techno-pragmatists like Patricia Wallace, in her book *The Psychology of the Internet,* view computer-mediated communication as both potentially useful and harmful.[1] We techno-pragmatists adhere to Marshall McLuhan's tried-and-true adage that the medium is the message and, like McLuhan, believe that new media are both extensions and amputations of man. To say that the medium is the message is not to discount the relevance of the content of the media, but rather to recognize that the medium by which we absorb and exchange information is as, or more, significant to our psychic and physical landscape. The same information broadcast by different media (the same activities performed by different methods) have profoundly different effects. A medium is any technology that makes communication possible, but may escape notice as a medium because it appears to have no "content." An example of such a medium is the automobile. Before the car, people relied on horses or their feet to move from point A to point B. As the car became the most common mode of transport (in privileged areas in the world), people

[1] Patricia Wallace, *The Psychology of the Internet* (Cambridge: Cambridge University Press, 1999).

SOURCE: Heidi Nelson Hochenedel, "Love and War in the Global Village: A Techno-Pragmatic Perspective," conference paper originally delivered at the "Medium as Message" conference at the University of Windsor, Windsor, Ontario, February 2000 (specially edited by the author for this volume). Used by permission of the author.

were able to travel and relocate more easily while remaining in physical contact with distant friends and family. By all accounts, the car is an extremely useful medium—it can be viewed as an extension of human legs and feet. But while it extends our lower extremities, within it our legs and feet are quite useless. Hence we experience what can be described as a virtual amputation of our bodies. The car at once extends and amputates our lower extremities.

The automobile has had a profound impact, not only on human culture, but on the planet as a whole. One might have predicted that the new facility of locomotion would have resulted in people devoting much less time to travel, freeing them to pursue other more creative activities. The reality, however, is just the opposite. As locomotion became more convenient, people began moving around much more, profoundly impacting the structure of cities by creating a commuter culture. Henry Ford could not have foreseen urban sprawl, the depletion of the ozone layer, global warming, and road rage. This is not to suggest that life on earth would be better without cars; rather, the car, like any new medium, has had many unanticipated consequences, and these, like the obvious calculated benefits, should be taken into account.

## Hot and Cool Media vs. the Tepid Internet

McLuhan divided media into two categories, "hot" and "cool." In his view media that require little interaction from the consumer or that engage only one sense are "hot," whereas media that demand more active participation are "cool." Participation does not refer so much to intellectual involvement as engagement of the physical senses. Media like radio, print, and photographs are "hot" because they demand little engagement of more than one of the consumer's physical senses. Text, for example, is hot because it only engages the reader's eyes. Cool media like the telephone, speech, and seminars engage more than one sense and require the consumer to participate more fully in the experience. According

to McLuhan, hot and cool media have very different effects on the consumer, altering human sense ratios differently, and influencing the way we react to our environment and to the content of the media in question. In general, hot media contribute to modern linear, alienated, and independent culture, while cool media encourage group participation and "tribalism." Oddly enough, McLuhan did not speculate that there could be a medium that was at once hot and cool. Nevertheless, this is precisely the case with the Internet. Not only does the Internet contain a mixture of hot and cool media, electronic text closely simulates speech (a cool medium) because of its immediacy and its demand for participation. E-mail, chatrooms, and video conferencing are at once hot and cool, or "tepid." The effects of this new medium are profoundly different from anything we have ever experienced.

## Life in the Global Village

McLuhan believed that electronic media have radical "tribalizing" effects, and that they would create a world in which political boundaries drawn on the world-map would cease to matter as much as local alliances and conflicts in "the global village." According to McLuhan, the global village was conceived by the intense interaction between different people all over the world made possible by film, radio, video, and television. The global village was in its embryonic stage of development during McLuhan's life, and is still only in its infancy. Yet now people all over the world are interacting with each other in ways that would have been quite unlikely ten years ago. Today the global village is mediated not only by traditional media like television and radio, but also by chatrooms, newsgroups, multi-user dungeons, e-mail correspondence, and video conferencing. Within this village ideas are being shared, people are comparing cultures, forming friendships, and falling in love. The global village is at once harmonious and fraught with conflict, as reflected by the name-calling referred to as "flaming" by the cyber-community. As often as we befriend some villagers, we make enemies with others. McLuhan's utopian vision of the global village was tempered by the realization that increased communication would lead to more conflict. In his famous *Playboy* interview in 1969 he notes:

> The global village conditions being forged by the electronic technology stimulate more discontinuity and diversity and division than the old mechanical standardized society; in fact the global village makes maximum disagreement and creative dialogue inevitable. Uniformity and tranquility are not the hallmarks of the global village; far more likely are conflict and discord as well as love and harmony—the customary life mode of any tribal people.[2]

Techno-skeptic David Shenk has argued in his book *Data Smog* that we ARE becoming tribalized—but not into ONE big global village, as McLuhan suggested.[3] Rather, he posits the existence of multiple fragmented and specialized villages, unaware of or hostile to each other's existence. The world is becoming more diverse, and techno-clans are becoming more alienated from each other. We are not all coming together in one virtual town square; rather, those of us with similar interests and ideologies are now able to communicate more easily, resulting in less diversity within specific subgroups. Shenk also argues that as we become more connected with minds all over the world, we are more alienated from our local, face-to-face relationships. As virtual tribes are formed, "real" relationships dissolve.

From the techno-pragmatic perspective, it does not matter whether we describe the virtual community as one big global village or many smaller virtual villages, since McLuhan's global village has never been characterized by homogeneity, but always by conflict and diversity. As in any village, we know our friends and family best, but we can visit our neighbors any time we care to. Moreover, it is not clear whether the "problems" Shenk describes are entirely neg-

ative. If people invest less time in face-to-face relationships as a result of computer-mediated communication, it can only be because these new relationships better fulfill intellectual and social needs. If people are more fulfilled by "virtual" relationships, then they SHOULD invest less in face-to-face relationships. Obviously birds of a feather flock virtually together, causing ideologies to reinforce themselves as people offer each other support for particular lifestyles and convictions. Nevertheless, it is also true that people have easy access to more alternative points of view than ever before. A curious Christian connecting with other Christians on the net can easily click on a Hindu site. Moreover, she can do so in relative privacy, without fear of reprisal from her Christian community. She can at once strengthen her own beliefs and sense of community as she educates herself about others. Life in the global village is not without its unintended consequences, but they are not always negative.

Unlike the printed text media of the past, speedy electronic text allows and even demands commitment and interaction. Effectively, tepid electronic text is a totally new kind of medium, and its full effects have yet to be understood. Electronic text, like the phone (a cool medium), is an extension, amplification and amputation of speech. It allows one to gather information quickly, and to instantly interact with the authors of that information. Like traditional text (a hot medium), it is usually linear and logic-bound, engaging only the eyes. Hypertext demands participation, while it discourages physical trips to the library and investment in face-to-face relationships with people who do not closely share one's interests. It is, at once, tribalizing and alienating. Tepid.

"Tepid" electronic text is different from traditional "hot" text because of the speed with which it can be transmitted over the net. Mark Kingwell has argued that our addiction to ever increasing electronic speed is careening the human race down the fast track to nowhere.[4] Yet

[2] Marshall McLuhan, Interview with *Playboy*, March 1969, p. 21. Available online: http://www.nephridium.org/features/indymedia/mcluhan_interview.html
[3] McLuhan, Interview.

[4] Mark Kingwell, "Fast-Forward: Our High-Speed Chase to Nowhere," *Harper's Magazine*, May 1998, pp. 37–48.

clearly electronic speed is the glue that bonds people separated by physical distance into a solid community. Like the airplane, improved electronic speed has effectively decreased the physical distance between people, while it encourages the formation and solidification of new relationships all over the world.

## The Ramifications of Tepid Media

There are many important features of computer-mediated communication. It is convenient, requires no postage, very little physical exertion, and, like the phone, it is immediate: there is often little or no lag-time between a message and a response. This medium is therefore something between a phone call (a cool medium) and a letter (a hot medium). Computer-mediated communication, however, is much less intimate and invasive than a phone call or face-to-face communication. It is now possible to e-mail people one would never dare to call or bother to write. As a result, people all over the world are exploring relationships that would have been impossible during the Phone Age. Since computer-mediated exchanges are still usually text-based, they have the potential for being higher quality than ordinary conversations because people have time to think before they write. This is less the case with synchronous media, like MUDS (multi-user dungeons), chatrooms, and video conferencing.

Computer-mediated communication is often anonymous, and has the potential to be a breeding ground for deception. People can easily swap genders or take on fantasy personae. In most cases, however, this does not occur, and it seems that the feeling of safety, distance, and anonymity encourages more honest self-disclosure than wanton deception. The opportunity to get one's point across without interruptions and without the need to worry about one's physical appearance is a tremendous advantage to a-synchronous computer-mediated communication like e-mail. As a result, people often disclose more about themselves over the Internet than they would over the phone or face-to-face. Patricia Wallace notes in her book *The Psychology of the Internet:*

> The tendency for people to disclose more to a computer—even when they know that a person will be reading what they say—is an important ingredient of what seems to be happening on the Internet. Yes, it can be an impersonal, cold-blooded medium at times. Yet it can also be what Joseph Walter describes as *hyperpersonal.*[5]

Computer-mediated communication is not consistently impersonal, as many suppose; rather, following Wallace, it can be *hyperpersonal.* It should be noted, however, that the tendency to self-disclose to the computer can foster both intimacy with and alienation from the people on the other side of the computer screen. The ease with which some people self-disclose on-line may falsely communicate emotional instability, scaring away potential friends or lovers. Moreover, virtual friends often disappear over night, as there is little if any consequence to ending such a relationship. Nevertheless, as a result of the heightened tendency to self-disclose, Wallace has shown that people often form committed relationships with others on-line, and that these relationships are far deeper and more common than many believed possible at the dawn of the age of computer-mediated communication.[6]

Many people have suggested that cyberspace is cold, sexless, and genderless, resulting in users who are unable to conceptualize themselves as living, breathing, human beings.[7] Nothing could be further from the experience of many Internet users, who frequently find both support and love on-line. Sexual attraction is alive and well on the Internet: Wallace reports that 7.9% of the relationships formed on-line are romantic liaisons.[8] Computer-mediated communication has rede-

---

[5] Wallace, *Psychology of the Internet,* p. 151.
[6] Wallace, *Psychology of the Internet,* p. 134.
[7] Mark Kingwell, *Dreams of Millennium: Report from a Culture on the Brink* (Boston: Faber and Faber, 1996), p. 182.
[8] Wallace, *Psychology of the Internet,* p. 134.

fined sexual attraction in the postmodern world. Unlike any other era, we are living in an age where beauty can be less important than other qualities that account for sexual attraction, although this may be a temporary condition which will probably change when video cameras become common-place accessories.

A potent disadvantage to computer-mediated relationships is that they may change expectations one has for face-to-face relationships. On the Internet one can talk to any number of interesting people. But off-line, one's choices for socialization are considerably more limited. Parents, children, husbands, and wives do not typically share the same specialized interests that often absorb an Internet user. As a result, the Internet junkie may feel under-stimulated and bored with life off-line. She may also become too dependent upon on-line relationships and begin to socialize primarily on the Internet. Internet dependence is a problem that psychologists are only now beginning to address. In the next section I will look at why this problem is taken so seriously by so many, and how we might change our attitudes towards it.

## Real and Virtual Relationships

Many people believe that computer-mediated interpersonal interaction is not real. There is an assumed distinction between authentic and virtual relationships, one which privileges face-to-face or "real" interaction. Many people warn of the dangers and futility of spending too much time on-line interacting with "virtual" people. Moreover, people who spend significant amounts of time on-line are branded "geeks," "nerds," or "weenies" and assumed to be emotionally incapable of forming authentic relationships in the real world. It is no exaggeration to say that such people suffer stigmatization at the keyboards of techno-skeptics, who believe that life on-line constitutes a puerile fantasy. Kroker and Weinstein write:

The geeks have over-identified with the Net and have become in consequence INCEPTS. . . .

The geeks have embraced that fate in a Nietzschean data-dance. . . . They mutate it [the Net] with everything from the data trash of e-mail messages that lack the presence of speech and the discipline of writing, to the most subversive data games.[9]

Here the authors assume that e-mail is neither "present" like speech nor "disciplined" like writing. It is a trashy hybrid, devoid of any REAL value. People who use it are termed "geeks" and their value as human beings is called into question. In the same vein, Kingwell describes the Internet as "coma inducing mind-floss." He writes:

The new medium of electronic communication has become, in the event, candy floss for the mind—quick, sweet, lacking in nutrients. Like television it actively discourages coherent thought. And it has the added danger of providing the illusion of interaction. . . . The hacker culture is no longer the preserve of the nerds and weenies.[10]

Kingwell and Kroker are clearly fearful of and hostile to computer-mediated communication, and have not hesitated to resort to the basest of rhetorical techniques: name-calling! Their criticism of electronic media (and those who use it) is suspicious because of its gratuitously intolerant tone and striking lack of originality. Throughout history, conservative knee-jerk reactions against new media have been common place. We rarely trust new media, and never fail to work up nostalgia for the old methods they replace. Reading and writing are two media that took their share of abuse in their early days, and the printing press remained the object of hostility centuries after it became part of the fabric of everyday life. Like Kroker and Kingwell, the Luddites of old did not lack for names to call the "victims" of a new medium. Emerson is reported to have said: "Instead of Man thinking, we have . . . the *bookworm*, meek young men who grow up in li-

[9] Arthur Kroker and Michael A. Weinstein, *Data Trash: The Theory of the Virtual Class.* (New York: St. Martin's Press, 1994), p. 155.

[10] Kingwell, *Dreams of Millennium*, p. 153.

braries." [11] This spirit of hostility to new media continues to have a voice today in the works of the techno-skeptics.

While much techno-criticism was and is warranted, we have rarely regretted the price paid for new media. The printing press is probably responsible for the bloody Protestant Reformation,[12] yet in retrospect, we can hardly regret its result: widespread literacy. What is to be lamented is the lack of insight people had about the power of the printing press, one which resulted in so much bloodshed. In any case, it is useless to bemoan the realities of our new techno-environment: the changes are coming whether we like them or not. As McLuhan has noted, there is no possibility of a world-wide Luddite rebellion: resenting a technology cannot halt, or even slow, its progress. By understanding media, we gain some control over them. But lamentations and name-calling yield no such understanding.

If the techno-utopian view of technology is ludicrous, the techno-skeptical stance is sterile. Both views have contributed to widespread myths about the nature of computer-mediated communication and its resultant human relationships. In an attempt to understand computer-mediated relationships, let us look at some of these myths.

## Debunking the Myths of the Electronic Age

**Myth #1**—*The written word (on computer screens) is inferior to the written word on paper because it lacks "discipline."*

Some e-mails are mediocre or poor. But high-quality e-mails are exchanged on a regular basis. As I have already pointed out, e-mailers can think before they write, potentially raising the quality of personal interaction.

**Myth #2**—*The written word (on computer screens) is not immediate, like speech.*

This is only partially true. Synchronous media, like chatrooms and video conferencing, ARE immediate. It is, however, true that facial cues are not yet widely present over text-based electronic media. I believe that this is actually an advantage to e-mail because of one's freedom to disregard physical appearance while exchanging information. In face-to-face exchanges, anxiety about physical appearance and articulateness may prevent one from focusing on the message. If lack of immediacy is a problem, surely it is balanced by the fact that one can carefully consider one's thoughts before committing them to the screen. It is interesting that Kroker and Kingwell are not inciting people to stop communicating with paper letters, which are far less immediate than e-mail.

**Myth #3**—*Computer-mediated communication discourages coherent thought.*

This claim is so preposterous that it hardly merits attention, yet it is a prevalent attitude. If anything, e-mail exchanges enhance coherent thought because it is possible to get immediate feedback about ideas from a variety of different people. While newsgroups abound with fighting and flaming, ideas are shared and people learn. Many people report being very influenced by the ideas communicated over the Internet.

**Myth #4**—*Computer-mediated communication creates only the illusion of personal interaction.*

For techno-pragmatists, this idea is absolutely absurd. People are talking to REAL people on the Net just as surely as they are talking to people over the phone or by letter. The Internet is a new medium, not a fantasy world. There is no such thing as a virtual person, and there is no such thing as a virtual relationship. Unless people are consciously playing fantasy games on-line (like

[11] Quoted in Mitchell Stephens, *The Rise of the Image: The Fall of the Word.* (New York: Oxford University Press, 1998), p. 35.

[12] Leonard Shlain, *The Alphabet vs. the Goddess: The Conflict between Word and Image* (New York: Penguin, 1998), pp. 333–340.

MUDS etc.), there is nothing illusory about computer-mediated interaction. In no way does it resemble television. Kingwell's suggestion that electronic media are comparable to television seems to be at the heart of confused thinking about e-mail and chatrooms. The television engages the senses, as McLuhan noted, but it does not demand intellectual commitment and participation. While one can learn from television, there is no exchange of ideas. Moreover, television is used to broadcast fantasy. While computer-mediated communication can also be entertaining and escapist, this is NOT its primary function. The purpose of e-mail and other electronic communication media is to facilitate the exchange of ideas. The primary purpose of television is to broadcast ideas and to entertain viewers.

**Myth #5**— *Users of electronic media are losing touch with their physical bodies and are experiencing something called the "discarnate effect."*

This is perhaps the most exaggerated lament of techno-skeptics. Kroker writes:

Human flesh has been left behind, abandoned by virtual reality. So it puts on the electronic garments of the Internet body, and warp jumps beyond nostalgia for its own disappearance.[13]

As I have pointed out earlier, communication over the Internet is neither sexless, nor genderless—on the contrary. Flirtation, sexual innuendo, and affection abound on the Internet, just as it does over phone lines and in letters. The distinctiveness of sexual attraction on the Net is that electronic media tend to mute the dictatorial power of physical appearance, and that people cannot physically have sex unless face-to-face visits are scheduled. I would argue that the myth of the "discarnate effect" is the only pervasive fantasy of the computer-mediated communication age. Everybody is talking about it, yet no one has experienced it. This fantasy is being played out with great enthusiasm by intellectuals, who are both afraid of new media and frustrated by the fact that while things are changing rapidly, they are not changing fast enough to be really dramatic.

## Conclusion

It is clear that we are living in a global village and that its effects on our cultural, physical, and psychological landscapes are profound. These changes are at once good and evil, delightful and painful. As electronic media continue to alter our sense-ratios, we struggle to adapt to an everchanging environment. In general, the global village is a force for good (although certainly it has its problems). Now, more than ever, we can communicate effectively with people all over the world. More interaction means greater understanding and increased dialogue, but also introduces conflict where there was none before. This is to be expected. We do not fight with people we have not met. And now, in spite of niche marketing and the tendency to retreat into one's specialized communities, there is, at least, the potential for knowing our neighbors better than ever before.

We are in the Medieval period of the Information Age. The far-reaching effects of computer-mediated communication, which continues to evolve at a break-neck speed, are probably still unimaginable. The Information Renaissance looms invisible, far below the horizon. All we can do is study the immediate effects of computer-mediated communication and cautiously speculate about what may be around the corner. For the time being, the Internet is text-based and, for the most part, electronic information is typed. In the near future, we can predict the rise of the Image (and of the Voice), and the fall of Text. The evolution of computer-mediated communication will have dramatic and undeterminable effects on the psychic landscape of cyber-culture. What future alliances, skirmishes, love affairs, and wars our global village will witness, I leave to the prophets to predict.

---

[13] Kroker and Weinstein, *Data Trash,* p. 160.

# POSTMODERN CULTURE

## *What Is Postmodernism?*

"Postmodernism," with or without the hyphen, has become a buzzword in the last decade or so.* What does it mean? How can I use it at trendy parties without sounding silly? There follows a ten-minute primer in the meaning of the term, both as a concept and as a current reality.

It's important to appreciate the diversity of postmodernism. But at the risk of trivializing a complex historical phenomenon, here's a roller-coaster ride through some of its main manifestations.

If we engage in a bit of broad historical situating, we find that the postmodern shift has been located as early as the late fifties to as late as the early seventies, but for the most part changes in the 1960s led cultural critics to see us as entering a new historical period (especially in the worlds of art, architecture, literature, and ideas). Some observers have identified this shift with the full onslaught of consumer capitalism: Frederick Jameson, for one, calls postmodernism "the culture of late capitalism." Others, such as J. F. Lyotard, see it as the product of a crisis in the legitimacy of science.

In architecture and visual art postmodernity witnesses the return of classical elements embedded in modern techniques, materials, and styles. The clearest expression of postmodernism as a coherent phenomenon is found here. In architecture we see the reappearance of the column, of classical motifs and of decoration, ornament, and color, as opposed to the soulless gray, silver, and black boxes of modernist architecture. The postmodernist architect celebrates pluralism, difference, and eclecticism; he or she recollects the past, recycling or parodying it.

In visual art, as Kim Levin points out, the past is ransacked for clues to the future. Postmodernists attempt to remedy this feeling of alienation by scavenging the past and by bringing back the human body, long absent from modern art. These artists are tolerant of ambiguity, playful, and full of doubt. They revel in pastiche and the collage.

In literature and literary theory, postmodernism is a cool response to the triumph of modern technology and science, especially electronic and communication technology, over older or more isolated worldviews. Postmodernist literature showcases the disjointed, the nonlinear, the out of whack. From Umberto Eco's exploration of the medieval spirit in *The Name of the Rose* (1983) to William Gibson's skewed vision of the future of the computer revolution in his cyberpunk novels from *Neuromancer* (1984) on, postmodern fiction wanders through dark worlds and alternative paradigms, worlds foreign to the modern faith in science and technology, paradigms alien to the modern belief in the unity of truth, reason, and order.

Roland Barthes, along with other French literary critics, has heralded the "Death of the Author." Meaning is now supposed to come from an interaction between the

*This discussion is a slightly edited version of Doug Mann's article "What Is Postmodernism?" published in *Philosophy Today* [Society for Applied Philosophy Newsletter] 23 (September 1996), pp. 1, 3. For a more neutral account of postmodern thought, read the introduction to this chapter and the commentaries on Lyotard and Baudrillard.

text and the reader: The reader of literature *constructs* the text from his or her unique perspective. Under postmodernist theory, everything can be read as a text, and all readings of each text are equally meaningful, if not valid. Meaning and truth are thus plural, changing, and subjective. To give privilege to one truth over another becomes an act of psychic terrorism.

Following the death of the author is the death of the "canon," the body of writing seen as defining modern Western literature. We are now faced with a pluralism of narratives: of stories told by formerly "marginalized" groups, by women and blacks, by the Third World instead of the First, by the prisoners instead of the wardens. We are urged by postmodernists to abandon the "privileging" of the stories told by dead white Europeans and their spiritual offspring abroad, to substitute a multicolored weave for the old monochrome one.

In philosophy and politics the postmodernists see reason, progress, scientific truth, and democracy as (to use Lyotard's expression) "meta-narratives," big stories the Western world has told itself to convince itself that it's better than the rest of the world and has a right to its resources and leadership. The belief in objective Truth is a product of the rationalism of the Enlightenment, of a faith in economic and technological progress, and is expressed in the optimistic humanism that ruled the modern Western world for so long. Derrida calls this faith "logocentrism," the West's centering its philosophical and political vision on universally valid rational beliefs. The postmodernist wishes to take apart this faith, to substitute local stories for these meta-narratives, to make truth an individual rather than a social phenomenon.

Philosophical and moral ideas, social values, and political beliefs become constructs, ways of interpreting a reality that has no inherent meaning. The postmodernists' preference for "constructivism" in interpreting ideas, social values, and political assumptions lead to the more radical notions of *hyperspace* and *hyperreality.* Hyperspace, a science-fiction term, is a space that exists only as a construct, as an idea; hyperreality is a place where a model of some part of the world is more real than the world itself. The postmodernist sees the reality of our selves, our values, and our science through "hyper" sunglasses. The result is *relativism* with respect to truth, values, and reality (both personal and scientific): The door is opened to diverse truths, moral codes, and views of what is real.

The philosophical method of choice for many postmodern thinkers is "deconstruction," a term made famous by the French philosopher Jacques Derrida, meaning a taking apart of the belief structures of Western science, philosophy, and art. More specifically, Derrida seeks to take a text apart, to reveal its inner contradictions, its hidden assumptions, its moral and political hierarchies, its "warring forces of signification." His preferred approach to the discovering of meaning is *différance,* which means "to defer, postpone, or put off" a text's meaning, given the central postmodernist premise that we should avoid forcing a given interpretation on a text or person (which is itself based on the further beliefs that all the world's a text and that many distinct readings of these texts are valid).

Postmodernists are skeptical about politics. Michel Foucault sees Power and Knowledge as Siamese twins joined at the hip: This assumption leads postmodernists to be by and large cynical about even *talking* about political change, never mind engaging in it (except perhaps at the local level). The average citizen in postmodern societies gets his or her political knowledge already cooked by the mass media (television being the central producer of postmodern political hyperreality) and drifts into a general noninvolvement in an amorphous mass politics run by anonymous elites. The consumer economy keeps the masses happy, reveling in their narcissism and hedonism. Bread and circuses replace the public political realm.

Even within media and pop culture we see echoes of the postmodern mindset. Anything fast, image-centered (as opposed to text-based), without a linear narrative, and that shocks or alienates the traditions in its field can be seen as having a postmodernist flavor. Also, paralleling postmodernist architecture's somewhat ironic appropriation of the classical column, we can identify a "postmodernist" pop music when we hear it borrowing from a tradition and reworking it into a new artistic form (Kula Shaker, Dead Can Dance, and Beck being typical examples of recent pop artists borrowing from traditional musical forms to create something new and interesting). Media now attempt to enter more directly into the process of news making or artistic creation and are increasingly dependent on the hyperreal, virtual world of computer graphics, all as part of an effort to prove that McLuhan's prophecy that the medium is the message has finally come to pass.

Postmodernism addresses a growing reality in our culture, a reality that's both liberating and worrying. On the positive side, it leads us down roads previously unexplored by Western rationalist humanism. Insofar as power is based on manufactured ontologies, postmodernism opens things up politically by deconstructing these ladders of being.

But by making truth relative, social beliefs and systems constructs, and everything a text, it runs the danger of putting all social and personal values on the same plane, thus opening the door to profoundly antidemocratic forces, at least within literary and artistic circles and within academia, and perhaps by extension, within the wider world also. And it runs the risk of generating a deep cynicism about our culture and its future: It denies us the right to believe in the superiority of our own way of life, while at the same time offering no solid grounds from which to critique that way of life.

How can egalitarian, liberationist movements, such as social democracy or feminism, embrace a metaphysic so profoundly relativistic? If anything goes, don't exploitation and oppression in some sense of the word "go" too? Also, slipping for a while into a neo-Marxist point of view, can't postmodernism be seen as yet another attempt by Western consumer society to eclectically absorb both its own scattered cultural hinterlands (such as native communities in North America or traditional Celtic culture in Britain) and those of the Third World into the great central cultural-economic maelstrom that is global capitalism? Thought and culture should not be seen as floating, like Swift's Laputa, high above the social and economic realities that nurture and shape them. The cultural and social critic has to take these and other questions seriously before unreservedly championing the postmodern condition.

## Our Postmodern Condition

Jean-François Lyotard (1924–) was born in Versailles, France, and has taught in Algeria, Brazil, California, and at the University of Paris since 1968. He is a prolific writer and has addressed many philosophical issues over his long career. In the 1950s and

1960s Lyotard was a member of "Socialism or Barbarism," a Marxist group that rejected the authoritarianism of Soviet communism. The May 1968 Paris revolt of workers and students against the government of Charles de Gaulle disillusioned Lyotard with leftist politics—the revolt was a great show, but accomplished little. In the early 1970s Lyotard rejected Marxism, in part because of the "systematization of desires" that Marxists tried to impose with their emphasis on industrial production as the ground of culture. He became more and more associated with the French poststructuralist school of thought, rejecting what he saw as the rigid structuralist approach of Marxism.

*The Postmodern Condition* (the source of the reading that follows) was commissioned by the Council of Québec Universities as a report on the status of science and technology. In this short book, Lyotard defines *postmodernism* as an "incredulity toward metanarratives," a lack of belief in the master stories that formerly powered Western culture. These meta-narratives include those of Christian Salvation, Communism, Darwinian Evolution, and Freudian psychoanalysis. But the two meta-narratives Lyotard sees as really powering Western culture are (1) the Enlightenment narrative of Reason, Progress, and revolutionary emancipation (originating mostly in the French Revolution of 1789–1795) and (2) the German Idealist narrative of the speculative Unity of all Knowledge and the self-conscious march of the World Spirit (Hegel is the principal culprit here). Within the last generation or two we've had a loss of faith in these meta-narratives of the March of Liberty and the Unity of Knowledge, resulting in a loss of faith in science's search for Truth.

In *The Postmodern Condition,* Lyotard outlines how knowledge now and in the future will center on information processing. He argues that very soon, all knowledge will have to be convertible into computer data for it to be considered valid. Knowledge is *the* postindustrial force of production. Further, the central criterion for scientific research is now *performativity,* roughly economic utility. Knowledge is produced to be sold. An equation between truth, wealth, and power has thus established itself in our age: Research that doesn't pay off, isn't performative, will slowly fall through the cracks (with destructive effects on university life, says Lyotard).

Lyotard sees forms of discourse as governed by rules such as Ludwig Wittgenstein's language games. Wittgenstein speculated that the meaning of a word is determined by the way it is used, which in turn depends on what language game is being played by those who use the word. For example, players in a rough football or hockey game might use very foul language, language they would never dream of using with their families or in a television interview. In fact, the same swear words used in the latter two contexts would have a much stronger and different meaning than they would during the game.

For Lyotard, what counts as a valid statement (a "good move") in a given form of discourse depends on what language game one is playing. Lyotard sees two types of discourse in the West: *traditional narrative discourse* (e.g., storytelling around the tribal campfire) and *scientific discourse.* Each has its own rules. Modern scientific discourse has to legitimize itself: It does this by turning to the very narrative discourse it had previously discredited, describing its research as an epic tale to conquer ignorance and disease, to unlock the secrets of nature, and so on. *The Postmodern Condition* is largely the story of how modern science has attempted and failed to find a new source of legitimacy, one that doesn't depend on tribal chanting around a campfire.

# The Postmodern Condition

## JEAN-FRANÇOIS LYOTARD

### Introduction

The object of this study is the condition of knowledge in the most highly developed societies. I have decided to use the word *postmodern* to describe that condition. The word is in current use on the American continent among sociologists and critics; it designates the state of our culture following the transformations which, since the end of the nineteenth century, have altered the game rules for science, literature, and the arts. The present study will place these transformations in the context of the crisis of narratives.

Science has always been in conflict with narratives. Judged by the yardstick of science, the majority of them prove to be fables. But to the extent that science does not restrict itself to stating useful regularities and seeks the truth, it is obliged to legitimate the rules of its own game. It then produces a discourse of legitimation with respect to its own status, a discourse called philosophy. I will use the term *modern* to designate any science that legitimates itself with reference to a metadiscourse of this kind making an explicit appeal to some grand narrative, such as the dialectics of Spirit, the hermeneutics of meaning, the emancipation of the rational or working subject, or the creation of wealth. For example, the rule of consensus between the sender and addressee of a statement with truth-value is deemed acceptable if it is cast in terms of a possible unanimity between rational minds: this is the Enlightenment narrative, in which the hero of knowledge works toward a good ethico-political end—universal peace. As can be seen from this example, if a metanarrative implying a philosophy of history is used to legitimate knowledge, questions are raised concerning the validity of the institutions governing the social bond: these must be legitimated as well. Thus justice is consigned to the grand narrative in the same way as truth.

Simplifying to the extreme, I define *postmodern* as incredulity toward metanarratives. This incredulity is undoubtedly a product of progress in the sciences: but that progress in turn presupposes it. To the obsolescence of the metanarrative apparatus of legitimation corresponds, most notably, the crisis of metaphysical philosophy and of the university institution which in the past relied on it. The narrative function is losing its functors, its great hero, its great dangers, its great voyages, its great goal. . . .

The decision makers, however, attempt to manage these clouds of sociality according to input/output matrices, following a logic which implies that their elements are commensurable and that the whole is determinable. They allocate our lives for the growth of power. In matters of social justice and of scientific truth alike, the legitimation of that power is based on its optimizing the system's performance—efficiency. The application of this criterion to all of our games necessarily entails a certain level of terror, whether soft or hard: be operational (that is, commensurable) or disappear. . . .

Still, the postmodern condition is as much a stranger to disenchantment as it is to the blind

SOURCE: Jean-François Lyotard, *The Postmodern Condition: A Report on Knowledge,* trans. Geoff Bennington and Brian Massumi (Minneapolis: University of Minnesota Press, 1984); originally published in French in 1979 as *La Conditione postmoderne: Rapport sur la savoir.* Selections from the introduction and chap. 1, "The Field: Knowledge in Computerized Societies," pp. xiii–xv, 3–6 (edited; footnotes omitted). Original French-language edition copyright 1979 by Les Editions de Minuit. English foreword and translation copyright 1984 by the University of Minnesota Press. Reprinted by permission of the University of Minnesota Press.

positivity of delegitimation. Where, after the metanarratives, can legitimacy reside? The operativity criterion is technological; it has no relevance for judging what is true or just. Is legitimacy to be found in consensus obtained through discussion, as Jürgen Habermas thinks? Such consensus does violence to the heterogeneity of language games. And invention is always born of dissension. Postmodern knowledge is not simply a tool of the authorities; it refines our sensitivity to differences and reinforces our ability to tolerate the incommensurable. Its principle is not the expert's homology, but the inventor's paralogy.

Here is the question: is a legitimation of the social bond, a just society, feasible in terms of a paradox analogous to that of scientific activity? What would such a paradox be? . . .

## The Field: Knowledge in Computerized Societies

Our working hypothesis is that the status of knowledge is altered as societies enter what is known as the postindustrial age and cultures enter what is known as the postmodern age. This transition has been under way since at least the end of the 1950s, which for Europe marks the completion of reconstruction. The pace is faster or slower depending on the country, and within countries it varies according to the sector of activity: the general situation is one of temporal disjunction which makes sketching an overview difficult. A portion of the description would necessarily be conjectural. At any rate, we know that it is unwise to put too much faith in futurology.

Rather than painting a picture that would inevitably remain incomplete, I will take as my point of departure a single feature, one that immediately defines our object of study. Scientific knowledge is a kind of discourse. And it is fair to say that for the last forty years the "leading" sciences and technologies have had to do with language: phonology and theories of linguistics, problems of communication and cybernetics, modern theories of algebra and informatics, computers and their languages, problems of trans-

lation and the search for areas of compatibility among computer languages, problems of information storage and data banks, telematics and the perfection of intelligent terminals, paradoxology. The facts speak for themselves (and this list is not exhaustive).

These technological transformations can be expected to have a considerable impact on knowledge. Its two principal functions—research and the transmission of acquired learning—are already feeling the effect, or will in the future. With respect to the first function, genetics provides an example that is accessible to the layman: it owes its theoretical paradigm to cybernetics. Many other examples could be cited. As for the second function, it is common knowledge that the miniaturization and commercialization of machines is already changing the way in which learning is acquired, classified, made available, and exploited. It is reasonable to suppose that the proliferation of information-processing machines is having, and will continue to have, as much of an effect on the circulation of learning as did advancements in human circulation (transportation systems) and later, in the circulation of sounds and visual images (the media).

The nature of knowledge cannot survive unchanged within this context of general transformation. It can fit into the new channels, and become operational, only if learning is translated into quantities of information. We can predict that anything in the constituted body of knowledge that is not translatable in this way will be abandoned and that the direction of new research will be dictated by the possibility of its eventual results being translatable into computer language. The "producers" and users of knowledge must now, and will have to, possess the means of translating into these languages whatever they want to invent or learn. Research on translating machines is already well advanced. Along with the hegemony of computers comes a certain logic, and therefore a certain set of prescriptions determining which statements are accepted as "knowledge" statements.

We may thus expect a thorough exteriorization of knowledge with respect to the "knower," at whatever point he or she may occupy in the knowledge process. The old principle that the acquisition of knowledge is indissociable from the training (*Bildung*) of minds, or even of individuals, is becoming obsolete and will become ever more so. The relationship of the suppliers and users of knowledge to the knowledge they supply and use is now tending, and will increasingly tend, to assume the form already taken by the relationship of commodity producers and consumers to the commodities they produce and consume—that is, the form of value. Knowledge is and will be produced in order to be sold, it is and will be consumed in order to be valorized in a new production: in both cases, the goal is exchange. Knowledge ceases to be an end in itself, it loses its "use-value."

It is widely accepted that knowledge has become the principle force of production over the last few decades; this has already had a noticeable effect on the composition of the work force of the most highly developed countries and constitutes the major bottleneck for the developing countries. In the postindustrial and postmodern age, science will maintain and no doubt strengthen its preeminence in the arsenal of productive capacities of the nation-states. Indeed, this situation is one of the reasons leading to the conclusion that the gap between developed and developing countries will grow ever wider in the future.

But this aspect of the problem should not be allowed to overshadow the other, which is complementary to it. Knowledge in the form of an informational commodity indispensable to productive power is already, and will continue to be, a major—perhaps *the* major—stake in the worldwide competition for power. It is conceivable that the nation-states will one day fight for control of information, just as they battled in the past for control over territory, and afterwards for control of access to and exploitation of raw materials and cheap labor. A new field is opened for industrial and commercial strategies on the one hand, and political and military strategies on the other.

However, the perspective I have outlined above is not as simple as I have made it appear. For the mercantilization of knowledge is bound to affect the privilege the nation-states have enjoyed, and still enjoy, with respect to the production and distribution of learning. The notion that learning falls within the purview of the State, as the brain or mind of society, will become more and more outdated with the increasing strength of the opposing principle, according to which society exists and progresses only if the messages circulating within it are rich in information and easy to decode. The ideology of communicational "transparency," which goes hand in hand with the commercialization of knowledge, will begin to perceive the State as a factor of opacity and "noise." It is from this point of view that the problem of the relationship between economic and State powers threatens to arise with a new urgency.

Already in the last few decades, economic powers have reached the point of imperiling the stability of the State through new forms of the circulation of capital that go by the generic name of *multinational corporations*. These new forms of circulation imply that investment decisions have, at least in part, passed beyond the control of the nation-states. The question threatens to become even more thorny with the development of computer technology and telematics. Suppose, for example, that a firm such as IBM is authorized to occupy a belt in the earth's orbital field and launch communications satellites or satellites housing data banks. Who will have access to them? Who will determine which channels or data are forbidden? The State? Or will the State simply be one user among others? New legal issues will be raised, and with them the question: "who will know?"

Transformation in the nature of knowledge, then, could well have repercussions on the existing public powers, forcing them to reconsider their relations (both de jure and de facto) with the large corporations and, more generally, with civil society. . . .

# The Reign of Simulacra

Jean Baudrillard (1929–) is a French philosopher and cultural analyst who started his academic life as a Marxist sociologist interested in consumer society (he completed his Ph.D. thesis in 1966). He concluded that Western societies, which had once been societies of production, in the post–World War II period became societies of consumption.

Becoming slowly dissatisfied with Marxism, he went on to incorporate structuralism and semiology into his analysis, seeing the objects we consume as a system of signs or code that had to be decoded, this system as embedded in structures of consumption and leisure that he felt could be analyzed sociologically. He laid out his semiotic analysis of consumer society in his books *The System of Objects* (1968), *The Consumer Society* (1970), and *The Mirror of Production* (1973). His most important earlier work is *For a Critique of the Political Economy of the Sign* (1972), in which he rejected Marxism as the only valid way of analyzing consumer society.

Marx said that objects all have a "use value": for example, a hammer is useful for hammering nails into a board. But under capitalism, all objects are reduced to their "exchange value," their value or price in the marketplace (e.g., the hammer might cost ten dollars in the local hardware store). Baudrillard agreed—so far, so good; but he added that, at least in advanced capitalist countries, consumer goods also have a *symbolic value*—they symbolize distinction, taste, and social status. A BMW or a gold watch can certainly have both use and exchange value—we can drive the BMW to work or sell the watch to a dealer in used jewelry. But, says Baudrillard, we also have to understand their status as signs in the code of consumer values—they signify *social distinction*. As you drive your BMW down the main street, you're saying to the unwashed masses, "I'm no longer one of you—I'm distinct, a member of the wealthy and discriminating classes." It's the BMW's symbolic value, its *cachet,* that makes it so irresistible to these classes.

In the 1980s and 1990s, Baudrillard turned away in a large degree from both Marxism and structuralism to post-structuralism. He became the high priest of postmodern culture, turning toward an extreme version of McLuhan's communications theory. He was fascinated by how media affect our perception of reality and the world. He concluded that in the postmodern media-laden condition, we experience something called "the death of the real": We live our lives in the realm of hyperreality, connecting more and more deeply to things such as television sitcoms, music videos, virtual reality games, and Disneyland, things that merely simulate reality.

Early in this new phase of his work, Baudrillard reflected on love. In his book *On Seduction* (1979), he claims that there are two modes of love. The seductive female mode, which is artificial and symbolic, involves flirtations, double entendres, sly looks, whispered promises, but a putting off of the actual sexual act. It involves the manipulation of signs such as makeup, fashion, and titillating gestures to achieve control over a symbolic order. On the other side is the male sexual mode, centered on the phallus, which is direct and natural, seeking to master a real order—to complete the sexual act. On top of each of these modes is now layered the "cool" seduction of media images pumped out by television, radio, and film.

He continues this theme of cool seduction in his book *The Ecstasy of Communication* (1988, in translation). Here Baudrillard discusses how we surrender ourselves in an "ecstasy of communication" to the seductive power of the mass media— television, ads, films, magazines, and newspapers (though Baudrillard is an avid film fan). The luminous eyes of television and computer screens penetrate into our private spaces in an ecstatic and obscene way—our secrets disappear, and the images we consume become more and more pornographic.

In the mid-1980s Baudrillard hit the road. His travelogue *America* (1986, in French) creates a simulacrum of the America he traveled across. He talks about the violence of the Wild West, jazz, the empty deserts of the Southwest, the neon lights of motels at night, tribal warfare between gangs in New York City, and much more. Baudrillard saw America as a glittering emptiness, a savage, empty nonculture—in short, as the purest symbol of the hyperreal culture of the postmodern age.

In his lecture on film given in Sydney, Australia, in 1987, *The Evil Demon of Images,* Baudrillard claimed that although the United States lost the Vietnam War on the ground, they won it in the hyperreal realm through films such as *Apocalypse Now* and *Platoon,* which fantastically replay the war not as the story of defeat by a determined enemy but as that of internal division. Cinematographically, the Americans defeat themselves.

Before the Gulf War of 1991, Baudrillard wrote an article in *Libération* in which he claimed that the war wouldn't take place. Afterward, he claimed that it hadn't taken place, for the Western audience was aware of it only as a series of hyperreal images on our TV screens. There was no real enemy—Saddam Hussein was a former U.S. ally in the Middle East—and the outcome was entirely predictable. Despite the horrible loss of life (mostly on the Iraqi side), the war was at best a hyperreal war. Baudrillard's work in the 1990s continued to focus on this theme of the hyperreality of postmodern culture, his writing becoming more disjointed and aphoristic, perhaps echoing Nietzsche's style.

Going back to the beginning of his "postmodern" phase, Baudrillard starts his important essay "The Precession of Simulacra"—taken from the same work, *Simulacra and Simulation* (1981, in French; 1984, in English), as the reading selection below—by recounting the feat of imperial mapmakers in a story by Jorge Luis Borges, who make a map so large and detailed that it covers the whole empire, existing in a one-to-one relationship with the territory underlying it. It is a perfect replica of the empire. After a while the map begins to fray and tatter, the citizens of the empire mourning its loss, having long taken the map—the simulacrum of the empire— for the real empire. Under the map the real territory has turned into a desert, a "desert of the real." In its place, a *simulacrum* of reality—the frayed megamap—is all that's left.

The term "simulacrum" comes from Plato, who used it to describe a false copy of something. Baudrillard has built his whole post-1970s theory of media effects and culture around his own notion of the simulacrum. He argues that in a postmodern culture dominated by TV, films, news media, and the Internet, the whole idea of a true or a false copy of something has been destroyed: All we have now are *simulations* of reality.

Indeed, in some cases these simulations *precede* the reality they are supposedly simulating: The TV family becomes a model for "real" families, or news reporters create the news they are supposedly just reporting by playing up a minor political scandal. In our culture, claims Baudrillard, we take "maps" of reality such as television, film, and so on as more real than our actual lives—these simulacra (hyperreal copies) precede our lives. Our television "friends" (e.g., sitcom characters) might seem more alive to us than their flesh-and-blood equivalents ("Did you see what Jerry/Rachel/Frasier did last night?"). We communicate by e-mail and relate to video game characters such as Lara Croft better than to our own friends and family. We drive on freeways to shopping malls full of identical chain stores and products, watch television shows about film directors and actors, go to films about television production, vote for ex-Hollywood actors for president or governor (Is he really an actor? or a politician? It doesn't matter). In fact, we get nervous and edgy if we're away too long from our computers, our e-mail accounts, our cell phones. Now the *real* empire lies in tatters, while the hyperreal map of it is clear and bright. We have entered an era where third-order simulacra dominate our lives, where the image has lost any connection to real things.

Baudrillard's later philosophy of culture can be mapped in terms of three things: (1) the orders of simulacra, (2) the "phases of the image"—the four levels at which art represents reality, and (3) the three phases of utopian and science-fiction writing outlined in the short essay that follows. The following chart illustrates how these three sets of distinctions parallel each other (a few examples from high and popular culture have been added to the ones Baudrillard himself gives in his works).

## ORDERS OF SIMULACRA

1. Symbolic Order: Society is organized as a fixed system of signs distributed according to rank and obligation (e.g., in the feudal era a peasant couldn't become the king). The question of reality doesn't arise: The meaning of signs is already established in advance (by God or power structures).

2. First Order of Simulacra: The early modern period, from the Renaissance to the Industrial Revolution. A competition for the meaning of signs starts. Simulacra aim to restore an ideal image of nature. Fakes and counterfeits enter the scene: baroque angels, concrete chairs, theater, fashion. But true originals underlie the fakes.

3. Second Order of Simulacra: From the Industrial Revolution

## PHASES OF THE IMAGE

1. Art reflects a basic reality (see "The Precession of Simulacra" for an extended discussion). Example: Gothic paintings depict the birth of Jesus as the true son of God, replete with signs of his divinity (the Three Wise Men, a halo over the Madonna's head, etc.).

2. Art masks and perverts a basic reality. Example: baroque paintings of an impossibly beautiful Jesus ascending to the heavens like Superman, with the Madonna watching with a blissful look on her face.

3. Art masks the absence of a basic reality. Examples: pho-

## UTOPIAS AND SCIENCE FICTION

1. No need for utopian or science-fiction writing: The utopian order already exists in the here and now.

2. Utopias: Transcendental or romantic dreams, counterfeit copies of the real world. "If only we could get everything right, life would be beautiful!" Thomas More's *Utopia;* Francis Bacon's *New Atlantis.*

3. The classic science-fiction of the Age of Mass Production:

| ORDERS OF SIMULACRA | PHASES OF THE IMAGE | UTOPIAS AND SCIENCE FICTION |
|---|---|---|
| until the mid-twentieth century. Mass production of copies or replicas of a single prototype: cars, planes, refrigerators, clothes, books. Liberation of energy through the machine (Marx's world). Copies more or less indistinguishable. Reproduced things aren't counterfeits: they're just as "real" as their prototype (though we can still recognize the prototype). | tography and the mechanical reproduction of paintings (see Walter Benjamin's important essay "The Work of Art in the Age of Mechanical Reproduction"); a framed reproduction of a Renaissance painting of the Madonna hung over one's bed, right beside a velvet image of Elvis. | robots, rocket ships to Mars, space exploration, alien invasion, intergalactic wars. Present technology projected into the future and outer space. Robert Heinlein's *Starship Troopers;* Isaac Asimov's *I, Robot;* Fifties Hollywood sci-fi films (e.g., *Them, It Came from Outer Space*); the original *Star Trek* television series; Borges's imperial map. |
| 4. Third Order of Simulacra: The present age—dominated by simulations, things that have no original or prototype (though they may parallel something). Era of the model or code: computers, virtual reality, opinion polls, DNA, genetic engineering, cloning, the news media make the news, Nike sneakers as status symbols, Disneyland. The death of the real: no more counterfeits or prototypes, just simulations of reality—hyperreality. Information replaces the machine as the basic mode of production. | 4. Art bears no relation to reality at all. Examples: A virtual reality female talking head reads news headlines to us over the Internet. Is she real? a fake? The question has lost its meaning—there is no original to compare her to; Madonna (the singer, not the mother of Christ) made up like Marilyn Monroe vamping it up with a troupe of lithe male dancers in a music video on MTV. | 4. The end of science fiction: the real absorbed into a hyperreal, cybernetic world. Not about an alternative universe, but about a simulation of the present one. Philip K. Dick's *Simulacra;* J. G. Ballard's *Crash;* William Gibson's *Neuromancer;* Ridley Scott's film *Blade Runner;* Paul Verhoeven's *Total Recall;* David Cronenberg's films *Crash* and *eXistenZ;* the Wachowski brothers' *The Matrix;* the Borg, the holodeck, and VR characters (e.g., *Voyager's* doctor) in the later *Star Trek* television series. |

In the following essay from *Simulacra and Simulation,* Baudrillard applies his theory of orders of simulacra to one specific field: science-fiction literature, taken in the broadest possible sense. He argues that the three types of utopian and science-fiction writing parallel the three orders of the simulacrum that have ruled our culture since the Renaissance, with the cutting-edge utopian writing of today no longer being, strictly speaking, "sci-fi," but merely an extension of our own technological and cultural landscape (e.g., Ballard's novel *Crash* or William Gibson's cyberpunk stories).

Baudrillard's writing is difficult, and for starting philosophers is best taken in small doses. As you read through this short essay, refer back to the chart to find your bearings. Remember that Baudrillard's central claim about postmodern culture (though he claims that he himself is *not* a postmodernist) is quite simple—we live in a "desert of the real," a cultural space where television, film, and computer images are more "real" to us than the nonmedia physical reality that surrounds us.

# Simulacra and Science Fiction

## JEAN BAUDRILLARD

THREE ORDERS of simulacra:

simulacra that are natural, naturalist, founded on the image, on imitation and counterfeit, that are harmonious, optimistic, and that aim for the restitution or the ideal institution of nature made in God's image;

simulacra that are productive, productivist, founded on energy, force, its materialization by the machine and in the whole system of production—a Promethean aim of a continuous globalization and expansion, of an indefinite liberation of energy (desire belongs to the utopias related to this order of simulacra);

simulacra of simulation, founded on information, the model, the cybernetic game—total operationality, hyperreality, aim of total control.

To the first category belongs the imaginary of the *utopia*. To the second corresponds science fiction, strictly speaking. To the third corresponds—is there an imaginary that might correspond to this order? The most likely answer is that the good old imaginary of science fiction is dead and that something else is in the process of emerging (not only in fiction but in theory as well). The same wavering and indeterminate fate puts an end to science fiction—but also to theory, as specific genres.

There is no real, there is no imaginary except at a certain distance. What happens when this distance, including that between the real and the imaginary, tends to abolish itself, to be reabsorbed on behalf of the model? Well, from one order of simulacra to another, the tendency is certainly toward the reabsorption of this distance, of this gap that leaves room for an ideal or critical projection.

This projection is maximized in the utopian, in which a transcendent sphere, a radically different universe takes form (the romantic dream is still the individualized form of utopia, in which transcendence is outlined in depth, even in unconscious structures, but in any case the dissociation from the real world is maximized, the island of utopia stands opposed to the continent of the real).

This projection is greatly reduced in science fiction: it is most often nothing other than an unbounded projection of the real world of production, but it is not qualitatively different from it. Mechanical or energetic extensions, speed, and power increase to the nth power, but the schemas and the scenarios are those of mechanics, metallurgy, etc. Projected hypostasis of the robot. (To the limited universe of the preindustrial era, utopia *opposed* an ideal, alternative universe. To the potentially infinite universe of production, science fiction *adds* the multiplication of its own possibilities.)

This projection is totally reabsorbed in the implosive era of models. The models no longer constitute either transcendence or projection, they no longer constitute the imaginary in relation to the real, they are themselves an anticipation of the real, and thus leave no room for any sort of fictional anticipation—they are immanent, and thus leave no room for any kind of imaginary transcendence. The field opened is that of simulation in the cybernetic sense, that is, of the manipulation of these

SOURCE: Jean Baudrillard, "Simulacra and Science Fiction," in *Simulacra and Simulation*, trans. Sheila Faria Glaser (Ann Arbor: University of Michigan Press, 1994), pp. 121–127. Reprinted by permission of the University of Michigan Press.

models at every level (scenarios, the setting up of simulated situations, etc.) but then *nothing distinguishes this operation from the operation itself and the gestation of the real: there is no more fiction.*

Reality could go beyond fiction: that was the surest sign of the possibility of an ever-increasing imaginary. But the real cannot surpass the model —it is nothing but its alibi.

The imaginary was the alibi of the real, in a world dominated by the reality principle. Today, it is the real that has become the alibi of the model, in a world controlled by the principle of simulation. And, paradoxically, it is the real that has become our true utopia—but a utopia that is no longer in the realm of the possible, that can only be dreamt of as one would dream of a lost object.

Perhaps science fiction from the cybernetic and hyperreal era can only exhaust itself, in its artificial resurrection of "historical" worlds, can only try to reconstruct in vitro, down to the smallest details, the perimeters of a prior world, the events, the people, the ideologies of the past, emptied of meaning, of their original process, but hallucinatory with retrospective truth. Thus in *Simulacra* by Philip K. Dick, the war of Secession. Gigantic hologram in three dimensions, in which fiction will never again be a mirror held toward the future, but a desperate rehallucination of the past.

We can no longer imagine any other universe: the grace of transcendence was taken away from us in that respect too. Classical science fiction was that of an expanding universe, besides, it forged its path in the narratives of spatial exploration, counter-parts to the more terrestrial forms of exploration and colonization of the nineteenth and twentieth centuries. There is no relationship of cause and effect there: it is not because terrestrial space today is virtually coded, mapped, registered, saturated, has thus in a sense closed up again in universalizing itself—a universal market, not only of merchandise, but of values, signs, models, leaving no room for the imaginary—it is

not exactly because of this that the exploratory universe (technical, mental, cosmic) of science fiction has also ceased to function. But the two are narrowly linked, and they are two versions of the same general process of implosion that follows the gigantic process of explosion and expansion characteristic of past centuries. When a system reaches its own limits and becomes saturated, a reversal is produced—something else takes place, in the imaginary as well.

Until now we have always had a reserve of the imaginary—now the coefficient of reality is proportional to the reserve of the imaginary that gives it its specific weight. This is also true of geographic and spatial exploration: when there is no longer any virgin territory, and thus one available to the imaginary, *when the map covers the whole territory, something like the principle of reality disappears.* In this way, the conquest of space constitutes an irreversible crossing toward the loss of the terrestrial referential. There is a hemorrhaging of reality as an internal coherence of a limited universe, once the limits of this universe recede into infinity. The conquest of space that follows that of the planet is equal to derealizing (dematerializing) human space, or to transferring it into a hyperreal of simulation. Witness this two-bedroom/kitchen/shower put into orbit, raised to a spatial power (one could say) with the most recent lunar module. The everydayness of the terrestrial habitat itself elevated to the rank of cosmic value, hypostatized in space— the satellization of the real in the transcendence of space—it is the end of metaphysics, the end of the phantasm, the end of science fiction—the era of hyperreality begins.

From then onward, something must change: the projection, the extrapolation, the sort of pantographic excess that constituted the charm of science fiction are all impossible. It is no longer possible to fabricate the unreal from the real, the imaginary from the givens of the real. The process will, rather, be the opposite: it will be to put decentered situations, models of simulation in place and to contrive to give them the feeling of the real, of the banal, of lived experience, to reinvent the real as fiction, precisely because it has disappeared from our life. Hallucination of the real, of lived experience, of the quotidian, but reconstituted, sometimes down to disquietingly strange details, reconstituted as an animal or vegetal reserve, brought to light with a transparent precision, but without substance, derealized in advance, hyperrealized.

In this way, science fiction would no longer be a romantic expansion with all the freedom and naïveté that the charm of discovery gave it, but, quite the contrary, it would evolve implosively, in the very image of our current conception of the universe, attempting to revitalize, reactualize, requotidianize fragments of simulation, fragments of this universal simulation that have become for us the so-called real world.

Where would the works be that would meet, here and now, this situational inversion, this situational reversion? Obviously the short stories of Philip K. Dick "gravitate" in this space, if one can use that word (but that is precisely what one can't really do any more, because this new universe is "antigravitational," or if it still gravitates, it is around the *hole* of the real, around the *hole* of the imaginary). One does not see an alternative cosmos, a cosmic folklore or exoticism, or a galactic prowess there—one is from the start in a total simulation, without origin, immanent, without a past, without a future, a diffusion of all coordinates (mental, temporal, spatial, signaletic)—it is not about a parallel universe, a double universe, or even a possible universe—neither possible, impossible, neither real nor unreal: *hyperreal*—it is a universe of simulation, which is something else altogether. And not because Dick speaks specifically of simulacra—science fiction has always done so, but it played on the double, on doubling or redoubling, either artificial or imaginary, whereas here the double has disappeared, there is no longer a double, one is always already in the other world, which is no longer an other, without a mirror, a projection, or a utopia that can reflect it—simulation is insuperable, unsurpassable, dull and flat, without exteriority—we will no longer even pass through

to "the other side of mirror," that was still the golden age of transcendence.

Perhaps a still more convincing example would be that of Ballard and of his evolution from the first very "phantasmagoric" short stories, poetic, dreamlike, disorienting, up to *Crash*, which is without a doubt (more than *IGH* or *Concrete Island*) the current model of this science fiction that is no longer one. *Crash* is *our* world, nothing in it is "invented": everything in it is hyperfunctional, both the circulation and the accident, technique and death, sex and photographic lens, everything in it is like a giant, synchronous, simulated machine: that is to say the acceleration of our own models, of all models that surround us, blended and hyperoperational in the void. This is what distinguishes *Crash* from almost all science fiction, which mostly still revolves around the old (mechanical and mechanistic) couple function/dysfunction, which it projects into the future along the same lines of force and the same finalities that are those of the "normal" universe. Fiction in that universe might surpass reality (or the opposite: that is more subtle) but it still plays by the same rules. In *Crash*, there is neither fiction nor reality anymore—hyperreality abolishes both. It is there that our contemporary science fiction, if there is one, exists. *Jack Barron or Eternity,* some passages from *Everyone to Zanzibar.*

In fact, science fiction in this sense is no longer anywhere, and it is everywhere, in the circulation of models, here and now, in the very principle of the surrounding simulation. It can emerge in its crude state, from the inertia itself of the operational world. What writer of science fiction would have "imagined" (but precisely it can no longer be "imagined") this "reality" of East German factories-simulacra, factories that reemploy all the unemployed to fill all the roles and all the posts of the traditional production process but that don't produce anything, whose activity is consumed in a game of orders, of competition, of writing, of bookkeeping, between one factory and another, inside a vast network? All material production is redoubled in the void (one of these simulacra factories even "really" failed, putting its own unemployed out of work a second time). That is simulation: not that the factories are fake, but precisely that they are real, hyperreal, and that because of this they return all "real" production, that of "serious" factories, to the same hyperreality. What is fascinating here is not the opposition between real factories and fake factories, but on the contrary the lack of distinction between the two, the fact that all the rest of production has no greater referent or deeper finality than this "simulacral" business. It is this hyperreal indifference that constitutes the real "science-fictional" quality of this episode. And one can see that it is not necessary to invent it: it is there, emerging from a world without secrets, without depth.

Without a doubt, the most difficult thing today, in the complex universe of science fiction, is to unravel what still complies (and a large part still does) with the imaginary of the second order, of the productive/projective order, and what already comes from this vagueness of the imaginary, of this uncertainty proper to the third order of simulation. Thus one can clearly mark the difference between the mechanical robot machines,

characteristic of the second order, and the cybernetic machines, computers, etc., that, in their governing principle, depend on the third order. But one order can certainly contaminate another, and the computer can certainly function as a mechanical supermachine, a superrobot, a superpower machine, exposing the productive genie of the simulacra of the second order: the computer does not come into play as a process of simulation, and it still bears witness to the reflexes of a finalized universe (including ambivalence and revolt, like the computer from *2001* or Shalmanezer in *Everyone to Zanzibar*).

Between the *operatic* (the theatrical status of theatrical and fantastical machinery, the "grand opera" of technique) that corresponds to the first order, the *operative* (the industrial, productive status, productive of power and energy) that corresponds to the second order, and the *operational* (the cybernetic, aleatory, uncertain status of "metatechnique") that corresponds to the third order, all interference can still be produced today at the level of science fiction. But only the last order can still truly interest us.

# UNCONSCIOUSNESS AND SOCRATIC REASON _____

John Ralston Saul (1947–) is a Canadian philosopher, economist, novelist, journalist, and cultural critic who has rejected an academic career to be free to think and write critically (indeed, academic organization and language are among his targets). The son of an officer in the Canadian Forces, he was born in Ottawa, Ontario, and educated at McGill University and at King's College, University of London, where he received a Ph.D. in economics and political science in 1972. He is a critic of the modern ideology of the market trumpeted by the New Right, of technology worship, of advertising, and of what he calls "corporatism" (more on this topic later).

After finishing his doctorate, Saul went to Paris to write his first novel, returning to Canada in 1975 to work for PetroCan, the national oil company. The French version of this novel, *Birds of Prey* (1977), became a best seller in France. Saul has written four more novels and is a prominent literary figure, at least in France if not in North America, thanks to the popularity of his novels in translation. In 1995 the Utne Press dubbed him one of "100 Visionaries Who Could Change Your Life," his own life being shaped at least in part by his travels and adventures in North Africa, Burma, Thailand, and elsewhere (his novels are usually situated in exotic locales, which he is well known for getting "right").

Later in his career Saul turned to philosophical writing, emulating the broad interests, wit, and suspicion of power structures shared by Enlightenment philosophers such as Voltaire, Diderot, and Hume. His 1992 book, *Voltaire's Bastards: The Dictatorship of Reason in the West,* puts forward the idea that Enlightenment ideas about reason have been corrupted by power elites in the West, who in using them to shape our institutions have turned these ideals into bureaucratic nightmares. He continued his theme of attacking power elites in his pseudo-dictionary, *The Doubter's Companion: A Dictionary of Aggressive Common Sense* (1994), in which he offers witty and sarcastic definitions of terms such as "global economy" and "neo-conservative," to the detriment of these same power elites and their ideological self-justifications.

The excerpts included here make up the lion's share of the first lecture of Saul's 1995 Massey Lectures for CBC Radio (the same series that is the source for Taylor's *Malaise*), *The Unconscious Civilization.* In these lectures Saul argues that our culture, our civilization, has become dangerously unconscious in its acceptance of corporatism, an ideology that can trace its origins back to fascist Italy and Germany in the 1920s and 1930s. Under corporatism, individuals no longer see themselves as citizens of a democracy but as members of a corporate entity, whether a multinational business corporation, a government department, a lobby group, or a university department. As members of such corporate bodies, good corporatists pursue their corporate self-interests, ignoring the public good, which, under the corporatist model, either doesn't exist at all or is no better than the sum total of all the individual self-interests of competing corporate bodies. Corporatism has also caused us to embrace ideology (including both advertising and explicit propaganda) over reasonableness as the dominant mode of public discourse.

This has led over the last decade or two to Western culture's turning to the marketplace as a magical solution to most (if not all) of our social and political problems, even though, as Saul all too clearly points out, the great innovations in Western political and economic life—a stable, managed economy, the welfare state, workers' rights, minority rights, even liberal democracy as a whole—have been the products *not* of pressures emanating from the marketplace but of democratic political struggles. At the end of his lectures Saul urges us to return to the tough life of Socratic questioning of those with power and of their ideological distortions of reality, to being once again "conscious." In returning to Socrates and his image of the philosopher as a gadfly stinging the lazy beast of the *polis,* as one who questions the received wisdom of political leaders and public opinion, we have come full circle in philosophy's attempt to understand the human condition. A life in which there are no easy answers is a difficult life, Saul tells us. Yet, as Socrates did himself, we have to keep telling ourselves that "the unexamined life is not worth living."

# The Unconscious Civilization

## JOHN RALSTON SAUL

"WHO IS MORE contemptible than he who scorns knowledge of himself?"[1]

A true question—a question seeking truth without expecting to find more than a fragment of it—will remain clear and unforgiving over hundreds of years. John of Salisbury raised this problem of self-knowledge in 1159. As you will see, much of what I'm going to say in these pages will be an amplification of his question.

John of Salisbury was far from the first to centre "the life worth living" on self-knowledge. What today we should call consciousness. Self-knowledge; the life worth living; individualism; humanism; a civil society. The list of terms describing the best and most interesting in the human experiment can be very long.

Not only was John of Salisbury not the first, he was surrounded in the twelfth century by a surprisingly large group of writers and thinkers, spread out across Europe—many of them monks or teachers—who were busy rediscovering the concept of the individual, perhaps even discovering for the first time what the modern Western individual could become if he, and later on she, wished.

Nowhere in all of this questioning, then or before, was the individual seen as a single ambulatory centre of selfishness: That idea of individualism, dominant today, represents a narrow and superficial deformation of the Western idea. A hijacking of the term and—since it is a central term—a hijacking of Western civilization.

One of the things I am going to do . . . is describe that hijacking. The end result will be the portrait of a society addicted to ideologies—a civilization tightly held at this moment in the embrace of a dominant ideology: corporatism. The acceptance of corporatism causes us to deny and undermine the legitimacy of the individual as citizen in a democracy. The result of such a denial is a growing imbalance which leads to our adoration of self-interest and our denial of the public good. Corporatism is an ideology which claims rationality as its central quality. The overall effects on the individual are passivity and conformity in those areas which matter and non-conformism in those which don't.

Given the importance that John of Salisbury attributed to friendship and community, it is hard to imagine that he would not have asked the same question of society as a whole—particularly of ours, which is so determined to claim the individual as its anchor.

What is more contemptible than a civilization that scorns knowledge of itself?

I'll be more precise. It is taught throughout our universities, expounded in our think tanks, repeated *ad nauseam* in public forums by responsible figures—that democracy was born of economics, in particular of an economic phenomenon known as the Industrial Revolution. And that democracy is based upon individualism. And that modern individualism was also a child of the Industrial Revolution. (The less determinedly superficial of such voices will give some credit to the Reformation, which makes them only marginally less inaccurate.)

The point of these received wisdoms of the second half of the twentieth century is that the very heart and soul of our 2,500-year-old civilization is, apparently, economics, and from that

[1] John of Salisbury, *Policratus* (Oxford, 1909), vol. 1, 19. CC. J. Webbs, ed.

SOURCE: John Ralston Saul, "The Great Leap Backwards," chap. 1 of *The Unconscious Civilization* (1995; New York: Free Press, 1997), pp. 1–3, 5, 7–9, 15, 18–20, 27, 30–37 (edited). Copyright 1995 by John Ralston Saul and the Canadian Broadcasting Corporation. Reprinted and edited with the permission of the Free Press, a division of Simon & Schuster Adult Publishing Group. All rights reserved.

heart flowed, and continues to flow, everything else. We must therefore fling down and fling up the structures of our society as the marketplace orders. If we don't, the marketplace will do it anyway.

The only problem with this whole theory is that much of modern individualism and democracy found life in Athens, some time before the Industrial Revolution. And both grew slowly, with ups and downs, through a series of key steps until the twelfth century, when the pace accelerated. Every important characteristic of both individualism and democracy has preceded the key economic events of our millennium. What's more, it was these characteristics that made most of the economic events possible, and not vice versa.

. . . One-third to one-half of the population of Western countries is today employed in administering the public and private sectors. In spite of having a larger and better educated elite than ever before in history; in spite of knowing more than we have ever known about ourselves and our surroundings, we actively deny the utility of public knowledge.

In the nineteenth century, Alessandro Manzoni opened his great novel, *The Betrothed,* with another one of those unforgiving resumés of our condition: "History may truly be defined as a famous war against time."[2] But you cannot wage this war if you deny reality. If you cannot remember, then there is no reality.

To know—that is, to have knowledge—is to instinctively understand the relationship between what you know and what you do. That seems to be one of our biggest difficulties. Our actions are only related to tiny, narrow bands of specialist information, usually based on a false idea of measurement rather than upon any knowledge—that is, understanding—of the larger picture. The result is that where a knowing woman or man would embrace doubt and advance carefully, our enormous, specialized, technocratic elites are shielded by a childlike certainty. Whatever they are selling is the absolute truth. Why link child-

ishness to certainty? Quite simply, as Cicero put it: "He who does not know history is destined to remain a child."

. . . The technocracy has developed an argument that now dominates our society according to which "management" equals "doing," in the sense that "doing" equals "making." They have hung this argument on such things as a redefinition of the service economy, of financial speculation and of the new communications technology.

But of course, "managing" is neither "doing" nor "making." As Adam Smith put it: "There is one sort of labour which adds to the value of the subject upon which it is bestowed; there is another which has no such effect." The former is "productive," the latter "unproductive" labour. Smith clearly places management in the unproductive category. "The labour of some of the most respectable orders in the society is, like that of menial servants, unproductive of any value, and does not fix or realize itself in any permanent subject, or vendible commodity, which endures after that labour is past, and for which an equal quantity of labour could afterwards be procured."[3]

Smith, of course, is realistic: "But there is no country in which the whole annual produce is employed in maintaining the industrious. The idle everywhere consume a great part of it."[4] His argument is that the industrious produce the fund which finances the whole community. The idle—those not engaged in "useful labour"[5]— live upon the industrious. This includes the unwillingly idle—the unemployed. But he is not talking about them. They are not in a position to cost society a great deal.

He is referring above all to the managerial class of his day—the aristocracy, the courtiers, the professionals, the land and property owners (who live off rent income), the bankers and so on. In other words, he is talking about our technocratic managerial elite. It must exist. But how much of it can the industrious among us support? The answer might be that 30% to 50%—

[2] Alessandro Manzoni, *The Betrothed* (London: Penguin Classics, 1972), 19.

[3] Adam Smith, *An Inquiry into the Nature and the Wealth of Nations* (London: Penguin Classics, 1986), Books I–III, 421–431. First published in 1776.
[4] Smith, 157.
[5] Smith, 104.

the current level of the managerial class in our society—is far too high; that the management of business along with the financial and consulting industries—all of which are extremely expensive and increasingly so—are a far more important factor in keeping the economy in depression than is any overexpansion of government services.

Some of you will be surprised that I am invoking Adam Smith, the god of marketplace worshippers and of the neo-conservatives. Well, I am going to make a point of quoting both Smith and his friend David Hume, the demigod of the same contemporary Right, for two reasons. One is to show that the reigning ideologues of our day base their arguments upon a very narrow use of Smith and Hume. That they seriously misrepresent the more balanced message of the two men. And that the late industrial, global applications of Smith and Hume, which are now being pressed upon us, bear no relationship to the reality of what either man was talking about in an extremely early industrial and very localized situation.

Many are surprised that this management elite continues to expand and prosper at a time when society as a whole is clearly blocked by a long-term economic crisis. There is no reason to be surprised. The reaction of sophisticated elites, when confronted by their own failure to lead society, is almost invariably the same. They set about building a wall between themselves and reality by creating an artificial sense of well-being on the inside. The French aristocracy, gentry and business leadership were never more satisfied with themselves than in the few decades before their collapse during the French Revolution. The elites of the late Roman Empire were in constant expansion and filled with a sense of their own importance, as emperor after emperor was assassinated and provinces were lost. The Russian elites of the two decades preceding 1914—both the traditional leadership and the new, rapidly expanding business class—were in a constant state of effervescence.

One of the tricks which makes this sort of closet delusion possible is that the very size and prosperity of the elite permit it to interiorize an artificial vision of civilization as a whole. Thus, ours takes seriously only what comes from its own hundreds—indeed, thousands—of specialized sectors. Everything turns on internal reference. Everything is carefully measured, so that heartening "body counts" of growth or job creation or whatever can be produced. Truth is not in the world, it is the measurements made by professionals. . . .

. . . A managerial elite manages. A crisis, unfortunately, requires thought. Thought is not a management function. Because the managerial elites are now so large and have such a dominant effect on our education system, we are actually teaching most people to manage not to think. Not only do we not reward thought, we punish it as unprofessional. This primary approach to utility—a very limited form of utility—is creeping now into general pre-university education. The teaching of transient managerial and technological skills is edging out the basics of learning.

But there's another reason that knowledge of this crisis seems to have so little effect: the income of the elites at the upper levels has continued to grow and at the middle levels has not declined.

As Adam Smith put it, "The authority of riches . . . is perhaps greatest in the rudest age of society which admits of any considerable inequality of fortune."[6] By rudest, Smith means crudest, a term not often used to describe themselves by technocrats, specialists, managers and the professors at the Chicago School of Economics. Yet they do enjoy invoking Smith. Nor does "rudest" suggest a high level of civilization.

But what could be cruder than a human being, who is limited to a narrow area of knowledge and practice and has the naiveté of a child in most other areas? This is one of the elements that accounts for our clinical state of unconsciousness. . . .

Everything I've said so far revolves around an apparent inability to deal with reality. I would say that what we suffer from is a fear of reality.

[6] Adam Smith, *An Inquiry into the Nature and the Wealth of Nations* (Indianapolis: Hackett Publishing Co., 1993), 178. This edition includes edited versions of Books IV and V.

Who are "we"? Frankly, there is little difference in this mental state between those inside the elites and those outside. We have all by our actions or lack of them—in particular over the last quarter-century—agreed to deny reality.

The question is—Where does this fear come from? It isn't simply a vague taste for romantic illusions. We suffer from an addictive weakness for large illusions. A weakness for ideology. Power in our civilization is repeatedly tied to the pursuit of all-inclusive truths and utopias. At the time of each obsession we are incapable of recognizing our attitude as either a flight from reality or an embracing of ideology. The unshakeable belief that we are on the trail to truth—and therefore to the solution to our problems—prevents us from identifying this obsession as an ideology.

The history of this century—demonstrated in part by its unprecedented violence—suggests that our addiction is getting worse. We have already swept through the religion of world empires based upon the intrinsic superiority of each nation or race of empire builders, on through Marxism and fascism, and now we are enmeshed in the glory of a new all-powerful clockmaker god—the marketplace and its sidekick, technology. I would suggest that Marxism, fascism and the marketplace strongly resemble each other. They are all corporatist, managerial and hooked on technology as their own particular golden calf.

Along with these great ideological passions, we have also suffered and continue to suffer from what might be called fashions—nationalization, privatization, debt financing, debt as the devil, the killing of inflation.

Fashion is merely the lowest form of ideology. To wear or not to wear blue jeans, to holiday or not to holiday in a particular place can contribute to social acceptance or bring upon us the full opprobrium of the group. Then, a few months or years later, we look back and our obsession, our fears of ridicule, seem a bit silly. By then, we are undoubtedly caught up in new fashions.

But the wholesale, unquestioning embrace of political policies does consist of more than wearing blue jeans. Each of these miniature ideologies will disturb and often ruin many lives. Each

will also make the fortune of those who wait patiently to feed off human credulity. Each, in the oppressive air of conformity which ideologies create, will force public figures to conform or be ruined on the scaffold of ridicule. In a society of ideological believers, nothing is more ridiculous than the individual who doubts and does not conform. Think of the truisms of our day. Pay the debt. Embrace globalization. Which public figure of which stripe can stand up against these without committing political suicide?

Tony Blair, leader of the British Labour party, goes out of his way to fall into line. He tells *The Financial Times* of London: "The determining context of economic policy is the new global market. That imposes huge limitations of a practical nature—quite apart from reasons of principle—on macroeconomic policies."[7]

These two sentences may sound familiar. They should. They have been uttered in varying forms by hundreds of public figures from the Right to the Left.

Globalization and the limits it imposes are the most fashionable miniature ideologies of our day. Mr. Blair's statement means two things. One: "I am in fashion so it's safe to vote for me." Two: "The ideology is in charge, so don't worry, I won't be able to do much."

I myself would say that neither of these sentences is in the least bit accurate. They are declarations of passivity before the inevitable—before what is said to be inevitable—a standard reaction to ideology. And passivity is one of ideology's most depressing effects. The citizen is reduced to the state of the subject or even of the serf.

There is a certain terrifying dignity to the big ideologies. With the stroke of an intellectual argument the planet is put in its place. Terrifying. Only the bravest or the most foolish of individuals would not become passive before such awe-inspiring Destinies.

But the minor ideologies are almost always meanspirited and egotistical in the most straightforward way. They offer two choices—no more. And those two are really only one. Accept the

[7] *The Financial Times* (London), 22 May 1995, 6.

ideology or perish. Pay the debt or go bankrupt. Nationalize or starve. Privatize or go moribund. Kill inflation or lose all your money. We have suffered from this "either-or" sickness for a long time. . . .

Let me widen the focus here by briefly reintroducing the subject of corporatism.

First, corporatists from the 1870s on began laying in the idea that liberalism was guilty of a great sin because it had ". . . granted political and economic equality to individuals who were . . . manifestly unequal."[8] In other words, the corporatists were reviving the medieval hierarchical order. Contemporary corporatism has a more professional approach, focused on training, meritocracy and organizational structures, which are inevitably pyramidal, but the intent is exactly the same. This message is put out in a rhetorical, ideological manner through corporatism's mouthpieces—the disciples of market forces, the courtiers of neo-conservatism and, of particular importance, the authoritative voices of the social science academics.

Second, the denigration of such democratic, individualistic concepts as equality and justice has required from the very beginnings of corporatism a new set of social headings to put up over every doorway. This new approach was best evoked by Maréchal Pétain, the leader of collaborationist, corporatist France during World War Two. His slogan replaced *Liberté, Égalité, Fraternité* with *Patrie, Famille, Travail:* Nation (or rather, Fatherland), Family, Work. Other fascist, corporatist governments produced similar slogans. . . .

Let me slide the focus still wider. If I wanted to know what kind of society I was living in, I would begin by asking—Where does legitimacy lie? The source of legitimacy is at the very heart of civilization. From that assumption about ultimate authority flows much of the rest: power, organization, attitudes both private and public, ethics admired or condemned or ignored. I can

[8] Peter J. Williamson, *Corporatism in Perspective: An Introductory Guide to Corporatist Theory* (New York: Sage Publishers, 1989), 26.

identify only four real possibilities in Western history as the sources of legitimacy. God. King. Groups. Individuals. There are many variations on these sources. Many kings have claimed direct inspiration from God and so combined the two. Modern dictators, from Napoleon on through Hitler, have claimed to inherit the legitimacy of a king. The groups have ranged from medieval guilds to modern corporatism.

Now, the peculiarity of the first three sources —God, king and the groups—is that, once in power, they automatically set about reducing the fourth, the individual, to a state of passivity. The individual citizen is reduced to the state of a subject. That is, he is subjected to the will of one or more of these other legitimacies.

In other words, the first three are not compatible with the fourth, because they require acquiescence while individualism requires participation. Either one or more of the first three is in a dominant position or the fourth dominates.

I would argue that our society functions today largely on the relationship between groups. What do I mean by groups? Some of us immediately conjure up transnational corporations. Others think of government ministries. But this is to miss the point. There are thousands of hierarchically or pyramidally organized interest and specialist groups in our society. Some are actual businesses, some are groupings of businesses, some are professions or narrow categories of intellectuals. Some are public, some private, some well intentioned, some ill intentioned. Doctors, lawyers, sociologists, a myriad of scientific groups. The point is not who or what they are. The point is that society is seen as a sum of all the groups. And that the primary loyalty of the individual is not to the society but to her group.

Serious, important decisions are made not through democratic discussion or participation but through negotiation between the relevant groups based upon expertise, interest and the ability to exercise power. I would argue that the Western individual, from the top to the bottom of what is now defined as the elite, acts first as a group member. As a result, they, we, exist primarily as a function, not as a citizen, not as an individual. We are rewarded in our hierarchical meritocracies for our success as an integrated function. We know that real expressions of individualism are not only discouraged but punished. The active, outspoken citizen is unlikely to have a successful professional career.

What I am describing is the essence of corporatism. Forget the various declared intentions of the successive generations of corporatists—from the old Catholic groups to the fascists to the spokesmen for pyramidal technocratic organizations to the well-intentioned neo-corporatist social scientists of today. What counts is what they have in common. And that is their assumption as to where legitimacy lies. In corporatism it lies with the group, not the citizen.

The human is thus reduced to a measurable value, like a machine or a piece of property. We can choose to achieve a high value and live comfortably or be dumped unceremoniously onto the heap of marginality.

To be precise: we live in a corporatist society with soft pretensions to democracy. More power is slipping every day over towards the groups. That is the meaning of the marketplace ideology and of our passive acceptance of whatever form globalization happens to take.

Our only serious reactions to this phenomenon have come in the form of angry populism, which I will argue later is largely false populism focused on such anti-democratic mechanisms as referenda and what is called direct democracy.

For the moment, I would like to expand on the particularity of gods, kings and groups. They cannot function happily within a real democracy —that is, within a society of individuals. They are systems devoid of what I would call disinterest. Their actions are based entirely upon the idea of interest. They are self-destructive because they cannot take seriously the long-term or the wider view, both of which are dependent on a measure of disinterest, which could also be called the public good or the common weal.

The society in which legitimacy lies with the individual citizen is quite different. It can happily tolerate gods, kings and groups, providing they do not interfere with the public good—that is, providing that they are properly regulated by the standards of the public good. The citizen-based

society can do this because it is built upon the shared disinterest of the individuals. What's more, this has a tempering effect which can actually be beneficial to the other three forces— the gods, kings and groups. It limits their self-destructive nature by focusing them onto the longer term and the wider picture.

I believe that our ability to reassert the citizen-based society is dependent upon our rediscovery of the simple concepts of disinterest and participation. Both of these are a protection against our seemingly unconscious desire to take refuge in ideology. But the policies now being put in place throughout the West are based upon exactly the opposite assumption. Everything, from school education to public services, is being restructured on the self-destructive basis of self-interest.

I spoke earlier of three parallel oppositions or struggles—humanism versus ideology; balance versus imbalance; equilibrium versus disequilibrium. I can now add two more: democratic individualism versus corporatism; the citizen versus the subject. In the next chapter I'll deal with language versus propaganda and consciousness versus unconsciousness.

At this stage of our civilization, late in the twentieth century, I would say that we are losing each of these struggles to the darker side within us and within our society.

Am I exaggerating? Are we truly living in a corporatist society that uses democracy as little more than a pressure-release valve? Clearly the democratic mechanisms are still in place and the citizens do occasionally succeed in imposing a direction upon the elites.

But then, I am not making an absolutist argument. What I am talking about is the direction our society has taken and about how far it has gone along that path.

A simple test of our situation would involve examining the health of the public good. For example, there has never been so much money— actual money—disposable cash—in circulation as there is today. I am measuring this quantity both in absolute terms and on a per capita basis. Look at the growth of the banking industry and the even more explosive growth of the money markets.

There has never been so much disposable money, yet there is no money for the public good. In a democracy this would not be the case, because the society would be centred, by general agreement, on disinterest. In a corporatist system there is never any money for the public good because the society is based entirely upon measurable self-interest.

What then is the great leap backwards announced in the title of this chapter? It is our leap into the unconscious state beloved of the subject who, existing as a function in any one of the tens of thousands of corporations—public and private —is relieved of personal, disinterested responsibility for his society and thus gives in to the easy temptation of embracing the passive certitude that every ideology offers.

Let me close with two final oppositions. The first is that of permanent human patterns versus the temporary. Most of what is presented to us today as the inevitable forms of human relationships, given the dictates of such things as the market and technology, are in reality rather recent phenomena of a temporary—even incidental— nature. These are passing relationships because they are directly dependent upon the evolving forms of crude power. To develop theories about human nature and the nature of human society based upon variations of this sort of power— as we have often done from Adam Smith on through Marx—is to waste a lot of time on the service roads of economics.

These phenomena can be seen in their truly ephemeral nature when compared to the essential propositions which have been with us virtually unchanged for 2,500 years. Solon's ideas of public justice; Socrates' view of the citizen's role as a persistent annoyance; Cicero's "The good of the people is the chief law";[9] John of Salisbury's "Who is more contemptible than he who scorns knowledge of himself?" There are thousands of

other examples—in language and in action—of our efforts to improve ourselves by developing a responsible sense of self and society.

There is also a record of the ephemeral phenomena of self-interest. The trail is equally long —personal gain, violence for personal advancement, clever manipulation to get and hold power. The political figures who used their power for narrow purposes are often remembered, but generally as unfortunate examples of human weakness. The interesting thing is that nowhere in our active memory is this record of selfish acts in fact admired. It stands rather as a record of our failures.

This leads me to a final opposition. You might believe from the negative nature of my comments on us, the human, that I myself am one of those who looks down contemptuously from the advantaged position of the elite and who therefore also suffers unconsciously from self-loathing.

But the confronting of reality usually is a negative process. It is ideology that insists upon relentless positivism. That's why it opposes criticism and encourages passivity.

I would argue that confronting reality—no matter how negative and depressing the process —is the first step towards coming to terms with it, which is what I will attempt to do in a small way over the next four chapters.

This evening I have simply been exercising my right as a citizen—my Socratic right—to criticize, to reject conformity, passivity and inevitability. What encourages me in this process is the "delight" that I take in the human struggle.[10] Delight in mankind—that was the idea launched or rather relaunched in the twelfth century by the forces of humanism as they woke society from its Dark Ages.

The Roman poet, Terence, had said long before: "I am human and nothing human is foreign

---

[9] Cicero, *De Legibas III,* 3.8, trans. C. W. Keyes, Loeb edition, 467.

[10] Colin Morris, *The Discovery of the Individual,* 1050–1200 (Toronto: University of Toronto Press, 1987). More than this quote, many of the attitudes expressed throughout these pages on the rebirth of the individual are drawn from this remarkable book. I would also recommend Walter Ullmann's *The Individual and Society in the Middle Ages,* although I differ somewhat with his interpretations of early individualism.

to me." It was an attitude the humanists embraced in what they saw as a struggle between delight and self-loathing—delight in your fellow man and woman, sympathy for them; in other words, a sense of society.

This was then as it is now a profoundly anti-ideological idea which takes the human for what the human is and believes it is worth trying to do better.

## Study Questions

1. How did Matthew Arnold and Oswald Spengler define culture (see the Introduction)? What are the weaknesses of each of their definitions?

2. How does Lasch define a "narcissist"? Can we extend a psychological concept such as narcissism to a whole society, as he does? Why or why not?

3. Is Lasch right to see advertising as a "propaganda of commodities" designed to create a feeling of alienation in the individual consumer, to get us to buy more and more goods? Explain your answer.

4. Does the consumer economy and culture of narcissism make people more cynical, self-aware, and self-conscious, make us always (at least when in public) on display, leaving us feeling like an actor playing a role in the theater of everyday life? Why or why not?

5. Are human relationships today—those connected to work, family, love, and sex—more centered on narcissistic self-fulfillment than they were in the past? If so, how? Is Lasch right to criticize our culture along these lines? Why or why not?

6. Has feminism played a destructive role with respect to male-female relationships, as Lasch claims? How has it affected the institution of marriage and the stability of the family?

7. What three malaises of modernity does Charles Taylor outline in the reading selection? Does he think that we can avoid these malaises? If so, how? Do you think we can avoid them?

8. What does Taylor mean by "instrumental rationality"? Outline a few ways in which it governs our everyday lives. Does the dominance of this type of thinking have any negative effects on our culture?

9. What does the Unabomber mean by the "power process"? Why does he think that it has broken down in contemporary industrial society? What does he think we've lost due to its breakdown? Is his analysis sound?

10. Why does the Unabomber think that there can be no compromise between technology and freedom? Is he right that individual technologies such as the car and telephone seem innocuous when first adopted but later become necessities that we can't live without, making us dangerously dependent on them? Can you turn off your cell phone for a week (if you have one)? your computer?

11. Does the entertainment industry (as the Unabomber claims) serve up huge amounts of sex and violence in order to relieve our stress and pacify us, thereby better integrating us into the industrial-technological system?

12. Are the ideas expressed by the Unabomber by definition morally flawed, given the fact that he's a murderer? Should we refuse to publish or read his work, given his crimes? Why or why not? Is what he did morally different from what revolutionaries fighting against tyrannical regimes do?

13. Why does Marinetti think that his futurist comrades should embrace technology? How is this related to what he thought of Italian culture of his day? Are there significant moral or political problems with the futurist position?

14. What did McLuhan mean by his saying that "the medium is the message"? What basic effects did McLuhan see communications media as having on human beings? Is he overestimating the power of the media to change human nature?

15. How did McLuhan distinguish "hot" and "cool" media? How did he categorize each of the following: print, radio, television, films? Was his categorization right, based on his own definitions? How would he have categorized the World Wide Web and e-mail as forms of communication?

16. What did McLuhan mean by "the global village"? Do we today truly live in McLuhan's global village? Can we say that McLuhan was a good prophet with respect to the impact of communications technologies on global culture over the last twenty years?

17. What are some of the main manifestations of our speed-driven culture that Mark Kingwell discusses in his article? Can we realistically "slow down" our culture as a whole, as Kingwell suggests that we should, or is this a hopelessly utopian project?

18. What five myths of the electronic age does Heidi Hochenedel put forward? How do these myths relate to Kingwell's skepticism about modern communications technology? Evaluate Hochenedel's criticism of each myth.

19. Based on the readings in the section "Our Technological Culture," briefly evaluate the impact of the computer revolution (including the Internet) on our culture. Are we slowly moving toward a culture where virtual relationships replace face-to-face ones? If so, should we care?

20. What does Lyotard mean when he says that the postmodern condition is characterized by "an incredulity toward metanarratives"? Is he right?

21. Is Lyotard right that today information processing has surpassed industrial mass production as the central economic force in our society? If so, what effects will this have on our culture?

22. What are Baudrillard's three orders of simulacra? How do they map onto the history of utopian and science-fiction writing? Is he right that science fiction in the traditional sense is dead, and that instead the most advanced writers today are merely extending what already exists?

23. Do we live in a postmodern culture, one that is distinct from all previous cultures? Why or why not? (Discuss Lyotard, Baudrillard, and the introductory article "What Is Postmodernism?")

24. What does Saul mean by "corporatism"? Should we be worried about it? Why or why not?

25. Is Saul right that if we return to the Socratic project and ask hard questions about the current dominant ideologies of neoconservatism and the globalized marketplace, we will find them to be distortions of reality? If so, should we wake up from this distorted dream? Why or why not?

## Bibliography

Adorno, Theodor W. *The Culture Industry: Selected Essays on Mass Culture.* Edited by J. M. Bernstein. London: Routledge, 1991. Adorno was a member of the Frankfurt School of critical theory, which combined the insights of Marxism and psychoanalysis in its analysis of culture.

Appignanesi, Richard, and Chris Garratt. *Postmodernism for Beginners.* Cambridge, UK: Icon Books, 1995. Comics and text, good on the art and culture of postmodernism.

Arnold, Matthew. *Culture and Anarchy.* London: Cambridge University Press, 1932.

Bell, Daniel. *The Cultural Contradictions of Capitalism.* New York: Basic, 1976.

Benjamin, Walter. *Illuminations.* Edited by Hannah Arendt. New York: Harcourt, Brace & World, 1968. Benjamin was another member of the Frankfurt School. Contains the important essay "The Work of Art in the Age of Mechanical Reproduction."

Borgmann, Albert. *Crossing the Postmodern Divide.* Chicago: University of Chicago Press, 1994. A calm critique of modern hyperactivity and the culture of virtual reality from a mildly religious perspective.

During, Simon, ed. *The Cultural Studies Reader.* London: Routledge, 1993. A standard reader.

Eagleton, Terry. "Capitalism, Modernism, and Postmodernism." *New Left Review* 152 (1985): 60–73. A difficult but rewarding Marxist critique of postmodern culture.

Fekete, John. *The Critical Twilight: Explorations in the Ideology of Anglo-American Literary Theory from Eliot to McLuhan.* London: Routledge, 1977.

Foster, Hal, ed. *Postmodern Culture.* London: Pluto Press, 1985. A collection of essays.

Franklin, Ursula. *The Real World of Technology.* Concord, Ontario: House of Anasi Press, 1999. A series of short, very readable lectures by a prominent philosopher of technology.

Freud, Sigmund. *Civilization and Its Discontents.* Edited by James Strachey. New York: Norton, 1989. Freud argues that the meaning of civilization is the repression of Eros and Thanatos, our sexual and aggressive drives, for which we all suffer. One of the best books of the twentieth century.

Gibson, William. *Neuromancer.* New York: Berkeley, 1984. The founding novel in the cyberpunk genre.

Gordon, W. Terrence. *McLuhan for Beginners.* London: Writers and Readers, 1997. Lively comics-and-text introduction to McLuhan's ideas.

Gramsci, Antonio. *The Antonio Gramsci Reader: Selected Writings 1916–1935.* Edited by David Forgacs. New York: New York University Press, 2000. An Italian Marxist who thought that the ruling class rules not only through the state and economic life but also by means of a hegemony over cultural forms of expression.

Grant, George. *Technology and Empire: Perspectives on North America.* Toronto: House of Anansi, 1969. Contains the important essay "In Defence of North America."

Hall, Stuart, and Tony Jefferson, eds. *Resistance through Rituals: Youth Subcultures in Postwar Britain.* London: Hutchinson, 1976. The founding document of the neo-Marxist Birmingham Centre for Contemporary Cultural Studies, whose general position is that popular culture represents a field where the ruling and oppressed classes battle over cultural hegemony. Contains a long theoretical introduction and essays on the Teddy Boys, Mods, skinheads, reggae culture, girls' subcultures, and style as an expression of social class.

Harvey, David. *The Condition of Postmodernity.* Oxford: Blackwell, 1992. Harvey discusses how changes in the way that space and time are perceived led to a fragmentation in postmodern art, literature, and culture as a whole.

Hebdige, Dick. *Subcultures: The Meaning of Style.* London: Routledge, 1979. An important study by a member of the neo-Marxist Birmingham School of Cultural Studies on how working class and black youth in Britain expressed their discontent with the class structure in their country through the "oblique" medium of style (e.g., the Mods and Rockers, reggae, punk).

Hutcheon, Linda. *The Politics of Postmodernism.* London and New York: Routledge, 1989.

Innis, Harold A. *Empire and Communications.* Edited by David Godfrey. Victoria and Toronto: Porcépic Press, 1986. First published in 1950 by Clarendon Press. Innis was an important influence on McLuhan.

Jameson, Frederic. *Postmodernism, or the Cultural Logic of Late Capitalism.* Durham, NC: Duke University Press, 1991. An important Marxist critique of "postmodern" culture.

Kroker, Arthur. *Technology and the Canadian Mind: Innis/McLuhan/Grant.* Montreal: New World Perspectives, 1984. To quote the first line of the book, "Canada's principal contribution to North American thought consists of a highly original, comprehensive, and eloquent discourse on technology."

Kroker, Arthur, and Michael Weinstein. *Data Trash: The Theory of the New Virtual Class.* Montreal: New World Perspectives, 1994. Difficult but rewarding postmodern theory on how the human body is disappearing into a wilderness called virtual reality. Much wilder and woollier than Kroker's earlier book.

Kujundzic, Nebojsa, and Doug Mann. "The Unabomber, the Economics of Happiness, and the End of the Millennium." *Ends and Means* 3, no. 1 (Autumn 1998): 11–20. Also available online: http://www.abdn.ac.uk/philosophy/endsandmeans/vol3no1/kujundzic_mann.shtml

Leavis, F. R. *Mass Civilization and Minority Culture.* Cambridge, UK: Minority Press, 1930. Leavis argues that the Industrial Revolution helped to create a crass mass civilization alongside a minority culture that tries to preserve the "best that has been thought and said" (i.e., culture in its true sense).

Marchand, Philip. *Marshall McLuhan: The Medium and the Messenger.* Cambridge, MA: MIT Press, 1998. A biography of McLuhan, with a foreword by Neil Postman.

Nicolson, Linda J., ed. *Feminism/Postmodernism.* Routledge: London, 1990. A good collection of essays on the relations between feminism and postmodernism.

Postman, Neil. *Amusing Ourselves to Death: Public Discourse in the Age of Show Business.* New York: Viking Press, 1986. Postman, a prominent American communications critic who died in 2003, argues in this book that television has cheapened public discourse into a collection of trivial sound bytes uttered by pretty men and women with perfect hair.

————. *Technopoly: The Surrender of Culture to Technology.* New York: Vintage Books, 1993. Postman's manifesto claims that technology has conquered our political, economic, and spiritual lives, to the detriment of each.

Powell, Jim. *Postmodernism for Beginners.* London: Writers and Readers, 1998. Comics and text from Icon Books' rival company, this work is good on the theorists of postmodernism, especially Baudrillard, Lyotard, and Frederic Jameson.

Rosenau, Pauline Marie. *Post-Modernism and the Social Sciences.* Princeton, NJ: Princeton University Press, 1992. Very fair-minded, careful analysis of the main trends in postmodern theory as it applies to various issues in the social sciences, with an excellent bibliography at the end. Rosenau makes complex, muddled issues in postmodernism quite a bit clearer (perhaps clearer than they really are!).

Roszak, Theodore. *The Cult of Information: A Neo-Luddite Treatise on High Tech, Artificial Intelligence, and the True Art of Thinking.* Berkeley: University of California Press, 1994. Roszak attacks the idolization of the computer in contemporary culture.

Sale, Kirkpatrick. *Rebels against the Future: The Luddites and Their War against the Industrial Revolution: Lessons for the Computer Age.* Reading, MA: Addison-Wesley, 1995. The title says it all.

Sardar, Ziauddin, and Borin van Loon. *Introducing Cultural Studies.* Cambridge, UK: Icon Books, 1999. Comics-and-text introduction to the field that focuses on cultural studies' British origins and its spread throughout the world, notably South Asia and America.

Shenk, David. *Data Smog: Surviving the Information Glut.* San Francisco: Harper, 1998. Shenk objects to the clouds of data spewed from our modern information systems that obscure civil discourse, democratic politics, and clarity of thought.

Storey, John. *Cultural Theory and Popular Culture: An Introduction.* 3d ed. Athens: University of Georgia Press, 2003. Storey reviews the main theories of popular culture, from Matthew Arnold and the "culture and civilization" tradition through structuralism, Marxism, feminism, and postmodernism. Parallels in structure Storey's reader.

————, ed. *Cultural Theory and Popular Culture: A Reader.* 2d ed. Athens: University of Georgia Press, 1998. The companion volume to Storey's *Introduction,* this valuable volume contains fifty-five readings on cultural theory edited into digestible bites.

Strinati, Dominic. *An Introduction to Theories of Popular Culture.* London: Routledge, 1995. Similar to John Storey's *Introduction* but a bit broader in its focus, Strinati's work covers structuralism, Marxism and neo-Marxism, the Frankfurt School, feminism, and postmodernism.

Wallace, Patricia. *The Psychology of the Internet.* Cambridge: Cambridge University Press, 1999.

Williams, Raymond. *Culture and Society 1780–1950.* Harmondsworth, UK: Penguin, 1963. An early cultural studies classic on the development of the idea of the artist in Britain from the end of the Enlightenment to the middle of the twentieth century.

# Internet Resources

The Center for the Radical Advancement of Postmodern Sophistry:
http://home.comcast.net/~crapsonline/main.html
This site, which doesn't take itself too seriously, contains a number of essays by Doug Mann and others on the philosophy of culture, including "Evil Demons, Saviours and Simulacra in *The Matrix*," a Baudrillardesque reading of the 1999 film.

Contemporary Philosophy, Critical Theory, and Postmodern Thought:
http://carbon.cudenver.edu/~mryder/itc_data/postmodern.html
Links to other sites featuring articles and reviews on theorists such as Marx, Marcuse, Foucault, Derrida, Lyotard, Baudrillard, Rorty, and Taylor.

CTheory: http://www.ctheory.com/
This is an online journal on theory, technology, and culture edited by Arthur and Marilouise Kroker that features a series of short and punchy articles, including a few by Baudrillard. Unfortunately, many of the articles are written in dense "postmodernese" impenetrable to non-insiders. A valuable resource all the same.

Futurism Page: http://www.unknown.nu/futurism/
This page contains a good collection of futurist manifestos and links to other pages on the movement.

K.I.S.S. of the Panopticon: http://www.geneseo.edu/~bicket/panop/home.htm
Dougie Bicket's page on cultural theory and media literacy. It contains usually short entries on thinkers and terminology, pictures, links to other sites, and so on, with something of a British edge. Good on Baudrillard and all things Baudrillardesque. High marks to Bicket for his lively site (though there are a few minor errors here and there).

Sarah Zupko's Culture Studies Centre: http://www.popcultures.com
Links to other pages on all the major theorists and critics of culture, a comprehensive list of

journals, conference listings, publishers, links to articles, and more. Features a funky, easy-to-use interface.

Saul, John Ralston. "Democracy and Globalization": http://www.abc.net.au/specials/saul Saul delivered this lecture at the University of New South Wales in Sydney, Australia, in January 1999.

Also see the general philosophy Web sites listed at the end of the introduction to this book.

# Index